St ANN'S
NOTTINGHAM:

inner-city voices

St Ann's Nottingham:

inner-city voices

by Ruth I Johns

First published 2002 by Plowright Press, PO Box 66, Warwick CV34 4XE

ISBN 0 9516960 9 2

A CIP catalogue record for this book is available from the British Library

Cover design: NHP, Warwick
Page setting and printing: Warwick Printing Company Ltd, Warwick

To Thomas, Tarn and Adam

Contents

including more than 940 photos and index

Introduction

AIMS OF THIS BOOK

- To gather, from individuals and groups, the history of St Ann's in living memory.

- To share this history within St Ann's and beyond.

Background

From 1965-76, I knew St Ann's very well. After I left Nottingham in 1976, my friendships, and work with the Action Resource Centre, often brought me back to the City. I have spent a regular part of my life in St Ann's since the early 1990s.

When I worked with young people in St Ann's in the 1990s, I found they knew little about the recent history of their area. They were very interested when offered an opportunity to find out. They resent St Ann's bad reputation.

In the 'new' St Ann's, many people have worked hard for their community but, for all sorts of reasons, a shared knowledge of St Ann's history is missing. Thirty thousand people were compulsorily displaced at the time of the area's redevelopment in the late 1960s and early 1970s. Many had to move to other areas of the City. Inter-generational family and neighbourhood networks were broken up. The new St Ann's started with fewer people, many being the elderly who stayed, or new people who moved in to an area cleared of its focal points. There were few of the facilities that are necessary for social cohesion, especially in areas where many people live on low incomes.

In history terms, there was a gap between the recollections of the elders who remained and the experiences of the new people who moved in. In time, many former St Annies moved back. Gradually more family and neighbourhood networks have formed. Because of the way the district was redeveloped, the history of St Ann's has tended to reside as fragments in the memory of particular people and particular groups. They hold their history in the context of the outside community viewing St Ann's as an area with a bad reputation.

I wanted to try to open up St Ann's history in living memory for the solid social history story that it is. It deserves more recognition.

Method

This book covers much of the 20th Century and up until the present. There is also some background of St Ann's history in earlier times[1].

I interviewed, talked with and corresponded with people who live or have lived in St Ann's; also with people who work or have worked in St Ann's. Individuals read the text of their interview except in the few instances where someone could not be traced or, sadly, where someone has died or become incapacitated.

The Press was helpful in asking people to contact me. Many leaflets were distributed in St Ann's inviting participation in this book. I wrote to a comprehensive list of organisations and groups. Word of mouth worked very well as people told other people about the project. I spent over three hundred hours interviewing individuals and groups, usually using tapes, and many further hours talking with individuals or groups, including six open sessions held at St Ann's Library. Some information came from people I met quite by chance out and about. I visited organisations, community centres, projects, pubs, schools, churches, the Mosque and more.

People found news cuttings, leaflets, photos, booklets and all sorts of material they kept about some aspect of their life in St Ann's. They phoned to ask if I knew about this or that, and they were generous with time and effort when I asked for more information or clarification. The extent of participation in preparing this book exceeded all my hopes.

The few contributors who wished to remain anonymous are known to me.

I have deliberately avoided the pressure from certain professional sources to write 'conclusions'. People in St Ann's are tired of pronouncements *about* them. However, in the course of the book, I have made several suggestions concerning the built environment as it affects St Ann's people.

I have used the language individuals used rather than editing all speech or text into a uniform style. It is valuable to see how the use of words and phrases changes over time.

---

[1] For example, Appendix I on the history of St Ann's Well by Patrick Fleckney. Two helpful and readable history books on Nottingham are *History of Nottingham* by W Howie Wylie and J Potter Briscoe [Frank Murray, Nottingham. 1893] and *A Century of Nottingham History 1851-1951* [University of Nottingham. 1952].

For example, the phrase 'coloured' people was used in the 1950s and 1960s. I have not changed this to Afro-Caribbean, African Caribbean, black or Black people which are used now.

Views expressed by participants in this book are not necessarily my own.

I hope this book may encourage others to research more aspects of St Ann's history. I have tried to lay down adequate clues to facilitate this. Indeed, the process of gathering material for this book has already sparked off other projects. St Ann's has a history that should be known.

Thanks

Warm thanks to everyone who participated in this book. Acknowledgements given in the text are not repeated here. I valued the support I received in the lonely weeks of 'writing up' behind my computer in the West Midlands, when people would drop me notes or phone and simply say 'keep going Ruth!' To one person who forgets names, I have become The Book Woman! Thanks to my long-time friend and sometimes collaborator, Anne Bott. We have spurred each other on with our respective books.

Ellie White   *E James Smalley*

Thanks to Ellie White, E James Smalley and Alan Hardy (seen later!) who took photos voluntarily for the book and to everyone who found photos from their personal albums. Fewer photos were taken pre-1970s. The photos which exist tell us much about both St Ann's and the period in which they were taken. I was given a tin of photos that someone took from an empty house at the time of demolition.

As planning blight took hold of the district in the 1960s, a few people started to take photos of the 'old' St Ann's before it was demolished. Such photos offer a valuable record for the future. These people included Peter Garner; David Wilkinson, Rob Davis and David Strickland

(three fourth-year student architects): and members of the Nicholson family whose photos are used courtesy of the Nicholson Photo Archive[2].

Other photo sources include Nottingham Local Studies Library, Central Library (Angel Row, Nottingham) and the *Nottingham Evening Post* Photo Archive. Thanks go to Dorothy Ritchie and Ben Thomas respectively. I took photos to fill in some gaps.

Transcribing the many tapes before the interviews could be written up was a major task. My thanks to Christine Davies and Gulrukh Iqbal; to St Ann's Library staff whose interest and humour has been steadfast; to the *Nottingham Evening Post* for use of quotations: and to Nottingham City Council, especially Tony Thorpe, Service Manager, Property Records and Land Surveying, Design and Property Services Division, and (after his retirement) to his successor, Carol Miller. I looked up some of the Compulsory Purchase Orders affecting the 'old' St Ann's to confirm my recollection of the events of those years. Thanks to George Mann, Service Manager (Policy), Housing Department, City of Nottingham, for providing facts about the sale of council properties.

Funding this book has been difficult. I insisted that it should be independent and not beholden to funding sources with strings attached. The Lottery *Awards for All* made a small grant. All my time has been given. All the time of contributors has been given. That all adds up to a lot of time!

Finally, warm thanks to my husband who sees me setting off to St Ann's, Nottingham, for several days most weeks and accepts this as totally normal. Which it is! St Ann's has had a huge hold on my affections since I first knew it in 1965.

Ruth I Johns

2002

Money is stated in pounds, shillings and pence by many interviewees. Decimalisation of currency started in 1971. One pound = 100p. Ten shillings = 50p. There were twelve old pennies (12d) in a shilling. Half a crown was two shillings plus six old pence, so there were eight half-crowns to one pound. Old money included six-penny pieces, three-penny pieces, halfpennies and farthings (quarter of a penny).

---

[2]   Joseph (Joe) and Jean Nicholson have interviews in this book. Photos in the Nicholson Photo Archive have been taken by three generations of their family. Many of the photos which appear in this book were taken by their son William. Anyone wishing to find out location details about particular photos taken by members of the Nicholson family will be able to do this at Nottingham Local Studies Library in the near future. The photos were exhibited there earlier this year.

Setting the Scene

THE NAME AND SIZE OF ST ANN'S

The term St Ann's for the whole district, as we now know it, was used from the time of its redevelopment. For many people who lived in the 'old' St Ann's, the name usually referred only to the area around the St Ann's Well Road and not to the whole district.

However, for the purpose of clarity (except in two interviews at the request of the interviewees), I have used the name St Ann's for street names in the whole of the 'old' district. This will enable present and future readers to know that these streets were within the district of St Ann's as we now know it.

I have used the spelling St Ann's. The spelling has changed over time. For example, it has been Sentans, St Anne's, and - in recent years - it is often St Anns. For example, look at advertisements, the phone book, letterheads, common usage in letters etc. Indeed, in 1998, I used the St Anns spelling for the book *Elliott Durham and St Anns, the Comprehensive School on the hill in inner-city Nottingham*. It felt right to use that spelling in that context, and nobody even commented on it.

But, when it came to deciding how to spell St Ann's for this book which goes back to early in the 20th Century, on balance it seemed right to use the St Ann's spelling.

In fact, it is interesting how, in the 'old' St Ann's like anywhere else in which oral traditions were very strong, the spelling of names was often phonetic on the occasions people wrote them down.

This has led to some ingrained inconsistencies of spelling. For example, King's Hall Methodist Church was sometimes Kings Hall Methodist Church. I have publications with both versions featured side-by-side. The brochure launching the opening of the Kings Hall New Testament Assembly in 2000 uses both versions. Such name anomalies are common and I have have not imposed a 'correct' spelling.

Most people think Peas Hill Road is the correct spelling. So why the Pease Hill Centre on Abbotsford Drive? The spelling Peasc Hill Road is in a Ward Lock & Co Guide to Nottingham 1918-19.

One St Ann's street has different spellings on the street signs at either end, though somebody has now blacked out the name at one end!

Ransom Road is often spelt Ransome. And it used to be Coppice Road after it ceased to be called New Road!

Hungerhill Gardens are often referred to as 'the Hungerhills', or Hungerhill allotments. Often, people include the allotments at Stonepit Coppice and Gorseyclose Gardens (sometimes spelt Gorsey Close) in the overall name of 'Hungerhills'.

And, of course, in the 'new' St Ann's, many of the 'old' St Ann's street names were reused. And some of the streets which remained had their names changed! For example, Sycamore Road became Hungerhill Road, a road which already existed in a nearby location. The maps will help to locate names and name changes.

What area is included in St Ann's today?

Well, it depends on which source you look at! For example, the St Ann's area of the City Challenge initiative differs from that of the recent Sure Start 2 project. Electoral wards do not correspond to any popular understanding of the district's boundaries. Parishes and police areas straddle boundaries. People who live in St Ann's, however, usually have a clear idea of what it includes. But their idea may depend on where they live and who they are talking to! A St Ann's address can suddenly become 'Mapperley' for the purposes of commercial transaction, because of the reputation of St Ann's. Mapperley and St Ann's share the post code NG3 which makes this possible.

The varying definitions of the St Ann's area makes estimating population difficult. Inspector Howick refers to the police area of St Ann's and Sneinton having fifty-five thousand people. This gives us some idea of the reduction in population density after 30,000 people were removed from the substantial part of the 'old' St Ann's that was redeveloped. Fewer were housed in the 'new' St Ann's. There has, of course, also been a general loss of population from city areas in recent decades.

The maps will help those unfamiliar with St Ann's to find their way around. For the purposes of this book, the district of St Ann's runs between the Carlton Road end of Stonebridge Road, Robin Hood Street, Bath Street,

Huntingdon Street, up Elm Avenue, down Corporation Oaks, up the Woodborough Road, Hungerhill Road, up Ransom Road (including Caunton Avenue), across by Elliott Durham School, down The Wells Road (including Pearmain Drive, Colborn Street and Ball Street), up St Bartholomew's Road, turning along Gordon Road and cutting across toward the Carlton Road, but not including quite all the area nearest Carlton Road. The Hungerhill Gardens are also included.

MAPS

History can be exciting or boring or anything in between. How we approach it is up to us. One thing is certain, most people need to have a sense of place, a sense of belonging somewhere, even if they choose or need, to move away. Our 'place' is not necessarily the place where we were raised, but one we adopt. People often have roots in more than one place; I do.

As many voices in these pages testify, individuals and families find it traumatic to be uprooted peremptorily.

One way to look at 'our place' is to see how it has changed over time. Maps are useful.

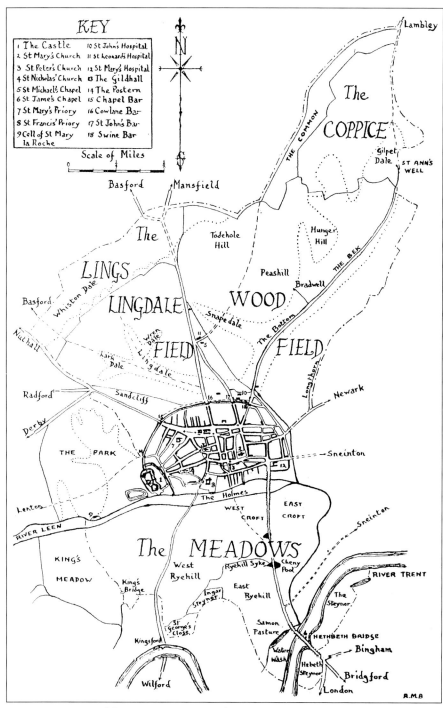

On this map c1480, Nottingham is small and surrounded by Common Lands. It was only after the Enclosure Act 1845, that it was possible for Nottingham to grow. The Common Lands were built upon, and became the 'suburban' sought after areas away from the poor and often unsanitary housing conditions of the 'old town'.

St Ann's was a pleasant place to move to, more space, better housing, improved and clean water supply and opportunities for business. The shape of St Ann's can be seen in this map. The Bottom/The Bek became St Ann's Well Road. The embryonic Woodborough Road is the dotted line on the left of Peashill and The Common. Longthorn demarked a future well-known route the other side of The Bek. Peashill, Hunger Hill, The Coppice are names still in St Ann's. St Ann's Well has been lost[1]

NOTTINGHAM AND ITS COMMON LANDS, c.1480
(Drawn by R. M. Butler and reproduced with the kind permission of the Thoroton Society of Nottinghamshire.)

---

[1] *See Appendix 1 for details of St Ann's Well.*

St Ann's Nottingham: Inner City Voices by Ruth I Johns • ISBN 0951696092

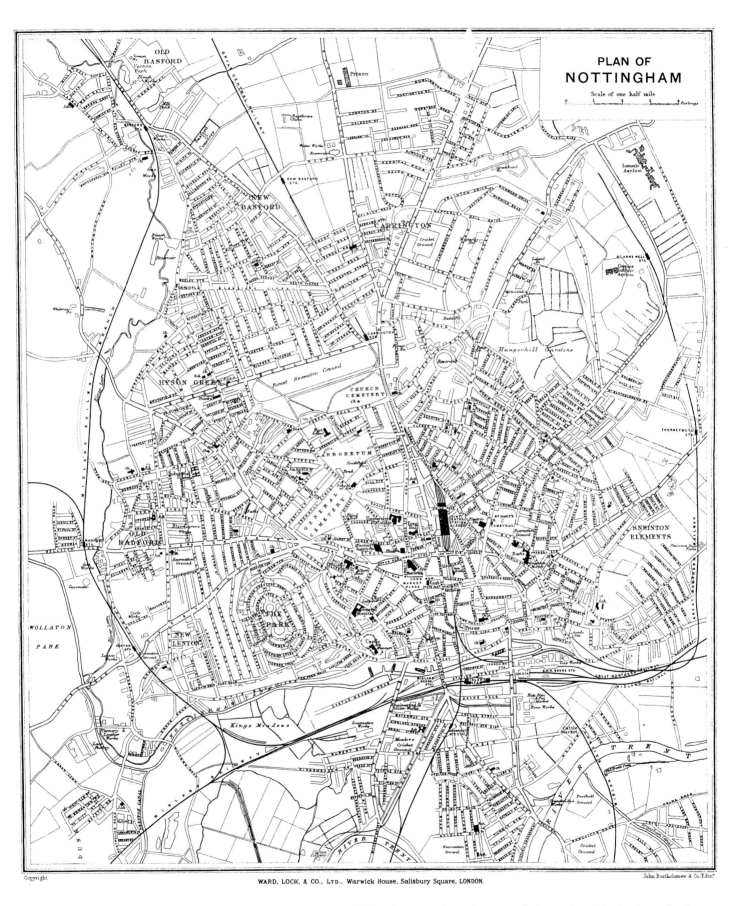

PLAN OF
NOTTINGHAM

Scale of one half mile

WARD, LOCK, & CO., LTD., Warwick House, Salisbury Square, LONDON.

John Bartholomew & Co. Edin.

Copyright

This map, published in Ward Lock & Co's illustrated guide-book Nottingham [1918-19] shows how St Ann's and other districts spread out over the former Common Lands. St Ann's, as we know it today, is easy to locate because of the Hungerhill Gardens. The covered round Reservoir is on Todehole Hill, and the shape of the district follows the previous map

This map is an Ordnance Survey one (revised in 1919) and offers more detail of St Ann's. Scale 6 inches to 1 mile. Source: Nottingham Local Studies Library

This is a 1968 map, just pre-demolition of much of St Ann's. Scale 6 inches to 1 mile. Reproduced from Ordnance Survey mapping on behalf of The Controller of Her Majesty's Stationery Office. Crown Copyright. Licence Number MC 100015493. Source: Nottingham Local Studies Library

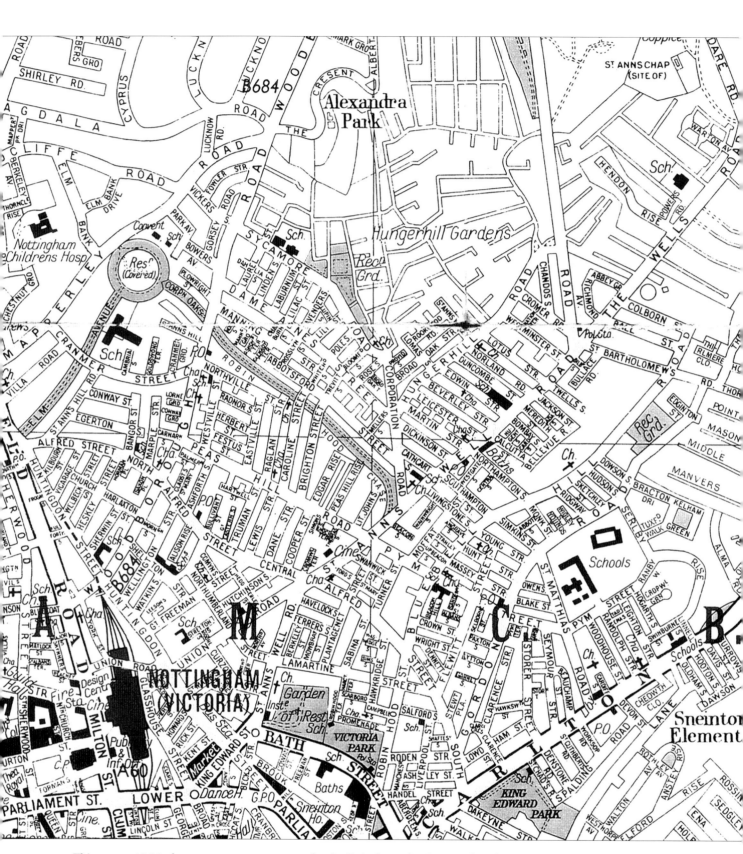

This map c1966 shows street names more clearly. It is from the Geographia detailed street plan of Nottingham, 1.5 inches to 1 mile. Reproduced under Ordnance Survey Crown Copyright. Licence Number MC 100015193

This 1989 map shows the 'new' St Ann's. Scale 1: 10,000. Reproduced from Ordnance Survey mapping on behalf of The Controller of Her Majesty's Stationery Office. Crown Copyright. Licence Number MC 100015493

It is difficult to find a map that gives someone who is unfamiliar with St Ann's an accurate sense of its layout now. The map on t previous page offers a bird's eye view of the position of buildings and this map gives clarity of road names. But if you look at, say, Robin Hood Chase on the previous map and then on this map, you may think this is not the same place! The previous map shows many building blocks with ends facing Robin Hood Chase, and the buildings do not all synchronise with the street layout on this m The answer to this riddle is the nature of the walkways through St Ann's. Many people refer to these in this book. This map does for example, show walkways in Marple Square. It does not show the Caunton Phoenix roads at the Alexandra Park end of Caunton Avenue following demolition of the Caunton Avenue flats in 1993.

It does not show all churches, including St Ann with Emmanuel Church (opened 1974). It shows a long-disused Baptist Church (now the Pakistan Centre) on Woodborough Road, but not the 'new' Chasewood Baptist Church (opened 1978). There are other errors (for example, Acacia Court should be on St Ann's Well Road), so, whilst the map is useful for locating road names, particulars on it need checking before using it for any research

ST ANN'S 'NEW TOWN'

St Ann's was built after the Enclosure Act of 1845, which took a long time to become fully operative. The district then was called New Town. Its new housing was far superior to much housing then compressed into a very tight area in the City Centre.

There was still a New Town Inn in St Ann's when St Ann's was demolished in the early 1970s because it was deemed to be a 'slum'. That reputation was fiercely rejected by many of its inhabitants.

Until the Enclosure Acts, the Lammas pasture lands could not be built on. New Town was built on the Clay Field part of the Lammas. It benefited from a restriction that a specific amount of open space was preserved for the use and enjoyment of local people, and thus the broad avenues of Robin Hood Chase, Corporation Oaks, and Elm Avenue could never be built upon.

There is historical material in Nottingham Local Studies Library and St Ann's Library for those wishing to investigate more about 19th Century St Ann's. There are Appendices at the back of this book with some detail about St Ann's Well (from which the district gained its name) and the Maze near St Ann's Well.

How extraordinary that a place of such local historical interest as St Ann's Well has never been celebrated in living memory! No public building/heritage centre/leisure gardens - no Millennium project!

To give a flavour of New Town, here is a 1920s voice, with the nom-de-plume Historicus describing the St Ann's of his childhood in the 1880s. *Nottinghamshire Weekly Guardian.* 17.4.24. Thanks to Brenda Smalley for drawing my attention to this.

Historicus wrote:

"When that part of Nottingham known as the Clay Field was built upon in the 'sixties [1860s], the streets off Woodborough-road and Union-road were known as 'The New Town'. The public-house sign of the New Town Inn in Great Freeman-street, is a reminder of this, and for some years St Ann's Rose Show was known as the 'New Town Wakes'.

"Part of the Clay Field is still unbuilt upon, extending from half-way up Brighton-street to the Chase. Most of the streets on St Ann's Well-road, as I first remember them, were in this unfinished condition, only more so. All Sycamore-road was open fields, and some fine old sycamore trees were still flourishing.

"At the top of Norland-road, before Duncombe-street and Edwin-street were built, were some fine fields adjoining the top of Hunger Hill-road, upon which we played shinny, goose and cricket at no great distance to the police lodge, which, I believe, was 'Bobby' Lakin's domicile. This officer was seldom met without a cane, and must have been something of a terror to the youngsters, for the following bit of doggerel was extremely popular:-

"Old Bobby Lakin
Put him on a pole and shake him.

"It may be news to the younger generation that policemen in those days usually carried canes. They did, and did not hesitate to apply them like true limbs of the law.

"I remember when the old Flower Show Field was all hedged around and the St Ann's Rose Show was held within. All the streets were decorated with streamers, even such dingy thoroughfares as Trumpet-street and Cyprus-street hanging garlands and decorations window to window.

"The show lasted two days, and the first band came marching from the Market-place at 2.30 in the afternoon, headed by the resplendent banner of the St Ann's Floral and Horticultural Society. A Crimean veteran named Smith, who was a coal dealer in Bombay-street, assisted to carry the banner for many years. He wore a silk hat and white waistcoat for the occasion and with his flowing grey beard looked a picturesque figure.

"Families gathered together at the Rose Show and St Ann's Well-road was thronged by itinerant vendors selling from barrows. There were all sorts of sports in the field, and a greasy pole to be climbed for prizes was fixed up on Norland-road. I think the first prize was a pig.

"At holiday times, there were always shows and roundabouts on old St Ann's Well-road. Rayner's Show once pitched at the end of Martin-street for a season. Cheap-jacks often occupied available pieces of waste ground. They sold "Brummagem" hardware, Sheffield cutlery and Staffordshire pottery. Concertinas, accordions and melodions were very popular in those days and the cheap-jack would sometimes be able to coax a tune out of one or the other of the instruments. At all events, he knew how to tell the tale. The last one I remember pitched on a piece of waste ground in Dame Agnes-street, now built upon. He stayed there a week or two and held singing competitions. . .

" . . . The New-road, as Coppice-road [now Ransom Road] was called in my boyhood, still bore traces of old times, having broken-down toll-gates at the top and bottom. The police lodge had originally been the old toll-house. We used to go up the New-road to watch the Robin Hoods at firing practice on the old Rifle Butts. But it was none too safe, for splinters of lead were always flying about, and we picked up scores of such 'spatters' from the road. Sergeant Alvey was at the Rifle Butt Lodge then, and a little man acted as marker. He used to point at the targets out of a pit. Some of the butts were like brick forts and Adjutant White's horse used to be stabled in the last one which, I think, shot up to 1,000 yards.

"Building was going on along St Ann's Well-road all the time, and the streets were very clayey, which is why all the old houses had scrapers. It is quite interesting to trace the old houses from the new up some of the streets by the scrapers that have generally been filled in. I noticed this up Manning-street recently.

"There were several springs - St Ann's Well, the spring marked by the drinking fountain in the wall at the tram terminus and Rag Spring just behind a stone wall up Coppice-road. Then there was a spring ran through the watercress garden on the other side, which some people say was the real Rag Spring, but that is an open question.

"I have been turning up in my memory some of the old shopkeepers on St Ann's Well-road in the early 'eighties [1880s]. Commencing from Commercial-square, there was Bramley the butcher, one of the best judges of beasts there was in Nottingham. He used to buy for the other butchers, and could be depended upon to judge the weight of an animal to a few pounds. When he left the shop he went to live at Mapperley.

"There was George Kirk, the draper and lover of gardening, and one of the most popular men in the neighbourhood, who lived to a good old age.

"At the corner of Alfred-street where the bank now stands was a chemist's shop first kept by Mr Huskinson and then by Mr C W Warriner. Mr Huskinson was once a passenger in a balloon which ascended from the Arboretum. It came down on some waste ground off Hunger Hill-road, and we had a fine view of it. That was about the time that the St Ann's Board Schools were being built. Although I was quite a boy, I remember them being opened by the Right Hon A J Mundella. At that time, Mr Philip Lowe kept the Oliver Cromwell. Mr George Sergent, greengrocer, and Mr Charles Redmile, who kept the hay and corn shop next door, were well-known shopkeepers.

"Passing the old Midland Lace Co. we came to Gillott's confectioner's shop, which still carries on the same business. Mitchell's barber's shop, Wilson's ironmongery shop, and Bullivant's shoe shop followed. Then there was Mr William's news-shop, and a baker's before we reached the St Ann's Well Inn. Giniver the grocer was on the other side of Peas Hill-road, in a row known as Malvern-terrace.

"James Pashley kept the Garden Gate for many years and let out handcarts. The landlord of the Scots Greys at that time was Mr Thomas Cotton. Attewell, greengrocer, Walker, hairdresser, and Mr John Radford, draper, who belonged to the Robin Hoods, were well-known shopkeepers. Crofts, the bakers at the corner of Beverley-street, had a public bakehouse, and there were several pyclet makers on the road.

"Mee Bros., masons, had a stoneyard at the corner of Norland-road, and almost opposite running up the left side of Jackson-street, was an open ropewalk belonging to Coates and Sons, Mr John Copestake kept the Queen's Arms, and Maria Foster kept the Westminster Abbey, which had a tea gardens attached. On the other side of the road were just as many well-known names, including Hobster,

An early motorcycle and sidecar used to deliver the produce of J Leigh & Co, Pyclet Bakery, 2, Robin Hood Chase. Photo: from 'Sneinton and St Ann's on old picture postcards' by Grenville Jennings [Reflections of a Bygone Age, Keyworth 1997]

plumber; Fox, chimney sweep and omnibus proprietor; Dr Marriott, Dr Dunn, Bycroft, baker, and Moses Ford, fishmonger. I ought to add that the Livingstone Coffee House stood at the corner of Livingstone-street. Not proving successful, it was afterwards turned into shops.

"A striking military figure often to be met with in the uniform of the Robin Hoods was Sergeant-Major O'Callaghan, who resided on St Ann's Well-road. He had served with distinction in the Connaught Rangers and wore a breastful of Crimean and Indian Mutiny medals."

In a copy of **St Catharine's Parish News**, St Ann's, for April 1901, I saw a letter from Lord Roberts entreating local people not to tempt his 'exemplary' soldiers when they returned from the Boer War but to aid them: "to uphold the splendid reputation they have won for the Imperial Army". How times, perceptions and the use of language change! There are still people who knew someone who fought in the Boer War and who remember celebrating Empire Day in the schools and churches of St Ann's.

Some of Historicus' statements illustrate a continuity that lasted until the time of St Ann's demolition. For example, the affection of St Ann's people for the diversity of their shops and those who ran them.

St Ann's Nottingham: inner-city voices by Ruth I Johns • ISBN 0951696092

Life Stories – Part I

In the two Life Stories sections are many, but not nearly all, of the recollections collected for this book. Social history asserts itself through the detail told. I asked for contributors' year of birth, so we can place their experiences accurately in time. Thus, we see the continuities over many decades - and the differences.

Up to the time when the area became blighted, from the mid-1960s, prior to demolition, there is a strong sense that children's and adults' lives were closely intertwined in a way that has not occurred - as a generality - since. The words of older people I interviewed are memorable. When as children, for example, their street games began to get out of control, grannies would appear in doorways and rein them in.

Redevelopment of St Ann's often separated elders from the younger two generations of their family who moved to other areas of the City. And the grandparents who stayed behind were afraid to check 'new' children they didn't know. And the cost to the Local Authority of elder care in redeveloped inner-city areas like St Ann's rose[1].

Now, there <u>are</u> less things for children to do out and about in their neighbourhoods, fewer adults watching out for them and fewer adults who know them well. And there are, perhaps, fewer adults prepared to tolerate children's legitimate energy and noise. In most of St Ann's, there is not much space inside homes for children's activities with friends, and the streets are no longer safe for play. And many families are on a low income, which precludes their being able to spend too much on outings.

In the 'old' St Ann's, there were a large number of what I call 'useable small dollops of neighbourhood public space' which children as well as adults frequented, including shared backyards, busy allotments and over six hundred shops. Children mixed with people walking to and from the many workplaces in St Ann's or nearby. There were the uniformed organisations and youth clubs, free after-school clubs, and different church teas and parties to attend without necessarily belonging to any particular Sunday school. In the three-generation neighbourhoods, children from an early age called alone or with siblings/friends to see members of their extended family who lived near. This provided them with activity and interest. Even children, whose own home life was unhappy,

Top of Festus Street, Westville Street. Photo: Nicholson Photo Archive

usually had access to many known adults. But the shops, in particular, are vividly remembered. Some were a front parlour supplying one item (like eggs): others were thriving businesses.

They provided children with a large number of adults who saw them regularly from the time they first went out in a pram, and the adults also knew their parents. Children would run errands to shops and for shops. Shops are a recurring theme in recollections of the 'old' St Ann's. Almost all streets had one or more corner shops, and usually a shopping street at one end. What is the modern equivalent of these shops in children's lives today?

Where now are what I call 'useable small dollops of neighbourhood public space' inhabited by people with whom children can relate over many years?

There are adults in St Ann's working very hard indeed with the area's young people and they deserve support, the affirmation of the Press, and the pro-active interest of more people of the older generations. Some of the facilities used by young people appear in these pages. But the modern trend for facilities is towards big projects, rather than local ones in particular neighbourhoods. St Ann's is even in danger of losing its local swimming pool at the Victoria Leisure Centre.

[1] Inner Area Programme City Council Report 1978.

There is now a gap in which the cement which binds children from a young age to their community is missing. Relationships thrive in the small-scale 'useable dollops of neighbourhood public space'. Many St Ann's young people in the past twelve years or so have told me how useless many of the small patches of green in St Ann's are because 'you are not allowed even to play with a ball there'. Many of these patches have now been - and are being - integrated into gardens in a succession of estate improvements since 1992.

Somehow, we have got to get better at making children from a very early age feel they belong. If they get to 12-14 and feel they don't belong, it cannot all be their fault, or all their parents' fault or all their school's fault. There is that vital extra dimension of 'belonging' to the place where you grow up. And where you are known to many people of all ages: people who you meet frequently and with whom, over time, you develop relationships with two-way responsibilities and support.

From the life stories collected and many other conversations, one thing in particular became very clear to me. Up to the mid-1960s when planning blight was rampant, without the benefit (for many) of more than a very basic education, children in St Ann's nevertheless usually acquired life skills which enabled them to develop lives full of interest, talent and concern for others.

Why is it that, with better educational opportunities, a greater understanding of childhood needs, homes with modern labour-saving devices, and less extreme poverty, we are experiencing so many children deemed 'problems'? It is too simple to say it is due to family break-up or single parents or . . .

Families have always been complex, as many of these life stories show.

But, I am optimistic because there are an increasing number of three-generation families again taking root in St Ann's, there are strong networks, people do look out for each other once they know each other. But there is urgent need for many more 'useable small dollops of neighbourhood public space', so - from an early age - children can navigate their community and confidently feel a part of it.

E HALLAM

Born 1908

From letters 1999

I was born in Crown Street, Carlton Road and the family went to live at 17, Conway Grove, St Ann's, when I was four and I was there until I was sixteen. My childhood was around that area. At the top of Marple Street were steps up to Cranmer Street, where the Gordon Boys' Home was. My aunt used to collect eggs for the Home every Easter.

Marple Street ran down to Alfred Street North and St Andrew's School, where I went for ten years, was just around the corner on the right. Because of the steep hill on Woodborough Road, our parlour was on 17, Conway Grove

[off Woodborough Road] while the living room and kitchen were downstairs looking on to Carnarvon Street and were reached by passing all our neighbours' living rooms and that was where all the wcs were. I think one day, when in the backyard, we saw a zepplin and mother rushed us to the coal cellar. Our parlour, much to my mother's chagrin, was my father's workshop in second-hand motorcycles. I rode a Calcott Motor Cycle (which nobody seems to have heard of now) when I was about thirteen.

At St Andrew's School, I reached Standard four or five. They smacked my face if I forgot things. It was a hard life at school especially if you were backward. Indeed there were one of two sadists who said: 'This will hurt me more than it will hurt you'. That was a myth. Still I should thank them. I became ambidextrous which was very useful in my working life. For half a day a week we went to Shelton Street School for woodwork lessons.

I think there were more things for children to do than now. There were Boy Scouts, Boys' Brigades, Bands of Hope run by the churches, boxing classes . . . I belonged to St Andrew's Boys' Brigade No 1. We used real rifles in the games room to shoot at proper targets. As the oldest member I was invited to the Centenary Dinner Dance. I was also in the Boy Scouts situated in Bullivant Street, Alfred Street South. Alfred Street, from Mansfield Road to Carlton Road, was the longest Street in Nottingham. The 15th troop was led by Stanley Hooley and his brother Leslie Hooley. Their firm, Hooley Motors are now one of the biggest car dealers in Nottingham.

'The photo is of two classes at St Andrew's School. We did sit close together but not like the sardines shown. Also there are two teachers present, and there are some pupils standing up. My schoolgirl sweetheart, Agnes Richardson, is not there. She was probably with me in Class Seven, which was a mixed class ready to leave school. She sat right in front of me. In this photo there are gas brackets hanging from the ceiling. Burt Johnson was once swinging on one like these when we went for woodwork lessons in Shelton Street School half a day a week. He was caught by the schoolmaster. Didn't he cop it with the strap soaked in glue to stiffen it!'

In camp, we used to take the light shutters and signal in morse code to each other from distant hills. I remember sitting on the kerb to watch the Royal Party go by.

I remember the trams going up Woodborough Road in the winter when the driver used to pump sand on the line for grip on the rails, his foot always stamping away. Also the food kitchen on Woodborough Road next to Mr Pearson's Clothing Shop. I used to queue with my brother for soup in the First World War. I think Mr Pearson was a councillor.

One of the places where boxing classes were held was the St Bernadette Booth. Micky Mee and I once went there. We sat watching billiards. A youth came up and said: 'What do you two want?' Daft Micky said: 'We go to Percy Dexter's'. That was on Alfred Street South. 'Right,' he said 'you come with me.' We went through a door to the boxing area. He said to Mick: 'You take your coat and shirt off'. Mick was put in the ring and bashed about. He said to me: 'You're next,' and I did a runner. But we went back afterwards and they were kind to us. The other Booth in St Ann's was on Union Road run by Jack Britton. I wonder if he was a relation of today's promoter Jack Britton?

At the Band of Hope at St Andrew's Church, we had the basement for athletics. The children today have nothing to do. Of course, they have vandalism and the mighty Pops. If only I could bring back some of my school pals and challenge the sixteen year olds today. We would slaughter them! We were brought up the hard way. Theirs is thousands of robots herded together waving their arms in the air listening to a loud noise, with musicians plucking the string of their instruments like monkeys de-fleaing their neighbours!

At that time there was a Co-op Bakery on Marple Street. Mick won't forget that, for that is where his father was burnt to death in the boiler house. I understand some hot cinders from the overhead belt fell on him. Of course we played on the streets: marbles, tin lurky, statues, rounders, tick and run and cigarette cards.

My school days sweetheart, Agnes Richardson, lived on Marple Street near Mr Pick's Grocery Store which was opposite a pub. I once called her a Zulu and she never spoke to me again. If she were still alive, I would go on my knees and apologise at last. Agnes and I used to take her granny to the Mechanics Picture House on Mansfield Road. Agnes used to read the words to her from the picture. In the meantime, granny would be nibbling at a black pudding, which she took every time she went. If the Picture House was busy, you had to sit behind a huge round column supporting the roof or in the last seat or two in the balcony where the figures on screen were just long streaks! The building must have been constructed for religious purposes. I wonder how much the outings cost granny?

The last time I saw Agnes was in a pub on Aspley Lane. I had been to a dance on my own. She, I guess, was with her husband. She did give me a smile, but I hadn't the gut to speak to them.

I can remember my brother taking me to the Robin Hood Picture Palace when I was about six. He took me by the hand down the full length of Peas Hill Road and it was near the bottom of Robin Hood Chase. There was a film called Majiste. He escaped from the villains by putting his feet on the wall one side and his hands the other side and walking upwards to escape the trap door to feed him to the crocodiles.

When I was working at Thackeray's Cotton Mill on Alfreton Road when I was fourteen, my brother Ernest was killed on his motorbike. He was nineteen. He worked at Campion Motor Cycle Works on Robin Hood Street, St Ann's. He was killed by hitting a plank of wood which was on a lorry backing out of Radcliffe Road. My parents never got a penny. What if that happened today? A year or so afterwards we left Conway Grove. I think we left because of his death. Bad luck house.

By the way, the girls at Thackeray's had a name for being naughty, but three of them came to the cemetery to see Ernest buried. One was Ethel who I courted a bit. We used to have a cuddle in the cotton frame alleys. In fact, at the dinner hour, I was put in charge of the frames to stop them when bobbins were full. I had rapid promotion and two near death experiences while dealing with machinery.

I used to go to the boiler house for grease to oil the spindles. The first time the boiler man said: 'Get out of here'. But when I showed him the grease can he said: 'Who uses the grease'. I told him I did. So he said come in but wipe your boots. Afterwards, he showed me the huge engine and the horizontal piston, which travelled quite a way. The spring clips were called travellers, clipped to the spindles driven by strings from a round cylinder. If I was not dodging, changing full bobbins for empties, my job was to re-string them while sitting on a stool with strings around my neck and a knife to cut the string after knotting it to the spindle.

At first I was ordered to do this when the frame stopped. Eventually I did it while in motion. It was dangerous when the cylinder was turning toward you. You had a hooked steel rod and the string had a weight, which you tied on, and dropped it over the cylinder catching it underneath with the cylinder turning towards you. If the cylinder was a bit brown by the heat and you were a bit slow . . . I had the weight whizzing by my head a time or two.

Once, on the ground floor, I was oiling the two wheels, which drove the cylinder for both sides of the frame. I was standing on top of the steel guard when my foot slipped and I fell on the belt travelling upwards, which threw me on the floor. What would have happened on the downward side of the belt?

I worked as a bricklayer and then at a Petrol Depot where I ended up as General Foreman. I started filling two gallon cans and then as a lorry boy for Carburine and Gligo on Carlton Road. We unloaded petrol from trains at Thorneywood Station. When a tanker truck was almost empty, we had to pump like mad to keep the suction. I was one side of a two-handle pump and my mate the other side. If suction stopped we could lose gallons of petrol. Even so we never emptied the tanker. The foreman used to go and use the tap on the tanker to drain it.

When the Colwick sidings took over the Petrol Depot, I became a lorry mate. It was a four ton Caledon lorry but we only took two gallon tins. The biggest tanked lorry took 400 gallons. My journeys with Jack Hopper would be a story in itself. Jack used to let me drive. I was only fifteen and a half. The foreman at the Petrol Station then was Claud Ridgard.

People should be interested in history.

FLORENCE RHODES

Born 1908

Interviewed in her home 5.5.99. All photos from Florence Rhodes

I was born on Manvers Street, Sneinton, but moved to St Ann's in 1908 or 1909. We moved into the Chase Tavern on St Ann's Well Road. They told me I first walked there.

My parents, Harry and Elizabeth Reeve, were always in public business. I was number six in the family, out of seven. One of my earliest memories in St Ann's was my brother being born three years later, and then going to St Ann's Church School. The teacher said: 'Is there anyone you know?' And I said yes and I said the girl's name. I found out years after it was only her nickname.

I remember Bobby Biddle at the Police Lodge. He loved children, but he wore a leather glove. If a child was misbehaving, he would give them a clout with the leather glove.

'That's my father in the Trilby hat, left of the woman in white. My mother has the tallest hat. Lottie, my sister, put the cross on: that's her. I'm on the cart with younger brother Bill, who was killed in the RAF in the Second World War. We used to decorate these carts and we'd go round the streets on Sunday and collect for the Children's Hospital. My father would organise this. It said 'decorated by the Coachmakers Arms'. All the family was there, and some others. I reckon this was 1919. I had one brother killed in the First World War. There's my sister-in-law on there and she went out to India to meet my other brother. Then they married. I reckon this photo was taken on the bottom of the Chase'

'That's how we used to do it about 1916. We didn't have a horse and cart. We had this chappie: he used to get all the little ones together and we used to pull this cart. But it was still collecting for the same thing. We used to go round the streets one Sunday morning. And can you see my hair bow drooped again. I was always the one with the droopy bow!'

Then we moved out to Cotgrave and then we came back to St Ann's. Dad had a beer-off, bottom of Bombay Street and I know we were there in 1916, then we went to Radcliffe, then back to St Ann's, and we had the Coachmakers Arms on the corner of St Ann's Well Road and Union Road.

This chappie, his name was Joe Lane, and he used to drive the big mail van. It was a van and horse and it didn't fit anywhere. Bamfords, the funeral people, used to have it in their stables and he used to fetch it out at 12 midnight every night to go to the Station to collect the mail. It was a huge mail van. Bamfords had their place on St Ann's Well Road. I don't know where he took the mail.

We went to Sycamore Road School. During the First World War, this school was a hospital. So we went to St Ann's Board School half-time. We went mornings one week and the St Ann's Board School children went in the afternoons. Then next week we changed over. Sycamore Road School had a swimming pool underneath. We all learned to swim in there.

'This is taken in the Sycamore School yard in 1921 just before I left. I'm sixth from the right in the back row plus droopy bow! Miss Windley is on the right of the photo and Mr Cotterill on the left'

I left school at the Christmas as I was 14 in the January. There was eleven years between me and the next one. They had all married and gone. I was an after-thought, so that made it that I'd got to work so I just did pub work, and housekeeping in the family. I hated it. Hard work. Scrubbing, cleaning, washing, cellar work.

Then we moved from there and went to a place, the Woolpack on Sussex Street. That's where the Broadmarsh Centre is now. Then I went into factory work in the hosiery business. I didn't like the machine part. When I got into the offices, it was better. They moved me around. I seemed to do that for the rest of my life.

I got married when I was twenty-two and a half in 1930. I was the one that got away from St Ann's. The whole family was all married, buried, christened, churched: all the lot in St Ann's. But I still always seemed to come back to St Ann's.

In the War years I went into a gun factory in the Meadows. I was on turning. I'd got a huge lathe and some castings fell over and crushed my feet. That's what's the matter with this [pointing at foot] now. It just didn't get right and now I've got trouble with it. The Orthopaedic bloke told me it's due to what happened then. During the War, I worked eleven and a half hour shifts. There wasn't enough room in the air-raid shelters if we were all caught at the change over, so there was always half an hour to get one shift away and the other one in. It was interesting work, but very heavy. I was only seven stone twelve. I enjoyed every minute of it.

On the turning lathe, we would do anything to do with big guns. It was called a Herbert Nine Turret I think. There were three of us and one man. He was what they called a Setter. He set the thing up and you did the work. He said do it like this and you did it like that and it was like a knitting pattern. You'd have that, and then you'd bring another drill around that did something else, and, oh I says I can't reach that when they showed it to me. They built me a board to stand on. It was very interesting.

I've often thought, when did I do my shopping? It's a complete blank. But I must have gone somewhere to get me rations.

After the War, I went to Chilwell Ordnance and stayed there till I retired. I was on machine accounting. I did a little computer work. They wanted me to go away and train on computer work. I said I only had another two years and didn't think it fair to spend on training me when it could be a young person training that's going to have a lifetime. So I went on to clerical work until I retired.

My husband was a motor engineer. He worked in West Bridgford, so after we got married we got a house in Bridgford. My husband worked for the Ministry of Defence in the Second World War. He was in a reserved occupation. I left Bridgford in 1947. I didn't have children. I don't want to talk about my husband. We were together eighteen years.

For a little while, I went to live with a niece of mine in Sherwood and then a cousin had died in St Ann's and I wondered if I could get her house. So I nipped smartly down to the house agents on Abbotsford Street at the back of the Chase.

There was a row, they called them the Cottages and they were originally built for the servants in the Chase and they were lovely little houses. Pity they were pulled down. They could have been converted. I came back about 1956. And I loved it. Then, of course, it all had to come down. I retired in 1968. I wanted to stay in St Ann's but I was Phase One [of the Council's demolition plan] so everybody had to get out. After that, when they rebuilt, people could move in but Phase One people was out. They gave me a flat at Hyson Green. Oh, it was dreadful.

They've pulled Hyson Green flats down now. Finally the lady from the [City Council] housing came to see me, and I said I want to go back to St Ann's. So she said: 'Well would you like to go into Marmion Court?' So I says no, I'm not going to go into one of these old people's homes. I says I want a proper flat. She says: 'They're warden aided'. Finally they didn't call it Marmion Court, they called it Ogdon Court.

So I came to have a look and couldn't find it. It was only a little bit off the ground! I had to go to the Police Station on St Ann's Well Road to find out where it was. They'd been told down at the housing that it was finished. I came back every week to see how it was growing and I came here when I was sixty-seven.

[The flat has a pleasant hall, roomy sitting room with archway to the kitchen with door to the hall, a walk in airing cupboard, bedroom, box storeroom and good size bathroom.]

I like it here. I have a job with the stairs now but I don't want to go downstairs. The thought of moving gives me the wim-wams. I live from day to day and if anybody sees the door open, its liberty hall! If the door's closed, it's mine.

Folks bring me their wool and I crochet. I do lap rugs, I sent half a dozen to the Hospice on Woodborough Road at Christmas. I used to do squares but I hated sewing them together. So I thought I'd do it this way [Mrs Rhodes' crochet work and use of colour combination is beautiful].

Up to a few years ago, I used to travel quite a lot. I love holidays and seeing people and places. A friend who retired at the same time, we were very compatible for holidays and we used to go off for a month somewhere. I've been all over Europe, been as far as Australia, I've not been to America and I don't want to. I've been all along the North African coast, Holy Land, Greece, you name it, I've been there.

A lady I worked with said she was going to Australia, one of these family things and she said we've got some vacancies. My nephew had just gone there after he came out of the Fleet Air Arm. He said come out and if you like it you can go home, sell up and come back and be my housekeeper. I went to Perth. My friend went on to New Zealand then I met her coming back and we came back in 1970. We stayed three months.

I went abroad when I was working. I had a passport in 1932 and it ran out in 1992. I kept it up-to-date all those years.

With dad and mother working in the business, Lottie more or less brought me and my younger brother - the after-thoughts - up.

'This is my sister, my eldest sister, Lottie's wedding. There's me with the droopy bow! That was taken in the backyard of the Coachmakers Arms in 1922 I reckon. She made all the dresses. She was ever so clever and a very hard worker'

Lottie was a family name we've found out. We've just had a new baby in the family, a niece, Alice, that's just had a grandaughter. She's called Charlotte. And she's number five or six in the family with that name. But she was christened Lottie.

I'm the only one of the family that lives in St Ann's now. I'm also the last of my age level, all the rest are in their seventies.

There are twenty-four flats at Ogdon Court plus the Warden's flat. That's Sue Edwards.

Everything in my flat is mine. You do your own shopping. You live your own life. You can join in anything that Sue's doing like Bingo or a concert. She puts a dinner on Tuesdays, it's the only day she does. You can go if you wish. We have a Christmas Fayre, new cakes and things like that. They queue to get in and within an hour we've perhaps made £400. We don't have jumble sales. With the funds we raise, we have our outings. Last week, they went to Peterborough Cathedral and next week Lincoln. I can't walk far enough now. Sometimes we have a little morning thing, like a run into the country and stay at some pub for lunch and then come home for tea. I can manage that. Maybe a film show in winter.

Sue's been here seven or eight years after our previous warden died. Sue is so full of life.

She pops by every day. The Library man is coming any time now: from St Ann's Library. We have a chiropodist, optician, dentist and doctor if we wish them to come in.

I remember the Chettle's. Cecil (Cis) Chettle, the original Chettle, was a great friend of my brother that was the barber on St Ann's Well Road, George Reeve.

When Cis died his son Norman took over the [dental] business. Now the last time I'd seen him they'd moved into the new premises. In his waiting room, he'd got these two pictures. One of St Ann's Church and one of the

surgery which he'd just left because both were going to be pulled down. He says I thought we ought to have something left. The old surgery facing the Church was on the Fothergill style, it was a beautiful house [no photograph of this house has been found so far]. Oh, so you are going to see Norman Chettle, please remember me to him won't you. He always used to call me Auntie 'cause he played with my brother George's lads and they said Auntie so he said Auntie.

George, my brother who was the barber, lived in St Ann's all his life. Dad bought him his business in 1912 and he had it until it was pulled down in the 1970s. He worked on until he was real elderly. They [the City Council] put him in a flat somewhere, Bestwood I think. He died. He was too ill to bother.

For us in Phase One: there was a bit of disgruntlement. They didn't want to move out of the area but they'd got to and they [the Council] put them in various places.

Rent day. Florence Rhodes and rent collector at Ogdon Court

90th Birthday celebration at Ogdon Court. 'My friend made the cake. The flowers were for another ninety year old who died a few days earlier but they were added to my picture'

In 1999, **Cyril Trout** who was born in 1909, told me that he remembered when the circular Nottingham Suburban Railway - Nottingham Victoria Station, Thorneywood, St Ann's, Sherwood, Victoria - had a 'courting couple special' on Sundays: 6.00pm train in St Ann's Station.

There was subsidence some twenty years ago where he lived in Dowson Street and the Coal Board said they could not do any effective repairs for five years because: "We were above where they were now digging. Subsidence stopped at our street.

"You can still hear the culverted River Beck through the covers on parts of St Ann's Well Road. It drains all the land around St Ann's Well Road to Beck Street and comes out into the River Trent at Trent Street."

———

Around the 1930s, St Ann's characters remembered included Mrs Mee, chimney sweep of Dixon Street; a rag and bone woman at the bottom of St Ann's Well Road; 'a cripple chap' about sixty who had a three-wheeled barrow and sold soap and wash powder (c1938) and a Police Inspector called Black Prince who had a cane and was very strict if you were standing in a shop corner.

———

ELDEST AND YOUNGEST BROTHERS

RICHARD [REG] BEAL

Born 1911

Interviewed in his home, 8.6.99, and other conversations

I was born at 30, Westgate Street, St Ann's, the eldest of eight, three boys and five girls. My youngest brother, Arthur, is twenty years younger than me. My mother and father were William and Ellen Beal. She came from Old Basford and he from St Ann's.

With having a large family, I lived with my grandparents at 30, Westgate Street, when my parents moved to 2, St Bartholomew's Road. There, they had trouble with water. Water used to flood their cellars and they had gas meters there. They had to get on a dolly tub and float to the meter. So they moved to Norland Road until 38, Westgate Street became vacant and then the whole family moved together. My grandparents moved from 30, Westgate Street, and my mother and father from Norland Road: all to 38, Westgate Street.

Then, there were no buildings above Westgate Street. There were six or seven houses on a short street, Central Avenue, and beyond that was fields known as the flower show. It was the same across the way before the Boys' Brigade and the Council houses were built there. All there was at the bottom there was a placard where they used to advertise, and there was a Boots the Chemist there.

Arthur Hawksley's mother and father had a shop at the bottom of Westminster Street. Richard Keetch's father, also called Richard, was a haulage contractor with horses and carts. When we used to go from school, we used to go into this stables and sit there and eat the carrots. It was very cold one day and Dick (as we called him) got some straw and lit a fire. It got on to the bales of straw at the back of us where we used to sit. So we ran out. I went home. My father came home at lunchtime and said Keetch's is on fire. At the bottom of St Bartholomew's Road there was a Police Station and a Fire Station. The fire tender was horse drawn. There was not a lot of damage. They got it under control. There were no horses in the stables which was a good job.

I belonged to No 6 Boys' Brigade with my brother Joe. The Captain in charge was Les Palmer. I used to go and visit my parents at 2, St Bartholomew's Road. Around the corner the Palmer's had a fruit and grocery shop all combined. Charlie was Les and Mabel Palmer's eldest, then came Mabel, then Les. Next door to them was a Mr Marshall. I wasn't very old and I used to be frightened of him as he used to stand there in his apron.

Arthur used to belong to the 20th Nottingham Boys' Brigade which was on Northampton Street. When I was in Boys' Brigade Nottingham 6th, we used to meet outside a place on Coppice Road. It was called the [Canon Lewis] Memorial Hall. In there, they had a billiards and snooker table. And we went to a place up Edwin Street. There was gymnastics and everything there.

We would meet about twice a week. And then on Sunday we used to parade on Coppice Road and march with a bugle band down to St Ann's Church. We used to turn up Corporation Road and then file in to Church. We did the same on the way back.

At the time I was born, my father worked for the *Evening Post* and he used to deliver papers from Forman Street. He used to take them to the Midland Station and Victoria Station. He used to go about six or seven times. I remember his horse was called Dolly.

He did that till he got another job with dyers. I think it was better money. Then at night he used to work at the Westminster Abbey Hotel.

Mum didn't work outside the home. She had too much on. She occasionally did lace work at home. We had to help mother, perhaps turn the mangle for her. Woe betide if you didn't do your job because we used to get tuppence every week spending money. My dad used to come home on Saturday and he'd say: 'Now then, have we had any trouble during the week?' And if she said: 'Yes, I had some'. She used to call it chelp. We were reduced a penny.

Facing our house at the top of the yard was a coal place. We didn't have a place near the house. Us kids round about used to put cinema shows on with magic lanterns and things. We'd charge halfpenny to have a look at the show. There were about seven in the coal place one day and my mother came for some coal and says: 'OUTSIDE!' We had some lovely times during our young days.

Once, we came out of the Robin Hood Cinema, near The Chase, with bows and arrows. I shot an arrow and caused a puncture in a grocery delivery bicycle. There were groceries all over the place then.

People did lots of things for poor children. A gentleman called Seely Whitby held a party every year at the River Trent Pleasure Park. It was through Pearson's Fresh Air

Fund, a charity for poor children. We used to have potted meat sandwiches, cakes and ice cream: a real treat if you were lucky enough to get a ticket.

There was a girl called Gladys Lane, about twelve or thirteen. I was around six or seven. There were several of us that used to play, and she took us down to the Pleasure Park on the Trent. We used to sit and watch the boats. Coming back one or two of the young ones started to cry. She said: 'I can't carry you'. So she says: 'Come on, we'll get on the tram'. We got on the No 4. There was about seven all in a row. Seats were different then. You were facing each other. When the conductor come along, she says: 'One half please'. He says: 'Nay, I can't have this, you will get me the sack. You will have to get off at the next stop'.

It wasn't laughable at the time because we still had to walk so far with these young ones. Who could carry, did. We used to get to the [Victoria] Baths clock and then walk up Blue Bell Hill. We had some lovely times. School's a long time ago. We moved from the Board School to Morley School.

There was George Gunn and next door to him up Westminster Street was Cyril Stapleton, the violinist who eventually worked for the BBC. Westminster Street and Lotus Street were noted for bonfires.

Board School was a lovely school. There was Miss Newton and Mr Reynolds, he was the Headmaster. There was Mr Lindop, Mr Allen, Mr Newington . . . now the lads were a bit crafty with Mr Newington because when it was poetry we had a lovely afternoon. He used to love to read the poems and tell you stories about them. We used to keep him at it: 'What happened then, sir?' It was a good school. It was very strict. Miss Newton was a teacher. When we were having dictation, she would walk up and down the rows and woe betide if you lifted your head. She would rattle a ruler. She never gave you the strap, she used to send you next door to Mr Allen if you had been bad.

Aye, I did get the strap. One day, three of us decided to go to the races at Colwick instead of going to school. Teachers sent word to our homes to see where we were. That evening, mother never let on. Next morning at school, there were three strokes on each hand from our teacher and then three on each hand from the Headmaster. It never killed us. Look at me now, nearly eighty-nine. I believe in this punishment when you're young. I don't mean violent punishment.

At school, I was best at mathematics. I left at fourteen. Mr Williams was a keen cricketer and knew my dad because he worked at the Westminster Abbey pub. My dad said he had a lad looking for work and Mr Williams said: 'Send him up'.

So, I went to Steven and William's Lace Machine Builders, on The Wells Road. When I used to get in, I mashed the tea and took the cans round to everyone there. Then they put me on to the lathes, the drilling machine which was big lathes. You used to clamp them down and drill holes right through. Hundreds of holes and these used to fix on to the lace machine for the cotton to go through. That was all right but my mother used to moan about me

coming home smelling of oil. She said: 'I've got you another job'. By the way, I only got eight shillings a week, from eight o'clock in the morning and until one o'clock and then two o'clock until half past five every weekday. Saturday eight until twelve o'clock. Eight shillings a week! I kept sixpence out of that.

When I moved to Meadow Dairy, I got ten shillings and I got one shilling for myself. I was fifteen when I went there. I was an errand lad. There used to be the Manager, the first hand, then the chap who had been the errand lad had moved on to the counter and I used to do the errands. I was good at figures. We used to reckon things up in our head, three pence halfpenny and farthings even. Now with only three items, and the girls put it down on paper!

We used to have some laughs. But it was hard work. We used to knock our own butter up and margarine. We had to do bags of sugar, bags of rice, everything used to be weighed on the premises. I wasn't long as errand lad because I was quick at reckoning up. We used to have a woman come in. I think she lived on Meredith Street. She was a big woman. She had a brooch on and it said dragon on this brooch. Of course, we used to know her as dragon, not Mrs Smith. We'd say: 'Watch out, it's dragon coming!'

The Meadow Dairy was facing Beverley Street. And of course at the bottom of Beverley Street was the pawn shop. On Monday, there would be a queue taking pawn.

Jack Redfin was a bit of a comic Manager. When Mrs Smith came in, she wouldn't have any bits and bobs. When cutting corn-beef or ham you had to use your common sense and put some little bits in. One chap had come from another shop to relieve someone on holiday and after Mrs Smith had been in he said: 'I've got rid of the bits'. Mr Redfin says 'all of it?' And he says 'aye'. Redfin says to me: 'Why didn't you tell him?'

She was back in a few minutes. She played hell. She was a very strict woman. Her husband was a very little chap and she used to say 'watch for my old man coming by would you, I'm not going to carry these while he's an able-bodied man'. She used to make him carry the things. One day she came in with a pair of boots fetched from the pawn shop. She says to her husband: 'Come here I want you'. She put a biscuit tin on the floor for him to sit on and she says 'try these boots'. He didn't want them but he got them!

Meadow Dairy was a big firm, actually it was Allied Supplies. It was Maypole, Home and Colonial, Meadow Dairy and Sherries. I used to do holiday relief at different shops. I worked at Lipton's, then Meadow Dairy at Wheeler Gate, then I went to Shirebrook and I went to Alfreton.

Meadow Dairy were crafty. They stopped those available to be called up and put women in their places, so I got stopped. I got a job at Beeston with Mr Clarke, a grocer. I was Manager and Mr Clarke used to go round and get orders. He used to do a lot with the military people.

Dad was very strict. My sisters liked dancing and had to be in by eleven o'clock. If they weren't, he'd lock up and go to bed. I crawled downstairs to let them in!

I was called up in 1941 and I went to the Royal Air Force. I went to South Cerney, Cirencester, a flying training

St Ann's Nottingham inner-city voices by Ruth Johns • ISBN 0951696092

school where they had air speed Oxfords. From there I went to Scampton, that was Bomber Command, then to Dunholme Lodge and then to Firsby. I was in the Safety Section, dealing with Mae West parachutes, harnesses, tailor suits . . .

There was WRAFs as well. When OPS were on, we were next to the briefing room. They used to come out and pick things like parachutes up. We'd pack them. There used to be the doctor there to see if anyone wanted aspirins or were not well enough to fly and the Padre. I used to see a lot of terrible things. I can remember once when about sixty-two planes left Firsby and we only got about five or six back.

One of the remarkable things was that next day, there was stuff coming in quickly, new parachutes . . . there were women pilots bringing in Lancasters to the 'drome on their own. About seven Lancasters would come in at one time. Then the women got into a Hanson aircraft and went back wherever they came from.

When you had been on nights, you could go out and do farming. I used to go and help Frank Copeland stack the corn up, turning peas, anything like that. When you'd finished, I used to get a good meal. Out would come the ham and eggs. I enjoyed that. There was one airman, a Mr Sparrow, he was a London policeman in civvy street. One of the gunners said to me 'his wife's just had a baby. When we come back off the OPS, we've got leave. Do you think you could get him a chicken?' And I says aye I think so. Frank Copeland said of course and his wife dressed the chicken and I took it to him. Then he got killed, oh dear. They had been over and done the job and he got killed over the 'drome when a Lancaster from East Kirby and one of ours crashed.

I came out May 1946 and got a job at Boots at Island Street. Of course it's all been knocked down now. I worked in maintenance, doing plumbing. I worked for Denis Topliss. I didn't know anything about plumbing then, so I was a plumber's labourer to start with. There were about seven plumbers because there was a lot of work on because of the bombing.

The biggest mistake I ever made was to leave Boots after thirteen years and take over a shoe shop after an uncle who ran it died. My aunt was used to going to the till and going into market everyday. I had to make my money count.

My brother Joe worked at the Robin Hood Cinema in St Ann's as an operator. In those days, you could get carbon poisoning from that job and you were supposed to drink a lot of milk to help prevent this. He got carbon poisoned and died. But it was a long time later. He worked at the Gaumont Cinema, the Odeon and the Empress and finished at the Regal at Langley Mill. That's where he died.

I got married at twenty-three to Emily Breakspear and we lived at Lenton Abbey. She was born in Yorkshire. Her father was killed in the First World War. Her mother had four children and lived hand to mouth like we did when we were young. She came to Nottingham, remarried and lived on Dowson Street, off Blue Bell Hill. We were married at St Bartholomew's Church, St Ann's. That's pulled down now.

We would work a whole year for one week's holiday. One year, we went to Austria on a bus sleeping through the night for our holiday. She said next time, we'd do it by plane!

We had two children. A grandson is a vet in Frome. My grandaughter is a doctor. Her husband's a surgeon. We have great grandchildren. We've had our diamond wedding.

I've been connected to the British Legion since I came out of the Forces.

[A certificate states: 'This certificate is presented to Richard (Reg) Beal, Service Committee of the Mapperley Branch, British Legion. Though this may appear to be just another piece of paper, the award recognises the tremendous amount of good work which few people would undertake, and endorses the feeling of many to whom RRB became case members. Members of the Branch are proud and privileged to associate with you and the successes you have achieved.']

I got the gold badge, the highest award. I'm President Chairman. People don't realise how much work the British Legion does. This Branch covers St Ann's and Mapperley. There are a lot of ex-servicemen in both. Yesterday, I visited a man with no legs. He needs to go in a convalescent home at Skegness and his wife has got to go with him. There are a lot of people to visit. Everyone is a volunteer. We need more people to collect for the British Legion.

Richard [Reg] and Emily Beal

My wife has done a lot for the British Legion. I'll show you her certificate for twenty-five years' service. *['The Royal British Legion Poppy Appeal, 28th September, 1989 Certificate of Appreciation to Mrs Emily Beal in grateful recognition of distinguished voluntary effort on behalf of the Poppy Appeal. Upon such service fully and freely given, the success of the annual appeal depends.']*

Reg Beal later said his darling wife died May 23rd 2001. They were married for sixty-six years. The Mapperley Branch of the Royal British Legion has now closed and he is a member of the City Branch

ARTHUR BEAL

Born 1930

Interviewed in his home, 23.6.99, and other conversations

I was the youngest of nine children. The oldest is Reg who you've met, then Joe, May, Mary, Gladys, Francis, Hilda, then another baby, Connie, who died of whooping cough when she was a few months old. We lived at 38, Westgate Street, St Ann's. Times were a bit rough but we were a close family. There wasn't much money and you had to make do, but as kids we were always playing. We enjoyed ourselves. For forty-three years, my father, William Beal, was a bar and cellar man at the Westminster Abbey, St Ann's Well Road. Then he worked for Boots at Island Street.

I started at St Ann's Church School. In the War, we only had about three hours school and came home. There was another group in the afternoon. Then I went to the Board School and then to Morley School.

At the Board School, we had a teacher called Whittaker. He'd been in the 1914-18 War. We used to get him talking about the War, so we didn't get sums and writing. Eventually he cottoned on to what we were doing! He was very fond of the strap in those days.

I had the strap quite a few times, mostly for talking. There were some evacuees from London. I was talking to these evacuees asking them what it was like with bombs dropping. The teacher caught us talking and he thought it was the other lad, fetched him out and strapped him. It was my fault really for starting it. We became big friends. There were quite a few evacuees in Dickinson Street, some with their parents and others in digs.

Then I was evacuated to Lowdham to a place facing the Borstal. The people lived in a railway carriage on a plot of land. Me and another lad called Eric Marriott lived in the caravan at the side. Before we moved in they had chickens in the caravan. The first morning when we woke up, there were chickens trying to get back in! Then the other lad went to Burton Joyce because his parents didn't like him staying in a caravan. I carried on for a bit then went back home.

Most of the houses had outside shared toilets and a tin bath kept in the yard. Ours was a more modern house and had an inside bathroom and toilet. That room was added on. The awkward thing about being a large family was that there was always someone in the bath. So we had an arrangement with an auntie who lived on the opposite side of the street, to run across there if we wanted to go to the toilet.

Five times out of ten, you rushed out, crossed the road and there was somebody already in there. Then you were really desperate, and rushed down the hill to the public toilets at the bottom of Robin Hood Chase.

There were tar blocks laid as a road surface in some streets. When there was a coal shortage, people used them as fuel. All the washing was black then! It taught them to lay cobbles on roads.

We used to play out a lot, and quite late. You were supposed to be in for nine. If the police saw you out at that time they'd tell you off and told you to go home to bed, which they don't do now. Up the road from where we lived, there was quite a big field. We used to call it the flower show and they used to break in horses on there.

We played tin lurky. You could kick a tin down the hill and then somebody had to bring it back to that spot. We used to put a circle round that spot. All the kids used to run and hide. If the person bringing the tin back saw them he'd say one, two, three and he'd say go and sit near the tin. While he was looking for somebody else, if someone kicked the tin the others were released and ran to hide.

And there was Ducks Off. You used to have six bricks made up and a big stone ('duck') on the top. There would be seven or eight used to play, and used to have one throw to try to knock the bricks down with the 'duck' on top. And if you did, the lad at the side used to stack the bricks up and put his duck on top and he's got to dobb somebody before he gets back to the line. And if nobody knocks them down, then he used to do a kind of forfeit. And he used to say 'right, knock my duck off the top'. You had to knock it off without knocking the bricks off. We were that skilled at doing it, playing it every day. Sometimes we'd knock it straight off the top or perhaps with my 'duck' on one of your feet. There were hundreds of games.

The girls used to skip and there'd be songs with the skipping. My wife still does this skipping now.

When I was twelve, I went to camp with the Boys' Brigade. It was twelve shillings for the week at Papplewick (aged thirteen), and then next year at Chapel St Leonards. I was in the 20th Nottingham Boys' Brigade. At Chapel St Leonards the day ended with the singing of: 'The day thou gavest Lord is ended'. That was about 1942. A chap gave each of us sixty lads two shillings because he was so moved by our singing. They were going another time to North Wales but it was too expensive and I didn't go.

My sister Hilda was evacuated longer with some people who were very old fashioned and religious. When she used to come home at the weekend, she'd got one of these fur capes like older women used to have, and I laughed at her.

I went to Morley School. Teachers at Morley School were very strict, always strapping you. There was Mr Henson the Head Teacher, then a Mr Butler, Mr Cragg, Miss Owen and a Miss Twe, an unusual name. She used to do needlework with us. Then Mr Jackson was very fond of the strap on both hands when you misbehaved. Even some of the women teachers gave you the strap. Miss Redmile did. Miss Harrison the Art teacher used to get Mr Jackson to do the strapping for her.

But I think I learnt more away from school than what I did at school because it was so rough at times. I liked art. I thought I'd like woodwork but the teacher was very nasty and I used to hate going into that class. Now I really love woodwork, I'm always doing things. If I'd had a nice teacher at that time, I think I would have got a bit further.

St Ann's Multiracial Inner City Voices by Ruth I Johns · ISBN 0951696092

I was always running errands for my mother. She was called Ellen (nee Singleton). I still do the shopping now. All the meters used to be emptied by a chap who used to have a bag, like a Gladstone bag, on his shoulder. To me it was like a work of art the way he rolled the pennies up. He had a brown piece of paper and he brought all the pennies together and made them into rolls, stacked them and put them in his bag. All the kids used to run home when the gasman came because they'd think 'we've got a penny coming here!' Yes, we used to get a penny.

We used to get pennies for taking empty bottles back. There was a beer-off at the bottom of Dickinson Street where all their empty bottles were stacked in the backyard. We often used to climb over the wall and take him his own empty bottles back! Until he cottoned on to us. But that's nothing to the days we now live in.

We used to go scrumping at the back of Coppice Rec. I got shot at on the Rec. We used to climb steps and go down the slide. We used to say: ' Run sticky bummy here I come' when we came down. I don't know where that comes from. When at the top of the slide we used to pretend to be shot. I actually was. I felt a numb pain in my head and I thought 'crikey'. Apparently it was a lad with a pellet gun fired at me as I was coming down. My sisters thought I was mucking about and then they saw the blood.

My dad took me to the General Hospital. My mother was out at the time and saw an ambulance and said to my sister: 'Oh look that poor soul at Christmas time'. And it was me!

I made a bike by finding bits and pieces. It was all home made. Then I painted it. It was my pride and joy. People used trams and the Pleasure Park at the side of the River Trent for outings.

I started work at fourteen. A week's wages were twelve shillings and six pence. My Londoner friend got a job at the Institute for the Blind on Chaucer Street and he said he'd get me a job there. I went as driver's mate. It was mostly stacking a lot of the canes. I was there about a year.

Pub entertainment was good in St Ann's. They had pianos and they brought singers in, sometimes ones who appeared at the Empire in the City Centre. There was a flower show every year. You could buy puppies at the flower show. There was a chap there who would bite off a puppy's tail if you wanted it docked. He'd then wrap the tail end with a cloth.

You could get a good meal at Clarke's Fish and Chip Shop and Supper Room, opposite the bottom of Southampton Street. It was one shilling and one penny for fish, chips, peas, bread and tea. He brought sticks of rock back from holiday for the local kids.

I've had loads of jobs, lorry driver's mate, painters and decorator's mate, I was down the pits and I've driven a dumper on building sites. I finished up at Boots for twenty-six years. I was down Gedling Pit about nine years. I did my training at Bestwood Pit. I worked on the screes on the top, then underground on haulage working with the ponies. Then packing, working behind the colliers, and then I went on the coalface. When you started at the coalface you would do three yards and then help the collier; then you'd do six yards and then help the collier, and then you would do nine yards on your own (nine yards was called a stint). After nine yards you're whacked. You would be really tired and sleep in the bus back. Coal seams could be 4'6" thick. The foreman was Tommy Fox. He was 18-stone and 6'3". He could pick up a tub of coal single-handed. It would take three of us.

And you used to think to yourself: 'Crikey, I've got all that again tomorrow'. It was very hard work. Skills buses used to run from the bottom of Northampton Street in St Ann's to Gedling Pit but most of the time I would bike it. It could be very foggy. There were shifts, mornings, afternoons and nights. Nights was when they'd move the conveyor belt and the packers used to go on at night.

There was a lot of poverty around those streets at that time in St Ann's. Some of the houses did want pulling down, but some were very good. It was heartbreaking to see it all go. My father died at Westgate Street. My mother got a little bungalow at Clifton.

Miners used to get a free coal allowance every other month. I was still living at home so my parents got the benefit. You were left a ton of coal outside your home every month. If you wanted it bagged, you paid a bit. If your coal allowance was too much for you, you could sell it back to the Coal Board for £2 a ton.

Arthur Beal with his mother at home in St Ann's

A coloured man lost his knee in the mine in 1950. Accidents were often not reported. There was a high accident rate. The pit bottom was supposed to be sprayed with water but the spray was often not working and there was dust everywhere.

I nearly had a bad accident. A bar bent and a collier pushed me out of the way. I nearly got buried twice at work and when I was getting married, I thought I'd pack it in. I got married to Joan King at St Ann's Church in 1955. Gedling Pit closed in 1986.

We got engaged and it was a five-year waiting list for a Council house at Clifton and we waited quite a few years. We started off with my parents. I'll never forget, we went to the pictures one night and we were near the Guildhall. I said: 'I think our house is about due'. She said it would be a while yet. But I nipped in and the chap at the desk asked me my name and then said I should be getting a letter tomorrow. So we moved to Clifton.

I have two daughters, Sharon who is a teacher at a school in Mapperley, and Lesley who's training to be a nurse.

When I married and got a family, then we started going to different places. We had a touring caravan. Then we exchanged it for a 22' bigger one that we kept at Chapel St Leonards. We liked it down there but the rent kept going up and up so we packed it in and we started going abroad quite a bit, from about 1965. The rent for the caravan would be over a £1,000 p.a. now. I used to let it out but I wasn't very happy with that because there is always somebody who leaves it in a bad state. When you sold, you had to sell to the site owners. I didn't get a proper price for it.

Abroad, we went to Austria, Spain, Russia. It was still a Communist state but I've always liked Russian music. I play the accordion. Moscow was like the 1940s over here, everyone in uniform. You remember when it was the American's, the Polish Air Force and our soldiers all in uniform.

The rooms weren't very big in the house in Clifton and no way could I have got a piano in, but an accordion is handy.

I was about fifty when I learnt computer skills. I often look back and think when I was on the coalface with my shirt off sweating like I don't know what, if somebody had said I'd be working with computers, I'd have said 'what's a computer?'

Boots taught me the basics but the rest I picked up myself. I organised the delivery fleet, tracing the trailers and ordering drivers . . . Mistakes could happen. For example, a driver delivering to Cardiff might nip off and when he returned think the trailer was unloaded and bring it back full! I was working mostly nights.

Now I'm retired. I've got a nice bit of garden out there. I do the vegetables and the lawn and my wife the flowers. I've been in Arnold thirty-five years now, not all in this house. I like doing painting, art, woodwork. I've just made a doll's house. Well it's not a house, it's a Co-op shop. It's a copy of an old Co-op shop and it's going to have lights in. I've got two grandchildren.

I think childhood was happier in a way when I was a child. There were so many things to do. Even during the War when they built four air-raid shelters in the nearby field, we used to have sing-songs in them and serve cocoa or tea. And if there was an air-raid at night you didn't have to go to school next morning. And in the morning, you'd be looking around for shrapnel from bombs. There were a lot of comics to read and we used to play cards. Each cigarette packet came with a card and there used to be quite a few games with those.

ERIC

Born 1914

Interviewed in his home 29.6.99

I was born at 22, Lotus Street, St Ann's, just at the beginning of the First World War. I was the younger of two boys. My brother, Cyril, was nine years older than me. He died 20 years ago. He went to the school attached to St Ann's Church. When he left he went to work for Raleigh. When it came to me, I went to the posh school on Sycamore Road in the building which is now the Afro-Caribbean Centre.

My father, Harold, came from Garibaldi Terrace, Alfred Street Central, St Ann's. He was one of six boys and one girl. Four of the boys were footballers. My father played for Forest Wanderers on the Forest, one played for Nottingham Forest, one for Notts County and I don't know who the fourth played for. My grandfather came from Birmingham and was a wheelwright.

My father was a gas fitter. He started as a plumber and worked with Sir Albert Ball for a long time. Then he went to the Nottingham Gas Corporation on the corner of Huntingdon Street and Woodborough Road.

My mum came from Stonehouse in Gloucestershire. She was one of six. I've never found out where her father was born but her mother was born at Holland's Yard off Glasshouse Street, Nottingham. My mum went out scrubbing houses. One of them was at Milner Road, Sherwood. The man of the house was a perambulator manufacturer at Basford. She had to go out because my father went down with an illness when I was about seven. Eventually he lost the use of his legs.

They hadn't got medical facilities in those days and it was hit and miss. They said he had rheumatism but it wasn't. He died in the City Hospital when I was sixteen. We didn't have an easy life.

I can still remember my mother taking me to school for the first time and leaving me at the gate. It was a big shock. I was never brilliant on the maths side and a poor scholar at English. Now my grandaughter, she's the tops in English. I enjoyed sports. I went on to Morley School at the age of eleven. And I met up with Cyril Stapleton there. He lived on Westminster Street. At Morley, I was good at running.

When Cyril was about twelve, the Headmaster asked him to form his own little band at school and he did. Nottingham Corporation sent him to Czechoslovakia for about a month to develop his talent. He was brilliant all right. It comes out however poor you are. His father was a plasterer.

Our house had three bedrooms, two rooms downstairs and a scullery, a toilet inside and an outhouse.

I belonged to Boys' Brigade No 6 at St Ann's Church. My father was a staff sergeant there. It had a very good band and won numerous prizes. I was never in the band. I was never in the boxing team because I didn't like boxing. Parades to Church every first Sunday of the month.

Most parents made their children go to Sunday school in the afternoon and we had Bible classes. We had little concerts and put on the odd concert on a Saturday night, things like that. Outside, we used to swing around gas lamps and played all the tricks kids did then.

My father belonged to St Ann's Church, but my mother was Caretaker of the Hungerhill Road Baptist Mission, so of course I had to go to the Baptist Chapel. There were lots of Baptists in Nottingham, including Marsdens the big grocery people. He had five or six big grocery stores around Nottingham, including three in St Ann's, on Union Road, St Ann's Well Road and Woodborough Road. He also had a big bakery on Union Road and he gave quite a lot of money to this Chapel.

Mr Coombes from the Woodborough Road Baptist Mission produced Coombes Self-Raising Flour. We used to call him Father Coombes but he was just an ordinary Baptist chaplain. The other big Baptist who used to come was Mr Whatmough. Do you remember Whatmough the sweet people? He used to have a little factory in Paddock Street, where the Broadmarsh Centre is now. He used to bring a bag of sweets for the kids.

There was a shop at the bottom of Lotus Street, a tobacconist shop, all pipe tobacco and cigarette tobacco. Then Mr Fox who ran it started brewing beer in old stone bottles. This became quite popular and then he started brewing ginger beer, one penny a bottle. If you had a penny, then you came out of school steaming and were in there like a shot for a bottle of pop.

We were lucky if we had a joint on Sunday, because my father was a cripple. There was no State pension. The only money that came in for him was a sort of pension. I used to have to go to a place on Parliament Street, where the Elite Cinema was. It was called the National Deposit. If you were sick, they paid out monies through these different insurance companies. I would go and fetch nine shillings a week from there in my lunch-time on Thursdays. On Monday morning, the rent man wanted seven shillings and eight pence, so if mother hadn't been working we were struggling.

We had a local landlord but the house was in an agent's hands. The landlord was Hanbury's the decorators on St Ann's Well Road. They had a very small place but there were four or five people working for them. They were actually in Commercial Square where the bank was, the butchers, the pub, the Church, Boots the Chemist and F W Farnsworth (which became Pork Farms).

Lots of people let out houses but, of course, as kids we never took any notice. There was Bavin who owned quite a lot. A few on Robin Hood Chase, like the Hopewell family who started the furniture business, owned their house. I never knew the father but I knew two of the sons, Eric and Claude. The firm started on Alfred Street and then moved to St Ann's Well Road and they built it to what it is today [branches on Huntingdon Street on the edge of St Ann's, and in Derby]. John, Eric's son, is at the top of it now. I didn't go to school with Eric. He was just that bit older than me. But I knew him through traipsing up and down St Ann's Well Road so many times. That piece of furniture over there [pointing] belonged to him, it came out of his house.

Eventually, I joined a gentleman's club on Goldsmith Street. We were both sitting having a coffee and looked at each other and said 'Snap!' We talked a lot, and I mentioned I was wanting a new piece of furniture and he said: 'I've got just the thing I think you want, it's in my house. It's only been there three months'.

My brother started working and thought he was keeping my mother and me, but he got a bit big-headed and he left home early, got married and started a family before he was on his feet properly. Miners' lads were earning a fair amount of money, so he went down Gedling Pit. Hard work. Then he left and became a deputy foreman at a pit just outside Doncaster and then he came back and worked for Boots where he finished his life.

I started work at fourteen but jobs were scarce at that time. I worked for a chap on Chesterfield Street who made wooden frames for the insides of three-piece suites. I used to have to get there half an hour earlier than the other chaps in order to make the fire to put the glue pots on. The wood had to be glued, framed and clamped. The frames were very well made. I worked five and a half days a week. I think I started at nine shillings.

My mother wanted me to work for the Gas Corporation, the same as my father had. He was in hospital. She wanted me to have a permanent job or one where I was apprenticed. I started there a week before I was sixteen and was indentured until I was twenty-one. I stayed there until I married in 1936. Then, of course, War broke out a few years after. I was expecting to be called up but some gas fitters and plumbers were Reserve Occupations because of the damage done in raids needing attention.

At the Nottingham Gas Corporation Depot on the corner of Woodborough Road and Huntingdon Street 1934. Eric is second from the right in the back row. Photo from Eric

One morning, the boss stood outside and said: 'You, you and you go down to the Labour Exchange. You're being transferred. There's been a bad air-raid on Sheffield. You're being sent there to help.' At the Labour Exchange, on Castle Boulevard, we stood outside for about two hours, then told to go back as they had enough people. So back to the Woodborough Road and the boss said: 'They fetched you and you'll have to go back again!' We didn't know what we were supposed to be doing.

Then we were sent to the training centre in Leicester where I learnt a new trade. I was there fifteen weeks and got the top prize of the whole class for welding. A firm making smoke screens in Leicester had a number one priority so we went there to make smoke screens.

There was trouble bringing in aircraft on the runways because the lights were down (so Jerry couldn't see). So they brought out a new thing called radio location, made by Marconi or BTH as it was in Leicester. The Government never allowed the manufacturing of the whole of one article in a factory. A bit was manufactured here and a bit there. Because of my welding skills I was put on that job and stayed until the end of the War.

I went back to the Gas Corporation with my tools for about two years. Then I got itchy feet and wanted something different. I tried for jobs but didn't have the experience to get them. Then the Gas industry was to be nationalised and I was asked to be Service Manager for the East Midlands Gas Board at Lincoln but I must move to Grantham. My wife, Irene (nee Attenborough), and I had worked for two years building our own bungalow at Carlton and she said she wasn't moving. My wife's family lived in Carlton. Her father, a builder, had built his own house.

One of the advisers came and tapped me on the shoulders and said: 'You've made the biggest mistake of your life'. It was seven or eight years until I got another good chance, as Commercial Sales Representative, then eventually Senior Commercial Sales Representative, for Nottingham.

I went down to London to Watson House, which was the mouth-piece of the Gas Board. Any course worth going to was at Watson House. We were trained by chefs from different hotels. You would be told for what purpose and how you would sell a certain oven to a hotel, the ways you calculated the size of the oven, the size of the burners, how many burners you needed, how many meals had to be prepared . . . If you sold them the wrong appliance, you were talking hundreds of pounds. You were in trouble! I retired in 1978.

Irene and I had one child and we have a grandaughter. As I said earlier, she's good at English, and the viola. She's just finished her 'A' Levels and is looking for a University place. She has the chance of Lancaster, Hull and London. My son-in-law, her father, works for the Gas Board, well it's Transco now.

After I retired from work, for a while I went part-time selling houses for a local estate agent. I'm a good cook today! I do the gardening. We enjoy living out here. My wife is eight-five now and I'm eighty-four.

My mother lived on Lotus Street until she died in 1953. We then moved from Lily Street for Carlton.

Before the Cavendish Cinema was built on St Ann's Well Road, there was a firm there, Lewis's. They made all the Meridian stuff before they moved up to Hadyn Road. I remember very well when the firm was there making for

Meridian. On Lotus Street, there was a big factory which used to be a Maltster. Then Somnus Bedding came in and took that over. Then there was Keetch's Transport and Kelham's Cattle Transport. Old man Kelham was the bloke who used to go up the Cattle Market and buy cattle and then sell them. He lived in a place called Twells Street, the opposite side of St Ann's Well Road to Lotus Street, and he had a big yard at the back.

Just imagine, St Ann's Well Road full of people and one bloke coming up and he's got thirty or forty cattle and all he's got is his stick to drive them! You'd see women scarper into shops and they didn't laugh. Once I was with my mother coming down the road towards the Central Market and along comes this Kelham with his cows. My mother was scared.

He would take them up his yard and take some of them back the next day and sell them. Later he got transport and his sons used the transport. Has anyone mentioned Strecker? He turned out to be a speedway rider. They were Germans and had a rough time in the First World War. The father was put in a camp. Of course the kids, including Fred, were born here.

I was only just born myself in the First World War but I used to listen to stories that my mother and father used to talk about. We used to fetch our pork from Strecker's, pork chop, pork dripping and plenty of jelly in the bottom. Strecker's had some friends who kept a pork butcher's shop at the bottom of Dame Agnes Street and their name was Abel. Our Friday night treat was Abel faggots, a penny each. They were delicious.

Then I remember Bill Hopcroft who used to be one of the directors of Notts County Football Club. He used to keep Victoria Car Dismantling on Mapperley Top. He came from a very ordinary family. Anybody mentioned Shepherd's shoe shop? That used to be on the corner of Curzon Street. The son and I went to school together. He used to walk all the way home for his lunch at Curzon Street right to the top of Hendon Rise and back again. They were a very religious family. If you wanted a good pair of shoes, you went to Shepherd's.

St Ann's was a good shopping area.

Cyril Stapleton started a little quintet at the Old Ritz which is now the Odeon in the City Centre. Then he got in with Henry Halls Band, but to be a permanent member you had to master two instruments. I don't think he ever mastered two, although he was a brilliant violinist. He started to play with a lot of the big bands. He played for the RAF Squadron he was in during the War.

Irene and I used to go old-time dancing quite a lot at one time. There was the occasional dance at Grantham Town Hall. Avelin and Barfords which used to manufacture the big rollers which went on the road had a big place just outside Grantham. We were going to a dance there one Saturday night. The lady behind the bar said: 'You should have been in here last night, we had Cyril Stapleton'. She said he was poorly and had to conduct his band sitting down in a swivel chair, and it wasn't long after that he died.

CYRIL STAPLETON

Details from 'Local Boy Makes Good' [Dennis McCarthy & Radio Nottingham 1971], based on a BBC Radio Nottingham Series of radio interviews by Dennis McCarthy[1]

Cryril Stapleton was born on Woodborough Road over a Laundry at Mapperly in 1914.

He used to live in Westminster Street off St Ann's Well Road. He told Dennis McCarthy: "From there we moved, as I began to work a little. We went to Robin Hood Chase, where I well remember living at 134. I stayed there until I was fourteen, having won a scholarship to Trinity College of Music, and later on from there I joined Henry Hall's Dance Band at the BBC . . . "

He played the violin ever since he was about seven. When he was about fourteen, the Nottingham Education Committee gave him a minor scholarship of £25 to have some violin lessons in Czechoslovakia. He had to pay it back by the time he was twenty-one.

He first went to school at 'the old Bath Street School' in St Ann's, then on to Morley School on St Ann's Well Road.

One of his first jobs was in the pit of a Nottingham cinema, playing with a small orchestra that accompanied silent films. He formed his own band early in his career and eventually became the conductor of the BBC Showband taking part in hundreds of radio and TV broadcasts.

CICELY R TRIBE

Born 1916

Contribution sent in 2000

I was seven years old in 1923 and lived in Peterborough. My mother, who was forty-three years old, was expecting her third child and was not too strong to begin with. So my aunt who lived in St Ann's, Nottingham, took me for the last three months, while my brother spent most of his time with my grandmother.

My aunt lived in National Terrace, off Westminster Street, which went down to the St Ann's Well Road. There might have been other like terraces but I don't remember too clearly, nor can I remember much about my aunt's house. She was bringing up four children on her own as my uncle was in a hospital for incurables. He had been a baker and was suffering from some disease caused by, I believe, contact with flour. I do remember my aunt was too poor to live anywhere better at that time.

My memories were of rooms that were barely furnished, gloomy and dark. The doors opened on to a sort of lane between the rows of these dwellings. There was no sign of anything growing as there were no gardens as far as I can remember. It was all so different from my own home,

although we were quite poor too. At least we had gardens where our food could be grown.

On the other side of the St Ann's Well Road, the streets ran up a fairly steep hill. I remember three of these streets, Donkey Hill, Blue Bell Hill and Ball Street. My aunt had a friend who lived right at the top of Ball Street. Here my memory is a little keener. I was an asthmatic and, as we spent much of our time in that house on Ball Street, the effort of climbing that hill was very stressful for me. However, when we made it to the top, it was worth the climb.

My aunt's friend's name was Olive Newton, one of a family of a baker's shop somewhere in the town, quite a good business. Mrs Newton had two daughters, Margaret and Jessica, Margaret being about the same age as my cousin and Jessica about the same age as myself. My aunt's name was Elizabeth Rose and her children were Kathleen, Kenneth, Sidney and Gordon Rose.

I think the Newton's were quite well off and they befriended my aunt, as my cousin and I always seemed to be playing with the Newton girls. The house was very nice and there was a garden and trees and, once I had recovered my breath, the air seemed much cooler and clearer than in the dusty streets below in June, July and August.

I don't know what my boy cousins did when not at school. But we four girls seemed to spend happy hours playing our favourite game which consisted of cutting out pictures from redundant catalogues and arranging the 'furniture' into rooms and the 'figures' into families, giving them names and telling stories about them. These little catalogues were printed in black and white, no gaudy colours then, and I can't imagine children today being so absorbed in a box of bits of paper cut-outs of our own making. We had imagination!

Sometimes we played outside and I remember hopscotch, skipping rope games, shuttlecock, battledore, and ball. Woe betide if we let the ball fly from our hands for off it would go rolling and bouncing right down the hill and across the road at the bottom, followed by the best runner among us to bring it back. A ball cost money and we could not afford to lose one.

I went to school for a few weeks and it terrified me! I can't tell you what school it was, but I remember a huge two or three storey building, red brick, so very different from my own school at home which was a small single storey complex of two buildings and two playgrounds. It was a Church school and looked it with its little bell tower and lancet windows [St Ann's Church School]. We were taught the scripture and classics and quite a lot about proper behaviour.

The School at St Ann's seemed totally strange. There seemed to be hundreds of pupils, most of them being what now we would call streetwise and quite rough. Some of them told me a teacher wanted to see me one day after school when I was waiting to see my cousin coming to take me home. They pushed me through a door and banged it shut. I found myself in a little lobby kind of place and nowhere was there any teacher or anyone else. I remember to this day the scream of terror that tore from me.

---

[1] Dennis McCarthy spent his childhood in St Ann's after his family moved up from London in the Second World War. He became a well-known and much liked Nottingham broadcaster and writer. He died in 1996.

They had guessed I was a greenhorn, not used to such trickery. I was too scared to speak most of the time with unfortunate results. One day we were at lessons near home time and the teacher had told several other pupils they must wait until it was time to go. I daren't even ask and consequently ended up with a puddle under my seat. My cousin scalded me all the way home.

One day, my dislike of that school was mitigated a little for we were lined up in a crocodile and marched for what seemed to be miles, out of the dusty streets, and up to somewhere called the Coppice [Coppice Rec]. I can't say where it was exactly but, oh bliss! There was beautiful green grass and shady big trees there. I felt almost as if I was at home among the green fields that I loved so much. There was a wooden hut there but we did not need to use it as we sat on the grass for lessons and, later, we were given large mugs of milk and some enormous currant buns before marching all the way back again. No school buses then. We had legs, hadn't we?

My aunt was a member of the Salvation Army. Our Sundays were spent at the Citadel. Sunday school in the morning, usually marching somewhere or other in the afternoons with the collecting boxes and evening service back in the Citadel. I remember those endless marches in the afternoon heat. Looking back, I think that was a bit much on a seven year old who was so short of breath.

People did not seem to be so concerned about child asthma then: it was something that you grew out of. Only I never did. One day we went to a rally or something to a place called Eastleigh. I don't know if I have that name correctly, but it was a sultry day among crowds of people and their rattling collecting tins. A few years later, the Salvation Army was good to my aunt and her family during the great Depression after my uncle had died. They helped her to emigrate to Canada where they all did very well and she continued as a preacher until she died aged seventy-four.

Other outings I dimly remember were to a place called the Arboretum where there were lots of trees and a picnic on the river bank somewhere near a bridge where there seemed to be long stone steps to sit on [Trent Bridge]. I also remember how scary those great stone lions outside the Town Hall were to me.

I wish I could remember more about St Ann's but it was all a long time ago. I can remember going to a corner shop with a jam jar for a pennyworth of piccalilli for my aunt. Also giggling every time I went past a greengrocer named A Onion on St Ann's Well Road.

My mother, worried by a notion that she might not survive childbirth at her age insisted I return home as she wished to see me again. Happily she survived her ordeal and my sister was born alive and well. I never returned to Nottingham. In those days, only those who could afford it could do any travelling unnecessarily. By the time I could have done so, there was no one left there to visit.

BESSIE LAWSON

Born 1918

Interviewed in her home 11.8.99

I was born at 47 Plantagenet Street, St Ann's, as Bessie Childs. My father worked in the Eastcroft [Refuse Depot], London Road, and my mother was a machinist making clothes in a factory in the Lace Market. I had one sister, Joan, three years younger than me. I went to Blue Bell Hill Elementary School.

These two photos, believed to include members of the same family, were found in an empty St Ann's house at the time of demolition. The group of younger people are in First World War uniforms. These photos were among a number handed to me when people knew I was preparing this book

St Ann's Nottingham: Inner-city Voices by Ruth I Johns • ISBN 0951696092

It was a lovely school. It's not what's on the outside of a school that counts, it's what goes on inside. I can remember standing in front of the class when I was about seven and showing the children how I could knit on two meat skewers[1]. My mum taught me to knit on these.

It was thundering and lightning very badly one day, when I was about the same age, and my mum came to meet me from school. She said: 'Are you frightened?' I said no, there was no thunder and lightening, only fairies waving their wands!

We used to play all sorts of games. The cobbled stones in the street had gas tar on and we used to pop it, where we played marbles and snobs and things. Parents used to cover you with lard, which stopped the tar sticking. It was mostly my dad who did the lard thing. He used to work shifts and, if my mum was at work, he'd cover us with lard so that we didn't get a good hiding when she got in from work.

She was a machinist making clothes and used to work eight to eight, a very long time. I used to have to take the washing to the Victoria Washhouse where you did your washing. I'd wait for her coming in and she used to do the lot and the ironing as well. She was there until about ten o'clock.

My dad was good about the house. He used to have dinner ready for us when we came home from school if he was there and not on another shift. When they were both working, there was a very nice old lady next door and we used to go there.

When my mother was eight days old, her mother died. Her dad was a police sergeant and before that a grenadier guard, so my mum went to live with her granny, her dad's mum. Her dad got married again but her stepmother wasn't very nice to her so she stayed there. Grandad was Police Sergeant Flinders at St Ann's. He used to live in a police house up Corporation Road, corner of Sycamore Road. I never knew him very well because he died when I was young. But I was never afraid of policemen because of him. I saw the house. We used to have a walk up there sometimes.

Police then were stern, very stern but good. They used to stand and watch you go after talking to you.

I belonged to Brownies and then Guides.

The teaching was very good at Blue Bell Hill School. It enabled me to go to Bluecoat School [Church of England School]. I passed the scholarship exam, aged ten. I didn't want to go. My mum made me go. I didn't know anybody who was going.

But I was glad I did go. The teaching was very good. I was good at writing, English not so good, history, geography, not maths. I loved sport. There was a Mrs Kendall and Captain (later Major) Merles. He was very strict and, of course, it was church at St Peter's Sunday morning. Sunday school in the afternoon and church again in the evening. My mum was a very big church goer. From school, we went to St Peter's, otherwise to St Catharine's

on St Ann's Well Road. It was very high church. The Brownies carrying the candle.

One thing used to annoy my dad. Every Sunday afternoon he used to go and have a drink Sunday dinnertime at the Criterion on the corner of Alfred Street and Plantagenet Street. Then he used to come home. He used to have dinner and used to sing, then nod off. The Salvation Army would come outside the door every Sunday afternoon. Mum didn't mind because she used to hum along with them, but he couldn't stand them. My dad he wasn't a religious man at all. He was a lovely bloke. He came from Cambridge and his dad was a shepherd.

He didn't go on pub outings but sometimes went on an outing from work. He came home after an outing one night and my aunt sat there. She said she wasn't going 'until Jack comes home'. He came home worse for wear, of course, and he'd got a bag full of rock. She sat there and says: 'Come on Joe, let's have this rock'. And he was handing it all around and we were putting it back in the bag and he was going around again with this rock! He wasn't nasty, he was funny.

I had a cousin round the corner on Havelock Street. We used to do all sorts of things like send my sister in a shop to ask how much the two penny bars of chocolate were. And the woman would say: 'You naughty little girl'. And we'd laugh. And we'd stand and look into Musson and Royle's shop at the bottom of Ford Street St Mary. It was like an Aladdin's Cave at Christmas. It was a good childhood, it really was. We weren't rude, we weren't cheeky, we were taught not to be cheeky. All the grannies and aunts lived round about and children could always go there if there was something wrong. And the policemen used to walk by.

There was this old girl who lived opposite. She used to take her jug down to the beer-off at the corner and have it filled. She'd go outside, drink half of it, take it back, fill it up again and go home.

My friends in St Ann's didn't quite know what to say when they used to see me in my Bluecoat School uniform. I used to swank a little bit you know with a tennis racket. It was a second-hand one because they were so dear. They didn't say much. I used to go out and play for a while, and after that I couldn't because of homework.

I was learning to play the piano. My dad won sixty pounds, a heck of a lot of money then. He won the money on a sweepstake at work. He bought my mum a piano because she used to play. She used to play all the musical comedies and I do wish I'd still got that music.

I learnt the piano for three years. I was made to practise in the front room with gloves on because my mum couldn't afford a fire. I was going for my Intermediate exam but I couldn't. I had so much homework. She was talented. But she hated anybody to listen to her playing the piano. She had three lessons, that's all she had. I went for three years and can't play a note now!

I can remember when it was snowing my dad used to light a candle in the loo across the backyard to keep it warm. And light a lamp. Of course, before then, there were what we called the ten o'clock horses. They'd come to

---

[1] Long metal pins with an 'eye' head, used to put through meat to hold joints together.

empty the tubs at ten o'clock at night. They did make a noise. They used to wake me up. My first recollection, I don't know how old I'd be, was screaming and running down the passage to my mum's room saying: 'What is it, what is it?' And she explained. Fancy having a job like that [emptying tubs of human sewage into carts].

My dad stood under one of the little lamps we used to have and his hair caught fire. I'll always remember that. He was tall. My mum was shouting: 'Jack, oh Jack, your hair's on fire'. She sort of banged it. Then later, they came and wired us for electricity. No candle-reading in bed any more, but put the light on until your mum came along and said: 'Put that light out'. We didn't realise the cost. A candle would burn all night. We read School Girls' Own and all the books. We read an awful lot, Joan and I. She lives down in Wiltshire now. There was the loveliest big library along Shakespeare Street. My mum, Joan and I went every Saturday afternoon because my mum used to like books and music. You could get music from there as well.

My mum was very particular with cleaning. She worked so late. One day she said to me: 'I wish you'd help me more'. I said but I want to go out and play and she said she had so much to do. My dad had a talk with us, and we used to set to and scrub the back kitchen, do our bedroom and take turns with things. Mum was very pleased.

She could go to Sneinton Market on a Saturday morning, get a piece of material, come home, cut frocks out and we used to go out in them in the afternoon. It was her work in the factory. She used to do that. The frocks were very nice, plain but nice. One had got a frill, a square frill and fastened at the nape and little puff-sleeves. Once she made me a coat with a cape and fur all round the edge of it. I don't know how she could afford all that, but then she was working all those hours, and she used to do an awful lot at work I think in her dinner hour. She didn't come home.

In those days, you got your Matric [examination] if you were lucky before you left school, but I didn't. I left school at fifteen and my mum asked me what I wanted. I said I want to be a nurse. She said, sorry, the kitty can't afford it. She took me down Clumber Street and she said they want a junior in there. She waited outside while I went in and got the job.

I was in the coat department. I hated it. I was there five years and, then, I said 'no more'. At Easter, you were there until nearly ten at night putting clothes away. Everybody used to have new clothes at Easter you know, shoes and everything. My sister went to work at the Dolcis shop, which was then on Long Row. It had just started. It was a new shop and she loved it.

When I left, I saw they wanted someone at the General Hospital, an orderly, so I told my mum I was going. I got thirty-two shillings a week. I loved every minute. One of them said: 'I don't know why you don't come and be a nurse'. I said my mum couldn't afford it. She said I was old enough to leave home but I didn't want to.

I was there about five years. It was hard work but it was nice. It was during the War and we'd got soldiers coming in. I was so tired, but I loved every minute of it.

I'd get there about half past seven in the morning until five, half an hour for lunch. Half a day off a week and a day off a month. Christmas Day I was there.

When I got there, I'd get jugs of water and refill them for patients. I'd go round with the nurses and help make the beds. I couldn't do anything tablet-wise or anything like that. I'd help with the lunches and dinners. I can remember one man, he was diabetic, and he couldn't have the same food. He had bed boards at the side of him to stop him wandering around. He said he wanted some food another man had, and I said he couldn't have it, so he just threw an orange at this man and it went right across his nose. I'd help feed some of the men who were so ill.

Some were badly injured from the War. You remember the round wing at the General Hospital with the children's ward on the top? They took the children away and put soldiers in the top ward. They had a very good sister on that ward. The matron could walk down the ward and she didn't look as if she was looking. When she came back, it was: 'Those trolley wheels are the wrong way round, the bed wheels want to go in' and you've not done this, that and the other! Wonderful really. If it was like that now, it would be better.

I got married in 1945. My husband came from the Meadows and we lived at 41, Plantagenet Street, St Ann's. In those days, mothers got houses for you. You know, your aunt lived across there and mum got us this house near hers. It was only a small terraced house but we were quite happy there. All together, I was on that street for fifty-three years, up to the time of demolition.

It was hard work bringing up a family. I always did my washing at home at first because I couldn't leave the children. But my mum still went down to the washhouse. I used to have the dolly tub outside, my mangle, ponch, get the big copper going early in the morning and then get the kiddies sorted and saw my husband off to work. I used to do a big wash once a week including blue and starch. I did kiddies washing nearly every day.

David was in the Cubs at St Ann's Church, Anita in the Guides. That Church was pulled down. Anita was confirmed there.

I used to love the Library. When we were older we could go on our own. We used to trot up Union Road and through the bridge by Victoria Station and on to Shakespeare Street. And when I was a mother, I went with my kids. David went to Mundella School and was studying a lot so he went to the Library a lot.

When the Council man came round and told us that they were going to knock Plantagenet Street down, we were all flabbergasted. None of us round there wanted to move. Joan Priestley will tell you the same. We'd bought that house by then. My son, David (born 1951), was at University. We'd had a shower room put in the back room and we were quite happy. We had a son-in-law (Anita was married) who did all the decorating. I'd got a part-time job in a wool shop, Thomas was on nights and I wasn't scared being on my own in that house.

Then we were all miserable. We used to go every Sunday afternoon and look at them knocking other people's houses down. The Council man said we can have three choices. I always wanted to go up Bakersfield. But the choices were top of Ransom Road, and up on Valley Road. We went to look at these two and we didn't care much for them. Then we only had one more choice. Then we had a letter saying we'd got this bungalow [Wollaton Park] and we didn't want to go, because of leaving Planagenet Street.

All our friends went different ways. We came here. I cried for a fortnight. This is not my home, that's my home [Plantagenet Street]. The people were so friendly, knock on any door and you'd get: 'Come in duck, what's the matter. All right I'll see to her.' And if anybody was having a baby, you know the people would be there, the washing would be done, the husband would have a meal, you'd get all that. Well, when we first came here, it's like this all the while. Quiet. There isn't a thing.

They're good the neighbours round here, I've only got to ring them especially Dolly at the back. She came here because they knocked her place down. She's the same and you know we sit and talk about what used to happen.

My husband, Tom, died six years ago. He was an engineer with Trent Engineering. David, my son, works for Lucas Engineering in Birmingham at present. He goes by car every day. My two daughters live in Bulwell. His previous employer wanted him to move down south and he didn't want to. You know, with kiddies at school.

My sister Joan, who worked at Dolcis, married and had two children. She lost a third. She divorced and got married again to a nice bloke. But he's dead now and she married a Scotsman. She's happy down in Wiltshire. Her eldest daughter lives down there.

My hobbies are sewing and knitting. I love doing tapestries. I have help every Thursday with the cleaning. I make pies at the weekend for family because I've got three apple trees out there, but I can't eat any fruit.

I didn't go back to work except part-time in the wool shop because, with Tom on nights, I had to come home and get a meal for him. For a while when David was about four months, I went back to the General Hospital five to eight every night. I'd leave David with my elder daughter, Kathleen. I had Kathleen some years earlier. My parents were very supportive. I did enjoy the work. I still have regrets at not being able to do nursing.

I sit here sometimes and think all about St Ann's. My mum used to go every Saturday afternoon to the Market on King Edward Street. Walking from the top, they'd got everything. Slippers, shoes, material and then Ivy's Wool Store. Straight to the bottom and get the fish if you wanted some for tea, after the greengrocer's and the *Evening Post*. Go home and we'd have tea, then clear away and sit. No television. We hadn't even got a wireless to start with. The kiddies would get ready for bed. After radio, we sat and listened to the play in the evening. There was always a play on the BBC then. Then, later on, we used to have Rediffusion: one and six a week.

We thought it was wonderful to listen to the wireless. The other night I was telling my daughter that I had a wonderful dream and she says: 'Oh yes, where were you?'

I said I went shopping on St Ann's Well Road. I started at Asher's Fish Shop, wet fish shop, then the greengrocers. Going a bit further up to the pork shop, back again to Farnsworth on Alfred Street for different things. That was really, really good. And I thoroughly enjoyed it.

You know when I used to go shopping properly up there, I never thought that the friendly people wouldn't be there any more. There was the beer-offs, there was all the lot. There was Hopewell's across the road, the furniture shop where we got our first dining set, sideboard, table and four chairs at £40. And then we had a bedroom suite at £80. We'd really saved and saved and saved and bought them cash down if you please. They gave us a carpet, a full-sized carpet, because we'd paid for them cash.

Of course we would walk up The Chase and then on to the top where the reservoir is, where the kids could play round and round. And we used to sit there talking or doing something you know, we felt quite safe. My son, he always laughs and says: 'Go on tell me again mother, when you used to go out and leave your door unlocked and nobody bothered you'. I say it's true we did, nobody bothered you. There was some crime. But there was no radio, no television so nobody got to know about anything, did they? They took it as hearsay. Oh, there were robberies, definitely, but no stabbings. I can't remember anything like that.

I've three grandaughters and one grandson. My grandaughter Emma got married about three weeks ago at the Church of the Good Shepherd up at Woodthorpe. She lives in Essex now. They are all doing well. My family's often here.

Bessie Lawson died in 2001

DENIS N ENSER

Born 1922

From letters and a tape sent in December 1999

I was born in a two-bedroom house in Manning Terrace. I had a brother Maurice and sisters, Peggy and Beryl. My dad was employed in the lace trade at Birkin's factory in the Lace Market. Along with so many Nottingham people, he lost his job when the lace trade collapsed in the late 1920s.

Although dad looked for work, life must have been a struggle with four children to feed. The family existed on twenty-eight shillings per week dole money. Even that was reduced after so many weeks. Nevertheless, I remember my childhood as happy. Some were worse off.

To earn a few extra pence, mum, along with other jobs, took in washing. Early Monday morning dad would light the coal-fired copper in the scullery and fill it from the communal tap in the yard. The dolly tub and ponch were brought out. These were kept with the wooden roller wringer in the yard. Even that was second-hand so it had no guard on the cogs on the outside.

Whilst mum was feeding the clothes through the rollers and dad was turning the handle, I managed to trap my hand in the cogs resulting in the loss of my finger ends.

My brother Maurice and myself at 7, Manning Terrace 1930

Maybe that's why I'm left-handed. I was rushed to the Children's Hospital in Chestnut Grove near Mansfield Road: no waiting for an ambulance in those days. Dad ran all the way carrying me.

My first school was Shelton Street, then Huntingdon Street Juniors. Before I went to the seniors, I had another accident. Coming home from school, I was larking about on some railings, fell and broke my leg badly. As a result, I changed schools and went to St Ann's Church School. It was nearer. I loved that school. There were smaller classes and it was much more friendly. I joined the Church Choir. One teacher was Miss Pulver. (We called her Miss Pullover!) Among other things, she taught us country dancing. I can't see children nowadays doing that! I'd missed schooling because of my accident, so she gave me extra tuition, and I managed to catch up and pass the scholarship and so on to Huntingdon Seniors.

After school, we played a lot of the time on Abbotsford Street: tin lurky, Rum-stick-a-bum, conkers and games like that. One of our best games was to tie a skipping rope round the lampost to swing on. Not too popular with the neighbours though, as we kept breaking the gas mantle putting the street in darkness.

The local Bobby would chase us, and if we did get caught - which was not very often - he would clip us round the ears with his gloves. We reckoned he had marbles in the fingers of his gloves. The clip didn't half sting. No good telling dad, I'd only get another clout!

The days before bonfire night, we would collect anything that would burn, old settees, mattresses and the

like. We went round the local shops scrounging cardboard boxes. I was dared to go into Bamfords, the undertakers on St Ann's Well Road, and ask if they had any empty boxes! I came out a lot quicker that I went in. Anyway, our firewood would burn for several days after November 5th.

We didn't have pocket money in those days, so to buy mum and dad something for Christmas, we went carol singing to the posh houses on Mapperley Plains. We sang one or two carols and knocked on the doors. We collected quite a few pennies and in some places we were invited in to sing a bit more. We went to the same houses for several years.

Our special treat was to go to the movie pictures at the Robin Hood Picture House at the bottom of Robin Hood Chase. It was there before the Cavendish Cinema was built. It only showed silent films. There were three in our gang: Wilf Gilliatt, Den Bilbie and me. We would collect jam jars, which were returnable for half a penny, until we had four pence. One of us would go in and let the others in the side door.

But our favourite place to play was Sycamore Recreation: Licky Rec to us. There were iron swings, roundabouts and a slide. We used to go down the slide rubbing a bit of candle wax behind us. It was supposed to make it more slippery. It certainly made a mess of our trousers - another telling off from mum! After dusk the swings were chained up and the gates locked. That was more of a challenge. We squeezed through the railings and clambered up and down the slide on the chains. But that had to stop. One night Wilf got his head stuck in the railings and we nearly pulled his ears off getting him free. He was known as Wilfred the Rabbit after that.

Next to Licky was Hungerhill Gardens. We knew every path in that maze of alleyways and spent hours chasing the girls round there. I can't remember what we did if we caught them. Well, we were only ten at the time!

Another Park we went to was Coppice Rec where we held school sports. I wasn't very good at games but I did enjoy cricket. My brother was a good player and I followed behind when he played for works and church teams. I helped carry the bags of pads and stumps. If we were lucky, sometimes we had tea and sandwiches afterwards. Football

My parents William (Bill) and Rachel (Ray) Enser at 79, Manning Street c1938

ST ANN'S NOTTINGHAM: inner-city voices by Ruth I Johns ● ISBN 0951696092 was played on a field on Mapperley Plains. The whole class would get on a tram at the bottom of Woodborough Road, each of us stamping on the foot bell, driving the conductor mad and the same again when the forty of us got off coming back.

Swimming lessons were taken at Vic [Victoria] Baths. We were in such a hurry we never seemed to dry ourselves before teacher was marching us back to Hunto [well-known nickname for Huntingdon School].

The Chase Mission Baptist Church played an important part in my younger days. This was the church near Raglan Street. We went every Sunday afternoon. That gave mum and dad a rest from the kids. I couldn't miss because my Uncle Fountain was the Sunday school secretary and mum would soon learn if I missed any time.

We had Anniversary Sunday, when we learned new hymns, Harvest Festival, Christmas party and once a year we went to camp with the Life Boys. That was the lads equivalent of Girls' Brigade. We went via train from Victoria Station and it was quite an adventure. Sleeping away from home was an added thrill. Our Sunday school teacher took us in turn to Lyons café for tea and cream cakes. Oh, so posh for a child!

One memory which crossed my mind was seeing the R101 airship flying across Manning Street. It filled the whole sky. Only a few days later, it crashed on its maiden voyage and with loss of all aboard. I believe it was 1930.

Rev F J Legg, and his wife Audrey, who were at the Chase Mission 1935-40

When I was about seven we moved from Manning Terrace to Manning Street. We hired a handbarrow from Hopewell's. We loaded up and pushed up the hill to our new home. All the wardrobes and beds were hauled in through a bedroom window with a clothes-line.

My brother and I now had a bedroom of our own. Even though it was the attic, it was ours. Previously, we had to share with our sisters.

We now had a little garden which mum loved. She was born in the country and grew quite a variety of flowers. She made it quite pretty. I liked that house. I stayed there until I left to join the RAF at the beginning of the War. Later, I married at Holy Trinity Church.

Dad would go to the butchers on Beastmarket Hill late on Saturday night after the pubs were closed at ten o'clock. There he would buy our joint of meat for the week. There were no fridges, so the meat was sold on the cheap via a Dutch auction. This would mean we would have roast beef on Sunday. Cold on Monday. Stew on Tuesday and soup made from the bones on Wednesday. We knew how to stretch a penny. On Sunday, we had Yorkshire Pudding first to fill us up, so we didn't eat so much meat. If things were tight we would have a four-penny rabbit: the joint of beef being two shillings.

But there was always homemade bread, toasted on an open fire with lots of dripping from the joint. We'd not heard of cholesterol in those days. Mum was a very good cook and made all her own bread. She made a currant loaf we called barm bread. She sold a few loaves, but I think gave away more than she sold to those not as fortunate as we. I can still remember the smell of that bread rising in front of the coal fire, lovely!

I had a thought. The house where I was born in Manning Terrace, the house where I grew up in Manning Street, the schools I went to on Shelton Street and Huntingdon Street, the Church I was married in: they have all been knocked down. It's a good job I'm not famous. There would be nowhere to hang the plaque!

Betts the butcher was on Manning Street and I knew that family quite well. Avills the pork butchers on the bottom of Corporation Road. There was the pub that we used to call the Adelphi which was quite a big hotel. Of course, we were not allowed there as children. Preston's the greengrocers, Foster's the haberdasher, that was on the top of Manning Street. Pennel's the chemist, that was well known on Dame Agnes Street. Dr Davidson was quite a character. He lived in Robin Hood Chase. A no-nonsense Scottish doctor but he did a lot of good. I can never remember him sending bills but we had to use him frequently. The Coachmakers pub was on Union Road.

One character stands out in my memory. Albert Clay who kept a shoe repair shop on Corporation Road. Mr Clay was blinded in the 1914-18 War. He was totally blind and learnt to repair shoes at St Dunstan's and he kept his own business and brought up four lads. Two he never saw. But he could tell a tale. As a boy I used to help him deliver his shoes and he used to recognise the addressee by the feel of the shoe and he could recognise his work. An intelligent man he was. He used to entertain us.

Albert Clay at Mapperley War Memorial

Walking home from school was quite an education. I walked a lot. I went home to dinner from school on Huntingdon Street and back again, all in an hour. On the way home, on the right hand side of Woodborough Road there was a brewer's yard, which belonged to Rock Ales. You could see through the windows where they used to steep the mash for making beer. A beautiful smell. We often used to peep in. Across the road they made the barrels and I watched for ages as they shaped the staves and where they steamed them into shape and forced the iron rings around the barrels. I watched complete barrels being made: wonderful skill with quite elementary tools. They made lovely waterproof barrels.

Another way walking home was up Robin Hood Chase. I can't remember the name of the little street that came off. There was a slaughterhouse. We watched the cattle there being slaughtered in an open yard. We didn't find it horrific as they might do now. We sat on the wall and watched the poor cows being pole-axed and then dragged into the yard, being skinned and chopped up. Quite an entertainment for young kids! It didn't seem to bother us.

In my schooldays, things like Shipstone's horse deliveries, where they had a four-in-hand delivering the barrels of Shipstone's ales, were quite a common sight. These horses knew exactly where to go, they knew the route. And sometimes they used to feed them beer and they knew exactly where to stop to get a drink! Colossal huge dray horses they were in beautiful condition.

One building on St Ann's Well Road was the Public [slipper] Baths. In the terraced houses we had, there was no hot water. So once a week we'd go down to the baths where they had no shortage of hot water. I don't know what it cost but it couldn't have been much. They provided

Outside the Chase Mission 1940. Left to right, A Preston, W Wright, C Standeven, ? , and my brother, Maurice

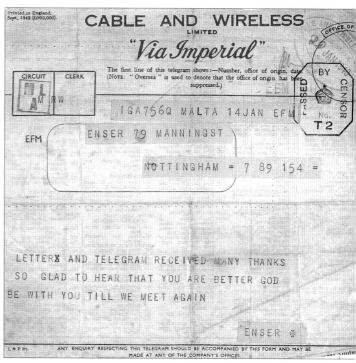

War-time cable, January 1943

My dad with grandson, 79, Manning Street 1949

you with a little bit of soap and we took our own towels. That was a once-a-week ritual to go and have a soak in a big deep bath instead of getting into the bath tub that was kept in the yard and filled from a kettle.

NB By coincidence a later occupant of 79, Manning Street also appears in this book. See John Bailey

NORMAN CHETTLE

Born 1922

*Interviewed in his home 8.6.99. Norman Chettle, and his father before him, ran a **Dental Practice** on the St Ann's Well Road for over six decades*

I was born over my father's dental practice in St Ann's. It was 180, St Ann's Well Road, opposite the old St Ann's Church. He served in the First World War and I think he started the practice in 1919. He was born in Leicester overlooking the Clock Tower and over Cook's Travel Agency. He married Winifred Comery who lived in St Ann's.

I went to Shelton Street School and then to High Pavement. I was lucky to get there. My House Master had been in the War with my father so I was popped into his House. When I was a small boy, I used to watch the Boys'

Brigade from my bedroom window. They would play the bands and march down with banners flying. Outside the Church they'd all stand to attention and then eventually march in.

We were Congregationalists in Union Square. It was a big chapel. It closed before the time of demolition. We joined St Nicholas Church which, of course, is Church of England. My mother's cousin played the organ there.

I didn't play out with the kids a lot. I had one very good friend. He was the grandson of the Hopewell's, the furniture people. The old lady lived at 17, The Chase and we used to go and see her there. Phil, my friend, went to High Pavement too, so did his brother.

I have one sister but she is a lot younger than me. She was too young for me to associate with when we were young and then I went to Edinburgh to study. I met my wife, Sibyl, up there and then the Second World War came. My sister later moved to London to work at St Bartholomew's Hospital. She still works there.

I was a dental surgeon in the Royal Navy in the War. I was in the East Indies Fleet. I married Sybil in 1944. I had a surgery at Chatham for the invasion and they gave me a day to get married and a day to get back after the invasion. So we've been making up for lost time ever since!

It was always understood I would take over the dental practice, and that's what I did when I left the Navy. My father then became semi-retired. I ran it and he got in my way! I always say my father started after his War and I started after my War!

Ever such a lot of us were demobbed together and they became my patients until I retired. They brought their families. In fact, one family I saw for four generations. Many patients became friends. Some didn't like me but mostly we had very happy relationships.

It was quite a nice house, a big tall-fronted house. It had been Dr Cram's and he moved into Robin Hood Chase and he'd got it from a Dr Dunn and eventually we were paying rent to Dr Dunn and then we bought it from him. At the back it had stables and a little coach house for the original doctor's horse and trap.

We were I think just about the last place in St Ann's to be demolished. Everything else went. It was the most dreadful, dreadful time of my life. Everything around was smashed. I used to have nightmares. It was awful, and people were setting fire to things.

There was a milliner down the road and he used to sell the most superb hats very cheaply. He stood marketing in Newark some days of the week. He said: 'I won't leave until you leave because they won't pull it down as long as you are there. And until you've got somewhere else to go, they won't pull it down.' So I stayed and he stayed and the whole of the rest of the place was a desert. When I left my car outside, it was covered with brick dust the next day.

Yes, patients still came. As I said a lot of the families had started after the Second World War and then as they progressed, they moved away. But they continued to come back to me. In fact, after I moved into the new practice, the very first patient to come was Mrs Fish from Epperstone. The ladies from the pickle factory used to come and they all

The premises from which Norman Chettle created his 'new' dental practice after his had been demolished. Signs were not allowed then: now they are. Photo: E James Smalley 2000

smelt of vinegar. The factory was up Dame Agnes Street somewhere. Of course they couldn't help it. I used to make domestic visits to some of the older people, some had been in the First World War. They would show me their scars and tell me their War stories. And I used to come home to Sibyl and say I've been seeing some of my old warriors today.

My replacement practice was 6, Cardinal Close, a couple of hundred yards up the road. It was really a Council house. Now it has a big sign up but we weren't allowed to put signs like that up. I saw enormous changes in St Ann's and not for the better a lot of them.

People said the houses had to come down, but they got rid of a lot of low rental businesses that employed a lot of people. We did all our shopping down there, low costs and super shops. When we were talking about you coming the other day, my daughter said she remembered Edna's the big greengrocer at the bottom of Peas Hill Road. They were great.

One thing that sticks in my mind. One year at Christmas I came into St Ann's shopping with my daughter who was about twelve then. As we went along everyone said: 'Hello Mr Chettle, is this your daughter?' And then chit-chat. After, my daughter said it's just like being in a village.

Demolition broke up families. It was dreadful. That was when I was sad about it because Bill married the girl next door and Aunty Flo lived across the road sort of thing, and this whole community was destroyed. Very sad.

Nobody I know was consulted. The only thing that happened was that a chappie came round and asked how

long my dental practice had been there. I said fifty years, and off he went. So we went on from there and that's why they had to find me fresh premises. I hung on to the very end but I feel I was absolutely robbed. For the house and the practice and moving I got £12,000. In those days, I couldn't buy any sort of comparable practice at that price, apart from the move and having to refit a surgery. The unkindest cut of all was when I was taxed for Capital Gains on that £12,000.

There was a film on television about St Ann's at that time, showing how awful it was. They picked absolutely the worst possible building they could, everybody said it was dreadful. Of course, my memory is really about the people. When I was a boy, most of them like my father had been in the War. There was Vicker's down the road. He was a tailor and he had a steel plate in his head from the War. He had two daughter's, one my age. Have you heard of the Ashers?

They ran the greengrocers on St Ann's Well Road. Their brother ran the fishmonger down the road, they were all inter-connected. Smith the saddler, he was down the bottom. He was always being called up for Jury Service, a great nuisance to him. He asked his solicitor what he could do to stop it, and he told him he had to become a criminal! Smith asked how. His solicitor said: 'Well you don't pay your taxes and you don't pay your local taxes'. So he didn't and was taken to court and found guilty. And they never had him for Jury Service again!

When you went into his saddlers shop, it smelt of leather, that beautiful smell of leather when they made saddles and things. Then there was Adams the Seed Merchant. He was just below Hopewell's. He was just off a very narrow street, can't remember its name. He sold everything from horse food to everything you could think of. His whole place was divided into bins and you went in and bought whatever you liked and he shovelled it out.

For years we lived over the practice, then we moved to Hoveringham and then here. We moved long before the surgery was demolished. There was so little traffic then, I could get in very quickly to the practice. My father died but my mother lived over the old surgery until we knew it was coming down and then she moved out.

I was only in the new practice about nine years. I retired about sixteen years ago.

After I retired I continued to go in to St Ann's to the Bank. Of course, they knew my face. And to the Library. Then the Bank closed which was a great shame and it became a bit difficult to get into the Library. Tell Diana [Reynolds], in the Library, that we haven't forgotten her.

There were quite a lot of changes in dentistry during the years I practised, but much, much bigger ones since I've retired. I did a day a week for the School Dental Service as they used to call it. The Senior Dental Officer was desperate for people to work on that job. He was a really nice guy. I went mainly to Chaucer Street, the main School Clinic. Then I used to go to school clinics including my old school at High Pavement.

I haven't any photos of the St Ann's days. My mother destroyed all the photos.

Sybil Chettle died 2001

St Ann's Nottingham. Inner-city voices by Ruth I Johns • ISBN 0951696092

VI BOOTH

From a recollection at a St Ann's Library Reminiscence Day

My dad was a stoker at Wilford Power Station. We always did the washing on Monday mornings. My dad got up at five o'clock in the morning at our home in Northumberland Street. There was an open yard where at least a dozen houses shared lines. People fell out so they had to stagger which days they used the lines. But my mother always had Mondays. She also had her own line. She was a bit particular. In fact she was strict. She was a perfectionist.

The toilets were right at the top of the yard, one for each house, down a little passage, about twelve back to back.

Then we lived on Northumberland Terrace where we had a front garden. The landlord pulled the old kitchen down and built a bigger one. We paid 12/6 a week for that which was expensive in 1932. I went to Bath Street [Victoria] School and then Pierrepont School.

When I left school, I worked at Boots in the packing department on Island Street. I worked through the Second World War packing nepocrine and acroflavin for malaria, to send off to the War zone. The bright yellow wouldn't wash off. I went dancing all covered in yellow to Jephson's on Coalpit Lane. I met my husband on a blind date there. He was in the Airforce.

In the last stages of preparing this book [2002], I asked an organisation for permission to use a photograph. The woman, who phoned to say 'yes', told me she was born in St Ann's. She said her grandmother: 'had been taken screaming from her house' when she had to leave it because of demolition. All over Nottingham there are people who still find it hard to understand the reasons for the *wholesale* redevelopment of St Ann's in the early 1970s.

This woman told me it was hard to see why her family home was demolished when the nearby police houses in Westgate Street were left and were built around.

Houses in Westgate Street which pre-date the redevelopment. Photo: Ruth I Johns 2001

ROSE AND VERNON HAWLEY'S LIFETIME IN ST ANN'S

I interviewed Rose and Vernon Hawley in their home on 2.2.00 and have met up and exchanged letters on other occasions

ROSE HAWLEY

(nee Smedley)   Born 1922

I was born at 20, Havelock Street, St Ann's. My grandparents, Alf (a train driver) and Keziah Garner, lived at 8, Havelock Street. My granny, my mum's mum, had three daughters and two sons. One was killed in the First World War. We left there when I was five. My father decided we ought to get out of the cluster of St Ann's and for a while we went to live at what was then called New Lenton. But we visited our granny because it was on the tram for a halfpenny along Castle Boulevard, Lenton Boulevard and back again to St Ann's. My gran died in 1940. She was then living with my uncle at Seymour Terrace off Carlton Road because my auntie died and left him with three children.

I've got an older brother who is eighty and a younger brother who is seventy. My dad came back from the First World War wounded. He'd been gassed. He was in the Robin Hood Regiment. They advised him to get an outdoor job. Before he went in the Forces, he'd trained at Liptons as an apprentice grocer. So he joined Burtons the grocers, on Exchange Walk, a beautiful shop, and he was their Head Traveller. He started with a bicycle and an empty book! He had to find his customers. He cycled all round South Nottinghamshire. Eventually they upgraded him to a motorcycle and he ended up with a Morris Minor car.

He used to go one week and get the orders and the customer would pay for the previous week. He'd return the orders to Burtons. They would parcel them up and send them to the customers. He loved the job and people loved him. He went to villages, to farms, Saxondale Hospital [a psychiatric hospital]. When I was a girl, he'd sometimes take me with him.

My mum didn't work after she was married. Before she married she was a jennier in the Lace Trade. My granny used to do lace work at home. One of the first things I remember was running to the lady who distributed the lace work and taking it back to her. Sometimes it was perhaps only an hour or so later when it was a 'special'.

My father's mum and dad lived on Alfred Street, St Ann's, with my auntie, who had lost her husband, and little girl named Doris Skinner. Now Doris was an only child and she went to a private school and she lived with grandma and grandad all her life really until they died. And then she went to live near my father's sister in Forest Fields. My grandpa Smedley was a lamplighter and I think he was one of the last lamplighters. He carried a ladder on his shoulder and his little black and white dog would sit at the foot of the ladder while he went up and did the gas lamps, and changed the wick elements.

We used to visit them once a week and have a halfpenny cornet. Then, of course, dad had a lot of trouble travelling because there was a big strike. We weren't ever so rich but we used to manage on his weekly wage. Twice a year he used to have what today we call a bonus. That's when we got our new shoes and our new clothes. There was nothing extra but we had a happy childhood.

We came back to live in St Ann's, because gran and grandpa wanted help. We lived at 63, Pym Street. They were big houses facing Blue Bell Hill schools. That was in the late 1930s. Grandad died in 1938. I remember queuing in the Blue Bell Hill yard with my granny and the rest of the family for a gas mask and my gran was ever so frightened. I remember my mum saying: 'Go and stand with your gran because she isn't very well'. She would be in her late 60s then. My auntie died of TB and it shook gran very much. After gran died, we moved to 2, Abbey Grove, The Wells Road, St Ann's. We were surrounded by allotments. There was just a horseshoe of the old houses. I was married from No 2, fifty years ago.

When dad decided to take us to Lenton, I went to Lenton Council School and then I went up to a brand new school called Cottesmore. When we came back to St Ann's for gran, mum and dad still sent me to Cottesmore. So for my last two years I travelled from St Ann's to Cottesmore to finish my education. Then I earned eight shillings a week in a boot and shoe shop on Union Road in St Ann's. I left school at seventeen, which was ever so late to stop at school in those days. Mum was always ailing and when I should have been looking for work or writing for interviews I'd look after mum and the family, which I enjoyed doing.

The shoe shop was called Stevenson's. A lady and her daughter ran the shop and down below was her husband who was a deaf and dumb fellow and he used to do all the repairs. I used to go up and down those cellar steps: all for eight shillings a week!

I saw the boot and shoe shop through Christmas and then I got a job in the Player's offices. They sent me from the office in No 2 Factory, on Radford Boulevard, to the Cigarette Boxing Department and I was the stock girl there.

All the big boxes of five hundred cigarettes went down onto the transport and I had to keep a tally of everything that went down. And my boxes had to tally with theirs at the bottom. Believe me it was difficult when you'd got ten lads working on the trolleys. They used to bring the boxes up in fives, five by three. And I worked there quite happily but one Friday, the Territorials were called up. All the lads had joined the Territorials [Territorial Army], along with the Foreman. When they were all called up, we were in a mess. It was down to about three lads to collect from all the machines.

I belonged to St Ann's Church Fellowship. Vernon went to St Matthias Church. It was all in St Ann's. He had girlfriends and I was courting and engaged to a fellow in the Royal Wiltshire Yeomanry but sadly he got killed. I used to go to what they called an After Meeting after Sunday evening service and Vernon's friend used to go to St Ann's Church. They used to go to school together. And

one day they brought Vernon to our Fellowship, but it was quite a long time before we started really to get together. It was just after he joined the Air Force. But I never called him Vernon. I couldn't get my head around Vernon! I used to call him 'tiny' because he was head and shoulders taller than most people we knew.

I stayed on at Player's until I was called up and then I was called up to work in the Children's Hospital on Chestnut Grove as a Nursing Orderly. I had to live in.

It must have been just before my nineteenth birthday. I really wanted to go into the Forces because my brothers had already gone. But they exempted me. Albert was in the Army and Alf, the younger brother, was in the Navy. I volunteered for the Fire Service and had my medical and intelligence test and passed it all. Then the Government wouldn't let me go. I was told I'd have to do what they wanted me to do. So I landed up at the Children's Hospital with a case in my hand and I didn't know what was confronting me. I was there until Vernon came home in 1948.

I've always been in the Guides. I joined at Lenton when I was eleven. We came back to St Ann's when I was fourteen and I joined with St Ann's Church and I went into the eighty-third company, St Ann's Church Guides and the Guide Captain was Miss Hollingsworth. Her mother kept the little beer-off on St Ann's Well Road where St Thomas's Close is now. She got called up in 1940 and the Tawny and Brown Owl got called up or went away to do War work in 1941. It left Miss Terry the Lieutenant and it left me with a Brownie pack and no leader. I was sixteen at the time.

I was very young but took over St Ann's eighty-third, St Ann's Church own Brownies. Fortunately when I got called up, Matron at the Children's Hospital was very sympathetic and let me off at four o'clock every Friday to go and run those Brownies. That was wonderful. We met in the School Hall at the side of St Ann's Church. But that building was 'condemned' and they built a Church Hall – a glorified Nissen Hut – round the corner on Corporation Road in what used to be the School's playground. And it wasn't really big enough.

After a little while they decided that all youth organisations should be in one hall and we went to what we called Hungerhill 'Tin' hut but it was a nice hall. The only thing was we had to provide everything, we loaned it off the High School. We had a lovely time at this hall, kept these Brownies going. The Guides had to go to the companies that were left after leaders were called up. The twenty-fifth St Ann's was like one open group, just for church people. So there we were in this hut, Scouts, Guides, Cubs and Brownies. We had to do a lot of work because we had to pay the rents, electricity and ground rates . . .

During the War, we did all sorts to make do. I got bandages from the chemist and dyed them to the right blue for the neck ties of the uniforms. For the Christmas parties, we made the Brownies their first jellies. You couldn't get jelly in the War. I made jelly with gelatine crystals dad got from Burtons. I boiled a bottle of Cherryade and put it in moulds and they thought it was lovely. I took them to Elton camp one Saturday. There was only one who'd ever

St ANN'S NOTTINGHAM: inner-city voices by Ruth I Johns • ISBN 0951696092

been on a train. We got the train from Victoria Station for two pence return to Elton. And they thought it was heaven. We did our campfire cooking at my dad's allotment garden where the houses are now on Botany Avenue. We were all poor but we had a marvellous time.

In the winter we used to go up to Hungerhill Gardens and sledge down. In the spring we'd go round the gardens and do woodcraft and things like that. For a hike we said let's invite the Church Fellowship as well and unknown to me they invited Vernon as well. So we got together and started courting.

I loved everything at the Children's Hospital. We were woken at six in the morning. We had to do half an hour's duty before we went to breakfast. The kiddies were awake at four, and they would be washed and given breakfast. In my half-hour duty, I had to clear up and wash the dishes from the kiddies breakfast and set trays for their lunch-time drinks. Then I went for my breakfast which would be a boiled egg or a kipper, toast and marmalade, cereals. Only one slice of toast, one butter-ball and one drink, but we always had to go to the dining room.

From there, I'd come back and sweep the ward and the floors were oak, dark oak. The nurses used to come from all over. Some of them were called up and they were ladies' daughters. They came to our Hospital because it was in a safe area. If they were washing the children and they put a spot of water on the floor, the wood went white. So we had to go around with a mop, not an ordinary mop, we used to put dusters on the end of a brush, put a bit of polish on . . . And once a week we had to do the whole ward polishing, two of us, then buffing it up with a buffer on a handle.

After sweeping the ward, I'd give a drink to all the children who could have one. I was mostly on a surgical ward and I saw some nasty sights. It broke my heart really. And then I would wash the children's bandages. They were called 'many tail' bandages. They used to wrap over and expand when they'd had an operation on their stomach. I used to wash them by hand and iron them. Then at half-past eleven I would get the trays ready for the children's lunches. They all had a knife and fork and spoon. Babies had to be fed. I didn't do the babies at first until I got into it. I did the M J Player Ward. The children had mince from

leg of beef, it was always mince. I used to mash the potatoes for them. They were always steamed. They used to be in a big steamer in the cookhouse and sometimes they were lumpy. I used to get a drop of milk and mash it all to make it better for the kiddies. A lot of them just had mashed potatoes. Sometimes we had to have 'Pig Potatoes' - little potatoes with skins on - and they used to steam them. When they got to the Ward I used to skin them, because all the kiddies didn't like skin, and mash them. It was mostly mashed potatoes and gravy and rice pudding or egg custard.

And then we'd wash the dishes and go for our own lunch which was half an hour, back again and we'd be cleaning then, probably helping with the beds to get them nice in the afternoon. Nurses did them in the morning. We washed all the lockers, cleaned the bed rails. Of course, parents weren't allowed to visit children in those days. It was horrible, the state some of the children were in, they didn't know their mums and dads. The mums and dads cried at us saying: 'What shall we do?' I used to say: 'Well for a day or two wear a handkerchief on your head so they'll think you are another nurse, and they'll soon get used to you again'.

Parents weren't allowed in the Hospital at all. Sister saw them once a week on a Saturday at two o'clock. It was called Trolley Day and mums and dads would queue to see Sister, each Ward Sister, and she would give them a report.

Children taken out to get the air

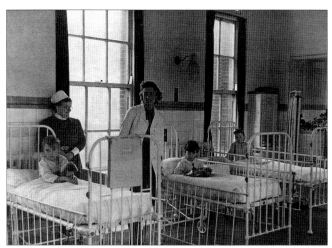

M J Player Ward when Rose Hawley worked there. Left, Sister Roberts and a doctor who went to be a missionary

. . . Rose Hawley with a small patient on the roof of the Children's Hospital

Parents were allowed to ring up but they couldn't see their children, because they used to cry you see. That was the thinking then. They would get upset. If parents brought them some apples or a bar of chocolate, we'd put their names on it and put them on a trolley and take them up. I got to know a lot of the parents, I used to feel for them. All the time I was there, parents weren't allowed to visit. I think it changed after the War. Of course, if children were very, very ill we'd have to fetch the parents and put them in a side ward where the other children did not see them. But parents weren't even allowed to look in the windows.

Downstairs at the Hospital were the medical cases, asthma, bronchitis and all that. Upstairs where I was, Margaret Jenny Player Ward, they had appendix problems, hernias, scalds, burns, hare lips and cleft palates, emphysema, draining of the lung, anything that was surgical went on ours. The other ward across the passage they did all the orthopaedics dealing with arms and legs and heads. Ours was a very busy ward. It used to be spotless. As you can see, my home has no brass in it! Because every morning there I had to clean the brass taps and the baths and anything brass.

The Hospital was privately funded, mainly by the Player's family. J D Player used to come in every morning. Player's still paid my wages. When I was nineteen, it was one pound, ten shillings a month. My dad had to pay for my clothes and my stockings and shoes that I wore on duty. The Hospital did provide uniform. If anyone had told me I was going to work in a hospital when I left school I would have said 'not on your nelly!'

The operating theatre was sponsored by the 504 County Nottingham Auxilliary Air Force Squadron. And beds were sponsored. The big factories, especially the Lace ones, had their name across the top of a bed. A bed would have Cooper and Roe or something on it. One bed was sponsored by a printers. They used to give so much a year toward the beds and, of course, there was big turnover with linen. I used to have to count the linen going in and out. It was a lovely little hospital, it didn't smell like one.

Yes, they had collections in St Ann's for the Children's Hospital. There used to be a certain day in the year when people would collect for the Children's Hospital, and one for the General Hospital and City Hospital.

Matron fetched me one day and said in a deep voice: 'I must remind you that you can go back to Player's where you belong'. So I looked at her and said I didn't want to go back. She said: 'What with all that money in front of you?' She said Sister Tutor had always been upset that she hadn't been able to train me as a nurse. She asked if I'd like her to have a word with her friend who was Matron of the City Hospital. She said: 'Go and be a midwife Rose and bring all the babies . . . you love babies, look how you have looked after our babies'. So I said no thank you, I'm waiting for Vernon, until he comes out of the Forces and within months he came out.

Vernon and I got engaged at Goose Fair 1949. We got married at Easter 1950 at St Ann's Church. After Vernon and I got married in 1950, we lived at 35, Hawkridge Street, on the corner of Sims Street. We made a garden in

Rose and Vernon's wedding with a guard of honour for the Captain. St Ann's Church April 8th 1950

the front from a load of rubble. It was a little terrace house. We did quite a lot of alterations. We were there two years. Our eldest son, Tim, was born there and then we moved up to 14, Richmond Avenue, St Ann's, and we had Christina and Philip. We lived there for thirty-one years.

In the Tin hut I mentioned earlier, Vernon and I set up a club for kiddies. We found that a lot of kiddies on Saturday night were sitting outside pubs. We ran a club for girls and boys for about ten years.

The first year we got married, the Vicar, Rev Little, came and said to us: 'Captain, do you think you can help us?' I said it depended on what it was! I only worked part-time doing a little cleaning job for a friend who was a nurse at the Children's Hospital when I was there. She had two babies in ten months and asked if I could help when she had the second baby. Her husband was a solicitor. So I went to Forest Fields to look after her first child.

Captain Rose Hawley leads the parade from Coppice Road [now Ransom Road] to St Ann's Church. The parade was on the first Sunday of every month. Half-hidden by Rose is Pauline Gilbert. Carrying the Union Jack is Betty Goodman. On her left is Dorothy Gilbert and, in the marching line behind her, Jean Gadd, Sylvia Dawes, Nellie Goodman, June Gadd and Betty Gilbert. The girl behind Dorothy Gilbert's left shoulder is Sheila Merriman

St Ann's Nottingham inner city voices by Ruth I Johns • ISBN 0951696092

Robin Hood Rangers camp at Sherwood Lodge 1957

Anyway, the Vicar said they wanted someone to look after the Scouts. Vernon said he'd never been a Scout and the Vicar said: 'Well, what have you got to say about that Rose?' So, I said I'd teach him all I knew, if the present fellow could stay on for a couple of months while I get Vernon into it.

When my own girl got into the Brownies, I moved on to the twenty-fifth Company Guides and when she got up into Guides I moved on to Rangers. I was the District Ranger Captain for years. Then I was District Secretary and for eight years I was a Commissioner. And it was all in St Ann's. It's a rule of guiding that when you have done it for so long, you move to another district. After forty years, I didn't want to move out of my own district. I said there wouldn't be another district like St Ann's.

There were many Continentals in St Ann's during and after the War. The Poles, Lithuanians, Ukrainians and so on, some of them 'displaced' persons. They could read English hesitatingly but could not write it. So I helped with all their forms and did everything in confidence. The Poles had a Guide unit of their own on Hartley Road, Radford. They had grey uniforms. When I was Assistant Commissioner, the Polish Guides said they'd love to come on one of our parades. Every month, all these organisations marched down to St Ann's Church on the first Sunday of the month. The Scouts had a band and the Boys' Brigade had a band. All the kids and all the mothers came out. They were big parades.

Anyway, they wanted to march on the St George's Day march near the 21st April. I went to the County Commissioner, Mrs Hanson, and asked permission. It was strict in those days, all navy blue and they had grey uniform. 'We'd love to have them,' she said. And I said: 'Well there's some Ukrainians as well and they have a flowered top.' And she said: 'Bring them all. They are all

welcome'. In the end we had a very big party. We all got together in the Sycamore School Hall and they did their traditional things. It was beautiful.

We all paraded and went to the Albert Hall on Derby Road and they joined our District, so, with all these friends, we had a very big District. They got a very big clap in Market Square, which we were thrilled about because this is what guiding and scouting is all about. They came every year while I was Commissioner and then they broke away. In those dark days, they hadn't heard from their relatives back home and didn't know if they were alive or dead. I used to urge the parents to teach their children traditional things and they used to think that was wonderful, because they said: 'One day we're going back'. And I've seen it happen in my lifetime. Some went back but there are still many in Nottingham.

I think a lot of these Continentals lived in St Ann's because property was cheap and it was near Gedling Pit. They were lovely people.

When the new St Ann's Church was built after the St Ann's demolition, the Guides and Brownies went back there. The Rangers stopped after I stopped. When St Ann's district was pulled down, a lot of the children moved from the area, to Clifton, Aspley and Bilborough, Strelley, they went everywhere. It was a pity really. And now, children with anything about them go to College.

All the years I did Brownies, Guides and Rangers in St Ann's, I never got a door slammed in my face. Everybody knew when we were away [at camp] but we never got robbed. Parents used to say to me: 'Any cheek Rose, give them a damn good hiding' because they knew you wouldn't do it unless they were really naughty. But I never did of course. But the children knew what their parents had said to me, and we never got the cheek that mothers got. I was always made welcome by parents.

Our house wasn't affected by the demolition time in St Ann's. Our children were born 1951-1958. So Philip was still quite young at that time. I brought up a little black lad with him almost. Dukey's dad was a road sweeper when they first came over, and he died suddenly. The son was with our Philip at school and he used to spend more time in our house than his.

The Vicar of St Ann's Church had a nervous breakdown when they told him they were pulling his church down. He daren't tell us at first. It was a very traditional church. At the time, a woman worker, Pam Harvey (she's a Reverend now) was left in charge on her own. The Bishop knew the church was coming down.

At first, they said they were going to make a communal church in the new St Ann's where the Roman Catholics, the Methodists, the Baptists and Church of England would share one building. We all said that was silly, we'd be falling over each other getting in and out for morning and evening service!

Miss Harvey asked if I would go with her to the Planning Office of the Council. So I left my lad with my mum and we went. We found that the proposed Eastern By-pass was going through St Ann's Church. The planner said there would be a bridge over St Ann's Well Road and

Demolition of St Ann's Church. *Photos: Vernon Hawley*

ST ANN'S NOTTINGHAM: Inner-city voices *by Ruth I Johns* • ISBN 0951696092

St Ann's Church was going to be below it. Our bell would be 'that much' below it. I said we'd never get anybody there. When I saw this planning proposal, I said to Miss Harvey: 'What are they going to do with St Ann's Church?' Houses would be going. They were slapping on compulsory purchase orders. Then they slapped one on St Ann's Church. So somebody ripped it off. The PCC [Parish Church Council] went to London. The PCC went everywhere to try to save our church. But they said they wanted a Health Centre there. But we wouldn't let them pull the Church down until we had permission to build a new one. They promised us that. We went to no end of meetings. We were always at it.

Then they said Emmanuel Church was going to join with us. So our Church is now St Ann with Emmanuel. But it was only joined after the foundations of the new Church went in. The money from both churches built the new one. What was given in compensation for one church wouldn't have built a new church. The PCC decided that nothing from the old churches would go in the new one, or it would be a museum. Emmanuel weren't bringing any of their staff and our Miss Harvey who had taken us through that awful time had to leave. And we had to start afresh and the Rev Roy Williamson came in.

That time was a very sad time for St Ann's people. It's atrocious if you stop to think of it. If that happened now there'd be a riot. We didn't leave. The population changed. Older people were left. Years ago, I did a survey with Rev Mattie MacQuillan and we found that, then, eighty per cent of people in St Ann's were over seventy. The people with families left and went all over. When the older people died, younger people came in but there was no continuity. All the chaps who had little workshops went. The area could be beautiful but the Council won't let it be beautiful because we get problem families sent in. And, now, there isn't the same variety of housing. And there's nowhere for children to play. There are little green areas where you can't play with a ball.

The redevelopment time caused a lot of heartbreak and a lot of people, the old people, died. They got in their new flats and they just collapsed. It was because they couldn't go out and knock on the lady next door. In the old St Ann's, if a woman who was having a baby had nothing, by the time the midwife came in and the woman had her baby, that baby would have a cot and everything. Neighbours went round and collected things, they weren't new but they were clean. If anyone was in trouble, the street was in trouble. People were accepted as newcomers came in.

But after I finished guiding, I did five years as a volunteer for the Probation Department on Robin Hood Chase, St Ann's. I helped with their crèche one morning a week and I went and baby-sat for a few of their clients. But then they said we weren't going to be insured so it was a bit risky. We'd got our own children and Vernon and I felt they should have covered us better than that. It could be tricky, a woman on her own.

Our Deaconess from St Ann's Church, Rev Mattie MacQuillan went to be Chaplain at the new Queen's Medical Centre. With the Rev David Stoter, they set up a

Sycamore Scout and Guide Band, Sunday morning after the Church Parade to St Ann with Emmanuel Church, Chase Precinct. 1988

Guild, and even before that I went up to help as a visitor. There are Ward Visitors through the Chaplain of the Chaplaincy and the Guild. The Guild sponsor literature and so on. As each ward was opened, there was a Visitor. You used to go round once a week and talk to patients and ask if we could help in any way. We had to have training for eight weeks. I still had my mum and dad at the time, so they didn't send me to the older people, they sent me to maternity. Well, I had the time of my life except for the sadness of those who lost their babies. I did that for ten years until about 1983, about the time we came to this house.

Then they asked me if I could help at 48, the Ropewalk. I'd never heard of it. It came under the Queen's Medical Centre and the General Hospital. There was a service once a week. It was for people with cancer, who had chemotherapy or radiotherapy and stayed there during the week and went home at weekends. I was asked to go and talk to women there like I did previously on the Maternity Ward. So I did that for about fourteen years until it closed when the City Hospital set up its Cancer Unit.

That work had a sad side but I loved it. I talked to the patients. But when it closed six years ago, I was seventy-one and felt I should give that up regularly. But I still go up every fortnight flower arranging which is one of my hobbies.

My daughter got married and got a house in St Ann's and came to us one day and said the house next door to them was for sale. She said it was a lovely house. We'd just modernised the house in Richmond Avenue but there'd been a lot of trouble with mining subsidence. My Tina was washing her hair one night and the ceiling fell on her. It's a wonder we weren't killed. You couldn't close the windows, you couldn't close the doors. So we moved up here in 1983. This house is well-built and our daughter still lives next door. The owner of the factory at the back lived here. Eventually that was sold off. When we came it was a Builder's Merchant. Now, it's a training centre.

Just up the road is the Hendon Rise Club. Everybody in St Ann's knew the Hendon Rise Social Club because all the young couples and the young marrieds used to come up here dancing on a Saturday night. They loved it. Happy Days.

2002. The Hendon Rise Social Club is for sale

National Savings

Rose Hawley's mother, Miriam May Smedley (third person from right), is receiving the banner of the League of Nottingham Street Groups 1942-43. It says: Awarded to St Ann's Well Road and Blue Bell Hill District Committee. Miriam Smedley was Secretary of the St Ann's Well Road Group and the woman (top left) Secretary of the Blue Bell Hill Group. The banner was awarded to the District Committee with the highest savings achievement for the year. The man behind the banner was Manager of the Cavendish Cinema where the Awards Ceremony took place. Others in the photo were members of Nottingham National Savings Committee

Nottingham had over 800 Street Savings Groups, 95% of them run by women, according to *Women and County, the Journal for the Women of Nottingham and Nottinghamshire*: May 1946. The City's National Savings Committee enlisted a van in an effort to expand saving even further and to 'get everyone saving'. Manned by voluntary helpers, the van 'went into action seeking to initiate groups in, as yet, unconquered streets'.

VERNON HAWLEY

Born 1928

I was born on 3, Serlby Rise, on the Gordon Road estate, St Ann's. It's the estate just over the hill toward Carlton Road. Then my mum decided she wanted a change and went over to Hereford Road for about six months. It was too windy so she came back to 4, Serlby Rise. Apart from

my time in the Air Force, I was there until I got married. I had one sister but she died before I was born so I was an only child really. On my mum's side, my mum and her sister came from Arnold but they used to work in Nottingham. Mum worked for a firm called Boulles's, French pastry cooks, on Clumber Street and that's where she met my father. Grandma, her brother and sister emigrated to Mablethorpe on the East coast and bought a boarding house and eventually they got two houses. My mum used to spend time out there in the summer and come back to Arnold in winter.

There was a good train service from Nottingham to Mablethorpe. We've still got some relations out there. The person we'd call big grandma [great grandma] lived in Arnold. We used to go over most Sundays to see her. We used to walk all the way. Big grandma died around 1937 when I was young. After that we didn't go to Arnold very much. We've always visited Mablethorpe.

On my father's side I never knew my grandma and grandad. He died around the time I was born and she died a year or so later. They came to Nottingham from Derbyshire (near Youlgreave) for work. They were blacksmiths and farriers on Carter Gate. My father had five brothers and two sisters: quite a big family. They were all blacksmiths and that sort of thing, they had horses and carts and used to cart coal about. Well it was in barrows to start with.

My father used to tell me stories. Because there was a pub next door to the blacksmiths, there was a hatch through the wall to the pub next door. My grandad used to drink a lot because of the heat of the fires and then all of a sudden he stopped drinking. My father went to Sneinton School. There were allotments up there and he had to feed pigs before he went to school. He was in St Mary's Church Choir. They did work for the wholesale fruit markets. If the police got in trouble, they would send for grandad and his six sons to help sort matters out! When Broadmarsh, Carter Gate and all round there was cleared[1], my grandma and the lads went to live at the top of Storer Street, St Ann's. They had a coal yard at the top and they had horses and carts to do haulage.

In the First World War, my dad's three older brothers were all in the Army. Two of them got wounded but they all came back. They bought an ex-Army lorry and that's how they started with motor haulage. They had a yard on Hermit Street near Penny Foot Street, Sneinton. They finished up with quite a big firm with about twenty lorries at one time.

The three older brothers owned the business and the three younger brothers worked for them. Dad was number four. The older ones came back out of the Army and put their bit of money in. During the 1926 Strike, the firm carried on working with a dispensation from the Mine Workers Union because it used to take food, only food. The mine workers were, of course starving. They used to go to the banks by the pit and rake coal out and bag it up. So what the family haulage firm did was sell them food and then they were allowed to carry the coal back.

---

[1] These were clearances of overcrowded slums made possible when the City was able to extend after the Enclosure Act of 1845. St Ann's was one of the improved areas that was developed.

St Ann's Nottingham: Inner City Voices by Ruth I Johns • ISBN 0951696092

Things went downhill a bit in the 1930s and it ended up with my Uncle Bill and my father being in the firm. During the Second World War, none of their drivers got called up because they were all working on airfields. They were on Reserve. Their best lorry was commandeered. Dad later met a soldier who said he set fire to dad's lorry at Dunkirk to save it falling into enemy hands. He could see the name under the paint. All the drivers had to maintain their own lorries, they all had to be cleaned and greased. I used to go with dad and play in the yard on Hermit Street. My dad was in the Home Guard and mum got a job at the Co-op Bakery. She and her mate used to do deliveries three days a week in a petrol wagon. When rationing came in, she had to deal with coupons. They often came back with bags of potatoes from customers in the country areas.

I went to St Matthias Church in St Ann's and was in the Church Choir. I went to the St Matthias School on Carlton Road and then when they closed it my mum didn't want me to go to Manvers so I had to traipse all the way over to Sneinton Boulevard School.

Then I went to Mundella School. I was always mad on aircraft, still am, and the school had an ATC [Air Training Corps] squadron so I joined. During the War all us lads used to do jobs as well. I delivered meat for a shop on the corner of King Edward Park. Two sisters ran the shop after the butcher's lads got called up. It was a family business. On a Friday night I used to cycle, delivering meat to West Bridgford and the end of Trent Boulevard. Another night I went to Sherwood. I did all the long distance!

When I left school I went as an apprentice toolmaker at Claude B Barton's engineering on Union Road, St Ann's. It had to move and is now at the top of Winchester Street. There's a big car park on one side and on the other a factory which still says Claude B Barton. Never anybody working there. On odd occasions you see the lights on. It's all laid out with exactly the same machinery as when I left school.

I started there in 1944. There was a night shift as well. Like a lot of engineering firms, they used to do a lot of specialised work, machine tool accessories, things called 'V' blocks and we used to do jigs and fixtures and things like that including for guns and turrets. We would also do maintenance. The boss had broken his arm doing something factory inspectors wouldn't allow now. They didn't have guards or anything. He was in hospital a long time and studied radio. When he came back, above his door said 'Radio Doctor'. So he did radios in the shop as well after that.

I started on twenty-one shillings a week. You had to provide all your own overalls and everything and they stopped you two and six a week for tool club. You had to buy all your own tools and he used to sell them to you through his shop. At that time Rose worked at a nearby shoe shop and we didn't know each other then.

One thing we lads had to do was to go down the 'black hole of Calcutta' to the coke stoves. During the week it wasn't too bad but on Monday morning in winter when everything was frozen up, the first job was to clean the stoves out and start the fires. The firm did a lot of stuff for the Air Ministry. We used to do electrical work and maintenance for factories. These days, factories would have their own maintenance staff but not then. We were working Bank Holidays because when hosiery factories were closed, we'd go in and see to the line shafting. They probably had an electric motor or a donkey engine one end and all down would be a set of shafting with pulleys on. And that was line shafting. Then they'd send for us if belts down to the different machines broke. We had a kit for mending them. We had line shafting and so on in our own works as well. We did Printing firms, including Windsor Press on Huntingdon Street. And across the road from us was Marsden's the Grocer's warehouse. We used to maintain all their tea packing machines and things like that.

There wasn't the same safety awareness then. The belt used to come off the top pulley, so you would stand on a stool and the belt was still around the shaftings: with everything still working, you could go 'whoosh' and pull the belt on again!

Whichever lad was last to start work had to go five minutes to knocking off time and take a bucket down to the shop at the front of the works where they had an Ascot heater, fill the bucket and take it back. So there was one bucket for everyone to wash their hands in! We used to have grease solvent stuff like grey pumpice stone. You wiped your hands on some cotton waste or your overalls.

There was a lot of dust because a lot of work was in cast-iron which makes powdery turnings. We had some large machines called Planers. The jobs were bolted down on to the machine bed which moved to and fro, whilst the tool head moved across on a bridge unit. A lot of the work was high precision and had to be passed by an inspector who came to the works. Everybody had a hand brush or paintbrush to sweep all this stuff on the floor. Fridays at three o'clock the lads had to clean up right through the workshop.

All this blooming cast-iron dust was everywhere, you couldn't use anything to dampen it down. My hands were all right but, very often with cast-iron, you could tell who had done the job by the fingerprints. They'd do a machine, or an item, and next day it would have their fingerprints on because hands could get moist and it caused rust marks.

Rose and I knew each other through St Ann's Church Fellowship where I went along with a friend from school. All the churches had their clubs and I used to go across to St Ann's Church. She used to collect the subs and I'd go for two pennyworth of chips and a fish from Clarke's on St Ann's Well Road opposite Southampton Street. It was there we started to be attracted to each other.

By the time the War was sort of finishing I went into the RAF as an engine fitter. I did my training in Hereford. It was blooming cold there one winter. There was a row of hangers in the middle of Bulmer's Cider Orchards. No airfield because everyone was training.

Aircraft came in on lorries and you'd do the engine work. You'd take engines out of aircraft, strip them down and put them back, and wheel it outside and start it up. There were also about a dozen huts and a little compound where we all lived. We would start in the morning at six o'clock, and have a wash if you felt like it. You had a side pack for your knife, fork, plate, overalls, books and shaving kit. You'd go for a run and then form up in your training entries. We'd march to the camp with our stuff and then come back at dinner-time and go back to the site and then back again for your tea. So you left your billets all day. But there was one lane from the main site up to the cookhouse. You weren't allowed to knock off early but had to form up in your entries. The Corporals or whoever was in charge lined you up. You weren't allowed through the gate until a certain time but whoever was first through the gate got to the cookhouse first. Nobody could overtake you and it was quite an experience seeing all these different lines of men all marching slow, sometimes in Wellingtons in a foot of snow!

At night, the Cider people sent a bus up and you could go and get a bit of cash shovelling apples into vats and things like that.

After training I went to Cottesmore and then spent most of my time at Coningsby in Lincolnshire, where they had two pathfinder squadrons and a trainer unit for pilots and 231 OCU [Operational Conversion Unit] aircrew training. I was always interested in engines and aircraft particularly Mosquito aircraft. Sometimes I'd get over to see my grandma at Mablethorpe because the station was near there.

When I was discharged, I went back to my old firm. Rose and I didn't tell anybody we were getting engaged until we got to Goose Fair. Bill and I took Rose on the Big Wheel. We all went as a group to Goose Fair, walked down Alfred Street and over the top. When we married, we lived on the corner of Sims Street, St Ann's. I can see the streets there.

We'd got a little bit of garden at the front, blue brick yard at the back. We were the end house so it was bigger than the others because our front door was actually on Hawkridge Street. We did quite a lot to the house because my dad was in building and lorries used to call round with bits and pieces. But we didn't stay there very long.

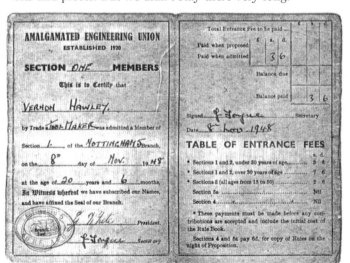

Vernon Hawley's admittance as a Tool Maker to the AEU on November 8th 1948 aged twenty

The family haulage firm site was bought out by Boots, which had already expanded over most of that area. So the family firm moved to a garage on Daleside Road. The firm was 'B' licenced, which meant it could do general haulage but were restricted to a sixty-mile radius of the Council House. But they got a special dispensation to go to Skegness for the Nottingham Co-op which had a branch there.

'B' licenced firms did not get nationalised. It would have been too much of a headache and expense to take them over. Father's firm used to do building and demolition as well as haulage. Eventually the firm was sold to Beardsley's.

Of course, just down the road from where we live now in St Ann's there's a garage called Kelley's and that used to be Keetches. And across the road in the brickyard bottom used to be their garage and they were nationalised. British Road Services' main Nottingham workshop was there and the yard was where they kept all the BRS lorries. The little office block on the front on The Wells Road was built for BRS offices.

We moved to Richmond Avenue, St Ann's. We came back off our holiday one year and found a crack had gone two inches and the Coal Board came and shored the houses up. It was like that for ages. It wasn't a strata fault. The miners said what happened was that in August when the pits closed for two weeks the maintenance men did the conveyor belts. But because the coal had stopped being taken you don't get a strata fault but a difference in level. Gedling Pit is under there. Miners have told us they had to leave a pillar under Mapperley Hospital. The pit came as far as our street but not much further. The Coal Board re-did the houses eventually. Then the floors were level but the ceilings weren't!

This is a much sounder house. We moved here in 1983. When the place was built there was a vehicle access at the side as access to the then hosiery factory. Over the years it changed.

The Hendon Rise Club is in the old Horticultural Hall up the road. When it was all allotments round here, all the gardeners used to have flower and fruit shows and sell the stuff from there. As the allotments were built on, the Hall became an ordinary club. For a while the Gladstone Club used it. They used to be on St Ann's Well Road. Now the Hall is an ordinary social club again. It's privately owned.

When our family came along, well before we moved up here, Rose finished work and I carried on at Claude B Barton's for a while. One of the things we used to do there was maintain a lot of hosiery machines, the big machines. We had some special shapers used to machine the main beams. The shaper stood still and the beams were moved across concrete pads set on the floor after each top section was machined.

I used to go to night school three nights a week and Saturday morning and did my National Certificate. Then a job came up at Nottingham District Technical College. I got a job in the Production Engineering Workshop, a sort of laboratory, but it was a funny place to work. I used to go one day a week to carry on with my National Certificate, then they stopped overtime but we used to work most evenings a week. Theoretically you got time off in lieu but the wages were not liveable. One of the things I did at the Tech was teach mining students because they had to do Electro Mechanical courses.

As happened then in engineering, there was plenty of work, so I went to a firm called Peerless Engineering on Nuthall Road, a small firm. They used to do work for Broughs the motorbike people and a lot for Furse Electrical Lightning Conductor Department. A lot of weather vanes on churches are lightning conductors and they came in for renovation. We used to do work for Elastic Yarns, on Castle Boulevard, which also included subsidiary firms, Fine Wires Ltd and Clutson and Kemp Ltd.

They used to do knicker elastic. The rubber came in on hanks and the cotton came in on hanks. Then it was wound off hanks on to bobbins, then on to bobbin machines and they wound on to cones. Some were pineapple cones. We used to build our own machines. Everything was covered with French chalk and you were supposed to wear masks. They used to make bell wire which was copper wire covered with cotton as an insulator. Plastic took over a lot of that. We used to do a lot of experimental work.

Then I saw a lab job advertised. I was always interested in laboratory work. When I was doing my National Certificate course work you had to do laboratory work on engines, steam engines and oil engine castings and all sorts of things. During wartime air-raids on Nottingham, the Technical College on Shakespeare Street got bombed, including the engines' lab. After the War they rebuilt it and that's why it looks so nice now, opposite the Registry Office. When you were doing Laboratory Classes, you went to use the Univeristy's engines' lab at Highfields.

Professor Pope came to Nottingham University from Sheffield and he was quite go ahead and jobs were advertised for a grade of staff he introduced. He eventually became Chancellor of Aston University. He got a lot of money for engineering and chemistry. He paid us more and we used to work overtime and be paid properly. Everybody else was laboratory stewards or technicians. When he left, it took them a little time to steamroller us into their system! We were in the main workshops of Civil and Mechanical Engineering. We did work for Rolls-Royce and all sorts of people.

I got promoted and used to do part of the week in the laboratories and part in the workshop, then gradually it all became laboratory as the work expanded. We used to do work for people like Shell, on Civil Engineering, specimens for Tarmac for roads in frosty weather, work for British Rail and so on.

The University got the land where the Government Buildings used to be on Clifton Boulevard and Professor Pope built up his own Department with his own staff. So we had a sort of aircraft hanger and we had five ton travelling cranes, wind tunnels for wind power work and water tunnels. Civil Engineering split off but we still had the fluids lab. All the basic experimental work for the Water Sports Centre at Holme Pierrepont was done in our labs.

Vernon Hawley (right) and Bob Beale in Main Bay L4, Mechanical Engineering Department

Vernon Hawley (centre) with Ian Cooper and Reg Creasey in Main Bay L4, Mechanical Engineering Department

I ended up as Laboratory Supervisor in the Thermodynamics, Fluid Mechanics, Heat Transfer and Nuclear Engineering to give it its full name! We'd actually got a Neutron generator and a nuclear lab. Eventually that was given up because of the insurance costs when people started to get worried about nuclear and, of course, there's houses nearby. Then we did nuclear engineering and the basics, and then have to go to nuclear power stations for the rest of that work.

We used to do a lot of development work for Fords, Government work and for Rolls-Royce. At one time I did a lot of work on breech blocks for eighteen pounder guns.

We did work for the Queen's Medical School. They've got an engineering department at the School now. We did artificial limbs, mechanical aids and that sort of thing. We did some heart pumps. There was a lot of trouble before the Peristaltic Pumps. In the early research days, we used to go down to the cattle market and come back with containers full of blood to use in testing! And then afterwards, the gardeners used to take it home for their allotments. We used to do testing on knee and hip joints. In earlier days they were made out of stainless steel. We did materials testing. They used to send us bones, joints and we'd glue them. In the early days they were bolted weren't they? There have been big advances.

We did a lot on carbon fibre and plastics and they started a Glass Reinforced Plastics lab.

I remember when our son Philip did Pole Vaulting. When he was fourteen or fifteen the teachers at Elliott Durham School were on 'no external activities'. They stopped doing athletics. I ran the local Scouts on Ransom Road, the 69th Nottingham Company: a new open Scout Group and we registered ourselves as Robin Hood Athletic Club. Phil bought a glass fibre Pole from Redmayne and Todd.

Professor Pope and Professor Smith weren't in the ivory towers of universities because they'd been in engineering. Professor Smith had been Professor of Aircraft Propulsion at Cranfield College. We did wave power. There was a long water channel, hydraulic channel set in the floor. It was deeper one end and could be drained and it had removable concrete slabs. We had a wave machine and everything. They worked out that the energy required to build wave power machinery, for example in steel making and in lorries transporting fuel and so on, would never be recovered by the amount of energy created by wave power. It would be a false economy. And wind power has serious environmental effects. And there's high maintenance. The blades are fibreglass but they flex and eventually crack and when they are eighty feet up, maintenance problems are difficult.

I retired in 1993. The Departmental Supervisor, Cliff Baldwin, did a lovely painting of a Mosquito aircraft which was presented to me.

Tim, our eldest child, went to St Ann's 'Board' School and then to High Pavement School. He was a Social Worker in the City. Tina and Philip also went to the St Ann's 'Board' School. Tina went on to Mundella and Philip to Morley School and then on to Elliott Durham School.

Rose has told you about using the Hungerhill 'Tin' hut for Brownies, Guides, Scouts and Rangers. We used it – it was painted galvanised steel – until it came down. We got planning permission to build a Scout and Guide Hut up Ransom Road for the Nottingham 69th Scout Company and 25th Guide Company. It was the time when St Ann's was being pulled down. They were pulling the Empire Cinema down. There was loads and loads of brick rubble. Some would be sold. But if it was near dinner-time or going home time and they had a short load they would tip it where we wanted to build and the land needed filling in. We hired a vibrating roller and flattened it. And we actually got a grant, I think from the Department of Education and Science, to concrete the site. Frost and Leatherlands, who used to be at the bottom of St Bartholomew's Road, St Ann's, put in the drains before the concrete and then we had the place slabbed. But we still didn't have a building.

We used to go to Mablethorpe and wander through Lincolnshire looking at prefabricated buildings. Then we saw an advert in the paper. Somebody was selling his prefab, £800. There were people going round Army camps pulling them down. We got a grant for that. It came on two lorries one pouring wet night and we had to get everybody living on Richmond Avenue out to help! All these neighbours helped with assembling and that. Then we had to line the building.

A man who worked for Wimpey's, who were building the new St Ann's, asked Headquarters and they said let us have enough timber because, in the long run, it would probably save them having to make another hall (because they had pulled ours down!).

Then I got in touch with British Plasterboard. It was when things were beginning to go from Imperial to Metric measurement. They had a warehouse full of Imperial stuff and we used to go and collect it in our old London taxi and trailer. We opened the new hut in 1968 and the children were thrilled. And the Over-Sixties Club met in there for years. Eventually that's where the Metrazone Community Centre is now, though they moved 'our' building a bit further up and rebuilt it.

Then I transferred to the 4th Company Nottingham Scouts which met in the hall just below the Sycamore Centre[2]. I still go there as honorary scouter and secretary. The 4th used to meet in the Sycamore School, which closed when they opened Elliott Durham Comprehensive School in 1966. The Ukrainian Guides met in the hall as well. On Richmond Avenue, there was a Mrs White, Mrs Black and Mrs Green opposite us. Then it was Rechinko's, Skabaski's and Jamas's. A lot of Lithuanians, Ukrainians and Germans came to live round there as the older people died and the houses came on the market. A lot worked down Gedling colliery. A bus used to pick up for Gedling Pit at the bottom of Ransom Road where the filling station is now. A lot of the houses below Richmond Avenue were Council owned and these people couldn't get on Council Housing lists. A lot of the privately owned houses had people who needed to walk to work to places like the Bus Garage on Manvers Street or the Post Office on Huntingdon Street.

The Richmond Dairy was originally on the corner of Richmond Avenue. They made cream cheese.

Then a doctor came to Richmond Avenue, Dr Boroski, who was Polish. There used to be a skin clinic on Parliament Street next to News House and he worked there, and he wanted to set up in General Practice. We were about first on his list. We sponsored him. You had to have enough people to sponsor you before you could set up as a GP. He used to turn his front room into a waiting room and his back room into a surgery. He was a good doctor. He was a Scout.

His friend was also a doctor of Mechanical Engineering at Nottingham University, Dr Lichtarowicz, but his wife was a medical doctor. He was also in the Polish Scouts. They had their own uniforms with sort of diamond shaped hats.

Our home wasn't affected by the demolition of a lot of St Ann's. But there were all the little shops up and down the St Ann's Well Road that went. We were always in and out of them and everybody knew us because of the Scouts and Guides, and we also ran a football team with the various lads round about. One lives down the road now and is retired!

---

2   This hall was refurbished mainly with City Challenge funding in 1995.

At Home in Nottingham: inner city voices by Ruth I Johns • ISBN 0951696092

Lotus Street just before demolition. Photo: Vernon Hawley

There used to be a hardware shop, Mrs Trott's, on the corner of Lotus Street. She had a paraffin tank in the backyard. A lot of people used to have paraffin heaters. In the winter she had to go outside to fetch the paraffin, so I rigged up a pump and a pipeline into her shop so she could switch it on and fill people's cans in the shop.

We used to go up and down a lot with the Scout and Guide band. We could take the band in our old London taxi, and there was a trailer for the drums. Bonfire night was often before a parade Sunday when we would be up and down the streets and some of the bonfires were still burning. When they started to pull St Ann's down, we collected street signs. We've still got one or two. Most went in the Scout hut and when it was moved they disappeared. They'd be collector's items now.

The 'old' London FX3 taxi which served the Scout and Guide band. Son Philip stands in front

The taxi is still doing well in 2002

We used to take the Scouts and Guides camping, Guides one week, Scouts another. We didn't charge them much. We picked a spot on the map and then wrote to the Vicar at Colston Bassett. We found out he'd been in the Army with a Vicar from St Ann's. We went to see him and he said he didn't have anywhere suitable for camping, but that the next field belonged to Sir Dennis La Marchant. We got a letter back from him: 'Dear Hawley!' But he was very good to us. We went down there for years and had a hut down there. He provided the milk and sent a bag of potatoes. We were all right for water because he had a cattle trough in the field and the water was mains. Half the village were still drinking from pumps.

While camping at Colston Bassett, the Guides and Scouts entertained children from a nearby Roman Catholic orphanage

We used to collect all the camping equipment together and my father would come down with his lorry and collect it. We piled in the equipment, the kids used to climb on top. All the way down St Ann's Well Road mums and dads would be waving to them. A lot of them would never have had a holiday otherwise.

There was going to be an inner-ring road right across St Ann's, from Gregory Boulevard, by the Children's Hospital, Cranmer Street then by Emmanuel Church, across St Ann's Well Road, to Carlton Road and Meadow Lane. They compulsorily purchased Emmanuel Church and pulled it down. I think they ran out of money but they decided St Ann's Church had got to go. There was quite a fad at the time for round churches. But we had a planning committee and the Diocesan Architect came down and after quite a few meetings he came up with a multi-purpose building which at that time was unique, the Church and a hall in the same building.

The last Service at the old St Ann's Church was on Easter Sunday. We went in on the Monday to take down things that belonged to the Church, like the War Memorial. We are still looking for that. We haven't tracked it down yet. We took brass plaques off the walls and they were all in the Church. We went for dinner and when we got back, somebody had pinched everything.

The Roman Catholics had two Churches either side of the valley. St Edward's on Gordon Road and St Augustine's on Woodborough Road. People in St Ann's and in other areas don't go over hills. If you're on one side of the hill you'll come down into the middle. But if you are down in the middle, you won't go over the hill. It's always been like that. So the Roman Catholics decided wisely for them that they had a church on both hills. Whereas the Church of England lost three churches to compulsory purchase: two hill churches, Emmanuel and St Bartholomew's, and St Ann's in the valley. Nothing from the three lost churches went in the new one, St Ann with Emmanuel in Robin Hood Chase. It would have been a museum. Odd bits were saved. I've got the bell rope from St Ann's.

One of the Hopewell's lived in the house on Robin Hood Chase that is the Vicarage now. Bernard Hopewell was Choir Master at one time. My father joined St Ann's Church Choir for a while and they used to have Choir outings up the River Trent. We still attend St Ann with Emmanuel Church.

There isn't the variety of housing now. Some beautiful houses came down. The Henson's, who were connected with the Scout group, lived on Hungerhill Road as it was then. They were beautiful three-storey houses. A few people managed to stay here but everybody was being shipped to Clifton and so on. Families were broken up. At that time people didn't have cars. You'd have a street like Westminster Street where half the people were related to one another. They'd all do their lace work, the jennying and the drawing, and come with bags of hairnets. Mrs Carnelly used to do hairnets. But all that died off when the houses and shops came down.

When new people came from abroad, they all mixed in and everybody spoke to each other. Now different cultures can be more in little enclaves.

Before demolition, I did a report on Scout groups in the City. In St Ann's, there were groups at Blue Bell Hill Schools, St Catharine's Church, the Congregational Church in Commerce Square, St Ann's Church, Sycamore School, the Baptist Church on Woodborough Road, St Andrew's and groups all up and down the St Ann's Well Road.

Scouts and Guides got harder. In the original families in St Ann's, you knew the grandmas and grandads and you knew the young ones that grew up, so they would carry on as families. There were always contacts. Immediately after redevelopment, St Ann's had a lot of older people who refused to move away when the families left. And when the older people died, younger ones came in. Many families in St Ann's now don't appear to have contacts with anybody. Their grandma's and grandad's may be anywhere and you haven't got the same family support.

In the old St Ann's you had nice big houses, you had close houses, and some Council houses, a wide variety of shops with living accommodation above, and you'd got a public house or beer-off on every street corner. But these were meeting places. Now the area is very bland and the open plan idea hasn't worked. It looked nice for the first year or two but when the older people died and younger ones came in there wasn't the same parental control. Gradually over the years it's become like a fortress, a maze. Sometimes, I go and visit parents of Cub Scouts or somebody and I think they are on such-and-such a road but you can't get down it, or you can't walk through because of little fences. So people are even more isolated. The housing itself is getting better now the Council is three-quarters of its way spending a fortune on it, making it decent.

The open plan was wrong and they were cheap houses but the leafy green areas they left were right. Now they've been built on, like there's a row of bungalows on what was a leafy green patch on Hungerhill Road near St Ann's School. I think Sycamore Rec is only still there because it's part of the Bridge Trust. Well that's another story (see Appendix III). The City Council is a Trustee of the Bridge Trust and one fine day the Charity Commissioners came along and found that land belonging to the Bridge Trust had been built on by the Council without permission or payment.

Rose and Vernon celebrated their Golden Wedding on April 8th 2000 at the UNAS Club, Nottingham University Park. Behind Rose and Vernon are, left to right, their son Philip; Danielle, Philip's daughter; Michael, Philip's son; Rose and Vernon's daughter Tina; Laura, Tina's daughter; Rebecca; Rose and Vernon's son, Tim and Simon. Rebecca and Simon are Tim's children

JESS PHELPS

Born 1923

Interviewed in her home 19.4.99

My father lived on 8, Eastville Street, St Ann's. His name was John Charles (Jack) Mace. He went to Huntingdon Street School. I've still got books the Boys' Brigade presented to him. He went to War [First World War 1914-18] and finished up a Sergeant. He was in the trenches, of course, as all young men were in those days. The Germans poisoned the water and he always had a dicky sort of tummy thereafter. He went home to Eastville Street and got a job with Howitt's the printers on Ashforth Street, St Ann's. It was just across the road. A very large factory: one of the biggest printers in Nottingham at that time. In those days, of course, towns were for people and work was in towns. People lived near their work. Suburbia was unheard of.

His younger brother was Herbert who also came back from the War. He was a lace designer and took a big part in the designing of the Battle of Britain panel of Nottingham Lace which was commissioned about the Second World War. Dad's youngest brother, Horace, was killed in the First World War.

Before she married, my mother (Gertrude May Walker) lived on Peas Hill Road, St Ann's. She went to Shelton Street School. Although they lived near each other, my parents met 'on the parade' so to speak. People spent their Sunday afternoons with this walk up Mansfield Road which was the 'in' thing. The parade of the ladies all in their Sunday best and they used to walk up and down Mansfield Road as far up as the Rock Cemetery.

Just at the bottom of Peel Street on the Mansfield Road, Tom Asher had a tobacconist shop. He used to sell loose snuff and Player's Weights by weighing cigarettes. He was a very famous man. He used to put football results up outside. This is before there were many papers or much traffic. That's where my mum and dad met and then eventually they married at Emmanuel Church on the Woodborough Road.

My mother was the seventh child. Her mother, my Grandma Walker, had a hell of a life. Mr Walker really fancied himself, a ladies man. He'd always got a fresh buttonhole and he was rather tall and elegant. But he didn't like babies very much. The day my mother was born, he wouldn't look at her. He just packed his bags and went. So my mother never saw her father. My mother was very close to her mother and when they lived at Peas Hill Road they both used to do lace work, sometimes all through the night they were finishing lace to earn a bob or two because Grandma Walker was sort of destitute. My mother's brothers were older, so they weren't all at home except Archie the next youngest to Mum.

The lace work was brought to Grandma Walker. My mother I suppose was brought up a bit as a man hater. That's why she wiped the floor with my father. She never pulled any punches with me, she would always make my

heart palpitate. And it was very unfortunate that she had me a year and four months after the light of her life, her son Jack. And she called me Jessie and her father's name was Jesse Walker. It seemed odd that that was what she called me. I had jet black hair and was swarthy looking.

Grandma Walker's sister Rose was a bit of a gypsy, rings on every finger. She married a wealthy man so we used to call her our rich aunt. She used to go to Skegness and sit on the pier and tell people's fortunes in spite of all the money she had. My mother always used to go and see Aunt Rose. One day she told my mother she was going to have another baby girl. My mother didn't want me let alone another baby girl. She said the girls would be as different as chalk from cheese and that it would 'be a life for a life'. Someone dear to her would die when the baby was born.

My mother found out she was pregnant. Grandpa Mace was as fit as a flea but into the February time he became ill. And got worse and worse. I think it must have been cancer. My dad was torn whether to be with his dad or my mum. Grandpa died just before midnight on July 11th and Betty was born at midnight. My mother registered Betty as born July 12th. Grandma stayed at 8, Eastville Street.

Have you heard of Jem Mace the boxer? The bare-fisted, 99 rounds boxer in long pants. As kids, we were told he was our great great grandfather. But in fact we found out he was our great uncle. It appears he was very much a gypsy and he used to like to travel with the gypsies and his other hobby was violinist. We always said that Jem left me his muscles and my sister the violin. Years later, she settled in Germany and played violin with the Detmolder Landes Theater. She's nearly sixty-nine now but they still call for her when somebody is sick and they can't play. Betty's first violin was a five bob [shilling] school violin.

After my parents married, they got a little terraced house and when I was three months old, they moved (1923) to Park Avenue, Thackerays Lane, just as suburbia was being built. When we moved there, Thackerays Lane was in fact the Day Brook. Eventually that brook was culverted. When we moved there, it was the wilds of the country. Grandma Walker lived with us. The trams stopped at Sherwood Depot so it was a walk from Sherwood Depot all the way up and over the hill down by Woodthorpe Grange to Thackerays Lane. Eventually they moved the terminus nearer. When we moved out there, there was no school at Woodthorpe and we went to Hazel Grove School at Mapperley. To get there, Breck Hill Road was just a rut track. I've got a big scar on my leg to prove where I fell. We just had to walk. From then on, of course, suburbia just grew and grew.

We used to go to Grandpa and Grandma Mace at 8, Eastville Street, St Ann's, every Friday for our tea. You stepped off the road up two steps into the front room and it was a typical terraced house in St Ann's. There was a chenille sort of thing on the mantlepice and little ornaments. Then you walked straight through the front room to the back room which was where you lived. It had a black-leaded grate. In the corner was the door where the stairs went up to two bedrooms upstairs. Two rooms up and two rooms down, with the small kitchen off the living room. It had the copper, a brick built copper in the corner. When she washed the clothes, grandma had to build a fire underneath it.

You went out the back door and down a yard with blue tiles. I remember them vividly. No garden. You walked down the yard to the loo. It was a water loo then. I suppose it had been a privy. The toilet paper was very neat cut squares of newspaper which had a hole drilled in one corner and string through to hang up.

When I was three or four and Jack was five or six, for our teas on Friday at Grandma's we ate bread and jam, possibly a bit of jelly. It was all very dark and dreary and then Dad used to come back from work at Ashforth Street and he would have his tea. He had a bit of ham, or perhaps a boiled egg. Grandma Mace's birthday was on March 6th. I always think of her on March 6th. She always said it was the first day she could have her tea without the light on. Grandpa sat in his own chair, oak with stave high back and a red cushion. He sat there with his lovely one eye blue and one eye brown and his white hair. He was the same shape as my father, very much so. Grandpa was an engineer at Jardine's. Granny didn't work. She was a pampered lady. She had pure white hair and wore a little black scarf as a shawl. She must have died when she was about seventy. And I look at myself now and my mind boggles! I first remembered her when I was about four and even then she had pure white hair and a little black shawl as a little old lady.

And then it would be time for us to go home, around seven o'clock. To get to Mansfield Road, you didn't go round by Woodborough Road but to Victoria Station over a sort of bridge. There was always a blind man sat there begging and I would never pass him until Dad had put money in his hand. Mum used to get mad. Whether it was a half-penny or a penny, I don't know. Then we'd cross Mansfield Road to get the tram which would clank to the terminus. We got to know the conductors. Old Mr Turner was one. And then we used to trudge home.

Grandpa and Grandma Mace's next-door neighbour was a coal merchant. They used to deliver a bag of coal at a time to somebody. But they finished up very wealthy people. They had a daughter Jessie too.

Grandma Mace used to visit us from St Ann's every Wednesday for lunch. She felt she had gone into safari because it was miles away. We would find tuppence under our plate at teatime. That seemed to go on for years.

My dad worked at Howitt's in Ashforth Street, St Ann's, until after the Second World War. When War broke out, he had to Fire Watch sometimes. I mean this enormous factory and my dad was only a little man. I think he and Jack Howitt, the boss, used to do it together but I don't think Jack Howitt would stay all night. Dad had to be there in case there was an incendiary bomb. Fortunately there never was.

I used to love to go in and see dad in the factory. His Day Book was a book as big as that [showing how big] and there was a special stand that it stood on. It was enormous this book and he had a little step that raised him up to do his booking. His handwriting was gorgeous and he had a natural flair for figures. He went into estimating. I think he

went to Forman's first for a couple of years and then went to Howitt's as an estimator. He told me that during the War, Mitchell and Butler's, the beer people, sent an enquiry into Howitt's for a very large number of beer labels. He'd work out how many sheets of paper it would take, how many upon a sheet, how many you could print at a time and then the cutting out of them etc. And he lost this order for one-eighth of a penny (old money) on one thousand labels.

I left school on July 26th and became 14 on August 10th (1937). On the Monday after I left school, my mother marches me down to Boots in Station Street where they interview girls for shop work. I wouldn't have dared not do as she said. She told me thousands of times that she'd taken everything in the world to get rid of me. But there we go, she takes me by the hand to this woman sitting behind an enormous desk. I answered her questions timidly. She said you, Jesse Mace, are not good enough to work in a Boots shop. Well I mean can you imagine you're only thirteen and you feel only as big as a fly on the carpet. My mother goes all hufty and takes my hand and we finish up in some other office in the same building where they took on girls for the factory. I was all right for that. So two days later I started at Island Street which they've just pulled down. I'm quite upset by that. I used to go there to work.

I went to the insulin department, this dreadful Mrs Finney who was the Overseer of the room sat me down, I had a white overall on and a net on my head and they sit me on a belt moving in front of me all day. The first girl erected the carton and put a bit of glue on one end and put it back on the belt. It came to me and I had to wrap the little vial of insulin in a leaflet and put it in the carton, then back on the belt for the last girl to take it off and glue the end. Then it went back on the belt for a girl at the very end who was packing them in dozens or whatever. A girl on the first end was on the little labelling machine. She picked out a vial of insulin and the machine came down with the glue on and stuck the label on.

And then the next couple of days I'd be the first girl opening the cartons and then I'd be the last girl, but always on this belt for two years, just with the belt always moving in front of you. And you did that from eight in the morning until six at night. I got twelve shillings and six pence for Monday, Tuesday, Wednesday, Thursday, Friday and Saturday eight till one. My mother only gave me my tram fare and kept the rest.

By the time I went to work, the trams went to the end of Thackerays Lane. I used to get off at Milton Head, walk all the way down Parliament Street, then Lower Parliament Street, to the bottom of London Road where Island Street was. And that was a big area once you were there. Our part was right at the bottom. I'd get up about six, cut myself a sandwich or two for my snap.

I thought to myself, there must be more to life than this One day I didn't get on the tram at Milton Street but walked up Mansfield Road to Shakespeare Street. I'd heard there was a Gregg Shorthand and Typing School there. A very nice man, Mr Meakin told me it's sixpence a lesson, an hour the shorthand or an hour the typing. I couldn't afford it every week. He said you can just come, but tell whoever's in the office when you come. I got off the tram a few stops back and saved the money, so some weeks I could afford either a sixpenny shorthand lesson or sixpenny typing lesson.

About fourteen years ago, I'm on a Barton's bus going on a tour of Scotland. On Derby Road, the bus picked up a man and I thought I know that face. It was an old Mr Meakin now. At Pond's Hotel in Glasgow I went across to him and told him he had changed my life. I told him that when I finished at Gregg's, I could do forty words a minute typing and forty words a minute shorthand and I was able to give up packing insulin and apply for an office job. He smiled. I took his picture on a Polaroid camera on the way back and gave it to him.

My office job didn't last long because the [Second World] War came and I had to work in a factory making parts for four-engine bombers. I used to get up at 5.30am and go to the far end of Netherfield. I went back to an office job after.

My dad was fifty when he started his own business after the War, still in print. He was in Black's factory on Sherwood Street until the demolishing of Sherwood Street, and then he found premises at an old upholstery factory after the owner died. It was at the side of Spray and Burgess factory on Eastwood Street, Bulwell. Dad wanted me to go into his business. I fought him for a long time and didn't, but eventually my marriage had broken down and I had Druscilla. When she was about six, I did go into dad's factory and I finished up as Work's Director. And all that sort of started in Eastville Street, St Ann's. He died in 1981.

I was there twenty-five years and some of my boys still come and see me and say you've been retired long enough. Now why don't you come back! Now, I'm in a Trust retirement home in Alexandra Park and I can go travelling without the responsibility of a house. My brother lives in Vancouver, my daughter is in Spain, my sister is in Germany and my other brother in the Scilly Isles. I don't have any photos because when I moved in here, I threw them away. That was naughty wasn't it? I just didn't have room for so many things.

I do voluntary work. I go to St Peter's Church in the City and do the coffee room each Monday and one Thursday in the month. There's always people who are glad to see you.

But there you go, life could be a tragedy in parts and other parts you remember as fun.

"We all belonged to gangs. During the 1930s, I lived in Dame Agnes Street, St Ann's. When I wasn't playing or swapping football stars and comics I would be out with the gang round the back of the orange gate that shut off the ironworks. Often we were expected to do six dares a week and break one window in the month to carry on with membership, but dares were broken and the offender was usually rolled down the railway embankment or locked in the coal house." S Archer in *Bygone Days and Memories from Nottingham* 1930s – 1950s [Stylus Press. 1992]

JOAN PRIESTLEY

Born 1926

Extracts from her contributions to St Ann's Reminiscence Days 1997 and 1999 at St Ann's Library and correspondence

I was born at Broad Oak Terrace off Rose Street up Dame Agnes Street, known locally as Damey. I attended Sycamore School up to the age of nine when we left the district. My father worked for the Co-op for 52 years, when a job with the Co-op was a job for life. He started work at thirteen, looking after the horses in the stables on Great Freeman Street, St Ann's, and worked his way up to be Transport Supervisor at Meadow Lane making him one of the longest serving employees.

During his younger days, he drove heavy goods lorries delivering to the Co-op grocery branches. Due to his lack of education and to improve his handwriting he would write all the branches and their number over and over again. There were about sixty Co-op shops in and around the City at that time. Thanks to him I have the addresses of the local St Ann's Co-op Stores: 6, Union Road; 9, Alfred Street North; 29, Robin Hood Street; 23, St Ann's Well Road and 50, Dame Agnes Street.

After an absence of thirteen years, I returned to St Ann's in 1949 and was married at St Ann's Congregational Church by the Rev Ronald Ross. Owing to the acute housing shortage, we were lucky to share my mother-in-law's house in Plantagenet Street. In her earlier days, she helped babies into the world and laid people out when they left it. Most streets would have a lady like her.

The first improvement we made to the house was to take the old brick copper out of the tiny scullery and we bought a gas boiler. In 1950, my mother-in-law died and we were offered the tenancy of the house. It was scrubbing brush and black lead for the grate. These old grates had many uses, hot water on one side of the fire, and the oven on the other side was handy for stews and rice puddings with a lovely brown skin on top.

The oven shelf, wrapped up in paper, warmed the bed on cold winter nights and had a certain smell. The alternative was a stone hot water bottle, or an aluminium one, which was lethal, but useful, if you'd had words with your 'other half', by slipping it down his side of the bed. You waited for the yelps of pain and naughty words. It brought a whole new meaning to bedtime!

Washdays were always a challenge. Although I had a gas boiler, I still had a dolly tub, ponch, and enamel bath in the sink for rinsing and bluing whites and making starch. And outside the back door in all its glory stood a huge cast-iron mangle, snuggling up to our motorbike under old macs and tarpaulins, which attracted the ginger tomcat from next door and all the other moggies in the area. The air was quite strong in warm weather and my husband reckoned we could smell it in the custard on Sundays!

Later on, I went up market and bought a second-hand wringer with rubber rollers for twenty five shillings. How we ever got sheets and blankets dry in those tiny backyards, I'll never know, but we did with the help of props to keep them off the dirty brickwork.

I was working full-time in various offices 1941-51. In 1951, I became a full-time housewife. To keep the housework in order we had certain days for certain jobs. Listening to the radio was a great asset whilst doing all these chores. There was Housewives' Choice at nine o'clock, Music while you Work at 10.30. The Archers began in 1951 at 11.45. I can remember it well as our daughter was on three-hourly feeds. After dinner at 2.00 was Woman's Hour and 4.15 Mrs Dale's Diary. Mrs Dale was always worried about Jim! After tea, while doing the ironing was Journey into Space, the Goons, sometimes Hancock's Half Hour or a play or concert and 10.00 was bedtime.

Most of my shopping was done on Saturdays. Here are just a few of the shops I used, starting with Alfred Street South: Farnsworth's Pork Butchers (pre-Pork Farms), Barnes Dales little dairy sold Colwick Cheeses etc. Barber Len for son's haircut, Coupe's Furnishing and round the corner into the Square was Plunkett's Gents Outfitters, Atkin's Wine Shop, Winfield's the Butcher. If you'd had some coal delivered, it was up to Brown's the Coal Merchant to pay the bill on Union Road, down again to the Square, there was Carnill's Pork Butchers, Briley's Ladies' and Children's Wear, past the imposing Westminster Bank. Crossing over and passing the Cromwell Pub to the Co-op Butchery and Greengrocer's, Morley's Cake Shop, Dean's for Ladies Fashion, past the Cavendish Cinema, then there was Mr Ash, an excellent Fishmonger for many years.

Butler and Morris Gents' and Boys' Wear, then a hardware shop and round the corner on Peas Hill Road was Edna's Greengrocer's shop. She always seemed to wear a turban and have a cigarette on the go, always busy mostly serving people outside. Suddenly, she would shout: 'Let's have a sale!' That would attract more people than ever. Jean and Peter Barton had a lovely sweet shop on the corner, next to Pilkington's the pork butchers. On Friday nights during the winter, their windows would be steamed up with hot black puddings and roast pork. Patrick and Green's came next, Ladies' and Children's Wear, Stoppard the Pawnbrokers and T.S.B. [Trustee Savings Bank]. Along to Northampton Street, known as the Flower show, the Public Baths were on the corner, there was No 23 Co-op Grocery Store, the Post Office, Meakin's the cobbler, Marsden's, Mr Chettle the dentist, Ridgards for cookers, Mr Clarke the Chemist, Hopewell Furnishers and Wayne's Poodle Parlour and Pet Shop.

Such a variety of shops, there was no need to go into town, and then only a short distance to the Central Market. Sunday mornings, whilst cooking the dinner and the family were out either at Sunday school or visiting grandparents, I listened to Two-Way Family Favourites, when the wireless still reigned supreme. Over lunch we enjoyed the Billy Cotton Band Show. In the afternoon, we would get dressed up, even if it was only a walk to the local park and there were always Sunday school Anniversaries to look forward to.

In 1953 came the Coronation. Every Friday evening for weeks a shilling was collected for the children's party. It was to be held in a neighbouring backyard but it was rained off and held at the Gladstone Liberal Club at the corner of Lamartine Street. In the evening, neighbours crowded into the only house in the street with a TV to watch the ceremony. After that, most houses got a TV set. The Black and White Minstrel Show on Saturday night and Sunday Night at the Palladium were very popular.

Bonfire night had its excitement. Children would be collecting rubbish for weeks and as soon as they came out of school on November 5th, they would be scurrying round like demented ants, piling up the bonfires. By five o'clock, it was well alight. As more and more rubbish was piled on, it got bigger and nearer to Hardwick's Picture Framing and Glass Cutting shop. Mr Hardwick would come out ranting and raving, and then the fire engine would appear. They made a half-hearted attempt to put the fire out amid boos from the crowd. Of course, when they had gone it was started up again. Next day the children would poke the ashes into life again until the dustmen cleared it away.

Another occasion when the firemen were called was to chimney fires. Gathered round a roaring fire, after red-hot soot began to fall, caused panic stations and efforts to try to damp it down and then to book a sweep as soon as possible. Everything was covered up the night before the sweep came at around 6.00am. Hoping he would arrive on time, his barrow would be heard rumbling up the entry. The poor man's face was already black. He must have started very early. Later on, my husband acquired a set of sweep's rods. Then there was some fun and games, especially if he turned them the wrong way round and lost the brush up the chimney. More naughty words!

There was a huge fire at the Marathon Factory opposite the Criterion pub around the late 1950s. The factory was gutted but eventually rebuilt.

Joan Priestley sent in this picture she took of the Marathon Factory on fire 'one Friday morning'

ST ANN'S, NOTTINGHAM: INNER-CITY VOICES BY RUTH I JOHNS • ISBN 0951696092

As Christmas approached, thoughts turned to when the Diddlem [a local saying for a Christmas Club] would be paid out and how much to give the postman, milkman, dustman and paperboy as a Christmas box. Christmas Eve, people would be out early. There would be queuing at Pork Farms and bread shops (no freezers then). Then Winfield the Butcher would have a huge mound of sausage meat in the window with the message 'Stuff the Bird'. After dinner, girls from the local factories would run through the streets singing and laughing with balloons and wearing paper hats after celebrating at the local pubs.

There would be finishing touches to the front room, probably only used once a year and, at three o'clock, I would make a start on the mince pies whilst listening to the world famous carol service from King's College Chapel, Cambridge. It was an early start too on Christmas morning. After opening their presents, children on the street would be trying out their new presents such as roller skates, scooters or showing off a new doll and pram.

Getting the front room fire to start was a major issue. Either it would smoulder, sulk or go out, or fill the room full of smoke. Both front and back doors had to be wide open even in the coldest weather until the fire took hold. The bedrooms smelt of smoke for days after. In time, gas fires made it so much easier and cleaner.

Toward the mid-1960s, there were rumours of redevelopment and, with the coming of SATRA [St Ann's Tenants and Residents Association], Ray Gosling, Margaret Behrman, Arthur Leatherland, there was good co-operation with the Council. One of their plans was to build high-rise flats, but the people stuck out for what they wanted, houses with gardens. Another plan was for an Eastern By-pass to come from the Carlton Road across St Ann's Valley to Woodborough Road. You can imagine with the volume of traffic now what pollution and noise it would have caused. Thankfully both plans were scrapped.

The Clearance was done in Phases. Ours was No 7 and we decided on a relet at Sherwood in 1972. If my husband was making anything and couldn't find what he wanted,

he'd say: 'I know where I could find it, in the cellar at Planto'.

We tend to look at the past through rose coloured glasses. It did have its down side. But, when you think about it, it was part of our social history. There was bad publicity on the TV and in the National Press. I wrote a letter of protest. Of course, I didn't get a reply. But it was an insult to all the hardworking people struggling with bad housing etc.

We won't see the like of those times again or the numerous little corner shops and beer-offs open all hours and selling almost anything from bundles of firewood, to bacon, Beechams Pills, to corn-plasters, where the cat sat alongside the boiled ham and fly paper, no pressure selling or loyalty cards, folk had goods on tick and paid at the weekend.

Then there were the elderly ladies trotting along with their jugs for their supper beer and grumbling about the bad lace work they had been lumbered with. If the beer wasn't up to standard, the man behind the pumps soon knew about it. The colourful characters around the streets, like the ladies coming from the washhouses Friday teatime with prams piled high with clean laundry, neighbours helping each other in times of need. They really were some of the happiest days of my life.

ETHEL LILIAN MUSSON

(nee Wilson) Born 1926

From a reminiscence of Ethel Lilian Musson (nee Wilson) at a St Ann's Library Reminiscence Day

I was born in Cathcart Street, St Ann's, in 1926. My education was at St Ann' Church School. I started there in 1929. My first teacher was Miss Wilson and we were at school all day, but in the afternoons we had a rest on camp beds. The other teachers were Miss Pulfrey, Miss Pygott, Mr Parnham, Mr Bagguley and Mr Morrison the Head Teacher.

Though the classes contained more than forty pupils, the teachers had full control of the classroom. Yes, corporal punishment was in force but you only received the strap for very serious breaches of discipline. There were also classrooms at Coppice Road [Canon Lewis Memorial Hall[1]]

On Empire Day, pageants were organised and all pupils took part, each section representing some part of the Empire. On May Day there was dancing round the Maypole and parents were well represented at these events. We were taken swimming either to the Victoria Baths or to the swimming bath at the old Sycamore Road School. There was a Gala and Sports Day for the children.

Kenmore Gardens where Plantagenet Street was before. Photo: Noel Priestley c1972, Nottingham Local Studies Library

---

[1] Much later, the Boys' Brigade owned the Canon Lewis Memorial Hall [see Index]. Rose Hawley told me the Boys' Brigade let out the basement, where a Mr Shipley ran a billiard hall. He lived in one of the gardeners' 'houses' in the Hungerhill Gardens. He had no electricity or gas, and water from a well. "We were hoping City Challenge might have renewed the now disused building for community purposes," said Rose Hawley 2001.

Three nights a week in the winter, there were after-school activities at the St Ann's Board School. On one of these evenings silent films of Laurel and Hardy and Charlie Chaplin were shown. On the other evenings, various activities took place.

St Ann's Church was well supported and had a flourishing Sunday school with about seven classes. I still have books given as prizes dating from 1932. The first Vicar I remember was Rev Caley who became Canon Caley, then Rev Bromham followed. There was a Christmas Party each year for the Sunday school and this was held at the Memorial Hall on Coppice Road [now Ransom Road]. There were so many children that the Party took place on two consecutive Saturdays. There were strong Scouts, Guide and Brownie packs and Church parades, also a Young People's Fellowship group run by Miss Pygott two evenings a week.

ALAN SWIFT

Born 1926

Interviewed in his home 13.9.00. Alan Swift went into **Veterinary Practice** *on the Woodborough Road, St Ann's. There is still a Veterinary Practice there*

The large house at the right-hand corner of Corporation Oaks and Woodborough Road, St Ann's, had been empty for some years. There had been squatters in it at some time, and it was vandalised. But previous to that, it had been a Doctor's Surgery.

It was in a very poor state when we got it. It was either 1956 or 1957. Unfortunately, I cannot find anything now which tells me the actual date. Tom Denholm purchased

The house renovated for the Veterinary Practice. Corporation Oaks is on the left. Plowright Street is on the right. The block the other side of Plowright Street was demolished some years after the area's redevelopment. Photo: Alan Swift c1958

the building. The Practice, which was called Denholm and Swift, leased it from him.

I joined Tom Denholm's practice straight from college. Tom Denholm was in Partnership with somebody else and, when they split up, I went into partnership with Tom Denholm. So, obviously, we had a nucleus of clientele and some clients went to the other Practice. Woodborough Road was the administrative base of our Practice. We did a lot of farm work.

At that time, we had a branch Practice in Ilkeston and one in Hucknall. They were lock-up premises where we held surgeries. We chose the Woodborough Road premises because the price was reasonable and it was a very good position from the point of view of clientele. There was a big area to call on because there was no other veterinary surgeon in that area. There was Smythe in the City but nobody just out of the City. And it bordered very closely on to the farm part of our work, which geographically started on Mapperley Plains.

We had a sixty per cent to forty per cent bias toward large animals then. That changed over the years when small animals predominated.

There were a lot of cattle, pigs, horses and general farm work, riding stables, riding schools. But, of course, the farm situation grew difficult and the farms went. The farmers let fields for horses to graze on rather than rearing stock on them, and the farm work dwindled away. I retired in 1986 and we were still doing a certain amount of farm work in the early 1980s, but the horse population had grown. Children were having ponies whereas years ago only very well off people had ponies. The change was due to increasing prosperity. City people went to riding schools . . .

The small animal work changed with advancement of professional skill, the technology of the work. But not nearly to the extent that it has changed since I retired in 1986. There's a lot of veterinary stuff on TV these days. They are anaesthetising all sorts of animals. Once upon a time that wasn't possible. And they are doing replacement hips and eye operations. We didn't have the anaesthetics or the tools now available.

At Woodborough Road, we had a kennel man and his wife, Alma and Harry Siggee, who lived on the premises. They were there until they retired. By then, of course, we had animal nurses and there were usually two or three of them living up there.

In our early days there, much of our work was home visits. From the Ilkeston and Hucknall surgeries, there would be about a five-mile radius. From Woodborough Road, we'd go out to Hoveringham and Gonalston. Yes, it was mostly home visits for small animals as well. We would do tremendous mileage.

Gradually it changed and more people came into the surgeries and home visits became more rare. People cannot afford to have them now. It was all private work except for the Ministry of Agriculture work, testing cattle for Tuberculosis, Swine Fever vaccinations when necessary, that sort of thing. But apart from that it was private work for farmers and residents of the area around us.

St Ann's Nottingham. inner-city voices *by Ruth I Johns* • ISBN 0951696092

I started work in 1951 and Veterinary Surgeons weren't very thick on the ground then. In our early days, you were looking almost at a James Herriott type of work with the majority of farms being one man and perhaps a couple of workers, not the vast places that they are now.

At Woodborough Road in the 1960s there were us two Senior Partners and a Junior Partner, two qualified assistants and the kennel man and his wife. She did the cleaning. The Junior Partner, Andrew Wilson became a full partner. This team visited the other surgeries for certain hours each week on a rota system. We used to have a morning and an evening surgery at Ilkeston and Hucknall twice a week. And a secretary, Betty Jackson, co-ordinated everything from the Woodborough Road Practice. Later, Brenda Moffatt did this important job.

You could start work at half-past seven in the morning, or six o'clock, going out on a milk fever visit, and not finish until virtually the next morning if you happened to be on duty at night. We worked very long hours and weekends, Saturdays and Sundays. There are many more veterinary trained people now. Some practices have six to eight people in them. And, of course, quite a few people are specialising in exotic species. They may do some other work as well. If you need specialist advice now, it's there. We were reliant very often on places like Universities if you needed to send anything for analysis.

We used to get called to do unusual things. There was a Chipperfield's Circus on the Forest grounds and they had a lioness who was in labour for a day or two when they got to Nottingham. We had to do a caesarean section. I can't remember how many cubs there were but unfortunately we lost her. In those days, there were not the anaesthetics. We had to give the anaesthetic to start with by mouth. We gave it to her in a drink and she didn't feel like drinking. The operation went all right but she died a day or so later.

Now, there are all these pre-med injections, which make an animal docile before anaesthetising it. Imagine trying to put a gaseous anaesthetic mask over an animal without a pre-med. Most of our anaesthetics in the early days were intravenous and that was easier but it carried quite a high risk. But, looking back, it's amazing what we managed to achieve. We used to do quite a lot of cattle caesarean sections under local anaesthesia or epidurals.

Many of the houses in St Ann's before redevelopment were kept like new pins. The ladies worked their fingers to the bone. Manning Street was almost opposite with small houses coming on to the street but they were beautifully built. We lost quite a few clients with redevelopment, and there was a different clientele afterwards but it didn't affect our business too much. In the local area, the usual pets were a dog or a cat, a canary or budgerigar. The children had mice and guinea pigs, and then over time people started having two dogs. And then toward the end of my working life the exotics started coming in. We had things like snakes and various reptiles, birds of prey, quite a lot of people had birds of prey.

I'd never been trained in exotics, so we had to seek advice. We had a certain amount of poultry work but not a lot. It was a lovely life, you met all sorts of people, had all sorts of experiences. People became your friends. You perhaps treated their dog over twelve to fifteen years you see. People would phone in for us to call, but people from the St Ann's area would call and say: 'Can you come to see the dog?' There were a lot of crossbreeds, little dogs which roamed the streets, quite a lot of people kept greyhounds because, of course, there was a big stadium in Nottingham for racing them. There were Terriers, Boxers came in and a few had big dogs like Airedales or even Great Danes.

In the sixties and seventies, breeding puppies seemed to be developing, like Poodle puppies and Dachshunds. I think people made quite a lot of money out of it. And showing became more popular. It was in the late sixties I think that dog training classes started. Before that most training was only gun dog training.

We came across certain cruelties but I don't think it was anything like the cruelties that are done now. Then, a lot was due to lack of knowledge and lack of thought. But sometimes, a dog was left tied up to a chain which grew into its neck. Such things were usually brought to our attention by the RSPCA [Royal Society for the Prevention of Cruelty to Animals] or the police. We had call outs from the police at night if an animal had been injured in a road accident and the driver was hurt and couldn't afford a Veterinary Surgeon. You could go to a police call at Broxtowe at two o'clock in the morning and when you got there the dog had gone. But often the police were with it.

There was never anything I wanted to do except be a Veterinary Surgeon, ever since being a small child on the Wirral.

What would I pass down to a young person fifty years on? That's a tough one. It's a bit of a cliché, but I would say follow your heart. Have a goal, try to achieve it, don't give up on your dream too soon because it does sometimes come true. And do a job you enjoy however hard it is and however tired you get. However crotchety you get, you also get the good times. The most satisfying part of my job was seeing new animals being born and holding them in my hands, it's just a wonderful experience. New animals are so perfect.

There is, of course, still a Veterinary Practice in the same house on Woodborough Road. It started as Denholm and Swift, then it went to Denholm, Swift and Wilson and then, when we took a fourth partner in, Martin Grace, we decided to call the Practice the Oaks Veterinary Practice because Corporation Oaks runs down the side of it. But it's not called that now.

I was standing at the bus stop on the Woodborough Road just below the Practice in 1995 when a car knocked down an Alsatian dog, which was in a lot of pain and badly injured. It screamed and was heard. Within seconds, two white-coated people rushed out of the Veterinary Practice and tranquillised it.

EILEEN SELBY

Letter 1999

My grandfather, Frank Hallam, had an undertaker's business on St Ann's Well Road in the 1800s. He died when he was forty-seven years old. He was a member of the St Ann's Rose Show and roads were named after three members of the Show: Hallam Road, Robinson Road and Lees Road. [These were then the new roads on the Porchester/Mapperley side of The Wells Road.]

When he died, the funeral business was sold to Bamfords Funeral Co.

I can remember being taken by my mum's family to allotments on the Hungerhills. There was a lovely little hut where you could sit. I think we had a drink of water from a well. Later on, we used to go to the Cavendish Cinema. During the War I danced at the Victoria Ballroom and re-met my future husband there: happy days!

PEARL HANDS

Born 1926

Conversations since 1994 and interview in her home 12.10.99. Photos from Pearl Hands

I went to live in St Ann's in 1954 after a spell on the Alfreton Road after I came from Jamaica. Alfreton Road was nice, you could come in from work and do all your shopping down there. It was very lively. Music both sides of the road. But the room we were living in was not very satisfactory, so I went to St Ann's, to 5, Flewitt Street because I had two rooms there.

There was a grocery shop in front run by a German woman and we became friends. It was the usual accommodation of the time. There was no bathroom and an outside toilet. I used to go across the road to my friend and have a bath or the public baths were about a ten-minute walk away, Victoria Baths.

As soon as I came over [1953], I got a job. I went to a firm with a vacant sign, making lace. This chap came out and he talked to me nicely but said he couldn't employ me because they were all elderly people there and they'd never seen a coloured person before so they might not be very pleased if he employed me. So I went straight across the road and rang the bell and got a job with Mr Ball putting lace on chair backs. He said: 'You'll have to do some good work Pearl because most of my work goes to Jamaica, Princes Street'. He was a nice man and the ladies were very good.

But there was a woman there doing the pressing for about £3 a week and, because I didn't have anybody to talk to, I was getting on well with my work and began earning £4. I don't think she liked that. For a month I worked there and no work came back to me. Suddenly a lot of work was coming back to me. I told somebody about it and she told the Foreman and a security check was made. It was found that while the woman was pressing the work she was pulling the lace from the linen. Mr Ball called her into the office and she said I'd just come to this country and was earning more than other people.

I left. Mr Ball asked me to come back but I told the girl in the office to tell him not to sack the woman because she'd been there a long while. About six or seven months later, I heard she died of cancer so she was probably an ill person at that time. That was the only nasty thing I came up against. I didn't look for prejudice. It was there, but I didn't look for it. At those times you could walk and get a job easily. I found another job at Marsdens in Chilwell.

When I was living in St Ann's I was working at Plessey and from there I went to the City Hospital.

St Ann's was happy. It was known as a slum but I had happy memories. You didn't have to go into the City to shop unless you were going to a department store like Jessops, Griffin and Spalding or the Co-op. Everything you'd want was in St Ann's.

I enjoy city life very much and I couldn't live anywhere else than Nottingham. When I go on holiday, as soon as it ends I want to come home to Nottingham. It's a shame St Ann's had this bad name, I loved it. I went to live at Clifton when I was rehoused and then I wanted to come back into the inner-city. I came to the Meadows. St Ann's is very pretty now. I love to go on a bus down there. I've got friends there.

I was very, very ill while I was working at the City Hospital. I received wonderful care under the consultant Mr Cochrane and everybody was so good to me that I decided I would do voluntary work when I retired. And that's what I ended up doing eventually. But after I had my baby, I went back to work at City Hospital as an Assistant Nurse. I was there seventeen years. Back in Jamaica, I had sometimes helped in a Clinic. I always said if I ever won a fortune I would give it to the City Hospital, but not since it got Trust status.

On my spare Saturdays, I would sometimes go from St Ann's to Mapperley [Psychiatric] Hospital and work in the Coffee Bar voluntarily. My first husband left after ten years so I brought up my daughter alone, without state help except Housing Benefit.

Since I retired, I've been busy!

Day trip with the Group to the Tramway Museum at Crich, Derbyshire. Pearl Hands with Mrs Simms

One of Pearl Hands' co-volunteers, Augustas Benjamin, at the Bridgeway Hall lunch club

I helped at a pensioners luncheon club at Bridgeway Hall, Meadows. I have always believed strongly that pensioners should have non-chipped cups, straight clean forks, proper tables and tablecloths. On purpose I dropped and broke one chipped cup per week! I was amazed when the woman who criticised me breaking the cups suggested I should replace the retiring organiser. That was 1986. They had faith in me, so I developed faith in myself.

The Princess Royal talks with Pearl Hands 1995

Meadows Community Centre lunch club trip to the American Adventure 1996

I had also been running a luncheon club for Afro-Caribbean elder women at the Meadows Community Centre and about forty-five attended. I had an opportunity to get a keep fit class for the Afro-Caribbean Club and I would only accept it if the same was offered for the 'white' club. I persuaded Social Services to bring proper tables, cloths, crockery and cutlery for the Bridgeway Hall Club.

Pearl Hands with her 1997 Race and Community Relations Award. Photo: Nottingham Evening Post

Yes, I was awarded the Nottingham City Council Achievement Award 1997. [It says: 'First prize presented to Pearl Hands for Achieving Excellence in Race and Community Relations in the Voluntary Sector.']

My second husband was a wonderful man, Richard Bazil Hands. He sadly died in 1998. He worked with British Rail from the age of sixteen for forty-five years and did many jobs on it.

In 2001, Pearl Hands received a Citizen of Honour Award from the Lord Mayor

BARBARA LEVICK

Born 1927

From a Reminiscence Day contribution at St Ann's Library in the 1990s

After the best part of 100 years, in which the dwellings so hopefully put up in the Industrial Revolution to house workers cheaply and - at that time - the height of luxury, were to be pulled down to make way for the new Utopia: new St Ann's. They were not only clearing St Ann's Well Road and the nearby streets, but stretching over to Carlton Road and Woodborough Road, parts of Nottingham which didn't consider themselves part of St Ann's at all at that time.

In view of the confusion, rumour and uncertainty, several people joined together to form a Residents' Committee. Ray Gosling, the TV Presenter, and Arthur Leatherland, who lived on Cromer Road, spearheaded the Group. They recruited a few other interested individuals and so St Ann's Tenants and Residents Association [SATRA] was born.

I went to a few of the meetings which were held in an old shop turned into an Information Centre on St Ann's Well Road, just below the old St Ann's Well Inn, and my interest was fired by the fact that we, the people of the area, were able to say what *we* wanted when the dream came into being. We didn't want tower blocks of flats, but low blocks, so people were not cut off when the lifts broke down, and were able to sit or stand on the balcony and chat to their neighbours and passers-by.

We could speak out against busy roads. The original plan showed a motorway cutting the estate in half from Woodborough Road to Carlton Road. We didn't want that. We could suggest names for the streets, instead of the old names being used like Bombay, Calcutta, Ladysmith, Livingstone, Gordon, which when first used reflected the Glorious Empire.

Well, the Empire had gone! We wanted something different. A friend of mine wrote to the *Evening Post* Letters Column suggesting that only the names of Rose Street, Lily Street and Lavender Street should continue to be used. The Planning Department applauded this suggestion and so was born Aster Road, Lavender Walk, Tulip Avenue, Heather, Lobelia, Rose and Primrose Closes. I think they ran out of flowers after Phase Two and reverted to some of the old names for Dane Close, Hutchinson Green . . .

Apart from the planning of St Ann's, we had the people to consider. Those who owned their own homes couldn't afford to buy again. Although they were promised a current market price for their homes, this figure was so low it was laughable if it hadn't been so tragic. No one but the Council would buy the property, so the price plummeted.

The only option was to accept a new Council house at around £4 a week. Those who had rented previously had been paying less than £1 a week. Older people in particular were upset and worried. Many had been born in their old homes and lived there 60-70 years. They didn't want to be uprooted. So SATRA had another problem to sort out.

It was decided to employ a full-time worker who would visit people in their homes, gee-up the Authorities, get local people involved in groups to do things and make things happen. At this stage, in came Margaret Behrman, sent to us by the United Nations Organisation [UNO]. After a few months, we had to pay her wages. How could we, in a run-down area, raise cash for a full-time worker. The SATRA Tote was born. Membership was sold at 12p a year and it grew. People had raffles, jumble sales, and we held a Sale of Work. Members of the public made, sewed, knitted, and cooked various items for sale at a Coffee Morning to be opened by the Mayor.

Gosh, the things we had! Someone said: 'Come and pick my raspberries'. And somebody else said 'I'll give you some sugar'. So there was jam! Jam jars came from an old lady who had hundreds of them in her cellar, along with two-dozen cats whose scent permeated even the glass jars. They had to be washed a few times before we could use them! Rugs, hand-made, dolls and soft toys galore, baby clothes,

kids jumpers, embroidered dressing table sets, homemade wine and sweets, cakes, pictures and lace mats galore. The stuff left over was sold the next night at a Hall in the area and a couple of hundred pounds were raised toward Margaret's wages.

SATRA lobbied councillors, planners, Social Services, the churches and any agency that could help in any way. We started a Care Group to help the old people, to make the move as smooth as possible, get them settled in, arrange for new doctors. Street stewards were elected. St Ann's got settled. The need for a Tenants' Association dwindled. A Club had been built but was never a success, and was taken over by a brewery and so SATRA died. But, it will be remembered by quite a few people with affection, because we [now] older people tried to hold the community spirit together.

We organised fun things too, it wasn't all serious. We had a Carnival on the Chase in 1971, we had another in Coppice Road in 1972 with a march through the estate with a jazz band, Robin Hood and kids in fancy dress. In 1973 we took part in the Palio Race at Wollaton Park but our horse dropped dead an hour before the race was due to start. Typical! But a good time was had by all. Chase Chat [community newspaper] was another spin off. January 1973 was the first issue. Copies of Chase Chat have been donated to St Ann's Library by Colin Haynes and can be consulted there.

Barbara Levick lived in Gordon Road, St Ann's, 1956-71 in a house bought from Kathleen Pole between Pym Street and Paxman Street. 'I wasn't aware that I was poor,' she said. Barbara Levick brought up a family and ran a clothes and wool shop from her front room. A girl came on Sunday to get some socks. When asked why she didn't come to the shop on a Saturday when it was open, she said: 'We've got to see how much is left after daddy has been drinking on Saturday'.

ALAN ROYCE BLOOM

Born 1928

Interviewed in his home 29.9.99

I was born in Aspley and moved to St Ann's when I was four. We were on the first row of houses to be built on the Aspley Estate, on Ledbury Vale. Unfortunately, there was a domestic upset and my mother and I left and returned to her parents at 113, Robin Hood Chase in St Ann's. I spent my life there until I was twenty. Although the Chase thoroughfare is still there, the houses were demolished.

Soon after my mother returned, my grandmother died. My mother's sister and brother were also there. My mother helped out. My grandfather was beginning to ail at that time. He was getting the same age as I am now come to think of it!

My grandparents had lived in St Ann's since they were young, in Heskey Street at that time, just off Robin Hood Chase. He was a master plumber. She was a housewife. Her brother was in clerical work.

St Ann's Nottingham: inner city voices by Ruth I Johns • ISBN 0951696092

I went to Shelton Street School and then Huntingdon Street Junior and Huntingdon Street Senior. I did get a grammar school scholarship but we were too poor for me to take it up.

By that time, my mother's brother was married and her sister had taken a place in Wales knowing there was somebody to look after Grandfather. My mother had to support him and me. It was more unusual in those days to have a one-parent family. People did talk.

A studio photograph of Hilda Maud Bloom (nee Shacklock), Alan Bloom's mother when she was a child. The other child is her brother Fred

Alan Bloom's Great Aunt Grace Shacklock, his mother's sister, is in this St Ann's Church School photo of 1892. He does not know which child she is

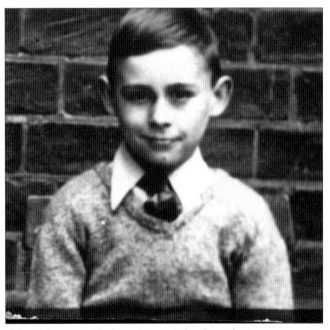

Alan Bloom at Shelton Street School aged nine

We were just talking about whether there was any bullying at Huntingdon Street School in those days. I can remember two occasions where somebody jumped at me from the toilets. One was Ken and the other Peter. One lived in a shop on Peas Hill Road and the other on Woodborough Road. There were two gangs in the district, one on Eastville Street and one on Westville Street, they were all red heads, that's how I can remember that one!

Hilda Bloom

My mother eventually worked at Simon May, the lace manufacturer. She was a jennier. She worked right up until her fifties. She was finishing, scalloping . . . She did that before she was married and she went back into it.

When my father came out of the Army, he couldn't get a job, then he got a job as a salesman in wines and spirits. It was his downfall. He became an alcoholic, got into trouble and lost all sense of reason.

It's only in the last few years that his side of the family traced us and got in touch with me. I didn't know he had any relatives. It appears he had about thirteen brothers and sisters. He came from London. We've exchanged histories.

We discovered some amazing things, especially about his name. His mother's surname was Shacklock, the same as my mother's maiden name. She never told me about her past but I reckon she married a cousin. Her name Sedonia Shacklock comes up again in my family history. It's unusual. I can't imagine there being two in the Nottingham area unless they were related.

I was brought up in the Baptist Chase Mission because it was the nearest I think. I've still got my prizes from Sunday school. The Minister was the Rev Owen. He was blind. He was there all during the War.

There was Christian Endeavour on Thursday night. We did walking and hiking and things like that. Also, before that, the Lifeboys in little sailor hats and that. Then later I joined the Air Training Corps.

In the War, down Robin Hood Chase, they put air-raid shelters. There was one every few yards as you went down. And there were smoke screens down the centre and up to Corporation Oaks. My mother said the shelters made the whole place look a mess and she hated the smoke screens. The smoke came in the house and everywhere. The Pioneer Corp lit the smoke screens every night when there was a raid. They were like a chimney with a flat top on a paraffin base. You could always tell when they lit them because of the smell. They used to come down lighting them up, and two or three would blaze up and you thought it was more of a target than a prevention.

We had several bombs around us. If we didn't go out, we sat on the stairs with grandfather. Mother used to have a scarf round her head because we had an anti-aircraft gun on what we called top Chase and it was very loud. It used to shake the whole house. If that went, you could hear the planes coming over. Someone would get it. There were searchlights up there and several more at Mapperley, criss-crossing the sky.

The night of the Nottingham blitz [1941] we were over at Bobbersmill with a friend of my mum. The sirens went early so she said stay in the spare room and we couldn't believe it next day how close it had been. It was Westville Street and one a bit further down.

One day a plane came over, we saw the markings on it. I was on my way back to school after lunch. It came down and let off his guns somewhere. They gathered us up in the school hall and let us off early once things subsided. It brought it home to us, things we'd heard about Coventry . . . Some friends of mine were evacuated. They went to live in villages.

The air-raid shelters were flat horrible looking things, concrete and brick. Each one took about four families, two from each side of the Chase. My mother used to get us up when the siren went, always about half past two in the morning. We were half asleep and she used to make us get dressed and insisted I wore my school cap. My aunt lived next door and there was an elderly couple. They were all their life in St Ann's. So it was a mixture of people.

I used to have to do the errands. I can remember queuing at the Co-op in Dame Agnes Street with ration book and coupons. Two ounces this, two ounces that for just me and my mother. Grandfather had died by then. We didn't get much between us. The first time we got a bit extra was when I joined the RAF and I used to bring a 48-hour pass rations over. I got home once a fortnight.

At fourteen, I started working for J Hardy and Company, wholesale furnishers in the City Centre. They were very well established. I had a lot of responsibility. I was cashier and bought sales ledger clerk. I had to go to the bank with thousands of pounds every morning. I worked from half past eight in the morning until six o'clock at night with one hour for lunch. Seventeen and six pence a week. I was there until I was drafted into the Royal Air Force in 1946.

Alan Bloom in the RAF c1946

I was in the first lot of National Servicemen after the War ended. I had been in the Air Training Corps (Sherwood Squadron, Haydn Road), that's why I got accepted for the RAF. Otherwise it would have been Army or Navy. We took a lot of stick from servicemen being demobbed. They thought we were having it easy. They put you through some tough training. In the Air Training Corps we did two evenings a week, and parades: good training.

I finished up at Gloucester Records Office. I went in as trainee aircrew because I'd done my exams and things in the Air Training Corps. But I only did fifteen hours of flying before they made the course redundant and they put you on general duties. On demob, I went back to St Ann's until I got married for the first time.

It was ages before we went on holiday. First, it was a day out. We went mad looking forward to it. The first holiday I had was with my mother's sister who lived on the coast in North Wales at Porthmadoc. She had a cottage on the moor and you could see the sea. Like my mother, she was very strict.

When I came out, I went back to my old job for a while. When I married, I got a house at Clifton, a new estate, the biggest in the country I think. That would be around 1952.

There were a lot of people from St Ann's up there, including a friend of mine just down the road. We remained friends until he died a couple of years ago.

And then I got interested in photography and saw this job with a firm called Tempest down the Meadows. They still exist. They take pictures of schools and school children. It was black and white then. Now the children have a blue background. They put me in the commercial department and I learnt a lot from them.

I didn't set up business on my own but I used to do it as a hobby. I'd do weddings and portraits which were popular after the War. Then I got a part-time job in a studio on Saturdays doing weddings.

Occasionally it got me back to St Ann's. There was a wedding at St Andrew's Church. That was where mother was married. One at Emmanuel Church, one at the Baptist . . .

Then I went into the NAAFI at the Audit Branch where we used to do the accounts for BAOR [British Army on the Rhine]. Then I changed to something quite different through a friend of mine. I became a Representative. The attraction was that once you 'made it', they gave you a car to use, a good car, Vauxhall Victor. It was for a firm up in Newcastle where I travelled once a week. They sold stuffed pork roll and steak and kidney pies and things like that. It was commission only and hard going but I stayed quite a time. They sold up North better than in the Midlands. Easier to sell Pease pudding in Blackburn than in Leicester or Bristol!

St Ann's became a very mishy-mashy place because people who lived there had all gone different places, and people moved in temporarily knowing that it was going to be demolished. It wasn't a settled area at that time. I had gone to the Chase Mission and kept in touch for quite a long time.

In 1958, I started with British Gas for two weeks stop gap and stayed until I retired. That was administration.

I only had one child with my first wife, common-law wife, Joan. She disappeared to Ireland and took Lorraine with her when she was about four. I couldn't get over it. After five weeks and hearing nothing except a postcard, I took a boat from Holyhead to Dublin and I traced a friend of mine. I went round everywhere, post offices and shops, with a photo of Lorraine: 'Have you seen this little girl?'

I wasn't making progress, so I called at the Gardai. I thought I've got to do something before I go back. They stamped the photo. Very helpful the Irish. So I was able to go to the Irish Press and give them a little interview and the photo. I'd only been back forty-eight hours when the police knocked on the door saying a teacher had recognised her and would I make contact. So then I got on

a 'plane and found out where they were living and confronted her mother. She had met somebody else, and was living in an attic. Lorraine was overjoyed to see me. Joan asked if she would like to go with her Daddy, so I arranged to bring her back for three weeks. Joan agreed to her stopping afterwards. The environment where she was over there was not too good for her.

By then, I'd moved to a Victorian house in West Bridgford. My mother came and looked after Lorraine while I worked, until I met and later married Margaret. Lorraine was born in 1960, and has been working in Majorca now for eighteen years. Of course, she never knew St Ann's, but my mother was a very good storyteller and, of course, could go back further than me. She used to make Lorraine laugh. She used to show her pictures.

When she was very elderly, a friend of the family looked after my mother. She was a good age when she died, ninety-two. She had some years of terrible health. I don't know how she got through that time.

Now my main hobby is DIY [Do It Yourself] and videoing. I had cancer diagnosed in 1994 and had major surgery. I always set myself a target. I've got that much to do, I can't get through it in a day.

Alan Bloom was given this photo of Mrs A Bestwick who ran the newsagent at 26, Dame Agnes Street. Her son George came into the business after the Second World War and is seen here with his mother

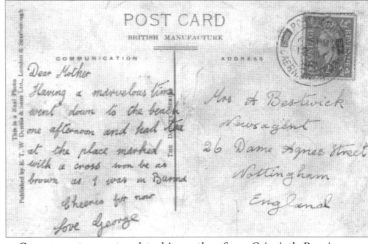

George sent a postcard to his mother from Criccieth Bay in Wales in May 1947. This is the message on the back

GLADYS FAIRCLOTH

Born 1928

From letters of Mrs Faircloth who, with her husband Alan, celebrated their golden wedding in 1999. They were married at St Batholomew's Church, St Ann's

My Great Aunt Ginny was a Mrs Johns and her three sons were Horace, Alec and Gus, who became Johns Painters and Decorators [now at Mapperley]. They were my father's cousins. My father and his two brothers were brought up by Aunt Gin. My father was only nine when his mother died at the age of thirty-nine. His father was Ben Walker, Aunt Gin's brother. My grandfather was a lithographic artist. I was born on Turner Street, St Ann's and was one of eight children.

I remember how cows and sheep used to be driven through the cobbled streets to the slaughterhouse on Little John Street off Peas Hill Road where my father helped, as he was a butcher by trade. As a child, I used to take little packets of tea for them to brew up, and hide behind the gate as I was terrified when I saw the cows coming up the street. One man used to bring a bull through the streets on his own. It had a brass ring through its nose tied to a very thick rope. I also remember a big vat of hot water and a pig hanging over it. I was only a little girl and I thought they were cleaning it.

They were the days when you could get five caramels for a halfpenny, or a little bag of sweets off the tray if you were lucky enough to have a halfpenny, because people were poor.

I went to St Ann's Church School, a nice school that was sadly demolished.

My grandmother, May Stafford Archer (born 1879), used to help her friend in a small house where the parlour was turned into a shop. All they sold was pickled onions, red cabbage, and toffee apples covered in treacle and rolled in coconut on a stick for a halfpenny. When the children came out of the Cavendish picture house on a Saturday morning (that was known as the 'twopenny rush'), that's where they went if they had any money left.

We used to make choc-holes in the middle of the street in between the cobblestones to play marbles, and put a skipping rope round the old-fashioned lampost to swing around. On bonfire night, you could always hear a fire engine somewhere because some of the fires were too big in the middle of the streets.

I remember Sally Slick Slack who used to go down to the Central Market and bring back old wooden boxes to chop up for bundles of firewood. You could often see her walking up St Ann's Well Road pushing her old pram with her stockings all wrinkled round her legs. I saw her once sitting at the bottom of the Chase when I came out of school. I ran across the road and gave her a sweet and she said: 'Thanks me duck'. She was a nice old lady.

Then came the War. I was eleven years old. We had shelters in the streets as a lot of people didn't have cellars to go in. Everything was rationed. Some things we didn't

Grandma Archer. On the back of this photo, she had written: 'This is the cook. How many tarts can you eat? (signed) Mother'.

see at all, like bananas, until they were put on the children's green ration books.

I met my husband when I was seventeen on St Ann's Well Road. He was home on leave from Germany just after the War. There weren't any houses to be had anywhere. The Local Authority offered us a prisoner-of-war hut to live in on Colwick Woods until we got a Council house but my husband refused it. It was terrible. We lived with my parents for a while until we found two unfurnished rooms.

We waited six years on the Council Housing list until a house came up on the Clifton estate in 1953 and we are still here [2002]. We have a son (David) and daughter (Ann). My parents lived in St Ann's all their lives so I didn't really leave because I was visiting them twice a week. They were moved to Clifton in the early 1970s due to St Ann's redevelopment, but my mother soon got an exchange back to St Ann's where she was happy. My father agreed.

Gladys Walker (later Faircloth) aged 19

This is Gladys' sister Violet (on the right) and Aunt Dorothy (Dolly) Archer walking down St Ann's Well Road in the late 1930s. Violet Walker was born June 2nd 1923 and she married Geoffrey Lucas. Aunt Dolly was born December 16th 1919 and she married Frank Potter

Gladys marries Alan Faircloth, a Normandy veteran, at St Bartholomew's Church, St Ann's, on March 12th 1949

Gladys' father, Ben Walker (in bowler hat). Her brother, Benny Walker in front, and George Archer on the left. Taken in the backyard of the Walker family home on Turner Street, St Ann's

Ben Walker, fourth from the left front row, Gladys Faircloth's father

Emily Walker, third from the right middle row, Gladys Faircloth's mother

Pub weekend trips to Blackpool from the Coachmaker's Arms at the bottom of Union Road/ St Ann's Well Road. The women went one weekend and the men went another. Gladys Faircloth dates these outings in the 1960s.

HOWARD ATKINSON

1929 – 1994

Howard Atkinson

EGG

Crack in the shell;
hush, it's breaking.
What is inside?
Me
Breaking out.

Howard Atkinson

It is amazing; this little poem made such an impression on a young visitor from Germany. Isabell visited the exhibition at Brewhouse Yard Museum, Nottingham, in 1997 to pay tribute to a man of great courage. In writing a thank you for the exhibition, she wrote:

*EGG. Crack in the shell. Hush, it's breaking.
What is inside? He.
Breaking Out.*

*Breaking the waves. Starting new.
    Every Morning. Every day.
    Until I found myself to share with you what I am.*

One example of his courage was to marry a girl from Germany, from East Berlin, at the height of the Cold War in 1961. Howard wrote later: " . . . but have learnt not to waste time in regrets, and my divorced wife and I still meet and in our small ways work to keep this world one".

Indeed they stayed friends for the rest of his life. After one of Marianne's visits to his flat in St Ann's, Howard wrote:

YOUR DAFFODILS

When I got back
the daffodils were
in the brown mug on the table
where you had left them,
by the bowl of fruit.
Some had come out
like slow golden explosions.

I see you waving
as the train draws out.

Without your bubbling talk the flat
was silent. I miss your gentle, incessant
commotion about the place.

Come again, come soon.
Come while the daffodils
are still in bloom.   March 1984

And Marianne came again and again. She met some of Howard's neighbours, and some neighbours and friends she gets to know better now, when reading his many poems, letters and stories:

"The Villain tapped at my door last night. I do not know what time it was, but I woke up. The bedroom door was open and I could see his shape through the glass like a moth moving outside. I remembered it was Wednesday - the day he draws his dole and supposed he was drunk. I just lay still. After a moment I saw his shape bend down to the letter-flap which he opened and stared through. He must have seen that I was in bed but could not tell if I was awake. He flitted away."

Yes, Howard was seen as a friend by all his neighbours; Alf used to call every day: "Alf has just called for cocoa and sandwich. He puts ten p in a begging bowl each night now."

Although Howard had a lot of courage – he had very little money. There were friends who liked to invite Howard to tea: "That means letting the boys win chess and watching ITV".

The circle of my friends is small:
It is because I am not tall.
I could easily entertain them all
in the circumference of my hall.

I hope my friends die after me
So they will always come to tea
And the people will not say:
'Poor thing. All his friends have gone away.'

By now, of course, some of his friends have gone away, moved up, moved on. But there are many who remember Howard. Alan still remembers him, he has shown me this letter:

Howard Atkinson, 21, Duncombe Close, Nottingham, NG3 3PH. Thursday 2 April

Dear Alan,

I expect you don't get many letters, so there's one from me. The thought crossed my mind this morning that you might welcome someone on whom occasionally to call and exchange conversation with. This morning I visited Horace Blanchard, a 78-year-old almost blind, crippled scandal monger who lives 35, Courtenay Gardens, just by St Augustine's RC Church on Woodborough Road, who loves talking to people and never has audience enough. He will always offer you a cup of tea, perhaps a tot of whisky and maybe a sandwich - though some of his visitors are rogues and take unfair advantage of his hospitality.

He is in most days, most of the day. If you want something to do which would be an act of Christian charity, go and spend an hour with him one day and see how you get on. Say you are 'A friend of Howard's!'

I look forward to seeing you again soon, perhaps at the YMCA, and to a drink in the bar of the Theatre Royal. Long live poetry! Read and write from time to time – and <u>do</u> call on Horace,

Yours Howard.

A fervent letter writer, Howard made friends and enemies. There were also many letters to newspapers, often written on behalf of the wider community or in his role as editor of 'Poetry Nottingham'. But it is the many loving letters he wrote to his son Peter, to his ex-wife Marzi as he used to called Marianne, and to some close friends which will be read again and again, both for the content and the style. Descriptions of shared experiences with friends and neighbours, such as the cleaning of Fred the goldfish's tank have an unforgettable charm:

"I have just been helping Syd to clean out his goldfish tank. The goldfish is named Fred. Fred is very particular about his tank, as he is used to have Margaret clean it out, and she takes two hours and washes the stones at the bottom with Dettol. While the big tank is being cleaned Fred skulks at the bottom of a little tank nearby where he can keep an eye on how things are going."

Howard's wish was to stimulate and inspire those around him. He said: "If life is to continue, we must be bigger than that in which we believe, and smaller than what we believe ourselves to be".

This has been taken on board literally by the ex-wife Marzi who has put up exhibitions of Howard's work in Nottingham, London and Oxford. She is hoping to continue this cycle of exhibitions to include Brighton, Bristol and possibly Berlin, to be returning to Nottingham with a final show and the completed set of ten themed booklets before the end of the year 2004.

For it is here in Nottingham, specifically St Ann's, that she remembers Howard, with his example to do better, to do

more – for the community. For her teaching German, for three years as a volunteer at the Neighbourhood Centre, has been a great joy; Howard would not only approve another course being run, he himself would be involved with the activities at the centre!

Would he be missing one of our beautiful cherry trees?

THE CHASE

a shopping precinct
squat concrete drabness
cheap tasteless little shops
people badly dressed
above ground littered with petals
three cherry trees in bloom –
exiles.

May 1985

I have begun to plant a patch of lavender in every city the exhibition will have been to. Will there be a suitable place in St Ann's? In The Chase?

To keep those two remaining cherry trees company?

Marianne Vera Atkinson 2000 and 2002

<u>KATH PRICE</u>

Born 1929

From conversations, letters and Kath Price's writing. Kath Price was brought up just out of St Ann's on the Sneinton side with two brothers, Arthur and Joe, and a sister June. She published a collection of childhood memories in 'Looking Back' in 1980. After marriage, she moved across from Carlton into St Ann's, which she already knew well. In 'Looking Back' she writes:

"My mam took in washing for a family who kept a fruit shop. They were named Jones, and I remember having to fetch this washing every Monday from up the top of Alfred Street North, St Ann's. A distance of two miles seemed two hundred to me and I tried to keep the large bundle on the rickety old push-chair. Many's the time the lot fell off and I'd be struggling, trying to tie up the bundle and lift it back on to the pram again, and when it got to Wednesday and it was all washed and ironed, the excuses I made about having a belly ache or toothache were to no avail. I still had to cart it all back again. It was nice though coming back. I ate the shiny red apple given me by Mrs Jones and rode part the way in the push chair, holding on tight to the two half-crowns for my mam for doing the washing."

When Kath Price met her future husband, Sam, they were both fourteen. Kath, a busy waitress with many GI customers at the Milton Café near Victoria Station, was getting off the bus on her way home. After working long hours five and a half days a week making munitions, he volunteered to do wartime fire watching at the factory of Universal Engineering Company on Leighton Street.

Their marriage lasted over fifty years. Sam died May 19th 1999. Kath has four children, eight grandchildren and four great grandchildren. Kath says: "Responsibility at an early age was the best thing for us".

Kath's wedding day April 5th 1948. Left to right: Kath's dad, brother Arthur, sister June, Sam, Kath, cousin Joan, Kath's mam, sister-in-law Kay. The baby is nephew Tony

Kath's brother Arthur Smith and his wife Kay reached their Golden Wedding in 1996. They married in 1946 after knowing each other for just ten days. They met in the Empress Eugenie Pub in Alfred Street, St Ann's, just after he returned home from War service with the Royal Signals Regiment in the Middle East and Cyprus.

At a Reminiscence Day at St Ann's Library in 1998, Kath (who has written many letters to the *Nottingham Evening Post* and articles in *Sneinton Magazine* about her recollections) said:

"My first little house in 1950 was on Dawson Street, near the area known as The Mounts. My rent was six shillings and sixpence weekly. The house was very small and in the ten years I lived there, I had three little girls. The bedroom was so small, my girls all slept together; no bath, outside toilet, no hot water.

Brother Arthur's wedding to Kay (nee Body) 1946. Extreme left, Kath's dad. Sister June in front. Mam and Auntie Polly on the right

Kath says: This was my first little house and my babies in the 1950s

"My landlord offered me a tenancy of Harcourt Terrace, Lamartine Street, a house with bath, hot water, and a new rent of thirty shillings. My husband's take-home pay was then £7.00. I wondered how I would pay the new rent. Luckily there were many factories in St Ann's, so I got a part-time job in hosiery. My boss was good. He let me have school holidays off.

"My new home had three bedrooms, also a bath, hot water and a small yard for my kids to play in, and a cellar where the coal man dropped my coal through a grating. In my old house, the coal place was inside, dust everywhere. When the coal man came, he always came after I had scrubbed my kitchen floor!

"The cellar head was where I kept my food, no fridge then, and food kept cool here, milk, meat etc. There were lots of shops, a beer-off on every corner, fruit shops, newsagents, fish and chip shops. We lived hand to mouth. Every quarter of cheese, a packet of biscuits, bread and milk . . . I saved pennies for my gas and electric meters, rented a wireless for one shilling and nine pence a week from Rediffusion. Our simple pleasures were a walk to Trent Bridge and the Arboretum, a night out at Cavo [nickname for the Cavendish Cinema] or the Empress on St Ann's Well Road."

Many of the women from St Ann's, Kath told me: "Took their weekly wash to the [Victoria] washhouse on Bath Street where we could obtain all the hot water, drying and ironing facilities needed for less than three shillings.

"My Sam was very well-known as a butcher at Dewhurst's on the St Ann's Well Road opposite Robin Hood Chase and the old St Ann's Church during the 1950s and

Sam Price (left) and colleague John at Dewhurst's, St Ann's Well Road, 1950s

Dewhurst's Victoria Centre closure 1993. Sam Price (in hat) at the back with his hand on son Steve's shoulder (front right)

Son Stephen's wedding to Donna Bird at St Matthias Church on October 7th 1995, the same church where Kath and Sam Price married in 1948. Donna is the youngest of eight sisters and three brother from St Ann's

60s. He also worked at many of the Dewhurst shops and became the Manager of their branch in the Victoria Centre after it was built. Everyone knew Sam Price.

"From 1972-98, we lived on Abbotsford Drive in St Ann's, and were very happy there.

"Linda was our eldest, then Patricia and then Kathleen. Then we had a son, Stephen, born at Harcourt Terrace in 1966. Linda was then seventeen, Patricia sixteen and Kathleen[1] fourteen. When Stephen started school at Bath Street School, he told his teacher he had four mams at home and two television sets!

"Stephen was a pupil at Elliott Durham Comprehensive School 1978-84 when Mr Bratton was the Head Teacher. I am still in contact with Matt Lidgett, one of his teachers who helped Steve obtain his Bronze, Silver and Gold in the Duke of Edinburgh's Awards. I have a soft spot for Elliott Durham and the teachers at that time. Steve went from Hunto [Huntingdon School] to Elliott. I was a dinner lady at Hunto for sixteen years. Steve married Donna who was in the same class at Elliott Durham and she did the Awards too."

---

[1] Kathleen [Kath Brown] is interviewed for this book.

While living on Abbotsford Drive, Kath wrote this poem:

Cold geriatric walls.
How I hate your rubber doors
that close behind me
with a sickening thud,
and melancholy fills my mind.
Stone-faced nurses stare
as I gaze around
for a face that should not be here.
I see her among the frail and feeble bodies.
Her eyes find me:
she smiles and I know
she's still my mother.

Kath Price recalls that you used to know the day of the week by the food on the table in the days when the family ate at the table together. Monday was leg o'beef stew day. The big brown earthenware stew pot went into the oven at

Kath and Sam Price's Golden Wedding Day celebration April 5th 1998. Grandaughter April on Sam's right and grandaughter Georgia on Kath's knee

the side of the coal fire and, when it was put on the table and the lid came off, the lovely aroma of carrots, onions, turnips and taters wafted over you. There were arguments about who would have the lovely brown skin off the top of the rice pudding.

Tuesdays was sausages and mash, mushy peas and thick brown gravy with onions cooked in the frying pan. Chunks of bread cleaned up the plate. Wednesday was meat and tater pie day. Thursday was tripe and onions (not so good!). Friday was hot faggots and gravy. Saturdays, when dad got his wages from Britannia Cotton Mills, a fresh rabbit went into the stew with a cowheel. For tea it was fresh crab and mussels. Dad and grandad had a cod steak for tea. Sundays were special, lamb and mint sauce with Yorkshire pudding.

JOSEPH (JOE) NICHOLSON

Born 1930

Interviewed in his home 6.7.00. All photos from Joseph (Joe) Nicholson

The Nicholson family came to Nottingham in 1897. That year, my father was born in the Meadows, Nottingham. Within about two years, he was packed off to his Aunt and Uncle in Wakefield. I think there were so many children, so he was sent off. But in 1911 he came back. After a visit to his parents, he refused to return. He became an apprentice plumber and went into the Army in the First World War. He was gassed during the last German offensive and put into hospital. After he had recovered, he was sent to the Russian Caucasus until he was demobilised in February 1920. He then finished his apprenticeship.

All the family moved into Whitehead Street, 1914-15. Grandfather died in 1925 so I never knew him.

My mother's family had probably not been in the area for quite so long. The first family member to come was probably her Aunt who came into domestic service. She married a cab driver and they settled in Marple Street. It was a strange street off Alfred Street North and parallel to Woodborough Road. The street was on a steep hill and had steep steps at the top leading to Cranmer Street.

It was a strange sort of house. Being on a hill, you went into the front door off the street and then downstairs to the lower living room and back door. My mother's elder brother went to live there when he came out of the Forces, because he had his left hand shot away and couldn't work with farm horses any more. He got a job as Commissionaire at the *Nottingham Guardian* office. They used to have a system at the *Guardian* office where telegrams were delivered quickly because there weren't so many telephones for gathering news. He married one of the Post Office telegraph girls. These girls used to run between the Post Office and the newspaper office.

When they started to have a family, she had to leave and my mother came up from the Lincolnshire Fens to take over from her. She lost that job when the telegraph boys

came back from the Forces. I've got the letter thanking her very much. She went to work for Forman's the Printers, then on Hucknall Road.

She lived with the family in several different houses around Nottingham, finally in Raglan Street, and eventually met my father. They married after he finished his apprenticeship. They started in an old house in Carlton, didn't stay long and moved to 19, Festus Street. And that was where I was born in 1930. My parents were keen theatre goers before I was expected and, after they couldn't go out at night so much, they bought a radio.

I was told the electricity was put in the house on Armistice Day, 1930. My father was ill and he and the electricians sat down and listened to the Armistice Day parade. I've got some photographs of me on my christening day. I was christened at Emmanuel Church, Woodborough Road. When Emmanuel Church was demolished, some of the stone was used to build the Vestry in Holy Trinity Church, Lambley.

My father died in 1933 of the after effects of gas poisoning. He was thirty-five. It said bronchitis on his death certificate and stated his profession as plumber with War Pensioner in brackets, so my mother didn't get a War Pension only a Widow's Pension.

We stayed in Festus Street for a while. My Aunt and Uncle lived in 53, Raglan Street, and then got a better house in New Basford, and my mother and I moved into Raglan Street, with Granny too. My mother stayed there until the Council pulled it down and they gave her a Council flat near the bus terminus on The Wells Road, more or less on the site of St Ann's Well. It was a new flat and she thought it was marvellous. It was upstairs which was a little inconvenient but she managed all right and she was there some ten years.

I can't remember much before I went to school. I can remember from about the age of three or four, there was the weekly walk to Sneinton Market: down Peas Hill Road, along St Ann's Well Road, up Alfred Street South, along Sabina Street, through the Bath Street Park to the Market. Mother was a country girl from Thurlby-by-Bourne in Lincolnshire and when she left school she worked as a children's maid on a farm. She lived on an isolated farm. She took the children for a walk every day and she used to tell me how the geese followed them round the lanes.

She thought everybody should have a nice walk every day, so I used to be pushed in my pram every day from Festus Street to the Arboretum, even if it was snowing. And that's why we've got a lot of photos in the Arboretum! I went to St Andrew's Church of England School on Alfred Street North, which went of course with all the clearance. It stopped being a Church of England school the day I left, in 1941. It was financed by Sir John Player, the tobacco magnate. I think at that stage he gave up spending a lot of money on it and the Council took it over and it became the Alfred Street North Temporary Council School, and it was temporary until the area was demolished!

When I was there, there were fifty children in Form 1. I remember most of the teachers. Miss Dyer was a terror. At least two cousins of mine warned me about Ma Dyer when

ST ANN'S NOTTINGHAM: inner city voices *by Ruth I Johns* · ISBN 0951696092

I started: 'Oh, you wait until you get in Ma Dyer's class, she don't half shout!' She was in the youngest class of the Juniors. There were Infants and Juniors, and Senior Girls. Ma Dyer never hit me but I can remember her giving a lad a caning. She bent him over and whacked him and a big cloud of dust came out of his trousers and we had a dreadful job not to laugh. She would pick on anybody who was awkward.

There wasn't bullying but I can remember having an argument with Bobby Batterham. We didn't hit each other but he took a tremendous kick at me and his shoe came off and sailed over the wall into a garden on Marple Street. The Headmistress of the Infants had to go along Alfred Street and up Marple Street and say: 'Please can we have our shoe back?'

The teacher in the first class in the Infants was Miss Quarton and she was very gentle. We used to have a sleep in the afternoon. We had beds provided by Sir John Player with steel frames and canvas on top. In the Juniors we had visits from the Vicar of St Andrew's. He gave us a pep talk every now and then. We only had to go to a Church Service once a year, on Ascension Day. I got a scholarship and went on to Mundella Grammar School. One boy in my class failed the scholarship but achieved it the next year. In those days, you had two chances. One brilliant girl got the chance of a scholarship but her dad wouldn't let her do it.

In Mundella, they put you in any old how for the first year and then sorted you out according to what you were good at. In the second form, I did science, chemistry, physics, biology, maths and French. I got into the fifth form, got a good School Certificate and then school ended and work began. We didn't have much money.

I went to work in Boots laboratories and went to night school, got an inter-BSC and then packed it up because of health problems. I continued working in the labs. I did various things, starting with streptomycin and penicillin. I was in the Technical Development Department for a while, trying to develop drugs which the firm either had information about or found, and trying to get them into the production stage. We did this for some but not for streptomycin.

After a while, I moved into production and worked in the labs doing assay work and on the fermentation plant. I married Jean in 1952 and we lived with my mother at Raglan Street for a while. Caroline was born in 1953 and we moved to Lambley in 1954. This was our own house, although when we moved here it didn't have a toilet inside or mains drains. I used to cycle about seven miles to work.

I don't remember very much about the Hungerhill Gardens. My grandfather always looked after a garden up there, but my father, as I mentioned earlier, was not very fit and he couldn't be sure of getting up there in the winter to light a fire so he never had a greenhouse. As a little boy, the Hungerhill Gardens seemed enormous.

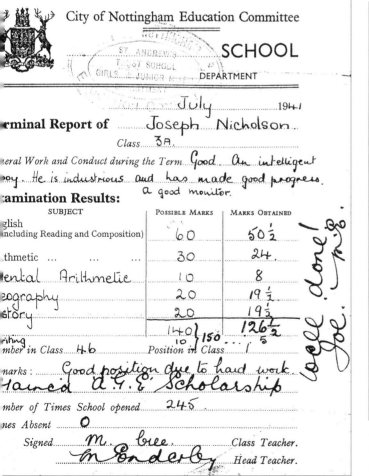

Joseph Nicholson's report from St Andrew's School, July 1941

Father, Joe Nicholson, and brother, George Nicholson, in step-brother Leslie's garden c1911. Note that Joe is working and has clothes and watch chain that befits his employment. George is still a schoolboy in knickerbockers and stiff collar

The area started as an upper working-class area and, as it got older, people moved out when they could afford to. My Uncle Charlie and Aunty Flo must have had about six houses in their life and every time they went up a bit.

The worst thing the Council did in the redeveloped St Ann's was the street plan. It became the kind of place where crime could flourish because of poor street planning. The maze-like pattern of closes and alleyways make it difficult for the police, especially in cars, to get around the area quickly.

Joseph Nicholson pushes his son Joseph Edward Nicholson in Nottingham Arboretum, 1930. There is a mongrel dog, Mick (female) on the end of the lead!

Hungerhill Gardens c1924. Uncle Joe Davis (left) and grandfather Jacob Nicholson

Joseph Edward Nicholson in 'our' garden. Hungerhill Gardens 1930

Hungerhill Gardens c1924. From left, Annie Ainger; Aunt Bertha Lorriman; grandfather Jacob Nicholson; Cousin Ernie Lorriman; mother (then Lilian Ellis); Cousin Renee Lorriman; father Joe Nicholson; Aunt Annie Nicholson and Uncle Joe Davis

Joseph Nicholson and Lilian Sarah Nicholson, Skegness, after 1925 and before 1930

St Ann's Nottingham, inner city voices by Ruth I Johns • ISBN 0951696092

Joseph Edward Nicholson with Granny Ellis (Ann Elizabeth Ellis) at 19, Festus Street. This is probably a christening picture April 1930

Nancy and Marjorie Ellis (cousins of Joseph Edward Nicholson) 49, Raglan Street c1928-30

Joseph Edward Nicholson, Hungerhill Gardens (not 'our' garden) c1932. The jacket is interesting: a 'reefer' jacket, the precursor of the Duffle Coat. It was navy blue with brass buttons with anchors embossed on them

Joe Nicholson with daughter Caroline on her Christening Day, December 1953. Photo taken at the rear of 53, Raglan Street

Lilian Sarah Nicholson in her garden at 53, Raglan Street. There were many attractive small gardens like this in St Ann's

. . . and her garden after demolition started. Photo taken by her grandson William, March 20th 1972

Lilian Sarah Nicholson who moved to Wells Gardens, St Ann's, after Raglan Street was demolished. Photo taken by her grandson William June 6th 1973. Lilian Nicholson was born in 1900 and died in 1976

DOREEN BACON

Born 1930

Interviewed in her home 25.5.99

When students at Elliott Durham School were helping to prepare 'Elliott Durham and St Anns' [Plowright Press 1998], they were especially interested in the brief profile of Doreen Smith. I showed them this from the St Ann's community newspaper 'Chase Chat' of October 1974. They wanted to know what happened to Doreen. Well, I found her!

When my mother came to Nottingham, she worked in a pub as a housekeeper-cum-barmaid. When her employers found out she was pregnant by the son of the house, they threw her out. 'Mammy' Langham took her in. She was a Salvationist, the whole family were Salvationist. Mrs Langham's son was called Tommy and he was in the Salvation Army Band. Mrs Langham lived on Alfred Terrace, St Ann's, No 12 I think. The Terrace started on Dame Agnes Street as an entry and then opened up as a terrace, with little gardens in front, to Abbotsford Street.

Through Mrs Langham, my mother met my father who lived further down the Terrace, and when my sister was two months old they got married. He was a widower and twenty-one years older than my mother.

My mum's mother was born in North Muskham near Newark. My grandfather was born in Redmile and he worked for the railway. They got married and moved around with his work on the railway. When they met he was a porter. Eventually he was a Guard. They moved to Leicester when my mother was born. Then they moved to the Meadows in Nottingham and my Uncle Percy was born there. When my mother was five, her mother died of diphtheria, which left her father with two young children and a boy, Fred, who was ten years older than my mother. Two years later he died of pernicious anaemia.

Although there was an extended family in North Muskham and an aunt in Nottingham who kept a babyware shop in Carrington Street, none of them would take the children in. They were looked after by my grandfather's housekeeper and a man on the railway who took it upon himself to save them going on the Parish. He wrote to the Muller Homes in Bristol and the children were accepted. It was a religious institution. I've found out all the details. Muller Homes have been very helpful.

Mum stayed at the orphanage till she was seventeen and Uncle Percy until fourteen. Mum went into Service in London and Uncle Percy was put to a job in London. He misbehaved and the orphanage (which kept in touch once children left) got in touch with an uncle in North Muskham and Uncle Percy worked on a farm there. I suppose that's why my mother moved to Nottingham. My sister was born in 1912 or 1913.

My brother was born in 1920 and I was born at 41, Broad Oak Street, St Ann's in 1930. In St Ann's, I was like a gypsy. My mum used to point to a big house on Robin Hood Chase with a conservatory where we moved, then somewhere down Hyson Green and then somewhere else. We went lots of places. My sister reels them off. I can't remember. Then we went to Peas Hill Road, St Ann's, and that's when I started school. My sister was widowed when her son, Fred, was ten months old, so he was eleven months younger than me and we were brought up like twins. I went to the old St Andrew's School on Alfred Street North, St Ann's. Dad took us on the first day because he was retired by that time and my mum worked.

Fred wanted to start school with me but he was only three and they said no. So he did his favourite trick when he wanted his own way. He got down on the floor and kicked and screamed until he was told he could start school! We stayed there until my father went into hospital about 1936/37. My mum took me to a foster home and she paid them five bob [five shillings a week] to look after me. She bought my clothes.

Fred went to live with his Grandma on Stanley Road, Forest Fields. My father died in June 1938. At that time I was living with foster parents in Lotus Street, St Ann's, with a family called Hunt. I was very unhappy there. I used to run away. He used to drink and throw pots. One Bank Holiday, we all went to Burton Joyce and had a lovely time, but then Harry, the man of the house, had too much to drink which was usual at the weekend and came home. He was throwing pots and hitting her with a poker. I was upstairs looking down. He said: 'You come on down you little so and so and I'll give you the same'.

I was in my nightie. I ran from Lotus Street all along St Ann's Well Road, up Alfred Street and down to Sherwin Street. Nobody stopped me. It didn't occur to anybody to stop this child who was running, obviously terrified. My mum took me back to Lotus Street. It still hurts.

My mum used to arrange these private foster carers. She used to say: 'I could put you in a Home the same as I was, but I won't'. But I used to think I wish you would. One place I stayed, when she was living in Sherwin Street, was a family up the street. I had never seen a miner with a dirty face. I woke up one evening and went downstairs and this man of the house had just come home with his black face and I just screamed and ran home.

This was the story of my life. Something spooked me wherever I was and I would run home. I was in Lotus Street when my dad died and after that mum took me home. After that I gravitated between my mother and my sister who had remarried and had another family.

Then the War started. There was a bus outside school on Duncan Street and we were being evacuated. We had a little case and were given a carrier bag of what they called rations. Fred was going with me. He changed his mind and got off. My mum was saying: 'You stay on'. She was glad to get rid of me. Then I went to Fiskerton. I was there two years.

In spite of everything, I wanted my mum. But it was a real home in Fiskerton. They were an elderly couple. Their son was a signalman on the railway and Pop Smith was a ganger on the railway. He also had the village cycle shop and it was wonderful. He fitted me up with an old bike with solid wheels. I used to cycle up the lane (it's called

ST ANN'S NOTTINGHAM: inner city voices by Ruth I Johns • ISBN 0951696092

Gravely Lane now) to Morton every day to school. Back at lunchtime and then back again. I was so proud of having this bicycle.

After two years, they asked if I could be taken away because they were getting too old to manage. I was eleven by then. I went home and everybody had just moved up to Morley School. So I started at Morley School and stayed until I was fourteen.

The public [slipper] baths on St Ann's Well Road, bottom of Southampton Street, had a men's and a women's entrance. You sat on a bench waiting your turn. I think you paid six pence. Friday night and Saturday were very crowded. Everybody was poshing up for the weekend.

I lived with my mum. There was just the two of us. My brother Cyril was in the Air Force. Then she took this girl in. Mum was good at taking people in, except me. This girl eventually married one of my brother's friends who was in the Navy. Then my mum took in a Bevin boy. She said he needed somewhere nice to stay. He was introduced by Uncle George (later my stepfather) and came from Bridgenorth. My brother was stationed there and mum said if he needed a good home, she hoped someone would take him in.

Then mum got married again and didn't tell me until the night before. I went off on a bike all upset, fell off and split my chin. My stepfather lived on Edwin Street with his brother and family.

He was a widower and had a son Ken. He said he wanted to live with his dad. So there was no room for me, so I was sent down on Hungerhill Road to stay with a friend of my mother's. I used to call her Aunt Phil and she was another proper mum. Her husband was in the Army. My brother, in the Air Force, got married and came to live with them. Ken went into the Navy at sixteen. I sort of went home then but never really settled back home.

The really bad winter of 1946/47 I remember. The factories were closed. My brother, my sister-in-law's brother and my stepbrother had all come back from the War. One from Italy, one from Africa and my stepbrother from Malta. They used to sit around the old black fireplace at 38, St Ann's Valley. I used to go down to the old St Ann's School on Corporation Road, get a quarter [of a hundred weight] of coke with my friend Brenda. We used to take the sledge, socks over our shoes, and drag it back up Hungerhill Road and St Ann's Valley right to the top, then as soon as I got back mum would send me off again to go and queue for another quarter. When I did eventually finish, I couldn't get near the fire because all of them were still near it. The old story where they say: 'What are you having for your tea? Well, I'll have toast and make it myself.' This didn't work in our house!

I left school just before I was fourteen and started work at William Gibson's on Thurland Street as errand girl. That was fun. After the War they moved back to the Ashforth Building on Ashforth Street as T W Hardy. I was there until I was eighteen.

Then I went nursing at the Coppice Hospital[1] until I was twenty-one. I started as a scullery maid. I liked the elderly

ladies. I was on a ward they called the Wing. Some of the time I lived in, some of it with Gran, my sister-in-law's mother-in-law at Forest Fields and then as I got older into bed-sits on my own.

I got married the day after my twenty-first birthday. To a Royal Marine from Nottingham. I was in a state. I tried to call it off but my brother said no because my mother had put so much into the wedding. It only lasted six months.

At twenty-six I went to work at the GPO as a telephone operator and then to the City Police doing the same. I didn't want to be a telephone operator for the rest of my life, so joined the Army to get an education. I was there nearly three years and got Second-Class. I was going for First-Class but they didn't want me to do it. I wanted to be a driver, passed all my written tests and map-reading and everything else, and was told I would make a good driver. But the driving instructor told me I wouldn't pass my exam because I was too feminine. So I became a clerk and, because I wasn't allowed to take my First-Class education, I left.

Doreen Bacon in the Army c1956

---

1 Coppice Hospital was on the edge of St Ann's. It is now flats and called Hine Hall.

I was nearly twenty-eight and worked in Manchester at Lewis's store in the office on the first floor, then at Gestetners as a demonstrator, then a demonstrator instructor for Hartley Electromotives. I travelled with the job all over the country. Home in Nottingham on Goose Fair weekend, I met Tub Smith, an American airman, who became my husband. It was the same time my stepfather died in Ransom Hospital near Mansfield. We became better pals after my mother died. He used to come and stay with me in Manchester.

After I married, we went to America. I worked in a hospital in California on the Information Desk. Then, Tub got transferred to the Air Force Academy in Colorado Springs. My son, William Brett, was born there. He's thirty-three now.

Later we adopted Donna when she was nine days old. Then I was ill. I was in hospital for Donna's first birthday. We prayed so hard for me to get well and the Church prayed so hard. Tub said if his wife got well we would accept what came and it was a posting to Vietnam for him.

I came home. My sister got me a house on Crown Street back in St Ann's and my brother decorated it. I felt like an immigrant. Brett didn't understand a word anyone said to him! There were Pakistanis, a family of Sikhs, a family from Dominique: they were a lifeline.

I met people like Barbara Levick and Margaret Behrman and I joined SAMPH [St Ann's Mentally and Physically Handicapped Association] to do voluntary work. The Blue Bell Craft Centre came and I got to know Jill McGuire and Mike Stroud.

When Tub came back from Vietnam, our marriage was in trouble. It was the things he'd seen in Vietnam and he was drinking. We were on the American Air Force base in Essex. He got orders to go to Germany and I said I wasn't going. I bought a house on Spalding Road, and went to work as an office manager. People were very helpful.

Ray Gosling asked me to take part in the St Ann's Festival. I moved to Bakersfield which is where I met Brian. We've been married twenty-one years and everybody said it would never last. At that time I worked at the Probation Service on Robin Hood Chase in St Ann's. Maggie Smith, Senior Probation Officer, knew of my voluntary work with SAMPH and asked if I would like a job.

After Brian retired from the Police Force after twenty-five years, we ran a guest house in Beeston Rylands for five years. I had a heart attack, got over that and then got Rheumatoid Arthritis. I was feeling better, Brian was only forty-nine and feeling too young to retire, so we bought a coffee shop in Mapperley. It was called *Bon Appetit*, right opposite the War Memorial. When I was ill because of Arthritis, Donna used to help out. We had the coffee shop four years. I got so ill we couldn't do it.

[Doreen and Brian moved to Cleethorpes for some years and now live in Ilkeston and are actively involved in Church life. They attend the Church of Nazarene, a blend of Pentecostal and Wesleyan.] Brian Bacon is also interviewed for this book

TONY BURT

Born 1931

Interviewed in his home 25.11.99

I was born at 5, Bilberry Street, St Ann's, the next street to Donkey Hill. My mum was born up at Whitehaven in Cumberland and her family moved down to St Ann's in the early 1920s. He dad was a coal miner and went to work at Gedling pit.

Tony Burt and his sister playing at the back of Donkey Hill, St Ann's 1933

My father was born at West Bromwich. His parents, my grandparents, originally came from Plymouth. My grandfather was a photographer journeyman when photographs first started. Then he was a grocer in Nottingham on Daisy Road, off Porchester Road.

My parents married in 1929, the same year as my sister was born. That's why they got married I believe. They lived in Bilberry Street. I had a younger brother and I've got a half-sister. My dad left us during the War for another woman and they had a child. I still see her. I treat her as a sister. My dad and his new family lived on Festus Street, St Ann's.

My half-sister and I are still in St Ann's. My brother died when he was twenty-three of heart trouble. They found that out when he went to the Air Force. Today, he would have been operated on and have been all right. He was invalided out of the RAF. My sister lives at Hayling Island and I go down there for a week every year. She

St Ann's: Nottingham Inner City Voices by Ruth Johns ISBN 0951696092 married up here, they were both in the Air Force, and lived with us in Bilberry Street for a bit.

In 1939, when the War started, the Corporation had just built Bestwood estate and that's where my mum and dad moved to. In one of the houses lower down, a couple moved in and their gas boiler exploded. They came to live with us for a bit and that's the woman my dad carried on with and they left us. And my mum and us went back to Bilberry Street, St Ann's, No 7 next to No 5 where she used to live and where I was born. It was my grandad's house and there was my Aunt Jen and twins there. We were only away at Bestwood about three years.

My mum worked at Luxford's factory. When you grow older you realise how hard she must have had to work to keep us.

I went to Morley School. We used to play a lot in the brick air-raid shelters in Bilberry Street. After the War was over, it was a long time before they pulled them down. They'd got bunks in and we went in whenever we liked. They were in the middle of the road with just enough room for cars to get by, but there weren't many cars then.

I was good at drawing at the time, so from Morley School I went to Nottingham Art School for two days of tests. Five of us went and I was the only one who passed. But I didn't go to Art School because I was the elder son and needed to earn. My sister was in the Land Army. I went to Raleigh for a bit and then down Gedling Pit. I would have liked Art College. I was always interested in that sort of thing which is why I took up printing and design as hobbies.

When I went to the pit, they wanted men underground and on the surface. Because I was little, they wouldn't let me go underground. I went into the baths for a bit. After three or four years I did go down. I tried cycling to work for a bit but I mainly went on the pit bus, until I started courting when I got a motorbike. When I went down the pit, I became an Electrician.

At the pit, they were always asking for volunteers for St John's Ambulance Brigade. As I said, I worked in the pit head baths to start with and the chap who ran St John's worked on top as well. He kept encouraging you to join. Once you were in, it was all right. We used to go on weekend holidays to Skegness every year to The Derbyshire Miners' Home. You went on a Friday until Sunday and they had a big parade. You were treated for being in St John's.

I got married in 1952. My wife, Gwen, came from Arnold. We lived in Arnold for two years and then there was a shop for sale at the corner of Donkey Hill and I bought that. I mean we bought the business and rented the shop. We had it until it was demolished. It was a general shop. We sold toys, tobacco, groceries . . .

I kept my job and my wife was looking after the shop. As luck would have it, I'd got a printing hobby. I'd got a treadle machine and a lot of type and everything off Permberton on Canal Street. They dealt in printing machinery. I used to print letterpress. So when the shop trade got bad, I bought an automatic machine, and put it in the back and we turned over mainly to printing.

That went well. In fact, I packed my job up for six years. I rented the old Scout hut, where the shop by the Police Station is now [Ransom Road], for £3 a week. I was printing until the shop was pulled down. When they started to do the new St Ann's, the worst thing was they pulled all the houses around you down first so you hadn't got much trade.

We printed invoice books, leaflets, all sorts. I printed a lot for SATRA [St Ann's Tenants and Residents Association]. When I saw Ray Gosling at the sessions you ran at St Ann's Library, I hadn't seen him for years. He recognised me but couldn't remember where from. So I told him and he said: 'Oh! Do we owe you any money?' I said no. I didn't take any part in SATRA but I knew Arthur Leatherland because he came into our shop at the bottom of Donkey Hill. We used to allow a lot of tick which you'd got to do. They would pay you at the weekend because everybody hadn't got money all week.

When we knew the shop was to be pulled down, we looked for somewhere else to live in St Ann's. The people in this house were moving to Australia so we bought it and moved in about 1969 but kept the shop on until it was demolished. My mum was upset about moving, she wanted to stay in St Ann's. The Council found her and her sister places in Luther Close, St Ann's, next door to each other. My mum was there until she died [1995]. She had wanted to stay in Bilberry Street. A lot of people wanted to stay in their houses but of course they wouldn't let them. But she did settle in. A lot of her friends moved away from the area and they lost touch.

I was working all hours and not getting much money in. I went back to the pit, this time to Cotgrave and I was there until I was made redundant in 1986. Then I 'retired'. I used to print a bit. I only sold that automatic machine this year. I decided to do my garage out and make it into a room. I'd been doing draw tickets for churches, that sort of thing.

Five generations in Tony's Burt's family. His mum Maggie (bottom left); sister June (behind); June's daughter Susan (right back); Susan's daughter Louise (front right) holding her daughter, baby Coral c1993. Photo from Tony Burt

You can't retire when you are an electrician! I still get asked to do electrical jobs. My hobby now is machine knitting. I do jackets and all sorts, mainly for the family. When I was made redundant, I got bored and the wife had a knitting machine that she didn't use. So I started to use it and then I went and took a City and Guilds in Machine Knitting at South Notts College. I use a computer with it as well. You can design something on the computer and couple it up to the machine, put the programme into the memory of the knitting machine. I don't do all my own designing. Some designs you buy are good.

Tony Burt at work on his knitting machine. Photo: E James Smalley 2001

I'm a member of the Nottingham Guild of Magicians. One year I was president and I was a librarian for several years. I started magic soon after I left school. The Guild used to meet at the YMCA. We used to entertain in clubs. I met my wife at one of her relations' wedding where I was giving a magic show. I didn't see her but she saw me! A mutual friend arranged for us to have a date. I did magic until about ten years ago.

We've always had a dog. We used to keep one in the back of the shop. There were break-ins even at that time. Sam, this dog, is a Japanese Akita. I still get free solid fuel as part of my redundancy payment. It comes every five weeks. When I was young at the pit and still living at home, I went to tell the man that my dad had left so I got a coal allowance which helped my mum. If I had had a dad going to work I wouldn't have got it.

We have two sons, one had polio when he was eight months old. We have three grandchildren. My son who lives here has an allotment on Hungerhill Gardens. And he races pigeons. My other son lives in Wollaton and is married. My wife has gone in next door to see our neighbour. There's a good community around here.

At the back of Tony Burt's house is a patio then a sizeable drop where there used to be a quarry and a brick works. This is an unusual aspect of St Ann's, with houses high the other side of the hollow. At one time the quarry was a British Road Services Depot

FRED HUDSON

Born 1932

Interviewed at his home, 27.1.00

I was born at 4, Cromwell Terrace, Commercial Square, in St Ann's. It was right at the bottom of Alfred Street Central and behind the Oliver Cromwell pub. I had an older brother Arthur and sister Joan.

My mum came from Somercotes, in Derbyshire, and was in domestic service before she was married somewhere about 1921. My dad was a private gardener to a quite wealthy Bleacher and Dyer, Weldon, who lived at a house built by Watson Fothergill on Mapperley Road.

My dad originally came from Arnold. His dad was at one time the stoker at Papplewick Water Works. They moved to Papplewick to the firm's housing. My parents came to St Ann's after they married because they wanted cheap accommodation and by then my grandad was living in Nottingham.

When I was about three we moved from Cromwell Terrace to Bangor Street just off Alfred Street North. It was nearer dad's employment. He used to come home for lunch. At the time, we didn't consider Bangor Street as St Ann's! St Ann's was in the bottom [in the valley].

I went to school at St Andrew's School. It was over the road from where we lived. That was the Infant and Junior School. I moved when I was eleven to Huntingdon Street School. 7 x 7 = 49 is impregnated on my hand today by a three-pronged strap! I think it was called Senior Boys' School. Oh, it was a tough school. I always called it Huntingdon Street Academy for Young Gentlemen! Corporal punishment was handed out freely. To start with there was a Head called Mr Davis and then Mr Keeble.

I wasn't good at much in school. I left when I was fourteen. If you were any good you were in the 'A' Class and I was in the 'C'. I have often thought that if I could have gone to school until I was sixteen I would have learned something. At fourteen, you were only just starting to develop.

As kids, we were threatened with brimstone and treacle if we didn't go to the toilet regularly. There was California Syrup of Figs on Friday night to ensure that we did!

You used to come home from school, grab a slice of bread and treacle and then go out and play. Invariably all you were doing was running around the area playing cowboys and Indians or something like that. When I was about eleven, Mrs Keetley the local ironmonger wanted me to run errands for her. All I used to do was go and fetch the bread daily for her and then do a few errands on Saturday. And I used to get seven pence a week.

One day, my mother went to Mark Shaw the Chemist at 143, Woodborough Road, and he asked her if I could take his dog for a walk. So I got a dog-walking job once a day but not at weekends: four shillings a week. All I had to do was take the dog up Woodborough Road on to Robin Hood Chase, right down to St Ann's Well Road and then bring it back. It used to take me three quarters of an hour. I walked

St Ann's Nottingham: Inner City Voices by Ruth I Johns   ISBN 0951696092

the dog for about nine months and then it died. You lose your job when the dog dies!

We were in a terraced house at the bottom of the yard. The person who lived at the top of the yard had an allotment on Woodborough Road. He grew flowers there. I had to go round to certain customers to ask if they wanted any flowers. I got about a shilling a week for doing that.

When we were at school, it had two allotments, one up the Woodborough Road and one, would you believe it, in Walter Halls School, Mapperley. About once a fortnight if the weather was nice we'd go up there with this gardening teacher. I don't know who tended the gardens otherwise, but we used to go up there and all we did was weeding.

I didn't do it very often, but sometimes we used to go down to the Cavendish Cinema on the St Ann's Well Road on the 'tuppeny rush' on a Saturday morning. And I used to like swimming at the Victoria Baths. On a Saturday morning I invariably ended up there. During the War my mum and a friend next-door-but-one used to go down to the Cavendish and we used to go down there in the blackout, with a number eight torch.

During the War, our cellar was reinforced as an air-raid shelter. A section of the wall adjoining our next-door neighbour was altered so that there was a division only one brick thick. The idea of this was that, in an emergency, the bricks could be knocked through giving an escape route from one cellar to the other.

In Conway Street, they had two brick shelters with concrete roofs on one side of the road. They had wooden seating in them all the way round. I wouldn't have liked to go in them. My dad was a shelter warden. As soon as the siren went, he used to have to go to Egerton Street where there was a shelter for the factories on Egerton Street. He was responsible for anybody who went into it.

There was a Co-op on Alfred Street. It was grocery, butchery and greengrocery. Butchers did their own slaughtering in those days. Our yard came out into Egerton Street. Next-door was the Co-op slaughterhouse. There were several slaughterhouses round the area but this one was being used right the way through to redevelopment.

They used to bring the cows and sheep there. When there were cows they were going: 'Hu, hu, hu . . . ' and when they were sheep they were whistling. They were in a yard no more than five yards from where our back window was over a wall. You could go to the bedroom upstairs and see all the steam rising. On a summer's night, you could see all the rats running inside. I can remember a rat trying to get in our cellar grate.

On Bangor Street right at the top there was a slaughterhouse on the left-hand side and that one became a fire lighter factory and was burnt down about 1948. And then coming down the street on the left-hand side there was a slaughterhouse for Pells, the butcher's on Mansfield Road. And go on to Egerton Street and you could see them with the carcasses up there and ripping them down and taking out the intestines and the bag out and everything. It did smell, sometimes more than others.

Everybody would do their washing on a Monday. When I came home for dinner, I used to get the job of putting the sheets, as thick as possible, through the mangle. Then they would go on the string of lines across the yard. There was a big chimney from a factory on Heskey Street and if the wind was in the right direction the smoke used to puffer down on the washing.

My dad had been pensioned out of the First World War with shellshock. He was very nervous. I don't know how he managed to get his gardening job but it was the best job he could have got. On that bad air-raid in 1941, we had to sleep in the cellar. We put boards across, then blankets on top of the boards. You could hear the aircraft thumping away and the bombs dropping. I said to my dad: 'How far is that one? Is it Market Square?' And he says that one dropped within two hundred yards of where we're living. There was one that came up Peas Hill Road with a string of bombs. Either the first or the last one dropped on Lorne Grove within two hundred yards of where we were living. If they had dropped a bomb before or after, it would have landed in our street.

The bomb that fell was unexploded and it landed right at the side of a petrol station on Lorne Grove with a petrol tank underneath. My brother found it. He was a messenger boy and he used to have to go to these different ARP [Air-Raid Patrol] posts taking messages. He was cycling up there and suddenly realised there was a hole in the ground and he reported it as an unexploded shell. And of course it was a bomb.

The following morning of course everybody had to go to work. I can't remember if we went to school. The buildings had tumbled down and not far from us along Mansfield Road, Sherwood Street where the Bluecoat School was, there was an unexploded bomb which went off about eight o'clock in the morning. It was a tremendous noise. The bake house at the Co-op at the side of the River Trent on Meadow Lane went as well.

I don't know if it was on that night but there was a shelter under the Oliver Hind Boys' Club on Dakeyne Street and it got a direct hit and a lot of people died. We only had one severe night raid.

Can you remember, there was no lighting? Everything was pitch darkness. Even the buses had little five watt bulbs in and they were painted blue. Buses stopped running about nine o'clock at night.

I was in the Life Boys just up the road at St Andrew's Hall. I thought I'd mark time in the Life Boys until I could join the Scouts like my brother at the YMCA on Shakespeare Street. He really enjoyed it. I went down there on my own to join the Scouts and the first night it's: 'Well, we'll see if we'll accept you'. But as soon as the Group's Scout Master knew who I was and knew my brother had been in the troop, I was in. I was about eleven. I stayed until I was eighteen, through Senior Scouts and Rover Crew. Rover Crew had to disband because everybody was going into National Service.

In the Scouts, we had some great camps. The first one I ever went to was at Oxton and we pushed a trek cart all the way to Oxton. There was a Point-to-Point horse race one day. We were standing there with semaphore flags. If somebody fell off, we had to give certain signs. If an ambulance was wanted, send a signal. And after the race we had to pick up rubbish in sacks. That's the main reason we were there! That was a patrol camp, with patrols in the corners of a four-sided field.

The next camp was at Wirksworth in Derbyshire. The following Whitsuntide was a Midland Counties jamboree at Walesby. We went to Holyhead one year, another to Denbigh in North Wales. We went to Botley in Hampshire on the River Amble. And then an August one at Worth Matravers, near Swanage. It was lovely weather. For two nights we camped without tents. The last one we had was at Sands End near Whitby.

I was in apprenticed engineering so I was deferred until I was twenty-one, so I was three years behind going into the Services. At seventeen, I took to cycling, not in a club, just with friends. Occasionally, we'd go youth hostelling. We took our bikes to London and then went out to Kent and Sussex. The following year, myself and two friends did over a thousand mile Youth Hostelling tour in a fortnight. That was the first fortnight's holiday I'd ever had. It was the year before I went into the Forces. I was twenty-one.

We went down to Oxford, Southampton, Dorchester, Exeter, over Exmoor to Lynmouth, down to Ilfracombe and across to where the paddle steamers went to Swansea. Then right up through Wales almost to Holyhead and back through Shrewsbury. Three is an ideal number, two in front and one behind and taking turns to take the draught off the one following. It was really good.

When I left school at fourteen the signpost said 'Factory'! I went into hosiery engineering. The factory was just turning over from War work. It was 1947. I went into apprenticed engineering and learnt how to work lathes, milling machines and grinding machines and bench work. It was a little firm called Kent and Dring on St Ann's Hill Road on Alfred Street North. I stayed there until I was just short of eighteen and the floor gave way, one of the beams across cracked, we so moved out to Draycott in Derbyshire. I got fed up with that place, having to travel either on the bus, but mostly on my bike, eleven miles there and eleven miles back and sometimes not getting back until eight o'clock at night. I knew every bump along that road to Draycott.

From about sixteen or seventeen, I used to go dancing at the Victoria Ballroom. That was another place I went on my own. I must have been discussing it with my brother. He was out of the Forces by then and said he'd take me down. And I said I didn't care whether he'd take me down or not, I'd go on my own.

And I went to Hanford and Richards the dancing school in Trinity Square for three or four years and then graduated to the Victoria and the Astoria. And I used to go down to the Ice-Rink and learnt how to skate. But of course you were short of money so when you were doing these things you weren't spending money on anything else. If you were doing ice-skating and dancing you weren't going to the pictures. And even though they had a little canteen at this dancing school I never went up there for three or four years. People used to go up for the coffee.

I decided that as I had to go in for National Service for two years on the minimum rate of money, I would go for three years instead on the top rate of money. And I went in with my trade so that put me a rank up to start with. I went down to Cardington to get kitted out and from there to West Kirby for square bashing. That's the routine training. From there, I was posted to a camp at Hullavington near Chippenham in Wiltshire and I was there six years.

What happened was a very unfortunate thing. I'd been in the Forces just over two years when I developed a cataract in my right eye, so I was only looking through one eye. And I thought that if I could somehow sign on - which was going to be very hard - that I'd be all right, I'd be looked after. I'd had different reviews on this eye. When I first had it I was A4G7 that means Air 4 Ground 7. G8 and you were out, so I was very unfit.

I went up to Wendover for the operation. They either moved the top part or needled it somehow and then just used atropine drops. This is not the inplant operation which is done today. Six months later they put me up to A4G4 which was OK. When I told the Medical Officer who was a Wing Commander that I was thinking of further signing on, he says: 'You won't do that on A4G4: I'll put you up to A4G2, how's that?' So that was a fix that was. Because I couldn't see properly! In the RAF, you have still got to shoot a rifle and my right eye was faulty. Because they were short of the trade that I was in, I was able to sign on for a further seven years. So that made ten years in all.

When we were at Hullavington, the last four years we managed to get RAF accommodation. At the time I was married. I had three daughters in that marriage. Then in 1959, I was posted out to Germany near Cologne and stayed there until 1962. In Germany I bought a new car, the first member of the family to buy a car. For the last part of my Service I was at a camp in Warwickshire near Stratford-on-Avon and I was living near Rugby and used to travel every day.

About four years after I went into the Forces, mum and dad moved into Alms Houses on Derby Road. My sister married in 1949 and two years later my brother married. When he married, they had to go and live on Robin Hood Chase, St Ann's. Before the War my sister was a milliner, then in the War she went to work for Eriksons and married somebody she met at a drama group there. He'd studied at RADA [Royal Academy for Dramatic Art] and they were very ambitious. They went to London to make their fame and stayed at Boreham Wood. They went into repertory for about a year, and then he did different things like teaching on night school courses.

When I came out of the RAF, it was fairly easy to get a job. I could more or less pick and choose. The RAF give you addresses of employment agencies. I got a job tool making at Universal Engineering at the end of Castle Boulevard. It wasn't very well paid. I stayed there a year and then went to Bentley Engineering which was hosiery engineering again and about five or six pounds more a week than doing my ordinary tool making.

I wasn't in St Ann's at the time of demolition but I saw it all when flattened. I stood where we used to live and

ST ANN'S Nottingham inner city voices by Ruth I Johns • ISBN 0951696092 thought there had been thirteen houses in an area not much bigger than our present garden. I thought how did they ever manage to get thirteen houses on that little site?

I stayed in engineering - not all at the same place - until I retired. I remarried.

For the past twenty years, I've been a Civic Society guide around the City and that's created my interest in history, archaeology, architecture and everything that goes with guided tours. We've got about seven walks altogether.

PETER GARNER

Born 1932

*Written contribution 2000. This includes facts Peter Garner researched about the **Nottingham Suburban Railway**, which played an important part in his St Ann's childhood and influenced his decision to become a locomotive Fireman at Colwick Depot. St Ann's Station was on this line. Peter Garner has given slide shows of his photos of the 'old' St Ann's Well Road at St Ann's Library*

I have many memories of St Ann's, some fond, some not so fond. A very memorable one happened just before Christmas 1944.

I had just come out of Morley School at about 4.30pm. It was quite dark owing to the blackout. I was making my way to the No 40 route bus terminus at Kildare Road to go to town to visit the Library. Whilst waiting at the bus stop, the sound of a railway engine slipping and restarting reached my ears. I ran to the railway embankment at the side of Somnus Bedding works, opposite Kildare Road, known locally as Three Corner Field.

On climbing the embankment I observed a train struggling to climb the gradient out of the tunnel in the heavy snowstorm. Thorneywood Tunnel, 400 yards in length runs under Thorneywood Mount from Thorneywood Station on a heavy gradient of 1 in 50 to the Three Corner Field. The train was emerging from the tunnel and climbing towards St Ann's Well Road Station situated at the top of Kildare Road just beyond where the Gardeners' Public House now stands and where the old St Ann's Well once stood.

I shall never forget the eerie, ghostly sight of the engine struggling to grip the rails, climbing the gradient out of the tunnel in the darkness. Sparks belching from its chimney, its wheels constantly spinning and making little progress, and its oil lamps on the engine front buffer beam flickering in the driving wind and snow. I was hypnotised and spellbound.

The locomotive fireman began sprinkling sand from the engine sandboxes with his firing shovel on to the rails in front of the engine. The engine intermittently began to grip the snow covered rails and the goods train from Thorneywood passed over the girder bridge across The Wells Road, taking its train on to St Ann's Well Station towards Sherwood tunnel under Woodborough Road. The train would then pass through Sherwood Station just off

Winchester Street, Mapperley Rise. It would then pass through Woodthorpe Park to join the LNER [London and North Eastern Railway] line beyond what is now the B & Q store at Daybrook. After reversing, the train would pass through Gedling eventually ending up at Colwick Sidings, Netherfield, where there is now Victoria Business Park, Halfords, Miller Bros, MFI, Allied Carpets and Morrisons.

Kildare Road/The Wells Road Bridge, Nottingham Suburban Railway c1900. Photo source: Peter Garner

Why was the Nottingham Suburban Railway built? Before Nottingham Victoria Station was built and opened in 1900, all trains on the Great Northern Railways from London Road Low Level Station to the west (not to be confused with the Midland Station on Station Street) had to journey via Netherfield, Gelding and Daybrook. Also, some trains went via the Leen Valley line to Bestwood, Butler's Hill, Hucknall, Sutton-in-Ashfield and, later, to Shirebrook using the same route.

These passenger trains became subject to delays between Gedling and Daybrook due to the number of coal trains from the Nottinghamshire and Derbyshire collieries bound for Colwick Marshalling Yard. As a result of these delays, in 1886 the Nottingham Suburban Railway Company was formed by a group of businessmen including the Nottingham Brick Company and Nottingham Corporation. The proposed railway would shorten the journey and provide transport for people living on the eastern side of the City. The first meeting was held on 7th August 1886. Mr Edward Perry, the County Surveyor, who lived at Woodthorpe Grange was appointed Engineer of the line.

The construction contract for the line was awarded to Mr J P Edwards. The company received royal assent on June 25th 1887 and work began on the line. The total cost was approximately £300,000. Kildare Road was made to provide an access road to St Ann's Well Station. The finished line was inspected for the Board of Trade by Major General C S Hutchinson on November 22nd 1889.

The first train over the line left London Road Low Level Station on December 2nd 1889 at 7.45am to Daybrook and returned at 8.15am to Nottingham Low Level Station. The opening service consisted of ten trains from Nottingham Low Level to Daybrook, and some running to Derby, some to Stafford, some to Pinxton, some to Sutton-in-Ashfield via Bulwell Forest, Butler's Hill, Hucknall, Newstead and in 1900 the line was extended to Shirebrook. There were nine trains in the reverse direction from Daybrook to Nottingham Low Level. There was no Sunday Service.

The Carlton Road Station, Thorneywood, was used during the 1st World War to bring wounded servicemen to Nottingham because it had easy access to the platform for taking wounded men into ambulances. Wartime economies in 1916 forced the closure to passengers of Thorneywood, St Ann's Well and Sherwood Stations. During the Railways Grouping Act on January 1st 1923 the Nottingham Suburban Railway became part of the LNER.

St Ann's Well Station, looking to Sherwood c1900. Photo source: Peter Garner

A memorable occasion in this line's history was the visit of King George V and Queen Mary on July 10th 1928. They came to Nottingham to open the Royal Show at Wollaton Park and the new University. First their Majesties went to Woodthorpe Park where they reviewed 17,000 school children. A total of 6,500 children together with 284 teachers arrived at Sherwood Station in thirteen special trains from Basford and Bulwell, Thorneywood and Nottingham Low Level. This occasion meant that Thorneywood and Sherwood Station had to be overhauled after twelve years of disuse and reopened. The line was made single track in February 1930 and the last passenger train to run over the line was in September 1931.

After this date, only goods trains used the line calling at Sherwood, St Ann's Well and Thorneywood Stations: bringing building supplies and coal to Sherwood, coal and supplies for making firelighters at a factory situated in St Ann's Well Station yard, and coal and building supplies to Thorneywood Station. On May 8th 1941, a bomb fell on the line at Colwick Road necessitating all traffic to enter the line from the Daybrook end. A special train chartered by the Railway Correspondence and Travel Society consisting of four coaches was hauled by Engine 67363 on June 16th 1951 and was the last train over this line.

My grandparents, with whom I lived after the death of my mother in 1935, frequently travelled on the line. During the 1940s, my grandfather, as a special treat, would take my cousin and me for Saturday night train rides from

Nottingham Victoria Station to Basford and Bulwell via Netherfield, Gedling and Daybrook, returning a different route via New Basford and the 'Rat Hole' (a tunnel connecting the Great Northern Line with the Great Central Line) to Victoria Station.

All these experiences had a great influence on me and inevitably led me to become a locomotive Fireman at Colwick Depot. Fate decreed I was never to travel over the Nottingham Suburban Railway, which was still open to goods in 1948. It was during my National Service that the line closed. Many times my father, my cousin Alan, and I would take a walk to Colwick Woods along the Suburban Railway track bed from Carlton Road and back, usually at weekends and as a Christmas treat.

Centre right, Kildare Road (off The Wells Road), built as an access Road to St Ann's Well Station. Photo taken from the former railway embankment by Peter Garner 1965

I remember having a picnic with my grandmother on Three Corner Field, gathering wild parsley and riding home on trolley bus No 330. I would be six or seven at the time. Later I would spend days in school holidays at St Ann's Well and Thorneywood Stations observing the shunting operations.

Peter Garner's mother, Ethel Taylor, in a formal studio family portrait c1920. She is sitting (left) with her mother Minnie Taylor; brother Thomas Taylor (behind her) and her father William Thomas Taylor. Minnie and William Taylor, his grandparents, brought Peter Garner up after his mother's death

When my mother died in 1935, my father and I went to live with my grandparents William and Minnie Taylor at 13, Bombay Street, St Ann's Well Road. I could not have had a more loving and caring childhood, perhaps different from many today where materialistic possessions count and false image play an important part. Whilst attending the Edwin Street [St Ann's 'Board' School] and Morley schools during the War, the whole country adopted a wartime measure known as blackout. It meant no streetlights, shop lights or household lights showing.

My grandparents fixed a large sheet of hardboard to the living room window frame each evening to ensure that no light escaped. Should any light be showing, you could risk prosecution. ARP [Air-Raid Patrol] Wardens, and police, patrolled to ensure no lights were showing. Motor vehicles had their headlights blanked off with just a narrow strip of angled light showing. All buses had inside lights covered in dark blue dye, the windows were shaded with the same colour.

During bright moonlight nights, American soldiers would light the smokescreen burners on Northampton Street. These would emit a thick black smoke to help obscure the sky. Other smokescreen burners were situated in various parts of the City including Robin Hood Chase in St Ann's. I remember going with my grandfather, in the inky darkness of the blackout armed with a torch, many times to his allotment garden on Ransom Road to make up the fire for the night in his greenhouses. On a few occasions, it was thick fog and we would make our way through the cold darkness to the garden.

We would unlock the gate to the steep garden path and make our way up the path to grandad's garden. There, we would clean the ash from the fire-bars and make up the fires for the night with coal before returning through the darkness to listen to the wireless and then to bed. To listen to the wireless was fascinating. I would also listen in bed on a crystal set: no batteries were required but a good pair of headphones.

My father bought the crystal set and headphones from the bottom of Union Road, St Ann's. The components were mounted on a bakelite sheet about 12" x 9" which was fitted to the top of a beautifully polished mahogany box. One of the most popular programmes was ITMA [It's That

Rear of 13, Bombay Street 1970. Photos: Peter Garner

Man Again!]. It starred Tommy Handley, Jack Train (Colonel Chinstrap: 'I don't mind if I do'), Derek Guyler ('Don't forget the diver, Sir'), Dorothy Summers (Mrs Mop: 'Can I do you now Sir?') and Dino Galvani ('Senor So-So').

Later programmes to be enjoyed were Merry Go Round, Waterlogged Spa with Eric Barker and Jon Pertwee, who played the part of a Cornish postman who said: 'What's it matter what you do, so long as you tear-em up?' I would also listen in the dark to An Appointment with Fear with the cultured slow-speaking voice of The Man in Black, Valentine Dyall, as the storyteller. I would be listening in bed and end up terrified under the sheets.

On some Saturday nights, my grandparents, cousin Alan and his mother and myself would be taken to the Empire to the Variety Show. One item that never failed to bring tears of laughter to my grandfather's eyes was Wilson, Kepple and Betty with the Egyptian Sand-dance routine performed to the music of Ballet Egyptien by Luigini.

For as long as I can remember my grandfather held the post of Caretaker at the Scout Headquarters at what is now Black's Camping shop in Shakespeare Street. I would go many times and help him to arrange tables and chairs for meetings and various other functions. The rooms upstairs seemed to be booked every night. I would help him in many ways and always attend to the central heating boiler before locking up for the night.

Bombay Street, off St Ann's Well Road 1966. St Bartholomew's Church in distance

During the 1941-42 period when Nottingham was involved with enemy bombing, school children were detailed to have lessons in people's homes. This involved teachers taking lessons all day with several changes of pupils. This was to negate multiple casualties should schools be bombed. I was allocated to Mrs Stackhouse, whose house was on the bottom of Bombay Street on St Ann's Well Road. This was home from home for most of us and held nothing like the rigours and discipline of the classroom.

St Ann's Well Road near Calcutta Street. The house by the car was Mrs Stackhouse's. The whole house was used for school lessons 1941-42. The corner shop was the one hit by a swerving Trolley bus in the 1940s. This photo was taken by Peter Garner before the road was demolished after some years of planning blight 1971

Right to left, the Misses Duffty Corner Shop (closed), Mr Hodkin Newsagent still open, and Mrs Ware's Confectioner (closed). Photo: Peter Garner 1969

I well remember the Duffty's shop at the bottom of Edwin Street opposite Bombay Street. The shop was kept by two elderly spinsters, two white-haired bonny ladies who wore their hair pinned up in buns at the back of their heads. The shop was intriguing. It was mainly a general grocer's and sweet shop. They also sold vegetables and motor car parts. These were displayed in the Edwin Street shop window and comprised speedometers, ammeters, spanners, motor car horns and various other items and tools appertaining to motor cars. The shop was also a beer-off and many a person could be seen entering with a jug and leaving with it full of ale.

A few yards down St Ann's Well Road from the Duffty's shop lived Barry Howard at his father's butcher's shop. Barry is a famous actor now. Next door to the Howard's lived Dennis McCarthy (who became the well-known Nottingham broadcaster) with his parents. For a time Dennis worked for his father in his decorating business. I would occasionally see them on St Ann's Well Road setting off or returning from a job and we'd pass the time of day.

On the opposite side to the McCarthy shop I remember one summer's evening when a trolley bus coming up St Ann's Well Road and crashing into the shop at the corner of Calcutta Street. The driver swerved to avoid a child crossing the road. Nobody was seriously hurt.

The slipper baths were situated at the bottom of Northampton Street. I regularly visited them. Whilst bathing you would be entertained by someone crooning in another cubicle! These baths were normally very busy, especially on Fridays and a waiting room was provided to wait your turn.

Opposite the slipper baths was the Kings Hall Methodist Church which was bombed on the night of May 8/9th 1941 by the German Luftwaffe. My grandparents woke me up during the air-raid and we sat in the living room and could clearly hear the bombs being dropped around us. I remember my grandfather going to have a look on St Ann's Well Road and coming back and saying the Kings Hall had been hit and was on fire. Later when the All Clear siren sounded, we all returned to bed.

I remember one encounter with the local police when I was caught riding in the front carrier of a butcher's bicycle being ridden by Alan Martin, the son of a local butcher. We were stopped at the bottom of Bilberry Street by a policeman and had to give our names. We would be about twelve at the time.

One sunny evening just after the War, I remember hearing a clattering and rumbling on St Ann's Well Road. I was amazed to see travelling showmen moving up the road with their amusements on trailers, being pulled by their steam traction engines. They were making their way to the Ransom Road Park where the St Ann's Rose Show was held that year.

At the age of ten, I went for four years for piano lessons with Mr Roxburgh who lived at the top end of Robin Hood Chase. I remember two couples who lived at Ransom Road Gardens, just below what is now Brewsters Avenue. They were Mr and Mrs Alsebrook. The other couple, Mr and Mrs Slack, lived about 200 yards below on the same side of the road. They were the only people living on that side of the road. My grandfather would visit both of these couples regularly on the way home from his allotment garden.

In the War, I remember going to film shows at the tin Church on the corner of Norland Road opposite the Sir Rowland Hill pub. The films, all in black and white, were Charlie Chaplin, Laurel and Hardy, cartoons and westerns. When I came home during the lunchtime from school, one of my jobs would be to stoke up the fire underneath the copper in the scullery. Grandma would be doing the washing and I would help with the ponching of the clothes. The most sincere friend I have ever known was in my St Ann's schooldays, Peter Mulligan. A friendship always remembered.

My other very special friend was my grandparents' dog Lady, a black and white terrier who was my constant companion. We were great pals. I remember so many times sitting on the front doorstep with Lady on my right, both of us looking down Bombay Street watching the world go by on St Ann's Well Road. A frequent sight was the red Trojan vans delivering Brooke Bond Tea. Their depot was at Hendon Rise. Lady would accompany us on visits to grandad's garden. When she died, I remember her gently laid to rest in grandad's garden, his eyes moist with tears. In this he was not alone.

Here is one of my grandfather's quotes that could equally well be applied to our life today:

If we live and care about our past,
Our past will surely care for us.
If we live to forget our past,
We will surely lose our souls
And live to fear the future.
Those who ignore the past
Are destined to relive it.

My thanks for help with this contribution to Nottingham City Archives, Freda Wilkins, Helen Blackmore, Mandy Morris and my wife Ann for typing the draft.

A few of Peter Garner's other photos of the area leading into and along St Ann's Well Road area when planning blight had taken hold and before demolition

The Lodge, Coppice Recreation Ground, Ransom Road. The Recreation Ground was formerly The Robin Hoods, Volunteer Regiment, Rifle Range 1967

Bottom of Norland Street (with advertisement hoarding). Duncombe Street and Edwin Street either side of the 'Board' School 1969

The Westminster Abbey Hotel at the junction of St Ann's Well Road and Ransom Road 1967

Corner of Bombay Street and St Ann's Well Road. Many shops already boarded up 1969

Bellevue Road (boarded up) looking toward Northampton Street 1971

The former Robin Hood silent Cinema, at the side of Robin Hood Chase on St Ann's Well Road, used as a small factory. Houses boarded up pending demolition 1971

'Twichel' to Northampton Street (a small area of newer housing) from Bellevue Road 1971

Bombay Street 6.00pm of July 18th 1969. Mrs Spencer on the doorstep and Mrs Booth on the chair

ANON

Born 1932

Written impressions sent in 2000 (name withheld on request)

Nowadays there don't seem to be youth clubs like we had as teenagers during the 1940s and early 1950s. We had regular meeting places.

- On The Wells Road at the junction of St Ann's Well Road and Ransom Road, there were a few shops, round the corner from the old Police Station. One of these was owned by Mrs Wood: Flo to her friends and a few cheeky lads. These she didn't look kindly at, perhaps thinking they were taking a liberty. It was a regular meeting place for sometimes up to twenty local, and some from farther afield, teenagers. Although, when the age of eighteen was reached, lads joined the Forces for National Service (and on their first leave a noticeable improvement was apparent in their bearing) and others started to meet in pubs.

During their teenage years, the shop was full to overflowing, with crowds outside, buying (when they had any money) one or two cigarettes and a match, 3d fruit cordial drinks - hot in winter, cold in summer but not ice cold. Sweets were still rationed. This shop, although we didn't know it at the time, kept us off the streets and created some sense of community spirit.

- Other meeting places were The Cavendish (Cavvo) and The New Empress (Empress) Cinemas, particularly on Sunday nights. A tactic often used was to pay 9d to sit in the front seats, but move back to the one shilling (1/-) seats where the main meetings were. The only bit of bother was one night when some were too rowdy, so 'Cliff' the doorman, who seemed to have bad feet, cleared out the entire back three rows. Some people came from quite a distance. Other districts had cinemas, but The Empress was a general favourite. I met a girl there. We are still in friendly contact.

- Cattle herded along St Ann's Well Road. There used to be an abattoir in Alfred Street. People stood in doorways out of the way.

- Boys' Brigade Band leading the Brigade, Boy Scouts, Cubs, Girl Guides and Brownies once a month on Sunday morning to St Ann's Church. On meeting a horse, the Band stopped playing except for a single drumbeat every other step (left foot).

- Sledging in winter down various steep local streets, among which was Donkey Hill (favourite), Ball Street, Colborn Street and various avenues in Hungerhill Gardens. The best runs were passed around by word of mouth. Many accidents happened. I remember knocking a lad through a garden gate in Hungerhill Gardens.

- The 6th Boys' Brigade Headquarters was at the bottom of Ransom Road [Canon Lewis Memorial Hall]. In the basement was a snooker/billiard room heated by a coke burning stove and manned by a small, elderly man with one leg shorter than the other. His name was Tom, he smoked a pipe and he lived in a two-storey garden house in Hungerhill Gardens. Many lads who frequented Mrs Wood's shop also came to this Hall. Some football and cricket teams of Morley Youth Club were selected there.

- Morley Youth Club, at Morley School on The Wells Road was in use five nights a week. Monday and Fridays, boys; Tuesday and Thursday, girls: Wednesdays being mixed. I'm not sure what other lads did, we played ball games. In summer we arranged cricket matches with other youth clubs, played football and/or cricket using the Air-Raid Shelter to mark a wicket on, playing with a tennis ball. In winter, we played handball in the School Hall. This game was played using a football, which could only be hit by the hand and not rise above two or three feet. This game, played in kneeling and stooping position resulted in many skinned elbows and knees. The lads played the girls at Netball and I'm pretty sure the lads lost. On Wednesdays, we also had our first dancing lessons.

- Sometimes there were differences of opinions, which resulted in fights. One was between two brothers on Coppice Rec. One had taken the other's football boots to play in one of the usual 20-or-so aside games. A side was picked to start, then whoever came along was added to a side, generally by whoever's ball was being used. If anybody had a football, they were 'somebody'. The fight between the brothers who lived on Lotus Street was very bloody.

Another bloody fight was between two girls who attended Morley School. They were slugging it out with fists on St Ann's Well Road. I saw it between Meredith Street and Bombay Street. In those days, we left school at fourteen.

- St Ann's Well Road, along with other major roads, had a full diversity of shops, doctors, dentist etc. So the road was always well-frequented on foot so one didn't go far without meeting somebody known, as most had been at school or in a youth organisation together.

- Before the Second World War, the only Cinema open for children on Saturday morning was the Majestic on Woodborough Road at Mapperley just round the corner from the top of The Wells Road. This was quite a walk, there being no buses, also no money for bus fares. Not many took the trouble to walk up. When the Cavendish Cinema on St Ann's Well Road was being built, a teacher at Board School suggested we went down on Saturday morning to see it going up. When it opened, it was a regular visit on Saturday mornings if we were lucky enough to be given the money.

- At Board School, Mr Buxton, a teacher, taught us how to swim. He had us lined up in the Hall and showed us first the arm movements and then lying down (us not him!) the leg movements, which he did with his arms! For practical swimming, he took the lads from at least two classes and walked from Board School to Victoria Baths. If we had a halfpenny, we bought a cob from a corner shop. We always seemed hungry after swimming. The cob was shared if necessary.

To get the 3d entrance fee to the swimming baths on Saturday mornings, we asked our parents if we could take the bottles back (1d on each beer or lemonade bottle). More often than not, there'd be only two so we'd have to wheedle the other penny. One lad, big for his age at thirteen, had to take his Birth Certificate and found out he was adopted.

At the Saturday morning bath, in the mixed 'Exhibition' pool, lads used to depth charge girls by jumping from the top board, hug their knees and try to land near a girl. It took some fine-tuning because some girls stood together on the side, so a jumper had to be careful not to hit the pool edge.

- When the Second World War started, all schooling was suspended, then restored by small groups of children meeting in the house of a volunteer resident who allowed them in, up to ten children for a short time just to carry on as normal as possible. The reduced number of teachers went to many different houses.

Board School had a thriving garden on land between Blue Bell Hill Road and Gordon Road, now the site of St Edward's Roman Catholic Church. This land was shared by possibly two other schools. Sometimes, selected trustworthy pupils were asked to go unaccompanied to do jobs when weather allowed or sometimes to bring produce back. The intention of the garden was to help with the War effort. I cannot remember anything being stolen. Fun was had with lads, from one or two other schools on a similar errand, by hiding in the rows of whatever was growing and throwing lumps of earth at each other, sometimes the occasional stone.

The Headmaster was Mr Ludgrove, the teachers Miss Tuck (who unfortunately had a voice whistle when shouting), Mr Buxton, Mr Whittaker, Miss Brown, Mrs Anderson and Miss Probart.

The School had a Woodwork Room not used during my time during the War. During one of the School's Christmas Concerts, one of the lads had to sing (not his choice!) Billy Boy. At the line: 'And Nancy tickles my fancy', he couldn't sing for laughing. At these concerts, each class had to perform something. Also, some adults came along and helped out. One of the teachers had a friend who was a magician. He whipped off the braces of a volunteer lad. Then, Empire Days were an annual feature.

We didn't have any organised sport at all: none at Junior School or Senior School Morley. The lads from two classes walked from Morley School up to the top of The Wells Road to the Walter Halls School, in Mapperley. Those lucky enough to have football boots changed at the side of the pitch. On the way up, sides had been picked and two games were played, together on the same pitch, coats for goals. The teacher, Mr Jackson walked round the pitch reading a newspaper. Although Mr Jackson was more interested in cricket, I can't remember any practice sessions, although we did get to play other schools in friendly matches.

- One lad was sentenced by the Court to have the birch[1]. Afterwards he said: 'I will never do wrong again'.

- Cycling straight up Donkey Hill, without toe clips, was always a challenge regularly beaten.

- Running as many errands as required by neighbours for 6d a week.

- Children and grown-ups, who used Hungerhill Gardens, would collect in buckets the droppings left by Shippo's horses, Shippo's being Shipstone's Brewery dray horses delivering barrels of beer to pubs and off-licences.

- Being at the bottom of Edwin Street, and hearing a commotion I looked out and saw a standing bloodied man and was told that he had snatched a child from under the wheels of an oncoming bus.

The bus conductors were a varied lot, some quite surly, others cracking jokes and having fun with the passengers. St Ann's Church was the 'Hatched, Matched and Despatched' stop! If you were on a trolley bus and a little late and the poles came off, it was aggravating. The conductor had to take out a long pole carried inside the bus body and replace the poles on the overhead wires. Possibly most kids tried to get off without paying at some time or another, also trying to get away with paying juvenile rates for the first weeks of work.

- A lot of children were together right through their school and teenage years. Friendships were forged and cemented and still in place.

- No doubt there were petty criminals in St Ann's. But I can't recall any individual actually suffering. The occasional gas or electric meter was broken into, mainly by the house occupant who was short of money.

Occasionally someone related how somebody got into a house through the cellar grate: this was a small steel plate hinged to the outside wall, so coal could be chucked down into the cellar from the street. In many cases, next doors and mine, the front door key was hanging on a piece of string hanging past the letter plate. Back door keys were left on a hook in the outside lavatories across the yard. The lavatories had 2" or 3" gaps top and bottom and were a bit nippy in winter. When a pipe burst, there were sheets of ice and icicles.

- St Ann's on bonfire night was quite a sight cycling home from work after six o'clock at night. Every street passed had at least one bonfire going, most had two, some had three. I never heard of any damage, but there was the occasional call out of the Fire Brigade. The morning after, every house that had been round the fires took their share of the ashes. There were

no fireworks during the War. VE and VJ nights were very good nights.

- Just about everybody had relatives living locally. I had five houses to visit with uncles and aunts. I was born in the bedroom of Clarke's cobbler's shop on St Ann's Well Road, opposite The Havelock pub, which became Halliday's the Barber's.

What did it mean to be 'posh' in the old St Ann's circa 1950-60s? Members of a group respond:

• People who could afford toilet rolls. "We were posh, we had a bathroom." People who had a hot water Ascot in their kitchen.

• "I remember saying I'd seen Morecambe and Wise while having a bath and the listener thought I was posh and had TV in the bathroom. I was watching from a tin bath in front of the fire!"

• "Jack Dunnett, one-time MP, was a multi-millionaire who owned Notts County and a string of shops which operated the Tote. He had favourite people in the shops who wheeled themselves on to the City Council. Dunnett had a Rolls-Royce but he would meet Len Maynard, his agent, at a car park and be driven in an *appropriate* car to a function. Dunnett didn't respect people. He tried to make himself common and it doesn't work.

"Whereas Councillor Olive Moss, Conservative, of Manvers Ward, with a hat, and addressing a meeting with airs and graces, was genuinely concerned for people and they respected her for it."

• "When I was an apprentice, we'd go to houses in Mapperley Park with one or two servants. It brought about a situation where we were more class conscious than the people who were the boss. We'd try and keep ourselves working-class. We were called trash and

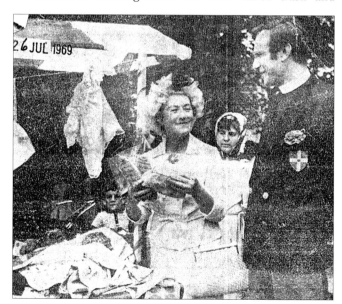

Councillor Mrs Olive Moss, after opening a Garden Party at St Catharine's Church, St Ann's Well Road, talking to the Vicar, the Rev D P Keene. Photo: source, two different people had kept this, believed to be Guardian Journal

---

[1] Birching became illegal in 1948. Internet.

they'd tip us! They were middle class people trying to be posh."

- "I once gave my aunt's address as a reference as it was a 'good' one at the time. Now that area's gone down and it's one of the worst. Times change!"

On holidays

One interviewee told me she had a passport from the early 1930s. I asked a group [1999] how unusual this was then. VERY! Skegness, Cleethorpes, Chapel St Leonards camping with clubs, and increasingly over the years with families in caravans to the same places and Mablethorpe: that was the meaning of holidays for those who went. And many didn't.

Three pre-War holiday photos found in an empty house in St Ann's prior to demolition. On the back, the place names are written. Two are at Mablethorpe and the one with a row of wooden huts in the background is at Sutton on Sea

Before the War, one week's holiday from work a year was normal. By the 1950s, it was two for some people before it became a statutory right. Many St Ann's people never went away on holiday, but spent 'time-off' with outings in Nottingham. Several people mentioned the day trip special trains to Skegness from Nottingham Victoria. The Pleasure Park on the River Trent and the Arboretum were often mentioned. For some, Hungerhill allotments were a green space to enjoy and picnics were taken, and this is a custom which is now strongly developing again.

There is a lot of interesting history around the links between places like St Ann's in Nottingham and the East Coast resorts. One interviewee told me he sold two caravans he had at Chapel St Leonards around 1965. He paid a fee for the plot and slabs around the caravans but, toward the end of his time there, the charges kept going up. There was a contract whereby you had to sell your caravan on site. Site owners began to see opportunities to make more money as caravans were modernised and began to attract more people. People who had been using sites for years at very modest cost disliked the new approach.

At one time fixed caravans were not assessed for rates [annual local tax on property which preceded Council Tax] by local Councils.

Another remembered a railway carriage at Chapel St Leonards just after the War. "We had our own bedrooms and it was all electric. Electric kettle and cooker."

In 1972: "We bought a caravan at Mablethorpe and went down every Friday night until Sunday night for thirty bob petrol".

The links between the East Coast resorts and St Ann's, and other parts of Nottingham, are still strong and some people have now inherited bungalows or purchased one: some retire to these permanently. Others prefer to live in the City except for seaside breaks.

Several interviewees remarked that holidays abroad started in the 1960s. Ray Gosling said: "In 1964, three of us went to Spain for £15 each. It was dreadful. Nobody told us Spain was warm. We went dressed up as you did in this country!" By the 1960s, a few St Annies were travelling to Australia and Russia, as well as nearer destinations, for holidays. But, as the card below shows, travelling did not start with the 'package' holiday.

This is one of several postcards, from a woman friend to a woman in Conway Street, St Ann's. This card was sent from the Grand Hotel, Moscow, in 1936. The picture is of blocks of 'worker-houses'. The cards were found in an empty house in St Ann's at the time of demolition and handed to me in 2000

Allotments

HUNGERHILL GARDENS
and other allotments

Allotment gardens are mentioned by many people I interviewed and spoke with. I wish there were more current photos of people working their plots but, when people are enjoying their plot, it would seem an intrusion to appear with a camera! If anyone has photos they would like to go 'on the record', please send them to me.

Allotments on the north/northwest edge of St Ann's are the largest complex of detached allotments in England. Thanks to sustained campaigning, in 2000 these allotments, known as Hungerhill, Stonepit Coppice and Gorseyclose Gardens were put on the Register of Parks and Gardens of Special Historic Interest in England by English Heritage[1]. This is similar to a Grade II listing of an historic building. In 2001, the listing was upgraded to Grade II*. The whole allotment area is often described as 'the Hungerhills'.

Hungerhill Gardens from Thirlmere Close, Thorneywood Mount. The rows of houses in the foreground are on Ransom Road, Chandos Street and Hungerhill Road. They escaped demolition. The block in the far centre is Alexandra Court which, when I first lived in the area in the mid-1960's, was a block of rented apartments for professional people. The apartments did not have their own kitchens and gradually became less attractive as people's requirements changed. Also see Alexandra Court in Index. Photo 1978: Nottingham Local Studies Library

View of Stonepit Coppice Gardens and Hungerhill Gardens from Alexandra Park. A field on the left of these allotments was excavated for the building of Caunton Avenue flats (see Index), which were demolished after a sustained campaign by tenants. Photo 1974: Nottingham Local Studies Library

The area of allotments was once in one block. After Sycamore recreation ground was formed from some of the allotments in the early Twentieth Century, Gorseyclose Gardens was separated from the block.

The role these allotment gardens have played in the lives of St Ann's people has changed over time. The Hungerhills have always been within the boundary of the City. From 1605, they were divided into thirty parts, each part to be leased to one Freeman, until the 1830s when, on the petition of the Nottingham Independent Cottage Garden Society, they were made into allotment gardens.

As well as to its traditional users, the allotment gardens became increasingly important as productive and easily accessible green space to working-class families who moved into St Ann's as it developed in the latter half of the 19th Century. Older people who lived in St Ann's prior to the period of demolition in the early 1970s often speak of this. Men came home after a heavy day's work and, after a meal, walked up to their allotment; even when it was icy and snowing in order to stoke their greenhouse boiler. All the family made visits on summer weekends. Surplus produce was often sold in local shops.

---

1 There are only three other allotment sites on the register: in Birmingham, Warwick and Coventry.

Hungerhill Gardens 1978. Abbotsford Drive with 'new' houses in the centre. Photo: Nottingham Local Studies Library

Mr D Sharpe in his allotment. Note the sheds made out of bits of old houses. Photo: Nottingham Local Studies Library

But, by the mid-1960s decline in the allotments had taken hold and escalated during the years of redevelopment of St Ann's and long after. But, there are gardeners now who have been tending their plots over many decades.

By the mid-1990s, a growing number of people were campaigning for improvement to the allotment site which had become insecure and vandalised. Funds have been made available for essential perimeter fencing, clearing and other work on the large site. Allotments are being renovated, and taken up not only by individual gardeners or families who love their green plot 'in the country' but by a variety of local groups who value working together outdoors and developing knowledge of gardening and food production.

Some of the Hungerhills has been lost to housing, but the large existing site is a triumph. It will be harder in future to claim any of this site for housing because of its Grade II* status. And dedicated people in STAA not only work practically on site, but they read the small print on past and present documents very carefully.

Tony Hallam, Nottingham City Council's Horticultural Officer told me [2001] that 96 out of 179 allotments at Stonepit Coppice were let, 330 out of 449 at Hungerhills and 29 out of 31 at Gorseyclose Gardens.

Mr Harry Beadles in his garden 1976. Source Nottingham Arrow, Nottingham Local Studies Library

Coppice Gardens allotments 1986. Photo: Nottingham Local Studies Library

Office and stores of the Hungerhill Garden Holders Association, looking NE from the main drive, May 1978. Photo: Reg Baker, Nottingham Local Studies Library

John at work on Hungerhill allotments, spring 1999

Terry Brady, third generation in his family to garden on the Hungerhill allotments. Photo: Nottingham Evening Post April 1996

. . . and pulling leeks winter 1999

Allotments from near the entrance of Gentleman's Avenue to Hungerhill Gardens, also showing the improved housing. Photos: Ruth I Johns 2001

"Not my door: someone else's" says Anne Sharp. "Many of these have now been replaced." Photos: Anne Sharp

St Ann's Rose Show

This was an historic society. In 1860, it was the only one of its kind in England. The General Cathcart Hotel on the Hungerhill Road was the scene of its first activities and the exhibition was staged as the St Ann's Rose, Floral and Horticultural Society's Show.

The judges at the first Show included Dean Hole, a clergyman and national rose expert, who was unbelieving that roses could bloom for show in April until he realised they grew in the 'tiny glass-houses' on the Hungerhill Garden Allotments. As he returned home with a glorious bouquet of roses with the rose growers' 'best respects to the Missus' he remarked: 'I felt ashamed to think how little I had done, and how much more such men [as the allotment holders] would do, with my larger leisure and more abundant means.'

In the 1960 St Ann's Rose Show brochure, it states that the early Shows soon moved to a large field on St Ann's Well Road, facing Dickinson Street. In 1864, the Show became the St Ann's and All England Rose Show. In 1895, it was held in a field known as Donkey Hill facing the Westminster Abbey Hotel. 1896 saw the Show being held at the City Centre Market Place. The next year in the Market Place, it was a disaster due to a violent storm, and the weather was bad when it was held in St Ann's the following year at the Coppice Recreation Ground. And then the St Ann's Rose Show lapsed until 1925.

However, the roses growers of Hungerhill Gardens continued, as the St Ann's Floral Society, to exhibit elsewhere, including at the Royal Horticultural Society Exhibitions. After 1925, the Nottingham Garden Holders' Association reorganised the Show and it was held at the Coppice Road Recreation Ground.

Some interviewees refer to Flower Shows as well as Rose Shows.

Rose Hawley's father **Horace Smedley** and her brother **Albert Smedley** shared an allotment where the Elliott Durham School [Ransom Drive] was built in 1966. Albert Smedley says they used to pay their rent to The Asylum. They grew flowers and vegetables. They also had a second allotment where Botany Avenue is now between Abbey Grove and Hendon Rise. Rose and Vernon Hawley also had 'the first allotment in' on this site. Their allotment included a spring. When it rained, a lot of water ran down the path to the gate. The rent for these allotments was paid to the City Council.

On Horace and Albert Smedley's allotment at this site, they kept pigeons. Vernon Hawley says about five allotment holders on 'their avenue' kept pigeons. Albert Smedley cannot remember their full names but they included Stan 'who had a fair turn of language', Johnson and old man Robinson. They raced their pigeons in the Midland Federation and met at a pub on Glasshouse Street where the former footbridge over the Victoria Station used to be. Later they met at the Peacock on Mansfield Road.

A man called Bains kept pigeons on the next avenue. He trained all his birds for the RAF. They were trained to fly at night which is not normal for pigeons. Vernon Hawley says that bombers going over Germany in the Second World War sometimes carried them.

One morning [2001] in Hungerhill Gardens: a grandfather, who said he originally came from Jamaica, and his son were walking from their homes up to their allotment. The older man said that, on good days, he spent most of his time gardening on his allotment. "There's no place on earth like it."

ALAN SCHOFIELD

Born 1959

Voluntary Secretary of STAA. *Alan Schofield was interviewed at the Chase Neighbourhood Centre, St Ann's 29.11.01. STAA is a group dedicated to looking after the historic Hungerhill Gardens and promoting them*

Originally, STAA started as the St Ann's Allotments Campaign in 1993. It became STAA in 1998. STAA is its name, it is not an abbreviation of anything.

It was a new experience for me when I got my allotment at the Hungerhill Gardens, St Ann's, in 1990. I had never had an allotment before. Looking around the site, it was clear that it was in a state of decline and that it was likely to be lost. There were threats and rumours about large sections of the allotments being sold off for housing and development. There was a proposal within part of the City Council to sell off Stonepit Coppice Gardens en bloc. I don't know whether they would have developed the land themselves or sold it off.

At that time, I had contacts with the Nottingham Garden Holders' Association which had been on the site since the 1880s. They were selling peat, fertilizer, seeds and things on the Hungerhills site, and they still do, but they did not seem to be strongly involved with the campaigning issues.

The campaigning group, formed in 1993, was a very small informal pressure group. We drew up a plan for how we thought the gardens could be. We called it a Vision for the Future and it gained a fair amount of positive support from allotment gardeners and from the City Council. But the big question was: would the City Council think it worth paying for? We kept badgering away. In 1994, we did a survey of gardeners which got a big response and confirmed our views that most of them were not happy with how things were.

We prioritised by trying to get security fence around the site. In 1995, Nottingham City Challenge and Nottingham City Council paid for a new fence around the perimeter. It was important in the security sense, to stop vandalism, but it had a big effect on morale. It was a way of saying: 'This site is one whole area, we are not going to have it parcelled off and we are confident that it can stay and flourish.'

ST ANN'S NOTTINGHAM: inner city voices *by Ruth I Johns* • ISBN 0951696092

After that, in 1997, we managed to raise funds for a part-time worker with the St Ann's Allotments Project as it was then called. The worker was Julie Scott and she started to do a lot of work around take-up of gardens. She showed people around, introducing new gardeners to the site. It was frustrating, because we raised the profile of the site but didn't have a budget to do some necessary things. But as the profile was raised, we made connections with other groups and a lot more individual gardeners and we obtained grants.

STAA Ltd is now a company limited by guarantee. The membership is entirely of allotment gardeners on the site. If anyone gives up their garden, they are no longer a member of STAA. STAA is still fairly small with a membership of about fifty. The number of gardens on the Hungerhills at the moment is 670. There are over three hundred gardeners. We don't claim to be an association of all the gardeners. We are a group interested in promoting the gardens and looking after them. Obviously, we are in touch with most of the gardeners through Newsletters and informally and we try to represent their views. Recently, there has been more work around clearance on the site and security gates.

Yes, that ties in with the work that NECTA [Nottingham Environmental Construction Training for All Ltd] are doing and also with the St Ann's Allotments Consortium. We are part of the Consortium which includes STAA, the Renewal Trust, TANC [Technical Aid to Nottinghamshire Communities], Ecoworks, Groundwork Greater Nottingham, the City Council Allotment Service, and the Social Economy Development Officer of the City Council, Lynne Taylor.

The Renewal Trust is now working as a lead body in terms of the Consortium, and the Consortium is planning a big bid to the Heritage Lottery Fund. We hope that will assist major infrastructure work on the site for the first time in some one hundred years.

We need to preserve the Hungerhill Gardens historic site. The Hungerhills are unique. It is the oldest and largest site in the world. The gardens were first laid out in the 1830s. But we also have to make the gardens relevant for the 21st Century. The whole site is now on the Local Plan as Open Space and listed by English Heritage and recently it upgraded the listing to Grade II* which puts the Hungerhills in the top 40% of listed gardens which is very significant. The Listing covers the whole of the Hungerhill Gardens including Stonepit Coppice and Gorsey Close Gardens.

The Listing is very important because, although it doesn't change the legal status of the site, it does mean that any planning application has to be referred to English Heritage and normally it would not grant permission for something that was detrimental to the historic gardens. In theory, without the protection of this listing, though the gardens have been there since the 1830s, allotment holders could be turned off them with a year's notice for no stated reason.

The site is technically owned by the Bridge Trust and Chambers Estate. The City Council rents the site even though the site is managed by the City Council. So, as the site is not owned by the City Council, under allotment law it is known as a Temporary Allotment Site. We lost five plots two years ago on Ransom Road. They were part of the bigger complex years ago. They were sold and we contested this with the Council. The Council argued that the money from the sale would be used on improvement on other allotment sites.

They sold the site to Metropolitan Housing Trust and it still has a metal fence around it and nothing has happened. We hope that was the last time plots were lost. We missed the fact that those plots were not in the Local Plan Open Space Network and it was before the Listing Grade II* status. We have done a lot of work reading the small print to make sure other allotments cannot be lost.

It is amazing that I can look at a 1830s map and still see my allotment with the same pattern of hedgerows as there was then, and we don't want to change the pattern of hedgerows. We want to look after the old fruit trees and some of the existing buildings. There needs to be a lot of repair to infrastructure, retaining walls, roadways, and maybe - thinking of the 21st Century - we should be thinking of toilets. Should there be sewerage? Should there be lights? Do we need to have parking places?

Originally, the gardens were set up for upper and middle class people from the City Centre to come out to a Leisure Garden. That use changed over time but there is still a tradition with people, who don't have gardens, coming from other parts of the City and who treat coming as a trip to the country. Which means they may be gardening in a way that some of the people you have spoken to who were gardening to grow produce in the mid-20th Century might not recognise. There are people now who are literally leaving their plot wild and just cutting a patch of grass. It is a safe place for their kids but they don't see themselves as vegetable or flower growers.

The Annual Rent now is 9p a square yard a year. So the very big plots may cost £60 a year and a small one £20. The average is around £40-50, which is about a £1 a week for a place in the country which is not bad.

Members of STAA are about 50% from St Ann's. The others come from places like Sherwood and Forest Fields where there are no allotments and some from Stapleford and the Meadows. Members include people who have been gardening on the site for twenty or thirty years and newcomers. We find there is a close link between occupied plots and vehicle access. When people have manure or a shed to load, they want to use their car even if they don't usually.

In September this year, ten plots were taken up for a community orchard and we are hoping to clear them this winter and plant one hundred fruit trees. There are also some existing fruit trees. Depending on interest, it is a project that could be extended. We wanted to get plots which were in danger of being overgrown because an orchard is a good way of maintaining plots easily. And if, in the long-term, they revert back to conventional gardening, nothing is lost.

We hope it will be a way of introducing access to the gardens to new people and to people who wouldn't want a

One of the side lanes leading to individual plots, off Gentleman's Avenue, Hungerhill Gardens. Photo: Ruth I Johns 2001

A garden near the centre of Hungerhill Gardens. Photo: Ruth I Johns 2001

I was in Broad Oak Close one day in 2000 and saw a hole in the fence from which I could take a photo of the Hungerhill Gardens from that aspect. As I was looking through the fence, two boys - aged around ten - approached me on bikes. They asked whether I had lost a dog through the fence and I said I hadn't. I said I was about to take a photo of the allotments and was asked why. I said because they had been there a long time. Quick as lightning, one boy said: "We've been here a long time, will you take a photo of us?!" The photos reveal two views, one into the allotment mass and the other shows St Bartholomew's Road rising to the top of the hill on the right of the photo. Photos: Ruth I Johns 2000

Allotments abutting Ransom Road on the left going down and showing a garden holder's 'house.' Photo: Wilkinson, Davis and Strickland 1967

Houses now occupying that situation on Ransom Road. These make a pleasant change of design in the area. Photo: Ruth I Johns 2000

Another aspect across the Hungerhill Gardens, from the edge of the Metropolitan Housing Association estate on Brewsters Road - once also allotments. Alexandra Court in the middle distance. Photo: Ellie White 2000

Horticultural Hall on Hendon Rise is mentioned by several people. It has been a Social Club in recent years. Photos: Ellie White 2000

This was a wonderful 'find' in Wilkinson, Davis and Strickland's photos taken in 1967. I asked Peter Garner who asked a number of people to help locate it. It was The Lodge, marked with a circle on the map, between the path to Sycamore Recreation Ground [Sycamore Rec to locals] and one path to Hungerhill Gardens. The occupier was Mr George Hebb. The Lodge was demolished. The detail of this building, including the weather vane, is beautiful

plot of their own. The idea is for people to come along and help with cutting the grass and hedges and sharing the fruit. Local people will get the fruit anyway. Obviously, the value of the fruit won't show for ten years or so, but if you don't plant the trees, nothing happens. The orchard has already had a couple of school parties visit.

There is one couple, the Westbys, who have a plot. They have grandchildren at a local school and the children visit their plot from school.

Other projects who have allotments include Ecoworks and the Nottingham Women's Training Scheme [NWTS]. NWTS has been around for twenty or so years and have had an allotment for about eighteen months. There is an organisation called SPAN which has a plot used by the Mental Health Service. The Porchester Day Unit have done very well over the past two years and the Chase Action Group have a plot, as has a group called Back to Roots which is two Asian organisations with a plot.

These projects either need a very good group of volunteers or they need somebody who is a worker on a regular basis to keep things going. People don't always have the skills at first to manage everything needed in running a plot. As we know from individual gardeners, it's a lot to take on. It would be good to be running some training courses, or informal support, so - in the early stages of gardening - people could get help with what to plant, when to plant and what to expect when things grow.

STAA would like to set up a Community Composting Scheme. We would like to do more distributing produce to local people and them bringing back the green waste for composting. We have ideas for a couple of plots as museum pieces. One could be restored to the Victorian tradition and maybe another to the Dig for Victory Second World War style. We will continue to be interested around issues of oral history and want to do more projects around food and cooking and culture.

We ran a project with Colin Haynes[1] last year where we worked with Caribbean elders and local primary schools which came to the Chase Neighbourhood Centre, cooked food, sang songs, did artwork and it was a really good mixture of young and old. The culture of allotments is very broad and very deep rooted locally. Other organisations are beginning to feel it.

It would be great to have some sort of building or centre on the site or near the site that could be a clubhouse with bar and cups of tea, with exhibition space for traditional shows and somewhere where there could be a tool store and where people could get together. But, maybe the fact that this hasn't happened before . . . St Ann's is different, I don't know why. But I think the idea has a lot of value.

I think the thing we still haven't shifted much is the City Council's sense that the allotment service is something they should invest money in. The Council is happy for us to go out fund raising, but they are not shifting in terms of committing real capital money. They don't seem to see the

mixture of education, economic, social and community benefits of allotments. Allotment gardeners don't have gardens for these reasons but that is what comes out. But we are still struggling to get the Council to see that. They want to prioritise education or other issues in the inner-city but maybe don't think as broadly as we would like.

I find the contrast between allotments and built-up areas remarkable. And the way the Hungerhill Gardens exist in St Ann's which has such a negative reputation. It is an asset for St Ann's we need to be shouting about and proud of. I hope STAA has contributed to making this happen.

I moved to Nottingham in 1981. I got an allotment because I had a small flat without access to a garden. Without a car, it took me forty minutes to walk to the Hungerhills. Often it was a struggle because I didn't want to go up there, but I came back feeling better every time. Once I realised that, it became a pretty important part of my life. For a long time when I was unemployed, I would be there two or three days a week on a regular basis. These days, I am self-employed. I do a mixture of gardening, building type work and community arts work. My work for STAA has all been voluntary except for a spell last year when Julie Scott took a break.

At the moment, there is funding for Colin Haynes, Nick Lipton and Val Moore, all part-time but that all comes to an end in March 2002. It is very uneasy and difficult for the workers to be continually on short-term contracts.

It is a constant struggle. At the moment we have received some money from the Chase Action Group Social Economy Development Fund which will go toward the STAA co-ordinator in March. We will ask the City Council's Allotment Service to fund some of our work on site but I guess it will only cover a day a week in the next financial year.

We will be applying to the Lottery for a two year project, Growing Together, from the middle of 2002. This project would help to get people on site and, as I mentioned earlier, to offer support and training linked in to issues around art and history and food. But, the funding applications take time.

What would be my message for fifty years' time? Don't look back! I think you have to look at the past and see what happened. We can learn from that. It is interesting. But we have to live now and whatever we are doing has to make sense now. STAA found it frustrating that there are no allotment records from the 19th Century in the City. They were thrown away. It is incredibly frustrating. But there comes a point when those facts won't help the gates that are broken and the tap that doesn't work. We need to get on with those. And we need to embrace new people, new cultures, new approaches.

If we say the allotments used to be like this and we have to keep them like that, then we are excluding everybody who has come in. Although, as I said earlier the first allotment holders on the Hungerhills were settled shopkeepers and professionals from the City Centre, since then it has always had immigrant communities. When the factories were set up, people moved here from farmland

---

[1]   Colin Haynes wrote an article on Nottingham's Hanging Gardens [the Hungerhills] in Nottingham Civic News, November 1971.

Nottingham inner city voices by Ruth I Johns • ISBN 0951696092

areas. And there have been different groups since, including Eastern European and Caribbean, and we have continually to look forward.

But the framework of the 1830s allotment site at the Hungerhills should not be lost. That framework is the important bit to hang on to.

ADRIAN HORSLEY

Born 1948

*Interviewed at **Ecoworks** Garden Hut, its 'Show Home', on the Hungerhill Allotments, St Ann's 1.2.01. Photos from Ecoworks*

Adrian Horsley (left), Terry and John on Valley View plot c1998

Ecoworks was started around 1991 by a coalition of people. Some from MIND were interested in mental health voluntary sector initiatives, some were interested in environmental issues and especially interested in setting up an alternative technology type project. These people came together and Ecoworks was born.

It is a non-profit making company limited by guarantee. In the early days, there were discussions about all sorts of things including the regeneration of the Gedling Colliery site but it was finally decided that it was best to start fairly small and this garden project began. I was employed part-time on a consultancy basis to start the project, coming up here just two days a week. It's grown over the years. There's now a full-time post which Paul Payne and I job share.

Paul was a volunteer for quite a long time before he became an employee. We started off with one allotment and now we have eight. It's sometimes called the Garden Project and sometimes the Permaculture Project. Things are done in an environmentally friendly way and gardening is a wonderful recreational, therapeutic and learning activity. Our first funding came from Nottingham Health Authority

to enable the project to work with mental health service users. That funding lasted for two years and then we had funding from Opportunities for Volunteering, which is Central Government Department of Health funding.

At that point, it became a full-time project and we were able to take people from all different sections of the community and it wasn't limited to mental health issues. And that was always part of our aim, the integration and de-stigmatisation of mental health.

There are many routes through which people find us, including statutory departments, doctors . . . we also put on courses which we publicise quite widely and we have a regular newsletter each quarter and the *Evening Post* run little articles on us sometimes. Ecoworks is the contact point for the Nottingham Permaculture Association so anybody interested gets in touch here.

At the moment (mid-winter) we come up twice a week, Tuesdays and Thursdays. And we have around five or six regular volunteers coming up, maybe more on a Tuesday because there's a craft project going as well. Numbers change over time. If people last for over about one month, they tend to keep coming. Trevor [who was stoking the stove] has been coming for three or four years. One volunteer has been coming for six. The stove came from Nottingham Castle. It was found in an old room and we happened to hear of it when we needed one. [It was a bitterly cold day and the garden hut needed that stove!]

Although the Hungerhill Gardens are in St Ann's and we have strong links with the Chase Community Centre, people come here from any part of the City. We used to have our offices in the Sycamore Sports Centre, St Ann's, before they started doing it up. There was a verbal understanding that we would be able to move back but the rent doubled [it is now the Sycamore Millennium Centre]. At present our office is in the International Community Centre on Mansfield Road. I think we'll stay there for the foreseeable future.

A lot of activities take place up here. The main emphasis is that it is a recreational project. So it's not necessarily about doing lots of work and growing masses of food to sell or to feed a huge number of people. People come up here to enjoy themselves and for some that may mean sitting around and having a chat and a cup of tea.

It's a magical place. People really enjoy gardening and growing things and learning about gardening. So we have informal teaching. If people want to learn, then Paul and myself pass on knowledge of gardening and Permaculture.

I'm also a Director of STAA and Paul's on its Management Committee. They sometimes participate in some of our festivals and have stalls up here. And Ecoworks as an organisation is part of a loose knit Hungerhill Cornsortium interested in the regeneration of the gardens.

Soon we're hoping to have more of a public face with an Information Centre somewhere in St Ann's, maybe at the Chase Community Centre, so we see our future as being more closely linked to the St Ann's area.

I lived in America for a number of years and returned in 1992. I developed a strong interest in gardening and did a Permaculture course. When I came back, I became involved in Ecoworks and it's been my life for the past eight years. I see lots of possibilities for the future here and the growth of activities. At present we are building a straw bale structure.

The walls are being constructed of straw bales and the structure will become an important activity centre where we're able to run more courses and do more events. This is such an unusual place. I mean we're only a couple of miles from the City Centre, and yet as you look around you, you could be in the middle of Alaska. It is a real oasis in the urban landscape. This site often produces the effect on people that they come up here and discard their worries and return to a different way of thinking. We want to keep that kind of atmosphere.

I see allotments as very important because, these days, people can feel so limited in the sense of power they have over their own lives. If you live in a rented Council house, you can't make modifications, but when you have an

Activities at Ecoworks.

Mosaic making, rear of 'Showhome' c1997

Weekend plot c1997

City Centre in distance. View from Thorntop plot 1999. 'Totem pole' on right

Sue, Nathan and Roxy c1998

The hole on Thorntop with Brian, Leslie, Jon M, Trevor, Nathan and Little Jon

Marianne Atkinson (third from right) celebrates her 1999 birthday at Ecoworks

St Ann's International Inner City Voices By Ruth Johns • ISBN 0951696092

ft: In glass-house by 'Showhome'. Top middle: Willow plot 1999. Middle bottom: Nathan c1998. Right: Christmas Party 1998

allotment you can decide: 'Well, I'm going to plant cabbages now, I'm going to put a little hut here and I'll plant a tree there. And there's this tremendous feeling of power and I think that's so important.'

There are individual allotment holders around us. There are two volunteers who come up on a fairly regular basis and have started up small plots of their own.

On Tuesday there was a pole lathing course here, turning wood on a lathe operated by a bendy pole. Recently we had people come in to run special weekend projects, art activities, small build and alternative technology activities. Our usual volunteers come and events are open to anybody. The more diversity the better. At present, regulars include someone who lectures in computers and people who are long-term mental health service users and people with learning difficulties. It's a wide cross section.

Inside the house, February 2001

A Victorian gardener's house which Ecoworks will renovate

Straw bale structure beginning, February 2001.
Photos: Ruth I Johns

I suppose we're following the tradition that gardeners since the 1830s have had here. You take care of the land. I hope in fifty years time, there will still be allotments here. We won't personally see the benefit of some of the things that we're doing now for the future. I think this site is absolutely brilliant but I'd also like to see smaller sites dotted throughout the area, because if people can just walk fifty yards to a little plot of land where they can grow stuff, it's much more useful than having to get on a bus or walking half an hour to get up here.

One idea that Alan Schofield, of STAA, has is a community orchard using some of the derelict allotments. Many still have good fruit trees on. We could gradually start clearing those allotments, leaving the fruit trees for the community orchard and involving local groups or schools to keep the grass mown and to harvest the fruit. It could be a wonderful area for people to have picnics. And,

at some future time if needed, the area could always revert to individual allotments.

March 29th 2002. Adrian Horsley writes: Today is the last day for Ecoworks employees of the garden and crafts project. We have been unable to secure further funding despite bids to numerous funding bodies. There is so much competition for a limited amount of funds in the voluntary sector. For some Ecoworks volunteers the closure of the project could be quite serious as it has become an integral part of their lives for a long time. It is ironic that now there is more energy and enthusiastic volunteers than ever before. The project workers have committed themselves to carry on voluntarily for the next two months at least, and will continue trying to secure funding. I think that one way or another there will continue to be a gardening project here

ST ANN'S NOTTINGHAM: inner-city voices *by Ruth I Johns* • ISBN 0951696092

Things we did then: many we still do

Whilst preparing this book, I have been struck on the one hand by the huge differences between life in the 'old' and the 'new' St Ann's and the changes over time, some of which would have happened - albeit much more gently - even without the massive redevelopment. And, on the other hand, there is substantial evidence (which has been too little recognised) that the population in the 'new' St Ann's has, over three decades, nurtured many of the things needed to create a community. It has been a struggle because there was very little legacy of buildings or landmarks (either physical or social) left when 340 acres and 30,000 people were cleared in the late 1960s and early 1970s.

This section includes activities 'we did then' which do not appear elsewhere in the book. They are mentioned often in individual recollections. Many of these activities have been rebuilt in the 'new' St Ann's, like St Ann's Library. There is a later section which includes organisations which started in the 'new' St Ann's.

Employment, of course, is part of a continuum, albeit seeing huge changes over the years both in extent and content.

STREET GAMES

These are mentioned many times in individual recollections. Here are two accounts. One is by Grenville Gibson who lived on a newer part of St Ann's, Serlby Rise. The other is by John Wheeldon, who lived in the middle of the 'old' St Ann's. Street games are seldom possible now, mainly because of traffic. What has taken their place?

GRENVILLE GIBSON

Born 1934

Sent-in contribution about boys' street cricket c1947

It was a fine day so, after breakfast, I went to see what my pals wanted to do. They weren't really bothered so we decided to play cricket. There were no white flannels, no pads, no stumps or balls: just a cricket bat that had seen better days and a well-worn tennis ball. We only had one wicket, which was as well as we only had one bat! The wicket was the lampost at the corner of Serlby Rise and Tuxford Walk. Each of us batted for himself, there was no team. The others took turns to bowl and field. The batsman who made the most runs was the winner. We kept our own score. Bowling was not easy.

Most of us hadn't mastered the art of over-arm bowling and we didn't have the benefit of TV. So we bowled from the pavement on Tuxford Walk, mostly under-arm, over the road and up the slope, trying to hit the wicket, which was the bottom section of the lampost. Batting was not much easier. To the left of the wicket and only a few yards away was the shrubbery; a hedge encircled collection of bushes, many of them of the holly variety. A similar obstacle stood in the way if you were tempted to hit the ball over the bowler's head, another shrubbery. The penalty was severe. Not only was it: '6 runs and out.' But it was your job to climb the hedge and find the ball lost in a dense tangle of overgrown bushes. 'Have you found it yet?' was the oft-heard cry: 'I'm going home if you don't hurry up.'

The shrubberies weren't the only problem. The best place to aim was down Serlby Rise. If you hit it hard enough, the ball would speed off down the hill towards Gordon Road. There were no boundaries, you kept on running, making as many runs as you could before the ball was returned. If your sense of direction was wrong, the ball could end up in one of the dense privet hedges, which surrounded the front gardens. At least the fielders had to help to look for it. If you hit the ball over the hedge into the front garden it was the batsman who had to knock on the front door to ask permission to look for it. We soon got to know how our knock would be received!

The match was not without its interruptions. Vehicles and bicycles wishing to pass caused a problem. 'Delivery van stopped play' has never been a problem at Trent Bridge!

Ladies deep in conversation on their way to the shops on Carlton Road seemed totally unaware of the bowler waiting to deliver the ball as they walked across the pitch. Still, we had plenty of time, that is until play ended for the session with the call: 'Grenville, dinner is ready!'

I hear they are now experimenting with floodlit cricket. They are fifty years behind the times. Our afternoon matches went on until it was time for bed, another advantage of using a lampost as our wicket.

JOHN WHEELDON

Born 1951

Formerly of 22, Cathcart Street, St Ann's 'and proud to say so' sent this poem in. His family moved out of St Ann's due to demolition in 1968, but: "we never settled after we moved."

A GAME OF FOOTBALL

Dedicated to all the budding Bobby Charltons of Cathcart Street, St Ann's, and the shoe shops

Four coats, ten lads, a patch of land,
Imagination and a ball in hand.
Concrete, cobbles, grass or clay,
It didn't matter: our Match of the Day.

Twenty eyes would stand and stare
As the ball was thrown high in the air.
The game had started, all was well
When it would finish, no one could tell.

Players bounced off fences and walls
To try and get to kick the ball.
Tackles flying, high and low,
No quarter given that you know.

Friendships gone, left behind,
Once nice lads, no longer kind.
'Pass it here' you'd hear one cry.
A crunching tackle, then down he'd lie.

The ball flies over someone's gate.
The match is stopped, we'd stand and wait.
'Watch my windows,' we'd hear him shout.
He throws the ball, we clap and shout:
'Thanks Mister.'

Grazes and cuts on legs and shins
Caused by kicks, and walls and bins.
School shoes are ruined, what will mam say?
But nothing could stop our Match of the Day.

The light is fading, it's nearly gone.
The lads leave limping one by one.
The Match is drawn, no one will win.
But, come tomorrow, we will start again.

A HISTORY OF THE BOYS' BRIGADE IN ST ANN'S DISTRICT

by **Keith W Vinerd** [1999]

Born 1938

Photos: Boys' Brigade Archive, Northampton Street, St Ann's, unless otherwise stated

Keith W Vinerd, a Boys' Brigade Training Officer, with special responsibility for the Duke of Edinburgh's Awards within the Nottingham Battalion which [2002] holds 154 Gold Awards and 1020 Duke of Edinburgh's Awards at all three levels. Keith Vinerd's brother, Brian Frederick Vinerd was elected in 1967 as a councillor to represent St Ann's Ward on the City Council. He died in 1981

Five years after its founding in Glasgow[1] the Boys' Brigade came to Nottingham and the 1st Nottingham Company was started at St Andrew's Church, on the edge of St Ann's, in October 1888 through the efforts of John A Dixon JP. The first Captain was Dr W Windley and subsequent Captains were W Newham, H H Bradfield, Rev A H Hatfield, W R Bryan, W Paling, A L Nichols, R T O Hawthorne, David Harvey, D H Richardson, G W R Harvey, D K Mills, M Cahill, J Caunt and D Odam.

Around 1950, the 1st Company welcomed to their ranks boys from the Gordon Boys' Home on Cranmer Street, St Ann's.

The 1st Company celebrated its centenary in 1988, when the Boys' Brigade President, the Rt Hon Viscount Thurso, attended a Thanksgiving Service in St Andrew's Church. The Centenary booklet recorded a donation of a full set of brass band instruments by John D Player of John Player and Sons after the First World War. Two years later, he gave them a cinematograph, which was operated for many years on a 'penny rush' on Thursday evenings giving 300 local children the chance to enjoy the adventures of Charlie Chan, Fu Man Chu and other idols of the silent screen.

Until recently, the Company continued to meet in their premises on Alfred Street North but sadly the Company closed in 1998.

---

[1] The Boys' Brigade was founded by Sir William Alexander Smith on October 4th 1883 at the North Woodside Mission in Glasgow. After the first year, a uniform of pillbox, belt and haversack was introduced at a cost of one shilling and six pence. By the third year, membership numbered 2,000 boys and had spread from Scotland to Cornwall and eventually to the Channel Islands, Ireland, America, Africa, Canada, Australia and New Zealand. The BB was the first organisation for boys and the first to take boys camping.

St Ann's Nottingham: inner-city voices by Ruth I Johns • ISBN 0951696092

Two companies were formed in the heart of St Ann's, the 6th Nottingham Company and the 20th Nottingham Company. The 6th was formed on May 8th 1891 and based at St Ann's Church [later St Ann with Emmanuel Church after the district's redevelopment] and it met in the Canon Lewis Memorial Hall on Ransom Road. The first Captain was A Scrimegour and later Leslie Palmer and E H Ley. The last Captain of this Company was Mr D Chambers. The 6th Company closed in 1998.

The 20th Company was formed originally on September 11th 1919 at the Wesley Chapel on Broad Street in the City Centre. It moved in 1932 into the newly built East Nottingham Boys' Club on Northampton Street, St Ann's. The financing of this Company Headquarters, known as the Boys' Club, was entirely due to the efforts of the founding

The Boys' Brigade premises on Northampton Street viewed from Westgate Street: the building just past the washing hanging out. Photo: Ellie White 2000

Captain, Ralph Carr, a veteran of the First World War where he saw service in the RFC. The premises cost £3,000 donated by local businessmen.

Despite the redevelopment of the entire neighbourhood [late 1960s and early 1970s] around the Club, it is pleasing to note that it kept going with a few members. Currently, it only has a Junior Section and credit is due to Mrs Gwen Hirst who is Officer-in-Charge. The Company[2] is currently attached to the Nottingham Central Methodist Mission formerly Parliament Street Methodist Church. A lifelong member of the 20th Company was John Rowland Jacques who was the first boy to be enrolled. On October 10th 1935, John and Nora Jacques were married and held their reception on the Club premises on Northampton Street.

John Jacques eventually became Nottingham Battalion Life President but sadly died at the age of ninety-one in 1997. The first Chaplain of the 20th Company was Rev Strongman and the first Company Bandmaster was Mr R B Mills.

The Duke of Edinburgh's Award started in 1956 and the first Gold Awards to be gained in the County of Nottinghamshire were gained by three members of the 20th Company, Barry Booth, David Newton and Peter Hill who passed through the Bronze and Silver Standards before reaching the Gold Award in 1959. Over the ensuing years, the Company has gained 34 Bronze, 27 Silver and 10 Gold Duke of Edinburgh's Awards.

With the close proximity of the River Trent, Len Adey of the 20th Company started a seamanship activity in 1958 with the help of John Jacques and Bernard Pottinger. With finance from the Nottingham Battalion of the Boys' Brigade [BB], a North Atlantic ship's lifeboat was acquired and named Steadfast and a Dinghy kit, Sure (in accordance with the BB Motto 'Sure and Steadfast'). These were fitted out in the extensive basement workshops of the Club in Northampton Street. To the present day, boys are trained in this activity. Len Adey left the area in 1963 and sadly died

---

2 The Company closed in 2001.

The Boys' Brigade Building. Photos: Ellie White 2000

Barry Booth, David Newton and Peter Hill 1959. Barry and David attended Morley School, St Ann's, and Peter attended Huntingdon School

Captain R T O Hawthorne with the 1st Nottingham Company, St Andrew's Church, 1930

shortly afterwards as a result of injuries sustained in a plane crash.

The Nottingham Battalion Champion Sergeant Competition started in 1902. 1941 was the only year there has been no appointment. The post is mainly a ceremonial one. The incumbent is appointed following competition open to the whole Battalion and the medal is currently presented each year at the Battalion Service, usually by the Lord Mayor. In 1951, Colour Sergeant D Swale of the Northampton Street Company won this Competition and held office for the years 1951/52.

In 1988, the Nottingham Battalion found it necessary to vacate its Headquarters on Castle Gate in the City and their office was incorporated in the premises on Northampton Street, St Ann's, which is now known as the Battalion Headquarters and Activity Centre coupled with the Headquarters of the 20th Nottingham Company. The refurbished premises were opened by the Lord Mayor. There is now one full-time member of staff supported by voluntary workers and a caretaker.

In the early hours on Tuesday April 21st 1992 (the Centenary of the Battalion in Nottingham) the premises in Northampton Street suffered serious damage. A burglary seems to have led to property being ignited in the office area. There was a good deal of fire, heat and smoke damage to the office, shop, main hall and sports equipment. No electricity supply was left, much of the wiring having been burnt through. All meetings had to be re-sited. However, led by the Battalion President of the day, the late Roy Wadd MBE, the Battalion rallied and was able to carry on with the Centenary celebrations that autumn.

New and smaller Company units, some of which are outside the inner-city, have replaced the large 100-200 Boy Companies of the past. However, despite the changes over the years, particularly in St Ann's where most of the members of the older and well-established Boys' Brigade Companies were split up and rehoused elsewhere when the area was redeveloped, the BB has also moved on and still has something to offer.

The Rt Hon Lord Trent opening the East Nottingham Boys' Club in Northampton Street in 1932. On his right is Captain Ralph Carr. At the opening ceremony, Captain Swain (Captain of the Nottingham Battalion of the Boys' Brigade) said: "There would be very little work for our probation officers, and the Borstal treatment would not be so much required if we could keep all the boys off the streets."

Members of the 1st Nottingham Company, St Andrew's Church, 1988

Mrs Janet Barlow, St Ann's, is Nottingham Boys' Brigade Battalion Vice-President with special responsibility for the Junior and Anchor Boy Section

John Irons, Field Officer of the Boys' Brigade, Nottingham, based at Northampton Street in St Ann's told me [2001] that Gwen Hirst was leader of the Juniors of the 20th Nottingham Company based in St Ann's for over thirty years until August 2001 when this Company closed. So far, nobody has been found to take over the leadership.

A new Company started at the Chase Baptist Church, St Ann's, in 2000, and works closely in co-operation with the Girls' Brigade there.

Tim, Anton and Steven at 20th Nottingham Lightweight Camp, Edale 1997. Photo from John Irons

---

Things in my life have a way of leading back to St Ann's. I am Series Editor of Plowright Press' 'Ordinary' *Lives Series*, which in 2000 included Geoff Raynor's autobiography, *Geoff: 44 years a railwayman*. Geoff, born 1922, started work on the railway in 1939 as a Messenger Lad at Victoria Station on the edge of St Ann's. He gave a talk about his work at St Ann's Library. But it wasn't until 2001 he told me that as a boy he regularly cycled from his home in nearby Carlton to Northampton Street, St Ann's, to join the activities of the 20th Boys' Brigade Company.

GEOFF RAYNOR writes [2001]

"Sunday morning Parade was compulsory [c1933] as was Monday night Drill Parade. The drill was based on the Army Drilling Manual and we had great pride in achieving the Drill Cup for the best Company in the Nottingham District (four out of five times while I was there).

"To say that I played an instrument in the Brass Band would be a bit over the top. I would rather say I blew into a cornet and hoped for the best. We did play quite a lot of music both in the Northampton Street Headquarters and also on the march. The great event was when all the companies in Nottingham marched to the Albert Hall once a year.

"The march for us would begin at Northampton Street, go along the St Ann's Well Road, other companies joining en route until the march reached Parliament Street. Then, the most wonderful thing was when one marching column reached near the Palais de Danse, the other companies would arrive bang-on the tail end. The timing was perfect I never knew this to fail.

"We would go to the Albert Hall and take our place with our instruments near the organ and play fanfares and the National Anthem. When the Service ended, the Band had to make a hasty exit, then march to the Council House where we took up our places to the rear and at the side of the Lord Mayor who took the salute as the other companies marched by.

"It was great fun but I had to leave the BB at the age of fifteen and a half because my father became ill. My brother and I had to tend the family allotment so were unable to attend Sunday Services and drills. Captain Carr was in charge of the 20th and Mr Fisher and Mr Jacques[3] were the two lieutenants."

THE NEW VICTORIA BALLROOM ON ST ANN'S WELL ROAD

LES CRIPWELL

Aged 94. [2000]

*Les Cripwell often played at the Victoria Ballroom, starting in **Billy Merrin's Commanders**. Photos from Les Cripwell unless otherwise stated*

At one time this Hall was called the Power House because the building and the one adjoining were owned by the Electricity Board of the time. The long, narrow hall had been used for many purposes, boxing, skating, conferences and exhibitions. When let as a ballroom, it was on a

---

[3] John Jacques was fifteen when he became the first member of the 20th Nottingham BB Company. "My father volunteered me because he was an officer," Mr Jacques told the *Nottingham Evening Post* September 5th 1992. "He didn't insist but he would have been disappointed had I said no." The following year the Company had its first camp, in a field at the side of Bingham railway station. In 1922, he was commissioned as an officer and worked his way through the ranks to the post of captain in 1964. In 1992, he was 88 years old and an honorary life president of the Nottingham Battalion. It was thought girls would be admitted to membership within a couple of years, said the Press report.

nightly basis, those booking the Hall supplying their own band.

My diary for 1928 when I played there shows that on October 8th was the occasion of the Chilwell Nursing Association's Old Time Carnival Ball 8.0 pm – 1.0 am at a cost of one shilling and sixpence. The season's first Military Ball, the Notts Field Battery, was on the 24th. Other bookings included the Basford United Football Club Dance, the Old Berridgians FC Dance and the Nottingham Corporation Benevolent Dance.

I played saxophone with Billy Merrin's Commanders which became a well-known band. In 1933, Mr Lazzerini decided to run the Victoria Ballroom in opposition to the Palais de Danse on Lower Parliament Street just outside St Ann's. He started by booking Billy Merrin's Commanders to be resident band after their successful season at the Royal Opera House, Covent Garden.

Billy Merrin's Commanders. Victoria Ballroom, St Ann's 1933. Left to right: Billy Merrin, Alan Massey, Stan Howard, Geo Rawlinson, Teddy Desmond, Eddie Pullen, Ron Bradley, Roy Wallis, Les Cripwell, Jan Castelli and 'Cod' Hill

Tea dances were held five afternoons on weekdays. Friday was the exception. There were six evening dances in the week. At this time, Roy Richards and his Commanders were resident at the Palais de Danse. Roy and four other members of the Billy Merrin's Commanders had left this Band to play at the Palais de Danse with a ten-piece band. Billy Merrin had to make quick replacements and managed to open on time. And so there were two Commanders' Bands! This could not last. With Billy Merrin's Band doing regular broadcasts, dancers flocked to the Victoria Ballroom. When Roy Richards' short contract ended, the original Commanders won the day!

We opened at the Vic - as it was called - with a bandstand halfway down the hall. Beer crates covered with green baize were used as an efficient bandstand built in two days. Large velvet curtains were hung across the hall, the rear part of the hall being used as bars and for whist drives. Professional dancers were employed at the Vic as at the Palais. Freddie Carlisle was employed as organist to play during the Band's break and at the usual Interval.

When Billy Merrin started his Search for Talent Night, the Vic was packed. At one of these talent contests, a

Al Washbrooke Band at the Victoria Ballroom 1956. Left to right back: Ken Hand, Colin Cox, Dick Ramsden. Front: Les Goff, Les Cripwell, Syd Goldsmith

young man called Ken Hodgkinson from Radford won first prize. He was a bricklayer by trade. Billy Merrin gave him a place in the band but changed his name to Ken Crossley. He later went on to be a vocalist in Henry Hall's and other bands.

When Billy Merrin's contract ended, the Fullerton Wills Band followed at the Vic, then Jack Padbury's. Jack was a very experienced musician. Jack brought a very fine pianist with his band, Al Washbrooke. Al was one of the finest pianists in the dance business, also being an accomplished accompanist and arranger. In fact, Al Washbrooke's Band was resident at the Vic Ballroom for many years during the 1950s.

During much of the 1930s, the Vic Manager was Eric Pilkington. His policy was to give top price attractions and facilities at a small admission fee. He booked famous bands for one night stands, Lew Stone, Billy Cotton and others. During the War, Reub Sunshine supplied a band. After the War, Jimmie Honeyman took over again with the men who had been in the Army but had now returned to Civvy Street. I joined him in 1945.

Jimmie Honeyman's Band, Victoria Ballroom 1945. Al Washbrooke at the piano. Jimmie Honeyman far right. Les Cripwell second from left (front)

While I was playing in Jimmie Honeyman's Band at the Vic in 1957 for a student Rag Ball, a strange incident occurred. A student picked up a fire extinguisher, and aimed it at the Band. We made off in all directions. The drummer went out the back through the curtains, gave them a tug as he went and down came the battleship grey curtain. They had been up since 1933. There were clouds of dust and dancers made a run for it. That was the end of the dance. Next night, the curtain was back in position, gold in colour again and, for once, we could see the monogram on the curtains which was VB. The Hall is now used for Bingo.

The former Victoria Ballroom, now enjoyed for Bingo. Photos: Alan Hardy 2001

Les Cripwell has written an account of his life, which includes information about personalities and dance halls in Nottingham and elsewhere. His manuscript is held at the Nottingham Local Studies Library.

*In 2000, Les Cripwell told me that he knew **Cyril Stapleton** who lived in Franchise Terrace, Westminster Street, in St Ann's, the son of a plasterer's labourer. Through the help of Nottingham Education Committee, he obtained a loan of £25, repayable in two years, to go to Czechoslovakia for a course of lessons under Professor Sevic. Cyril Stapleton played lead violin in Henry Hall's Band and became a well-known musician. Later, he formed his own band and Frank Sinatra said it was the best band in Britain. Cyril Stapleton died February 26th 1974.*

THE CINEMAS OF ST ANN'S

RICK WILDE

Born 1939

Chief of Projection, Savoy Cinemas, Nottingham and a local cinema historian, Rick Wilde wrote the following for this book about the three cinemas of St Ann's. He worked in one of them in the 1950s. Photos from Rick Wilde

NEW EMPRESS CINEMA

From my very first job at the Orion, Radford, in 1953, to my present one at the Savoy, Lenton, represents almost half a century of showing films to the Nottingham public. I have worked in many well-loved places, with wonderful nostalgic names, including the New Empress, St Ann's Well Road.

Many ask: 'Why *New* Empress?' It's simple! It replaced an older hall that existed 1913-27 in King Edward Street. My time at the New Empress was in the 1950s. So, for those of you who attended its weekly minors shows - or did courting in its back rows - I offer a few memories.

The New Empress 1944 showing an Ingrid Bergman and Gary Cooper double-bill 'Saratoga Trunk' and 'For Whom the Bell Tolls'

Looking through my log books, I see it was the time of The Dam Busters (Richard Todd), Underwater (Jane Russell) and Land of The Pharaohs (Jack Hawkins). An age when you paid to see your favourite star regardless of the picture, in an era of fads and crazes: like watching 3-D through a pair of cardboard specs with green and red lenses.

Now, who will own up to jiving in the isles to Rock Around the Clock or The Big Beat or sneaking in the back exit to ogle Brigitte Bardot or Sophia Loren in a steamy adults only saga, made all the more exciting because you knew you were under age?

Kids had their own Saturday Matinee. For a tanner [sixpence], you were able to join-up, get a card and a badge, fight your way in and shout yourself almost hoarse. The lights would go down to a cheer that could often be heard outside.

Frequent visitors arrived to judge competitions, and there were plenty. Best belly dancer, balloon blower, whistlers, clogdancer, conker, fancy-dress, even Guy Fawkes! Prizes were awarded by local footballers, boxers, actors from the Theatre Royal or entertainers from the Empire. If a Circus was in town, a clown would come and perform.

Programming could be awkward. Singing cowboys were avoided (not enough action) and swashbucklers of the Captain Blood variety were dying out. Hopalong Cassidy was OK and so was Tarzan, but the best received appeared to be the comedies. Abbott & Costello were good - especially on the weeks when they met Frankenstein, Dracula or the Invisible Man. Likewise, any Old Mother Riley film would be repeated again and again.

My records also show what Serials you were watching: King of the Congo, Superman, Zorro, Nyoka, Flash Gordon, Bomba, even a fifteen-week saga called The Mysterious Dr Satan.

In the middle, Ben Warris (half the Jewel and Warris act) and film star Shirley Eaton at an Empress matinee. Both were in the Theatre Royal Panto. With them is Metropole Manager, T F Chapman who was also a guest. December 12th 1959

The Cinema drew most of its patronage from the Shelton Street/Plantagenet Street areas, as well as from around the Sneinton Road districts which then still had avid cinemagoers. It was not unusual for the New Empress to re-run box office hits. And every so often, a special show for OAPs would be given. All they had to do was to produce their Pension Book to enjoy Showboat (Howard Keel), I Died a Thousand Times (James Cagney) or Love Me or Leave Me (Doris Day).

Opened in 1928 when films were still silent, the Hall had eight musicians augmented by a Mustel organ. It had 1,600 seats, 500 contained on the balcony. The 'talkies'

Lapel badge of the ABC Minors. The New Empress kids matinees began in November 1948 ending in November 1960

arrived in September 1929 making the musicians redundant. That same year, the New Empress was sold to the nationwide ABC circuit, which ran it until it closed in November 1960.

I was promoted to their Carlton Cinema, Chapel Bar: it had none of the character and atmosphere of the New Empress. Happy days, or maybe I should say Happy daze!

ROBIN HOOD PICTURE HALL

This long vanished silent Cinema will be recalled by those who grew up around the Robin Hood Chase area of St Ann's during the 1920s. It occupied the ground floor of what later became Cooper's factory. Originally, a brewery storage depot, the interior was converted with little alteration at minimal cost.

The Cinema opened in 1911 with a mixed bill of short films, and claimed in its advertising to seat 500, although the plans clearly show 300. Two shows nightly and two changes weekly was the general pattern. Admission was 3d, 6d and 1/- (children 1d, 2d and 3d). On Saturday afternoons all kids could get in for a well-washed jam-jar!

Accompaniment was provided by a solitary pianist, who had to extemporise as best they could to the action and moods unfolding. If their playing was not liked, or

The days when pictures flickered, pianists were pelted, and silence was not so golden. This was the district's first cinema, the Robin Hood, that occupied part of a building erected in 1880 and was demolished in the St Ann's redevelopment

worse still, if they forgot to play at all, they would very quickly be brought down to earth by a barrage of jeers, orange peel, apple cores and monkey nuts. One pianist suffered from a well-aimed pomegranate. No mucking about in those days!

Since the Robin Hood Picture Hall had no competition, its business remained good until the late 1920s when bigger and better cinemas emerged. First came the New Empress, St Ann's Well Road, in 1928, then the Majestic up Woodborough Road in 1929. Times were changing. Those who once found the intimate interior of the Robin Hood so inviting were now switching to these elegant spacious palaces with their fine orchestras.

By the spring of 1930, cinemas everywhere were scrambling to install Talkies and appease a clamouring public. As rival cinemas trumpeted their all talking-singing-dancing blockbusters to packed houses, the tiny Robin Hood with its upright Joanna, wind-up gramophone and worn seats suddenly looked obsolete and old fashioned. Its patronage evaporated and finally in December 1931 the proprietors announced that it would be closed and sold. The projectionist, Teddy Watts, would take up a similar position at the Globe, Trent Bridge.

The auditorium was converted into a Billiard Hall and would flourish until 1952. Cooper's, who occupied the remainder of the building, took it over. They made children's clothes. The property fell in the sixties redevelopment programme.

CAVENDISH CINEMA

Built to serve a thickly populated working-class district, the Cavendish made its debut in December 1938 having been blessed with a Civic and VIP send-off. Its first film was Will Hay in Convict 99, and 1,700 witnessed it.

On a bitterly cold December morning 1938, the Cavendish doorman has the unenviable task of snow-clearing. What a pity the Jack Buchanan musical comedy couldn't have had the title 'Break the Ice' instead of 'Break the News'

Never overtly elaborate in design, it nevertheless covered some ground. A huge barn of a place, it was affordable and luxurious, integrating quickly into the community. It soon began a quest to raise money for the district's poor with a cheque from the Directors for 25 guineas. That Christmas, a Director saw several barefoot children paying 6d to see the Disney film Snow White so he promptly refunded their money.

Gardeners at the St Ann's Rose Show in July 1939 were able to compete for the Cavendish Cup and a campaign for used books and papers brought in several tons, which were pulped and the money used to buy children's shoes.

Throughout the Second World War, entertainment continued to boost morale and the Cinema's stage was used for many recruitment drives as well as concerts, when locals could get up and join in whatever the show. The Cinema held many shows for the GIs based at Wollaton Park, and was itself hit by incendiaries during one air-raid. One landed in the front stalls making a mess, another dropped backstage, another in a storeroom and the remainder of the stick of bombs fell in the rear yard and Cooper Street/Enoch Terrace at the back of the Cinema.

Worthy of note are two indelible impressions recalled from the 1950s when the place was still challenging the tide of closures, which would soon begin to wash away many of our local cinemas. In December 1954, after many weeks of rehearsals, the children put on their very own pantomime. Tickets went like hot cakes, prompting the Manager, Bernard Rains, to say: 'We could have sold out twice over.' It left many in tears.

Perhaps the best memory was the day the Lone Ranger rode into town in the form of Clayton Moore. Arriving to plug his film The Lone Ranger and the Lost City of Gold, he was greeted by about 7,000 children lining St Ann's Well Road and another 1,700 crammed inside the Cinema. It was August Bank Holiday 1958. Afterwards he paid a visit to the Children's Hospital.

The last reel unwound in September 1969 and for a decade afterwards, the building operated as a Bingo Hall. When that waned, wrestling and pop concerts were held there until a blaze destroyed the stage end. The ground floor is presently in use as a store: a sad reminder of happier times.

ST ANN'S LIBRARY: new and old

A public library has been in St Ann's since 1885. The present Library in the Chase Precinct, Robin Hood Chase, was opened in 1972. The current staff write [1999]:

No staff from the time of the new Library's opening in 1972, twenty-seven years ago, still work at the Library. But Pauline Ridgard and Diana [Di] Reynolds joined in 1974 and Diana is still working here. She has seen many readers come and go and young children returning as adults, often with toddlers of their own. Two readers were heard recently trying to guess how long she'd worked here, though they had to give up in the end and come and

Di Reynolds, who joined the staff in 1974, and Jill Blyth outside St Ann's Library. Photo: Ruth I Johns 2001

ask. It's generally agreed, however, that she doesn't look a day older!

Tricia Leonard, Helen Blackmore and Jill Blyth are relative newcomers, having all joined the team in the last seven years. All staff agree that what makes it such a great place to work are the readers, young and old. 'Readers' join in their pushchairs, clutching their board books (chew resistant!), join in summer activities making dragons and giants, listening to stories and having their faces painted as tigers, then they come with their school class to borrow books to look at the old photographs and later they bring their homework questions. Adults come in to read the newspapers, borrow books and magazines, look up crossword answers, find books for the wide range of courses they're studying (childcare is especially popular at present), and they come with their children and grandchildren.

It's our readers who make St Ann's Library special. You forget the occasional rude or difficult customers (and maybe there are those who find the staff awkward or unfriendly!) as St Ann's folk display their generosity.

After a Library visit, a primary school group walk up Robin Hood Chase toward the underpass at Abbotsford Drive. Note how the buildings on the 'new' Robin Hood Chase do not overlook it. Photo: Ruth I Johns 2001

People who bring in goods from their allotments and biscuits from the market stalls, including the ninety year old who bakes apple pie for us, are not wealthy but are friendly and appreciative of their library service.

There are three features of St Ann's Library, which we think make it a very special library. The first is the memory of its old people. Up till recently, the history of St Ann's has lain buried in people's memories. For the past five years at the annual Reminiscence Days at the Library, people have been coming from all over Nottingham and from far beyond to share their memories and old photographs and slides. Some of these – and much more - will be in Ruth's [this!] book. St Ann's deserves its own history.

St Ann's Library also has quite a good Black Roots collection. This was the area in which many Jamaicans settled in the fifties and the collection aims to reflect something of the literature and heritage of the Caribbean (there's a reasonable collection of black romances too). We've had some excellent storytellers from the Caribbean. We have enjoyed working with elders from ACNA [Afro Caribbean National Artistic Centre] and other agencies to produce *Trailblazers*, a collection of reminiscences about the experience of coming from Jamaica to Nottingham. Children from Sycamore Junior School came to the Library to hear Dave 'Stickman' Higgins perform poems based on those reminiscences. His drumming was great!

And thirdly, 1999 is National Year of Reading, and St Ann's Library has been wanting to set up a Readers' Group to talk about books and share enjoyment. People can be scared that this is a bit 'high brow' and literary and for

In August 1999, a plaque was unveiled in the entrance of St Ann's Library in recognition of Alma Lucy Reville who was born at 69, Caroline Street, St Ann's, in 1899. She became Sir Alfred Hitchcock's wife in 1926. Their daughter, Patricia Hitchcock O'Connell, said she was glad Nottingham was paying tribute to her mother's talents as screenwriter and film editor. Alma had been in the shadow of her husband: "though he didn't make a move without her," said their daughter. She is researching her mother's life for a book she is writing about her contribution to the film industry. Photo: Ruth I Johns 2001

ST ANN'S NOTTINGHAM: inner-city voices *by Ruth I Johns* • ISBN 0951696092

other people. But what has been lovely is how supportive library friends and colleagues from other agencies have been. Who can forget the last 'Food for Thought' session when readers from the Library, METRA [Metropolitan Housing Tenants and Residents Association], Blue Bell Hill Community Centre, Mellors Lodge [housing project], the Housing Department, the Health Centre, and the Pharmacy all read foody poems and extracts down at the Chase Neighbourhood Centre.

So keep reading alive in St Ann's, keep coming to the Library to borrow and consult the books, magazines, books on tape, and keep talking to us. And here's to another twenty-seven years or more of St Ann's Library. We think it's the best library in Nottingham (but we may be biased!).

In 2000 Tricia Leonard retired from St Ann's Library and Liz Hayto joined the team. Helen Blackmore moved to a new job. In 2001, six public access Internet computers were added to the Library and create a busy atmosphere as St Ann's people gain free access to the latest technology

Early days. The existence of a library in St Ann's goes back to January 7th 1885. There was a Reading Room and Library on the ground floor of the unlicensed Adelphi Hotel on Whitehead Street, St Ann's. In March 1887, a reference in the City Council's reports stated the St Ann's District Reading Room had been removed to a handsome building in nearby Dame Agnes Street. The premises were enlarged, sold to the Council and renovated so that in 1909, it was reported that: "Situated in the centre of a most populous district, there is little doubt that the extended facilities for intellectual entertainment and pursuits will be appreciated. . . . Upon the death of the owner, the Estates Committee made a wise purchase. Two shops occupied the ground floor, and with a view to future usefulness, the partition between them was knocked down, and used as an Institute for St Ann's Church."

At the opening ceremony, Councillor C Foulds, Vice-Chairman of the Public Libraries Committee, said he was sure it was a right thing to cater for those of the working-classes who desired some better form of recreation than that provided at the public houses and places of amusement.

Alan Guest was in charge of the **Dame Agnes Street Library** during some of the 1950s. At one time a portrait by his uncle Joseph Jackson of Walter Briscoe, a City Librarian, was stored at Dame Agnes Street but nobody knew what happened to it, said **Alan Guest**, speaking at St Ann's Library on the 110th anniversary of the opening of the Reading Room. While he was at Dames Agnes Street Library, he said all the regulars regarded him as the junior assistant and Mrs Pearce, who had been the library assistant for many years, as the Librarian. "In fact we got on well and she did make exceedingly good cakes. I remember her as an old lady but it occurs to me now that she must have been younger than I am now or we wouldn't have been employing her.

"Of the building itself, I remember there was an outside lavatory and the coke boiler had been replaced some time prior to my arrival by a gas boiler but it was still situated in the middle of the staff room in a large sunken area so one had to be careful when walking near it. In 1959, I left to become the Librarian of the new People's College of Further Education."

The Library closed on August 30th 1969 and a Mobile Library served the area until the opening of the existing Library in 1972. From a News Sheet provided at the opening ceremony.

St Ann's Library on its opening day 25th August 1972. Photo: Alan Guest, Nottingham Local Studies Library

St Ann's Library 1973. Photo: Alan Guest, Nottingham Local Studies Library

Barbara Levick was at the opening of the existing Library on August 25th 1972. She told a Library audience twenty-five years later:

"When the new St Ann's was being planned, apart from houses, shops and pubs, we, the Committee of the St Ann's Tenants and Residents Association [SATRA] felt we wanted something more than just the bare necessities of life. We wanted a bit of culture, somewhere to get information on what was happening in the district and a meeting place. We had hoped to build a community centre, but that was not to be until some time later. A library seemed the best option. The Council approved the idea, and twenty-five years ago, this library that so many of us use came to be opened."

After the opening ceremony at the Library, guests were taken by a Lilac Leopard coach to the Council House for lunch and Councillor Betty Higgins arranged a tour of the building.

"Sadly quite a few of the people who attended the opening are no longer with us: Arthur Leatherland, Frank Glassup, Alec Birks, Councillor Ronnie Griffin and John Ingle. Others are scattered now: Margaret Behrman, Ray Gosling, Audrey Lighton, Lillian Taylor and members of the [Blue Bell Hill] Craft Centre.

"The Library we fought so long and hard for is now taken for granted. But due to the hard-working and friendly staff, the Library goes from strength to strength and is as popular and well patronised as ever by individuals, schools, pupils doing their homework and others who just want a quick look at the daily newspaper in the hope of picking a 'winner'.

"Long may you continue to serve us so well. We would be lost without you and the books you provide us with. Without your being there we would be condemned to watching TV instead of improving our minds on travel, history, adventure, mystery and, best of all, love."

GLADSTONE CLUB

COLIN SHIPSTONE

Born 1937   and

TERRY LIMBRICK

Born 1934

Secretary and Chairman of the Gladstone Club, Manning Street, St Ann's. Interviewed at the Club 3.1.00

Terry Limbrick The Club is about one hundred and twenty years old. It originated at the corner of Lamartine Street and St Ann's Well Road and it was there until all the demolition and new housing came about. We had to move because they told us it was going to be a traffic island [for the aborted Eastern By-pass road]. The Seventh-day Adventist Church is now on that site.

Gladstone Club at Hendon Rise Social Club c1973. Photo: Gladstone Club

When we had to get out quick, we moved up to the Hendon Rise Social Club [built as the Horticultural Hall], on Hendon Rise up The Wells Road. We went there February 1973 and we stayed there until Home Brewery decided we were making too much money. They introduced a rent that was about twenty times what we were paying.

In 1977, these premises on Manning Street had been derelict for some years. It had been St Augustine's Catholic Church Club. They wanted to get rid of it and the price was good and we would have been foolish to turn it down. So we moved here in 1977.

The compensation we received from the Council when we had to leave Lamartine Street/St Ann's Well Road was absolutely naff. I think it was just over £300. And considering we owned four or five little shops on the St Ann's Well Road as well, the Club was robbed but it was a case of Compulsory Purchase. But we were fortunate to be able to rent the Hendon Rise Social Club. A guy called Bob Moran wanted to sell the tenancy. But we couldn't sell any beer except Home Brewery, whereas before we used to sell a lot of breweries. We weren't so restricted.

The Club was started around 1880 by the Liberals. It is still a Liberal Club but like most Political Clubs now we don't do the 'hard and fast' rule as they did years ago. I remember at one time an important Liberal lady from Matlock came in here. There was no Liberal Club in Matlock, so she was a member of the Conservative Club there. There was a time when you had to state on an entry form that you were a bona fide Liberal but that has gone now. Up North, it's more political. Halfway through Saturday night entertainment, somebody will stand on stage and tell you about the Liberal Party and you've got a Party Political broadcast at half past nine just before you play Bingo!

I mean if you want to be in politics, that's okay, but don't stuff it down everybody's throat, that's my way of thinking. It's the same with churches. You don't want the Church of England or the Catholic Church knocking on your door every five minutes trying to convert you.

Colin Shipstone There's a waiting list for membership. Once you are on the waiting list, you have one person to propose you and another to second your application. The first year of membership, if the new member steps out of line, then the proposer and seconder will lose their membership as well as the new member.

Terry Limbrick The Club was a Limited Company up to 1973. It was a men's club and the only time women were allowed in was on a Saturday or Sunday. When we went up to Hendon Rise, I pointed out that the law had changed, women were getting equal rights and they were entitled to membership, which didn't go down very well at the time. Some of the people running the Club at that time were still somewhere around 1900 in their thinking, they hadn't moved on and they hadn't got a tremendous number of members.

When we went to Hendon Rise we got a lot more members and more still when we moved here in 1977. There were some well-known people who were once members of the Club, a lot of professional people like

St Ann's Nottingham: inner-city voices by Ruth I Johns • ISBN 0951696092

surgeons from the old General Hospital. St Ann's became somewhat derelict, but prior to that posh people lived here as well, like doctors and matrons of hospitals, the Hopewell family . . .

So we bought the premises off the Catholic Church and we've gone from strength to strength. A lot of hard work has gone into this by the various Committees and, since we've been here, we've only had two secretaries before Colin and only two Chairmen before me. The two previous secretaries and chairmen sadly died[1].

Gladstone Club Table Skittles Team end of season night out 1980. Photo: Gladstone Club

Colin Shipstone We have just under one thousand members. And the Club also owns the house on the corner of Manning Street and Woodborough Road. That's John Moore's, the Steward's, living accommodation. The Assistant Steward is Bill Wright. I lived in St Ann's for fifteen months after I got married but I don't now. About half our members come from the St Ann's area and the others from farther away. But often not far out of the area.

Terry Limbrick They like coming here because we don't have any problems. If you step out of line in this place, you step outside the door and you don't come back in. I know that might sound harsh, but we've got a rulebook and you've got to obey the rules. Then it's not going to be like it was when it was the St Augustine's Club. It more or less shut down because there was a fight every night sort of thing.

You wouldn't catch anyone in here selling drugs because they know we'd phone the police. People know they can come in and sit down nice and comfortably with good shows at the weekend. Older people feel safe in here. But we get some younger ones as well. Almost half are aged forty plus.

Colin Shipstone We like to keep it as a good family club. On Mondays, Wednesdays and Thursdays we're open normal licensing hours in the afternoons and evenings.

Tuesday night we have a Bingo night. Monday night there is long alley skittles, and Thursday is table skittles. Then on Friday we have a Bingo night and a games night where they can play snooker, pool, darts . . . well, you can play darts any night. On Saturday and Sunday we have entertainment plus Bingo.

Terry Limbrick We've had all sorts of artists, most of the sixties groups like the Bachelors, and the sixties bands. Duncan Norvelle started here, Dilly Pearce . . . People who are household names on TV now. Even Torvill and Dean came in the early 1980s. They wanted money to go to the European Championships, for accommodation etc. We put on a Charity Night for them. In this country, training will be paid for but there won't be money in the early days for things like accommodation. He was a Policeman at that time. I don't know what she was doing.

We do one Charity Night a year for some cause. We've done it for Cancer Research, Guide Dogs for the Blind and so on, and we often get people who are appearing locally. They'll come in and sign a few autographs.

Colin Shipstone If any of the members is running any sort of sponsorship or charity event, we give them permission to go round the Club. The membership fee is £5 a year.

We've just had a £55,000 extension put on the front and we've one or two other improvements in the pipeline. The people prior to Terry and myself could have had a piece of land at the side for the Club but they didn't know how big it would become. We could really do with that now. The new extension includes new toilets, a toilet for people who are disabled, a kitchen extension and some storerooms and it's been done so that we can build over it later on if we need to.

What happens here kills the myth of St Ann's, doesn't it?

Terry Limbrick I don't think St Ann's is any better or any worse than anywhere else but it's got that reputation.

Colin Shipstone You'll find there's a lot of camaraderie, people stick together. If you've got any scheme or anything like that, they will put their act together and help you out. I've always found that since I've been associated with the Club.

A group at the Gladstone Club's two week holiday in Marmaris, Turkey, 1999. Photo: Gladstone Club

---

[1] Michael Jordan, one-time treasurer, secretary and licensee of the Club died in 1999. He was President of the National Union of Liberal Clubs and he used to live in St Ann's near the Club at one time.

Terry Limbrick If I announced that we were going to have a Charity Night for little 'Nell' down the road on a Thursday night, the place would be packed.

Colin Shipstone There would be volunteers straight away and I'll come and sing a couple of songs. Yes, I do sing. We also run a couple of trips each year and we go on holiday. We went to Turkey last year and are going again this year.

Terry Limbrick Forty-three go every year. It will be the fourth year we've been to Turkey. They liked it so much. This is the third year in the same hotel.

Colin Shipstone Last year, my wife and I tried it and afterwards my wife said: 'We're going again, aren't we?' There have also been holidays to Cornwall and the Isle of Wight etc. I've been a member of the Club for something like fifteen years and this is my eighth month as Secretary.

Terry Limbrick I've been a member for many years and Chairman for about five years.

Colin Shipstone We always look after the members. The senior citizens have a party every year, free. And there's a kiddies Christmas Party, for the children of members. There were about a hundred and twenty at the last one. One of the lads will be Santa Claus. We always have a summer outing to Skegness or Blackpool.

We don't serve food here now. The members don't want it.

Terry Limbrick With most people being fairly local, they're not going to come in to buy a cob, they may as well make it up at home before they come out. When you come in on a Saturday night, people bring out sandwiches and all sorts, maybe mussels. They pass them round and don't just sit there scoffing the lot! If it's a Birthday Party, they will come in with all their own food and we don't mind. All we say is don't leave too much of a mess.

Colin Shipstone We've got a room downstairs which seats about forty people and members can use it.

Terry Limbrick Most use it for family events, just family and friends, so they might put three tables together and twenty people come and they'll all have sandwiches. They will say to the Steward: 'It's our Gert's birthday on Saturday night and we'd like to use the room . . .' And that's fair enough. They'll set it up themselves so you don't have to worry about it. And they clear up and put everything into black sacks. It's far better to have a party amongst your friends.

Colin Shipstone If they're not members, we charge them £25 for the use of that room, the private room downstairs.

2002. Colin Shipstone has retired as Secretary. Roy Pearce, who was Assistant Secretary for fifteen years, is now Secretary. John Moore, Steward, has now retired and Bill Wright, Assistant Steward, has left. The Stewardess is now Mrs Dawn Slaney. Club members continue to have an annual holiday in Turkey

FAMILY CARE

SUE JONES

Born 1952

Interviewed at Family Care, Warren House, Sherwood 27.6.00. Family Care was formerly at Warren House, Plantagenet Street, St Ann's

I'm a senior social worker at Family Care. It's full title is Southwell Diocesan Council for Family Care. It was formerly the Southwell Diocesan Board of Moral Welfare at 1, Plantagenet Street, St Ann's. I joined the agency in 1983 and worked there for about three years before we moved over here.

When we were based in St Ann's, quite a percentage of our work came from the area because we were known and people just dropped in. They dropped in to seek help through our family support services or sometimes they were giving to Family Care. Maybe they'd received some support years before and were coming back and saying: 'Can you use this equipment, toys and so on'?

There was a lot of mutual support. We moved to Plantagenet Street around 1964. I think the name changed soon after that to Family Care. We're a family support agency and an adoption agency, with origins back to 1886 as a Diocesan Board of Moral Welfare. There were other Moral Welfare Boards around the County. In time they closed and the work came to be vested in one agency, now called Family Care.

My understanding about the reason why the Headquarters came to be in St Ann's was because we had been around that area for many, many years. Previous addresses were The Pilgrims House, 3, Pepper Street and 16, Gorsey Road, just inside Mapperley. Yes, there was a Mother and Baby Home there but it had been the Headquarters at one stage. I think at one stage we were in a building in or near the then Kings Hall Methodist Mission, St Ann's Well Road. [Was this the building on Commercial Square nicknamed 'The Welcome'? Over the entrance it said: 'Mothers and Babies Welcome' and free advice was given to mothers and babies before the start of the National Health Service.[1]]

When I went to work in Plantagenet Street in 1983, I was very conscious that the street was such a mix. Our building, Warren House, stood on the corner of the road. It was the old Vicarage for St Catharine's Church. It was a house built on numerous half-levels with cellars and attics and all sorts. It was a very old established house that used to have tunnels through to the City, like other parts of Plantagenet Street.

Across the road there was accommodation which used to be some sort of alms houses[2]. Further down the road where the old St Ann's had been totally flattened were all the Council houses that had been built in the 1970s. Then

---

[1] Kathleen Shaw in *Elliott Durham and St Anns* [Plowright Press 1998]
[2] Working Man's Retreat, built 1852, now general needs housing managed by Nottingham Community Housing Association.

ST ANN'S NOTTINGHAM: Inner-city voices *by Ruth I Johns* • ISBN 0951696092

some new houses were built in the 1990s and it felt a real kind of mix of an area. It intrigued me. Families of all ages, from newborns to people in their nineties.

We were a fairly small group of social work staff when I joined in 1983. Vera Hall was the Principal Social Worker. We had an Administrator who was then Christine Russell who was associated with the Board of Social Responsibility as well, and later with Macedon [housing trust for homeless people]. And as well as Vera who was very much involved with the 'hands on' work, there were three of us. Marion Ashmead had been there for years and I guess would be quite well-known around St Ann's. I replaced Ruth Robertson who again had been around the area for a long time. And Valerie Knowles. We were a small team, which has certainly grown in size. The secretaries at the time were Sandy Truman and Sheila.

I'd previously worked with a local Authority in Yorkshire for some years and came here with a special interest in family support and adoption work.

In St Ann's, we were conscious that we were working with people who had a lot of relations in the area, who were rooted. And maybe some parts of the family had moved out or were on the edges of St Ann's but who still had rooted connections in St Ann's itself. People got to know us through Health Visitors, Health Centres, lots of word of mouth. People came in because so-and-so recommended we might be able to help. Or a friend would bring somebody in who had a particular difficulty.

We've certainly missed out coming here to Sherwood in a sense. There, people felt comfortable coming in a door to what was essentially a house with a living room where you could sit and talk. Obviously the professionalism was there but the services were available to people in an accessible way. They didn't have to knock on the door or go through an intercom system. They could just say: 'Can I come in, can I talk?'

We moved because the house itself needed a lot of renovation. And sadly we were experiencing quite a lot of break-ins and we had to take account of the adoption records we needed to protect over the years. Adoption records legally have to be kept for seventy-plus years. Obviously that information is very precious to people whose lives may be identified in just one piece of paper and nothing else. We had to take stock of what services we were offering and how we could best deliver them. Although St Ann's was important to us, the Agency by then was serving the whole Diocesan area.

We try to make ourselves continually accessible. We still have a tie with Yellow Pages. We leaflet Health Centres, schools, general notice-boards, shop windows, post offices. We have display boards up in different places. We've got displays on the buses at present. Statutory agencies refer people.

We are a Christian based agency, that's our roots. We're still seen as the Diocesan Social Work Agency and are supported as such. So we get grants from the Southwell Diocese, we get a lot of donations from Parishes and Churches. We're registered as a Charity. We get aid from both City and County Local Authorities. We get money

This photo was taken outside Warren House [formerly St Catharine's Vicarage], Plantagenet Street, St Ann's before Family Care moved. Left to right: Pat Morrell, Paula Smythe, Ann Fletcher, Sue Jones, Sandy Croule, Deirdre Offord, Sue Smith, Bernard Driver*, Chris Savage, Dorothy Driver and Sherile Mitcham

from different sources for particular projects. For example, our Young People's Counselling Service which had been going for four years was supported by Children in Need and then by the Lottery. That's the only service that we know locally which is specifically for children affected by separation and divorce.

We work with anyone who has a faith or no faith. We work with anyone who voluntarily wants to make use of our services because we can only work with people who choose to do so. A family, from my point of view, can be anybody who identifies themselves as a family. Family support is a term that feels unspecific but it covers a very wide variety of possibilities, including teenagers who are struggling to assert their independence.

I remember a situation where somebody came in having experienced a termination and who was very distressed by the trauma around it. She came in and talked for two hours and all I ever knew about her was her first name. Now that's not on offer in many places because you usually have to go through the red tape of names, addresses, dates of birth and all the rest. We're tied in very properly with the services that protect children in our society today. That's important. But we can start where people are.

Not long ago, someone rang and said she remembered this Sister in St Ann's who came to help her mum when she was struggling, was she from our Agency? My answer was that she might well have come from us, but we don't have the paperwork to prove it. But we'd had a presence in the area that was meaningful. I'd like to think that will continue.

*__Bernard Driver__ died April 7th 2002. He was born August 24th 1916 in the area. His funeral was at St Catharine's Church, where he became a Churchwarden in 1956 and served under seven clergy. One of them, the Rev

Canon David Keene told me: "He was a man of great determination and everything had to be 'just right'. I particularly remember on one occasion after the men had used scaffolding to re-paint the Church: Bernard, who hated heights, coming down from a ladder and kneeling at the Altar to give thanks that all was finished.

"On one occasion, his arm was broken when he took one of our homeless to the Salvation Army Hostel for the night and Bernard was pushed down the stairs. In the War, he was a staff driver to Brigadier General Clarke. He also was a driver to Field Marshal Montgomery as they planned the invasion and Bernard went over on 'D' Day.

"When he retired, he was a traffic warden. No one was allowed to get away with it however exalted their position!

"As members of the congregation dwindled and the Church Hall had to be demolished, a community room, with kitchen and lavatories was built within the west end of the Church, a useful place for meetings and for worship. The main Church is used only for major services. The link with St Mary's in the Lace Market - the old Mother Church - was much valued with the congregation and servers going there once a month to worship in St Catharine's style. As Bernard would say; 'They had the full bag of mashing.'

"Dorothy Driver was Church Secretary for many years."

GREYFRIARS PIPE BAND

Michael Masterson says the Band was formed in 1956 by Pipe Major Michael Walsh, a Limerick man who: "in his spare time, twice a week trained us to play the pipes and drums. The band progressed and was soon up to championship standard in advanced piping and drumming. Most of his pupils went on to become world class pipers and Pipe Majors in various organisations and top pipe bands."

Greyfriars Pipe Band in Nottingham City Centre 1966. Photo: Terence Balchin. John B Hibbitt took a photo of the Band in St Ann's 1959 [see Index]

The band disbanded in 1970, but in 2000 Michael Masterson, himself a Pipe Major, was approached to lead the first St Patrick's Day Parade in Nottingham. Still recovering from illness, he got together with Michael Walsh and John St John and they led the parade. Michael Masterson was inspired to start up the Greyfriars Pipe Band again. The Greyfriars Club, set up in 1959, has helped to raise funds. The Club is on the complex of the Church of Our Lady and St Edward, Friary, School and Club on Gordon Road.

"Here we are practising and training once again. However, the band is now mostly formed of young children. I hope before long to have once again the great band we had in the 1950s and 1960s," says Michael Masterson.

BLUE BELL HILL CRAFT CENTRE

There are as many stories about the Blue Bell Hill Craft Centre as there are people who knew it. Several people mention it in their recollections. Ray Gosling wrote about it in *Personal Copy: a Memoir of the Sixties* [Faber & Faber 1980], there are stories for and against it in *Chase Chat* the community newspaper which was run for a few years.[1] The thing I most remember about Jill McGuire and Mike Stroud were the way they quickly adapted their ideas to suit the local situation when they moved into the area. But they retained their idealistic approach of working for nothing and being supported by the local community: shopkeepers in particular offered food including surplus stock.

The raison d'être of the volunteers was not to speak for the community but to serve it, not in any patronising way but in a very practical way. Maybe it was unsurprising that their motives were often misinterpreted. They were sometimes seen as 'spongers'. Young people I have spoken

The Blue Bell Hill Craft Centre on Blue Bell Hill Road/Young Street, where items were exchanged and some craft sessions run and - most importantly - where people met up. Photo: Margaret Behrman's Album, Nottingham Local Studies Library c1972

1 Colin Haynes has given copies to St Ann's Library.

to about this project usually want to know more, and they feel it had much which could be of value in the present time.

For every task the 'Craft Centre people' were seen to do, they did many unseen and earned a lot of respect (for example, among local elderly for whom they would do house repairs to make a home habitable long after landlords didn't care because of planning blight). Members of the Craft Centre were the driving energy in pressing the Corporation to set up an Adventure Playground and - as Marion Wallwork and Barbara Halls pointed out in *Leisure Activities* [Nottingham Consumer Group 1966] - St Ann's was a pioneer in adventure playgrounds. For several years when local children in an area under planning blight urgently needed a playground, members of the Craft Centre ran imaginative daily sessions using all manner of materials. After St Ann's was redeveloped, members of the Craft Centre moved on into different work, some allied to the same objectives, others not.

After St Ann's was redeveloped the Adventure Playground site moved - but not far - and it has had a varied history depending on priorities and funding at any time. The site stands back from the main St Ann's Well Road and needs imaginative leadership to work well.

The Westminster Bank: looking down Alfred Street Central from Commercial Square on St Ann's Well Road. The Oliver Cromwell pub is on the right. This photo was taken in 1969 when the Bank was already doomed for demolition. Photo G L Roberts, Nottingham Local Studies Library

HOLIDAY HOME

Patricia A Wood [1999] wrote: "Due to circumstances, I found myself living in St Ann's in 1968-71. I was involved in a number of community projects. I moved out to start and run a holiday home in Collingham in the country for kids from the area. The idea was that, when home life was difficult, it would be better if children had a holiday than be taken 'into care'. We were supported by the NSPCC [National Society for the Prevention of Cruelty to Children], the Probation Department and Social Services. We grew our own vegetables, bred pigs, had a house cow, goats, hens, rabbits etc. Children would often adopt a pet for a week."

EMPLOYMENT

Much about the history of employment in St Ann's is told in the recollections of its people. The Index will guide people who wish to find details specifically about employment. It is such an integral part of life for those who experience it, that it cannot be seen in isolation, any more than people can be defined only as 'unemployed'.

Recollections show clearly the patterns of employment in St Ann's. For some, there were severe hardships in years prior to the Second World War. The War brought different employment patterns. Many men in St Ann's worked in Reserved Occupations, including mining and skilled trades: others joined the Armed Services. One man interviewed was a 'refuser'. Some young women joined the Services: others did war work 'on the home front'. After the War,

employment gradually became easier and there were many years when 'you could leave a job on Friday and start another on Monday morning'.

St Ann's men worked in coal mines, for Raleigh Cycles, on the railway, for British Road Services, in factories, local firms (from management to odd-job boy), pubs, shops, and as labourers. When they advanced in their work, they did not necessarily leave St Ann's. There were professional men and women living in the area, like doctors, teachers and midwives. Many women worked in local factories, did cleaning jobs, ran or worked in shops or pubs, and did lace work at home. Some, like Jess Phelps, found ingenious ways of getting away from work they disliked into work they enjoyed.

Before and during the War, St Ann's was largely self-reliant. After the War, when material circumstances gradually improved for many families, it remained self-reliant. In all sorts of practical ways, people in 'better circumstances' continued to help those who needed it. For example, Harry Bramley, the successful butcher, sold flowers and tomatoes grown by people on the Hungerhills: the proceeds all going to them. Many shops were run 'for that little extra that makes a difference'. The stately building of the Westminster Bank, which came down as part of the area's demolition, was proof of the enterprise going on in St Ann's, through its factories, workshops and shops. And it was not the only bank in the district.

Wages earned in St Ann's were largely spent in St Ann's. Money earned outside the district by St Ann's people was largely spent in St Ann's. People from outside the area came in to shop, to work, to the pubs and cinemas and much else.

Nobody now would want slaughterhouses in residential areas, but there were several in St Ann's (mentioned by interviewees). The slaughterhouses supplied many of the twenty-two butchers in St Ann's. Some of the bones were collected from butchers for a local workshop which processed them, as Ray Alexander tells below. The local community had this very close connection with supplying its own needs and, therefore, a close involvement with the ways things were done, who did them, and how much was paid for products and services. Transactions could be in kind as well as money.

From the 1970s, people in St Ann's felt the increasing loss of jobs in the outside workplaces (for example, the mines and Raleigh). The textile industry shrunk severely. These national influences reducing employment could not be avoided, but they were felt acutely in St Ann's because, by the early 1970s through massive redevelopment and population transplant, it had lost much of its ability to be as self-reliant, adaptive and able to help itself as it had in previous hard times.

Those St Annie's who lost their work when, for example, the coal mines closed often adapted and embraced new work, including computer-based employment. By that time, many had either moved from St Ann's because of impending redevelopment or at the time it happened.

Some made staying in St Ann's a priority, like Harold Smith and Tony Burt, and worked out employment choices. They moved to St Ann's roads/streets which were outside the area to be demolished.

The majority of the 'new' St Ann's population lacked established networks of inter-generational families, neighbours and colleagues nearby. And the 'new' St Ann's lacked a range of flexible buildings available cheaply so that people could test new employment opportunities with products, services and ideas. And houses were houses and nothing else. No eggs from Lincolnshire being sold from a front 'shop' parlour once a week . . .

There is such a close link between the kind of buildings which are available and the employment which results: as Islington Borough Council found out in 1977. It asked me to investigate via Action Resource Centre how its compulsory purchase programme of workplace buildings could be prevented from continuing a haemorrhage of jobs. The Borough wanted the land for housing. To cut a long interesting story short, it was found that 11% of enterprises in the buildings to be demolished were 'Way of Life' companies. They provided goods and services, often on an inter-trading basis. Their employees were often family members. They included people who would find alternative employment difficult to find. These Way of Life companies had small profit margins, but the enterprises provided a very satisfactory way of life for those involved. Compulsory demolition of premises was indeed a death-threat to such enterprises.

In its 1970 publication, *St Ann's: Renewal in Progress*, Nottingham Corporation said there were over 200 firms and over 700 shops in St Ann's prior to redevelopment. It said the industries were mixed in with the housing 'often causing nuisance to the residents'. Yet, I have not heard anyone who

lived in the 'old' St Ann's express this view. The publication said industry would be limited to three areas (on the edge of the district). Houses in part of the largest industrial area (around Watkin Street) "are in good condition and will remain for about fifteen years. When they are cleared, the land will be used for industry." Photos of streets in this area - still in existence - are shown in The Built Environment in the 'new' St Ann's section of this book.

In its outline of firms, Nottingham Corporation made no distinction between workshop type firms and industries with big factories.

The new Wimpey estate which filled the bulldozed 340 acres in St Ann's did not include flexible workspaces, though there were professional voices at the time who stated the need and showed how it could be met. They were not suggesting factories but flexible small units, as described by David Wilkinson.

St Ann's has been an area of high unemployment for several decades now. Successive Government programmes for unemployed people have been taken up through local organisations, but few people have commented on them. Special schemes and projects came and went. Some individuals clearly benefited. Others commented that those who benefited left St Ann's as soon as they found employment, because they had no roots in the district: then, other young people who were unemployed moved in. It is hard to establish the correct facts because the complexities

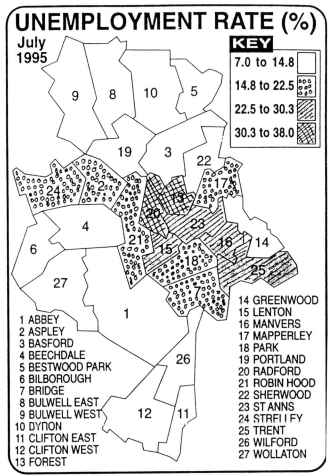

Unemployment at July 1995. St Ann's falls into some of area 23 and some of 16. From October/November 'Nottingham Arrow'

of 'community' and the availability of training, employment and accommodation are all intertwined.

It is evident that the large area of St Ann's that was redeveloped lacks flexible small buildings which are multi-purpose and inexpensive. Workshop schemes have been introduced in recent years (see, for example, the Ashforth Workshops). But, to quote one interested party: 'they are not cosy.'

It is not appropriate to have workspace which can only be used during 'normal working hours'. Most people building up enterprises work extraordinary hours! We are led to believe these days that the ideal life is one without anything or anybody impinging on our personal space. But, my understanding of St Ann's after talking to people and asking questions for several years, is that many people would welcome more 'real' things happening on the patch, more people doing 'real' things out and about during all waking hours and more adults visible for young people to relate to: there is an earthy understanding that if 'real' things are absent, undesirable activities - like drugs - thrive.

Below are a few photos of workplaces in St Ann's before redevelopment.
Others, including many shops, appear elsewhere in the book.

This is as close as big factories got to housing. Nobody would recommend this. I believe this is Lincoln Terrace off Alfred Street North? In which case it was part of the Phase 10 redevelopment area. Photo: Wilkinson, Davis and Strickland 1967

Photo: Wilkinson, Davis and Strickland 1967

Tidmas Factory, demolished early 1973. Photo: Reg Baker 1972, Nottingham Local Studies Library

*A factory being demolished.
Photo: Nicholson Photo Archive*

*Grandad and grandchild walking the gauntlet of a St Ann's urban landscape awaiting destruction. **Is there anything wrong with workspace on this scale mixing with residential?** Photo: James Snowden*

Fred Hoyes Workshop in its last days. Photo: Wilkinson, Davis and Strickland 1967

St Ann's Nottingham: inner-city voices by Ruth I Johns • ISBN 0951696092

Flexible workspace on the corner of Alison Rise and Alfred Street Central. In use here as wholesale footwear distributors

Flexible workspace. Workshop, shop, pub or house?

Flexible workspace. In use here as P R Cooper and Co Ltd, Children's Wear Manufacturers. All these buildings were demolished. Photos: Wilkinson, Davis and Strickland 1967

Flexible workspace for church hall, workshop, residence . . .

TWO HOUSES AND A WORKSHOP AT THE BACK

RAY ALEXANDER

Born 1932

In 1927, Bill and Gladys Alexander, my parents, moved into 26, Northumberland Street, St Ann's with two small children, Dorothy born on 28.3.26 and Arthur, born 15.8.27.

26 and 28, Northumberland Street were two houses with an archway running between them, at ground floor level, for access into workshops at the back. When my parents moved in, Mr and Mrs Ford were already living at No 28. Both houses were laid out with a front room and a living room in which the fireplace was an oven and a boiler, set with a brass tap fitted to the boiler. There was also a back kitchen with a copper built in.

Each house had a double cellar. Upstairs there were three bedrooms plus a top attic. The toilet was in the backyard. The split between the houses was in the archway. My parents had the front bedroom and Mr and Mrs Ford had the back bedroom.

These two houses had workshops beyond their backyards. It was originally built as the Snowdon Laundry around the 1860s. The Ford family had a stall in the Central Market selling poultry food, dog biscuits, bone meal and ground oyster shells.

This photo shows the archway between 26 and 28 Northumberland Street. Photo: Ray Alexander c1951

The layout of the workshops at our end of the building consisted, on the ground floor, of a room with a blue brick floor with a grate in one corner. In the middle of the floor stood a circular saw used for cutting up bones collected from the local butcher's shops. In the wooden ceiling were some large hooks.

Two large doors opened onto our backyard and to the right of these was a double trap-door. The central part of the workshop contained a large flour mixer and also a large oven for baking the dog biscuits, also for cooking the bones before grinding them into bone meal. On the opposite side was a workbench. At the other end of the workshop was the grinding machine, using the bones to make poultry food. After being ground, it would be carried upstairs and spread out on the floor to dry. The upstairs was also used for grinding oyster shells for poultry grit.

The layout of the upper floor was as follows. As you came up the stairs, above you was the start of a large workbench. In the middle of the floor was the machine for grinding oyster shells. To the front of the building was a set of double doors with a hoist above.

There were quite a lot of windows right across the workshops into both our backyards.

I was born in our house on 5.1.32 and my younger brother Roy on 16.5.36. On May 9th 1941, my father who was a Wartime Reserve Policeman was killed during the bombing of Nottingham. As far as I know, he was the only policeman killed in the City during the War. It happened on Shakespeare Street when the College was hit.

Bill Alexander, Ray Alexander's dad

Like many other families in our position, we carried on. We grew up and moved to other parts of Nottingham. My mother remarried and lived in the house until around 1970 when they were rehoused at Clifton 'with an indoor toilet and a bathroom.' She did want to leave. But mam went and watched them pull down the old house brick by brick and cried all the time. The whole premises were demolished with the rest of the area.

On the subject of slaughterhouses, Ray Alexander told me: "Animals were driven up Northumberland Street, where I lived, to Alfred Street. Most butchers had a yard at the back. For example, Richardsons on Alfred Street. They would kill animals collected from the cattle market and driven through the street half a dozen at a time. This was in the 1930s and 40s. I remember a knacker's yard on Huntingdon Street and on the bottom of Pym Street."

ST ANN'S NOTTINGHAM: inner-city voices *by Ruth I Johns* • ISBN 0951696092

The Coppice Rec sometimes called Ransom Road Recreation Ground, photographed here in 1967 by Wilkinson, Davis and Strickland with houses visible on Ransom Road and Caunton Avenue

And a more recent photo by Peter Garner 2000. He says this was sometimes the venue for the St Ann's Rose Show in years gone by. It was formerly the site of the old Robin Hood Rifles' Shooting Range. The road was then called Coppice Road. The old Rifle Range Lodge on Coppice Road became the Lodge of the Recreation Ground

Public Water

When doing some work about the 1960s, I was challenged when I said how many people still depended on slipper baths and washhouses at that time. My own experience came from St Ann's. Very few people put in bathrooms and other improvements to St Ann's houses in the decade leading up to demolition. So many remained dependent on slipper baths and washhouses. Then the argument was used that St Ann's needed to come down because so many homes lacked amenities.

As stated elsewhere in this book, many homes in St Ann's needed to be replaced, and many could have been modernised into fine homes. It was, in fact, a discussion I had with people at the Housing Corporation in the late 1970s which eventually led to my looking up the facts, given here, about slipper baths and washhouses.

The Slipper Baths on St Ann's Well Road the year they closed 1971. Photo: Peter Garner

SLIPPER BATHS

[also called private baths[1]]

The St Ann's Well Road Slipper Baths, at the bottom of Northampton Street, opened on July 27th 1927 with 16 male and 8 female baths, the discrepancy having much to do with 'dirty' jobs done by many men, e.g. mining before workplace baths were introduced.

In 1946, 35,501 bathers were reported to have used these baths in a year at a cost of nine pence a time and only two pence for old age pensioners and blind persons, this reduction continuing [and becoming 1p after decimalisation] until the Baths were closed. But the actual number of people who had a bath was rather more because adults, who used these baths as children, will speak of two or three siblings using the same bath. Interviewees also spoke of having to wait for a bath on Friday evenings and Saturday mornings.

In 1957, 37,440 users were recorded, which meant each bath was used 1,497.9 times in the year. In the Baths and Parks Committee Annual Report for the year ended March

31st 1971, it was stated that the St Ann's Well Road private baths were closed down on the last day 'of an eventful year' and have since been demolished. It referred to this establishment, known as the cottage bath, having 25 private baths no longer required. However, in its last year (whether to the actual year end or the Baths and Parks Committee year end is not clear) there were 14,262 bathers recorded.

It was a matter of some interest to the Public Baths and Laundries Committee in 1957 and restrained irksomeness in later years that: "Many towns are experiencing a considerable falling off in attendances, but this is not the case in Nottingham (1961)."

In 1961, the Committee announced that it was having the suites at the St Ann's establishment modernised. In 1965, the Committee announced the highest attendances for six years. Their Report for this year states: "It is generally thought throughout the country that attendances of persons for this type of bath are lower than in pre-War days. This is not the case in Nottingham." The possible reasons given were a larger

---

1   The use of the word 'private' now tends to denote private enterprise. These baths were 'private' in the sense of being for personal use. They were always run by Nottingham Corporation.

population (but there were also more houses with baths); the value of cleanliness was greater; there was fuller employment in industry and an influx of immigrants. Whatever the reason, the Committee felt its policy of renovating baths had been justified.

In 1967, the Committee refers to there being: "a tendency in some quarters that this service is barely required . . . but it would appear to be needed for some years yet." By 1970 a drop in numbers at all, except two, private bath establishments in the City was noted, the most significant being at St Ann's (21,159) where: "an extensive redevelopment scheme is being carried out."

The other private baths used by St Ann's people were the Victoria Private Baths, built as 'slipper baths': 20 for males and 10 for females. These were opened on June 15th 1896 (the same day as the Victoria Exhibition and Victoria Small swimming pools). The private baths were modernised in 1959. In the year ending March 31st 1958, the Committee reported 58,762 bathers representing 1,958.7 per bath. In its 1956 Report, the Committee conjectured that the high use of 'private warm baths' in Nottingham might be the number of people attracted to employment and living in rooms or lodgings.

In its 1973 Report, the Committee noted a drop in attendances at the Victoria Private Baths from 29,284 to 22,682. Whereas two years previously the combined attendances of Victoria and St Ann's Well Road Private Baths had been 52,000, there was 'now' a drop of 30,000[2] in that area of the City. This was a 'most welcome sign' and one which the Committee hoped would soon be repeated at the other four Private Bath suites in the City.

It is interesting to note that in the 1960s the services offered at Private Baths increased and included not only hire of towels and soap, but bath cubes and Luma, shampoos, Brylcream, chocolate machines, hairdryers, weighing machines and ironing machines.

VICTORIA WASHHOUSE

In 1946, there was recognition that a washhouse was needed in the centre of St Ann's and from time to time Nottingham City Council Public Baths and Washhouses Committee [later Public Baths and Laundries Committee] referred - for example in its Annual Report of 1959 - to the possible development of a public washhouse adjoining the existing slipper baths in St Ann's Well Road. It never happened. The time was past because, slowly, machine washing was gaining popularity. The time of Launderettes had begun, although much family washing was still done at home by hand and the Victoria Washhouse was still to be much used for more than another decade.

In St Ann's, trips to the Victoria Washhouse on Bath Street were a regular feature of many women's lives from the time this Washhouse was opened on October 25th 1928. And children often helped, sometimes, for example, by taking the washing in a pram or pushchair to the

washhouses where their mother would meet them after she finished work if it saved her a double journey, first home and then to the washhouse.

The Victoria Washhouse had 60 washing stalls. In 1951, the Annual Report of the City of Nottingham Public Baths and Washhouses Committee recorded that 44,461 hand washers used the Victoria Washhouse, representing 125,304 hours of washing in twelve months.

Most families who used these facilities would only go once a week, so these figures give some idea of the importance of these facilities still remembered by older people today.

In 1946 washhouse charges were four old pence an hour with two pence for every additional half-hour or one shilling for use of a washing machine (soap provided). By 1952, the Committee was reporting that the hand washing facilities did not have the 'same attraction' for the housewife as previously because of the advent of machine aids to washing. In 1955, there were 28,507 hand washers, and 27,823 machine users of twelve washing machines newly installed in 1954.

The year before the Committee boasted: "It is now possible for users of washing machines at Victoria Washhouse to leave the building with the weekly washing done, the clothes dried and ironed, at a cost of little more than two shillings and six pence in less than two hours. This time compares most favourably with that submitted to the Government Committee of Enquiry on Air Pollution by the Electrical Association of Women when 7 hours 51 minutes was given as the average time spent by housewives in industrial areas on completion of the family weekly wash."

These facts about washing provide a useful backdrop to the importance in older people's recollections about washing. Stories of boilers, dolly tubs and ponches, for example, are sometimes wrongly treated merely as nostalgic reminiscing. Some interviewees recalled helping their mother do the ponching. It was hard work. Keeping a family clean was a major task. Going to the washhouse

Victoria Washhouse machines 1973. Photo: G L Roberts, Nottingham Local Studies Library

---

[2]   Much of that drop was due to the closure of St Ann's Well Road private baths.

ST ANN'S NOTTINGHAM: inner-city voices *by Ruth I Johns* • ISBN 0951696092

once a week, and dolly and tub for the rest was quite normal for many women. If money was very tight, washing everything at home was the only 'choice'.

And, despite, all the difficulties of home washing, 'taking in washing' from better-off people was a much-practised way of supplementing family income.

If washing was not done well, there might be serious health and other consequences. The generations who endured this necessary discipline sometimes looked askance at later 'scruffy' youngsters (who were, thanks to washing technology, usually also very clean!).

In 1957, the Committee reported that a slot-payment ironing machine at Victoria Washhouse meant: "a queue of patrons is almost continually in being and your Committee has ordered another machine."

1959 being the driest and sunniest year since 1943 adversely affected attendance at washhouses in the year ending March 31st 1960 because clothing could be dried quickly in the open. One of the greatest benefits of public washhouses was stated as being quick drying facilities.

The 1961 Report added that garments made of quick drying synthetic fibres were playing a part in reducing attendances. In 1962, it cost ten pence an hour for hand washing and to use a washing machine cost three shillings (soap included plus two drying racks for one hour). However, by 1963 there was an increase in hand washers: "against all modern thought which for years has been that mechanical washing is taking over from the laborious older-fashioned method of performing the family wash."

But that increase was a blip described in 1964 as perhaps having been due to a hard winter. Both hand washers and machine users reduced although: "the laundries continue to give good service to the gradually decreasing numbers of the community who do not have facilities for washing clothes at home and who are appreciative of the provision." In that year, there were 14,551 hand washers and 13,881 machine users.

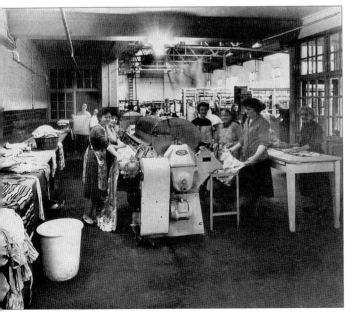

Victoria Washhouse 1973. Photo: Nottingham Corporation, Nottingham Local Studies Library

By 1967, it was clear the Committee wanted the space that would be freed if the washhouse facilities at Victoria were closed, to make way for Turkish, Russian and Sauna baths. In 1968, the financial situation precluded that happening. Things drifted on. By 1969, there were 7,868 hand washers and 12,394 machine users. By 1970, Victoria was one of only two city washhouses that still had washing stalls and in 1972 it was reported that it was impossible to get spare parts for the washing machines installed there in 1954. The machines at another city laundry: "could possibly be kept open a little longer if Victoria closed and usable parts transferred."

With a mixture of seeming pride and also exasperation, the Committee reported: "There can be few Local Authorities in the country that continue to provide such a service." But even in 1972, Victoria Washhouse was used by 3,088 hand washers despite the state of the stalls and by 9,792 machine users. This was the time when the 'old' St Ann's was in its death throes.

VICTORIA POOLS
now VICTORIA LEISURE CENTRE

The Victoria Oval Bath opened on December 16th 1850 and was 100' x 42' in size. The Victoria Exhibition Pool opened on June 15th 1896 and was 110' x 35' and the Victoria Small Pool opened on the same day and was 70' x 30'.

City baths were covered over during the winter for a variety of events, but by 1963 only the Victoria Exhibition Bath was covered seasonally because of the growing demand for all the year swimming including school use. Nottingham City Council Annual Report of its Public Baths and Laundries Committee[1] in 1964 said the Exhibition Hall was used in the winter for meetings, exhibitions, cat and dog shows, wrestling, boxing tournaments and badminton.

The Victoria Baths were not only used by the people of St Ann's and Sneinton, for whom they were easily accessible, but also by those from a wider area. By the mid 1950s, by arrangement with the Education Committee, school children suffering the results of polio attended Victoria Baths for weekly swimming practice as swimming was the only exercise possible for them. As years went by, the use of swimming for people with disabilities developed both in scale and in other city baths.

By 1963, the facility of cheap admissions for old age pensioners at private [formerly known as slipper] baths was extended to swimming baths, though the Committee for that year stated: "Whilst it is not thought likely that great use will be made of this concession, your Committee felt that every encouragement should be given to those pensioners who wish to remain physically active."

For many years Free Passes were issued to promising young swimmers. For example, in the Report for 1963, it

---

[1] In 1961, the Committee changed its title from Public Baths and Washhouses to Public Baths and Laundries thus reflecting the increased use of machines for washing of domestic clothes and household items in place of hand washing at stalls.

Victoria Leisure Centre 2001

Sports Hall 1999

states that 163 passes were issued, 120 of them on the recommendation of the City Schools' Swimming Association (60 boys and 60 girls).

Many people have spoken to me of using these pools but nobody from St Ann's has spoken to me of having this award.

In 1965, the Committee reported a full-scale conversion of a swimming bath water filter at Victoria Baths, thereby increasing the life and efficiency of almost obsolete equipment. In 1968, the Committee name changed to Public Baths and Parks when two committees were amalgamated, and the focus on 'leisure' as a major activity was dawning. In due course, pools became part of Leisure Services responsibility and then Leisure and Community Services.

The Victoria Baths [Pools] on the edge of St Ann's and Sneinton were untouched by demolition of St Ann's. However, the usefulness of Victoria pools held their own as

Fitness Adviser, Richard Francis (left), in discussion with a client in the Fitness Room

Aerobics in the Bedford Room, 1998

Special Event at the Gala Pool 2001
Photos: Victoria Leisure Centre

a growing awareness of keeping fit became recognised. And the pools continued to be used by schools. Huntingdon Primary, Elms Primary and Blue Bell Hill Junior schools in St Ann's now [2001] use the pools as do five schools from Sneinton and beyond.

In 2001, the Exhibition [now called Gala] and Small Pools were in use, the Oval Pool having been covered over to become a Sports Hall. The complex is now called Victoria Leisure Centre. There is a Health Suite, still with Turkish Baths, and sauna and hot rooms. The sports hall use includes trampolining sessions, pre-school gymnastics and movement classes, gymnastics for five to six year olds and for seven to eight year olds, martial arts, 50+, squash, basketball, table tennis, and badminton. There are fitness classes and a fitness suite.

In recent years, people working in the City Centre have increasingly used the Victoria Leisure Centre before work or in their lunch hour. More people now live in the nearby Lace Market district of the City Centre than ten years ago. But the Leisure Centre's value as a local amenity for St Ann's and Sneinton cannot be over-emphasised.

There was angry local reaction to the announcement in 1999 that Victoria and Noel Street (Forest Fields) baths would close.

The City Council plans a flagship £12m swimming centre on the Forest Recreation Ground. John Truscott, Chair of Manvers Labour Party, St Ann's, in a letter to the *Nottingham Evening Post* said St Ann's and Sneinton were the areas with the lowest car ownership in the City and accused the Council of doing a 'bogus' consultation exercise.

Protesters objected to the valued green space of the Forest Recreation Ground being lost for an amenity which most people would need a car to reach at a time when the City was trying to reduce traffic congestion. Councillor Jon Collins, who represents St Ann's, believed the new swimming centre would be popular with the people of St Ann's and Sneinton and pledged local pools would not close until it was built.

In the Press, Clive Wheeler wrote on behalf of regular users of the Victoria Leisure Centre: "We are writing as long-time users of the fitness suite, specifically the sauna and Turkish Bath facilities . . . Some of our number have been using these facilities on a weekly basis for well over twenty years." He said the proposed closure seemed: "in complete contravention of the stated aims of the Council's policy and strategy - the Leisure 2000 Strategy – of providing facilities citywide, district and neighbourhood."

Save the Victoria Baths Campaign Group has found a possible legal life-line in the Nottingham General Inclosure Act 1845. Under the Act, they believe councillors were allowed to use five acres of land for baths and washhouses. The Act states that the land must be for the use of the inhabitants 'for ever'. The campaigners say the City used the Act to build Victoria Baths.

Currently, Victoria Leisure Centre is open 6.30am to 10.30pm and shorter hours at the weekend.

I met Jill Edwards at the Centre in November 2001. Her family has been helping to look after Nottingham's pools and leisure centres for one hundred and seventeen years. Her grandad was once Manager of the Northern Baths, Carrington (recently closed with local protest). Her father was, in turn, Manager of Beechdale, Victoria and Clifton Pools. And she is now Duty Officer at Victoria Leisure Centre.

Faith

What has struck me most when putting together information offered to me about faith communities in St Ann's is their adaptability. The pre-demolition map of St Ann's shows many churches and chapels.

The role of the small 'Tin', 'Iron' or prefabricated building is an interesting one historically. Faith communities often begin in a location with a small basic building. Some return to basic buildings.

One of the most used 'Tin Churches' was the one on the corner of Norland Road and Hungerhill Road, sometimes called a Mission Hall. It served different groups over its lifetime, the last being for St Ann's Church people after their Church was demolished.

We will never know, of course, what would have happened if so many places of worship in St Ann's had not been pulled down at the time of redevelopment. The loss was not only of places of worship, but centres of social service and activity. With the knowledge of hindsight, of course, it is easy to see what other uses might have been made of some of the better buildings if they were no longer needed for their original purpose. Assuming that some buildings needed to be replaced, it was a bad mistake - socially and, in the long term, economically - to do everything at once rather than on an evolutionary basis.

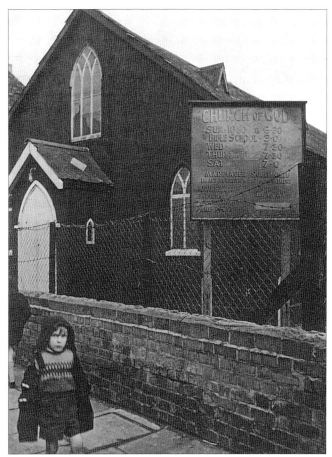

The same Mission Hall 1967. The sign says Church of God. Photo: Wilkinson, Davis and Strickland

Photo c1972 of this Mission Hall, from Margaret Behrman's album, Nottingham Local Studies Library. She remarked: "One of the last places of worship left to serve the dwindling community for a little while longer."

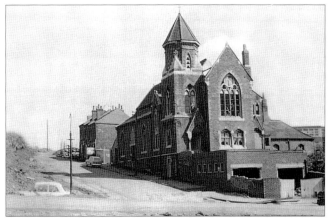

The Chapel at the bottom of Raglan Street just before demolition. Photo: Nicholson Photo Archive

It is easier to break than to build. Photo: Nicholson Photo Archive

There are still knowledge gaps to be filled about some churches or groups. Here are photos of two of the church buildings demolished in St Ann's. Nobody I've met has mentioned these.

1) *Gospel Hall (and/or school?), junction of Liverpool and Salford Streets, demolished 1972. Photo: Reg Baker, Nottingham Local Studies Library*

2) *Morley Memorial Hall (Methodist Church), Blue Bell Hill Road at the top of Pym Street, demolished c1971. Photo: source Mr Thornton, Nottingham Local Studies Library*

Does anyone have a photo of the Campbell Street Methodist Chapel, St Ann's, which was used [1968] as Nottingham's first mosque for a time before the building was demolished? If you can help fill in any gaps over this, or anything else about St Ann's, please write to me at the address on the inside cover.

Several people mentioned attending the 'big' Congregational Church.

Congregational Church looking toward Alfred Street South from Commercial Square, St Ann's Well Road 1971. Photo: G L Roberts, Nottingham Local Studies Library

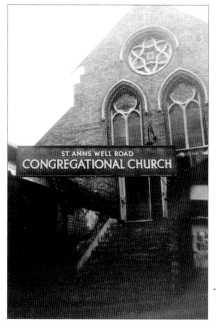

This photo from Ann Reddish shows how the Congregational Church was entered from between the shops. The Church was demolished

St Ann's Nottingham: inner-city voices *by Ruth I Johns* • ISBN 0951696092

The number of people involved in any particular faith community does not necessarily determine the extent of their practical social service to the wider community. All social services provided by church communities in the 'old' St Ann's were self-financing, or supported by better-off people (often from other parts of Nottingham) or sometimes by local and, occasionally, national trusts. Now, of course, funding can include statutory agency support.

There are people in St Ann's who belong to faith communities besides those mentioned in this section. For example, I have talked with Hindus in St Ann's who attend the Temple on Carlton Road, nearby St Ann's.

ST ANN'S CHURCH (demolished 1971) and ST ANN with EMMANUEL

The first Anglican Church to be built, in the area of St Ann's as we know it today, was St Ann's Church in 1864 on the St Ann's Well Road near the entrance to Robin Hood Chase.

When it became possible to purchase land on the former Lammas Land called the Clay Field, plots were gradually purchased where churchmen thought a church or mission room would be needed in a fast growing area.

Prior to the building of St Andrew's Church, St Ann's parish stretched from Carlton Road to Mansfield Road. At the time St Ann's Church was built: "there were no houses in Robin Hood Chase, not a score on the eastern side of St Ann's Well Road, and there was pasture land where Abbotsford Street, Dame Agnes Street, Manning Street, Sycamore Road, Coppice Road [now Ransom Road] and The Wells Road now stand. Brick yards occupied the slopes leading up to Blue Bell Hill and the land between Caroline Street and Woodborough Road." *St Ann's Church Centenary publication 1964.*

While the Church was being built, services were held in a mission room at the bottom of Robin Hood Chase. The Church Schools were built and opened in 1866 and the Vicarage was built on Woodborough Road. The population grew so quickly that St Ann's Vicar, Rev H J Tebbutt soon started to promote the building of St Andrew's Church and he became its first Vicar in 1871.

St Ann's Church, facing down St Ann's Well Road c1969. The prefabricated Church Hall can just be seen behind the Church. Photo: Nottingham Local Studies Library

St Ann's Church had to be enlarged five times during the second Vicar's appointment and the schools, the largest in the City, had seven extensions. The Vicar, Rev J D Lewis, was also Chaplain to the Coppice and Mapperley Hospitals and became an honorary Canon when the new Diocese of Southwell was created in 1884. He remained at St Ann's Church for twenty-nine years until 1900. He died in 1905. The Canon Lewis Memorial Hall in his memory was built on what is now Ransom Road. Rose Hawley said her mother had once recalled how people made collections to pay for the hall which was built 1908/1909. Both Rose and Vernon Hawley[1] were Sunday school teachers in the Memorial Hall in the 1940s and 1950s.

In 1961, a new prefabricated Church Hall was erected in the playground of the demolished St Ann's Church school buildings. The Church had transferred the school buildings, land and the Canon Lewis Memorial Hall on Ransom Road to the Nottingham Co-operative Society in exchange, at no charge, for the new hall capable of seating one hundred people.

---

[1] See Index under Rose Hawley and Vernon Hawley.

Photos, from the Rev Jim Neill, of St Ann's Church inside and outside, facing up St Ann's Well Road

The new hall could not cope with the Church Boys' Brigade Company, the Nottingham 6th, in addition to other demands made on it. The new owners offered to rent the Canon Lewis Memorial Hall to the BB so they could continue using it, with an option to purchase it which they achieved in 1964. The Canon Lewis Memorial Hall first became the 6th Company's HQ in 1940. The Company was founded in 1891. The Lifeboys, the junior branch of the BB, also met in the Canon Lewis Memorial Hall. The BB Company closed in 1998, and the future of the building is currently uncertain. It is for sale [2002]. Few people in St Ann's now associate it with being the Canon Lewis Memorial Hall.

John Irons, Nottingham Boys' Brigade field officer and secretary, has expressed concern about the future of the plaque, which records the death of eleven men in the 1914-18 war, and which is neglected in the building's basement. The plaque was made at a time when the Memorial Hall was used by St Ann's Church Men's Institute.

St Ann's Church also at some time loaned a 'Tin Hut' on Hungerhill Road, St Ann's, for Scouts and Guides and other activities. This was sometimes called the Church Hall, not to be confused with the Church Hall built near the Church in 1961.

At the time of the Church's centenary in 1964, as well as the BB, its youth work included the 25th Nottingham (St Ann's) Girl Guides, led by Mrs S Raven and Miss P Fowles; the Church Brownie pack, the 83rd Nottingham, led by Miss S Deane and Miss J High; the 97th (St Ann's) Scout Troop, led by Gordon Raven the Scouter: and the 97th Wolf Cub

The present staff (from left to right)
Mr. H. Smedley, Mr. A. L. Walker, Rev. H. W. E. Sanders, Mr. G. Gibson, Miss P. B. Harvey, Mr. S. Adams, Rev. L. A. Rawlinson, Mr. G. H. Raynes

This photo is taken from St Ann's Church Centenary publication 1864-1964.

Pack, led by Miss Margaret High. The Adventurers' Club was started in 1964 for girls and boys of seven plus. The aim was to use informal and recreational methods to teach the scriptures. Average attendance was over fifty.

St Ann's Church is mentioned in individual stories. Several people have told me that they still feel distress on behalf of the Vicar of St Ann's Church, Rev L A Rawlinson,

The Canon Lewis Memorial Hall in a dilapidated state. Photo: Ruth I Johns 2000. This is, potentially, a very interesting building and it is sad to see it in such a state

Joan Priestley sent in this photo. It was taken after the last parade of Scouts, Cubs, Guides and Brownies, when they marched around the streets, before the Church was demolished

St Ann's Nottingham: Inner-city voices by Ruth I Johns • ISBN 0951696092

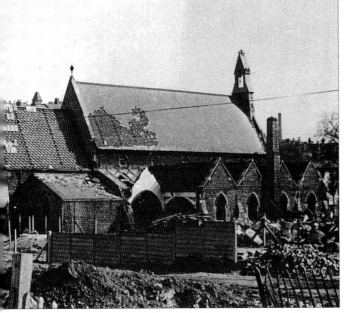

St Ann's Church being demolished 1971. Source: Margaret Behrman's album, Nottingham Local Studies Library

View of the tower as you approach the Chase Precinct from the car park. Photo: Ruth I Johns 2001

at the time leading up to demolition of the church (1971). With the new Church Hall next to the Church and a very active congregation, many people felt his positive work in St Ann's had been betrayed. He left in 1968. He later visited the new St Ann with Emmanuel Church several times.

During 1957, the Vicarage on Woodborough Road was taken over by the Vicar of Emmanuel Church and St Ann's Church Vicarage became 17, Robin Hood Chase, once home of the Hopewell family, which had long associations with the Church. This house is now the Vicarage for St Ann with Emmanuel. After demolition of St Ann's Church and its daughter Church, Emmanuel, a year later, the two Churches combined as St Ann with Emmanuel on Robin Hood Chase one side of the Precinct.

The Vicarage on Woodborough Road was demolished, though considerable improvements had been done including turning part of it into a separate maisonette. It was an interesting, sturdy, building.

After St Ann's Church and its hall were demolished, their Scouts, Guides and Rangers moved to a hut which was built for them on Ransom Road.

Between the time of St Ann's Church demolition and the opening of the new St Ann with Emmanuel Church on

April 6th 1974, St Ann's Church congregation worshipped and held their activities at the St Ann's Well Infant School on Hungerhill Road, St Ann's. The Rev Roy Williamson was the first Vicar of the new Church and was appointed before it was built.

At the tenth anniversary [1984] of the new Church, the Rev Jim Neill remarked: "This is the most concentrated parish of elderly people in Europe. So the stories of elderly people not liking change is a myth."

Partly because of the Residential Homes in the area, there are many funerals at St Ann with Emmanuel. Below is a list, from the Parish Magazine, of funerals at the Church in August and September 1999

St Ann with Emmanuel Church has a 50ft tower with a large white fibreglass cross facing the Chase Precinct and another facing the playing fields behind. The crosses are illuminated at night. Photo: E James Smalley 2000

PARISH REGISTERS

BAPTISM:
SEPTEMBER 26th   **AURELIE ELIZABETH CARRINGTON**

WEDDING:
SEPTEMBER 18th   **RORY TYRONE PITTER** and **CATHERINE CLAIRE LYNCH**

FUNERALS:

AUGUST 19th	**BARRIE WHITCHURCH** *Aged 59 years*
AUGUST 20th	**SIDNEY PARKES** *Aged 63 years*
AUGUST 23rd	**BARRIE FOSTER STURMAN** *Aged 49 years*
AUGUST 23rd	**PATRICIA MARY SNOOK** *Aged 61 years*
AUGUST 27th	**CYRIL ORME** *Aged 87 years*
AUGUST 27th	**JOHN HENRY COOK NUGENT** *Aged 81 years*
SEPTEMBER 2nd	**VIOLET WARREN** *Aged 84 years*
SEPTEMBER 3rd	**ANNIE TOWLE** *Aged 88 years*
SEPTEMBER 3rd	**JOHN HENRY WORTHINGTON** *Aged 87 years*
SEPTEMBER 6th	**JOHN FOSTER** *Aged 74 years*
SEPTEMBER 6th	**DORA DUFFTY** *Aged 80 years*
SEPTEMBER 6th	**CYRIL WESTBURY** *Aged 90 years*
SEPTEMBER 7th	**CHARLES ALFRED BERRY** *Aged 76 years*
SEPTEMBER 7th	**LAVINIA FIDLER** *Aged 89 years*
SEPTEMBER 7th	**WINIFRED HOULT** *Aged 89 years*
SEPTEMBER 8th	**VERA WINIFRED HARROP** *Aged 87 years*
SEPTEMBER 9th	**LINDA JEAN SHAW** *Aged 54 years*
SEPTEMBER 9th	**ETHEL MAY AUSTIN** *Aged 57 years*
SEPTEMBER 9th	**FLORENCE GRIMMER** *Aged 78 years*
SEPTEMBER 9th	**ELIZABETH ROSE SALMONS** *Aged 64 years*
SEPTEMBER 10th	**LILY CARTWRIGHT DEXTER** *Aged 79 years*
SEPTEMBER 13th	**JOHN SHEPHERD VINE** *Aged 86 years*
SEPTEMBER 14th	**DAISY BEATRICE HANNON** *Aged 79 years*
SEPTEMBER 14th	**PAUL CHRISTOPHER PAYNE** *Aged 41 years*
SEPTEMBER 15th	**FREDERICK GEORGE WESTCOTT** *Aged 77 years*
SEPTEMBER 17th	**MURIEL NORAH McKENNA** *Aged 74 years*
SEPTEMBER 17th	**EDNA FELTHAM** *Aged 79 years*

We gratefully acknowledge the legacy of £500 left to the Church by the late Ellen "Nellie" Danvers who used to come regularly to the Sunday Evening Service from Fountaindale Court.

REV JIM NEILL

Born 1941

*Interviewed in the Vicarage of **St Ann with Emmanuel Church**, St Ann's 28.9.99.*

St Ann with Emmanuel Church was built to replace two of the three Anglican Churches which were demolished when St Ann's was redeveloped: St Ann's Church on St Ann's Well Road and Emmanuel Church on the Woodborough Road

Rev Jim Neill

I came as Vicar to St Ann with Emmanuel Church in Robin Hood Chase early in 1977. I came excited about the prospect and I still am after all this time. I love the area, I love the people and I am as happy here as I was the first day.

The Church was built and it opened in 1974, so I followed the man who had seen the job through. I can always remember on my first night as I went around the congregation, people telling me: 'I'm old Emmanuel' or: 'I'm old St Ann's.' It was a kind of rivalry still lingering, and they wanted to make sure I knew which they belonged to as it were. But that sort of thing went quite quickly fortunately. And I've always insisted that although we are in the District of St Ann's, we are St Ann with Emmanuel, not one or the other.

There were five Anglican Churches. There was St Catharine's Church which is still standing with about half a dozen who go to one service a week, there was St Matthias which still stands and has probably the smallest congregation in the Diocese. There was St Bartholomew's that came down and the whole name has been lost, and many people still talk about it with love and affection. We do have people who were brought up there.

I came from a church family. Both my grandads were Vicars, my father was a Vicar, I had two uncles who were Vicars. I was one of five children and the only one to carry on the clerical profession. The others are involved in

church life. I started off my ordained ministry in the beautiful town of Kendal in the Lake District. A very live church with a large congregation and youth work four nights a week. At the end of three and a half years I wanted something completely different. So I went to Sheffield. It was Park Hill flats, which are quite infamous today. They were built after the War to solve social problems and they created a lot more. There was no church building. I inherited a congregation of about six and I built it up in the Bingo Hall. I enjoyed it there.

After three years, I was offered a church which had a vicarage and a school in St John's Street in the centre of Mansfield. As soon as I got there, plans were put before the Pastoral Committee to close it and I said: 'Over my dead body. I've come from a place where we had to worship in a Bingo Hall and they promised me a church if I built up the congregation. I did that but still no church. I come here into this Victorian Church holding a thousand and then after three months they want to close it.' But we fought for its survival and it's still very active. I was there six years.

I was offered about six parishes in about eighteen months and I turned them down one by one, partly because I was frightened that St John's would be swallowed up and I didn't want the church to close. I inherited it with a gap of two and a half years without a Vicar. I was convinced that was the place for me. When I turned down the last offer I thought that's cooked my books and chances, but a few months later St Ann with Emmanuel was offered and it felt right.

My predecessor, Roy Williamson, who is now a retired Bishop, did a wonderful job of marrying the two congregations together, which is a brave thing to do in church life especially in those years. You had all sorts in the congregation, Roman Catholics, Chapel people, Anglicans middle, high and evangelical and they all live happily together today.

Originally, a lot of the congregation came from outside the area because the congregation had been scattered due to demolition. They had to travel in to church. At that time, that would include most of the church officers. Then it swung very much the other way and now it's about half and half. There's slightly more maybe from just outside the parish but very near. About half of the congregation walks to church. The majority of the congregation that I inherited has died, sadly.

There are about one hundred and twenty-five people on the electoral roll of the church. An ex-colleague came back only on Sunday and said the church looks in good heart. It's lovingly cared for. He was impressed by the Choir, by the worship and the state of happiness of the people worshipping together.

We have Sunday schools. They are smaller than they used to be. One of the problems of this area is youth work. When I got here there was a lot going for the under elevens, little for the over elevens and the congregation I inherited was 55% or more pensioners. So there was a dearth of teenagers, young marrieds and that is still true today. We still have church families and young people coming.

ST ANN'S NOTTINGHAM: inner-city voices *by Ruth I Johns* • ISBN 0951696092

The Boys' Brigade folded up, the Scouts are just about surviving but this is the day in which we live. There is very little in St Ann's for young people. There's a crying need for it, but we live in a different generation than when I was brought up and the church was our life. It supplied everything for us. It was also people's social life. But now there are computers and videos and entertainment is sophisticated, we can't keep pace.

We have a very good mid-week course at present, the Emmaus course. We've averaged thirty to forty every Wednesday night for the past two years. It brought in adult and young people who came at the beginning and who are still coming. It started as a confirmation class. We looked at Alpha, the popular course internationally, but we decided we would rather do the Emmaus course that was written by John Finney, a retired Bishop back in this Diocese.

We've got Brownies, Guides, a very good Choir, we've had line dancing, a women's group which is devotional but this afternoon they've been preparing stuff for the Harvest meal tomorrow.

Every month, I run a bereavement service for all those who have been bereaved that month. When people come to a service like that, they meet people they were at school with and they still remember their face and their voice. The atmosphere before and after the service has been incredible. So there is something of that spirit and unity of St Ann's that lives on. I occasionally do a bereavement visit in, say, Bestwood Park if that's where the relatives are. But the people will say to me: 'We were brought up in St Ann's, and they will name the old street. Or, if I do an out of Parish funeral, people can get excited at having someone from the area in which they were brought up. Their heart is still very much in their roots here.

I visited a young woman, who used to come to our church when her father died. I told her I knew her dad because I tried to help him when his marriage broke up when she was a toddler. I spoke to her about this bereavement, and she said nobody had spoken to her after her dad died about the need for care and follow-up. She was pleased we were still there for her if she wanted it.

The bereavement service is chiefly for those for whom we've been responsible to take the service. We give them a date of the service when we go and see them about the funeral, and a little leaflet, a card with a prayer in times of bereavement. We say we do hold this service at the end of the month, and we call out the name of your family member who has died and pray with you and for you in that service. Most months, and we've been doing this for twenty-one years, we have someone at that service because it is a bereavement service.

And some come month after month because it's that service that first brought them here. One month can be packed, another have a very few people. Sometimes families come, sometimes two of a family, anyone can come. If it's Christmas time, we will always include them in our carol service. At other times we use it as an opportunity especially to pray for the bereaved and give a service, which is easy to follow and we hope helpful to enable them to carry on.

When I first came here I couldn't get over the number of funerals that I had. The majority in those days went up to Wilford Hill Crematorium. Now more people will come into church.

The problems in St Ann's? Boredom, unemployment, single parents and most of the crime which is to do with the theft of cars and with drugs.

The good things? Just the people. I think it is a lovely estate. People call it and I ask them: 'Have you been down Abbotsford Drive recently or up St Ann's Well Road?' It's just beautiful if you've got eyes to look. The houses are smart, some of the gardens are beautiful, some of the trees . . . I love the fact that I can walk from my house into the City Centre in five to seven minutes and cross only one main road. To me that is tremendous. But I do get cross when I go to the other end of the Parish just a mile up The Wells Road and you can't sell a house and put St Ann's. You have to put Mapperley and it's not Mapperley. It's St Ann's. I'm proud to be here.

Recently, I challenged a young couple who got married and moved out of St Ann's. I asked them: 'Why don't you move back in?' They did, they took up that challenge. Alas, sadly he died very young but I remember them taking up that challenge. I don't think people realise sometimes how good it is to be central.

MARTIN DAVY

Trainee organist **St Ann with Emmanuel Church**

Martin Davy

I have always attended St Ann with Emmanuel Church. Since the age of six or seven, I have been playing musical instruments from the recorder, tenor recorder, keyboard and then piano. I did not start playing the organ until I was made trainee organist at St Ann with Emmanuel in 1997. I started having lessons. Shortly after, I also went back to the piano because I wanted to improve further. When I play at Church, I use both the organ and piano.

I play regularly once a month for an evening service and at other times when I am required. I am currently studying for A-Levels at Nottingham Bluecoat School and will be leaving soon to go to University to study Law. *2000*

St ANDREW'S CHURCH

Canon H J Tebbutt, who was first Vicar of St Ann's Church on the St Ann's Well Road, was responsible for building St Andrew's Church, Vicarage, schools and Parish Room. In 1903, St Andrew's Church Magazine said: "It is difficult to over-estimate the value of such a collection of buildings." St Andrew's Church opened in 1871. It was built on a site where once gallows stood, at the corner of what is now Mapperley Road and Mansfield Road. It is on the edge of St Ann's but has been closely associated with it; as it is now.

The Parish magazine started in 1903, replacing Parish Notes. The Magazine gives a comprehensive account of church activities. Copies of some of them are held by the current Vicar, the Rev Richard Clark. It is interesting to get a sense of the important part St Andrew's played in the life of St Ann's. For instance, we learn that 'Daddy Shaw' commenced a children's service in the schoolroom on Bangor Street, St Ann's around 1870. In the Parish Magazine, we learn there was a regular Children's Sunday Evening Service in the school buildings, with an average attendance of two hundred.

A Sunday Morning Children's Service was also held for many years in the Church's Mission Room in Bullivant Street, St Ann's. This Mission Hall in the heart of St Ann's was well used.

The Boys' Sunday school was attended by 260 boys in 1900 with eighteen teachers. In 1904, there were 143 girls on the books of the Girls' Sunday school with eleven teachers.

In 1902 there were 248 men on the Men's Institute Register with activities including billiards, football, cycling, swimming, and much more.

St Andrew's started the 1st Nottingham Company of the Boys' Brigade in 1888. The November 1903 Parish Magazine states that forty to fifty lads went on annual camp each year; that year to Thoresby Hall. The Company started an Ambulance Class, which was receiving instruction from Dr Rowe who: "was kind enough to find time." At Whitsun 1904, the boys camped at Welbeck Abbey at the invitation of the Duke of Portland.

There was an active Girls' Friendly Society and Band of Hope. Nearly 100 girls' names were registered with the Band of Hope and 50 boys'. The Magazine states: "In addition to the ordinary programme of addresses and recitations, we hope this session to have some lessons on drink and its relation to crime, as well as lectures on the effects of excessive use of alcohol on the human body." Dr G A Ferraby was to give a lecture on 'Alcohol on the Brain.'

I was interested to find in the April 1904 Parish Magazine a story about a Nottingham lady who took her 'little girl' to a football match. In this issue there was also a lament that for each voluntary worker: "there are ninety-nine people who are content to sit and watch and wait, whilst golden opportunities of doing good drift by to the Land of Might-Have-Beens." I have found such remarks, in changing speech forms, in documents shown me from various sources and from dates throughout the Twentieth

Century! A salutary reminder that human nature is constant!

A 1904 letter to the Parish Magazine Editor (William E Radford for many years) stated that more people didn't go to church: "Because of the apathy, indifference and indolence of the majority of people, and also because of the growing tendency for Sunday pleasures; the taste for sensationalism, and the engrossing cares of commercial and social life." Sounds very contemporary?

In 1904 it was reported that a burglar had robbed St Andrew's Church of the contents of the Poor Box and other items and: "I understand that St Catharine's [St Ann's] was also burglariously entered a few days ago and from all appearances it looks as if there is a gang going round engaged on this particular class of shady work."

There may still be people who remember the special series of Organ Recitals for which St Andrew's was noted.

Taking a huge step forward to 1945, in the publication of St Andrew's Church to celebrate victory, people were reminded that seventy-four years before, there were a couple of houses in the new Mapperley Road and along Red Lane. But a few thousand very poor folk lived in the area behind Cranmer Street [now the Phase 10 area of St Ann's]. There were no rich folk to give large sums. There was no parochial organisation. "Yet, these folk, the fathers and grandfathers of many of our present worshippers, were not dismayed." In a few years they had raised £12,000 out of wages of just 'a few shillings a week'. Pew rents were introduced to pay the Vicar's stipend.

Over time, more houses were built for better-off people and: "the feeling between the folk at the bottom of the hill [St Ann's] and up the hill had started." By 1945: "The folk at the bottom of the hill are starting once again to come up the hill, the old feeling of estrangement is rapidly vanishing."

During the Second World War the BBC reckoned about 100,000,000 listeners had heard services from St Andrew's and the church was used 'by thousands of men' in the Forces before setting off abroad. *Light from Gallows Hill*. St Andrew's Church. 1945.

ATS Girls on Church Parade at St Andrew's Church during the War

St Ann's Nottingham. Inner-City Voices by Ruth Johns • ISBN 0951696092

Troops attending service at St Andrew's Church before being posted overseas

Demolition of St Ann's some twenty-five years later meant a brutal severance of contact between St Andrew's and 'the folk down the hill'. However, Phase 10 people in the 'new' St Ann's have struggled hard for their community and the current Vicar of St Andrew's, the Rev Richard Clark, is rebuilding strong links between his Church and St Ann's.

REV RICHARD CLARK

Born 1960

*Interviewed in the Vicarage of **St Andrew's Church** 5.7.00. The Vicarage is on Chestnut Grove and the Church on the corner of Mansfield Road and Mapperley Road*

St Andrew's Church is on the edge of St Ann's and has been closely bound up with St Ann's history. In the latter 1860s, another church was needed on the north side of St Ann's to deal with the increasing population of St Ann's. The Vicar of St Ann's Church on the St Ann's Well Road, Rev H J Tebbutt, decided to create St Andrew's Church on its present site. It had a parish population in those days of seven thousand, which reflects how densely people were packed into terraced houses in the parish area. Rev Tebbutt was so enthusiastic about the project that he moved and became St Andrew's first Vicar [1871].

Rev Tebbutt's vision for the Church was that it would be a blend of rich and poor. Some original houses in the area belonged to very rich people. The house opposite the Vicarage was designed for a former Lord Mayor. The bottom end of the Parish (now the Phase 10 area of St Ann's) was dominated by Alfred Street. There was a collection of buildings to serve the area, including the Boys' Brigade Hall on Alfred Street North, and a Mission Hall on Bullivant Street. There was the St Andrew's Institute, which probably occupied part of the Boys' Brigade Hall.

The people from the top of the hill who were well-off paid pew rents at St Andrew's Church. They would go down to the bottom part of the Parish on Sunday afternoons and be involved in Christian activities. That was the way Rev Tebbutt set it up. He also set it up as a Missionary Church, which is why it is called St Andrew's (nothing to do with Scotland). It ran like Rev Tebbutt planned it until between the wars. Then from the time of about the fourth Vicar, it became a very, very posh Church taking people from a wide area who came particularly for the beautiful organ music and choir music. It also had the barrier for poor people that there were pew rents, which went toward the stipend of the Vicar right up until 1967.

So, in those days you would typically be met at the door by a Church Warden in a morning coat and he would show you to your seat. Ten minutes before the service was due to start, the bell would be rung. The church was designed to have eight bells but it has only got one because money ran out when building the Church, which is why the spire is too short for the tower. And the tower, therefore, is built in a weak way and can only support one bell. So they'd ring the bell and, if you had your seat booked under the pew rent system, you had to fill it in the next five minutes otherwise it could be made available to anyone.

The spire of St Andrew's Church.
Photo: Nikola Voce 2002

A small addition was built at the back of the Church about ten years after it was consecrated in 1871. The addition was for poor people's pews. Later when they took out the original pews of the Church, the pews in that added area were found to be worthless and poor quality, whereas those in the main body of the nave were oak.

A Children's Service was held in the middle of Sunday afternoon and an eight o'clock Holy Communion Service. Today, older people who like the Book of Common Prayer and who get up early mainly inhabit this early Service. But in those earlier times, it was something of a pioneering Service available to servants, because servants couldn't go to the main morning service because they were getting dinner ready for their employers. The early Service was pioneered as a way of reaching poorer people. That's basically the way St Andrew's was up until the time of redevelopment except for the fact that St Andrew's Church School had been lost.

The other feature of St Andrew's was that John Dayne Player, one of the sons of John Player and Sons, propped the Church up financially for a long time. His wife was a patron of the Children's Hospital at the bottom end of Chestnut Drive and she would visit daily in days before the National Health Service.

The Institute movement provided masculine activities to keep men out of drinking houses so it was fundamentally teetotal. A men's golf club came out of that and it was later passed on to the YMCA. Later it passed to the members and it became Mapperley Golf Club. The Church had a sporty curate who went on to be Vicar of Emmanuel Church on Woodborough Road, St Ann's, and he started the Magdala Lawn Tennis Club.

St Andrew's was always active in the community and between the wars ran workshops for the unemployed, and had a projection hall for showing movies. It had its own amateur dramatic group up to the 1960s.

St Andrew's was fond of medical mission work and at one time employed a Parish nurse to tend to the needs of members of the Parish. It also pioneered what is still a practice of the Mothers' Union to send poor people on holiday. It did that from the end of the Nineteenth Century.

What happened at the time of redevelopment was that the old community boundaries were broken down. Phase 10 was the last phase of demolition and that was the part of St Ann's in St Andrew's Parish. When Phase 10 was put back together again it wasn't based on the people who were living there before. They put in everybody who hadn't answered letters or were rootless, so any concept of the original Alfred Street North community was out of the window.

Redevelopment of Phase 10 had a bad effect on the Choir which had drawn its junior members from the Alfred Street North area and that community contact was broken.

The former Church building in the remnant of Alfred Street North. Over the left-hand door it says Parish Hall and over the right-hand one Boys' Brigade. Behind (left) is one of the few remaining large factory buildings in St Ann's. It is on St Ann's Hill Road. Photo: E James Smalley 2000

St Andrew's had the first ever Nottingham Boys' Brigade Company. And that was a very big thing in the Church up till the time of redevelopment of St Ann's. There was a major decline in the St Andrew's Company and it closed down in 1995[1].

In 1992, the Parish Hall, which was also the Boys' Brigade Hall, in Alfred Street North was sold to the Council for £1,000. The building wasn't actually owned by the Church but by Trustees who were basically Boys' Brigade people. There was an attempt at one time to use it for business workshops but there were not the right sort of Government Schemes then. Recent work has improved the Hall to a much better standard and it is used mainly by a dance school at present.

The Trustees are still able to dispense money for some Church activities particularly those to do with youth. It is currently giving a grant toward a part-time worker.

A Church Hall, which is now St Andrew's Community Hall, was built at the side of the Vicarage on Chestnut Grove around 1938 to replace a former building. It was designed more as a meeting room with beautiful wood panelling and a wood parquet floor. In the Second World War soldiers were billeted in the old Roller Skating Rink which is now Neales Auction Rooms [at the corner of Villa Road and Mansfield Road] and the officers were billeted in the Church Hall. They left it in fairly poor condition and it was later renovated.

It is one of the challenges for this Church that people don't see themselves as living in a community area, a single community area. Mapperley Park as an address has gradually moved up as far as Mapperley Road and Mapperley Park people don't think in terms of community areas. Mapperley Park is divided between three parishes, St Andrew's, St John's [Carrington], and St Jude's. The St Ann's side of the Parish used to have the Mission Hall on Bullivant Street and the Boys' Brigade Hall. Both have been lost.

The St Ann's part of the Parish includes a massive collection of flats on the hill running down from Cranmer Street, known mainly as Cheverton Court, which has an amazing sloping roof usually known as the 'ski slopes'. At the bottom, there is Marple Square which is a shopping precinct theoretically. All but one of the shops have closed. Nottingham City Council has conceded in recent years that the shops are unlettable so they have turned the former housing office over to Phase 10 Action Group and residents, and established a new housing office in the precinct.

There is a wholesale baker in one corner but almost none of the industrial units under the residential units are used. The nine to five time restrictions on use are not suited to running businesses. A lot of the housing stock is run down and there are no facilities for children over eleven. The playground area is on a slope so it's difficult to establish adequate play areas. A lot of the open grass area isn't fit for any activity. There are discussions in progress about how the area can be redeveloped.

1   At the time of the centenary of the 1st Nottingham (St Andrew's) Company in 1988, there were only fifteen boys and eleven officers, including Hindus, Pakistanis and Chinese. The influx of people with different faiths from Christianity led to a more flexible membership. A parade was organised through St Ann's and a specially designed commemorative flower-bed designed in the Arboretum Park during the summer. Nottingham Evening Post

St Ann's Nottingham: inner city voices by Ruth I Johns • ISBN 0951696092

Other than Mr Hussain's shop, there is no shop or Post Office; for example, nowhere where you can buy vegetables. The nearest supermarket is in Victoria Centre. Again, local action is trying to seek solutions. One of the two pubs in the area closed, the Craven Arms. The police objected to the renewing of the licence. It was pulled down. Kwik Save opened on that site and soon closed. Now the building is part of Hawk's Cycles. The other pub is an Irish pub.

It doesn't appear to be a very settled community. Cheverton Court is almost entirely single person units. There are a lot of people in the area who move in and out of this part of St Ann's. The solid part of the community is women with children. There are people who have lived in the area for a long time. But there are no people who were born and grew up there, who have any sense of cultural heritage as a result of being in that area.

There is a substantial Jamaican community, which relates to the Jamaican community across the City. If there is a Jamaican funeral at St Andrew's, there can be four or five hundred people attending. There is a network. If I do a white funeral, there may be only thirty people present. There are several smaller minority groups and there is a Pakistani Centre in the parish, but there are not many Pakistani people living in the area.

The old Ukaidi Centre in Marple Square is to become one centre for the Sure Start Programme in St Ann's. The International Community Centre on Mansfield Road is being managed by the YMCA on a ten year lease but doesn't have any outreach into St Ann's Phase 10.

I was born in Nottingham and have been here as Vicar for over eight years now. In my last year studying Law at Cambridge University, I decided to go into the Ministry and left. I did a year at Chester Law College subsequently whilst going through the process of selection for the Ministry. Then I did a year at London City Missions in dockland and learnt a lot about inner-city Ministry. When I was working in London, my patch for six months had sixteen tower blocks. I wasn't planning on coming back to Nottingham but when this post became available, it fitted in many ways. I see myself staying here.

This Church is known locally as the Church with the notice board, because that is what people see when they travel around this area. The parish at present is not a community area. About seventy per cent of accommodation is flats and bed-sits and about one-sixth of the population move every year. There are very few family homes, so when

Rev Richard Clark 2002.
Photo: Nikola Voce

people look for a family home they move away but may still keep coming to this Church. Others come because they see the Church and come from places like Foxhall Road and Waterloo Crescent. Sunday morning attendance averages around seventy-five people including around seventeen children. We did Harvest and Carol Services for St Ann's Phase 10.

It's a very unusual Parish with every sort of social situation except rural. There will be eight to twelve nationalities at Sunday Services. At present I think we have the youngest Parochial Church Council in the Diocese. We see the Church being very much as a training situation in many ways. It's a Church with a future. There was a stage when the choir was running down and everybody was getting older and it looked as though it would be the last person who hadn't died locked up!

When Rev Ron Lacey died, the Bishop suspended the patronage [1983] and put in somebody who would modernise extensively. He obviously put some backs up and some people left for other churches. But it saved this Church. There are inner-city churches that will close in the next twenty years because of non-viability and St Matthias [Carlton Road side of St Ann's] could close within five years.

Things which St Andrew's is doing at present include a partnership with Youth with a Mission praying on Forest Road and Mapperley Road at night. The police told the prostitutes what was happening. They didn't feel anyone was out to get them. We just asked if there was anything they would like us to pray for on their behalf. We've had responses like: 'pray for my children.'

St Andrew's is in partnership with the Cherish Fund which is active in the Phase 10 area. We have coffee mornings which anyone can go to. Irene Moses, a Malawian woman and nurse, runs the Cherish Club and is at the coffee mornings on Tuesdays. Then there's activities for children organised by Kirsten Rosslyn-Smith who is a prospective ordinand from St Andrew's and a graduate from Trent University. Her husband teaches in prisons. Kirsten assisted Su Townsend from Phase 10 Action Group in taking children on holiday to Derbyshire. I went up there too some of the time. Water was dripping through the ceiling and it was a riot but the kids loved it. Everything was an event, cows walking down the lane, cows being milked. Walking down the Tissington Trail, I was chatting to one of the kids and asked if he had been on anything like this before. He asked what I meant and I said: 'In the country.' Oh, yes, he said, once on a primary school trip.

We've tried to assist by putting in other volunteers. It took a long time after the Phase 10 Action Group got cracking before the Council put in any personnel resources. The youth work was operating for a long time with untrained volunteers alone. Opportunity knocks for Phase 10 at present with the proposed improvements to the housing.

I'm about to start doing evening classes lecturing at the New Testament Assembly Church, at King's Hall, on St Ann's Well Road, for people who want to work toward a Certificate of Theology. I'm having lunch with Pastor Joan Richards from there on Friday. The Course is University of Wales accredited. It means people can demonstrate an ability to reach a certain academic standard. I believe one of the issues around social exclusion is providing quality education. There was an awful situation in the Meadows recently where there was community computer training, but people were training to use a software programme that was already obsolete.

At the YMCA at the moment there is a young man from Phase 10 who in his late twenties thought: 'Wait a minute, I haven't got a single qualification. I've got to start again.' He's now doing an Access Course at New College. He's studying Community Sport and he is very good which is why he's got the placement at the YMCA. But, with the right start, he could have been doing that ten years ago.

We're now looking more toward community sport because only the best-behaved kids now would be going to youth clubs. It's interesting to look at the boarding school model. Boarding school kids are kept civilised by having a high level of activity while they are there. There are a vast number of activities on tap, which is why boarding school kids are friendly and good at sport. That seems to me to be a correct model for any teenager.

We're looking at basketball coaching. There aren't enough Phase 10 kids for an age-group soccer team, but they want a team. So what we need to do is to line them up with a similarly small group elsewhere, because the League structure doesn't take into account these sort of community areas. Last summer, Phase 10 Action Group through Su Townsend got some community sport going on the Huntingdon School playing field. They got forty kids over there on the football pitch. They just needed the opportunity.

Another big issue for the inner-city is to have facilities that are economically viable for the participants. I really hate the idea of the proposed fun pool at the bottom of the Forest. It would be totally divisive. The people who used it would come from outside the ring road. It will be expensive to use. It won't be suitable for the local community, and it's more inner-city space that won't be available for inner-city people anymore.

If there was a suitable site in St Ann's (like Huntingdon School playing fields) and it had Astro turf, there could be a community sports programme eighteen hours a day, seven days a week. Crime would be cut that way. Last summer when we stopped the summer youth programme, petty crime went up.

I think it's fair to say that it doesn't take very many people for an area to get a reputation. For example, if you get a few people with guns who have a go at each other, Radford, Meadows, St Ann's, Bulwell, whatever on a fairly small scale, every single incident is a big incident. It therefore infects the attitude for the whole area.

I would like to tell people in fifty years time that 1999 was a turning point for Phase 10 area. Because that's when the Council agreed to put in capital funding into the area and when the residents got a centre at 8, Marple Square. My fear is the thing, which the City Council's Social Exclusion Unit has recognised, that changing the physical environment will not in itself create community. Phase 10 area will probably have to remain because of the way the streets were planned at the 1970s redevelopment when the

artery of Alfred Street was lost. It used to run right across St Ann's. The Council hate cutting across anything! All roads and bus routes go into town. But Phase 10 has the potential to become an urban village. It's the right size, it's got focal points and it's a question of making them what they should be.

People in St Ann's are very experience orientated. They are into the visual rather than the written. With the coming redevelopment, it's no good showing a plan, but you've got to show them something and then ask what they think about it. That has been a difficult barrier to get through to the Housing Department people, because they are used to working in terms of meetings. They are in a different world to the residents.

One day a colleague and I were looking at a similar development to Phase 10 where houses had the back garden at the front. I asked what kind of person would design a house like that. And he said: 'Someone who doesn't have to live in it.' Somewhere like Cheverton Court, which I mentioned earlier, would be regarded as wonderful, Mediterranean Italianate, if it was in Chelsea or Kensington and people would pay vast sums of money to live there. But, in St Ann's, people's economic situation and their personal difficulties affect the area.

I'm married to Sue and we have a son who is fourteen. Sue is Church Treasurer, which she has been doing voluntarily for five and a half years. It's a characteristic of an inner-city church that you don't have formal skills: there isn't an accountant in our congregation, or a solicitor. There is one teacher. The presumption that the Church of England is full of professional people doesn't stick in this sort of environment. We went through a period where we didn't have a Parochial Church Council secretary for two years.

People come to the door a great deal. We try to provide services and not money and food: not food because we got the idea that people were coming for food and then spending money on something else. For example, I gave somebody a lift to an endoscopy appointment the other day. Highwood House, the Homeless Families Unit, is near us. It's a minefield trying to provide effective care for people and, you're right, it is a distinctive factor about Church of England Ministry that you are living where you work.

War Memorial

A War Memorial in St Andrew's Church includes the names of many men from the Alfred Street North and Alfred Street Central areas of St Ann's. The Rev Richard Clark has been researching their fate. One hundred and eighty-eight people of the parish died or perished in the 1st World War and around two dozen in the 2nd World War.

He says: "The most cataclysmic day for the City in the 1st World War was undoubtedly July 1st 1916, the first day of the Battle of the Somme. As part of the 46th North Midlands Division, the 7th Battalion of the Sherwood Foresters (known as the Robin Hoods) launched a diversionary attack in an area, known as Gomme-Court, to the north of the main Somme battle. But the attack was

ST ANN'S NOTTINGHAM: inner city voices *by Ruth I Johns* • ISBN 0951696092

The War Memorial in St Andrew's Church. Photo: E James Smalley 2001

The Iron Church purchased in 1879

expected and achieved little. But the Battalion suffered 662 casualties, not all from Nottingham, as people from other parts of the country - especially Scotland - liked the idea of serving with the Robin Hoods. Nottingham lost more men on that day than any other day in the War.

"After the War, two war memorials were constructed in the Parish. The main memorial stands in the specially constructed memorial chapel in St Andrew's Church. The second memorial, in bronze, was placed in the St Andrew's Institute in St Ann's and unveiled by Colonel Brewill on November 20th 1922. I have been unable to ascertain whether this memorial still exists."

Does anyone have any more information?

EMMANUEL CHURCH

Emmanuel was a Watson Fothergill designed church on the Woodborough Road below St Augustine's Roman Catholic Church of a later date. Emmanuel Church was demolished in 1972

The development of this Church was owed to the efforts of members of the newly formed Nottingham Church Extension Society. Its inaugural meeting at St Andrew's Vicarage in 1877 included the indomitable Rev Henry Jemson Tebbutt who was first Vicar of St Ann's Church before launching St Andrew's where he moved to be its first Vicar. And here he was - with others - proposing new churches.

Eventually the land on which Emmanuel Church stood was purchased and vested in the Ecclesiastical Commissioners. More land between Woodborough Road and Westville Street was purchased in the hope that the congregation of the future church would one day buy it from them as a site for vicarage and schools. On the front portion of land, an Iron Church was soon erected.

The Iron Church had a ready-made congregation. Many years previously, the Rev Tebbutt, with the assistance of Mr W Windley bought a Mission Room in Bullivant Street, St

Ann's, which was built and used by the Methodist community then worshipping in the Alfred Street Chapel. In Bullivant Street, he established a mixed junior day school and a Sunday school which paved the way for the erection of St Andrew's Schools in Alfred Street North. From *'Emmanuel' Nottingham. The Story of a Nottingham Parish and Church*, told by their Vicars. 1913. This was shown me by Rev Richard Clark.

For some years prior to the dedication of the Iron Church, the Bullivant Street Room had been the scene of Sunday Evening Services conducted by the Rev Oliver Rice, then Curate of St Andrew's.

In 1880 the plans of Watson Fothergill for the permanent Church were accepted and the building continued in phases until finally completed in 1901.

In 1885 the Iron Church was removed by the Church Extension Society to Blue Bell Hill, St Ann's, at first to be St Bartholomew's Iron Church and later St Bartholomew's Parish Room.

The Church's Boys' Brigade Company, the 16th Nottingham, was founded in 1893. In 1913 it was sixty strong.

In 1960, the Church celebrated its 75th anniversary which was attended by the Lord Mayor and Lady Mayoress of Nottingham, Councillor and Mrs John Kenyon. The Vicar at that time was Rev G Muxlow [1956-1962].

An Iron Parish Room was built by Emmanuel Church in the time of the 'sporting' Vicar, Rev Llewellyn Gwynne [1892-1899], later Bishop Gwynne of Khartoum

In 1908, a Mission Room and Men's Institute was built in Lilac Street to serve the North East corner of the Parish

On December 2nd 1968, the City Council issued the Nottingham (St Ann's Well Road No 5) Clearance Compulsory Purchase Order which included Emmanuel Church and its adjoining Parish Hall. Objections were pursued at the subsequent Public Inquiry on behalf of the parishioners, although the Southwell Diocesan authorities were not opposed to its acquisition. I remember local people at that time who felt they were not being heard.

In its latter years, Emmanuel Church had an all black choir of 20 Jamaican children who became widely known, presenting recitals of an exceptionally high standard including works by Bach and Handel. 10th Anniversary scrapbook edition of the Parish Magazine of St Ann with Emmanuel. Choirmaster and organiser Bill Vasey also formed a young vocal group known as Bill's Boys. They raised money for the Save the Children Fund and to pay for their camp. The choir produced several talented musicians including Michael Cummings who appeared in Flint at the Theatre Royal for three weeks.

The last service in Emmanuel was on May 21st 1972 conducted by the Rev Roy Williamson who came to St Ann's in 1971 and was to be Vicar of the new St Ann with Emmanuel Church at the bottom of Robin Hood Chase.

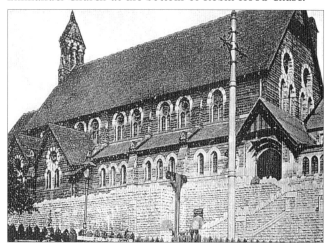

The last days of Emmanuel Church. View from Woodborough Road. Photo: Nicholson Photo Archive

And a view from Peas Hill Road, looking NW. Photo: Nicholson Photo Archive

ST BARTHOLOMEW'S CHURCH

In 1885, the Iron Church was removed, by the Church Extension Society, from Emmanuel Church on the Woodborough Road, St Ann's, to Blue Bell Hill, St Ann's, as the first St Bartholomew's Church. In *Emmanuel Nottingham, the Story of a Nottingham Parish and Church*, 1913, the Rev F W Paul wrote: "For twenty-eight years now the time-worn edifice has stood on Blue Bell Hill, at first as St Bartholomew's Iron Church, and in later days as St Bartholomew's Parish Room."

St Bartholomew's Church is recalled by several people in this book. One man told me that, as a Roman Catholic child in the neighbourhood, he would often go to St Bartholomew's Church with his friends and vice versa.

The Church was a landmark on the hill, visible from all around. Peter Garner says the Church was built in 1894 and demolished in 1971. Several people 'in the know' have suggested that what happened to Church of England Churches in St Ann's at the time of demolition [i.e. which were demolished and which stayed] was as much to do with Diocesan politics as with Local Authority politics.

St Bartholomew's Church. Photo: G L Roberts, Nottingham Local Studies Library

ST MATTHIAS CHURCH

This Church, on St Matthias Road, was mentioned by several people but nobody produced any historical detail. I had no reply from suggested 'obvious' local sources of information. From what people tell me, the church used to be regarded much more as part of St Ann's. It is reported to have a tiny congregation.

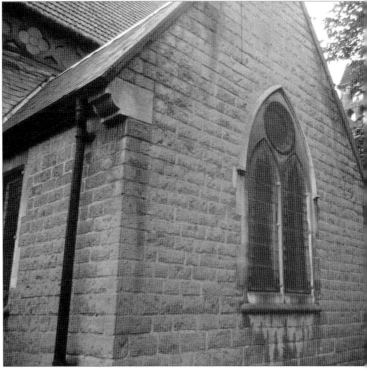

Ellie White took some photos of the exterior of St Matthias Church (2000) which included broken glass panes and a hall, partially boarded up, at the back

ST CATHARINE'S CHURCH

St Catharine's Church was built on the St Ann's Well Road in 1896. The Architect was Robert Clarke. An Iron Church nearby St Catharine's served as a church in the Parish since 1884.

In 1902, there was a large St Catharine's Church Bazaar held at the Victoria Hall and opened by the Duchess of Portland. The aim was to pay off the building debt of £1,050. The Church Wardens had hoped to pay off the debt by sale of some church land to Nottingham Corporation for street improvement purposes but the scheme fell through.

St Catharine's Parish was formed in 1888 causing the boundaries of St Luke's Parish to be modified (see map below). Formerly St Luke's stretched to St Ann's Well Road. When St Luke's Church was demolished [mid-1920s], there was confusion over the resultant changed parish boundaries because many people at first felt 'they belonged' to St Catharine's Church because of its proximity but it couldn't visit them because they lived in another parish. In the late 1920s there was dispute over the possible demolition of St Mark's Church and the distribution of that parish.

It is interesting to note how the changing parish boundaries around that part of St Ann's influenced local life. In 1929, the then Vicar of St Catharine's, the Rev J M F Lester, wrote[1]: "This map shows the original Parish

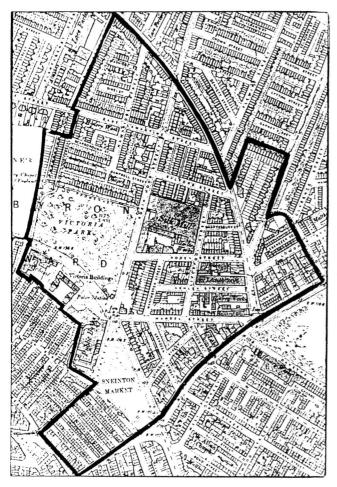

Source: St Luke's Jubilee Book 1863-1913

marked round with a black line and the addition made from St Paul's Parish in 1924, marked round by dotted line." The houses he marked in black are those which had been demolished or disused and he puts some dates on the clearances. The covered market was built 'last year' and replaced the prison. "In 1924, a vast clearance began and is now going on, already half of St Paul's district has gone."

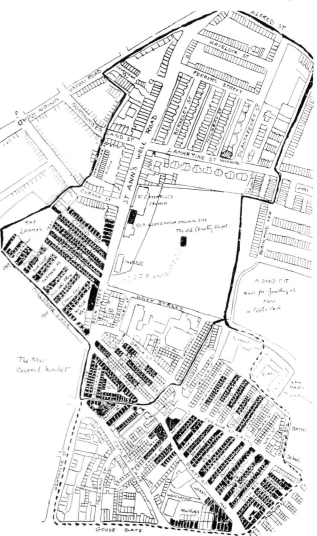

Map referred to above

When the 1920s clearance was happening, people looked to the newer St Ann's 'in the suburbs' as desirable.

The *Nottingham Evening Post* March 5th 1969 reported a lot of criticism by St Ann's church members when news broke of the impending doom of five churches as a result of the St Ann's redevelopment. It said the Rev Kenneth L Barnett of St Matthias reacted in a very hostile way whereas the Rev David Keene, Vicar of St Catharine's, expressed a different approach.

He said he was told the new church building would be up before the others were pulled down, except for St Ann's which was needed as a site for a health centre. He said: "Far from being an attack on the church, the plan was an attempt to enable the church to operate where the people

---

[1] *Dear St Catharine's, Nottingham. A Pilgrimage and a History* by the Vicar. Printed by Hill & Tyler, 91, St Ann's Well Road, Nottingham, 1929.

would be living as well as providing land needed for other development.

"St Catharine's parish is at present made up of part of the former St Paul's and St Mark's parishes and the whole of St Luke's. Now in turn we are invited to join with other neighbours. We may even have the opportunity of joining with other denominations in a united Christian venture."

In the event, St Catharine's and St Matthias remained. St Ann's, Emmanuel and St Bartholomew's were demolished.

A logo at the end of a St Catharine's Church publication, 1929

S. Catharine's Girl Guides + Brownies Sept. 1921

S. Catharine's, Nottingham. Christmas, 1926.

Wishing you all a happy Christmas, with affection, from J. M. F. Lester. Christ's-Mass at S. Catharine's will be at 7 and 8 a.m.

Interior of St Catharine's Church, as on its Year Book 1958

REV CANON DAVID KEENE

Born 1932

*Interviewed in his home 18.5.00. Canon Keene was Vicar of **St Catharine's Church**, St Ann's Well Road, St Ann's, 1964 – 1971. All photos from the Rev Canon David Keene*

I was brought up in a church family. My father came to the faith at about thirty and accused his parents of child neglect because he'd been deprived of this experience earlier! He was determined I wouldn't suffer in the same way. He was highly involved in politics and the church. I was an only child.

As a child I attended St Paul's, Lorrimore Square in London. It was one of the famous tractarian churches in its heyday where the actors and actresses from the Old Vic would go. The Church was bombed during the War so people then worshipped in the Vicarage until a hut was built.

I was evacuated in the War to several places. At one of them in Parkstone, Dorset, I learnt housebreaking. I went down with my school and then the children were boarded out. This woman had many evacuees. Her daughter was kept home from school to do the cooking. Her husband worked at Portland all hours. In the evenings she dressed up and entertained American servicemen in Bournemouth.

Sometimes, she took us boys and the baby in the pram (a good cover for jemmies and housebreaking tools) to the expensive area, Canford Cliff. And she'd have us climbing into houses. If a grown-up tells you to do that, it's very exciting. I was given the job of looking after the baby instead of the exciting things like breaking-in. There was a very large bar of chocolate which was broken up and distributed as a reward for the enterprise. I'm sure the staff at the school had no idea their precious children were on housebreaking expeditions.

Until you become a parent, you don't realise how awful it was for parents having children away and then visiting and discovering this sort of thing going on. I was reunited with my parents about the age of ten. I was away three years.

I passed the Eleven Plus and went to Alleyn's School in Dulwich. I was at a meeting there Tuesday night because I'm becoming President of the old . . . well, we can't say boys' association now because it's become co-ed; now called the Edward Alleyn Club.

When I was about eighteen, I heard a sermon about the ordained ministry. I called on the Vicar and he said: 'I'd wondered when you were coming David.' I went forward in the selection process and was recommended to proceed after I'd done my National Service for two years. I went in the RAF and finished up as Adjutant of a camp living in a Mess as a Senior Officer. After that, I went to Trinity Hall, Cambridge and read Theology for three years, and then Theological College at Westcott House, Cambridge.

I went to Radcliffe-on-Trent to serve my title as we call it. I lodged with a widow and then a family with four children who treated me like an elder brother. We're still friends. Then I went as a curate to St Peter and St Paul in the middle of Mansfield.

I had this invitation to go to Louvain, the Roman Catholic University in Belgium. They liked having at least one Anglican Priest and one Orthodox because they said being Ecumenical is difficult without somebody to be Ecumenical with. In those days it was all a bit cloak and dagger because they didn't want the Roman Catholics in England to know what was going on in Belgium because it was very progressive.

Places in the country were suggested where I might go to be a Vicar. Being a townsman I had this thought that the real work goes on in towns. You discover later that it's no easier in the country. So they offered me St Catharine's, St Ann's. I remember going on this foggy night and being met by the Church Wardens. One of them had broken his arm so he was driving me through these cobbled streets in St Ann's with his one good arm off the wheel when he changed gears. It was an electrifying journey and my introduction to St Catharine's.

10 Downing Street
Whitehall

December 30, 1963.

Dear Mr. Keene,

In the absence of the Ecclesiastical Patronage Secretary I write on behalf of the First Lord of the Treasury to inform you that The Queen has been graciously pleased to approve your appointment to the benefice of St. Catharine, Nottingham; and to say that you will hear further regarding the customary formalities from the Home Office.

I will arrange for a press notice to be released this week.

Yours sincerely
Philip Woodfield.

The Reverend D.P. Keene.

Letter of appointment

I married Muriel [nee Cockayne] after five years at St Catharine's. She was a Church Army sister and came into the congregation through another sister who worshipped there. Muriel was brought up in a very Evangelical Church and St Catharine's was exotic and enjoyed its religion, so she tried the Evangelical churches and not a soul would speak to her. When she came back, everyone said: 'Where have you been sister?' She said she decided to put up with the smells and bells for a bit of affection! She was from Derbyshire.

St Catharine's was in the Catholic tradition. It called itself the English tradition. There's Latin tradition and English tradition. There is a great solidarity among churches like that in Nottingham. St George's in the Meadows, St Matthias, St Stephen's; parishes in what people called tough areas were nearly always in the Anglo-Catholic tradition.

St Catharine's seemed an exciting venture. The Parish Priest who was there before me, Father Thompson, began life as a Plymouth Brother and Northern Irishman. He was the right man at the time because things were a bit at low ebb and people a bit depressed. He introduced one of these giving schemes. People from the church went out knocking on doors for support. For example, one of the factory owners, Tommy Bow, in Lamartine Street went to St Jude's Church in Mapperley but he felt an obligation to the factory's neighbourhood church and covenanted £4 a

Wedding pictures after the marriage 27.12.68 of Muriel Cockayne and Rev David Peter Keene at St Catharine's Church, St Ann's Well Road

week. Father Thompson had terrific determination and it meant the Church paid its way. He persuaded me to go there. I think my salary was £7.50 a week.

I went there in April 1964 and was there about seven years. It was a twenty-four hour parish because it included Sneinton Market and the Telephone Exchange and Post Office Sorting Office. The Parish included some of the former St Luke's Parish. We had friendly relations with Parliament Street Methodist Church and also Campbell Street Methodist Church which closed, the Congregational Church and King's Hall Methodists. St Ann's Church on St Ann's Well Road would have nothing to do with us. They all thought we were too high.

Then they put in the Rev Roy Williamson to St Ann's Church. He went on to be Bishop of Bradford, then Bishop of Southwark. He was a Northern Irishman and an open Evangelical and they thought we might be able to work together. We were friends. But, at the time of St Ann's

On January 30th 1966 eight children of the Logan family were baptised by David Keene at St Catharine's. He said one of their neighbours, the woman in the hat, introduced the family to the life of the Church. The children were James (19), William (17), Ann (16), Kenneth (13), Susan (8), Victoria (6), Christopher (5) and Jane (2)

Two photos of David Keene with his parents Charles and Nellie Keene in the garden of St Catharine's Vicarage

redevelopment, St Ann's Church quashed any idea of our joining one central church, where St Ann with Emmanuel Church is now and keeping small worship centre outposts and vicarages (for example where our Church and vicarage was). It wasn't the City Council that was responsible for the closing of churches, but the Church Authorities. But they would have had negotiations with the City. I've still got my file from the time when I thought the Methodists and Anglicans would unite, it's one of my saddest files. I saw it this morning when I was sorting out.

One of the things I was doing was getting the parties from the Methodist and Anglican churches together so that, for instance, people who look after local preachers met our people who looked after lay readers. We were confident of the need to plan ahead. We had to allow for where churches would be planned, you wouldn't want a great duplication of buildings and we needed a united front with the City Fathers so we could negotiate for land in the middle of a development.

There would have been negotiations for the plot of land where St Ann with Emmanuel was built. What surprised us was the concentration of churchiness where St Catharine's is. The planners plopped the Seventh-day Adventists next to St Catharine's and the Mosque evolved on land across the road.

A local authority can compulsorily purchase church land. Father Thompson had St Catharine's Church yard at the back, which had been closed, re-consecrated to bury ashes because he said that if the planners were thinking of putting a roadway through there, that ki-boshed them because they would need an Act of Parliament to do anything with consecrated land.

I've got articles that I wrote at that time which I will show you. St Matthias didn't want to join the scheme either. They were the spikey end. So the churches that were eventually closed and united were Emmanuel on Woodborough Road, St Bartholomew's on Donkey Hill and St Ann's Church. We had very good relations with St Edward's, the Roman Catholic Church. Our Mothers Union and their Union of Catholic Mothers used to have joint meetings. And there was the Salvation Army. We didn't do things with the Salvation Army.

The odd thing was that Salvation Army officers used to visit me pastorally. They'd say it was hard in the Salvation Army structure to admit they needed help. It would be thought a sign of weakness. One of the glories of the Church of England is having a Priest on the spot. It is the shop that never closes. You are busiest after five o'clock because all the other professionals have skidaddled off into the countryside and closed down till the next morning. I hope that doesn't sound unkind?

There was a great mixture of trades in St Ann's. For example, all the textile factories I used to go visiting. There was Bancroft's who made for Ladybird and they made souvenir stuff for Scotland and Wales. We used to laugh that people going to Scotland from Newark and Nottingham would buy tartan made in St Catharine's parish. There was Pork Farms. I knew the boss Ken Parr. They had a directors' dinner every day and I was invited to

go anytime. So I was like an Honorary Chaplain. I used to visit the Telephone Exchange and Sorting Office sometimes at night. When we had our Harvest Festival, I tried to bring in the produce of the Parish, so we would have a headset from the Exchange. The men from the Sorting Office brought in stuff they had grown. The undertaker would produce something in wood (not a coffin!). A textile factory would have a drawing, a head piece from a piece of machinery, the different textiles and then the piece they'd chosen with a picture from Vogue of something made in the Parish. Pork Farms always put in a display.

There would be sixty or seventy people in Church on Sunday mornings, and we had a Sunday school. The Russians used the Church and had an altar there. Then the Greeks wanted a home. So on Sunday mornings, we'd have our eight o'clock and ten o'clock communion services, twelve noon it was the Russians and three o'clock the Greeks. All of us use incense, so when it got to Evensong, you could scarce see across the Church because their services lasted about three hours. The Archdeacon at the time, the Venerable Michael Brown, said it was the most used church in Nottingham.

A visit of the Russian Orthodox Bishop, Bishop Nikodim (left), of the Russian Church in exile to his community in Nottingham 7.1.68. This is the feast after the Mass. David Keene (right) said the eating only began after a long grace and endless toasts! In the middle is the Rt Rev Gordon Savage, Bishop of Southwell

I had a Pole who came to see me regularly. He did time for attacking somebody with an axe. My wife used to be slightly worried when he was in the study with me. He used to show me his Army card with a picture of him. He said: 'When I came to England I was a Polish hero. Now I am a bloody Pole.' That was sad.

The West Indians used our Church Hall for worship so that was another community. After Service, we would have coffee in the Hall and they'd come in about twelve noon. They worshipped the whole afternoon. One day this West Indian called at the door. He was a bus conductor and he was being blackmailed. When he left Jamaica, his father had said: 'If ever you are in trouble, find a Priest and he will sort you out'. I must say on that occasion the police acted with immense discretion and agreed to meet him in

St Ann's Nottingham: inner-city voices by Ruth I Johns • ISBN 0951696092

my house. They warned his blackmailer off because he didn't wish to make a charge.

And for a while, St Catharine's Hall was the Mosque. It was not entirely popular with the Verger because he had to cover the floor with rolls of wallpaper so they could prostrate themselves, and getting rid of all the wallpaper was not an easy task. The Imam was a good friend. He brought me presents back when he went on the Haj and he'd say: 'Of course, you've been to the Holy Land?' I said I couldn't afford it, and he said: 'But your congregation would send you surely?' We had good friends in that community in the Parish.

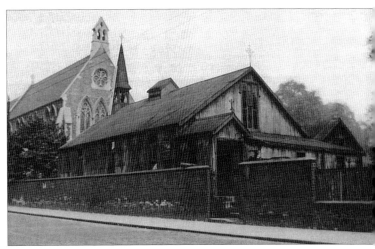

The 'Tin Tabernacle' was the original Church building until St Catharine's (next to it) was built

St Catharine's Church Hall, seen here on the right, replaced a 'Tin Tabernacle' or Iron Church: the original church. The Hall was used as a Mosque, a West Indian Pentecostal Church, by the 'Little Theatre,' Nottingham Harmonic Society, Nottingham Operatic Society, the Church youth clubs, a playgroup, many social occasions including Brahmin weddings and Muslim funerals, and the Church had its own small printing press

Yes, the demolition began while I was there. I felt betrayed. I thought by then planners would have learned their lessons about breaking up communities. I used to hold meetings in the Church Hall and go off to the Planning Department. There were, for example, those houses on St Ann's Well Road. In parts of South London where I came from, you might get a long street like that and they'd cut off a group of houses at intervals and make a little green or put in a few shops, so you didn't get such a long stretch and all the houses were restored with bathrooms and things. It brought places back to life. At first in St Ann's, they said they were going to save what was good.

In some of those courtyards off Alfred Street, there were three generations living there and they were sent off to Broxtowe and Strelley. I remember when the first buildings went up at the bottom of Carlton Hill and they were wooden and people asked me if people would be put to live there. I said I was sure they were builders' huts, but they turned out to be houses. And they put people in high-rise flats in some areas.

One of the characteristics of a funeral at St Catharine's was that you drove down the street where the person had lived. All the people would turn out and the blinds would be drawn. Sometimes they'd put black boards around the house. The men would take their hats off. The person who had died would be given a good send-off.

When we had a funeral from the high-rise flats in Sneinton and you kept up the tradition of driving past and there'd be a woman in a green coat, the cleaner, who would be the only person who'd turned out. There were some nice complexes in the new St Ann's eventually for the older folk but their children had moved away and, once they lived on the outskirts, they couldn't pop in to see mum and dad in the lunch hour. It was harder to keep an eye on mum after she was widowed. So the families were stranded from their families and their old friends.

SATRA [St Ann's Tenants and Residents Association] had meetings at St Catharine's. I felt we were bamboozled. Whenever I had suggestions, the planners said: 'Do come to the Planning Department' and they'd get a large book out and make notes. Then after they'd started all this bulldozing, I saw the Architect and said: 'I don't know why we need a City Architect.' And he said: 'Nor do I.' I said: 'It looks as if they've just invited Wimpey in.' And he said it went to the lowest tender. That's how he put it.

St Catharine's had an Institute. Earlier last century most such churches had an Institute which was a place where working men could meet for relaxation and improvement. They would have a library and snooker tables. My predecessor, Father Thompson, had women coming in saying their husbands were gambling away all their money in the Institute. He found that, though he was President of the Institute, it was run without the Church and he had to go to

Court to get rid of the Committee on the grounds that they weren't running it according to the Title Deeds. This action, of course, caused a certain amount of bad blood among the men. But he said it had to be done for the sake of the wives and the reputation of the Church. It took a bold Irishman like Father Thompson to have the courage to do that sort of thing. From correspondence long before, I'd seen that other Vicars had been worried but not known what to do.

Because of this history of the Institute, when I talked to people at Church House about using the Institute Hall as the Ark Coffee Bar, they nearly had a fit. It was for young people. So we had to have one of those special agreements where it was let to a Management Committee for 364 days a year and on the yearly renewal, the Vicar would be the Chairman (not the President) to make sure the Church didn't lose control.

Other churches and SATRA were invited to join and we canvassed all sorts of folk to help refurbish it. St Ann's Church wouldn't join because they didn't think it was spiritual enough. The Methodist Minister, the Rev Derek Kendrick, had been a joiner before he was ordained so he took on the joinery. We got the bar from Griffin & Spalding. Hopewell's whose original shop was in St Ann's Well Road didn't help. Someone painted wonderful murals of the Ark and someone else, a sign-writer, did a big board with a rainbow.

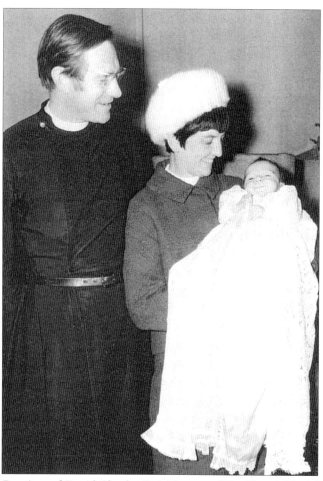

Baptism of David Charles Patrick, son of David and Muriel Keene, March 1970. Muriel Keene became a Deaconess in 1987 and was ordained in 1994 when this became possible for women

I learnt fast that you could hire a snooker table, which people put coins in and a man would come and empty, so you didn't have to worry. He gave some coins back if there was over a certain amount. I learnt how to have a juke-box with a control hidden behind the counter so you could adjust the noise! And that was service free because the coins paid for it.

We needed about ten people on duty every night. We had a pool of thirty Church people and we ran it four nights a week and SATRA ran it three nights a week. And, of course, the bar and everything behind it had to conform to hygiene rules. For example, we put in double sinks. On the nights the Church ran the Ark, we would have a gospel slot half way through the evening. With all the local lads there, it took a certain amount of courage to get up and speak about why we were there and what we were aiming to do. All sorts of conversations would ensue from this. Some said: 'You can't ram religion down people's throats.' We said we were providing an agenda for different sorts of conversations. At first the police were on our side but then they got naughty and just walked in without a 'bye your leave' and started addressing the young people.

I thought this was very 'off'. They began suggesting to me that it was a sort of Fagin's den where plots were hatched. We were offered the help of a solicitor who was willing to be phoned at any time if any of the lads were hassled by the police. You could be picked up for standing there sometimes. The solicitor was a lawyer from a local firm. It's still on my conscience that I didn't investigate more when a young West Indian chap was roughed up in the Parish. I was not sure about it but as a Priest I should have tried to find out more.

There were a lot of young professionals who would organise things for young people. For example, they'd pin up a piece of paper saying: 'I've booked a football pitch on Saturday three o'clock, sign your name if you're interested in coming'. And we got a football team going in a wonderfully relaxed way. And some went to Holme Pierrepont Water Sports Centre. We had a marvellous combined Committee running the Ark from the Church and SATRA, including a transvestite who was super.

Yes, the Ark did get burnt down after I left. I was so sad. The wonderful paintings went too. The Ark was also used on Saturday mornings for teaching English to newly arrived people from abroad.

And do you remember the Blue Bell Hill Craft Centre? There were these young people who arrived with such recherché ideas that they were going to teach folk how to spin yarn and use a loom. But of course they found much more urgent priorities and they were prepared to learn. One of the things they did was a pensioners' lunch one day a week in the Ark. They cadged all the food from shops in the area. They did all the work voluntarily and were respected for that. Some of them were Quakers. We didn't charge them rent. They found a lot of the older people had talents and they had them singing and doing all sorts of things.

David Keene told me: "This is Sarah Anne Best, who lived at 7, Cooper Street, St Ann's. She was a lace outworker (drawing and scalloping). She scrubbed the sanctuary floor of the Church. One night she was so tired, she scrubbed round the Altar but not under. Back in bed, she couldn't sleep, went back to Church, fetched out the scrubbing materials and scrubbed under the Altar. On one occasion, she had arranged the flowers. After the service, someone remarked: 'Couldn't see your flowers very well Sarah Anne.' 'They weren't for your benefit,' came the reply! After the demoliton of Cooper Street, she moved to purpose-built flats for the elderly on The Wells Road, and gave me her grandfather clock."

Sometimes I'd have old boys call and I'd take them to the Homeless Hostel on Boston Street because they were frightened of going in on their own because of bullying. I'd take them to their cubicles. I knew some of the Market people. Two men from Victoria Market would set up their stall early and then come to Communion on a Wednesday and they'd come into the Vicarage for a cuppa.

When I first arrived, I called at Victoria School opposite the little Park. It had an awesome Headmistress. She would have her door open, you'd knock and she'd carry on writing. On one occasion she saw me when she had a mother with her and she said: 'You can come in here and be a witness.' She was quite fearsome. We made friends in the end but it was hard work. Father Thompson was a great pub person but I wasn't a pub person. I'd been brought up next to a pub in South London and father had a drink problem when he was young, so he didn't drink.

St Ann's had a wonderful variety of shops. The shop next to the Church, he was a motor factor. I think he was a Mormon and didn't even drink tea or coffee. He sent his children to a private school where he said he could tell the teachers what to do rather than be told. The nearby greengrocer thought this man was very religious. When I asked why he said: 'By the amount of orange squash he drinks!'

Some people who moved away came back to Church on Sundays because that's where their roots were. Sometimes they'd meet up with family still in the area. Sometimes someone in the bus station would hear the Church bell being rung and simply come to Evensong because they had an hour to wait for a bus.

Of course, earlier last century, the gentry felt a great sense of duty toward places like St Catharine's. I've got printed cards when the Duchess of Portland and the Countess Manvers would be holding stalls at the Church bazaars. In my day, there was still one left, a Miss Wharton who would come from West Bridgford. Toby Wharton would drop his Aunt off at St Catharine's in his Rolls Royce car, which was about as long as the Church! This diminutive Aunt would treat him like a little boy and tell me: 'Father, instead of dropping off, he ought to be coming in,' and this poor man who was 'big' in the County would blush. She was the last of that generation of such ladies.

Sometimes I'd go to West Bridgford and see her and she'd say: 'Now, Father, my stocks and shares have gone up so I've got this money to spend. How can we beautify St Catharine's?' She insisted that when she died, she wished to be cremated and buried just outside the Church steps: 'so you tread on me every time you go in!' Her ashes, and those of others, are buried on the reconsecrated ground I mentioned earlier. Sometimes she'd have a party and invite everyone from the Church along, so she would have her County friends and people from all along Alfred Street, St Ann's. We'd give them lifts there and back. And she'd say: 'If my County friends want me, they'll have my Church friends as well.'

St Catharine's ran a number of clubs when I was there. We had the Kittens for the small children, the Kit Kat Club, and a youth club, which eventually folded as they couldn't agree what to do. Then we founded the Catharine Wheelers which was a Square Dance Club.

Two journalists from the People called one day and said their Editor had sent them grubbing to get a story. Did I have anyone in the Parish living below the poverty line. I said: 'Probably everybody'! I introduced them to some of our Church people and the journalists came back several days later and said they wanted to write a different sort of story. They didn't know people could live so triumphantly in such adversity and they wanted to come to the Square Dance on Saturday night. When the newspaper came out, it had grubbing stories from Birmingham, Manchester and Glasgow and nothing from Nottingham because the journalists hadn't told the story the Editor wanted.

When St Ann's was being portrayed on the box, people would say to me: 'Father, will you look around my house, it's not like that. We don't know those people being interviewed. They've probably only lived here three weeks.' The Council had this policy of putting the problem families into the area toward the time of demolition. Ray Gosling of SATRA said it was done to make folk want to leave rather than having to leave.

Once a month social workers, from statutory and voluntary agencies, who worked in the area met at the Vicarage. They liked coming there because it was neutral ground. There was one chap who used to sleep in doorways and we gradually coaxed him into our drive and finally into our garage. He was so cut off from society. My wife's mother went in and washed him down once and shampooed him and he looked like a patriarch. Various people would call with things for him, but he seemed to live on water biscuits and lemonade.

Once I asked him into the house and after a while, he said: 'Can I leave now Sir?' What I thought was being kind was too much for him. He liked his world in the garage. One day when I went in to see him at night, a man passing by said: 'It's not fit to put a dog in there.' And I thought if only he knew how long it had taken to encourage him in there. If a large van appeared, he would scuttle away because, I think, he thought it was coming to take him away. The police said: 'If he gets too smelly, let us know and we'll get him hosed down,' but he never had to be hosed down. But one day when we'd been away and came back, he'd died.

We gave him the best funeral we could. When my mum sorted out his clothes she found a wadge of notes in his back pocket. They were given to Social Services and they returned one note saying it was no longer legal tender because the number had been rubbed off.

The social workers and Church decided something should be done and some University undergraduates searched for people sleeping rough in the Parish and found forty-eight. A soup run was started in the Huntingdon Street Bus Station. Then, Help the Homeless Association[1] was inaugurated. I've found my file about the inaugural meeting. Then the nuns from the Convent Hospital were left a house on Nottingham Road and the Cyreneans ran it. Other premises were gradually acquired. Including, finally, the one on Canal Street and the Diocesan Board of Social Responsibility managed to persuade the City Fathers they should put some money into the enterprise. At the grand opening, you would have thought it was the City Fathers who had thought the whole thing up.

And do you remember the young Jewess Margaret Behrman, a qualified social worker, who worked in St Ann's on SATRA's initiative? She was good at getting people working in the area to come together. Some of the young women had to call in some very difficult places. She was paid for half by Christian Aid and half through a local tote. People would go to her for help and advice.

Then there was Sue Kirton from the Southwell Diocesan Board of Social Responsibility on Plantagenet Street. She

was amazing. She always had a cigarette drooping out of her mouth and one eye half closed because the smoke came up. In fact, one side of her glasses was brown with nicotine. I was Chairman of the Case Committee there. Imagine trying to chair the committee of which she was a member! I felt so much the new boy. My wife, Muriel, helped at the Board's hostel in Gorsey Road. Miss Kirton was still there when I left. Of course the Board is now called Family Care. Our daughter Sarah was adopted through Family Care.

One day I had a request from Mary Ward College, a Roman Catholic Teachers' Training College at Keyworth. The students wanted to send in a bus for me to fill with poor children and they'd give them a Christmas Party. I wrote back saying certainly not! How could I choose the busload? Then I had an invitation to go and talk to them. I told them about the clubs we ran at the Church and suggested they might like to help. They would meet families and build relationships with them, whereas pouring jelly into children would do nothing for the children or themselves.

They did come and help on a Saturday and it was an effort to come from Keyworth. I remember one student coming to see me one Saturday and saying: 'My family don't want to see me today.' And I said: 'That's how real life is. You can't just do good when you want to and it's tough, but come and have a coffee.' Many of the Mary Ward students came from Ireland and before they went back we had a most exotic jumble sale of all the things they daren't take back for mum to see: lurex galore!

A playgroup used the Church Hall, run by someone independently, and the Health people thought we ought to have miniature toilets. We managed to get some low washbasins. And then we had battle with the Fire people who wanted all the doors open to get on to the stage to get out quickly if there was a fire, and the playgroup people worried in case the children would fall off the stage. Then there was a drama group called the Little Theatre that used to meet there. They came from away. I enjoyed acting in classic plays like *Hobson's Choice*.

As a complete contrast to my work in the Parish, I taught Religious Education at Hollygirt School, an independent school for girls. I would take some of the girls with the produce from the school Harvest Festival to the Salvation Army hostel in the Parish.

There were those almshouses in Plantagenet Street[2]. It was always a job to fill those because once people could get rent paid if they couldn't afford it, there wasn't the need. Some of them were left empty. There were conditions that were hard to comply with; conditions which would have been sensible in the days they were set up. There was another Charity, the Sanderson Charity. The solicitors who managed the Trust which handed out ten shillings to people at Christmas sent the money for me to manage.

We used to publish a Church magazine every month. It would be typed by a woman who worked in the wages department at Boots and she went in early to type the magazine. Her husband kept a corner shop on Alfred Street

---

[1] Help the Homeless Association combined with the Macedon Trust to build a brand new hostel on London Road. I was privileged to have been invited to the opening on December 7th 2001. It is a splendid building and should give dignity to those living there. David Keene 2002.

[2] See Working Man's Retreat.

A group of photos which appeared in a St Catharine's publication 'You need the Church and the Church needs you' during David Keene's ministry

and would never refuse food for folk. He used to keep a tally book and when he died she found that some people owed quite a bit of money. She went out to work to subsidize the family while her husband was letting people have food without payment! I tried to get some of the money back and I called at one house and said: 'Is this the Batty family?' And the chap replies: 'No we're Daft!' They were both common Nottingham names.

I remember a West Indian man whose employers wanted him to work on Sunday and he said he couldn't work on Sunday. It was a matter of principle. And his employer made life difficult for him. And he set himself up as a picture framer on Alfred Street South, and then he got a place in Victoria Market which thrived. It took courage to stand up for what he believed.

One day a woman arrived with a young man to see me. They'd got rooms over a café on Alfred Street and were troubled by a ghost in the boy's room. So I went round and they got various people there interested in this ghost including the Italian landlord. In the end I went to the boy's room and exorcised this ghost. A few days later when I was walking by, the woman was scrubbing the step in front of the café and she said: 'Hello Father, thanks for coming. It's worked.' I thought that's splendid, that complete trust that, if Father came to get rid of the ghost, it would go.

I discovered in St Ann's that when you knocked on a door, you didn't wait to be invited in, you went in. If you wanted to sit down, you moved whatever was on the chair and sat down. And then when you sat down, the kettle went on.

By the time I left in 1971, the demolition and rebuilding of St Ann's was still in progress. I went to Bingham as Rector for ten years. Then I went to Southwell as Canon Residentiary and Director of Ordinands for seventeen years until I retired. We have two sons and a daughter. I remember my St Ann's days with great affection.

2001. St Catharine's Church now has a tiny congregation

This is the view [2002] of St Catharine's from St Mary's Rest Garden, Bath Street. Photo: Ruth I Johns

WOODBOROUGH ROAD AND CHASEWOOD BAPTIST CHURCHES

by **Douglas Wooldridge** [1999]. *Archivist, East Midland Baptist Association. Photos from Douglas Wooldridge and the Rev Steve Mantle unless otherwise stated*

One of the most striking buildings in St Ann's now is that of the former **Baptist Church, Woodborough Road,** which is now the Pakistan Centre. This Church was opened in February 1895 on the corner of Woodborough Road and Alfred Street North and could seat 1,000. The Iron Chapel it replaced was built over a brick built basement containing schoolrooms, and when the new Church was built, the Iron Chapel (which seated 500) was re-erected in Arkwright Street, the Meadows.

This aspect of the former Baptist Church on Woodborough Road was not possible before the area's redevelopment. Photo: Alan Hardy 2000

In 1903, the Woodborough Road Church became responsible for the Edwin Street Mission Room where services were held, and Sunday school was held in the nearby St Ann's Well Road Board School. Despite the depletion of numbers caused by the loss of young men, including Sunday School teachers, in two World Wars, and other wartime restrictions like blackout and the necessity to hold services in the schoolroom for fear of air raids, membership still numbered over one hundred post-1945. The Church served an active role in the community through its services and many other activities over the years, including a Young People's Institute on Saturday evenings. But by 1958, there was a feeling that it had outlived its purposes in that neighbourhood. In 1963, there was a call to unite with another church and sell the property.

Arthur Mee, who founded the Children's Newspaper and wrote the Children's Encyclopaedia and the King's England series on the Counties of England, was associated with the Woodborough Road Church as a boy. His father, William Mee, editor of the *Nottingham Journal*, was a Church Deacon.

ST ANN'S NOTTINGHAM: inner city voices by Ruth I Johns • ISBN 0951696092

In the 1960s when Nottingham Corporation decided to clear the area and redevelop it, both the Woodborough Road Baptist Church and the St Ann's **Baptist Chase Mission** were threatened with demolition. The East Midland Baptist Association decided to bring the two congregations together in 1970. There was a gradual coming together of the two Woodborough Road and Chase Mission congregations, meeting in each other's church alternatively. The Chase Mission premises closed in 1971, and services continued to be held in the Woodborough Road Church until the opening of the new **Chasewood Baptist Church** in 1978. The building of the new Chasewood Baptist Church was delayed due to difficulties in obtaining planning permission and compensation for the Chase Mission.

The present membership of Chasewood Baptist Church is seventy-seven with thirty-four children and twenty-seven young people over fourteen. It is interesting that the number of church members is the same as in 1909, when the former Chase Mission on the same site was opened. But the number of children has drastically decreased. In 1909 there were two hundred and sixty-nine children in the Sunday school which had a teaching staff of twenty-five. Those were the days of big Sunday schools with many children being sent by parents who did not attend church themselves. One of the big events of the year was the Sunday School Anniversary.

The congregation today is also very different as its members are largely of West Indian origin and they have contributed some of their own culture with a much more free style of worship than would have been the case ninety years ago.

The origins of the demolished Chase Baptist Mission went back to 1880 when a group of friends from the Tabernacle Baptist Church (also known as Exeter Hall) with their Minister, the Rev H E Stone, started meetings for worship in a joiner's workshop over some pigsties in Westville Street, St Ann's. The congregation expanded and a move was made to Herbert Street, where two shops were

The Chase Mission

A group of members and workers, Chase Mission c1909

The converted shops which became the Herbert Street Mission

purchased and converted into a place of worship. This was known first as the Herbert Street Mission and later as the East Nottingham Baptist Mission Church.

In 1900, a site was purchased at the top of Raglan Street, fronting Robin Hood Chase, for the Chase Mission. It was decided no building works should begin until £1,000 was in hand. A special effort to clear the remaining £250 of the debt was made in December 1914, the 34th Anniversary of the founding of the Mission in Westville Street.

The local church was, for many people, the focal point of their weekly activities. The Chase Mission News in 1918 lists weekly meetings for all ages. On Sundays, there were adult classes at 10.45 am and at 6.30 pm, Bible Classes for young men and women (these would have been conducted separately) at 2.30 pm and Sunday School at 10.00 am and 2.30 pm. On Tuesdays there was a women's meeting at 3.00 pm, and a service at 8.00 pm. On Thursday the Senior Young People's Christian Endeavour met and on Saturday there was Bible Reading and Prayer at 7.00 pm. In addition, by 1922 there was Band of Hope on Monday evenings. On Wednesday evenings there was Boys' Brigade and also a Social Literary Class.

One man was largely responsible for the success of the Mission. This was Mr W A Coombs who became Honorary Pastor a few months after its foundation in 1880 and served in that capacity for fifty-three years. A much loved figure, at the Jubilee Celebration in 1930, he was presented with a framed portrait in oils which now hangs in the Chasewood Baptist Church. The current Minister is Rev Steve Mantle.

Sources: *Woodborough Road Baptist Church 1875-1975* by R Ward and *The Nottinghamshire Baptists* by F M W Harrison

Chase Mission 1st Nottingham Girls' Life Brigade members outside the Mission on Robin Hood Chase c1960-61

Mr W A Coombs, second left, and friends 1909

Laying the Foundation Stone for the new Chasewood Baptist Church c1977

Mr W A Coombs and friends on a much later occasion. Photo from Denis N Enser

STANDING: MISS A. M. LEACH, MR. W. WRIGHT, MRS. H. BOOTH, MR. J. FOUNTAIN. CENTRE: REV. B. W. OWEN, MRS. B. W. OWEN. SEATED: MR. D. STANDEVEN, MR. R. PRESTON, MR. W. ELLIOTT.

Minister and officers 1940. Photo: The Chase Mission Diamond Jubilee Souvenir Booklet

Extract from *Woodborough Road Baptist Church 1875-1975* by R Ward: "It was suggested by Nottingham Corporation that since Chase Baptist Mission and ourselves [Woodborough Road Baptist Church] would both be involved in demolition, the two congregations should unite and have a new church in the area. Thus it was that in 1968, the East Midland Baptist Association began proceedings in an effort to bring this to fruition. . . . Much delay and frustration, first in obtaining planning permission and then over re-negotiating the compensation, due to increased costs, have been the means of this Church attaining its centenary. All things being equal, many feel that the new Church should now have been built . . . Instead our present building is still standing, and we have no indication of when we shall obtain satisfaction from the Corporation."

In the end, the Woodborough Road Baptist Church building remained and became the Pakistan Centre. The building, designed by Watson Fothergill, is one of the few architectural landmarks that survived in the area.

St Ann's Nottingham: Inner-city voices by Ruth I Johns • ISBN 0951696092

Girls' Brigade, 1st Nottingham, outside the old Woodborough Road Baptist Church, mid-1970's

Val and Gloria Murray, both members of Chasewood Baptist Church, married there on July 11th 1998. Also in the photo are left, Mrs Olive Davis, Church Treasurer for many years who acted as registrar and, second left, Rev Steve Mantle

The Rev Steve Mantle told me that the first Minister at the 'new' Chase Baptist Church was the Rev Ron Collett. In 2000, I met members of the congregation who provided me with valuable help. Steve Mantle left Chasewood Baptist Church to become Regional Minister for the East Midlands, 2001.

KINGS HALL METHODIST CHURCH, St Ann's Well Road, now KINGS HALL CHRISTIAN CENTRE (New Testament Assembly)

The first church building on this site was a tin chapel known as the **St Ann's Well Road Wesleyan Chapel**. It was built of wood on a brick foundation and covered with corrugated sheeting. It opened in May 1883. This site on the corner of Martin Street and St Ann's Well Road was 'waste land' when it was first selected and open-air services were held. The response led to the building of the chapel. In the meantime, prayer meetings were held in a room over a shop near the corner of Livingstone Street not far away.

Whilst the brick church was being built, the tin chapel had to go, and temporary accommodation was found in Dame Agnes Street under the first floor Free Library, a building also used later by St Ann's Church. The **King's Hall Methodist Mission** was opened on May 21st 1903.

On the night of May 8th and 9th 1941, incendiary bombs lodged in the roof of the church and the building was severely damaged by fire. A poster was immediately placed outside saying 'Bombed but not beaten.' The officers of the East Nottingham Boys' Club in nearby Northampton Street quickly offered use of their premises. The still useable parts of the church building were back in service and re-dedicated in June 1951.

Left to right: Mrs Joyce Mantle, Girls' Brigade Captain for many years, Ms Sally Plackett (ex-Girls' Brigade, in her Women's Royal Army Corps uniform) and Mrs Margaret Plackett, current Girls' Brigade Captain (2001). Mrs Joyce Mantle (not a relation of Steve Mantle) died in 1998. She was a great-grandmother and lived in St Ann's. Photo: early 1990's

The Tin Chapel

The new King's Hall Methodist Mission Church. Note the sheep being driven in the road

The interior of the Church

Early in 1951, a small chapel in Sycamore Road joined forces with King's Hall, which was rebuilt as the building we see today, including three shops facing St Ann's Well Road. The spire had to be taken down. The Sycamore Road chapel building served the youth club until the new building was complete. Grants to assist rebuilding were received from two Methodist connections: The Joseph Rank Benevolent Trust and the Johnston Yapp Trust, and the War Damage Commission. The Church opened on February 28th 1957. It escaped the later redevelopment of St Ann's. *The King's Highway.* brochure prepared for the opening of King's Hall Methodist Church, St Ann's Well Road. King's Hall Methodist Church was part of the Methodist Church Nottingham Mission which, in 1965, included the Albert Hall Central Mission (661 members), King's Hall, St Ann's Well Road (98 members), Aspley Hall (241 members), Bestwood Hall (54 members), Broxtowe House and Braddock House (member numbers not given). Nottingham Mission Plan and Directory January-March 1965.

In the 1970s, during Rev John Stacy-Marks' Ministry, a lot was happening at King's Hall in addition to the regular Sunday Services and Sunday School. For example, Women's Fellowship Group, Brownies, Football Practice,

The bomb damaged Church

The rebuilt Kings Hall Methodist Church. Late 1950s

Junior Youth Club 8-14 years, Bible Study, Junior Girls' Choir, Senior Youth Club 14+, Senior Citizens' Group, weekly Guild (talks on different subjects), Guides, Swimming, Choir, 17+ Badminton, Modern, Old Tyme and Sequence Dancing, Discos and the Bi-Thursday Grub Club. The latter was started by John Stacy-Marks for senior citizens and the Church Newsletter appealed for help with donations of salt, rice, custard powder, sugar, tea etc. Meals for elders had to be funded by the church community. No Council subsidy then! The Club's prayer was 'God bless this bunch, as they munch and crunch their lunch!'

Arthur Watterson tells more of the King's Hall Methodist Church story.

Leaving Church. Car Park of King's Hall Methodist Church. c.1990

Kings Hall Christian Centre (New Testament Assembly) was officially opened on August 19th 2000 by the Mayor of Nottingham, Councillor Ian Malcolm. The Welcome Address was by Bishop D Greaves. In the Opening Brochure the past history of King's Hall includes the history of placing of King's Hall on the market in 1993 and being purchased by visionaries Pastor Joan and Deacon Newton Richards in 1994. Projects planned were Parenting Groups, After School Club, Breakfast Club and Youth Club. Users would reflect the ethnic mix of the area.

Pastor Joan Richards tells more of the Kings Hall Christian Centre N.T.A. story.

The Church when it was no longer a Methodist Church and before being renovated by the New Testament Assembly. Photo: Ruth I Johns 1999

Outside the Kings Hall Christian Centre before the 2000 exterior renovation. Photo: New Testament Assembly. A photo of the new name board can be seen over some shops (in the Shops section)

ARTHUR WATTERSON

Born 1914

*Interviewed in his home 25.5.00. Born in St Ann's, Arthur Watterson recalls the start of his working life at Bancroft's factory on Robin Hood Street and his long association with the **King's Hall Methodist Church** on St Ann's Well Road: and much more.*

I was born at 8, King's Lynn Terrace, off Turners Street, St Ann's, where my grandmother lived. I don't know how long I lived there but after that it was Eaton Street, Mapperley, next door to my grandmother and grandfather. Then we moved to Cathcart Street, St Ann's, in 1917. I remember the morning we left Eaton Street because I was crying that I wanted some breakfast. My mum gave me the toasting fork and a slice of bread and she said: 'The fire's not quite out, do it yourself.' So I made my first round of toast!

I was the eldest of seven children. After me were twins Violet and Mabel, then Ellen, then Tom, Elsie who died as a child, and Ken. Mother died at the age of thirty-nine. One sister died with meningitis, before mother died, so six of us were left. My mum had tuberculosis, bronchitis, asthma . . . she could hardly draw breath. My father was a coal miner.

I went to St Ann's Church School and I got on pretty well. When it came to scholarship time, three of us got through and were going to be transferred to Mundella School. When I told my mum and dad, they said I wasn't going there, I was going to work when I was fourteen. This was quite a bother to me. Next day, I told my teacher who went round to mum and dad to talk to them, but they were quite adamant. Then my teacher said: 'If I can get him into a school where he can leave at fourteen, will you agree to that?' They agreed providing I did not stay until sixteen, but left at fourteen. So I went to Huntingdon Street School.

Most of the boys there came from better class families. My parents were poor, the family was big and I went with patches on my trouser bottoms with little or no heel on my shoes. And I was ashamed. I used to stand against the wall in the school playground and nobody would have anything to do with me. But one day there came a turnround. I was delivering newspapers to try to earn a shilling or two for mum and dad. When I was going round with the newspapers, I saw: 'Rutherford splits the atom' and it stuck in my mind. There were forty-eight of us in class and in the Science class, the teacher asked if anyone could tell him something remarkable that had happened that day. No hands came up and, then slowly, I dared put mine up and said 'Rutherford's split the atom.' From that day, teachers' and scholars' attitudes toward me changed.

King's Hall influenced my life from the time, at the end of the First World War, when my mother and I went round from Cathcart Street to watch a parade and she went round to Mrs Truswell who was interested in King's Hall as well. They weren't very involved but my mum asked if there was a Sunday school and I found myself in the primary at King's Hall. The first real job of work I was trusted with early on was numbering the envelopes for the Church collections. So we knew how much folks had put in. They made promises to give a certain amount and I had these little square envelopes to get ready for people.

I remember Bernard Hughes Smith putting his hand on my head when I was fourteen with a certificate: 'King's Hall Wesleyan Mission Sunday School awarded to Arthur.' Signed Mr E Frankton. Mr Frankton used to have a fruit stall on Sneinton Market and he lived on Blue Bell Hill, St Ann's. And the Secretary was Mr C L Gough.

When Sunday school finished we had a young men's class because they didn't want to lose you. And then there was the men's class. When I was fifteen, Arthur Revill who was Superintendent of the Sunday school came up to the young men's class and took me downstairs. We had a big Sunday school in those days, over two hundred. He said someone had given up their class so now it was mine. I said I didn't know anything and he said: 'You'll learn!' He said if I had any troubles I should go to him. He was a man you'd trust with your life. He lived in one of the terraces at the top of Gordon Road.

So I became a Sunday school teacher and eventually as the years went on I became Superintendent of the Sunday school. I also became a Society Steward. Then Arthur Revill came along and said he'd got a double appointment as a local preacher and could I take one of the services. And that's how I got involved with local preaching.

In the old building, when the prize giving was on for the children, there must have been six hundred parents in the place. It was a big Church with a balcony all the way round. Marsden the grocer was very interested in the Church. They had a big shop across the road. He saw we were in a pickle space-wise and he put another floor on the side for us. We took part of that floor to start the Men's Institute. There were two billiard tables in there, and the young lads when they got to fourteen and fifteen didn't run off because they got people they knew and

were able to congregate in there. We had some great times.

I stayed at school till I was fourteen in 1928. Then mum took me round looking for jobs. I didn't know what sort of work I wanted or could do. At Bancroft's factory on Robin Hood Street there was a notice outside saying they wanted a boy for the cellar. Mum wanted the money thinking she was going to get ten bob a week and it was seven and six pence. It was a filthy job, sweeping the floor and taking the dirt down and putting it in the boilers and that sort of thing. I wasn't happy, but I got along with the fellows there and most of them were kind and helped me. I worked with an old chap, Tommy Flint, who lived on Massey Street. He was about seventy years old.

One day a notice went up in Bancroft's that they wanted a boy for the counting house. Mr Radford[1] took a liking to me. He had lost his son early. It was Armistice Day, November 11th, and I stopped when the buzzer went. He came across the yard after and told me I'd done the right thing. I'd been going to night school until my mother died and I got that job adding up figures and it was right up my street, balancing up the totals.

There were about eleven departments and a manager in each. Bancroft's produced ladies' and children's clothing. Mr Radford sent for me one day and was pouring out quite a tale about his own life and his son and his wife and his daughter, Joyce Radford. He said Carver in 'S' Department's got a week's holiday next week: 'I want you to go in the Department and see that the goods are sent away, see that the orders are entered up and see that the counting house gets information so they can send the invoices off.' That was another step up the ladder.

After that week, he said I'd done very well, and from then on when somebody was away I took over in that department. Then eventually Florrie Richardson, who was in charge of the department making tea aprons and café things, was thinking of leaving and setting up her own business. She wasn't a too kindly woman and she was a real tinker to the girls. I learnt a lot up there, poked my nose into a lot of things.

Anyway, I eventually got my own department. I was about twenty-one and I was making progress in life and that was a great feat for me. I was dealing with people in Switzerland and so I had to get along with the cost of the Swiss Franc. My department made babies wear: rompers and tunics, suits and dresses.

Nan [Nancy] and I met on the street! She was an Anglican and had been to the watch night service at St Ann's Church on January 1st 1936, and I came out of King's Hall after their watch night service. Three of us stood and talked and that was the beginning of our relationship. She worked at Cooper and Roe's on Carlton Road until we got married. During the war, because we didn't have children then, Nancy had to work and went on a milk cart delivering milk.

---

[1] Arthur Watterson said that when William Bancroft died, he left two executors, Mr Radford and William Harlow, the estate agent. Mr Radford, a Society Steward at the Methodist Church at the junction of Mansfield Road and Gregory Boulevard, was someone employees could approach without fear.

Wedding of Arthur Watterson and Nancy at King's Hall. The bridesmaids Ada Nicholson (on her left) and Amy Brough, sisters of the bride. Minnie and Alfred Brough, Nancy's parents are standing behind her and Ada. Behind Arthur Watterson are his father Thomas Watterson and an aunt, Nellie Saxby. The tall best man and lifelong friend is Alfred Bourne. The Reverend on the left is a friend, Harry Breakspear, and next to him, Harry Watterson, an uncle. The girl is Helen Saxby, a niece

We married on August 19th 1939, just before the outbreak of War. We got married at King's Hall. There were so many people, including girls from the factory, outside the Church afterwards that they had to stop the traffic on St Ann's Well Road. We had a really wonderful wedding. We didn't want a drinking wedding. So we hired one of the Anglican rooms on Coppice Road [now Ransom Road] and had the reception there. There were some wooden buildings there. It was in one of those.

Then the Second World War came along and I was a conscientious objector, a refuser. Before I was called up, I'd always gone to these public meetings. Captain Popkess was Chief of Police in Nottingham and I listened to what he had to say. At work we were making suits in iridescent cloth in a reflective yellow, which aircraftmen wore, so if they were shot down they would be easy to spot. When I was called up, I said goodbye to Nan, and caught the train to Liverpool and they sent me to an old housing estate waiting to be told what we would do. I was selected for clerical work and sent to Nottingham. I couldn't believe it. I checked in to the Pay Office on Hucknall Road where Lewis's Factory is and the chap in charge said they'd find billets for me. I said: 'Sir, I live in Nottingham and could live at home.' He looked at me and said: 'Right, Watterson, the first time you're late, we'll post you.' Nan couldn't believe it when she saw me.

In the Pay Office, we did all the ATS accounts so I learned what to do, including when they were on Ak-Ak gun sites and got killed and things like that. There was quite a lot of correspondence with the War Office. I would write letters free hand and then the Officer in Charge of the Section would read them and sign them. I was in the Pay Office for a long while. Near the end of the War I was issued with a fresh uniform, it wasn't new and I caught meningitis from it. They sent me down to Oxford and this doctor got me over it, and then he asked if I could stay and help him for a bit until I said I thought Captain Langford would like me back in Nottingham.

After the War, I returned to Bancroft's. I had the job of preparing all the clothing for children who were going to dance for the Queen during her visit to Nottingham [1955]. William Bancroft came to me and said Bancroft's had an invitation to meet the Queen and he said: 'Arthur, you've done all the work, you're coming with me.' And so I met the Queen.

Soon after, I thought I'd start my own business making babies' dresses, boys' tunic suits, rompers, things like that. And all those years I was a Sunday school teacher at King's Hall Methodist Church on St Ann's Well Road, though I didn't live in St Ann's then. We moved to 308, Foxhill Road, Carlton. I've been retired now from business for some thirty years. We have two children, two grandchildren and one great grandchild.

Arthur Watterson's Diploma for thirty years' work with the Sunday school at King's Hall. He wrote on it: 'This continued for something like another 20 years'

The Church was badly damaged by an incendiary bomb in the War. Ralph Farringdon from King's Hall and a great friend of mine had a friend who was a builder. So we sat down and talked things over. Finance was the problem. Eventually it was decided to put a floor where the balcony was so we would have a place for young people there and the Church would be big enough. We didn't close the Church except for a very short time.

Like a lot of organisations, we lost a lot of the young men in the War.

The official re-opening of King's Hall, in 1951, following refurbishment after the bomb damage. Anthea Watterson holds a bouquet to give to Lady Belper. The key was presented to her by L A Thraves (left). On the right are Rev Ken Waights, Rev Ezra Sellars and Rev G H Taylor

King's Hall started in 1883, so in 1983 it was the centenary. And we celebrated. The President of the Methodist Conference came down and talked to us. And we had an open-air meeting and he asked for questions. And I said: 'Mr President, I've a feeling that you want to close this place.' He said: 'No, take my word for it, this will stay open.' It wasn't long before it closed. That was the President of the Conference breaking a promise.

The original Manse was 272, Derby Road before we bought a Manse at Dean Road, which isn't in St Ann's. King's Hall was in the Albert Hall Circuit.

Towards the end of my time at King's Hall, membership size was becoming a little bit difficult. When John Stacy-Marks, the Minister then, first came to Nottingham he was a young single man who didn't know how to put his bed up when his furniture moved in.

But he built up a tremendous youth following. He got a bus and used to take them out, he got them all interested. One day he told me the phone had rung at two o'clock in the morning. He mentioned the name of the lad who phoned him from the bottom of Robin Hood Chase on St Ann's Well Road and told him he'd pinched a car. John got up and went down there, and they took the car up to the Guildhall and he made the lad explain. John got him out of trouble and that's the sort of person he was. His next move was to Cardiff.

Previous Ministers at King's Hall included Derek Kendrick. While there, his wife left and they divorced. He

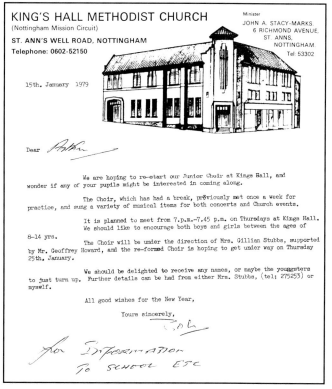

As the above letter shows, for a time the Minister, Rev John Stacy-Marks, lived in Richmond Avenue, St Ann's

later remarried. He was a bricklayer before training for the Ministry. I'm a great friend of Derek's. He's now in Camborne, Cornwall, and retiring this year.

I've been tracing my family tree and found this uncle, my father's brother, who went to America via Canada. He walked from Eaton Street to Liverpool, found a job on a sailing boat and got to Canada. He didn't tell anyone he was going though he got in touch after. He married a farmer's daughter and had three children. One is still alive and lives in Texas.

Nancy (Nan) Watterson died March 27th 2002

PASTOR JOAN RICHARDS

Born 1957

*Interviewed at **King's Hall Christian Centre** (New Testament Assembly), St Ann's Well Road, St Ann's 14.9.00. Kings Hall was formerly Kings Hall Methodist Church*

The official opening of our Church was August 19th 2000. We purchased the building from the Methodists in 1994. I think by then they had an ageing congregation and the building wasn't very well maintained. I think they had their last service here October 1993.

We were worshipping at St John Evangelist Church Hall, Watcombe Circus, for about a year before that. But we had a vision of owning our own property, to have our own keys. We wanted to set up a multi-cultural church where

ST ANN'S NOTTINGHAM: inner-city voices *by Ruth I Johns* • ISBN 0951696092

Pastor Joan Richards

children's choir and they take part in the service. We have some Sundays when the children are in charge and decide who speaks. It's been very good.

We have a Wednesday Service, a Tuesday Pastor's clinic for new Brethren who have just taken affiliation. They ask questions. On Wednesdays we have a Prayer Clinic for spiritual needs. We deal with different things, like depression. And we're just about to start a Bible School for Brethren and people outside the church, who want to get a qualification in Theology. There will be opportunity for ordinary Theology Certificates, to Masters' Degrees and Doctorates. We have a Bible School set up in our London Headquarters Church. It's linked to the University of Wales. We've been lucky to find a teacher in Nottingham, the Rev Richard Clark from St Andrew's Church. He knows quite a lot about St Ann's as well.

We have a vision eventually of having another building at the side of the Church for educational purposes, to involve the community. The Council has promised us the plot of land at the side.

At present about six or seven of our congregation come from St Ann's. But now we've had the launch, we've got our sign up, we've got a state of action . . . a lot of people didn't know this was still a church. Now we are going to start a lot of publicity and go out and talk to the people in St Ann's. We're looking at having an After School Club and a Youth Club. We are starting a Luncheon Club at the end of September for the elderly, which is going to be a little different from the ordinary luncheon clubs. We're going to call it a Prayer Fast and offer spiritual guidance as well as a meal.

There are other things in the pipeline, like women's issues, mental health and so forth. We're even looking into a drug clinic because we recognise that St Ann's is really in need of help. Some young people tend to be hooked on a lot of different drugs. The vision is to be the church of the community, like John Wesley, and we believe we are not doing anything different from what the Methodists were doing. We believe we are extending the work here. Whereas the Methodists had an ageing community, which couldn't continue, we believe we're offering some younger people.

The King's Hall Brethren here you know were bombed in 1941. Then a few Brethren got together and said something like 'we are cast down but we are not defeated.' There was always that community spirit to keep things going, and I think that has been lacking over recent years. The six years I've been here, I've got the feeling that the people of St Ann's have felt intimidated by the problems of crime and social problems. And I think they need to come out and be a bit more of a voice.

We're working closely with the police and the police are very interested in the fact that we're working with them. I've asked them to get CCTV cameras put around the Church because we've had reports of people exchanging drugs in the car park.

All I've ever known is Nottingham. I came over from Jamaica in the West Indies when I was three. My parents brought me over. My dad had a brother in Nottingham.

there would be a lot of facilities, including for both young and elderly. This building seemed ideal for us and, thank God, the Lord brought together the finances.

It was sold to us for £75,000 and the Methodists took £6,000 off, which was originally for the organ but they wrote that £6,000 off, so they gave us the organ. It would have cost a lot to move it out so, after consultation, they let us have it.

I started Pastoring a year before I received a word of prophecy from the Lord in May 1993 that He was going to give us a building. Derby and Nottingham New Testament Assembly Churches came together in March. Headquarters believed that it would utilise the building more to close a church that was not really profitable at the present, and put our resources together. This building is mortgaged so we need to use it.

We have just under thirty adults and about thirty kids. At present, we have one quality service on Sunday instead of two services. We come in at twelve o'clock and have our Sunday school between twelve and one o'clock and then we have our midday service from one o'clock to three-thirty. And then that's it for the day.

It's something we've never tried before. But people are really saying it's good, because we spend time socialising more because everybody's not running home to get back for the evening service. People with children can go home and sort the children out for the next day at school. At Pentecostal we used to come back in the evening and have long drawn out services and a lot of parents said: 'You know the children are suffering.'

The children now have their Sunday school where we minister to their needs. And they come into the main service in which they also take part, doing dances and

Wherever I go in England, there's nowhere like Nottingham. I was brought up in Radford, a similar sort of area. I've got three children, two girls and a boy, and two grandchildren. My grandchildren come to Sunday school.

I was brought up in Church. My dad is a Pentecostal Bishop. I was with my father's Ministry for quite a number of years working with the Youth Department. I Youth Pastored for about four or five years and was an Evangelist Minister.

ST AUGUSTINE OF ENGLAND CHURCH

From 'St Augustine of England, Woodborough Road, Nottingham. A Centenary Handbook 1879-1979.' Compiled by Rev Neil McLaughlin, Robert Mulholland, John F Hay and Ian Wells

St Ann's area was part of the new suburban development of Nottingham made possible by the release of land for building after the Enclosures Act of 1845. The houses were a considerable improvement to those of the old town: they had sewage and piped water. Fears that the inhabitants would steal the lead pipes of the plumbing were not realised; the water pressure discouraged this practice. In 1873, the overall death rate per thousand in the old town was 31.1 per cent whereas in the more salubrious area of St Ann's it was only 17.6 per cent. Infant mortality, too, was only half that of the old town.

In 1880, there were two lace factories fairly near the site of St Augustine's Church and a large engineering works on the other side of the Woodborough Road. Further up Woodborough Road, there was some development but Mapperley Park was still a park. Down the hill was the Union Workhouse.

An Iron Church was erected in 1879. It was of iron and wood and the foundations of natural skerry. There was no drainage except for surface water to Woodborough Road, no water supply and therefore no water closets. Tub closets were supplied.

Fr Joseph Gernon took charge of the mission for ten years and saw the opening of Nottingham's first Nazareth

St Augustine of England Church, looking down Woodborough Road, St Ann's, c1978. From the Church's centenary booklet 1979

House, known as the Convent of St Ann, on Cranmer Street, St Ann's. Nuns stayed there for three years only but provided great financial assistance to support a resident priest at St Augustine's.

The Iron Church was used for a school and, at the end of the first year, seventy children attended each week. The Sisters of St Joseph of Peace took over the running of the school in 1889. In 1892, the building was condemned for school use as insufficient and unsanitary and the nuns raised the money to build a new school in Northville Street, close-by.

Less than fifteen years after the Iron Church was opened it was inadequate in every way. It could not accommodate its congregation, but it soldiered on for another thirty years. But for the last couple of years before the new church opened in 1923, services had to be held in the Sacred Heart Convent and St Augustine's School. The new church was designed by John Sydney Brocklesby, is Romanesque, and unique in Nottingham.

In the period after the Great War, the parish had a wide cross section of society, although it lacked the very poorest among the townsfolk; these people lived in Broad Marsh and Narrow Marsh [old town] areas between the Lace Market and the Meadows, and were served by the parish of Our Lady and St Patrick.

In St Augustine's parish were large numbers of neat, modest terraced houses which were well kept by what Canon Bird [Curate at St Augustine's 1919-1921] described as 'good, stable working-class families'. There were somewhat grander houses in Robin Hood Chase, Mapperley Park, Alexandra Park and Corporation Oaks. These homes were occupied by relatively prosperous folk who could afford resident staff. Among those in service were a number of Irish girls who came to England to work as maids, and young men from the same country who were employed as grooms.

The priests lived in a house on Woodborough Road on the corner of Manning Street. The Curate 1925-1930 was Rev Edward Ellis, later to become Bishop of Nottingham. As Bishop, he returned to St Augustine's in 1964 to open the Social Club built in the garden of the Priest's house. There are still many people who remember Rev Msgr Canon Maurice Parmentier who was rector from 1927-1962. When he first arrived the new church was still a shell and in debt.

Rev Joseph Wakefield was rector 1965-1972. The 'winds of redevelopment' were already blowing about St Ann's when he came and: "As early as 1967 the Catholic population began to diminish as the old housing was cleared . . . In 1970, the demolition men caught up with the presbytery at 240, Woodborough Road and, after much negotiating with the local housing authority, Fr Wakefield moved to 1, St Ann's Valley, a new council house."

The Council's original plan was to demolish both the presbytery and the Parish Hall [Social Club] and to rebuild them on the site of the school next to the church. But when the diocese applied for a licence to use the proposed new hall as a social club, the Council had reduced the size of the site and refused this use.

£22,000 was received from the City Council for loss of the presbytery and land at 240, Woodborough Road. With

St Ann's Nottingham. Inner-city voices *by Ruth I Johns* • ISBN 0951696092

the transfer of the school, the church lost its heating system so the winter of 1972-1973 was endured in an unheated church. By April 1974, the new presbytery and sacristies, with meeting room, above were completed at a cost of £50,000. In 1975, for £48,000, a new parish hall [not licensed] and youth club with new boundary walls were completed behind the church facing Westville Street, and the original plan for redeveloping the parish was completed.

The former parish hall/social club was sold to the Gladstone Liberal Club in 1977.

The Diocesan Year Book 1994 reported that Fr C F B Cossins [Rector 1920-1925] and John Brocklesby "would be hard pressed to recognise the lower end of Woodborough Road today, but they would recognise St Augustine's even if a little grimier on the outside than when they built it."

In 1995, the Parish Priest, Fr Philip McBrien, told me that St Augustine's parish stops at St Ann's Well Road. It also included parts of Mapperley, Carrington and Sherwood.

He said two of his parishioners had been very involved in the campaign to get the St Ann's Caunton Avenue flats demolished. There was a St Augustine's Tenants and Residents Association for the area bounded by Woodborough Road, Robin Hood Chase, Abbotsford Drive and Peas Hill Road. Linbird Green was Chairman.

Fr Hannigan did much to support the new Vietnamese community in St Ann's. They are: "very faithful to St Augustine's School. Many now live in St Edward's Parish (Fr Michael Copps)." St Edward's Parish is the other side of St Ann's Well Road.

Father McBrien left St Augustine's in September 2000 and is now [2002] at Bishop's House in the City. St Augustine's Parish is looked after by the Cathedral priests.

Fr Philip McBrien blesses the statue of St Augustine after it was unveiled at the Patronal Feast on May 27th 1993. Nottingham Diocesan Year Book 1994. The statue stands on a plinth on one side of the main church doors with the statue of the Sacred Heart, from the old Mapperley Convent of the Sisters of St Joseph of Peace, on the other

QUENTIN JACKSON

Born 1930

*Interviewed at St Edward's Friary, Gordon Road, St Ann's, 3.2.00. The Friary is next to the **Church of Our Lady and St Edward***

St Edward's Parish currently covers an area from the St Ann's Well Road up to Mapperley Top and down the Carlton Road, so more than half of it is within the general area of St Ann's. The Parish originated about 1886 and a school was founded. Possibly it had existed before, but it went into premises on Hunt Street, St Ann's. Hunt Street doesn't exist any more. It was roughly at the top of the present Southampton Street. This school served as a church at weekends, and there was a Priest's house nearby.

The Parish was not doing very well and in 1930, the Bishop asked the Head of the Franciscans if they would come in and take over the Parish, which they did. Then things started to improve, but the area was very poor. That was partly why the Friars came here, we go to the poorer parts of cities.

On a Friday evening, people laboriously took away the desks, brought out Church furniture and made it look like a little Church until Sunday evening when the reverse procedure happened. They managed to have dances and socials in the school premises. But from the early days of the Friars being here, they purchased an open plot of land which was used for allotments higher up the hill.

Then in the 1950s, they built the Church, which is now the Church of Our Lady and St Edward. It was very difficult to scrape the money together. It was raised by public subscription. Next they built the first stage of the building to replace the school which was very old. Then they built a Social Club and that was a good source of revenue. So that paid off the debts that had been incurred and provided money for the completion of the school. Last of all, they built a house for the Friars which is the present Friary. It's all on this site now. So the early Friars here had a long vision in purchasing this site, and now people have a very good set of buildings. People cared very much for their Church.

Some of the older people, and there are many who still remember the 1950s, expressed wonder that this was their church. They remember the old church in the school. I would have just seen the old school, but I don't really remember it. I would have seen it when visiting the Friary in the 1960s. The house was notorious among the Friars in this Country. The local Friars took the line that they were soon going to move out of the house, so if a floorboard goes we won't replace it. The house was in a dreadful state but money was very short. There was never a lot of money.

This building [the Friary] is good and comfortable to live in but it's hard on maintenance because a cheap building makes expensive maintenance. But that's not true of the Church. The Church is built to a good quality. But the school is expensive to maintain because the initial building was cheap.

The Friary is the flat roofed building in the foreground adjoining the well-built Church. The School and Club are behind the Church. Photo: Ruth I Johns 2001

We Friars are mobile people. Every three years, we have a general move around. Superiors are appointed to each house and communities change. In the course of the general movements, I came here in 1981. There were several of us youngish Friars in those days and we engaged in the work of the Parish and also quite a lot of other work. Chaplains went to the Youth Custody Centre at Lowdham as it was then, to Nottingham Jail, to the hospitals, and we work in Emmanuel House working ourselves and also involving the lay people of the parishes to a certain extent.

Shortly afterwards, the Bishop pushed me into being Chaplain at Trent Polytechnic [now Trent University]. So while we were here as animators in this Parish, we also did these other things, often with the less fortunate, the marginalized. Some work is done with the Sisters, the Youth Agencies and so on. The Youth Custody Centre is now a Private Prison at Lowdham and I spend a lot of time there. I have other national responsibilities.

For example, I'm the Religious Assistant to the Poor Clares. They have eleven monasteries throughout the country. They are enclosed communities. I do a certain amount of translating for the General Curia. I receive documents by e-mail, translate them and send them back by e-mail. We've got very modern!

I've been in the Order for over fifty years and have seen tremendous changes. I was more in academic teaching in my early days so I didn't see the real poverty but you hear these stories. In 1994, I remember Mrs Kiddy reminiscing about her cycling club days and how a Friar came here and didn't have a bicycle, so they managed to raise sixpence a week between them to buy him a bicycle. There were stories of Friars looking in the cold room, before there was a fridge, and discovering that the remains of the joint they were relying on had disappeared because somebody had taken them to a local family.

There was a marvellous old Friar here who died at the age of ninety-four. He was still stomping around the streets and was frequently to be found scrubbing the floor for some old lady. He'd go round 'his' old ladies and take them

tea if they weren't well and tidy up for them. He called them old ladies but he was probably ten years older than they were.

A Friar told me he saw a young man going down the street with a towel over his back. He said: 'Are you going for a swim?' Without any irony, he said: 'No, I'm going for my weekly bath.' Now to those of us who had grown up with indoor bathrooms, we just hadn't thought that if you wanted a bath you had to go down to the Victoria [Slipper] Baths.

The houses had outdoor toilets and no bath. Things have improved immensely, though the District Heating Scheme in the new houses has always been a bone of contention. I think it's largely replaced now by individual gas heating units.

There is still poverty but it is a very different kind of poverty. The kind of poverty which exists now is more a difficulty with managing money rather than the absence of money.

We don't give money now unless we know the person and know their circumstances. We don't give money without questions; there are always those who are looking for money for drink and drugs. People in need come to us largely for food. It's always better to make mistakes in giving food than to send somebody who's really needy away. That's the principle we work on.

There are five Friars here now. A couple of us are already 'retired'. About four hundred people worship in Church on a Sunday. There are a lot of families. There is close working between Parish, School and families. We visit families, we still keep up that tradition. It's very important. We have some extremely good lay people who come and run catechist programmes of preparation for Baptism, Communion, Marriage, and parenting.

The Social Club is open every night from seven until elevenish. It has a Management Committee and a steward. It's not doing as well as it was. They have a dance every week but interest has waned. Bingo a couple of nights a week is a good service to the local community because there are quite a lot of elderly people who don't go far and it just provides them with an alternative to looking at four walls. There's a Mothers and Toddlers Club at present, Irish Dancing, there has been Karate, Youth Clubs. Some are doing all right but it's more difficult today.

When this club was built, there were a lot of people who saw it as their recreational place and they went regularly. Nowadays they want variety so sometimes they will come here and sometimes go to other places. We have volunteers, including young ones. For example, all Catholic Parishes have a St Vincent de Paul Society. It's quite active. Every couple of months, it takes a group of people out for a meal. They may not always be the most materially poor, but the housebound, and it's an occasion for socialising and being affirmed.

It was our St Vincent de Paul Society that established Ozanam House on Blythe Street, Mapperley about ten years ago. It's got its own Management Committee but we are still much involved. We've given quite a lot of money to it this year because they are extending.

A message for fifty years' time? Franciscans believe that it is out of poverty that really valuable things come. We Franciscans came in because it was a limping Parish really. Now at the moment we are seeing a really lively Parish which has come out of that poverty and which is still trying to address itself to that poverty. We Friars are looking more closely to see what we should be doing. We're not content simply to continue the things which we are doing at the moment or the way we're going about it. We're looking very hard to see what are the real needs of the locality. Circumstances change and we must move with the times.

When people have everything they want in their lives, they want that to continue, and that's death, absolute death.

In times past, priests were always addressed as 'Father'. Our role is better expressed now by the title 'Brother'.

We are Francis of Assisi people. You will know something of him? Born just before 1200, he saw that the poor people were being neglected. He gathered a group around him without any preconceptions about where he was going. But he wanted to be of service. Somebody said to him: 'You had better go and get approval.' So he went to the Pope. You could go straight to the top in those days. The Pope tried to steer him in the direction of conventional religious life and thought Francis's ideas were too vague and would lead into heresy.

But Francis insisted he wanted to stay with the poor, not to have any power, have no possessions but to live the Gospel. So that's where it started, with no preconceptions. Among the first people to join him were some Priests and so from early days they diversified in their work. Francis was concerned to be with the poor. The lepers were a big concern in those days. But very early on, Friars got into the Universities and founded some great medieval Universities. And we are a Missionary Order and are in most countries of the world. But we are always being tugged back, come back and keep aware of the original vision of Francis. Go to the poor and live with them, be Brothers to them.

Brothers can be trained lay people. In this community in recent years we had a Brother who was a highly trained Paediatrician. He was the Charge Nurse on the first Infants Oncology Ward at the Queen's Medical Centre for seven years. An interesting Brother here at the moment joined us a little later in life. He had been an Insurance Assessor in the Aircraft Division, so his job was to go round to air crashes and sort out insurance. He would come to me and say: 'Quentin, I've just discovered this liability needs to be insured against.'

Yes, we work in schools. Our school here is the feeder school for the Becket School and some go to Christ the King School. There's so much to be done in school besides just the immediate teaching. There are a lot of children who don't have a daddy at home but they need men that they can relate to and who are safe.

People don't go to their Priests so much now, they go to their doctors, or - if they are posher - to their counsellors. If they are American, then they go to their analyst. What they really want is to find a wise person, wise and sympathetic. And I think that probably is one of the things we're trying to be.

When I first came here from London, there were representatives through several generations of a family still close at hand. People had grannies nearby. People hadn't scattered so much. But, some of the people who talk about the old back-to-backs on Dowson Street, Sketchley Street and so on are still in the area. And a considerable number of those who moved out still come back because they have members of their families in St Ann's.

This was an area of considerable Irish concentration. There was a considerable influx in the 1960s and this continued. The Parish was a good meeting point to mix with the older generation of native Nottinghamiens. The Irish content has been considerably diluted now, but it's still there. But the Irish themselves are second and third generation. It's a happy mix.

My hope is that we would keep close contact with the local community and be part of it. The danger is that religion will become an isolated, separate activity from the ordinary life of people. Technology brings a sort of self-reliance. Or, if I can't do it myself, at least there's a Government that will do it for me, or Social Services. Or if something dreadful happens to me, I will get money to make it good for me like the dancer last night who got £8m. There's that belief that there's security all the way around and at least I'll get money. And that has replaced the real belief in God. People are not asking what is life, what am I, what is my life about? Those questions are too scary so let's get on with the immediate.

CHURCH OF CHRIST

Mrs Edith Sharp, interviewed below, told me that all the Churches of Christ in the Nottinghamshire District sprang from the Brethren who met in the warehouse of Brother Jonathan Hine. By 1839, there were too many members to accommodate and a redundant building on Barker Gate, in the Lace Market, known as Salem Chapel, was purchased.

In 1881, the Salem Chapel was sold because it was in the middle of a business area and the Brethren felt it would be better to go where more people lived. They chose a site in Long Hedge Lane, St Ann's, and purchased sufficient land to build a Chapel and schools. The schoolrooms were completed first and the Church held its first meeting in the Upper Schoolroom on June 24th 1882. Opening Services were held at the Chapel itself on Sunday, September 17th 1882. Extra seats had to be brought in to accommodate everyone at the Evening Service. The next day there was a tea and social meeting for 250 people.

Churches of Christ in the Nottinghamshire District spread as far as Leicester, Loughborough, Lincoln, Horncastle, Louth and Spilsby.

The St Ann's Church of Christ was demolished at the time of St Ann's redevelopment and the current small church building was opened on May 20th 1978 and shared with the Independent Methodist Church from Carlton Road.

EDITH SHARP (Nee Haywood)

Born 1926

*Interviewed in her home 17.5.00. Mrs Sharp told me about the **St Ann's Church of Christ** which was a discovery for me. I did not know of this church before except from a caption on a photo of Mr and Mrs Robert Halliday [of Sherwood Church of Christ] found in an empty house in St Ann's at the time of demolition*

I was born on Wigley Street, St Ann's. There were six of us in the family. I had a sister and two brothers older than me and a younger brother and sister. My mother came from Brinsley to be a domestic worker for somebody in a shop who lived on Blue Bell Hill, St Ann's. My father was born in Nottingham and worked for Skinner and Rook [Provision and Wine Store] on Long Row. And they had a factory bottling beer, wines and spirits. My father went out delivering. In those days, there were big houses and those people made orders and everything was delivered to them.

We moved to the top of Flewitt Street, No 158 I think, but the family got so big we moved across the road to 101, Flewitt Street, St Ann's. St Edward's Roman Catholic Church used to be on Hunt Street before it went to the top of Gordon Road. I lived just over the wall from the old St Edward's Church playground. Quite a lot of children around us were Roman Catholic. There was only a little wall between the playground and us and I used to talk to them over the wall. It was quite an interesting life. The Franciscan Friars lived at the top of Hunt Street and when their accommodation got demolished they moved to the top of Gordon Road.

I went to St Matthias School and then to Pierrepont School. When I was a child, the Pierrepont School was Rose Hill Farm. I can remember cows, sheep, grass, crops... My grandmother, Hannah Shelbourne, who lived with us used to be a worker on the farm when she was young. After the farm was taken over in the 1930s, my grandmother used to fetch lace work from the Lace Market. She had a great big square barrow made of wicker-work, and she would take it up to the Lace Market and get it filled with lace work for clipping and drawing. As a little girl, I used to take parcels of this lace work round to women in Young Street, Gordon Road, Young's Terrace and Wigley Street for the women to do this work for my grandmother.

She was the matriarch who organised this work locally. I would fetch the parcels back when the work was done and then my mother would write out the bills of how many drawings, how many this and that people had done, and I would take the money round. It was probably only two or three shillings a week they would earn for it.

I liked Pierrepont School. I was only telling my husband the other day that - at school - I made my own school dress and my own school jumper. Miss Moultby was the Headmistress. Miss Norman was the music teacher. Miss Bickers was the PE teacher. She was a little tiny person. I can't remember her name but I liked the teacher who took maths. She was very strict. I enjoyed maths.

I can remember the Cavendish Cinema being built in 1935. It was wonderful to have that Cinema at the bottom of the hill.

I attended the Church of Christ on the corner of Young Street and Gordon Road from when I was a toddler. It was opened on June 24th 1882. It was all built with member's subscriptions. The Church never had money from anywhere else. It was knocked down with the St Ann's redevelopment. It was a big church building and a big schoolroom and they completed the schoolroom first. The present Church is on the same site. It was opened May 20th 1978.

They redeveloped all the way around the old Church, which was a building that took a lot of upkeep. When I was young there were sixty or more members and at least six classes in the Sunday school. The members decided to try and keep the schoolroom and demolish the Church. But something fell on the structure and in the end we had to take the lot down. The new Church is a little Marley building.

I married in 1947 and moved to Clifton but we only stayed there for a year and a half and then moved to Broxtowe and after six years we did an exchange and came to this house in Bestwood Park. My father died in 1941. He was wounded in the First World War and in 1941 he had to have a leg off and died soon after. They didn't know much medically then. My mother, younger brother and eldest sister were still living in St Ann's at the time of demolition. They moved out to Somersby Road, Arnold, to a house they bought.

At Church, the thing I remember most are the Anniversaries. Sometimes, there were one hundred children, all tiered-up in the Church singing the Anniversary songs. We used to practise for week after week. The Church of Christ was mainly in the Midlands and started in 1836 with a meeting in a warehouse of Jonathan Hine where the Broad Marsh bus station is now. It came out of the Scottish Baptist tradition and believed in baptism by immersion. I can't remember now exactly when it was but there was a division in the congregation. Some people wanted to join the United Reformed Church [URC], and a ballot was held. I was only young at the time. And the Church of Christ Churches decided whether to join or to stay in its own right. Quite a few people went into the URC. For instance, there's a URC in Bulwell that was a Church of Christ, in fact there were two Churches of Christ in Bulwell. There was one in North Sherwood Street. That was the one you wrote to me about, saying you'd found a photo of one of their religious plays. When I was young, there were thirteen Churches of Christ in the Nottingham District, including Underwood, Ilkeston . . .

We had an Arts Festival for all those thirteen Churches of Christ at the Albert Hall on Derby Road in the City Centre. You could enter contests for scripture reading, poetry, singing ... and religious plays and so on. We used to have a Sports Day. I can remember being in the Nativity Plays year after year and everyone had some job to help.

The Church sent out Missionaries who had a skill like teaching or medicine. We had a Mr and Mrs Mottershaw who went out to Africa somewhere. They brought this little girl back home with them and, in the Sunday school, we thought it was lovely to meet a girl from Africa that we'd helped to send pennies to. She went back home when they returned to Africa. There was a lot of co-operation from the American Churches of Christ, which are mainly known as the Church of Christ Disciples. There are a lot of such churches in America and Australia.

I would say the main appeal of the Church of Christ was simplicity. When I was first in the Church, they didn't have Ministers. All the work was done by Lay Ministers and Church members and everything was done voluntarily. In those days, ladies weren't allowed to do much in the Church. They had to sit back and listen, same as St Paul said. But gradually the ladies did take part.

It was a non-denominational church. During a wedding ceremony led by a Lay Elder of the Church, you had to have the Registrar of Weddings sitting in the Vestry listening to the service. We believe that there is no such thing as denomination.

After the Second World War, it gradually became harder to be a Christian because everybody tended to be rather critical. You were regarded as a goody goody if you went to church. My own brothers and sisters were very kind-hearted people but, after they were about fourteen years old, they thought they were too big to go to church. And I would say I was sorry but I couldn't go out with them in the evening because I'd got a meeting at Church. In those days we had Prayer Meetings and Youth Meetings perhaps three times a week.

When we opened up our new Church after the redevelopment, it was not just our Church but also the Independent Methodist Church from Carlton Road on the edge of St Ann's. They only had a few members and whilst we were waiting for our Church to be built, we worshipped in their Church. Then eventually they sold it to another church, it's a Black congregation now.

When we first went into the new Church in St Ann's, we had a nice Sunday school and youngsters. And we'd have mid-week meetings. But gradually people got cars and took the children out on Sundays. And people grew up and moved out of the area to probably what was thought of as a better area. There are only three Churches of Christ in the Nottingham District now, at Riddings, Selston and St Ann's, where there are only about seven of us who worship at the Church on Sundays.

There's the St Ann's fraternal as we call it. It consists of our Church, the Chase Baptist Church, St Ann with Emmanuel Church and St Edward's Catholic Church. We keep in touch and have meetings together. We have a joint Songs of Praise occasionally, we've had hunger lunches during Lent where you have a bowl of soup and cup of tea and give your money for famine relief. At special times in the Church Calendar, we get together in each other's churches and it's very uplifting. This is something that started after the redevelopment of the area.

I don't go back to St Ann's except on Sundays now. All the people who actually lived around moved away when it was redeveloped you see. They were just scattered about to different areas. I can remember them demolishing that lovely St Ann's Church on St Ann's Well Road. I don't know why they had to demolish it. There used to be a St Bartholomew's Church on top of Blue Bell Hill and they took that down and I don't know what happened to it. My youngest sister got married there. It was a beautiful church. Street names in St Ann's are very confusing because of the way they were changed or re-used at the time of demolition.

Where people live now, people always have their curtains or blinds drawn sitting watching television. In the old St Ann's, the women used to sit at their front door doing their lace work and watching children. They used to keep a sheet or something under the lace work to keep it clean. It was difficult keeping it clean; there weren't any vacuum cleaners then.

When I left school, I went to work in the office at Skinner and Rook, the firm where my father worked. I worked there for two years and was sixteen and the War had been going awhile, and I asked for a rise. They said I was earning enough for a sixteen year old. So I found a job at W J Furse, an engineering factory in Traffic Street. I spent most of my time in their office until after the War and enjoyed it very much.

I got married in 1947 to Les who was born in Basford. He's one of twins. We have three children, two daughters and a son, and three grandchildren. My son and his family went to live in Australia just over two years ago. I've visited them once. I never believed I would go to Australia on an aeroplane.

Edith and Les Sharp after their wedding at the Church of Christ in St Ann's, 1947. Frank Sharp, twin brother of the groom, is on the far left, front row. The mother of the groom, Edith Sharp, stands behind him. His father, Samuel Sharp, is far right of the second row. The bride's mother, Ellen Haywood, stands behind the bride, and her grandmother, Hannah Shelbourne is next to her mother. The bride's brother, John Haywood, is far right of the first row. On the Church notice board, it says: 'Keys 101, Flewitt Street'. 'That was my mum's house. She used to clean the Church,' said Edith Sharp

Another family wedding. Edith Sharp's elder brother, John Haywood on his special day outside the Church of Christ

At the 'new' St Ann's Church of Christ, Reenie Wilkins (nee Merrin), left, and Edith Sharp. Reenie Wilkins was related to Billy Merrin, one time dance band leader at the Victoria Ballroom, St Ann's Well Road

Left to right standing, Joan Pare and George Burke and sitting, Reenie Wilkins and Edith Cumberland (nee Gent). She lived in one of the houses facing the former Church and seen in the photo of John Haywood's wedding

ISLAMIC CENTRE

I visited the Islamic Centre, Curzon Street, St Ann's 4.4.95

The Islamic Centre. Photo: E James Smalley 2000

I was to see Sufi Ramazan, the secretary, but he could not be there. It was agreed that the treasurer, Haji Karim and a colleague would take me round the Mosque after prayers. I was taken through the main hall, where ten men were praying, to the floor where women pray and from which you see the Imam.

The new Mosque cost over £1m. It is a beautiful building and I was struck at the unusual open views offered up St Ann's Well Road through the lattice grilles in Islamic arches. When prayers finished, I was shown the main hall and the downstairs hall which has facilities for funeral services. It is an immense size and can get very crowded. At funeral services everyone stands.

Downstairs, a vehicle can drive up to a large garage-sized door at the back of the building and the deceased person taken into the mortuary. The body is prepared for prayers and taken into the funeral parlour. Burial is in space reserved for the community at the Wilford Hill Cemetery, West Bridgford.

Mr Karim said the new Mosque was built little by little: "We did it ourselves." There was a wire hanging down from the dome roof awaiting a chandelier when funds allowed. And a minaret is still needed, but an extension is in progress at the back. "Sufi Ramazan was a leading spirit to get the Mosque built. We're still paying the debt." £75,000 had been given by City Challenge and £75,000 by the City Council in recent times.

Many who pray at the Mosque are from Kashmir. Haji Karim told me that more of the Pakistani Kashmiri community lived in St Ann's before demolition of the area. He lives in Sneinton. Others come from Carlton and Forest Fields. It is the biggest Islamic Centre in the area. There were 400-500 at Friday prayers. At prayers five times a day, there were some 30-40 men.

There are classes for boys and girls under ten for one and a half hours in the evenings and for two hours for boys over ten. There is always someone in the office to offer advice. Often it is Sufi Ramazan. Mr Karim said: "People visit each other and try to help each other. We want people to have a fair deal: young people to behave themselves, no drugs. There's bad unemployment in this area."

The founding of the Islamic Centre, opened in 1992, was not without its problems due to the power struggle between various groups of Pakistani Muslims in the City at the time [1968] when the Campbell Street mosque in St Ann's was the only mosque in Nottingham. It was an old Methodist church awaiting demolition as part of the clearance of St Ann's and rented to the Mosque Committee by the City Council.

In 1975, there was a confrontation by two groups outside the Campbell Street mosque which Akhtar Hussain likens to a scene inside the Stoney Street Baptist Chapel in the Lace Market in 1817[1].

"To those Pakistanis and Kashmiris who lived in Nottingham in the 1970s, 1980s and 1990s, the description of the trouble in Stoney Street Chapel in 1817 would seem so familiar with their own experiences of infighting among Muslims in their Nottingham mosques."

Before the present site of the Islamic Centre on Curzon Street was available, it was to be built on Carlton Road/Stonebridge Road. Events in the mid-1970s surrounding the Centre are complicated and are outlined in Akhtar Hussain's book.

At Curzon Street, a temporary mosque was built in 1978. The temporary building, built by the community itself, was used for fourteen years. I was told that it would eventually be pulled down. However, in the meantime the temporary mosque was converted into a large modern hall. When I visited the new Mosque in 1995, the old building was still very plain outside but, as shown in the more recent photo, it has been renovated.

Raja Mohammad Azam [Chairman of the Islamic Centre Management Committee] told Atkhtar Hussain that: "Anyone can come and pray here. The issue that Imam must be of Barailvi sect is right. Imam leads the prayer. This is normal that each mosque has an Imam. The

The original temporary building and building work in progress. Photo: E James Smalley 2000

question of conducting funeral services was a big problem. With the help of friends I have established that the relatives of the deceased should be allowed to choose any person of any sect to lead funeral prayer in the Islamic Centre. This is being done in practice, and this will continue."

The Nottingham Evening Post June 17th 1977 stated that the City Planning Committee had approved plans to build a mosque and religious complex on land owned by the City Council at Curzon Street, St Ann's. The Chairman, Oscar Watkinson said the outline planning permission did not prevent other applications. A number of representations from different factions of the Muslim community had been made to him and other city councillors. But the validity of different groups to represent the community was not within the committee's province.

The go-ahead for building the Mosque was given by the Planning Committee in June 1979. Evening Post June 15th 1979 The Planning Officer, Stephen Byrne, said the requirements that it should face Mecca had not posed any problems. The Mosque, complete with dome and minaret, would make an interesting addition to the City skyline. One condition imposed was that the minaret should not be used: 'for any kind of live or recorded music, speech or invocation.'

The foundation stone was laid in 1981. By 1984, progress had been stop-go due to funding. Mr Hussain Bhatti, Chairman of the Islamic Centre, made many trips abroad to fund-raise. Nottingham Trader March 14th 1984. Gifts included £50,000 from the Iraqi Government, £12,500 from Saudi Arabia and 42,000 Rupees from the Pakistan Government, as well from the community in Nottingham and other parts of the country.

By 1987, the Mosque was still half built. Nottingham Evening Post November 18th 1987 reported that the Home Office was concerned whether there were political overtones associated with cash being given to mosques in Britain by countries like Libya and Saudi Arabia. Mr Bhatti stated that gifts were gestures of goodwill to help a community realise a dream.

Nottingham Evening Post September 5th 1989 reported that Hanson Engineering, the Heanor structural steelwork group, had completed placing the dome on the Islamic Centre.

Nottingham Evening Post March 2nd 1992 reported that Muslims from around England joined Nottingham's Islamic community to celebrate the opening of the new Mosque in St Ann's. Centre secretary Sufi Ramazan said: "It has been a long wait but it has been worth all the effort." Religious leaders including the international figure Pir Sayed Manaver Hussain Shah led the celebrations. Labour's prospective parliamentary candidate for Nottingham East, county councillor John Heppell, promised £75,000 towards the completion of the adjacent community centre. Sufi Ramazan said £225,000 was still needed.

The Pakistan Centre on Woodborough Road, St Ann's, is also available for Muslim prayers, and it is a social centre for many other activities. See under Pakistan Centre

1   *The Four Tribes of Nottingham: the story of Pakistanis and Kashmiris in Nottingham* by Akhtar Hussain [Awami Publishers, Karachi. 1999]. Available from 96 Newgate Road, Sale, Manchester M33 4WY.

SEVENTH-DAY ADVENTIST CHURCH

At the Seventh-day Adventist Church, on the corner of St Ann's Wells Road and Lamartine Street, St Ann's, I was made welcome at the Over Sixties Lunch Club 9.11.99. I spoke with James McNeill, Sam Nugent, Murelda Elson and Sister Patricia Douglas.

Previously, the Church was located in North Sherwood Street until 1975 when the present site was offered to the Church as part of the area's redevelopment programme. The first Pastor of the new Church was Pastor H Parkin who moved over with the membership from North Sherwood Street. He was followed by Pastor G Harris 1979-84, then Pastor P Rhodes who was succeeded by Pastor Eric Lowe. Pastor Curtis Murphy, the present minister, came in 1992. This Church, the Nottingham Central SDA Church, is one of three Seventh-day Adventist Churches in Nottingham.

The Church was dedicated on June 19th 1976. The Mayor of Nottingham, Councillor S J Rushton, attended. Brother James McNeill, who previously lived in Radford, was present at the opening of the Church. In 1978, he moved to St Ann's and lives close to the Church. Its present membership is one hundred and eighty.

James McNeill said: "More than ninety per cent of the congregation is made up of people of Afro-Caribbean origin. There is also a large percentage at the Chase Baptist Church. Afro-Caribbean people play a great part in the churches in this community. I think black and white people get along very well in St Ann's. In the social field they get on well too. The young people get on together. Some of the older Afro-Caribbean people, both men and women, work allotments. They spend a lot of time gardening on the Hungerhill allotments in St Ann's."

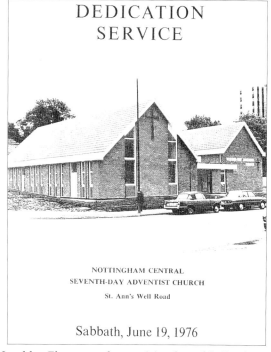

DEDICATION SERVICE

NOTTINGHAM CENTRAL
SEVENTH-DAY ADVENTIST CHURCH
St. Ann's Well Road

Sabbath, June 19, 1976

Murelda Elson used to visit the old St Ann's for shopping and visiting relatives. Now she comes from Wollaton to St Ann's primarily to attend Church for worship and other meetings. The congregation comes from Beeston, Rise Park, Clifton, Carlton, Sherwood and Bakersfield, as well as St Ann's.

The main worship is on Saturday, beginning with Sabbath School for Adults and a children's Sabbath School, followed by a Service for adults and children. The Adventist Youth Society meet later in the day, and during the week there is a Prayer Meeting. As part of the Church's work for the community, on Thursdays food is cooked on the premises to take to homeless people in Market Square, City Centre. This is funded by members of the Church.

Christmas dinner 1978, organised by the Church's Community Services team, and held in a hall in Beeston

ST ANN'S NOTTINGHAM: inner-city voices *by Ruth I Johns* • ISBN 0951696092

Holiday at Skegness organised by the Church's Community Service team

Murelda Elson said the Community Service Department of the Church had been active for many years. At Christmas, a proper Christmas dinner is prepared for the homeless. An anti-smoking clinic has been held on the premises for the local community 'with quite a lot of success'.

Murelda Elson was the Community Services Leader for a considerable time with a team of twelve members. From 1976-94, senior citizens from St Ann's and Beeston were taken on holiday to Skegness or Mablethorpe. The Local Authority Social Services Department was asked to suggest people who needed a holiday with help and support. Later in the year, in October, they would have an outing to Derbyshire for tea and an opportunity to show photographs to each other. At Christmas they would come to Church for Christmas dinner. One result of this programme was that a couple, both in wheelchairs, met each other and were later married in St Ann with Emmanuel Church, St Ann's, by the Rev Jim Neill.

Four members of the Church's Community Service Team. Left to right: Doreen Wood, Murelda Elson, Mary Worbey, Sonia Collins

A Christmas, dinner for senior citizens of the local community is still provided. Students who are studying away from home and who live locally are also invited.

Sometimes, Pastor Curtis Murphy takes School Assemblies at Sycamore Junior School, where he's also a Governor, and at Bluecoat's Secondary School.

Murelda Elson said: "When we first came here, people didn't understand our religion. They thought we were a strange Sect, and I think some said we were a cult. And we had to stay here and prove that we were not. And now they come and ask to be married here and to bring their babies to be blessed. And some of them pop in and worship with us."

James McNeill added: "And even now, some people think we had connections with the disaster which struck the Davidian cult in Waco, Texas, some years ago. The only connection we had was that some of our young people were misled by a representative of the Davidians in Wacco. We tried to dissuade them from going, pointing out the dangers, but they didn't listen and sadly they died in the disaster."

Murelda Elson: "They broke all ties with us when they went. Nevertheless, we were deeply grieved to lose our beloved members in such tragic circumstances."

There are a number of clubs. The Over Sixties Lunch Club on Tuesdays is for both Church and the community at large. There is a meal and recreational activities. On Wednesday, there is a Prayer Meeting in the evening. There is a Youth Choir, called United Voices, because sometimes they sing with young people from other churches. They practise on a Monday night and take part in services and events. Sometimes they visit local residential homes. There is a Pathfinder Club for 9-16 year olds and an Adventurers Club for 5-9 year olds. They meet up with other such clubs once a year at camporees. In school holidays, there are holiday schemes for children; at least once a year for a couple of weeks.

James McNeill notes that since 1976, there have been some changes in the Church. "Then, many of the major offices in the Church were held mainly by white people. Now they are shared. Another change is that women are nominated to the eldership of the Church. And now there is inclusion of different types of music in the worship services, including guitars, saxophone, trumpet, drums and so on. It used to be organ and piano."

Leadership of the Church is through the Pastor and a number of Elders. Elders, and other church officers, are voluntary. Patricia Douglas is the present ministerial intern at the Church.

She has completed five years' training at the Seventh-day Adventist Seminary, Newbold College in Bracknell. As part of her advanced training, Patricia Douglas became an intern assisting Pastor Murphy for a year. Then she will have a second year in another place.

Patricia Douglas said: "I think this is very much a community church. Everyone is welcome. We see ourselves as a family of God and we don't like to ostracise anyone. We try to cater for people of all age groups. And the Church tries to respond to both local and international need."

2002. Sister Patricia Douglas went on to serve the second year of her internship in Leicester and, from June this year, she was licensed Pastor serving the Tamworth, Walsall and Cannock churches. She is the first woman to be given this position by the North England Conference of the SDA Church. From 2001, Pastor Curtis Murphy has been President of the Irish Mission

Lunch preparation and some of the other activities at a Tuesday Lunch Club get together at the Seventh-day Adventist Church on the St Ann's Well Road. Photos: E James Smalley 2000

Shops

Shops are mentioned many, many times by people who lived in or who remember the 'old' St Ann's. The Index will help readers to find shop references. This section includes recollections of people who ran or run shops in St Ann's, or who worked in them. Recollections of one family shop includes two generations. One recollection is of a fourth generation member of a shop which started in St Ann's. One is of someone who still runs a shop in St Ann's after losing two at the time of demolition.

It is sad that we have few photos of shops whilst the area was still colourful and bustling. Long after starting this book, I was glad to learn that members of the Nicholson family had taken many photos of the 'old' St Ann's, mainly just prior to redevelopment. They were sorting the photos for an exhibition at Nottingham Central Library 2002.

In 1967, Tom Lynch, President of the National Union of Small Shopkeepers, urged Nottingham's planners to reconsider plans to replace 650 small shops in St Ann's when the area was redeveloped and to replace them with only fifty. In the event, there were less than fifty, and some of the new ones that were built were soon shut because of their position (for example, in Marple Square Shopping Precinct). A few others were provided in response to campaigning (for example, at the bottom of St Bartholomew's Road).

Mr Lynch said many of the shopkeepers did not own their properties but occupied them on a weekly rental, so consequently the only compensation they would get would probably be two years' rateable value. Evening Post 8.9.67.

He said some shopkeepers had sunk up to £5,000 in their businesses and, because of the redevelopment, would

These four photos depict an experience I often saw: the sheer grit of elderly people or mothers with prams and/or small children walking the gauntlet of boarded-up or demolished properties to do their shopping. For some people, this went on for many months. Some were rehoused from accommodation about to be demolished and placed in that with maybe only a few months to go. Photos: Nicholson Photo Archive

have no chance of selling. He doubted they would be able to afford the rents of the new shops when built.

His Union urged Nottingham Corporation to slow down on the pulling-down, to have another look at their long-term redevelopment plans and to pay more attention to improving existing property in the area.

Mr P L Allerton, Assistant Planning Officer, said no really firm decision had been taken on the number of shops to be replaced but agreed Mr Lynch's figures were within the broad bounds of their policy. "The thing one has to remember," he said, "is that so many of these shops are merely providing pin money for the wife while the husband goes out to work.

"When one undertakes the redevelopment of run-down areas, these little shops have to go, and the tenants are often in no position to pay higher rents for new accommodation. It is one of those unfortunate things, which rob a family of earning a little extra money. These little shops are just not economic units on their own."

JOHN GOODMAN

Born 1921

Letter received 1999

I was born on St Ann's Well Road at 154 opposite Robin Hood Chase. My father kept a Butcher's shop there until he died in 1927. We then still lived at the back and my mother rented the shop out, finally leaving in 1936.

I have pleasant memories of St Ann's Well Road. It was a friendly community of shopkeepers who got on well together and helped each other out.

We were at the end of a little block of five shops. Next-door was the Maypole Dairy, then a Beer-off, then Holden's Hat Shop, then a Fish and Chip Shop and then Beacon Street. The other way was Hopewell's Furniture Showrooms, a ladies' hairdresser, then a chemist.

As a young lad, I was often taken for rides around the area and Nottingham by one of Hopewell's drivers, Tommy Roberts. He was a great friend of my father's. At the other corner of Beacon Street was the Chase Tavern, kept by the Brentnall family. Their son Jack later kept a Music Shop opposite the Hippodrome in the City and was a committee member of Nottingham Forest Football Club.

When the trams were running, it was great fun for us lads to put pennies on the tramlines and let the tram put a groove in them.

I had the attic bedroom at 154, and one of the joys of a winter evening was lying in bed and watch the lights of the trams move across the ceiling as they passed up and down the road.

There was the Robin Hood Picture House at the bottom of the Chase and we enjoyed many a matinee there on a Saturday afternoon, silent films of course, it never got to talkies.

My father stabled our horse in stables at the top of Little John Street. The horse delivered meat during the week, but all the family went for a spin on Sunday afternoon in the trap. Happy days!

HAROLD SMITH

Born 1924

From conversations. Harold Smith is one of very few people who ran shops in the old St Ann's and also in the redeveloped St Ann's

At the time of demolition, the Council took land off everyone. They only wanted Shipstone's and Home Brewery pubs in the new St Ann's. I was displaced from two shops in St Ann's due to demolition. The planners have a lot to answer for. Precincts are no good. Shops should be along a road. Precincts lead to crime. The

The tram terminus on St Ann's Well Road looking toward the City Centre. Trams would pass Robin Hood Chase round the corner. A postcard published by C & A G Lewis c1923 and found in a collection of old picture postcards: 'Sneinton and St Ann's' by Grenville Jennings [Reflections of a Bygone Age, Keyworth. 1997]

Harold Smith was born on Girsby Terrace, off Pym Street. He used to be a paper boy at this shop on the corner of Pym Street and Gordon Road. When the owner retired, he bought the business. Photo c1965

St Ann's Nottingham: inner-city voices by Ruth I Johns • ISBN 0951696092

Harold Smith's wife, Alma, 1968

Shop interior, 215, The Wells Road, 1970s

Alma's mother, Sarah Parr, at the shop at 215, The Wells Road, 1971. She was born in 1899

Harold and Alma Smith, 215, The Wells Road, June 1979

Council has spent a fortune trying to make Robin Hood Chase right.

When it was built, they decided to place a bookmaker's in the precinct. But, in 1973 in St Ann's, there wasn't a single butcher or hairdresser. There are the same people in the 'official' jobs now who made the mistakes then. If I'd made such mistakes, I would have been *out*. I felt sorry for the old people who didn't want to move away from St Ann's. Being left on their own could send them senile. My dad never got over leaving St Ann's. That was a crime.

When I had to give up the two shops I rented, I arranged to buy an existing one at 215, The Wells Road. It was then a bungalow shop. The Council only allowed 5 x the rateable value for the shops I left. That was nothing. I came to see the owner here [215, The Wells Road] and arranged to buy the shop for £4,000. I didn't have the money but I said I'd pay him 10% interest over four years. I think the usual rate of interest then was 7%, so both of us were happy. The shop quickly established itself. Over the years we extended it and I built garages on the end.

If we get any trouble in the shop, we bar the culprit, then they have to take a bus journey to get gas and electricity cards. Eventually, they ask to be let back as it's a long way to the Chase and I say: 'Yes, if you write me a letter of apology.' We have a tough policy on youngsters who steal. Some parents won't do anything if their child steals, and those kids don't stand a chance, and other parents take it seriously.

I employ ten part-time people, mostly middle-aged women. Once two young blokes came in and abused the woman behind the counter. One of her sons came in and said: 'That's my mother you're talking about.' People being abused by yobs need to see strength or they will come back. They are really cowards. But there is no more crime than there was 20-30 years ago. Nobody's ever offered me drugs. I've never seen any although there must be places where people can get them.

This year [2002] I'm handing over to my great-nephew, Carl Smith, who started by helping out and then became a partner. His mum, Gillian, does the books. I won't retire. I'll still be around for help and advice. Doreen Clark, who you met, used to look after my mother and she looked after my wife. Now she comes four times a week to look after me!

Harold and Alma Smith and her mother (behind the counter)

Alma at the back of 215, The Wells Road, 1979. 'That's where the garages now are' said Harold Smith [2002]. He said Alma died seven years ago

The Wells Road shop in the mid-1980s. The new building next door is a home for the frail elderly

Alison Thomas behind the counter at The Wells Road shop, early 1980s. 'She started as a paper girl. Her family were born on Pym Street. Her brother Chris also started as a paper boy. He became a partner at one time. Now he has his own business (wholesale milk and bread) and he has Beardsall's old factory let out as business units,' said Harold Smith

Chris and Harold's van c1982

Harold Smith over the shop at The Wells Road. 'The premises were built in the 1930s as just a barber's shop. The 'bungalow shop' had a lounge which he gradually opened up into what is now the main shop

St Ann's Nottingham: inner-city voices By Ruth I Johns • ISBN 0951696092

The shop 2002. The end portion is let off as a Barber's shop. This photo by E James Smalley for Plowright Press. All the others courtesy of Harold Smith

I still see Ray Gosling occasionally. We go back a long way.

In the mid-1960's I stood for Council once, in Forest Ward. It was when I was working with Raleigh. Betty and Frank Higgins asked if I would stand and they were my agents.

I remember Oliver Hinds, Patron of Dakeyne Street Boxing Club [in nearby Sneinton]. He bought land at Chapel St Leonards so kids could go camping. You used to have to be twelve before you could go, but I went from aged ten. The last time was two weeks before the War broke out. There was a big field with a brick cookhouse and a horse trough where we got ducked. Oliver Hinds and his wife lived at Edwalton Hall and there would be outings there, with soft drinks and gymnastics.

In 1940, I was going on a week's holiday to Blackpool. We got as far as Manchester and had to turn back because of the War. A lot of Forces were billeted in Blackpool and there were queues waiting to get there. In the building trade, I had a week's holiday and also one at Christmas. Calverton Lido, Papplewick Lido and Lowdham, places just outside Nottingham, were popular for visits.

LES TOWNSEND

of Butler Morris Ltd, St Ann's Well Road branch

by **A Sheldon**

and letters

A Sheldon writes, 1999, about Les Townsend, Manager of the St Ann's Well Road branch of Butler Morris Ltd, men's, youths' and boys' clothing and outfitters shop. Les had been there for some seventeen years when A Sheldon, a local lad, started working there aged fifteen just after the start of World War Two

The shop was situated in a row between the Cavendish Cinema and Peas Hill Road. Ash's wet fish shop was on one side and Les Shaw's ironmongers on the other. Butler

Morris Ltd was a three-windowed shop, which had grown to occupy 163, 165 and 167 St Ann's Well Road, having started at 163 and this forever being known as 'the old shop'. Les started work there at the age of nineteen and soon became Manager. The shop was opposite Dr Adams' house, another well-known St Ann's venue.

A stream of callers came into the shop for a chat, not only customers. At times people used him as an agony aunt. Many times, a worried elderly lady clutching an ominous looking manila envelope marked OHMS [On His/Her Majesty's Service] would arrive for Les to give his reassuring advice on how to deal with it.

He was a very good salesman, not a high-pressure type but people trusted his judgement on their purchase. One of his junior staff would deliver goods. In 1940, I was one of these and we covered many miles by bicycle. Les too used a bicycle with some painful looking drop racing handlebars. Most days, we had a pile of trousers to be shortened and after closing time Les would set off uphill home to The Wells Road with a large parcel of trousers. These garments were shortened, hand-sewn and pressed, mostly by his wife ready for the following morning. Les would never refuse this service, although there was no charge for the alterations.

Mrs Townsend was a pleasant, glamourous lady known as Aunt Lil to younger staff. They had two children, Jean and David. Les also had a largish 'family' of canaries in breeding cages and kept chickens in his garden, as many people did during wartime.

He became a special constable early in the War and later entered the RAF Police Section, known as the 'Snowdrops' because of the white headgear.

Many police officers on the beat would drop in for a chat and a cup of tea. There were so many mirrors around the various rooms of the shop that, from the back room, we could see anyone entering the shop. In the back room there was a large cupboard which had a six foot by three foot mirror as a door. I remember an Inspector walking in the shop while a young policeman was enjoying a cup of tea and chat. Les shoved him in this mirror cupboard still clutching his tea. Les then managed to get the Inspector into another room whilst we smuggled the policeman out.

During the air raid on Nottingham in which the area around the Cavendish Cinema had several bombs, all our shop windows were shattered. When daylight came, Les was in the window areas knocking out large pieces of glass whilst I kept passing people away from the falling glass. I spent many a night on fire watching and ARP [Air Raid Precautions] duties with Les and we were back to open the shop as usual the following morning. No stress counselling or compensation in those days!

Les's daughter Jean owned a sweet and confectioner's shop on the corner of nearby Peas Hill Road and St Ann's Well Road. Most local traders would purchase their needs from other local shops and a 'trade discount' system was an incentive.

We accepted what were known as trading cheques whereby many people would take out a cheque from firms like the Progressive Supply, Provident or City and

Butler Morris shop on St Ann's Well Road, at the time of its final closing down sale 1970, when demolition was creeping closer to the shop day by day. Photo: A Sheldon

Suburban, who charged one shilling for each £1 value. These cheques could buy goods at many shops in the scheme and were big business in the 1940s, 1950s and into the 1960s.

Les would often cut a few corners with customers, not in any bad way but for the benefit of those customers. For example, a made-to-measure suit with a try-on fitting would entail adjustments being marked and returned to the makers for finishing. Delivery times were haphazard in wartime. So Les would order a suit ready-made and sew on large basting stitches with white cotton and scatter a few chalk marks. The customer would try the suit on for fitting and, after disposing of the cotton and chalk marks, the suit would be ready next day without fail for the special occasion! Les never slipped up; always a perfect fit.

Sadly, Les died in 1962, aged fifty-nine. Aunt Lil later moved from The Wells Road home to one of the flats over the shop, which had been modernised when the shop was

Bill Ward's newsagents shop at 194 and Handley's Drapers at 196, St Ann's Well Road seen here from a house in Dickinson Street c1970 as demolition approaches. The Shipstone's notice is on the wall of a shop on the corner of Cathcart Street. Photo: A Sheldon

A Sheldon's maternal grandmother's house at 16, Dickinson Street (middle house) c1970. Photo: A Sheldon

refurbished after the War. This was full-circle because Les and Lil had lived over 'the old shop' many years earlier. Their son David had been delivered by Dr Adams.

The demolition of the 1970s sadly crept toward the shop. I had the sad task, with a nephew of Les's who was also a member of the firm, of closing down the shop with a Final Sale in 1970. As the shop succumbed to the bulldozers, we all remembered 'our Les', rarely seen without a tape measure around his neck.

I moved away from St Ann's in 1955 after I got married. My widowed mother was moved later to a flat in Clifton.

THE 'PROVERBIAL' CORNER SHOP:

recollections of Mumtaz Khalique who, with her husband, started a pioneer Asian shop in St Ann's. Three of her children add their memories of that time

MUMTAZ BEGUM KHALIQUE

Born 1934

Interviewed in her home 19.4.00 and 9.5.00 and conversation. Mumtaz Khalique was born in Lahore. She was living with a brother and sister-in-law in Meerut when the troubles leading to the partition of India and Pakistan in 1947 started. She experienced a difficult train journey to Chaklala, Rawalpindi, in Pakistan and lived in a tent for new arrivals for a time.

Her life in St Ann's began ten years later, in 1957, with her husband, three children and pregnant with her fourth. Mumtaz Khalique has eight children: Javid, Shanaz, Parvaze, Robeena, Samina, Jabeena, Abraze and Nageena. Here, she talks of her early years in St Ann's when her husband, Abdul, and herself built up a successful shop on Woodborough Road. All photos: Mumtaz Khalique

We came to 30, Bangor Street, St Ann's, off the Woodborough Road. We paid half-a-crown a week for one room for all of us. There were two beds and one settee.

St Ann's Nottingham: Inner-city Voices by Ruth I Johns • ISBN 0951696092

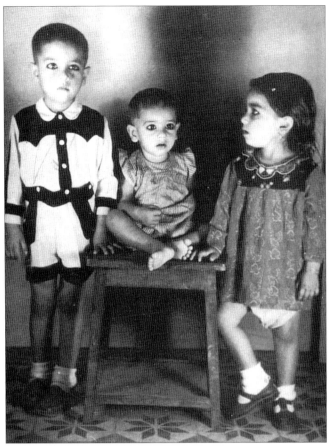

'My husband and I travelled from Rawalpindi to Nottingham with our three beautiful children looking ahead towards a bright future,' said Mumtaz Khalique of this picture

Mumtaz Khalique's brother, Nazir, in 1958. He qualified as a Homeopathic Doctor in Karachi. He couldn't find a professional job in Britain and became a bus conductor. At first, the newly arrived Khalique family stayed in the same house where Nazir lodged. Later, he stayed with them once they became settled. He married and had a family, moving to Peterborough. He has died

A friend of my husband's father was living here and my brother, Nazir, was his lodger. The friend made a cup of tea for us and bought food for us before we arrived. He showed me the kitchen.

There was a big West Indian man six-foot tall in the kitchen. He was the first West Indian I saw and he was very polite and gentle. He lived with Pakistanis before and knew a lot about us and called me 'sister'. I could not speak English at that time. His name was Jim. He was a really good man. He helped me a lot. He was also a lodger. When my husband started work and my brother went to work, they said: 'Don't worry, Jim is here to look after you.' He was fifty-five or sixty at that time.

A few weeks later, I saw a lady in shalwar and kameez. It was snowing, but I put my coat on and walked very carefully and followed her. Nobody told us there was an Indian family living nearby. There were not many Asian people at that time.

Mumtaz Khalique, October 1958

I called to her but I didn't know what her language was. I spoke Urdu, Punjabi and Mirpuri. She knew English too. Her husband had told her about us. She helped me a lot. She said: 'Don't worry. You are pregnant; when you go into hospital tell your husband to leave your children with me.'

My third brother, Dr Ayub Mirza, came back from Pakistan after two months. My husband started a job. My brother put the children at the Elms [Infant and Junior School], Cranmer Street. He said he could not take them and bring them back. He was going to Hull. He had a job there. He was a doctor.

The Indian lady took them and looked after them when my fourth child was born a week early. In my country when a woman gets labour pain, she makes loud noises to ease the birth. The doctor told my husband to tell me to keep quiet. I was in pain all day long. I gave birth to three children before and did not suffer so much. It was a very painful delivery. My husband helped me a lot.

In those days mother and baby were kept in hospital for twelve days. They looked after me well, but I wanted to come home and see my other children. We stayed for another month in that one room.

My husband's relatives in Birmingham and my father-in-law's friends in Nottingham were old people. They came by ship on work permits and did not go home. They were sailors. When I came to this country, everyone came to see us. There were not many, ten or twelve. Everybody gave me £5; at that time £5 was a lot of money. When our baby came, people from Birmingham and Sheffield came to see her. They gave me £5, £10. My husband said: 'You can keep it, they gave it to you and your daughter.' I saved nearly £200.

I remembered that my mother knew a gentleman. She was like a sister to him, a 'munh-boli' which means adopted sister. I asked my husband to see that uncle. His name was Ismail. He was pleased to see us. We had dinner there. I told him that living in Bangor Street was not bad at all. Every facility was there, a co-operative store next to the church. I did my shopping there. My friend brought my children from school. The launderette, fish shop and wool shop were close-by too. From my house, you could catch the bus No 31 to town. At that time the baby clinic was far away, near where the Bingo Club is in St Ann's.

We told Ismail we had £200. If he saw a house for us and, if we needed more money, we would return it back. I could get it from my brother or my family. He laughed and put his hand on my head and said: 'Puthar (which means daughter), don't worry.'

There were four people in a house at 145, Peas Hill Road. The Pakistani owner was going back home for good. The money people got for rent they sent to their families back home. He wanted to sell but he had lodgers who did not want to leave. It was convenient for them to go to the City and to Beeston Boilers to work. He asked if any of them wanted to buy the house.

My mother's friend, Ismail, asked him how much money he wanted for the house. He said: '£400, but, if you buy it, I will take £300. I want to go back home. I am homesick now.' He had been here for many years. He had been a sailor on a ship. He never went to see his family. He was an old man and had children back home. He put the house for sale.

My 'Uncle' Ismail came and I asked about the house. The lodgers were two Jamaicans and two Pakistanis. They were nice people, he said. The house had three storeys. The attic was rented as well. In the cellar there was a kitchen and the toilet was outside at the back. He said: 'You can have two rooms on the first floor and share the kitchen with the lodgers.' I asked to see it. My husband agreed to see it.

I thought, if I kept the lodgers, there would be ten shillings a week for each of two rooms and three people in the attic paid £1.10s. If I borrowed money, it would be paid back after three months. We talked about it and bought the house. At that time we were not able to pay a mortgage because we had children and our income was not enough. My husband's wage was £10 a week.

So we moved to Peas Hill Road. I got pregnant again and I told my husband: 'If we are progressing nothing else, we are expanding our family!'

The children, Javid, Shanaz and Parvaze and our little girl, Robeena, were growing up. Two went to school. They used to go out through the back door and back entry, because from the front door there were cars on the road. Robeena was born in 1957 (and later qualified as a School Teacher from Darlington Teacher Training College. She has taught in Derby and Nottingham).

My husband worked at Beeston Boilers. It was hard work. He was an educated and professional man back home. He loved his children very much. When I was eight months pregnant with our fifth child, my husband was feeling pain for a week but he never went to the doctor. He was a healthy man, but at last he went to the doctor and took painkillers for three or four days and was still in pain. He was losing weight and could not go to work.

I wrote to my brother in Hull and sent it first class. He is a doctor. He came to Peas Hill Road. My brother took my husband to the doctor on Woodborough Road. He called for an ambulance to take him to hospital. During this period of his illness, I gave birth to a little girl, Samina, at home (she later qualified at Oxford as a School Teacher and has taught in Nottingham and overseas, including Africa). My bed was booked in hospital, but I told the midwife my husband was not well and there was nobody to look after the children. The midwife saw the situation, everything was all right, every kind of help was available to me and I gave birth at home.

Khalique went to the General Hospital, had a small operation and was sent to the City Hospital. They kept him for three weeks. He was very upset because of his illness. My baby was a few days old, but I walked from Peas Hill Road to Mansfield Road, caught the bus to the hospital and then walked from the bus stop to the hospital, every day. He told me not to, but I wanted to see him happy. It was another bad winter.

His younger brother, Karim, came from Birmingham for a visit and found Khalique was in hospital, so he went with me regularly for two weeks to visit him. When his brother came out of hospital, he was keen to go home to Pakistan.

When my husband came back from hospital, he was still very weak. My village people told me to give him chicken soup as it gave strength. At that time, there was no Muslim shop, no Halal meat. The poultry farmers used to come by van to sell whole alive chickens door to door. We bought three or four chickens and slaughtered them. I cooked the soup which made him feel better. The doctor told him he must not do any more heavy work.

At that time, life was not easy for us. There were not many people for my husband to see. A Pakistani family was living near Robin Hood Chase. She was a villager and never came out of the house. Her husband used to work from six in the morning until six at night. We hardly met them. My husband became very thin. He could not do any job. West Indians, Pakistanis and Indians, we were all struggling for a living.

ST ANN'S NOTTINGHAM: inner-city voices *by Ruth I Johns* • ISBN 0951696092

Preparing one of the chickens. Mumtaz Khalique with (left to right) Robeena, Javid and Parvaze

My brother in Hull came when I needed his help. There were no relatives living near. There were some single men but they were old. I started to go to the grocery shop across the road. Two men who were brothers were working there. It was a very small shop but everything was available. I left the children with my husband.

One day, I went to the grocery shop, it was eleven o'clock. There was a long queue, no cash till, no self-service. I was the third person in the queue. One Pakistani was in front of me. He asked for bread, then started looking round for something. He wanted eggs. The eggs were at the back in a cool place, there was no refrigerator. The shopkeeper was looking at him and asking what else did he want. He used body language. Though I did not know much English yet, I could understand a few words. I kept

quiet. At that time, I was very shy. In our country we are not allowed to speak with strangers. The shopkeeper laughed at his body language. He gave him the eggs and he left. I came home and told my husband. I felt sorry for that man.

My husband's family in Pakistan was in business or in the Army. One day Khalique said to me: 'What do you think if I start a business of some kind?' There was no telephone in our house. I wrote to my brother, Dr Ayub. He came and we went to see 124a, Woodborough Road. It was for sale. My brother asked how we would manage. I said if he could help with money, it could be done.

At that time people were coming from India and Pakistan. I thought if someone wanted a job, we could get help in the shop. At last my brother said: 'Go on Monday, and ask about it.' We went to the estate agent. He said we could buy the shop any time. The previous owners had gone. The man was dead and the lady had now left. The price was £1,300. We offered £1,100 and he accepted it. My brother said he could give us £150 for a deposit.

My daughter, Shanaz, told her teacher at the Elms School that her parents were looking for a shop. The teacher came to me at Peas Hill Road and told me about a good solicitor, Mr Quellian, and told me he knew a lot of Pakistanis. We went to Mr Quellian and he started the work.

We moved from Peas Hill Road to Woodborough Road August 1958. The children had summer holidays. At that time, my husband had started a job. When he was on sick leave, he got a Diploma, and he got an office job in Long Eaton. After six months, he went in there from six o'clock to nine o'clock in the evening.

When I first came here, I felt the loss of the taste of food and air. Home was Jasmin-smelling. On Peas Hill Road with five children and a husband working, I was - at first - depressed. I am an imaginative and thinking woman, and I was sitting in the downstairs kitchen thinking. I would 'go over' the smell of home and decided to put it in an imaginary freezer in my heart where it was safe. This is

At the back of 145, Peas Hill Road, Mumtaz and Abdul Khalique, after his illness and considering a new career direction

Far left, Abdul Khalique, with friends from his village and his brother-in-law Yacub Mirza (in white coat), Robin Hood Chase, St Ann's, 1959

my country, my people, now. I won't go back now. Khalique thought my ideas were good. We keep our country in our heart.

What we bought was a shop at the front, with two storeys on top of it and a small kitchen at the back and there was a cellar. We bought it as a home. That was good for us as we did not pay anything to take over a business. It looked like a chemist's shop. It was boarded up outside. The shelves were set like a pharmacist shop. We took the shelves out. We borrowed some money from our friends, bought some wood, and found a carpenter who started to put new shelves.

I was pregnant again with Jabeena, my sixth child (who later qualified as a School Teacher at Nottingham University and has taught mainly in Nottingham). We borrowed money from my second brother, Nazir, to help buy the shop. My husband said we will keep the lodgers in our old house, which we hadn't sold, because it will keep income coming. Then we started cleaning and decorating. My brothers came and stayed for visits.

We did not have a car at that time, so his English friend helped him to bring groceries to the shop. Some friends told me to get addresses of wholesale dealers. I went to ask at the shop over the road. The shopkeeper laughed and said: 'You are not going to pinch our customers are you?' But his elder brother had left and gone to Sheffield and he was going as well.

Abdul Khalique with Robeena, Mumtaz Khalique with Samina, and Dr Ayub Mirza: 'My brother who helped me in so many ways'

I started learning a little more English. He gave me the address of Lawson and Gibson, wholesale dealers. My husband phoned them. They came next day, asked what we wanted and they delivered. If we could not give the money, they told us to do it next time. In the morning Gibson delivered the groceries, my husband came from his job and asked if any customers came. I told him four or five. Two were English and three Pakistani. I told him lots of people came and stopped, then laughed and smiled.

He said: 'Let's go round and see how it looks.' When my husband looked at the things I had put on the shelves, he said: 'No wonder people were laughing. You put things up-side-down!' I put things like Carnation Milk, tins of baked beans, custard and sugar all up-side-down. A few things were in right order. When the children went to bed, we put the things right.

The business was going on well. The Asians living here started bringing their families through immigration. There was only one other shop with Asian food and Asian language. We used to order food from Birmingham, London and Manchester. The wholesalers bought in bulk. Asian food was in demand. Asians and West Indians came into the shop. English people came too. They thought my husband was English as he was well-dressed and fair-skinned. They thought he was married to an Indian lady! They bought English food. We kept West Indian food like yams, green bananas, salt fish, okra and mackerel in brine.

'West Indian friends had been on holiday, and showed us their hats. We decided to go round to Palmerston Street and pose for a holiday photo!' said Mumtaz Khalique

My elder brother, Yaqub, came in 1959. He was retired from the Army. He got a job as a supervisor at Raleigh. He helped to take the children to Christmas parties, Nottingham Goose Fair and garden parties.

He stayed with me, then went to the Peas Hill Road house, and took charge of that house and the rents. We established our shop. I never let my children come into the shop at that time. It was a hard time but I never thought of it as a hard time. I adjusted. A few Pakistanis asked how I coped when there were not many Pakistanis. I never felt lonely. I made friends from every nationality

There was a wool shop across the road. The owner was about forty years old and I was young. I used to buy wool from her. She treated me like a younger sister. She helped me with patterns when I could not read them. I felt very comfortable with her, and all my children remember the jumpers I used to knit as they wore them to school.

ST ANN'S NOTTINGHAM: inner-city voices *by Ruth I Johns* • ISBN 0951696092

Abdul and Mumtaz Khalique with their daughters (left to right) Shanaz, Samina and Robeena in their St Ann's backyard

The next addition to our family was our son Abraze in 1960. He secured a scholarship to the Boys' High School. He played rugby, was a prefect and is now a GP in Nottingham. He helped a lot after my husband died.

All different nationals were like family members to me and it gave me strength. I never faced racism but there were some people who told me they had. The man I spoke about before, who used the body language in the English shop, he started buying things from my shop. He was happy. He could speak his own language. I stayed most of the time in the shop while my husband had a job to earn money to pay the bills. After some time, my husband started to run the shop and I stayed home more. We made our shop self-service.

We had a big sitting room and the shop was on the front. We made it as one big room. We bought baskets, made a counter and put a cash till in. When the women came from Pakistan, they did not talk to my husband. In our country, women don't talk to men freely and their husbands did not like them to gossip. When I was alone in the shop, the women used to sit in the kitchen and have a cup of tea. In those days, I used to cook a lot of Asian dishes and enjoyed eating them with the women. I made so many friends. Sometimes their husbands came and they talked to my husband. They stayed at the counter and I always made for his friends. I took the ladies in the kitchen. It was a social gathering.

At that time Pakistanis and Indians lived together and loved each other. I remember a man who was about the same age as my husband. He used to work with my husband on night shift. He brought me his wage packet to save for him. He lived on Cranmer Street with other Asians. He wanted to save and bring his family to England. He trusted me. The next time he brought his wage packet, he took £1.10s. I asked if that was enough and he said: 'Ten shillings for rent and a £1 for food.' He got £9 a week and never took out more than £2. The families came by ship.

They couldn't afford the airfare. That man died about six years ago and his son is a Doctor.

When the families came from Pakistan, their wives became pregnant. They had to go to clinics and hospitals for check-ups. There were no clinics back home. Their husbands could not speak English often, and they asked if I could go with their wives to hospital or clinic. I asked them to make the appointment at one o'clock. It was my routine to feed my young children and put them to bed at around 12 o'clock and they woke at 2.00 pm.

We didn't have a car then. The bus stops were not good for the hospital. The Health Clinic was far away. We had a long walk from Woodborough Road, Union Road, Market and Bingo Club where there is now a Mosque. After the visit, the mothers and myself would walk back the same way. The Clinic was very good at that time.

Village people came to the shop to ask for help with tax problems, problems with wages, in finding jobs and going for interviews. Sometimes, I would have a word with a husband to ease his understanding of the benefits to his wife and family if she went out and, possibly, even start driving.

Nowadays, shops are open twenty-four hours a day and seven days a week. Then shops were shut half-day Thursday and on Sundays. That was the law. I shut on Monday half-day and all day Sunday. After I put my children to sleep, I took the pram and my purchase card and went to Gibson's store near the main Post Office in the City. The Post Office is still there. I repeated this two or three times.

Following Abraze came the arrival of Nageena, in 1961, the youngest who completed our family. She gained a scholarship to Nottingham Girls' High School and qualified as a Dentist at University College, London. She worked for five years in hospital dentistry. Then she studied law and was called to the Bar in 1994. She practises as a Barrister specialising in personal injury and clinical negligence.

Abdul Khalique and son Parvaze, middle son of the family

Next door neighbours. Helen (back left) and Peggy O'Grady (front right) with Mike behind her. Robeena (back middle), and Samina and Abraze (front left and middle)

Mike, Javid, Parvaze and 'Hugo' from next door

Mrs O'Grady and Mumtaz Khalique

My fourth brother, Dr Jamil Ahmed arrived in 1969. He has always been surprised by my life. He asks: 'How did you manage with a big family, work in the shop, and helping your other relatives as well as the community?' He once gave me a two-week break with all expenses paid. I enjoyed having a local holiday.

Dr Jamil Ahmed (left back) with Javid and, in front, Abraze

Sometimes the wholesaler delivered groceries and sometimes I would take Robeena's pram to bring them from Gibson's store. My brother said: 'Khalique you need a car now. Let's go on Saturday to see a car'. They went to buy a second hand car but my husband never moved from the showroom as he gazed at a new Vauxhall car. Dr Ayub, my brother, always helped us money-wise and gave the £150 deposit.

My husband started using the car straight away. The children were young, the business was good. For ten years we had a very good business. West Indian, Asian and

Nageena 'feeling like a princess' in £5 pair of shoes and a dress her mother made

St Ann's Nottingham: inner-city voices *by Ruth I Johns* • ISBN 0951696092

English people came. Right at the bottom of Woodborough Road was a newspaper shop. The owner was Mr Onion. We used to buy newspapers, magazines and the *Evening Post* from him. The grocery shop opposite closed. The owners went to Sheffield, one came back. Their mother was disabled and they looked after her very well.

At first, we did not know the education system here. Our first child, Javid, took the 11-plus test. The next year my daughter, Shanaz, sat it. They passed. We got a letter about Javid. I told my brother and he came at the weekend. He helped me a lot in my life. We had love and respect for relatives. We lived like a joint family.

My husband told my brother that Javid was going to High Pavement School. We did not know what this meant. He took the letter to one of his patients who read it and said: 'You are the lucky one. Your child is going to a good school.' We bought uniform and shoes for him. Javid was a House Captain of Rugby.

My third child, Parvaze, was Head Boy of Claremont School. He is now a GP, practising in Nottingham. All the children did well in school. They all started at the Elms School. Shanaz went to Haywood School. Shanaz helped me a lot with my young family. She trained to become a School Teacher at Doncaster Teacher Training College. She has taught in London and Nottingham.

We went to all the parents' evenings in different schools. We used to close the shop when we were invited to schools. At High Pavement, I was the only person in a sari. I used to wear saris, now I wear shalwar kameez because it is comfortable. Javid was in his third year, then an Indian boy came. At High Pavement, an American exchange teacher was doing some research for some project. He asked at what age did we have our Javid. I was sixteen and my husband was nineteen. He said: 'No wonder your child is so intelligent.'

We heard that Woodborough Road would be demolished in two or three years, but after one year they told us about demolition. We got worried. We got a house

On the Woodborough Road, St Ann's, Mumtaz Khalique says goodbye to family and friends as she starts a journey to Pakistan to see her parents and family for the first time since leaving. The tall man on her right is her husband's brother, Mohammad Saddique. I called him 'Uncle Chacha'

Her brother, Dr Ayub Mirza, greets her in Pakistan. There was civil unrest at home during the time of her stay: 'And I sent my husband a note saying that if anything happened to me, he should marry someone nice to look after the children. I helped in a hospital and a camp while I was there, and came back when flights started again'

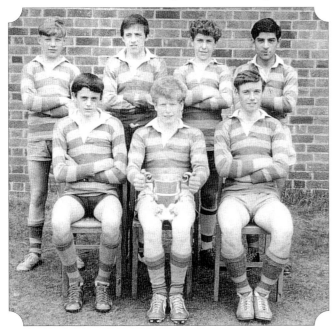

Javid (back right) during High Pavement school days

Two nieces, a sister and Mumtaz Khalique's mother (right) were among family members awaiting her arrival home

on Grouville Drive, Woodthorpe. We moved there in 1970 but still had the business on Woodborough Road. We had two cars then. I had an Escort as I had passed my driving test by then.

My younger children continued at the Elms School. In those days, we closed the business at six o'clock in the evening. In the morning my husband used to go to the shop before me. I took three children to the Elms by car. At ten o'clock I finished mopping and cleaning. I put biscuits and juices on the table and came to the shop at 10.30. If my husband wanted to get groceries, he went out. I cooked the dinner for the children at Woodborough Road. At three o'clock I used to go to Grouville Drive and gave them tea. They watched TV and did their homework. Sometimes my husband wanted me back at the shop, otherwise I stayed home with my children. We did our duty at the shop like a rota system.

On Sundays I cooked at home at Grouville Drive. My daughter said it takes a lot of money to get the groceries, how did we manage? I said God gave me the shop! I took all food from the shop and that was the advantage of the shop. I spent money on clothes and shoes for the eight children.

All of the eight children started their education at the Elms School. Robeena is 7th from the left in the second row from the front

Jabeena is 2nd from left in the second row from the back. And Abraze is on the front row at the left

We had to leave the shop in 1972. The Council gave us three months notice to empty the shop. We were looking for a place. They offered us something but it was not what we wanted. On Alfreton Road someone closed a business. One Pakistani wanted to open a restaurant, but people did not want it there. Now look how many restaurants are open on that road!

The estate agent said we could buy the shop for a grocery and butcher's shop. The surveyor came and the Council came to see if the community there had any objection. They did not. We went to see Mr Quellian again. The Council did not give us much money for having to leave.

We never thought of any hardship but, when my husband's health was not well, it was a bit hard. The children helped when we closed the shop. We did not know much about many things. I learnt many things later when I went to Community Centres.

Khalique was worried because he had to develop the business again, but it picked up in about six weeks. All people from the area around used our shop.

People did not like to move from St Ann's. They said they were settled there. They used to go to work by No 31 bus, the doctor's surgery was near, a telephone booth was on the road, and a fish and chip shop. The Police Station was three shops away at Woodborough Road. It was not a big Police Station. It was a small room with a window. Two policemen were always there. It was opposite where the Pakistan Centre is now. I went three or four times with somebody to translate. It was a community Police Station. School was not far away.

After my husband died on January 16th 1975, Javid helped me a lot in the shop. He finished his education two years before. The others helped. But I didn't keep the business for long after.

My community work started from the shop on Woodborough Road. People came and asked about Urdu classes and religious lessons for their children. It was mostly educated men who were involved with it, like my husband and brothers. I found a few ladies. We went to our community and told them about our programme. The community rented a small room near Bath Street. The men taught boys the Quran and the ladies taught the girls.

Then there was a house where Muslims started to pray. The children started their religious lessons. I took my children. It was a very old three-storey building. Downstairs was for small children, second floor was for men to pray, third storey was used for a store. We organised a ladies' group.

Then later came the Pakistan Centre on Woodborough Road. First it was the Pakistan Friends League Centre. They put me on the public relations side because I had the shop and knew people and was interested in social work. I knocked on the door of Pakistanis and asked them to become a member. We started the Pakistani Ladies' Circle, the first group to be set up.

Then Urdu classes started at Bentinck School. They were run by two ladies who were literate in their language and could read and write. Things started like that. Now there is a lot going on all over the place.

The last photo taken (26.12.74) of Mumtaz Khalique with her husband before he died

I do a lot now. I work with disabled people near Forest Road. I go to a few Centres if they need help to encourage others in adult education. I helped People's College with an advertisement. I did an Urdu exam there and I was asked to advertise for adult education to encourage more Asian women[1]. Zee TV asked me to be a judge for a cookery class in the Asian Women's Centre.

Some parents find it difficult caring for their children nowadays for all sorts of reasons. Society starts from home. Parents should change. If they do not change there will be lots of problems. Some families have adjusted themselves, because back home they had English influences in the Army and some are educated. People in their home country have a different lifestyle from here. That clashes with the new generation, and is East meets West.

Bus outing to Skegness for the day c1971. 'A few women in the Pakistan Ladies Circle decided to organise the trip, and the men said, if Mrs Khalique goes, they would send their family.' Mumtaz Khalique was a founder member of the Pakistan Ladies Circle

This picture, taken in 1974, is of Nottingham's first Pakistani Student Society, which was mixed. Sitting together (left to right) are daughters Sabina, Robeena, Jabeena and Shanaz

A poetry evening at the Pakistan Centre c1975, with poet Hafese Jelundry. 'They made me sit in front next to him,' said Mumtaz Khalique

My advice to other people is: change with the society and keep your own culture and values. That is best, but, where you live, accept and respect their values and culture as well as your own.

I have always wanted to thank all those who supported me through that time living in St Ann's, especially my late husband Abdul Khalique. We both encouraged one another to survive in the 1950s in Britain, working alongside each other. My thanks to all my children, who were all hardworking and supported me. They all work to help other people.

[1] Mumtaz Khalique is an active member of the Asian Women's Project in Nottingham where she promotes education amongst Asian girls. She has taken many education courses herself including passing Urdu GCSE and A Level. Mumtaz Khalique has often been called upon to act as interpreter and for other support, a process which began many years ago when the shop she and her husband ran in St Ann's was a focal point for help and advice in the community. Mumtaz Khalique spoke of the importance of education in an interview during those years, with Jean Davey in the *Evening Post* of October 20th 1964. Jean Davey asked her who had taught her English and she replied: 'My children.'

Mumtaz Khalique's father, who came to stay with her at the end of his life

Mumtaz Khalique (centre back) with her five daughters, 1976. Sitting (left to right) Shanaz, Robeena, Samina and Jabeena and (in front) Nageena

Mumtaz Khalique has received several awards in recent years. Here she addresses an audience at Nottingham Playhouse after receiving a Millennium Achievers Award, 2000; a Community Award for her help in schools and community organisations in Nottingham. The event was organised by the Muslim Women's Organisation. Mrs Khalique told the audience that it is never too late to learn. She was currently studying Maths and English at People's College

After taking part in a sponsored Fun Run for charity 1993, Mumtaz Khalique is met by daughter Robeena. Mrs Khalique took part with some of her grandchildren. She has twenty-four

ابھی ابھی میرے دل اور دماغ نے ایک فیصلہ کیا ہے
جیسے تو میں فیصلہ کرنے میں دیر لگاتی ہوں ۔۱ مگر فیصلہ کیا ہے
وہ یہ ہے جو مجھے ابھی یہ Award ملا ہے ۔اب مجھے یقین ہو گیا ہے
یہ مجھے کبھی بھولا نہیں ہیں یہ نے دیا اور نئی ہیں مجھے ہمت ہار نہ دیا
اور اب مجھے لپ بڑی امید ہے ساتھ خدا ایر بھروسہ ہے کہ نئی
آنے والی نسل کے لیے ہمیشہ زندہ دل زندہ آباد رہے گی
انشااللہ آمین تم آمین ۔
خدا حافظا ۔شب بخیر اور گڈ نائٹ

To get a flavour of shopping in St Ann's at the start of the 20th Century, here is a selection of advertisements from St Catharine's Church Parish News 1901. Source: Rev Canon David Keene

T. HENSON,
PLUMBER & GLAZIER,
GAS AND HOT WATER FITTER
(Registered by the Worshipful Company of Plumbers, London),
2a St. ANN'S WELL ROAD.
ESTIMATES ON APPLICATION.

For GENUINE
English Beef & Mutton
Pickled Tongues & Corned Beef,
TRY
THOS. HALL, The Old-established Butcher,
57 St. ANN'S WELL ROAD.

T. BROWN,
Newsagent and Stationer,
153 Gt. Alfred Street South.
Orders taken for all kinds of Papers and Periodicals.
N.B.—A Choice assortment of Birthday and other Cards.

B. CHARLES,
HATTER AND OUTFITTER,
124 St. Ann's Well Road.
Latest Styles. Good Value.
SILK HATS Ironed and made Fashionable.

Commercial Square Millinery Establishment.

· · MRS. BATES · ·
Begs respectfully to inform her customers that she has returned from buying a choice selection of
LONDON AND PARISIAN NOVELTIES,
and solicits a continuance of your esteemed patronage.
Yours faithfully, B. BATES.

TRY **A. SNOWDEN'S**
Celebrated Bread & Confectionery
93 Saint Ann's Well Road.
Wedding and Birthday Cakes made on the shortest notice.
CREAM BUNS—A Treat.

JOSEPH ORCHARD,
English & Foreign Fruiterer,
II *St. Ann's Well Rd., Nottingham.*
Opposite Saint Catharine's Church.
FRESH FISH DAILY.   Orders promptly attended to.

Do you want a Smart, Stylish Dress ?

A Pair of Good-fitting Corsets,
P. & S., C. B., or other makes ?

A Pair of Guaranteed Kid Gloves
at 1/11½ ?

Linens, Oilcloths, Shirtings,
Carpets, &c. ?

Try **George Kirk's**
General Drapery Stores, 182 Alfred St. Central.

S. GRIFFIN, Maker of the Celebrated
"Griffin" Cycles
Cycle Accessory Depot,
170 Great Alfred St. South.
4 PLANTAGENET STREET, NOTTINGHAM, February 11th, 1897.
SIR.—I have great pleasure in expressing my entire satisfaction with the machine you built for me last year ; in fact for finish and easy running I have not seen its equal. I have ridden it over all sorts of roads daily, and have not had any alteration to the machine whatever.   Yours truly, T. BAKER.
Mr. S. GRIFFIN.   Capt. St. Catharine's C.C.

J. WEBB,
FASHIONABLE TAILOR
18 Great Alfred Street South.
SCOTCH TWEED SUITS FROM 50/-
GOOD WORKMANSHIP.   STYLE and FIT Warranted.

CHEAPEST AND BEST **Funeral Director** in the Neighbourhood.	**FRED E. TEMPERTON,** JOINER & BUILDER, CURZON STREET. *Residence : 18 Berkeley Street.* Alterations and General Repairs to Property personally attended to.

H. EVERETT,
General & Fancy Draper
79 & 81 St. Ann's Well Rd.

Largest Selection and Value Unequalled.
DRESS AND MANTLE MAKING
A SPECIALITY.

All garments made on the premises by experienced workpeople.

C. H. CUNDY,
GROCER, TEA & PROVISION MERCHANT,
37 St. Ann's Well Road.

Agent for Coombs' Aerated Flour and Specialities.

WILLIAM SLEATH,
COAL MERCHANT
Offices : GREAT NORTHERN COAL WHARF, NOTTINGHAM,
And 8 Wesley Street, Cotmanhay, Ilkeston.
For Prices, &c., **Henry Pearson,** Rent and Debt Collector,
apply to   29 Plantagenet St., Nottingham.

Black Vicuna Frock Coat & Vest
from £2 10s.
Blk. Vicuna Morning Coat & Vest
from £2 2s.
All Wool Indigo Serge Suits
from £2 10s.
Tweed Suits from £2 2s.
MOURNING ORDERS EXECUTED AT A DAY'S NOTICE.
YOUTHS' AND BOYS' CLOTHING.
Style and Fit Guaranteed.

H. Tomlinson, TAILOR and General Outfitter,
ESTABLISHED 1871.
◁ 80 ▷
UNION ROAD.

JAVID KHALIQUE

Born 1949

Interviewed in his home 9.11.99. Javid Khalique is the **Service Manager for Nottingham City Social Services** *responsible for the Training and Development Service*

My parents ran one of the first, probably the first, Asian shop in St Ann's. I think the other nearest one was in the City Centre. Ours was at 124a, Woodborough Road on the corner of Palmerston Street. It was near Alfred Street. It was a fairly large shop opposite the old Baptist Church which is now the Pakistan Centre. I grew up looking out at this beautiful old Church where there used to be all sorts of activities.

The shop had two fronts, one on to Woodborough Road and one on to Palmerston Street. It was a three-storey building, with cellars as well. My father extended the back of it because business grew very, very quickly and it started to sell Halal meat as well. So it was both a Continental greengrocers and a butcher's shop later on. I think it opened about 1961 and it carried on until the compulsory purchase order arrived from the Council when St Ann's was redeveloped.

My parents were first generation here. My father, Abdul, first came to England about 1955 and went to Birmingham to work in the steel industry there, for a couple of years. Then he went back to Pakistan. He hadn't made his fortune. He wanted to bring his wife, my mother, and children over and he came back but didn't settle in Birmingham but came to Nottingham and worked in the Stanton Staveley Iron Works. He got ill with pleurisy after a couple of years and needed time to recover. My mother already had five children. Three of us were born in Pakistan, the others here.

My uncle, Dr Ayub, who was a Doctor in Pakistan and a very political socialist person, came over and saw that my father was struggling. My father was an educated man and had been an engineer in the Pakistan Air Force and my uncle suggested he should open some sort of business. My mother saw that my father wasn't going to be able to do heavy factory work, so they followed my uncle's suggestion and he guided them. They did the right thing at the right time. A large number of people were coming from the Caribbean islands, from India and Pakistan working as labourers, in the Health Service, on the buses, for John Player's or as trades people. The immigrants in St Ann's brought with them different cultural needs for foods and spices, for vegetables that were from abroad as well as many other things that everybody liked, cornflakes, sugar and things.

I remember the first thing that arrived in the shop. My father asked me to unpack a box of Tate and Lyle sugar, and I put the packets on a shelf. The second thing that arrived was butter, Anchor butter, half-pound packets of it. My father must have been about twenty-four at that time. But he had developed this poor health and diabetes. He was a big strong fellow, and very handsome, and he liked people tremendously.

When we arrived we didn't understand City ways at all. We'd come from a village. My uncle luckily was here for a short while and he took me with my father to the Elms Infants School on Cranmer Street and got me registered there. I didn't speak English at that time. My grandfather back in the village had said: 'Aeroplane!' And that was about the only English word I knew!

Luckily, we had some lovely teachers at Elms Infants and Elms Juniors. The Head Teacher was Mr Baker and my class teacher was Mrs Tetley. They really were very helpful, got excellent additional English classes and I learnt English very, very quickly. We were eager, my sister and next brother went as well and learnt quickly. I think what happened to us children in terms of an introduction into the education process was excellent. I'll always remember Elms Infants and Elms Juniors with a great deal of love and affection. The teachers were sensitive.

I think my parents and other members of the community could have done with some kind of welcome to England, some kind of opportunity to learn English. I know people who are our elders, who came maybe in their twenties, and fifty years later in their seventies they still have poor ability to speak English. They don't feel confident, for example, in dealing with forms.

I am the eldest child and it's always been an Asian approach to life that the eldest son takes a lot of responsibilities. But we all helped and grew up in that shop and were strongly formed by it. My parents owned the property. People used to borrow money from each other, a kind of unspoken credit union, and return it as soon as they could. The ground floor was the shop. The cellars underneath were converted into rooms, the first floor had a small bathroom and later a toilet (the loo was originally

1958 at Peas Hill Road before moving to the shop on Woodborough Road. Mother, Mumtaz Khalique, holding baby Samina with her other children (left to right) Shanaz, Robeena, Parvaze and Javid

outside) and there were two bedrooms on that floor. One was large and looked out over the Baptist Church and one was on the side overlooking houses behind the entry.

There was a yard outside with a wall, which must have been about six foot tall, separating us from next door. We were the end of the terrace. Then on the next floor was a very large attic converted into a room. My brother grabbed that. It was very luxurious space! I always felt there were ghosts up there. My sisters took the large bedroom on the first floor and myself and another brother shared the smaller room. My parents slept downstairs where they'd converted the cellars. There were two cellars and they managed to put a little kitchen on the side and there was a small kitchen on the first floor so they could have a cup of tea in there when resting from the shop. We were cramped but I never felt cramped.

Once, about the age of nine, I gave myself an adventure. I told my parents I was going to take a walk up the Woodborough Road. I put a haversack on my back and put in some crisps and sweets and a bottle of pop. I'd been up to Cranmer Street to school and I'd played with my Sikh friends a little further up the road, but I had never been further.

There was no worry about a child in this area, a black Asian child, which is what I called myself, from a Pakistani or liberal Muslim family, taking a walk. I carried on walking from almost the bottom of the Woodborough Road right up, looking everywhere, past Alexandra Court flats. On further to the Porchester Road. I didn't realise Mapperley Hospital was a mental hospital and I saw all those green lawns and flowers. I hadn't seen these except in the Aboretum. And I stopped there and had my lunch and thought it was a nice place.

Through my work, I was involved in the decommissioning of Mapperley Hospital some thirty years

Parents Abdul and Mumtaz Khalique holding baby Jabeena and in front (left to right) Parvaze, Javid, Samina, Robeena and Shanaz, 1960. Woodborough Road in the background

later. And then I carried on walking to Mapperley and almost to the countryside. I thought this was the end of the world! And, tired, walked all the way back. I was away two or three hours. And that's how a kid from St Ann's saw the world, St Ann's being the centre of it.

I think the first generation that came here, myself included, had just come out of the post-war experiences where Britain's colonies were becoming independent as part of the bargaining that took place for our contributing to Britain during the War and it's anti-fascism struggle. Those that came had a great love of Britain and saw it as the Mother Country even though they came as immigrants. I don't think there was an open acceptance of ourselves as Black and Asian people and there was discrimination. But it was at a much more overt level than sometimes occurs these days.

I think the first generation had a better understanding of how to deal with it because they'd been members of the Empire. And they accepted it, as perhaps the norm. It was maybe some twenty years later, when the associations of various communities developed, that the challenge to discrimination was better organised within the community.

I'm conscious that there were some events in my life in St Ann's where things were sad. Which only later on rankled a little bit. Like going into a sweet shop and standing waiting to buy some toffees. A friend of the woman shopkeeper said: 'Well, don't you want to serve that little boy?' And she replied: 'Oh no, he's just a blackie so he can wait.' I can remember feeling very angry about that. Not a good experience for a child.

I was quite a clever little fellow and I was coming back from the Central Library carrying a book of the Old Testament stories which had some big pictures in. And I loved those sort of stories. I was walking home and there was a white boy, Trevor, who wasn't too smart and he came to me and said: 'You can't read that book, you're a Paki.' And I remember feeling, oh dear, what's going on here. So even though I was only eight or nine, there were all kinds of social dynamics that worked within those who came as immigrants, who wanted to improve their lives, who were eager for opportunity and who really wanted to go back. My parents' intention was to go back after five or six years, but circumstances didn't allow enough wealth to develop. And once the children were here, we were going to be part of this society and we wouldn't have choices to go back.

I remember two of my relatives from the same village. They were not direct relatives but because we were from the same villages we regarded people as relatives. They were uneducated and young fellows of about twenty and they've done extremely well now. I met them on my way home from the Elms Junior School and we walked up Alfred Street North and there was a TV repair shop on the corner near to the Mansfield Road. It said apply within for jobs. There were about twenty people working there and, as my relatives couldn't speak English then, I went in and asked if they could have work. And I was told, yes, they did have jobs but: 'We haven't got any for you lot.' This was at an adult level, but as a child I was involved within that.

As Asians, we quickly produced our own little internal community to support each other. But I think for other societies which were of a Christian background, there was a tension. Particularly for Caribbean people who were more used to going out in the evening, for whom music and dance was fine whereas in my community it wasn't for a very long time. They had problems of who could go into what, where and who couldn't. I was conscious of those things happening for some of the people who were sharing the same street with us.

When we came here worship was mainly in people's homes. It was a long time until the Pakistan Centre, Indian Centre, Caribbean Centres came forward. For Black Christians finding a place of worship where they were accepted was actually very difficult. I find it sad that in the early days Black Christians, when they went to an Anglican or main street church to join a congregation, would be told this church is not for you.

In my attic I found letters of the old Pakistan Centre constitution when it was starting up and people had this need to be together. But initially, worship was a domestic thing. It was a very young community. Britain wanted young fit labour so it had a disproportionate number of men and relatively few women until a decade or so later. It had few people who were disabled or elderly. It's only now that we're seeing a representation of all kinds of physical, emotional and age states within our community.

My father died when I was young. He worked very, very hard. He wasn't a manager otherwise he would have recruited people to help him with the business and expanded it. Nor was he greedy, he was content. The shop in St Ann's was very successful within five or six years and it met his needs. It met social needs for the community, it met economic needs not only for ourselves but of people who came to the business. It was a place where a lot of social exchange, chat, gossip, help, advice took place. It was vibrant, it really was. It wasn't just a transaction of the buying and selling of something, it was much deeper than that. That shop for at least a decade filled a far greater role than just a place for buying goods.

My mum, Mumtaz Begum, worked in it as well. She was a very strong woman indeed. She had a definite idea of what she wanted to use our immigrant experience for. She strongly believed in education and she was very skilled, though she was uneducated. She was a skilful leader type of person and a lot of the community, particularly where women's issues were concerned, came to her for help over many years. And they still do today.

She had a lot of experience of dealing with human problems. Long before there was Social Services, there was an informal social welfare system and my mum was helping not only the Pakistani community but also the Indian and Caribbean communities. She was a source of help, advice and information and a problem solver for family disputes and difficulties.

Quite a lot of people came from our part of the world, Mirpur side of Kashmir. They were largely from very small villages. We weren't a very educated people, it was our labour that was wanted. My father had education and was a resource in terms of reading letters and newspapers and letting people know what was happening. That's a tradition that exists in our community.

My mother was very strong about us getting an education, but when we started getting queues outside the shop on a Saturday morning then I had to help. My father would bring the boxes of food in, I'd unpack them and put them on shelves and, at the end of the day, I'd clean the place up. I'd mop the shop down every Thursday, Friday and Saturday evening. My dad used to look absolutely exhausted. My mother was managing eight kids and helping in the shop. She was one strong person. I don't know how she managed it because we find it difficult to manage with three kids! How did they manage it?

He would open up about eight in the morning and close about six-thirty most evenings and seven-thirty on Saturdays. It took a lot of cleaning up. I didn't have to do it but I wanted to help my parents. Instead of watching Crackerjack, I'd go upstairs and help. After the shop was shut, on Thursday, Fridays and Saturdays, my dad would spend another two hours delivering groceries because people didn't have cars. He had an old Ford estate and put the groceries in the back and deliver them: Goldswong Terrace, Cranmer Street, up the sides of Woodborough Road, Peas Hill Road, St Ann's Well Road. He'd maybe do twenty deliveries and sometimes he'd take me along for company. We used to have a good chat. And, of course, it was early up for him in the morning, five-thirty at Sneinton fruit market.

I can remember when I was about sixteen years old and nearly ready to do my 'O' Levels and he was needing me to help more, as he was growing tired. We came back from doing a delivery and he used to smoke, he took out a cigarette and lit one for himself and then looked long and hard at me and he offered me one. I think he'd found out that I'd been pinching a smoke! I felt very close to him that evening.

My father found, with the shop, what he was happy with. He loved people. When, years later, a compulsory purchase order came for the shop, the City Council offered I think it was £500 for our home and an astonishing successful business. And an opportunity to move to Victoria Centre, which was a different style of running a business. He was offered a stall, a space, in an open market area being built in Victoria Centre. That signalled a lot of unease for him. He had the strength to run the business in St Ann's. It was hard, very hard work. But when St Ann's went, his place in the world, his sense of harmony and comfort with how he earned his living went forever. He was at ease there. I loved him for his lack of greed. He was content and that is a wonderful gift to achieve in your life. Briefly he was Chair of the Labour Party East Constituency. He was conscious that suffering and poverty was more than just down to self and circumstances.

I think people forget how beautiful St Ann's and its people were. Black, white whatever, there was a closeness and a need for each other. A genuine sharing. I have books upstairs in my attic where there are perhaps over a hundred names of people who couldn't afford to pay for food but who had families to look after. My father would say: 'Well, fine you take the food.' I treasure that book.

ST ANN'S NOTTINGHAM: inner-city voices *by Ruth I Johns* • ISBN 0951696092

After he lost the shop, my father opened a shop on the Alfreton Road and he died there a few years later. He was forty-two. Alfreton Road was different. The population had been uprooted. We were seeing more anger, demoralisation, a sense of alienation within an uprooted generation of settlers in Britain. That was never the case in St Ann's where there was a sharing atmosphere. In St Ann's, there were some bad people around but, overall it was a wonderful place to be.

My mother lost interest in the business after my father died. I ran the business with my mother for a couple of years. She had other challenges to face. She was left with substantial responsibilities because some of the eight children were quite young. I think her running the business with my father was *their* life and she didn't see it as her life with her children or as a widow. So within two years, she said: 'Javid, I don't want to continue this way.'

I think if she had had an education, her life would have been remarkably different. But I'm not sure if it would have been any richer. She created wealth in different ways. She drove us kids quite hard for an education as many immigrant mothers did. I eventually qualified as a doctor. I went back to the old country for about seven years to do this, but I missed Nottingham terribly and realised this is home as well. I'm the Service Manager for Nottingham City Social Services responsible for the Training and Development Service.

I could have been economically better off had I stuck with being a doctor, but I am much more content working around issues that have meaning for me. Part of the training function is working with communities, working with families as Social Services, and as an education service in Youth Community Services. It includes developing individuals who may be experiencing distress or difficulty in their lives, to be able to speak for themselves and take charge of their lives.

All my brothers and sisters have done well and have children too. I guess we're looking at how we get our children to be balanced, good people who can make a contribution and achieve to the best of their abilities. We stay close but we don't have the closeness that I think my parents had with their brothers and sisters. It was a much more close community and broader than just immediate blood relatives. People felt they belonged to each other. I think we've lost a little bit of that two generations on. And the haste of life doesn't give you the time to develop the depth of social relationship that my parents' generation had. That will cost us a lot in the long-term culturally and socially and in terms of inter-dependency. I think that is happening generally and is not only the immigrant experience.

In the house next to our shop in St Ann's lived a Caribbean family. I remember they had two sons and one of them, Hugo, became a social worker too. And the house on the other side had an Irish family. The people mixed in, Greeks, Turks, Pakistani, Indian, Caribbean. Once we saw difference and recognised difference, we loved the difference.

I sometimes see people these days who say: 'We must promote diversity.' Well, in St Ann's in the 1960s, there was diversity. It was a natural process, a willingness to come to each other's aid and to support each other. I don't know whether we valued that moment in our lives for what it was, which was wonderful, despite the environmental and sometimes the economic poverty.

At some stage, official people would have said that St Ann's housing is past its sell-by date. Much of it was excellent housing, but maybe past its sell-by date in terms of people's ability to maintain it. I don't think people had adequate resources to upgrade their houses. There would have been a sociological explanation as to how the poor could be directed to be 'better' people. There could have been Council interests involved because there were multi-million pound investments at stake. And Council decisions must have been made about removing this Victorian 'blot' called St Ann's and replacing it with modern models of housing. Nottingham has always had a housing problem. Immigrants had to rent or purchase their housing because they couldn't get into Council housing.

When St Ann's came down, I was not fully aware, but I was conscious of all of this reducing the environment. I look at the modern housing that came to replace St Ann's and I think to myself it's Balsa wood. I look at the flats they created off Cranmer Street and I think they are damaging to people's health. Who gave away this wonderful history? My parents were very angry that their business and living were taken away. I think their compulsory purchase order, and I remember seeing the letter and what was being offered, came as a very, very great shock. The power of Local Government was seen as unquestionable in those days. And there was no way of refusing.

In fifty years' time, I'd like there to be some understanding of those times. St Ann's was poor, it had some gorgeous old buildings and a familiarity and a smell and a diversity of people in it which was rich beyond belief. It was a joyful place to grow up. I played with kids from every possible background. We fought each other, loved each other, supported each other, we played jokes and we played tricks and we got up to mischief. Some of us ended up in prison because of the dislocation or we ended up working for communities. A large number of people I grew up with around Palmerston Street ended up doing some community orientated work. Was that the only work we - mainly Black and Asian people - could get or was it because what life had taught us in St Ann's was useful? Some people went on to run businesses. There was a desire to go ahead, to progress, not to be defeatist, to explore the world but from safety of belonging. That's what St Ann's offered us and what it means to me. I'll never forget it.

I would say to an increasingly traumatised generation that may not know about belonging and about purpose and about serving others and being served by others, and not trusting others, that the destruction of St Ann's didn't help society at all. If, at some stage, we could recapture a fraction of what it offered, I think we would do well.

We have three children who, unlike me, don't have a split. Part of me belongs to Pakistan and always will. They belong here. They are British and whilst they are culturally different, they are culturally British as well.

Woodborough Road with the City behind. Baptist Church on the left and Emmanuel Church up the hill on the right. The Khalique family shop is not visible, but was situated on the right-hand side between the two churches. This is the neighbourhood where the family was rooted

The same shops boarded up ready for demolition

. . . and demolished. Up the hill on the right, new homes are already in position. The Craven Arms was built on the site opposite the Baptist Church and later demolished because of user problems

Further up the Woodborough Road on the left with a car coming out of Cranmer Street. This is part of the area which has become known as Phase 10, because it was Phase 10 of the redevelopment programme

. . . and on the right looking up Woodborough Road. Buildings in both photos were demolished including Emmanuel Church

A view from Peas Hill Road looking toward Woodborough Road. This demolition phase included the Khalique shop, off the picture to the right. Photos: Nicholson Photo Archive

ST ANN'S NOTTINGHAM: inner-city voices *by Ruth I Johns* • ISBN 0951696092

SAMINA KHALIQUE

Born 1958

From a letter 2000

Going to school meant so much to me. I had a succession of lovely teachers. There was Miss Hanson, Head of Elms Infants School, St Ann's. She told me and my friend, both biscuit monitors, that it was her birthday and she invited us into her office to share a piece of cake. We felt really special and privileged. I have never forgotten her kindness.

At Junior School, Miss Pengelly sent me a letter from Scotland enclosing a piece of heather, telling me it would bring luck. Imagine that! Then there was Miss Dickinson and Miss Crow. I really believe the teachers instilled a sense of friendship alongside the pupil/teacher relationship which stayed with me in later life in my decision to become a School Teacher.

Samina near the shop, St Ann's

Elms Junior School adjoined Elm Avenue, which was a natural setting with dreamy trees lining the Avenue majestically. It's a shame they were later struck with the Dutch Elm Disease. As children, our journey to school led us through a labyrinth of roads through St Ann's. We felt we could explore different routes to and from school and not repeat the same way home, not like today where my children, Zarina (15), Elisha (14) and Jahangir (10), catch buses or get dropped off for the school run.

It was a bit mischievous of us sisters and brothers, but sometimes on the way home down St Ann's Hill Road, towards the bottom end, we would hover by the textile factory. I think it is still there today. It had a chute which looked so tempting. We were intrigued by the prospect that the chute could have a second function as a slide, but soon learnt that it was too steep an angle to conquer; it hurt the backs of our legs to climb such a gradient, judging by the bruises and wooden splinters we'd get.

It's a funny thing about childhood, but we remember where and when an injury occurred, how it was sustained, treated and dealt with. I recall sitting on my mother's knee on the back step, the outside door leading to Palmerston Street was open. A bee stung me on my forehead. I can remember lashings of vinegar thrown somewhat hysterically at me, resembling someone throwing a bucket of water to put out an urgent fire!

On another occasion, after being chased by twins down Cranmer Street, I turned round, only to bang my forehead on a lampost. I was making my way down the Woodborough Road when my dad met me halfway up the hill, scooping me into his arms and covering the bleeding wound with a huge square cotton hanky. He took me to the Children's Hospital near St Andrew's Church.

My mum and dad's shop on the corner of Palmerston Street (yes, it was the proverbial corner shop!) was the centre of my universe. For me, it was an imaginative place to be in. At school, we'd have a Wendy House where you could pretend at playing shop, but I had a real shop to play in.

I was always intrigued by the packaging of various products such as tins and packets which had 'made in . . .' stamped on them. It was the countries they originated from that captivated me. I did wonder about them. I thought Tibet cream was actually made in Tibet! I drew tremendous pleasure from seeing bottles of cream soda with their metallic crown-shaped tops, arranged in symmetrical formation in their crates, clinking and clanging as they were set down on the floor.

I took some vegetables to school to be used in our class lesson: green bananas, yam and plantain. These were some of the foodstuffs stocked, which filled a gap culturally in those late 1950s and early 1960s. On the shop counter was a weighing scale, with pounds (lbs) and ounces (ozs) on it, with the corresponding price in shillings (sh) and pennies (d).

Further down the road was a launderette, not far from our shop. With mum having eight children, there was no shortage of laundry! A lady used to come and help. I remember being fascinated with the mechanics of a mangle. You fed the garments through two rollers on a stand by turning a handle. After going through the two rollers, the garments rid themselves of excess water. It looked hard work, requiring a lot of effort. Vivre washing machine today!

My ears would prick up on a Sunday morning when you could hear the band of the Boys' Brigade, a tinkling procession from afar, which gradually loudened as it drew nearer to the large church building, near to our shop on the Woodborough Road. (It is now the Pakistan Centre.)

Samina at work

J G Grant, Butcher, 59 Peas Hill Road, 1920-58. Photos: Source Mrs Scully, Robin Hood Chase, Nottingham Local Studies Library

Four of the shop photos taken by David Wilkinson, Rob Davis and David Strickland as part of their thesis 1967

JABEENA S KHALIQUE

Born 1959

From a letter 2000

I remember:

- A five-storey house on the corner of Woodborough Road.

- Four in a bedroom with a storage heater so hot you couldn't sit on it.

- Our neighbours, including 'Peggy' and the Irish family we played numerous imaginary games with.

- A family business of Halal butcher, mixed with Continental foods, managed by mum and dad; a young couple, burdened by yams and mutton, with eight kids in tow.

- Nights filled with reggae music and traffic from a main road into the City Centre.

- Street where kids played and never worried about bogeymen or drugs.

- A 'dragon dress' made for an Xmas party at school; mum adept at making each of the girls feel like a princess.

- Mr Flannigan's, a pot-bellied newsagent with no space but for adult magazines alongside 'Bazookas' that you could chew for eternity.

- The journey uphill to school, through 'entries' partitioned by metal poles that made us gymnasts working on asymmetric bars.

- Dogs and cats fighting over territory.

- The Library, a good walk on Saturday mornings, building up a thirst for books, and then returning via the chip shop on the way home.

- Local shops well used by the community, shops for every item available, no chain stores or supermarkets.

- Lasting memories of well used streets and houses built for families that would move on to brand new estates.

ALBERT GODFREY

Born 1936

From a talk given at St Ann's Library Reminiscence Day 1999, a letter to the Nottingham Evening Post and conversation 2001. Albert Godfrey recalls **Price and Beal's** *shop, Commercial Square, St Ann's, in the 1960s.*

Mr Malcolm Price, a local JP and well-known Nottingham businessman, Chamber of Commerce and so on, was a men's retailer. In 1965, when I was married and wanted to add to my income as a general commercial traveller, he asked me if I would like to work Saturdays in Price and Beal's shop in Commercial Square, St Ann's, for £2.50 plus commission and spivs[1]. I had an entry into Price and Beal through working as a textile warehouse lad in 1953. It was a successful firm with several shops, all sadly gone now.

The Commerce Square shop was long and narrow with a 2' x 2' wooden till. The Manager, Gilbert Bacon was 5'5'' tall, immaculately dressed in a Bruddersford cloth suit with a tape measure around his neck. On my first Saturday, he showed me the duster, the sales book, the weekly payment book, the till with handle and bell noise and I awaited my first customer.

He was a Jamaican: 'Man, I want a suit please. The best but not too dear.' This meant bespoke patterns from cloth bunches from £60 to £100. They liked to dress well. After the pattern was chosen, I would watch Gilbert use his measure for about thirty minutes, check over and over again, and then say: 'Left or right dress, Sir?' I thought he was asking what side of the bed the guy got out of!

A small deposit was taken, the order sent off to Leeds or Manchester to be part-made. It usually came back in two or three weeks. Then the customer would come for a fitting and Gilbert would literally mark crosses all over the place with his tailor's chalk, indicating where the suit needed letting in or out to ensure a perfect fit. In another two weeks, the finished suit would come back and the customer was usually very satisfied.

Gilbert showed me how to measure and fit. He also taught me how to shorten legs and sleeves, seven shillings and sixpence a time, in the tiny back kitchen where there was a sink, tea table, chair, sewing box, and 'lavie' outside at the back.

At 5.30pm sharp, Mr Price in bowler hat in his 1934 Bentley would arrive. 'Had a good day Bacon?' he would ask and acknowledge me tidying up. He would go off to the main shop on Parliament Street.

I was born and bred in Bulwell but worked there in St Ann's for three and a half years, from age thirty-one. It was an interesting life. The other side of the perk for me was that Ted the main branch's buyer would always find me an order for school wear which I sold doing my Monday to Friday repping job.

There was never a dull moment on Saturdays with Gilbert's many customers, coloured and white ones; all great people. Next door was Jimmy and Hazel running Brierley's the drapers. Pownall's the pawnbroker was opposite.

I saw Malcolm Price at his Edwalton home a few months ago and showed him something I had written about the shop. He was very interested. I first knew him in 1954. He was always very fair to his staff. He died peacefully in his sleep recently [2001]. I think he was eighty-nine.

---

[1] Cigarettes

Tuesday morning market in the Chase Precinct, *St. Ann's. There have been rumours that it will cease. Local people wish it to continue. Photos: Ellie White 2000*

St Ann's Nottingham: Inner-City Voices by Ruth I Johns • ISBN 0951696092

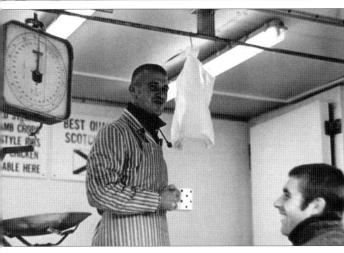

IVOR LEONARD

Born 1936

Ivor Leonard lived in St Ann's from the 1930s until 1956. He sent in these recollections of some of the then many public places, which became indelible in local people's experience and memory

I lived in Beverley Street just across from Calcutta Street off the St Ann's Well Road. Starting at the beginning of St Ann's nearest the City at Bath Street, the first pub on the St Ann's Well Road was The Admiral Dundas, then came the Oliver Cromwell which was on the corner of Alfred Street. Then on the right-hand side was The Chase Tavern, followed by The Cathcart which was at the corner of Cathcart Street. A little further along was The Scot's Grey's, known locally as Cocky's. At the corner of Meredith Street was the Meredith pub. On the opposite side was The Havelock Inn. The last pub was The Westminster at the end of St Ann's Well Road and beginning of The Wells Road where the Police Station was. St Bartholomew's Road, which used to be Donkey Hill, is still there today.

Now for the people and the shops. There was Mr Sales who owned the butcher's shop next to the Bank and Clarkies Fish and Chip shop, which used to be filled with American Forces personnel during the Second World War. Next came Ward's the paper shop and Pownall's the second hand shop. On the right hand side came Mr Fletcher, the barber who had a parrot. When you went in for a haircut, it perched on his shoulder.

Just past the Public Baths was Mr King the off licence, and at the corner of Leicester Street was Mrs Mellor's the greengrocer. Then you came to Beverley Street and just past there was Mr Martin the butcher. Across the way was Winky Watson's the Chippy, his name being so because all his potatoes had eyes in them! Next-door was Strecker's shop, owned by a German family. They suffered quite a few hardships including Mr Strecker's internment during the War. They sold homemade cooked meats. Today their shop would be called a Delicatessen.

On the opposite side of the road was another butcher called Mr Howard. Next-door was Mrs Weir's the sweet shop, then Hobson's the paper shop and Mrs Dufty's the beer-off. Next door was St Ann's Board School where most of the children of the area went. Then came the fruit shop owned by Mr Pearce. Across the road was Lee's the sewing machine shop. He had a sideline charging accumulator batteries for radio valve sets, which were all the rage in those days. Mr Lee's son became a well-known violinist.

Across the road was the pawnbroker's, owned by Mr Anderson, which did a very brisk trade every Monday morning. Then came Barnaby the rag and bone man who also had a business selling coal and firewood. These are some of the characters I remember.

Other places popular in those days were the Victoria Ballroom and the Empress Cinema. I spent many happy hours in both. The Cavendish Cinema was a well-known haunt of the younger generation and most teenagers went there every week. A little higher up St Ann's Well Road was Robin Hood Chase, which was a tree-lined avenue of Victorian houses where a lot of influential people of the time lived. In St Ann's Church the Annual Rose Society Awards were held.

STUART BRAMLEY

Born 1939

*Interviewed at St Ann's Library 23.6.99. Stuart Bramley talks of growing up and working in the **Harry Bramley Pork Butcher** business*

I was born in St Ann's at 359, St Ann's Well Road and I lived there for six months and then the family moved to Mapperley. But the family business carried on there for the next thirty years. It went on until it was closed and knocked down because of demolition. There used to be twenty-two butchers in St Ann's.

There wasn't enough room for the family above the shop. It was only two-bedroomed accommodation. Very small. I had an elder brother seven years old, and a twin sister.

So my personal connection with St Ann's started when I was about fourteen. At that time I was attending People's College on College Street in the City, and I used to work before I went to school and after I left school. I would come on the bus from school to St Ann's Well Road and then later go home on my bicycle. This was for about two years before I left school.

Stuart Bramley's parents Harry and Nellie Bramley at 359, St Ann's Well Road c1966-67

I would help with all manner of things in the shop and in the workshop at the back, all to do with pork butchery. After leaving school, I did one week's work in an architect's office but didn't like it and went to work with my father and stayed in the business. I was the errand boy. I had a carrier cycle.

I can remember, when I first started, I had to go to the slaughterhouse on Monday mornings. We sold pig's tripe and pig's tripe had to be cleaned properly. We couldn't rely on slaughtermen to do it. It was my job to do it. I got there on the carrier bike and I had a big basket on the front. I had to sit on the bike and ask two slaughtermen to lift the basket full on to the cycle because it would have tipped over if I wasn't sitting on it. Then I asked them to put a bucket of blood to swing on the handlebars. Then I would ride up London Road and all the way up St Ann's Well Road. There was no other means of getting it there.

In those days, if you wanted something, you did it yourself or you didn't get it.

In 1956, when I was 17, I was determined to get my driving licence. I was the first in the family to have a licence. I got a 1931 Austin 7. Driving lessons were less than ten shillings a time. Twelve lessons and I passed my test. There was no waiting for a test. You applied one week and got it the next. Then I got rid of my carrier bike.

It altered the shape of the business. There were no regulations in those days and we could deliver to country pubs, although the pub trade wasn't like it is now but it was beginning to develop, pork pies, sausage rolls and things like that.

I worked with my father, mother and brother prior to going into the Forces, Conscription in 1958, I did three years and used to come home and help them at certain times when they were busy. When I left the Forces, we heard from the Public Health Department that things were afoot with an idea of demolishing the area and they hinted that the business would not be there in about eight to ten years. We had a family get-together. Dad said he was stopping there. That would be his premises. My brother and I thought we couldn't stop because we had a lifetime in front of us, so we decided to buy our own property, move the machinery and supply my father from our new premises. Then if the day came when the old premises were knocked down, father could come and join us.

Our new premises were on Colwick Road near St Christopher's Church, Sneinton. That was around 1963. About a year later, the trade wasn't enough to sustain my brother and me in the kind of wages we wanted. So I bought a van and then went out delivering wholesale to other shops. There were literally dozens around the City. And we built up quite a round and it expanded and expanded. My father came to work for us after 1969 when the St Ann's Well Road shop was shut for demolition. We still kept expanding. In the mid-seventies, we decided to shut the shop on Colwick Road and concentrate on wholesale butchery. In 1982, my brother wanted to leave the business and we found a man to buy his half share of the business. We worked together for two years and then left the area and moved to Bingham to a proper factory on an industrial estate and it's grown and grown. It's called Bramley's Sausages. All we do is make sausages, frozen and fresh.

My father was one of the few who got adequate compensation for his premises in St Ann's. We had a very good shop there, a lot of class customers used to come, monied customers and one of those was a solicitor who he talked to about these things. My father talked to the Council and it said he could engage anybody he liked to litigate to determine what compensation he was entitled to. Mr Ball the solicitor did this for us. I can remember him coming up July 1968 because it was Bank Holiday the weekend after. He said: 'Harry, you've got to shut the doors on Bank Holiday Saturday.' And that's what we did. He had received the cheque from the Council, and when you received your cheque that was the end of business.

My father didn't start the business. It had belonged to one of the Carnills. They were Pork Butchers on Commerce Square. There were beef butchers and pork butchers. The two were distinct in those days. If they were beef butchers they sold beef and pork but not pork products. Pork butchers sold pork and pork products only. Percy Carnill had two shops in Commerce Square, one a beef shop and one a pork shop. My father got his shop about eight years before I was born. My mother worked in the business as well as bringing up a family.

There was no slaughtering done on the premises but everything else to do with the pork trade. We made pork pies, black puddings, polony, haslet, faggots, sausage rolls, potted meat and everything conceivable. What we sold from the shop was made by us.

The meat was slaughtered in Nottingham. We dealt with firms in the Cattle Market. It was 1954 before meat rationing ended. Prior to that it had been a long struggle because you could only get your allocation depending on the number of customers who were registered with you.

When I was fifteen, of course, it didn't register the kind of people we were dealing with. On reflection, you think it was an enjoyable way of going on. My father was a big character in the area and our shop was always full of

Photo of one of the sturdy bags provided for customers

characters. One particular fellow was a bookmaker and boxing promoter, Reg King. Nowadays there are only about two boxing promoters in the world! This chap put on local boxing matches pretty regularly at the Ice Stadium. He had three or four bookmaker's shops, consequently he was looked on as having money. He was a good customer to us. He'd come into the shop and he'd see people in front of him, little old ladies with no money. And he'd say: 'Harry, give them what they want.' And when they left, he'd pay for them. But he'd take money off them in another direction! Through the bookmaker shops. We saw what went on but we didn't tell people.

Dad used to display flowers. Someone would grow them in the allotments on Hungerhill Road. He would put a bunch in the shop window. We would probably sell twenty bunches a day and that was pocket money, not for my father, but to those who grew them and had nowhere to display them. We sold tomatoes in the same way. They were grown in greenhouses on the Hungerhill and other allotments. That's what went off in St Ann's but it no longer goes on. There was a demise of the allotments.

There were all sorts of characters. There was Dennis from Dame Agnes Street. He used to come round on his bike and say: 'Harry, does your blind need mending?' It was a canvas sunblind and he'd come round twice a year and sew it for you. And when it wore out, he'd make you a new one.

There was another fellow who came around. 'I've come to do your sign, Harry.' He'd come every two or three years. He'd scrape the sign off your windows from inside the shop and write Harry Bramley inside out so it could be viewed from the outside. He'd do it freehand and then gild it. He'd travel round different towns. He'd probably do two shops on St Ann's Well Road. Not everybody had the quality of business that we had generating the cash flow.

One character was called Billy Hardtimes. He was a little old man. He had an allotment up The Wells Road. He kept pigs there. Nobody knew his name and that's why he was called Billy Hardtimes. Now my father was Bill's bank. Bill used to feed his pigs with swill that he used to push up the road twice a day in a barrow. Then he took his pigs to the slaughterhouse. We'd fetch him and take him there and he'd get paid by cheque. He had no cheque book and he couldn't read or write. Dad cashed the cheque for him and that's how life went on.

There was a Butcher's outfitter on Trent Lane which was off Daleside Road. I had to go there to fetch skins and all manner of things. On the way there was a scrap yard. On the top of a shed in the gateway was a three-wheeler bike and, I thought, I fancy that. But he wouldn't sell it to me. I went in everyday for a month and he still wouldn't. In the end I got another fellow with a scrap yard down there, called Fred Strecker, and he purchased it and I bought if off Fred. Fred had a sister, Ollve, who also had a Pork Butchers shop in St Ann's Well Road. Fred was a bit of a Jack the lad. He was a speedway rider in the late twenties, early thirties. There was a speedway track down Daleside Road. I knew Fred well because he lived right against our house. We were neighbours.

I think their family had great difficult at the outbreak of War. But they did carry on. You see pork butchers originated from Germany. Everybody thought my father was a German at one time, but he wasn't. There was another pork butcher in Nottingham called Wagner (of Wagner and Allsopp). He had to leave the country at the outbreak of War. My father learnt his trade from a German pork butcher. He called himself Blanch.

There were a lot of little shops on the Road that were owner occupied. The man went out to work and the shop was to supplement the living. But we were a business. Most of the pork butchers were.

There was great sadness as the time of demolition came. People didn't realise what they were living in.

Behind our shop was Westminster Street. It would be no more than two to three hundred yards in length and either side was terraces. There were eight hundred people living in Westminster Street and it is hard today to believe that that number of people existed in such a small area. They enjoyed it. It was the only life they knew. When the time came to be moved, they were in fear as to what was going to happen to them. A lot of the older folks went into Homes and that was the time of building Balloon Woods, Top Valley and all the big Council estates expanded to take people, many from St Ann's. They had to go somewhere. People got dispersed to different areas and the community just died.

We never had any bother with Health people until the early sixties. There was no empire of civil servants. They all operated from one little office in Nottingham. Then they decided it was a good idea to expand, jobs for the boys, so to warrant the jobs they made their own rules and regulations, nationally as well as locally. There's an army of civil servants now. I don't think the end product is any better.

From somebody who has been adequately trained, or been in the job all his life, there is no food poisoning. In recent years, we've had outbreaks of food poisoning. It's down to food not being cooked properly. We used to boil hams and sell ham off the bone for years and years and years. No problems. In the late fifties and sixties people started wanting cheaper food.

This fellow comes along and says he can save us 'x' pounds a week. He introduced slow cooking for hams, pork and legs of pork. These joints were slow cooked all night long and brought to a temperature of 180F, not boiling, and then left for an hour and then brought up to that heat again, then shut down, insulated. When you get there in the morning and lifted the lid, they were cooked. But what we think is cooked these days, *isn't* cooked. We used to boil things and you could see the water simmering or boiling and that killed the bacteria. But it doesn't get killed any more.

There's no skills left in the trade now. We've got eight employees at Bingham. Apart from my partner and myself, nobody can cut up a pig. They can make sausages but they don't know what a pig looks like. But now we buy meat, lumps of meat. We deal with a firm on Meadow Lane, meat distribution people. They get sides of pork come into the factory. It is chopped up and what we call Cryo-Vac'd. That's a machine that seals it with polythene, airtight. They cut legs, shoulders, loins, chops . . . and they sell to the supermarkets. In the process, there's pork that has to be trimmed off the bellies and one thing and another and all that goes into a big tub and we buy it. It comes ready for the mincer.

The supermarkets want the stuff that can be cut straight away, no waste. They can undo the polythene, a butcher puts one knife through and that's it, it goes on the counter. The distributor gets the waste.

The generations that ate polony, black pudding, faggots, tripe and whatever have died and the younger generation do not eat it. Nobody makes pork pies in quantity like we used to. Pork Farms have no shops now. Yes, Pork Farms started in Alfred Street South. Ken Parr bought F W Farnsworth when he got demobbed from the Forces. He bought F W Farnsworth because it had a big allocation of meat and he expanded that firm from probably one shop into about ten little shops. He joined them altogether between Alfred Street South and Commercial Square. And all the little shops behind were converted into a factory and he went across the road and it went on and on.

And can you remember T M Parrs? They were another pork butcher. They were out at Beeston. But they originated on the Mansfield Road and I think Samworth Brothers who owned T M Parrs bought Pork Farms. Then it was sold out to Northern Foods and now it's a Division of Northern Foods. They've gone the way of every other pork butcher, they're mainly into fast food, pizzas and savoury foods.

I still meet people who bring back memories of St Ann's. In fact, I was in Arnold on Saturday and did. I can't remember their names but I remember their faces.

I retired three years ago at the end of this month. My involvement is going in now when my partner rings me up: 'Will you come and do this, because we're a driver short?' or 'I'm going on holiday.' As far as anything else is concerned, I'm retired.

DENNIS CARNELLEY

Born 1950

*Interviewed at **St Ann's Well Road Post Office**, Robin Hood Chase, St Ann's 5.5.00*

I've been working here since 1974 when I was twenty-four. At that time, I was working for my parents. They already had a Post Office in Wollaton when they decided to buy this one. So I came down here with my mother. Then about six years later my brother, Bryn, came in as well. Then my mother retired and my father sold Wollaton Post Office and came down here and worked with us for a few years and then he packed it in. Now it's my brother and me.

This is the only Post Office in the area, though there's Thorneywood Rise, right at the top of the hill. When I first came here, there were two banks on the block, one was TSB and the bank at the bottom was the National Westminster Bank. Now they are both closed. Now for some years this has been the only financial transaction place.

Nottingham sub-postmasters lobbied Parliament a few weeks ago. The lobby was organised by the Sub-Postmasters' Federation from all over the country including Scotland and Northern Ireland about the threat of closures.

The Government wants to modernise the payment system for benefit payments. They want to do it electronically. By 2003, they say it will be ACT - Automatic Credit Transfer - into a bank account. If they do that, it will take away 70-80% of my business. As you probably realise this is a big benefits office. They will virtually take away my salary overnight. So we're campaigning with the Government for some sort of plan which has a Post Office based solution for electronic payments. There's about two years in which to hammer something out. Tony Blair said he would talk to the Federation and Post Office and all interested parties . . .

There are a lot of people who don't have bank accounts and might have problems getting one. We've got to persuade the Government to come up with a simpler accounts system so beneficiaries can have an account of some sort. Banking rules are so strict now.

This Post Office is very much part of the local community. In the mornings it's especially busy. Some people come in because they don't see anybody else during the rest of the week. They will come purely to queue and chat to people, catch up on the gossip. There's a lot of people who come to us first, because they've got no money to get breakfast or whatever. We provide that sort of service. It also caters for the rest of the shops. People collect their money from us and go to the various shops on the Chase. If there was no Post Office, they would have to go into the City Centre to a bank.

Some of the shops do their banking here. In this respect, they are paying my wages and I'm paying theirs! Part of the proposed Government idea is I think that shops will provide a range of services offered by a Post Office.

I've dealt with the public for such a long period now, it's like family. I've seen children grow up to men sort of thing. People come and talk to you about some of their problems. We're a listening ear. It's a family community. I find people here a lot easier to get on with than the people in Wollaton. I did work at my parents' Wollaton Post Office for a time. There were some very nice people at Wollaton, don't get me wrong, but there were one or two who would read the Post Office Guide and then come and tell me my job!

What is the attraction of St Ann's people? It's a hard question to answer. They are down to earth. You can have a row with them one minute in the morning. In the afternoon, they come in and buy your stamps! They'll do anything to help someone out. I suppose it goes back to the old St Ann's where neighbours used to help each other out, socialising, chatting and catching up on gossip. There is a sense of that even now in this modern day and age. People look out for other people.

The area people come from to here is bounded by Woodborough Road up to Alexandra Court, down Hungerhill Road, right the way up St Ann's Well Road, Brewsters, some from Blue Bell Hill area. And some from the private estate off The Wells Road. Some come just for Child Benefit. We cover a big area.

I gather from what I've been told that before the area was redeveloped there were at least five sub Post Offices. Then after, there was just this one. Before demolition this Post Office was actually on St Ann's Well Road, that's why we have that name although we are in Robin Hood Chase. People get mixed up. It's called Chase Post Office or Robin Hood Chase Post Office but that's not the official name.

In fifty years time, I would like this to be remembered as the hub of the community, providing friendly service. People relying on it and coming here for advice and hopefully getting the right advice. People respect the place and the service. That's important for the history of the area and the history of the Post Office.

It's nice to think that a Postmaster still counts for something. For example, for passports, the counter-signing has to be done by somebody reliable in a community and people come in and ask me to do it. Advice can be needed over all sorts of things. For example, how to post certain things, what currency to have when going abroad, driving licences, about free prescriptions, how to fill in various forms, about paying bills, lots of things.

ADAM HOPEWELL

Born 1960

Interviewed at **Hopewell's the Furnishers**, *Huntingdon Street 17.5.00. Adam Hopewell is Managing Director of Hopewell's, a family business. His great grandparents started the business in 1885 at 279, Alfred Street Central. Photos courtesy of the Hopewell family*

Yes, I'm called Mr Adam because with three Hopewells here, it is the simplest way of avoiding confusion. My father, John Hopewell, was taken ill recently but he's hoping to come in this week, but he won't be back full-time. It's in the family tradition not to retire but just keep going. There's Gordon Hopewell and myself here at present. We're the only three Hopewells in the company now.

John Hopewell is the son of Eric Hopewell. Gordon is the son of Bernard Hopewell and his second wife. Myra Hopewell was on the Board and she died in December 1999. When I started in 1981, there was my grandfather and Bernard as well. I have an elder brother and younger sister who don't work in the firm, and the rising generation, well it's too early to say whether any of them will be interested.

I'm intensely proud of what has been achieved here and its history. I thoroughly enjoy it.

I came here after University and a degree in Economics and Geography, which wasn't very furniture or business orientated.

The original Hopewell family lived in St Ann's and there was a Hopewell's shop in St Ann's up to the time of the area's demolition. The family house was at the bottom of Robin Hood Chase. There were certainly cousins and a lot of family in St Ann's. I vaguely remember the construction work in the area. Our links with St Ann's are much more limited than they used to be. We have warehousing in St Ann's. This shop is on the City edge of the area.

Hopewell's is described as General House Furnishers. We do mainly three-piece suites, dining room and bedroom furniture for domestic houses, also carpets and fabrics. We have a contract side as well but it's principally general house furnishing. We have customers all over the country and we do a small amount of export.

Our long-distance customers tend to be people who have lived in Nottingham and have not found anything in their area they are comfortable with. We deliver, for example, to East Anglia and Cornwall and south of London. Old customers account for a high percentage of our business. Word of mouth is very important in this business.

Hopewell's moved out of Parliament Street to here. It was impossible to maintain a store which requires a lot of showroom space in the City Centre, and there was also a need for car parking. We have to advertise more here. The last generation of Hopewells obviously felt much closer to St Ann's than I do, not having lived there and only drive

The Hopewell family in 1906. Back row standing (left to right): Ernest, Frank, Jim. Middle row: Edith, Frank E Hopewell, Claude, Eric, Annie E Hopewell (nee Buxton). Front row, Bernard and Connie. Eric, seen here on his mother's knee, was Adam Hopewell's grandfather. Annie Hopewell played a very active role in building up and running the business. She died in 1943, some six years after her husband was killed in a motor accident

ST ANN'S Nottingham. Inner-city voices by Ruth I Johns • ISBN 0951696092

279, Alfred Street Central, where the Hopewell business started in 1885. The building, to which a new front was subsequently added, was demolished at the time of St Ann's redevelopment. The business first moved to 180, Alfred Street Central and, in 1898, it had prospered sufficiently to move to 176, St Ann's Well Road. In the first decade of the 1900s, it moved again to the double-fronted shop at 156 and 158, St Ann's Well Road. Hopewell's opened other shops in the City, lost the shop on St Ann's Well Road and the warehouse at Dame Agnes Street (due to the area's demolition) and eventually concentrated its Nottingham retail and warehouse operations at Huntingdon/Great Freeman Street. The Hopewell family have published Hopewell's the furnishers: A short History 1885-1992

book, get in the best selling lines and typical interior design. But you've got to keep your own identity. You don't want to lose that thing which makes Hopewell's different from any other store. You can't take blueprints from another company and superimpose them. You've got to strike you own path.

Including our store in Derby, we have about sixty-five staff including part-time ones.

Hopewell's is unusual, because so many family businesses evolve over two or three generations but to last to four generations is a rarity. They are fragile unless there's a continuing generation to take up the next step, they dissolve or get absorbed by larger companies. So Hopewell's is unusual and I'm very proud of it.

An early photograph of Hopewell's shop on St Ann's Well Road

through. But there still is an affinity with St Ann's on the basis of that's where the company had its roots. We look to support projects in St Ann's. For example, schools and St Ann with Emmanuel Church. My great grandfather went to St Ann's Church [which was demolished].

St Ann's is not an area we would focus on for customers but we should keep some strong connection with it. Not many of our staff come from the area now.

Is the family history being handed on to the next generation? Probably not enough. I have a daughter. My brother Steven has five children but doesn't live in Nottingham. IIe lives in Wakefield. And my sister Emma lives in London.

To run a company like this, you either have to have the right people or be able to do it yourself. And because you can't possibly do it all yourself, you need a combination of both. You have to have your own handwriting on a business. The simple option is to do everything by the

1922. An early motor vehicle replacing the horse-drawn vans. Claude Hopewell is the driver

A glimpse of some of the St Ann's shops at different stages of planning blight. The Ladder Shop was once Hopewell's shop on St Ann's Well Road. J G Grant, Butcher, on the corner of Peas Hill Road and Cooper Street, also see earlier photos. Photos: Nicholson Photo Archive

Boam Brothers (of Northumberland Street, St Ann's), confectioners. George Barton is the roundsman with the delivery cart on Gordon Road, c1930. Photo: Nottingham Local Studies Library

Marsdens of Union Road, St Ann's, with Les Oliver delivering groceries on Beverley Street, 1960. Photo: Nottingham Local Studies Library

DENNIS DIXON

Born 1932

*Interviewed at **Hopewell's the Furnishers**, Huntingdon Street 17.5.00*

I'm in my fifty-fourth year working for Hopewell's. I am Despatch Manager and I started work with the firm when I was fourteen. I started on August 19th 1946.

I was born slightly out of St Ann's on the Carlton Road. But when I was four we moved to Edwin Street off the St Ann's Well Road. At first, I worked for Hopewell's Removal Section from the St Ann's Well Road. I never worked in the days of horse and carts. When I started, Hopewell's had Thorneycrofts, Bedford and Leyland vehicles. They were all petrol engines.

As a child, I suffered from bronchitis and I had to have an outside job, which is how I started at Hopewell's. I was in the old St Ann's Church Choir. The choir master then was Jim Hopewell who had his own business in Nottingham. He was a brother to the Hopewell's furnishers in St Ann's. I asked Mr Jim, I said : 'You've got connections in business' and I told him what I'd got to do. And he introduced me to his brother Mr Claude Hopewell. And my mum came along with me to the interview.

I was an only child. I started at thirty shillings a week, which was good then. I wasn't supposed to work overtime but in those days you could be out two or three nights at a time. Anything over a forty-eight hour week and I had to go and see Mr Claude who then gave me an extra shilling per hour worked extra. Long distance delivery was all over the country. At that particular time I & R Morley had a lot of fabric factories in Nottingham and they were removing a lot of their managers back to London after the bombings, and we did the removals.

We were allowed eight hours to reach London because the vehicles were limited to twenty miles an hour at that time. The biggest change I've seen is with the roads. The biggest change in vehicles is that you had to have them serviced every thousand miles, now they go for twelve thousand miles before they are serviced. We're using Mann vehicles - it's the Volkswagen Group - diesels.

I've enjoyed my working life. When you work for a family business, you feel you know who you are working for. You're not a number. You meet a lot of people ... happy people, naughty people at times and ones that can be nasty on the phone!

I continued living in St Ann's after I got married and then moved to where we are now, at Thorneywood, just outside St Ann's and nine-tenths of a mile from here. We moved to Thorneywood forty years ago before St Ann's was demolished. I still sing in the church choir: St Ann with Emmanuel, the church which replaced two that were demolished.

My parents were in St Ann's at the time of demolition. They were moved to Sneinton Dale. That was a traumatic time for my parents and relatives. My mother had brothers and sisters in St Ann's. Practically every street had a brother or a cousin, and it meant that in their old age they were separated and in various parts of the City. And when they needed each other, they hadn't got each other. That was really sad.

It had been a very close community. There were a lot of nice houses pulled down. Nowadays, they would have kept those houses: good houses, villa type houses.

There were also some awful houses where you had to walk down the road to the toilet and they needed getting rid of.

Dennis Dixon has now retired [2002]

St Ann's Well Road with a no 47 trolley bus c1964-65. Photo: Nottingham Local Studies Library

Nos 167 – 171, St Ann's Well Road, near the corner of Peas Hill Road (where Acacia Court now stands) c1970. No 167 was Butler Morris Men's Outfitters; No 169 was West and Bradley, hardware shop, previously Shaw Bros; and 171 was Frank Ash, greengrocer's (his brother owned Ash's Wet Fish Shop off the photo to the left). Photo: Geoffrey Shaw. Nottingham Local Studies Library

Three photos taken in 1969 by G L Roberts: Nottingham Local Studies Library. Judging by the lack of traffic, these must have been taken at a quiet time

The last days of the 'old' St Ann's Well Road. The grand building of the National Westminster Bank coming down. Behind it is some of the new housing. Victoria Centre high-rise flats in the City Centre in the background . . . and close-up of the Bank's end. Note how people still used the shops 'hanging on' until the last moment. Photos: Nicholson Photo Archive

St Ann's Nottingham: Inner-city voices by Ruth I Johns • ISBN 0951696092

A small row of shops on St Ann's Well Road. They were built by the King's Hall Methodist Church in the 1950s when the Church was partially rebuilt following damage by a bomb in the Second World War. The shops are now owned by the Kings Hall Christian Centre N.T.A. Photo: Ellie White 2000

Robin Hood Chase Precinct shops after a 'face-lift' and the start of the Lottery, and before the Chase Neighbourhood Centre was built. Photo: Ruth I Johns mid-1990s

Chase Precinct supermarket. There is a Fish and Chip shop in the Precinct, off photo. Photo: Ruth I Johns 2002

Fish and Chip Shop on the corner of Pearmain Drive and The Wells Road. Photo: Ruth I Johns 2002

The Hawk Cycle Outlet on Woodborough Road on the corner opposite the Pakistan Centre. After the Craven Arms was pulled down, Kwik-Save opened but did not stay and Hawk Cycles moved in. Photo: E James Smalley 2000

The Kwik Save sign on the Woodborough Road. Photo: Alan Hardy

St Bartholomew's Road, which escaped demolition. Shops were put in after local protest at lack of amenities following the redevelopment of St Ann's. Photo: Ruth I Johns 2000

The unwelcoming entrance to [Phase 10] Marple Square Shopping Precinct facing Woodborough Road

The only shop open in the Precinct is Mr Hussain's, shown here

All the others (some seen here) closed long ago. This Phase 10 area is being redeveloped (again!) and there is hope that shops (including Mr Hussain's) will be brought back on to the Woodborough Road frontage. Photos: E James Smalley 2000

St Ann's Nottingham: Inner-city voices *by Ruth I Johns* • ISBN 0951696092

The Transition Years

The photos on these four pages show a variety of St Ann's housing in an advanced stage of planning blight. It is still easy to see which needed to come down and which improved. The economic and social cost of small-scale neighbourhood redevelopments (as outlined by the three architects David Wilkinson, Rob Davis and David Strickland) would have been much more effective over the years than the extensive wipe-out that occurred. And consequent expenditure of many millions of pounds making good the 'new' St Ann's. All properties on these pages were demolished

Photos: David Wilkinson, Rob Davis and David Strickland who were amazed how people steadfastly carried on with their lives 1967

St Ann's Well Road (Birkin Terrace) from Union Road 1970. Photo: Nottingham Local Studies Library

Photos: Nicholson Photo Archive

ST ANN'S NOTTINGHAM: inner-city voices *by Ruth I Johns* • ISBN 0951696092

Photos: Nicholson Photo Archive

Photos: Nicholson Photo Archive

ST ANN'S NOTTINGHAM: inner-city voices *by Ruth I Johns* • ISBN 0951696092

THE TRANSITION YEARS

Being deliberately run down, planning blight, demolition which caused the displacement of 30,000 people, and redevelopment of St Ann's was a crucial slice in Nottingham's history. The transition years peaked in the decade up to1976. Their effects are still being felt: evidence exists within this book. For example, in individual life stories and in the improvements [as in Phase 10] still happening to make good mistakes that were made.

It is, however, important to realise that the policies and actions of Nottingham Corporation in St Ann's were not significantly different to what had happened and was still happening[1] in cities elsewhere in the UK at the time the bulldozers started rolling in St Ann's. But, by then, doubts had arisen about redevelopments elsewhere which should have caused Nottingham's planners to think again.

When I came to know St Ann's in 1965, it was a district in which many were living as third, or even fourth, generation St Annies, where work was plentiful, where shops and pubs attracted people into the area, and where there were many different people, including Poles, Pakistanis, Indians, West Indians, Italians, Africans, Irish, Ukrainians and many others. Some had settled for many years, others were more recent. In particular, people from the Asian subcontinent and the Caribbean responded to British Government post-war campaigns to attract them to this country to fill job vacancies. These newcomers to Nottingham often settled in St Ann's because accommodation was inexpensive. Sometimes, initially, they lodged with someone from their home country who was a pioneer settler in this country, probably owning their house in St Ann's.

In 1965, I started Family First Trust [FF], a community housing association and self-help organisation, on the fringe of St Ann's. I have written about the early years of FF[2] but did not single out my St Ann's experiences, some of which appear below. My work made me acutely aware of the way in which housing was *the* key factor that determines much more than whether someone has a roof over their head, essential though that is. Well-being also depends on being accepted in a neighbourhood which must have reasonable public amenities, shops, public transport . . .

In the mid-sixties, housing redevelopment was being used as a means of raw social control. For example, the City Council only wanted FF to purchase houses in run-down areas with no guaranteed future. I insisted that FF would only convert and improve older housing into modern flats and maisonettes in areas of mixed housing with shops and transport nearby. Homeless families did not deserve to be dumped in run-down areas. FF ran into fierce planning obstruction. We never gave in. It was a hard struggle for some years, after which the City Council admitted with good grace that FF's policies worked and it was then possible to co-operate with the Council.

But the 1960's City Council policy meant that FF was unable to improve any of the large houses in St Ann's. Nor was anybody else.

There were influential 'outside' people who studied St Ann's. For example, Elizabeth Burney studied housing as it influenced immigrants. She said even the active Pakistan Friends League in St Ann's did not know of the rule whereby single men could put their name on the List[3]. "No official effort was made to inform immigrants of the normal council housing procedures, even at the stage, early in 1965, when the 'live' waiting list had shrunk to only 2,000 and slum clearance had not begun to take up the slack."

In 1966, there were several ways of getting Council accommodation in Nottingham. A young man could put his name on the List at age eighteen and get a house any time after five years if he was married. Nobody could remain on the List if they were living in self-contained accommodation whether rented or owned, unless they had a large enough family to qualify for a place on the overcrowding register. The five year waiting list applied to everyone on the general List. This policy was to change a few years on.

Elizabeth Burney states that one reason for the absence of coloured people on Nottingham Council housing estates was the deliberate policy of housing them in old terraced houses acquired specially for the purpose. Once a coloured family received the keys of a terraced house, they were not eligible for council accommodation. "As long as these are virtually the only houses offered to coloured people, it cannot be said that Nottingham's housing policy is free from discrimination," she said.

In my experience, one-parent families [predominantly married mothers whose husbands had left], and larger families, were two of the other groups discriminated against in the same way.

Local people who wanted to move out to a Council estate were encouraged to sell their houses cheaply to the Corporation. Ms Burney said the Council spent the minimum on keeping these houses habitable and some streets, especially where the Council put its problem families, have a 'sullen air' in sharp contrast to the "paint box colours of those which obviously belong to immigrant owner-occupiers". St Ann's, she said, was one of Nottingham's main centres of coloured settlement.

In the St Ann's redevelopment area of some 300 acres, Ms Burney said there were 4,900 jobs in about 200 different firms. Much of the employment - about 2,600 jobs according to a survey carried out by the Town Planning Department - was in clothing and textiles. About 75% of the people, mainly women, working in these firms lived within five minutes walk of their job. "Such is the socio-economic weave which has somehow to be unravelled and knit up again."

---

[1] "Between 1958-70 in the towns and cities of England and Wales, new homes are likely to be built on sites where no less than half a million older houses now stand or stood." So said Henry Brooke, Minister of Housing and Local Government, in his Ministry's publication *Flats and Houses 1958: Design and Economy* [HMSO 1958]. He spoke of layouts, housing densities, design and costs but there is not a single word about people!

[2] Life Goes On ISBN 090789500X.

[3] *Housing on Trial: A study of Immigrants and Local Government* by Elizabeth Burney [Oxford University Press. 1967].

In fact 340 is usually the acreage quoted for the St Ann's redevelopment. The housing policies mentioned above give us clues how St Ann's housing was deliberately down-graded. This down-grading, the processes of planning blight and the inclusion of good buildings for destruction (for reasons of redevelopment convenience), represented a major shift in the Council's thinking about St Ann's over a relatively short period of time.

For example, the 1952 Written Statement of the City of Nottingham Development Plan, which forecast up to 1972, estimated that St Ann's had 11,500 dwellings of which 3,000 would need to come down by 1972. This represented 80 acres. In fact, 10,000 dwellings came down and 30,000 people displaced from them.

When I first knew St Ann's, redevelopment was still only rumour. By the time it was known to be a fact, there was generally an acceptance of its inevitability but a lot of resentment. By the time the bulldozers were months into creating what looked like a war zone, the momentum for wanting to get it all over with grew. Life in St Ann's had been rendered intolerable.

In 2001, I met a woman who spent over a year in St Ann's in the late 1960s when the City Council put her into two 'condemned' properties in turn. At the time she was experiencing many problems due to severe post-natal depression and was admitted to Mapperley Hospital. She came through eventually and today is well. There were so many people like her who were treated like flotsam in a disaster not of their own making. Some were broken by the trauma. People mention relatives who died soon after having to move.

Many people who experienced the redevelopment still feel upset about it. Some because they lost 'fit' properties. Others welcomed the idea of better housing but resented the way things were done. For example, some didn't realise they could have three choices of where they were re-housed by the Council and took a first offer thinking it was that or nothing.

Others were very happy about moving if they were allocated a new home in a neighbourhood they liked. But common bonds of belonging were being destroyed. People were involuntarily separated from each other not only geographically but in far-reaching much more subtle ways. "Why did they get that new house, and we only got …?"

Attempts by St Ann's people to influence the Council at that time were made and are recorded in these pages, but they did not include the majority of residents.

There was a significant intervention in the fate of St Ann's due to a Survey. It was done in 1966/67 by members of an Adult Education Class under the auspices of two Nottingham University lecturers, Ken Coates and Richard Silburn. The BBC made a film of St Ann's as a follow-up to the Survey. This film is still deeply resented by many St Ann's people. It showed part of the area in its worst state of pre-demolition blight. "We were told we lived in a slum, but we lived decent lives and had pride," is a typical comment. More about this Survey later.

There was some structurally very bad housing that needed to come down in the old St Ann's. There was much housing that could have been maintained and upgraded; similar housing in some areas is now much sought after. There were many houses and other buildings that were demolished purely to satisfy 'easy' clearance. Some buildings that were 'fit' could have been left to create variety and interest in the new St Ann's. For example, some of the pubs and groups of shops on St Ann's Well Road were deemed 'fit' buildings and came down for planning convenience. The former library on Dame Agnes Street was 'fit'. so was the Robin Hood Club at the corner of Corporation Road, and the Theatre Club and premises on Hutchinson Street. The latter three examples are used solely as an indication that it would have been possible to leave some 'public' buildings.

Many people have said to me: "Mr Chettle's big house should never have come down. It was beautiful." I have not managed to find a photo of this house. Mr Chettle was 'the' dentist on St Ann's Well Road. There are very few buildings in the 'new' St Ann's that offer variety.

A few people I interviewed for this book still have their copy of the Nottingham Corporation's 1967 pamphlet *St Ann's Towards Renewal,* prepared by Nottingham City Planning Department. And/or its successor pamphlet *St Ann's: Renewal in Progress, 1970.* It stated that there were about 10,000 dwellings in the redevelopment area. In 1961, 65% of houses had no piped hot water supply, 75% had no bath and 25% had no toilet within or attached to their house. 15% of families had the exclusive use of both hot

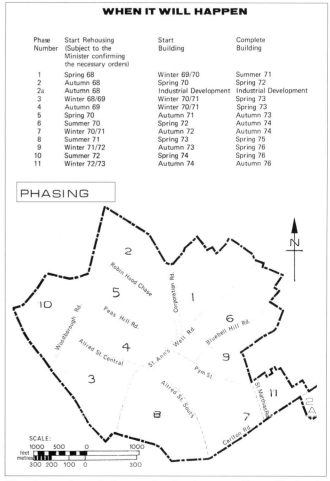

The timescale and phases of redevelopment. From 'St Ann's: Renewal in Progress' [Nottingham Corporation 1970]

and cold water taps, bath and toilet. Nowhere was there a thought about how many of the better houses without baths and toilets could have had them added. Some owner-occupiers had added bathrooms before they knew about demolition.

Here are fragments from my memory of planning blight in St Ann's:

- Landlords ceasing to do any improvements except the bare minimum and sometimes not that. There were some substantial landlords in St Ann's, like the Foundation of Nottingham High School and the Council. Companies of different sizes owned groups of houses as did some individuals (or their trustees). It was a complex pattern of ownership. The indigenous population did not have a tradition of buying their own house. More could have afforded to do so than those who chose to. As stated earlier, some settlers from other countries did.

- Some better-off people in St Ann's left before they had to. Those who could buy their homes on mortgage often moved to nearby areas like Thorneywood, Carlton and Mapperley.

- At the time, there was little detailed knowledge of what was happening outside the immediate streets affecting people. Life became a struggle for individual families and generations were split up. The bigger landlords must have done deals with the City Council. I don't know what they were. But rumours from 'those in the know' abounded.

- Authorised and unauthorised individuals and 'firms' scavenged for lead, furniture left behind, all sorts of items like brass handles, iron features, tiles, anything that could be sold. Much of this 'enterprise' was organised from outside the area, sometimes by people coming from a distance. Because ownership of possessions for their material worth was not usually an issue for people in St Ann's, they left behind some pieces of Victorian furniture which - over the years – had become 'valuable'.

- Familiar haunts closed week by week: shops and workshops, schools, factories and churches went. Pubs, still open, would sometimes hang on standing

The Garden Gate, St Ann's Well Road, corner of former Cathcart Street, standing alone in a landscape of demolition in front and building work behind. The pub was demolished. Photo 1971: Nottingham Local Studies Library

alone in a flattened landscape until they were finally flattened too. Street lighting failed. Water ran from water mains. Phone boxes didn't work.

- Streets were increasingly boarded up but people still had to walk down them, including children going to and from school.

- The sound of the area changed. Silence and darkness took over at nightfall and the noise of demolition or re-building by day. The smell was often of burning wood from demolished buildings. For example, when Emmanuel Church on Woodborough Road was being demolished, massive oak beams were burnt. Even in those less environmentally aware days, this sight was very distressing. That timber could have been re-used. I asked if I could take a short piece and struggled to put it in a car. It travelled to London when I moved there in 1976 and it is probably still a feature in the small garden we had.

- For a considerable number of children, some or all of their first seven years were spent in a 'bomb-site' environment. They would play in streets only partially peopled, on building sites not adequately protected (at least two children died as a result). Many were children of those temporarily housed in the district; children who desperately needed security.

- On one occasion, the police brought a young lone mother to Family First after the Local Authority sent her to temporary accommodation which was a brothel in St Ann's. She walked out with her baby. She felt she could not return to the Council department that sent her there. The policeman thought she looked 'lost' and brought her to FF. I looked at the accommodation list she had been given. Obviously it had not been checked out. This is one example of an event that hugely affected a family but which seemed of little consequence to the responsible authorities. The scale of the movement of thousands of people led to this dehumanising.

- The first family who came to FF's attention in St Ann's due to planning blight and demolition was a three generation mixed-race family whose settled way of life was severely affected by feeling they were no longer able to influence their own future. FF could sometimes arbitrate satisfactory outcomes. I still have a lovely photo which they gave me of the little girl in this family. She must be 35+ now!

- Families placed into temporary accommodation in St Ann's often needed practical help, like more warm bedding to make the accommodation bearable. Through a network of volunteers, FF provided friendship and support. Some friendships made then are still strong. Some families placed into temporary accommodation did have loving extended families but not locally. Without car or telephone, keeping in touch was difficult.

Many organisations including the St Ann's Tenants and Residents Association (SATRA), the Blue Bell Hill Craft Centre, some of the churches and groups from immigrant communities, tried hard to lessen the trauma experienced in St Ann's. Though helpful for those involved, these efforts only scratched the surface of what was needed. St Ann's experienced large-scale 'wartime' devastation but without a sense of common purpose. This struggle was built on the bureaucratic belief that the means justifies the end. "It will be worth it in the end", was a typical statement of officials when I was trying to find out the housing prospects for a particular family. Ever since, there have been expensive attempts to improve the housing, the environment and local amenities.

What was overlooked in the bureaucratic view of housing the 'slum' dwellers of St Ann's was any comprehension that the majority of people in St Ann's were talented, multi-skilled, inventive, problem-solvers, community focused, family orientated and - in general - tolerant. That *doesn't* mean there were no problems or no trouble-makers but the area was not defined by them.

In the planning blight years morale declined. One scheme to try to help was launched on March 10th 1969. It was the Nottingham Fair Housing Group, financed by the Gulbenkian Foundation. It closed four years later. Its prime aim was to try to assist in giving equal and fair housing opportunity for all groups, this being an initiative setting out in particular, but not exclusively, to assist immigrant groups at the time of housing redevelopment in Nottingham. As well as its central advice centre, it quickly opened advice centres in two main redevelopment areas, St Ann's and the Meadows.

Its work brought to the surface some of the special problems affecting immigrants. For example, a landlord gave a West Indian family notice to quit three months before they were due to be re-housed. The landlord wished to do this so he could sell his house to the Corporation with vacant possession and secure better compensation. Once the matter was 'taken up' it was resolved quickly by the Council offering to house this family ahead of the sale.

The Fair Housing Officer, Mr M Ajeeb, reported (1970): "The majority of Asian immigrants from the St Ann's area are now moving to areas which may well become General Improvement Areas under the Housing Act 1969. Therefore, the opportunities to improve their houses in these areas will be available and the [Fair Housing] Group intends to make information available to them in due course.

"A substantial number of West Indian immigrants from St Ann's area are also moving to the suburbs and the desire amongst them to disperse into the larger community is even greater than the Asians. However, both groups often face discrimination when seeking either home ownership or rented accommodation in some areas of the City. The tactics of practising discrimination in this respect are so subtle that even the Race Relations Act has proved powerless to prevent it . . .

"The problem of rented accommodation is becoming more acute by the day in the City. The clearance of St Ann's and some other parts of the City will undoubtedly add more strain to an already insufficient supply of available rented accommodation in the area. In this particular field, the plight of large families is serious as the

supply of large, older houses is decreasing . . . " These families faced strain, depression and confusion, he said.

This report made clear that, as a consequence of redevelopment, 'mistrust and misunderstanding' was felt by many immigrant owner-occupiers in the cases of compensation.

Among the European settlers was a group of Italian families on Dane Street. At the time of the Compulsory Purchase Order (1968) which included their homes, owner-occupiers in Dane Street included Rocco Loscalzo, Nicola Farino, Vito Cerabona, Paolo Lorenzo, Pietro Bamonte, Mario Sabetia, Giovanni Cacciato, Guiseppe Pilieri, Rocko Labbatte and others in nearby streets, like Antonio Puglietti on Cooper Street. The effort and satisfaction represented by these - and other - families who worked hard to be able to own their own homes was very considerable.

"This was a very difficult period for all our family as we had been living in the area for over fourteen years," said Tony Cerabona[4]. "Mum and Dad owned the house at 40, Dane Street, off Alfred Street Central. They had worked very hard and made many financial sacrifices to achieve this. It was very disconcerting that our home was being taken away and demolished."

Dane Street 1972. Photo: Nicholson Photo Archive

I do not know what each owner occupier received in compensation, but I personally knew owner-occupiers in houses which were kept in good repair and well cared for who received as little as £50 and thereafter became Council tenants for the rest of their lives. The amount of compensation seemed a more arbitrary process than would be permitted now.

People have spoken to me of 'haggling', getting representation by solicitors, knowing 'the ropes' but more usually they spoke of accepting what was offered believing there was no opportunity for discussion.

A few people who were not owner-occupiers spoke of removal or inconvenience payments including new carpets/curtains but no clear pattern emerges in people's memory. When I suggested to some people that payment had been available for carpets/curtains, the idea was

---

4   In Elliott Durham and St Ann's, the Comprehensive School on the hill in inner-city Nottingham. Edited Ruth I Johns [Plowright Press. 1998].

ST ANN'S NOTTINGHAM: inner-city voices *by Ruth I Johns* • ISBN 0951696092

usually regarded with amazed disbelief. Was it only for long-standing tenants? Yet, I know someone who received payment who was relatively short-term. It is hard to come to any conclusion other than that, to a considerable extent, compensation was negotiable but that most people neither realised this nor knew how to set about negotiating. Today, compensation would be a central issue.

No sooner had St Ann's been rebuilt than it started to feature in official reports as an area of deprivation and the problem of small firm relocation was recognised. The people of 'the slums' soon were perceived as part of the 'urban problem' or the 'inner-city problem'. The means of redevelopment had not justified the end. There was no Utopia!

In 1976, Nottingham City Council considered a report on *Industrial Relocation* which, for example, drew attention to the serious decline in Nottingham's industry and problems faced by small firms, many of which were affected by clearance activity.

In an *Inner Area Programme City Council Report, 1978*, it states: "Slum clearance activity over many years has reduced the choice of housing available in the inner-city through reduction in the privately rented sector and owner occupation, and has also displaced a large number of small industries."

The same report states: "The City Council has undertaken a substantial clearance programme for many years and this has caused particular disruption and environmental problems in areas subject to redevelopment over the of years."

The Report further stated that:

- In the inner-city area there was a greater concentration of one-parent families, immigrants, isolated elderly and young people with problems. The large number of elderly, in particular, placed demands on the home help and meals-on-wheels service[5].
- An increasing problem of vandalism and other anti-social activity from children of primary school age, with whom the law could not deal because they were below the age of criminal responsibility[6].
- Social and physical upheaval due to clearance activity has been a factor in the decline of population in the inner-city.

There have been reports galore about the new St Ann's that - to the present time - outline St Ann's 'multi-deprivation'. Often these reports are linked to funding for Special Schemes, Projects and Programmes.

It is not my purpose here to go through these reports. Interviewees mention some of them. It is, however, important to place on the record how - since redevelopment - the people of St Ann's have been observed, sometimes planned for and sometimes forgotten but seldom affirmed. If you mention St Ann's outside it,

you are almost invariably asked questions about drugs, crime and vandalism. It is as if the normal life of St Ann's is invisible.

However, something important has changed in recent years: the need to consult local people about their own ideas for their own community has taken root. But consulting can only work when there is a guaranteed outcome as a result of that consultation. If nothing happens, people again feel let down and cynical, as the people of Phase 10 did until recently because the upgrading of their part of St Ann's was put on hold again and again after pots of funding ran out.

But, despite all the trauma of the redevelopment time, St Ann's *has* survived. It has soaked up millions of pounds to improve the housing that replaced what was demolished. And one major improvement scheme - in Phase 10 - is only now in progress.

There is much in this book about St Ann's survival. I believe St Ann's people need much more recognition for the fact that they have made something good out of an inauspicious 'new' St Ann's as laid down in the early 1970s.

WHO SPOKE FOR ST ANN'S PRE-DEMOLITION?

Nottingham Corporation made a redevelopment plan for the district of St Ann's and carried it through, though not entirely in the form at first planned. For example, the plan for the Eastern By-pass that would have split up the area was dropped. And the Council's original idea of developing the district itself was ditched and the redevelopment handed over to Wimpeys. But the Council spoke on behalf of the area. The area was discussed by various departments, for example, Housing and Planning and in full Council.

Reports appeared in local papers: letters for demolition, letters against it, and letters saying why were good houses being pulled down before many bad ones? But, considering the size of the project, the biggest housing scheme ever for Nottingham Corporation, there was little fuss about the Corporation's imposed plans for the area. And there was no vision of consulting the 30,000 people involved.

A view from St Ann's c1972, after the bulldozers had arrived, toward Sneinton's tower block mentioned on the next page. Photo: Nicholson Photo Archive

---

[5] Many elderly people had insisted on staying in St Ann's when their children and grandchildren were re-housed in Aspley, Clifton, Bestwood . . .

[6] Families settled into the 'new' St Ann's from other areas usually did not have grandparents nearby to keep an eye on children. The many St Ann's elderly people who stayed in the district did not know these families and the elderly people were often grouped together.

Nottingham Civic Society and Nottingham Junior Chamber of Commerce arranged a joint visit for their members in 1964 to see the St Ann's Well Road district and then the new high-rise Manvers Court, Sneinton's tower block. The invitation to the tour stated: "We will see for ourselves the environment of this 'legacy of obsolete development from the industrial revolution' and then inspect Manvers Court." This is an example of how St Ann's was 'talked down' years before the bulldozers arrived.

Below, I outline the part played in speaking for St Ann's by **SATRA** [St Ann's Tenants and Residents Association]; by a Survey of St Ann's undertaken by two Nottingham University lecturers and an Adult Education class; by the work of three architectural students, and by Allen Cunningham, employed by the City Council's Architect's Department.

Ray Gosling, author, journalist, TV and Radio programme maker, was largely responsible for SATRA's birth. SATRA was very important by reason of its exceptional presence when St Ann's was under threat rather than because of the size of its support from the people of the area. But it did make a difference. In Alan Sillitoe's 23.10.80 review in *The Guardian* of Ray Gosling's book *Personal Copy: a memoir of the Sixties* [Faber.1980], Sillitoe said the efforts of SATRA were certainly justified but not much was achieved. Sillitoe was brought up in Radford, Nottingham, and knew about inner-city areas.

Perhaps the most important thing achieved by SATRA in the long-term was its role in helping to create a growing political (small 'p') self-awareness of what could happen to large numbers of people in their own communities without their consent or consultation. The age of accepting what was handed down was ending.

Ray Gosling talks about SATRA in this book and other people recall SATRA.

Nottingham Evening Post and News, April 8th 1966 reported: "Residents of the St Ann's Well Road of Nottingham protested last night when plans for the phased redevelopment of the district were outlined at a meeting at St Catharine's Church Hall [called by SATRA].

"Some of them, who claim their houses are decayed and infested with insects, were disappointed when they learned the phasing might mean several more years before they were re-housed.

"Others protested when they were told that their homes, which they consider have at least thirty years life left, were scheduled for demolition in the first phase. Of the 500 people at the meeting hardly any seemed to express approval of the proposals for redevelopment.

"They supported Mr Arthur Leatherland (66) a retired engineer of Cromer Road who said: 'We must fight for our rights'.

"Ray Gosling (25) said that Cromer Road, with lots of the better houses, was in the first demolition phase. Little John Street, one of the worst rows in the area, came in the sixth phase.

"Before they left, the residents were grouped according to the phasing, and each group appointed street committees as an initial step in the campaign. Then they left . . . some

Arthur Leatherland c1972. Source Margaret Behrman's Album: Nottingham Local Studies Library

to return to the homes they do not want but are likely to keep for some time, and others to homes they wish to keep but which are likely to disappear soon in a pile of rubble."

Arthur Leatherland, an active SATRA member and Council tenant, had already sent the Council a protest petition signed by 200 residents from Cromer Road and Hungerhill Road. He had lived at 3, Cromer Road for twenty-seven years and said many of the properties had been improved with Government grants less than four years before. Bathrooms and indoor toilets had been installed to give tenants a better standard of living.

Nottingham Evening Post and News, March 1st 1967 reported: "Some of the worst slums in the St Ann's Wells Road area of Nottingham are to be pulled down under a clearance scheme approved yesterday by the City's Housing Committee. About 1,274 properties are involved."

In fact, the homes affected included streets, including Cromer Road, Hungerhill Road and part of St Ann's Well Road in which the houses were 'fit' and only included in the clearance scheme for planning convenience. After a well-managed campaign - and a twist of City Party Politics - Cromer Road was reprieved and it still exists as proof that some of the talk about 'worst slums' was far from true.

Snippets from SATRA Minutes which give an insight into its work at the time:

News of the World. No reply from either the Editor or Mr Roxon to our distress at their slur on the St Ann's area.

28.10.67. [At a meeting with Alderman Derbyshire] We talked of [the Council] handing out control to package dealers and worried that the people as client would have no control over their future.

St Ann's Nottingham: Inner-City Voices by Auth Johns • ISBN 0951696092

28.10.67. Messrs Gosling and Leatherland went at 4.30 on Monday 18.10.67 to the Housing Department, King Street, to meet Mr Lee, Housing Manager, and Alderman Derbyshire. Mr Leatherland said Lee had already done some moving of dirty people into Ransom Road. Mr Lee said we have to house DP somewhere. Mr Leatherland said we don't want to single DP out: no ghetto. Derbyshire said NO NO we won't let that happen. Leatherland said again, don't dump DP. Lee then said, well but everyone must have their share, quota, which is 3%. Leatherland said we can stand 3% but not 50%. Lee and Derbyshire gave categorical assurance there would be no dumping of dirty people in older property.

We then talked about where people were going, the overspill, and Lee mentioned Aspley and Sherwood. Mr Gosling mentioned Clarence Street as a very bad street and Derbyshire said it always had been, and told a funny story. We talked again of overspill and Mr Lee brought up the problem of publicity and Mrs Hamilton. It had embarrassed his department. He was thinking in future of limiting choice to three [offers], and people would have to take one of the three. Lee also suggested that if we have particular cases we write on official notepaper of SATRA to Mr Lee for him personally to take up. We agreed.

28.10.67. A box number was seen in the *Evening Post* offering houses at £150 each in St Ann's.

28.10.67. Do we need Hungerhill Gardens and Brewsters all for cultivation? City against taking any of the gardens for housing. Why doesn't SATRA fly a kite? Miss Smith said let them dare touch Hungerhill but agreed about Brewsters [later built on by Metropolitan Housing Association]. Also said why so many garages? In future we'll need flat roofs for helicopters!

30.11.67. The Public Inquiry for Phase One was held at the Police Assembly Rooms on Wed 22nd November. Gosling and Leatherland attended. Attached is a report[1]. Mr Mann suggested that the Corporation's insistence on being the only agency capable of doing redevelopment didn't tie in very well with the Victoria Station project [Victoria Centre: a large housing/shopping development on ex-railway land undertaken by a private developer on the City edge nearest St Ann's]. Why couldn't the Great Central Railway tracks be used for the motor-road [Eastern By-pass] instead of Peas Hill Road? And, the inspired thought that, due to down-grading, the longer the scheme is held up the cheaper it becomes.

14.12.67. Mrs Hamilton, Simons Terrace now gone to Bestwood. Two others from the Terrace to Ransom Road [i.e. well ahead of demolition].

From a private note from Ray Gosling to friends circa 1967 and later printed: "The society around St Ann's is horizontal, the world on your doorstep. Cheek by jowl live the quiet and the noisy; student and spastic; celibate and promiscuous; young, old, black, white, grown; teetotal and alcoholic; the poor, the middling and the rich. Dogs have plenty to sniff, children playmates. There is town greenery, smallholdings and in the railway cutting a primeval forest. All human life within the walking distance of a one-legged man . . . To me, having been over so much of this England, St Ann's seems a remarkable place, where against all odds live – so far, so lucky – in harmony, humour and happiness all manners, creed, colour and fancy, but not fashion."

In a publication after the new development of St Ann's had been completed[2] Coates and Silburn said that SATRA, whatever its limitations, showed real initiative and encouraged an active response on social and individual issues by those residents it was able to organise. They said that Margaret Behrman, a full-time SATRA community worker, told them in 1971 that: "The Association was most successful in fields like the organisation of playgroups, the maintenance of citizens' advisory services, and the offering of help, particularly to old people who needed representing in their disputes with the local authority."

The authors added: "When the Ministry vetoed the planned [Eastern] by-pass road and one large area was therefore given to understand that its clearance might be indefinitely deferred, SATRA *was* able to organise meetings throughout that zone [Phase 10 of the overall scheme] in order to insist that its inhabitants be re-housed according to the original schedule.

"This successful campaign proves (if proof were needed) that the people of St Ann's were perfectly capable of defending themselves; but by the time it [the redevelopment] was undertaken, not only had all the major planning decisions already been made, and sometimes remade, without any real consultation, but a large part of the old St Ann's population had already been re-housed, often far away from the demolition areas."

This comment some years after the completion of redevelopment did not accord with how the authors reported St Ann's at the time of planning blight in the late sixties.

In the preface to the **Coates and Silburn 1968 report of their St Ann's Survey**[3], the authors thanked Ray Gosling of SATRA: "who has maintained a running commentary of adverse but stimulating criticism."

This Survey was done of part of St Ann's. It started in October 1966 under the auspices of an adult education class of the Adult Education Department of Nottingham University. The adult students, who did the interviewing, were not of the area. St Ann's was chosen because it was an area: "not only being represented for slum clearance, but which also had the clear appearance of being run

---

[1]   Gosling and Leatherland's report included information that a 'large number of objectors including the Co-op and Nottingham High School Foundation had withdrawn'. The inquiry was finished in a day though it was booked for two. The report records: 'There was a horrid viciousness towards objectors from the officials, not publicly but in their private scowls and tut-tuts.' Objectors included several who wanted their homes to be 'grey' (i.e. fit) instead of 'pink' (unfit). The report stated: 'Most objectors would say their property had a 10-15 year life. When one man said his had only been up some eighty years, everyone on the top table laughed.' Two objectors were West Indians owning their house. Others included Bramleys Butchers Shop on St Ann's Well Road.

[2]   *Beyond the Bulldozer*, by Ken Coates and Richard Silburn. Department of Adult Education, University of Nottingham, 1980.

[3]   *Poverty, Deprivation and Morale in a Nottingham Community: St Ann's. A Report of the preliminary findings of the St Ann's Study Group* by Ken Coates and Richard Silburn. Department of Adult Education, Nottingham University. 1968.

---

down. Students began to familiarise themselves with it." The Survey was based on 176 interviews with householders.

I have strong memories of this Survey and its aftermath. Together with publications following, the study gained much publicity and those outside St Ann's increasingly believed the view of St Ann's and its people indicated by the Survey.

When the BBC made a film of St Ann's following the study, I was approached by Coates and Silburn to inquire if I could introduce BBC reporters to people in St Ann's. I refused and felt angry that those whose names appeared on the study, and whose career reputations were considerably enhanced as a result, did not feel they naturally owed St Ann's people their own involvement in this introduction process. I wondered how many people in St Ann's they actually knew.

An important reason why the Survey was an incorrect assessment of the people of St Ann's was that it was started after planning blight had taken hold of the area. Evidence of this was included in some of the comments people made to survey interviewers. For example, a forty year old woman stated: "The area has changed in the past two years - the Council are moving problem families in as other people die or move out. People who can't afford new house rents move in. I like the area because I have always lived here, but I don't like the new people."

Coates and Silburn recognised in their 1980 publication that: "a large part of the St Ann's population had been re-housed" ahead of demolition.

Their original Survey area included streets which were marked 'for Social Services use' on the relevant Compulsory Order Schedule[4], and these were the streets used as temporary accommodation, sometimes from an early stage of the area's planning blight.

The school included in the Survey probably had the highest ratio of children [among all schools in St Ann's] from homes on extremely low incomes and the author of the chapter on schools states that 42% of the children came from broken homes. And that many children arrived at school without breakfast either because their mother went off to work before them or because the family got up late. At the time of the Survey, what was found was not a true reflection of St Ann's before planning blight, but a reflection of an area in severe environmental and social crisis. Most readers coming to this Survey were not aware of this and they would accept the Survey as a 'scientific' description of the way the 'old' St Ann's was.

There are many subjective comments in the Survey. For example, about home background: "Many of these children are emotionally retarded, lacking stability in their family lives and suffering from inconsistent handling." The Survey left St Ann's with a public reputation which people who had lived in the area all or much of their lives resented. Many still do.

The authors became involved with the Survey because

of academic interest in poverty and they had ideas about its resolution which, to my mind, had more to do with trying to fit the people of St Ann's into their socio-economic analysis than with understanding the people of St Ann's. There *was* poverty in St Ann's. That is a fact, but its people were infinitely more than 'poor people.' Poverty needed addressing then. It needs addressing now as an issue of social justice. Now as then, 'poor people' need to be seen as owning many positive qualities and skills and not as statistics of 'multi-deprivation'.

Concurrent to the St Ann's Survey, **three final year students from the Department of Architecture and Civic Planning**, Nottingham University, did a joint thesis on St Ann's. I interview one of them, David Wilkinson, for this book. The others were Robert Davis and David Strickland. Two of them were married with family and lived in or close by St Ann's. Their thesis was accompanied by plans and models which went on public view in an empty shop on St Ann's Well Road.

The students realised, at first hand, the value of much in the St Ann's community. Their work in the community led to their recognising three aspects of the 'Client' (St Ann's). Firstly, the inhabitants wanted comfort, amenity, safety and commodity without pain or loss. Secondly, there was the sponsor, the Council, which demanded value through efficiency, and which determined the physical standards to which residents have a right on the basis of an overall cost and a general economy. And thirdly, there was humanity, requiring long-term value through positive growth, stimulus and meaning. As architects, they were responsible: "to humanity for creating a form for a settlement which instead of causing sterility, restriction, banality and laziness encourages the positive evolution of mankind by its vitality, freedom, meaning and stimulus . . ." The idea of 'humanity' [or, as we would now say, 'society'] as part of the client body was far-sighted.

I will touch on some points of the thesis. The students stated: "At present, the inhabitants of the district [of St Ann's] are not involved in any decision as to the form or manner of the redevelopment of the area. All know that the redevelopment by the Council is imminent. This is due to the Press, visits by councillors and general rumours.

"There are many, varied - and no accurate - accounts that we have heard of concerning when and how and to what degree this action will be. This is not unusual, for redevelopment proposals are only published when final.

"St Ann's is very large, it is twice the size of Cumbernauld, half the size of Mansfield, and the City has a scheme to replace it. As architects involved in St Ann's, we consider that the organisation of the loosely knit City [Corporation] departments will be unable to produce a satisfactory solution to a problem of this magnitude and involvement . . .

"At present the City [Council] is horizontally divided into departments. We feel that a united group working outside this departmental set-up, but with direct links (as members of the group belong to different departments) could form a suitable design team, comparable to the Commissions for the new towns. The multi-disciplinary

---

[4] For example, in the Nottingham (St Ann's Well No 5) Housing Compulsory Purchase Order 1968, handwritten over various streets is: "Passed to Social Services." These streets included Northville Street, Raglan Street, Caroline Street and Brighton Street. In order to be 'handed over', the houses were obviously already emptied of their residents, some for a considerable time.

St Ann's Nottingham: Inner-city voices by Ruth Johns • ISBN 0951696092

group would include not only members of the departments concerned, architects, planners, treasurers, estates, housing and engineers, but also an economist and sociologists . . .

"Within the group, involved particularly with the housing would be a public relations section. They would act as an approachable front to the project, presenting work both to the public and to the Council at various stages, and to bring in all manner of inquiries, so that the problem of St Ann's becomes one of interest and stimulus to all concerned . . ." They made a case for this approach as saving money as well as being more suitable.

"The people of St Ann's live in the district, generally because it is a cheap place to live, or it's a nice place to live, or because it's the only place to live. Most of the rents are low: fifteen shillings to twenty-five shillings. In the new flats which the Corporation have recently put up, the rents are from £3 - £4 pw, the highest being for the larger flats . . . If, therefore, the district is developed in this way, although all would have a right to a new flat, few will be able to afford them."

The proposal the architects put forward in detail was for small-scale demolition where necessary, not exceeding around 60 houses in any one neighbourhood in St Ann's at one time. This would involve some 200 people and the pattern of their lives, which: "would seem to us complex enough to deal with at any one moment".

In contrast, the Council's redevelopment scheme was a rolling programme of areas of around 1,000 houses and 3,000 people in each phase, including commercial and public buildings. This scale was incompatible with the architects' practical vision of the resettlement of the district in which good buildings would remain and properties needing improvement for an extension of useful life would get it. Schools and nodal public amenity areas could be improved by opening them up with landscaped space and trees around them. The small-scale demolition areas would not create: "a vast relocation problem".

A scheme which offered both new and upgraded housing would offer people moving out of bad accommodation the choice of a slightly increased rent (for improved property) or higher rent for new. Careful planning of amenities would mean, for example, that a car park could cater for people at pubs in the evening, schools during the day and allotments or church on Sundays. Small-scale industry could be integrated in the newly built areas and provide convenience, life, character, personality, identity and direct sources of labour. Various types of shopping, pubs, entertainment, open spaces, care in provision of pedestrian routes were important. The danger of through traffic and heavy traffic would be removed. Buildings could alter their functions i.e. shops to houses and houses to shops. "Our initially imposed diverse pattern will thus be able to settle and find its own balance, due to the pattern of the district as it evolves," stated the architects.

"Because the present [i.e. the 'old'] St Ann's was built at the same time, with similar materials and patterns, it forms a unity. It has the same feeling running through it, a feeling of its era, its people. Our feeling is not so far away from this. We still believe in small houses, in churches that

The following are three illustrations from many prepared by Wilkinson, Davis and Strickland for their thesis

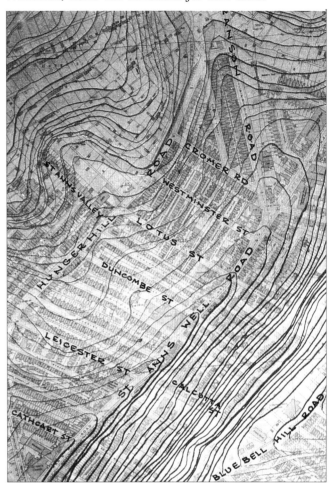

Contours showing the St Ann's Well Road valley and hills up either side. The students prepared a detailed plan for the area bounded by Leicester Street, St Ann's Well Road and Robin Hood Chase which is off the drawing at the left corner (where St Ann's Church can be seen)

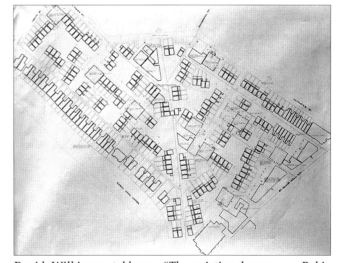

David Wilkinson told me: "The existing houses on Robin Hood Chase, together with a group on Martin Street, the Church and commercial properties on St Ann's Well Road, were to be retained and incorporated into the new housing development. The plan illustrates the proposed form of the new terraced houses, and the squares and spaces between them. And it shows the group garage buildings, which were also to house small local businesses and light industry."

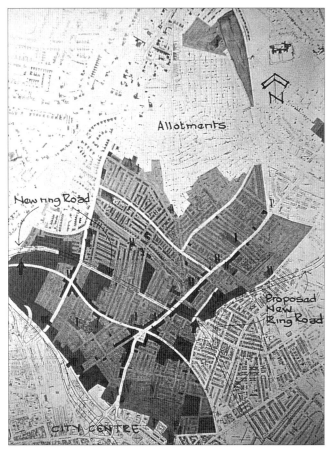

This map covers all the proposed redevelopment area. The students indicate their ideas for possible land use and major service road layout following redevelopment. The darker areas indicate industry: both to be retained and possibly expanded. The white lines indicate proposed major service roads. The line of the City Engineer's new Eastern By-pass road proposal can be seen cutting across the valley from the top of Blue Bell Hill

look like churches and factories that look like factories. Such trust in human scale and a natural symbolism we intend to exploit, with our modern architectural scope and morality, making it more meaningful, more vivid, rather than expounding form for its own sake (like dwelling blocks of sixteen floors)...

" . . . St Ann's Well Road will develop differently to Alfred Street and Commercial Square and the base of

This scene on St Ann's Well Road would still exist if the Wilkinson, Davis and Strickland proposal had been heeded. Photo: source Liz Edge, Nottingham Local Studies Library

Robin Hood Chase, bringing colour and meaning to the heart of the district."

There is, of course, a lot of detail in the thesis mentioned above. For example, the students produced a housing decay survey, grading property into: chronic, terrible, bad, poor, fair, good, valuable and immovable. In their scheme, there was no reason why buildings which are important to people - public houses for example - should not become focal points of a redesigned area.

To cater for the wide variety of accommodation in the new neighbourhoods, a small component system was envisaged, using existing bricks, crushed: "as aggregate for modular concrete blocks, pre-cast floor and lintel units and a special pre-cast roofing beam system . . . "

After they gained high distinction for their joint thesis, the students' work went on exhibition at the City Architect's Department. It was some sort of recognition after having not been taken very seriously, David Wilkinson told me. They were convinced that the City Council's phased redevelopment plan was too inflexible and it assumed it was necessary to scuttle good property along with the bad.

Letter to the Royal Institute of British Architects

The three architectural students mentioned above wrote a letter to the RIBA Journal, May 1969, expressing dismay at a previous issue's 'glib architectural' criticism of the new Housing Bill. The criticism mentioned two sociological surveys, one of which was the St Ann's Survey, also mentioned above. Their letter included:

"We spent a thesis year studying the problems and their possible solutions in this area, while working in parallel with the two sociologists: It seems so simple: an extended slum . . . 74% unfit . . .

"St Ann's is being systematically run down by the Council as part of the economics of wholesale redevelopment. An entire district of which in one year of shopping, drinking and living there, we only saw a glimpse. That glimpse was not a scientific analysis: it included the pub that gave out free drinks when the team won, the shop turned into an Indian library, the boat-builder, the picture-frame maker, the unfit house with no room to park the two E-types [Jaguar cars], the lady who sold eggs in her front room on Wednesdays, the Polish group sitting outside the abandoned church painting pews in the sun, the streets of children, the man who lived in a slum that was a palace inside . . . Many things that defied analysis. How can one easily categorise and give statistical percentage to these things? To analyse and categorise all the facets of living is impossible - and wrong."

Allen Cunningham was the Architect employed by Nottingham City Council to supervise the City Architect's Department's plans for the redevelopment of St Ann's. After the City Council ditched its own plans in favour of Wimpey, he resigned as a matter of principle. I traced Allen Cunningham in 2001 to seek his agreement to publishing his letter of resignation, which had been passed to me earlier. His reasons explain a lot of what was happening at that time. Allen Cunningham became a University Head of Architecture for over twenty years and a Visiting Professor since: in London.

In his reply to me, he said he frequently had Saturday lunch with Ray Gosling "during my period trying to create an enclave of which Nottingham might have been proud."

"What you will not know are the reasons which my letter of resignation could not reveal . . . " He outlined the 'tie-up' between the parties. I cannot mention these without, first of all, independently researching them and that is outside the remit of this book. But, he is not the only voice stating these things which are similar to rumours of the time.

Allen Cunningham continues: "I wonder too whether the record of the Housing Committee meeting which voted for the Wimpey proposal indicates that the scheme prepared under my direction was cheaper, quicker to build and offered higher living standards according to the City officials reporting on the two alternatives for the benefit of the councillors. I was present and remember the episode vividly . . .

" . . . The Poulson Newcastle scandals broke soon afterwards which put St Ann's in the shade."

Letter of resignation to the City Architect to take effect 31st March 1969

Allen Cunningham wrote his letter of resignation to the City Architect, David Jenkins, on February 27th 1969. Cunningham said he had hoped to work in the City for five years but had been unable to accomplish what he set out to do. He wrote:

"On Monday, July 11th, 1966, I was asked by you, City Architect, to supervise the preparation of proposals for the redevelopment of 340 acres of neglected and rotting city fabric consisting largely of dwellings classified as 'unfit for human habitation', but nevertheless inhabited by 30,000 real live people.

"1976 was concocted by the City Council as the date by which fairy godmother must complete the transformation. The task was immense. For me, it became a form of crusade for my conscience. We were to be responsible for uprooting a social as well as a physical fabric. I have been haunted, not so much by the creation of the physical buildings and environment (which is difficult enough), but by the replacement of 'community' which consists of buildings and people. I became convinced that this can only be achieved if the people for whom we are building are able to participate in the process. Society reflects itself in the physical environment by creating it. This principle starts as an interaction between dwelling and occupant, which has been described as the stimulus of 'natural relationship', and it extends to the entire built environment. I wanted to put this principle into practice.

"In the autumn of 1967 we set down, in association with all the other involved departments of the City, a very carefully considered set of proposals with costs. A programme giving significant dates for the whole redevelopment was compiled by the Project Co-ordination Section in the office of the Town Clerk. All these proposals were approved by the Chief Officers' Group and then submitted to, and approved unanimously by, the Housing Committee. Our brief was thus finally established.

" . . . In addition, we succeeded in providing covered arcades linking the houses, segregated bicycle tracks, corner shops and individual dwelling plans which, I believe, deserve to be tested at least in prototype form in order to establish their merits and defects. Let the people judge. Some plans have been designed to allow different arrangements of rooms and we had hoped that future tenants, having discussed the proposals at the formative stage (already done) could:

a) choose a room arrangement
b) decide the colour for the outside paintwork
c) have the option of making extra built-in cupboards or fitments in a co-operative workshop and
d) plant their own surroundings with trees and flowers.

"By the autumn of 1968, our proposals had been drawn up and costed and they accorded completely with the instructions of the Housing Committee.

"On Thursday, October 10th, however, after twenty-seven months work on the project, the Housing Committee, against the advice of the Chief Officers' Group, instructed the departments to commence negotiations with a 'package dealer' of their choice, who was to design and build the first two phases comprising nearly twelve hundred dwellings. The reason given for this decision was that the houses would be completed more quickly, although more expensively, than by employing traditional builders selected through competitive tenders. Since then, as you know, three package dealers have been asked, by the Housing Committee, to prepare plans and submit costs. Three months have been allowed for this procedure.

"This change of policy occurred when the Ministry of Housing and Local Government advised the Corporation that the spending of nearly three million pounds without some form of competitive pricing violated the canons of public accountability. The new programme anticipates the completion of the first two phases no sooner than the competitive tendering procedure we originally recommended.

"I am opposed to 'package deal' housing. It is not possible to reconcile citizen involvement in the building of their own environment with an invading force of imported 'packages' which take no account of local idiosyncrasies; contractors who, in their remote offices, pull their standard 'types' out of a drawer (architecture), rapidly draft up arrangements of the types on the allocated land (planning), arrive in town, build the diagram, 'hand over' the goods to the faceless people, pocket the profit and de-camp to scatter the same types in Timbuktu with, perhaps, modified cosmetic trimmings to add 'local' flavour. This method of building our environment is chosen because (illusory) low price and (real) high speed are given precedence over quality. Future generations will judge the product only by the positive contribution it makes to their existence and will thank no one for the compromises surrounding its creation.

"I hope that both the proposals prepared in your department and those of the 'winning' package can be published to enable a fair appraisal to be made of the two methods of approach toward planning our future cities.

"I do not think that the 8,700 hours that were spent preparing our proposals in your department have been entirely wasted. Some of the ideas put forward will achieve fruition in St Ann's. Some will not. I hope that our experience, if not fully used in St Ann's, will benefit other areas of the City and the country.

"Finally, City Architect, after thirty-two months in your department there are five points concerning redevelopment projects which ought to be pinned up somewhere:

- Thorough pre-development research and analysis is required before any plans or proposals are made.
- Citizen participation is essential before, during and after redevelopment through open dialogue with Local Authority representatives involved on the work.
- Multi-disciplinary design groups should replace individuals who, at present, operate inefficiently from segregated and autonomous departments.
- A formula is required which will enable rental and ownership to mix in compulsory purchase areas.
- All developments should be analysed after occupation in order to verify or correct theoretical assumptions.

"I suspect that the confusion and resultant waste, epitomised by the curious decision making methods so far employed in the redevelopment scheme for St Ann's, are not uncommon in Local Authorities' dealings countrywide. This thought does not give rise to overwhelming optimism . . ."

I have seen the drawings of Wilkinson, Davis and Strickland and Allen Cunningham's proposals for St Ann's. They would need far more space to reproduce than is possible here.

POLITICS OF THE REDEVELOPMENT

I found little detailed recollection of the raw politics in Nottingham at the time of St Ann's redevelopment. But, there still exists a lot of sturdy emotional hurt, a feeling that things were not done right, that redevelopment should have been better, that respect was not shown. A few people produced newspaper cuttings which they have kept.

In 1967, there were three Conservative councillors for the St Ann's Well area, Ron Griffin, Brian Vinerd and Stan Rushton. The redevelopment plan for St Ann's covered four wards, Market, Mapperley. Manvers and St Ann's, but increasingly people called the whole area St Ann's. Local councillors found themselves in a difficult situation. In 1968, Councillors Vinerd and Rushton publicly criticised SATRA for "stirring up trouble". Councillor Vinerd challenged Tom Lynch, President of the Small Shopkeepers Union, to prove his figures when he claimed that the existing shops in St Ann's would only be replaced by fifty [far fewer than fifty were built]. But Councillor Vinerd was also reassuring people in St Ann's that they would not be housed in 'monstrosities' like the Hyson Green flats.

On 11.10.68 the *Guardian Journal* reported that Nottingham Housing Committee had rejected the City Architect's scheme for building the first 1,200 homes in redeveloped St Ann's and had chosen George Wimpey & Co for the contract, with work to start October 1969.

Guardian Journal 3.12.68 reported that the Ministry of Housing and Local Government had stepped in and stated that a contract of such size must go to selective tendering. Ron Griffin said it was the biggest shock of his political career and it would cause delay for thousands of people waiting to be re-housed. He asked for assurances from Housing Manager, Mr M C Lee, that clearance would continue and he said it would. Alderman W Derbyshire said the first two phases of the redevelopment had been registered with Wimpey's to get the scheme off the ground. The delay should be laid at the door of the Labour Party.

A delegation of the Housing Committee went to see the Minister, Mr Anthony Greenwood.

The *Guardian Journal* for 6.12.68 said the three Conservative councillors for St Ann's were not taking part in a public debate about the Minister's decision to insist that the Conservative City Council had to advertise for tenders for the first two phases of redevelopment. The debate had been called for by John Carroll, Labour candidate for St Ann's. The Conservatives said a highly satisfactory contract had already been negotiated with Wimpeys [*Guardian Journal* 9.12.68] and the ruling would cause delay.

The *Guardian Journal* of 30.12.68 reports the Minister's response to the delegation insisting on tenders. His letter stated tendering would not cause any delay.

"It is the people I am sorry for" said Councillor H Wilson. Councillor Vinerd said it was a slap in the face for the people of St Ann's [*Guardian Journal* 31.12.68] and even SATRA deplored the Minister's decision. Wimpey's cost for Phases One and Two was in the region of £3m.

Guardian Journal 3.1.69 reported the Labour Group's statement that: "The many attempts by people who should know better than to criticise the Government for delay of Phase One of the St Ann's clearance scheme, to mislead the occupants of St Ann's and to create general confusion on what is now actually possible, is to be deplored". The Group called on Housing Committee Chairman, Councillor H Wilson, publicly to withdraw his previous statement stating that if Wimpey's had the contract the development would have started 'next month.' "This has never been even remotely possible".

On 8.1.69, the *Guardian Journal* reported that Councillors Stanley Rushton and Brian Vinerd had written to Anthony Greenwood, the Housing Minister, placing on record their: "amazement and complete disgust" at the Minister's recent decision. "You will no doubt recall that quite recently, while your own Party were in control of the City, a similar development was embarked upon in Bulwell and you, as Minister, allowed a negotiated tender to stand . . .Your decision is not in the interests of the people we represent."

Wimpey's tender for Phase One was accepted [*Guardian Journal* 3.5.69] being the lowest of three tenders. "This completely vindicates the Committee for negotiating in the first place with the people who have now got the job," said Alderman Derbyshire. He hoped the completion date of the Phase One would still be August 1971 in spite of the delay caused by Government intervention.

St Ann's Nottingham. Inner-city voices by Ruth I Johns • ISBN 0951696092

On 30.1.70, the St Ann's redevelopment was officially launched and was called the largest housing programme ever undertaken outside London. The *Guardian Journal* of 31.1.70 reported Alderman Derbyshire stating that the first phase of the scheme was being undertaken by George Wimpey and Company and would be for 518 homes and the second phase would be for 559 homes. Eventually the Corporation hoped to provide homes for 17,000 people by 1976. The plan to get the scheme completed by that date was largely, he said, the work of Councillors Griffin, Rushton and Vinerd. "At the opening ceremony yesterday Labour and Conservative members sank their differences to give the scheme a united political send-off," said the reporter who added that a Housing Department spokesman stated that about 7,000 people had already been moved out of St Ann's.

The first completed houses were officially handed over to the Corporation by Mr D Macpherson, a director of George Wimpey and Company Ltd, at a ceremony on 21.12.70. Mr Julian Amery, Minister of Housing, was present. Forty families had already moved in and homes were being handed over at the rate of fifteen a week [*Guardian Journal* 22.12.70]. Wimpey's were constructing Phases One and Two and would start on phases Three and Four on 1.1.71. and were negotiating the tender for Phase Five.

A section of the audience watching Mr Julian Amery, Minister of Housing, officially opening the St Ann's redevelopment. Photo: Guardian Journal

At a civic luncheon on the day of the launch [*Guardian Journal* 22.12.70], Mr D Macpherson of Wimpey's presented the Lord Mayor, Councillor Oscar Watkinson, with a piece of silver plate to mark the occasion.

As we have seen from the above, 7,000 people had been removed from St Ann's eleven months before the time when only forty families were re-housed in the first of the new houses. This fact brings some scale-perspective to the human/social cost that St Ann's people bore at the time of redevelopment.

An article in the *Evening Post* of 24.12.70 echoed many sentiments of the time, and it demonstrates the way St Ann's people were talked about as if they were faceless beings to be fitted into a planned 'Utopia'. The writer said: "Of course, the haunting thought that must be in many people's mind is will the new St Ann's become the slums of the year 2000 and beyond? Will our brave new world come crashing to the ground in less than fifty years?

"Somehow I doubt it. The old St Ann's grew up as allotment owners each developed their land [in the latter half of the 1800s] with as many houses as possible. The resulting district became very densely populated with little public open space or gardens. It was a baby born not of love but expediency.

"If there was a spirit about the old St Ann's in the later stages, it must have been one of bravado, a kind of strange togetherness that comes to people in trouble. It is best summed up with a phrase like 'We are all in this hole together, so let's make the best of it.'

"On the other hand the new St Ann's is the product of no fewer that nine major Corporation departments. The homes are built to the very highest specifications, including such extras as built-in linen and drying cupboards, and a second toilet and washbasin in the three and four bedroom houses."

The *Evening Post* on 6.8.71 reported that Wimpey's were asking for an extra £10,000 on an £800,000 negotiated contract for work on Phase Five. Some councillors expressed concern. Councillor F C Woodward (Con), for example, is reported as saying: "Contractors should be given the test of competition." After the Chairman of the Housing Committee, Councillor H Wilson, pointed out that a refusal to pay the increase would mean a year's delay in the development, members decided to defer the matter for one month to allow the City Architect to see the firm and 'test their feelings'.

And so it went on, but Wimpey's stayed the course.

During the time of St Ann's demolition, there were substantial changes in Political structures due to Nottingham City Council losing its Unitary Status in 1974, which it regained in 1998. So, for over two decades, the City Council had lesser powers. One of the changes meant that funding for many voluntary schemes became the responsibility of the County Council.

There were political rows about who was responsible for the way the new St Ann's turned out. Labour gained control of the City Council before the St Ann's redevelopment was complete. One dignified argument was when Labour Council candidates for St Ann's Ward, Betty Higgins, Peter Burgess and John Carroll, wrote to the Press and said: "We are surprised that the Conservative candidate for St Ann's has not been informed that St Ann's was planned by a Tory Council.

"The provision of houses, though essential should not have been the only consideration. There were no provisions made for community facilities, neither shops, meeting rooms, privacy or seats for elderly people except in the shopping precinct. The Labour Council are having to make good this omission by putting up fences, providing shops, and meeting rooms to make life more enjoyable."

Yet, as outlined above, there were skilled people in the 1960s who knew how St Ann's could be redeveloped in a way which respected its people. From the time St Ann's redevelopment was completed until now and into the future, millions upon millions of pounds have been, are being and will continue to be spent to put right the shortcomings of the redevelopment.

The 1970s saw the development of community centres like ACNA and the Pakistan Centre with premises in St Ann's. The Chase Neighbourhood Centre came much later. Each had its own struggle within Nottinghamshire (County Council) and Nottingham (City Council) politics. Each is mentioned elsewhere in this book. There have been several major, and many minor, projects to improve housing and the general environment in St Ann's.

During the 1970s, political mud-slinging was not only inter-party but also, for example, within the Nottingham Labour Party (including the East Nottingham Branch). The strategies of Jack Dunnett, MP for East Nottingham, were one cause of dissent. These strategies were sometimes called the 'Dunnett-Machine' and St Ann's was part of his active territory.

St Ann's people remember people and feelings of the 1960s and 1970s, but seldom much detail of the events which so affected their lives. Talk about redevelopment and you are quite likely to get one or two descriptive sentences coupled with body language which says much more.

Today, if the area were to be massively redeveloped, it would be different. People would demand to be consulted and the political process would have to be much more equal. These are different times. Indeed even as the 'old' St Ann's was coming down, there was increasing national public debate and legislation emphasising the value, in areas with older property, of Housing Improvement Areas. It influenced Nottingham but too late for St Ann's.

Reports in the Press during those years confirmed the political point-scoring over the St Ann's redevelopment, its people being guinea pigs. The Coates/Silburn poverty story of St Ann's provided oil for the cause of leading local politicians and the public to think about the 30,000 displaced people as 'poor people' and 'slum dwellers' not as competent individuals, as members of families, as human beings with diverse outlooks and needs.

But, although in the 1970s the age of community campaigning was only just dawning, St Ann's people had no lack of political nous. It had been exercised for generations in helping themselves, their families and their community not only to survive but also to develop traditions and shared enjoyment. The stories told by many interviewees are proof of immense skills in utilising opportunities and inventing them. But there was no precedent for a community response to imposed compulsory removal of 30,000 people and their homes.

However, I have met more than a handful of people now living in St Ann's who thought they and their families would have to move away from the district when their homes were demolished and who found ways of staying. They found individual ways to put pressure on decision makers in order to obtain a maisonette or house of their choice and - even now - "you must not mention this by name!" I have been trusted with many secrets!

Either they knew someone who knew someone of influence, or, when a London politician or bureaucrat was visiting the area, they made sure they met them and made

their case, which was then 'taken up' as a means of political point-scoring. "After I spoke with the visiting would-be MP, he took my case up and I was soon told I could select which house I wanted," said one. "I'm still in it. I picked a wonderful position."

In 1975, W Osborne of Cromer Road, St Ann's, wrote to the Press stating that SATRA had received a letter from the Corporation dated August 21st 1973, saying that the Housing Committee had agreed that two prefabricated shops should be erected near the junction of St Ann's Well Road and St Bartholomew's Road as quickly as possible. A year and nine months later nothing had been done. Councillors Betty Higgins and Peter Burgess had tried to help as well as the SATRA Committee.

Councillor Bob Birch had collected a 183-signature petition for shops to be built in this area. They would save housewives, particularly old people, a half-mile journey carrying heavy shopping from the proposed precinct at Robin Hood Chase. They wanted a supermarket, chemist, fish and chip shop, newsagent, butcher, grocer and greengrocer nearer home. Failing that they wanted shops of their choice in the new Precinct said Councillor Birch, the young Post Officer engineer representing Manvers Ward [which includes part of St Ann's].

By 1975, Ray Gosling told SATRA - of which he was chairman for seven years - that St Ann's had changed utterly. "There is only one landlord - the Corporation. There is no need for any outsider to come down St Ann's Well Road any more. SATRA is failing to measure up to the promise it once held of binding the community in St Ann's together. That's what has prompted me to think the Tenants Association cannot do it without the politicians' leadership." He called on local representatives to do more.

A selection of photos of when the bulldozers started their work. Photos: Nicholson Photo Archive

St Ann's Nottingham: inner city voices by Ruth Johns   ISBN 0951696092

Photos: Nicholson Photo Archive

Soon after Family First Trust [now Family First Ltd] started in 1965, the children of St Ann's wised up to the fact that people donated it prams and push-chairs no longer needed. Most were serviceable but some were not. BUT the wheels were good! After the first two children who called went away with an old pram, the avalanche of children requesting wheels started. So I said: "No need to call. When we've got something which can't be used by a baby or toddler, we'll put word out." When we did, children always came to Family First in Alexandra Park for their trophy. I asked who would make sure their homemade cart or trolley was safe when they'd made it, and I quickly discovered the dads, uncles and older brothers who were helpful in this respect.

In January 2001, an *Evening Post* photographer looked out of my window and pointed: "That's where we lived before demolition." He married and moved away before the family house was demolished. His father moved to Aspley and "like many older people who moved away, he died soon after." He recalled the immense variety of employment in the old St Ann's, and boys from the Gordon Boys Home on Cranmer Street marching around St Ann's in their special uniform. As a child, he went for a seaside holiday to the Nottingham Poor Boys Home. (In his autobiography *Bill of Bulwell* [Plowright Press. 1995], Bill Cross describes a week's holiday spent there.)

Photos: Nicholson Photo Archive

Photos: Nicholson Photo Archive

In 1972, Mr and Mrs Terence Gough, Flewitt Street, had their own toilet in the backyard knocked down by demolition contractors who left a note on their door saying: 'Please use toilet at no 72.' They were one of only two families left in the street. They had been offered a new home but not until Mrs Gough had her baby. She was eight months' pregnant. Mr Gough told the *Nottingham Evening Post* that the toilet they were asked to use didn't flush, was used by meths drinkers who had installed themselves in empty properties and his wife had to climb over ten yards of rubble to reach it. St Ann's Councillor Peter Burgess took up their case and the family were immediately offered a new Council house in St Ann's.

Such stories of hardship of people being left in mainly unoccupied streets were not unusual. Most didn't get into the headlines but a few did. Harry Fletcher of Wright Street, Blue Bell Hill Road, complained that the Corporation had cut off water supply to his toilet when they cut off the supply to the (empty) house next door. He had to take buckets of water to flush the toilet. He had to ring the Corporation five or six times before they came to board up the house next door and take away the rubbish that had been dumped.

The only other occupants left in Wright Street were a couple with four children between one and eight. The spokesman for the Housing Department said it would be half way into the following year before Wright Street was demolished. "Only in unusual emergency cases can families be offered other accommodation before their own houses are pulled down." From *Nottingham Evening Post* cuttings given me by local people.

GETTING INVOLVED

Ray Gosling and David Wilkinson were not obvious candidates to get involved with St Ann's politics. People who look at the world around them in a different light to the reigning fads and fashions and image-making of the day are often regarded as maverick at the time. But events tend to prove their analysis of events worthy of respect. I interviewed both Ray Gosling and David Wilkinson for their recollections of events leading up to St Ann's demolition and beyond.

RAY GOSLING

Born at some time which makes him around a decade past a half-century

Interviewed in his home, 15.2.00, and conversations. Ray Gosling was a young writer/broadcaster when he first knew St Ann's and became involved in setting up **St Ann's Tenants and Residents Association [SATRA]**. *He is an author and has created a substantial body of TV, radio and Press work*

Back cover of Ray Gosling's 1980 book Personal Copy. Reproduced permission of Faber and Faber

I was born in Northamptonshire. My father worked in a garage mending cars for other people. My mother was a bit genteel. She came from Cambridgeshire, from a peasant family who worked on the estate of a local Lord. When she was fifteen, he said she could teach in the local school.

I went to Northampton Grammar School, 'C' stream material, and then to Leicester University for a year. I absolutely hated it. I ran Rock and Roll bands in Leicester and all the usual things of those days happened. I can remember being thrown through the window of the Boot and Shoe Club in Hinkley, bodily thrown through the window. I walked past it the other day. They've got one stained glass window which says Boot and Shoe Union Operatives and the other window is plain. I thought nobody's gone through the other one!

I was Chez Ray Rock. We ran dances at the Co-op Hall on Belgrave Gate in Leicester, sometimes two a week. The lead singer was a guy called Ray Chapman. He became quite a famous cult singer in the seventies and eighties particularly in Germany and France. The whole thing turned into a club. And it all sort of collapsed. I came to Nottingham because I was being threatened with guns in Leicester. I was petrol bombed in my flat.

I was about twenty-three by then. I didn't want to go to London. It was too far in case I regrouped. So coming to Nottingham was a good thing. I got a flat on Shakespeare Street. Then I went to Hartley Road in Radford. Things went wrong in the flat, it sometimes happens when you are young. I found a flat opposite the Grosvenor pub on Mansfield Road, it was a lovely, lovely flat, and I was writing a bit.

Writing most weeks enabled me to support myself. It was for little Nottingham magazines and eventually the BBC. The BBC started with a fifteen minute programme called Shire Talk run by a very left-wing guy called Gerald Nethercott. He was very posh. Then eventually the BBC in Birmingham, Manchester and London. Nottingham was very convenient.

How did I get to know St Ann's? Drinking had always been a large part of my life. It's a tragedy now for me to go back to St Ann's. I wish the world would change but I can't see that it's going to. But in those days [pre-demolition] St Ann's was one of the most fantastic drinking places in the world and it was a fantastic place for shebeens. There were pubs with pianos and music and sing-songs. There were two gay pubs on Union Road opposite each other, one was the Napier and I think the other was the Union, again both with pianos. When the pubs shut, the West Indians and Caribbeans had shebeens.

There would be after hours drinking in some pubs but you had to be 'well in' and I was not. I was a tourist in St Ann's. It's fun to think of St Ann's having tourists. Going to St Ann's for a good night out was terrific. Over fifty pubs. And different people, all friendly. I used to go down and smoke a bit of dope. And there would be wonderful chicken and rice. There was a shebeen on Manning Street, back of Manning Street and Miss Josie was the lady. She cooked the most wonderful chicken and rice I've ever had in my life. You'd stay there until about two o'clock in the morning.

In the shebeen, it would be sort of early Reggae music, sometimes old jazz. The police did raid these things. I remember sitting in a tree on Robin Hood Chase. I never got caught. The shebeen was in a big cellar. You went in from Manning Street but it was in fact a cellar of a big house opposite. There would be a few blacks, a few older whites, mainly young whites. People of my own age group.

It could be students from the Park. I used to go there with a Jewish girl called Viva who was a doctor's daughter. You could just stand there and bop, bop, bop and eat this chicken and rice out of a saucer. And we'd buy cans at enormous prices. Aston was the guy who ran it.

Every pub in St Ann's used to have a room off the pub which was hired out to various groups like the Foresters and the Royal Antediluvian Order of Buffaloes. In St Ann's Well Inn this bloke said he wanted to propose me for membership of the Buffs, a sort of secret society. He liked the things I'd been doing in St Ann's and thought he'd get kudos by proposing me. So he goes to the meeting and doesn't come down for ages and ages. Eventually, ashen faced, he came and said something's gone dreadfully wrong. So we went down the road to one of the pubs on Commercial Square. He said: 'I don't know what you've done to them, but they're not going to have you in the Buffs!'

How did I get involved in politics in St Ann's? I first became involved in Radford. There was a whole left wing/anarchist coterie that used to drink in the Black Lion on Willoughby Street in Lenton until two or three o'clock in the morning. Bob Gregory, who died recently, urged me to put myself up as an Independent candidate in the Council elections. I put myself up as a Madman and Billy [Richard] Silburn, who later wrote a book with Ken Coates, was my agent. I got something like 13% of the vote and had a page devoted to me in the *Manchester Guardian* as it was then! I had a letter afterwards from a pop singer called David Such saying he liked the way I talked about things and he might try it himself. So I'm the founder of the Monster Raving Loony Party!

We're talking about the 1960s and you could do loony things and get away with it. We're not talking about some proto-fascist time like today. I gave a talk on anarchist subjects to a group of architectural university students from Nottingham University at the Bell Inn. We got thrown out by David Jackson, grandfather of the present owner, because he was proud of the University having groups and talks there. When I started having a go at the City Council he said : 'Out!' So several followed me out and we became friends and one of them, Dave Wilkinson, lived off the Woodborough Road in St Ann's.

I then started going to some of their lectures and we went to one by Professor Buckminster Fuller from Illinois and we followed him to Paris where we kipped out in the Tuiluries Gardens at some counter protest against the World Architects' Federation.

The three architect students I'd got to know worked in the City Architects' Department office doing summer work. At the time, there was general public talk that redevelopment was on the cards for St Ann's, the Meadows, Hyson Green, Radford . . . Knocking down of slums was on the agenda but the students discovered this amazing scheme for St Ann's. It showed a great motorway was going to cross the middle of St Ann's.

Just around the corner from where I lived was Professor Harold Wiltshire, Professor of Adult Education for Nottingham University. His wife, Hilda, was a live wire and would occasionally come out drinking with us in St Ann's. On his staff, Harold had Ken Coates, so we would all meet and talk about things. St Ann's was soon on our agenda.

So Ken and Billy got Professor Wiltshire's permission to run a session of classes at the WEA [Workers Educational Association]. They enrolled people to go out and do a survey in St Ann's. They fixed on the subject of poverty as well as redevelopment. I was never keen on poverty being an issue. I've never forgiven Ken and Billy for the way they did that survey. It became a sore thing that marred our relationships a bit.

They did it that way because it suited their political agenda. They were asking for new definitions of poverty and the people of St Ann's were used as guinea pigs along the way.

They were making points like the equivalent today would be the minimum wage should be raised because people can't live on what they've got. But the measurement of whether you have a colour television or not should not enter into things.

They used me at the beginning of their survey, because they didn't have the human connections with St Ann's people which I had. I knew all sorts of people. As well as pubs and shebeens, I used to shop there. At Pork Farms the jelly used to run down the cobbles on the street, but the bloody pies were terrific. Occasionally I'd go to church at St Catharine's and knew Father Keene. I'd wander about talking to people. David Keene wore full cassocks and a funny little hat in the streets. He let SATRA have St Catharine's Church Hall for free.

So we arranged a public meeting there and we gave enough detail for people in the City Council to know we might have got hold of information. It was a spectacular meeting. On the advice of the troublemaker Bob Gregory, we organised it so that the people from the Council were feeling important at the top table, and then we turned the whole meeting around so they were in the back and we ran the meeting with the maps and plans and everything we'd got from the front.

It was headlines in the *Evening Post*. We made sure we'd leafleted not just the core area affected by redevelopment plans but also fringe areas like Thorneywood and up The Wells Road. These were scare mongering tactics. But we felt justified because they planned to take away over five hundred shops, over fifty pubs, put a motorway across St Ann's and that would affect everybody.

Then we found Arthur Leatherland, 3, Cromer Road, St Ann's. A man who spent most of his day on the Hungerhill allotments and he and me became the mainstays of SATRA. His life was walking up the road, going on the allotment, going back to his house which the Council owned, looking after his wife and children. It's where he'd grown up and he didn't want his house pulled down. Cromer Road is still up because of our efforts. Arthur was teetotal, a Nottingham Conservative, he didn't approve of things like shebeens or my raffishness. But he had a great respect and affection for me.

After that meeting, with the Municipal elections coming up, I said I will stand as an Independent Tenants Association candidate. I thought they would support me but they divided into two camps. Arthur Leatherland and others thought I was doing a disservice to the cause. On the side that supported me was a quite remarkable woman, Dorothy Smith who lived in Westminster Street in a terrace that was dreadfully bad and it did need to come down. She didn't drink but she was a friend of drunks and rabble-rousers, the exact opposite of Arthur Leatherland.

We did some amazing things in the run up to the election. I remember burning half a derelict car off Enoch Terrace. I didn't get many votes, about 12%, less than when I had stood as a Madman. It's important to remember the politics of St Ann's at that time because the City Council was Labour. It was Labour which wanted total redevelopment. And it wasn't peculiar to Nottingham. Labour did that in Leeds, Sheffield, Birmingham. In most of the London Boroughs Labour had a policy of knocking down and redevelopment. Now St Ann's was marginal. It's difficult to believe now but St Ann's was always swinging between Conservative and Labour. So was Manvers Ward on the south side of St Ann's Well Road.

Enoch Terrace awaiting demolition. Photo: Nicholson Photo Archive

St Ann's had a Conservative Councillor who was a great friend of all of us, Ron Griffin. He had a stall on the old Central Market and a peg leg so he could never move very fast. He sold knick-knacks, brass monkeys, three ducks for the wall . . . Ron had plenty of time to talk. Some of the information the students built up, they got from Ron. They had a connection with John E Wright's, Huntingdon Street, which reproduced architects plans and things like that. So with St Ann's being a bit Conservative and the Conservatives being in opposition, you can see how these two camps came about.

After my defeat, I realised the error of my ways and said sorry to Arthur Leatherland up on his allotment and I said I'd leave. And he said: 'No, you're not leaving. You're going to be our Chairman and we're going to get on and put this behind us.' He took me up to see Councillor Ron Griffin up on the Market and he made my apologies. Ron said: 'The next thing you'll be telling me is that you've got Labour sympathies.' Well, a lot of people on the SATRA Committee had Labour sympathies. Anyway, with me writing and travelling away a lot, I said I'd be Co-Chairman. Mick Waplington who was about my age and a shop steward at Raleigh became Co-Chairman too.

After the Coates and Silburn poverty survey on St Ann's, when Mick went to work, there was half a boot lace on his lathe and he said 'what's this doing?' And his mates said: 'It's for you poor f....., as you live down St Ann's don't you.'

I've been used to nasty things, they don't come as any surprise to me. But I could never forgive Ken and Billy because, after their survey, they wouldn't come and be shouted at by the people of St Ann's.

Mick lived at 36, Calcutta Street with his wife and two kids. He was very left wing. He left Raleigh and went down Gedling Pit and was one of the very few people in Nottinghamshire NUM who supported Arthur Scargill.

It was a good mix of people in SATRA. Dorothy Smith's concern was social issues. Dorothy lived with Joanne. They wanted to do playgroups and an Adventure Playground. We ended up running the first crèche in the Victoria Centre. It's still there run by other people. So all these social things came along, the encouragement of the Blue Bell Hill Craft Centre, the urban farm . . . And SATRA had a shop, an advice thing. The shop moved several times. The first one was east of where Hopewell's was. It had been a shop but when we had it, it was somebody's front room. We kept the shop going on small bits of money. Harold Smith let us have a bit. It was used for meetings on Sundays.

SATRA shop when it was at 94, St Ann's Well Road c1972. Photo: source Margaret Behrman's album, Nottingham Local Studies Library

St Ann's Rose Show went to Chilwell, to Gregory's the rose growers. Their Head Gardener, Ken Bates, lived in St Ann's. Gregory's were one of our secret sponsors as we set up playgroups, an adventure playground . . .

The bigger houses had multi-occupation. Mr Fox, the Alfred Street Postmaster bought several houses which he let as rooms to new immigrants. He was the second richest man in St Ann's.

One man in a big house at the back of the Board School didn't want to leave. He was born there and bred dogs. Bulldozers moved him off. Arthur Leatherland and I slept there with him at the end. It would be different now. It was a stitch up then. Dealing with St Ann's enabled the Council to get the Victoria Centre done. It was wicked. The only way to make it work was to see that St Ann's didn't exist. For example, almost no shops. At that time the fashion was for big.

Then the Conservatives were in and they said they'd see if the City could build the St Ann's redevelopment. So, as a sample, at the top of Westminster Street a little block of terraces were taken down and a new block put up by a local builder. And then Wimpey was also invited to put in their scheme. Wimpey won, their costs and timescale were heartbreaking for me. Not only did Wimpey win but, once on board, the argument to save good houses had gone. Wimpey needed cleared sites because they had standardised pieces. The argument to pull everything down, which was Wimpey's, included all the nice, good houses like North Hungerhill Road and Broad Oak Street. They all went.

St Ann's lost the variety that could have come into the new development. There were all those pubs with things going on in them. A deal was done between the brewers, only three in the new St Ann's. There used to be many different ones. Pubs got big compensation, home owners a pittance. The new area had one landlord [Council] and one form of heating [the District Heating Scheme].

In those days, some days I was away doing research for something I was writing or interviewing somebody or something for Radio Four. But I was in St Ann's with SATRA most days. Some people wanted Wimpey because a movement had started of getting out quick. For example, someone saying: 'I'm in Phase Six, I should be in Phase One'. It had become an unstoppable flood. And on the social side things could get out of hand. I remember being in Lavender Street one afternoon and someone said a perv's been spotted at the bottom of the park. They were about to march on the matter. It was some chap taking his trousers down behind the bushes. I was able to tone things down and say we'd put up with these things for years, nobody had ever been hurt, and to move things on in a positive direction. We had public meetings for every single Phase [of demolition] in St Ann's, from One to Eleven including 2a.

The motive to do good is very strong. It was also an exciting time. I remember the Public Enquiry which was at the YMCA on Shakespeare Street. It took weeks and I was there every day from morning to night. All the other parties had barristers and lawyers to represent them. I did it on behalf of the tenants in St Ann's on my own. The fact that I've done jokey things doesn't mean I'm not a serious guy. I had been taught by Arthur Leatherland in no uncertain terms that if we were going to succeed we'd got to be serious.

But Arthur could be fun too. He said could we have Jack Dunnett MP in and I said we don't need him. And Arthur insisted and Jack Dunnett came, and Arthur went berserk telling this MP not just about the issues to do with St Ann's but with every issue on God's earth. So we all have our moments!

Jack Dunnett was a bit of a rascal. He was interested in football and he bought or acquired the control of Notts County tote and he needed agents to run the tote. So Jack acquired or leased a whole series of small shops in St Ann's whereupon he put in his tote agents . . . So by the time the Tories were losing favour on the City Council, there was a new Labour party coming in who were Jack's cronies.

I can remember John Carroll, who I became very fond of. John and his wife were selling vegetables and tote tickets and touting for the Labour party all at the same time. It was a very efficient organisation. I think Jimmy Green was local to the area, but not the others, they came in. I'm not sure if Jack Dunnett was ever interested in politics, he certainly wasn't interested in St Ann's. It was a hunting ground for him to sell tote tickets. He was interested in Notts County and the glory of football.

I was with SATRA all through. There were a couple of years when I stepped down from being Chairman, and Frank Glassup from Phase 10 did it. I was there from the first meeting until the opening of the Club, the Pint and Pot. Margaret Mann took over Dorothy Smith's sort of social role. And we had community workers. The United Nations Association paid for a £15 a week worker. Margaret Behrman was the first one from Essex University. She stayed about six years and was brilliant. Everybody was very fond of her. Then Ann Littler, who came from Kent, for about three years before she did a home for battered wives around the corner. Then she went to the Meadows. She sadly died of Motor Neurone disease. The last was Julie Hilling but things were more settled in St Ann's by then. That work ended when the Club happened, that was a moment of triumph and turned out to be a disaster for some.

SATRA wanted this Club. Similar groups had clubs in Strelley and Clifton. I wanted the Club not just to be only a tenants club and boozing club, but also to have a place to produce *Chase Chat*, the monthly newsletter, and to be able to hold meetings in the afternoons, be available for a playgroup and all sorts of other functions. A bit like the hut with the grass roof in the Precinct now [Chase Neighbourhood Centre]. There was always conflict between those who thought the Club could only work as a boozing club and those who thought it could only work as a community centre.

We missed a really good deal from Mansfield Brewery by one vote of our committee. That was a great pity. By the time the Club [Pint and Pot] opened, St Ann's was much more like it is today. The redevelopment was completed by then. The social mix had been whittled down. The middle class were weeded out. The monied bits and the work bits went. The old St Ann's had a much wider social mix. So when the Club opened, a lot of very bright, quite wealthy shopkeepers had gone. Some of them if they were attached to Jack Dunnett's tote and his political machine had reasons to weave in and want to be coming into a Club. There was a Tenant's Association Club to curry favour, to show face. That's gone. But by the time the Club opened, the shops were gone, the world was changing.

There was a poet I knew, called Doris Louisa Heath. She was slightly mad. I liked her a lot. She used to write to me sometimes three or four times a day. She lived off Norland Street in the old St Ann's. I organised an Afternoon Tea with Nostalgia event at the Kings Hall [St Ann's Well Road]. We had some terrible failures but this was an enormous success. I was picking people out to tell their stories. Then, I saw Doris at the back of the Hall and said come on, give a big hand for Doris Louisa Heath, and the whole audience turned against her and me and said : 'Out, get out, get out!' I've really no idea why, except she was regarded as a bit of a pestilential person because she was always going up to people and you couldn't shut her up. We do sometimes get moments of terrible intolerance.

I don't spend much time in St Ann's now. I buy my notebooks and soap from that enormous Cash and Carry that used to be the [Cavendish] Cinema. They're quite good for value. I go to the Library to change my book. I make an effort to pop into a pub and have half a pint. Last time it was the Sycamore and I was the only person in. Very sad.

St Ann's was killed by greedy capitalists like Wimpey in league with greedy politicians like Bill Derbyshire and really stupid Labour politicians like Alderman Foster who was supported by the Co-op. If things had been done properly, St Ann's today would be an area of some shopping, some quality works where employed people could feel proud. And a wide mix of housing and people that every district should be. If you go to Spain and look at the Spain that people love, like Barcelona, you'll find districts which are a mixture of all classes of people. And if you have that, you get the pubs full of people you want to talk to. And you find cafes. It's not all the fault of Nottingham politicians because there are world forces, like the rise of the big supermarkets and the Internet, which have changed things. But the City Council and greedy big builders destroyed what was and I can't forgive them.

Ray Gosling (right) talks with David Wilkinson at The Bell Inn, Nottingham, November 2000 on the occasion of David's retirement. Photo: Ellie White

DAVID WILKINSON
Born 1943

Interviewed at my home in St Ann's 18.10.00. David Wilkinson, from Warwick, was one of three architectural students at Nottingham University who made a study of St Ann's, pre-demolition, with proposals, for their joint thesis in 1967. The other two students were David Strickland from Middlesborough and Rob Davis from Birmingham. They were awarded a First Class degree

The study of architecture requires the final year to be a study of a building, the design of a building. Three of us were interested in housing and housing was always frowned upon by architectural lecturers as being too involved and potentially politically 'loaded': a building like a swimming pool or town hall was thought to be much more appropriate. Three of us persuaded the staff that we would do housing and that we would do it co-operatively together. Two of us were married students with children and living in St Ann's at the time. We were about twenty-two, twenty-three.

David Wilkinson, the student architect

St Ann's was an intriguing place, smokey atmosphere, very tight density urban living. We were fascinated by it. It was special because just above St Ann's was this huge area of allotments, Hungerhill Gardens.

In the 1960s, slum clearance was all the rage and had been for some years. The solutions were system-built concrete panel buildings mainly designed by the French and taken on board by the British. The Park Hill and High Park Schemes in Sheffield were the things you went and studied with awe as young students. At first, it seemed to us that what we needed to do was simply build this new Utopia on the allotments, which, by then, were under-used. And that St Ann's could be flattened and the problem would be solved.

But, then it became very clear, particularly to our wives who pushed the children to the shops in St Ann's, that here was a vibrant community. For all the dereliction and misery in certain parts, there were places in St Ann's that were delightful. There were ten thousand houses in the valley of St Ann's, thirty thousand people.

The huge scale of the thing gradually began to dawn on us. How on earth could you actually begin to do this when these were all human beings, all of whom had their own lives to lead and their own thoughts? So, in conjunction with Ray Gosling, who was a chum of ours, we thought we ought to ask the people of St Ann's what they felt. We discovered that my wife and his sister used to be at school together! Ray was the older intellectual wizard who appeared on radio and the television and had a sense of charisma. With funding he provided, we distributed leaflets and, twelve months on, the St Ann's Tenants and Residents Association [SATRA] had been firmly established.

During that year we spent much time studying and analysing the area, finding out what was there, what was good, what was bad, what made people tick, what needed to be kept and what needed to go immediately. We evolved a process where we felt improvement grants ought to be immediately offered in the area. I remember Lord Kennett (the Minister responsible for Home Improvements) coming to promote improvement grants and the Ministry of Housing had a caravan on Slab Square [nickname for the Market Square in Nottingham City Centre]. We went and berated him because nobody in St Ann's - or I think in the Meadows - were allowed improvement grants because somebody had decided these areas were beyond the pale.

We felt that the better houses, which could be left for at least twenty years, ought to be improved immediately. People's lives would be improved enormously. And the worst should be immediately demolished. The process of resettlement or redevelopment of St Ann's could be an evolutionary process. You could take the worst out first and build little houses with gardens designed in such a way that the community could continue to thrive amongst the existing industries and work of the area.

David Wilkinson said he was struck that many people, in spite of years of planning blight, still attempted to keep their homes in good order even though landlords had given up doing so

Still attempting repairs

House in good order next to an empty one

Making a statement that 'this is still my home'. Photos: Wilkinson, Davis and Strickland 1967

One of the fascinating things about the area was that it was full of little backyard industries. There were some big factories as well. But there were many things going on in individual people's houses and small backyard industries. None of it made noise or nasty smells so it was perfectly sensible to keep it within the development of the area. But, of course, in those days the planned ideal was to clear everything and zone the City. There would be an industrial zone, so these business owners would be pushed out into shiny new factory units which they couldn't afford, so their businesses died.

There were lots of corner shopkeepers, they lost their livelihoods and nobody ever addressed those issues, terrifying really.

We evolved the idea of providing two and three-storey buildings within the housing area. These buildings would provide secure parking near people's homes and also small industrial units. Of course, we're talking about the sixties when not many people had cars and why on earth would you need a car when the City was so near? But transport routes were important and people with cars wanted them parked nearby not, as was done at that time, the use of the Radburn System where you had cars parked away from housing areas. These schemes have created huge problems of vandalism and theft. We are now spending vast amounts of money, undoing this car separation, bringing cars into dedicated spaces next to each house.

So industry would continue within the redevelopment. We spent a vigorous twelve months and were very committed. We produced drawings and models and put on an Exhibition. At that time the Tenants and Residents Association did not exist except for a handful of people. Our Professor ticked us off for being involved politically. It was Professor Arthur Ling who made his name rebuilding Coventry after the War, but he was a planner more than an architect. But we were young and we had a passion and he wasn't going to deflect us.

Came the day when we mounted our thesis Exhibition and met our examiners, practising architects from around the country. We had a difficult time because the two who

were assessing us were architects who wanted to get on and look at the buildings. What have you *done?* We insisted, however, they went through our analysis of how we had arrived at our design solutions, before they looked at our final designs and models. It was the process that was important, the process of working with people. Before 1966/67 nobody had done that. We got 1st Class degrees.

After University we all needed jobs and were all taken on by Liverpool City Housing Department. It was not easy. I spent two years and then moved on and worked for Shelter, the campaign for the homeless, which had set up a project within the Granby area of the City. I started my own practice in 1975. Dave steadily moved back North and now runs a practice in York. Rob moved to rural Worcestershire and has run a 'one man' practice for thirty years.

My work in St Ann's had an enormous influence on my future. When we worked for Liverpool City Council, the Housing Department was appalling. Like other cities, it was arrogant, it had a huge housing programme, it had standard house types and would cover the land with those and, if not those, then they would bring in the big builders 'to do a real job'. Housing is one area of architecture that desperately needs the involvement of the community.

Housing is very special. Whereas a swimming pool or an art gallery can be something people love or hate, people need to feel at home and have a house they wish to nurture not that they wish to abuse. Sadly, history has shown that estates built in the fifties and sixties have been continually abused because they were alien, completely alien. I have just completed the total demolition and rebuilding of over 1200 homes in Runcorn, as designed by James Stirling in the 1960s.

When I was working with Shelter, Peter Walker then Shadow Minister for the Environment talked to us. The problem with politicians is they want an easy answer. I talked about what we learned in St Ann's. There isn't an easy answer. It's hard work.

My practice now employs architects over six or seven offices. Housing is our mainstay.

Ten to fifteen years after I left Nottingham, I think housing got a lot better. Housing Associations became a force for good, there was a lot of missionary zeal in people. But they have sadly grown to a size which isn't good. Thirty-five years ago, in places like Nottingham and Liverpool, all the social housing was built by one Authority, the Local Authority. That was bad. We then got the smaller Associations, community based in local areas. But they have now grown, been encouraged to amalgamate. So, in Liverpool, for example, you have them all snapping and snarling at each other for bits of land to develop. They've all got Chief Executives, Directors of Finance and Directors of this and that, they all drive large motor cars. The bureaucracy that has been established is enormous. I feel saddened that we've now moved back to where we were those thirty-five years ago.

We've got rid of the monopoly of Local Authorities in building social housing, now we've got lots of monopolies which are even worse in a way. It's driven by money now. Housing Associations are looking for fancy projects, things

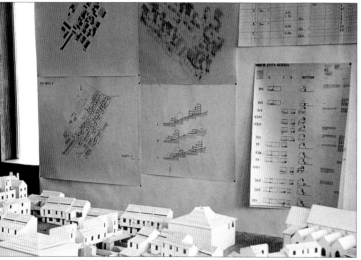

Part of thesis Exhibition mounted by David Wilkinson, Rob Davis and David Strickland. St Ann's Church was left intact (bottom right-hand corner)

that will get them into the Journals, things that will get them brownie points. What they are not doing is looking after the old housing stock and the poor people they were set up to look after. They're all fighting over redundancy payments and larger cars and better deals . . . If you go to the Housing Association Conference at Harrogate, it's the most appalling spectacle of people in the trough I've ever seen. I know many hardworking housing professionals who are still working to provide new and improved homes for the most needy. But, sadly, there are many more whose agenda is failing very badly to address the real issues of poverty and deprivation, which are still very much a part of our inner-cities.

So where are the people with the passion now? I don't know, I don't see them. As I've said to you earlier, I would like somebody to come and kick my door in and say: 'You are an old fool and you don't know what you're doing and this is what we should be doing'. Nobody's doing that. I'm not seeing Housing Associations questioning ideals. In the Thatcher years, I didn't see many of them standing on street corners saying this is an outrage and we should not be doing this (i.e. increasing rents, building houses for sale, reducing improvements to existing houses, government investment reduced).

We came up with a solution for St Ann's after careful analysis. If we had followed the gurus of the time, we would have produced whacking great concrete towers on Hungerhill Gardens which we'd see from this window.

Of course, at the time St Ann's was demolished, there was a respect for authority or even a fear of authority. Town Halls were fairly sinister establishments, designed to intimidate weren't they? People in St Ann's were intimidated when somebody came along and said: 'We're going to give you a brand new property'. Then, that had to be good and people just went along with it.

It was interesting that, in all our analyses, nowhere was there a concern for ownership. I think that was a symptom of the incredible arrogance of compulsory purchase. Ownership was irrelevant if you were going to knock it down. All that was important was that it was deemed unfit, wallop, the machine rolled over.

David Strickland (left) and David Wilkinson at David's retirement party at The Bell Inn, Nottingham 21st November 2000. Photo: Ellie White

Regeneration has remained one important facet of David Wilkinson's work throughout his working life. He retired from the Wilkinson Hindle Halsall Lloyd Partnership in 2000 'except for occasional work!' He was based in the Liverpool office. There was a farewell party for the Nottingham Office at the Bell Inn, Angel Row, Nottingham, on November 11th 2000, when **David Strickland** *was also present. Rob Davis was hoping to be. Ray Gosling was among the guests. David Strickland told me he lived 'somewhere near the bottom of Robin Hood Chase' for part of his student time in Nottingham. He remembers making a model for their thesis project and putting it out the back to dry, only to find local children clambering over it!*

"To start with we had such grandiose ideas of putting flats across St Ann's Valley, Corbusier-style, and then we learned we needed a different approach," he said.

Children's lives go on despite planning blight

Three of the photos taken of children in St Ann's 1967 by Wilkinson, Davis and Strickland

Going to school

A break from street games to have our photo taken

He's bigger than me!

Built Environment in the 'new' St Ann's

With 340 acres and 30,000 people cleared, what happened next and what was left? This section focuses on the built environment and what happened after the transition years of planning blight and demolition.

The Wimpey houses arrive! Photo: source Philip Everett, Nottingham Local Studies Library

Wimpey fills the empty space. Photos: Nicholson Photo Archive

Photos: Barbara Dexter

There wasn't a rush for cameras when the district was rebuilt, though plenty of people expressed concern at the 'sameness' of the architecture.

This photo appeared in Nottingham Corporation's 'St Ann's Renewal in Progress' May 1970. The Church on Blue Bell Hill Road is St Bartholomew's in its last months

Lindsey Adams, class teacher at the Elms School is taking a group of children down Robin Hood Chase for a visit to Stonebridge City Farm. The new housing has ends facing Robin Hood Chase in place of the houses facing it either side. Many of the complaints about the 'new' St Ann's over years has been that housing was 'back to front', and that blind ends of buildings looked on to thoroughfares where pedestrians need to be seen. Photo: Barbara Dexter c1973

This shows much of the new housing facing into the St Ann's Well Road valley. The photo, taken from cleared land [where St Bartholomew's Church stood] at the top of Blue Bell Hill Road, is a 1973 Nottingham Evening Post photo. It was reproduced in 'Elliott Durham and St Anns' [Plowright Press 1998] and, with permission, we use it again here. St Andrew's Church steeple is the biggest one in the distance

ST ANN'S NOTTINGHAM: inner-city voices by Ruth I Johns • ISBN 0951696092

By the 1980s, there was a growing concern that 'something should be done' to improve the housing and environment in the district. Although trees and plants improved things, especially during the summer months, the fabric of the housing offered a drab environment. There were already serious problems in Phase 10 Marple Square area and with the Caunton Avenue flats. They are mentioned in more detail below.

Housing on Robin Hood Chase being improved mid-1990s. Photo: Ruth I Johns

Part of central St Ann's in the 1980s. Photo: Nicholson Photo Archive

Government Ministers were so impressed with the City Housing Department's pilot Estate Action improvement schemes that they approved an additional £15m bid for work on a further 937 homes. Nottingham Arrow October 4th 1993. The money was used for improving houses and flats with thermal cladding, new doors and windows and work to cut energy costs. "Crime will be tackled by tidying up derelict land, re-organising footpaths, improving lighting and replacing locks. Residents will benefit from new gardens with parking, helping to cut car crime. The area will be landscaped with new walls, trees and planted beds."

Off Westgate Street, 'plain' houses have their new look. Photo: Ruth I Johns 2000

Nottingham Arrow, a Nottingham City Council publication, published these photos (below) of housing in St Ann's before and after the improvements. Gradually, improvements have taken place in more of the district as areas 'left out' pressed to be included.

Photo: Nicholson Photo Archive 2001

Before

After

Site of the former St Ann's Board School 1995. Photo: Ian Brown, Nottingham Local Studies Library

Site of the former Cathcart Hill 1995. Note house ends face the walkway. Photo: Ian Brown, Nottingham Local Studies Library

St Ann's Valley from Westgate Street, looking across St Ann's Well Road where the bus is heading away from the City. I found people like living in St Ann's Valley, partly because of its proximity to the Chase Precinct shops and easy public transport. Photo: Ruth I Johns 2000

This was Cathcart Hill in 1969. Photo: source Liz Edge, Nottingham Local Studies Library

E James Smalley took these photographs 2000

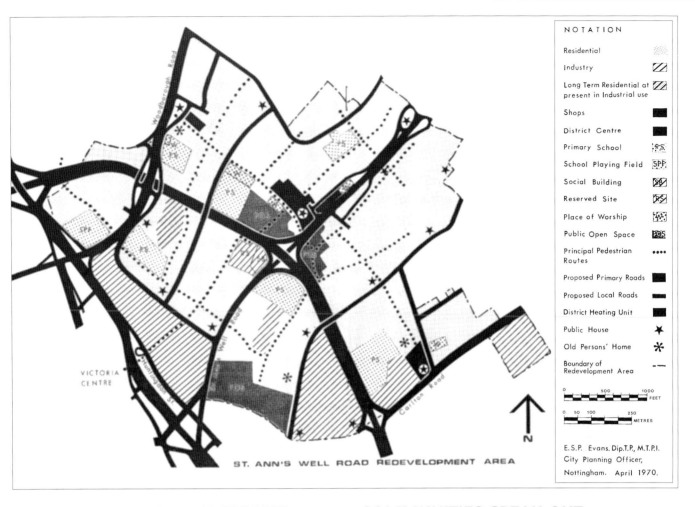

NOTATION

Residential

Industry

Long Term Residential at present in Industrial use

Shops

District Centre

Primary School

School Playing Field

Social Building

Reserved Site

Place of Worship

Public Open Space

Principal Pedestrian Routes

Proposed Primary Roads

Proposed Local Roads

District Heating Unit

Public House

Old Persons' Home

Boundary of Redevelopment Area

E.S.P. Evans. Dip.T.P, M.T.P.I.
City Planning Officer,
Nottingham. April 1970.

ST. ANN'S WELL ROAD REDEVELOPMENT AREA

EASTERN BY-PASS PLAN STOPPED

This map shows the plan for the Eastern By-pass road, which would have cut St Ann's up and created huge noise in the area.

In January 1970, the Civic Society [Newsletter 22] expressed misgivings that the City Centre was being planned primarily for traffic and not people. "If an opportunity arises for the Society to question any major planning proposal, we must make sure that it is taken. To this end, it is the Society's intention to object at the Public Inquiry concerning the Eastern By-pass, which is a new road through the middle of St Ann's."

In June 1971 [Newsletter 26] the Civic Society described the Minister's rejection of the Eastern By-pass and Sheriff's Way - announced May 11th 1971 - as 'the greatest landmark in the history of planning in this City'. The Minister, Peter Walker, was praised for upholding the Inspector's recommendations. The Civic Society said the Traffic Plan was never submitted to the full Council, yet the Planning Committee proceeded as if it was official policy. The plan was never submitted officially to the Ministry. The Society made these points 'time and again' - for instance in a letter to the Town Clerk March 18th 1969.

The St Ann's Tenants and Residents Association [SATRA] were of one voice against the By-pass plan.

The Eastern By-pass plan was killed off well after St Ann's redevelopment started and altered land use on certain sites at short notice. Several interviewees mention this.

COMMUNITIES SPEAK OUT

As we saw in the section on The Transition Years, although there were voices concerned for St Ann's, the wholesale redevelopment of the district happened without huge public outcry and with minimal consultation. The complaining and the determination to be heard came later. In the years after redevelopment, people in St Ann's and other redeveloped areas began organising much more assertively.

Local voices make good sense

An undated joint paper prepared by the St Ann's Tenants and Resident Association, the Meadows Association of Tenants and Residents, the Sneinton and District Tenants Association and the Meadows Group was given me in November 1994 by Arthur Oscroft, Director of Housing, Nottingham City Council. The paper was called *Problems of Redevelopment in the Meadows*. The paper was based on the experience of all participating organisations. The Housing Department, or certain people in it, obviously kept the document because it was helpful.

It is four tight-text pages of obvious common sense from people who found out about redevelopment the hard way. They hoped that lessons could be learned about how to stop areas getting into bad planning blight long before demolition, how properties could receive basic maintenance as long as people were living in them (although not major improvements): all practical, sensible stuff. People needed clear information, needed to know who they could talk to for clarification, needed to feel involved. The relevant departments needed to keep a close watch to prevent accumulation of rubbish as people moved out of an area. The Council needed to know, ahead of time, the number of large families to be rehoused and to reverse its attitude that people must fit into what is built.

The paper stresses: "The Local Authority is not simply replacing old houses with new houses. It is replacing a complex of different types of dwellings, shops, businesses, community facilities, pubs etc with new housing . . . We suggest that someone be made responsible for assessing the effect of the removal of existing resources, and that for this purpose an accurate survey be undertaken into the existing facilities of an area. This should also include recommendations as to how such facilities may be replaced in an area or, if this is impracticable, how their removal may be ameliorated . . . We believe that the onus is placed on the developing authority to show why they cannot replace existing facilities, rather than on voluntary organisations to show why and how they should be replaced."

CAUNTON AVENUE FLATS:
built and demolished within 25 years

The field behind Family First Trust in Alexandra Park suddenly became a hive of activity in the late 1960s. Earth removing equipment started digging close to the boundary, scooping out the land so there was a sheer drop. We were expecting the housing but not the excavation. Wildlife fled the field. The development was completed in 1970. This small estate was a cul-de-sac at the end of Caunton Avenue, a road of solid early Council houses. The new development comprised sixty one-bedroom flats and bungalows, seven two-bedroom flats, nine with three bedrooms and thirty-five four-bedroom maisonettes. The estate was largely deck-access.

When, in 1975, Family First opened a purpose-built Day Nursery and Family Centre, we suggested a pedestrian link with this estate which was already suffering major problems. The Local Authority would not agree to this, which was disappointing.

By 1979, the Caunton Avenue tenants campaigned with recommendations to the Council about dampness, inadequate heating, and inefficient ventilation.

By the mid-1980s people living on this estate were angry on many fronts. Housing conditions were awful, the environment was lousy, and there was no clear way of making their voice heard. The rights culture had grown and led to expectations of getting help but there was no on-the-ground help. Residents watched their children getting into trouble, saw the problems but felt bereft of opportunity to change things. At one time, two tenants' groups were competing to address problems, and squabbling. The first community worker sent to 'help' seems to have made matters worse. Grants were being

made by departments both from the County Council and City Council in support of applications from both tenants action groups. The Caunton Avenue Flats Tenants Association [CAFTA] was the main group.

The cover of a Caunton Avenue Flats Tenants Association booklet

In 1985, CAFTA received a 90% result from a tenants' survey. The demands were that families, the elderly and people 'at risk' were no longer allocated housing on the complex. And that people in those categories already living on the estate should be found more suitable accommodation.

CAFTA wanted politicians to set up an urgent public enquiry into why, having had over £400,000 spent on improvements to the estate earlier in the decade, conditions had not altered significantly. There were calls for a more efficient heating system to be installed, that all asbestos be removed safely and for the Environmental Health Department fully to investigate the nuisance caused by insects. Other demands included that problems of condensation be properly evaluated, that the Area Health Authority investigate tenants' health, and so on . . . ending with the suggestion: "Or would demolition be more appropriate?"

Noise proved a major cause for complaint. Eight out of ten tenants said they were disturbed by noise. The design of the estate acted as a noise-enhancing machine. There were large concrete 'tunnels' which drew children from all around as a play area. Noise echoed and magnified.

Papers I have been shown state continuing problems around organising self-help on the estate. At one time, for example, the Chair of the Action Group wrote: "We felt the

St Ann's Nottingham: Inner-city Voices *by Ruth I Johns* • ISBN 0951696092

The approach to Caunton Avenue flats. Photo: Reg Baker, Nottingham Local Studies Library 1985

One of the accesses. Photo: Reg Baker, Nottingham Local Studies Library 1985

County Council's Community Support Team. *Changing Nottingham: the first ten years of the Community Support Team* [Nottinghamshire County Council 1994] states that with the Team's support, the Association contacted solicitors who agreed there was a case for suing the City Council for breach of contract on the basis that the estate was mismanaged. Reports were commissioned which condemned the flats as a fire risk and reported health risks because of the condition of the flats. Other independent reports found problems, highlighting twelve design faults likely to make crime more prevalent.

The tenants' case was sometimes presented in novel ways. The publication says: "The most effective of these was presenting a slide show of the worst repairs, poor lighting, and general dilapidation, to a group of councillors and officers of the Council, who were expecting to attend a normal committee meeting. This 'visibly shocked' some of those present, who had denied the problems were as bad as claimed by the group."

After ten months, the Council gave way and agreed to rehouse the tenants.

In 1993 the flats were demolished.

The flats being demolished. Photo: source 'Changing Nottingham', Nottinghamshire County Council 1994. Believed to be a Nottingham Evening Post photo

Association was more concerned with their own social rights than the problems concerning the tenants. Our aim is to hear the problems concerning the tenants, take what action is possible for their resolvement and liaise with the Council whenever possible to mutual amicable satisfaction and convenience."

It was small accountancy discrepancies which led in 1988 to the last management committee members of CAFTA relinquishing their role to Valerie Moore, Community Accountant, Community Support Unit of Action Resource Centre, and Fiona Robertson, Community Support Worker, Robin Hood Chase, St Ann's: 'until a properly constituted committee is formed'.

In 1991, the Association renamed itself the Coppice Tenants' Association and secured the backing of the

Government restrictions did not allow new housing to be built using Council money. An agreement was made with three Housing Associations to provide mixed, self-contained accommodation. The newly built area was re-named **Caunton Phoenix**. John Heppell, MP for Nottingham East, officially opened the £2.5m housing development of fifty-five new homes in 1994.

Caunton Phoenix was part of the City Challenge programme. When Nottingham City Council made its bid for City Challenge money, it described [all of] St Ann's as

Some of the Housing Association houses at Caunton Phoenix. Between the houses is the bank where the land was excavated at the border of Alexandra Park in the late 1960s before the Caunton Avenue flats were built

Another view of Caunton Phoenix. Photos: Ruth I Johns 2001

"a largely 1970s Council Estate, lacking defensible space - an unpopular living environment which contributes directly to social problems." This was the St Ann's which the City Council redeveloped only twenty years before making this statement!

In 2000, Dr Ron Blake, Senior Lecturer, Department of Building and Environmental Health, Nottingham Trent University, met me in St Ann's and offered any of the material prepared by the **City Challenge Evaluation Unit** of the University. City Challenge ran 1992-97 and is mentioned by a number of interviewees.

This map is helpful as it shows St Ann's (as defined for City Challenge). It is a 'structure' map from the City Challenge Evaluation Unit's 'Nottingham City Challenge Area: Baseline Report on Land Use and Environment' 1994. Not all the projects marked happened. For example, Marple Square. St Ann's is the City Challenge area above Carlton Road excluding Sneinton Square and some of the adjoining land to its NW. And it excludes some of the land marked 'Industrial Zone' around and NE of the City Challenge HQ. The map clearly shows the relationship of St Ann's to Victoria Centre and the City Centre, and the important area covered by the Hungerhill allotments

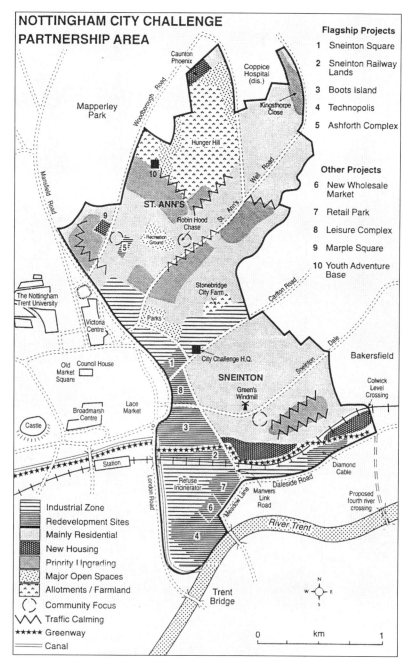

KINGSTHORPE AND KILDARE TENANTS ASSOCIATION

In 1976, the City Council started making housing cuts. By then the Nottingham Federation of Tenants Association was setting up the Nottingham Housing Action Group. In *Housing Action* June 1977, the Action Group's stated aims were: "To inform everybody what is going on concerning housing cuts; to conduct a public education programme on the whole system and finance of council house building and to actively fight and organise for better housing conditions."

The Group applauded the City's 54,000 Council dwellings. But: "In the last year, the foundations of council housing in Nottingham have been slowly chipped away, opening the door to anybody who has the money to buy a council house."

Voices were growing. For example, the Kingsthorpe and Kildare Tenants Association, St Ann's, reported dissatisfaction at the way repairs were being carried out: "What the Council finds hard to admit is that when they solve problems of their own making, they are not doing us any favours."

In 1987/88, the Kildare Road Tenants Action Group, in an application for grant to Nottinghamshire County Council's Community Support Unit, said that it had been set up: "for the purpose of getting tenants together on the estate, many people feel isolated and cut off, so provisions such as Welfare Rights facilities, crèche and general support for tenants is much needed. Also the group will campaign around issues of importance to tenants e.g. Heating System, dampness and condensation repairs and the environment. Service will be available to all tenants on the estate [72 flats and 129 maisonettes] five days a week Mondays-Fridays." The Action Group was a voluntary group seeking £400 administrative costs for a year.

In 1995 a Government-funded housing office for tenants was opened on Kingsthorpe Close. Professor Alice Coleman, of the London School of Economics and author of *Utopia on Trial*, supervised the DICE [design, improved, controlled experiment] project funded by the Department of the Environment.

Kingsthorpe Estate suffered many social problems and was 'stigmatised' before the recent improvements, according to Nottingham City Council. Nottingham Evening Post 9.10.95. A spokesman said: "The new-look estate is a much better place to live and the City Council is committed to making it a decent place to live."

It was 2000 before there was serious commitment to putting in a playground for children up to age eleven.

The new-look Kendale Court. The flats are not as elegant from The Wells Road side [see John B Hibbitt's photo soon after they were built]. But the improvement to both housing units and environment is impressive. Photos: E James Smalley 2002

JM on Kendale Court

from letter sent 1999

Even in the early 1970s, St Ann's had a bad reputation. But, for me in 1971, with a three-month old baby, it was a blessing to be offered a Council flat on Kendale Court, The Wells Road, which I shared with another mum.

The flats looked like a prison from the outside, but could be made lovely inside and it was my first real home at eighteen after leaving my Yorkshire home at sixteen. I lived in St Ann's for a year and then I became an Army wife.

At Kendale Court, I found no problem with neighbours. I think it wasn't so much the area, but the company one kept, which is true of any area in which one lives.

St Ann's was a handy area to live, being close to town, and the flats had a shop and a pub. I found there was a caring side to the community and I was happy living there. Sadly, one always hears the worst and not the good deeds.

St Ann's could do with a break, maybe more money spent on it to modernise homes and shops, though I haven't been there for some years now. Money doesn't solve all problems, but it helps if spent in the right way. My son, now twenty-nine, was born in Nottingham and is now a proud Nottingham Forest supporter. I haven't been to St Ann's for years since we now live in Mansfield Woodhouse, but I feel in a way that my roots started there. I've always liked Nottingham and find it a lovely City.

JOAN TROUT

Born 1935

Reprinted from a special commemoration edition of Chase Chat 1995. Mrs Trout still lives in the Blue Bell Hill area of St Ann's. Mrs Trout's husband, Cyril (born 1909), has lived in St Ann's all his life

The biggest change to me has been the Blue Bell Hill Road over the years since I first came to Nottingham in 1958. Blue Bell Hill was the road I used most when walking to and from Hockley.

The bottom end of Blue Bell Hill always appeared to be very high. Most of the houses round its meeting with Alfred Street were three floors high. On a dark and damp day, they seemed to touch the sky.

The houses in the middle of Blue Bell Hill, around Young, Massey and Simpkins Streets had not got the height, only two floors and bay windows.

One day, after being to town, I was returning home later than usual up Robin Hood Street and Blue Bell Hill. It was dusk, during the winter. I passed between Young and Simpkin Street. I was the only person on the road. All the houses had been pulled down, the street lamps all removed. What a lonely, sad place it was.

Watching the rebuilding of the houses, only one shop this time. It didn't seem the friendly place of the past, more green and gardens about, a wider road, more traffic, my old Blue Bell Hill, gone for ever.

THE OUTER RING OF ST ANN'S UNAFFECTED BY THE REDEVELOPMENT

The housing which survived outside the redevelopment area created a ring around the 'new' St Ann's. Some photos in other parts of the book show, say, Bracton Drive and St Bartholomew's Road. Here we take a quick tour of some of the other housing which escaped demolition on the edges of the redevelopment area. The oldest housing is Park View.

PARK VIEW
[formerly Victoria Buildings] Bath Street

Long before Local Authorities were permitted to provide housing for the general population, Nottingham's built Victoria Buildings for Corporation work-people, especially employees of the Health Committee. The Corporation's Industrial Dwellings Committee recommended the site between the Board School [on Bath Street] and the Victoria Baths. Compensation of £100 was paid to a Mr Richards for loss of the Turkish Baths on part of the land needed and £10 to Mr Richards (Jnr) for the same reason. The matter of replacing the Turkish Baths was considered for many years by the Council.

Victoria Buildings, designed by Bakewell and Bromley were completed in 1876 and only the next year it was decided that not only could Council work-people be housed there but anyone else as well.

By 1970, there was concern over the state of the five-storey flats, still with only stone staircases, sculleries with stone sinks, no baths or showers, and improvements were made toward the end of the 1970s when the flats became Victoria Park View. For more details see Stephen Best's article in *Sneinton Magazine*, Summer 1984, from which the above information was found.

Park View flats next to the Victoria Leisure Centre. Photo: Ruth I Johns 2002

ST ANN'S NOTTINGHAM: inner-city voices *by Ruth I Johns* • ISBN 0951696092

In *Sneinton Magazine* Summer 1988, Ian Wells, Secretary of the Victorian Society, said the history of the flats were full of good intentions, but only four years after their completion, the police were describing them as the: "worst houses in Nottingham". Some of the 'worst' tenants were removed and 'a better class of person' installed, but major problems were being caused by the overcrowding the flats had been designed to eliminate.

A century later, in 1988, tenants were complaining about poor conditions despite the 1970s improvements. And the question was whether to refurbish or demolish the flats. Now, Park View flats – which have been refurbished – will sometimes be seen advertised for sale.

Views vary over time as to whether Bath Street is St Ann's or Sneinton or half and half, the dividing line being the road. The buildings on Bath Street were certainly viewed by people in the old St Ann's as much more 'their patch' than do most current residents in St Ann's due to the shift in population density within the district following redevelopment.

VICTORIA BUILDINGS

by **Barbara Levick** 2001

Born 1927

When I was Secretary of the St Ann's Care Group, an offshoot of SATRA [St Ann's Tenant and Residents Association], it was suggested that we go to Victoria Buildings on Bath Street and try to talk to some of the elderly residents who live there. It was believed that quite a lot of old people were living in appalling conditions. As we were on the brink of creating a new Estate with all mod cons, this was a chance to do something for these people.

We were warned that quite a lot of these people were slightly eccentric. They had lived in their own little world for so long that their life - in some instances - bore little resemblance to most people's lives. So, off we trotted to knock on doors and see what we would see. The first thing that alerted us to the terrible conditions was the state of the staircase with broken stone steps, which were a hazard to frail elderly people. The first person we met was an old lady of ninety-one years who had lived in this flat for most of her life, with no hot water or storage for coal except a small space under her sink. There was no lift, so coal had to be lugged up three flights of broken stairs. She said she longed to get away, but was afraid she would never be able to pay the rent of a more modern place. She was paying eight shillings and six pence a week.

This was in 1970. We assured her that if it was possible to get her out, we would see that she got extra money to pay for a better standard of housing. We tried hard but, unfortunately, she died before we could help her attain her dream.

Another resident we visited had very little furniture, just a bed in a corner, a couple of chairs and a rickety table, but the walls were covered with evening gowns on wire coat hangers, along with wedding dresses and bridesmaids' dresses. This old lady (a bit like Dickens' Miss Faversham) had never been married. Her fiancé had been killed in the First World War and she had lived in a dream world, requiring nothing but the basics of living and spending all her money on second-hand finery.

With the help of Social Services, we got her a grant to enable her to get a bit of decent furniture. We had a contact on St Ann's Well Road, a second-hand dealer, who helped us enormously and we felt that we had done a good job.

A few weeks later, news filtered through to us that she had burnt quite a lot of the furniture and was far from well. We went round to see her and took some nourishing foods. But it was too late. She died shortly afterwards. Some time later, on idly looking through the *Nottingham Evening Post*, I noticed that her Will had been published. She had left something in the region of £15,000 to a local Church. And she had been living in such squalor, scrimping and saving. It did teach us to try and make a few enquiries about the financial status of people before we dived in feet first.

Another quite different case came to our attention. This lady was much younger than most of the residents. She was perhaps in her late 40s and her flat was the epitome of comfort. She had had a gas fire installed to save carrying coal, had a lovely Turkey red carpet covering the old stone floor, comfortable easy chairs and an assortment of occasional lamps to give a soft glow instead of a harsh overhead lighting fitment. She told us she only had to pay nine shillings and six pence a week rent, whereas if she lived in a more modern house the rent would be about £4 a week. She saved her money to go abroad for a few weeks holiday every year. She was quite happy living there and didn't mind not having a bathroom. The [Victoria] Public Baths were nearby. It proved to us that it was not what you had in life but how you used it that mattered.

A social worker phoned me and asked for my help in talking to a lady who they were trying to move out to a more convenient dwelling. This lady was being very stubborn in letting anyone in. I went to try and reassure the lady we meant no harm but were there to help her. Eventually she let us in. We explained that a much better home awaited her and she did not have to worry. We would attend to everything, pack up her belongings carefully and get them transported to the new place and help unpack and get her straight before taking our leave.

After a lot of persuasion, we finally got her to agree, and we arrived two days later to help her get her things packed up. In the bedroom we found a number of old shoeboxes. She shouted at us and told us not to touch them. They were private. Luckily for us, we never went anywhere in someone's home singly, we always went in pairs, and the Social Services lady persuaded her to let us pack the boxes up. She had a peep at the contents in case it was just rubbish that she could perhaps get her to throw away. Imagine her surprise when she found the shoeboxes contained unopened wage packets, dating back to the 1930s.

Apparently, this lady had lived firstly on her husband's wage, and saved her own, then as time went on she drew the Old Age Pension, then a Widow's Pension, still saving the wages she got from when she worked as a cleaner in a factory and putting them in shoeboxes. She had got into the habit of saving the unopened wage packets from various places of employment and it ceased to be any concern to her. She had no family as far as we could ascertain, having had no children, she outlived her brothers and sisters and it seemed she was alone in the world. But there was all this money that was in notes that were out of circulation, old white £5 notes that crackled when you touched them and written in beautiful copperplate, each one was a work of art, but no bank would accept them.

The lady from Social Services told us she would need us to stand by and witness her counting them and sign to say we agreed the amount. It would have to be taken to a bank's Head Branch in Nottingham where a receipt would be given for it. Then it would be sent to the Bank of England, which would be the only place to get it changed. They would arrange for a local bank of the lady's choice to issue her with a bank-book for the full amount. She was most upset about this as she did not trust banks but it had to be done and she accepted it with bad grace, calling us interfering do-gooders.

Eventually, we got her moved but she refused to go to the bank and draw any of the money deposited. She said that had we left her alone she would have been able to take some of her money and buy new things, but you couldn't spend 'a bit of a book'. She had no idea what to do with a bank-book and would not listen to advice. She eventually just faded away and nobody knew what became of her money. It could still be in some bank earning interest for some non-existent person. Such a sad ending!

I have not put names in for obvious reasons, but these were all cases that we looked into way back when we were trying to make St Ann's a better place to live in. At least there are no more old people forgotten in that Victorian monstrosity on Bath Street. Many people have tried to get better conditions there, but I'm happy to think we were the first to start the ball rolling.

GORDON BOYS' HOME

Founded in 1855, the Nottingham Gordon Memorial Home for Boys moved to Cranmer Street in St Ann's in 1904. The 'Home' was named after General Gordon, noted for 'his stand in Khartoum'. The new building was financed by public subscription. The boys were destitute or 'from an unwholesome home environment' and entered the Home around age 10/11, attended local schools and after leaving school stayed at the Home until they were sixteen. Then they were boarded out with foster parents. It was not until 1950 that the boys were able to stop wearing the military type uniform and hat which so marked them as they went out, quite often in

The former Nottingham Gordon Boys' Home. Photos: Ruth I Johns 2000

crocodile formation. People I have spoken to remember seeing them and sometimes became friends with one or more of them.

The Home's 1950 annual report says: "The boys are now encouraged to join outside organisations. Each Monday and Tuesday evening, twenty boys attend the 1st Nottingham Company, the Boys' Brigade. Others are members of the 1st Nottingham Life Boys [junior branch of the Boys' Brigade] and of the 83rd Nottingham Troop of Boy Scouts.

"Boys of school age again attended the Pipewood School Camp near Rugeley, a Staffordshire beauty spot, for a month where they were visited by members of our committee. Our thanks to the Nottingham Education Department who organise the Camp. The senior boys went for ten days to the 1st Nottingham Boys' Brigade Summer Camp at Heage in Derbyshire. Many good friends of the Home continue to invite the boys to the cinema, theatre, tea-parties etc . . . Church attendance also receives special attention. Boys attended Elms School and Huntingdon School.

"The question of the provision of suitable outdoor and indoor recreational activities is one of our main problems and the Committee are constantly seeking ways and means of extending these facilities."

In 1955, one boy was doing so well at school, the Local Authority made arrangements for him to stay with local foster parents so he had better facilities for quiet study. He was seen as University potential.

"Boys go visiting locally one Sunday afternoon and evening a month, and judging by the waiting list of homes who want a Gordon boy, their behaviour is obviously good; one result of the untiring efforts of our Manager and Matron (Mr and Mrs Routley) to instil manners into the boys at the Home [1955]."

In 1958 the Gordon Boys' Home left Cranmer Street and the substantial building with its name in stone over the front door and they moved to a large house in Alexandra Park for a few years before closing. Times change and foster homes became the preferred home to boys on their own.

The building on Cranmer Street, with Nottingham Gordon Home inscribed over the front door, was afterwards used as a Teachers' Resource Centre and later still as student accommodation. In 2001, it was sold by Savills (in the region of £750,000) as a freehold property creating income stated on the sale particulars as £110,160 p.a.

The site is 0.773 acres. The property has been converted in recent years to provide 72 student bedrooms. These are arranged in eight flats in the main four-storey building providing 58 student bedrooms. A modern annexe at the rear of the site provides another 14 bedrooms in four flats. Each flat comprises study bedrooms, with shared shower rooms and wc's, and separate kitchen/living room. The flats have an independent central heating system. There is an ample car park.

The complex is freehold subject to an existing tenancy agreement with Nottingham Trent University for a term of twenty-one years and one day from September 20th 1996, subject to five year break clauses.

This complex is in front of the Elms School.

The **Gordon Road Estate** seemed very new to the people of the 'old' St Ann's. It included Bracton Drive (where Clare Williams lived in 1943) and Serlby Rise where Grenville Gibson describes playing cricket as a child on the corner with Tuxford Walk (which went through to Bracton Drive via Kelham Green).

Serlby Rise from the Gordon Road end. Photo: Ruth I Johns 2001

From Bracton Drive looking across Gordon Road down Dowson Street with Blue Bell Hill Road the far end. Photo: Ruth I Johns 2001

Dowson Street and its neighbouring streets have some very long-term residents who have been there since before the redevelopment. They include Mr and Mrs Cyril Trout.

Another area on the edges of the redeveloped St Ann's is the **Promenade** facing Victoria Park and the area behind it.

These photos were taken by Ellie White 2000 around the **Campbell Grove** *and* **Promenade** *area*

ST ANN'S NOTTINGHAM: inner-city voices *by Ruth I Johns* • ISBN 0951696092

*Looking at The **Promenade** from Victoria Park. The path leads into Robin Hood Terrace. Photo: Ruth I Johns 2001*

*A terrace on **Woodborough Road**, St Ann's Hill on the left, just before reaching Corporation Oaks on the left and Robin Hood Chase on the right. Photo: Nicholson Photo Archive*

*The small area around **Wellington Street and Watkin Street** (which run between Shelton Street and Huntingdon Street near Woodborough Road) mentioned by Barbara Dexter as the 'railway houses' and part of the catchment area for the new Huntingdon Infant and Nursery School at the time of St Ann's redevelopment. In 1970, Nottingham Corporation said these houses had a further 15 years life. The land they were on would then be developed as an extension to the adjacent industrial area. Photos: Alan Hardy 2002*

. . . looking down Corporation Oaks, across the Woodborough Road to **Robin Hood Chase** where the houses were demolished. The pub is the Dame Agnes Mellors before it changed to The Woodborough. Photos: Ruth I Johns 1995

A substantial block on **St Ann's Hill Road** converted into modern housing units by Tuntum Housing Association. Photo: Ruth I Johns 2002

Old meets 'new'. Looking up **Corporation Oaks** which remained. The first building on the right is still a Veterinary Surgery and . . .

Looking up **Cromer Road** toward Hungerhill Road at the top. Chandos Street on the right just before the one-time corner shop with a 'To Let' board. This area was reprieved from redevelopment over thirty years ago. Several of the people I spoke with and/or interviewed live in this patch. Photo: Ruth I Johns 2000

St Ann's Nottingham: inner-city voices by Ruth I Johns • ISBN 0951696092

1852 BUILDING STILL IN GOOD USE

In 1978, Nottingham Community Housing Association [NCHA] discovered the disused **Working Man's Retreat** in Plantagenet Street. This terrace of six brick-built cottages was built in 1852 for "the reception and occupation of Aged People of the working-classes, who are not Paupers . . . and that the objects of such charity shall be Married men or Widowers of the age of Sixty Years or upwards . . . and that such objects shall be of good moral character and be possessed of . . . four shillings by the week at least, but not more than ten shillings a week . . ."

As each resident died or moved away, his property was left empty. This coincided with the years of planning blight and the redevelopment of St Ann's, and anything valuable was ripped out or smashed. The trustees of the charity administering the block sought to improve it but, even with local authority improvement grants, they had insufficient resources to do so. Eventually permission was gained from the Charity Commissioners for the NCHA to acquire the premises on a 150-year lease on payment of a premium administered by Nottingham Elderly Persons' Trust for the benefit of old people locally.

Thorough renovation into modern self-contained homes was completed in 1982 and the property maintained well since. It is still managed by NCHA and used for general family housing [2002].

The former Working Man's Retreat. Photo with an unfortunate punch hole mark on the middle window: NCHA

METROPOLITAN HOUSING TRUST ESTATE

The Metropolitan Housing Trust [MHT] Estate in St Ann's - with 516 homes - was opened in 1976. This Estate is known as the Ransom Road Estate, The Metropolitan Estate or Brewsters. The estate's central road, Brewsters Road meanders over the hill between Ransom Road and The Wells Road with side roads leading off. The estate cost £7m. Half the tenants were nominated by the City Council's Housing Department.

The City Council's Estate's Committee Report on April 19th 1973 said the total site area of the scheme was around

*Just around the corner from Cromer Road, looking up **Ransom Road**, St Ann's Well Road behind. Photo: Ellie White 2000*

*A few of the substantial houses on **The Wells Road** built by Nottingham Corporation after Local Authorities were allowed (from 1919) to start building their own housing stock. Photo: E James Smalley 2002*

Photos taken from near the Pearmain Drive, Pippin Close, Woodlane Gardens junction looking across to the Metropolitan Housing Trust Estate beyond. The mast near Elliott Durham School in the distance. Photos: E James Smalley 2002

33.768 acres. 12.316 acres of it came from the former Coppice Hospital land owned by Sheffield Regional Hospital Board. And 21.452 acres was allotment land of Brewsters Gardens, The Wells Road Gardens and part of Hungerhill Gardens. Of the allotment land, 14.858 acres was held by the Chambers Estate, 6.265 acres held by the Bridge Estate and 0.329 acres held by the Housing Committee.

A view across Hungerhill Gardens, to the City Centre in the distance, from the Brewsters Road (Ransom Road end) edge of the estate. Photo: Ellie White 2000

In October 2001, the estate celebrated its 25th birthday. The Estate has an active Tenants and Residents Association[1] [METRA] which assisted in drawing up priorities for improving the estate with a programme of regeneration starting in 1996. Tenants wanted easier access to their homes, more privacy, greater security, better car parking, traffic calming to improve safety and a play area for children of all ages. £3m was spent on improving the district heating system, increasing insulation (both to reduce fuel bills), new doors to all homes and building the play space on Brewsters Road.

A programme of £6m further expenditure is in progress which includes demolishing 20 homes and most of the garages to improve access; turning some houses around making the back door the front and main entrance; creating hard standing for a car in the gardens of many

Estate improvements in progress. Photos: 'The Estate News', newsletter for residents February and September 2000

---

[1] See interview with Carol Bacon, METRA's Voluntary Secretary.

St Ann's Nottingham: Inner-city voices by Ruth I Johns • ISBN 0951696092

properties; making some gardens bigger and fencing gardens in; placing road humps on Brewsters Road to reduce traffic speed; closing some footpaths; replacing old kitchens and renewing wooden windows and repairing roofs. Improvement should be completed by the end of 2002.

From 1998, to help deal with the antisocial behaviour of a minority of tenants MHT, which runs an office on the estate, only issues Assured Shorthold Tenancies for the first twelve months. If there are no problems within this period, an Assured Tenancy follows. This is a step which makes it easier to evict troublemakers early on, a step supported by METRA.

Like the City Council in the main part of St Ann's, the MHT has built some bungalows. Tenants include people already on the Estate.

MHT supports METRA. For example, in donating money toward the cost of Metrazone, the Community Centre on Ransom Road, and three part-time employees. METRA has a close connection with the Morley School [now St Ann's Junior School]. For example, summer 2001, the School and METRA held a joint Summer Fair at the School.

The Tenant's newsletter for July 2001 highlighted the previous year's Buddy Scheme at the School, which was repeated in the autumn with Year 5 children trained to support Year 2 children new to the School. This was part of a GRASP project initiated with the help of the Divert Trust to work with families on the estate whose children attend the three local schools. GRASP [Gaining Real Achievement Stimulating Potential] started on the estate in 1999. The MHT Social Investment Foundation granted £67,000 over four years toward the cost of an 'achievement' coach, Debbie Pearson, to work with the children, their families and local schools.

DISTRICT HEATING SCHEME

The District Heating Scheme introduced in the redeveloped St Ann's failed for many years to bring the benefits forecast. Instead it created problems, both in terms of obtaining proper heat and hot water supply, and cost problems. People mobilised locally and campaigned. Having had no say in the redevelopment of the area, people were no longer willing to be planned for.

The District Heating Scheme, introduced when St Ann's was redeveloped, is a Heat and Power project run from the Eastcroft Incinerator on the London Road, between St Ann's and the Meadows. The Scheme was conceived in the late 1960s and was based on the burning of domestic and commercial refuse, using the heat produced for the provision of heating and domestic hot water to some 4,000 City Council dwellings (mainly in Victoria Centre and St Ann's), schools and other establishments. At one time, it was proposed that the Scheme extend to the Meadows after it was redeveloped, but this did not happen although many of the pipes were laid.

There is a considerable amount of useful recorded material about the District Heating Scheme. It is not appropriate for me to research it thoroughly for the purposes of this book, except to flag up an outline and hope that - at some time in the near future - someone will do a thorough piece of independent research into all aspects of this pioneer scheme. As well as very complex environmental aspects, there are myriad contract, maintenance, administration and financial aspects. Who gains and who, if anyone, loses?

A 1993 Consulting Engineers Report [Kenneth Lewin & Associates] estimated that there were some 20 to 30 miles of underground Secondary mains (those between sub-stations and domestic dwellings, schools etc). The underground mains system includes Primary mains (those between the London Road Heat Station and commercial properties and sub-stations). The steam generated at the Eastcroft Incinerator is conveyed to the Heat Station at the junction of London Road and Canal Street.

Here, states the Report, the steam is first used to generate electricity which is sold to East Midlands Electricity. The generators reduce the steam pressure and low pressure steam from these goes to direct injection heaters which produce medium pressure hot water.

This is conveyed in underground mains to serve the Broadmarsh Centre, the Victoria Centre (commercial and residential), the Civic Centre, three buildings of Nottingham Trent University and a number of sub-stations. These sub-stations serve all the domestic properties and other buildings such as schools and elderly people's homes in St Ann's.

The Report sets out to describe the complex District Heating Scheme and reasons for the 'very excessive' heat charges being levied on domestic consumers within St Ann's and the Victoria Centre flats.

Originally, Associated Heat Services (AHS) were appointed by Nottingham City Council to operate the Scheme, and it was later passed to the National Coal Board.

If you mention 'Clorius Meters' [later Mainmet] to some longstanding St Ann's residents of the 'new' St Ann's, you can still get a reaction of outrage, now softened by the humour of time and more recent experience of the improved system.

Just one of the problem areas which was indicated in the 1993 Report: "Evaporative meters, even where located in well lit areas, are very difficult to read and a high standard of meter reader is vital bearing in mind that once his job is done, no evidence of the actual meter readings remain. The consumer is required to sign the meter reader's sheet but, in general, consumers have no knowledge whatever in regard to meter reading procedures, the heating charge systems etc."

There were serious problems with leakages, breakdowns in supply and 'who was responsible for maintaining the secondary mains?'

As early as 1972, SATRA [the St Ann's Tenants and Residents Association] was protesting at the number of breakdowns in heating supply. The Scheme was heralded as creating a cheap source of heat, and SATRA at one point called on tenants to protest at a 20% increase by the

National Coal Board for the cost of heating. Some SATRA members went to London to lobby Shirley Williams, the Government's 'Prices Secretary'.

In 1973, explaining 'teething troubles' of Nottingham Incinerator at Eastcroft, a National Coal Board spokesman said: "There is no other incinerator in this country where the heat is being reclaimed by burning rubbish. So there have been very few people we can ask for advice and help in solving the technical snags."

In 1975, residents were campaigning against paying an all-in-rent that included heating charges, rather than paying for the heating separately. One tenant applied to withdraw from the Scheme as a test case. There were complaints of having to pay for heating even when it wasn't working and there was either insufficient or none.

In 1976, Councillor Peter Burgess lost his fight to take legal action against the National Coal Board over the last increase in District Heating charges in the City. Nottingham Evening Post 8.7.76. He was refused legal aid because his case was a 'representative action'. Councillor Burgess, who lives in St Ann's, said he was denied help because other council tenants would benefit from any success he might have in the courts. He had already spent £100 and could not afford to take action without legal aid.

In 1977 an increase of 7.8% was the second increase in six months. The *Nottingham Evening Post* of March 22nd 1977 said: "There must be sympathy for tenants who are faced with a 'pay up or else' situation. They cannot just opt out of the system and switch over to gas, oil or coal. It is an integral part of the letting. . . It would seem sensible for an outside consultant body to be called in to examine the cost and efficiency of the Scheme."

Also, in 1977, the Sociable Theatre Company put on a production called 'Hot Air' after interviewing members of SATRA. In one scene, an actress was seen preferring to be thrown out of her home into the snow because it was warmer!

In April 1984, the Victoria Tenants Association [just outside St Ann's] produced a special Newsletter about the 'Clorius Struggle'. In 1986, the Nottingham Heating Project produced an informative booklet about the Scheme. It also produced a Report, for the St Ann's Heating Group, specifically on the Scheme as it affected St Ann's. It stated that the Standing Charge had to be paid 52 weeks a year, making it £159.38 for a 2-bedroomed house in St Ann's on the District Heating Scheme, compared with Gas £36.80 and Electricity £32.20.

There have been numerous Press reports over many years about the Heating Scheme. People in St Ann's have produced cuttings to show me. Opinions still vary a lot about the Scheme, though the cost of supplying heat and hot water for domestic use is no longer a major issue. Improvements to the District Heating Scheme have been costly.

Following writs issued by British Coal against some 17 consumers for arrears in payments of heat charges as levied, in 1991 British Coal accepted the Defences issued and chose not to proceed with the court case(s) and settled out of court.

In the Consulting Engineers Report (1993) referred to earlier, it states that British Coal and Nottingham City Council asked Judge Heald to set aside the first week of the hearing in order to hear arguments and to rule on the various responsibilities. "After some 20 years operating the Scheme, that situation appeared remarkable."

The St Ann's Heating Group [STAHG] reported that: "Years of hard work and pressure by STAHG finally paid off. In April 1995, British Coal are pulling out of the Scheme to be replaced by a new company comprised of Nottingham City Council and a private partner. £12 million has been committed by the City Council to upgrade the Scheme."

Following British Coal's role in Eastcroft, there was a controversy about whether it should be owned publicly or privately (1995). Potential purchasers were asked to bid.

Improvements have been made to the System and most people now seem content with it.

In 1999, there were discussions about using existing pipes in the ground for linking up some more homes in the Meadows to the District Heating Scheme. EnviroEnergy, a joint venture between the City Council and Dalkia - which runs the Scheme now - said the average district heating costs across its 3,600 St Ann's properties was £175 a year. Nottingham Evening Post 7.6.99.

There was controversy when White Rose Environment applied to the Environment Agency for a licence, which was granted in 1998, to run a clinical waste incinerator at the Eastcroft site. Later it was granted a licence to burn low-level radioactive waste. Accurate monitoring of emissions and disposal of ash are key environmental concerns, voiced by individuals and groups like Friends of the Earth.

"As part of 'Celebrating 75 years of Council Housing in Nottingham', a postal survey was sent to all City tenants. 11,069 responses were received, a turnout of 30%. Asked whether they would prefer to stay with the City Council as landlord or have their home managed by a private company, **98.7% voted to remain with the City**." City Council Labour Briefing, July 1996. The Briefing for May 1996 stated: "The City Council is proud of the fact that it has built, or managed, over half of Nottingham's total housing stock."

SALES OF COUNCIL PROPERTIES

I asked Councillor D Liversidge, a Manvers Ward[1] Councillor and Chair, Housing and Social Services Strategic Board, Nottingham City Council, for up-to-date figures on housing stock in St Ann's. What proportion of properties built by the Council in the redeveloped St Ann's are still owned by the City Council and how many have been sold under the Right to Buy legislation? He passed my enquiry to George Mann, Service Manager: Housing Policy at the Housing Department.

[1] Manvers Ward covers part of St Ann's.

Figures in the three tables below are for housing within the boundary of Carlton Road, Stonebridge Road, Bath Street, Huntingdon Street, all Phase 10 area, Woodborough Road, Hungerhill Road, up Ransom Road, across by Elliott Durham School and down The Wells Road, up St Bartholomew's Road and back to Carlton Road.

Table 1.
Local Authority Stock within your defined boundary of St Anns Managed by the Housing Department

Type	1 bed	2 bed	3 bed	4 bed	5 bed
House	1	419	1197	62	3
Bungalow	56	5	1		
Flat	1113	465	6		
Maisonette	68	276	5	90	
Bedsits	62				

Table 2.
Elderly Housing Provision

Local Authority Residential (not included in Table 1. above)

The Oaks	50 units
Long Hedge	48
Mellors Court	30

Local Authority Sheltered (included in Table 1 above)

Bellevue Court	27 units
Bullace Road	27
Courtenay Gdns	24
Curzon Court	27
Dane Court	24
Fairholme Court	24
Fountain Dale Court	26
Furze Gardens	16
Mowbray Court	40
Ogdon Court	24
Welland Court	33

Table 3.
Sales of dwellings formerly managed by the Housing Department Within your defined boundary of St Anns

Dwelling Type	Number of Sales
Houses	1426
Flats	86
Maisonettes	20
Bungalows	7

I asked a supplementary question for the figures for Pearmain Drive and Caunton Avenue. The reply was:

Question 4 – (a) The Council owned dwellings at Pearmain Drive and Caunton Ave are as follows:–

	Size			
Type	1 bedroom	2 bedroom	3 bedroom	4 bedroom
Houses	0	99	36	7
Flats	59	0	1	0

There are no right to buy sales in Caunton Avenue, but 63 houses and 2 flats have been sold in the Pearmain Drive area. These sales are included in Table 3 above. The houses, which replaced the demolished Caunton Avenue flats, are all Housing Association owned.

Of the 62 bedsits listed above, 59 are at Cheverton Court in the Phase 10 area, 2 at Kingsthorpe Close and 1 at Welbeck Walk.

Outside the area of the figures above, but pertinent to St Ann's, is Alexandra Court which is still owned by the City Council. It is currently used as a hostel with a closure date set for March 2004. The future of this building has still to be determined.

COUNCIL HOUSE PURCHASER

This purchaser, who wished to be anonymous, told me [1999] that she and her husband bought their Council house about five years ago when the Council was encouraging people to do so.

"My husband is long-term St Ann's. We were Council tenants for fifteen years before that. Now, of course, we can't sell. Earlier in the year, the Council improved the houses next to us (double-glazing, new cladding etc) but, of course, ours wasn't included. Although, in order to do the external landscaping improvements, bulldozers went through our garden as well as the rest.

"Council tenants won't do anything to help themselves and it was months before the fronts were improved. This meant that some people got more garden as, for example, some six entrances and exits from our Close were sealed off. But if we wanted to have the extra space that was logical for our house, we would have had to buy it. In the end, we had to put back our own fences, grass etc so our dogs would be safe.

"At one point, we incurred solicitor's bills when trying to get redress from the Council. We felt we had been misled by the Council into purchasing our house. We've been out of pocket all the way along."

I have spoken with a handful of people who told of the same type of experience. I don't know how general this dissatisfaction has been. At the time Council properties were being improved it became apparent which properties were owner-occupied (i.e. the unimproved ones, except for the owned ones which were already improved).

PHASE 10 MARPLE SQUARE

The information I received 19.12.01 from the Housing Department stated plans to revitalize the two neighbouring areas of St Ann's: the 1970s-built Cheverton Court and Marple Square off Woodborough Road. There was a proposal to appoint a specialist housing partner to help progress the project. These two complexes "have been earmarked for redevelopment as part of the City Council's award-winning St Ann's Phase 10 regeneration scheme. The Cheverton Court premises will be demolished and replaced with new homes and nearby Marple Square partly demolished to make way for new housing, shops and community facilities. If all goes to plan, work could start in eighteen months time."

In 2001, Nottingham Housing Department won an Institute of Housing/Inside Housing Magazine award for the regeneration work taking place in St Ann's Phase 10 area.

Councillor Dave Liversidge joining in the celebrations. Photo: City of Nottingham 'Life' newsletter for City Council employees. The accompanying article in 'Life' said Phase 10 has suffered from a number of problems over the years, including a high crime rate, antisocial behaviour and other social exclusion issues . . .

At the award ceremony Councillor Liversidge said: "This is a fantastic achievement and a tremendous reflection on all the dedication and innovation going into this project.

"Turning around their most troubled estates is an aim for most local authorities, but we have taken the idea literally. The Housing Development section, with their partners in the Council and the local community, have been working to turn around St Ann's Phase 10 in more ways than one. The estate, which was Phase 10 of the redevelopment of St Ann's in the 1970s, is made up of a series of cul-de-sacs with paths running along the fronts and backs of people's homes."

In 2000, the City Housing Department said that at the start of the Phase 10 scheme around Heskey Walk, improvements included walkways being closed off and altered into private driveways with wrought iron gates and surrounding brick feature walls; old fencing being removed and replaced with modern walls and stairways up to front doors; new pvc windows: and gardens being turfed, fenced and tarmaced to provide a more secure front garden for family and children.

There is more on Phase 10 Marple Square under Phase 10 Action Group in the section on Community Organising after Redevelopment. The public relations summary given by the Housing Department about the background to the current Phase 10 regeneration states:

"The Marple Square and Phase 10 estate lies on the north-eastern fringe of Nottingham City Centre in the St Ann's District. It covers just over half a square mile and comprises 455 properties.

"The original development of St Ann's resulted in little public or private open space for the residents. 80% of the

Before improvement

After improvement. This photo shows the same location with some of the new boundary wall and wrought iron fencing and gate. Photos: Nottingham City Housing

ST ANN'S NOTTINGHAM: inner-city voices *by Ruth I Johns* • ISBN 0951696092

A pilot scheme encompassing 16 homes incorporating the ethos of "turning houses around" and defining private space was completed in April 2001. The work for this scheme is now underway and subsequent stages across the estate are scheduled for completion by the year 2005.

Consultation and option appraisal work is ongoing and some major redevelopment is planned for the community shopping and residential area at the heart of the estate.

'Turnaround News" (the quarterly newsletter) is delivered to residents on active stages to keep them informed of physical work issues.

- 'Residents Selection Booklets' are produced for each stage to give residents individual choices on a range of physical works options.

- A 'Fear of Crime' survey is currently underway to assess the positive impacts of physical improvements.

- 61 properties completed and currently being improved, a further 44 from August.

- Training organised for over 80 local people with driving lessons for a dozen.

- 10 computers built by local people with 7 installed in houses and 3 in the St Anns Resource Centre .

- Youth Services now being planned by local young people co-ordinated by two NSPCC workers and local volunteers.

- Other youth services agencies now active in the neighbourhood.

- Contract Partnering (M4I – Movement for Innovation) being developed for future physical work.

- Developed a logo for neighbourhood with resident Artist in Regeneration.

- Sponsored an interactive CD ROM Millennium Map for neighbourhood showing the changes of the past 100 years.

- Recycling bins provided at Marple Square.

- Car abandonment closely monitored and improved response developed with CCTV, Environmental Services and local Housing Office.

- Consultation Meetings held with over 100 households.

- A successful Year of the Artist project saw a resident artist work with young people across the neighbourhood and design new signage as well as other installations exploring identity and regeneration.

- Training organised for jobs in Call Centres – strong support from employers including Capital One.

- Eight editions of the local newsletter delivered door-to-door across neighbourhood.

- Weekly job information provided for local people.

- Weekly Welfare Rights Service providing six appointments a week.

- Two local people working at the Resource Centre, further vacancy due to be advertised locally.

- Three formerly unemployed local people now working for NECTA (a Social Economy construction training company) with a further seven more places available in helping to do the physical work.

- Local people are meeting to plan a local website and a community radio.

- In four months over 2,000 people have used the Resource Centre.

"I moved to St Anns in January of this year. I arrived here with a low sense of self-esteem, lacking in confidence and alcohol dependent. After visiting the St Anns Resource Centre I was bombarded with a lots of training courses, job opportunities, advice, support and guidance.

I'm currently taking part in courses in Information Technology, Communications, CV Writing, Job Search, and Driving Training. As a result my confidence levels have increased remarkably. My time is occupied constructively, and I now feel I have a purpose and many personal goals to fulfil.

Subsequently, I have become heavily involved in community issues and joined the 'St Anns Phase Ten Action Group' as the Vice Chair. Through the success of my own learning I now act as a motivator and go-between to help other residents achieve as much from life as possible.

The Resource Centre has certainly made me realise my potential and has given me a sense of pride and community spirit in the area".

Damian Hendry
Vice Chair
St Anns Phase Ten Action Group

"The Resource Centre is excellent, the staff are so approachable and trustworthy. I visit the Centre quite often and meet other residents and new people. I feel a lot safer in the neighbourhood as meeting more people from around the area has increased my sense of security"

Wendy Holt
Vice Secretary
St Anns Phase Ten Action Group

"I chose to come here. I was put on priority due to the racial harrassment I was experiencing. I chose the house that I wanted… I love it here"

Resident
Sherwin Walk, St Anns

"When I arrived in St Anns 20 years ago, I thought what a nice area, as we got out the car in the car park everyone said Hello and Good Evening…. As soon as we got in; the lady next door shouted, 'Would you like a cup of tea?' ".

Resident
Sherwin Walk, St Anns

For further information please contact: Paul Amann, Neighbourhood Manager on (0115) 91 51948 or email paul.amann@nottinghamcity.gov.uk

City of NOTTINGHAM

achievements

Nottingham City Council Housing Department

Neighbourhood Regeneration
St Anns Phase Ten

A page from Nottingham City Council Housing Department's Information Pack on Neighbourhood Regeneration at St Ann's Phase 10.

original housing was built between 1845-1880. The remainder was constructed in the 1900s.

"The area suffered from a lack of modern amenities, public open space and poor environmental conditions of housing, leading the City Council to develop the whole area from 1966. The redevelopment was implemented in 11 different phases. In the spring of 1974 work started on developing the area of St Ann's estate known as Phase 10, with 87% of the dwellings in low-rise two and three storey housing'

"Nottingham City Council based the new design on the principles of the Radburn layout. Cul-de-sacs set aside for garaging and car parking were linked to the nearby houses by small pedestrian alleyways that ran past the front and backs of people's houses.

"St Ann's experienced a number of problems once the remodelling was completed. Residents were transferred to various locations around the City. The period of time taken to clear the area and rebuild the estate meant that it was several years before residents were moved back into the area.

"The result was a break with the traditional ties and connections binding together the old community due to an inability to reassert the sense of community found within the old estate. The re-establishment of community ties within the neighbourhood was problematic, and did not develop fully for another several years.

"Residents initially saw the new housing as a good answer to their existing problems. But within 10 years however their view had changed. Unemployment, a spiralling crime rate, and a 'bad image' had ensured that Phase 10 was seen as one of the worst Council estates in Nottingham."

I find this summary problematic in quite a few ways, not least because many residents who were moved away never thought they had a chance of returning. Through individual applications, some did later return. To anyone unfamiliar with what happened, it would be easy to read phrases like: 'inability to reassert the sense of community', and 'within 10 years however their view had changed' as placing the onus of Phase 10's failure on its residents. But, as is evident in Cheverton Court's design, the failure was literally built-in.

CHEVERTON COURT

Cheverton Court, built for single people, is part of the Phase 10 area which will almost certainly be demolished. The housing units are very small. Cheverton Court's design reflected the not unusual arrogance of the 'experts' in planning for people without taking into account their basic needs, background and social culture. Its design was written up in the professional journals. Here is a quote from the *Architects' Journal* May 10th 1978. It suggested that contact between flat occupiers would be difficult and that "architecture can and ought to allow meetings between individuals in a subtle way."

The article further stated: "The feeling of security within each dwelling is very pronounced, with three enclosed walls, and although orientation is direct to the City below, including the Victoria Centre housing slabs which are a prominent landmark, it is difficult to imagine where the other flats are in relation to one's own due to the nature of the sloping section. This reinforces the independence of one flat from another." This sounds like a recipe for personal disintegration for people culturally used to friendly neighbourhoods.

Cheverton Court. Photo: Architects' Journal 1978

SHELTERED ACCOMMODATION FOR ELDERS

A list of the City Council's sheltered accommodation in St Ann's is given earlier. I spoke with elders from several complexes and interviewed Florence Rhodes who lives in one.

The City Housing Department told me [2001] that the Social Services Committee of July 2000 approved the refurbishment of one wing of The Oaks to provide specialist facilities for 12 men over 55 who have complex care needs and require a planned rehabilitation programme.

"The development is designed to provide a more appropriate service than traditional long-term care for this socially excluded group who make up a substantial percentage of residents at The Oaks. This wing of The Oaks has been renamed Acorn Lodge and residents of this wing are referred from Hospital or from the Community if they have become too frail to maintain their previous lifestyle. They need twenty-four hour support initially and a per od of recuperation pr or to starting a rehabilitation programme designed to enable them to move into their own accommodation after 3-6 months.

"The Salvation Army have worked closely with officers to identify the need for this provision for this older age group and to offer their specialist advice on how to promote independent living for this group.

"In April 2001 the Housing and Social Services Board agreed to the closure of Long Hedge as from 31 August

2001 Whilst the former residents have all been rehoused, Long Hedge is being used on a temporary basis to accommodate the residents of the other wing of The Oaks as it is now closed for refurbishing. Following refurbishment, this wing of The Oaks will be opened again, the temporary residents of Long Hedge will return to The Oaks and Long Hedge will then close."

The **Bullace Court** Community Centre of the City Council's Bullace Road complex, from Westgate Street/St Ann's Well Road. Photos: Ruth I Johns 2001

*Acacia Court is one of **Tuntum Housing** complexes for elders. The building design offers a pleasing post-redevelopment design. It is a sheltered scheme for active elders over fifty-five and is suitable for single people and couples. It is primarily, but not exclusively, for African Caribbean elders. It has 32 one and two bedroom flats and good communal facilities*

HOMELESS families and single people

There is provision for people in need of a home in St Ann's, but I do not think it would be helpful to them to publish photographs of specific locations.

CLOSURE OF THE PSYCHIATRIC HOSPITALS

Mapperley Hospital and Coppice Hospital are shown on the 1968 map. In previous times both were called Lunatic Asylums. St Ann's Women's Hospital, also a Psychiatric Hospital is just off the map, also on Porchester Road.

Mapperley and St Ann's Hospitals were beyond St Ann's, though historically there was a close link because of proximity. **Coppice Hospital** was within the district. With the changes in Mental Health legislation and practise, large hospitals have given way to smaller units and community based services. All three hospitals have closed.

The Coppice Hospital in recent years has been converted into private housing apartments, called Hine Hall, see below. Mapperley Hospital and grounds are also largely being taken over for housing. There are still units and clinics involved with mental health in the same vicinity. There is also the Priory Clinic on Ransom Road, within St Ann's, which is a specialist clinic, founded in 1990, for patients suffering from alcohol or drug problems. It works with both the private and public sector patients.

The Priory Clinic

People have talked about mental health experiences in confidence. There are a lot of good things happening in service provision and many things which need more understanding. I used to visit all three of the hospitals regularly when I worked for Family First and one or more of its tenants were hospitalised.

There is a history project needing to be done around Mapperley Hospital, Coppice Hospital and St Ann's Women's Hospital and the services which have come in their wake. The issues around mental health are huge and urgent.

PEASE HILL CENTRE

by **Margaret Smith**,
Administrative Assistant and Secretary 2001

*Pease Hill Centre, Furze Gardens, off Abbotsford Drive, St Ann's, is part of the Nottinghamshire NHS Trust, **Health Care of the Elderly** Directorate.*

Pease Hill Centre was opened in September 1993 to provide residential, day-care and community services for older people with mental health needs in the City Centre South and East areas of Nottingham City.

The Pease Hill Centre. Photos: E James Smalley

The building was originally a Nottingham County Council old persons' residential home, which has now been considerably refurbished. It has been extended to provide a main kitchen, which gives all on-site catering. The residential unit has a large lounge opening on to a screened garden area, the day hospital also has a conservatory opening on to a landscaped garden. These facilities were opened to provide a more appropriate setting for staff and patients moving from Mapperley Hospital, as part of the programme of transferring resources from hospital based to community settings.

The **day hospital** is a twenty-five place facility, which provides assessment and support to older people with mental health problems. It is envisaged that the facilities provided will develop to fulfil needs of its client group and reflect the multi-cultural society of Nottingham's inner-city areas, thus increasing the contact between the services provided and the local community.

The **residential unit** provides long and short-term care, assessment, treatment and support in as homely an atmosphere as possible. It strives to provide the best possible quality of life for patients in a safe and supported environment and provides twenty-four residential places, two of which are reserved for respite care, for people requiring long-term NHS continuing care. All patients at Pease Hill are under the care of a Consultant in Old Age Psychiatry.

The multidisciplinary community team based at Pease Hill provides the services of Community Psychiatric Nurses, Physiotherapists, Occupational Therapists and Social Workers, who visit people in their own homes to provide assessment, advice and support to both patients and their carers.

Changes in recent Government legislation recognise the complex health needs of many older people and our service continues to develop and change to meet these changing needs in today's society. We welcome feedback from all users of our service so that we continually maintain our standards of care delivery.

HINE HALL

The Coppice Hospital, now turned into apartments under the name of Hine Hall, was designed by Nottingham's well known Victorian Architect T C Hine in 1857-59. It was built as the County Lunatic Asylum.

Looking over Kendale Court, the long block of flats backing The Wells Road, to Hine Hall. This gives some idea of the size of the building. Between Kendale Court and Hine Hall from this angle, we see a small private estate where most people would say St Ann's ends. St Ann's is to the left and Hine Hall from its front face overlooks it. Photo: E James Smalley 2002

Ken Brand[1] writes: "It has all the Hine characteristics: patterned brickwork, large mullioned windows and Elizabethan gables. The hospital provided accommodation for thirty male and thirty female patients. A feature of the interior was Hine's patented device for gas lighting combined with a complex form of air-conditioning.

"In 1890, at the age of seventy-seven, Thomas Chambers Hine retired. His son George had just moved to London and had started to build up what was to become a highly specialised practice designing lunatic asylums. Earlier, in Nottingham, George had supervised the extension of the Coppice Hospital (1880) and produced the award winning design for Mapperley Hospital built in 1887. It was this success which resulted in G T Hine being appointed as Consulting Architect to H M Commissioners in Lunacy."

The Lodge of the former Coppice Hospital on Ransom Road bears a plaque Hine Lodge. There is no longer any access to Hine Hall from Ransom Road. Photo: Ruth I Johns 2001

Peter Garner wrote to me stating that the Coppice Hospital was built on part of the original Alexandra Park, on a projection overlooking the valley of The Wells Road, on land occupying seventeen acres. It was for patients of the upper and middle classes but for those unable to pay the cost was covered. It was funded from a charity founded in 1789. With the advent of the National Health Service, of course, organisation of hospitals changed.

Some of the Coppice Hospital land was sold to Metropolitan Housing Association for its 1976 estate.

---

[1] *T C Hine. Architect of Victorian Nottingham* by Ken Brand. Getting to know Nottingham 6: Nottingham Civic Society. Undated.

PEDESTRIAN ACCESS
from St Ann's to the City Centre

The question of pedestrian access from St Ann's to the City Centre arose when Victoria Station was demolished and the high-rise Victoria Centre developed on its site.

The Chairman of Capital and Counties Property Company Ltd, Mr Leslie Marler, reported that the development of the Victoria Centre would include a pedestrian overbridge to the [new] St Ann's Well Road development area which would house 20,000 people within a few minutes walk of the scheme. Architecture East Midlands, August/September 1968.

The Victoria Centre opened in 1972. In a comment published in response to Mr Marler, 'CJM' said: "Pedestrian tunnels and bridges are the walled and fenced retreats of compromise and do not in any way form environmental links with the rest of the City."

There wasn't a bridge. The pedestrian approach and underpass to St Ann's leave much to be desired.

After leaving the Victoria Centre, crossing Huntingdon Street and walking down Union Road, you enter this pedestrian access to St Ann's. The road over the underpass is Shelton Street

The underpass in close-up

View after leaving the pedestrian path, walking from St Ann's down Union Road to the Victoria Centre. Union Road is an area of light industry. Photos: E James Smalley 2000

I have spoken with people who believe that St Ann's shops were so drastically reduced in number, even on the fifty initially planned for the redevelopment, because 'in influential corridors' it was thought that the St Ann's population would boost trade in the Victoria Centre.

SYCAMORE NURSERY

One interviewee mentions this former Local Authority Nursery. I remember it well because, from 1966 until 1975, the one-parent family tenants of Family First Trust who worked, took their pre-school children there. It was on Sycamore Road [which became Hungerhill Road after the redevelopment]. It was a happy nursery, but it was a marathon to walk there and then take one, sometimes two buses, to work. And do the reverse in the evening and, at the end of the week, probably only be less than £2 better off materially than staying home.

Family First built a Family Centre in Alexandra Park in 1975 for tenants and neighbourhood. It included a 30-place Day Nursery including a baby room.

The Sycamore Nursery eventually became the Phoenix Centre, a Social Services Department run Family Centre, with a remit to provide support and advice for parents and vulnerable children under five. In 2001 it was closed despite local protest. Councillor Betty Higgins said only 60% of places at the City's ten Family Centres were taken. The Larkdale Family Centre on the City edge of the St Ann's area was reprieved for the time being and St Ann's Family Centre in Magson Close, on the Carlton Road edge of the area, was never under threat and continues. The Sure Start scheme is one factor deciding changes of under-school age amenities in St Ann's.

On the monkey climber, Sycamore Nursery 1962-63. Photo: Pat Bostock, Nottingham Local Studies Library

The Phoenix Centre shut and boarded up. On the left of it is the Sycamore recreation ground and behind are the Hungerhill Gardens. Photo: Ruth I Johns 2002

*The former **Cavendish Cinema** (much mentioned in this book) escaped demolition when all around it was redeveloped. It is now a discount store. Its size is seen in sharp relief to the houses facing St Ann's Well Road. Photo: Ruth I Johns 2001*

St Ann's Nottingham: inner-city voices by Ruth I Johns • ISBN 0951696092

The **Medical Centre**, a doctors' surgery, is post-redevelopment on the St Ann's Well Road. The King's Hall Christian Centre (New Testament Assembly) is just seen on its left. Photo: E James Smalley 2000

Eyesore on St Ann's Well Road for too long. This former garage site is near the Chase Precinct. Photo: E James Smalley 2001

The **Chase Neighbourhood Centre**, self-built by the Chase Action Group, and written about elsewhere in the book. On its left is the Launderette run by the Chase Action Group and the Precinct's Fish Bar. The Neighbourhood Centre introduces a different style of design to the area. Photo: E James Smalley 2000

In Jon Collins' and Des Wilson's leaflet campaigning for St Ann's Ward in the May 4th 2000 City Council Elections, Debbie Hall of Robin Hood Chase said: "With their help we got the **playground** at the back of Robin Hood Chase cleaned up, new lighting and railings to stop cars getting onto the playing fields." The playground seen here in the 1980s at the back of St Ann with Emmanuel Church. Photo: Nicholson Photo Archive

WORKSPACE

Some workspace was left on the edges of St Ann's after redevelopment, including a small industrial zone (shown on the City Challenge Partnership Area map). Leaving St Ann's by the pedestrian access (photos in this section), you walk through this zone to reach Huntingdon Street and the City Centre.

There are other pre-redevelopment workspaces, including around Kilbourn Street and St Ann's Hill, and the lower end of The Wells Road. Most have been well-used. Some may soon make way for modern developments.

This is **Bancroft's factory** on Robin Hood Street. Look also at the small building on the right: Brown and Skevington, Printers. Photo: Ruth I Johns 2001

There isn't now the close connection between local workspace and the local population that there was before redevelopment. But there are local ventures in local space and shops run by local people. How local workspace can be relevant to local communities is a big subject for the future for social, economic and environmental reasons. There were people in the 1960s (e.g. David Wilkinson) who understood this.

Interviewees often describe local work pre-redevelopment. This subject, under the heading Employment, is given more space in the 'Things we did then: many we still do' section. Also see Shops. There needs to be more debate about how to introduce relevant and flexible workspace within/adjacent to largely residential areas like St Ann's.

These homes on Peas Hill Road, a short cut off road since St Ann's was redeveloped, look over the Business Centre and, rather bleakly, have the blind ends of housing at the end facing them

*Come down Colborn Street and you see Kelley Commercial Vehicles Ltd/Prime Self-Drive on **The Wells Road**. Photo: Ruth I Johns 2001*

It would be a useful project to find out what goes on in the workspace left in St Ann's. Who works there? Why? What are the linkages between people who live in St Ann's and the workspace now available?

ASHFORTH BUSINESS CENTRE

and its environment

The Ashforth Business Centre opened in 1997. It has twenty purpose-built managed workshop units designed to meet the needs of start-up and expanding businesses with flexible monthly licences. It is one of four managed workspace sites [2000] developed by Nottingham City Council's Business and Technology Group.

The Ashforth Business Centre and the new bungalows, on the Alfred Street Central side of it, are on the former site of the Ashforth Factory. They sit uneasily (in planning terms). The small business units are an attempt to bring back small workshop units. They are attractively built and maybe when Phase 10 area is redeveloped there will be some more overall 'community planning' to link up space in a friendly way.

Entrance to the Ashforth Business Centre showing wall with the new bungalows beyond

The Ashforth Business Centre with Pakistan Centre in background

Inside the Business complex. Photos: Ruth I Johns 2001

Across the Woodborough Road from the Peas Hill Road is the **Phase 10 Marple Square** area which is about to be partly demolished and regenerated. The **Welbeck Workshops** were introduced on the City side of Marple Square to try to improve work/environment but the workshops have not all been taken up.

The Welbeck Workshops in the Marple Square complex, seen from the City side. The photo was taken from the car park on the opposite side of the road. Photo: Ruth I Johns 2001

If you walk past the Workshop entrance to the left of this photo, you come to **Balisier Court** on your right-hand. Run by Tuntum Housing, it is a sheltered housing scheme for frail elders. It is stranded between Marple Square and the walkway to Welbeck Close through to St Ann's Way.

Balisier Court looks like this from the front. There is no housing facing Balisier Court, only a car park. Photo: Ruth I Johns 2001

This is what it looks like behind. Photo: Tuntum Housing. Which raises the question of whether we can reclaim an urban environment which is friendly on the public side?

*And here is **Welbeck Close** from the St Ann's Way end. The Pakistan Centre is just visible. To get to the Woodborough Road, you walk down Welbeck Close, through the pedestrian way, then you come to Balisier Court on your left, then the City side of Marple Square where Welbeck Workshops are. Photo: Ruth I Johns 2001*

It is hard to see from these photos that this is quite a densely housed area. But where is the feel of friendly public space? Young people grumble about the 'bits of green' - as in front of the Welbeck Walk sign - because they cannot use them for any activity. And should a group of youngsters congregate just to chat, they tend to be viewed as threatening.

SYCAMORE BUSINESS CENTRE

See under Sycamore Millennium and Business Centre. This recently opened centre on Hungerhill Road uses part of the premises of the former Sycamore School. The premises survived St Ann's redevelopment.

SMALL FACTORY OUTSIDE REDEVELOPMENT AREA

From its start in 1965, Family First Ltd (formerly Family First Trust) was primarily a housing association and it still is. From the start, it developed a range of community services including a Furniture and Clothing Service. By the 1980s, the Service needed larger premises. Around 1983, it moved to small factory premises in Kilbourn Street, St Ann's. These premises were outside the St Ann's redevelopment area. The factory space was flexible.

The Furniture Service has developed steadily over the years. In 2001 it was used by some 100 statutory and voluntary agencies. It has recently developed a white goods section which repairs electrical equipment. In the first year of this new endeavour, FF supplied more than

This is the central isle in Family First's Kilbourn Street premises after they were renovated by supervised trainees. In the background, one of the few 'original' large factory buildings remaining after redevelopment. Photo: Ruth I Johns c1983

Phil Moody, FF Manager responsible for organising the opening of the Kilbourn Street premises. Photo: Ruth I Johns c1983

Left, Ernie George, Workshop Supervisor, instructs trainee Allan White on a white goods repair task at Kilbourn Street. Photo: Terry Campbell 2001

Volunteers sorting clothes at Kilbourn Street. Left, Joan Harris, and Joan Webster. Photo: Terry Campbell 2001

500 items to referral clients or for sale in FF shops. This activity is an important social economy activity. It benefits those on low incomes who obtain electrical equipment which meets stringent safety requirements; trainees who learn important skills; agencies which save time (= money); the environment and staff.

The replacement value of furniture supplied by FF in 2001 was £1.85m. FF's Kidstuff collects and distributes children's clothing and equipment. It had 764 clients in 2001. And the FF shops, staffed by volunteers, help to underpin the Furniture and Kidstuff services.

The areas of St Ann's which escaped redevelopment still attract versatile use. For example, in 1999 Eddie Izzard, comedian and dyslexic himself, opened Nottinghamshire Dyslexia Association Resource and Lifelong Learning Centre in St Bartholomew's Road, St Ann's. In 2000, more than 4,000 people accessed these services, said Dee Caunt, General Manager.

Family First moved its administrative offices to 375, Alfred Street North, on the same site a few years ago. One of the fleet of vans, which are a familiar sight in the City, in front of FF's offices. Photo: Ruth I Johns 2002

ST ANN'S NOTTINGHAM: inner-city voices *by Ruth I Johns* • ISBN 0951696092

THE FUTURE?

What will happen to St Ann's built environment, and therefore its social environment, in the future? There is already tension between those who want to exploit St Ann's nearness to the City Centre for upmarket housing development, and those who want St Ann's to be an inner-city area in which a wide range of people, many on limited incomes, can have a decent life in community with each other.

Much energy and finance has been soaked up in recent years to bring the 1970s St Ann's housing up to standard. There is a danger that people will relax their guard and future built environment decisions may be made before local people see what the consequences are likely to be for them. What do I mean by this?

Around the edges of St Ann's, there are buildings which developers are already interested in or may become so. And there are areas of St Ann's - also on its edges - which escaped the major redevelopment of the late 1960s and early 1970s, but which are now seen by some as needing redevelopment.

There is the possibility, therefore, for St Ann's being reduced to its central 'Wimpey core', hemmed in by expensive property by people whose lifestyles would not bring them into St Ann's. There would be unpleasant social consequences.

The Metropolitan Housing Trust estate could be separated from the core of St Ann's if unbridled market economy redevelopment took place around lower Ransom Road/Cromer Road and some of the Blue Bell Hill area, thus linking up to the existing private housing on, say, Ball Street, Colbourn Street, Richmond Avenue, Abbey Grove, Botany Avenue and Hendon Rise with consequential increase in prices. One of the severe problems in the St Ann's District is that there is very little affordable property for purchase. It cannot lose the affordable houses it has without bad social consequences. Many people, who live in these roads now, are an active part of life in St Ann's.

Maybe the older areas will be allowed to remain or, if they are redeveloped, they could be developed in some way

Looking down to St Ann's Well Road. The empty site straight in front was a garage. The photo shows part of the 'Wimpey core'. The line of trees at the left is Robin Hood Chase, reaching Woodborough Road at the top of the hill. Photo: Ruth I Johns 2002

as co-operative ventures for the benefit of St Ann's people including existing owners. Owners in the 'old' St Ann's were treated badly at the time of the major redevelopment. This was spoken about in The Transition Years section.

Readers of this book can be left in no doubt that there are many people who like inner-city living, not to be confused with City Centre living. When St Annies were forced to leave in the late 1960s and early 1970s, many eventually came back to an inner-city because they liked the lifestyle. Although some people in St Ann's would move out if they could afford to, very many would stay. Some who could afford to move out choose not to. There are skilled people who choose to work in St Ann's even though they could be earning much more using the same skills elsewhere.

Being on a modest income is not a character defect. Affirmation is needed of people in communities who value aspects of their social culture more than judging it only in financial terms. Of course, this view can be misrepresented. It is <u>not</u> a justification of poverty. But, we live in times when many people from the affluent sections of society seem unable to grasp the fact that not everybody wants to live like them.

The Victoria Centre from St Ann's. Photos: E James Smalley 2002

Photos at the beginning of this section show the Wimpey core of St Ann's.

The idea that St Ann's could be diminished to its Wimpey core never occurred to me before starting this book, even though I had been harassed by a developer who wanted to purchase the flat I have on the edge of St Ann's. He had the idea of buying up several small ones and making them into redesigned expensive ones. I told him this idea wouldn't go down well in St Ann's. He said: "Well if development takes place, it needn't be St Ann's." I replied that I wanted to be in St Ann's. And I wouldn't change my mind. St Ann's needs its edge areas to create diversity of built environment, including affordable owner-occupied accommodation.

The Victoria Centre makes a wall along one side of St Ann's on the City Centre side. This is now a familiar feature, compensated for because St Ann's is not hemmed in on its other three sides: yet.

Plans for a 13-storey 'apart-hotel' on the site of the former postal sorting office on Huntingdon Street were approved in 2001. The plan includes 144 rental apartments and 193 residential flats. This building will be a further 'wall' on the City Centre side of St Ann's.

In the *Nottingham Evening Post* of April 23rd 2001, a £2m scheme was shown for a 40-flat scheme in the grounds of St Catharine's Church and next to St Mary's Rest Garden. This scheme is in St Ann's and I anticipate the flats will be high-cost.

The flats already built at The Marlborough on Cranmer Street are, as the agents say "on the outskirts of the City Centre close to Mapperley Park." Arguably, they are just outside St Ann's but they are part of the trend. These were selling in 2001 for £135,000 - £185,000. Some are no larger than my St Ann's flat: value £29,000. That is the extent of cost difference between inner-city and City Centre prices. St Ann's must remain inner-city not City Centre.

The former Coppice Hospital is already - as Hine Hall (see earlier) - apartments, with its access into St Ann's closed off.

There are substantial buildings that could become high-cost apartments depending on City Council planning policies and the actions of others involved. The Gordon Boys' Home on Cranmer Street?

Alexandra Court will soon cease to be a Hostel for 160 people. Some have been there for over ten years. The Council has stated it cannot afford the cost of modernisation of Alexandra Court and has yet to decide on its post 2004 future. Although just outside St Ann's, Alexandra Court has always been closely linked to St Ann's through decades of its residents.

Alexandra Court. Photo: Nottingham Evening Post 2000

Bancroft's elegant factory on Robin Hood Street survived the redevelopment. Will it become expensive loft-style apartments?

I could go on! The question arises, will the St Ann's community - and those working with it - take action in time to ensure that a substantial part of future development remains accessible for people who want to live in inner-city St Ann's? The consequences of diminishing the district to the Wimpey core would be socially disastrous. If that happened, some years on planners would conclude that St Ann's should be taken out. And redeveloped as what?

An artist's impression of the proposed flats viewed from King Edward Street. The headline above it reads 'Flats scheme for inner-city churchyard.' The site is at the junction of Bath Street and St Ann's Well Road. From Nottingham Evening Post April 23rd 2001

Bancroft's factory from Victoria Park. Photo: Ruth I Johns 2001

By the time the 1960s redevelopment plans for St Ann's were made, there was already plenty of evidence from other parts of the UK that such schemes were very problematic. Yet, by dint of much effort, struggle and helping each other out, St Ann's people have - despite the problems - made St Ann's a place worth striving for. All the investment to help make good the buildings and amenities has helped, but money alone doesn't make for a sense of community. Or, as Bill Chambers said: "They can come and paint it, put chandeliers on all the lamps, but it's only the people in the area that count."

There is now much evidence from other areas of the UK that if inner-city areas are taken over for upmarket development, then there is a desperate dearth of affordable central housing for people on modest incomes. The consequences of this, socially and economically, are dire.

As it becomes necessary to redevelop or develop sites in St Ann's, can we see some of the good practice, now known to be socially and economically valuable, take place? St Ann's could then become an inner-city which, to use the modern jargon, reaches its potential.

Pubs

The number of pubs in St Ann's now, shown in photos in this section, is a fraction of the number in the 'old' St Ann's. A list of St Ann's pubs in 1956 is given below.

Some of the pubs on the 1956 list changed names in the following decade but almost all disappeared at the time of demolition. A few escaped demolition because they were on the edge of the area, for example, *The Lord Alcester*, the *Mechanic's Arms* [now the *Pride of Erin*] and the *Foresters' Arms*.

I contacted several of the large breweries which own pubs in St Ann's to see if they wished to provide any history of particular pubs. The responses? Either nobody who could offer a thought on the subject or I was told they had nothing. Or they: "were too busy running pubs to worry about their history." Short-sighted?

It is hard to come to any other conclusion than that there must have been some agenda to the wholesale demolition of these community landmarks. I have spoken to knowledgeable people who were sure there was a plan to limit pubs in the 'new' St Ann's to specific breweries. Many pubs were 'fit' buildings as shown in the City Council schedules at the time compulsory purchase orders were made. Some were interesting buildings. Retaining the good pub buildings would have offered 'character' to the new St Ann's.

At the time, the reason given for their demolition was because it was easier and cheaper to develop a totally cleared site. But many readers will recall from their own experience of other redeveloped areas around the country that pubs were often left standing.

Many older people talk of the 'old' pubs and the events which took place in them, including piano playing and singing, outings, annual celebrations, workplace events and family celebrations. Today, outings, entertainment and/or events are still on offer in some of the current pubs. But running a community pub is harder than it once was because of the pressures placed on licensees.

Most St Ann's pubs do not provide food: "because locals go home to eat". In 2000, *The Woodborough* started providing food and Sunday lunches in particular. These days, as a generalisation, people don't come into St Ann's to pubs except those who once lived in the district who come back to drink with friends, or those who live in nearby areas. The Gladstone Club on Manning Street has members who come from a wider area.

Harold Smith [1999] told me that pubs and clubs used to do trips down Gedling Pit [now closed]. Tony Burt said it was up to the Pit Deputy to decide who was going down.

The wife, of a husband and wife team, who kept a pub on the edge of St Ann's for fifteen years said [1999]: "We were never offered any drugs. My son-in-law is in the Police Special Branch and says high-class villains are worse than the locals."

A few pubs with large car parks have experienced problems (e.g. drug trading) and different solutions have been found, for example locking off the car park. Pub car parks in St Ann's are little used, unless near to the City and used for near-city parking. Some years ago because of problems, the Craven Arms was shut down and demolished [where Hawk's Cycles now stands on the Woodborough Road]. In 2002, the *Welcome Inn* was temporarily closed after a police raid as part of its Operation Real Estate set up in 2000.

> In 1968, Truman's Brewery, owners of the **Robin Hood Social Club** on the corner of Corporation Road and Dame Agnes Street, appealed against a Compulsory Purchase Order. Mr A W Congdon for the brewery said the Club building was only forty years old and the Club had a large membership. It was unique in having its own skittle alley. Mr E W S Martin, Corporation Estates Surveyor, said the Club was modern and in good condition. But if it was left standing on its corner site, redevelopment plans would have to be revised. The Corporation had no obligation to find alternative premises for commercial enterprises. *Guardian Journal* 25.7.68.

ALICE THEAKSTONE

*Contribution given by Alice Theakstone at the 1998 St Ann's Library Reminiscence Day. Alice Theakstone has since died. From 1958-1972, Alice Theakstone and her husband kept the **General Cathcart**, St Ann's*

The Cathcart was owned by Home Breweries. It had a large stained glass window of General Cathcart on horseback. Previous to that we had the Cricketer's Rest, then the Nag's

Head in the Meadows. After we closed [time of demolition in the area], we went to the Lord Alcester [edge of St Ann's] for four years.

The people were wonderful. They were always busy. On Mondays, the women would sit there shelling peas. And they'd bring their lace work too. There was Bill Marriott, who delivered for Shipstone's; lots of pubs gave him a pint on his way round, then he'd come into us on his way home, singing. Some had a garden up at Hungerhill and would bring in chrysanthemums etc to sell round, always a bit for me. There was Elsie Pace, she'd come in every day: 'Give us a jar!'

There was a sweet factory on Abbotsford Road and a chap used to bring in a bag of chopped sweets for the kids. There was Billy Fewkes, we called him 'Conchie'. A lot of the old chaps always wore a buttonhole (a carnation or a rose) from the garden.

We didn't know a soul before we went to the Cathcart. But everyone was so friendly. As soon as we arrived, Mrs Sewell next door, who used to keep the pub, said: 'I'll do the cellar while you get sorted out.' Dolly Calladine said: 'Come across for bread.' There was never any bother on Cathcart Street.

It was hard work though. The beer was all hand-pulled, and you'd be struggling in the cellar. When we closed at night, we had to soak the pumps in salt to clean them. We emptied all the ashtrays (people smoked a lot then). Then we did the sweeping. We'd do the mopping next morning. During the week we opened 10.30 till 3.00 and from 6.00 until 10.00 (and then 10.30). On Sundays we opened 12.00 till 2.00 and from 7.00 till 10.00. The police were strict about closing time.

We sold mainly beer, not shorts. Catering was my own little sideline. I put aside the money for the kids' bikes, then a butcher's van for Donald when he passed his test. I did ham rolls, pork and stuffing rolls, potted meat rolls, a dish of pickled onions. One time when we ran out, I got 3lbs of tripe, washed it and cut it into pieces and the darts team tucked in. I did hot pies and Cornish pasties and kids queued up at the back door on Fridays, then went on for chips. You could eat for one shilling and nine or eleven pence. On tote night, which was about every three months, it was a free night until 9.00. I cooked legs of pork, chickens and did sandwiches and crackling. I cooked all day long for that and borrowed the dishes off Sid Shaw at the butcher's.

We had table skittles and a good darts team. When we left, the skittles team bought me a large canteen of cutlery with wooden handles. The darts ladies gave me a blue vase.

On Easter Monday, we had an Easter bonnet competition. People made their own. They were very fancy, even real eggshells with chickens in them on their hats. On bonfire night they used to have a bonfire on the street with furniture, mattresses and dressing tables. Next day, there was a hole in the road where the tar had burnt.

Most Christmas and New Year's Eves, after we closed, they used to hang around Cathcart Street waiting for us to come out and let the New Year in. We'd put three or four gallon jugs outside on the table in the yard. Danny, with his piano accordion would be dancing round the lampost. We had a Conga from the Garden Gate pub up to our pub. There was a great spirit.

The General Cathcart Skittles Club Outing 1958. Photo: source, Alice Theakstone's family via Les Oliver, Nottingham Local Studies Library

ST ANN'S NOTTINGHAM: inner city voices by Ruth I Johns • ISBN 0951696092

LIST OF ST ANN'S PUBS

from Kelly's Directory 1956

Adjutant White, 16, Hungerhill Road
Admiral Dundas, 62, St Ann's Well Road
Alfred the Great, 15, Alfred Street South
Barley Mow, 2, Clarence Street
Bath Inn, 1, Handel Street
Bay Horse, 185, Alfred Street Central
Blue Bell Inn, 90, Robin Hood Street
Broad Oak Pool Inn, 39, Corporation Road
Chase Tavern, 140, St Ann's Well Road
Coachmaker's Arms, 109, St Ann's Well Road
Craven Arms, 108, Woodborough Road
Criterion, 147, Alfred Street South
Curzon Arms, 23, Curzon Street
Dame Agnes Inn, 44, Dame Agnes Street
Devonshire Arms, 39, Hawkridge Street
Duke of Cambridge, 1, Clarence Street
Earl of Lincoln's Arms, 70, Woodborough Road
Empress Eugenie, 105, Alfred Street South
Enterprise Hotel, 176, Woodborough Road
Foresters' Inn, 183, Huntingdon Street
Foxhound Inn, 95, Union Road
Freeman's Arms, 209, Alfred Street Central
Garden Gate, 223, St Ann's Well Road
General Cathcart, 48, Cathcart Street
Hero of Waterloo, 27, Hutchinson Street
Hop Bloom Inn, 38, Blue Bell Hill Road
King Edgar, 20, Peas Hill Road
Livingstone Hotel, 123, Blue Bell Hill Road
Lord Alcester, 100, Pym Street
Lord Belper, 76, Robin Hood Street
Mechanic's Arms, 373, Alfred Street North
Napoleon, 55, St Ann's Well Road
New Inn, 56, Union Road
New Town Inn, 75, Northumberland Street
Old Bricklayers Arms, 14, Lewis Street
Oliver Cromwell, 127, St Ann's Well Road
Prince Leopold, 29/31, Moffat Street
Princess Royal, 89, Northumberland Street
Queen's Arms, 345 & 347, St Ann's Well Road
Robin Hood Arms, 41, Robin Hood Street
Royal Foresters, 111, Peas Hill Road
St Ann's Well Inn, 173, St Ann's Well Road
Scots Greys Inn, 245, St Ann's Well Road
Sir C Campbell, 11, Robin Hood Street
Sir Garnet Wolseley, 9, Gordon Road
Sir R Clifton, 22, Bath Street
Sir Rowland Hill, 80 & 82, Hungerhill Road
Stanley Hotel, 126, Sycamore Road
Sycamore Inn, 20, Sycamore Road
Union Inn, 17, Union Road
Unity Inn, 86, Peas Hill Road
Victory Inn, 69, Alfred Street South
Vine Inn, 26, Handel Street
Westminster Abbey, 387, St Ann's Well Road
Zetland Arms, 44, Welbeck Street

Hero of Waterloo, corner of Hedderley Street and Hutchinson Street. Sunday morning outing, May 1952. Photo: source, Mr Sleaford, Nottingham Local Studies Library

Among the **Compulsory Purchase Orders** I have seen, the pubs which were deemed 'fit' - but demolished in St Ann's redevelopment for planning convenience - included the Garden Gate, 223, St Ann's Well Road; the General Cathcart, 48, Cathcart Street; the Scots Greys Inn, 245, St Ann's Well Road; St Ann's Well Inn, 173, St Ann's Well Road; the Oliver Cromwell, 127, St Ann's Well Road; Napoleon Inn, 55/57, St Ann's Well Road; New Inn, 56/56a, Union Road; Foxhound Inn, 95, Union Road and the Coachmaker's Arms, 109, St Ann's Well Road.

The St Ann's Well Inn waiting to come down. Photo: Nicholson Photo Archive

The General Havelock, on the corner of Meredith Street and St Ann's Well Road, waiting to come down. Photo: Nicholson Photo Archive

FORESTERS ARMS

This is one of the few St Ann's pubs that escaped demolition.

The Foresters Arms as it was 1936-1945. Photo: Nottingham Local Studies Library

St Ann's Street 1976 and the Foresters Arms escapes demolition. There used to be a footbridge from St Ann's Street over the former Victoria Station (behind the camera)

The Foresters Arms 2001. Photo: E James Smalley

JUNE HUMPHRIES

Born 1944

*Interviewed at the **Foresters Arms**, St Ann's Street, St Ann's 29.9.99. June Humphries is Co-Manager of the Foresters Arms*

I manage this pub with my partner. We've been here two years. But I've been a regular here for thirty-odd years.

Before St Ann's was knocked down, this pub on St Ann's Street was on a thoroughfare from the City, when you could walk from Huntingdon Street right through Alfred Street down to Carlton. It used to be quite nice you know. All the big houses and that. With all the demolition and development, it's changed. Union Road used to be across the road where the motor dealer now is.

Now the pub's between the Victoria flats and the St Ann's industrial area. We do get a flux of people during the day but at night it is definitely a gay pub. They also come from Leicester, I've known them come from London, Birmingham and Manchester. Saturday is our busiest night.

I was born in Wrexham, North Wales. I joined the Army when I was seventeen and came to Nottingham when I was twenty in the mid-sixties. I was living on Lenton Boulevard with a friend and came to this pub because it was a gay pub. It's always been known as a girls pub.

On Tuesday, we have a Karaoke night, Thursday night line dancing which my partner teaches and then a disco. Friday, Saturday and Sunday we have a disco. Monday night we play darts. It's only Wednesdays that's quiet really.

Before we were working for a holding company. Holding companies buy run-down pubs, put a manager in to see if they can make anything of it. They hold a pub until they decide to make a go of it and keep it or until it's sold. We got moved from here to there and

June Humphries 2001

ST ANN'S NOTTINGHAM: inner-city voices by Ruth I Johns • ISBN 0951696092

everywhere. I had the Nelson on Hockley before I came here. That got sold. I heard this was coming up and went for it. I live above the premises but I've got a house in Sneinton as well.

This is a Scottish and Newcastle pub. I'm quite happy with them and settled now. I've got the pub I wanted. Jeff and Carol who ran it before were big friends of mine. Carol died unfortunately. Jeff's retired.

It's hard work but worthwhile. I get up at about nine and it's a twenty-four hours a day, seven days a week job, but we enjoy it. All my friends are here, all the regulars, so it's nice.

In the sixties everything was hush-hush you know. This is the oldest running gay pub in Nottingham. There was the Napier (Dog and Partridge as it was then) and here. When I came to Nottingham, nobody was supposed to know were they? The police never gave any trouble, it was just understood. Now it's not even a topic.

At the time of St Ann's demolition, I lived in the Meadows. We used to go to these two pubs in the evenings. But I knew St Ann's quite well. We used to walk from the pub at the top of Alfred Street [now the Pride of Erin] and you could walk right down through to all the old pubs. It was a very close-knit area then. At the moment there's drugs over the Huntingdon Street end which is a shame really. Here it's lovely.

I'd like this to be known as the oldest gay pub in Nottingham because there are people who have been coming in for over thirty years. I don't have any old photos. Jeff had loads of them on the wall and when he left, somebody took them. I really wanted them. He said, when he left I could have them.

This [the back patio area with tables] used to come up to an entry with ladies' toilets and men's toilets. It was only a little yard then and an 'L' shaped room in there. You can see changes have made a big difference. I would imagine the pub was built about one hundred and fifty years ago. As far as I know it's always had the same name. There used to be a little paper shop next door.

This is the only pub around here that's got a yard. You could be in the country couldn't you? [Though very near, the Victoria flats aren't visible.]

We advertise all the venues and whatever's on in different pubs. We do a lot of crazy nights like dress up nights. We support charity a lot. I have been known to have three charities going at once. We might have a charity night and all proceeds to charity. Not long ago, we raised £250 for Comic Relief. We had one or two who had their hair shaved off. We do our bit.

Since September 2001, the Co-Managers of The Foresters Arms are Lorraine Hatton and Debbie Law. June Humphries decided to take early retirement after years in the pub trade and [2002] she says: "I'm thoroughly enjoying the quiet life."

Two other pubs which escaped demolition.

The Pride of Erin on the corner of Alfred Street North and St Ann's Way. Photo: E James Smalley 2001

The Lord Alcester on St Matthias Road. Photo: Ellie White 2001

'NEW' PUBS

The Gardeners on The Wells Road with Kendale Court behind it. This is the pub linked to the site of St Ann's Well [see last two paragraphs of Appendix I]. Built in the early 1960s. Photos: E. James Smalley 2001

Sycamore Inn on the corner on Hungerhill Road and Abbotsford Drive. Opened 1971

ST ANN'S NOTTINGHAM: inner city voices by Ruth I Johns • ISBN 0951696092

The Welcome Inn, St Ann's Well Road, formerly the Pint and Pot started up by SATRA [St Ann's Tenants and Residents Association]

The Chase, Chase Precinct. Opened 1973 replacing the Garden Gate

The Peveril on the corner of Dennett Close. Opened 1975

NB Some individual recollections may also include references to pubs. See Index.

THE WOODBOROUGH

TINA COX

Interviewed at The Woodborough, formerly the Dame Agnes Mellors, Woodborough Road just above Robin Hood Chase, St Ann's 9.9.99

It's a locals pub. It's people who live on the estate who come in here. I'm the licensee, I own the premises. It doesn't belong to a brewery. I took it over about two years ago. I've been brought up in pubs all my life. My parents had a pub on Alfreton Road. So it was just something I thought: 'Right I'll go for it'.

The Woodborough opened 1973 as the Dame Agnes Mellors. Photos: E James Smalley 2001

I thought it's something that gives me a job and home all in one go, though I don't still live on the premises now.

We changed the name when we bought the pub and it no longer belonged to Greenalls. It sits on the Woodborough Road so we called it The Woodborough. But everybody calls it the Damey. When customers ring for a taxi they say they're at the Damey and they are asked: 'Where?' And then they say The Woodborough.

When I left school at about seventeen, my dad was running a pub. My parents had split up. I couldn't serve behind the bar but I did other bits and bobs, bookkeeping, cellar, stocking the shelves up, all the bits I could do legally. Then my dad came out of the pub, had a break, got married again and had a family. And we bought this. It's just me now.

We have a Karaoke on a Friday evening and before that we have an auction. Two women run it. Everything you can possibly think of comes in, from garden furniture, televisions, household things, clothing, to bits of everything . . .

Customers come from all around St Ann's, this side and the other side of the estate and the other side of The Wells Road. Most walk. They don't park their car because they are having a drink. Sunday afternoon we have Karaoke as well in the bar. We've had a couple of ladies' nights when we've had strippers and drag artists which goes down quite well.

I don't know much about the history of the area myself. Most of the customers are men and they talk about what everyone knows men talk about: work, booze and women.

When we bought the pub, it was really run down. Greenalls were selling it so they never really bothered. This room, the lounge, was the first to be done. We ripped out the seating and put the stage in. We completely ripped the back of the bar down. The bar's been done for four months now. It was really tatty but some liked it because it was a typical working man's pub. The tarmac lads came in at half past five with filthy dirt boots and clothes. It was getting on my nerves because I wanted a really nice pub.

Many have said why do you spend so much money on your pub because, at the end of the day, it's St Ann's. Well I don't agree that because people class St Ann's as a bad area that you've got to let everything get run down. So we refitted it, did most of the work ourselves, working through the night sometimes.

And now people really love it, they absolutely love it and they say it's nice to see somebody putting so much effort into their pub. For a long time before, nobody had loved this pub. The brewery kept putting in relief managers for six months. Now I've been here two years and it's the same face all the time, and people love it.

The pub has fantastic potential sitting where it does. Even the breweries want the pub off me now.

In recent years, food has been served at the pub. It's unusual for pubs in St Ann's to do food. The pub has been sold to a brewery and Douglas Reid took over as the Landlord at The Woodborough in August 2001

THE WISHING WELL

TONY CROSS

Born 1962

*Tony Cross, Manager of the **Wishing Well**, Cardinal Close, St Ann's interviewed 11.8.99*

I was born in Doncaster. My dad was in the Army. Our family moved all over including Singapore. We ended up in Nottingham. My dad's a manager of a pub in Nottingham. He's been there eight years.

When I used to live in Birmingham, I delivered cars for Rover. I've worked at Butlins, Skegness. I've worked on the land. I moved to Nottingham when my dad got the pub. I went on a brewery trip, and I was going to ask for in-house relief so that I could take over when my dad went on holiday. But this pub came up and I got this. I've been here since July 3rd 1995 as Manager. The pub is owned by Kimberley Brewery.

I didn't know St Ann's before then. The people that's been born and bred here have told me about it. They've said the old St Ann's was brilliant, shops all down the St Ann's Well Road and lots of pubs. Most of my customers are the older generation, over 50s, but some younger ones come in now. They're mainly local and walk here.

The older customers think the problem families are being sent to St Ann's, but I don't get problems here. I don't know whether the 'good old days' were better because I wasn't here! They bring me in the *Bygones* [from the *Evening Post*]. They used to go to the pub with their dad, do odd jobs for them and get crisps, pop and whatever, that's what I hear.

Here we play pool and things. Last Tuesday we had a trip to Skegness, two busloads, and they do that at The Westminster too. I run brewery trips. Customers look around the brewery and see how things are done. The head bloke talks about hops and how they are used and so on. After the trip, you get a free bar and that's why they go!

It's getting darker [eclipse of the sun] but it's only two minutes isn't it? Mind you, it's a good money making scheme isn't it? A lot of them round here are not bothered about the eclipse.

The Wishing Well opened 1978. Photo: E James Smalley 2001

They finish work, then come in for a pint. Lunchtime trade isn't bad. Since the *Pint and Pot* shut, they come up here. We don't do food. I'm just going to open up now.

I went on a course, a week away, on how to become a manager. It's about bookkeeping, the beers, how to tap them and all sorts, how to clean . . . They are always sending memos because things are changing all the time. If you want to be a trainer yourself, you have to go on a course on how to train. My dad does that.

Managing a pub is hard, hard work. People think it's easy. They just see you this side of the bar. They don't see you earlier in the morning. Up at eight o'clock and all the things needing to be done including the books, tills and so on. It's all go. Every Sunday I have to turn the pumps. The cellar's a roll-in one so it's easy.

Jeffrey Davis said he took over as Tenant for the same owner of the Wishing Well in April 2000

THE WESTMINSTER

STAN BIRCUMSHAW

Born 1926

*Interviewed at **The Westminster**, St Ann's Well Road, St Ann's 14.9.99. The Westminster opened 1971*

Harry Carnell was the landlord here when I took over in 1972. He left that picture [pointing to a picture of the old pub in the magazine *East of the City, Autumn 1999*] on the wall here. About four or five years ago, it disappeared from the pub and it's turned up in this magazine.

The photo of the former Westminster Abbey Hotel

1970 photo with landlord Harry Carnell (in white shirt) and landlady Doll Carnell who previously owned a corner shop at the bottom of Calcutta Street. Photo: Nottingham Local Studies Library

There used to be a sign Westminster Abbey outside. It was about the only pub named after the Abbey. About twenty-five years ago they changed the name to the Wheeltappers. The big Westminster Abbey sign, which cost £3,000 and came second in a championship of the best signs in England went. They ruined the pub, made it an entertainment pub and it went down and down. And then they couldn't afford the entertainment and let it go tenanted. I came in as Manager.

I was here two and a half years, and Shipstone's then asked me to open up a brand new pub at Rainworth called the Sherwood. I spent five happy years there, and then the brewery asked me to come back here. It had been run down by management. I've been back here eighteen years. Shipstone's sold out to Greenalls about 22 years ago and Greenalls sold out to Nomura over two years ago. It's a Japanese bank!

When I first came here in 1972, the estate was still being knocked down and the new estate being built. My first wife used to stand on this doorstep in the morning when the workmen were coming in off the site and ask them to take their dirty boots off.

There was sludge everywhere. There were still two pubs left on the estate, one of them was across the road, The Havelock, and the other was the old St Ann's Inn. A smashing chap in there, he worked for our brewery for nineteen years and he had the new St Ann's Inn on Shelton Street. The old St Ann's Inn was the last pub to be knocked down. Before demolition there were over fifty pubs on this estate. Many of them Shipstone's. And there were four or five good little breweries here as well, but they all lost their licences. The Council gave them to the big three, Home Brewery, Shipstone's and Mansfield Brewery.

Maybe there was a bit more behind that than we knew. The man in charge of Shipstone's at the time was a big man on the Council. So maybe he had something to do with it.

But Shipstone's was a very good company to work for, a close-knit company. My Managing Director used to come every week and if I didn't have my light on by nine o'clock on a dark night, he'd phone up the next morning and tell me.

We had only been back at the Westminster Abbey, St Ann's, for about six months when my wife, Isabelle, died. She had the biggest funeral you ever saw in St Ann's. That room over there was chock-o-block full of wreaths. They had to put on five extra cars for the wreaths. She was a very well-liked woman.

We used to have the Chrysanthemum and Dahlia Show here, it was the biggest show in Nottingham. We had a marquee on the car park on a Friday, Saturday and Sunday with licence extensions from the Council to stay open. When Greenalls took over, they closed it because it wasn't bringing in enough extra trade to the pub. The trade became just money, money, money. They don't think about communities anymore.

The flowers were grown up on the Hungerhill allotments. They used to show them all over the county actually. The Committee met here. In the end one man, Len Page, more or less ran it and he died the morning he was going on holiday, a smashing chap, and that room over there died the day he died. After that the others let some young kids from the Wheatsheaf at Bingham take over. All the trophies went there. One was bought for £500 thirty odd years ago and stood six-feet high, a beautiful trophy. It was bought by Shipstone's.

Len Page used to run a tote and raffles and every year pensioners got £8.50 worth of groceries at Christmas from the money. He lived on Ransom Road.

The majority of pubs had pianos in those days. I bought a piano from one of my gaffers. I think it was £666. Eventually I bought an organ and then another organ. I've still got two organs upstairs. I lent the piano to our brewery and they lent it to somebody else. The last time I saw it, it was in the Sherwood pub at Rainworth. It was a wreck. All that money down the drain. Nearly all the pubs had a piano or organ and at weekends every little pub was buzzing. There was no television of course.

Pubs are bad off today. Last year, 10,000 closed down, the same the year before and this year, because the big breweries, well the companies are taking over whole estates and they are putting the rent up that high that people are leaving the trade.

The rent for this pub is £18,000 plus 3% of trade, so you are talking £25,500 for rent alone. Then you've got Council Tax, water, gas, electricity, staff, maintenance and you finish up working a lot of hours for next to nothing. I would say in the next five years, there will be at least three pubs close on this estate.

Pubs used to be centres of community activity. People now just can't afford to come out and pay the prices the brewery charges for beer today. I mean I could go down and buy my beer from a place down the Trent - a wholesale warehouse - for £65-95 a barrel cheaper than my brewery is selling it to me and I have to buy from them. My brewery must be buying it for that price.

I don't know if you saw that article in *The Sun*, an article by Littlejohn who writes every week. This article was about Wetherspoon's pubs and how they can undercut anybody. Now how can they undercut everybody and the man that runs it made £368m in six years? That shows he's buying his beer very cheap from somewhere. Now our brewery can surely buy in our beer as cheap as them. But they are not selling it as cheap to us and that's what's killing the trade.

When you think the average pint of bitter now is £1.60-£1.70 in town, out of town is dearer. My mild is £1.50 but I've been in a pub not far away, £1.64 for mild. When I first came into this trade it was one shilling and nine pence [under 20p] and one shilling and ten pence for bitter.

We used to take four busloads away from here on holiday each year. We still do trips. There's seventy-eight people going to Skegness on Saturday. We do that as often as we can arrange it. We still have Christmas parties for the children and Christmas parties for pensioners, but money is not as free as it used to be. The pub down below, I think they've run about three trips so far this year.

I'm seventy-five next year and I'm packing up. I was born in Hucknall. I was down in St Ann's 1947-49 as an insurance man. When I came out of the Army in 1947, I went back to Raleigh to work. I was Foreman when I went into the Army. When I came back, I fell out with the Managing Director. He wanted to sack some staff. I wanted to work less hours, but he wouldn't agree to this. He told me to go and sack them, so I told him to sack them himself and I packed up. Then I went on the milk round for the Co-op on Meadow Lane. I started at six o'clock and was finished by eight, so I took a part-time job collecting insurance for City and Glasgow Insurance.

I bought a house at 82, Portland Road with sixteen rooms and I used to come down St Ann's collecting insurance. Quite an experience that was. Knock on the door and a little girl says 'mum's not in tonight'. Mostly it was penny policies and endowments and things like that. I used to collect in St Ann's, Carlton, West Bridgford and Meadows. I went all over this estate on my bike.

I can remember on old lady on Denman Street, Radford. When collecting her insurance, I could never understand it because she was nearly ninety years old. I remember reading on the policies, that at seventy-five they become paid-up policies. I asked her one day why she was still paying it. It was only a penny policy. She says: 'I've paid it all my life.' I went back to the gaffer and said this old lady shouldn't be paying this policy, so she got all her money rebated. Smashing old lady she was. Every time I knocked on the door, I'd got to go in for a cup of tea.

After that I went to a firm in Hucknall called Byron Engineering, a small company building greenhouses. Seven men and five directors, but everybody worked. We would build a greenhouse and then take it out and erect it. It became quite a big company. They built some of the biggest greenhouses in the world, some on Guernsey and Jersey. They did greenhouses for one man on the south coast and all he did was grow mushrooms.

I was there three years and would have been longer. But we went to build a greenhouse in Ditchley, Surrey, for a multi-millionaire and we were there from January 4th until August 11th. When I came back Mr Bonsor of Byron Engineering gave me my cards. I said what's that for and he said: 'Your wife put in your notice last week'.

Then I went down the pit for sixteen happy years, Linby Pit, Hucknall. I started on the conveyor belt and finished at the coal face as a cutter driver. I nearly had an arm off in the machine. So I went to a Union meeting and got on a committee and then two and then three, then eleven committees and I was rarely down the pit. I had six years like that. I opened the Miners' Welfare at Hucknall. It was a good Club. George Berry, the Head Magistrate in Nottingham was on the Committee.

But that wasn't how I got my pub experience. When I joined the Army in 1943 at eighteen, I only weighed seven stone two pounds. They sent me down to Bradbury Lines in Hereford, to put some weight on and we lived on sausage, sausage, sausage. If you were caught out of bed between two o'clock and four o'clock in the afternoon, you were put on a charge because you had to rest. Otherwise it was all exercise. All the people down there were professionals including the hangman at the time.

I spent time in Glasgow Maryhill Barracks. Later in Chester, I met the Commander of Western Command and we did a party for him at Chester. Me and two friends had volunteered for the Palestine Police and we'd passed our tests. While we were waiting we were shoved in the Officer's Mess. The Palestine Police disbanded and they wanted us to join the Jordan Frontier Police. The War was nearly over so we said we were not bothered, so we stopped in the Officer's Mess and finished up in the Officer's Mess at Sandhurst. There were 600 officers.

Toward the end of the War, I was in charge of the bars and the accounts. Happy days! I never drew my wages all the time I was working in the Officers' Mess, I sent it all off to my mam. She died and my dad spent the lot. She was only thirty-nine and I was twenty-one.

While I was down the pit, my wife took a part-time job at the Wagon and Horses pub at Hucknall and she liked the trade. I'd never even thought about the trade but the Manager at Shipstone's at the time, Percy Chambers, kept asking me to take one of his pubs. I'd been married twenty-one years and had this party at the Wagon and Horses, and he talked me into taking the dirtiest, filthiest pub you've ever seen in your life. £16 a week for me and £3 for my wife. The Pot Makers at Sutton-in-Ashfield. And I packed up a job where I was on £9 odd a day, plus I got a percentage of all we took at the Miner's Welfare on the Bingo and other entertainment.

But we did all right up there, we'd got it a nice pub. Then a friend of mine died at the Nags Head in Mansfield and I went to look after his pub. Another friend in Mansfield at the White Hart died and I went to look after his pub. At one time I had five pubs, all Shipstone's. Five wages. Five £16s; a lot of money in those days. Eventually, the gaffer said which pub do you want out of the five and it was the Wagon and Horses.

After the Wagon and Horses, I came to The Westminster for the first time. It was the second biggest pub in the Brewery.

My sister had the pub now called Byron's down Church Street. She and her husband had that for eleven years. My first wife had a friend who worked there behind the counter and as a waitress but she never drank. So we used to take her a pint of milk down when we went, just for a bit of a laugh. Anyway she fell out with my sister and left.

About six months later, she answered an advertisement for bar staff and her and her sister came here for a job. Three years later we were married and we've been married twenty-four years.

I've two daughters who help me one day a week. The Government says they're allowed to earn £15, so four

Stan Bircumshaw 2001. Photos: E James Smalley

hours, that's all they are allowed to do. And my wife Linda works here. They are all out this morning. Tuesday mornings they all go down the Market [on Robin Hood Chase]. My two eldest daughters live in Bestwood and Hucknall.

I'm ready for packing up next year. I can see this trade going down and down and down and I've seen some very good friends, if they haven't gone bankrupt, they haven't been far off when they've come out. And even the Managers that have got reasonable jobs are not happy these days. When I was on Shipstone's Brewery as a Manager, I used to go round collecting for all the managers when they retired. One even now sends us a Christmas card because I collected for their son when he got leukaemia.

I've lived over the pub all these years. Everybody knows me. Between five hundred and a thousand come in here every week. From all over St Ann's, as far as Carlton, up to the Woodborough Road right over to Sherwood and down to the City. Most walk, some come by bus. Few by car. There's not a lot of passing trade.

I've locked the car park off because cars would come and people were selling drugs. Only one person ever tried to solve this out there, and that was Sergeant Williams. She got rid of it while she was local. Then there was noise and locals phoning and asking me to turn the music down near our property, so I've locked the car park off. I don't think drugs are any worse here than anywhere else, but I hate it.

When I retire, we're moving to a council house in St Ann's. I've got my daughters here, so we won't move far away. If we win the Lottery, I might buy a bigger house. A lot of landlords don't like ex-landlords coming back as customers but my wife plays in the Women's Darts team, so we'll be back. There's entertainment at weekends, usually discos. Artists are too expensive.

Two years last October, when I was made redundant when Greenalls sold out I went down to the Council because I've been on the list for thirty-one years. The following day, I got an allocation, three bedroom house. Then, of course, we stayed on for Nomura.

In the 1970s, this pub used to do twenty hog's heads a week [a hog's head is 54 gallons]. That's one thousand and eighty gallons a week, the second highest pub in the Brewery. There's only one that used to take more, and that was the Grey Mare at Clifton. But with the prices going up as I said earlier the trade has dropped. Before it used to be traditional beer. It's nearly all keg beer now. I like this keg beer myself and a lot of my customers like the keg mild. But it's the prices.

We have to buy from our company now. They buy from about six companies usually. Here it's Bass Worthington, Whitbread, Carlsberg Tetley, Scottish Courage, Guinness, Bulmer's, Matthew Clark and Schweppes.

It's not allowed in your contract to buy except from your company, with us, Nomura.

The only way you could buy yourself is if you bought a pub lock, stock and barrel, become a Free House. Then you could go to these companies yourself and buy beer yourself. There are no Free Houses in St Ann's. The Gardeners is owned by a small company. The others by

breweries, firms or In Partnership. In Partnerhip is a part of Nomura. As I said, Nomura has got 5,500 pubs all under different labels. In this country a company cannot brew beer and have more than 2,600 pubs, but that company brews beer and has 5,500.

They brew overseas. They've got three breweries in Czechoslovakia and they can get away with it. They shouldn't but this Government lets them. Nobody wants to know what's going on. I've asked *The Sun* to inquire how much these companies are paying the breweries for their beer. People think landlords are making a fortune and they don't know what they are talking about.

I mean I work on 45% gross profit. Out of that I have to pay Council Tax, rent, gas, electricity, staff . . . you are lucky to finish with £20,000. I was getting more as a Manager, but I enjoy the trade and always have done. I've signed for three years this time and we've invested quite a lot of money in it out of our redundancy from Greenalls. My wife had twenty years in. I had already 'retired' you see so I hadn't got a lot. The person who is now my Area Manager came and asked me if I would take this pub on for them, and said they'd let me have it at a cheaper price because we'd been here so long. I think the reason nobody else would take it is because it has always been known as a trouble pub. It's *not* a trouble pub at all, so eventually I got it for quite a reasonable price.

What we actually buy, as a tenant for a period of years, are the fixtures and fittings. We signed for three. Then retirement. A nice rest and maybe we'll see a bit of the world.

As I see it, for some reason St Ann's and the Meadows have a bad reputation. Even when I used to come down here and play darts in the 1940s, it had a bad reputation. People used to have a fight now and again in those days. They'd have a good scrap and then go back in and buy each other a drink. For a small while I had a pub at West Bridgford and, of course, earlier I'd delivered milk down there. It was no better than St Ann's. But down in West Bridgford they keep it under wraps.

The Westminster. Houses on the left are post-redevelopment ones on St Ann's Valley. Photo: E James Smalley 2001

ST ANN'S NOTTINGHAM: inner-city voices *by Ruth I Johns* • ISBN 0951696092

The Westminster sign. Houses on the left are on Cromer Road, which was not demolished. Photo: E James Smalley 2001

We've got about 4,000 houses on this estate and the local Police Station shuts at five o'clock. You phone up Carlton, then it goes to Sherwood Lodge, then back to Carlton . . . I phoned 999 two or three weeks ago and forty minutes later someone walked across from the Police Station. They had two cars on the road. I won't stand for any trouble in here.

Very nice Inspector we've got here. At one time we had two Inspectors. When they both retired, they came and thanked me for never calling the police out in five years. They didn't use to shut at five o'clock.

Every bit of green we had here has been built on. [A customer interjected and told Stan that building houses had started on gardens - allotments - at the back of him.] I'm surprised they haven't started building on the park up the road. There used to be a bit of green on Hungerhill Road but they built four bungalows on it [customer's voice: 'Six'].

ST ANN'S INN

*I went with Alan Hardy to his local on 1.12.99 and - with permission of Landlady Christine Wilson - recorded some conversations with customers. **St Ann's Inn**, Shelton Street, opened in 1973. Christine Wilson manages the pub for Scottish and Newcastle*

*A long time regular is **Bill Huthwaite**, a well-known flower seller on Lister Gate in the City Centre for many years until his recent retirement. He is moving to a flat near Robin Hood Chase, St Ann's. Bill Huthwaite at St Ann's Inn 1999. Photo: Alan Hardy*

- **Anon I** I was born on Caroline Street, Peas Hill Road, St Ann's. We moved to the Meadows before the time of redevelopment because our house caught fire. I was about sixteen and it was 1942. I worked in St Ann's as a window cleaner on all the roads off Woodborough Road. I fell and hit my head. They made a mistake and put me in Mapperley [Psychiatric Hospital] and then they found a haemorrhage so they rushed me to Derby. I live in St Ann's now.

- **Sam** I worked at Stanton and Staveley Iron Works, Ilkeston, for very many years. I've lived in St Ann's all my life since I came to England in 1960. It was hard work. Every time I pass here, I nip in and have a pint. St Ann's is a wonderful area. Warm friendly people. I've lived amongst them for years. I'm welcome by them and they are welcome by me. I'm eighty soon.

Four years ago, I was knocked down by a madman driver who went right over my foot on a pedestrian crossing but I never received any help or compensation, even though I worked all those years, hard work. The police took a statement but it was dropped.

I'm a member of a Baptist Church.

- **Patrick Murphy** I've lived in St Ann's for forty-two years. My dad was from Ireland. I was born here on Storer Street, on the Carlton Road side of St Ann's. I remember outside toilets, tin bath, small front room, two bedrooms for six people. I went to Manvers Pierrepont Bi-lateral School and loved it. It's closed down now. My dad died when I was about nine. The family moved to

Abbotsford Drive, St Ann's, near to where my mum now lives. I live in Sneinton now. I'm a postman in St Ann's, all over St Ann's. At present I'm doing the fringe of the area on North Sherwood Street. I work from the Central Post Office. This is my local pub. I always come back and visit pubs and friends, weekends and when I've got the day off.

In my spare time, I spend a lot of time with my little boy who's three and a half. I watch a lot of sport, follow Nottingham Forest and do a lot of reading. Before I worked for the Royal Mail, I did a lot of travelling abroad.

St Ann's is like any housing estate, say like the Meadows, Clifton, Broxtowe, Bilborough. It's got some crime, all estates have. But with it being close to the City Centre, anything that happens here hits the *Evening Post*. It gets bad publicity through the *Evening Post*. Eighty per cent of the people who live here are genuine and they'll help you out. They are much the same as they were years ago, a lot of them. My mum lives here by herself and has no problems. She's got a dog. She's not as well as she used to be, but she walks the dog, reads, watches telly, and still has neighbours and friends around her. Her second husband died a few years ago and she wouldn't move even if she won some money.

- ***Anon II*** I used to live in St Ann's up near the Police Station about ten years ago. I live in Sneinton now. I come into this pub about once a week. St Ann's is as mundane as everywhere else, though each place has its characteristics. You get to find your friends and acquaintances.

- ***James Kitchen*** I was born in 1933. I was born in Carrington and, when I was seven, we moved to Queen's Drive, the Meadows. When the Meadows was knocked down, we were allocated a house in St Ann's. We were walking around on mud, no paths for ages. But I've been in the same house since it was built.

I wouldn't want to live anywhere else. My son is in the Army in Kosovo at the moment. He phoned his mother last night and said he was going to pick up the mail for the rest of his Army pals but they wouldn't let him because there was rioting in Pristina. He was born in St Ann's. He's nearly twenty-one. My other son lives in Northampton. He was born in the Meadows. My wife gets up at five o'clock in the morning. She's over sixty but she wants to continue working. She's a supervisor in a knitwear factory.

I worked for the railway for thirty-five years. I was on Victoria Station. Victoria Station closed in 1966. The doors were closed but actually the station wasn't closed until 1968 because they were still running trains through. When they closed the doors to the Station, I was the one who gave the keys to the police to close it up. And I had to go to work at what they called Nottingham Yard just off Wilford Road.

Shutting the Station was what they called a 'Beeching axe'. Beeching had three or four jobs as well as the railway one.

I was a wheeltapper, a carriage wagon examiner. If I said a train couldn't go, it wouldn't. If I thought it was unfit it wouldn't go. Yes, I'm wearing a twenty-five year Service Award, but they still owe me two awards. There's

St Ann's Inn. Photos: E James Smalley 2001

ST ANN'S NOTTINGHAM: inner city voices by Ruth I Johns · ISBN 0951696092 only two jobs I've ever done, at Raleigh and on the railway. I worked for thirteen years at Raleigh. When Tube Investments took Raleigh over, they went down the pan as well.

I enjoyed myself on the railway, it was a passenger safety thing. I remember one instance when a train was due to go to Skegness, and two or three of my mates were on it going on a fortnight's holiday. They said to me: 'Don't dare to do anything with these carriages!' I said the carriages had come from Nottingham Midland Station and were supposed to have been examined by three different people. When the train came to Nottingham Victoria, I could only go down one side at a time, so I jumped down on the line with my tapping hammer. I've still got my tapping hammer at home.

On one of the wheels the tyre was coming loose so I went to the Inspector and put a red card on the coach, stopping it. It took half an hour to shunt that coach out with all the passengers on the platform, because you are not allowed to shunt with passengers on board. And my name was mud! The people at Nottingham Midland would come under scrutiny, because the tyre wouldn't have come loose between Nottingham Midland and Victoria Stations.

I used to come to this pub when it was on the St Ann's Well Road so I followed it round! I know the Landlady, Christine Wilson.

I used to play football. I signed on for Nottingham Forest just before I went into the Army. When I came out, I only got as far as the Reserves. I broke my ankle and that did me with football. I played for Notts County Cricket Club.

When I worked at Victoria Station, every Wednesday two of us had to go up the Clock Tower [which is still there at the front of the Victoria Centre] and we had to wind the clock with a cranking handle. The weights used to go down to the ground floor and we had to wind it up to the top. We used to have to wind it at eight o'clock every Wednesday morning. And the clock was always kept two

The Victoria Station clock tower remained after the Station was demolished The clock tower became part of the Victoria Centre complex, which is just outside St Ann's. Photo: Alan Hardy 2000

St Ann's Inn 2001. Photo: Alan Hardy

minutes fast. There was a reason for that. When people were running around for a train at, say, six o'clock, and the clock is two minutes fast, they think they've missed it and look for the next train and see they have time in hand!

I did that clock for about seven years before Victoria Station was closed down. When the Station closed the clock in the tower went automatic. The tower was made into a restaurant with different floors. I don't know how they did that because the rooms weren't as big as this one. And there was a steel spiral staircase all the way up. When I went up with an Inspector who was six-foot plus tall, every time he went round a corner he banged his head. Me being short, I didn't have that problem!

- ***Dennis Dilks*** I live in St Ann's on the Carlton side. I'm a postman delivering in Thorneywood on the edge of St Ann's. I've lived around this area all my life, for forty-five years. I was born at the Hollow Stone at the back of the Ice Stadium. My grandparents brought me up. When I was about four, we moved to Carrington Terrace on Salford Street, which is about five minutes from where I live now. I lived in Carrington Terrace until I was about seventeen.

I went to Manvers School on the Carlton Road and left at fifteen. The careers teachers were absolutely useless. I wanted to take up office work, something clerical. Their suggestion was to go in to engineering, something like that, but it didn't interest me. I'm useless at anything like that. I went out and within a week of leaving school I found my own job: clerical! I started off as an Office Junior at Hickling and Pentecost. It was a very big company on Station Road. My mate was the Stationery Buyer. He was leaving to join the RAF and he trained me up on his job, and told me to apply for it. I got the Stationery Buyer's job at seventeen. But I didn't stay so long as it was a bit tedious.

For a while, I drifted from job to job. You could leave one job one week and go to another one the following week, no problem at all. I stayed mainly in the Lace trade firms. I worked for Simon May on Weekday Cross, then Jersey Kapwood on Alfreton Road.

Then I had a spell of unemployment. Then there was a Government Scheme if you had been out of work for a certain time. I went on a scheme with the Council, putting fences and draining ditches and the like. After that year, I was unemployed for about five months and then eleven and a half years ago, I saw a job for the Post Office and applied and have been a postman ever since. I'm a single man.

I like the part of the job when you are out on delivery meeting people, but I don't like the indoor part where the management are always badgering you. But I do like the independence of the job. They are piling more work on postmen all the time, cramming in extra for no extra pay. And, of course, it makes you late going out because you're doing more sorting and taking more. About eighty per cent of our delivery is what most people call junk mail. We don't mind, but we're having to carry the weight of it. It's heavy. You are supposed to complete your first delivery round by half past nine. But if you've got four bags of mail and you don't get out delivering until seven o'clock, it's very difficult to do four bags of mail in two and a half hours.

Then you go back for sorting and take your second delivery out. And you've only got an hour to deliver that and, on my round, they've added another five hundred houses on the second delivery. You don't go to every house on a second delivery.

This has been my local pub for the past few years. The first six or so years with the Post Office, I didn't have a regular area. I could be one or two days on one area, maybe the Mapperley posh area, and one or two days on another area and so on. But, now I'm on my own delivery, and I've made this my local base, where I come when I finish work. It's a very good pub. The other side of it has been refurbished and they've got a stage area for anyone performing or for a disco. I don't go to those, because I work six days a week and I get up at three o'clock in the morning, go to work about half past four until twelve-fifteen in the day, and then I come in here. Then I go back home and have something to eat and go to bed about ten o'clock, five hours' sleep and up again. So I don't go out in the evening. This is my night-time!

There's a fellow over there near the bar, he used to be a window cleaner. He said in the old St Ann's around the late 1960s there used to be fifty-eight public houses. Everything has changed now. It was a terrible area to live in because of all the coal chimneys. And the smog and the fog was terrible. Central heating has made the atmosphere more healthy.

- **Anon III** I've been living in St Ann's about six or seven years. Before that I was nearby the area. They were good days before demolition, all different shops, different pubs. Beer was cheap, everything was cheap. A pint of beer in the City Centre now is around £2, it's cheaper here.

I was mainly in the building trade, as a labourer working for firms including Wimpey's who built this estate. The rate went up to £5 per hour. But I'm sixty now. I've finished work now.

I'm helping the Landlady, Christine Wilson, collect money for the children's Christmas Party. It's the first time I've done it this year. The party every year is for local children. The landlady is very good. It's good for the children to enjoy themselves. I come in here about three times a week.

THE BEACON

MICHAEL MASTERSON

Born 1951

*Interviewed at the **Beacon**, Blue Bell Hill Road, St Ann's 10.8.99. Michael Masterson came to St Ann's aged twelve when his parents, who came from Ireland, moved to Nottingham. He is tenant of the Beacon. His parents still live in St Ann's. The Beacon opened 1974*

The Beacon. Photos: E James Smalley 2001

I was born in Dundee, Scotland. I was about one month old when we went back to Ireland. When I was five we came to Lincolnshire, around 1956. My father bought a little house in Lincoln. Then he got work up here and we came to St Ann's in 1963. I was twelve years old.

Our family came from Achill Island off County Mayo in Ireland. I have four brothers, Patrick, Gerry, Brian and Hugh.

St Edward's Church used to be our Church on Hunt Street, St Ann's. The Church and the school was all in one building there. The Church is now on Gordon Road, with the school and Friary.

We used to do a lot of work with the Franciscan Priests at that time. We helped people. We went out and helped people at night, that's not done now. We had food parcels for the people who were old and couldn't get out and we'd do their shopping, we'd do their gardens. Most of St Ann's was terraced houses, outside toilets and backyards. At the time, we thought those days were bad but as you grow older you'd give anything to go back in time just to have a few weeks of the way it was.

You'd give anything to have a Christmas you had thirty years ago. Now it doesn't mean anything. The kids don't even look forward to it. Then, you waited for weeks and weeks to get something for Christmas. And everybody bought everybody something, whatever it was.

As a kid, I used to work for someone down on Lamartine Street. I used to collect lace and bring it round to people's houses in bags and they did the work at home. A lot of people were doing homework at that time.

I had a paper round, a heavy paper round, down there with George Smith. Ray had a haberdashery shop next door. Just along the road was Ted Bulman, he was a barber and he had all sorts of knick-knacks in the window, cheap and nasty, but if you had pocket money you'd go down there and say: 'I want a Boston please'. And he'd say: 'What does your mother say?' I'd say: 'She said I could have a Boston'. And he'd whack you around the head and just give you a 'short back and sides'. Ted, he was a character. He was the cheapest barber in town. I think we paid nine pence.

And then we'd go to the Cavendish picture house, there were loads of things to do. As we got a bit older, we'd go to a coffee bar in Trinity Square in town. You met at that coffee bar on a Sunday afternoon, expresso coffee. And as you got older still, Friday night was special. By then most people didn't work Saturdays or, if you did, only until twelve o'clock. You'd finish work on a Friday and you'd follow the pubs. There was one at the top of Union Road, it was called Room at the Top. At the White Hart upstairs there was a kind of disco, well it wasn't disco at that time, but they had music, skiffle groups.

Another highlight of the week, I played in the Greyfriars Pipe Band and we were out every weekend. We had a good pipe band. It was probably classed as one of the best pipe bands in this country and the Gordon Highlanders supported us. They sent us uniforms and things like that. It was great when you marched along with all the pipers and the drums and their own dancers. You don't see things like that any more.

Of course all the fires were coal. You could get paraffin sticks, or Zip lighters. I was taught how to clean out the ashes and then pack the fire grate with paper and timber and put a paper across the front to draw the fire up the chimney. Nine times out of ten, the paper caught fire on me. The house was freezing until you'd got the fire going. It was an awful chore at the time.

I went to St Bernadette's School on Sneinton Dale. It was not a good school. I would stand by that statement.

I became an apprentice plumber with H Cooper and Son, a jobbing firm at 125, Alfred Street South, St Ann's. We'd get a list of jobs to do in the office in the morning and load up the handcart with ladders, slates, sand, cement, paint, putty, lead, tools and, of course, the mash-can (kettle-teapot) and anything else we needed. We'd be out for the whole day all around St Ann's. In the winter, we were mostly on outside toilets where the main appliances were bursting all over the place, because we had bad winters then. We did roofs a lot. You'd have your snap and you'd make up your own tea at the side of the road. It was all cobbled stones at that time. And you'd get tea everywhere you went. People in general were very good, nice people, poor to a certain extent but not poor poor, they survived. People were cleaner even though the facilities weren't there.

I remember when I was a kid, Clifton was a new estate and many moved out there. But the nicest place that was ever around was at the top end of Alfred Street South on the verge of Carlton Road, called Stewart Place. It was beautiful. There were little cottage-type houses and I thought how could they knock that down. We went everywhere with the handcart, it was up and down and it was worse going downhill than pushing it up.

And we used to put it to the kerb to rest it. If the governor was passing, he'd have a van and if he saw you, you would get what for! If we had no work, we'd have to whitewash the stables. Our yard was like a mews where the stables had been. That's where we kept all the materials and the vans and the handcarts: opposite the Timmis Factory.

I have fond memories of Nottingham when I was a youth: the cobbled roads, the trolley buses, the smoke from the early morning chimneys, people out early going for the bus, calling into the paper shop for *The Mirror* and five Park Drive or ten if you could afford it. When I was young I assumed all adults smoked. All the workers were out early in the morning. The men had ex-Army shoulder bags for their lunch, hobnailed boots and, generally, a flat cap. The women wore long Gaberdine coats and headscarves. The men went to the pit or building sites and the women to the factories. When the factory sirens went, bicycles came from everywhere!

I remember cafes early morning, with mugs of tea and toast and dripping (you've never lived if you've never tasted toast and dripping); chatter about the night before; and the juke box in the corner playing Rock 'n Roll while you're slurping tea and eating well-done bacon sandwiches or cobs, waiting for your 'pick up' for work.

I finished my apprenticeship and went down to London in 1970 for twenty-three years. In those days, I chanced everything. I worked on the tunnels on the Victoria Underground line with a firm called Kinnear and Moody. I bluffed my way as a tunnel man. The guy I went with *was* a tunnel man. He was from Kingston, Jamaica, and he kept me with him for two years. He was a good man to me. I earned quite a lot of money and I went into business as a builder for twenty of those years in London, had work off the Westminster City Council. And then I got the feeling coming back, and I came back to Nottingham in 1993.

I didn't get married until I was thirty-three in 1983 and Eileen and I had been together for fifteen years. She comes from the same place in Ireland as I do. We have a daughter, Margaret. We didn't want Margaret growing up in London so we came to Nottingham. I'd been coming back and forth all the time I was in London to see my parents in St Ann's. My parents still live close by here along the road. That bit wasn't pulled down. It was actually quite a posh area in those days. We weren't rich or anything but we were quite proud that we were up here. Some neighbours are still here from years ago.

I was glad to be back. Some things never change: Sneinton Market, Goose Fair, Bancroft's Factory in Robin Hood Street where I had once done maintenance.

I went back to my old trade, plumbing. I posted letters all over the area, I was prepared to re-washer a house for £9, anything that would bring in the money. I've never signed on, I'd always find something to do in the week and bring money home. And then a job came up as Steward of the Greyfriars Club, the Catholic Club. Somebody said: 'Go for it'. I didn't know enough about it, so for a few days I went down to a pub, The Earl Howe run by Kevin Quinn on Carlton Road. Kevin was a childhood friend of mine and he showed me the basics.

Anyway I got the job. I said I was going to be honest and I don't want paying for a month because I don't really know a lot about the trade. And I said, if I can't hack it, you can have your keys back and you won't have lost anything. But they did give me £50 a week and then I did well, because I agreed terms if I doubled takings in six months and I did. I was there for two and a half years and went on to bonus and was able to get enough money to get this place in 1997.

I bought the tenancy of the Beacon. It's good here but not great. But I'm working and it's what I want to do. I've had staff here and I've said: 'If you don't enjoy your job, find something you enjoy. It's bad enough having to work for a living without being miserable as well!'

It's a wonderful view from here [across St Ann's to Woodborough Road hill]. The pub was built in 1974. It took the licence of the General Havelock which was on the St Ann's Well Road. It was exactly twenty-five years ago on June 19th and the following Saturday we celebrated with tickets for £7-50 and beer 30p all day. Our clientele comes from St Ann's. We have arguments here about which was such-and-such a street and where this and that was. I've got a great memory of St Ann's Well Road and Blue Bell Hill. When we came from Lincoln the trolley buses were a novelty for us. We'd sit amazed at these trolley buses on St Ann's Well Road.

My customers are pensioners and middle-aged people. I run a very strict pub as people will probably tell you. People say I've barred enough of the good drinkers and I say I'd rather have an empty pub than have blaggards. We do Bingo three nights a week. It keeps the pensioners going and they spend a lot of money here.

For Bingo nights, I buy a fridge, a washing machine, a TV, something like that. Every month I do a Big Bingo night. We have skittles, long alley skittles with a nice alley out the back; it is an old traditional thing in Nottingham. We have pool, ladies' darts, darts: just the things we used to do years ago. We used to have entertainment on a Saturday night but I've stopped it as it wasn't paying. So I got a CD player in there and customers bring in their own music and it's made things better. People like to come into a lounge for quiet chat and a drink. When you've got a band it's no good. I don't do food here. There's a chip shop at the top of the road and people eat at home.

The view across St Ann's from the Beacon car park. Photo: Ruth I Johns 2000

Left to right, Eileen Masterson, Robert McGinty, Sean Masterson, Michael Masterson and Linda Grey of the Evening Post. Sean Masterson became the youngest licensee in Great Britain [1998] and Robert McGinty became the second the following year. Photo: source Michael Masterson, Nottingham Evening Post

I've never seen anything worse in St Ann's than in any other area. There are problems with children but that always was. We just didn't realise it when we were kids. But the Press emphasises everything. At one time, you wouldn't walk by someone on the streets who needed help. Now, no wonder people don't want to help anybody because, if you report something to the police, you're scrutinised yourself. If somebody's all right with me, I'm all right with them. I'm not prejudiced.

The thing we got publicity for is for having two of the youngest licensees in Britain. I put them both through an apprenticeship. One is my nephew, Sean Masterson, and the other is related to me as well, Robert McGinty.

They worked for me since they were sixteen. Later they got their City and Guilds and I put them through a course as well. They are in the Institute of British Innkeepers. As soon as they were eighteen I put them on the course. They've got their National Licence Certificates.

We'll probably stay in Nottingham until we retire and then go back to Ireland.

Michael Masterson left the Beacon, which reverted to the brewery in February 2000, due to sudden severe ill health. By March 2002, he was recovered and hoping to run a pub again in the near future. He is busy with voluntary work, including forming the new Greyfriars Pipe Band. The previous band disbanded in 1970

Schools

SCHOOLS IN ST ANN'S

Schools and names of Head Teachers [1999] as listed by the City of Nottingham Education Department.

Schools for under-11s

- Blue Bell Hill Infant and Nursery, Gordon Road. Mrs Maureen Jarvis.
- Blue Bell Hill Junior, Gordon Road. R Alan Smith.
- Elms Primary and Nursery, Cranmer Street. Ms Jacqui Smith.
- Huntingdon Primary and Nursery, Alfred Street Central. Steve Clarke (Acting).
- Morley Junior, The Wells Road. Andy Fox.
- St Ann's Well Infant and Nursery, Hungerhill Road. Ms Lynda Barrett.
- St Augustine's RC Primary and Nursery, Park Avenue [on the edge of the area since it moved]. Bill Lewis.
- St Edward's RC Primary and Nursery, Gordon Road. Miss Helen Farrell.
- Sycamore Infant and Nursery, Abbotsford Drive. Mrs Chris Castleden.
- Sycamore Junior, Abbotsford Drive. Mrs Linda Claxton.

Secondary School

- Elliott Durham Comprehensive, Ransom Drive [on the edge of the area but the only 'Neighbourhood' Secondary School]. Mrs Kathy J Yates. Elliott Durham School was opened in new buildings in 1966. It amalgamated secondary age pupils from Sycamore Girls, Morley, and Huntingdon Boys schools.

Special School

- Rosehill School. School for age 3-16 pupils with Mild Learning Difficulties, St Matthias Road. John Pearson.

While preparing this book, I visited ten of the twelve schools listed above after writing to all of them inviting them to take part. During this time, two Headships [Elliott Durham and Huntingdon] changed, one school changed its name [Morley Junior School], two were about to amalgamate into one [the two Blue Bell Hill schools] and the remit of one extended [Rosehill]. These changes are noted in the text about particular schools.

During this period, two of the schools, Morley and Huntingdon, came out of 'Special Measures' [a euphemism for stating they were under-achieving set against Government criteria]. Both schools made a robust and successful effort to achieve, which meant that all St Ann's schools [2001] were deemed satisfactory schools. Some are in the top 25% of achieving inner-city schools nationwide. From 1997-2001, teachers in several schools expressed their belief that St Ann's would see closure of one or more of its schools 'soon'. But, during this period, no closures have taken place. St Ann's schools care deeply for their children and there is great loyalty to particular schools.

When the Adopt-a-School scheme started in 1998/99, staff of firms and organisations who volunteered to read with primary school children at first often expressed surprise that St Ann's schools were so good. It was not as they expected. Adopt-a-School covers much more than reading as is evident at Elliott Durham School.

A few years ago, I spent considerable time in Elliott Durham Comprehensive School and, with the help of past and current pupils and staff, prepared *Elliott Durham and St Anns* [Plowright Press, 1998]. The material in that book is not reproduced here, but I include an interview with the School's new Head Teacher, Rob Boothroyd, to bring the Elliott Durham story up-to-date.

Huntingdon Primary and Nursery School is the under-eleven School in the district with which I had most contact 1965-1976. When I first contacted the school about this book, it was in 'Special Measures' but its Head Teacher, Diana Owen, was very willing for the school to co-operate. Most other schools were also very pleased to be participative.

As well as the material about St Ann's schools in this section, many people mention schools in their recollections. See Index.

ST ANN'S CHURCH SCHOOL

The Rev H J Tebbutt, the first Vicar of St Ann's Church, established a temporary day school in which he had two hundred children at the beginning of 1865. A new school was erected by November 1866. Until 1870, the only free education was provided by the churches and then the era of the Board Schools began until the 1902 Education Act, when the Local Authority took over responsibility.

In 1935, the senior [eleven plus] scholars were removed, leaving Infant and Junior Departments. The school closed on January 16th 1938, and the buildings demolished in 1963. Notable Head Teachers were William Wheatley, John Neil Colleypriest, E J Morrison, the Misses E Baker, A Litchfield, A Glover and Lawrence. From sources including *St Ann's Church centenary publication 1964* of which a remarkable number have popped up in the hands of people I've spoken to. Which proves the value of recorded people's history handed down [even though dates do not always precisely agree!].

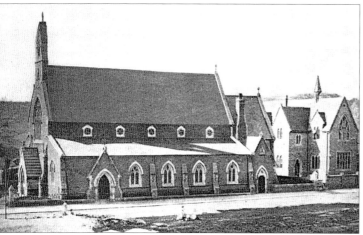

St Ann's Church and School 1866. From the publication mentioned above. Several people told me they attended this school

ST ANN'S WELL ROAD SCHOOL

Known locally as St Ann's Board School until it was demolished in 1970, it was replaced with St Ann's Well Infant and Nursery School on Hungerhill Road. The Juniors had moved to the Morley Junior School, which [2001] has been renamed St Ann's Well Junior School.

NELLIE HAYES

Born 1909

*Interviewed in her home 14.4.99. Head Teacher at **St Ann's Infant School** from c1951 until after it moved into its new building, post-redevelopment of the district*

I was born in Hull on the Humber. My father was a Pawn Broker's Manager. I was born in a bedroom over a pop shop. When I went to school the kids used to call me 'Nellie Pop Shop', which I found rather amusing and I think they did. Eventually, of course, I went to the local elementary school. I used to have to come home every Monday morning with all the bank money and my mother objected. She said a child of my age should not be allowed on the streets with a whole bag of money, so I was not allowed to bring it home any more unless someone was with me, which was rather a shame. My father had epilepsy.

I had a scholarship and went to Newland High School, which was a High School for girls the other side of Hull and it meant taking two bus journeys which tickled me to death. I had never been off my mother's apron strings before.

I liked English best. I found French rather harrowing because the French mistress did not like me and I did not like her, which makes a lot of difference. I always wanted to be a teacher. I used to teach the flowers we had in the house! We had a big round table and it had an oil cloth on it. On the oil cloth there was a pattern of a huge white daisy and red rose, and they were called Rosy Ruler and Daisy Ructions. Every morning, I used to take a stick and wallop them both. Poor old Rosy Ruler and Daisy Ructions! Later in life I met a girl called Rosy Ruler but I never told her this.

After I left school, I had a year on a cash desk in Hull City Centre. I wasn't just the cashier but also the errand girl. Mother objected and she went to see my old Head Teacher. She said I think you ought to know that if you

The 'Board School' St Ann's Well Road just before demolition. Some of the new houses can be seen in the background. Photos: Peter Garner

ST ANN'S NOTTINGHAM: inner-city voices *by Ruth I Johns* • ISBN 0951696092

Some of the close-built St Ann's houses. Edwin Street (left) and Duncombe Street (right) seen from the rear of the Board School c1969. Some people said the substantial building of the Board School could have been kept with more space opened up around it. Photo: source Liz Edge, Nottingham Local Studies Library

recommend your girls to this particular firm, they are not going to do the job they specified, they are going to be glorified errand girls. So the Head Teacher said: 'Well I'm not having that for my girls, particularly not this one who has potential, so let her come back and I'll put her in as a student teacher.'

So for twelve months, four days a week I went to my elementary school where I was student teacher and the other day of the week I went back to my grammar school in my gymslip.

After that year, I went to Teacher's Training College, Hull Municipal, and I had to live in College. After two years, I qualified, and then was appointed to a little infant school in Hull where I stayed twelve months. Then I got married and there was the marriage bar[1].

Of course, when the [Second World] War came it was married women with experience of teaching boys who were asked back. So this married woman did not hesitate. I remember I went to the Education Office one Friday morning and stood on the steps opposite a window overlooking Nottingham Old Market Square and filled in my particulars, and sent it in. A man came back with a paper: 'Please report to Sneinton Boulevard on Monday morning.'

So I went up to Sneinton Boulevard and there they sat. There must have been forty odd. They were big classes in those days. The Headmaster put me there and he said: 'Now this is Mrs Hayes . . . ' and a broad grin spread all over their faces, oh a woman, here is fun! So I thought, I shall wipe that off your faces! When he'd gone, I said: 'Now let's get this quite straight, you play me up and I shall play you up, do we understand each other?'

'Yes, Sir.' And I said: 'I'm not Sir either.' So I was 'Yes Miss' thereafter. I was there seven years and, then, back

[1] Women were officially barred at that time from certain jobs if they were married, a practice which didn't finally end until after World War Two.

came the men teachers for boys. So the organiser came to see me. He said he'd got a nice class of girls for me. I said I don't want to teach girls. So he said: 'I will send Miss . . . to see you.'

She said: 'Where will you go?' I said: 'I will go to Sneinton Boulevard Infants' and she said there wasn't a vacancy and I said then you must make one. And she did!

I remember the first morning. All the poor little devils were standing outside and they were weeping because they heard me routing at the boys you see. One said: 'I went to a party last night.' I said: 'Did you have something nice to eat?' 'Yes,' he said, 'a cake with ball bearings on.' So that made me laugh and so they all laughed and we got on well. We became good friends. I spent a long time there until a temporary vacancy came up at Jesse Boot School. I always wanted a foot in Jesse Boot.

The first morning they had a sweepstake for something or other, and I won it, seven shillings and sixpence. So I took myself to a little shop on Arkwright Street, Meadows, a second-hand shop, and bought myself a blue and white pottery jug, which I still have. Years after when I'd been at St Ann's Infants for some time, I went to a second-hand shop, and lo and behold, they had three jugs, the other three of the set. So I bought these and they are on the sideboard if you'd like to go and look.

After about a year at Jesse Boot, I went to William Crane and I didn't like the job very much and they didn't like me. Then, about 1951, I went to St Ann's Well Road School [formerly the Board School on St Ann's Well Road] as Head Teacher of the Infants. That was my spiritual home of course. My father having been a Pawnbroker, I'd lived amongst those people and knew their language. I was there a long time.

Classes were fifty in those days. There had been a discipline problem. It had been a free activity school where kids went about doing their own thing, which often amounted to kids putting things through the floorboards which were riddled with large cracks. I went in one morning

Thanks to Vernon and Rose Hawley for this Cub Pack photo of Nellie Hayes in the Hall of the Board School 1960 with the 69th Nottingham [Robin Hood] Scouts. The back row line-up from the left is, ? , David Lawson, Tim Hawley (son), David Sheperd, Nellie Hayes, Stephen Rawson and Geoff Carnelly

and there was a little girl on her knees, chin on her hands and her backside in the air. And I said to the teacher: 'What's the matter with her?' 'Oh, she's facing Mecca and she'll get up in a few minutes,' and she did and went about her business. I thought that was rather interesting.

We had seven classes, big ones. There was an upstairs and a downstairs. The first morning I was there, I distinctly remember somebody went tearing down the corridor with a newspaper, and I said: 'What's the matter with him?' 'Oh,' I'm told, 'he's a gladiator and this is his flaming torch.' So I said somebody had better put it out. One youth apparently climbed up a lampost and put his feet over the cross bars and flicked peanuts on people going past. He was a little devil.

The worst thing was that the classrooms all led into each other. There were no sinks and no water inside at the start. There was a corkscrew staircase. One of the staff ran down it with paint water and slopped it on the stairs. Then a little boy went down for a wee and said: 'Miss Young, someone's wee'd on the stairs.' 'That's all right,' she replied 'I did that!' But there was a bath in one room, possibly because the building had been used in the War as a rest centre.

There were seven outdoor toilets. They were so old and damp, there were ferns growing up the walls. They were there until the old school was pulled down. We kept spare knickers at school in case of accidents. They weren't allowed to come to school without knickers. We also kept boxes of plimsolls for PE, and the girls had to tuck their dresses in their knickers.

At my window was an old piece of curtain hanging on someone's corset lace. I got new curtains up. I had a funny little office. If parents came at playtime, there would be a cup of tea for them. I grew up in areas like St Ann's so I took everything in my stride.

Most of the changes in the School were my own organising, because I couldn't deal with free activity. I didn't think those children were ready for it. So we went back to programming and time-tabling and what have you. The Staff didn't like it very much. They all left in the first year and I had completely new staff. As there was no whole set of reading scheme books, the Supervisor gave me 48 copies of *My first story book*. We had some little story books too. Then we got *Janet and John*. John was fussy

Head Teacher's room looking south, December 1970. Photo: Peter Garner, Nottingham Local Studies Library

and Janet not much better! We had no capitation and all the money was spent until the following March. My husband, who was a painter, got a punch and made hundreds of counters out of cardboard.

We had the first coloured boy at our school, Maurice Pannikin.

It wasn't a bad school at all. They were all happy years. I was back in my spiritual home. Those people knew all about pop shops and what not. They realised they'd got one of their own kind.

I would meet people after who remembered being taught by me. Some I'd follow through when they went to other schools, like Julie who became a Head Teacher herself. She still comes to see me.

We took the kids out every Election Day because the School was a Polling Station. Mums would come too. Once it was at the Zoo and one of them said: "Eeh Miss Grainger, come and look at this bloody great pigeon!" It was a vulture!

Once at Dudley Zoo, it poured with rain, but there was a grocer's exhibition so most of the mums found their way to that. We had the kids and we took them on the water chute, as if there wasn't enough wet in the sky! We went down this water chute with shrieks of laughter when we got to the bottom. Everyone was soaked, but it didn't matter. We got dry.

I enjoyed my years in St Ann's. I was just over 65 when I retired. I saw St Ann's being knocked down. There were steps going up to the School, do you remember? There was a big window at the corner. Incidentally, I have some of those bricks, they were Queen Victoria Jubilee Bricks. You see . . . with the whole diamond on it. I've got some in the garden.

Underneath some of the houses on, it must be Rushworth Close, there are five old pianos! Because we just knocked a hole in the hall floor and shoved them all through and eventually they were buried.

All the Education Archives of the City of Nottingham were kept in the School's cellars. There were boxes and boxes of slides in the cellar. It all got thrown out. The coal-fired boilers were down there, they got a lovely fug up. Coke was delivered regularly. And we had gas lamps. The keys were on the end of a long stick and the Caretaker lit the lamps with it.

John Salt was Headmaster of the Juniors [which moved into Morley School buildings a few years before St Ann's School was demolished]. He kept himself very aloof. I remember him saying: 'Get out of this office, woman, you demoralise me!' We shared a School Secretary. The School motto Aim Higher was over the staff toilet!

The day we moved all Hell let loose. The pipes flooded. We had old desks with inkwells. Then we got tables and chairs in the new School. We moved on the last afternoon before Christmas.

I sometimes go down to St Ann's Library when they have functions, but I'm not very good on my feet now. Someone has to take me. I'm well looked after. One of the fathers of one of the kids I taught comes Wednesdays to help with paperwork. I can't see very well. They were happy days at St Ann's School.

St Ann's Nottingham: inner-city voices by Ruth I Johns • ISBN 0951696092

ST ANN'S WELL NURSERY AND INFANT SCHOOL

All photos from the school

The *Evening Post* on April 4th 1881 reported: "A set of schools on St Ann's Well Road, built under the auspices of the Nottingham School Board, and which will accommodate about 1,100 children were opened yesterday by Mr A J Mundella MP, Vice-President of the Council of Education in the presence of a large number of people assembled in the principal room of the building". The School then comprised a senior, junior and infant school.

The junior section of the school transferred to the buildings at Morley School when - in 1966 - Huntingdon Street Boys School, Morley School and Sycamore Girls School were amalgamated in the new Elliott Durham Bi-Lateral [later Comprehensive] School on Ransom Drive.

The *Nottingham Evening Post* of November 6th 1970 reported: "The rapid changes in the St Ann's area of Nottingham means that homes, streets and schools of which thousands of people have fond memories are suddenly disappearing.

"Mrs N Hayes, Headmistress of St Ann's Infants School for the past nineteen years has been surprised at the large number of people who like to catch a fleeting glance of the school they once attended – and which is soon to be demolished.

"Mrs Hayes opened the doors of the school on November 26th in the evening so that former pupils could browse around and take a last look at the place where they spent much of their childhood. The school, she said was designed by an eccentric architect in the shape of a ship. She would be sorry to see it go, as a family atmosphere had been built up in it." Many of the older people still called it the 'Board School'.

The new St Ann's Well Infant and Nursery School was built with its entrance on Hungerhill Road. After Nellie Hayes left, Pat Wakeling was Head Teacher from 1974 until 1998. The present Head Teacher, Lynda Barrett joined the school as Deputy Head in 1980 and became Head in 1998.

The school celebrated its twenty-fifth anniversary in November 1996, the same year as the Ofsted inspectors described the educational achievement of its 220 pupils between three and seven as a 'major success'. Chairman of the Governors, Peter Rumney, said he was thrilled the hard work, skill and dedication of staff had been recognised. The Inspectors commended staff for their strong commitment to the spiritual, moral, social and cultural development of the children.

The School has a reputation of involving parents: never more so than when the parents were the first in any Nottinghamshire school to take over running of school meals in their school at the start of the Autumn Term 1985. This was due to the closure of the school meals service in the Summer Term due to Union action, refusing teachers to supervise meals. Mrs Dawn Vernon, of Pearmain Drive, St Ann's, led a protest on County Hall on July 11th and was the volunteer organiser when the parents took over the midday meals service for some 200 children.

The mums made it clear they were fed up with being 'mucked about'. Children coming home at lunchtimes meant eight school journeys for mums each day. After lengthy negotiations they persuaded officials to let them run the service and a team of thirty backed up kitchen staff and supervisors.

At the time of the 2000 Ofsted Inspection, the school had 139 full-time pupils and 97 children who attended the nursery part-time. 59% were entitled to free school meals. 20% came from non-white European families. The Inspection Report said the School had

The entrance on Hungerhill Road

maintained its high standard of behaviour and positive attitudes since the last inspection [1996] and had made good improvement overall. The school had good links with parents who supported the children's learning well and: 'pupils are secure, happy and want to learn'.

Two members of staff [2001] were once pupils at the school. One is Emma Cooper, the senior Nursery Nurse. And the other is Devern Gordon, the Caretaker, who lives nearby. His parents emigrated from Jamaica and returned there nine years ago. His mother visited at the end of 2001. Linda Jordan is the school's longest serving teacher,

Party to celebrate Ofsted[1] 2000

---

[1] Office for Standards in Education.

Glimpses of life in school

Devern Gordon, Caretaker as DJ at post-Ofsted disco 2000

Keyboard practise. Kieran Moran and Dariel Marvin

having been there for thirty years in January 2002. She is City Secretary for the NUT.

Local historian Gill Tanner spends time in school with each year group on separate themes. For example: Reception Year 'Each Peach Pear Plum'. Year One 'Bath-time and Bed-time' and Year Two 'Seaside holidays'. The school employs a Music specialist, Rachel Arblaster and is well known for its Art, Design and Music. The school has After-School Clubs.

The school's allotment on the Hungerhill Gardens is tended by Mr and Mrs Westby, grandparents of one of the pupils [Joseph Westby] and nursery children make frequent visits.

St Ann's Infant School and Nursery received excellent SATs results in May 2001 for Key Stage One pupils [age seven]. Reading had improved 13% to 76%, maths up 11% to 89% and writing up 9% to 51%.

'Each Peach Pear Plum'. Adele Twigger

Visiting the School's allotment

St Ann's Nottingham. Inner-city voices by Ruth I Johns • ISBN 0951696092

Emerald Crown 2001. Khara Gray

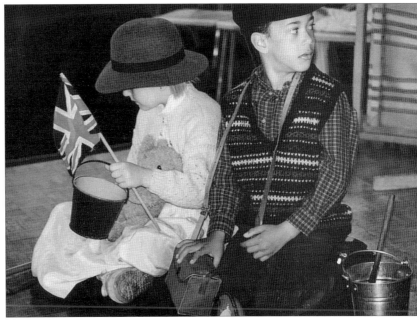

On the beach. Carla Notman and Ishmail Daniels

Bath-time and bed-time in days gone by. Left to right, Devern Gordon (Caretaker), Leone Brown, Suraj Singh Ratour and Emma Cooper NNEB

Lynda Barrett and **Maureen Jarvis** are sisters, both of whom are Head Teachers of Infant and Nursery Schools in St Ann's [2001]. Maureen, the elder sister, is Head of Blue Bell Hill Infant and Nursery School, and Lynda is Head of St Ann's Well Infant and Nursery School. Both schools are achieving excellent results, being commended for subject attainment and the quality of schooling, pupil behaviour and social development, and parent participation. Both attribute the success of their schools to good teamwork. Their father, Alan Barrett, used to be a policeman in the St Ann's community. Clare Williams, interviewed elsewhere in this book, is their aunt who did her district midwifery training in St Ann's in 1943.

Time off together. Left, Maureen Jarvis and Lynda Barrett

BLUE BELL HILL INFANT AND NURSERY SCHOOL

Mrs Maureen A Jarvis, Head Teacher since 1994, wrote the following in 2000. All photos from the School

Blue Bell Hill schools' building [the Junior School is on the same site] was built as a girls' secondary school in the 1930s: the Pierrepont Girls' School. The original Blue Bell Hill Elementary School building was on Beacon Hill Rise. We have a painting of that school in this school, painted by Mr K Yarwood who was the Art Master when our school caretaker, Brian Aram, attended that school.

The School building was adapted in the early 1970s to be used as separate Infant and Junior Schools. Some members of staff can remember carrying piles of chairs from one building to another when the new School opened.

The building, soon after completion, that was eventually to become Blue Bell Infant and Nursery School and Blue Bell Hill Junior School

In 1984, a new Nursery Class was opened in a part of the main School that had been converted.

In 1987, Ruth Thompson wrote a book *My Class Likes Dancing*, published by Franklin Watts, featuring photographs of the children dancing inside and outside the school.

The Infant and Nursery School was extended in 1992 to provide two extra classrooms and improved administrative areas and the children had great fun watching the diggers and builders.

In 1995, we worked with British Conservation Volunteers to create a garden at the front of the School. The children planted a tree to remember the previous Head Teacher, Audrey Aslin, who worked here for eighteen years before her death. Parents raised money in 1996 to plant a tree and rose buses in the garden to remember the Head Teacher and the children of Dunblane.

Over the years, we have worked hard to create a beautiful conservation site in the middle of the City. In 1997, the Caretaker and Groundsman, Sam Humphries,

made nesting boxes and the children in each class adopted a tree and a nesting box. Every year the children wait with excitement to make sure their particular nesting box is occupied, and they always are. Foxes, rabbits, squirrels and a huge variety of birds (including pheasants) are regularly seen on the school site. One teacher, Debbie Reynolds, worked with the children to create a bog garden in an area of the grounds where a natural spring emerges from the hillside. We were runners-up in a local award for this work.

In 1997, we began a series of free classes for parents and members of the community, run in the School with a free crèche. These have been very popular and the classes have ranged from computer training to line dancing.

In 1998, we received a grant from the Emerald Necklace scheme in Nottingham City and we planted an orchard on top of the hill where it overlooks the City. The orchard consists of forty native fruit trees which blossom and bear fruit each year. In a few years time, this will become a sensational Spring vista from many parts of the City overlooked by the orchard.

We were featured in the *Evening Post* as 'bringing the bluebells back to Blue Bell Hill'. A lady who read the article has kept contact with the school ever since and has given us donations of bluebells from her garden.

The Ofsted Inspection in April 1998 described us as a 'school at the heart of its community' – a title of which we were, and are, very proud. They also expressed astonishment that we were a school in the inner-city with no litter and no graffiti, and wondered how we did it.

With the new Unitary Authority in 1998, we became part of Nottingham City Local Education Authority once again after twenty-four years merged with the County. The Current Chief Executive, Ted Cantle, initiated a scheme for local businesses and organisations known as Adopt-a-School. We were pleased when his Department decided to adopt us.

In 1994, we were one of the original schools to run an NVQ [National Vocational Qualification] Early Years Care and Education training scheme. This two-year scheme trains parents and members of the community to work with young children. This year [2000] we were excited to be national finalists being awarded one of fifty-two National Training Awards. We were invited to attend a ceremony in London where we were one of only five businesses and organisations to receive a special National Training Award from David Blunkett [then Secretary of State for Education and Training]. We were the only school in England and Wales to receive this recognition.

AIM HIGH

TRY VERY HARD

CELEBRATE SUCCESS

RESPECT AND CARE FOR EACH OTHER

ST ANN'S NOTTINGHAM: inner-city voices *by Ruth I Johns* • ISBN 0951696092

The idea of our School Mission Statement is that by achieving the statements, you will get to the top of the hill and pick the bluebells of life, whatever those might be for you.

———————

From September 2002, Maureen Jarvis will be Head Teacher of Blue Bell Hill Primary School. Blue Bell Hill Junior School will amalgamate with Blue Bell Hill Infant and Nursery School on the same site

Glimpses of life in Blue Bell Hill Infant and Nursery School

Road safety games

Toffee apple making. Autumn Fair 1998

Games in the newly furbished playground 1997

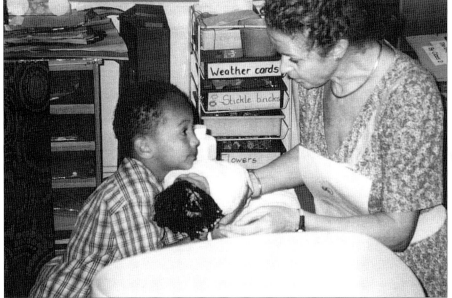

Parenting skills in the Nursery

PE in the Nursery 1998

Local involvement 1998

*Members of Parents Group
organising The Balloon Walk 1999*

Festival of Light dances 1997

*Children in school grounds looking
toward the City 1993. Photo:
source the School, Nottingham
Evening Post*

*Children painting the School Hall mural. They designed the mural assisted by Community Artist, Joe. Maureen Jarvis
explains the mural to different children*

MORLEY JUNIOR SCHOOL now ST ANN'S WELL JUNIOR SCHOOL

The Junior Section of St Ann's School, St Ann's Well Road, transferred to Morley School buildings after the Morley School children amalgamated with Huntingdon Street School senior boys and Sycamore Road School senior girls to form the new Elliott Durham Bi-Lateral School (later Comprehensive School) on Ransom Drive in 1966.

Morley School was taken out of 'Special Measures' after the 2001 Ofsted Inspection. The Inspectors praised the children's behaviour and said they had a positive attitude to their work. Head Teacher Andy Fox was commended for his determination to turn things around after the School was placed under Special Measures in 1999. In 2001, Andy Fox said: "I cannot praise enough the efforts made by our staff, especially those who have come out of two years of Special Measures with their heads held high, eager to continue improving the education of children at Morley, a 105-pupil junior school."

In 2001 Morley Junior School changed its name to St Ann's Well Junior School so its name matched its Infant and Nursery 'sister' school on Hungerhill Road and helped to re-establish community links that were lost over thirty-five years earlier.

The School, situated on the corner of The Wells Road and Brewsters Road, has close connections to the Metropolitan Housing Trust's estate in that area of St Ann's. One of its disused buildings has for many years been a small community centre, The Wells Road Community Centre.

ST ANDREW'S CHURCH SCHOOL

The school buildings were opened in Alfred Street North in 1872. From their opening, they were used both for day schools and Sunday schools, the boys in the upper part of the building and the girls and infants in the lower. St Andrew's Parish Magazine 1904

Joseph [Joe] Nicholson said St Andrew's School stopped being a Church of England School the day he left in 1941.

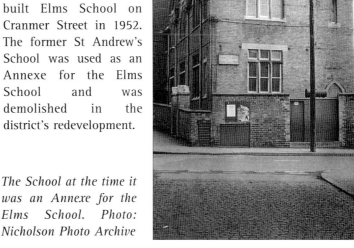

It then became the Alfred Street North Temporary Council School until its children moved into the newly built Elms School on Cranmer Street in 1952. The former St Andrew's School was used as an Annexe for the Elms School and was demolished in the district's redevelopment.

The School at the time it was an Annexe for the Elms School. Photo: Nicholson Photo Archive

ELMS PRIMARY AND NURSERY SCHOOL

All photos from the Elms School

The Elms Infants and Junior School was formally opened by Sir Hubert Houldsworth on September 21st 1953. He was described in the local Press as 'NCB [National Coal Board] Chief'. But children started attending the Elms School in the Autumn Term 1952. The Infants and Junior School later became the Elms Primary and Nursery School.

Miss D G Singleton, Head Teacher of the Alfred Street Temporary Council School, is seen here having a word with the children before breaking up for the summer school holidays in July 1952. She took charge of the new Elms School

Children leaving the temporary school for the last time

The site being prepared for the building of the Elms School. Elm Avenue in background is a wide pedestrian path up to the covered reservoir, formerly Todehole Hill

The covered reservoir from the air

The new School 1952

Class 6 1953-54

Class 7 acting the Robin Hood story July 1956

In rocking chair (left) teacher Cathy Holmes who set up the original Nursery at the Elms. Date of this photo not known

St Ann's Nottingham: inner-city voices *by Ruth I Johns* • ISBN 0951696092

Some years ago, but nobody can remember which year, children from the Elms School were taken to Robin Hood Bay for a break. They were so proud of their packed lunches in strong bags provided that they insisted on holding them all the time they played football! Seen with John Graham, Deputy Head

Jacqui Smith, Head Teacher says [2000] that Elms School is proud of the links it has formed over many years with the local community and feels itself to be a small but integral part of the vibrant, developing area in which it stands half a mile from the City Centre on the [Phase 10] edge of St Ann's. The backgrounds, abilities, religion and cultures of the pupils is wide ranging and: "something we often celebrate".

The school was built with three separate playgrounds for nursery, infant and junior children. Infants, five to seven years, are now known nationally as Key Stage One and juniors, seven to eleven years, Key Stage Two. Nursery places are available half-day from age three and full-time from age four.

Parents are encouraged to help in many ways, from swimming observation, to hearing children read, supporting educational visits, cooking, sewing, or helping out in After School Clubs.

The last Ofsted Report was very satisfactory, stating that the teaching overall is good and is a strength of the school. "The leadership of the Head Teacher and the governing body is strong and provides clear educational direction for the school. The governors play an active part in the life of the school and take their role as critical friend seriously."

The report said: "Pupils are encouraged to appreciate and develop their knowledge of British culture and traditions: for example, through visits to places of historical and cultural interest. Opportunities are also provided through teaching in subjects such as art, music and dance to gain an understanding of a range of cultures. The opportunity for pupils to participate in the Windrush celebrations by performing a traditional African dance is one such example."

A page from the Elms Primary and Nursery School Prospectus 1999/2000

Elms School staff February 2000. Back row left to right: Kim Stephenson, Lesley Sherriff, Alison Lord, Desrine Reid. Middle row: Heather Lea, Prya Vij, Lindsey Adams, Emma MacManus, Chris Smetham, Richard Stone. Front row: Jackie Evans, Michelle Enright, Sue Chivers, Jacqui Smith [Head Teacher], Sarah Woolford, Sukie Paddem, Judith Moore

Red Nose Day in the Nursery.   Cheer up children.

Parents listening to readers at school. Thank you parents for your support.

Christmas Production - we love to sing and dance.

Organiser System

Who is your favourite author?

Looking after friends.

Please! Please Mrs. Smetham no more walks!

A "Jessops" volunteer helping a child with his reading.

CHRIS SMETHAM

Born 1948

*Interviewed at the **Elms Primary and Nursery School**, Cranmer Street, St Ann's 16.1.01. Chris is a Learning Support Assistant at the school*

I came to this School in April 1969 until December 1975. I then had six years away when I was having my two children, and then came back in January 1982. Originally, I came from Yorkshire, moved to Grantham when I was ten years old. I decided I wanted to be a Nursery Nurse and came to the Nursery Nurses Training College [Waverley College] on Forest Road, Nottingham, for two days a week.

Do you remember Miss Wright? We had a reunion recently and it was wonderful to see her. That began my association with Nottingham. When I finished College, I became a nanny for a couple of years, which I really enjoyed and then the children became too old to have a nanny. I had an interview at the Council House with Mrs Cornish (she of the hats!) and it was like having a chat. She suggested a job at the Elms Infant School. I came along and saw Miss Hanson, the Head Teacher, and got the job.

I was with the infants not the nursery children. In those days there were eight infant classes and they each had at least forty children, and some more than that. Downstairs in the School, there are only five classrooms in the main building, so there was a class in the Hall. At lunchtime, all the equipment had to be put to one side while the tables came out for dinner.

The building was just as it is now except that it had an old nursery building, a three-room building, down on the drive. The Nursery used two of the classrooms and the Infants one of them. I was here when the Nursery opened but I can't remember the exact year. It was a sixty-place Nursery. There were also some portable buildings on the drive. There were two classrooms in there that originally the Juniors used and then the Infants took them over. And at the car park at the far end of school on Goldswong Terrace there were some portable classrooms and the Juniors had those. I think there were twelve junior classes then.

So it was a very, very big school with separate Heads for the Nursery and Infants and the Juniors. The only time the two schools met was when the Junior children came down the stairs to the dining room, which is very small so they had to have a couple of sittings. And, at one time, the Juniors had to hold some classes in the basement of the big building next door. It was then the Teachers' Centre. Before that it was the Gordon Boys' Home. Now it is student accommodation. Now teachers use the Sandfield Centre on Derby Road which used to be the Cottesmore School.

Then the numbers at the Elms started to drop away. In those days, families stayed in the area, so, as the children grew older, the numbers dropped and the portable buildings went. That happened whilst I was away having my children. When I went away, the area round the Elms was still very much the same. When I came back, the schools had amalgamated and became a Primary School, and all the rebuilding in the area had happened. It was sad because it did spoil a lot of the community. A lot of families moved away from the area, although there are still a lot of the same families here, but it just didn't have the same feel about it. Miss Hanson had retired and Tony Normington was the Head. And the power had changed at County Hall and Nursery Nurses were no longer used in schools. But then the power changed again and it became the thing to have Nursery Nurses back, which was lucky for me.

When my son was six and my daughter four, I attended this block interview at the Council House. My son, Tom, is now twenty-four and my daughter, Kate, is twenty-three.

Most Nursery Nurses wanted to work with nursery children. I preferred working with older children. They were starting to employ Nursery Nurses to work with Junior children and there was a job going here again. I'd kept in touch with the School and the Deputy Head, Audrey Moss, had been the Deputy of the Infants and some of the same staff were still here. I came and had a chat with Tony Normington and I became a Junior helper.

When I trained I could officially work with children from 0-5. Then they started employing Nursery Nurses to work alongside teachers in the classrooms with children up to seven years old. And then training took into account 0-7. Then I think the City realised we were quite useful people to have around in some inner-city schools in Junior classrooms. So my job description was Junior helper. The job has changed a lot since 1982 and from when I originally started in 1969.

In 1969, there was another Nursery Nurse and myself to assist in the eight infant classes. I helped in each of four classes for two days a week once a fortnight, and then on Fridays we would do all the dogsbody jobs around the school. So each class would have a Nursery Nurse for two days a fortnight. In those days, we used to mix the paints, mix the glue, do all the practical stuff which the teachers didn't have time to do, work alongside the children in the classroom and just generally help out. Miss Hanson always called us by our surnames. One of my jobs was to make tea for the staff, so a few minutes before playtime I would go to the staff room and make sure the kettle was on and then the teapot filled.

I had to go to Miss Hanson's room, where Jacqui Smith's, the Head's, room is now. I would take a tray with tray-cloth and cup and saucer from a cupboard and go and pour her tea and take it to her. I don't do that now of course! When I was working with the infants, there were classes for Asian women who wanted to learn English. That was about the time the Victoria Centre was being built. The classes were held in a building on Huntingdon Street, and I used to go and look after the children in a crèche while their mothers were at lessons. That was after school. About four or five mums came.

When I came back here in 1982, the job had changed. I wasn't expected to mix the paints or make tea for the staff and that kind of thing. It was more hands on with the

ST ANN'S NOTTINGHAM: inner-city voices *by Ruth I Johns* • ISBN 0951696092

March 1988. Back row left to right: Chris Smetham, My Dung, Anthony Walker, Fatima Tashbin, Marcus Laing, Shane Thompson [who was sadly murdered when a young adult], Terry Brown, Chartelle Holness, Bianca Brooks and Mary Hirst. Middle row: Emma James, Donna Bryan, Ben O'Connor, Jermaine Duffus, Majid Fazal, Zoe Wilson, Fitz Keeling. Front row: Yaseen Mohammed, Claire Mitchell, Donna Samuels, Nicholas Wright, Dalton Hodges, Steven Cotterill and Claire Inger

children. I used to do a lot of art and craft stuff which I really enjoyed. Those days were pre-National Curriculum of course. You worked alongside the teacher.

It was then recognised that there were children with special needs who would benefit from one-to-one teaching. I would withdraw children from the main class and work one-to-one or in a small group with literacy and maths and that sort of thing. Then, when the Community Teacher, Carole Keely, started we had our own room and we could take children there which was rather nice. She was absolutely brilliant. If there were problems within school, she would go and talk with parents and liaise with parents when children were admitted. We worked very closely together until there were cutbacks a few years ago and the School couldn't afford a Community Teacher. We really miss having somebody in that role.

My role has changed. From working in class some of the time and withdrawing children for specific things, I now work with special needs children all the time. With the City Council's Inclusion policy, I work with children who are Stage Two and Stage Three, sometimes withdrawing them working one-to-one or in a small group and sometimes working with the child alongside the Teacher. It's nothing like when I did my training, nothing at all!

I have named children who I support, around eighteen to twenty. Some are individual and some in small groups. I have had many more but we have more Learning Support Assistants in school now. That's what we're called now. There are two of us full-time permanent and four who are employed to assist specific children for so many hours a week.

Yes, I've seen a lot of changes. When I started, if a child had severe special needs they would go to a special school. And the children are different now. I know that sounds strange but they are. As I said earlier, we used to have classes of forty. There would be problems like inadequate clothing and food and that sort of thing. You do not often get those problems now. You used to get some children who didn't behave very well, but I don't remember it being as much of a problem as it is now.

I think possibly a lot of children don't have a stable home life now and I think the community is different. In general - and I don't mean just in St Ann's - people are a lot more self-centred and don't look out for each other so much. They've got their own lives to live and are very materialistic, which I think is very sad.

We lost the Community Teacher, but we now have EMTAG [Ethnic Minority and Travellers Achievement Grant] teachers, it's the post-Section XI funding to assist children from ethnic minorities. The teachers tend to have more contact with parents. My contact with parents is that I will take a child home if they are not very well. And I liaise with our School Nurse who works from St Ann's Health Centre. She also goes into Highwood House [for homeless families] so she knows many of the families in school, and she has had contact with this school for quite a while.

And, of course, I see parents when they come into school but I don't visit them at home, which I used to do. There used to be more contact with parents. We didn't have the time constraints of the National Curriculum and things seemed happier in those days. I know sometimes when you look back you have a rosier picture but I do think that's true. At the moment my timetable is full from the moment the children come in to the minute the children go home. I have one afternoon a week, which is my assessment and resourcing time but there is usually something else to do in that time.

Historically, there are all sorts of things I used to do, like making sure the bookcase wires are fixed and the plants sorted out, silly mundane things which made a lot of difference to the general smooth running and pleasant atmosphere. Doing those things is sort of inbred and when I see something that needs doing, it gets to me that I don't always have the time to do it. There's more and more pressure being put on, with more and more children with special needs coming into school, a lot with behavioural problems. You are trying to keep one step ahead about what you will do with the next child you are teaching.

Some children don't get enough support and are not at the same level as the rest of the class so a lot goes over their head. We do what we can but we cannot be with every single child and there are a lot of children on our special needs register. I feel I do my best but sometimes you feel that your best is not good enough. You'd love to do more but there just isn't the time. Because I support so many children, I sometimes feel that I'm not quite ready for the next because of the need to sort resources and things out.

If it's 'in class' support that's fine, because the teachers plan and differentiate their work. But when I take a child out of class it's up to me to sort the work out and I just feel

Tony Normington, Head Teacher, leading the pensioners' Christmas Party Bingo with the assistance of twins Maureen and Louise Wright

Party teatime for local pensioners in School

that I should be able to do all the things I've always done and there isn't time. It would help if there were fewer children but we haven't got enough teachers for that. The ideal would be to have a nursery nurse in every class, which would be wonderful. But it's never going to happen.

We have one or two parents who come in and help but a lot have younger children so it's not practical. Also, if they didn't have a particularly good time at school, they think we're going to eat them because they didn't have good relationships with their teachers.

The largest class size now is thirty-three and the smallest is the Reception Class with about fifteen. The others are in the high twenties. My load of paperwork isn't too bad. If it's class support, I report verbally to the teacher. If it's one-to-one, then I record what I've done with each child. I try to get it done in school but sometimes I take it home to do.

The Elms is a feeder school for Elliott Durham Comprehensive School but last year only a few went. They tended to go to Forest, Haywood, Manning. A lot of Asian girls go to Manning because it's a girls school. I think there were so few to Elliott Durham because in the past it didn't have a particularly good reputation. But I think some of 'my' children would do really well there. Elliott Durham has a really good special needs team.

Mind you, at one time, if you mentioned the Elms School, people would be: 'Ohhhh! You don't work there, do you.' But I love it, always have.

At Christmas, we used to have parties for old age pensioners from the local area. The children would invite their grandparents or neighbours. Some would find it hard to get up the hill so those of us with cars would go and pick them up. The highlight was the entertainment when Tony Normington, the Head Teacher, did the Bingo game.

They absolutely loved it. They would use the Unifix cubes that the children used for maths. It was a big competition and Tony used to love doing it. I'm afraid that fell by the wayside because of cost. We couldn't afford it, which was a shame. The children would entertain the pensioners and the older children helped to serve the tea and to find numbers on the Bingo cards. It was a really nice time.

And at Christmas some of the children would go and sing to pensioners at the Residential Centre in Courtenay Gardens. The old people really loved the children going and the children had mince pies and sweets and enjoyed it. That's also fallen by the wayside because of time constraints and releasing a member of staff to go with them.

My message to young people in St Ann's in fifty years time? To be proud and think, despite all you hear, in spite of all you might have heard on the radio and television and all the rest of it, think about your own experiences of a place. I can't think of anything negative to say about St Ann's except I wish the planners had done better. When they got to the area around here, they ran out of money and it was just all crammed in. I get lost when I walk in that area, I cannot find my way around.

One of the nice things about this School is the location. It's high and we have a good view of the City. It's set in nice grounds and we're lucky because we have two playgrounds,

ST ANN'S NOTTINGHAM. inner-city voices by Ruth I Johns • ISBN 0951696092

Margaret Conn

and a field just across Elm Avenue. The trees and the grass are lovely. The School was built in 1952[1] so that's before the time of demolition and redevelopment in St Ann's.

A tree is planted in memory of Margaret Conn who was a teacher in the Junior School when the Infants and Nursery, and Junior Schools were separate. When the schools amalgamated, she carried on teaching here. She died in November 1985. The tree is on the School drive near the Caretaker's house.

An impressive moment for Robin Towle, of Nottingham, when he received his certificate for securing most marks (90) in the pianoforte solo (age nine and under) test, from Mr. H. Stubbs, Fellow of the Royal College of Music, at to-day's opening of the 10th Beeston Musical Festival.

By the time he was nine years old in 1951, Robin Towle, of 27, Kilbourn Street, St Ann's, and a pupil of the Elms School, had won seven 1st and 2nd Awards at Music Festivals for his piano skills and had attained Grades I & II Royal Schools of Music Examinations with Merits and Distinction, and Grade I Theory (highly marked). In this Evening Post photo of May 18th 1951, he is receiving his certificate for most marks (90) in the piano solo (age nine and under) test from H Stubbs, Fellow of the Royal College of Music at the 10th Beeston Music Festival. What happened to Robin Towle?

[1] Elms School will celebrate its jubilee in Autumn 2002.

KATH BROWN

(nee Price) Born 1953

*Interviewed at **Elms Primary and Nursery School**, Cranmer Street, St Ann's 16.1.01. Kath Brown is Cook Supervisor at the School*

There are three part-time ladies and me at present. We cook about 140 lunches each day. Yes, last time you came in, I was making scones with cream. That was for a buffet. Sometimes we do scones for the children as part of their lunch. They love them.

We cook real food prepared on the premises for the children. There are quite a lot of schools where a lot, and sometimes most, of the food is bought in already prepared.

I was born at 9, Dawson Street, Sneinton, the year of the Queen's coronation. I was one of three sisters and a brother. Dawson Street looked out on what was called The Mounts. Mr Wells, the coalman, kept his horse on there, tied up of course. We used to spend a lot of time at my grandad's big allotment which he shared with my dad up on Cardale Road. I went to Hogarth Primary School on Carlton Road. I then went to Pierrepont Girls School on Gordon Road in St Ann's. I was just ready to leave school when it joined with Manvers Boys School as Manvers Pierrepont and now it's gone. I loved school. I never had much time off.

I liked history and religious knowledge. I hated cookery! I was rubbish at it. I used to make rock cakes and they'd be that much like rock that my dad said they'd break the wall! I'm the laugh of the family, because to think I could never do anything right regarding cookery and I've turned out to be a cook!

I don't quite know why I wasn't any good at it. I was pretty good in school and excelled in sports. I think because I wasn't doing so well in cookery, I tried too hard. Now I just don't have to think about it and it turns out superb!

When I first left school at sixteen, I worked for British Homes Stores. I was on Ladies Nightshirts. If you went into British Homes Stores then, and saw the state of ladies nightgowns; great big long things in horrible bri-nylon, and the women's pants . . . like my grandma wore. I thought, I can't do this for much longer! I was so bored. I gave my job up and my mum was saying: 'If you don't give me your board money next week, you'll be out!' You know how it is because of shortage of money.

I saw a job advertised in a chemist, the chap was lovely and the girls were nice, but the money was rubbish. I told him I'd take the job because he was in dire straights. I said I'd do it until I next needed a new pair of shoes. When my shoes started wearing out, I said I'd have to look for somewhere else. Then I went selling newspapers and things on trolleys at the General Hospital. I loved that job and stayed until the chap who owned the hospital shop, Mr Jones, sold it. I used to go round every ward, even the Pay-Bed Wing.

I used to finish about half past eleven and that was it until half past three in the afternoon for the *Evening Post*. So I had a bit of time to myself in the day, but I had to go in Sunday morning every other week. Mr Jones did every other week. I don't know what his first name was. In those days you never called anybody by their first name. We had some neighbours we were close to when we moved to Harcourt Terrace in St Ann's, and sadly the wife died. I know his name is Les Drabble but I still write to him as Mr Drabble.

I was about seventeen when that job ended and I went to work in a factory, but I wasn't there very long because I found out I was having a baby and I got married. It's my thirtieth wedding anniversary this month. I got married in 1971. I had a choice. Either I could have some money to put down for a deposit on a house or have the money for a big white wedding and go into rented accommodation. So I talked about it with my husband-to-be and we thought it would be more sensible to put a deposit on a house. It was in Forest Fields which was quite posh then, wasn't it?

Then we went to Arnold for about four years but I didn't like it very much and then we came back to St Ann's. And we've been here twenty-five years, and we had two boys and a girl. They are Julian, James and April. Julian is a Plumbing and Heating engineer like his dad. April followed my footsteps. It was her choice. She's Assistant Catering Manager for the City Council at the Sandfield Centre. It's the Education Offices for the City so it's got a restaurant. James went in the Forces straight from school and was in the Gulf War. The radio this morning was saying it was ten years since the Gulf War and I thought it doesn't seem two minutes. He came back all right and hasn't suffered like a lot of them. But he gets very depressed. And he wasn't the type to get stressed out over things.

I started in school meals because you are off when the kids are off for school holidays. I had a part-time job working in Victoria Centre in a jeans shop called Western Jean Company and I loved it. But when it got to school holidays, it was a bit of a problem. So I put my name down when the kids went back to school. Our eldest was about eleven, just started secondary school and they rang me the next day to go up to Elliott Durham School. And my brother was in the school too. He'd be about fifteen then: that was about 1981. So I'm glad to say that I started at the bottom end, washing pots. Then, I gradually started to do other bits and bobs and got a few extra hours. Then I learnt how to do the stores and weighing up the food and things like that. I'd been there about six years and was a bit fed up feeling I wasn't going anywhere, so I had a two year break.

I went to help somebody I knew who had opened a shop. I had a lot of shop experience because my family all had shops and I used to help out at night and weekends. Then I got a phone call from Mrs Wakeling at St Ann's Infants School. My lads and daughter had been there. She knew I'd worked at the Elliott Durham kitchen and she said she was really stuck. Could I give her a hand? So I went round and helped and, within a couple of months,

somebody left and somebody moved up and I was asked if I would like to take the job as Assistant Cook, because I'd got the experience. I did that for a year and then I saw an advertisement for Robert Shaw Primary and Nursery School at Beechdale for Cook Supervisor. It was a big jump. I went for interview and I was given the chance. I worked really hard. I was there a year. Then, because of dwindling numbers they started getting meals sent in instead of having their own kitchen.

So the County Council was going to redeploy me. At that time, they were making a lot of changes, which meant quite a lot of people were leaving their jobs and taking early retirement, or being made redundant, and things like that. I was sent to kitchens where women automatically thought that because their cook was going to leave and they were Assistant Cook, they would move up. And when I said I didn't have a kitchen, that met a lot of resentment.

I was one of the last people to find a job, where I knew I would be able to fit in without treading on anybody else's toes and make things awkward. That's when I picked Sycamore School in St Ann's and was there six years as Cook Supervisor before moving to Elms here. The lady who was here wanted to move on to a comprehensive. But, she needed the experience of the work I was doing at Sycamore, because we were also doing a pack-out meal for two other schools and sending them out. So I was asked to swap and she loved it that much down there and I loved it up here so we stayed. That was six years ago now. I usually get itchy feet, but I haven't got them yet!

Yes, I've been to quite a few schools in St Ann's and I went to Blue Bell Hill too not long ago because their cook was poorly. I went there for a week and the assistants here said it would be fine, they'd cover here.

Next week's menu is: Monday, quiche with chips, tinned tomatoes and Angel Delight or jelly and cream. Tuesday, roast turkey with carrots and broccoli with country diced potatoes, gravy and cornflake tart and custard. Wednesday is mutton and tomato pie, peas and sweet corn, creamed

Kath Brown (centre) with Shereen and Becky, who wanted their photograph taken to prove they made elegant salad platters. June 1999. Photo: Elms Primary School

ST ANN'S NOTTINGHAM: inner city voices *by Ruth I Johns* • ISBN 0951696092

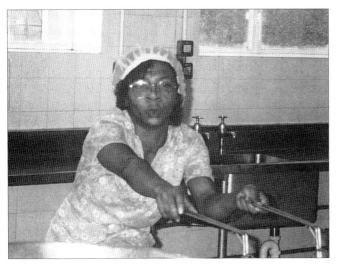

Hilary Chambers, Kitchen Assistant, June 1999. Kath Brown says she was practising boogie dancing for the Carnival while working

potatoes and gravy, and probably a chocolate crispy. They like them. Thursday it's tuna pasta with salad, coleslaw and potato waffles, with steamed chocolate sponge pudding and custard. Friday is chicken smiley faces, jacket potato wedges and probably pasta in tomato sauce and a muffin for pudding. I work to a three-week guide menu that comes from Nottingham City Catering offices, to make sure the children get a balanced diet.

The menus have definitely improved over the years since I was a child. I wouldn't stay for school meals! It was all stew and rice pudding. But my mum was saying that in 1953 there was still rationing so the stew mince was probably a Government subsidy thing. I used to go to my grandad who cooked my dinner.

Not many children bring sandwiches here. We provide for vegetarians. On the turkey day, for instance, there will be a vegetarian spaghetti bolognaise alternative. Instead of the mutton pie, they can have the pastry because it's made with vegetable shortening and they would have a vegetarian mince to make the pie. Most will eat tuna and eggs. We've got about twenty-five vegetarians out of the 140 who have dinners.

Staff have the same dinners. They can have a salad and we do jacket potatoes as well. They order their meal in the morning and come and collect it. Staff don't supervise children at lunchtime now. We have special midday supervisors. They are not called dinner ladies any more.

The children eat up pretty well apart from vegetables. They're not very good on vegetables. We do everything we can. We've got posters up: 'Eat your vegetables up, it will keep you fit and healthy' and we do competitions and all sorts of things to encourage them to eat everything.

A lot of children here do have a breakfast before they come to school, but they are hungry by lunchtime and they would have seconds of a lot of things - but not vegetables. If we've got anything over, we pick a table to have it. A different table each day to make it fair. I'm here to cook for children so I would rather let anything spare go to the children than to be wasted. Years ago it went to pigs.

The children usually sit on the same table each day, eight on a table with two servers. Our Head Teacher, Jacqui Smith, is very strict on table manners. Because she says not a lot of families sit down now at table and eat a meal together. And I think she's right. So they sit at table and learn how to eat a meal. They are allowed to talk as long as everybody's not shouting above each other. It's more like a family. Brothers and sisters in different classes are encouraged to sit with each other. So if there's an older one who you've encouraged to eat certain foods, which perhaps a year ago they didn't, then they will usually encourage the younger brother or sister. And so you get the benefit of that. So, it's not just education in the classroom.

We've got about seven midday supervisors. Some of them are mums. Yes, I do see children of people I knew as children and it makes me feel old! Last year I was walking down the drive to the Post Box and a woman came up and said: 'What are you doing here?' And I told her and she said: 'I can't believe it, you used to do my dinner at Elliott Durham and now you are doing it for my son. I now know he's in safe hands.' And I thought that was nice of her to say that.

Catering keeps you on your toes from when you come in the morning until you go home in the afternoon. When you come through that door in the morning, you've got to leave any outside worries on the doorstep and do what you've got to do, do your job which you're trained to do to the best of your ability. I cannot fault the City Council, they are brilliant at training. When someone starts in the kitchen here, they go down for a day's induction course, and then they get training from me, which is all documented. I've got a trainee now, a mum with kids.

I'll train her in basics over three or four weeks, then she goes for her induction day. I'll train her in general kitchen duties and basic cooking. Then she'll go for her basic food and hygiene certificate, and the rest of her training will be done with me. It includes food ordering, menus, there's a lot to learn. It can be done in a year. We order our food from designated suppliers, one for frozen food, one for fresh vegetables, one for stores and so on. There's a strict budget.

Occasionally, children need treats. My grandaughter loves McDonald's and you've got to have a treat every now and then. They always want a Happy Meal because they get a toy. If we could give a toy every time here, we'd be inundated wouldn't we?

What would I like to pass down for fifty years time? I don't regret anything. I don't regret getting married young, seventeen. I definitely don't regret having my children young because I've grown up with my children. I've been able to do a lot of things, even play goalkeeper when one of the lads wanted to play football and nobody else could be found. 'Mam will you go in goal?' I don't regret that because I've got my time now.

I'd like to say to young people that the opportunities are out there. They're a lot greater than when I was younger. You've just got to work hard and you can achieve what you want to. I would have loved to stay at school but the money was needed at home, that bit of extra money you could bring in. So you went to work.

When I was younger, the only thing I ever said I wanted to do was to be a policewoman or go into the Services. But, of course, I needed qualifications, and did not have them. By the time my kids left school, I was a bit too old to do those things because they've strict age limits so I lost out a bit, but I do love what I'm doing now. If I had been a bit younger, I would have gone to College and been a Health Inspector.

Sometimes my husband says my interest is to our disadvantage. For instance, if we go out for a meal and there's a dirty knife or fork or you go to the toilets and they aren't clean, you start saying: 'If they can't do that, what's happening in the kitchen?'

I work from half-past seven or quarter to eight in the morning until about three o'clock. Some days I don't get done and I stay a bit in my own time.

I enjoyed growing up in St Ann's. It got a lot of bad publicity. A lot of places further out are the same but you don't hear about it. People still help each other. I've got someone elderly on the street. If the weather's bad, I'll do their shopping. If they can't get the light bulbs in, it's done . . .

Yes, I live in a street which people protested about and it wasn't pulled down when so much in St Ann's was. The houses are well built and are standing the test of time [thirty years on]. A lot of the people who were moved out to the Meadows or Clifton have come back to St Ann's. When I was small, I can remember St Ann's Well Road, shops from top to bottom. Near where I live now, both sides were all shops then. It was nice. And Central Market was wonderful. They pulled it down when they put the market into Victoria Centre. You could get everything in Central Market[1], clothes, meat, fish, vegetables, even your pet goldfish! When they rebuilt St Ann's, they didn't think about pedestrian access to the City Centre. The pedestrian way from the Union Road is not very nice.

Kath Brown's mum Kath Price also contributes to this book

BILL CHAMBERS

Born 1943

*Interviewed at the **Elms Nursery and Primary School**, St Ann's 30.11.00. Bill Chambers is Caretaker at the School*

My earliest memory of St Ann's was my aunt who used to live on Wainright Street, off St Ann's Well Road. We would come up and see her and when I was a teenager I knocked around with some of the lads who lived around there. We got into this and that and went to picture houses and things like that.

I was born in the Meadows, Nottingham, and the Meadows and St Ann's were built very similar; alleyways, entries, go down an entry and then over somebody's wall and you were in a backyard and then the next street! You didn't have to walk all the way round as lads. There were lots of large houses in St Ann's, especially on Robin Hood Chase. My aunt's father-in-law used to live in a large house on Robin Hood Chase. I quite liked the way the old St Ann's was, though some of the houses were in a dilapidated state and needed to come down. It was very much a community and the community is still there but different.

As a lad in the Boys' Brigade I remember going to St Andrew's Church Hall on Alfred Street. When the Queen came to Nottingham [1955], she went down Goldsmith Street and all the Boys' Brigade lads lined the route. I was in the 9th Company down the Meadows. St Andrew's Church Boys' Brigade used to have a silver band.

I can relate to youth activities from fond past memories. There was rivalry between groups. For example, Boys' Brigade and Scouts. We used to run the legs off them. They used to run when we came to see them! And we used to chase them, but it was rivalry, it wasn't out and out violence. At school, one of them would say: 'We'll come down and see your lot off', and we'd go down. They'd come down another night and see us lot. It very rarely came to physical violence.

I got married at twenty-one to a Sneinton girl and we moved to Cathcart Hill, St Ann's, which was just off Hungerhill Road. We've been together a long while. When the Council started demolition of St Ann's, it moved us to Aspley. We had two children, a boy and a girl then. I wanted to go down Lenton because my mates were down there and we were poaching at the time, nipping around borrowing people's rabbits or whatever. We were offered a house at Clifton but I don't like Clifton and then we were offered a house at Aspley and spent a number of years at Tunstall Crescent.

Do you remember that film after the two University teachers[1] made a study of St Ann's before it was demolished. It was crap. St Ann's was basically taken over by the Council because landlords didn't keep houses up to scratch. And the film only showed the parts of the area which were run down. My mate's lad, Paddy, played football with me. His mum Liz Gately was a lovely, brilliant woman. Though they never had a heck of a lot of money. On the film, Paddy's older brother is actually standing outside when they're knocking a nearby house down. That was a bad documentary.

In Aspley, I joined back in the Boys' Brigade as an officer. When our son, Clive, was reaching eleven, I got this job as School Caretaker at the Elms. We moved up here [in the school house] and have been here ever since. I was appointed in 1978 but didn't start until February 4th 1979.

I'm seeing the third generation of children in the school! People who went through Infants, Juniors and Senior school are now bringing their children, and a lot of my early friends from when I moved up here are bringing their grandchildren! It's a big wheel that turns round.

If you take an overall view of St Ann's and the Meadows, they knocked them down and rebuilt them with quite nice housing with gardens. But there were the terrible

---

1   On King Edward Street at the City end of St Ann's Well Road.

1   See Ken Coates and Richard Silburn in Index.

St Ann's Nottingham Inner City Voices by Ruth Johns • ISBN 0951696092

years of the Tories who put people out of work. And then there were ten to fifteen years with people, especially from St Ann's if they were black or Asian, who couldn't get decent employment. I know at one stage I used to sit in my house ringing up Government schemes to see if there were any places for lads to go on.

We've had a huge decline in industry in Nottingham. We've lost Raleigh, Player's, the pits, some textile firms and lots of other light and heavy industry that used to be small firms. For example, I worked in a wood yard, Soresby on Castle Meadow Lane, before I came on this job. I used to deliver, for example, to at least five or six small joinery and plumbing firms who used to employ local people in St Ann's.

If you compare the amount of people living in the old St Ann's and you look at the amount of houses they put back in, it adds up to a massive movement of people. That was one of the reasons why the area declined because it seemed more sensible to keep people out of work than build the area up again. During the Thatcher years, a generation of children grew up who weren't going to get a decent job.

There's a small group of people doing whatever they're doing and giving the area a bad reputation, but there's lots of nice people here. In the 1950s when I was leaving school, the job market was easy. You could go from one job to another. Today they expect you to get qualified. You go to University and get into debt and then get a job and pay them back!

I got this job because the chap I was doing Boys' Brigade with was Caretaker of William Sharpe Comprehensive School, and he said: 'Why don't you come on our job'. So I did. I spent a year at Whitemoor Primary School and that was a nice, busy school, five nights a week lettings plus Saturday night. Then I got this job and I enjoy it.

I look after the building. We have a good cleaning staff. If there's something needing doing and I can do it, I do. I don't overstep the mark. I've always had a big sports interest, though I've never achieved a lot myself. I like being involved with the kids, some involvement with football, swimming, cricket . . . It's nice to see these kids having good chances in sport.

When I first came here, Miss Hanson was the Head Teacher downstairs because it was an Infant and Junior

Bill Chambers in school. Photo: Ruth I Johns 2000

school before it was a Primary School. I was shocked because there were several kids suffering from rickets which I'd seen when I was young. After a time those things seemed to go away and we seemed more affluent and later things declined and people were really hard up again. Things went backwards and now it seems they are levelling out. Kids question more now which is good.

It must be about twelve years ago now when we had Community Police Officers coming in and actually getting to know the kids in school, doing things with them like road safety and cycle proficiency courses. There was Mick Morrell, Chris Timms, Alan Barlow and several others. To my way of thinking it showed the other side of policing. Then the area they covered was hugely expanded, so they hardly ever came in. After that, I was told by the police that every Police Officer is a Community Police Officer, but there wasn't the same interaction.

As I see it, we're in the zombie years, sitting at computers and the competitiveness in achievement. Yes, they've got to achieve and to meet criteria which hopefully will take them on to get a job. But there's that element of time off where you play badminton, football, cricket, swimming, athletics . . .

When I came to St Ann's, I thought there would be a local football team, lots of lads playing football. I asked two lads where the football team was and they said: 'What are you talking about?' So I said do you fancy starting one and they thought I was joking. The lads were Pete Dunn and Andrew Cavelle and we started on the street. Then my son's friends, Malcolm and Martin, joined. We got a good lot of lads but nowhere to go apart from St Andrew's Church Hall which the vicar, the Rev Ron Lacey, let us use. Totally brilliant bloke!

We didn't have a team, we didn't have any money, we all just got together. If I wanted to sort out a game of football, I'd ring somebody up and say: 'Can you give us a game of football?' And I walked around the streets until we had enough players! There was a lack of youth leaders. Youth clubs seemed to decline. Partly due to the massive movement of people [when St Ann's was demolished] and, later, due partly to the cut back in money available through Government to Leisure Services.

I'm on Notts Youth League Committee. One of the blokes, Ernie Johnson, I first met at football when we were in the Boys' Brigade and we've been knocking around together for over thirty years. Up to age fifteen, the kids are in the Young Elizabethan League and when they're sixteen they come up to the Youth League. It's sponsored by Newcastle Brewery.

If you can get enough lads together to form a football club you have to register with the Football Association which affiliates you. Then you apply to join a League, and you've got League fees and insurances and things like that. And Newcastle Brewery put money into the community through Notts Youth League.

At present, there's nothing like this in St Ann's but hopefully we can start it up again. The old Sycamore Sports Centre, on Hungerhill Road, has been revamped by the Renewal Trust as a Business Park and a Youth Centre

[Sycamore Millennium Centre] and I hope they will develop this side of things. I've had some involvement there. Youth clubs have been declining for so long it is going to take the community a long time to get back into youth club mode and to want to run things. At one time the youth clubs' teams all played each other.

I'd like to give one or two nights at the Sycamore Centre to help get things going. But once it's going, it must have continuity and it's finding people willing to give that time.

When I was involved with football around St Ann's, I knew roughly what was going off. If people get to know the kids, they are pretty decent. There will always be the bad ones that's going to screw you. But I think today there's a lack of interaction between adults and children. You can build a building and put in it every conceivable thing you could think of from computers to table tennis, and in my opinion there will always be Jack the lad who's not going to want that. He will be out on the streets and get up to whatever he gets up to. There isn't a level of understanding between grown-ups and teenage kids, we've missed something along the line here.

I took some kids from around here and some from Hyson Green Boys' Club to play at Bramcote. There were four or five pitches. Because we had no transport we went on the bus. When we got there, Bramcote were a nice, well-organised team, established for a good number of years and had a number of teams. There was masses of parents around the pitch. I was gob-smacked. I'd not found a lot of parental support, two or three people used to help out and a couple of the lads' mums. I think now if we could get something going, there might be a lot more parental involvement because parents seem more aware or want to be more aware of what's happening to their kids.

One of the more derogatory things for St Ann's, and I've moaned to councillors about this, is that in order to get European money it has to be known as a deprived area. This is a terrible indictment on people and the area. If we get some regeneration money from the European Fund, it's flashed on television that it's a deprived area.

In fifty years' time I would like to think people would say St Ann's is a nice place to live. At the end of the day it's only people that make an area improve. They can come and paint it, put glass chandeliers on all the lamps, but it's only the people in the area that count.

There should be continuity. It might only be a small need in the community but an essential one. Money should be available because people are going to run things. Obviously a check has to be kept on money and to get value for money, but - as long as something is useful - continuity. Some of our local politicians do seem very hands on and they believe they know the needs of an area like this. But when it comes to small group funding, I don't think they actually get out and interact with small groups. If they did they might understand a bit more.

This school was built in the 1950s before the area was demolished. It could hold 400 kids. Now we're less than 200. Since Jacqui Smith has been the Head Teacher here, because there are no men teachers, I've been able to get

involved in some of the sporting activities in school and we've even run infant football which is brilliant. It's a happy school.

We have three children and five grandchildren. One daughter is living in St Ann's and her son is in this school. My other daughter is at Hyson Green and my son is at Alfreton.

School outing to Rutland Water when Bill Chambers' daughter Trina (centre) was at the Elms

HUNTINGDON PRIMARY AND NURSERY SCHOOL

The existing buildings, on Alfred Street Central, were officially opened by the Lady Mayoress, Mrs Dorothea Foster, on June 11th 1973. They were built for Huntingdon Junior School [Head Teacher G A Richardson] and Huntingdon Infant School [Head Teacher Mrs B E Dexter]. These schools replaced the then to be demolished Huntingdon Junior School[1] and Shelton Infants School[2].

Huntingdon Junior and Infant schools which came into use in 1972

---

[1] The senior boys section of the Huntingdon Street School was merged into Elliott Durham Bi-lateral [later Comprehensive] School when it opened in 1966. The Huntingdon Street Board School opened on January 31st 1876 with Mr E W Hemming as its first Head Teacher. He stayed until July 26th 1901. The first boy to enter Huntingdon Street School became Sir Albert Atkey, Member of Parliament for Central Nottingham and a Mayor of Nottingham. Arthur Mee, Editor of the Children's Encyclopaedia attended for three years.

[2] The original infants section of Huntingdon Board School grew rapidly and moved to its own premises as Shelton Street Infant and Nursery School in 1893.

The 'old' Huntingdon Street School. Photo: Peter Garner, Nottingham Local Studies Library.

Huntingdon Infant School equipment for physical education. Both photos from the City of Nottingham Education Committee's official launch brochure

The new Junior School was accommodated on the first floor of the building and the Infant School, at ground level, included purpose-built nursery facilities for sixty children.

A special room for community use, together with a kitchen store and cloakroom facilities was built next to one of the assembly halls. The school was built, using the Method System Building with brick walls with timber fascias, by Bodill and Sons Ltd at a cost of £194,765. Furniture and equipment cost £17,780.

Building commenced in February 1971 and the school was occupied in September 1972, some months before the official opening.

The Huntingdon Junior and the Huntingdon Infant Schools amalgamated into the current Huntingdon Primary and Nursery School in September 1996 with one Head Teacher, Miss J Carruthers. The school was registered to take 420 boys and girls aged 5 – 11 years with a Nursery Unit for 60 full-time equivalent children between 3 – 5 years. At that time there were some two hundred children on the school roll plus a sixty-place day nursery. The children came predominantly from the area of housing in which the school is situated at the bottom end of Woodborough Road. There were three infant classes and five junior classes and staff included two part-time Special Needs Support Teachers and 2.6 full-time equivalent Section XI Staff [the term then used for staff financed to assist the needs of ethnic minority children].

In 1996, approximately 45% of the school's children came from ethnic minority backgrounds, the majority being African Caribbean and of mixed race.

Another aspect of the 'old' School. Photo: Geoffrey Shaw, Nottingham Local Studies Library

A first floor classroom of the 'old' school in it last term of occupation, July 1972. Photo: Peter Garner, Nottingham Local Studies Library

The site of the new school

Building the new school

Children in the new Huntingdon Infant and Nursery School 1972

Photos: Barbara Dexter, Head Teacher

Moving in August 1972. The Ashforth factory in the background. Photos: Barbara Dexter

ST ANN'S NOTTINGHAM: inner-city voices *by Ruth I Johns* • ISBN 0951696092

Photos: Barbara Dexter

The Nursery playground 1975. Photo: Huntingdon Primary and Nursery School

The School taking part in the SATRA [St Ann's Tenants and Residents Association] Festival 1974. Phil Everett top left. Photo: Huntingdon Primary and Nursery School

The Hunto Steel Band played at the opening of Family First's Family Centre in Alexandra Park 1975. Left, Margaret Bramall, Director of the National Council for One Parent Families, the Band Leader and Ruth I Johns, Director Family First, right. Photo: Nottingham Evening Post

The Queen's Silver Jubilee and May Day being celebrated by the Infant and Nursery School 1977. Photo: Huntingdon Primary and Nursery School

The full Band playing on the same occasion. Photo: Ruth I Johns

The children wrote accounts of their visit to Nottingham Forest Football Club grounds. One wrote: "3rd February 1981, Mr Dick Williams from the Daily Mirror sent us these photographs [one here with Brian Clough] of our six-a-side team holding the European Cup."

And here are just a few photos from the School collection. Some are undated.

A class in Huntingdon Infants School 1996

1982

Prize-winners Caleb Stone and Shareen Iqbal, with the runners-up in the Homemakers' Competition sponsored by Nottingham Building Society 1994

SPEECH BY HEAD TEACHER, MRS BARBARA DEXTER[1], at official opening of the new building of Huntingdon Infants and Nursery School, Alfred Street Central, St Ann's, June 11th 1973. The school included the former Shelton Street School.

It is ninety-seven years since Huntingdon Infants School admitted the first 56 children. The school was conducted by a Head, one pupil teacher and four monitors. During their first week in school, the children were thoroughly examined and classified.

It was during these early years that the Head wrote in the School Log that: 'When children come to school at five and a half or six without any previous training, it is almost impossible for them to pass Standard One at seven-years. If anything could be done to induce the parents to send them at four or four and a half, so that they could have a few months training in the baby room, the necessity for over pressure, as regards infants, would be done away with. All children are wonderfully helped if they have good grounding in the baby room.'

The school enlarged and had a temporary class in Mansfield Road and this was obviously one of the reasons why in 1893 the school moved into splendid new premises on Shelton Street.

There were six classes for 458 children. One class had 101 children in it. It was staffed by a Head, three uncertificated teachers and six pupil teachers. Quite a different position to that in which we found ourselves many years later in 1968 when, with a similar number of children, Shelton Infants School was designated Top Priority Area School in the City, with the result that we had ten teachers, two qualified nursery nurses and extra accommodation in the old dining rooms on Huntingdon Street.

Nevertheless, over the years, the school built up a fine reputation as a happy school with sound educational practice and many have been proud to be associated with Shelton Infants School. It was a school staffed by enthusiastic and dedicated teachers who only left because of babies, promotion and retirement. Two of them are with us today: Miss Wallis, who was Head for twenty-one years, and Mrs Reynolds who taught the children of Shelton Street long enough for one of her five year old pupils to grow up and become one of her colleagues on the staff. Though now retired, Mrs Reynolds still comes every week to play the piano for us.

It was a school that always had good co-operation with parents, so much so that early in 1972, mothers spent weeks in school sewing, knitting and helping us to prepare for what we had all been waiting for. In September 1972, due to the redevelopment of St Ann's and to the foresight and planning of the Education Committee, we moved to this new building, surrounded by green grass and trees to complete the circle and become Huntingdon Infants School once more. And the school is fulfilling the wishes expressed by the Headmistress almost one hundred years

ago because we now have a splendid 60-Unit Nursery which, although only opened six months ago, is already helping the children of this area socially and educationally and the benefit should be felt not only in the next few months but for many years to come.

On behalf of the staff, parents and children of Huntingdon Infants, I express our grateful thanks to the Education Committee for our new school and to the Lady Mayoress for opening it so graciously.

Before the Infant School moved from Shelton Street to the new premises, Barbara Dexter took these photos of the school and of children playing in the school playground 1971.

Shelton Street School building 1971

The road sign is Wellington Street

Side entrance showing staff kitchen windows

---

[1] Also see interview with Mrs B E Dexter

St Ann's Nottingham: inner-city voices *by Ruth I Johns* • ISBN 0951696092

The toilets accessed from the school yard.
Photos: Barbara Dexter 1971

Outside the dining room. It was a street before demolition started

Shelton Street Infant School

Children's games. Photos: Barbara Dexter 1971

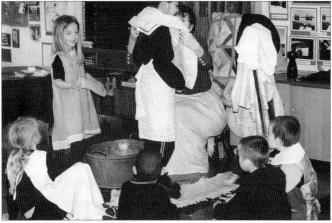

ST ANN'S NOTTINGHAM: inner-city voices *by Ruth I Johns* • ISBN 0951696092

Photos: Barbara Dexter 1971

MRS LES ROSE

Class Teacher, Shelton Infants and then Huntingdon Infants Schools wrote:

"I remember walking to the Forest [Recreation Ground] a few days before Goose Fair opened. Most of the children had not walked so far before. They were so excited and got as much pleasure from kicking up the leaves under the trees and throwing them at each other, as they did from going around the amusements. In the afternoon it was difficult to keep them awake, they were so tired.

"Another special occasion was when the Victoria Centre opened. We took the children to see the Emmet Clock. Their faces were alight with wonder as they watched the sculptured flower open to reveal the revolving animals when the clock played music on the hour. They just stood in awe and silence.

"The Stonebridge City Farm was also a source of great delight. Many of the children had not previously seen farm animals, and to be able to touch and feed them was magic."

BARBARA DEXTER

Born 1930

*Interviewed in her home 19.11.99, Barbara Dexter was a former Head Teacher of **Shelton Street Infants School**, St Ann's, before it was demolished as part of the St Ann's clearance and then, in 1972, of the new **Huntingdon Infants and Nursery School**, Alfred Street Central, St Ann's. Mrs Dexter retired in 1990*

I was born in Bakersfield, Nottingham, and lived there until I was seven. My father worked at Player's and my mother started whittling about him riding on his motorbike to Players when it was foggy. So we moved to Lake Street, Bentinck Road. I went to Edale Road School, then Jesse Boot School, then Bentinck School before I went to the Manning School. I have only lived outside Nottingham for the years I was at College in Coventry.

In 1950, I had a term up at Highwood Player Infant and Nursery School, which was then called Player West Infants. Then I moved to Coventry Road Infant School at Bulwell for two terms. Then to Glenbrook Primary School which was then a fairly new school. I learnt a great deal from the Head there, Miss Gill. She was really helpful and taught me a lot. Then I had my son.

I went back to Glenbrook and Miss Gill said: 'Now then, are you staying here or are you going to look for promotion?' Until that moment I had never thought of promotion. I was so happy at that school but she planted a seed. So, after a while, I applied for Deputy Headships and eventually got Shelton Infant Deputy Headship in St Ann's. That was about 1958. I was there five years as a Deputy Head. During those years things really began to move in Nottingham education. They took on things like vertical and family groupings in infants schools. We had all ages in one group.

After that I went as Head at Southwark Infant School, Old Basford. The children looked as if they were dressed to go to Sunday school compared with Shelton Infant School. I was there for four years and then I became Head of Shelton Infants in 1967. There were only two members of staff who had been there prior to my arriving. So it was six new teachers, new Deputy Head and new Head.

The School grew and had to have extra space in what had been our school kitchen in Huntingdon Street. Eventually it became a place where they did special work with teenagers. We had two rooms, which had been dining rooms, massive, they were really long huts. I opened one class in there and then a second. By then we had four hundred and seventy children.

Shelton Infants' School staff 1970. Back row left to right: Ruth Thomas (student), Di Heslop, Mary Clarkson, Alan Hickman, Lilian Blakely, Pat Hope and Dorothy Goodrich. Front row: Hilary Gibson, Lesley Rose, Mary Walton, Barbara Dexter [Head Teacher], Barbara ?, Sue Summerfield. Photo: source Barbara Dexter, C A Noble, 29, Shelton Street

When demolition started, we grew smaller but not as small as some of the schools in St Ann's. They started pulling down all the houses around us and the school was standing in splendid isolation, except on the City side of Shelton Street where the railway houses are. They are still there. We also took children from North Sherwood Street because that area hadn't been redeveloped at that time.

And then they started building our new school just below us. We couldn't go near the building so we watched from the edge and did a lot of work about our new school. We moved into it in 1972 and it was officially opened the following year.

The parents who were staying with us, from the railway houses, were excited and asked if there would be a uniform. I said yes if you want one. And we did. They were really interested and supportive. When we opened, we had families coming from all over Nottingham to the new St Ann's. Some came from the Meadows. It wasn't always the

ST ANN'S NOTTINGHAM: inner-city voices *by Ruth I Johns* • ISBN 0951696092

St Ann's families that were moved back into St Ann's. But the newcomers soon began to be part of our community and I felt the school was the centre of it. If they had any problems, it was school they'd come to.

I can remember one mother coming in high dudgeon. I said: 'Whatever's the matter, aren't you very well, come and sit down.' She was coming to say her child got dirty while he was painting, but we sat her down and got her a cup of tea. It was nothing to do with school. It was problems at home. She became a valued part of our community and became a crossing lady in spite of having bad legs and she supported the school very well.

She was a lovely mum and she was worried about her son. She kept taking him to the doctor and she said: 'They keep fobbing me off.' She went to the Ewing School for the Deaf and then back to the hospital and it turned out he had meningitis. Unfortunately he became stone deaf but he had already learnt to read so he was able to cope. He continued at hearing school.

I've heard of him since. A few years ago there was an article in the paper. He had all his certificates for swimming and life-saving and applied to be a lifeguard at a swimming pool. They refused him because he was deaf.

In those days, we rarely saw the dads. It was the mums. When we had an Autumn Fayre or Concert, or at Christmas for the Nativity or Christmas Carol Service, then we'd get dads. Prior to the development upheaval, the community was wonderful. They really did help each other. If one was ill, others would bring the children to school, do the shopping, look after the person who was ill, very supportive of each other.

By the 1980's, I felt that had come back with a lot of our parents. They did help each other and some very young mothers really supported each other. They had no extended family and were each other's support.

Dinner ladies at a later date (undated): all ex-mums at Huntingdon Infant and Nursery School. Back row left to right: Ms Sue Benton, Mrs Heather Sparks. Front row: Barbara Dexter, Mrs Jean Wells whose children went to Shelton Infants School, Mrs Carol Williams and Mrs Angela McPherson, Senior Midday Supervisor. These two photos from Barbara Dexter

The new school was called Huntingdon Infant and Nursery School, that was downstairs, and Huntingdon Junior School was upstairs with a separate Head. At that time, it was Alan Richardson who had been Head at the demolished Huntingdon Junior on Huntingdon Street.

The last time I was in the School was a few weeks ago when the new Head, Diana Owen, showed me round. The Nursery was only on one side, that's quite interesting because we used to be full to the brim, sixty in the morning and sixty in the afternoon in the Nursery but times change. Families become older and there are fewer children.

After redevelopment of the area, some families came back. I remember one family in particular. Some of the children were in my class when I was Deputy Head at Shelton. The mum said: 'I don't like it, they've sent me to Clifton. All my friends are scattered all over the place, I want to come back here.'

Some of the children were very bright. Of course, we also had children from families who were rehoused because they hadn't paid their rent. They [the Council] brought them into the same street, only it was now a Close, where they used to do the same as before. So new buildings, but little changed.

And then we had the excitement of people coming in to the new houses with the promise of a new beginning. We did all kinds of things in school to encourage parents. We had coffee mornings regularly, a mother and toddler group and so on and they became a school family. It was important the parents felt they belonged. They came in to help in the classrooms with the children or if their child was upset they could stay with them. It was wonderful to

Huntingdon Infant and Nursery School cooks (in the lighter overalls) and other staff. Barbara Dexter fourth left back row 1984

have the opportunity to do that in the Nursery, we hadn't had one before. The Nursery was from age three.

Of course when we opened we had no nursery children. So we had to find them! I could get children from the families already in school but we had sixty places to fill in the morning and in the afternoon. At the time they were pulling down the old Shelton School, members of our young staff went out looking for families with nursery age children. The workmen were whistling at these teachers and asked them what they were doing. They said: 'We want some children.' And the workmen said: 'We can sort that out for you!' I'll never forget the teachers coming back and telling me I sent them on some strange jobs! But the Nursery soon got known. A child would come part-time when they were three and then full-time in the fourth year.

Then they went on to the Junior School when they were seven plus. Before the children made the change, Junior teachers would come downstairs to see the children and the children would sometimes go upstairs to show the Head their work or for some activity. Being in one building made the transition much easier. Before, we had to cross the Woodborough Road from Shelton School and go to the big awe-inspiring building of Huntingdon School, which was for Juniors and Seniors. In 1966, the seniors went up to Elliott Durham School on Ransom Drive.

I was disappointed that they didn't do something with the old Shelton Street building. It had character. The hall floor was wonderful. When we first moved into the new school, every time it rained we'd get water leaking in where there were flat roofs over the hall and kitchen. That was troublesome for some time and the floor kind of lifted. Every time it did that I said I wished we still had the old Shelton School floor. I don't know what it was made of but Bill Stokes would. He cleaned it often enough.

That reminds me of an illustration of what I meant about community. I remember a family with quite a few

children and they lost their father. One of them right from age five wanted to help the caretaker, who took this child under his wing. Even as an Infant he used to help put the chairs up and down. When he was a Junior, he came back into school (the old building now gone). Then he went to Rosehill School and still came back and helped the caretaker, and, by now, he's emptying baskets and helping to sweep the floors and so on. By eighteen, he was our Assistant Caretaker. Eventually he became our Senior Caretaker and he's now Site Manager of a Comprehensive School. All his mum's children came to Shelton/Huntingdon, and so have her nephews and nieces and now the grandchildren.

And, in the new school, that began to happen quite quickly, ex-pupils coming with their children. I found that very good.

I retired in 1990. I'm still involved in education as Chair of Governors at our local Infant and Nursery School, Highwood Player Infants, and a Governor of the Manning School.

I enjoyed St Ann's. I could have made a move to the Inspectorate or an adviser's job. I thought long and hard but decided I was happier where I was enjoying work, with the families and the children. Families were always welcome in school. I think if you let them see what you are doing, they respect what you do. My husband, John, has also taught in the City Centre, seventeen years as Head Teacher of Bentinck Primary School. Previously, he was a teacher at the Elms Junior School in St Ann's and started its first after-school play centre in an Annexe on Alfred Street; then he went to Douglas Junior School on Ilkeston Road; he became Head of Victoria Primary School [sometimes called the Bath Street School] in St Ann's and then Head of Bentinck. He retired in 1989[1]. We both liked working with the families and children.

When I retired a grandma came with all of her daughters and her son and her grandchildren and said: 'We've come because you've always been here for us.' I really enjoyed their company.

We had more families with only one parent over the years and the number of children on free meals increased[2]. But they were better dressed, the change in that was incredible. When we were in the old school, some of the families were struggling. Some of my staff came from quite well-to-do families and I'd say to them that the mothers did really well with no running hot water, toilets outside. My grandmother's toilet was across the yard although it was not a shared one.

The majority of the children were well turned out even then. They may not have had new clothes every five minutes but parents had a pride in what was there. Some of our children were from the other side of the Mansfied Road and were still sharing a tap and outside toilets after St Ann's was redeveloped.

Families who came into the new houses worked hard to

Staff at Huntingdon Infant and Junior School 1990. Barbara Dexter second from left front row. First left front row is Di Baker. Photo: Huntingdon Primary and Nursery School

---

1   John Dexter died January 2002. Over 300 people attended his funeral at St Margaret's Church, Aspley, including many from St Ann's.

2   15.2.71 Huntingdon Infant and Nursery School Log Book records: "The use of decimal currency began today. 44p for five dinners. 9p for one."

get them beautiful. Some of them were very young when we were in the new School and I really admired how well they did because some of them were only girls themselves, sixteen, seventeen, eighteen. I'm still in touch with quite a few. One of the boys, for instance, was in the Gulf War. His sister was a child in the Nursery and became one of its Nursery Nurses. When she said her brother, Ian, was in the Gulf, I got his address and wrote to him. When he came home, I was invited to the family party. His mum became one of the dinner ladies, she became the senior one.

About six months ago, I was in the checkout at Marks and Spencer and I heard this young man say: 'Morning, how are you?' Handsome West Indian young man. He said: 'Mrs Dexter, we were all frightened of you.' He said he was naughty then and I said: 'No just a handful!' Now he's in financial services, he's not usually on the checkout. I see ex-pupils at Clarendon because I go there for lunch. Sometimes, it's the little tykes who turn out well.

I think of a school as a family. We had an outing to Skegness and this mum with two little boys plus baby came. We took buckets, cloths and everything in case anyone was sick or wanted to wee when we were miles out. I was worried whether this mum and her friend would get back to the bus on time because one of them was notorious for coming when they were ready! But they were back on time without having a watch. They said they kept looking at the tower. We had some good times together.

Educational bureaucracy? There's too much pressure on staff. So many papers have come out in my teaching career. If I counted all of them there wouldn't be as many as there have been in the last ten years. It's just horrendous. Each child is an individual and each has different needs and it hasn't changed. Each will learn at a different rate, not everybody can take everything in and it sink in straight away. I think the National Curriculum has put so much emphasis on reading that they've tended to forget the writing. The writing hasn't developed as much. To my mind reading and writing go hand-in-hand. Whatever you write should be able to be read back. Children's imaginations need to be stimulated so they write a story or draw a picture.

One of our Governors wanted to give a prize to the best child in the school each year before they moved on to the Juniors. So I said no! All the children going up to the Juniors had achieved something. Would he agree to give them all something? Ever since, he paid for them to have a book at the end of their Infant School years. It was a wonderful way of showing the children they had worked hard, and also of showing him that not everybody achieves to the same level.

The Infant and Nursery School, and the Junior School were amalgamated [1996]. So now it's joint administration, one Head and one Deputy Head, one Board of Governors. It used to be the Local Authority's Primary Education Sub-Committee that dealt with all Primary schools. When Boards of Governors were introduced, we first had the same group of Governors for Victoria, Huntingdon Junior and Huntingdon Infant Schools. Then Victoria closed and later the two Huntingdon Schools had separate governors.

And now they've amalgamated. In the 1970's there was a point where the cutbacks were so bad that we only had two teachers and one Nursery Nurse for sixty children. There was a lot of unrest.

We didn't want to lose the Nursery or to lose the numbers, but we needed help. It wasn't the nursery mums who came in to help, it was the other mothers who had already been helping and offered to go into the Nursery. One of those mothers is still helping in school twenty years on. Eventually we got the full quota of staff back but it was horrendous.

The 1970s and I still remember thinking of the nursery mums: 'Well you want your children here and yet you won't go on a rota, not every day, just a half-day every other week.' Then things changed. In the 1980s, if we were short staffed, I had literally to go and ask the mums who were standing outside in the morning if someone could offer back-up and they did. A grandma came in one day when we were short in the Nursery and a Nursery Nurse asked if she could come in. She said: 'I can see how bad you are fixed. Let me go and turn my washer off and I'll be back.' That's the kind of response we got from a lot of the parents. Some couldn't because they went to work. And some wouldn't no matter what! But you get that in every community.

In the 1980s they stopped doing some of the things I thought were important in school, like regular visits of the nit nurse. We used to have her regular visit and the regular visit of the nurse who came to check eyes, ears and things. In one family, the little boy wasn't flourishing and the school nurse said could I talk to the mother. This was in the Shelton School. She wondered what he was eating. He was so small. Eva Covington, the School Welfare Officer said she would have a word too. The mother said he always had a good dinner, because I asked why he didn't stay and have a free school dinner. She didn't want that because she gave him a good dinner of a packet of crisps and a cream cake. I said here he would get meat and vegetables and a pudding. She was one of several parents I persuaded to let their children stay for school dinners. They liked having their children with them. There was a lot of love, you could feel it all the time.

Every November we had an Autumn Fayre to make money to give the children a Christmas party and buy them a little present, only a little one because we had 200 plus children. Parents gave what they could and they'd bring in stuff and join in with everything. Originally, they would come with £1 and they'd spend that, then later it was £5 but we knew once that was spent we wouldn't sell any more because there was no more money. But they were generous.

We had lots of different people, Sikhs, West Indians, Italians . . . I'm proud of a lot of the children because they have done so well. The children who live in St Ann's have a lot of innate ability that's not always tapped, but at school we always tried to make the best of it so they would use it wisely. All the different nationalities, we used to call it a rich tapestry. Parents would come and talk and bring things in for displays.

Once we had some eggs in an incubator and the mums were coming in every day to see what was happening and lo! *the* day came when the chicks were born. Children were rushing out to bring their mums in. We always wanted to get parents involved right from the nursery ages. For example, giving a child something to take home to do. For instance: 'Take this matchbox and find five things which fit into it!' It was starting them off on maths and the parents really entered into the spirit of it. After all, parents are the best teachers.

The thing I was looking forward to in retirement was taking my two grandsons to and from school and to see them at school. They are fourteen and sixteen now.

LOG BOOKS

Entries from Huntingdon Junior School and Huntingdon Nursery and Infant School Log Books, and conversations

During the years of planning blight and redevelopment in St Ann's, caring teachers were at the cutting edge of social as well as educational help. It was contact, especially of young mums with each other at the school gate and in school, that helped to create the beginnings of community in the 'new' St Ann's.

School outings and holidays are important to all children, but for many St. Ann's children in the district's transition years from 1966-76 they were probably one of the most important aspects of their education at that time.

When the old Huntington School building was used as a polling station on Election days, children went on outings. For example on 12.5.66, the Junior School Log records: "Seventy-seven children of the third and fourth years and nine staff travelled to London for the day by special train at 8.05 am, arriving home a little late at 9.04 pm. Saw changing of the Guard at Buckingham Palace and visited Westminster Abbey, where we heard the London Symphony Orchestra rehearsing, went by boat from Charing Cross Pier to the Tower and, after looking around the Tower, went by bus on a sightseeing tour, finally arriving at the Zoo in Regents Park. Had tea there, bus to St. Pancras to catch the train. Good weather and lovely day. Meanwhile a small group of children of Class Five travelled with their teacher to Newstead Abbey where they enjoyed a happy day."

And on May 11th 1967: "School closed all day for Municipal Elections. Eight members of staff took sixty-two children on a visit to York. Visited the Railway Museum, walked along the walls, had lunch in the park, went to the Minster and up the Tower, walked through The Shambles to the Castle Museum, where we also saw the judge arriving for the Assizes, and then for an hour's trip over to Bishopsthorpe. End the day with excellent high tea at the Co-operative Restaurant."

And a snatch of atmosphere about holidays. The log entry 25.5.73 by G A Richardson, Head Teacher of the

Junior School: "Mrs Richardson (my wife) and I set out with eighteen children for a holiday in Scarborough. Both my own children accompanied us and we joined with Springfield Junior in the venture. This year we had the best weather of all our holidays so far. It was very pleasant to be able to spend whole days on the beach. We have previously often spent a good deal of time touring around the countryside in the coach to avoid the rain. It was a most educational and recreational trip. I especially enjoy the four children sponsored each year by the Edward Clarke Trust; their reactions make the whole thing worthwhile. What a pity we haven't more free places!"

There were twenty-four years in which City schools were run by the County Council before the City of Nottingham again became a Unitary Authority in 1998. Log Book entries indicate that Huntington schools followed guidelines. For example, in administrative organisation, teaching of ethnic minority children, and staffing and health and safety matters.

In the 1970s and the 1980s there was intermittent industrial action on the part of non-teaching and of teaching staff [not only in St. Ann's schools].

17.1.79 Junior Log, for example states: "No instructions regarding strike by caretakers and other non-teaching staff planned for Monday next." 18.1.79: "Phone call from Area Office informing Head Teacher that he would be responsible for opening and closing school. Chairman of Managers informed. There is grave concern as there will be no caretaker, no crossing wardens, no meals, no midday supervision, maybe no heat, and maybe pickets at school. Chairman of Managers contacted County Hall."

26.1.79 the Junior Log states: "Letters from the Director received regarding action to be taken in the event of 'lightning strikes' by manual workers (caretakers, dinner staff etc.). Copies of letters for parents and reply slips to ascertain numbers of children who could, or could not, go home instead of dining in school in the event of meals being cancelled without previous notice. The duplicating of a relatively complex reply slip at short notice proved problematic for a school with limited reprographic facilities."

18.1.80 the Infant and Nursery Log says the Chairman of the School Managers was phoned to inform him that all teachers in the school (all NUT) would be leaving school at 2.30 pm on January 23rd to attend a Union Meeting.

From my personal knowledge of the local situation, there was a strong feeling that inner-city schools were not appreciated 'from above' and were starved of funds. They did not seem a County Council priority, even though the County Council's Deprived Area Study [1975] highlighted the needs of Nottingham's inner-city areas. And the Government Education Policy didn't help.

Cutbacks took various forms, for example, the Junior Log Book 17.9.79 records a meeting attended by the Head Teacher to hear about proposed cuts. "Thirty-two proposed cuts will include loss of school pianist, Mrs Sheil; 10% cut in general allowance, 50% cut in swimming, school lettings to outside bodies will cease, no orchestra concerts . . . other cuts will have a knock-on effect."

ST ANN'S NOTTINGHAM: inner-city voices *by Ruth I Johns* • ISBN 0951696092

19.9.79 Junior Log: "Meeting of Head Teachers at Victoria Primary to discuss the inconsistencies of the proposed swimming cuts. This school will lose 10 periods per fortnight, being allocated 4 (two in the large and two in the small [pools]) while now we have 7 per week. Further, the lack of an instructor in the large pool will prevent us using that pool as we have no trained life-saver on the staff." Log Book 16.9.80: "Swimming 9.00am. No instructor available for large pool. Instructor late in small pool."

28.11.79 Infant and Nursery Log: "A meeting of nursery parents was held this morning to ask for committed help for the nursery. We managed to get enough help from the parents to make up a rota of helpers to cover each session. This is to begin immediately in view of staff cuts."

8.10.80: "Head Teacher to meeting with Assistant Director, Mr Addison, and other Primary School Heads regarding the effects of closure of Victoria Primary School in September 1980. We will gain about nine children." [Victoria School, Bath Street, was on the City side edge of St. Ann's.]

14.10.80: "Mr Gibney, Supervisor Caretakers, visited to discuss cleaning hours. These will be cut in total from 94 at present to 88 hours in both schools after half term."

The following Log Book entries give some idea of the practical day-by-day problems that beset staff because of years of maintenance neglect.

4.6.92 Infants and Nursery School Log Book: "Disastrous day! Ms J Wilson [Head Teacher after Mrs Dexter retired in 1990] and Mrs Baker had set aside time to update computer work. But, as soon as it was switched on, we were called to the Nursery where water was again pouring through the ceiling in three separate places, this time through electric wires. We covered the area with buckets, water trays etc and Mrs Breakwell ingeniously designed a method of ensuring that water flowed into a dustbin through plastic piping!

"Obviously the situation was dangerous so Ms Wilson decided to close Nursery North for the afternoon. Radio Nottingham was informed, also Rev J Neill (Chair of Governors), and County Hall Education Administration. We could not inform the Area Office as nobody was available (a training day for officers).

"DLO and building Surveyors were contacted. Two men arrived to clear blocked down pipes (with no ladders or equipment!), but no electrician had arrived to check electrical wiring by the time Ms Wilson left (3.00 pm to have physiotherapy). It was decided to inform parents available that Nursery North would probably be closed again tomorrow. The situation will be assessed early tomorrow morning.

"Two large holes appeared in the pavement outside school. We decided to refer the matter to the Highway and Environment Departments. Mrs Flatt (Health and Safety rep.) phoned this information through to them.

"Two midday supervisors were absent. Luckily we found a temporary (Mrs Lamb, a parent).

"During our attempt to work the computer, it became 'stuck' in the middle of a programme. On phoning Helpline,

we were told that there was a problem at County Hall. Despite several attempts to rectify this, we had to have special instructions to 'exit'. A whole day wasted!"

3.2.93 Infant and Nursery Log: "Mrs Baker and Ms Wilson struggled to complete new forms for the Area Office which proved very difficult as the instructions received were already out of date."

10.6.93 Infant and Nursery Log: "Ms Wilson attended a Section XI meeting at Sandfield Centre on behalf of the Elliott Durham family [of schools], to discuss government proposals and reductions in funding in the next two years."

11.2.94 Infant and Nursery Log: "Mr Bloor visited to examine rotten putty and window frames on the exterior of the building. Apparently, 'putty' is the school's responsibility although the 'wood' is non-delegated. He therefore agreed to repair the worst part of wood on two windows, but the rest would have to wait to be replaced!"

9.5.94 Infant and Nursery Log Book: "School broken into in the early hours of the morning. Mr Clegg phoned Ms Wilson at 7.00 am."

On a more positive note, on 25.7.94 Ms Wilson and Miss Carruthers had a visit from Mr I Vernalls from the City Council to discuss new updated proposals for the Ashforth Street Development across the road from the school.

25.10.95 Infant and Nursery Log Book: "Mrs Breakwell came into school on request of Site Manager, Mr Clegg. Due to storm last night, severe flooding had occurred particularly to the Infant Hall, electrical storage cabinet, Room I and stairwell. Other damage occurred in the Junior School. Electrician called out to look at the electrical cabinet, apparently very high risk of fire as circuits 'shorting'."

30.10.95: "Mr Clegg has done splendid work during the holiday to try and resolve problems . . . All staff except Ms Wilson returned."

Mrs B Breakwell was acting Head, October 1995 - July 1996, until the Junior and Infant and Nursery Schools amalgamated.

During these years of mounting difficulties, Huntington Schools retained close links with what they called the Elliot Durham family of local schools. Staff continued to do their best for children despite growing behaviour problems, which caused Jonathan P Hancock, Head Teacher of the Junior School, to write to parents 19.4.91 about children's punctuality, lack of attention, disrespect, mouthiness and lack of care for property.

A few days later, the School Log records that the initial response from parents was overwhelmingly in support of the school's statement. Whatever has happened, parents of Huntingdon Schools remained [with occasional exceptions] very supportive of teachers.

Parents and children in St. Ann's have, for generations, appreciated their under-11s schools. Testimony of many interviewees in this book affirms this. There were unhappy children at school, but even they usually found in some teacher or school activity something that fired their interest and enthusiasm. The promising young swimmer, for example, could be recommended for free tuition at the

Victoria Baths. Now these pools are under threat. If they go, another local facility within walking distance will be a serious loss to local people.

It may not be coincidental that behavioural problems grew in the years in which schools had to cut back on activities. And these cutbacks happened at the time when people in the new St Ann's were struggling to develop a community identity without - as a generalisation - the family networks of support available to many in the old St Ann's. Also unemployment was growing.

Teachers were concerned that standards were changing with regard to young people's behaviour. The Junior Log Book 25.9.79, for example, states: "PC Breeze, liaison officer for the Juvenile Bureau being set up by the police, to co-ordinate action when young people are reported for criminal activity. I expressed concern that there is no agency concerned with the child below the age of criminal responsibility who, through contact etc, is 'at risk' or who has been involved in 'criminal activities' for which they cannot be held responsible."

The nit question

The incidence of 'dirty' children was a matter of concern when a large number of properties in the school's catchment area were under planning blight for some years. A considerable number of children at Huntingdon and Shelton schools were from 'temporary' accommodation used by Social Services in the nearby streets after the permanent population had already moved or been moved. Keeping clean in the very run-down properties was difficult. It is also interesting to see plenty of references (only one or two shown here) in the School Log Books that indicate substantial continuing parental interest through these difficult times.

There used to be something of a stigma about having nits; a sign of less than capable parenting. Head inspections were stopped some years later, but nits are now cyclically epidemic nationwide in Primary Schools. Parents seldom now see them as a stigma and are, often not prepared to use chemical 'cures' because of potential side-effects and the nits often soon come back anyway. Regular conditioner and fine-combing is the order of the day!

But at 27.5.68, Mrs Din, Nurse's Assistant, called to look at [Junior] children, also on 28th and reported 18 dirty bodies, 18 dirty clothing, bad cases, 60 dirty heads. On July 11th there was an open evening for parents and about 100 came to look at children's work. This was followed by a concert, PE display and play. The hall was full. July 16th, sixty-five children visited Twycross Zoo. Torrential rain all day but somehow smiling faces when they returned.

Mrs Din visited on 5th, 6th and 7th February 1969 and inspected 325 [Junior] children. Of these, 76 had dirty heads, 16 had dirty bodies and 21 had dirty clothes.

10th, 11th and 12th September 1969, Mrs Din made a routine visit and saw 332 [Junior] children. 92 had dirty hair, 10 dirty bodies and 12 dirty clothing. 25.9.69: "Our

Harvest Festival Service. Rev Richard Crowson gave an address. Excellent display of foodstuffs. The gifts, mainly in tins and packets, were given to the Nottingham Council for Social Services."

27.9.74. Hygiene nurse reported 194 [Junior] children seen. 19 whose parents received letters and 6 children with dirty bodies or clothing. Further 16 under observation because of dirty hair.

28th and 29th January 1976. Hygiene inspection. 161 [Junior] children seen. 9 letters sent out, 8 others to watch.

9.1.80. [Infants School] A full cleanliness inspection was carried out today by Mrs Edwards. No children with nits!

By the late 1970s, Junior children received talks by a dental technician on dental hygiene and were given free packs of toothpaste.

Reading

Junior Log Book 19.10.70 records G A Richardson, the Head Teacher's concern "for my good readers that they should have better teachers (we already devote so much time to backwardness that the able could be forgotten)."

In April 1976, he wrote in the Log Book: "My term as Headmaster has been a demanding one, often exhausting. I recall an occasion, in the old school, when a West Indian Grandma sought to soothe an existing state of harassment I was experiencing, by saying: 'Never mind, Mr Richardson your reward will be in Heaven.'

"I feel fortunate in having a two-fold reward without having to wait! The first was a state of mutual respect and regard I shared with the children, and the second was the feeling of being involved in something worthwhile. When I looked back through the Log Book I spotted an entry for April 1968 detailing the current state of reading attainment. There was, at that time, an average of 68% of the school two or more years retarded in reading attainment. I have just compared this with January 1976 and find that the same figure has fallen to 26.6%.

"I said in 1968 that there was an enormous job to be tackled. The existing figure is still too high but does represent a significant improvement. At the other end of the scale 14% of the children are two or more years advanced with their reading. If I may be allowed to claim some part in this improvement, then I am satisfied. This is my reward!"

TONY NORMINGTON

Born 1945

*Interviewed in his home 18.7.00. Former Head of **Elms Primary and Nursery School**, St Ann's, and, in 1999, recalled from retirement to assist **Huntingdon Primary and Nursery School** (as acting Joint Head with Steve Clarke) for some months*

In 1963, I wasn't sure if I wanted to go into teaching. I was offered a place at Manchester University to do Town and Country Planning. I wasn't certain, so I did a year's

Tony Normington 1997

teaching in Grimsby to see whether I liked it. My older sister worked at a Teacher Training College at that time, but there were no other teachers in the family. Now my brother, two sisters and me are teachers!

I was offered a place at Clifton Teacher Training College, Nottingham, and did a three-year training and I stayed in Nottingham when I finished in 1967. It was still a fairly new College, which later became part of Trent Polytechnic and then Trent University. I taught at the Whitegate Junior School on the Clifton Estate for about six years and then became Deputy Head at Douglas Primary School in Radford where over ninety per cent of the pupils came from ethnic minorities, many (then called) Jamaican.

Three years later, in 1977, I was appointed to the Elms Junior School, St Ann's. The Head of the Elms Infant School, Miss Hanson, retired. She had been there since the School opened in the early 1950s. In 1979 the Infant and Junior Schools amalgamated and I was Head of the Primary School. It had a Nursery section.

Education in the City was under the County Council at that time and the Elms was the first school in the City to amalgamate. It was a school in need of some input and the Inspectors told me to take my time. The School had qualities but the children's learning wasn't necessarily a top priority. The staff were very, very concerned about the social welfare and well-being of the children. But academic development was somewhat neglected and there were some very able pupils at that time.

Yes, I went to the School after the surrounding area had been redeveloped. It was Phase 10a or 10b around there. I remember the pupils coming up and being admitted after their families moved into the new houses. I do remember the old Cranmer Street, because the Teachers Centre was

next to the Elms School. For ten years or so I'd been attending courses there and I remember those huge multi-occupied houses. The Teachers Centre used to be the Gordon Boys' Home and is now a Trent University Residence. At one time the basement of the Teachers Centre was overflow classrooms for the Elms School.

The housing in the area was very intense and there used to be some five hundred pupils in the Junior School and three hundred in the Infants and three hundred plus in the Nursery. By the time the School was amalgamated after redevelopment the total number was down to two hundred and eighty.

I think the whole culture in Nottingham in the 1960's training of teachers led to teachers not having great expectations of the children, and parents – and some teachers – felt the children's education was neglected. The culture was to work with children's experiences and if you haven't had many experiences, there isn't much to work on. There were a few teachers who quietly worked on the basis of what we now call numeracy and literacy. But it hadn't got to be high profile because, sadly, back in those days, if you concentrated in those areas you were unlikely to get promotion.

I felt the children had been let down. Some went on to University later. In time, the School changed. Teachers retired or moved on, and I was able to appoint younger teachers and train them in my vision. I feel guilty that some of the pupils didn't reach their potential at eleven. I think later we redressed that and children who wanted to achieve, and those that we could help, did achieve and succeed.

Tony Normington (right) when Head of the Elms Primary School. On his right is Ernest Wright, School Governor. He is now [2001] Chair of Governors

During the late 1970s, early 1980s, the Elms was a 'seventy per cent school'. About seventy per cent of the children came from ethnic minority backgrounds. At one time, there were seventy nationalities represented in school, not necessarily from where the children were born but where their parents were born, including North and South America, the Caribbean, parts of Asia, various parts of Africa, Middle East, middle parts of Europe. About seventy per cent of pupils were on free school meals, at one point about seventy per cent didn't have a parent in full-time employment, and seventy per cent of pupils were not living with both natural parents.

And when you consider that about a quarter to a third of the pupils at that time were from stable Asian (mainly Muslim) family backgrounds that gives an indication of the fragmented family life that some of the pupils experienced. One year, we had a seventy per cent turnover in school population too. That had a destabilising effect on the school. When it was first recognised, I attended a Regional HMI conference on the matter. At some point over thirty per cent of the families at school were under Social Services. One particular fortnight I went to six case conferences.

As well as a lot of movement in and out of the local area, there was a National Children's Home in our catchment area and children came and went. In the late 1970s a Homeless Families Unit opened nearby with lots of families coming and going. The record short-time stay was two hours. It could be two weeks, two months (which was average), and sometimes up to a year.

There were also lots of thriving supportive families involved in the school. They helped decorate, some painted woodwork, there were parent clubs and parents were very supportive of the children. And there were very able children, some of them are graduates in law, in engineering, doctors, teachers. Most of our successful pupils were from ethnic minorities, Vietnamese, Asian, Thai and African Caribbean. In my early days at the School, a lot of the children hadn't worked Stage One as it was then called in a second language. They had no English. Around 1980 external Section XI funding came in and a Section XI teacher (or second language teacher as they were then called) came in and children went down into the old Infants School for half-an-hour with this teacher before going back to their classroom. And that was that until half-an-hour the next week. It was nonsense.

Then a very astute Inspector ruffled a few feathers and realised that some of the money from Government to the Local Education Authority wasn't being used appropriately, and that Section XI funding meant schools should have extra staff. We ended up with two Section XI teachers and they worked alongside the class teachers, so children weren't withdrawn from class. They could plan together and support children. Toward the end of my working at the Elms, most of the children in school were born in this country. We had a little girl from Croatia who had some English. She was very bright.

In the early days, most of the children went on to Elliott Durham School although some of the girls went to Manning all-girls school. As numbers in school reduced we'd have thirty children leaving, rather than fifty and sixty, and parental choice in secondary school meant they were going to nine or ten different schools. Some parents wouldn't go and have a look at Elliott Durham, which was very unfair. Sadly, a lot of parents that went to Elliott Durham wouldn't send their children there. Elliott Durham was opened in an inappropriate way. There was no preparation for pupils coming from the three original

secondary schools in St Ann's: Huntingdon, Sycamore and Morley.

When I first started at the Elms, a lot of people said: 'My God! That has a hell of a rough reputation.' It wasn't tough, it was challenging, it was exciting, it was enjoyable.

All my career, I taught in inner-city schools because I enjoyed it. I retired in 1997. My own background was being brought up on a housing estate in Grimsby. I came from a very poor background so I could empathise with a lot of situations. My parents were supportive but my father was very ill and my mother had to go out to work. I was successful at Grammar School and had a chance to go to University. There was certainly something about the Elms that held me. I remember once applying for a job in a suburb and, in my application, all I could put was how much I loved the Elms!

There are five components to the catchment area of the Elms School. One is the nearby St Ann's area, one is the Aboretum (North Sherwood Street, Colville Street area on the other side of the Mansfield Road). In the early days the families from there were the most impoverished. That's now reversed and better off, supportive families are there. The third are children from the nearby Homeless Families Unit in St Ann's. The fourth is a handful of children from the Mapperley area from the other side of Mapperley Road, Villa Road, near to St Augustine's School and Gorsey Road.

The fifth component comes from outside the catchment area, either from elsewhere in St Ann's or from Sherwood, Bulwell, Beeston, Aspley, Top Valley. That's because a lot of those parents were educated at the Elms themselves and want their children to be, or families who used to live in the catchment area and moved out but wish their children to stay at the same school. For example, one Thai family moved and kept their son at the Elms and he went on to the High School.

I'd always promised myself that I would retire at fifty-five in the year 2000. Up to 1997, once you got past the age of fifty, you could retire if the Governors agreed and you got a pension, which related to the service you'd done. Then the rules were changing so I retired in 1997. Early in my career, my first wife died of a brain tumour and I became a single parent for some years with two young boys, which was challenging. When parents said I didn't know what it was like to be a single parent, I obviously did. But, of course I had employment and was reasonably well off. I'd always promised myself I'd retire a little early to make up for all that and that's what I did, except . . .

. . . yes, I went back to Huntingdon Primary School, St Ann's, when it was in Special Measures[1]. I didn't go looking for it! There was an initiative in Nottingham in the last five years of my career for raising achievement in the inner-city. Elms School did well and the project was highlighted nationally. A colleague, Steve Clarke at Jesse Boot School, was asked to assist Huntingdon School and he could only do it part-time half the week and he asked if I could go full-time. He said he'd only do the job if he could chose who he worked with. And I said Yes! The

---

[1]   The school failed an external inspection (Ofsted).

school neither had a Head nor Deputy at the time. So Steve and I went in as joint Heads January 1999 until July 1999. He knew a lot about the Elms School when I was there. We never discussed our role between ourselves, it just worked. It was one of the most enjoyable times in my career.

When I first went I wondered what I had let myself in for. Huntingdon School had been neglected by the County Council, all the Heads in St Ann's knew it was struggling and had been for some time. But my initial impression was changed because the children were lovely and had very supportive parents. I knew something about some third of the families through my links in St Ann's. The new City Council Education Authority were partly right in looking for rationalisation in schools but they needed to do a more in-depth study rather than take a knee-jerk reaction to an opportunity. But, there is one school too many in St Ann's for the number of children at present.

With a lot of hard work from the staff, a lot of support from the new Education Authority and a lot of endeavours from the children and their parents, the school was turned around. The parents were fantastic. When we had the HMIs coming around, the parents were wonderful, cleaning, helping us to clear out some of the mucky holes in the school. The quadrangles and gardens had been neglected over the years. The parents were very industrious.

I'm still involved in the School. Last week I went in to celebrate coming out of Special Measures. I've been going in on a regular basis to support the new Head. A new young top-quality Head was appointed, Diana Owen. I've been helping with things like background information on the School, budgeting, analysis of staffing. I've grown a strong attachment to Huntington in two terms.

If children are going on from Primary School into a lot of different secondary schools, what effects will that have on community life? I think it will have a massively detrimental effect. It is perhaps relevant to say that when I had occasional parents who wanted to take their child from the Elms, usually because of bullying of a particular child, I would say they'd find the same thing at the next school. I noticed that children were actually making demands that the parents were agreeing to, want to go to another school, try another school, the grass is greener on the other side.

I think it would be better if there was a local community secondary school where St Ann's children went, but that's perhaps not possible because of the historical problems that Elliott Durham has had. Nottingham is a prime example of the outward movement for secondary education, because it is perceived that if a catchment area is 'better' then the School is better. The schools are *not* necessarily better. They just have a more settled catchment area. Aspiring parents in the City want that sort of environment.

Education in the past few years has been blamed - by the media and Governments - for all the failings in society. I don't think education creates society, I think Politicians do. Politically there has got to be more input into education. There's got to be perhaps smaller schools, which would go away from my former suggestion of rationalising

school places in St Ann's. The central problem is that children haven't got the role models to be as successful as their abilities could allow. I think it's a matter of educating parents first. We have a generation of parents, perhaps two generations, who haven't proper parenting skills. They haven't had proper parenting skills, there's been a fragmentation in society, people moving away from the local neighbourhood.

The first Head Teacher I worked with had worked at the Blue Bell Hill School in St Ann's for many years. He used to talk of the strength of neighbours supporting one another. He said there was poverty and there was abuse, but people knew how to support each other. And when you had some activity in school, parents flocked in.

When the new St Ann's evolved, it was obvious there were tensions because people were just thrust together, not necessarily from the old St Ann's but from all over the City. To develop the kind of community spirit in the old St Ann's takes years and years and years. But you've also got a situation where you've got unemployment, more one parent family situations, more drugs and complicating things. I've heard it said that the solution is to shut all inner-city secondary schools and let all the children go out. I don't agree with that. It would be disastrous. But I don't really know what the answer is.

The long-term solution has got to be financial support for inner-cities. This afternoon in the Government's education statement, they're going to put more into inner-cities. Years ago, the Government used to have additional money for inner-city schools. Teachers who stayed in inner-city schools got a priority. It was only £275 p.a. but that was a lot of money then. The Government now expects inner-city Primary Schools to perform to the same level as Bramcote and Wollaton schools. Well, they can but at a cost. And the casualties in the teaching profession are much more than when I first started teaching.

My wish for the future in St Ann's is that people reach their potential in life.

HUNTINGTON SCHOOL SHOWS THAT TEACHERS, ST ANN'S PARENTS and CHILDREN ARE ACHIEVERS

In April 1998, Huntingdon School failed an Ofsted inspection and was put into Special Measures. In a letter to David Blunkett, then Secretary of State for Education and Employment, the parents and children of the school stated that in July 1998, at a packed parents' evening, the Local Education Authority assured the audience that although the school had difficulties, there was no reason why it should close. But on November 5th, parents and carers were informed that the Local Authority recommended closure of the school because it had surplus places and the school's children could be transferred to better performing schools with spare places in the area.

The parents letter stated: "We the parents at Huntingdon Primary and Nursery School strongly feel that the school has not been given a fair chance to get out of Special Measures and we feel that this school should be given the opportunity to prove that it can provide a better education for our children. The School is situated in attractive surroundings with CCTV cameras and provides a safe environment for our children and we are adamant that this school deserves a chance." The letter was signed by Ann Jack, Chris Larvin and Beverley Harper [leaders of the Action Group].

The Parents Action Group was formed the same day as news came of the possible closure. Letters and telephone calls were made to John Heppell, local MP, all local radio stations, the *Evening Post*, East Midlands Today [TV], a petition was organised and leaflets distributed. A meeting was called for November 6th partly in order to organise a protest at the Council House when the Education Committee met on November 9th to discuss the possible closure. Over seventy parents attended this meeting to make their feelings known, also Governors and Unions. It was felt strongly that parents had been betrayed by being told previously that the school would not close. Children wanted to help. They took letters in Braille and tapes to David Blunkett in London. The Royal Society of the Blind helped them with the Braille. Acting Head Teacher Rebecca Meredith said it was a wonderful experience for the children.

The Ofsted Inspectors critical report in 1998 praised the Acting Head, Rebecca Meredith, but said she had not had enough time to save the school from Special Measures. The previous Head was criticised. She wasn't present when the Inspectors visited. She resigned. The report said almost one-third of pupils made unsatisfactory or poor progress in their work.

Some eighty parents, staff and Governors demonstrated at the Council House on November 9th.

Many people I have spoken to in St Ann's deplore a lack of positive reporting in the *Evening Post* about St Ann's, there being much about the crime element of St Ann's news. But, with regard to the threat to Huntingdon School and its reprieve, the *Evening Post* coverage was extensive and positive. Huntingdon parents and members of the local community also wrote published Letters to the Editor to put their case across. Early on in the campaign, the Rev Jim Neill wrote: " . . . I am pleading, as pastor of this large urban priority area Parish, and as a co-opted Governor, for someone to listen to the people in the community and especially to those who are trying to make the school a better place. Things have dramatically improved including the numbers on the roll."

In the Press on November 19th, Councillor Don Scott, Chairman of the Education Committee, City of Nottingham, wrote " . . . It is because the Government and the City Council are determined to provide the best quality of education for pupils, that the consultation is taking place on the possible closure of Huntingdon. I should add that the school has received, and will continue to receive, major extra support from the LEA to ensure the best possible education for its pupils." On November 21st a letter appeared from the Huntingdon Action Group asking when

this 'extra support' would begin. On the same day A L Hancock, St Ann's, asked: "Has there been any support for this school since it was put into Special Measures? I know this school has a high percentage of special needs pupils. What is on offer to these children if we allow them to be scattered across Nottingham?"

Two meetings, for formal consultation with staff, Governors and parents, were arranged in school: November 26th and December 3rd. Staff made arrangements to keep children after school and to arrange a crèche to allow parents to attend these meetings.

Representatives and the Association of Teachers and Lecturers [ATL] accused the City Council of putting up a 'smoke screen' in its efforts to close the school. The ATL said the Council, post-1996 legislation, had been able to exercise consultation leading to closure, so why 'has Huntingdon suddenly been pulled out of the hat?' Councillor Don Scott agreed he would look at the criteria again.

On December 3rd parents were told by the Acting Head Teacher, Rebecca Meredith, that her maternity leave would begin in January and that Steve Clarke (a Head Teacher at Jesse Boot Primary School) and Tony Normington (retired Head from the Elms Primary School in St Ann's) would be coming to Huntingdon as a duo to head up the school as an interim arrangement.

January 1999, the City Council gave the school 'one last chance' to prove itself and closure plans were put on hold. Don Scott said: "We need the strongest commitment from the school and from the community to help us address the issue of poor standards." Dave Flatt, Chairman of the Action Group, said parents were committed to the task. "I'm convinced that the school will turn around if we get the right people at the top and the right resources and support."

A determination for the school to succeed included ten and eleven year olds going into school an hour early three days a week for extra maths, English and science. "All the children offered the chance to do this have taken it up," said Steve Clarke. By mid-year, Inspectors were saying the school was making good progress. Mr Clarke said children's performance had much improved and "the rise in self-esteem and expectation, among teachers and pupils, was there for all to see."

In September 1999, Diana Owen, previously Deputy Head of Mellors Primary School, Nottingham, became permanent Head Teacher of Huntingdon Primary and Nursery School. In January 2000, Huntingdon came out of Special Measures. Don Scott died suddenly in September 1999. The note he wrote only a few months before and reproduced here shows how he personally followed the school's progress in its determination to succeed.

A pupil, Cherie Croft, wrote to Councillor Jon Collins, Chairman of the City's Education Committee, and a St Ann's councillor, asking for help in planting a tree in Don Scott's honour because he had given the school a second chance. At the tree-planting ceremony in March 2000, Jon Collins said: "The School was in real difficulties but Don was so impressed by the case they put he decided to give

St Ann's Nottingham: inner-city voices *by Ruth I Johns* • ISBN 0951696092

To all staff at Huntingdon,

Congratulations on getting such an excellent report on the progress made in addressing the key issues for the school. This reflects tremendous credit on the part of all staff. Well done and have a well-earned break at Easter.

Best wishes,

Don Scott.

them a reprieve. It took real political courage to do that, and now you only have to look at the SATs results, the school and the children's faces to see the improvements."

Sue, Don's widow, attended the ceremony. As well as the tree, the children created a special garden. Sue said: "It's a lovely thought. The school made a promise to Don and it's nice to see what has happened." As part of a tribute speech, Cherie read: "Promises are meant to be kept."

With 240 pupils on roll, by summer 2000, the number of 11-year-olds reaching the level expected of them in science was up 52% to 96%, in Maths up 38% to 71% and in English up 6% to 50%. For the first time ever, the school had pupils one stage beyond what was expected of them at 11-years-old, said Diana Owen, Head Teacher. She paid tribute to all the staff, particularly the Year Six teacher Ann Lupson.

DI BAKER

Born 1945

Interviewed at **Huntingdon Primary and Nursery School**, *St Ann's, 24.11.99. Di Baker is School/Budget Administrator*

I have worked here for over twenty years, first coming part-time in the then Infants School. I come into St Ann's to work, but I live quite near. It was my first job when my children were old enough. It's been wonderful.

So I started some seven years after the new School was built. I worked then for Mrs Dexter who was Head of the Huntingdon Infant and Nursery School. The work was very different then. It was just a question of answering the phone, doing pupil records, dinner money and bits and bobs. I worked seventeen and a half hours a week (and even had time to tidy my office!) and do nice things like talk to visitors, watch children in rehearsals for plays and go out on school trips.

Gradually, the workload increased as schools began taking more responsibility for their own finances. I now work thirty-two and a half hours, just under full-time. I work from half-past eight until quarter-past four every weekday, which is over the time I officially work. I sometimes have a Friday afternoon off. Sue [Love] and I alternate so one of us is always here.

I deal with all the finances to do with the school. I do the School Fund, petty cash plus all the money that is in our budget which is a totally different issue from the School Fund. I'm responsible for all ordering, invoicing, paying invoices, reconciling our financial menu on the computer and so on. The School handles £470,000 p.a. I keep staff records including the forms for all the teachers and staff for their pay every week. These go to the City Treasurer's Department who pay staff. This afternoon, for example, I've got to fill in all staffing forms. If we've had extra work in school, any supply teachers, mid-day supervisors etc, it all has to be detailed.

I deal with all dinner money and make sure all statistics to do with that are completed, which takes quite a long time.

Diana Owen, Head Teacher, Huntingdon Primary and Nursery School, celebrates 2001 with pupils at continuing success in improved standards. The School ranked seventh in the 100 most improved schools in the country at Key Stage 2. Photo: Nottingham Evening Post

I chase up dinner money payments and make sure free school meal records are accurate. Some 60-70% are on free meals.

Children are eligible for free meals if their parents are on Income Support. If they get a job and their circumstances change, then we get a note saying free meal authorisation has ceased from a particular date. Meals are £1.34 per day.

We have a special programme called STAR for all the records of the children in school. I keep that up-to-date. Children need record folders, plus a file where we keep contact numbers . . . I am responsible for first-aid in school. There are about 200 children here.

There are forms if children transfer to another school and they have to be sent to the Admissions and Inclusion Service and to the school the child is going to.

After Mrs Dexter left, we had a new Head, Mrs Jenny Wilson. Unfortunately she retired on health grounds but I'm still in touch. She's one of my best friends. She was Head of the Infants and we had an acting Head in Juniors. Jenny didn't want to be Head of a joint school. Now we have a new Head, Diana Owen.

I've seen a lot of change over twenty years. When I first came I was very shocked because I suppose I had led a very sheltered life. I wasn't used to seeing children who only had one parent. I can remember sitting with the children one dinner time and saying: 'Oh, you'll have to tell your mums and dads.' One of them said: 'I haven't got a dad, Miss.' And then another would say the same. I wasn't used to seeing children who got upset over what I would call unusual things.

I think generally children are looked after better clothes-wise now. When I first came there was a child who hadn't got proper shoes to wear. He had some kind of material at the bottom of his foot. You never see this now. They have videos and computers. I think children have similar behaviour patterns, and a lot of them seem to need special help. That's a good thing. When we were a lot younger, we never heard of children getting special help.

School meals are very different from when I first came. In some ways good and some not. There's more convenience food. We still have fish and mashed potato but the fish is now these manufactured shapes or fish fingers. I would say the fish content is fairly sparse. And instant mash potato now. But we have pasta and rice, a lot more variety now. But we used to have proper roasts, proper meat, and now it's all this rolled meat which is sliced up, and beef burgers. We have salad every day which we never used to. Salad isn't very popular with the children. Staff like it.

Puddings are much the same but now there's also fruit. The children like bananas and things. Quite a lot of children bring packed lunches, a couple of sandwiches and then loads of chocolate and crisps.

I don't think children now have as much fresh air. They live sheltered lives watching television.

When I came here, there were still factories over the road. They came down relatively recently and made way for the bungalows.

I am married and have two grown-up daughters. One lives in London and the other at Oxton.

SUE LOVE

(nee Osborn) Born 1952

*Interviewed at **Huntingdon Primary and Nursery School** 24.11.99. Sue Love is Clerical Assistant at Huntingdon Primary and Nursery School. All photos from Sue Love*

I've lived in St Ann's all my life. I was born at 16, Young's Terrace which was on Gordon Road. I lived there until it was demolished when I was twenty-one and then I moved to the house where I am now. I moved there with my parents.

Sue Love's mum and dad and the handle of the pram with Sue in! Young's Terrace

Sue with her mum and cousins in the backyard

St Ann's Nottingham: Inner-city Voices by Ruth I Johns • ISBN 0951696092

Sue's mum with Blackie the cat

Some of the children from the Terrace on the peg rug Sue's mum made. Sue is the smallest child standing on the back row

I got married when I was twenty-one and went to Ball Street which was still in St Ann's. I lived there until I was divorced and then moved back to where I am now. The house was in my mum and dad's joint name and they both died and I became the tenant.

I went to school at the old Blue Bell Hill School which was a very old one on Blue Bell Hill. The Head Teacher then was Mr Leigh and the Deputy Head was Mr Lowe. And from there I went to Pierrepont Secondary Modern School and the Head Teacher was Miss Bridge. I passed my 11-plus and could have gone to Grammar School. But all my friends were at Pierrepont and I just wanted the community. I loved school. I did well there, was in the 'A' stream all the way up.

Everyone was so friendly. In the Terrace, it was only two up, two down. We had an outside toilet and a place to keep the coal. We used to keep our tin bath in the outside toilet. My mum was a bit on the large side and the tin bath was wider one end. One day she got in the wrong end. She was worried we might have to phone the fire brigade to get her out! But we got her out OK.

It was lovely, there were twenty-eight houses in the Terrace and everybody knew everyone. If the milk was on the doorstep of an older person for longer than it should have been, there was somebody knocking on the door to make sure they were all right. At Christmas, nobody was on their own. New Year was brilliant. We all came out and sang Auld Lang Syne. Everybody went in and wished each other a happy New Year and insisted there must also be the dark-haired person with a lump of coal. The atmosphere was wonderful.

I was the only child. I had cousins. But everybody was your relative, everybody was your friend. I can remember falling over, I tripped over the cat and there were about half a dozen people ran out of their houses to help pick me up.

I left school at sixteen. I could have left at fifteen, but I decided to stay an extra year. I've still got the paper my mum had which said I could stay on for an extra year, but if I left within that year she would have to pay £10 which was a lot of money in those days. So I made sure that I did well. I did the CSE [Certificate of Secondary Education] and passed. I've still got my certificates somewhere.

I don't know if you've ever noticed but there's a tiny section of the old Pierrepont School, which is now Blue Bell Hill Junior, Infant and Nursery Schools, which looks like a little cottage. In that little cottage a lady used to come from a College once a week to teach us basic office

Sue Love in the middle of the front row at a New Year's party in one of the houses on the Terrace

Sue Love at home on lunch hour break from school

skills, shorthand and typing. That was in that extra year at school. I passed everything there as well. It was something the school encouraged us to do. In the morning she came and did shorthand and in the afternoon it was a different lady for the typing. We used the old Imperial Typewriters. All the keys were covered so we became touch-typists.

I always remember we had a record, which was on an old gramophone. The record was really slow to start with and then it speeded up. They used to say: 'You've got your fingers on the home keys,' and it used to be ASDF, colon, space LJK and I can remember the actual exam. I'm really grateful for that opportunity because there weren't the opportunities which there are nowadays. People are really fortunate these days.

I remember the old Rosehill Clinic. The building is still there. There's this little building on the side of Rosehill School and it used to be Rosehill Clinic. The same tiny windows are there. It was a bit scary. Every time I walk past there, I shudder!

I used to go there for the dentist. He came in wearing this green gown. Your mum wasn't allowed to be with you. I can remember this black rubber thing being shoved in my mouth. You had an appointment to go. It was done through the school. Very different from now! I had this little abscess on my leg and I remember the nurse saying: 'Don't be a baby, you'd better not cry.' And she just jabbed this thing in the abscess. Nowadays things are much better for children.

The nit nurse used to come to our school and we had injections there. We were lined up in height order. Me only being tiny, I was always first for injections, for seeing the

nit nurse, everything! I can remember this girl coming and she was only very slightly taller than me. She was from Poland. We're a multi-cultural society today. When I was young, I'd never seen a black person. I can remember being on Gordon Road and I saw this gentleman and he was black. I was so scared I went running to my dad and said: 'Dad, there's a man and he's been burnt. His face is all black.' He came out and said he was an oriental gentleman and told me where he came from. I learnt there were other parts of the world from where I lived.

I'd be about seven. At Blue Bell Hill there was a girl called Lorna Osborn and she was a black girl and she'd say: 'We're sisters, aren't we?' My maiden name was Osborn. We used to act as if we were sisters. She was the only black child in school and we just thought she was wonderful. Eventually we had Pakistani people, one or two Polish, but nobody seemed to mind. Not like they do nowadays. Once we understood where they came from and found out they were friendly, skin colour didn't really matter. Now you can get even children victimised because of their skin. But a child is a child.

When I left school I worked at a place called Milwards in Lenton as the office junior. But I did shorthand and typing. I was there from sixteen until I had my daughter at twenty-five. She was born in 1977. She was born with a congenital heart defect and needed quite a lot of care so I worked from home. She had major heart surgery, so I was always at hospitals with her: the City, Queens Medical and Groby in Leicester.

So I did typing from home, including typing up syllabuses for students at Nottingham University, invoices and letters for an engineering company in Carlton and things like that. After my husband left for a man, I moved back with mum and dad with my daughter. Then I used to come to this school to do voluntary work every afternoon with the children, tie-dying, painting, collage work. Mrs Dexter, the Head Teacher, suggested I went in for nursery nursing, and I had an interview at Basford Hall College and was accepted for the September. Unfortunately, during this time my dad died from a brain haemorrhage. I found him and he died the same day.

My mum was an invalid and bedridden and my dad used to look after her. So I put my plans on hold and continued to work from home doing typing. I liked working from home. I nursed my mum for ten years. There was a lady next door who lost her husband at a young age with cancer. She used to come and sit with my mum for company while I came to school to help the children and give me a bit of a break. I'd help the children with any activity they might be doing, nursery, infants or juniors. My mum died in 1993 of cancer.

Up till that time, we used to take her out in her wheelchair. She thought the Tuesday Market on the Chase Precinct in St Ann's was marvellous. Our neighbour would come as well. Then I thought I better get a proper job. My daughter's OK. She's still under the hospital and always will be. She's now a qualified nursery nurse. She's done very well. Although she had something wrong with her, I never drew attention to it. I think children know

St Ann's Nottingham: Inner-city voices *by Ruth I Johns* • ISBN 0951696092

themselves how far they can go. If you are always saying don't do this and don't do that, you make them frightened and make them think they are worse than they actually are.

It was getting a bit late for me to train as a nursery nurse. So I started as a midday supervisor here. I also became a cleaner as well, obviously to get the money to survive. I had four jobs. I used to get up at five in the morning and go to C & A as a cleaner. I'd finish there at nine o'clock. I'd come down to school at half-past eleven as a midday supervisor and finish at quarter-past one. Then I'd go upstairs to the office and do two hours of administration support. I used to get changed into clothes I brought to school and then I'd clean the school and get home about half past six.

I did this for eighteen months. Then I gave up cleaning at the school. By this time, there was more and more work coming to school because of the amalgamation of the two schools [Huntingdon Infant and Nursery School, and Huntingdon Junior School], so much paperwork. So my hours stretched from twelve to four o'clock. I had to give up the midday job. Then I just had my morning job and the school office job.

Mrs Oaks, who was the Administrator for the separate Junior School, could only do one day a week when the schools merged and Di Baker was the other Administrator. One day when I was on holiday from C & A, I'd finished all my jobs at home and it was still only 9 o'clock so I phoned Di and asked if she would like some help in the morning. I proved to be such a help that the Governing Body asked if I could become full-time. So I've been doing this for two years now and I love it. I love the school. I've been a School Governor for seventeen years. I was a Governor for each of the Schools before the amalgamation.

Yes, I've seen some changes. But you can't beat the three R's. If people can read and write, they are halfway there and basic maths. They are the most important areas of the curriculum. When I was at the old Blue Bell Hill School, they were sticklers for handwriting, you had to do a sentence, know what a verb and a noun were.

I think education is reverting back to the old way and they are realising where it went wrong. Sometimes the old ways are better especially where children are concerned. My daughter attended Elliott Durham School. I was looking at an essay she had written. There were no full stops, no capital letters, no sentences. When it was parents' evening, I said: 'I'm not trying to tell you your job, but there's no capital letters, no paragraphs and I was nearly dying by the time I read it!' They said: 'So long as she understands what she is writing, that's all we're interested in.' And I thought that doesn't make sense.

I now work from quarter-past eight to quarter-past four. I'm supposed to work thirty-two and a half hours a week but we do a lot more and we get TOIL [time off in lieu]. Occasionally we get out for an extra hour or something, and every fortnight one of us will have an afternoon off. But because of our loyalty to the school, we end up working longer.

As you know the school was put into Special Measures after the Ofsted [Office for Standards in Education]

Inspection. One of the main areas of concern was its lack of resources for the children, even basic pencils and books. The children didn't have enough to work properly. So all of a sudden orders come in to Mrs Baker, there's so much work, so many invoices to pay . . . They've altered all sorts of things. I do most of the typing, filing, answering the phone, reception duties and generally assist Mrs Baker as much as I can. My job is called Clerical Assistant.

I don't have any time to belong to any Community Centres and things. St Ann's has changed. Years ago [after the redevelopment] it was still very similar to the old fashioned terraces because a lot of people from the terraces moved in to [the new] St Ann's. There were one or two who thought that now they had a bathroom, they'd gone upmarket and they changed. But most were basically the same. Where we were, most of the people were St Ann's but some were from Clifton. We were in one of the later Phases of redevelopment. All the houses were built along the front of St Ann's before we moved to where we are now. When I lived in Ball Street, I used to catch the 40 bus and see the building going on. My parents were grateful to have a bathroom.

To me the house is very tiny and pokey and all sorts of problems. You think: 'Who designed this, they haven't thought it out very well.' But when I first moved into it, it was a mansion to what we'd been used to.

Now a lot of one-parent families have moved in and a lot of homeless people have been housed in St Ann's. It's not as safe as it used to be. The lighting has improved, but there's still a lot of people hanging around. In the terraces we never locked our doors. When I see young people looking as if they might be aggressive, hanging around the streets, I always speak to them and say: 'Hello, are you all right.' And talk about the weather. I've found that if you talk to them, they're fine. And they call me by my first name now. They speak to me.

I think people are too critical of St Ann's. There are some wonderful people in the area, really genuine people. I think some people are 'place-ist'. I don't mean racist, I mean 'place-ist'. For example, a friend of mine went to hire a minibus, full driving licence, bus driver, no accidents and thirteen badges for safe driving. We were going to take a load of people to the seaside and the hire company said: 'Oh yes, no problem.' As soon as we said our address, St Ann's, it was: 'Oh no, sorry.' It was just after my mum died in 1993.

We went to another company and said Mapperley instead of St Ann's and we got one, no problem. I don't care where you live, you'll always find the same. There's good and bad in everybody.

There was a family in St Ann's recently victimised because of their colour. And there was an incident down the road from me with an elderly Polish lady who has been here nearly twenty-six years, living on her own. Her husband was dead. She was being victimised not by young people from St Ann's but some young people from another area. She lived on her own with her dog, never hurt anyone. They smashed her windows. The police phoned the Council to sort out her locks and windows. I was actually there when the Council person asked her if she had thought of moving. I said: 'Excuse me, she shouldn't have to move, she's been here a long time, this is her home, she's got memories here. Why should she move out?'

He said: 'The thing is, she's a target for being victimised and also it's a two-bedroom house and we could re-house her in . . . ' I thought it was awful, suggesting she moved when she's been there all those years and it wasn't her fault. The offenders were caught.

There's a lot of alleyways in St Ann's and a lot of little low brick walls. If some of the alleyways were blocked off it would be better. The way the houses are positioned, you couldn't see anyone in the alley because there are no windows either side.

When I was young, there was always a policeman walking around. They used to frighten us. They used to wear white gloves. There was one in particular, a very tall chap. In the corner of one of his glove fingers, he'd have a marble and if anybody misbehaved he'd get a flick with this marble, and you were scared. But you did respect the police. Some of the time they walked in twos along a certain route. It was called a beat.

CHRISTINE LARVIN

Born 1947

*Interviewed in the Parents' Room at **Huntingdon Primary and Nursery School**, St Ann's 25.11.99. Christine Larvin is a volunteer at the school*

I was brought up in Sneinton, Nottingham, until I was about twelve. I went to Newark Nursery on Newark Street. We used to go to bed in the afternoon. The beds came out after dinner. I was one of the lucky ones one day. I went shopping with one of the teachers. But I got lost in Woolworths. I can still remember it all these years later. It frightened the teacher.

At first we lived on Hampton Terrace. In the summer we used to dig a hole in the mud so we could have a paddling pool! We had a massive fire where we lived up Eldon Street.

After Nursery, I went to Sneinton Trust School until I was eleven. After the fire, we went to Dryden Street and then to Alfred Street Central in St Ann's. We lived there until it was knocked down.

I've got eight sisters and four brothers. After eleven, I went to the Sycamore Senior Girls School in St Ann's. My brothers and sisters went to the old Shelton Street Infants and Huntingdon Street schools. No sooner was mum starting one in school than one came out the other end!

Alfred Street Central was a very good shopping area. There used to be an egg shop across the road. She sold eggs from her own house. It was full of shops all the way up to the top and bottom of Alfred Street North and South, and all along St Ann's Well Road. When we had to leave because of demolition, we moved to North Sherwood Street, not far away.

Two photos from Shelton Street School days. Third from right sitting down is Janet Woodward (nee Larvin), twin sister of Christine Larvin

Fourth child from left back row in the dark shirt is Christine Larvin's brother Paul who runs the Fish and Chip shop on Chase Precinct. Photos from Barbara Dexter

Then twenty-five years ago, I moved back into St Ann's. I was about twenty-three and had a daughter. I've never been married. It was my mum's house and when she died I got the tenancy. There were about eight of us there then. Now there's only me, my sister and her son and one of my brothers.

My brother, Michael Larvin, used to help the Caretaker at the old Shelton Street school. He put the chairs up for Mr Stokes. Him and my sister did. Michael is now a Caretaker himself at Redhill Comprehensive. He used to be here [Huntingdon Nursery and Primary School] when Barbara Dexter was here, then he went to John Dexter's School before going to Redhill. He lives up there.

I've been attached to this school for twenty-six years. My daughter came here and my grandchildren come here. Well, one has left and gone on to Frank Wheldon School in Carlton. I've got three, two girls and a boy. My daughter comes all the way from the Arboretum to come here.

ST ANN'S NOTTINGHAM: inner-city voices *by Ruth I Johns* • ISBN 0951696092

Christine Larvin far right. Photo c1990. Others left to right: Rosemary Storey, one-time Junior School Lunch Supervisor. Her three sons attended Huntingdon Nursery, Infants and Juniors. Barbara Dexter, Head Teacher. Chris Kirk, parent, grandparent and childminder whose children went to the school. Photo from Barbara Dexter

We're sitting in the Parents' Room. We play bingo in the afternoon, we do a lot of work to help the school, like photocopying, running the tuck shop. At present we're getting ready for the Inspector coming and making sure everything is tip-top. We've just done all the SATs [Statutory Assessment Tests] papers, stapled all the thirty children's work. The children came in at eight o'clock in the morning to do extra work to make sure they were ready for the SATs and they are going to do it again in May this year.

The School is under Special Measures. They were going to close the School. Now we've got this two years to get things right. That's up till next summer. There is a School Support Group. Rev Jim Neill [Vicar of St Ann with Emmanuel] is in that.

I'll show you some bits and bobs about it after. We've all tried to save the School. The children and mums went down to London to see David Blunkett [then Secretary of State for Education and Employment]. The children wrote him a letter and we had it all in Braille. When we got down there, he wasn't in. He was in Sheffield. So they took us round to his office. It's a shame when you go all the way to London on a train. We had letters arranging the visit. In the photo here, that's my grandson and that little girl is crying because she didn't want her school to close. Glynis Johnson was organising the parents at that time. She is a grandparent.

I do a lot of fundraising for the School. As I said, I do the tuck shop. We can't have an Autumn Fair this year because the Inspectors are coming in just before Christmas so we're having raffles. We've just done one children's raffle and that raised £37. We're doing a doll raffle now, which will run on until the week before the children break up. We organise Christmas parties for the children. We're trying to get them Millennium mugs. We're hoping to give one to each child.

We usually do entertainment before the Christmas Party but this year, we're going to do Santa Claus instead and have the children's photograph taken with Santa Claus. The Juniors are going to the cinema instead because they are getting older and don't need parties. Normally we do a disco (that raised £150 last year), but we're going to have a big Millennium Party after Christmas this year.

There's about eight parents that come in here regularly to support one way or another. It's dwindled down a bit now. I'm in here [Parents Room] every day. I used to go into school regular, but I've had a hip replacement a couple of years back and am having a lot of trouble and cannot sit for a long while. But as soon as the School is out of Special Measures, we're going to have a massive party. I used to be in the classrooms helping the children with their reading, listening to them read. I've worked in the Nursery.

Things got difficult for a while here. I was really worried because my grandaughter could hardly read. I was in school every day. There's a new Head, Diana Owen, now and things are good. I think education is harder for children now. I mean the SATs we're looking at is like 'O' Levels from when we were at school. It's a good thing they are learning more. I think there's a hell of a lot more now pushed into them than we did. They've got to do science, they've got to do music, they've got to do religious education. The kids are getting there. But it's hard work.

Going back, my father died in 1969, when we were on Alfred Street Central. He was on Sneinton Market, fruit. A lot of the Larvin family are on the Market now. It was handed on. My brother Paul runs the Fish and Chip shop on Chase Precinct. My mum used to work for Stringers years ago doing lace work. We did it at home. We used to get all this lace work and sit up to two or three o'clock pulling threads just to get extra money. Your fingers used to be cut. It was delivered and then picked up in the morning.

When my mum finished work she was riddled with arthritis so she couldn't do any washing. So my sisters or my brother used to push the pram down to the washhouse at Victoria Washhouse with my flask of tea and my sandwiches, and I would go there straight from work. I'd spend two or three hours so it was washed, dried and

In this photo of a class of girls taken at St Ann's Board School 1929-30, Christine Larvin's mum is second from the right on the front row. Photo sent by Mrs V Fox to Nottingham Evening Post

ironed and taken home. I used to do that on a Tuesday and Friday.

My daughter Karen was born in 1969.[1] Where I live is friendly. I've got people's keys to hold when they go away. I live near the Cavendish. I go out to the Chase Neighbourhood Centre. I'm on their Committee. And we're doing an Autumn Fair for them at the weekend. The Centre does a good meal for Seniors on Thursday for £1.80.

I've just been to the Council and asked if we could have fenced railings for each alleyway because we're getting motorbikes. People coming into the area, using the phone on the bottom of our street for drugs, phoning people up and then they come. They used to go to the car park but it has cameras now. My grandchild that's just left here has just learnt about DARE [Drug Abuse Resistance Education] so she knows what to look for, and she'll say to me: 'Mama, I think they are dealing'. I mean it's not a nice thing for a child to be brought up with. It's only the last six months we've had them on our area.

I was talking to John Wheldon who used to be the Community Policeman and he said the only way to try and stop it is to get on to British Telecom and have the phone either monitored or removed.

It's a shame to give St Ann's such a bad name. It's a decent area.

ST AUGUSTINE'S RC PRIMARY SCHOOL

Fifty years after Catholic emancipation in England, a school was built in Northville Street, St Ann's. It was in an iron hut, which also served for the Church, on the site now occupied by St Augustine's Church. The School was opened on June 30th 1880. It soon grew and larger school accommodation was built on the site and opened on March 2nd 1895. The Sisters of St Joseph of Peace, who were already teaching in the St Edward's Parish of St Ann's soon became very involved with teaching at the new school.

During the years of the First World War, the School's Log Book refers to many Belgian refugee children who were admitted to this all-age school and free tram tickets were provided for those who lived at distance from the school.

On May 3rd 1923, the new St Augustine's RC Church was consecrated. Progress in the standard and reputation of the school grew during the years 1916-1934 when Sister M Loyola was Head. Sister M Stanislaus was Head from 1934-1957. In the Second World War, meetings for parents were held in connection with the evacuation scheme and some thirty-five children were evacuated to Ruddington. After the initial distribution of gas masks, there were numerous practices on their use and frequent gas mask inspections. An air raid shelter was provided and fitted out with first aid and other equipment. It was necessary to have air raid warning drills and on a few occasions the children used the shelter during real air raids.

---
[1] Karen came into the Parents Room midway during the interview.

Children from St Augustine's School outside St Augustine's Church soon after it was built 1923. On the right, Fr James Casey. On the left, Fr Edward Ellis who, in 1944, became the 7th Bishop of Nottingham. Also Sisters of St Joseph of Peace. Photo from 'St Augustine of England, Woodborough Road, Nottingham 1879-1979'

THE SCHOOL IN NORTHVILLE STREET

Built in 1895 as an all-age school in Northville Street, St Ann's, St Augustine's School building was demolished in 1972 to make way for the new Church Hall to serve the Parish. The young children still educated at Northville Street moved to purpose built premises at the corner of Bowers Avenue and Park Avenue on the edge of the district

Some of the 1960s children at Northville Street. Photos from 'St Augustine's Catholic School Nottingham. Centenary 1880-1980'

Numbers in the school continued to rise until the summer of 1962 when children of secondary age were absorbed into the City's new Catholic Secondary Schools. St Augustine's then became a Primary School catering for some 270 pupils from five to eleven. The school continued to grow and on November 16th 1964 the Junior children moved to premises which the Sisters made available at the Independent Convent School on Mapperley Road just outside the area. The Convent School opened in 1912. In 1959, the status of the Convent School was changed to that of Junior School with a Nursery in a house acquired in Corporation Oaks, St Ann's. By then, it was felt that the senior girls were adequately provided for elsewhere in the City. A number of Priests in the diocese received their early education in the School and the first woman Professor of Theology in the world, Josephine Ford, received her education until she was eighteen in the School.

By 1971, it became necessary to provide new premises for the Infant children as the building in Northville Street was considered inadequate. The thirty-place nursery unit, on the corner of Park and Bowers Avenues on the edge of the area, was completed on March 27th 1972. The new infant department was completed on June 10th 1972. In 1976, Sister M Francis retired after nineteen years as Head Teacher. [The School is now a Primary School and Nursery]

1979 – the International Year of the Child – was also the centenary of the Parish of St Augustine's and the School continued to keep close ties with the Church from which it grew. In 1980, the Rev N McLaughlin, the Parish Priest, was also Chairman of the School Managers.

"There is close contact with the child's home and out of school interests and a high degree of involvement in parish and neighbourhood activities – we were never designed to function as an island. Parents and teachers encourage our children to think about people less fortunate than themselves by praying for them and contributing to such charities as the Diocesan Rescue Society, Holy Childhood, CAFOD, and the Blind Institute. Our senior citizens are visited, offered gifts and are invited to school concerts. In this way, children are helped to create and love by sharing and caring."

From 'St Augustine's Catholic School, Nottingham. Centenary 1880-1980.' Compiled by Sister Margaret M Redmond, Head Teacher of St Augustine's 1976-1993, and school staff. I was offered this publication when visiting the school

---

In 1998, the Head Teacher, Bill Lewis, had been at the school six years and the Ofsted report said his leadership was a major strength in the school. It had 244 pupils in the main school and 52 children attended part-time in the Nursery. The Report said pupils from different cultural backgrounds mixed well together and respected each other's feelings and values.

On May 13th 2000, St Augustine's School held a reunion and included former pupils of the Sacred Heart Convent School. Mary Wade (nee Welton) said one of the oldest ex-pupils to contact her at the school attended from 1925-1934. She talked of a 'lovely little boy' and wondered what happened to him. His name was Thomas Tinkler. The next day Mary was talking to someone on the phone who wondered if he was too old for the reunion. His name was Thomas Tinkler!

The reunion day at St Augustine's School included the dedication of a special window by Monsignor Chris Fisher, Director of the Catholic Children's Society, and a past pupil of the School. The afternoon was spent renewing friendships.

SISTER PATRICIA

Born 1925 and

SISTER CHRISTINA

Born 1916

Sisters of St Joseph of Peace. Interviewed at the Sacred Heart Convent, Lucknow Avenue, Nottingham 11.7.95. Their work was connected with St Augustine's Parish, half of which is in St Ann's. Sister Patricia taught in St Ann's

Sister Patricia I was born in Leicester. I was twenty-two when I joined this congregation [Sisters of St Joseph of Peace] in 1946. Previously I had been nursing and I looked after my parents when they needed it. When I first came to Nottingham as a Noviciate, we lived in a large house at 30, Mapperley Road. Then I went to Rearsby and came back in 1949 and taught for two terms in Hyson Green, then went away and came back in 1951. Apart from one year in Yorkshire after that, I spent all my life in Nottingham. In 1976 we moved from Mapperley Road, which had been sold to the then Department of Technology and is now Trent University, to this much smaller house in Lucknow Avenue. It was built in 1877 with good Victoria brick, like the house in Mapperley Road, from a local yard, Mapperley Quarry (now built on).

Sister Christina I was born in Ireland, in the South. I was almost twenty-one when I first came to Nottingham in 1938, a year before the Second World War broke out. Things were pretty normal, a very busy City. I do remember the first Christmas I was here, hearing the bells of St Andrew's Church I think ringing out with the carol *Oh come all ye faithful*. It set a beautiful atmosphere compared to the following year after War was declared, when there was blackout and all the bells of churches were suppressed.

I was received into the Order on August 15th 1940 and I started preparation for the life of a Sister of St Joseph of Peace. I continued my education with one hour teaching in the Convent School every day. In my second year of Noviciate, I was assigned to the Convent School again to teach there 1941-42. That was before I went to College but I had a lot of help in my teaching methods from the Sisters, many of them Teaching Sisters, so I listened carefully to them and reproduced their ideas in the classroom.

Then I went to Liverpool to do my specific training at Notre Dame College, Liverpool, and after two years went to Hanwell, London, and then I wasn't based in Nottingham until I came back to do a course in Sociology 1970-71, when I studied this area with the help of some books, chiefly one called *Poverty: the Forgotten Englishmen*[1], which was an attempt to get into focus the fact that there was a great deal of poverty in an inner-city area of Nottingham [St Ann's], though I don't know if the term inner-city was known then. I'm aware that it was a very controversial book, but it was a great help to me because my experience in Nottingham had been a parochial one dealing with children in school and, even then, there wasn't much dealing with parents. You learned as much about the background of the children as you could from the children themselves. My study was called *A Community view of the School*.

I realised that even though St Ann's in sociological terms was quite a well-known place, that many people in Nottingham didn't know it very well. It was very poor and it opened my mind to that fact; the fact that part of our Parish of St Augustine's was in this area and it was important background for me. It really stuck in my mind that there was a line of demarcation between the poorer part of the Parish, St Ann's, and the other part where the upper middle class or those undergoing upper mobility lived.

I went away to London to teach and came back four years ago. Nottingham is a very changed place.

Sister Patricia   At the time of redevelopment of St Ann's, they [the authors of *Poverty: the Forgotten Englishmen*] gave it a name which almost became a term of derision. Before, St Ann's was, for us, the historic St Ann's Well. After the rebuilding, St Ann's became a derogatory name.

Sister Christina   I think those two men were trying to highlight something. Of course that could be offensive to many people in the locality because they were tarring everybody with the same brush. I found out the Sisters here didn't even know the term St Ann's. I was talking about St Ann's as I learned about it from those books.

Sister Patricia   They did a grave injustice to many people in the area because they weren't all down and outs and the children weren't running around in poverty. There was poverty after the hosiery factories, which were in the area, closed and there was unemployment. But there was a great sense of togetherness, and once you went into the houses, which came on to the pavements and went through to the back, some had beautiful gardens.

I taught in the Parish 1951-60. Some half of the Parish was St Ann's.

Sister Christina   It needs pointing out that our schools were selective because it was only Roman Catholics going to them.

Sister Patricia   In those days, there was no room for anybody else.

Sister Christina   Now you could get quite well-off Catholics going to those schools and maybe from St Ann's as well, as well as very poor children from St Ann's. It was very much across the board. When I was teaching at Hanwell in London, there were very few children from the neighbourhood who came to our school. They all trooped off to the school next door, whereas the Catholics came from a wide area and people used to say: 'Oh, your children are so well behaved.' They were better off than children in the neighbourhood school and their parents were aiming at middle class standards.

Sister Patricia   In my time teaching in St Ann's, our school was gradually changing. We were getting children from the Italian population, which started coming over in 1952. In the beginning just a dad came over, got himself a job - often on the railways - then perhaps two years later, or even less, dad got mum a job washing-up on British Rail in the canteens or something. Then she would come over leaving the children with Grandma, but, if they had children over ten, they would come too. And as soon as they could afford it, they went back to Italy and brought all the children back here.

In 1954, our first Afro-Caribbean's came over, mainly from the Bahamas and Bermuda. They came to fill the vacancies in hospital domestic service and on the buses and trams. So the children in school were gradually changing. Then in the 1960s when they [the Council] started to demolish the areas around St Ann's Well Road, they made what to my mind was the greatest sociological error. They parked people out at Clifton which was pure wilderness [then a new Council housing estate]. They started building houses in Clifton but nothing else, neither shops nor community centres. They shuffled everybody out there. When they rebuilt houses in St Ann's, where did they bring people from to live here? From the Meadows, and some of the Meadows people went out to Rise Park.

So the children we were teaching had completely changed and, what is more, very few of them had any roots. There was no background or extended families.

Sister Christina   There's a book called *Family and Kinship in East London*[2] and it's most interesting. It throws light on what happened there.

Sister Patricia   So, going back to the 1950s, most of the families were fairly large so economically it was a bit of a struggle, but everybody kept clean. There was much handing down and, particularly from the school, handing down of clothes from one family to another where the need was. The Sisters went out every Saturday to visit families in the whole of the catchment area of the school, and we were able to assess needs. It was done very quietly behind the scenes. I remember when Marks and Spencer stopped making double-breasted blazers, which were not so easy to pass on. I told Marks and Spencer and they said: 'That's why we've done it.'

In the late 1950s, we gave up the custom of going down

---

[1]   *Poverty: the Forgotten Englishmen* by Ken Coates and Richard Silburn [Penguin 1968].

[2]   *Family and Kinship in East London* by Michael Young and Peter Wilmott [University of Liverpool Press 1954].

ST ANN'S NOTTINGHAM: inner-city voices *by Ruth I Johns* • ISBN 0951696092

very early on a Saturday morning and collecting huge bags of fish, poultry and vegetables and distributing them to houses where they were needed. We used to go down to Sneinton Open Market at five o'clock in the morning. That was going on from the time the Order was founded locally in 1884, originally on Simpkins Street, Blue Bell Hill. Around 1890, the Order moved to a fairly large house on Elm Avenue, which became the nucleus of the St Augustine's School. We moved on to Mapperley Road in 1920 and the house we bought belonged to a Lace Merchant. The Elm Avenue premises were sold to the proprietors who started Hollygirt School that has since extended.

On Mapperley Road, there were two and a half acres around the original house built in 1875. We added an extension because there was not enough room for the Sisters. Then we built a Chapel in 1924 and the independent Convent School there started in 1924. The School was built on the proviso of the very large hall being available also to parishioners. It was called St Joseph's Hall, and there were partitions to make classrooms. When the partitions were turned back, the hall was used for a Social Club for girls on Saturdays and Sundays. They did Country Dancing, First-Aid, Pugilistic Studies, Martial Arts, Needlework . . . Everybody had to produce a piece of needlework during the year, which, of course, helped the Bazaar to raise funds to pay for the Church.

After I finished teaching at St Augustine's, I went to a School in Yorkshire as Deputy Head and left the following year to come back to Nottingham to open the nucleus of the Good Shepherd Primary School in Arnold that was opening. For ten years, our Sisters had run a non-fee paying School in the Church buildings while the Parish accumulated enough children to get permission from the Education Authority to build a school. We bought the land in 1951-52 but didn't get permission to build until January 1961. When we opened the School, we only had three classrooms, they built the rest around us over the years and, ultimately, I ended up with fourteen classrooms and three different buildings. I was Head Mistress for twenty-four years.

Of course, St Augustine's was an all age school until they built St Bernadette's Secondary School in Sneinton in the middle 1930s. It was an adventure for St Ann's children to go there when they had never moved out of their area. Well, they had moved to go to Clarendon College for woodwork and also for cookery, or to the Schools Clinic on Chaucer Street. We also had quite a connection with other schools in the area on a music basis, not competitive. We did choir, poetry, instrumental, joint percussion band and, as time went on, the Education Authority found money for children to have violin lessons and things like that. That's all stopped again. Nottingham had the most wonderful Youth Orchestra.

Sister Christina   Since I retired here, I keep the community accounts of the Convent. I have done quite a lot of Catechistical work, helping parents to understand what is going on in school and linking home and school, visiting old people and for a year I was very active in visiting the nearby Hospice. And I used to help at Emmanuel House once a week, which was very strenuous, helping homeless people.

Sister Patricia   Now I'm retired, I'm an Archivist for our own Community. For five years I looked after one of our Sisters here with terminal cancer. I belong to the Retired Head Teachers Association. We have a welfare scheme too. I also sit on the Education Committee to represent the Catholic Schools Commission once a term.

I'm still in touch with some of the 'children' I taught. Some send their children back to St Augustine's School. During the three months I was in hospital recently, I was inundated with grown-up 'children'. Some of them were on the hospital staff. I have a great affection for St Ann's. I say again, the greatest sociological mistake was moving people out of the area. I would have liked it done as it was in Elland, Yorkshire. They could have bought up some of the factories, pulled them down and built houses and moved people in, and gradually move people this way.

I think the authors of that book [*Poverty: the Forgotten Englishmen*] were trying to prove that the authorities were correct in getting rid of St Ann's but they weren't. There were beautiful trees demolished. All they did was just raze the whole area down. I wouldn't mind if the houses they had put up were good, but they're not anywhere as well built as the houses they pulled down. People were not asked, they were moved out.

In some of the families at our school in those days, there were eight or nine children in the family. When mum was giving birth - and most were home births - the neighbours would take the children or they'd come in to our Headmistress to report that their mother would soon be expecting another baby. We quite often kept children in School in the evening and fed them until somebody came to collect them. After the demolition of the area, we had literally to rebuild the school community as we had to rebuild the Parish because of the people coming in.

In Arnold when I was Headmistress of the Good Shepherd School we had to give some of the children breakfast because there were problems in the family. I sometimes found there were more problems with families there than there had been at St Augustine's. In the early 1960s, the coal mines in Lanarkshire were exhausted and many miners and their families moved to Calverton which was a small village then, but soon became a small town with houses built of Cornish materials.

The children were 'bussed' in to the school. The children found it difficult to adapt, but now the whole area is linked with two Catholic Schools: Good Shepherd and Christ the King Comprehensive.

The Sisters of St Joseph of Peace Convent on Lucknow Avenue, Mapperley Park, closed in June 2000. This ended a close connection between St Ann's and the Sisters which began in 1884. Sister Patricia and Sister Christina are retired in convents of the Sisters of St Joseph of Peace, Sister Patricia in Nottingham and Sister Christina in Rearsby

*The **Victoria Primary School** closed in 1980. The building, shown here in the foreground, was outside the redevelopment area. It is used now by New College. Photo: Ruth I Johns 2001*

*Another ex-school building just outside the redevelopment: the **Sycamore School** on Hungerhill Road [formerly Sycamore Road]. Part of the building is used today by ACNA [Afro-Caribbean National Artistic Centre] and part has become the new Sycamore Business Centre. The part shown in this photograph taken by Wilkinson, Davis and Strickland 1968 is the Business Centre*

***Our Lady and St Edward's RC Primary and Nursery School** on Gordon Road is between the Church and Friary [off photo left] and the Greyfriars Club right. This complex, starting with the Church, was built in the 1950s. Photo: Ruth I Johns 2001*

ST ANN'S HOSPITAL SCHOOL

A small school for up to sixteen children with psychiatric difficulties, St Ann's Hospital School, was only functional for a decade before closing in 1991.

In the Huntingdon Infant and Nursery School Log 30.1.95, it states: "Ms Wilson [Head Teacher] attended a Family Heads' Meeting at St Ann's Hospital School (pm)." Family in this context meant a family of schools in St Ann's so there was obviously a connection to schools in nearby St Ann's.

St Ann's Hospital, now closed, was a mental hospital for women opened in 1936. It was part of Mapperley [Psychiatric] Hospital complex on Porchester Road beyond St Ann's.

PIERREPONT GIRLS' SCHOOL

later Manvers Pierrepont Bi-Lateral School, then Comprehensive School

JEAN NICHOLSON (nee Pond)

Born 1931

Interviewed in her home 6.7.00. As a mature student, Jean Nicholson trained to be a teacher. She taught first at Pierrepont Girls' School, then at the amalgamated Manvers Pierrepont Bi-Lateral School which later became a Comprehensive School. Jean retired in 1983. She married Joseph (Joe) Nicholson, who grew up in St Ann's, and she lived in the district for some years. Manvers Pierrepont Comprehensive School closed in the early 1990s.

I was born in Everton, North Nottinghamshire. I went to the village school and won a scholarship to Retford High School. I stayed there in the sixth form and took my Higher School Certificate and was offered a place at Nottingham University. My stepfather wouldn't let me go. We didn't get on very well. He said it was time I went to work.

I had an interview in the morning at the University and in the afternoon I had one at Boots and they offered me a job in the Research Department. I took that and I went to stay at the YWCA for a short while. Then for a very short while I went to Beeston in lodgings and then I got a bed-sitting room on Oliver Street, near the Arboretum. In 1952, I married Joe and we had three children. In 1954-60 I was doing outwork for a firm which paid me seventeen shillings and six pence for hand embroidering one dozen dresses. Caroline was born in 1953. She is now a Consultant Pathologist. William was born in 1956 and is an Architect in London. Edward was born in 1957 and is a Community Policeman in the Park, Nottingham.

In 1960, Clifton Training College opened and I was accepted as a mature student. But, of course, there was no grant. So Joe saw me through a three year teacher training

ST ANN'S NOTTINGHAM: Inner-city voices by Ruth I Johns • ISBN 0951696092

Jean Nicholson [left] on Abbotsford Drive, St Ann's, on the approximate site of 53, Raglan Street, her husband's family home which was demolished with redevelopment. Photo: Nicholson Photo Archive 2001. See Index for Joseph (Joe) Nicholson

course which I did in two years. I got a job at Pierrepont School which was a girls' secondary school.

At that time, the Headmistress was Hilda Norman who was absolutely wonderful. She died a few years ago in her nineties. You always knew where you were with her. She had taught at the old Blue Bell Hill School when it was an all-age school. She told me one day that when she was a young teacher there, she found it very hard work and difficult. One day the boys waited for her and actually threw stones at her as she was coming out of school. She said she realised then: 'It's either you or them, so show them the length of your tongue Mrs Nicholson.'

She was really very supportive. You always knew the mood she was in by what she was wearing. If she wore her red suit and brogues you knew she was on the war-path and everybody had to watch out. She would walk around the school every morning and afternoon but you never knew what time.

She retired after I had been there a couple of years because her parents were ill and she looked after them. The Games Teacher, Miss Bickers, was very strict but practically every girl in that school could swim, and they won the City Swimming Gala year after year.

I taught all the Science throughout the school and we also had to teach Religious Instruction to our own form. I always got one of the difficult forms because I could mother them! At Pierrepont, the girls were really educated to bring the best out in them. We tried to make subjects mean something.

I think it was 1968 we amalgamated with Manvers School and became Manvers Pierrepont Bi-Lateral School, and a few years later it became a Comprehensive School. There was a joke about Manvers Pierrepont School for backward boys and forward girls! We were then teaching on two sites. That was horrible. The Pierrepont School was on Gordon Road and the Manvers School on Carlton Road. The women teachers were looked down on and rarely got graded posts. I taught all the Biology. When the children got their CSE and O Level options, all the best would be directed to Physics, the next best to Chemistry and I would end up with about forty-five doing CSE Biology, but one year I had to teach O Level Chemistry and my O Level group did the best of any group.

I sometimes feel I wasted twenty years of my life teaching because of the way things became organised and the problems it created. We were simply told the schools would amalgamate and we would just have to jolly well make the most it.

The men who had cars went between the two schools in their cars and people like myself without a car escorted the children. I can remember Mr Holder saying as I walked in soaked through: 'Your children are waiting for you Mrs Nicholson.' I said I needed to get dried first.

I had animals in school which was a good way of getting children interested in the subject. One day I was told I would have to take the school cockerel home because the men teachers said if it was there on Monday they'd walk out. So I said to the Headmaster Ian Craig: 'You know what I shall do with the cockerel because there is only one thing to do with a redundant cockerel.' So Joe necked it and we had it for Sunday lunch, but I also bought a cheap frozen chicken and roasted it. On Monday morning, I took in chicken sandwiches and said we were having a celebration in the staff room. We're having chicken sandwiches instead of cream cakes for a change. When they all had one I said it's not a celebration but a wake, that's Cocky you're eating! They said: 'We didn't mean you to *kill* him.' I could tell you the names of the men concerned but I'm not going to!

The children enjoyed having animals in school. One very naughty West Indian boy would come and ask if he could clean the rabbit out, and if he could bring it into class and nurse it. I would say yes, but while he was doing that, he would have to listen to the first part of the lesson then do his written work. The men couldn't understand why this particular boy would always do work and behave well in my class. One thing that really annoyed me was when men sent girls to me, as Pastoral Head, with a note on which was written 'please cane this girl'.

Well, I wouldn't! I asked them what they'd done and we'd talk about it. But I wouldn't cane them because I told them it was degrading for both of us. There was a particularly naughty girl who said, when I was off ill for several months, she wished Mrs Nicholson was back because although she was strict she was fair. Some years ago, one of the girls was killed when she was knocked down on the Carlton Road. As her Pastoral teacher in school, I attended her funeral at the Mosque on St Ann's Well Road. I was the only female there. It gives you a different aspect to male/female attitudes, the fact that you are shown respect. If people could actually look for the similarities between different people, we would all get on much better. There are so many more similarities than differences.

Also during my years of teaching, the police contacted me once because an Asian girl had run away from her home because she wanted to go to University and her parents insisted she work in a factory. I was her Pastoral teacher in school. We looked after her whilst the matter was being sorted out with her parents who eventually agreed to her further study.

I don't think we're going to get anywhere in education until we bring back school desks and all the children facing the front so they can see the teacher and the teacher can see them and have eye-to-eye contact. That desk should be the child's own space where they can put their belongings. If all the children realised that each of them had this place which should be respected, they would learn to look after their belongings.

I retired in 1983.

Several interviewees attended Pierrepont School. This is a group of girls at Pierrepont School c1953, a decade before Jean Nicholson joined the staff. Does anyone recognise themselves? Photo: Nottingham Local Studies Library

ELLIOTT DURHAM SCHOOL

Despite the fact that a third of Nottingham's secondary schools were, in 2001, officially stated as being among the worst in the country, Elliott Durham is making good progress toward its goals. National education policy, and the running of the City schools by the County Council before Nottingham City became a Unitary Authority again in 1998, left City secondary schools in a desperate situation. Kathy Yates, former Head Teacher of Elliott Durham, kept Elliott Durham's self-esteem together through the difficult years and retired on health grounds in 2000.

The latest Ofsted Report offers some positive pointers including that the attitude of pupils in lessons is satisfactory in 94% of lessons. 94% of teaching is satisfactory, 57% good or above and 13% very good or above. Good progress is being made on all of the key issues identified at the previous year's Ofsted Inspection, says Chairman of the Governors, Councillor Mike Edwards.

ROB BOOTHROYD

Born 1952

*Newly appointed **Head of Elliott Durham School**, Ransom Drive. Interviewed in school 31.1.01. All photos from the School*

This interview brings Elliott Durham information up-to-date following publication of 'Elliott Durham and St Anns' [Plowright Press 1998]

There are 450 pupils on roll. Numbers went up slightly since you did the book but then down again because of the threat of school reorganisation in the City. There are too many places in City secondary schools and we are in a zone that is being looked at. As the Education Authority has just appointed a new Head here, it probably is a good indicator for Elliott Durham.

Head Teacher Rob Boothroyd

St Ann's Nottingham: Inner-city voices *by Ruth I Johns* • ISBN 0951696092

We have staff equal to 32.5 full-time equivalents. And this year, we're recognised as the best improved school in the City. We've had the best results we've had in six years and we think they are a firm foundation for the future. A higher percentage of children are going into tertiary education and, in particular, to New College.

A high proportion of our pupils come from St Ann's but we are still losing pupils to the County schools and to Greenwood Dale, which is a grant maintained school and has extra funding and a different admissions policy. We are also losing to the City Technology College (CTC), but I believe that over the next five years we will grow to something like 750-800, and then be a real challenge as far as any city or county school is concerned.

This school is still living off a reputation which is fifteen or sixteen years old. I don't know how it got that reputation. I think people often see schools as being 'greener on the other side', e.g. the county schools. Government's benchmarks of A-C Grades do not take into account the value added factors. There is a public perception that if a school is in the 40-50% A-C grade bracket, then that is a school where a child will achieve. They don't recognise the rest of the results and they don't recognise the value added dimension of individual achievement over a five year period.

Value added looks at prior attainment on entry to the school and how the pupils progress based on their education here, rather than just looking at raw GCSE scores at the end of their school career. A high percentage of our children still enter school with a low level of literacy. And that is going to impact on their next stage of development, and this places them and us into a catch-up situation. So it is very important that we judge schools on the value they add to pupils' level of attainment rather than on the raw scores they achieve when they leave school at sixteen.

The reputation bias has an impact on Mapperley residents and their view of the school. They will quote acts of misbehaviour that I can honestly say, having visited other schools, are the same sort of acts of misbehaviour which occur in the community around those schools too. In other words, there may be a fight on the way home down Ransom Road and people make huge publicity of it. We deal with it instantly, the culprits apologise to the residents, but they still link that behaviour with Elliott Durham School. It happens outside Gedling School, I know it happens outside Arnold Hill School. I know it happens outside the CTC, but people somehow think, because they are a distance away that it doesn't happen there. But you hear people saying: 'Oh, I'm not sending my children to Elliott Durham because they fight on the way home.'

Certainly, we're into a period now when the Government is giving extra funding to schools and to city education in particular. So, for example, all schools received a grant of an extra £30,000 last year. Now we're involved in Excellence in Cities for the first year, which is targeting resources specifically at the inner-city schools. That is bringing extra funding to us and we've already appointed two learning mentors. We've got a learning support unit that's funded from that source. We're about to be linked to a City Learning Centre when it's built. It will be High Tec and we'll have virtual contact with them.

We're likely to become a small education action zone and, therefore, we'd have £250,000-350,000 spent on us over the next three to five years. That would look at raising achievement in families of schools through to the Elliott Durham, enabling achievement to be raised from 5 – 16. We could target youngsters and work on improvements from a very early stage, which would pay dividends by the

Two new members of staff at the Elliott Durham are former pupils. Wayne Parkes is teaching English and is Head of Year. He attended Morley Junior School before Elliott Durham. Beverli Taylor is Learning Mentor as part of the Excellence In Cities programme

time they reached secondary school, including things like attendance and behaviour. The Family School Heads are very enthusiastic about this.

Yes, I can fill you in with projects in school in the last couple of years. There's continuation of the ABC [Anti-Bullying Campaign] which is nationally and internationally recognised now. The Roehampton Institute list us as probably the No 1 School in the Country as far as best practice is concerned for peer counselling.

We're involved in the Adopt-a-School city-wide initiative. It brings people from business and industry into the school. Elliott Durham has been adopted by the Design and Property Services Department of the City of Nottingham. They provide learning mentors for pupils at age fourteen, fifteen and sixteen. And they provide key readers who work alongside pupils on Tuesday and Thursday mornings to improve literacy. They work within the curriculum in areas of geography, science and technology and they help us with publications. So it's a

Brian Kingfisher, Director of Design and Property Services, Nottingham City Council, presents reading skill awards as part of his department's commitment to the Adopt-a-School initiative. On his left is Helen Humphries, co-ordinator for the project

large initiative, it's well co-ordinated and it has been recognised by the City Council as an example of best practice.

The mentors are well matched including culturally. There is a link between ourselves and the Personnel Department of Design and Property Services and there is an interview process. Mentors are trained by ourselves and the Design and Property Services Department. The scheme has been going for two and a half years already and the first pupils with mentors have shown maturity and had improved exam results. I think some of the links will continue between mentors and ex-pupils. The present Year Ten and Eleven now have mentors attached.

We've talked about Excellence in Cities. Part of that is a partnership between Elliott Durham, Portland School in Worksop [North Nottinghamshire] and Nottingham University. We've established a core group that will focus on key areas for improvement in the school, mainly geared toward teaching and learning. We've got three staff going to Canada to look at best practice in Nova Scotia and then cascade that through the staff when they come back. And also through the cluster of schools that we work with. The teachers' brief is quite wide.

The DFES [Department of Further Education and Skills] is keen at present that we should learn best practice from within our own country and also from outside those boundaries. It's interesting because Senior Managers can't go abroad to do this. It is an opportunity for practitioners to go and find out, learn and come back and feedback to other staff.

We have pupils from Montserrat here and the Secondary School in Montserrat wants to do an exchange and to do e-mail and eventually video conferencing between the two schools. That is likely to take place in the autumn.

The Director of East Midlands BBC, Craig Henderson, and myself meet up on a regular basis and compare notes. We're finding out about each other's institutions and the idea is that we should share experience and help each other in our management and leadership styles.

There's a lot going for the School at present. We've been recognised as an improving school and we need to drive things forward now. The pupils are involved in the

IT and Music facilities in school

ST ANN'S NOTTINGHAM. Inner-city voices by Ruth I Johns • ISBN 0951696092

changes. They were involved in my selection process for Head Teacher. They have their own School Council and Ofsted Inspectors recognised that it was a School Council that works well. It is an important part of what is going on in the School.

In Assembly on Friday, I was talking about the Canadian trip and how that should impact on pupils and about all these other initiatives. So they are not isolated from them and are involved. Today, there's a staff interview in progress and the School Council is involved as part of the process. The School Council has an elected representative from each Tutor Group.

When the new Head was being selected, after its own process of selection, the School Council reported back to the whole Governing Body. The candidates were given a topic by the School Council and twenty minutes to address it under observation conditions. The topic was: 'To find out from the children about the things that hinder their progress as individuals'. It was a bit daunting but the pupils loved it.

My background? Twenty-six years in teaching. I started teaching at Hartland School in Worksop and spent seventeen years there. Geography was my main subject but I must have done near enough every job including pastoral roles, Head of Year and Head of House. When I left I was Head of Geography and Head of Humanities. I then spent three years at Alderman Derbyshire School, Nottingham, as Senior Teacher and came to Elliott Durham as Deputy Head six years ago. I worked my way up the hard way. I did a Bachelor of Education at Sheffield Polytechnic [now Sheffield Hallam University] two nights a week for three years. I enjoyed doing my first degree so much that I went on to do a Master's Degree at Nottingham University and a couple of years ago I got the National Professional Qualification for Headship.

What message would I like to pass on to someone reading this in fifty years time? How the warmth, caring and the multi-cultural aspect of bringing people together can make a school thrive. If we link that to the dreams and ambitions amongst ourselves, we can see Elliott Durham as a school, which had a wobbly period, but then became an improving school and propelled itself forward to something which the community in St Ann's and the surrounding areas are very proud.

We get quite a lot of involvement from parents. The distance of the School from the community is still a difficulty. It's a long trek up that hill especially when it's windy, cold and wet. We're looking at all sorts of ways of overcoming that. We've booked a school minibus to help parents and carers to get to parents evenings. We've got three excellent parent Governors who are taking a big interest in the school, Bernard Wilkinson, Paula Charlemagne and Michelle Hubbard. Sometimes we hold parent surgeries in the centre of St Ann's. I want people to feel our doors are always open and not to see the School as an institution. Once people are through that door, they have always recognised that it is a warm and caring school.

We have three after-school study centres. One is within the school itself, one at the Metrazone Community Centre on Ransom Road and the other at the Russell Youth Club just outside St Ann's in Carlton.

The member of staff being selected today is a musician being sponsored by Area Five Funding [a Local Authority fund for East Nottingham]. It will be a well-paid post for someone who will develop music in the School and also in the local community. There is a huge amount of raw talent in our youngsters as far as music and the arts are concerned. We have pupils who may be under-achieving at school slightly, but who have incredible self-confidence and can do things like rap, dancing and singing. There's no huge gap between them and what you sometimes see on stage.

The music teacher will teach for fifteen periods out of a twenty-five period week. Five will be for organisation and management and five will be flexitime in the community. We can use Metrazone, Chase Neighbourhood Centre and the new Sycamore Millennium Centre on Hungerhill Road. Also the Russell Centre. I think this post is a first, certainly within the County and City and it's very exciting.

We're just about to have a wind turbine and solar panel put on the roof. That has all been developed by my Site Manager, Patrick Belshaw. He has come up with sponsorship for the wind turbine and solar panel. It will power some of our computers and the Lord Mayor is going to open it on March 1st [2001].

This kind of enthusiasm goes through the School including the cleaners, secretarial staff, administrative support staff and teaching staff. The school is going into a new partnership with New College. They need sports facilities and we've got these lovely playing fields and facilities. The payback is that they will help us with our vocational courses: catering and hospitality, leisure and tourism, hairdressing and so on. And they've got a new centre at Clarendon for music and the arts that will also be open to us.

There is a possibility that we may have a children's nursery on site. It's a development opportunity the City Council is looking at. It would be on the left-hand wing of our House Block. The idea is to have learning skills in a woodland environment and a nursery facility with it.

The nursery would re-locate from the Victoria Shopping Centre. The idea has all sorts of spin offs. The nature trail could be used by this school and its Primary feeder schools. It would bring people into Elliott Durham from outside our catchment area and they would see what it is like. There would be an environmental classroom. At present this is at the planning stage with architects looking at costing, establishing funding . . .

The school may be housing an energy and technology exhibition that would be a working exhibition. Yes, we've got the space. I've already decreased the school's [official optimum] size from its original 1,132 to 932. If we could get to around the 800 mark, that would be the right size. It would still be friendly and caring. But it would also allow us to achieve and build and look to our vision. And, as I have mentioned, we can use the spare space to very good advantage.

The *Elliott Durham and St Anns* book you completed in1998[1] has been in the Foyer, in the Library and around school generally. I've got a copy at home, so have most staff members. I think it actually gave people a chance to reflect. We have had a very stable staff that have been here a long time. It was important to them that it was documented. Past pupils could reflect back and younger pupils see brothers and sisters within the book. And it brought a sense of humour and reality, didn't it? Come back in four years to record the next step!

I think we're getting better at recording things for the longer term.

2002. A pilot Tap the Gap scheme run by Nottingham City Council started in 2001. The scheme will be repeated in 2002 for more pupils who have just left school and are offered a four-week work placement in City Council departments (including in museums and sports and leisure centres) before starting to look for work or deciding to continue into further education. Students receive travel and lunch expenses. Elliott Durham pupils will be among those from only three other schools in the scheme and selected because of achievements in school and in the community.

In 2002, Rob Boothroyd added that the School has gone from strength to strength in recent months. The roll has risen to 500 pupils and Elliott Durham received a glowing report from HMI [Her Majesty's Inspectors]

---

[1] **Elliott Durham and St Anns** *was launched at St Ann's Library 1998. At a special School Assembly, a copy of the book was given to pupils to take home to each family or carer represented at Elliott Durham. Stewards at the official launch in St Ann's of this book will be pupils from Elliott Durham.*

GOING BACK

by **Craig Croly** [2002]

Aged 14

I was going to stay in Skeggy
Till I forced myself to come back.

I haven't been to school for two years
Nervous
Weird, in other words funny
First day I got on with everyone
Made a few friends,
Going to school every day then.

I might not go back
I'm not going back anyway.

ROSEHILL SCHOOL

Rosehill School on St Matthias Road, St Ann's, has always been a school that offered special educational provision. The nature of the provision has changed over time. The Head Teacher is John Pearson

In 1999, School Administrator, Wendy Quickfall told me the School was changing to concentrate on catering for pupils with autism and 'our numbers are a lot less'. Pupils came from Nottingham, and now from farther afield, including recently Rotherham, Leicester, Derbyshire and Nottinghamshire.

The 1999 Prospectus states that Rosehill is a day school for boys and girls aged four to sixteen years of age. It provides for a wide range of special education needs classed by the DFEE as 'Moderate Learning Difficulties' and 'Autism'. Rosehill has a specialism in autism. The Infant, Junior and Secondary Departments have their own buildings and the Post-16 Department (for students up to nineteen) has a specially converted area, forming part of the main building. There are twelve teaching rooms, a large hall/gym with adjoining changing and shower facilities, well-equipped specialist rooms for both Craft Design and Technology and Design Technology (Food). There is a Sensory Room, two Soft Play areas with music and light projection, an Exercise Room and some safe Outdoor Play areas. The School has its own kitchens and school meals are cooked on the premises.

The Prospectus outlined aims and objects for the pupils at different stages of their school life and for preparation for adult life. I hope a copy of this Prospectus - and previous ones - are deposited in Nottingham Local Studies Library as they are useful social documents, which help to track changes in approach to special education over the years.

In 2000, Rosehill School was among four Nottinghamshire schools which have been named by Ofsted Inspectors as among top flight schools. It was praised for the excellent education and guidance it offered pupils with autism and other complex needs. The school is now [2002] designated as a specialist autism centre with 70 places. It no longer educates children with moderate learning difficulties. It has pupils between the age of four and nineteen.

Part of the older building, seen from St Matthias Road. Photo: Ruth I Johns 2002

Photos from the Rosehill School Prospectus 2000

JIM MADDISON

*Head Teacher **Rosehill School** 1972-1991. In 1990, he wrote the following about the School's history*

Rosehill School was opened on November 5th 1931. Its history is one of continuous change - a fascinating reflection of the development of special education provision in Nottingham.

The Rosehill School makes special provision for boys and girls through the school age range who have difficulties in making progress at the normal rate. These slower learning pupils are drawn mainly from schools in the area to the east of Mansfield Road and the Meadows. The School being in the heart of Nottingham in the St Ann's district means that there are additional problems arising from city centre living. Learning problems are often associated with behaviour difficulties and disadvantaged family background.

An assessment unit concerned with the assessment of very young children was opened thirteen years ago. A unit for adolescents with autism has been operating for twelve years. The campus also embraces the district school clinic and at one time Nottingham's non-accidental injury unit (Social Services and NSPCC). If variety is the spice of life, it would be difficult to find a more piquant establishment.

The history of the School has its roots in the extensive general reorganisation of the City's schools in the 1924-33 period. This is reflected in the architectural similarities seen, for example, in parts of the Manning, Ellis Guilford, Haywood, Middleton, Crane and Rosehill schools. Rosehill's Open Air Department was designed to cater for two hundred handicapped and delicate pupils whilst the 'MD School' – as it was officially called – was built to absorb one hundred and sixty pupils.

This 'Mentally Defective' label was very unfortunate. Those who chose to use this term could not have foreseen how injurious it would prove to be over the years to sensitive children and parents as well as to the overall public image of the school. 'Each child admitted to the School must be certified as mentally deficient by a duly qualified medical practitioner' are cold words indeed. How times change! The name Rosehill in parts of the City still conjures up inappropriate and unrealistic pictures in the minds of some. Labels die hard!

The Log Book records that in the late 1930s, the School roll actually reached four hundred pupils. This is incredible when one remembers the huge problems being dealt with in those worrying days – multiple handicap allied to poverty and generally poor health (Tuberculosis being the scourge). Those who can remember the tiny isolated classrooms of the old Rosehill will wonder how this could be with crutches, sticks, supports and wheelchairs to contend with too.

Of course, the spectrum of ability was wide, many of the delicate and physically handicapped pupils in the Open Air Department being very bright and finding their way into higher education at a later stage. A friend of mine, an accountant and first class musician, remembers vividly his days at Rosehill. There have been many like him. All the senior pupils were boys in accordance with general policy at that time. The Director of Education, Mr A H Whipple wrote: "to separate the sexes in all senior schools is the only way education suitable to boys and girls can be developed."

In those early years, records emphasise in a significant way the importance attached to gains and losses in weight. The daily distribution of emulsion to each child was a feature and over many years breakfasts and teas were provided as well as a midday meal. Who did all the duties involved? There were definite afternoon rest periods. We have retained one of the isolated classrooms partly as a museum piece and the shutters behind which the beds were kept are still intact.

Log Book snippets include varied entries as " . . . poor attendance due to influenza, fog and generally defective footwear."

". . . a severe blizzard meant complete evacuation of the Open Air Classrooms. The central stoves were blown out."

". . . Mrs Smith, teacher, made a blot in her register which she unwisely removed by means of a rubber."

". . . two detectives took a pupil away after he'd stolen some fog signals. They lost him on the way to the station."

". . . the handicraft inspector was annoyed. He visited to find the children were attending a League of Nations meeting."

". . . the Director of Education was present at the delivery of a gramophone."

". . . Councillor Mrs Cattle was pleased to donate one ton of manure to the School for use in its garden."

". . . a local vicar appointed to inspect RI [Religious Instruction] in the MD School criticised the teaching staff for their lack of attention to modern Biblical criticism."

Since those early years, a great deal of change has taken place under only three Head Teachers[1] including the present incumbent. Recent years have witnessed the transfer of the last in a long line of physically handicapped pupils, the absorption of ethnic minority groups, the total mixing of the sexes, a change to being a small special school for primary aged children and the development into what is now a large (predominantly secondary) all age school with units meeting specific needs. Recent LEA and Government initiatives (1990), for example 'Children First' and 'National Curriculum', bring us to a decade of change where the School may have to decrease in size, become more specialised and even extend the age range. There will certainly be no lack of challenge and excitement.

Premises are a mixture of old and new. An extensive building programme in the mid-seventies demolished several classrooms, transformed older retained facilities, and introduced some most attractive new classrooms, library and recreational areas. The facilities for housecraft and woodwork are outstandingly good. The School lacks

---

[1] The current [2002] Head Teacher John Pearson is the fourth.

green space. If this was rectified we'd have a near ideal situation. [In another document it mentioned eleven classroom spaces, a large hall with adjoining kitchen, TV room, leisure room, CDT and housecraft area, library, indoor play space and computer room. It stated the School was adequately staffed with teachers, classroom assistants, cleaners and cooks and adequately equipped.]

The immediate area beyond the School was comprehensively redeveloped and the School overlooks and is surrounded by a large number of modern Council houses.

Our aim is to be of service to children, parents and other schools in the community. In educational circles we have a high reputation being used as a training facility by teachers, psychologists and social workers . . . How do youngsters come here? Parents, teachers in normal school, psychologists and sometimes social workers are all involved. The procedure is well established and with only an occasional hiccup runs smoothly. The machinery is oiled with care and concern . . .

What about employment after school? Our record here has been good but these are difficult days and the situation deteriorates. Work experience courses and further education extension play an increasingly important role. A specialist careers officer visits regularly to give invaluable help.

Do we have behaviour problems? Yes we do. Some of our children come to us from local primary and secondary schools because their behaviour absorbs so much of the time of teachers struggling with large classes. These youngsters are often unhappy and difficult. Helping them to adjust and make good social progress can be very satisfying although disappointment and frustration are daily companions.

The Head Teacher is always willing to speak to evening groups about aspects of the school's work. Individual members of the public with genuine interest in provision for youngsters with special needs are invited to make contact. The School seeks only to serve.

Midwifery

Kerry Anne Gifford, Sheena Prentice, Jo Moffett and Amanda Moult are four midwives who work in St Ann's, or have done so in recent years. They offered to meet up and be interviewed at **St Ann's Health Centre**, St Ann's Well Road, 14.6.00.

The entrance to Robin Hood Chase and Chase Precinct from St Ann's Well Road. The St Ann's Health Centre is the building on the right and stands where St Ann's Church used to be. Photo: E James Smalley 2002

*At the time of this interview, **Kerry Anne Gifford** had been a community midwife in St Ann's for about three years. She is also a relief midwife and connects with women in hostels and temporary accommodation. Kerry Anne was present for the whole interview session. **Sheena Prentice** worked as a community midwife in St Ann's for seven years until recently becoming a drugs liaison midwife based in the Meadows. She spends some of her time in St Ann's. Sheena was called out during the interview session. **Jo Moffett** is a community midwife based in St Ann's. **Amanda Moult** worked in St Ann's for four and a half years from 1994 and is now a community midwife in Wollaton. Jo and Amanda came in when work allowed during the course of the interview session. Community midwives work for Nottingham Community Health Trust.*

Sheena Prentice. When I was a community midwife working in St Ann's I was attached to a GP Practice and I did midwifery-led clinics so that women could access me and I could provide pre and post-natal care as a continuity. I had a very mixed clientele ranging from the inner-city mainly younger women with several children to women in Mapperley with partners in work in a more affluent situation. Women would book their pregnancy with their GP and then come to the midwives clinic. We provided continuity of care in St Ann's including delivery if births are at home.

For the past six or seven years we've done home births if women wanted that without it being an issue. If there are any problems we go straight to the hospital service without involving the GPs. The GPs I worked with were very woman-orientated and able to listen to what women wanted.

Kerry Anne Gifford. I'm based at St Ann's Health Clinic where I do midwifery clinics attached to a GP Practice. Well 'attached' is a funny word. I become the named midwife for pregnant women at that GP Practice. The model of care in St Ann's is the same model for the whole of Nottingham. It's changed recently. Women go to their GP to confirm their pregnancy and until recently their GP would make their referrals to the hospitals. In terms of place of birth, I don't think that was often even discussed. It was assumed a woman would be booked either with the City Hospital Maternity Unit or the one at Queen's Medical Centre. Women in the know, like some of Sheena's, would not discuss it with their GP and just wait and discuss it with the midwife. They could still connect with the hospital if there was need for any hospital involvement. For example, scans.

Now, GPs have the option of deciding if a woman needs referring to a hospital. If she is categorised as 'low risk', a woman can be referred to me for continuing care. She can decide the place of birth. Some GPs have embraced this new model of care and others continue to write a letter to the hospital whether a woman needs to be seen by an obstetrician or not. There's only one GP who springs to mind who would actively support home births on this patch. But, with the new changes, even GPs who aren't pro-birth at home now know that, if there is a home birth, they are not going to be called out in the middle of the night so they are not so actively against it.

Sheena Prentice. GPs who aren't against home birth would completely rely on the midwife and that's how my GPs were because they had me in their practice for so long and I gained their confidence.

I think home birth has gone from the culture. Birth has been medicalised. The assumption is that a woman will go in, give birth, and come home fairly rapidly. If women in St Ann's choose home birth, it's often because they haven't got any childcare and they can't think of a way of getting into hospital, having their baby and somebody else looking after the other children. But I think some of the fear stuff around birth at home affects them the same as any woman. Sometimes it's really hard to make choices.

Kerry Anne Gifford. I believe it also has something to do with the midwives' predilection. If, in discussion, you say: 'Have you thought about your place of giving birth?' or 'Do you know you have home birth as an option?', most women will say they don't want it anyway. The first woman who said she would like a home birth, the GP said: 'Oh no, you can't do that sort of thing.' I gave him some of the Changing Childbirth[1] material when talking to him so that he realised women do have control over these sort of decisions. Slowly but surely in the last three years, I've had two to three women, out of forty, who booked for a home birth.

Sheena Prentice. I think that sometimes women who have had children before, who've had an emergency delivery at home unattended, think it's more appropriate to plan their birth at home.

Kerry Anne Gifford. As a relief midwife doing other clinics, I have sometimes seen someone who has been thinking about a home birth, or had even mentioned it but felt that their request hadn't been taken seriously. Each one has an interesting story. Like one woman was someone I'd met as a student midwife years ago, who I knew had eaten her placenta post-delivery. So when I met her I was surprised she was down for a hospital delivery. She'd been told by her GP that she would be dicing with death having a home delivery. In fact, we facilitated her wish for a home delivery and I attended her birth and that was a particularly pleasant situation.

Jo Moffett. I am a community midwife based in the Health Centre here. I'm connected with two GP practices in St Ann's and with a GP who works on his own in Mapperley Park. He has a small caseload of between eight and fifteen women at any one time. The other two caseloads fluctuate a lot. It's probably better-informed women who ask for home birth, whilst some women want one because they hate hospitals. And I've attended home births because women have several other children at home who they don't want to leave.

The GPs I work for are fairly pro-home birth. Both of their wives have had home births. But I've worked at other practices where GPs are not happy about home births.

Kerry Anne Gifford. Of course home births used to be compulsory. There wasn't a facility like the City Maternity Unit or Queens Medical Centre. We're talking pre-1960

now and before that to give birth in Hospital a woman had to really make a fuss. So again, the articulate woman came off best. The women around St Ann's, they're not inarticulate but they don't make a lot of waves about most things. They just get on with stuff so maybe they accepted then that they had babies at home and now they accept that you have your baby in hospital. It's like St Ann's women carry the cultural norm.

Sheena Prentice. By the time it became the norm to have babies in hospital, the GPs who had expertise to support midwives in the community had gone. The new GPs were controlled by fear of litigation. The only reason over the last six years that GPs haven't felt they should control midwives is because we're responsible for our own practice. We're autonomous practitioners so if we make a poor decision it isn't their fault because they don't employ us. We're employed by the Community Health Trust.

Kerry Anne Gifford. Midwives are very accountable. Midwives have been under strict supervision since the turn of the twentieth century. Midwifery supervisors were always powerful. You've probably come across historical records where they actually went into the midwife's house to check her fire grate and her drawers and things. A serious inspection of her whole lifestyle in a controlling way by middle class women who were concerned about the type of midwifery practice that was going on at street level. It's not like that any more! But every year we get our practice assessed. Even if a little thing happens at a home birth situation, you still get interviewed. Our practice is incredibly well scrutinised by midwives, not by doctors. We've always fought for that.

Sheena Prentice. We're specialists in low risk women. Our capabilities are in assessing women's need. They may request a home birth but it may be completely inappropriate and it would be good to advise that woman that it wouldn't suit her.

Jo Moffett. The shortest time women stay in hospital for a birth can be six hours but in general they will come out before the baby is two day's old. Then we see them at home until the baby is twenty-eight days old. The first ten days we see them more regularly and after that a little less depending on the situation or if there are any problems.

Kerry Anne Gifford. In the last twelve months, I think the Caesarean Section rate for St Ann's has gone up phenomenally. Before, St Ann's women had the reputation that they would give birth naturally without a lot of fuss. In hospital there used to be the feeling: 'Well, they're St Ann's, they won't sue.' The Section rate has gone up in the City and in our area and it saddens me tremendously. Because one of the things I used really to like about working in the City was, if I wasn't doing home births, I used to know that the women I was looking after would experience a reasonably normal birth in hospital.

Now, they are talking about 18% Caesarean Section rate locally. I heard some figures yesterday that in January one of the Units, they had a primagravida Caesarean Section rate of 40%. And an epidural rate of 70%. That's just one month's figures. But to start the year in that way, it's frightening. You just think: 'What's going on?'

---

[1] Changing Childbirth, Part I and Part II, Department of Health [The Stationery Office. 1993].

Sheena Prentice. It works across the board. When I worked out my annual statistics for Caesarean rate in my area which includes Mapperley and St Ann's, the rate was 33%. It's distressing, extremely distressing.

Kerry Anne Gifford. As midwives we just think: 'Is there some way we can stop this?'

Jo Moffett. I think that a lot of the mums find the situation distressing. I think they are often made to feel it is something they had to have done at the time. Maybe a couple of months later when they sit down and think and they come back for their next pregnancy, they are then questioning what happened to them and why. I've quite a lot who had successful trial labours and end up having a vaginal birth after a Caesarean.

Kerry Anne Gifford. I sometimes get a sense from the grandmothers - the mothers of the mothers - what is all this fuss about? We just got on and had our babies. And going back further, midwives were called District Nurses and they were more authoritarian and rode around on a bicycle in uniform. And what nurse so and so said 'went'. A mother wouldn't leave the house until nurse said so, and information about the baby was prescriptive. We wouldn't dare! The language we use is about empowering, family centred care, woman centred. On the other hand you do get the feeling from some women that they want more prescription. They want to be told how long to feed the baby. I think mothers can be caught up in this culture of fear.

Recently, for example, in Coronation Street, the TV soap, a baby died soon after birth of Group B Strep. One of my mothers said she had a certain sort of discharge, the baby hadn't been moving, it was just about due and I could hear the anxiety in her. It was all about the fact she'd watched Coronation Street. And in situations like that, women are being wound up. There's a whole lot of stuff in the culture that winds them up.

You were asking about young mothers. We do get quite a few teenage pregnancies because we have two hostels in St Ann's where young women come from other areas of Nottingham while they're having their baby. But quite often they have parents who live in the Nottingham area who are supportive. I don't have many young women without supportive partners on my caseload. The women we see in the two hostels often don't come from St Ann's and they often have supportive partners.

Jo Moffett. Not including the hostels, maybe in a year I'll see two or three young mums and we're talking seventeen upwards. I've worked in other areas of Nottingham where they've been a lot younger.

Amanda Moult. At the moment I work in Wollaton but I worked in St Ann's for four and a half years from 1994, taking over from Kim who had been here about the same length of time. I know Kerry Anne and Jo very well. We've all worked together. [Sheena had to leave the room in answer to a call.] There are more young mothers than in Wollaton but not necessarily teenage. When we talk about support for young women, we always think of the support being a husband or partner. They might not have a partner or somebody they live with, but the support is often from

their family. And friends may be part of their support network. I'd say mothers in St Ann's have probably got better networks of support than in some other areas.

Kerry Anne Gifford. The women in Mapperley often take more of my time on the support side than the women in St Ann's. Because we share each other's caseloads when we're off duty, I do get to see women in Mapperley. Usually the husband is off work at home the first week and it's after this week that the women need support.

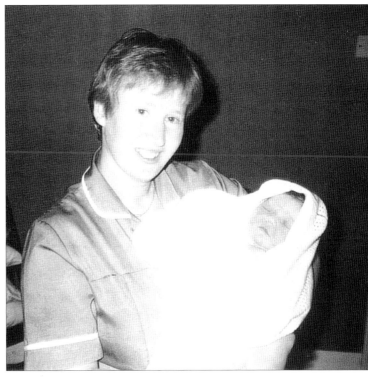

Amanda Moult with the baby she delivered at 5.22 am 19.8.95 in a home delivery in St Ann's

Amanda Moult. My experience of working in St Ann's is that, as a midwife, I was seen very much as a friend and I was just one of those who supported, who visited the house. I don't think it's that they didn't appreciate me as a midwife, but they appreciated other skills that I had. Like being able to talk to them and understand their problems in the area, particularly I think because a lot of people get moved into St Ann's.

With the bad name the area has, they think that it's a rough place to live, with lots of drugs, alcohol problems and everybody being bad. But when you're actually living or working in the area you discover that it's not the case. And so you then adapt to fit in with the area, with the rest of them. And I think because I worked here and I was here a long time you just ended up being one of the gang, one of the women in St Ann's. And you know it was a very pleasant thing to work in St Ann's with the women. I got questions, for example, around income support forms and queries about the physical things going on in pregnancy.

There's definitely been an increase in people taking drugs. On my caseload at any one time I'd say I would probably have two mothers on drugs.

Kerry Anne Gifford. Whilst Sheena was a community midwife, she did a survey about the number of pregnant women in Nottingham who were disclosing that they were on a range of drugs. And that's why she's become a drugs liaison midwife, because midwives felt a little bit out of their depth in knowing how to respond.

The amount of paperwork we have to do is incredibly stressful. Everything we say and do has to go down on record to the last dotted 'i' and crossed 't'. And what everyone else said and what you said back. There are eight midwives working in St Ann's, two of which are full-time posts. The others are job share or part-time. Today has been incredibly busy.

Amanda Moult. Yes, we have leaflets and things for new mums. I tend to pick my favourite things and choose what I give out carefully. We used to give out a booklet.

Kerry Anne Gifford. It was called *The Pregnancy Book.* But there's been a change at Government level and it's quite an insensitive change because all of a sudden this book has gone. Women used to really look forward to having it. We could only give one out for a first pregnancy. They were not going to go out and buy something so it was just a lovely thing to give someone. It was provided by the Health Education Authority.

There was a project in St Ann's we should mention. It was a community based peer group breast feeding project. It was started around 1990. It was to encourage people to breast feed. The La Leche League, which is a National Breast Feeding support group, and the Community Health Trust led a project. Twelve local St Ann's women were trained to become counsellors for breast feeding and they then held coffee mornings here at the Health Centre. And they also visited women who had a new baby to try to support them with breast feeding. One or two of those counsellors have gone on to do other things in maternity care. One is now training to become a midwife. She's got a large family, a lovely woman. She's had three children born at home in St Ann's. I delivered her last baby. And one of the women I think has started her own business.

Now, the Sure Start Project is about to begin. Now that's supposed to be using peer counselling as a way of attracting women who wouldn't normally get involved in groups. It's often said that St Ann's women are not group goers but I've never one hundred per cent believed that. If the ingredients are right, they will participate. But it has to be something down to earth. They don't play around with things that are a waste of time.

Last year we tried to get a post-natal baby massage group going. It worked for a couple of times and then faded. It always breaks my heart a little because in Sneinton they have a really well established post-natal support group run by Health Visitors, but the Health Visitors here - for whatever reason - don't see that as something which would work in St Ann's. I'm looking to Sure Start as a way of getting these extra things. Like Mandy said the women's lives are quite self-contained. They have support networks of family, neighbours, friends. They go shopping with one another, go to the pub. They see each other in the morning when they take the kids to school, go to coffee . . .

I think the housing regeneration scheme [City Challenge and City Council Estate Action initiated from 1992] helped the area a lot.

Amanda Moult. In the time I worked here, I could see how it was making the place feel better. I do firmly believe that if people have a nice house and their community is looking better, then they start to want to improve it.

Kerry Anne Gifford. The majority of the houses are incredibly comfortable. They're not luxurious but they've got all the basics, pleasant carpet, good-looking curtains, nice furniture. I wouldn't think twice about living there.

Amanda Moult. When I first started working in St Ann's, people said : 'Oh, you don't want to work there, it's awful, it's dangerous. What are you going to do at night, there are *no go* areas.' But there are no *no go* areas especially regarding midwifery. There was nowhere I wouldn't have gone, though there were places where my personal safety was not all it should have been.

I still miss the buzz that it used to give me working here. I'm sure people live here and feel that buzz. And maybe if they move out they look back and think of St Ann's in a nice way. I would come back but they didn't have a full-time contract since I've been away.

Kerry Anne Gifford. I'm a bit of a café society kid and because I've lived in inner-city areas and other parts of the world and watched them go from degradation to being Des Res. In a way I'm waiting for the day that happens to St Ann's, but I don't want it to be too up-market. I miss places to meet up with friends for a cup of tea at lunchtime.

Last year I thought it was really exciting that St Ann's Library was celebrating that Alma Reville Hitchcock, Alfred Hitchcock's wife, was born in St Ann's. My husband was involved in that ceremony. Hitchcock's daughter, Patricia, came and unveiled a plaque. What was disappointing was that there was hardly anybody there. It wasn't something locally that was recognised as an interesting thing.

The thing that is worrying everybody a bit has been the shootings. There is a little bit more anxiety in the air when I go round on my visits. In St Ann's, and probably in other areas, I get a sense that people have a little bit of an idea what's going on but they are not pointing fingers at anybody. Sometimes you get a bit frustrated. You think, is this keeping your eyes down and keeping yourself to yourself going to help the community in the long run? If you don't deal with the small element of quite young youths who have a penchant for guns, what will it end up like? I know that sounds like a negative thing from somebody who asked to work in St Ann's and I really like working here.

For anyone interested in **midwifery history** in Nottingham, including its inner-city areas, then *Delivered at Home* by Julia Allison [Stanley Thornes (Publishers) Ltd[1] 1996] is a good read. Julia Allison decided to train as a midwife after her second child was born at home in Nottingham.

The 'District Midwife' replaced the 'domiciliary', 'county', 'borough' and 'municipal' midwife. Julia Allison

---

[1]   Now Nelson Thornes (Publishers) Ltd.

ST ANN'S NOTTINGHAM: inner-city voices *by Ruth I Johns* • ISBN 0951696092

covers her subject from the start of the National Health Service in 1948 to its reorganisation in 1972; just twenty-four years in which birth took place in hospital under supervision of obstetricians and at home under the supervision of district midwives in about equal proportion. This represented 62,444 home births in the City.

Many women qualified - by social criteria - for a hospital bed but in fact delivered their babies at home because of lack of beds. But the outcome for their babies was no worse. Even if midwives reported that home conditions were 'beyond the pale', about half of the women were still delivered at home.

Describing one incident in 1962, a midwife told Allison: "I remember taking a white unmarried girl to see the consultant for booking and being turned away: no beds. This girl was very anaemic, unsupported, tiny room on Dame Agnes Street [St Ann's], no heating. Anyway, I remember saying to her not to worry, when she went into labour, I would say the fetal heart was unstable and admit her as an emergency. I did that more than once."

But if women in inner areas, including St Ann's, during the years recorded by Julia Allison were not able to make a choice about where they delivered their babies, there is now an assumption that they will opt for hospital births. As one St Ann's midwife, Kerry Anne Gifford, told me in 2000: "To give birth in a hospital (pre-1960), a woman really had to make a fuss. So, again, the articulate woman came off best. The women around St Ann's, they're not inarticulate but they don't make a lot of waves about most things. They just get on with stuff so maybe they accepted then that they had babies at home, and now they accept that you have your baby in hospital. It's like St Ann's women carry the cultural norm." My thanks to the midwives I spoke with in St Ann's for telling me about this book.

District midwife and transport in the 1960's. Photos: permission of Nelson Thornes Ltd, Julia Allison and Joyce Tarlton from 'Delivered at Home' by Julia Allison isbn 0748735003

CLARE WILLIAMS (nee Spencer)

Born 1918

*Interviewed in her home in Derbyshire 19.7.00. Clare Williams did her three months' **district midwifery training** in St Ann's in 1943.*

There are networks of people whose lives are profoundly linked to St Ann's. Clare Williams has two nieces who work in St Ann's now. Maureen Jarvis is Head Teacher of the Blue Bell Hill Infant and Nursery School, St Ann's, and Lynda Barrett is Head Teacher of St Ann's Infant and Nursery School. Maureen and Lynda are sisters, the daughters of Clare's sister Eva

I was born at 162, High Street, Scunthorpe, but I wasn't old enough for nurse training when I left school. So I worked in a sub Post Office until I could start training to be a nurse at seventeen. I started in an Orthopaedic Hospital for Children on the outskirts of Sheffield, then went to Lincoln 1939-42. And in 1942 I started my midwifery training in Nottingham, first at the City Hospital and then at the Firs Maternity Hospital in Sherwood.

My three months' district training was in St Ann's. That part of the training was compulsory if you wanted to do Second Part Midwifery. And you had to live with a midwife whilst you did this. I was living with two midwives, Miss Tomlinson and Miss Alexander on Bracton Drive. They were City midwives. They shared a Council house and each had a student. We students shared a bedroom. I was responsible to Miss Tomlinson.

We always knew them as Miss Tomlinson and Miss Alexander, we didn't use Christian names in those days.

Watching the premature baby midwife care for her low birthweight baby c1960

Clare Williams is fifth from the left on the second row 1943

On Bracton Drive, they were semi-detached houses with gardens. I think they were quite new at the time, and they are still there. I was very happy living there.

Being on the district was part of our training. We had quite a lot of responsibility. The first case the midwives took us to, they were there the whole of the time. After that, when they had a call, they would send one of us to examine the patient. If the patient was in the early stages of labour, we'd go back and give a report. But, very often, they were in the later stages by the time the midwife was called out. So very often, the baby arrived before the midwife arrived.

We got around mostly on foot over an area of a couple of miles. The area was full of terraced houses. I sometimes think of the people there: they mostly seemed happy. There is one terrace I remember very clearly and I feel sorry they knocked it down. It was a little cul-de-sac with about a dozen houses, very small houses. There was one room downstairs and a tiny kitchen. At the end of the room the staircase went up to just one room and a tiny landing. All those houses were the same. In the middle of the courtyard was a water tap they shared, no hot water just that tap.

Bracton Drive 2001. Photo: Ruth I Johns

Mostly, people were prepared for a birth at home. But I shall never forget one occasion. I'd finished my round when a little girl of six or seven came running up to me and grabbed my skirt: 'Please will you come and see my mummy?' And, of course, I couldn't resist, but I got in trouble when I got back because I was late for my lunch. This child took me to this house. There were three more children there and three dogs and I couldn't describe the conditions really. The mother was upstairs on this bed, just a bare mattress nothing else and she was just about giving birth. So I delivered the baby. She hadn't booked a midwife or seen a doctor or anything. After I delivered the baby, I dashed back to the midwife to tell her what had happened.

The first thing she said was I should have rung the police. They got in touch with the police, I don't know why really. I think they thought the police should sort her out. Anyway, I don't know how I would have rung the police in that situation. Even public telephone boxes were few and far between.

The other student with me didn't carry on training. She was married shortly after that three months and in those days married women weren't accepted for training, but it was soon after that all that changed.

Certain things in St Ann's were quite new to me at that time. I went to St Ann's because a list went up which told students which district they would be going on. We were paid as students but very little. I can't remember what it was when I was on the district, but I do remember my first year of general nurses training, it was £18, the second year £20 and the third year £22. When I was on the district, my board and lodging costs were taken care of and we got uniform provided.

After I finished on the district, I went back to see the two midwives quite a lot. My very first case on the district was twins. I was quite excited because they were 'my' first twins. The conditions at the house were very poor. It was only toward the end of the pregnancy that she knew she was expecting twins. I can remember asking my sister if she had any cast-offs that her daughter Maureen had grown through.

The twins were delivered at home in the room downstairs where half the window was broken with cardboard stuck over the crack. But all the people were always very pleasant and grateful. We did get first babies born at home but most of the deliveries on the district were second, third or fourth . . . We stayed in touch with a mother for fourteen days after the birth.

The first baby I delivered by myself was very early in the morning. The phone rang and Miss Tomlinson was still in her dressing gown. She asked me to go and told me there was a telephone just at the end of the road. She said: 'If she's ready for delivery, get the husband to ring me and I'll come.' So off I went. The woman was very close to delivery and I sorted her out upstairs. Downstairs there were two men playing cards. I looked at the husband and said: 'Please go and telephone the midwife and she will come quickly. I gave him the telephone number.' Well, I

ST ANN'S NOTTINGHAM: inner-city voices *by Ruth I Johns* • ISBN 0951696092

won't use the exact language he used but he said: 'No, he can go, it's his kid', pointing at the other man who was the lodger playing cards with him. They were obviously good pals playing cards together and I remember that shook me a bit at the time.

We had to write six cases up in our casebook as part of our course work for the examination. You can have the book, it gives some interesting background about living conditions in St Ann's. After the three months on the district, there was another six months back at hospital before you were qualified. I was back at the Firs Maternity Hospital.

After I was trained, I went to York Maternity Hospital and was very happy there. I married in 1949. We had two sons, Anthony and Robin. I did eventually go back to midwifery at Peel Street Hospital in Nottingham, the women's hospital. That's all gone now. Miss Jephson was the Matron then, she was lovely. They advertised that they were desperately short of midwives and were asking for people to go in one weekend a month, and that's how I started back in 1964. I was there ten years. My husband, Bert, died last year. He worked for Customs and Excise. We've been here twenty-six years now. I have two grandsons.

Lynda took me back to St Ann's for a look around about twenty years ago but it was nothing like I remembered. I would say it was a happy community when I knew it. It had all gone. I couldn't believe it because they'd built all the houses the other way round [not facing the streets].

Clare Williams' Case Book when she was a trainee midwife records births she attended at first at the Firs Maternity Hospital, Nottingham, and then for the three months **on the District in St Ann's** toward the end of 1943. The births recorded whilst she was in St Ann's are mentioned below. In St Ann's she attended, and assisted, a birth at which a district midwife delivered the baby: as Clare Williams described above, she was very excited at 'her' first twins. Her Case Book records the home was clean and in good repair. Tap water was available. There were four rooms and the front room downstairs was prepared for the delivery.

Preparations for the mother were noted as brown paper, bed linen, pieces of old linen, nightdresses and vests, cotton wool, sanitary towels, Dettol, towels, jug and bowl. And for the babies, three-dozen napkins, linen for cot, baby clothes, cotton wool, crepe bandage for binders, Vaseline, Zinc and Castor oil cream, towels and soap.

This mother first attended the ante-natal clinic at 24 weeks pregnant, after which she attended fairly regularly. A multiple pregnancy was queried at the 36th week and she was asked to return in a week, but she did not due to home circumstances. It was noted that: 'Her home was very poor, but she did her best and made adequate preparations.' And: 'although she had five other children, she was delighted with the twins. She was very anxious to breastfeed them both, but unfortunately her milk was insufficient.'

The father was a labourer, and they had six previous children, born in 1932, 1934, 1935, 1937, 1939 and 1941. One child had died of meningitis. All babies before the twins were 'normal spontaneous deliveries' at home and 7lbs or more at birth, and the twins were a healthy weight. The second twin was a breech birth. Both did well. The person named as a 'home help' was from the same street. The fee for attending the confinement was one pound ten shillings.

Clare Williams' second recorded St Ann's birth at home was to a 35 year old woman with two previous children born (at home) in 1933 and 1941. Her husband was a Maltster. This couple also had a four-room house 'clean and in good condition'. Tap water was available. The front room downstairs was where the delivery took place. Preparations for the birth were the same as previously mentioned above, except there were two-dozen napkins. The baby was 7lbs and was breastfed. The person named as 'home help' came from a nearby street. The fee for attendance at the confinement was one pound ten shillings. The mother was referred to as 'capable'.

The third birth was to a 23 year old who lived in a four-roomed house which was 'clean, dry and in good repair'. It had tap water. The front bedroom was planned for the delivery. This was a first baby. Her husband was in the RAF. The baby was 5lbs 8ozs and was breastfed. She first sent for the midwife after being in labour for ten and a half hours and was: 'very nervous. After constant reassurance she co-operated with us well and rested between her pains. The labour progressed satisfactorily.' The attendance fee was one pound fifteen shillings, this then becoming the standard charge. There was no named 'home help'. This mother first attended the antenatal clinic at 10 weeks and was told that her obstetric outlook was satisfactory in every way. Clare Williams, the student midwife, reported the woman was a proud mother, eager to breastfeed which she did without difficulty.

The fourth birth recorded was to a 24 year old first time mother whose husband was in the Army. Theirs was a four-roomed house which was 'clean and in fairly good repair'. There was tap water. On this report 'outside w.c.' was noted. This wasn't noted on the others above but most four-roomed houses had outside w.cs. The front room downstairs was prepared for the birth. The named 'home help' lived near. The baby was 7lbs and 12ozs. This mother first attended antenatal clinic at 16 weeks. Her obstetric outlook was satisfactory. The time after the birth was: 'a happy period for this mother who breastfed her baby and proved herself a capable mother. She passed the time in bed by knitting garments for her small daughter.'

The fifth birth was to a first time mother aged thirty-eight whose husband was a miner. They also lived in a four-roomed house. It was 'clean, dry and in good repair' with outside w.c. There was tap water. The front bedroom was prepared for the birth. The baby was 5lbs 8ozs and was breastfed complimented with Nestles. The named 'home help' lived near. This mother attended the antenatal clinic first at 12 weeks and attended at regular intervals. The midwife was called when she was in an advanced first stage of labour. She was delighted with the baby as she had wanted one for a long time. She was very eager to breastfeed but unfortunately her supply of milk was insufficient.

Another first time mother was the sixth birth which Clare Williams reported on as a trainee midwife with a district midwife delivering the baby. This mother, aged thirty-four, had diphtheria when she was five and again at fourteen, and pneumonia at nine years old. Her husband was in the Army. They lived in a four room Council house with outside w.c. The house was in 'clean, dry and good condition'. There was tap water. The front room downstairs was prepared for the birth. The woman next door was named as 'home help'. The baby weighed 8lbs and was breastfed. When visited at home before the birth, this mother had: 'made splendid preparation for the birth'. She first visited the antenatal clinic when sixteen weeks' pregnant and was told her obstetric outlook was good.

The above six 'Case Studies' of the births in St Ann's that trainee midwife Clare Williams attended were written up as part of her training and much detail is recorded day by day to do with the progress of mother and baby. All the mothers and babies were visited for fourteen days when, things being satisfactory for mother and babies, they were 'discharged'.

FRED SCOTT

Born 1925

*Interviewed at his home 13.1.00. When Fred Scott was a child, **his mother was a self-employed midwife in St Ann's before becoming a City Midwife**. His father was a shopkeeper. All photos from Fred Scott*

I was born at 32, Hungerhill Road, St Ann's, over a shop. Originally, it had been my paternal grandfather's butcher's shop. What we used as a counter had been the butcher's chopping area. My father sold cycle accessories, brake blocks, valve rubber, batteries . . .

I remember a boy coming in who wanted a new battery for his torch. It was almost dark and he said: 'I think the night's the best part of the day!'

I never saw my paternal grandfather because my father didn't marry until he was forty-five. My mother was thirty-two when they married and she was a nurse at the City Hospital, although I don't know if it was called the City Hospital then. My paternal grandmother lived with us. She ran the shop and I helped when I was old enough. We had a particular friend, Mrs Atkin, who looked after me until my mother got home. Mrs Atkin was in effect a child-minder and lived across the road from us. I have happy memories of that.

My father's name was Frederick Albert Aubrey Scott, but he never used the Aubrey. He had a shop in St James Street in the City Centre where he sold golf clubs and balls, not that he was a golfer himself.

My mother was Alice Mary (nee Sharman). She came from Suffolk. She came over for training in Derby and Nottingham Hospitals. My memories of my mother are of her as a midwife. I was an only child.

Fred Scott as a child

Fred Scott's parents on holiday at uncle's farm in the 1930s

179, Ransom Road, the Council house allocated when Fred Scott's mother became a City Midwife. He is on the doorstep in Scout's uniform

When I was a child, a man used to come round with a pole to light the gas lamps and he came back in the morning to pull down the supply of gas that put them out. I used to love going round with him to squeeze the thing that put the flame up.

My father also sold bicycles and battery radios. I had my first cycle when I was eight or nine. I enjoyed cycling and also having lamps and rear lights although you didn't really need them. When I was about twelve or thirteen I can remember cycling to Matlock with a friend. I never belonged to a club.

Every Sunday morning, I used to walk with my father from Hungerhill Road to his shop in St James Street to check that everything was OK. Then we often used to go to the weighing machine outside Marks and Spencer. We put a penny in. I got on first and weighed myself and then my father got on behind me and weighed us both and then he deducted my weight from the total to get his weight! Then we pulled out a little drawer and got a bar of Nestle's chocolate. We only had to put one penny in for weighing and getting the bar of chocolate.

In the 1930s there were day and evening train trips to Skegness in the summer. Evening trips started at four o'clock and cost two shillings and six pence. Steam engines of course!

My mother worked very hard. It was before the days of City Midwives. In other words she worked on her own account. There were other midwives in the area. Two on Blue Bell Hill and I think their names were Nurse Ashley and Nurse Skelham. And I remember my mother talking about a Mrs Healey on Dame Agnes Street.

As well as working on her own account, my mother helped at a private Nursing Home in Regent Street in the City Centre. She went in there most afternoons and she was also called out there when somebody was having a baby. They would send a taxi for her. In those days that was quite something. There weren't many taxis around. Sometimes she would be knocked up in the night to go there.

We didn't have a telephone at home then. Someone used to have to come and fetch her. Sometimes she would be called out and then came back because the baby wasn't anywhere near ready for being born. And she would be called out again later.

She covered a big area and walked. She didn't have a bicycle. So she walked with her Midwives' Case full of equipment. I've still got her tin case. We moved to a Council house in 1937 when she became a City Midwife employed by the Local Authority. We moved to 179, Ransom Road, which is near the top of the Road where it becomes Mapperley. She still didn't have any transport but was given bus tokens. My father's shop wasn't doing very well and my mother became the main breadwinner by the time we moved to Ransom Road.

For some years she had a bad eye that she couldn't see from. Before she became a City Midwife, she had to have it removed. She was only a City Midwife for a year or two at the most because the other eye started to go. After she finished, during the War she was a nurse at one of the Air Raid Warden's Stations, quite near to where we lived. We had to move from the Council house when she finished as a City Midwife and we rented a house on the Mapperley part of Woodborough Road near St Jude's Church. It wasn't nearly as good as the Council house that we left. She didn't work after the War, her health did not permit it. She was born in 1891, so she would have been about fifty-four when she stopped work.

After we moved to Ransom Road, I stopped going to the 6th Boys' Brigade Company, St Ann's, but still went to St Ann's Church and retained friendships there.

I went to Sycamore Infant and Junior School then to Huntingdon Street School for just one year prior to my 11-plus exam. They put me in the first form of the Senior School, which was not particularly helpful for getting the 11-plus, but anyway I scraped through and went to Mundella Grammar School. I stayed there until I was sixteen. One memory of my childhood is the funerals in those days, most of them had horse drawn hearses. I can remember my father saying that he didn't want that, he

As a child, Barbara Fairholm in her family's yard in Corporation Road, St Ann's, and aged twenty in the Arboretum

wanted a motor hearse and he did. He died in 1945 and was sixty-six.

My wife was Barbara [nee Fairholm] who lived on Corporation Road, St Ann's.

We married just after the War and although we lived with my mother, we continued to go down to St Ann's Church until we moved to a prefab on the Beechdale Estate in 1949. My wife's mother kept a grocery shop at 33, Corporation Road and next door, her father kept a cobbler's shop. We met at St Ann's Church Young People's Fellowship. We knew each other by sight over quite some time but we actually started courting the 10th January 1942. We married on 24th November 1945. Barbara was twenty-one and I was coming up twenty-one. I was in the Army so I took advantage of getting married and getting a wife's allowance.

When my wife left school she worked for PluPerfect, a high class crockery shop on Mansfield Road near Forest Road. I didn't know her then. Then she worked for Musson

Wedding day 1945. Fred Scott's mother is next to him

and Royle's on St Ann's Well Road opposite the New Cavendish Cinema, and that shop suffered some War damage. The windows were blown out. The shop sold drapery and clothing.

After that, she worked for her mother in her general grocery shop at Corporation Road in St Ann's and she got five bob [shillings] a week pocket money. Whilst I was in the Army, Barbara lived with my mother and went each day to help her mother in her shop. Later her mother gave up the shop and went to live with one of Barbara's sisters.

After I left school, I worked for the City Analyst's Laboratory. My job was mostly analysing water. I still went back and visited friends in St Ann's. I can remember one of my mother's friends saying: 'Do you know what I've got Bob for Christmas? I've managed to get him a bottle of tomato ketchup.' Things like that were very scarce indeed then.

Then, before I went into the Army, I had what was known as an Engineering Cadetship at Lincoln Technical College. It was a Government sponsored scheme because they wanted engineer officers, but they didn't want people who were already in engineering. Anyway I took the course but it wasn't very long before my mother became ill and I came out on compassionate grounds for ten months and was able to get a temporary job. I joined the Army the day before the War with Japan ended. I did six weeks in Northern Ireland and then went to Catterick and eventually came out of the Army in 1947.

I got a job which I didn't like but which paid well but I decided to get out and joined Nottingham City Council Mental Health Department on £260 a year. I worked clerically and then got a promotion I didn't really want as a senior clerk at the Council's Home Help Service. It had developed from five home helps to five hundred, and it needed some input. I took the original appointment to the Mental Health Department because, when the Mental Health Officer appointed anybody, he watched to see if they showed any aptitude to become Mental Welfare Officers. I was a Mental Welfare Officer from 1953 to 1966. Dr MacMillan was the Physician Superintendent at Mapperley Hospital and he was a real pioneer.

I became a Probation Officer in 1966 for six years. The Chief Probation Officer in the City was Leslie Palmer[1] who was a St Ann's man. But he didn't live in St Ann's then. In 1972, I went to the new City Social Services Department which came under the Notts County Council in 1974. I retired in 1990.

My wife died in 1983. I was blessed with a very unselfish mother and a very unselfish wife. Gems both of them. I have one son and he was born on Christmas Day 1951 and he's Head of Chemistry at a school in Northamptonshire. And I've got twin granddaughters who are twenty-one, both at University.

[1] A family photo album of Leslie Palmer is held in the Local Studies Library, Central Library, Angel Row, Nottingham.

Community Organising after Redevelopment

This section covers new organisations since the redevelopment. New organisations with obvious links to life before redevelopment appear in other sections: for example, Faith, Pubs, Allotments and Things We Did Then. There are, of course, no clear-cut 'before' and 'after' scenarios but, in order to present the material, it is necessary to have some shape.

When the 'new' St Ann's was built, there was a dearth of small, cheap, versatile meeting places. Church halls had been decimated, pubs 'with rooms' severely reduced in number and shops 'with back rooms' almost disappeared. These places accommodated small-scale informal get-togethers and arranged meetings. Adaptable small spaces, which could be a mission hall, a house, a shop or a workshop as needs required, became a memory. The new housing did not lend itself to versatile use, and planning approval processes tightened.

However, much community organising has occurred in St Ann's over the past three decades. The sense of loss of the 'old' St Ann's is still acute among some elders. They deeply regret the forced abrupt ending of a way of life. That has, on occasions, made it hard for them to recognise the efforts of the 'new' people. In the 'new' district bereft of amenities, the 'new' people set about improving their environment using available methods. But many of the 'old' St Annies, who were able to stay or who moved back, have put a lot into the new community.

After the mid-1970s, community organising would become far more dependent on grant funding, mainly from Central and Local Government programmes. The social and political environment in which individuals and groups set about organising was very different to the more informal arrangements of the 'old' St Ann's. These changes were happening nationwide wherever redevelopment of established communities took place or where new estates were being built (often without amenities for months or years).

BLUE BELL HILL COMMUNITY CENTRE

The Blue Bell Hill Community Centre was the only community centre provided at the time the 'new' St Ann's was built. As Steve Lack says in his interview, it was never going to meet the needs of all of St Ann's because it was on the brow of one of the hills overlooking the St Ann's Well Road valley. It therefore 'felt' very distant to large parts of the district.

But the Blue Bell Hill Community Centre nurtured - or provided early meeting space - for groups which developed community life in the new St Ann's. I'm sad now to see the neglected exterior of the Blue Bell Hill Community Centre, which still plays a very important role.

Blue Bell Hill Community Centre played a large part in the one-time St Ann's Festivals held in the 'new' community and was responsible for reviving the Festival in 1984. The Chairman then was Graham Hardy of St Ann's Probation Department; the Secretary was Carolyn Thompson, and the very active Treasurer/Warden was Mrs I Petgrave. She reported back to the Community Support Unit, Nottinghamshire County Council Social Services Department, which gave a £100 grant, that: "It was a marvellous day weather-wise and the event attracted 500 people.

"Individual stall-holders' expectations of income were realised . . . Thirty babies entered the Bonny Baby Competition, eleven Senior Citizens entered the Easter Bonnet Competition, and the number of children between 7-11 years who entered the Children's Easter Bonnet Competition was endless." Attractions planned included a marching band, Punch and Judy, children's demonstration of modern dance, kiddies roundabout and face painting, Pot-Pouri stall, the Pirate Ship (St Ann's Cubs and Scouts), Fortune telling, Tarot Card reading, Juvenile Jazz Band walk-about, fine art embroidery demonstration, cuddly toy making, Stonebridge City Farm home produce, Mobile Library (St Ann's Library), Welfare Rights [SAWRAG] information display, poster and badge making display, Nottingham Outlaws BMX Club, various stalls for neighbourhood groups, free games and activities organised by the Blue Bell Hill Youth Club, evening disco, The Red Circle Karate Club, the Robin Hood Society, *Nottingham Evening Post* roadshow, and Blue Bell Hill Junior School Scottish Dancing Team.

This 1984 St Ann's Festival, which was opened by the Lord Mayor, was a success following two years of trying unsuccessfully to get one off the ground. Thereafter, the Festival did not become a regular feature but 'Fun Days' have taken place occasionally in St Ann's organised by different groups.

The **Wells Road Community Centre** is a single storey building (with kitchen and toilet facilities) in the playground of Morley Junior School [re-named St Ann's Well Junior School in 2000] on The Wells Road. This space became available for community use when it was no longer needed by the school. In the City of Nottingham's list of Community Centres 1989, Mrs D Thompson, Brewsters Road, St Ann's, was listed as the contact and activities included Mums and Toddlers Group, After School Club, Senior Citizens Group, Karate, Bingo and Sequence Dancing Group.

In 2002, Mrs Christine Taylor is secretary of a Committee which arranges lettings of this space, currently regularly used for two bingo sessions a week and a church service on Sundays and also for occasional events.

STEVE LACK

Born 1956

Interviewed at **Blue Bell Hill Community Centre**, *Dennett Close, off Beacon Hill Rise, St Ann's 22.3.00. Steve Lack was the person volunteers at Blue Bell Hill CC suggested I should talk with. He was a Community Development Worker based at the Centre. Soon after this interview, due to Nottingham City Council reorganisation of services, two Community Development Workers in St Ann's, including Steve Lack, moved to other jobs*

When I was first appointed here in 1990, people doing my job were called Wardens to work specifically with a Community Association or to help set up a Community Association to manage their building. I'm now called a Community Development Worker and my job has changed. I don't spend as much time with the Community Association here but also with more groups in St Ann's offering help and advice.

The Community Centre here has been a centre for around thirty years. It was part of the old Blue Bell Hill Infants and Junior School. The hall here was the school's dining room and it's still got the old kitchen and the old caretaker's house. Subsequently added have been an office, a lounge and a playroom. So there's this mixture of old and new. Unfortunately we didn't get all the grounds of the old school.

Originally there weren't any houses in front of the Community Centre. You could see it from the main road. The houses were part of the new St Ann's when it was redeveloped. When the Community Centre started, it provided social activities for the community of St Ann's. Historically, I don't know if there was a particular cry for a Community Centre on the hill because it's been a bit of a divide having a hill here. There was a greater pressure for a Community Centre down on The Wells Road but that never came about and one was built here because the premises were here, and I think it was easier to tag on to an existing school.

So it provided social activities, activities for children, play schemes, youth clubs and activities for older people.

When the Centre was set up here, it was managed by the City Council[1]. The direction of the Centre has changed. Since about 1995, it has been managed by local people. Local people decide what happens here. Most Nottingham Community Centres were set up with a Management Committee from the start. But this one was somewhat different. It received all the money, for heating and lighting, etc. They were paid by the City Council. Now the City Council gives a grant and the Committee make up the rest in room hire etc.

When I started working here in 1990, I was working with people to get a Management Committee going, looking at Constitutions, looking at how we could draw people in. The Community Association is now a registered charity, which obviously helps when applying for funding. Activity-wise, the Centre isn't used to its capacity but I think St Ann's has so many buildings that are not used to capacity. But we do have a lot of activities going on here.

The great debate is whether buildings are offering the things that people want. But how you find that out is a difficult process. We've gone about door-knocking and asking people, and taken out questionnaires, and people have given us a list of what they want. However, there hasn't always been the uptake from local people. It's like a lot of places. People say they wish they had this and that, but it doesn't necessarily mean they would use it.

The average week is very much children focused. There's things like playgroups, after-school clubs, occasional dance groups use the building, training courses and we have an old people's day centre that use the place three days a week. Karate groups use it. The Community Association who manages the building has very much focused on childcare. So the training has been around childcare. Local people wanted that. It's given some local people some skills to take into paid employment.

People have come in as volunteers to work with playgroups and then gone on to get the training here without having to face the daunting prospect of going into College. And now a lot of the work here around childcare is enabling local people to go into the job market knowing there is affordable childcare on their doorstep.

For example, we do an after-school club [started 1999]. We pick up from local schools and bring the children here until 6.15pm five days a week. That is £2 per evening including picking up from school. The children are given some tea and they have a range of activities with qualified workers, most of them local. We can take up to twenty-four children at one time now. Some parents using the scheme are working full-time, some part-time.

---

[1] In the 1983 Nottingham City Council list of its Community Centres, the one at Blue Bell Hill was the only one in St Ann's, which was run by the Council. The Warden was Mrs I Petgrave. The Centre comprised a large hall, medium-sized lounge, small meeting room, kitchen and toilet facilities and had a car park. Activities were listed as Karate Club (Junior & Senior), Senior Citizens Lunch Club, Discos/dances, Religious meetings, Over 60s Club, TV Drama Workshops, Manvers 14+ Group, After Hospital Care Group, Slimming Club, Dog Training Class, Cubs and Scouts, Socials, Mother & Toddler Group, Senior Citizens Day Centre, Sunshine Corner, Chalfield Dog Obedience & Training Classes. At the time, the City Council gave some support to two voluntarily run Centres in St Ann's: the Afro Caribbean Centre [ACNA] on Hungerhill Road, and the Pakistan Friends League Centre [now the Pakistan Centre], 163, Woodborough Road.

Blue Bell Hill Community Centre 'old' and 'new' buildings and in need of some modernisation befitting the role the Centre plays in the local community. Photos: Ruth I Johns 2002

Every school holiday there's a scheme that runs between nine to five and obviously there's a charge for that.

The problem in this area is that the £3.60 minimum wage becomes the maximum wage and it affects the way you look at affordable childcare. In other more salubrious areas you will have people on a career ladder who can pay £6-£7 per session for their childcare. Here we charge £2 per session and that is impossible if people have two or three children. We only charge £1.75 per morning for the playgroup and people cannot afford to send their child every morning. You don't have people on career structures like teachers and solicitors living in West Bridgford saying: 'Now I must move back into St Ann's.'

All members of the Management Committee are local people. The only Local Authority representation is through myself as a City Council worker. The Community Centre Management has a Service Level Agreement. It gets a small grant and the rest of the income comes through room hire. The grant last year was £2,000 which covers a percentage of the heating, lighting, insurance . . . Then obviously there is a charge for the Social Services Day Centre that comes in to help the elderly as I mentioned earlier. The Committee organise some fund raising. They haven't got heaps of money but they survive. It's a big change from the days when the City Council paid everything and that the money from room rental etc went straight back to the City Council.

In some ways people resented that but in others it was easier because the building was managed by me. They didn't have any management responsibility. The dilemma now is that if you have a massive heating bill, you have to fund-raise for it. People have come to accept that and they do have more say in what goes on. They can direct things more.

I think when I first started I was able to attract more volunteers. Maybe that was because I had more enthusiasm but I think I still have the same amount. I just think people are asked to do such a lot now in volunteering and also working patterns have changed over the years. Whereas before you would get a traditional family made up of children, the father working and the mother at home, now more women are back at work and there are not the traditional roles for men. There used to be a lot of manual work. There's been a change in family structure. It has a knock-on effect for volunteering. There's a high proportion of one-parent families in this area, Manvers Ward.

I think the problem with the area now is that it's got such a bad reputation. A lot of the problem is that it tends to be the active members in the community who tend to get moved out first. There's a certain number of people who prefer to live in St Ann's and like living here, like its close proximity to the City etc . . . But there are a number of people who for some reason use it as a transit camp. They come in and the first thing they try to do is to get out again and it does unfortunately suffer from a stigma.

I think the area is very misrepresented by the media. It's the stigma that takes over. A lot of people that I work with at the Centre are great.

One of the other initiatives that I'm working on is Sure Start, a new initiative launched by the Government. I'm trying to get community involvement. It's based on the idea that early intervention can stop family breakdown, and can stop young people going into crime. It's based on working with families with children under four. It has had successful results in America. It's looking at what services people use, what they would like to use, whether a service is appropriate, how a service can best be delivered and what local people would like to see in the area.

I've been involved in trying to develop a Credit Union in the area. It's a slow process. I've been working on this for four or five years now. We seem to get so far with the registration and then get knocked back because certain things aren't right, and then the Registrar of Friendly Societies in London doesn't respond. It's difficult sustaining a group when you are all waiting. It's a daunting prospect looking after other people's money. And everything has to be legally covered and insured. But banks have withdrawn from St Ann's and a Credit Union is the kind of thing that would help pull communities together. But it is a lot of hard work. In its formative years it would be dependent on volunteers.

I act in an advisory capacity to the Renewal Trust. My role is to support the community representatives on that. It's a major initiative for drawing funding into the area.

2002. Steve Lack writes: "Since June 2000, I have been the Project Manager for the Urban Youth and Play Team, which covers the areas of Radford, Hyson Green, New Basford and Forest Fields. The focus of my work has therefore changed to that of managing services for young people in this area of the City." Steve Lack is still employed by the City Council, although the Project receives funding from the European Regional Development Fund

AFRO-CARIBBEAN NATIONAL ARTISTIC CENTRE [ACNA]

The Afro-Caribbean National Artistic Centre, on Hungerhill Road, St Ann's, was one of the first Caribbean centres in the UK. During the years people were being encouraged to come to Britain from the Caribbean, to assist workforce shortages after the Second World War, they often experienced discrimination in employment, in housing and socially. ACNA owes its history to the need of people from the Caribbean to organise their own social, political, educational and leisure activities.

The following interviews outline some of the ACNA and pre-ACNA story.

GEORGE LEIGH

Born 1928

*George Leigh is a founder member of ACNA and its President. He was interviewed at the **Afro-Caribbean National Artistic Centre** [ACNA] 21.9.00. Photos: ACNA unless stated otherwise*

I was born in Jamaica and came over here in the RAF. I joined in 1944 and was demobbed in 1948. I came to Long Eaton, just outside Nottingham, in 1948 and we formed the first organisation for black people in this country. It was the West Indian Carib Cricket Club. We called it Carib to personify one of the early races of people in the Caribbean. There were two such races, the Arawak who were mainly in Jamaica, but being Jamaican ourselves we tried to embrace all Caribbean people so used the name Carib.

Our Cricket Club started after the great West Indian Tour of England in 1951 with Weekes, Ramadin, Valentine, Worrell and Walcott and all those people. The first organisation was the Cosmopolitans Social and Sports Club. From 1952, the Cosmopolitans Social and Sports Club and the Caribs became one organisation and were known as the Colonial Social and Sports Club.

When the West Indian Tour came again, we approached Nottingham Co-op for premises at [no 279] Alfred Street Central[1], St Ann's. We got a three-year lease 1957-60. We changed our name to the Commonwealth Citizen's Association. The Co-op grocery shop was downstairs and we were upstairs. At that time a lot of people from the Commonwealth were welcome in Britain to help reconstruct it after the Second World War. In co-operation with Nottingham Council for Voluntary Service, we would meet new arrivals on a Saturday and help them. For example, they may only have had tropical clothing and we would help them get warmer clothing. And we planted the social seed there about them playing cricket at weekends.

We played cricket all over. In the latter part of the 1950s we went into the Nottingham Cricket League. On Saturdays, we would play in the English Cricket Team in various parks and on Sundays we would tour as the Caribs. We took the team around to Nottinghamshire villages where they had not seen black people before. It was a way of integrating people with the host community. We took our families around with us and were very successful.

Afro-Caribbean people settled in Long Eaton because it had big factories around which wanted people: Stanton and Staveley Ironworks, British Celanese, Concordia and Chilwell Ordnance Depot. Nottingham wasn't so hungry for labour and some places had a lot of stigma about employing black people. Nottingham City Transport didn't employ us until we mounted a big demonstration in 1954. It wasn't so easy to get into skilled work.

When we came to Britain, we knew all about it and its industries and where they were because our education system was the same as in this country. But people here did not teach their indigenous children about Commonwealth people. Well, it was the Empire then.

Every year, we played a cricket match in Nottingham Prison. In 1958, after we'd played the match and gone back to Alfred Street Central, St Ann's, there were some racial disturbances and the police told us to close and disappear. I was Chair of the Commonwealth Citizen's Association at the time. It included people from different countries, including the Asian community. By the 1960s people started to get their separate organisations like the Pakistan Friends League, the Indian Workers Union. The Caribbean Islands had some integration and we called the organisation the West Indian Nationals Association. We held some big functions at the Sherwood Rooms. When Jamaica got its independence in 1963 there was a big do and a High Commission was established.

---

[1] Photo in Shops: Adam Hopewell.

St Ann's Nottingham: inner city voices by Ruth Johns • ISBN 0951696092

21.6.98 George Leigh as Master of Ceremonies at Nottingham Council House for the 50th Anniversary celebration of S S Windrush

And, at the same celebration, back row left to right: George Leigh, Linford Stevens, Pastor James Stapleton, Milton Crosdale, Hilton James. Front row: Councillor Tony Robinson, Louise Dyer, John Heppell MP for Nottingham East, Dorothy McLaughlin

Around 1969, the West Indian Nationals Association [WINA] called a meeting with all the known splinter groups to try to found an organisation for themselves. And there were some conferences. Groups included SPADE [Solidarity for Protection against Deprivation and Exploitation], the Black People's Freedom Movement and the West Indian Student Association. At that time, the West Indian Nationals Association was losing a lot of their leaders. Eric Irons got a job, Vernon Clement became a community relations officer in Coventry, Neal Franklin went to Southwark, Gene Ewart went over to East Anglia University and ended up as something big there.

These organisations set up ACNA, the West Indian Nationals Association being the dominant partner then. It wasn't a revolutionary organisation. We might have had these revolutionary concepts, but we recognised that it was better to be in anything than to be out in the cold. We had strong links with all the City agencies including the City Council and the police. We ran Saturday schools. People from Nottingham University helped us.

In 1975, the Callaghan Government had Urban Aid to assist community development schemes. ACNA applied for a grant for premises. We had brought all our people together and we, as West Indian Nationals Association, decided to try and get premises for ACNA to show people that we could run something for ourselves rather than having English people run something for us, and our application was turned down by the City Council. There were demonstrations outside the Council House by Indians, Pakistanis and ourselves: all who wanted centres.

Some years before, the International Community Centre opened on Mansfield Road and we could all use it. We'd grasp any straw, but can you imagine how it was. It was one locker for Pakistani, one for this and that, one in that room . . . I said this won't work which is why we applied for Urban Aid. In 1976, we applied again. We were offered this place on Hungerhill Road, part of the old Sycamore School. It was so dilapidated, wet was coming through the roof. We turned it down at first and went to the place on Manning Street which is the Gladstone Club now, but we couldn't afford that. So in the end we came here. We had running costs for five years in our bid. After Alfred Street Central, we had been on top of Ben Bowers Restaurant at Canning Circus for some years.

So ACNA was opened here in 1978 by Lord Mayor Watkinson. Not all of our community have supported this place because, as you know, there will be people who support churches and other things, but we've survived.

On January 6th 1987, we had a terrible fire here but it rose like the Phoenix and re-opened in July 1988. During that eighteen months, the County Council allowed us to use next door, then the Sycamore Youth and Community Centre, to keep things going. And the pensioners went over to ACFF [Association of Caribbean Families and Friends] on Beaconsfield Street, Hyson Green. We went over there with our staff before they had their own. After the fire, the extension we are in was built for the young people. To start with I was Treasurer, then Manager in 1985. I retired in 1995 and am now President. I keep working. I've just done a big project for the Jamaican High Commission visit here.

When I was Manager, we had about seventy children at Saturday School, all ages. The elderly side was started in 1979 by the present Chair, Lynne Gilzean. She started the Luncheon Club. At Christmas we sometimes fed around a hundred and ten people. That was a big operation for a small kitchen.

The former Sycamore School buildings on Hungerhill Road. Photo: Geoffrey Shaw, Nottingham Local Studies Library c1971. ACNA uses the part of the building farthest from the camera. The nearer part has recently been converted into business units. And the entrance between ACNA Centre and the Business Units leads to the new Sycamore Millennium Centre

The police and ACNA organised a sponsored cycle ride to assist rebuilding and here a cheque for £1,700 is handed over in December 1987

The building after the 1987 fire

Photos taken, undated, but after the fire when previous photos were lost. Easter Fair fundraising

ST ANN'S NOTTINGHAM: inner-city voices *by Ruth I Johns* • ISBN 0951696092

We represented ourselves with all the agencies and kept abreast of what was taking place. Milton Crosdale, who used to be Chair here, he became Director of the Community Relations Council in Nottingham. It's now the Centre for Racial Equality. Then another organisation was formed with the help of the MSC [Manpower Services Commission]. It was called JIPAC [Joint Indian, Pakistani and Afro-Caribbean Community Project] and they operated from three centres. But when the funding dried up that was defunct. And we formed the Afro-Caribbean and Asian Forum. That started in 1983. It puts on conferences with Ministers, does common monitoring of racial harassment and so forth, and links with Government Officers, Probation Officers, we consult with the Health Authority, colleges and so on. So there's a lot of active work being done by the Forum but we have only a few paid staff and that is a problem.

Elders Luncheon Club cooks

Celebration cake made by a student of the Sugar Craft Class at ACNA to celebrate 25th Anniversary of Jamaican Independence 1988

I'm very proud to say that a lot of our younger people, especially the girls, are moving forwards. The girls' capacity for learning has outstripped the boys'. A lot of the men want strong jobs but they are not there anymore. Some are lawyers, accountants and doing development work in the City. I can remember the time when Eric Irons was the only black man working for the City Council. So there has been change and achievement.

I've always believed in keeping in the mainstream, you can't achieve anything otherwise. Yes, I did all the voluntary work here whilst in paid work. I was a high-pressure welder. I worked for Aitons at Derby. And British Celanese at Spondon. At Celanese, when every new black person came for a job, one of us went down to the interview room to make sure things were clear and he got the job. We started doing that about 1951 when the CARIBs just started. Can you see how that concept was driving things forward?

Very few people know the history of Afro-Caribbeans coming over from 1948. They show you the Windrush on TV and all these guys dressed up with a hat and black or white suits and the women all nice. This is how it was. You must come to the Mother Country looking smart. You can't come looking like a tramp because you're going to England where they are posh!

At that time to get a Council house could take five or six years on a points system. So people coming over weren't going to get Council houses. We had a word in our parlance, a partner. To get a house, you wanted a deposit and this is how multi-occupation started by people paying something to a partner. Terrace houses were going for £400-600. It was a way of getting a foothold, a way of clubbing together to get premises. And when demolition came along, this self-help was broken down and people became Council tenants when their houses were compulsorily purchased. They were owners before, afterwards tenants. Compensation was very little. We took issue on the matter with the MP, Jack Dunnett.

My message for fifty years time? I say to young people, you could be poor but you must grasp knowledge because knowledge will give you wisdom. It's a vision I have. A brain is a computer. You do not need everything in your brain at any one time. But at some time, it's ready in there and can be recalled and that's what I call knowledge. And if you've got knowledge, you've got wisdom.

I'm retired now and have left the education system. I used to help the teachers at Alfred Street and then here at the Saturday School. I would say that in the Caribbean the education system at the time I was a child seemed a little better than what we found here, except in mathematics. A lot of people found figures difficult in the Caribbean but soon learned to do sums over here when they went betting! I remember a chap saying that the Secretary at Alfred Street Central, Grenville Lawrence, advised him to go into the Betting Shop to learn to do sums quickly! He lost a lot of money but he could count well!

I'm married and have two children. I don't think people have so much civic responsibility these days. Everybody's hustling and wants to be paid for everything. Britain is too rich.

I think with a lot of our people, the shock that they didn't belong when they came here is still with them. We weren't welcomed with open arms. But I admire British people of that time for allowing all these people to come and they didn't revolt. They are still coming and there is no revolution. So I was right in my analysis that the people here are nice. They must have been. At that time in America, they were still stringing up black people. Even now, over there if you are black you live in this quarter or that quarter. My sister is in Florida and she tells me. She was in New York.

George Leigh has written two publications, now out-of-print but available at Nottingham Local Studies Library. They are 'West Indies Cricket Club: the 30th Anniversary' and 'Windrush'.

GEORGE POWE

Born 1926 and

DELROY BROWN

Born 1958

*Interviewed at the **Afro-Caribbean National Artistic Centre [ACNA]**, Hungerhill Road, St Ann's 23.5.00. George Powe is a founder member and Company Secretary of ACNA. Delroy Brown is Manager*

George Powe When the last Manager came here in 1995, she asked me if I would give her a little sketch about the history of ACNA because she didn't know its history and I'll give you a copy.

I'm married and have four children. My own links with St Ann's go back to about 1952. The black population then was very small. There were probably two West Indians for every African, from Ghana, Nigeria and Sierre Leone. The West Indians were mainly from Jamaica. Because of the

*George Powe.
Photo from 'Lest
We Forget'*

A panel from an Exhibition about service personnel from the West Indies who served in World War II which accompanied publication of 'Lest We Forget'. Photo: ACNA

difficulty in acquiring accommodation, there was a lot of multi-occupied accommodation, and we had the housing racketeers who used to sell slum property. Premises were difficult to get. The first black person to get a house in St Ann's was a guy called Aneke, and then came people like Soborasua. Because of our social situation at the time we tended to meet in areas where there were a number of black people. And that's how the Association started.

If you recall, one of the arguments was that St Ann's was one of the worst slums in England. So you could get a house for £200-300. Some of the racketeers said: 'Right, you can have a house off me and you can pay me £3 a week. And you can rent out rooms and put four people in a room.' When you talk to young people today, they do not realise how difficult it was to find £3 or £4. They think you are joking. Money value has changed so much.

I was born in Kingston, Jamaica. I came over here in the Air Force in 1943[1]. I was in Fighter Command. When I first came out of the Air Force, I went to Liverpool and then to Birmingham for a short period. The thing which brought me to Nottingham wasn't employment. It was

---

[1] George Powe is one of the ex-Service Personnel interviewed for *Lest We Forget: the experiences of World War II West Indian Ex-Service Personnel* by Robert N Murray. [Nottingham West Indian Combined Ex-Services Association. 1996] An earlier booklet began the process of putting Nottingham West Indian Ex-Service Personnel on the record. It was published by the Association in 1984.

more because I had friends who were politically minded like myself, and so we tended to follow each other. Birmingham was a better place for employment than Nottingham at that time.

When the City Corporation buses didn't employ black people, we formed groups and we agitated and went through the court system. Then we had to struggle for them to train black people as drivers. In those days, the majority of black people here were not so much engrossed in local politics but in international politics, about freeing home countries from colonialism. I applied for the job as a bus conductor and was told that I wasn't intelligent enough to be a conductor. When you tell young people of experiences like this, which my generation had, it sounds unbelievable.

The Co-op store on Parliament Street in the City Centre was the first shop in Nottingham to employ a black person.

We started to get involved in national politics when a lot of us wanted to get employment, because we met barriers. For example, it took a long time before they would employ black miners. The first foreigners that were employed as a group in the mines were the Italians. It was a struggle to get black miners accepted and that kind of struggle brought me to Nottingham.

In those early years the majority of black people here were not interested in the Labour Party or the Conservative Party. Trade Unions were not overtly racist but they practised racism. When there were the Closed Shops, you couldn't get a job if you were not a member of the Union. If you managed to get a job, they started questioning your credentials before you were admitted to the Union, and you might be thrown out of the factory.

I remember the first black woman from Jamaica was Mrs Mac. Her husband was living in St Ann's. He was a tailor and used to make suits on credit for the lads because many of them could not afford to buy suits. He sent for her and she came over. He lived somewhere around Festus Street. We're talking 1955.

The Communist Party was then quite strong in Nottingham. Then the Co-op Political Party was very strong. The Labour Party was quite strong. The Nottingham City Labour Party, East Section, was the first group that ever gave us anything material in our struggle. It was the time when Tommy Ives was the Secretary of the Nottingham City Labour Party. They gave us some office things like typewriters, duplicators and so on.

When the unemployment situation was bad, we had no meeting place as such. If we wanted to rent quiet premises for social occasions, it was extremely difficult. A number of people came around us and said they'd help, but when it came to the crunch they disappeared. So we said we'd try and do something for ourselves. We consulted the Consultative Committee for the Welfare of Coloured People, which Dorothy Wood set up from the Council for Voluntary Service.

At the time, France was carrying out dispersal: it didn't want too many black people in one area. It was tried here. The first batch of people that were sent from Nottingham were some Pakistanis. They were sent to Lincoln, didn't like it and so they came back.

We thought we would try and find premises to meet. But it was difficult to find anywhere to live let alone acquire premises for social purposes. And if you agitated at all, they'd say: 'Right you are a Communist' and then people don't want to know you.

Some of our own leaders did not want black people to develop any left-wing tendencies. Their argument was that we should be ambassadors, ambassadors for our home country. The only meaning I could put on that was that we should be docile and accept things as they were.

Sheila Patterson came and did some research and I sat in on her interview with Malcolm Lee, Director of Housing for the City Council. Very few black people at that time got Council housing. He said that a lot of people didn't want to live near black people because of the smell of their food and that sort of thing.

The only place we could get accommodation was in places like St Ann's and the Meadows. That encouraged us to meet in St Ann's and we started to meet at the Acorn, a pub which wasn't very far away from here. Then we would go to the Mechanics pub. Suddenly we found we were not welcome and there was a lot of agitation and they set up an anti-coloured campaign. It got so bad that Soborasua and I went to the Acorn and served ourselves and they had a demonstration outside the Mechanics. This was about 1960.

Pat Jordan had a book shop at 4, Dane Street, St Ann's, so it was another place where political blacks could go and chat. His tendency was to move toward Trotsky and he said we should find our own place. The old Bluecoat School became the International Community Centre. Milton Crosdale tried to organise a meeting to determine a review of premises and we decided that we would find our own premises. We worked it out that, at that time, it would cost about £30,000.

We wrote to various groups for support. The only group who helped apart from, as I said earlier, the Labour Party and the Co-op, was the Council of Churches which gave us £2,000 and specified it should be used for office equipment. Estate Agents said they would not rent us premises as we had no history of being tenants.

I went to see Mohammad Aslam for advice at the Pakistani Friendship League, which was near here and it was a company limited by guarantee. So I was asked by my group which was Tenny Lewis, Dorothy Smith, Louis Morgan and a few others to draft a memorandum in such a way that nobody can take it over. Even when we had a company, we still had difficulty with Estate Agents. So we set up a Trust and got a lease at 21, Derby Road for three years. At the same time we wanted to set up a supplementary school and the City Education Department let us use premises on the corner of Radford Boulevard and Ilkeston Road. It met on Saturdays and we had children of all backgrounds, white as well as black. Then the Director of Education, Mr Jackson, withdrew the premises because he said we were teaching the children about Communism.

The Saturday School moved to premises outside, but they weren't as accessible and the school kind of ran down until we got these premises up here. This came about because of the Urban Aid Programme which the Government was making available for inner-city development. The grant would be in two parts, part for capital and part for revenue. The limit for a project was £100,000. Overall we got £64,000 and then we had problems because we could not find premises. The only premises we could get was this place [part of the disused ex-Sycamore Road Secondary School]. It ate up all the money because inflation was rapid then.

We couldn't buy the premises. We leased it for fifty years. At first the Council wanted £2,500 a year rent and in those days, that was a lot of money. We said that was too much because we didn't know if we could make so much back. There was a lot of racism in the Council then. We negotiated and we got a lease with a premium and a peppercorn rent. And the Labour Council of the time said it would give us five years' running costs.

We had to borrow money - a ten-year loan - from the Bass Worthington Brewery to set up the bar for the Club. A lot of people questioned why we called it the Afro-Caribbean National Artistic Centre. The Artistic word came in almost by accident when Louis Morgan developed coconut art, and then we discussed the issue of youth and senior citizens and he said we could develop the coconut art, so the word artistic crept in!

It's the first organisation I know that was set up so quickly. With the structure that we have, it meant we could get a little group together to meet a particular challenge and then it would disappear when it was no longer needed. It wasn't just racism when we started but class prejudice as well.

Around the time of demolition of St Ann's, the first batch of black people to the area lost out. They were only paid for the land when houses were compulsorily purchased and didn't get any payment for the building itself [this was true for all private house owners]. Black people were dispersed into sub-standard houses, some went to Lenton, some to the Meadows. Many stayed in sub-standard houses for quite a number of years. It's when we started to agitate that a few got decent houses.

How do I think things would have shaped up if the old St Ann's had stayed? I think black people would have had disadvantage from the class point of view as I mentioned. Even if you were working a colossal amount and your money was so big that you can go and spend every night without even thinking, you could not get hire purchase.

I was living in Sawley at that time and had to stand surety for people in St Ann's because there was the stigma of living there. The bad reputation of St Ann's was there.

Yes, the WINA [West Indian Nationals Association] project was built at the back of ACNA. It's a separate organisation and they asked if they could replace our premises at the back with a purpose-built one for their project and we agreed. They approached Nottingham City Challenge and got the funding [for a Day Nursery and Women's Training Centre]. It was used until about nine months ago. It is only used for meetings at present. WINA is part of the same body of people as us but there are two administrations.

When ACNA moved up here, the supplementary Saturday School came here and we developed the Senior Citizens Luncheon Club, which had not met on a regular basis before. We have it three days a week now, Tuesdays, Wednesdays and Thursdays. We have the Club facility. We have dances. We offered West Indian culture by having West Indian artists, plays and patois and all that. Within a year of getting in here, we set up workshops training people in electronics, sewing, joinery . . . Then the workshops moved away.

When Mohammad Aslam became a County Councillor, we got some money from the County Council. He recognised the principle that there were three organisations: the Indian Centre, the Pakistani Centre and ACNA which represented non-white people. And JIPAC [Joint Indian, Pakistani and Afro-Caribbean] organisation was set up. It ran training like us, but on a wider scale, and education classes like English as a second language and things like that. It's gone now. JIPAC was run from here. We don't have the Saturday School any more but we run Easter and Summer Play schemes and the Robin Hood

The City Challenge funded building behind the ACNA Centre. Photos: Ruth I Johns 2000

Domino Club. We still have a surgery for advice giving and the Club is widely used. It is open every day.

Delroy Brown Because of its history, the ACNA Centre is well established with the first, second and third generation, whereas a lot of organisations just focus on the third generation rather than the older ones also. ACNA history means that we try to meet needs on that wide basis. At the weekends the Social Club provides a service for the younger element of our community and during the week we provide a service for the older element. We are working a lot in partnership with other voluntary organisations.

The nature of funding has shifted from the Local Authority to seeking funds from the Lottery and other sorts of agencies and that often entails working in partnership with other community organisations. We're involved with the Renewal Trust which is the main regeneration agency within St Ann's. The site next door is being developed into the Sycamore Millennium Centre. There are business units at the front and an excellent sports centre.

We try to have an invisible wall. People can come here and then go across there. It's important to hold on to the core value that this is a Caribbean Centre because it has always been a beacon for the Caribbean people who live outside the City and in the City and who want to express themselves here. The future depends very much on funding agencies. We have to look at how we can self-generate funds and maintain services which are relevant to our community.

It's important that this organisation survives. Listening to George, it is a legacy of how the work came about. I don't come from Nottingham in the sense of being born here. I came in the 1980s and worked in the Ukaidi organisation down the road [in Marple Square]. I think the 1980s was a high point of social activities in the City where people were very conscious of breaking down barriers, former barriers in the City. People were coming out of community organisations into the mainstream and now you find they are moving back into community organisations because that is where the real work is happening and where people feel comfortable.

George Powe When we started here, it was the only organisation of its type that existed in England. It was unique and we had people from different countries just coming to see what it was. It was designed for all age groups and sometimes we didn't get grants and we generated our own funds. Ukaidi started from here. The Cavaliers started from here. That was a cricket club which is now at the Marcus Garvey Centre.

To join the Club here you have to have a Proposer and Seconder. We have to abide by the Club Rules according to law. People assume that ACNA and the Club are one thing, but legally they are separate. People renew membership every year. We learned a lot from SATRA [St Ann's Tenants and Residents Association]. Do you remember SATRA? Instead of having two committees, we have one committee which controls ACNA and the Club and we have one membership card and one application form. It costs £3 a year to be a member. People join from age eighteen. And then we run things for youngsters.

Delroy Brown There are about thirty or forty at our Saturday playschool.

The whole nature of supplementary education is changing. One of the things we are conscious of is that, if we focus all our energies on dealing with social deprivation, what we tend to do is to exclude those who want to pursue excellence. So we are constantly fire-fighting, trying to dampen down people's destructive element and alienation and inability to want to do something constructive with their life. We've not had the necessary resources to do that. But we have to be conscious of how do we also pursue excellence? How do we draw out what is good for the community and use that as an example for those coming up?

So we are looking at the way there can be development for people to achieve their goals. And picking up on that, rather than constantly dealing with Social Services. They have more than enough resources. We don't. We do that out of the goodness of our heart because we have a social responsibility. I think we have to begin to think about how do we manage the right development rather than dealing with social deprivation?

George will bear me out I think. This organisation came out of listening to the struggle of his generation and the current issues of that time. There was much more motivation, more solidarity. If we look at the young people who have been brought up over here, they are much more confused about where they're at. Are they outside the host community looking in, or are they midway inside it looking inside and outside? Or are they inside it, with inability to self-actualise and do something for themselves in their own interest? It becomes difficult to determine what is their interest. We don't have the generation of the 1950s with pioneering motivations and wanting to establish something. What we have to do, and why my work is completely different, is we have to re-establish what the key goals are. We have to establish that sense of self-identity to say: 'Yes, we are here, we are part of the host, but also we have distinctive needs.' That is crucial now. It is a challenge.

George Powe What would I like to send down the generations for fifty years time? I'd like to say that they cannot develop themselves or develop their society unless they are prepared to contribute to that development. It does seem to me that we have a culture that has developed where people expect that something must be done for them, rather than they do things for themselves. They should believe in themselves and believe in their ability to make society a better place. They must realise nobody is an island. They cannot stand on their own. They have got to be united.

Delroy Brown Isn't it ironic, when I was born, if a black man looked at a white woman in America, he would have been hanged. Over here, social exclusion was rife. Now the tide's turned round in the sense of an absorption process. The images you see on TV aren't of successful black people and black people having a successful family. Absorption has come on the backdrop of social exclusion and life exclusion.

I was in a Leisure Centre jacuzzi yesterday evening with six white people. And your point about the law is in essence right, because it didn't matter who I was sitting next to because everybody had the space they were entitled to. The law enables a structure to do that. At the same time, there was no social interaction. So we have progressed, but there is still this vacuum. My question for fifty years time is will we, as black people, be around intact? Will we be around so we can trace our descendants, can trace roots and themselves all the way down to the young generation who came here? There were black people here in Tudor times.

George Powe   Unless we do something about it, we lose our heritage.

Delroy Brown   It's important to do things like your book. We need to record. The simple people need to record the simple history because the simple history is the intricate history of what really happened. Rather than historians telling what 'needs' to be told . . .

George Powe   It's a pity pubs like the Acorn didn't have photographs. Or the Mechanics. I mentioned these earlier. I was in the Mechanics with a white guy and the landlord came and took my drink away. We asked him why and he said he didn't 'entertain niggers in here'. We organised a sit-in protest with Margaret Gardner, did you ever meet Margaret? She was instrumental in helping to set it up. A photograph of that would have been wonderful. We never thought about it. If it was now I would be more conscious of recording things and then I would probably have a lot of photos. I've got photographs of demonstrations but most of them are outside Nottingham.

A few more facts about ACNA

In order to raise funds for the cost of running ACNA, the Afro-Caribbean Social Club was formed in the Centre in 1978.

After the Government's Manpower Services Commission came into being, by the early 1980s ACNA had set up a Youth Training Scheme (YTS) catering for the needs of young unemployed people by offering a number of courses. This later became a Youth Opportunity Scheme (YOPS). Eventually, Central Government changed the whole system and, because of the changes in the rules governing financial support for such schemes, we were unable to continue with this valuable activity. Instead we joined forces with the Indian Centre and the Pakistani Centre and created the Joint Indian, Pakistani and Afro-Caribbean Community Project [JIPAC]. After some years, financial constraints forced the closure of this project as well. *George Powe* 1995.

ACNA users in 1993/94 were 90% Afro-Caribbean and 10% European.

In the year 1998/99, there were nearly 4,000 attendances at the ACNA Elders Day Centre, with around the same number of Afro-Caribbean meals cooked at ACNA for Meals at Home. The Robin Hood Domino Club had around 3,000 attendances and the S S Empire

Windrush 50th Anniversary event 650. Tracing the Trailblazers Exhibition, compiled by ACNA users, continued to attract interest and groups hired the exhibition[2]. Around 320 people a week used the Social Club facilities. The Club provided subsidies to sporting, cultural, educational and other activities. The West Indian Carib Cricket Club played in the Nottingham Cricket League. In the 1998 season, it won the League. The ACNA Centre continued to support the Club which used the Carlton Forum facilities for their home base.

ST ANN'S RESOURCE AND ADVICE CENTRE

This Centre has come a long way since it started in the Blue Bell Hill Community Centre in 1983. It called itself **SAWRAG** [St Ann's Welfare Rights and Advice Group] and it needed funding.

Its objectives were:
- To help and advise claimants regardless of race, sex, colour, creed, sexual orientation or age, and to encourage the take up of their rights.
- To advance education of welfare rights issues amongst persons resident or working in St Ann's, Manvers or Greenwood Wards (the designated area).
- To carry out and/or assist research and study into rights issues in the designated area, and to publish findings of such research.
- The relief of poverty among people of the designated area
- SAWRAG shall be non-party in politics and non-sectarian in religion.

By May 1984, Advice Sessions were being held 10.30-12.30 Monday mornings, and 1.0-3.0 Wednesday afternoons at Blue Bell Hill Community Centre, and one afternoon a week at The Wells Road Centre.

Supporting the aims of the Group were these two Community Centres, King's Hall Methodist Church, Stonebridge City Farm, UKAIDI Project, Nottingham Centre for the Unemployed, Nottinghamshire Welfare Rights Team, Probation Service (St Ann's Office), Social Services (East Area, Hockley Office), Nottingham City Council (Councillors Betty Higgins and Peter Burgess) and St Ann's Library.

At a SAWRAG Management meeting 10.5.84 at St Ann's Library, two workers and one student on placement with the Nottingham Heating Project [NHP] attended. They explained they wanted to get a Heating Group started in St Ann's. Their brief was to work with unemployed residents of the area. The Committee thought the NHP could help with a take-up campaign on heating and the training of volunteers. It agreed the first step would be to deliver questionnaires to a sample area of St

---

[2]   The accompanying book was *Trailblazers, a tribute to the early lives of Jamaicans now living in Nottingham*. Edited by Andrina Louis. [Leisure Services, Nottinghamshire County Council. 1997].

Ann's to gauge reaction. Ron Bell agreed to liaise with NHP.

The Trading Standards Department of Nottinghamshire County Council refused funding in 1984 on the grounds that SAWRAG was 'not a new initiative'. The refusal came with a note from John Hannam, Senior Community Resource Officer, Welfare Rights Team, saying that the refusal was not a reflection on the quality of the group.

He suggested the group "should be funded at local level, which will give it a chance to run an advice service from a flat near the [Chase Precinct] shopping centre. The City [Council] are able to provide the flat at a peppercorn rent and would provide furniture and equipment. An ongoing grant of £1,425 will enable this group to run an advice service. The cost is greater than usual because of the rent, rates and heating which is inescapable in St Ann's because of the heating scheme [District Heating Scheme]. If this element is disregarded, the cost is in line with our usual £700 advice agency grant."

In August 1984, a grant of £100 was agreed towards volunteer training expenses. It was received in mid-October, this being the only grant received 1984/85.

The Heating Project in St Ann's quickly progressed. A leaflet announcing a Public Meeting of St Ann's Heating Group at the Sycamore Junior School stated that a survey of one hundred homes in St Ann's showed that:-

- 61% think their homes are not warm enough and need to use extra heating e.g. electric fires
- 88% think the standard charge is too high
- 80% complained of being without heat at one time or another due to breakdown or repairs
- 54% complained of draughts and/or damp
- 80% said they would like a Heating Group set up to campaign about these problems.

The Public Meeting was successful and a second planned with councillors and Coal Board representatives present[1].

By May 1985, SAWRAG opened the first St Ann's Resource and Advice Centre at 2a, Robin Hood Chase, moving to 14, Robin Hood Chase in 1990. And then on to purpose-built accommodation at the Chase Neighbourhood Centre in 1997.

In an Application for Grant to Nottinghamshire County Council in 1985, the St Ann's Resource and Advice Centre stated that the Centre: "set up by a group of local volunteers, provides a focus for local community activity. The Centre provides a resource room containing a photocopier, electro-stencil cutter, headliner, duplicator (on loan from the Social Services Department) and a typewriter; a room for group meetings and a base for St Ann's Welfare Rights and Advice Group [SAWRAG].

"Approximately twenty-five people a week are coming to the Centre for advice or welfare rights problems; the number of sessions is increasing from two to five per week. Nine local groups and approximately fifteen individuals have used the Resource Room since it opened a month ago."

By 1993-94, SAWRAG was very well established and groups using its equipment included; St Ann's Heating

When SAWRAG was at 2a Robin Hood Chase with Ron Bell (right), and volunteers Mary Stackhouse and Hughie Greenaway. Photo: from SAWRAG

Ron Bell leads a protest into the Trustee Savings Bank [TSB] branch office about its proposed closure on the Chase Precinct [1993]. The Post Office on the Chase Precinct is now the only 'money exchange place' in the area. Photo: source SAWRAG, courtesy Nottingham Evening Post

---

[1]   See Index for District Heating Scheme.

Group, Metropolitan Estate Tenants and Residents Association, Phase 10 Action Group, St Ann's City Challenge Sector Forum, Alexandra Court Tenants Association, Chase Action Group, St Ann's Community Initiative Project and the Broad Oak Action Group. These names include groups which have become [2002] dynamic independent groups in their neighbourhoods and others (e.g. St Ann's Heating Group) which played a major part in bringing about necessary changes.

St Ann's Advice and Resource Centre now receives some 45% of its enquiries from people living outside the St Ann's area. In 2000-2001, a total of 29,800 clients were seen and this generated 47,750 enquiries which were dealt with by Appointments, Emergencies, Home Visits, Telephone and enquiries at Reception.

Following a successful pilot scheme, SAWRAG have been given a franchise by the Legal Services Commission for Welfare Benefits and Debt Advice. During the year, the Welfare Benefits Advisor [Ron Bell[2]] has assisted clients to gain a total of £187,500 for extra weekly benefit entitlement and back payments totalling £136,396.

2,250 Home Visits were made in 2000-2001 to housebound people with referrals from Social Services, Warden-Aided Complexes, Health Centres, relatives and neighbours. The Centre's Annual Report states: "We targeted local complexes in St Ann's and Sneinton for pensioners to help maximise income, this generated 503 visits leading to extra income for the majority of clients." This take-up campaign was grant-assisted by the Renewal Trust in line with a Government Initiative Programme (Minimum Income Guarantee).

Two computers are now available at the Resource Centre in addition to other equipment.

There are now ten paid workers based at the Centre, which also values the work of its volunteers. The employees are Kath Ross (Supervisor), Elaine McElveen (General Advice Worker) and they have part-time clerical support from Trevor Wells. These posts are funded by Nottingham City Council and Nottinghamshire County Council.

Annie Smith (Elderly Disabled Outreach), Chris Shannon (Mental Health Outreach) and Sue Anneke (Reception and Information Worker), are funded by the National Lotteries Board up to the end of June 2002. At the time of writing no funding has been secured to continue these posts. Michelle Robinson (Debt) is funded by Severn Trent Water.

Ron Bell (Welfare Benefit), Maggie McCabe (Debt) and Jean Craxton (full-time Administration Worker) are funded by the Legal Aid Board.

Volunteers 2000-2001: Mel Bell, Sherry Davies, Julie Harrison, Nassim Iqbal, Monica Lindsay, Pat Robinson and Janet Thomas.

---

[2] Ron Bell has been committed to the Centre, both as volunteer and staff member, over two decades. When I visited the office in 1994, I was told: 'A lot of people want to see Ron.' He was first employed - when 'unemployed' - as a Welfare Rights Co-ordinator for 30 hours a week through the Manpower Services Commission's Community Programme, 1985.

PAKISTAN CENTRE

MOHAMMAD ASLAM

Born 1928

*Interviewed at the Pakistan Centre, 163, Woodborough Road, St Ann's 7.12.99. Mohammad Aslam was a founder member of the **Pakistan Friends League** and the **Pakistan Centre** in the former Baptist Church, Woodborough Road, St Ann's. In 1981, he was elected to Nottinghamshire County Council. He is a Chartered Accountant. Photos from the Pakistan Centre*

I lived in St Ann's from 1957 until 1963, then I moved to Lenton, then to Sneinton and then to Wollaton. In 1957, I lived at 18, Beverley Street, St Ann's. There were four terraced houses: 14, 16, 18 and 20. There was a passage you went down to the back of the houses, no gardens, a very small yard and toilets outside in the yard.

During my St Ann's years, I was studying to become a chartered accountant. I worked with a Chartered Accountant and learnt the trade and studied for exams in my spare time. I think the system is still basically the same. I qualified in 1962. I passed first time. During those years, I had very little contact with the local community and, therefore, I had no experience of racial prejudice.

I have three children, one girl and two boys. The girl is the oldest. She is married and lives in Surrey. She is a pharmacist. My elder son is married and a qualified accountant. He works with me. My younger son is a principal design technologist and works for Rolls-Royce. He is the one we live with. His wife is a pharmacist.

I come from Kashmir, Azad Kashmir we call it. When I came here in 1957 there were only between fifty to a hundred people from Kashmir here. Many were not able to communicate in writing even in their own language. I used to help them on a voluntary basis and word got out that there was somebody who would help if you wanted to write a letter, if you wanted a letter read, if you wanted to go to the Employment Exchange, if you had a problem with the Local Authority and this sort of thing.

That went on for a year or two. Every evening up to twelve people came to Beverley Street. I was married. My wife and children were in Pakistan when I came here. The man whose house it was worked at Stanton and Staveley. A friend of mine, Akhtar Hussain, from Karachi, joined me. He also wanted to study accountancy. So, three of us lived there. Rent was ten shillings a week at that time. I don't think that was too low because of the facilities there: obviously values are different now than at that time.

When we saw more people coming over to England, we would sit and talk and said we should have some sort of an organisation. Find the like-minded people in the community and have an office outside the house. People could go there and we could help at weekends.

We distributed leaflets when Indian and Pakistani films were showing on Sunday at the Savoy Cinema, Derby Road. Two or three said they were interested. As a result of that we called a public meeting to form an association for anyone living in Nottingham. Though most of us were married at that time, there were no women here.

The meeting was at the Broad Street Co-operative Society building. There was somebody from the Pakistan Embassy and Dorothy Wood who worked for the Nottingham Consultative Committee for Commonwealth Citizens. Names were proposed for Chairman, Secretary and Treasurer. The purpose of the organisation was to help people in an organised way. But people who were here before Akhtar Hussain and myself felt threatened, still they came and took part in elections. They lost and then decided not to co-operate. About two weeks later they had their own meeting with their own President, Secretary and all that.

It didn't go the way we wanted it to. We called it off while the dust settled. Ramadan was starting and during those days there was no Mosque or anywhere where people could go and pray. Today there are about twenty different mosques and prayer places. Then two or three people used to hire a hall for Eid prayer.

Akhtar, I and a few others thought it would be good if there was an Islamic Centre where we could combine religious and social activities. Because we were a small community, it was no good some people going round and hiring halls for Eid prayer and Friday prayer.

After all we all have Islamic background. There are those who are more religious minded and those who are more interested in the social side. We can live and let live together and make economical use of our resources.

When we had a meeting about it, some people said: 'You've got pictures of people who are candidates, Islam doesn't allow people's pictures.' Others said some candidates went into pubs and somebody who drinks cannot be a member of an Islamic Centre. That attempt is a long story and a failure.

Then we had another meeting and that didn't work. Then we reviewed the whole situation and came to the conclusion we should set up a separate organisation called the Pakistan Friends League. We wanted to accommodate Pakistani and Kashmiri. In the eyes of some people that was controversial. Because Kashmir is not part of Pakistan and it is not part of India. If it's a Pakistan Association, I don't fit in although I do have a Pakistan passport. Kashmir is still disputed.

After all, people who are acquiring British citizenship are no longer Kashmiri or Pakistani. We decided that Pakistan Friends League could include anybody who was a friend of Pakistan. So that suited people of the Kashmir Region, Pakistan, even white and black if they said: 'Yes, great idea, we support Pakistan and what it stands for.' That was a really good organisation which came into being in 1963.

We hired a room at St Catharine's Church on St Ann's Well Road, just opposite where the Islamic Centre is now. We had regular use of a hall every Saturday for two hours and Sunday for two hours. We were twelve people on the Management Committee. Every Saturday and Sunday for two hours, two people would go or make sure someone

else would go to offer help. That carried on until around 1973 when we moved to the International Community Centre, Mansfield Road, where we had similar arrangements. When we were at the International Community Centre, we had to abide by their rules like opening times.

In the meantime there was talk taking place about Mosques, Islamic Centre and that sort of thing. Because we were established in what we were doing, the people behind the Mosque project approached us and said why didn't we help them? We had already had experience of them. Some wanted to separate religious activity and social activities. Some said we weren't practising Muslims.

Akhtar and I and other good friends took the view that people should not dictate to other people. Indeed it is a good thing if you can pray. But that's between God and the person.

We agreed to help them on condition it was a secret ballot committee. Our group won. I negotiated with the City Council to buy land on Stonebridge Road and the City Council would make a grant of £10,000. They would also put in for Urban Aid money: Home Office 75%, City Council 25%.

I went to the other group at the Campbell Street Mosque [the first Mosque in Nottingham], off Robin Hood Street, on the edge of St Ann's. It was a disused [Methodist] Church. I negotiated with the City Council to have that. I said to them there is a piece of land and a grant and a possibility of Urban Aid and you can have an Islamic Centre. You know how in any religion you get sects, in Catholic Church, Anglican, in Islam. They said which sect will Islamic Centre belong to. I said forget about sects. If we can keep our children within the Moslem faith we will be lucky. But they wouldn't have it and said: 'We want Sunni Barailvi sect.' This is the majority sect.

So we had another meeting and another meeting, then I went to the Charity Commission, then we sat back and said what are we going to do? So we said let's concentrate on social side and forget about religious disputes. Being Muslim, wherever the community has a social centre you must have a convenient prayer facility. So then we saw this building [163, Woodborough Road] vacant. I went to the Bank and they said they needed security for a loan. Several people gave their house deeds and we borrowed the money. £10,000. We also got some grant from the City Council. We approached the Council for Racial Equality and they helped. The Pakistan Centre started here in 1977. Initially, I was Chairperson for the Management Committee. Mohammad Ibrahim is Chairperson now. You spoke to him on the telephone and he wanted me to speak to you because I've been in this community for more than forty years in this area.

I got elected to the County Council in 1981, from Lenton. I was the only Pakistani Councillor at that time. I proposed that the Council should give full funding to the Pakistan Centre, the Afro-Caribbean Centre [ACNA] and also Indian Community Centre, for compliance to the respective communities. They agreed.

Mohammad Aslam addressing a Conference on Education at the Pakistan Centre when he was Chair of the Pakistan Centre. The main speaker, on the language issue, was Mr Ralph Russell. The Conference was attended by Councillor F Riddell, Chair of the Education Committee, Nottinghamshire County Council, and John Fox, Director of Education

The Islamic Centre was built in Curzon Street, not on the site originally planned.

I didn't mind the Muslim community buying this land, instead of the land originally agreed, but I protested at the way it was done and Councillor Jack Green's part in it.

Akhtar Hussain has written a book[1]. He explains about Pakistani society. Apart from religious differences, there are social groupings. He just picks out four biradris in Nottingham and tries to explain how they react and interact with each other and he highlights how some looked down on others. Where I have a difference of view is that there are about twenty different tribes in Nottingham and in Islam there's no such thing as looking down on another. everybody's equal. When people go to Haj, whether you are Pakistani, black or white, everybody's got the same kind of piece of cloth and they are equal.

[1] *The Four Tribes of Nottingham. The story of Pakistanis and Kashmiris in Nottingham, England.* By Akhtar Hussain [Awami Publishers, Karachi. 1999] Available from 96 Newgate Road, Sale, Manchester M33 4WY.

Maulan Manzoor Alam addressing an Eid Congregation at the Pakistan Centre

He left some important things out of the book. I consider him one of my best friends. When he was here at some stage he worked for the Pakistan Centre. He became Manager. He moved to Manchester.

The Pakistan Centre was refurbished and, recently, we had a lift put in with a Lottery grant. But we still keep in mind that one day we will have a purpose-built centre. Whenever we have that, one thing is sure that it will be more about people's health education and social side of life. But we can't ignore religion but we keep religion in its place. It's a personal matter. I don't politicise religion but some people don't agree with me.

Every Tuesday and Thursday, there's a lunch here for people over sixty. They come from all over the City, between twenty-five and forty each time. They make their own way here. We plan to have a Day Centre. After Ramadan, we will start with those people who are severely disabled and who feel isolated. They will come from ten in the morning until three in the afternoon. Social Services will provide transport. Until yesterday, we've been providing the lunch free but Social Services expected

Pakistan Elders Conference. Standing left to right, Councillor Betty Higgins, Councillor Dennis Jones, Lord Mayor [1999/2000], and Mr M Ibrahim, Chair Pakistan Centre

Participants at the Conference

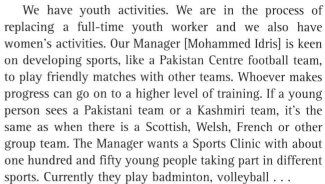

We have youth activities. We are in the process of replacing a full-time youth worker and we also have women's activities. Our Manager [Mohammed Idris] is keen on developing sports, like a Pakistan Centre football team, to play friendly matches with other teams. Whoever makes progress can go on to a higher level of training. If a young person sees a Pakistani team or a Kashmiri team, it's the same as when there is a Scottish, Welsh, French or other group team. The Manager wants a Sports Clinic with about one hundred and fifty young people taking part in different sports. Currently they play badminton, volleyball . . .

We have started a graduate training scheme. We found that Pakistani young people were not achieving good results so we decided to provide supplementary education. Three organisations got together, Muslim Women's Organisation, Pakistan Centre and Karimia Institute in Forest Fields. Muslim Women's Organisation has now left the consortium. We call it TEEP [Training Education Employment Project]. It helps young people raise their education level. If a young graduate person under twenty-five has been unemployed for six months or more, we have funding to give them £125 per week and link them to the Boots Company, or the City Council or police . . . organisations where they will work and get training for forty-three weeks. One day a week they will go to college.

We approached the European Social Fund and said Pakistani graduates are not getting jobs compared to other graduates. We want to give them some incentive. They gave us a grant out of which we pay the young people £125 per week. So far we have placed ten out of twelve.

Another project is working toward setting up a housing association run for and by Asian people. There's one member of the Management Committee who is interested in developing arts and music.

You ask what I would like to say to someone fifty years on. I think it is important that people of Pakistan and Kashmir regions should not forget about their background. Of Muslim religion, there's huge variety. Some think: 'You don't go to Haj, you don't pray, what rights have you to talk about Islam?' But I'm going to talk about Islam. Islam gives you certain values so you don't harm other people, you tell the truth and you do good to other people. Maybe same as other religions, but my religion's as good as anything can be.

people to pay £1.65 each day they come. We feel this is too expensive. I don't think you can expect an elderly person to come and pay £1.65: that person might think you can eat at home with other members of the family. So 50p to start with, maybe £1 later on.

We also have a Luncheon Club five days a week, which is a community restaurant. It's open to anybody. It's mainly white people who come. The original idea was to have it for unemployed people, disabled people, poor people, but you can't ask people if they work. Anyone can come, some are from Government departments, Social Services and people working in commercial organisations. So we set a menu price for the meal. £2.50 with meat and £2 vegetarian. It closes for Ramadan. The income generated here helps subsidise the meal for the older people.

Then a lot of the work is welfare advice. That background goes right back to 1957 as I explained earlier. The advice we provide is different from help and advice given by County and City Council services because we deal with legislation of two different Governments. We give advice on things here like, for example, Council Tax, health issues, unemployment issues. But we also cope with what goes on in Pakistan and Kashmir. We have to be aware of rules there and advise people. Then there's visas and passports and that sort of thing, what you can or cannot take with you when you visit.

Youth Conference at Pakistan Centre

Pakistan Centre Women's Council Sangeet Night

If they forget about their background and their religion, being in a minority they may be lost in society. Lost in the sense that other people may not give them proper respect and they themselves have nothing to hang on to and they would be losers in my view. They can be proud of their background and proud of their culture without getting involved in who belonged to this sect and that sect.

AKHTAR HUSSAIN is mentioned by Mohammad Aslam above and is author of *The Four Tribes of Nottingham*. He lived in St Ann's in the 1960s before moving to nearby Sneinton Dale and to Manchester in 1983.

Writing of Nottingham Pakistanis in the 1960s, Akhtar Hussain said there were three groups. Firstly the well-established ex-seamen who came in the late 1930s and early 1940s, the vast majority of whom could not read or write English. They mostly did unskilled jobs in factories and foundries. For the newcomers, the Nottingham areas of St Ann's, Arboretum, Hyson Green and Forest Fields were ideal. Some bought properties for letting, mainly to other Pakistanis. Secondly, there was the emerging band of shopkeepers, most of whom catered for the needs of a growing Pakistani population for Halal meat, Asian vegetables and groceries. There were exceptions like Mr L C Dean's up-market clothing shop on St Ann's Well Road. Thirdly, there was a handful of trainee professionals. There were few women at that time and the large majority of a population of some 500 Pakistanis in Nottingham in the early 1960s were from Azad Kashmir (District Mirpur). Among them were young men such as Mohammad Aslam, Mohammad Ajeeb, Raja Mohammad Azam and Munshi Khan who later became well-known for their political and community work.

Akhtar Hussain regrets Mohammad Aslam's defeat in Nottingham East Constituency in the 1987 General Election because: "He would have been as good a start as any recently arrived immigrant community can expect and hope for at that point in time . . . As the events during the decade between 1987 and the parliamentary election in May 1997 showed, the private lives of politicians at all levels were subjected to very painful scrutiny by the media which exposed and destroyed many political careers. I

believe Mohammad Aslam, or any other Pakistani first Muslim MP, would have been a target of special vicious attention by a section of the British media. I also believe that he would have had no difficulty in successfully defending himself."

NOTTINGHAM EAST

M. Knowles (C)	20,162.
M. Aslam (Lab)	19,706.
S. Parkhouse (L All)	6,887.
K. Malik (RF)	212.

● **Majority 456**

Poll 68.8%

1987 Parliamentary Election result for Nottingham East which includes St Ann's. Nottingham Evening Post 12.6.87

In his review of Akhtar Hussain's book, Robert Howard wrote in *Local History Magazine* No 76: "Akhtar Hussain came to Nottingham in 1960 after he graduated and worked as a labourer and bus conductor before becoming a community centre warden and an accountant. In 1983, he moved to Manchester where he became the City's Principal Race Relations Officer until 1993. This is his account and perception of events – which he has backed with masses of references and intimate detail. I know that some of his interpretations of events are disputed, but in the absence of other accounts, this is a remarkable work worthy of serious attention and consideration."

Some of the differences of opinion within Nottingham's Pakistani community have been played out within the context of St Ann's, either through Labour Party Politics or the disagreements over what organised provision was needed, i.e. a prayer-only facility or a social facility which included prayers facilities. The Pakistan Centre, on Woodborough Road, and the Mosque on Curzon Street resulted.

I often reflect why it is that, so often, members of any faith are expected to speak with one voice, be they Christians, Muslims, Jews, Sikhs, Hindus, Buddhists or any other. In putting together this history of St Ann's, I have asked myself, for example, how it was that in the old St

Ann's at the time of demolition there were six large Church of England churches[2] and some of these had additional Mission Halls in the District. The churches came from a variety of Anglican 'traditions'. In addition to the Anglican Churches were two Roman Catholic Churches and a fine array of different and large non-conformist churches and mission halls. Each of these many churches, chapels and missions came into existence to meet needs in a fast growing district. Their style of doing it offered a richness of variety. Should they all have spoken with 'one voice'? The quote at the start of one of Akhtar Hussain's chapters is: "Man can have Unity if Man will give up Freedom." History is surely proof of this.

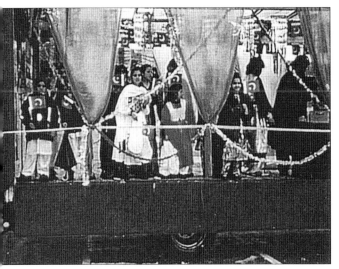

The Pakistan Centre participated in the Lord Mayor's Parade for the first time in 1997. In its 1997 Annual Report, special thanks were given to Tariq Lohar, folk singer from Birmingham who kept on singing throughout the parade; Mrs M Munir for the children's participation; Laiqat Latif, Abdul Waheed Khan and Tahir Azam, volunteers; Javed Choudhry, youth worker and Ajaib Khan, Care Service Manager. The float, representing Pakistani costume, folk songs and poetry, was prepared in the pouring rain and a colourful contrast to the grey, cold, wet day

---

2   St Andrew's, St Ann's, St Bartholomew's, St Catharine's, Emmanuel and St Matthias.

STONEBRIDGE CITY FARM

The farm is situated on three and a half acres of land. The letter below from Ken Bates establishes starting dates of Stonebridge City Farm. The Youth Opportunities Programme referred to in his letter was a Government Manpower Services Commission scheme: one in a long line of specially funded training or employment projects in St Ann's in the past three and a half decades.

Ken Bates (centre) discussing future plans

GUY JONES

Born 1961

*Community Gardener at **Stonebridge City Farm**, Stonebridge Road, St Ann's. Interviewed at the farm 5.9.00*

I have been here about six and a half years. Community Gardener is a very loose term. The resource of the garden is used to work with adults with learning difficulties, young people with behavioural problems and other people looking to get into employment situations. So it's a wide mix of people I'm working with. It provides useful work rather than training specifically for gardening.

The land the farm occupies had been earmarked at the end of the 1960s for a primary school as part of the redevelopment of St Ann's. But the falling school rolls meant that it never happened. So by 1978, local residents started agitating for something to be done with the site, and the idea of an inner-city farm came up and was mentioned in the Press. Local residents approached the City and County Councils, it was a combination of both in

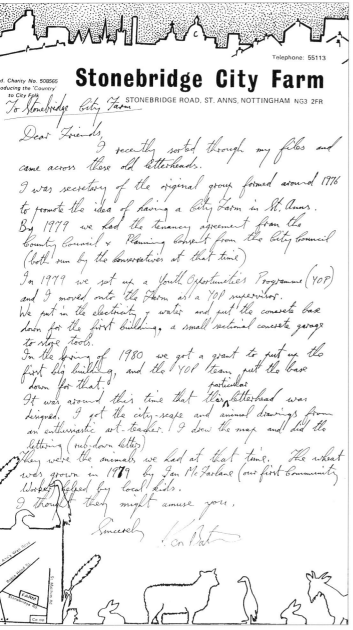

A letter from Ken Bates 7.5.97 about the beginnings of the City Farm

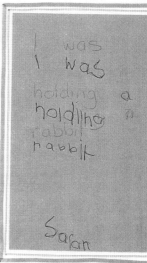

those days. The local authorities agreed and funded the clearance and paying of staff. The City Farm was officially opened in 1979.

At the start, it was a very open site, with a few goats which people would take back to their houses at night. A concrete shed was the first building on the site and it has only recently gone. From what I can gather, the farm developed fairly quickly with the barn being built so that animals could be kept permanently on site by being brought in at night.

In the early years the farm aimed at working with children in the local area[1], but something like fifteen years ago the emphasis started to shift more toward adults with learning difficulties and other special needs, and young adults having difficulties at finding work. So things have changed quite a lot.

An average week will start with me remembering that I've got to get in early (I live in St Ann's) because we're taking things to Sneinton Market. Over the summer, it has been plants that we've grown. As winter approaches, we may have to find something else to take down there. We go as casual traders, but we have the same stall every week.

On Mondays and Tuesdays, people with learning difficulties come from Home Farm Trust, that's a national charity. They've got an area of land they are working on and they help muck out the animals. We also have our own regular volunteers, who will be working in the garden and some will be mucking out. That kind of work goes on through the week. And we run a series of training courses which are mainly for our volunteers. Some are pre-vocational and some more recreational. For example, we've started a drama course at the moment, which includes building and costume design and writing as well as the acting aspect. Again, it's aimed very much at our client group.

---

1   The 1986 Rainbow Centre [180, Mansfield Road, Nottingham] Directory of Campaigning and 'Alternative' Groups in the City was published by Your Own Stuff Press. It stated the aims and objectives of Stonebridge City Farm as giving young people and children in Nottingham a taste of farm life plus increasing their awareness of animals and their part in the food production process. Regular activities included play schemes in school holidays, work experience, farm work with land and animals, and Intermediate Technology schemes.

Play scheme 1998. Photos: Stonebridge City Farm

On Wednesdays, we have an after-school club so the work with children goes on. It's for children from five to fourteen. It tends to be mostly Primary School age with a few lower Secondary school kids. At weekends, the atmosphere here completely changes and the farm reverts very much to how it was fifteen and twenty years ago, although it is open to visitors all through the week, except Fridays which is our Administration day. At weekends, people come and look at the animals and the kids can help muck out and that sort of thing.

We've had trouble over the years trying to get a café to function. With the size of the café and the number of visitors we get, it is never going to make money. In the past, we've had a grant to pay people to run it, but that ran out. We've also had volunteers running it but that tends to be unreliable. At the moment, we're exploring a relationship between Bestwood Bites, another organisation which works with people with learning difficulties. They're trying to run it as a project in its own right which doesn't have to raise money, but they don't work at weekends. At the moment the café only does tea and coffees.

The farm has sheep, pigs, a couple of calves, chickens, ducks, goats, rabbits, and guinea pigs. At present, we are reclaiming the garden because we recently had a new education building. And as part of the green ethos, we decided we wouldn't tip the spoil heap from the foundations. We would landscape it into the garden. But that's meant the garden being out of commission for about eighteen months. We've now done the main landscaping and we're putting in the paths and marking out the planting areas. As much of the work as possible is done by the people we work with. At the moment, there is a group of five or six out there finishing off a path.

The site is three and a half acres. We don't have an archive of the history of the project but we do have a file but it's not really sorted. Someone came and looked at the maps of the old streets which used to be on this site. And there are photos which aren't sorted but you can look through them. I noticed this letter [shown above] with Ken Bates' signature. He was one of the founders of the farm.

Vandalism has been a problem at times. The last time was because a young chap who lived near, and who had

been involved, used to climb over at night and wreck things but since he's moved away it's been better. There isn't a lot of involvement from local people now though a couple of the Management Committee are very local. There's less involvement now the project has changed its character and is filling a more specialist niche. It started off very much as a local community initiative. Though, as I said earlier, people do visit at weekends but it never gets terribly busy with visitors.

After about age twelve, kids don't want to be associated with the farm because they think it's kid's stuff and fluffy animals, but we may get them back when they are out of work or sometimes through the Probation Service.

Infant Schools have trips here and our Education Worker is looking at ways of expanding the age range, especially when the garden is up and running. We have four full-time and five part-time staff.

What would I want to pass down to fifty years time? What we've created here is an inclusive learning community, it's very supportive of people with a whole range of different abilities and disabilities. Nobody sees themselves as bottom of the pile. And people don't arrive at Stonebridge unless they've got nowhere else to go. I think we've shown that by using a bit of care and support you can actually get an awful lot from people that the rest of society's just rejected. I'm sure in fifty years time the same issues will be around, and if we can do this now then you lot in fifty years time can do it too.

We do tend to have a lot of parties which is helpful in building a sense of community, like trips to Skegness or celebrating people's birthdays and things like that. It's very important in a place like this. Many people would find it completely chaotic here because you've got to be doing about seven things at once and then allow for being distracted.

Before I came here, I worked for Conservation Volunteers, which was also working quite a lot with people with learning difficulties. I've also worked as a ranger and I used to be a Primary School teacher.

Some volunteers are referred to us by various organisations like Community Connections, which is very much about helping people to rehabilitate. Some people

Putting up the new building 1999, which led to the need to redesign the garden

come because their parents or guardians have heard about us. Some start coming on a college course as a placement and then, when the course ends, there's a negotiation for them to stay on. We tend not to charge for our services anyway, so 'negotiation' means asking us! We're funded by the City Council to cover the City so we have an open door policy. Local people don't tend to be more predominant.

At the moment we have to reapply for City Council funding. I think it is reasonably secure but until you actually get it, you don't know. I don't know what they call a top-up funding or a bridge funding from the European Social Fund. I hope in fifty years time that the bureaucracy of Europe has improved. Every so often we have a gap of about six months. What are you supposed to do while it's all being worked out? But I think those two grants will happen. We've also put in for a significant Lottery bid.

We're planning carefully ahead. In the next two or three years, we are not going to expand at all but to consolidate well what we have been doing because we have expanded a lot recently. Not so long ago, we were trying to do exactly what we're doing now but with only three staff and we didn't close on Fridays. The people who are funding us know what we are doing. Some members of the Management Committee don't actually know what they are managing. And a lot of people who know about the farm don't actually know what it's really doing. They see it as the City Zoo!

Being sentient creatures, the animals are a good point of bringing people together. The animal aspect is valuable for several reasons. A lot of people relate better to animals than they do to people so it's a way of bringing people out of people! There's the therapeutic value of handling animals. But some piece of legislation may turn up which means we can't allow kids to do some things unless they are wearing plastic gloves all the time . . .

With all the scares about E-Coli bacteria and all that stuff, I wouldn't be surprised if in ten years time we weren't allowed to have animals on the site. In which case we would have to think what we could do to replace the real practical work with animals. It is important to find useful work which could happen without the animals.

Since the above interview, Stonebridge City Farm suffered two vicious attacks on some of its animals, thought to be similar types of attack as at least one other in Nottingham. It also had to be shut-down for eight weeks because of the Foot and Mouth crisis in 2001.

In its consolidation orientated Development Plan 2001-2004, the farm is stated as opening 365 days a year to the public. The majority of its volunteers are adults with learning or other disabilities, and the project is now well-established as a training centre for them, though the Visitor Centre aspect of the Project is still vital. There are a variety of short courses, a full educational programme for local schools, play work and after-school work, and the project maintains an active link with the local community through the provision of green space in an inner-city area. The project offers opportunities to become involved in its management. In partnership with Nottingham University, an innovative project will be exploring volunteer needs via a Virtual Reality Farm

Photo: Ellie White 2000

Some aspects of volunteering at Stonebridge City Farm. Photos: Ellie White 2000

METRA [METROPOLITAN TENANTS AND RESIDENTS ASSOCIATION]

CAROL BACON

Born 1947

*Carol Bacon is **Voluntary Secretary** of the Metropolitan Tenants and Residents Association [METRA] and was interviewed in its office at Gedney Avenue, St Ann's 26.9.00. Metrazone is METRA's Community Centre on Ransom Road. The Metropolitan Housing Trust often refers to their estate in St Ann's as the Ransom Road Estate*

There are five hundred and forty homes on the estate of the Metropolitan Housing Trust. This estate was built from 1976-78. There's always been a tenants association, right from 1976, but until 1990 it was run very much on the 'looking after your neighbour' lines, which was no bad thing.

But in 1990-91, opportunities came the way of METRA, which the committee didn't feel able to take on board so other tenants were invited in. At about that time, both my husband and I left full-time work. My husband, John, worked in the building industry, for Nottingham City Council. He was invited to use his expertise to help the committee work their way through the myriad amounts of information on building your own community centre.

Funds came from Nottingham City Challenge and elsewhere, and the Metropolitan Housing Trust gave us the land to build the Metrazone Community Centre. At the same time, Nottingham City Challenge funded two workers for two years and that's when I became involved. John felt the committee needed someone with administrative experience to support the workers. And we've gone on from there. Yes, John's work is voluntary too.

We went through the stage of getting things going at Metrazone. It was a beautiful new building and now what's happened over the years is that we've outgrown it. It's now too small!

Yes, it was on the site of the old Scout hut. We were so successful in our first two years that City Challenge funded us for a further three years. I think Metrazone was one of the most successful City Challenge supported projects. Four years after City Challenge support ended and we're still going strong. The paid posts have always been a community development worker and an initial one was a youth and play development worker. But the woman in the job found it was too wide. In the real world you have youth workers and play workers for children. So she requested a job share.

After City Challenge, we got funding for one and a half posts from Metropolitan Housing Trust for a further three years. That meant three part-time workers. Since September last year, we've had no funding for workers except gifted hours from Nottingham City Council, and the Social Action Research Project funded a worker for six weeks during last summer. Because we're part of that project, we're into lots of other projects at the moment.

We've just been given £40,000 from the Sure Start programme to extend the Metrazone to have a room for the under-fours.

We're also part of the Learning for Life project which means, at some stage in the near future, we're going to get computers put into the Metrazone and it will be open five mornings a week from 9.0-12 noon for training local people. I'm not sure how the staff thing will work out. There will definitely be workers involved with the Sure Start programme. We're not sure how the IT project will pan out, whether there will be on-line support or a paid member of staff.

All the activities run by METRA are run by the Management Committee, all volunteers. They are a wonderful group of people who all live on the estate but we don't have a big pool of other volunteers. METRA is a 'no stars' organisation: everyone is valued for whatever they can do, and whatever time they can put in. I work the most hours but that's because I have those hours available. But I appreciate the ones who only have one or two hours available. Without them, we couldn't do what we do. For example, we run very successful after-school clubs. We had a summer play scheme that was funded by Nottingham City Council over a four-week period. Five hundred and ninety children came through the doors or out on trips. One day a week we went on a trip and all the trips were fully subscribed. We went to some lovely places and did some nice things.

We are being analysed by the Social Action Research Project - that's Government funded - which is about looking at, what's the word they use, 'social capital'. All these new words! They are all things we're doing all the time! They are talking about working with children and families, getting them to trust you. But, the fact that parents are prepared to put their children through Metrazone's doors means they trust you.

I love the work. I have a physical illness and am not supposed to work, but I find just staying at home makes me worse. I've lived on this estate - at the bottom - for twenty-four years. For the first thirteen, I was working full-time as an administrator for the Health Service. I've also got a nursing background. I trained as a State Enrolled Nurse. I've brought up three children on my own and now I'm bringing up two grandchildren.

I love every minute of my time at METRA. Every time you get a Christmas card or a little note from somebody you've done something for, it's like a pay packet. We're in the METRA office here. We've been gifted some shops by Metropolitan Housing Trust on The Wells Road opposite where the old British Road Services Depot was. I'm setting about fundraising to turn them into a more visible METRA office. Not for ego reasons but because, as you can see, this is up some pokey stairs and we're not very accessible here.

The building on The Wells Road, on the ground floor, will become a Nursery which is cost effective for local parents to encourage them to get back into work. The second floor will be a cyber café. I really do hate that term with a vengeance! But it's what people understand. And also a Credit Union office. In St Ann's there isn't even a

FROM NOTTINGHAM: inner city voices by *Ruth I Johns* • ISBN 0951696092 'hole in the wall' to get money out, and I'm anxious to get a Credit Union going because it is a wonderful way to help people financially. And there'll be a meeting place where people like Social Services, the Rent Officer, police, the local Councillor can hold surgeries. And the top floor will be METRA's offices.

The building on The Wells Road proposed for METRA's plans. Photo: Ruth I Johns 2000

The building used to be four shops and two maisonettes above. We're hoping to turn it into a real facility for the neighbourhood. METRA doesn't just work for the tenants that live on this estate. For example, the club we run for our elderly tenants has people coming from Bulwell, Basford and other inner-city areas. The after-school club we run includes children from Carlton, Broxtowe, Strelley . . . we reach out quite a long way. Some are from families who lived on the estate and then moved away. They want to come back and we say 'that's fine'.

We've been researched to death in St Ann's. There's a lot of feedback that the vast majority of people that live in St Ann's love living here. They don't have a problem. When I first came to live in St Ann's, I hated it with a vengeance but now I love it to bits. And I will jump to defend it at every opportunity. There is so much good going on in St Ann's. And I don't just mean here at METRA. There are small groups like ours doing lots and lots of things to try and make a difference in their community.

It gets a bad reputation because it's inner-city and good news doesn't 'do anything'. For example, four years ago in 1996, METRA got some funding together, about £8,000, and we put on what we called the METRA Festival. On foot, we distributed thousands of leaflets. On the day we borrowed Morley School and used the Metrazone and we had things going on across the estate. There were outdoor discos, the Army marched right through the estate, we had fire engines and tanks and a day that culminated in a £1,000 firework display. It was stunning how many people there were, about three thousand. Radio Nottingham and Radio Trent promised a presence. Not one line came out in the *Evening Post*. It was so hurtful. I wrote to the Editor and said so.

There were so many people and no incidents of any consequence. Had one window been broken in Morley School, it would have made headlines. We all worked so hard, I'd never done anything like that in my life, but no mention of this special day.

We were greatly helped by Penny Poyser at Nottingham City Challenge and by Metropolitan Housing Trust. It was a superb effort, a team effort with the METRA Committee. It was amazing. People keep saying: 'When are we going to have another Day?' There was a lot of feeling amongst local people. When City Challenge had its finishing 'bash', they asked us to help organise it.

The estate has all sizes of homes: houses, bungalows, maisonettes, flats and two sheltered schemes. The estate is just undergoing a £7m regeneration. It's only just over twenty years old: it speaks a lot for the original design! We've just had all new district heating, central heating, double-glazing, insulation . . . We've always been under the District Heating Scheme, from Eastcroft, but it's been upgraded and it makes a heck of a difference. On this estate, it's via radiators. Further down in St Ann's it's under-floor.

In a recent Government survey, St Ann's was stated as the tenth most deprived area out of four hundred in the City. Yet, we've got the most wonderful homes. Many have two toilets, up and downstairs. It's really an anomaly. We are in the heart of St Ann's but, in terms of Wards, we're in Greenwood Ward so half of the people in 'our' ward are home-owners. I don't have any envies about people owning their own homes.

It's low employment, benefit dependence, low educational standards that push St Ann's into tenth out of four hundred areas for deprivation. There's much to be done. But it *is* being done. All over this estate, we've got people working for the benefit of the estate.

We've got a very good area co-ordinator for the City Council, Jude Marks, who works out of the Renewal Trust offices. She's trying to go back to the old St Ann's Sector Forum days when people from every project in St Ann's met up to talk about what they wanted for St Ann's, so we all know what is going on and we're not each trying to re-invent the wheel. There's a very strong sense of community amongst groups at present.

We've got a number of good quality paid workers in St Ann's, along with voluntary people, who really want to see

St Ann's put on the map as a nice place to live, and to see much more positive publicity.

In the past, we've all tended to 'ring-fence' ourselves because there's been so little money and we've all wanted it and not wanted to share it. But now the Government is putting more money into inner-city areas and into communities, we find that if we get together and put in a really good bid we are more likely to get it. And we all have our little bit and, working together, we can achieve a lot more. I would like to see St Ann's become a beacon for the inner-city . . . it's achievable.

We were asked to go to London and do a stall about METRA for the Metropolitan Housing Trust Quality Fair for all its tenants across the country. So we outlined our progress all the way through, including the opening of the Metrazone in 1994. We won the British Telecom Award for disabled facilities and quiet garden and a Community Enterprise Award for the design of the building.

Metrazone is a difficult building to photograph. It stands high off Ransom Road. I couldn't get anyone else to take a photo! Through use of colour and imagination, it is a lot better than it appears here. Photo: Ruth I Johns 2000

In 1996 METRA was selected by the Civic Trust Regeneration Unit and they spent quite a lot of time with us after we lost the City Challenge funding and had to put a business plan to the Metropolitan Housing Trust. People from the Unit came up from London on a regular basis to help us put a business plan together. 1996 was the year we worked with the Housing Trust to secure £300,000 for estate improvements from City Challenge. That year we got our first recycling bins, for glass etc, for the estate.

In 1997 a multi-agency forum was set up on the estate with Metropolitan Housing Trust, METRA, local police, Councillors, local schools . . . And we got £140,000 for a play space.

METRA have been invited by Metropolitan Housing Trust together with three members of their Regional Committee to set up a steering group to oversee the £7m regeneration of the estate. This Regeneration Steering Group went down to London where the Metropolitan Housing Trust has many properties. They were doing stock transfers and, to tempt tenants to go with them, they set up

this show house. In one room were kitchens to choose from and in another were windows and in another . . . and I said: 'Just a cotton picking minute, if this is good enough for London, why isn't it good enough for Nottingham?' Up until then, if a new kitchen was needed, they would put one in by phoning you the week before and asking if you wanted blue or green!

They said they didn't have the space or staff in Nottingham. So I said, put the stuff in the METRA meeting room and METRA volunteers will staff it. And now tenants have an amazing choice. They can choose their units, worktops, floors, tiles, so each kitchen is individual. They are top quality and each new kitchen costs about £2,500.

Tenants make appointments and METRA volunteers staff the meeting room. Some people come in, and know what they want the minute they come in, but others take a long time. One lady came back three times, spending a total of seven and a half hours to choose her kitchen. But we didn't mind. I say: 'Come in and sit down, have a drink, don't rush because you won't get another new kitchen in your lifetime, so you want to be sure.'

The Regeneration Steering Group agreed that new kitchens would go to the hundred longest-standing tenants as well as the homes that were being 'regenned'. Not one of the kitchens look the same, they're redesigned and refitted. It's a fact of life, that those people who already had a new kitchen aren't getting one at this stage. But, such is the poor quality of what they got, we are campaigning to say that when the 'regen' kitchens are done, we go back and address this issue. We don't think it fair to have double standards, double quality across the estate. If there is the money, every house on the estate should have a designed and chosen kitchen.

Yes, in 1998 we had a Family Fun Day on Drug Awareness. It was a day of activity related to saying no to drugs. We had the police along and ran football competitions. We even got trophies that sit in the Metrazone.

John has been elected to the Housing Corporation's Tenant Consumer Panel. John applied for a paid post working with the Ombudsman and he didn't get that job, but some months later the Housing Corporation wrote to him, because Metropolitan Housing Trust are regulated by the Housing Corporation. They were looking for tenants in registered social housing to make up the Panel and inviting six people from across the country.

Our only income is John's part-time work apart from two small pensions. But last week, on Tuesday he was in London for a meeting with Metropolitan Housing Trust, on Wednesday he was in Birmingham for three days for a Housing Corporation conference. So that's four days working on behalf of tenants in one week.

In 1999 we got the second recycling plant opened, and the Homework Club at Metrazone. It's for pupils from Elliott Durham School. In addition to the grants for workers, over the last seven years, METRA has raised £40,000 to support our activities, and £140,000 to build Metrazone. For a little Tenants and Residents Association, it's not bad going is it?

When I first got involved, I felt the work had to be just for the people and children of this estate. But I pretty rapidly changed my mind when I realised it wasn't just people here that needed support. So now we reach out into the community and people come to us.

On a Monday we do an after-school club for five to eleven year olds which is social activity. On Tuesdays we do homework club for eleven pluses, on Wednesday we do a retired tenant group in the afternoon for people who are on their own. They don't have to be retired, they just have to want to come along. On Wednesday evening, it's the after-school club again. On Monday and Friday we have a youth group for twelve-pluses and the toddler group on a Thursday. That is all staffed by volunteers. We need more volunteers urgently.

A joint fund-raising day with Morley Junior School and METRA, July 2000

Summer 2000 play scheme. Pottery making at the Metrazone

A day at Bestwood Country Park summer 2000. Thirty-six children and thirteen volunteers

Katrina and Abigayle at Markeaton Park, summer 2000

A visit to Sherwood Forest. METRA summer play scheme 2000. Photos from Carol Bacon, METRA

Management Committee members aren't allowed to claim volunteer expenses. It's a rule we made ourselves. So all the money is spent on activities for the children. There are twelve people on the Management Committee. We've organised our own training at Metrazone on First Aid, equal opportunities, child protection . . . It builds up members' confidence. We've had a couple of members who have gone on into full-time employment.

I have people come to see me here about all sorts of problems and they'll say: 'I never knew you were here.' And I'll say: 'There's a nice glossy Newsletter comes through your door every three months, do you read it?' And they say: 'Yes.' So I say: 'Well, you should know we're here then!'

My message for fifty years time? That St Ann's is a good place to live. There are good people in St Ann's. There are some bad people, but there are those everywhere. I'm working with some lovely people, paid and voluntary, all over St Ann's. We hope to improve St Ann's image. We hope we're going to achieve that.

VIETNAMESE COMMUNITY

DIA LINH AU

Born 1960

*Interviewed at the **Vietnamese Community Centre**, Forest Fields, Nottingham 13.12.00. Dia Linh Au is Project Manager*

I was born in Vietnam and lived there until I was eighteen when I came to Birmingham and I lived in Coventry for one year. Then I came to Nottingham and lived on the Metropolitan Housing Association estate in St Ann's for one year and in another part of St Ann's for a year.

I remember the first day when I came to live with my Vietnamese friend who had a flat on the hill in St Ann's. In the evening I looked down toward the City Centre and it looked very nice. My friend had lived there two years before I came. It is a nice area to live in. I liked going to work in the morning on the crowded 42 bus down The Wells Road.

I've been Project Manager of the Vietnamese Community Centre here for over three years. Before that I was a Community Worker for the Vietnamese Centre in Birmingham.

Vietnamese people came over mostly in the early 1980s. Many of those who came to Nottingham came to St Ann's. Some of their relatives came over to join them. I think about 200 live in St Ann's. So some people have been here eighteen years or more and some under ten years.

A community group started in 1982 but the Community Centre here has only been open since 1989. It took years to establish. A group come here every week on Wednesdays to a Luncheon Club. It is special and tailor-made to meet the needs of the elderly and disabled people. The Luncheon Club has been here for ten years. There are about fifteen people each week, a large proportion from St Ann's.

We have Easter Play Schemes and Summertime Play Schemes for children aged from five to fourteen every year. We have annual day trips for everybody in our community to go to the seaside or to visit places of interest. There is the New Year Festival on the Lunar New Year and the Children's Festival in the time of the August Moon.

On a day-to-day basis, I help people with advice about Nationality, welfare rights and we accompany older people to hospital and doctors' surgeries and dentists' surgeries to translate for them. The elderly people have not always managed to learn the language.

English is a difficult language to learn. I did learn it at school. Most elderly people would speak French a little because of previous history in Vietnam. Even my dad, his first language was French. My grandparents sent him to a French-speaking school when he was five so that he would be an Officer of some sort, and later he could learn his own language.

When I was born in 1960, there was a long war and America was involved. I was in the South of Vietnam and

The Luncheon Club. Photos: Ellie White 2000

Dia Linh Au (third from left)

St Ann's Nottingham: Inner-city Voices by Ruth I Johns • ISBN 0951696092

we were fighting the Communist North Vietnam. When America withdrew their troops, for another two years we kept on fighting. But eventually the Communist North won and I lived under the Communist system for three years. My dad had worked for the British Embassy in Saigon so our life was very difficult after the war ended. My dad asked the former British Embassy if he could come to England and that's how we got here. The whole family came: mum, dad and eight sons. I'm the only son not married. One of my brothers married a British woman, the others Vietnamese.

The British people are kind people but occasionally, especially with the youth, we do have a problem. When I went to Stourport on Severn, youths looked at me and then vandalised my car.

We are teaching children born in this country to speak their own language. We have a Saturday School here and about twenty-six children between five and fifteen come.

Of the refugees from Vietnam in the UK, half are Chinese people who came to live in Vietnam. So they would want to speak Cantonese not Vietnamese.

CHASE NEIGHBOURHOOD CENTRE

The Chase Neighbourhood Centre. Photo: Chase Action Group Ltd

When changes were planned for the Chase Precinct in the early 1990s, the local community organised and decided they were going to have a community building they wanted. There were some surprised reactions (outside St Ann's) to the building's design.

It was a self-build project using the social economy approach. The project was supported by TANC [Technical Aid to Nottinghamshire Communities]. NECTA [Nottingham Environmental Construction Training for All Ltd] developed from its involvement.

I interviewed people directly associated with the Chase Neighbourhood Centre, TANC and NECTA. Community or social companies have been around for a long time, yet

they still get little recognition. It would be easy to reduce the story of the Chase Neighbourhood Centre to a few paragraphs, but the detail of individual accounts allows the full picture to be appreciated. The social economy (call it by any of a number of names) is a model which is little recognised by Government and major institutions.

There are direct historical links between the informal ways in which people in the 'old' St Ann's supported each other socially, through employment, and through networks of skill-sharing and caring, and the social economy approach which is evident in the story of the Chase Neighbourhood Centre.

The Centre was opened on June 13th 1997 by David Bellamy. The first enterprise of the Chase Action Group was the opening [1996] of a launderette in an existing Chase Precinct shop. The launderette is a community company under the Chase Action Group Ltd 'umbrella'. The launderette supports paid workers backed up by volunteers. The profit from any such venture is re-invested in the local community.

PHIL JACKSON

Born 1957

*Interviewed at **Chase Neighbourhood Centre**, Chase Precinct, St Ann's 15.3.00. Phil Jackson is a Community Development Worker in St Ann's*

I am a Community Development Worker employed by Nottingham City Council. Basically, my work involves working with local groups, individuals, and organisations in the area to look at ways of involving them in the process of change, in improving their area, in becoming self-organised so they can apply for funds and, generally, to support groups in developing their own initiatives and building solidarity.

I wasn't employed initially by the City Council. I've been a Community Worker in St Ann's since 1992 but I was involved voluntarily in St Ann's before that. I did some work with St Ann's Advice Centre when I first came to Nottingham at the end of the Miners' strike in 1985. I had been working with a Miners' Support Group in London as a volunteer. In St Ann's, I also did some work at ACNA [Afro-Caribbean National Artistic Centre], I then worked as a lithographic printer and I had other involvements politically. Then I went away to Ruskin College for a couple of years in 1989 and then came back and became a Community Development Worker. When I was a Community Worker, that was an Urban Programme post, and one of my tasks was to develop a neighbourhood centre here. Nine years on and we're sitting in it today!

I used to live in St Ann's on The Wells Road with my brother but I now live on the Strelley Estate with my family. I still work in the area and I've got ties. I was at a meeting last night with some of the children in the area. They were talking about their experiences, what worries them and what sort of things they'd like to see happen in the area. One of the points they made was that people come in from outside, who don't even live in the area, telling them what they want.

The brief for this Neighbourhood Centre was for a building right in the heart of the community to provide a number of services maybe differently from traditional community centres. In this building there is an Advice Centre, a project that deals with urban regeneration locally TANC [Technical Aid to Nottinghamshire Communities], there's a legal aid project, there's a community café, a training room with computers: so a whole range of services under one roof. My initial role was to set up a group of people who could move the whole thing forward.

We got a solid group together and the scheme really took off in 1993 when the Council and City Challenge put forward some proposals for changing the Chase Precinct and its surrounding area. Local people weren't very happy with the suggestions which included big flagship type changes, moving the health centre, and putting a supermarket on the front. So through TANC, we worked with local people to put forward their proposal for regeneration here with a self-build Neighbourhood Centre.

the local unemployment . . . At that time, about a thousand people had some sort of input in the scheme, from doing questionnaires to saving paper on the estate to make the fire-proof insulation for the building. They used to ask why the paper was needed and learnt about the project that way. It was sent away to a company who treated the paper, turning it into fibrous matter for insulation. Seven and a half tons were collected on the estate. The insulation is in the roof and all of the walls.

A lot of people who worked on creating the building were local people, and a lot of their mates would come along and ask questions. Some people who worked here found it difficult to be up for work at eight in the morning and coming on site in the middle of the winter. It was quite an achievement. The terms and conditions were good, union rates. For some it was a really positive experience and they have gone on to work with NECTA which is a company that was created as a result of what happened here. Those people are now supervisors. Others have got jobs in construction elsewhere. There were a lot of novel things that happened. For example, a lot of the timber used in the building was reclaimed from a factory in Lancashire.

COMMUNITY CONSULTATION

USING PLANS, MODELS & LOCAL PEOPLE WORKING OUT THE WAY FORWARD.

COMMUNITY CONSULTATION

Scale models were exhibited so local people could see exactly what was going on. Because banks and building societies had left, there was an issue about trying to make the remaining traders happy to stay and to tackle some of

'THATS MY MUM ON SITE'

'AND SHE'S BUILDING THIS'!!!!

ST ANN'S NOTTINGHAM: inner-city voices *by Ruth I Johns* • ISBN 0951696092

Once the building was finished, there was little money for staffing it. There was £2,350 from the Council toward running costs. The café ran on volunteers for a year and trying to keep it open most days of the week was difficult. The Advice Centre had gone in and a lot of the TANC projects went in so there was some rent coming in from them. The group running the Centre were also responsible for running the community Launderette opposite the Centre. So that was another asset.

It was a struggle for it to be self-supporting. There's a lot of talk about the social economy and intermediate labour market companies and the sort of support they need. But the support has not always been forthcoming. After a lot of negotiating, the Council agreed a reduction in the rent paid by the Launderette. After all, if the Launderette was not there, that space would be vacant. And there are three self-supporting jobs in there. And there will soon be a job in the community café. These kind of jobs can help to overcome some of the economic problems. There are six jobs now in the Neighbourhood Centre not including the Advice Centre and TANC or me - or the Launderette.

There are two part-time caretakers, an Administrative Worker, a Centre Manager/Co-ordinator Training Development Officer and part-time Volunteer Co-ordinator. Volunteers have been brilliant at keeping the café going. A lot of volunteers have come through here and gone on to get jobs. We have a key worker starting in the café on Monday. That should make a big difference and sort out the problem of continuity.

All the funding now is short-term. The year after a funded post has started, if the person wants to carry on working they have to start looking for funding and that takes time from the job they are doing. It's always difficult and makes long-term planning impossible.

Yes, we've got that room full of computers, but until very recently we've not had anybody to organise that space. But now we have Stan Norman. There's a class on Friday, there's drop-in sessions, we're hoping to get people to do a community newsletter. Stan wants to do stuff around a community web site. He's got a bid in to the Neighbourhood Support Fund to work with sixteen and seventeen year olds who have dropped out of education. It's a pity we weren't able to do that from the start. In reality, the computers have only been networked and joined up for the past couple of weeks, in the way that would allow ten people to sit around them with a machine that's functioning.

I think Stan is thinking how we can move forward in terms of the funding that's currently available. There's this New Opportunities Fund which is to do with IT centres and he sees a lot of opportunities. But he's saying to me, in a year's time these computers will be redundant. You will need hardware to bring it all up to date again.

Even if they don't do everything you want them to or they're not up to date in terms of all the latest technological development, then to me it's not a problem. But Stan says, if people go for jobs they will be asked what equipment they have worked on. He's looking at it from the point of view of people who have been historically disadvantaged so they can feel confident.

I still work with the Management Committee and the Manager/Co-ordinator on various issues around funding and support for the community businesses. I also work with Phase 10 Action Group, with Greenway in Sneinton and am going to be doing some work toward the Sneinton Festival. So although I focus on this project, I work across the area.

From my perspective, there's a lot of talk these days about social capital, human resources and capacity building and all these concepts around how local communities organise themselves. What relationships they develop between each other and how they are able to deal with the problems they face. In many instances these things are very serious in a community like St Ann's. For example, recently, there have been several incidents involving guns and gangs.

Solidarity can happen in a community for a whole number of reasons. A focus like the Neighbourhood Centre exists to encourage local initiatives and makes a positive contribution to what happens more generally in the community. People have criticised and said we've not done enough, it's never open all the time. Up to now there's been a problem about opening because there's just not been the staff to do all the things.

We have an amazing caretaker, Pat. Although in the last three days the kids were saying: 'Oh, he doesn't like us, he's always saying you can't come in.' He opens up and closes in the evening. If you looked at the list of organisations that have used the building for social and recreational purposes, and for meetings and conferences and seminars, it's quite amazing. All this can be built upon as the Centre moves on. It has taken a long time, it's been beset by all sorts of different hiccups and problems that have not necessarily been of the Management's making, but they have had to be dealt with. But the Centre has only been open two and a half years.

The fact that there were no staff here to begin with for lack of funding made it difficult, as I said earlier. And when we get staff, it's short-term. The last Co-ordinator we had here was on an 18-month contract, so after twelve months he found a job elsewhere because after twelve months he'd be thinking about what's next. So, on the surface things might seem all right with funding now, but it's short-term.

The Management group had big arguments with the Council. There was the capital grant to build the Neighbourhood Centre but no revenue support for the first five years which is the most crucial time for any project. It's taken until now to really make solid progress.

The group also had an ambitious scheme to develop the green space close to the Chase Precinct to build an all-weather pitch and to improve that little play area. It could be a sports area and a play area that was well looked after and attractive for local people. And the schools could use it. They wanted to do a self-build project - like here - to do the changing rooms. It was a bid for about £1m and the Lottery's Sports Council turned it down. It's frustrating when you see the Ice Stadium going up and that's £30m plus. What real benefits are local people going to get from that?

In 1999, Desdamona (Des) Armatrading, Administration and Finance Officer, was 'holding the fort' when I called. The Centre was struggling to find funding for key workers. Photo: Ruth I Johns

The Victoria Baths are under threat. There seems to be this move to build flagship projects costing millions of pounds, the Millennium Dome, the Earth Centre in Doncaster, the Music Centre in Sheffield: grand schemes which are struggling. There's this obsession with grandiose projects, while down the road our local baths are threatened with closure.

The group working here and proposing the sports project in the heart of a disadvantaged community is trying to do some of the things which the Government is always spouting about. But it's struggling to find resources and to do those things effectively. Sometimes my work can lead me down other paths but it is the community solidarity issue that I focus on, supporting people to feel that when they come together they can change things, question things and make a difference.

In the summer of 2000, Nottingham City Council reorganised the Community Services Division, changing the jobs of community development workers. I ended up looking for other jobs on the Council's redeployment register. You are on the register for six months. Then, if the Council can't find you a job, you are made redundant. After an interview in December 2000, I was offered the post of Assistant Area Co-ordinator in another part of the City. The job involves much less direct work with community groups and organisations. I am still involved with the Chase Action Group and St Ann's Advice Centre and participate in the management committees of both projects. Phil Jackson 2002

ALAN YOUNG

told me 2000:

I've lived in St Ann's since 1983 and I'm now a volunteer at the Chase Neighbourhood Centre. This place is going to be wonderful. I work with Stan Norman and I love what I'm doing. I feel it's making a worthwhile contribution. There's so much potential for the whole community.

I live two streets away from here and there have been big changes in the past six or seven years, improvements. We're about to get double-glazing.

In 1998, the Chase Neighbourhood Centre won a top award from the British Urban Regeneration Association [BURA]. The team who collected the Award. Photos: Chase Action Group Ltd

In Chase Precinct. Photos: Chase Action Group Ltd

NORMAN WHELBOURNE

Born 1940

*Interviewed at the **Chase Neighbourhood Centre**, Chase Precinct, St Ann's 5.4.00. He is Volunteer/Development Activity Worker*

I was born in St Ann's and lived here until I was seven, then the family moved to Radcliffe-on-Trent and came back to St Ann's when I was eleven. I have a brother and sister. We lived here until I was about fifteen. Then the family moved to Radford and I joined the Forces when I was about nineteen. I had aunties and uncles in St Ann's when they pulled it down and they went all over

Norman Whelbourne. Photo: Ruth I Johns 2000

The Chase Action Group circle in the centre of Chase Precinct. Photo: Ruth I Johns 2001

Nottingham. They said they'd move back but they never did. One auntie went to Abbey Bridge, one to Cinderhill. One moved from Alfred Street up to Blue Bell Hill, still in St Ann's, and then they pulled that house down as well, but she actually stayed in the area. I've got stepbrothers living in St Ann's and my mother-in-law lives on The Wells Road. I now live in the Meadows. It's a similar environment, inner-city. It's very much like St Ann's.

In the War I can remember being in a pushchair in St Ann's! There were all the shops. And I remember often hanging on to my mother's skirt when she was chatting with the neighbours, that sort of thing. 1947, the snow came. We had a yard. It was 1, Eagle Place, Alison Rise, off Alfred Street Central. I can remember VE Day when they had the bonfires in the old streets and everybody celebrated. I didn't know what it was all about, it was just a big party for me.

They used to herd the cows up Alfred Street to the slaughterhouse near us and we rolled cow's eyes or bull's eyes along the pavement. There was a butcher's on the corner with this slaughterhouse at the back and then across the other side of the road was British Drug House.

My mum used to do a bit of cleaning for the 'nobs'. She cleaned a doctor's surgery on the Woodborough Road.

I came out of the Forces in 1966, the year of the World Cup. Me and my wife lived in Broxtowe but didn't like it and moved back to Radford. Then they pulled Radford down like they did St Ann's and we moved to the Meadows and have been there ever since.

I was a long-distance lorry driver for years until I'd had enough six years ago. I got fed up with being made redundant and getting up at three or four o'clock in the morning. Then I worked for a driving agency and it was all right but you were never guaranteed an income. One week you would be earning £300 and the next week 'two and six'.

I've always been involved in voluntary work. I ran a Scout Group in Radford, I run a Scout Group in the Meadows.

I went to Clarendon and People's College to see if they did any courses in Youth Work and they didn't, and I was sort of stuck. I was walking through Forest Fields and Radford and I happened to come across BESTCO [Better Employment Skills Training Company]. I walked in on the spur of the moment and they interviewed me. I explained what I wanted to do. They said they couldn't get a placement, but could I get my own?

Well, I was working for Mencap eight hours a week as a volunteer on Saturdays, with the young kids in the Saturday Club, and I asked how many hours was needed to qualify for training. They said sixteen. So I went to Mencap and got another eight hours. Then BESTCO said would I like a placement with the Prince's Trust Volunteers and I started to help adults with learning difficulties, helping them how to read, how to write, how to spell. I'd never done anything like that and I loved it, and was apparently quite good at it.

So they said why didn't I go to college and get a Teaching Certificate.

I finally went to People's College when I was fifty-five and it was two years very hard work. It was the proudest moment of my life when I got my Teaching Certificate in 1998.

By the time I got my qualification, I had changed my placement from BESTCO and the Prince's Trust Volunteers to FOCUS, dealing with young people from twelve to sixteen with limited opportunities, along with adults with physical and learning difficulties. I was there four years and then unfortunately the funding ran out. I was very disappointed when I left FOCUS. I was paid only a pittance the first year, £75 a week but we managed because my wife worked. When the minimum wage came, I went on to that and it made matters worse because it affected my rent rebate and all that. It's sod's law!

Last year was horrendous, because I was supposed to finish in April, then it went to June and then to September and then I got a three-month contract to December. On New Year's Eve I was unemployed. And then I got this job at the Chase Neighbourhood Centre as Volunteer/Activity Development Worker. The Centre is a Company Limited by Guarantee, a non-profit making organisation. My job is funded by the Lottery. It's an eighteen-month appointment. I'm hoping it gets renewed. But if it doesn't, I still have my vision of how I'd like to leave this job so there's a good footing for people to continue.

My job is to try to see that there are activities, functions and things up and running for the local community and to encourage more volunteers. We've just got a young woman doing a dance group on a Monday evening for twelve girls, and I'm hoping to build up the lunch club for senior citizens except I don't like that word and prefer to call them over-fifty-fivers! It's a very small lunch club at present and I'm hoping we'll add bingo and ballroom dancing or something like that, along with volunteers.

The Community Café here comes under the umbrella of the Chase Action Group but is run independently. Any money it makes gets ploughed back into the café. There's a café co-ordinator who is paid and volunteers to run the café. The food is very good. Most of the café volunteers are St Ann's people, and also in the community laundry. But I

don't believe in turning down volunteers wherever they come from. I think it's good if somebody from the Meadows volunteers here and vice versa, because they all bring new ideas.

Now on a Tuesday and Friday morning there is a drop-in IT [Information Technology] Centre. That's run by Stan Norman the Community Development Officer. He's paid for by the Lottery like me, and also for eighteen months. He's helped by volunteer Alan Young, who I think you know. In fact the IT room is open most days for drop-in if there's someone there, but definitely Tuesdays and Fridays.

Stan is also running a basic IT course every Wednesday. On Friday afternoon there is an accredited computer course run in partnership with Clarendon College. This week, I have a basic Food Hygiene course running on Monday and Tuesday in conjunction with BESTCO and New College, Nottingham. There's a course next week on general health and safety in the home and office and that's also with BESTCO and New College.

Tuesday is Market Day in the Precinct outside and it gets quite busy in here, with people popping in for cups of tea. On Tuesday, the Nottingham Council for Voluntary Service runs a Volunteer Bureau here and one of their co-ordinators comes in. That's not only for volunteers for St Ann's and she looks at the board for our volunteer opportunities. On Monday and Tuesday mornings, someone comes in from the Carlton Job Club. There's a German Class on Thursday evening, which has been running some while. Wednesday not a lot happens but the hall is used for various functions, as a meeting centre, for conferences.

I'm trying to get a parent and toddler group up and running at present. There's a lot happening, but there could be more . . . I like working here. I like people. I've been inner-city all my life and I've seen a bit of the world. If you treat people with respect, they treat you with respect. I tend to think that the media only pick up on the bad things. There are young people out there who do a lot for their communities for no praise. These are the people who should be praised and mentioned, not the young people who are always getting into trouble.

Then why is there a myth about there being no community? I think it's because of the way they built the estates. I think the planners who planned St Ann's and the Meadows did a bad job. They used no thought. It's all very well having little grass areas. They just ripped the areas like this apart and thought people would like to see a bit of grass! I saw it when they pulled Radford down.

They destroyed areas where there was a community, like St Ann's and Radford. There were whole streets where people talked to each other and trusted each other. They ripped them down, broke that community up. When they built the new houses, they didn't replace the same people. You never tend to see anybody now and there's no shopping.

In old St Ann's, Radford or the Meadows whenever you'd walk down the street, you had houses either side and you felt safe. Now you're walking through these little jetties and you don't feel safe because you never know

The community café team on the day I interviewed Norman Whelbourne. He took the photo

what's going on round the corner. Two banks and a building society have been lost locally here and now they're talking of closing the Post Office. Now, if they close the Post Office, you might as well shut the Chase Precinct down. If people are going to have to use the Post Office on Carlton Road, they won't do their shopping here. It would shut the Co-op here down.

And as for the idea that all banking will be done on the Internet, I haven't got the Internet. And you get these humanless banks where you put your card in a slot and hopefully the money will come out. Banks and post offices and the Government don't think of the community. It's all greed.

Barclays shut a hundred and seventy-six banks on Friday, it's disgusting. I agree with the MP who says move your money. I'm paid by cheque so I have to use a bank, which means a walk into town which isn't too bad as it only takes ten minutes, but we're getting older. It's bad for old people and those with disabilities and young mums who want somewhere local where they feel safe and know people. They come into the Chase Precinct, get their Family Allowance or whatever, do their shopping and go home instead of traipsing all around town. We've started a campaign here to save the Post Office.

I'd like to see young people get more ownership over the areas where they live. I know there's not a lot for them, which is probably our fault. But they need to get things moving themselves, to take over from us old fogeys. There're some clever kids out there. And there are good places like the Blue Bell Hill Community Centre and Metrazone. But if more of them said: 'This is what we want can you help?' I'm sure us old fogeys would help them. But, what I won't do is to do it all for them. A lot of young people now expect everything done for them. I think if they realised things don't get done for them, they could take grasp and do it themselves. I think they believe that everybody's against them, more so than when I was that age.

I mean I was still wearing short trousers at fifteen. I got my first long trousers when I went to work and they were bloody overalls. I grieve when I hear these kids getting expelled or disaffected and things like that, because there's so much out there now. They've got the world at their feet and there's plenty of jobs. But it's not so straightforward. I've just been interviewing one young woman who has been offered a job, but doing it would make her £38 a week worse off. So it's a vicious circle and it's hard to break out of it. Children leave school at sixteen and believe they have no future. I think teachers have a lot to answer for. Children have got to have hope, so they are not just sitting in school doing nought, believing they will leave and be on the State on the dole.

The last time I spoke to Norman Whelbourne [2002] before going to print, plans were afoot for Jubilee celebrations. There was a plan to use the Neighbourhood Centre as a social centre for refugees living in the area

Dawn Henry, one of the three youth workers now working from the Chase Neighbourhood Centre with (left to right) MCs who go by the name of Smallz, Blender and Big Murder

On the right is Steff Webber, the Centre's Co-ordinator since November 1999. Photos: Ruth I Johns 2002. The other youth workers are Marc Bidmead and Jayne Richards, Youth Development Worker. Jayne Richards is currently working on a history project with young people

Steff Webber said they were hoping that the Youth Project would soon be able to use one of the empty shop spaces and that Sure Start could use two empty ones for a nursery and centre managed by parents

When Ellie White called in at the Chase Neighbourhood Centre with her camera, the team she photographed in the community kitchen were (left to right) Dave Mason, chef; Sean Highton, café assistant and caretaker, and Michael Pearson, volunteer. 2001

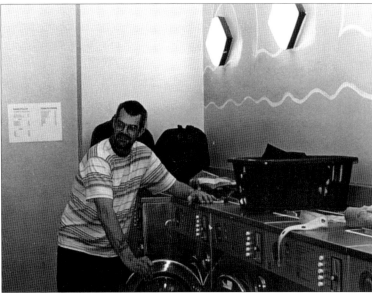

Over at the launderette, things were busy. Ian Bain, volunteer, helps to keep things under control. Staff at this time: Jo Brodsky and Sue Thomas. Photo: Ellie White

TANC [Technical Aid to Nottinghamshire Communities]

JUNE GREENWAY

Born 1965

*Manager, **TANC** [Technical Aid to Nottinghamshire Communities]. Interviewed at TANC'S office, Chase Neighbourhood Centre, St Ann's 17.1.01. The **Chase Neighbourhood Centre** was TANC's first project*

TANC started when a group of people from the voluntary sector got together around 1992. They included Community Development Workers, Community Action at Nottingham University and somebody working in a private architectural practice. They all felt that, from the experience of groups they were working with, there was need for technical help for building projects. As TANC developed it didn't only work on building projects. The common factor of all the projects was that they were in disadvantaged communities. The groups we work with have very little access to funding for the kind of service we offer. TANC's first attempt at raising funds from the Urban Programme failed. It then made a City Challenge bid for one worker and that was successful at the end of 1992, and that worker turned out to be me.

I was working in London when my job here was advertised in the *Guardian* and I just thought the job had my name on it! When I came for the interview, I wanted the job so badly, it was hurting my tummy! I was a town planner and an urban designer and now I'm a Jack and Jill of all trades. TANC helps groups, which have great ideas for projects whether they're about improving a whole estate or looking at particular buildings, or developing new services that weren't available.

Sometimes groups have a very good idea of what they think is needed to improve their community. Funders these days want a lot of hard information about why there is a need for a project. So TANC does a lot of survey work, door knocking and events to talk to people.

The Chase Neighbourhood Centre was the first project TANC was involved with. At the time City Challenge had a number of ideas for improving the Chase Precinct, including knocking down the Health Centre and rebuilding it about one hundred yards away from where it is at present. There was an idea that the pub might go, and an idea for some kind of community centre maybe in one of the shop units. There was an idea for a bucket-end supermarket, Aldi or Kwik Save to be where the Health Centre is now.

Local people really felt they had been 'done' enough in the past, and they didn't want to be 'done' again. So our task was to work with people, not just to be reactive against other people's ideas. But to find out what they wanted to see done, what were the issues that they wanted addressed.

There were a lot of things here already, a Post Office, a Chemist, a Health Centre, a Library, important things in people's lives. So we talked about what we already had here and what could be built from that. Issues were things like safety, the way people felt about access on and off the Chase area, and the lack of things going on after four o'clock when the Chase Precinct went very dead. Issues like jobs and training opportunities: unemployment was a key concern for people. There is a community centre on Blue Bell Hill, there was the church which was used for community meetings and so on, but they were either religious buildings or not in the centre of St Ann's, which the Chase Precinct is. There was the idea of developing a community focus, which was for everybody.

So we started to put all this information together with the idea that eventually we were going to have a community plan for this district centre. Some help was given by Oxford Brookes University. Phil Jackson who was a Community Development Worker in this area got involved. The City Council has recently sacked him because of a change in policy and he's working in Bulwell now. Good Community Development Workers make for good projects. With the current emphasis on active communities and social exclusion, getting rid of CDWs is completely contrary.

It was a very cold day when we did the first local consultation. There was this big bubble thing up outside and it was winter. I kept sending the volunteers into the Library to warm up. One of the volunteers, Nicola Knowles, now works with TANC. We planned everything around Market Day when there are a lot of people here. We try to catch people going about their business rather than expecting them to come and see us. The most difficult decision was around the Health Centre and the Supermarket. A lot of people liked the idea of a bigger supermarket, which was cheap rather than the current small Co-op Supermarket. But there was a majority of people against it.

A Chase Action Group design consultation for the new Neighbourhood Centre, held on Market Day in Chase Precinct 1994. There was a lot of interest. Phil Jackson, Community Development Worker front left. Photo: TANC

In the end the plan concentrated on making good what was here, improving routes on to the Chase and the car parking and looking at a new community building. We had funding to work with the Chase Action Group for five years which was a luxury. There were a lot of questions about what the community centre would be for and where it would go. One idea was looking at the side of the Library so there would be more use of the community room there. Also, there was some space between buildings at the back of the Library, or in a disused shop, or in the middle of the area: that is, we're not hiding but in your face. The Chase was the hardest place to build, because of the nearness of houses, flats, shops, and market day use. And a clear line where you can't build because of the legal bar on building on the green space which has been there since the Enclosure Act. So the space we could build on was much smaller than people thought.

But people wanted to build on the Chase. The Planning Department and the Design and Property Department and

Housing Department weren't very happy about it. So we dealt with those things when they came up. And then because of jobs and training being high on people's priorities we said the Centre could be built through an ordinary contract or as a self-built project. So the Chase Action Group went and had a look at a couple of self-build projects up and down the country, saw what they looked like, talked to the users. The Group consisted of workers, residents and traders. When all the information was gathered, we went out on Market Day and put all the information out.

Everybody went mad for it as a self-build project. Again the City Council weren't very happy. But we continued to develop the project so that it met all their regulations. Then the Group chose their architect and TANC looked at other aspects of the building, what it looked like, what it would be built out of. TANC is very interested in green design and using ecological materials but we couldn't just presume the Group would want to go with that. And again people were really keen, so it was organic paint and varnish, turfed roof, UK-sourced timber and so on.

There's a strange myth about what working-class areas are concerned about and it is so wrong. Everybody was up for the idea and it was seen as a way of making the building unique. For example, huge amounts of newspapers were collected by people in St Ann's and they were exchanged for newspapers which had been treated by Warmcel to convert them into insulation material. A large number of people were involved in this.

The Project Manager was appointed, Jo Brown [now at NECTA] and work started. Nothing as big had been done before in terms of self-build. Mostly, self-build is houses. Ten people were recruited. They could have come from Sneinton or St Ann's but most came from St Ann's which was good for the project. There was a good site atmosphere and people were very tolerant, for example shoppers and traders. There was hardly anything that was robbed from the site, there was no vandalism. In fact there's been very little since. The building is triple-glazed and there's quite a lot of glass.

It was a difficult project but it came in on time and on budget. The budget was £450,000. Originally £25,000 was put in the City Challenge plan. And we said you won't get anything for that. One of the biggest problems after the building was finished was that there never was any revenue funding identified. We did initial work on a business plan for the Centre and then Phil Jackson did a lot of work on fund-raising. Most of it came from Charitable Trusts including the Tudor Trust and Boots Charitable Trust. There was very little from the City Council. It's taken three years for the Centre to get on its feet. And now we're starting to see what is possible. The Manager now is Steff Webber. She's doing a good job.

After City Challenge finished, TANC went through six months of hell. We were desperate for funding. It's very hard to get money for a project like this because we do all the work that nobody else does and nobody thinks about doing. We're not the architects, we're not the landscapers doing the designs for new open spaces. We're working with a group, identifying needs, visiting projects and getting ideas, fact finding, working up good project briefs . . . It's not very easy to explain or for funders to understand. We don't work to Councillors or Council Officers but with groups. That causes a lot of perception problems but that's what the project is about and we make no apology for it.

TANC is a not-for-profit limited company. But at that time, TANC was just Freda Makki, who has gone to work with Carnell Green, the architect for this building, and me. Fran Younger who was a member of Chase Action Group was doing our administration. We were all made redundant because we had no money. But we kept coming in to work and eventually got some European money for three years. Last year we got some Lottery funding which will carry us on to November 2002. It's great that none of the funding is linked to councils. We're providing an independent service and a free service where it's needed.

We do fee-paying work but whatever profits we make get ploughed back. There is a voluntary management committee with a lot of the original members and the groups we work for have representation.

We're a team of five now. Jude Burgess is the latest member. She's on secondment at present from the City Council. Then there's Nicola who I mentioned earlier. Her background is architecture and urban design. She's doing an exam today. Cherry Jarvis joined us last year from Groundworks, which is a national project. Her background is working with community projects, arts and news projects. And Simon Spencer who is our administration worker and he's an IT whiz. It's a great team that's built up very slowly. We've always been clear about what we need and why and that's a lot to do with what groups are asking us for.

Now we're beginning to work for county projects as well as city ones. Other St Ann's projects have included the Pierrepont Family Centre, helping to develop their outdoor space for children with special needs. Because it was difficult to find funding, it became partly a self-build project. We had a session up on Hungerhill allotments doing a dummy run with willow work, testing designs and shapes, and then went back to the Family Centre and made a wonderful kind of willow igloo with a tunnel going through it. We had a couple of working weekends with as many volunteers as possible, including our Management Committee who did some path work and laid out some tiny allotments in car tyres so they are raised, little growing spaces. We begged from business for hardcore and timber, plants and so on and it all got done and it is lovely. If a project is great and plan 'A' can't happen, then there's plan 'B' and plan 'C'.

We've done work on Metrazone community centre on Ransom Road. That was one of our first projects in 1993. It was a burnt out Scout hut to start with. And there's another Scout hut on Hungerhill Road we did work on. We worked with Vernon Hawley who's been in this area a long time. We've been working in the Phase 10 Marple Square area for a long time with the Action Group. Work started with the tenants group 1993 or 1994 to get a community plan for the estate there because it's top of the disadvantaged area list for the whole of the County, and yet it is only just within sight of any real substantial injection of money.

June Greenway (in front) with children from Phase 10 Area. TANC devised a treasure hunt game to engage young people in the regeneration of their neighbourhood. Photo: TANC

The layout of the estate is turned in on itself and doesn't encourage getting to know people across the street and it affects the way people walk through the estate and how they feel unsafe especially at night. There was always a reason given by the Council why that area wasn't getting some decent money, until last year when the City Council decided they were going to use Capital Receipts money which is money from the sale of council houses.

The design of Marple Square hasn't been sorted out yet. It's very complicated to get it right. There are lots of different ideas about what should happen and what shouldn't. The onus is not only on the City Council and its officers, it's a partnership. It's a project I feel passionately about because of the amount of time we've spent there. We found out a lot about how long people have been there, what they have been doing. Some remember what the estate was like before demolition and some literally moved in the first day the 'new' houses were ready. All their information is really, really interesting.

As an urban designer, I always look at the old street maps and networks, and look to knit an area back into the wider City. A lot of modern design work doesn't pay enough attention to that I don't think. People talk a lot about how dense the area used to be, and how mixed it was with shops and living industry all on one patch. And it is deemed good practice now in cities to increase densities.

David Bellamy on the day of the Chase Neighbourhood Centre opening 13.6.97. Photos: Chase Action Group Ltd

The area has these signs up 'No ball games allowed'. You shouldn't have to put a sign like that up on any space, it should be clear what is appropriate and what not. I want to see the money being put into the area make a long-term difference, not a short-term kind of thing. It's potentially a great area. One man on Sherwin Walk had a great expression. He said: 'You fall out of bed and you are in the middle of town.' That's so true. And he added that the City couldn't afford to have the area looking like it did.

We've always done frontline work with voluntary and community groups. We would like to start to be more influential in terms of policy, to try to work back up the line to where decisions are made. We've been working when somebody else has set the policy and somebody else has decided what funding is going to be available and then groups respond. We would like to be a bit more influential on the strategic level but that's quite difficult.

The problem is often to do with who is setting the agenda. Even though councillors and council officers will say they understand that we work to the agenda of groups and say that is a good thing, that's not the way they want to work if things are not being developed in the way they wish to work. Then they can cause problems down the line.

People on the ground know what the issues are and it's then up to the professionals to work to that agenda. But professionals can't put the responsibility on people to know what the answers are. You've been to college, you've done all this work and got this experience and you've got

to work, in real partnership, at solutions which create a long-term solution to the issues.

My message for fifty years time? Oh that's quite hard. I think it's around the notion that it's easy to get ideas but the real hard work is putting them into practise. But if an idea is good, don't be put off, go for it, try and find people to work with you because there are actually a lot of them around. So do it rather than talk about it.

NECTA [Nottingham Environmental Construction Training for All Ltd]

JO BROWN
Born 1964

***Project Manager, NECTA Ltd** [Nottingham Environmental Construction Training for All Limited]. Interviewed at NECTA offices in Hyson Green 26.1.01*

NECTA is a non-profit construction training company borne out of the success of a community self-build project, the Chase Action Group's Neighbourhood Centre, on Robin Hood Chase in St Ann's.

The experience of constructing that Centre suggested ideas that would be successful city-wide in creating opportunities for socially disadvantaged people, by using construction as a vehicle to get people off the dole and into permanent jobs. NECTA's roots are right in the middle of St Ann's. NECTA was started by the Chase Action Group as a sub-department and it was then cut loose in early 1988 and formed its own limited company.

It is important for NECTA to be based in areas of multiple disadvantage. We now work on construction sites throughout the City. We try to negotiate jobs with social clients like community organisations who work closely with the City Council. So we're using bread and butter construction work as a vehicle to get people off the dole.

It's a complicated cocktail of funding we get from various sources. We run with the Government New Deal Programme so it helps them to pay wage subsidies. We've got another stream of wage subsidies through the Single Regeneration Budget [SRB] and we have a small amount of European Social Fund income. There's quite a lot of income through commercial payback from the practical jobs that we do. We get about 45% commercial income. And about 55% comes through the grants to cover the social and development work that we are doing toward social inclusion.

We have twenty full-time staff and anything up to eighty trainees. At present we've got about fifty. Permanent staff are engaged in three sections of the company. For simplicity we've divided it that way. The financial department runs all the finances of the organisation. There's a commercial department which controls the physical construction activities of the company, like any building company. It has a contracts manager and technical advisers, health and safety workers, and site supervisors involved on the front line with trainees on building sites. The other section is the welfare department, which generates evidence for funding and wage support mechanisms in the SRB. But actively and most importantly, it's involved in supporting individual trainees.

Trainees have to be six months unemployed, resident in an area of multiple disadvantage and they've got to express a determination for getting themselves into full-time work and in construction work. They have to get themselves to an interview and it's a real interview situation. And they've got to demonstrate that they are willing to put their back into it. We can support a trainee for up to twelve months.

NECTA challenges barriers to equality in the construction industry and tries to be a positive force for change. The construction industry in this country has a long and accurate reputation of being extremely difficult for under-represented groups: women, ethnic minorities and the disabled. We actively attempt to recruit from those groups.

I was doing a post-graduate housing degree at Leicester de Montfort University part-time when I got involved as Project Co-ordinator for the Chase Action Group through an organisation called TANC [Technical Aid for Nottinghamshire Communities]. I got involved in a voluntary capacity for a year or so before I was Project Co-ordinator.

Jo Brown (left) whilst working on the Chase Neighbourhood Centre during the construction of frame 4. John Frank (partially hidden) was a trainee on the project. Right, Phil Jackson, Community Development Worker. Photo: NECTA

Very early in the construction of the Chase Neighbourhood Centre, it was quite clear to the Group, and anyone else involved, that this was a very good way of achieving multiple outcomes. In the early 1990s, the project could have gone any way. The local population around the Chase heard the various options for a shopping centre, McDonald's, new Police Station, car park, whatever. To their credit the Group made a political decision and said: 'We're the experts in this situation. We will make sure that the ideas of the community around Robin Hood Chase are represented to City Challenge, whether it was what City Challenge Board want on their hidden agenda or whether it's a different thing.'

They were clear there was a need to represent all communities in the area and that's why it is called a neighbourhood centre, not a community centre. The Group made a decision to convert the actual building process into another means to an end and provide a social economy dimension to the project. People building the project would be local people, they would be getting an income and maybe spend some of it in local shops. They would be getting skills that would encourage their sustainable employment outside their Chase Action Group employment. Although we didn't know it at the time we were beginning to build the foundations of a permanent social company, which was later to become NECTA.

Let's face it, before this project, Robin Hood Chase was where you might find a burnt-out car on Monday morning because that's what used to happen on a Saturday down there. A fear of crime featured very heavily in people's perceptions of what went on down there. And the Chase Action Group managed to turn that completely around by building a timber framed building. The City Council was kind of reeling with: 'What do they think they are doing?' They thought the idea was mad. The whole place could get burnt down.

Site of the Chase Neighbourhood Centre. Photo: Chase Action Group Ltd

Of course, it didn't and that's because local people were building it, people that might have been vandalising it if it had been imposed on them. NECTA has carried on the whole issue of working with communities to realise their aims, have representation with NECTA and ensuring local people are recruited to work on such projects.

NECTA has three projects in St Ann's at the moment, and shortly a fourth. Firstly, we've been working on the Hungerhill Allotments for a year or so. The allotments are owned by the Bridge and Chamber's Trusts and controlled by the City Council who caretake them through the St Ann's allotments association, STAA. STAA had some money for allotment clearance and upkeep and asked NECTA if it could help by delivering a certain number of cleared allotments and that sort of thing. Hedgerows needed to be controlled, rubbish cleared, dangerous structures taken down. We did that on a piecemeal basis for some months and then a more formal relationship came about with STAA around March 2000 and the project has been widened.

However, simultaneously, the Hungerhill Allotments were granted English Heritage Status which is fantastic but it came at the time we were in touch with the City Council Planning Department, and - I think because of the Heritage Status - no planning officer was prepared to say: 'Yes, go ahead'. Our aim is to recreate allotments as they would have been and then they would be let. But there were some problems with planning which are still not quite resolved.

Of the Victorian sheds that were built on the allotments, many had fallen down particularly on plots that aren't cultivated at the moment. There was real opportunity for construction trainees to get some basic work to meet STAA's objective of getting plots renovated and the huts rebuilt. In one of these small huts, there's everything involved in terms of brickwork and timberwork. For example, there's foundations, sub-structures, brickwork, first and second timber fixing, fixed joinery, roofing, chimney building, lead work, glazing, hanging doors. In terms of learning about different trades and making

decisions about what kind of trade interests a trainee, there's all the learning experience in these small huts.

About the middle of last year, we started talking to Groundwork Greater Nottingham about a major scheme of access controls for these allotments, for example gates to the avenues, and for allotment clearance on quite a wide scale. On a three-year programme 2000-2003, NECTA won the competitive tender. Yes, NECTA's entrance to the site is now on Ransom Road.

STAA is a very small organisation run on commitment but with no full-time paid workers. It's nobody's fault but it is difficult to drive things along because there are so many different players in the programme. We are dealing with the City Council; we are dealing with STAA; Groundwork Greater Nottingham makes the decisions and provides specifications we work to.

As I said earlier, until March last year NECTA was working for STAA on allotment clearance. Every allotment we cleared was let. Some have gone back into non-cultivation but our remit was to get them ready to be handed over and then it was STAA's responsibility to find tenants.

From the plots we've done this year, it's encouraging to know people are coming forward for them. There are a lot of people who know Hungerhill allotments have been there for years. But, they don't really understand that allotments are still available and that work is going on to make them more consolidated and secure. STAA tries to make information available. With one member of staff, Alan Schofield, for a third of a week, there's a lot to do. STAA is there to defend the allotments.

Now there's also the Renewal Trust which is 'behind' the Hungerhill Gardens. It's a great force for change. The Local Authority are committed by default to look after the allotments [owned by the Bridge and Chamber's Trusts]. The general feeling up until recently is that some council officers and members would rather see the site built on. But those voices have quietened down.

Yes, there has been gradual encroachment year on year. But, that's not possible so much now. They can see that allotments are not just a pile of brushwood with old allotment holders hanging on until they are unable to garden any more. It's something that lives, it's young, it's new, it's part of healthy living, it's part of organic gardening. Allotments are becoming more secure and people aren't going to just go away. And allotments are now a vehicle for construction training.

Things are starting to come together. There's now a consortium group to discuss issues relating to allotments with representatives from organisations including the City Council, City Wide Construction and the Renewal Trust, TANC, NECTA and STAA. All stakeholders can attend and ideas can go back to allotment holders for consultation. Tony Hallam does allotment work for the Council for the whole City.

And it's not just about recreating allotments as they were forty years ago because there is the new angle about nature and sustainability. It's not STAA's intention to have all those six hundred or so plots relet to allotment holders.

Some plots need to be left as wildlife sanctuaries. There may be need for some public space in there with some infrastructure. It's not just harking back to the past.

Secondly in St Ann's, NECTA is working with Metropolitan Housing Trust [MHT] on their estate. We've got an open-ended programme of estate improvements. We're doing gates and fences and putting in new paths. There are other contractors up there, but NECTA has managed to make its own space there, in connection with MHT's commitment to social inclusion. And very much in connection with the estate residents. It's a partnership between the Housing Trust, residents and NECTA. But it's not the usual kind of relationship between client, contractor and client's agent.

We can recruit people from the estate to work on the estate. There's a greater chance of work being respected and protected by local residents if they know local people have done it. There's nothing more disheartening, and which increases vandalism and exclusion, than seeing major capital work going on in a community by a company from miles away. There's an officer, an architect Chris Francis, at MHT who has ensured that NECTA has a place there. It's never easy. Every project we turn our hands to has got issues, but that is the nature of construction. The MHT project is great and it introduces more technical construction skills for our trainees.

Hungerhill Gardens is the first point of entry for most trainees. We're not saying it's not a problem if they make a mistake there. But the first thing we need to deal with is basic work skills. We're talking about time-keeping, attendance, how they follow instructions, how they communicate with themselves as a group and with their supervisors. If they are going to have a day off, they should ring in: all those sorts of things that are often forgotten with work training. People concentrate on vocational training, but if the bricklayer can't get to work on time, they will be sacked. We also have to acknowledge that trainees coming in at the front end often don't have any tool skills at all. Some tasks on the Hungerhill

Hungerhill Gardens off Ransom Road where NECTA trainees are getting basic building training. Photo: Ruth I Johns 2000

Gardens, like allotment clearing are fairly straightforward tasks. With the MHT project things get a bit more technical, work is more in the public eye.

A third project in St Ann's is in Phase 10 Marple Square area. This is another example of partnership, in this instance between Nottingham City Council Housing Department as client, Nottingham City Building Works as the main contractor, the local Phase 10 Action Group and NECTA as a sub-contractor for some of the work. What we've done is negotiated with the client saying they should put their money where their mouth is. They are not just a cold buyer, but they should put some money into the social economy, to actively recruit people from the local area. We're talking to the main contractor saying the same thing. Residents come to us and demand that we address local employment.

Last year we found it very difficult to employ skilled bricklayers to do the supervision and we had to take brickwork down and rebuild. It was very frustrating for the trainees but it does go like that professionally sometimes as well. But we re-recruited and made absolutely sure of the management of the scheme. NECTA doesn't only exist as a means of getting people off long-term unemployment into work. It is also responding to a national crisis in construction, not only about equality of opportunity but, also, how the industry conducts itself within. There have been national studies that prove the industry is suffering a lack of investment and young active recruits at the lower end.

The building industry is now in competition with the Armed Forces for people who have good basic skills to enter trades at the bottom end. The only pool of labour for both is from the long-term unemployed.

If people have got a bit about them, they stay on at school, they go to college and they go into the Armed Services at officer level and the building industry at technical level. It encourages wage inflation, because those people in the construction industry command whatever wage they want. It is good for them in the short-term, but bad for the industry and bad for them in the long-term. It means that agreed prices can no longer be met because they can't get the labour to do it. It means the client either gets an over-priced job or a shoddy one. The whole process becomes disjoined because there isn't a wide enough pool of the appropriate skills at ground level.

NECTA is part of a process. We provide a year's training but aim to get people into the industry sooner if possible. We are a stepping-stone. We don't want to hold people back who are able to join the building market. And we don't want to push people out who haven't yet got the basic skills. Going back to what I was saying earlier, the building industry is being encouraged to recruit from the long-term unemployed, but the industry is finding those people don't have the skills. They recruit people who don't have time-keeping or attendance and are telling their supervisors to 'f*** off' as soon as they have been asked to do something. And they lose their job within a couple of weeks after their company gave them personal protective equipment, staff time, health and safety videos and the rest of it.

They might invest £500-600 in a trainee only to see them walk off the site at the end of the first week. NECTA takes the pain out of recruitment for a company and that's a good thing. If a trainee is ready to join a company within the training year, the subsidy goes to the company and they have a recruit with the teething issues dealt with.

Yes, that does make big demands of NECTA because the ones able to do best go first. It's the people who don't get the problems solved in the early weeks that our welfare support staff have to concentrate on, at the very least to help them understand what barriers they have to challenge so they can enter full-time work.

The fourth St Ann's job is a brickwork job at Pearmain Avenue which we're hoping to start soon. That too has Nottingham City Building Works as the main contractor. There's brickwork, pillars for fencing and so on, to help estate improvement.

We have been asked to work in places away from Nottingham but then we would be doing the same as any multi-national building company would be doing, taking people from one place to work in another. We're doing things in other parts of Nottingham like Radford. I think there is a finite size for organisations that are social economy organisations if they are going to remain true to their roots.

It's extremely important for NECTA to remember where it came from, like the rugged determination of the Chase Action Group and the people around St Ann's. It is important for NECTA to remember the whole line of experience going back to the time of St Ann's demolition. And the importance of people in their own communities having economic strength, to be able to be self-determining.

What would I like to pass on for fifty years time? I think what is happening through NECTA reflects a general theme, a kind of rediscovery of pre-capitalist kind of relationships and economic relationships. We've lived with capitalism for so long that it's quite common not to know there's anything else. I like to see NECTA as a positive force for change. I hope when people locally read this book in say twenty years time, that in some way NECTA was placing the building blocks for what exists then.

There's a danger that as an idea like NECTA gains momentum and kudos, strength and its own identity that it gets taken over by forces that already exist, rather than being a genuine grass-roots organisation that is there for the people. Local Authorities can be brilliant, terrible or indifferent. Nottingham City Council has been all three depending on which department you are dealing with. But it is fair to say that without the Local Authority, NECTA wouldn't exist in spite of all best endeavours of local action groups. And that's because of a few notable individuals within different departments of the Local Authority, most notably Pete McGuire of City Wide Construction.

I've lived in Nottingham since I was thirteen years old. I went to Claremont School, then A Levels at High Pavement College, studied plant biology at Newcastle University after travelling for a year. I worked on an organic farm for over two years, moved back to Nottingham and worked at Wollaton Park for a year doing work with the Nottingham

Biological Records Centre. After that, interspersed with periods of unemployment, I started construction work with the Tap and Tile Co-operative and was there for five years. I got tool skills in roof slating and tiling and, in the later years, with quantity surveying and management of the company. I left to do a post-graduate degree at Leicester and linked up with the Chase Action Group.

POW
[PROSTITUTES OUTREACH WORKERS]

SUE JOHNSON
Born 1957 and

MAUREEN McDONALD
Born 1953

Interviewed at **POW** *[Prostitutes Outreach Workers] 21.7.00 and conversations. Sue Johnson is Director and Maureen McDonald is Senior Outreach Worker at POW. All photos from Sue Johnson*

Sue Johnson I was born on Liverpool Street before the redevelopment. Liverpool Street was on the edge between St Ann's and Sneinton. When we moved, a lot of the houses along Liverpool Street were boarded up and we were one of the last to leave. I can remember a lot about that time. We moved into a new house in St Ann's.

Liverpool Street was a nice community, local shop and everybody knew each other. There was a big yard where people hung out their washing. And a washhouse down at

Back: sisters Ivy (left) and Sandra. Front: Sue and brother Jeoffrey outside their home in Liverpool Street, St Ann's c1962

St Ann's Nottingham: Inner-city voices *by Ruth I Johns* • ISBN 0951696092

Grandad and Grandma, Albert and Ciara-May Woodward outside their home in Alfred Street, St Ann's c1961

Victoria Baths. We used to go there for baths because there were no baths in the houses. I always ended up sharing one with my big sister, Ivy. We always used to have to 'two's up' because my mum had five kids. It was a luxury to go there. We used to go every Saturday morning and my mum used to pay. There were cubicles with baths in.

I can remember those times with a lot of fondness even though the houses were old and the toilet was outside and we were quite poor but we didn't starve. I was the sort of middle girl so I always had hand downs like vests that were too big for me. So even though I remember the downside of it, there's a lot of good memories because there were lots of kids and a sense of community.

Six parts of the family lived around Liverpool Street and Alfred Street. Around the time of demolition I can

remember being quite scared because as a kid you would be playing out at night and there would be houses boarded up. And the wino's started to go in, and there were the back alleyways to the houses where the toilets were. It became all run down and boarded with hardly anybody about.

Before that I felt comfortable. When people started moving off the street, some went to Bulwell or Clifton. But all our family stayed in St Ann's. When we actually got the keys to a house at 1, Broad Oak Close, I was dead excited when we went to look at it. It was a small house with toilets in it and it looked ever so posh, something out of this world. We were used to crumbling walls, wet patches and bedbugs.

They were still actually building the next lot of houses when we moved in and all the pavements were still up. My mum was a one-parent family then, so six of us moved in. My grandma moved into the flat across the road and five parts of the family moved into Broad Oak Close or Norland Close that was a bit further down. My mum was over the moon because we had indoor toilets.

Where I live now, all my sisters live on the same road. My brother sadly died in a car accident. He lived in St Ann's. I've still got lots of family in St Ann's. My eldest daughter lives nearby.

Sue and brother Jeoffrey (second and third from left) making papier mache models at Bath Street Primary School c1967

Mum Mayday arriving at King's Hall Methodist Church for her wedding c1973 with her brother Arthur Woodward. Note the new housing in the background

Afternoon girls' party at the back of Sue Johnson's house 1997. Sue Johnson middle of front row

My grandsons, Cyran (1995) and Tirrell (1996), my son Ross (1979) live nearby, also my nephews and nieces. Rochelle (1989), my youngest daughter, lives at home with me, so our family is quite big in St Ann's. There's quite a few big families in St Ann's, who have all grown up together. Watching their kids having kids gives you a sense of making things better in our community.

Left to right, nephew Shaun, eldest daughter Tanya and youngest daughter Rochelle, August 1999

Maureen McDonald   My mum and dad came from Ireland. It was very, very hard then because they were not letting out bed and breakfast places to Irish people. In the end after a couple of years, when they were staying in Ruddington, this house came up on Sherwin Street in St Ann's. I can vaguely remember it, definitely outside toilet. I was about two and a half then. Our outside toilet was in the middle of this block for four or five houses. My childhood there was very short because the houses were coming down.

My mum and dad went to Clifton. I lived between St Ann's and Clifton as my boyfriend lived in St Ann's. About fifteen years ago, I moved from Clifton to St Ann's. I have a twenty-five year old daughter. She is of mixed race and there is loads of family on her father's side which is my

family too. I've never regretted moving to St Ann's. To me there is a strong community. We just have to keep working together.

Sue Johnson   My children are mixed race and they mix with all parts of the community, black, mixed race, white. It was really worrying for me at that time, because it tended to be males that were targeted. I remember one shooting, it was not far from where my son lives. My children's father lives down the Meadows apart from when we were together in St Ann's. My eldest daughter went to visit her brother one day down the Meadows and then started to get slagged off in St Ann's from being seen down the Meadows.

Maureen McDonald   We can hold the scars for those that's gone and the way they've gone and the mums and dads will never be able to get rid of those scars. But I think if we all try to work together, things may get better. We try to communicate with everyone. So even if we seem not to be getting through, we're planting seeds because somebody is going to take a seed away and they are going to think about it. Those kids are growing, people are having babies now, so what do they want for their own children? Do they want their kids to grow up and see guns, see people shot, see people mugged, see people raped. And this leads on to the organisation we work for.

Sue Johnson   POW has been going for ten years now. Somebody from the World Health Organisation thought that people from prostitute communities can go back and work in the community. So we come from the prostitute community. That links into St Ann's for me as well. When I was growing up on Liverpool Street, it might have been L or M down the road, because prostitutes in those days used to go down to the Exchange pub in the City Centre. I knew some prostitutes and I'm not saying that's what sent me into prostitution, but I've always been involved around prostitution and there's always been working women in St Ann's. Even when we moved into our new house after demolition there was W, who is dead now, God bless her. When I first started, she said: 'Don't, because your mum will kill me if she knows I've seen you down here.' And then, years on, we got this invitation to do some research and, at first, we said no. Because at first it was suggested that it should be just about health needs of prostitutes because of the HIV epidemic.

If somebody works as a prostitute in St Ann's, there's not so much stigma as there would be in, say, West Bridgford. It's a lot more open. And I said, you can't just talk about health issues, you have to approach it from a different angle. If somebody has a black eye or they need somewhere to live, you can't just talk about health issues. To cut a long story short that's how POW actually started, and now we go out in the wider community as well as the prostitute community.

We get asked all sort of things, general advice. An old person in St Ann's will say: 'Sue, I've been trying to get this bath rail for ages, point me in the right direction because I'm going to the Council day in and day out and not getting any joy.'

Maureen McDonald   And it's important to get to know people and local shopkeepers on the Chase in St Ann's. As

ST ANN'S NOTTINGHAM: inner-city voices *by Ruth I Johns* • ISBN 0951696092

outreach workers, we go out on the road around the red light area two nights a week. They know when we are out there. There's a uniqueness in the credibility which works both ways. We talk about health issues, and matters of violence if there's violent punters, and if they want appointments, then the drop-in centre complements our work. We visit people in their own homes so, again, they open the door to us and discussion can be around childcare, or education because they may not want to exit but to cut down on the days they are working, so we can plant another seed . . .

We may visit people where they work, not in their own homes. They will rent places and keep work separate. You don't find many girls who work within their own homes especially with children there. Years ago you used to all get a baby-sitter. And then there are saunas that we target. For both sexes.

In fifty years time, I hope that people will treat everybody as you would like to be treated yourself, with respect. Don't judge people. Like someone might know somebody disabled up the road and totally ignore them. Or they can be ignored because they are facially deformed, I've actually seen these things. It excludes that person from the community.

Sue Johnson Everybody is an individual. If problems come up, educate yourself, don't ever stop educating yourself around issues when you are growing up. Go for that education, go for that support.

Volunteers get involved because, usually, they have experience of prostitution or of community issues. We have people who are not used to our sort of lifestyle and they can feel very threatened by it. For instance, if we are doing outreach one night, not only up Forest Road but it can be in St Ann's, and there's a drug deal going on or a fight, we would have to spend more time supporting a volunteer who doesn't have an overview of some of the dangers you can actually face. I'm not saying it doesn't affect us. We did stop a fight with baseball bats. Of course it affects us, but people sometimes say to me: 'If we're going out as a volunteer, how would you guarantee our safety?' And I say: 'Well, we can't.' We have always done outreach on street credibility.

Maureen McDonald You have got to have that unique down to earth approach, so the girls know there is no stigma. The person doesn't want to hear: 'I know how you feel' or 'I've been there'.

I believe violence is out there on the streets, not only in prostitution. What has helped is that girls communicate with us, so if there is a violent partner out there or a violent punter, or sometimes a girl robbing another girl for various reasons that may include peer pressure, they will come in and let us know. If they want us to get in touch with the police we do, and statements can be made at POW. They haven't got to be made in the Police Station. Again, it's us getting out there and making girls and boys aware of certain things. For example, if they are picking up punters, make sure you look in the back of the car. If there's a coat there, feel it before you get in. Is there anyone else there? That might

sound a bit silly to other people but it is education to keep safe. If they drink alcohol, try not to drink as much alcohol when you're working. Communication and passing over information has got better because of the trust in POW.

Sue Johnson I'm a great believer in people from the community working in their own community as they don't feel threatened by some of the issues, as a stranger to the community would. Being a community person, you most probably know some of their background when you meet people. I'll give you an example. Some years ago, when the project was run from my house - and that's why we've still got a knock-on-the-door aspect - a fourteen year old girl knocked on my door and said: 'I hear you help prostitutes.' I thought at first her mum had sent her for condoms or something and, I was thinking, how was I going to get out of that one. But it wasn't like that. Her mum was also working as a prostitute and I had to go to the girl's house. I didn't feel threatened by her step-dad and what he said. He told me to take her away and not bring her back, so I asked him to sign a paper giving me permission to act on the girl's behalf and he did. I didn't feel intimidated because I've been around people like him, with his big beer belly and breath smelling of booze, since I was knee-high to a grasshopper.

I just wanted to take this girl and to make sure she was safe. If you speak to some social workers, there would be the phone call to the police and lock this child up in care or something. I'm not knocking middle class backgrounds, but, straight out of University, they only know what they've learnt in a text-book. And they come out into the community and they basically haven't got a clue. There are no communication skills. There are some things you can't learn out of a book.

Maureen McDonald I sometimes think social workers' hands are tied, even the humane ones can only go so far. Because there are bosses at the top that are feeding down telling them how far they can go. It is important when one of our clients, who is within Social Services care, is on a review that a POW worker can be present. Because sometimes a client can feel they don't have a voice. There will be all those people around a big table and they're all professionals and it can be intimidating. So a POW worker is their voice until they've got the courage to say things for themselves. I think you ought to listen to kids, kids in care for whatever reason.

Sue Johnson There's a simple thing like swearing. I mean for some it's part of their culture. But if a teenager swears in front of Social Services, they automatically judge them on it. In certain areas of St Ann's, it's the norm. In different sub-groups of the community, I'm swearing like a trooper but not in a way that I'm thinking I'll use this word to be disrespectful. It's just communication. But if I didn't swear, they would think something very odd was going on.

There's a market trader who nearly always greets me with: 'Hey! How are you, fat bastard?' I reply: 'OK, you skinny c...!' I know it sounds daft but, to us, that's a term of endearment. A stranger might think there was an argument brewing.

Whatever culture we're in, we're all in it together and if we all started to live together we'd all get on absolutely brilliantly.

Maureen McDonald It doesn't matter if you're middle class, lower-class or whatever culture. We should all try and live together.

2002. There is now a youth outreach worker at POW to work with young people in St Ann's. So again, says Sue Johnson, this helps to build a sense of community with activities which build self-esteem.

POW will be relocated soon when its current offices off the Alfreton Road are demolished but it will stay in the same area. The future funding situation should be resolved by then

PHASE 10 ACTION GROUP

Marple Square is the centrepiece of the Phase 10 area. Phase 10 was at the end of the massive St Ann's redevelopment in the late 1960s and early 1970s. It is at the end of housing improvements which have been progressing in St Ann's since the early 1990s to put right some of the mistakes made at the time of redevelopment.

Whilst difficult decisions are [2002] still being chewed over about the future of Marple Square and of Cheverton Court, improvements are well under way to some of the other housing in the neighbourhood. Cheverton Court, often known locally as the Ski Slopes because of the shape of its roofs, was written up in the national architectural journals. Whatever the merits of its external design, the mainly one-person unit complex was not well-built and has met increasing fabric and social problems in recent years.

The daunting entrance to Marple Square from the Woodborough Road. Photo: E James Smalley 2000

Marple Square complex from the City side. Photo: E James Smalley 2000

Cheverton Court from the Marple Square side. Photo: Ellie White 2000

Once inside the Square, only one shop remains open. Photo: E James Smalley 2000

St Ann's Nottingham: Inner-city voices *by Ruth I Johns* • ISBN 0951696092

Two photos taken by Alan Hardy from his flat in Marple Square 1999. Overlooking the empty shops in Marple Square with Cheverton Court in the background

From the other frontage of his flat, there is a view of the Pride of Erin pub with Alfred Street North running up beside it to the edge of the Phase 10 area

This was supposed to be better than the demolished 'old' Woodborough Road which we saw in the Shops section. Photos: Ruth I Johns 2001

ALAN HARDY

Born 1937

*Interviewed at his home in Marple Square, St Ann's 15.9.99. Alan Hardy is Chairman of the **Phase 10 (Marple Square) Action Group** and is working hard voluntarily on behalf of the local community trying to get improvements to the Phase 10 area*

I moved into St Ann's in 1975 into the top end, Gordon Road area, Elgar Gardens on the top half of the Marmion estate. I moved in next to the show house. I was one of the first people on that estate and then it got built up down to the Carlton Road and they stuck a public house there called the Jubilee. I lived in Elgar Gardens until about 1982 when my marriage broke up and I went back to Sneinton to stay with my father.

I was one of three children. There was mum, dad, my sister and my brother in Sneinton. My sister was the eldest of the three. She has passed away. My brother went to Australia and has done quite well for himself. I looked after mum until she passed away and then dad passed away about four years ago.

When I first left school, my father wanted me to do painting and decorating. I didn't like it and got myself a job at Raleigh. It was a noisy, rowdy place. I joined the Transport and General Workers Union.

I did my National Service and, after coming out, couldn't settle back at Raleigh. Then I did a number of jobs. You could leave a job on Friday evening and start again Monday morning at a different place. As long as you had your P45 form following you all the way, you could get employment any time. We had three children, a son and two daughters and after my sister died we adopted her last baby, John, who was born a few months before she died. They've all got their own families and got jobs, touch wood, they are fairly well off in today's times.

I finished up with one of the best jobs I had, in Boots in the warehousing group. I joined USDAW [Union of Shop, Distributive and Allied Workers]. I became a shop steward. It really educated me into what can be done with the right approach. I was there about seven and a half years and loved it. I left because I had this arthritis coming on. Then I had a spell at an industrial cleaning job, which eased the pain because it was a warm dry atmosphere but the wage was no good.

I had a very understanding ex-wife who said while things were bad for me, and she was working, everything was OK. Then I started working for myself and I could push money over for maintenance. I built up a small fleet of vehicles and I was driving down to London three times a week in smallish lorries, three tons, four tons. I worked with the morning paper and evening paper deliveries, light haulage, furniture removing . . . But then again, the arthritis attacks came and you can't lift, you can't do things and you can't always rely on other people working with the same enthusiasm, and the business sort of dropped down and down. I finished up as a self-employed taxi driver.

I moved to Marple Square in 1989. Before that I had left my dad's place because we had an argument and I went into digs in St Ann's. That was a horrible part of my life. Coming here was good. Later on, I met Jan and we got married about four years ago. She's full of arthritis too. We're a couple of old codgers looking after each other! I've got some blood disorder, which nobody seems to know much about, but the blood clots. So I have to go to the hospital every six weeks for check-ups.

When I first came to Marple Square it was just changing from a nice place. It had shops, a launderette, a greengrocer, a baker, a fish shop, a bookmaker's, a hairdresser and a newsagent. The place was changing from being a place where middle-aged and retired people lived. You know it was no cats, no dogs, no children! Then, the flats weren't being filled. People were moving out or passing on and they [the Council] were bringing in younger people. When I got this flat, they sort of laughed at me because the area was going downhill, getting a bit rough. And I came and saw it and said it would do very nicely.

A nice big kitchen, a balcony where I could sit out, it suited me. The only difficult thing was the stairs. There was a public house, The Craven Arms, across the road toward the City when I came. I used to go in there at weekends. The best room was very nice. There used to be piano playing like in the old sort of pubs. They'd have a sing-song. And then it changed. It was just the opposite. It was full of rowdy youths who weren't from the area. And there was fighting and drugs and the police moved in and closed it down.

In the meantime, I'd got involved with the Phase 10 Action Group. A bloke called John Dunne was one of the Chairs at the time. The closed down pub was demolished and the site was either going to be a Police Station or a supermarket because that was needed in this area. It became a supermarket. The local shops were beginning to close before the supermarket, Kwik Save, came. The chip shop stuck it out and then left. The baker closed the shop, but still does the baking at the back. The Patel Bros opened as a double shop and they did late night shopping, and the supermarket put them out of business. After they left, the supermarket closed down and did us no good at all.

The only shop left was Mr Hussain's, the newsagent and he does a few groceries. We've always said that the Marple Square shops were in the wrong place, they needed to be on the front [instead of enclosed behind the front building]. We're hoping when the area is improved he'll have a mini-market on the front so he'll be able to sell everything including fruit and vegetables and, if needs be, meat, chicken and so forth. On the front, he'd get the business from the estate and from the passing traffic.

There isn't a fish and chip shop here and we're talking of there being one at the side of Mr Hussain's shop and run by the Phase 10 Action Group. It could feed money back to the estate to fund things like a week's camp for the children. We're talking about annual membership of the Tenants and Residents Association at £1. That could bring in about £1,000 a year and it could enable children and elders on the estate to use the proposed Healthy Living Centre, so they'd get a good deal for their membership.

We're talking about having a co-operative venture locally, where surplus stuff grown on the allotments is sold to people on the estate. You've probably seen the schemes, quite a few in London, where they go and spend £5 for a bag of fresh vegetables and stuff that lasts all week. We think this could be done through Mr Hussain's shop. We're hoping the Tenants and Residents Association could help organise this.

It's only going back to making sure people have proper food. Today if you ask a young person to provide a meal, they'd have to go to the supermarket and get cans of stuff off the shelf and open them up and make a meal. What we're talking about is getting a cabbage, cutting a cabbage and cooking it, or cauliflower and make a bit of sauce. They wouldn't know how to do it. And the old stewpot which used to go on for days. I still live like that.

We [Phase 10 Action Group] are talking about having a Healthy Living Centre in partnership with Tuntum Housing Association who want to be involved. There would be small group meetings, including for cookery and sewing. Tuntum has taken over Saddleworth Court round the corner. The Council sold it to them and now it's 24 flats for elderly people and it's now called Balisier Court. It's opening up for elderly African Jamaican groups but they wouldn't say no to a European person. There's going to be everything for them, a place where they can sit and play bingo or whatever, a launderette, a good security system.

I've got elected on to the Board of the Renewal Trust. It's creating the Millenium Centre where the Sycamore Sports Centre was on Hungerhill Road. The Greater Nottingham Partnership is involved, ACNA Centre, YMCA and Tuntum Housing Association. And they are saying the Healthy Living Centre could be there.

Renewal Trust was set up to finish the work left undone after Nottingham City Challenge. City Challenge was a sore point with Phase 10 Action Group. City Challenge really motivated everybody on this estate saying what could be done to improve it, own garden space, better car parking, turning houses back to front so the kitchen isn't looking out the front, and making entrances so people couldn't go into alleyways and mug people, and lighting and [CCTV] cameras . . . And then they ran out of money before our area was reached.

The Phase 10 Action Area is from one side of Huntingdon Street, Kilbourn Street, St Ann's Hill Road, Cranmer Street and Woodborough Road. The Group has been going long before I came here, from around 1974. When the Ukaidi Project, 9, Marple Square closed down, we approached Councillor Jon Collins to see if we could use that place as a base. But we didn't get it. Then we went for Lottery funding but that was refused because we were not a charity. Then we went for European money and were fairly successful. We ended up getting £184,000 from the European Social Fund. That's how we got our Centre started at 8, Marple Square.

Left to right, Richard Pope, City Housing Manager for Marple Square; Val Young, Phase 10 Action Group Committee member; Tony Curtain, Caretaker: and Alan Hardy, Chairman Phase 10 Action Group. The keys of the Group's Resource Centre are being handed over. The Group moved into it in January 1999 after doing it up

Councillor Jon Collins (left) and Hilary Armstrong MP, Minister for Local Government and Housing, visiting Phase 10 area in 1999. Photo: Alan Hardy

There was a lot of matching funding in that sum, people volunteering time and equipment. The Police Federation said it would give us £300 and we said we would much rather you came to our building once a week and talk to our children and sort out problems.

All the fitting out and painting of the premises was done voluntarily. Tony Curtain who became our Caretaker helped, so did Su Townsend who became our volunteer secretary. There was myself, there was Irene Moses who got in touch with an electrician who fixed us up with power points so we could put a cooker in. The Rev Richard Clark [St Andrew's Church] helped us out with getting the cooker. And Irene Moses helped out with people who volunteered to come along and help us on children's fun days to prepare food . . .

We have a full-time worker, part-time caretaker and we've got things up and running like an After-School Club, Toddlers Club, Citizens Advice, Legal Advice . . . Su Townsend organises children's fun days. She takes them boxing, and swimming, all over the place: trips away.

There's a real problem getting people back into work, because what they earn with one hand the Government takes away from their benefits with the other. Nobody seems able to help people over the hurdle of the first six months so that it can pay to be in work. If there were more help over that early period, I think more people could get back into work.

Four times we've been promised money for improving this estate and four times we've been let down. In 1993/94 Oxford Brookes University students were here for days on end, going around the estate doing questionnaires, doing plans and drawings. It highlighted everything that was wrong on the estate: single parents, low birth weight, bad eating, bad food, bad heating of the premises. City Challenge took this and said they'd do it and then pulled out because there was no money left.

We've missed other funding. They [councillors] would turn round and say it's earmarked for somewhere else. You can imagine the attitude of people here after being promised . . .

Alan Hardy took this photo of the Ashforth factory chimney being demolished, from his home in Marple Square

Close-up of the factory being demolished. This was one of few factories left at the time of St Ann's redevelopment. The others were on the edge of the area. Photo: Alan Hardy

We went to a few meetings. Councillor Jon Collins spoke highly of us, June Greenway of TANC [Technical Aid to Nottinghamshire Communities] did, two other councillors did. They knew something needed to be done on the estate. So they decided to spend from the Council's Capital Spending Fund. This is money which came in from the sale of Council properties which was frozen and now it can be released. There's soon going to be £12m spent on this estate.

They [the Council] have got the people on the estate involved and we've been talking about this for almost a year. Some of the money could be released in March 2000. We've had an upgrading of the heating system, but no windows. All the windows are rotten, so whatever heat comes in goes out. No insulation in the lofts. The estate needs double-glazing. We've got to have a better security system, well not better but more: more lighting and more cameras. When they first put some cameras on this estate people felt Big Brother was watching. We convinced them that it wasn't Big Brother but was for our protection and crime dropped. The security is run from a flat in nearby Cheverton Court. They've got all the screens and everything there.

Improvements are going to start on the estate with sixteen houses to begin with. So they've had the people from those houses to discuss and look at plans.

This is my second year as Chairman of the Phase 10 Action Group. We've got sixteen people on our Committee who attend regularly. There are a few more who can't because of commitments and work, but they will come to an emergency meeting if we can pick the time. We invite the police in to tell us what is going on, and the security people, Housing Department people, the local councillors, the Co-ordinator for Area 5 (this area), Jude Marks.

2001. Alan Hardy has now moved to a North British Housing Association bungalow in St Ann's because he and his wife, Jan, have severe arthritis. Although very near Phase 10 area, they now live outside it, and therefore Alan has had to resign from the Phase 10 Action Group. Living in the area is a condition laid down by the Phase 10 Action Group for being on the Committee. He is still a community representative on the Renewal Trust Committee

Alan and Jan Hardy in their new bungalow home 2001. Photo: Ellie White

Bungalows built by North British Housing Association on part of the site freed up by demolition of the Ashforth factory c1997. Photo: Alan Hardy

An 'open and transparent system'?

In 1998, local MP, John Heppell, was asked to take up the concern of the Phase 10 Action Group, St Ann's, and, in particular, their efforts to get a Marple Square Community Resource Centre. The letter below was a reply to John Heppell from the Regional Director of the Government Office European Funding Secretariat.

GOVERNMENT OFFICE
FOR THE EAST MIDLANDS

DENNIS MORRISON
Regional Director

John Heppell MP
House of Commons
LONDON
SW1A 0AA

RECEIVED
24 AUG 1998

The Belgrave Centre
Stanley Place
Talbot Street
Nottingham NG1 5GG
Switchboard: 0115 971 9971
Direct Line: 0115 971 2750
GTN: 6205 2750
Fax: 0115 971 2769

18 August 1998

Dear John

MARPLE SQUARE COMMUNITY RESOURCE CENTRE

Thank you for your letter concerning the Marple Square Community Resource Centre and issues relating to the St Ann's area in general.

I was a little concerned to read the suggestion in Alan Hardy's letter of 3 August to you that a request for information about how the project had been scored had been turned down by the Government Office European Funding Secretariat. The scoring and appraisal process for Objective 2 is intended to be an open and transparent system and applicants are free to contact us to discuss the scoring of their projects at any time. Indeed, we wrote to Nottingham City Council, who had written to us on behalf of the project sponsor, on 27 July informing it of this. This offer remains open and I will ask the Secretariat to contact Mr Hardy directly.

To avoid additional delays to an inordinately long approvals process, no structured appeals procedure is publicised for Objective 2. However, following receipt of your letter, I asked the Objective 2 Secretariat to check the scoring of this project. It has now done so and I am satisfied that the score of 48.88% represents a fair assessment of the project against the agreed selection criteria.

A project's score is not, of course, the only consideration when allocating ERDF grants. In the case of this project and others submitted under measure 4.1, the Objective 2 Programme Monitoring Committee agreed that to be considered for support project sponsors should confirm that all match funding was in place by 30 June 1998. Although the Marple Square project did not meet this deadline, I am pleased to see that match funding has now been confirmed and that it can be considered for funding if and when sufficient further funds are released through the appraisal, rejection or withdrawal of projects ranked higher in the scoring list.

Regarding St Ann's in general I am pleased to say that the European Funding programmes we administer have been able to support a number of initiatives which provide direct benefits to the local community. Principally, of course, St Ann's benefits directly through its participation in the URBAN Community Initiative which will be delivered in accordance with an Action Plan developed by a local community Partnership Council. In addition, a number of individual projects have been offered support recently. These include: First Enterprise Business Agency (funding towards running costs for two years); The Renewal Trust "Business Grants" and "Business Advice" projects; and two CHASE Action Group projects, "Business and Community Enterprise Support Grant Scheme" (£103,000 grant) and "Chase Community Childcare Service" (£140,000).

In addition, St Ann's has benefitted from over £13m Estate Action Funding over the last 5 years. This funding has enabled estate remodelling, security and energy efficiency measures to be carried out in the area as well as providing significant construction training opportunities for local residents.

Yours sincerely

DENNIS MORRISON

It is a classic example of how to wrap simple facts in bureaucratic mumbo-jumbo and how the last two paragraphs miss the whole point i.e. that the Phase 10 area's case rested on the point that it had been largely left out of the 1990s regeneration help offered to St Ann's. So listing that help served no purpose except to demonstrate the flawed thinking about the way major institutions think about local communities. St Ann's has many neighbourhoods. Each is very different.

In the past thirty-five years, I have seen many letters which fail to communicate clearly from statutory sources which not infrequently dare to suggest that people in local communities need to learn to communicate better!

JOSEPH MANDELA

Born 1960

Interviewed at the **Phase 10 Community Resource Centre**, *8, Marple Square, St Ann's 2.9.99. Joseph Mandela is a Tenant Participation Officer*

My family came to live in St Ann's on Raglan Street in the mid-1960s when I was about six years old. Like most people in St Ann's, we had to make do with what was available and I think that led people to become very creative in using their imagination and developing. We didn't have much but we didn't miss things.

I remember those houses for their cellars and outside toilets, cobbled streets right up the hills. When we played round as children we thought they were from Roman times! I had a brother and a couple of sisters and we played with most families up and down the street. I went to the old Sycamore Primary School. It was a woman Headmistress. She was a pleasant woman and she used to invite children into her office to show these Russian dolls and for tea and biscuits. We used to look forward to getting that invitation! You would sit there wondering what was going to happen, then she'd get the dolls and then open this one, and then that one, and discuss things with you. It was very good. Apparently there was a swimming pool under the school but we never got to see it. It was a liked and well-attended school.

I didn't go to Elliott Durham School but quite a lot of my friends did.

One of the games we played, we had what we called galleys with a rubber band fixed [catapults] and we aimed at targets with a stone. Sometimes we aimed at pigeons. We'd find old prams and stuff that had been dumped and built carts on the wheels. We used to go down Robin Hood Chase at what seemed a hundred miles an hour!

Then when the area was redeveloped, we went to live in Broxtowe. That was a bad experience for me. At the time Broxtowe Estate seemed like you were moving up in the society: indoor toilets, bathroom, front garden, back garden. I'd never had a garden. I tell a lie! In St Ann's, there was a garden path with a piece of green on and there was a big overgrown hedge, which separated the garden. We used to climb through there.

It's strange, but quite a few - like me - seem to be coming back to St Ann's in a professional capacity.

From 1992-96, I worked at the Ukaidi Project in Marple Square until it was closed down. The building the project used is now unused. We're looking at proposals to develop that building with a community housing association into a Healthy Living Centre.

When I left Ukaidi, I did some Leisure Management, then went into housing development. I was a Tenant Participation Officer paid for by the City Council and that's how I came into contact with local residents here again in Phase 10 Action Group. The Group had been working here for a very long time and almost disbanded because people had put in so much effort, trying to get resources to invest in the area to get a better quality of life. They had been promised this time and time again and they missed out on pots of funding that came into much of the rest of St Ann's. The money ran out by the time Phase 10 was reached. There had been reports, surveys, questionnaires done over the years, which highlighted the area as deprived. It was area No 1 on the Nottinghamshire County Council Social Needs Index.

There were shops in Marple Square Precinct. Then, for some reason, a Kwik Save supermarket was allowed just down the road and that saw off all the local trade except for one shop. Only one shop left now to serve the 450 households on Phase 10 area. A cycle store took over Kwik Save. And all the empty shops didn't improve matters. CCTV came in recently and has helped. But a lot of people were battle scarred because of the time they had spent campaigning and seeing promises reneged upon, then the general attitude became: 'We've seen it all before'.

My job was assisting local residents to organise themselves into tenants and residents groups, assist in training, assist with issues and how to get partnerships with statutory or voluntary organisations to improve the area. My loyalties lean more toward the residents though I'm paid by the City Council. People in residents and tenants groups are volunteers, they are not being paid for it, they do it because they care about the area.

Some officers in the City Council only see local people when they go in because something is wrong, and inevitably it's a confrontation situation. So when there's talk of tenants and residents groups they think: 'Oh no, they're going to give us some more work'. We try to help people to meet each other half-way. You know, stressing that people who live in an area aren't all bad, they're disadvantaged by the area they live in. People in more comfortable positions should realise that these people are not inferior or stupid or daft.

People here have been let down so much. It is evident here that services are non-existent. It's necessary to get education, Social Services, health agencies involved in partnership.

We've tried to work with the City Council and arrange site visits, tried at first to get some of the cosmetic stuff done like cleaning up the area and the drains to help make people think that, oh! somebody's noticing these things.

And we got funding to get all the children together and families and we had a very good fun day last year. It was packed. People got inspired by that, and wanted to get more involved and other people came in to help. We got a proper committee together looking at the wider issues and we needed a focal point in the area where people could get information and to meet. Everything was boarded up and closed. So we negotiated with the City Council and asked if we could use one of the units in Marple Square. It would give stability and ensure efforts don't fade away.

So this office was opened in January this year. I was fortunate to get this post when it was advertised. I started in April. The other paid staff person is a part-time caretaker. We would like to develop this place and you can see already, because of the layout and design, it is too small. This was the former Housing Neighbourhood Office. As you can see this is the main room, there are a couple of offices at the side, interview rooms and a reception office. From the Tenants and Residents Group there is a sub-group that looks at developing activities. They do a number of things like the recent Derbyshire camp, art club, music courses, Internet, football. That's in a very short space of time.

Su [Townsend's] job is voluntary. She has got about eighty-odd children on the estate interested and a youth and activities club. The amount of work, effort and response they've got from the children is brilliant.

Playworks on Alfred Street North in the old Boys' Brigade Building is a terrific resource. Nick Millington is there. You join them by paying £20 a year or something and you can go in once or twice a week for collage and stuff for art projects.

We're in the process of developing after-school clubs. We're looking at the academic focus, but incorporating social skills and personal development. Education is important and we're looking at getting the parents involved: help parents and help the children. We've got to do courses people can relate to. There are no longer the mines, Raleigh's and Player's where you used to be able to go in and get a job. And those days are not going to return.

Because of the limitations of this building, because of Health and Safety Regulations, we're looking at other spaces. We've created the demand but . . . We're asking other buildings in the area to rent out space. We've asked the Pakistan Centre.

And the Mount Nursery. Some people find it difficult to go on courses because of childcare. I get the impression they don't want local children. This is what the residents are saying. I'm currently negotiating some way to get access there. I'm willing to support the cost. We've got courses for women scheduled for next week and we can't facilitate creche facilities. If we could get a reduced rate, I could pay one of the volunteers to look after children over there, I mean just pay for the hire of the room or whatever.

We have a drop-in session every Tuesday morning where people can come in and have a coffee, something to eat and discuss tenants' issues. They bring their children here at the moment. It's not conducive to doing that and sometimes they want to get away from their children. So I suggested they could go across there and I pay for a volunteer to look after them. But I don't get a response.

I've put in a report that we've tried various facilities but there seems a barrier currently. I'll go on record and say that.

I've got no axe to grind with any other facility. But there's going to be a regeneration programme in the area and we need to look at how to tap into resources, how can we work together and develop a mutually beneficial working relationship. But some people have a different approach.

You know people here have got very good skills, but they need developing. And the youth activities, as I mentioned before, need more space. We're looking at a building over the other side of the Square, a similar sort of property . . .

Hopefully the City Council want to start housing improvement in the area by January 2000. Currently they are still in the consultation stage and that's important because previously it seems people haven't had meaningful consultation. TANC [Technical Aid to Nottinghamshire Communities] has done a baseline survey to identify what people would like to see. We had an open day here last month, which was well attended and we got considerable feedback.

We had architects down and the development section of the Council and they could talk to people and see what the problems were in the area and what were the good things. But I think people keep getting frustrated, because these things always take time. Some people don't fully comprehend the kind of money involved and what it can do. So the Council officers need to come up with proposals based on information. I've suggested to the Council that they hurry up and get signs up on the estate, big signs saying Redevelopment due to start January 2000. People hear about this money, then see nothing happening and so they think it will be the same thing over again.

The front design of Marple Square is one of the main things that needs to be done. It was identified by everybody and it's a major job. The perception that it gives off is that the space is dangerous. Taxis don't come in here, they say they will wait at the phone box. There's an option to bring the shop on to the front line, the Woodborough Road. It would attract passing trade and stuff.

The signs went up. Photo: Ruth I Johns

Phase 10 Action Group open evening 14.12.00. A large screen in Marple Square explained proposals so far. A City Council Housing Department caravan exhibition explained improvements to housing at the start of Phase 10 regeneration. Food was offered in the Phase 10 Community Resource Centre. Photos: Ruth I Johns

Outside in Marple Square watching the audio visual screen

. . . and inside celebrating that improvement will happen at last

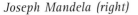

Joseph Mandela (right)   *Su Townsend (left)*

SU TOWNSEND

*Interviewed at the **Phase 10 Community Resource Centre**, 8, Marple Square, St Ann's 2.9.99. Su Townsend is Voluntary Secretary to the Resource Centre*

Phase 10 stretches from Sherwin Close up St Ann's Way up to Cranmer Street and along to Woodborough Road and down: just a small square. We work with eighty-eight children from this area so far.

We took thirteen children between eleven and fifteen last Monday for five days and stayed at a youth hostel belonging to the Wheldon School in Derbyshire. It's next door to a farm. The children saw calves being born, learnt how to milk cows and we went hiking. It was very good.

There were three adults initially and then the Vicar of St Andrew's, Rev Richard Clark, joined us and that made four. We had brilliant weather. On the holiday, we identified at least one child who is dyslexic just through playing Scrabble. It was the first time some of them had been on holiday, let alone without their parents. There was a lot of excitement in the dorms at night. They were too excited to sleep.

Here, on Monday we have a homework club and basketball at the YMCA. On Tuesdays we have boxing. Wednesday we have an art session and there are forty-six children in this room. I need a week off after the art sessions! We do all sorts. Recently, we had a big fun day over on the field and they all made their fancy dress and hats for that. They do pictures to take home and we've got

Phase 10 Action Group Children's Art Group. Photo: Phase 10 Action Group 1999

quite a lot up here. We do pastelling and painting and sticking . . . Thursdays they do music. That involved learning how to breathe properly and sing. They're learning scales, do hip-hop . . . On Friday we have a football team and practise over on the Huntingdon school field. On Saturday they go Go-Karting at Brake Away on Hungerhill Road.

We get funding from St Andrew's Church for three of the activities and volunteer support. We've got about seven volunteers now so it's coming on. They are parents. Initially it was just me doing it on my own every night.

Outsiders have got this vision that our kids are worse than the rest of the kids in St Ann's. So we can't get a youth worker. But they are not, they're quite good. If you ask them to do something, they'll up and go and do it. But they know who likes them rather than just pretending to like them. They won't have any respect for anyone who doesn't like them.

Only one of the eighty-eight children we are working with smokes, just one.

Yes, there are some changes coming to the Phase 10 area. We really need them. But, if they are going to be doing up the estate, they ought to look at the other problems like unemployment, training and youth facilities. Otherwise it's going to go back to where it was and the kids will have nowhere to go. I mean the other week they were on about putting hanging baskets of flowers up in Marple Square, but they don't want to change the humps and arrows in the park into a BMX track. If they had any sense, they would come over and say: 'Here's the compost, here's the seeds to be sown and here's the baskets, get your kids to do it'. They would be more than happy to do it and they wouldn't destroy their own work. The kids are willing to build and decorate their own place if they can get proper help to do it.

I live in one of the flats in Marple Square. I've been here eighteen months.

BRAKE AWAY

STEVE TAYLOR

Born 1954

*Interviewed at the **Brake Away Project**, Hungerhill Road, St Ann's 21.3.00. Steve Taylor is Manager of the Project. All photos provided by Brake Away*

Brake Away premises 1997 with (left) Jason Rimmel and Sean McCoy

I set up the Brake Away Project nearly five and a half years ago[1]. It was an idea to keep youngsters off the streets and doing something positive. It was instigated through Nottingham City Challenge, which was looking after St Ann's and Sneinton in those days. The City Council backed its organisation and setting up. I chose the premises and designed them and everything else.

Previous to managing the Brake Away Project, I worked in the field of young people's training and education for the City Council and I was particularly interested in youngsters' behavioural difficulties. I did that for about fifteen years and for about the same time before that I had been in the Motor Trade. This project was a way of combining the two.

The planning for the Project started on half a desk at the City Council. I didn't have an office or desk to call my own so I had to find premises. I saw this property, which was basically a garage shell, and negotiated an affordable rent.

Of the things that concerned the community, when City Challenge was aiming to help St Ann's and Sneinton, a major one was crime. When they looked at the crime statistics, 72% of the crime in the area was related to cars, the taking of cars, taking things from cars etc. So they decided it would be a good idea to have a Motor Project to try to help young people avoid that sort of problem. Instead of accepting the recognised remedial model of a motor project, there was a research stage and Trent University came up with various options which were studied by a Steering Group. Because they thought it was good to help disadvantaged young people, they tried to decide on a definition of disadvantage.

---

[1] The project was launched by Jack Straw, Shadow Home Secretary, on June 13th 1995.

St Ann's Nottingham: inner-city voices by Ruth I Johns • ISBN 0951696092

Steve Taylor, third from right

After going through about two pages of foolscap, somebody decided that any youngster who lives in St Ann's or Sneinton is disadvantaged in one way or another, even if it's only peer group pressure or whatever. So the project became available to any young person in the area. Most motor projects as you know are remedial and youngsters that have been involved in crime are directed to a particular project.

But this scheme was to be a diversion from crime and anti-social behaviour. We are fairly unique at Brake Away in the way we do things. Some motor projects only take a maximum of about twelve youngsters at any one time and they work regular hours. Brake Away Project here has got over eight hundred members from St Ann's and Sneinton alone.

We also service the whole City for various activities. We try to administer the project so we can offer the maximum amount of development to the maximum number of young people. It makes it difficult to administer and to manage but we end up doing a lot for a lot of people and are very cost effective.

In the early days, people thought the project was one that only took youngsters Go-Karting now and again and that they wouldn't be bothering the community when they were driving Go-Karts. I thought we had the potential to do much more than that. At that time, there was just myself, a part-time clerk typist and two-thirds time of another member of staff.

A lot has happened since then! The main aim of the project is the personal development of young people. We want young people to feel they have a worth in the area, so there's got to be enjoyment and excitement. We've added a lot of things which were never envisaged in the first place.

The project is heavily influenced by the young people themselves, whether they are members or from outside groups. We encourage young people to represent themselves on our committees and to have their own committee. All the staff have to be very flexible on the hours they work to meet the needs of the young people. If they come up with suggestions and ideas that are feasible, if they meet the project's objectives and we can afford it, then we'll do it.

We sometimes have to remind them that we don't have a bottomless bucket when it comes to finances, otherwise we would be doing regular trips to Barbados! But they can come up with very sensible ideas, suggestions about the Go-Karting, how the Go-Karts run, whether we do team races, endurance races, how they run their own satellite groups.

They organise the teams themselves, making sure everybody gets there on time, making sure they know who's servicing the Karts, who's marshalling, who is driving the Karts etc. We use two sites, Langar Airfield and once a month we can use a race circuit at Brandon near Newark. The faster Pro-Karts (two-engines) can be raced there.

1997

Racing at Langar [disused airfield] 1998

Fundraising Event at Langar 1999. Second left, Simon Hunt of Panthers Ice Hockey Team

Youngsters start as novices and go through all the various stages of training, including health and safety, to a point where we feel they are able to move on to the next stage and ultimately the racing of Go-Karts.

We actually take members as young as nine now but, because of the potential of the machines, they start driving at about eleven. Before they even get in a Go-Kart they have a practical training. And we can de-tune a Kart so they don't go so fast at first. We develop them slowly so they are aware of the safety principles long before they get into the racing principles. Everything we do is based on development, so they can see the next stage, maintain enthusiasm. But, Go-Karting is only one of the things we do.

We have a young women's driving programme which not only includes some driving lessons but the written test theory. We have safe off-road driving that starts at about fifteen. Both young men and women can get used to a car and what cars are about in a safe environment on the Airfield.

We have youth club sessions several times a week. In the training room, there is everything from pool to Sony play-stations, monitors, hi-fi television, video, cinema sound television, camcorder, all sorts of things. Young people come here because they want to, it enthuses them - that's a big requirement in development. While they are here we try and do the youth work, not in an obvious way by saying: 'You're coming in today to do a session on violence and drugs'. The youngsters are on a par with us so we do have conversations. We don't have levels of youngsters deemed to be less important because of their age.

Then we have satellite groups, up to twenty-three of them. They are a mixture of what we call disenfranchised groups and those linked to other organisations, like Russell Youth Club, Oliver Hind Youth Club, Elliott Durham School. Any group of eight or more people can form their own team. Because of lack of capital spending, we cannot supply a Kart to every team, but they can take responsibility for a Kart and make sure they are aware of the full cycle of maintenance, service and repair as well as the driving, marshalling etc. We used to have more than thirty Go-Karts but because of wear and tear and age we are down to twenty-two. Of the twenty-two, four are Pro-Karts, RAC approved race machines.

We are very health and safety conscious. If a Kart looks in pristine condition but it is not, we will not use it. When I first started the project, it became my whole life and I was doing about seventy-two hours a week. Now it's a little bit better, but I care very much about the project, our community here and the young people who use it.

I don't actually live in St Ann's. When I came here it was much better than I expected. But having said that the youngsters didn't have a lot going for them. Now there is not only this project, but others which show a lot of respect for the young people, try to get them to take some responsibility for their future and make St Ann's a better place for the whole community. If this book is read in fifty years time, these young people will be the grandparents won't they?

A lot of money is being spent up at the Millennium Centre [previously Sycamore Youth Centre]. Again, it's not only offering another site for people to use but showing respect for the community and the area. I think youth clubs and youth workers are very important. One of the problems currently is that, in politics, people think of things like education, social services, social security and employment. But something which might seem much more intangible is also very important and it affects everybody, and that's leisure and community services.

I think projects like Brake Away help young people discover their own abilities and gets their attention on to some positive things. Youngsters need to be enthused and you must value young people and help them recognise their own skills. Some youngsters see school as somewhere they've got to go. Here, it's somewhere they come because they want to. And parents are happy because the scheme is for everybody and not remedial. Having said that, I'm sure a few of the youngsters would now be somewhere different if Brake Away had not been here.

Vehicle Training 1996. Left, Simon Horton and Nickalas Green

One event sticks in my memory. One young man hated the police and we had this team event with the police. He was Captain of a mixed youth and Police team and, when his team won, the Police Officers carried him shoulder high. It changed his view of the police.

We have a summer programme including residential and day trips. Frequently, the young people will help raise the money. We hope to continue to move forward and have a lot of ideas for developing what we're all doing here.

In 2002, Steve Taylor said: *"The project has become more involved with training young people, both groups and individuals in motor vehicle repair and maintenance, bodywork and welding etc. The City Council refers to us as 'a centre of excellence for training'. We are used by many groups and organisations, such as schools, youth groups, Social Services, Youth Offending Team, Learning Gateway etc. We are popular because we have a simple philosophy: 'Youngsters come because they want to and stay because they enjoy it'.*

"The training and qualifications are organised and provided with their collaboration and are flexible so that their needs can be met and their enthusiasm maintained. The Project was recently reviewed by the City Council. It was a very positive report. All being well with finances, the Project is set to grow and provide many opportunities to more young people."

A sample of Brake Away activities 1997-1999

Trip to Wales

Sneinton Festival

Trip to Skegness

Steve Taylor and
Shaween O'Connor

Trip to the seaside

DARREN HAYNES

Born 1977

*Interviewed at the **Brake Away Project**, Hungerhill Road, St Ann's 21.3.00. Darren Haynes is Assistant Project Mechanic and a youth worker at the Project*

I first started coming in here when I was seventeen. I live just round the corner. I just joined with my friends, we came Go-Karting and all that. I went to Elliott Durham School. I left about fifteen. I used to nick off most of the time because it was boring. When I was a member here early on, there weren't as many staff as there are now, and I used to help out. And I also set up my own racing team as part of the Satellite Groups Scheme.

When I left school, I started doing voluntary work here, helping out where I could and then Steve Taylor, the Manager, said he would appraise me during the summer so he could put me on the payroll. Then I was a part-time worker for about a year and then I went up to full-time being paid the unqualified rate. But now I am a qualified youth worker. I went through a training scheme at the Radford Unity Complex, run by the City Council.

Brake Away Narrow Boat Trip, at Trent Junction. Left to right: Darren Haynes, Ryan McDevitt and Paul Smith

At Brake Away 1999, Darren Haynes and Celia Underhill, Secretary

Training Room/Club Room at Brake Away 1997

We've got about eight hundred members here now from St Ann's, Sneinton, New Basford and Sherwood Rise. We take the 11-18s Go-Karting out at Langar Airfield: just at the weekends in the winter because there's no lighting out there. In the daytime we do a lot with school groups out there. On Mondays and Thursdays we have a drop-in here in this club room we're in now. It's not very big. After school, they can play pool, with play-stations, listen to music, and work on school-related subjects. Anyone can come if they're a member, and you fill in a form for membership, £1 a year. And each time they go Go-Karting they pay £1.20.

We [staff] are here all the time. Youngsters who have left school and hang around the area also come in. They come in when they want to, work with us, talk to us.

There's seven staff, only three full-time. That's Steve Taylor, Simon Horton who is the Project Mechanic and me.

And Brake Away deals with young people from all over, including Clifton and Bulwell, who have left school and got no jobs. I'll be working with them for something like eighteen weeks on a scheme called Learning Gateway. It's giving them experience of what jobs are like.

Areas like this need schemes like this. When I was a youngster, I admit I used to go round terrorising people because there was nothing else to do. Here they come in, meet new friends, do what they want to do and enjoy themselves. I wish there was more of it when I was younger.

I grew up with all the people round this area. I know everyone who walks in and out the door. It's an advantage. Everyone's all right with me, I'm all right with them.

An average day? Fixing the Go-Karts over there, working with the youngsters out there [in the garage]. For example, some of them have just passed their motorbike test, so they will come in here and work on their motorbikes: fix their own brakes and stuff like that. We watch them and help them. Instead of them taking the bikes to a garage and paying expensive prices, they get the spare part, come in here and we'll show them how to do it.

St Ann's Nottingham: Inner-city Voices by Ruth I Johns • ISBN 0951696092

We get police and other people donating us things. We've got a couple of motorbikes in there donated by Clifton Police, one of my boss's friends donated a couple of bikes, and we got a caravan donated. We work on these with some of the youngsters, get them really good and sell them. The money goes into their [the youngsters'] budget for the long school holiday so that they can do trips, like a weekend on a narrow boat, sailing, canoeing. It's all organised from here, staff and volunteers. We've got three from BESTCO [Better Employment Skills Training Company] at present. And one referred from Social Services.

The car being worked on out there in the garage is the Project's car. We're working on it for the off-road driving that we do. From age fifteen and above, we take them to Langar and get them used to cars, like clutch control. Show them the basics so when they're seventeen, they can get their test and stand a good chance of passing. It's £1 a time they use the car and they get to understand cars.

We've got about twenty-five Go-Karts here, but we only use six at a time, only take six out for a track session. If something goes wrong with them and we can't repair it, it comes back in and swap it whilst it's being repaired or waiting for a spare part. It's fun working on Go-Karts.

We've got normal Go-Karts and then the bigger ones with two engines. They go twice the speed and that's Pro-Karting. They are called Pro-Karts because they are like proper racing machines and can go up to 80 m.p.h. And because they are so low on the floor, you think you are going faster. We use those out Newark way on a proper race car circuit, but not so often.

There isn't a proper racing circuit at Langar Airfield [disused airfield]. We've hired out a piece of land and we put tyres to mark out a track. In the summer school holidays we have sponsored events. Like getting the youngsters working with the police. When you do the Youth Work Training Course, that I've just passed, you have to do a project, organise it, do it yourself and do a full write-up, like an essay, about what you've done. Mine was getting the youngsters working with the police in an endurance race.

The police met us up at Langar. We take the youngsters up in our transport. The kids wanted to be in one team against the police. We thought it would be a good idea to mix police and young people in the same team. It was fun. Everyone enjoyed it. The youngsters thought that police were different from everybody else and found out they're really just the same.

Coming to work is walking round the corner for me. I really like it here. Everyone in and out of the door are my friends.

In 2002, Darren Haynes said: "Simon Horton left last October and I became the Project Mechanic. The Project now does a lot more training of young people and I am teaching them, as well as taking track sessions and being a youth worker. The Project has had an excellent report following its Review and we have high hopes for the future."

SURE START 2

SUSIE DANIEL

Born 1948

*Interviewed in her home 5.5.00 about the **Sure Start 2** Government initiative in St Ann's. Susie Daniel is an Independent Development Consultant and Trainer and has been supporting Sure Start schemes across the country. She has known St Ann's since the time of redevelopment and lives in the Arboretum area, which she says is often regarded as part of St Ann's, as it is for Sure Start 2*

Sure Start is a Government initiative based very much on the American Head Start. That was set up in the 1960s arising from people's concerns about children's development by the time they start school, in terms of education and communication skills and social well-being. So Sure Start is about addressing under-fives' issues in areas of deprivation. It's the first time the three Ministries - of Health, of Education and Social Services - have linked together for a programme.

A year ago, the Government had sixty Sure Start trailblazers across the country.

And then the second round has happened in Nottingham. Nottingham had one project in the trailblazer round, at Strelley. In the second round, St Ann's has been chosen. I heard about it at the end of January this year by being invited to a public meeting at the Chase Neighbourhood Centre, St Ann's, in February. Knowing these programmes had been decided two months ago, I went along to that meeting feeling like a stroppy local resident: 'Why have we heard nothing about it? Why haven't local people been consulted?' It was quite a well-attended meeting to the surprise of the Community Health Trust who were co-ordinating it.

There was a lot of anger at the meeting including from Councillor Jon Collins. It was anger around: 'Why haven't you come to see us? We're always getting initiatives happening in our area but nobody ever talks to us or involves us'. I had to get up and say: 'I came as a stroppy resident but actually my second hat is that I know a lot about Sure Start. And actually I think we have an opportunity here to bring together all of the needs of the under fours in the area.'

The Sure Start Unit at the DFEE notified Nottingham City Council that it had been identified as a Sure Start area and then the Council had to identify which area of the City Sure Start is going in, a choice based on deprivation levels and other indicators. St Ann's was chosen.

And a lead agency has to be identified. For the first round in Strelley it was NCH Action for Children. The lead agency for St Ann's is the Nottingham Community Health Trust. It had never really done anything in terms of community involvement, and with so many Government initiatives landing on their desk, they are running round in circles. Two weeks after the meeting, I got approached by the Trust and asked if I would Project manage the delivery plan in St Ann's.

I have to present them with a viable programme of how we are going to address the issues for the under fours, working within Sure Start targets for improving social and emotional health, the ability to learn, strengthening families and communities and increasing productivity of operations. I have to have a delivery plan for St Ann's to the Sure Start Unit by the end of this month, May 2000.

I've managed to get forty-nine proposals from local groups and agencies and I think it will make a really exciting Sure Start programme in St Ann's. Looking at the map of St Ann's, we've identified a cluster of 'villages'. So we'll have one central space where the Sure Start office will be, then we will be enhancing what exists at Metrazone [Metropolitan Tenants and Residents Association Community Centre], at Blue Bell Hill Community Centre, at the Chase Neighbourhood Centre and in the Phase 10 Action Area [Marple Square].

It includes part of the Arboretum area right up to Elliott Durham School at the top of Ransom Road. Within the St Ann's programme area, there are one thousand and thirty-eight under fours so we are slightly over the Government target of between five hundred and one thousand. They have provisionally agreed it so long as we can explain why we've done it.

Initially there is a contract for three years and the Government have found a way of doing it despite the fact that there will be a General Election in the middle. There is a commitment for ten years. They want to look at the long term. There's an enormous amount of baseline data that we have to set because it is not only what happens by three years time. It's about how, in ten years time, can we reduce the number of teenage pregnancies by the fact that life for children entering the educational system has been enhanced.

So we're looking at things like: what is done to young antenatal mothers? What do we do in their transition from hospital to the community? In addition to Health Visitor visits, they will have Sure Start visits. We're looking at a scheme of Community Parents to do some of these visits. The Community Parenting Scheme will be about parent peer support with other parents, but also getting something for themselves. It will be linked with New College so they can get qualifications if they want. And it's going to be a mixed economy of volunteers and paid people, because we have to keep in mind the Benefit System and whether people are better or worse off.

We're hoping to have a Project Manager and Community Participation Development Worker in post very soon.

The budget over three years is £700,000 to £1m. And there is the same for one-off capital payments. For example, the new Chase Neighbourhood Centre is wonderful but you can't do childcare there. The room where we could do childcare has doors off it which go through the main reception area and past the kitchen to get to the toilets. So Sure Start will have to enhance the building. I said to the Architect: 'How dare you build a building where you can't do childcare,' and his response was that it was supposed to be for the whole community. I think they have put in a bid for £25,000 for alterations and an extension so they can do childcare.

I have contacted 115 organisations in six weeks to get them on board this programme. The schools have been particularly weak. Though Diana Owen, Head Teacher at Huntingdon Nursery and Primary School, has put in a great bid.

Sure Start is building on what exists. City Challenge put all these new buildings up. W.I.N.A., the nursery [at ACNA, Hungerhill Road], do you know that one? It's like the Marie Celeste. You could walk in there and open a nursery tomorrow and it's stood empty for three years. It was built with City Challenge money. We would certainly like to see that as our Sure Start base, so we can have a drop-in place where parents can come, they can have childcare there and it's where staff will be located. There are very specific core services we have to provide: home contact; outreach and family support; good quality play, learning and child care; primary and community health and social care; and then things like housing advice, money advice and other practical support . . .

We're looking at Toy Libraries, and increasing Books for Babies and getting a core of, say, five play development workers who have their own patch. So they will be responsible, for example, for making sure that Metrazone have their own play worker and the staff necessary to do their sessions whenever they want. But also there are open spaces in that area so they will take responsibility for organising activities in these spaces. I was talking to Colin Haynes and I want to look at linking the [Hungerhills] allotments in. We'll have to build that into year two, but there's such wonderful open space there.

Sure Start hasn't felt it necessary to go out and ask parents what they want because Jenny Fleming of Social Action, De Monfort University, recruited local mothers to talk to parents about what they felt were the issues. They have been asked repeatedly and repeatedly. We're trying to draw all the reports together, including those done by TANC [Technical Aid to Nottinghamshire Communities] and then concentrate on going to parents and getting them involved. No longer saying what do you want but saying this is what we've got . . .

In my report I want to write a narrative about what St Ann's has to offer and then what Sure Start is going to offer, how it will look and how it will affect parents on the ground. All the data will be there but it will be Appendices so that the first part of the document will be something that everyone will want to pick up and read.

2002. Susie Daniel is now living in London

A CREDIT UNION FOR ST ANN'S?

FERGUS BRAZEL

Around 1995, local people came together with the vision of setting up a credit union for the St Ann's and Sneinton areas of the City. They formed Prosperous Credit Union Steering Group, supported by a City Council Community Development Worker.

A credit union is a financial co-operative providing savings and loans facilities, and other services, to its members. Members can also receive a return, known as a dividend, on their savings. The benefits of a credit union include:

- Low interest loans
- They are located in convenient places within your community
- You decide how much you want to save
- They are owned and controlled by their members, allowing you to have your say in how it is run.

Despite the hard work and commitment by the members of Prosperous, changes in regulation meant that it was going to be too difficult to register the Credit Union. The Nottingham Credit Union Development Agency [NCUDA], which is now supporting the group, recognised these difficulties and proposed that the members of Prosperous became part of the drive toward setting up a credit union to cover the whole of the City. They would then be able to run their own branch of the larger credit union.

Since then, much progress has been made and members of Prosperous are working with local groups and organisations and with NCUDA to register the city-wide credit union, with a local branch in St Ann's. Branches will be able to run their own collection points, hold local promotional events and have their own Loans Officer with the power to grant small loans. People wanting to get involved get in touch with Steff Webber at the Chase Neighbourhood Centre or me at NCUDA, Room 8, Clarendon Chambers, 32, Clarendon Street, Nottingham NG1 5HS.

SYCAMORE MILLENNIUM AND BUSINESS CENTRE

PAUL DITCH

Born 1954

*Paul Ditch is Manager of the **Sycamore Millennium and Business Centre**, Hungerhill Road, St Ann's. He was interviewed 22.1.02 at the Centre. It is in part of the complex that used to be the Sycamore schools: one of the original buildings [1886] and a post-1950 building. Some of the complex has been used since 1978 by ACNA [Afro-Caribbean National Artistic Centre]. The Sycamore Millennium Centre buildings were used for a time as the Sycamore Sports Centre and Adventure Base*

The Sycamore Centre, showing main door and Café on left. Army Cadets in the picture. Photo: Renewal Trust 2002

Paul Ditch. Photo: Renewal Trust 2002

This building used to be an outdoor activity centre called St Ann's Adventure Base. With the demise of City Challenge, there wasn't an exit strategy. No one quite knew what was to happen once City Challenge funding ran out. I think it was believed the site would go back to the City Council, and that it would pick up the running costs of the Adventure Base, the Youth and Community Centre. The

County Council would be aware that its status was about to change, and that many of its responsibilities would go back to the City Council. So the County Council didn't have any motive for either running it or for the upkeep, knowing that the City Council would be taking the responsibility. The City Council then acquired Unitary Status and acquired these buildings around 1998.

Out of City Challenge grew the Renewal Trust, a regeneration organisation that is keen to see St Ann's and Sneinton improve in housing, education and social fabric. Clearly, they saw these buildings as potential for regeneration, renovation and restoration. If the vision was there, and the partners they could pull together were there, then clearly a number of areas of interest could develop.

Yes, the buildings involved are part of the old Sycamore School complex. The Project has two parts. On the front, facing Hungerhill Road is the older building. That is now the Business Centre which attracted different types of funding to the newer back part of the complex which is the Youth and Community Millennium building. The two buildings run under different contracts with two quite separate funding regimes and two different management structures. I am Manager for both. I started in July 2000, two months before the official opening of the Millennium Centre.

The Business Centre attracted some funding from the Government Office East Midlands and the EMDA [East Midlands Development Agency] whereas the building we are in, the Millennium Centre, attracted some National Lottery funding.

The Business Centre works with a Board of Directors as the Hungerhill Trading Company, and is interested in business opportunities and lettings, and offering licences and leases to occupy space in the building. The units are let mainly to administrative and clerical-type organisations. So it includes people who work with computers, people who are meeting and interviewing people and counselling people. There are agencies involved in Health and Mental Health issues. There are two groups,

which are Government backed. One is Sure Start Plus, which is interested in young people of fourteen-plus. The other is Sure Start which is for the 0–4 year olds and is involved in pre-school provision. STAA, which promotes the Hungerhill allotments, has its offices in the building. The sixteen units are now all occupied and the revenue that's raised from the rent is a funding stream that flows into the Millennium Centre.

This Millennium Centre is one of nine centres nationally that the Government saw as an opportunity to celebrate the Millennium by making grants available either to improve existing buildings or to build new ones. We are seen as something rather different from traditional Youth and Community Centres. Newer technologies now available will come into this building. So we're becoming an information, communications and technology centre. There will be a lot of high-tech equipment, computers, all the software, modems . . . the Internet is a big thing obviously. We're looking to install a cyber-café. There will be Neighbourhood Learning Centre initiatives and Healthy Living initiatives which are ideas from the Government to include in Learning for Life principles.

Rather than being like colleges which assume what you want, we hope to put on what people in the locality want. On the sports side, the existing hall upstairs is too small to accommodate formal sporting activities. So we can't attract the five-a-side basketball and tennis that we would like. So we are negotiating with the City Council for the sports barn which is next door, just down the hill. We're at an advanced stage of agreeing a licence to operate that sports barn. It has stood empty for a year. It holds four full-size badminton courts, an indoor tennis court, a full five-a-side court and a basketball court. At weekends we could turn it into a roller disco court, archery and basically anything. It's probably one of the largest indoor arenas in the Nottinghamshire area. But it lacks changing rooms and toilets and a viewing gallery. Our vision with the Renewal Trust is to seek funding and build those things in.

Currently here, there's a range of sports activities including block bookings for clubs or associations involved with table tennis, martial arts, boxing, archery, aerobics and gymnastics. There are different sorts of dance activities and drama and theatre. There are all sorts of new things that have been developed since the 1970s under the heading of drama and dance. We've got a resident theatre group, Indigo Brave. Their work is varied and very interesting, including traditional theatre, mime and dance.

There was a recording studio in the other building years ago. They relocated when the building became semi-derelict. We're hoping the old swimming pool area in the basement could become a recording studio. The pool has been filled in. It's a large area and would be ideal for a recording studio.

But music already goes on here associated with the Youth Club, including traditional type disco evenings. Other things are based around individuals who have become involved: a lot of Afro-Caribbean and Indian influences, DJ skills, RAP, Garage, Hip Hop. A lot of it is to do with single beat and putting your own lyrics to it.

The Business Centre 2002 with (left) the entrance to the Sycamore Millenniium Centre. Off photo to the left is the other part of the old Sycamore School buildings used by ACNA. Photo: Renewal Trust 2002

Youth Club outing. Photo: Renewal Trust 2002

Manager of the Sycamore Community Café, Dave McLeavy. Photo: Ruth I Johns 2002

Yes, any young person can walk through the Centre's main door. They would be channelled into a Youth section for their age group. They would be offered membership if they were happy to join the Club after a few weeks. It's £5 a year. That includes invitations to subsidised events. Youth activities here include table tennis, pool table and music. There's a new range of ideas that have been developed about skills, counselling, therapy, beauty, and health issues. Issues are addressed through music, mime, theatre . . .

Yes, we liaise with as many schools as possible, but Elliott Durham School in particular because it has an outreach remit as part of its curriculum. And it has a community musician now. We've engaged the community musician to develop activities involving Elliott Durham young people.

Yes, the Scouts are still in the hut next to the sports barn down the road.

At the beginning of February, an Army Cadet Force detachment for St Ann's is starting here. When we get a licence to operate this hall as a bar, then they will relocate to the sports barn, and use the old Adventure Base outside area, which is two and a half acres of land, for their exercise and drill area.

A café has just opened on the ground floor. It's open Monday to Fridays at present but we are hoping it will operate in the evening when the Youth Club and the Army Cadet Force and those sort of things are being built up. Anyone can call in at the café. We're hoping people will come in from the local community. There are very few outlets for food, hot food, in the area. There's a lot of space there. It's franchised.

This building, the Millennium Centre, is managed under a liaison group which is a collective, representing bodies who funded the organisation and groups which now work within it. So, obviously, they come from the Youth Section as youth workers and sessional workers. Then there's a range of groups who send representatives including a theatre group, a music collective, counselling groups . . . They take control and arrange the developmental side of things.

My background? I'm from the North East of England as you will probably detect in my accent. I had an industrial background. Like a lot of youngsters I went to work in the shipyards. I served my time [as an apprentice]. I was also working part-time in a boys' club and was involved in the Scout movement. I made the transition to Youth and Community work as a full-time career around 1976 and did my placement in Nottingham with the Notts and Derby Boys' Club. I then went to the University of Ulster to take my Management and Administration degree and graduated in 1982. I worked for a number of Borough Councils and County Councils and eventually found myself managing Arts and Resource Centres, Community Centres and Boys' Clubs and Youth and Community Centres.

Boys' Clubs have now been assimilated into Youth and Community Services because of the need to broaden their remit. Youth and Community Services fall under different Committees with different local authorities. In Northern Ireland, it is Education and Libraries; in the North East, it is Education: here in Nottingham it is Community and Leisure.

The staff here, other than me, are an Area Youth and Community Worker, a detached Youth Worker, and an Outreach Worker specifically for abuse, drugs and sexual health issues. We've got Neighbourhood Learning Centre workers on part-time contracts and a full-time caretaker. We're looking to appoint a part-time cleaner.

On average, there are thirty-five young people coming in to each session. On a Friday evening, that would go up to fifty because of the attraction of the music. We have a zero tolerance programme here both for drugs and weapons. That's the way the vast majority of people coming into the building want it. It has to be a safe environment.

I don't think there is a problem of people getting here from around St Ann's. There are now certainly more cars available for people to be moved around, so I don't think transportation is the issue. It's about breaking the barriers about the sorts of areas that are perceived as somebody else's territory. That's where some of the stigma exists historically on buildings. It's about trying to break that down. And there are people coming here for the first time that wouldn't have gone to the Sycamore Sports Centre several years ago. The more things we are able to offer, the more diverse will be the people coming in.

The youngest age we can accommodate in the Youth Service is eight. People can continue coming as long as they can physically get into the building. If people feel comfortable coming in the building, that's where the Learning for Life theme comes in. The building still has a lot of the old staircases and corridors that haven't been designed out yet, but we're working on funding bids at present to allow us to increase accessibility to the building for everyone.

My wish for fifty years time? I wish we could move as fast as the ideas that are expressed to us. I think we are a very slow machine governed by other people's agendas. Young people's ideas aren't as high on agendas as they should be. I sometimes feel uncomfortable with the time we spend in deliberating whether something is a good idea or not. Then you see the huge sums of money being spent on activities and national pastimes that don't seem to have any rhyme or reason, and are not well thought out. Young people can have very short spans of understanding and once you've promised them something they seize on it. If we're not in a position to deliver, time goes on, they grow up and that moment was never seized.

I'm employed by the Renewal Trust. If someone or a group comes to me with an idea, I hear what people have to say and I would draft their idea and pass it on to our Liaison Group to have a look at. They would make a recommendation to a Renewal Trust directors' meeting. They refer their decision back to the Liaison Group who would decide the appropriate action in the light of that decision. It could take one or two months.

On the one hand there is the urgency to act. On the other, there's need to recognise the society that we now live in, which is about litigation and judicial recourse. Directors of Trusts are clearly concerned about the impact that any activity might have on buildings, on individuals and on themselves. History dictates that we are cautious.

What would I wish for the future? Well, youth have not changed throughout history. They are still the same rebellious group of individuals! I would hope that the partnership approach between an organisation like the Renewal Trust and formal organisations like schools, institutions and Government could - with youth - engage and co-operate with each other and respond quicker to requests that, on the face of it, seem to be a little difficult or strange or weird and wonderful. It's about having a more pro-active way of dealing with not only young people, but anybody.

We should be trying to address issues that some professionals and formal organisations still have to learn about. In future, there will be more young people with money and the kind of things that that attracts: more drugs, more violence, with the media, TV and music reflecting all that. As I said earlier about young people always having been rebellious, it's now about a generation who is looking at the things which seem threatening at *this* time. When we look back, there was a time when Mick Jagger looked threatening!

ST ANN'S NOTTINGHAM: inner-city voices *by Ruth I Johns* • ISBN 0951696092

When Things Go Wrong

This has been the hardest piece to write, because many people have expressed views but do not wish to be quoted by name.

In the past few years, there have been shootings in Nottingham, especially in the Meadows and St Ann's areas. There have, sadly, been shootings in other places in the UK. Many have been drug-related. Night-time police patrols in St Ann's and the Meadows became armed in 2000.

On February 19th 2002 in St Ann's, Brendon Lawrence, a sixteen year old student was shot in St Ann's. He was the fifth person to be shot in Nottinghamshire so far in 2002 and the first to die as a result. At the time of writing [April 2002], the perpetrator/s have not been found. St Ann's is stunned.

Several people asked me to delete from the draft text of this book what they said about previous shootings. After Brendon Lawrence's death, they felt it would sound unfeeling. They knew him and liked him. They felt his death was inexplicable in terms they had tried to explain previous shootings. Two young people, whose lives had been affected by gun crime, withdrew their interviews.

The shootings have added to the strain on St Ann's reputation. The vast majority of people in St Ann's are appalled when bad things happen, and they try to take steps to create a climate where bad things are less likely to happen. This needs to be recognised. The more the whole area is stigmatised, the harder it is for the majority of its residents to be self-confident. The more that young people grow up feeling that their area is regarded as 'bad', the harder it becomes to resist reflecting that image. Sue Love spoke of some people being 'place-ist': a good description of prejudice about St Ann's.

Community centres in St Ann's and the majority of individuals are standing up and being counted. But, yes, there will always be people who don't speak up when they should. They collude in crime. The balance of pressure in any community to stay silent or to speak up depends on many factors.

Collusion, however, is not only about shielding criminals. It is many things, including abandoning the young to their own devices and to institutional processes. From a very early age, young people need to be involved within their community, they need considerable responsibility, they need to be respected, they need to be involved near life-changing events in their neighbourhood: events which are too often happening behind institutional doors (including birth, serious illness and death). Young people need neighbourhood space for sport and other activities. I mention elsewhere in these pages the need for young people, in particular, to have access to 'small useable dollops of neighbourhood public space'. Parents and schools cannot provide the total environment needed for young people. Young people today speak - in their own way - very clearly about these things but seldom want to be quoted directly.

For family reasons, I spend my time between the West and East Midlands. When there is a murder or a shooting in my West Midlands area, the events do not define the place, they do not affect its reputation.

It is hard to report some 'incidents' in my West Midlands town because they are not found to be believable. For example, we usually have a lodger. A few years ago, our lodger was Baljit Takhar whose car was vandalised outside our home on three separate occasions in quick succession. Our car has been vandalised on one occasion, as have the cars of some of our neighbours on single occasions, but not systematically. I insisted that Baljit and I went to the Police Station and reported the incidents, only to be told that such things (i.e. the targeting of a young Asian woman's car): "wouldn't happen in your road because it is a 'good' area". I insisted the incidents were recorded and they were.

But, unlike this West Midlands town, whatever goes wrong in St Ann's seems to define it in the public mind: the many good things that happen in St Ann's sink into invisibility as far as its reputation is concerned. Why?

The Press speaks of increasing fear. Fear makes eye-catching headlines and helps to create a self-fulfilling prophecy. One G2 section of *The Guardian* in 2000 displayed a front-page 'photo' of the gun-holstered backside of a policeman in front of where I live in St Ann's. The headline was 'Mean Streets, UK'. I suppose the editorial staff thought it gave their story 'impact', but it was fanning fear as well as reporting facts. Nothing had happened at that place or within half a mile. My first job in the early 1950s was that of journalist. In Exeter at that time, it would have been hard to find a square half-mile without its sordid events, including murder and terrible deaths from barbarous back-street abortions, sometimes performed by people greedy at any cost.

Within one month in 2000, the *Nottingham Evening Post* had headlines like *Fear rising on city estates under fire*, and a letter from someone who lives near a previous incident in St Ann's. Jeremy R Dobbs wrote: "I have lived here for four years and the situation on the streets and in the houses has not materially changed. The people I have spoken to around here, and I have canvassed opinion, are not afraid . . . A large number of decent, honest people live here - through choice actually - and *Evening Post* scare stories do nothing to assist us in our day-to-day lives. A sober rather than a sensational appraisal is long overdue." In fairness, the articles are often more sober than the headlines but it is those that people remember.

Today, St Ann's adolescents grow up knowing that their home area is looked down on. They resent this. They say so over and over again. The wider community, or 'society', too often make inner-city districts like St Ann's a scapegoat without having any first-hand knowledge. For example, on the radio [2001] I heard a bulletin about heroin poppies being grown again in Afghanistan and the automatic follow-on comment that the heroin 'will flood our inner-cities'. Yes, heroin is around in inner-cities, but it is also around in most other parts of Britain too. I have lost a wonderful nineteen year old great nephew to heroin. He lived and died in rural Devon where there are big drug problems.

It is unjust automatically to couple drugs and inner-cities. But, yes, there are particular areas of some inner-cities, as there are particular areas of some other places, with acute drug problems.

Nothing excuses gun crime. Nothing excuses people killing or hurting each other. Nothing excuses violating other people's homes. Nothing excuses greed. But we must gain some sense of justice toward areas which are stigmatised, and realise that the problems of society are problems of us all. I don't totally trust crime statistics. I don't believe there is intention to report more crime in some areas than others, but it does happen: I see it through my own experience of living in two places.

The only long-term, certain way of limiting serious crime is to create confident close community networks of all age groups and backgrounds. When Brian Bacon described policing in St Ann's before the redevelopment, local knowledge was important in finding out who did what. It became harder when known communities were broken up.

The built environment is a major factor in determining how people can create a sense of community. Local Authorities have a key responsibility, through planning in particular, to put the needs of local communities before the needs of those groups/companies who may wish to manipulate events for their own self-serving reasons. For example, outside property developers.

No amount of police time and intervention will 'mop up crime' unless neighbourhoods are strong in their tolerance of diversity and intolerance of antisocial behaviour. This fact is recognised, though explained in varying ways by people of all ages and backgrounds. There is clear understanding in St Ann's of where neighbourhoods are working together to build community and where this still has to happen.

We get the police we deserve. They can, in the end, do little to protect us if we fail to protect not only our own close circle but also those who are our neighbours, and if we fail as adults to engage with young people (a point made by interviewees in these pages).

It may seem expedient in the short-term to stay silent when speaking out is needed. But, in the long-term, such expediency does not protect our neighbourhoods and leads to worse things happening. History surely teaches us that?

INSPECTOR IAN HOWICK

Born 1966

*Interviewed at **St Ann's Police Station**, Ransom Road, St Ann's, 22.6.00. Inspector Howick is the Local Area Commander. The Local Area covers St Ann's and Sneinton*

I have always lived in Nottingham and have been in the Police Force for twelve years: always in and around the City and for the past two years in St Ann's. So it's interesting, because I had a view of what St Ann's was like from outside which has actually proven to be very different from the way it is.

When I was working in the City Centre, a lot of the offenders for crimes committed in the City came from St Ann's. And so I was coming here for searches, to arrest people and all the bad things. So that started off my view of St Ann's.

Then I spent three years working on the Force Support Department. This is the group that works from our Headquarters at Sherwood Lodge across the entire County dealing with all the bigger issues, the more serious crimes, doing searches, firearms incidents, bigger raids, that sort of thing. So when I was coming into St Ann's, it was always for the wrong reasons. So I had the impression that it was going to be blood under the door every night working here.

Inspector Ian Howick (left) at a public meeting in the area. Photo: Kevin Mason, Annual Report of Nottinghamshire Police Authority 1999-2000

St Ann's Nottingham. Inner-city Voices by Ruth I Johns • ISBN 0951696092

But, now that I'm here, then yes, there are occasions when it is blood under the door, but it is by no means every day and clearly there are communities here. There are a lot of very decent, very nice people who have been here for a long time. And there is an element which causes disruption and commits crime, which is involved in violence, which is involved in drug dealing, which gives the whole area a very bad name. But once you are living here or once you're working here and you're here all the time, you can see it is a small minority.

This minority has a very high profile. As an example, you'll be aware of the shooting incidents that we've had around the City since Christmas. St Ann's has featured quite heavily in those, and there have been a number of very nasty incidents. But when you consider that there are fifty-five thousand people living in this area, we're only talking about a handful who are very violent people, using guns, dealing drugs etc, but it's very newsworthy. It's the sort of thing that gets talked about. People who are just living here minding their business, getting on with their lives don't get talked about, aren't newsworthy and so to an extent are invisible from outside the area.

Our area goes down the Woodborough Road including the Phase 10 area of Marple Square and Cheverton Court, Corporation Oaks then along Huntingdon Street on the City side, up Carlton Road to Porchester Road. And then I cover Sneinton as well. To me the boundary between St Ann's and Sneinton is very fluid. And the area we call St Ann's may be slightly bigger than the area people often think about as being St Ann's [for example, up the Carlton Road as far as Porchester Road].

When I first came here I just had St Ann's and then a year ago I took over Sneinton as well because they were merged as a police area. Whilst superficially they looked very similar, both inner-city areas, both got a lot of deprivation, both got a lot of social housing, both got a very diverse ethnic mix, to police they are very different. Sneinton as a whole is a community, it's got quite an Asian bias in terms of ethnicity and there are a lot of people who have been there for a very long time with a tight community spirit. They are very involved in improving the area themselves.

I don't think there is one St Ann's community. There are pockets of community around the different estates and different parts of the area. And pockets where there is no community whatsoever. In the area where there is community, it is a very strong community spirit but it tends to be people working for their own little area rather than for St Ann's as a whole.

And then also we've got a very large transient community. Obviously a lot of the housing is City Council housing and a lot of it is quite small, particularly down round the Phase 10 area. So it tends to be short-term housing for people, while they are finding them somewhere to live more permanently. These people have nothing in common so community spirit isn't there.

Some years ago, the police would have provided a response capability for people who were in trouble, and would have had a lot of Beat Officers out on foot on their beat, and they would have been known as the Community Police Officers. And they were the people who knew everything, knew everybody, spend all day going round drinking cups of tea, getting to find out what's going on in an area. Just by being there, police talked to children's parents, grandparents and knew people since they were a child, that sort of thing.

Because of changes in the demand on the Police Force and its funding, and issues I won't bore you with, we went away from that. The number of Community Officers were decreased and the number of Response Officers increased. With hindsight this had detrimental effects.

The Force restructured four years ago and has gone back to a concept of locally based, intelligence-led problem solving policing. That's where my post came from, so I am responsible for policing St Ann's. I am more community based than my predecessors would have been. Other people have got the responsibilities of the immediate response and mine is the sustained policing of St Ann's.

There are fifty-five officers who work here and in Sneinton, responsible purely for this joint area. Of those, five of them (three in St Ann's[1]) are the Beat Officers but in a more modern role. So the whole LAC [Local Area Command] is directed at local policing, but three officers in St Ann's have the specific responsibilities to replace the old beat officers. Of the total fifty-five officers, about thirty five would be in St Ann's.

Beat Officers are now called Beat Managers, but people refer to them often as community officers. Their role is to be seen and to provide high profile patrol for reassurance and to be a point of contact. Contact is a two-way thing. They get information out into the community and they pass information back to us. They are sent out to look at particular developing problems and issues in the area, with a view to resolving them by appropriate means, which may be a policing response or it may mean getting other agencies, voluntary groups, members of the community involved to resolve something early on before it becomes a police issue. It's called Problem Solving Policing. These officers also have links into schools, into the community centres and they know the movers and shakers in the area. They are more focused than the old beat officers used to be.

Yes, PC Jim Oaks is one of these officers. You saw him last time you were in. The others are PC Shaun O'Sullivan and PC Simon Helanor. In a lot of places, an officer has a specific area or beat but because St Ann's is quite compact, all three of them work as a team over the whole area and they have thematic responsibilities but will respond to anything that's happening day to day.

One of them is looking at crime trends and issues, picking them up early so we can intervene. One has got community problems, antisocial behaviour, neighbour disputes getting out of control, that sort of thing. And the other has tracking of offenders, victims and vulnerable people's problems. For example, there's a man in prison at present who has always committed a lot of auto crime

---

[1] There are now four [2002].

PC Helanor in the Chase Precinct 2000. Photo: Martin Ellis, Annual Report of Nottinghamshire Police Authority 1999-2000

when he's out. So we know from his history that the day he comes out, he will probably start committing auto crime and we need to be ready.

St Ann's Police Station is open to the public from eight in the morning until ten at night, that's when we have a front counter person. But staff work from here all the time, but at night they may well be out on the streets doing what they should be doing. Our control room is at Carlton and that is open twenty-four hours a day. If somebody in St Ann's needs the police when we're shut here, the call will go to Carlton and be relayed to the appropriate officer.

St Ann's Police Station, Ransom Road, 2000. Photo: E James Smalley

I think this Police Station was built in the late 1960s. It's in quite bad repair and we could do with better facilities but the advantage is that it creates a really good spirit among the officers who work here. They work more as a family than they do in some of the bright new Police Stations and I'm reasonably happy with it.

People hanging around telephone kiosks [drug dealing] can be intimidating to other people. Why can't more be done to stop it? That's a good question. If I had a solution to it, we could solve a lot of the problems in St Ann's. Like a lot of things, it's more complicated than it seems at first. When people are hanging around telephone kiosks or somewhere else, you know what they're doing and I know what they're doing. But in order to do anything about it we need to be able to prove it. In these days of accountability, we find it difficult to get enough evidence to take people to court. That's why we need help from the public.

Unfortunately the restrictions that are placed on the telephone companies means that telephone kiosks cannot be removed or re-sited somewhere else, or changed so they can't be used for drug dealing. Under the Government buy-out schemes, the companies were contracted to have telephone kiosks at particular places. What we are doing at the moment is trying to get the nature of the telephones changed, so that they are not used for drug dealing. But I cannot go into how we are going to do that, but there are things we can do to make them less accessible for drug dealing.

CCTV cameras can be superb and very effective initially when they are first put in. But offenders very quickly become aware of whether any action is taken as a result of something being recorded on camera. The important thing is the monitoring of the screens. If you go into the monitoring centre at Cheverton Court, they've already got about forty TV screens that they are watching. It's physically impossible for them to watch any more without cost implications, and a load more staff to sit watching TV screens, and that money is not available at the moment. There are possibilities of re-siting telephone kiosks within the area covered by an existing CCTV which we're looking at, at the moment. But CCTV is quite new and we need to show first that it's effective and then either extend it or move telephone kiosks into an area being surveyed.

It's the Meadows, Radford and St Ann's that have got problems with overt street dealing. People from the City and outlying areas will come into these areas to buy drugs. Most of the dealers are resident, with the occasional outsider coming in.

The DARE [Drug Abuse Resistance Education] project is aimed at helping children and young people to make informed decisions and know the consequences of the decisions they make. It's got heavy emphasis toward drug and substance abuse but it is wider than that and takes in cigarettes, alcohol and other activities. It encourages people not to do what they do not want to do sexually, criminally, the whole range really. It is a structured programme, which came in from America and has been running for about eight years now. DARE is run in all

ST ANN'S NOTTINGHAM: inner-city voices *by Ruth I Johns* • ISBN 0951696092

schools in the area. It's run by a team of officers who work from Headquarters and cover all the schools in the County.

It's a very good thing, but things don't get put into a local context. What we're trying to do at the moment, on a local basis, is to get that local context taken account of. So that the examples used when officers are talking in classes are local examples and the context is local. Particularly with the problems we've experienced lately, there are certain messages we are keen to get across. And DARE provides the ideal vehicle to do it.

The young people coming out of the DARE project graduate and get certificates. They are coming out with a lot more confidence, and better understanding of the consequences of decisions they will make in the future. DARE has certainly had a short-term effect. I think there will be a long-term effect but that's not been evidenced yet. The scheme has been running for a length of time now. There's a danger of it becoming mundane and it perhaps needs updating and freshening up to keep the momentum going.

What about fifty years time? It's timely to be talking about that because of the shooting incidents and the drugs misuse has all come to a head between January and now [June]. We've been doing a lot of work with the local community, with the Council and what I call the movers and shakers in the area. Where do we go from here? In the short-term to make sure that nobody else gets shot and, in the long-term, to solve some of the underlying problems which have caused the position that we are in.

If we get it right, we have the opportunity to stop isolated incidents degrading into violence and lawlessness as a worst case scenario. We can all turn it around, we can bring it back up, and we can promote all the positive things. As you know there's a boatload of money being spent in the area and there's a lot of good stuff being done and going on. And we've got an opportunity to make that normal in the area.

If we get it wrong and if we don't understand what the problems are, then people in the future will know that we've got it wrong because it will descend into lawlessness and violence. Of the nine shootings in the City, four have been in St Ann's. Three people have been shot. Obviously this has caused a lot of concern among local residents. The one thing that will be comforting them is that, although there are guns on the streets, they have been fired at people and pretty much contained within the criminal element of people who are involved in the drug dealing world.

It isn't just spontaneous incidents on the streets and people being shot indiscriminately, there's reasons behind it, which gives us a basis to do something. I can talk about some of the things we are looking at. Obviously, there's a law enforcement role for us in making sure that we continue to target and lock up drug dealers, particularly the high profile ones. We must offer treatment and diversion schemes to the users or use law enforcements against them if that is appropriate to try and reduce it.

And we're looking at the environment because there are certain parts of St Ann's which seem to be designed for drug dealing. This is easy to say with hindsight, but we've been left with a legacy and we've got to do something about it. So, we're looking at the geography of the area, changes that we can make to reduce opportunities for drug dealing. We've done quite a lot of that on an ad hoc basis as the problems have cropped up. Things like removing undergrowth and bushes, redesigning fencing, positioning of CCTV cameras and things like that. Every time we do something, it takes out another area which can be used for dealing. We need to continue that but in a co-ordinated way so that we're not creating other opportunities elsewhere.

Housing policy we have already touched on. It includes the transit population, the type of people coming into the area, consideration of the ethnic mix in the area. Obviously, with the vast racial mix in the area there's potential - if the strategy is wrong - to get large groups with different ethnic origins who are not going to get on for political or cultural reasons. We need to warn against that sort of thing. And to work with the community to build up community spirit in the area where it's lacking.

One of my personal concerns for the area is that it is being consulted to death. I've been on the fringes of some of the consultations. The impression I get is that although people are invited, or the various agencies think people are being invited to consult, they are not actually responding. The youth aren't responding. So whether they don't realise that they're being invited, or they think we're getting it wrong, I don't know. The Phase 10 Action area is one where I think the feedback is very good but I still don't know if the youth have a big input. But in relation to all the money available in the area like the European Money Management Area, SRB [Single Regeneration Budget] and Sure Start has just come along, it seems to me - as an outsider - that the same people always respond which is good. But there are those who are missing.

The other main policing difficulties in St Ann's? Burglary. It's one of the highest areas in the City, but reducing, which is comforting. And the reductions seem to be going in steps. With a lot of the regeneration that's just taken place, there's a lot of good security measures being put it which caused a rapid drop in burglaries. Fairly basic stuff like a lot of the front doors used to have a large plywood panel in the bottom, which took one kick with a boot which provided you with a three-foot gap to walk through, with a TV if necessary. A lot of those sort of things have been upgraded.

And the general design of the area. We're talking about blind alleys, communal spaces that have been changed quite subtly with the right sort of fencing, the right sort of lighting . . . And we've gone away from merely responding to burglaries to tracking and targeting burglars before they commit the crime with the aim of reducing the offences. This has been very successful. Things like Neighbourhood Watch and the Ringmaster System work.

The Ringmaster System is like an answer phone in reverse. We can put a message on this machine and it will ring up everybody who is part of the Scheme. People in the Scheme can be bracketed into different groups. For example, we might contact all shops and say: 'Watch out for this person who is shoplifting in the area.' We might contact Neighbourhood Watch co-ordinators and say: 'Keep a look-out, we've had this sort of crime or this car may be involved, let us know if this happens.' And there's a feedback loop where they can ring in with results. So that's reducing burglaries. But they are still a problem.

Auto crime can be a problem, not huge. Violence can be a problem, not huge but quite a lot of domestic disputes. Again I think we are getting more intelligent in the way we deal with those now. We try to intervene more than just arresting after the offence has taken place. We try to prevent future offences taking place.

Getting away from the crime side of things, there is a problem with young children out on the streets, especially on light evenings, with nothing they can do or they want to do, getting into trouble, being a nuisance, causing problems. Often it starts with nothing more than playing football in the street and ends up with somebody's car getting damaged, somebody's window being damaged, the ball going into somebody's garden and not being given back, or whatever. That is one of the biggest issues in the area for the police because it takes up so much of our time.

There are places provided where people can play football and other games to their heart's content. But they don't want to be in the places provided, they want to be in their own street, outside their own house.

I would like to go back to an example of what I was saying about the need to work on the community spirit in the area. Because it does exist in some parts, it's very strong in some parts, but there's huge areas where there seems to be little evidence of community spirit being there. Whether the desire is there or not, I'm not sure. But I can't believe that it isn't. We've been trying to set up Neighbourhood Watches in these areas and people aren't prepared to be involved. Because of the transit population, every street or block of housing is going to have a criminal element. It might be only one or two people.

But people don't want to be associated with Neighbourhood Watch or something like that, even though it's going to help them, because they are afraid of the consequences. That needs to be changed into a position where the community spirit on that street or block of housing is so strong that when the next new person moves in, they are given the message that criminals are not tolerated there. If you want to stay here, you are welcome but if you are going to be involved in causing damage, burgling our houses, assaulting people, you are not welcome.

All we've got to do is to make that jump and turn things around. There is an opportunity to do that now and that's why I say we're at a watershed. I'm hopeful, yes.

Yes, there are police officers living in St Ann's but they don't work here. We tend to have a policy these days that you don't work where you live.

In September 2001, Insp Howick became Chief Inspector, Community Relations, Police HQ, Sherwood Lodge, Arnold. **Inspector Michael Manley** *has taken his place as Local Area Commander*

BRIAN BACON

Born 1936

Interviewed in his home 25.5.99. Brian Bacon was a **Policeman** *in St Ann's at the time of the district's redevelopment*

It was about 1969 just before the amalgamation of Nottingham City Police and Nottinghamshire County Police. We were asked where we would like to serve. With St Ann's being the nearest to where I was living in Mapperley, I volunteered to work there. There was only one other police officer who wanted to work in St Ann's, Bill Lewis, because he lived at Mapperley.

Nobody else wanted to work in St Ann's because at that time it had a notorious name. All the villains lived in St Ann's, all the crime was in St Ann's, the so-called Race Riots were in St Ann's and so on. That was a load of baloney. When the two Police Forces amalgamated, I moved to St Ann's. They introduced Panda cars. St Ann's was divided into two Panda car areas, St Ann's Well Road being the dividing point.

St Ann's Police moved to the new Police Station at the bottom of Ransom Road. The old one was disused by the time I got there. There were at least four PC.s [Police Constables] and a sergeant each shift. There could be more. Two Panda cars went out and Beat Officers. On a Friday and Saturday night, there would be what we called the St Ann's Well Road Patrol. Two of us would walk up and down St Ann's to make sure there was no trouble. There always was outside one pub on a Friday or Saturday night. There would be a punch up at Commercial Square. It was always the same. They enjoyed it. You knew everybody.

We knew the villains that lived in St Ann's and they knew us. The method of committing a crime, like cutting lead piping off from the drain pipes, or sawing it off or hacking it off: it would tell you who had done the job. We would go and arrest them and they would say: 'all right you've got me'. Gas and electricity meters were piggy banks. If one of the occupants was on a suspended sentence or something, another one would admit to the break-in.

Everybody in St Ann's had pay-as-you-go meters. St Ann's was good in those days [before demolition]. I was there when they started to demolish it. They started to empty all the houses, whole streets at a time, empty, gone. And the stuff that was left in those houses: people just didn't realise what they had. We got a report of two kids playing in one of the derelict houses, and we'd go and kick the kids out and they would scarper. But when we looked round and saw the stuff that was in there. Looking back, there were antiques galore.

The people who left them had no idea of the value. They didn't want the stuff. Thought it was old. Most of it was up in the attics. Most of the houses had attics. One I went in had four antique sewing machines. I didn't know who owned them and just had to leave it. Probably the demolition men would know what to do with it. When the streets became empty the vandals moved in.

ST ANN'S Nottingham. Inner-city voices *by Ruth I Johns* • ISBN 0951696092

They moved all the people out and they all went here, there and everywhere. Some at Clifton, some at Basford, some at Hyson Green. So we lost contact with the criminals. And then things got out of hand crime-wise all over the City because it spread all over. Nobody knew who was doing what, whereas in the 'old' days we knew our own area. We had some fun in those days. It was nothing to go and find an old piano in a house at two o'clock in the morning and push it down the street playing it at the same time. Or find an old oil barrel and roll it down St Bartholomew's Road (Donkey Hill).

Then they started building up the new St Ann's and they made me resident Beat Officer and my boundaries were Robin Hood Chase, Woodborough Road, Huntingdon Street and St Ann's Well Road. That square area was my patch. It used to have every bit of industry you could think of. Ashforth Street factory and another one with individual units in it. If some people had known what was in that building, they would have broken into it years ago. But they thought it was just derelict. There was valuable stuff in there.

There were lots of little industries in St Ann's. On the old map, you see it. Like Somnus Bedding and Roberts Upholsterers. Rob's forte was repairing posh furniture. People used to bring in antique furniture, but to keep him going he made kitchen furniture for firms. He made the carcasses. He was suddenly taken ill and had to pack it up.

On my own patch, I could have sixty-nine cups of tea at different places! I was walking the beat. A lot of it was being a public relations officer. As far as I remember, there was only two crimes committed on that patch in the two and a half years I was there. Both were internal jobs, they'd done it themselves.

Life went out of St Ann's. I don't care what anybody says, it's people that make slums not only the environment. There was one house I went to just up from the Police Station. It had just been built. Three months after people moved in they were turned out. I went into the house because it was empty and there wasn't a door on hinges, there wasn't a corner left on any of the rooms. All the corners had been knocked off, the plaster smashed. Someone had gone up the wall with a hammer and had just gone bang, bang, bang. You could see it all up the walls, up the stairs and into the lounge. It was unbelievable.

People moved in from all over. I think they decided to move in a lot of problem families, give them a new house and say look you've got a new house and there's no need to be a problem.

Bill Lewis was on one patch and I was on the next patch. He got a job in Administration on a temporary basis. The Superintendent would on occasion come and have a walk around the patch. One day he came and I said: 'Can I have a nine to five weekend off job?' I was joking because I loved the work down there, it was great. One day he came along and he said: 'Do you want a nine to five weekend off job?' I said: 'Oh yes please!'

He said: 'Right, on Monday, Criminal Records Office'. It was filing, he said. They'd got so far behind they needed some help and it was a six-month attachment. I was there for eight years, so that's when I left St Ann's.

There was a memorable incident. Mary was a coloured lady, big built. She acquired Festus Street. It was derelict. She went to empty houses and got furniture and filled every house in Festus Street. One day there was a report of a fire at one of the houses on Festus Street. The Fire Brigade came along but couldn't get into the house because of the furniture that was in it.

Another time I went around there - she would always be behind one of those houses at night-time - and she had a great zinc bath and an open fire and there was this cow's head boiling away in there. She always used to call me 'Mr Government Man' and every time I went to see her she would ask if I would like some soup. I just said: 'No, I had had my supper thank you.' She had a black dog that followed her everywhere. One night I went to see her and it wasn't black any more, she had painted it blue. She said she wanted a different colour.

I got on with her really well. There was this time when I came on duty and there was unrest. They said: 'We're having trouble with Mary. This was in the middle of the afternoon. I walked up there. There was a Chief Inspector or Superintendent there, a Sergeant, two PCs that came from Canning Circus (because at that time we were linked with Canning Circus), and all the builder's people, the demolition people and Mary. I tried to tell Mary they'd got a new house for her, I think it was on St Ann's Hill.

They wanted her to move and she refused to go. And I thought with all those people around . . . I started talking to one of the demolition men and asked why all the fuss over Mary. He said: 'When you see a woman walking the street with an oven on her head, you don't approach her.'

Anyway I said to Mary they had a nice new house and would she like me to walk up with her and show it to her. She said: 'all right, no problem' and we went. It all depended on how you dealt with her. Her husband, I believe, had been a doctor and she came from a well-bred family, but she became disturbed, ended up in Mapperley [Hospital]. A lovely lady really.

St Ann's did have some characters. Did anyone tell you about the woman who used to walk along St Ann's Well Road with a pram? I don't know where she lived, she was always walking there. Her hair was matted and the kids would chase her. And then there was Lionel. He used to be on my patch. He lived on Flewitt Street but they moved him to one of the new houses off Abbotsford Drive. He was harmless.

Kelham's, a cattle haulier's firm had been going for years in St Ann's. One day, a workman came along and took someone else with him and they wanted to join the Union. So the boss said I don't want unions, I pay a good going rate, and he did. This chap said he was going to get the Union, so the Union said you will pay so much per hour to the workmen. They didn't ask what he paid! He said: 'You're not telling me how much I'm going to pay these men, I pay them myself.'

He was paying more than the Union was asking. The Union threatened to bring them all out on strike, and he said 'You call them out on strike and I'll shut the place down'. And he did. And that was it, finished.

Brian Bacon told me that his great grandad, who was called Little Billy Bacon because he was only 4'10" tall, used to own 2 and 2a, St Mark's Street and 4, 6 and 8, St Mark's Street, St Ann's. He was a horse dealer and ran stables at Bacon's Yard. Jesse Boot, founder of the Boots Company, used to hire a pony and trap from him when he went out collecting herbs.

The Young Bros, hauliers, used to wait for him at the station. His great grandad used to go to Wales and collect Welsh ponies to train. He'd drive them through the streets of St Ann's to some land he had. He broke them in to work as pit ponies.

On Sunday mornings, he would run horses up and down St Mark's Street, and all the dealers would come. Once he was asked to break in an angry 'hunter' horse. It would sidle up to a wall to crush its rider's legs. On one occasion, he saw a bottle on the wall as the horse got ready to 'crush' his leg. He hit it over the head with the bottle. After that the horse would do anything for him.

PROBATION, HOUSING AND NATIONAL ASSISTANCE BOARD OFFICERS RECALL ST ANN'S WORK

A meeting took place on 1.6.00 at Nottinghamshire Probation Department Headquarters, Marina Road, Nottingham, thanks to John Kay, Assistant Chief Probation Officer, and Barbara Granger, Chief Officer's Personal Administrative Officer, who facilitated a lunchtime meeting of the following people:

*   **Philip Everett,** *former Probation Officer in St Ann's;* **Charlie Harris**, *Probation Officer who worked in St Ann's;* **Janet Kenwood**, *ex National Assistance Board Officer in St Ann's;* **Richard Peet**, *former City of Nottingham Housing Officer in St Ann's;* **Joyce Peet**, *Richard's wife, who used to live in St Ann's and joined the Probation Service (not in St Ann's), and* **Helen Scott**, *Probation Officer who worked in St Ann's. John Kay was unable to be present. He was Assistant Chief Probation Officer for St Ann's from 1978 until the mid-1980s.*

The St Ann's Probation Office was opened in 1974 on Robin Hood Chase, just above the Library, as part of the St Ann's redevelopment. Margaret Smith was then Senior Probation Officer there. Barbara Granger remembered the Office being built. There was a sense of optimism about having a local office. I was at the Opening Ceremony. Some of the young people I knew well reported to that office

Philip Everett. I have been retired now for about eleven years. I was a Probation Officer [PO] for many, many years in St Ann's and was there when the new office opened. I stayed there until five years before I retired in 1988. It was the only area I'd ever worked in so I knew the old St Ann's very well and also the new.

The young Phil Everett   and more recently

Phil Everett at work in the Probation Court Office, with the late Jean Brown

When I worked in the old St Ann's, we worked from various places including the original City Probation Office on Broad Street, the one in Shire Hall and we had an office on Mansfield Road as well. When I first came to Probation work as a young man, I was the only officer covering the whole area of St Ann's. Everything that happened came to me. I took over from Reg Fairley.

That was around 1953. The Probation Service was very understaffed and over-worked in those days but it was a very enjoyable job. My background was in community work so I was interested in getting things going at that time. And there was a lot to do because there wasn't much going off in St Ann's. I mean now there are Youth Clubs and old people's groups, all sorts of things. Then, there was nothing so it was like virgin ground. There were plenty of good people like the Minister of the Kings Hall Methodist Church and David Keene, Vicar of St Catharine's Church. All sorts of people, like Margaret Gardner, who wanted to get involved. Then Ray Gosling, all kinds of people came along and community efforts started.

Janet Kenwood. I worked for the National Assistance Board from 1963. Then it was in Weekday Cross. It became the Department of Social Security and later the Benefit Agency. The sub-area for which I was responsible was St Ann's. I was the first female who had done that area. It was a large sub-area. I would start at the Salvation Army Hostel and sometimes used to have to say the prayers and read the lesson. Then I would go right up the Woodborough Road. It was a huge area.

Margaret Smith, Senior PO, and Michael Clough PO at the St Ann's Probation Office c1974. Photo from Phil Everett

I worked in the old St Ann's and the new. What I remember most about the old St Ann's was that there were elderly and young living next door to each other. The elderly used to help the youngsters when the children were ill and babysit and in return the young people looked after the elderly. And when they pulled it down, they [the Council] put all the elderly into one-bedroom flats on one side of the road and all the youngsters on their own on the other side. I think that was very sad.

Richard Peet. I worked for Nottingham City Council Housing Department as a Clearance Officer from 1970 to 1973. The Clearance Phases in St Ann's started about 1967. Every house had to be visited and details taken of residents and where they wanted to go. The most important thing was where they wanted to go, because they were being shipped off and being told to go. People in private property were given market value for their houses. The others, of course, didn't get anything except their removal fees paid. Sometimes one or two little extras. I visited thousands of houses back to back, outside loos . . . I left in 1973 and it was still going on. Then they started on the Meadows.

In those days Nottingham City had around 55,000 properties and we used to get the pick of any lettings because of pulling places down and rebuilding Council stock. Now I think there's about 30,000 left because a lot have been sold off.

When I joined, the clearance in St Ann's had been going for some time. They started on Woodborough Road and then moved down towards St Ann's Well Road and right down as far as Carlton Road. I did Phases 7, 8 and 9,

which were the lower end of Alfred Street South. All Alfred Street South and right the way up to Westminster Street which was off St Ann's Well Road, then down as far as Gordon Road and Carlton Road. Quite a big area.

A lot of people were very pleased about the clearance. There were one or two who didn't want to go, they had been there a long time and put up with the draughts and no baths and things like that. One particular man stood out in my mind. We moved him from an old house into a flat. And I asked him how he was getting on and he said: 'Well, my lad, I used to get up in the morning and put my legs into cold drainpipes. Now I've got central heating and it's wonderful to get up.' It made your day.

Most wanted to go but, when they moved, they didn't like it so much because of the change. All the facilities were there, not the warden-aided schemes then, but there were full packages of people together. We tried to move people street by street because they wanted to remain together. It was like any other place, there's villages within villages and close-knit families with aunties and mothers all round the corner.

Joyce Peet. I started working for Nottingham City Probation Office in 1968 just before it amalgamated with the County. I never worked in the St Ann's office, but I was brought up in St Ann's from 1932 when I was six. We came from Yorkshire. Work was difficult in Bradford so my father moved down to Nottingham and he drove lorries for Wilkinsons. They made furniture. All the family moved down. We lived on Sabina Street off Alfred Street South. I was married at St Catharine's Church on St Ann's Well Road. After we married we moved away for three years and then came back and lived on Sabina Street next door to my mum. My mum was in rented property but we had to buy ours. It was a very close-knit community. We did actually move out before they started clearing the area.

Charlie Harris. I'm Edward James Harris but everybody calls me Charlie, it's a very obscure nickname! I joined the Probation Service in 1960 after training and moved straight into Margaret Smith's team.

I worked in St Ann's from about 1968 and stayed until 1979. The work of a Probation Officer in those days was very much more community based and it wasn't so much criminalised. We had a whole list of things we had to do. I remember neighbours' quarrels were one of the things we could claim for on our monthly returns. And all sorts of things, like giving financial advice. Most Probation Officers dealt with people not in prison. When I arrived in St Ann's, there was only Phil Everett and one other person dealing with people in prison and after-care.

Most of my caseload was twelve year old boys. I remember doing a report on a lad who was charged with stealing an empty milk bottle. It was mostly things like meter breaking and stuff like that. Not the serious crimes we have today, no drugs of course. My memory of the old St Ann's when it was redeveloped was the high preliminary cost of compensating the numerous pubs and shops that disappeared. On the corner of every street was either a shop or a pub. There must have been dozens of pubs in the area [some fifty-six].

I used to go up Blue Bell Hill like a postman because I had so many clients. You know I had to knock on every door! And Alfred Street South where the Pork Farm empire began. They bought two or three shops and that sort of developed. They were all decorated in brown stain and wood grain effect. You could see a whole row of houses neatly painted all to do with Pork Farms and, of course, many of our clients worked there. It was a fantastic place to work.

One of the saddest things when I worked there was that people moved away and they didn't move back. So the new houses became occupied by people who didn't know each other as neighbours before. As we were sitting in the office we watched some move out. Streets decayed. As individual houses were vacated, people got into them to get the fittings to use in their own house. There was one old lady who went for a hospital appointment by ambulance. Some local boys must have seen her go and thought she was moving away. When she came back in the afternoon even her front door was off its hinges. The whole house had been stripped inside.

It was a crime of course, but it wasn't. It was just part of that time, the streets became very derelict and the feeling of people that they could scavenge became an epidemic. It gave us a lot of work because people were forever being picked up for stealing lead piping and things.

Helen Scott. I worked with Philip Everett and Charlie Harris. I joined in 1972 as a newly qualified Probation Officer. It's very difficult for me to separate the old St Ann's from my first job. I was twenty-one. I was very young, very enthusiastic I hope. It was my first job and I suppose to some extent it was just where I worked and I didn't fully realise how special St Ann's was. I didn't even fully appreciate the significance of what had gone on before and the redevelopment. I was right in the midst of a whole range of individuals and families with all of their needs and problems. My colleague, Brenda Boggild, and I used to go off into a huddle every so often because we felt quite discriminated against as female Probation Officers.

We had particular groups of people to work with, especially vulnerable young women with large families. Many of these young women had broken into their meters. We were let off Court duty one afternoon a week because it was expected that we would be doing more home visits. And we didn't get any exciting clients like lifers or anything like that because we were women.

Philip Everett. I'm not defending the situation, but at one time women were not allowed to deal with men or men with women. I can remember that changing.

Helen Scott. When I look back I think how dreadful the lives of some of those young women were. How utterly abused they had been and were being by their partners. Obviously now there is no crime of breaking into meters because electricity and gas aren't run on those systems any more. We had a number of prostitutes, some very successful, quite wealthy prostitutes to some very, very vulnerable under-age girls. During my time in the Probation Service 1972-78, I knew at least three young women under sixteen who were killed as a result of being a prostitute, at least two in St Ann's. These young women would be murdered and then they would be found to be under age.

I had quite a few young men clients between seventeen and twenty-five. I remember one interesting case. The young man had stolen a tomato from the Central Market just off St Ann's. The Church wanted him to go back to Ireland and he didn't want to go and I had to sit with him until he caught the night train. Six months later, he actually phoned me up to say life was great and he was glad to be there.

We spent some of our time in court, and a lot of it on home visits and visits to prisons or borstals. We did more after-care in those days and I think people did appreciate it. If you visited someone in prison before they came back they felt you'd made an effort to see them when in fact it was part of the job.

I remember families in the new St Ann's where the newness of their homes was wonderful to them. Everything was new and I remember some densely packed houses. Today it would be IKEA. They suddenly bought everything new and the whole of the downstairs of the house was probably only the size of this room we're in. Then there were other families and you'd go into the houses and there was literally nothing except a couple of chairs. The children would come home from school and all they would have was a loaf of white bread, and they would butter it. The money sort of went in and out of the home, on gambling and booze and all that stuff. The extremes of poverty were still there. It didn't particularly surprise me because I was brought up in a rural area where you had everything from aristocrats to people who were very poor.

Joyce Peet. I don't remember any crime when I was growing up in St Ann's.

Philip Everett. It was very localised. There were certain terraces and places where you knew everybody and there were other terraces where you never visited. I don't think Charlie was completely right saying that crimes were different. Some were serious. One of my clients murdered his niece for instance. There were occasional cases of incest and sex crimes but less than later because people were living at such close quarters that they knew what was going on. If a child was injured or hurt, they'd be there. There was tremendous community spirit so they couldn't get away with that sort of crime. I got the impression that most of the crimes were committed within the area. They would burgle a local factory rather than go out of the area to steal or burgle.

And there were different sorts of crime. I mean I can remember when attempted suicide was a crime. I knew a family man sent to prison for six months for keeping a dirty house. It was filthy admittedly. I don't know whether that's even an offence these days. He'd got two children. But yes, Charlie's right saying there were more petty offences. There were less warnings and people were prosecuted and put on probation for quite minor offences, mostly committed in the area.

St Ann's Nottingham: inner-city voices *by Ruth I Johns* • ISBN 0951696092

Charlie Harris. I was told my initial caseload wouldn't be more than forty-five in the first year. Then six months later it was ninety. That is a lot even today. Bill Jones used to have about twenty boys standing outside his office, a lot of them wore Brylcream on their hair. They lent on the wall and you could see this wavy line on the wall caused by their hair! I took over his caseload and things changed because not only did we work in St Ann's but all over the place.

Philip Everett. When I first started we dealt with boys from eight years old. Some of them went to Aycliffe as it was then. It was an Assessment Centre for placement in Approved Schools. And, then, of course, the age we saw people went higher and higher and eventually we didn't deal with children at all. Yes, when I started eight year olds were appearing in court and being placed on probation.

Charlie Harris. As a result of the 1969 Act, Social Services took all our under-fourteens. Then gradually, they took the under-eighteens. When the young people disappeared, we got the older ones with more serious offences. At one stage, the Chief Probation Officer dealt with these. It was 1976 before I got my first lifer and I was forty before I had a woman client.

Helen Scott. It was before my time that clients were of the same gender, but Brenda and I felt we still got the balance of the women.

Janet Kenwood. Once in the old St Ann's, I visited someone who had been released from prison. We were all there, the Children's Officer and everybody. He'd connected himself up to the next-door house's gas. He'd got no heating and suddenly his kettle started whistling and I looked through and there was his cooker that was supposed to be off merrily whistling his kettle! He used to do this regularly and connect the electricity to the street lights.

Once I found an old lady and I did something I should never have done, I opened the door. She was a recluse. And she was dead and she'd been there sometime. She was in one of the terraces that still had gas lighting. I fetched the police and her piano was stuffed full of £1 notes. It was about 1963. When I got back I had to report to the Deputy Manager and he told me I had disobeyed every rule in the book, not least by not waiting for someone to open the door. But I could have knocked forever! I used to visit her every week to check up on her.

We used to have a Welfare List and if we had a client we thought was at risk, we'd put them on that list and visit them every one or two weeks. Now it would be passed on to Social Services.

Philip Everett. Am I right Janet, that in those days it was a much more flexible system than now? I remember ringing you up and saying so and so needed a pair of boots and you would say: 'Come round and I'll give you a voucher.'

Janet Kenwood. Yes, it was very flexible. We used to give everyone who started work and who needed boots and socks a voucher to purchase them and a helmet if needed. There was this man called Whiting on St Ann's Well Road. He sold working clothes and was also a Pawn Broker. Some would take their voucher to Mr Whiting and he would

exchange it for cash, so they never did get their working boots. Mr Whiting also let out flats didn't he Phil?

Philip Everett. Yes, he was a landlord.

Janet Kenwood. They would call him a property developer now. He had a huge double shop. You could buy excellent watches there. He sold everything.

Things changed with the new St Ann's. It had a unique heating system. The heat came from an incinerator [at Eastcroft, London Road] which burnt all the rubbish. I think it was the first of its kind in the country. People didn't want to be on it because of the cost. So the problems changed. Before it was quite easy problems. After redevelopment, there was more debt.

But, I loved St Ann's so much that when I finished work, I opened a hairdresser's on Robin Hood Chase. That was in 1980 and we had it for three years. I needed to go back to where these people were. They are super people, salt of the earth. There is a lot of community spirit in the new St Ann's. They built their own Community Centre [Chase Neighbourhood Centre]. And Jim Neill, the Vicar in St Ann's, has been there for years and is super. He really is. Excuse me now, I've got to see an old lady in hospital and then go back to work.

Philip Everett. Today, they can't do the same things as Janet's role was. They are dealing with far more people. It's the same with the police. The police at one time lived in the area so they knew the people and they did control the trouble. If there was any, it was easier to deal with. It's all part of the community spirit really, isn't it?

Charlie Harris. I saw a snippet of community spirit in action. The troubles in Ireland started in 1968 and the Army was engaged in areas of Belfast, areas very similar to St Ann's. Around 1970, towards the bottom of Blue Bell Hill Road, the last part to be developed, the Army wanted to train the troops for street fighting and street patrolling in Belfast. The local populace got very upset that their beloved St Ann's was being used as a sort of battleground or a battle scene. I saw the first soldiers arrive from the training battalion. They wanted to train to see how they could effectively police an area of terraced houses. Before they got into action, the local people forced the Army out.

Richard Peet. I was born in St Ann's, moved away when I was five or six, then came back and we lived on the Woodborough Road. Then when I got married, we moved away and then came back as my wife said earlier. I remember one elderly lady who had been there for years. She used to sit in her backyard with a fire actually on the yard. She would go round dragging or collecting wood in an old pram and sit in the yard in a rocking chair. They were pulling the houses down around her and she wouldn't move. They had to Section her [commit her to a psychiatric hospital] unfortunately.

Philip Everett. One or two people were. One of my clients was.

I went to visit one client and the house was all boarded up and I thought they must have rehoused him. He lived with his mother and sister. He wasn't the brightest of lads. Then I heard this faint voice inside and they'd tinned him up while he'd been asleep. I saw an urban beachcomber coming round with a ladder and a van for taking lead stuff off the roofs. And he got him out and we took him into digs. The rest of the family had been rehoused in Sherwood and so just left him because he wouldn't go with them. He had no light or heat or anything.

He was in his forties and he said he wasn't going without his belongings that consisted of bags of rubbish. He was a coal heaver so he was filthy as well. In those days, we had some very good lodgings and we managed to get him cleaned up and fixed up.

Charlie Harris. David Keene [Vicar of St Catharine's Church, St Ann's Well Road] had an elderly man in his garage because he refused to be rehoused. They would have had him in the house but he wanted his independence and stayed in the garage and David took him dinner every night, clean socks and things like that.

Richard Peet. Elderly people - like my mother-in-law - on a street wanted to be moved near each other. We tried to get them within a block or so. But their attitude changed because everything was modern, everything completely altered, and they didn't like it. Some had family in Bestwood or Clifton and wanted to move to get closer to them.

Joyce Peet. Mother didn't want to go, none of them did. What upset them was the fact that a lot of the people who wanted to go elsewhere were moved out so that the street became a place where only the old people who wanted to stay in St Ann's were left. I used to tell my mother that it would be lovely because her new home would be warm and there would be a bathroom. But they missed the streets where they could knock on next-door and go in. Eventually there would only be four or five people left on a street and the rest boarded up.

Richard Peet. That was because they were waiting for new property and they had to wait longer than the people who moved away. So you probably ended up with a street of fifty houses and only a dozen left occupied by people waiting for the new homes to come off the production line.

Joyce Peet. But they [the Council] did try. I know when my mother moved, three or four people from the street were nearby. She got a flat in St Ann's. Very nice and comfortable.

Richard Peet. That wasn't so possible in the early Phases of the demolition because there was nowhere yet built in St Ann's for people to go. But as it got to Phases 6, 7, 8 and 9 it was different. I didn't want to get involved with moving mother, being close family, but I did say she wanted to move with her neighbours.

Philip Everett. There were a lot of street communities. I remember this terrace off Westminster Street. A lot of the families were related. Mother and father lived at one end, and they were all there. If a house became vacant, a married daughter would move in. And grandparents would be there. They could see everybody who was coming and going and there would be babysitting and support of every kind.

Helen Scott. How should the new St Ann's have been developed? I agree some people did stay on for ages and ages in properties they didn't want to leave. But I wouldn't

necessarily agree with what other people have said. I didn't feel so much of that community spirit. I tended to work with people who were marginalised even within St Ann's. Enhancing that marginalisation was the fact that sometimes they'd be put in houses other people obviously did not want.

So they were either very public where everybody could see in, or put somewhere terrible like Kendale Court [new St Ann's] which was damp and I can't think that anybody was happy there and it's now gone over to students.

I don't know if the redevelopment got all the community facilities right. There was the Chase Precinct but I don't recall there being much else other than these vast acres and acres of properties. The physical surroundings had changed, the houses were better, but some things hadn't changed at all. It was the most awful place.

Philip Everett. It's easy to say with hindsight, but I think they should have kept some of the older properties. I mean they fought to keep Cromer Road. They were nice little houses and one of my colleagues lived in one of them. There were a lot of other good houses, Robin Hood Chase for instance should never have come down. There was a beautiful old Vicarage at the top. It could have been converted into either family homes or nice flats. There was just too much demolition. They could have mixed the old with the new. OK, a lot of the houses were poor and no damp course and they needed to come down. But they should have thought about it more instead of the wholesale demolition.

Richard Peet. Talking about the properties that were pulled down, the Bank in Commercial Square was a magnificent building. I tried to get it stopped in my own small way. It was a shame because it was a central point. I think it was a Watson Fothergill building. But the architects had done their work and the Council sold everything off.

They would never be allowed to pull a building like that down today. A lot of that happened. Of course, you are not going to get this scale of demolition now, and today Nottingham City Council - any local council - hasn't got the sway they had then.

Councils don't have that monopolistic position now. I've worked for Broxtowe Borough Council latterly and they have sold so many houses off, and Nottingham City Council has done the same thing. The houses that have been sold are the better ones. The ones that aren't so good are still under management of the City Council and unfortunately they've got some of the bad lads and lasses in them. It would be difficult to do such a scale of redevelopment again. We did the best we could at the time.

Philip Everett. Having said that, originally they were planning high-rise blocks and there was going to be a great highway running through St Ann's [the Eastern By-pass].

Joyce Peet. I agree with Phil. A lot of properties in St Ann's were pulled down which needn't have come down. They were too good really. They could have been done up. We had a trip down memory lane a little while ago. We were at the bottom of Carlton Road and I suddenly saw Alfred Street South and I said let's go and see what's still left. I was at Pierrepont School and the building is still there. Quite a few of the little streets are still up there. We finished going down Robin Hood Street and saw the Promenade. When I was a girl, if you lived on the Promenade you must have had a lot of money. Campbell Grove is still there.

Philip Everett. They are mostly owner-occupied now.

Joyce Peet. They have improved them, put bathrooms in . . . (voice off) They are marketing for about £35,000 now. *Joyce Peet* Other streets could have been left. They kept some of the houses on Lamartine Street. Mr Farnsworth, with the Pork Butchers shop, had one of those big houses when I was a girl. He was a lovely man. Pork Farms took over his property when he left.

Richard Peet. And talking about Pork Farms, they started with the Farnsworth shop and then they took over other properties, as Charlie said earlier, on Alfred Street South and they went backwards on to Havelock Street. They gradually took over almost the whole block. Then they moved across the road on Alfred Street South and took over shops which became offices. Mr Parr had an office over one of the blocks of shops. And he could see everything that went off there and he had a big window etched with the Pork Farms logo. It had a farm cottage and fields and things on it. I had the unpleasant duty of having to go and see him and tell him that time was up and that he had to move. I had worked for him for ten years prior to my then job. I went to work for him for a week and stayed ten years. My wife worked for him for a while too. It was a very, very good business.

Charlie Harris. I have developed a thing about Public Housing, I don't think it works, putting people on estates with the same landlord. Unless the landlord is extremely intelligent, you can get the wrong mix of people. When I went back to St Ann's after an absence of fifteen years, the Chase Precinct looked like Dodge City. The Bank had closed and the shops had steel shutters up.

Something happened when all those people disappeared and a lot of new people came in. Wherever you go in Nottingham and you have a big ex-Council housing estate, there is this problem of bad neighbours and people being afraid to walk the streets. I wouldn't go into St Ann's at night now to socialise. I'd go to a country pub if I wanted a drink. Whereas I used to feel quite happy about coming back into St Ann's after working there even though I might be running into people I knew as criminals. Planners get it wrong with urban social engineering. You've got to get the right mix of people.

Richard Peet. That was proved with Balloon Woods wasn't it [a sixties Council development on the City outskirts which has been pulled down]. That was a big development. The bad lads used to get shipped up there.

Charlie Harris. Like Kendale Court [St Ann's] which seemed to be full of unmarried mothers.

Philip Everett. But how could they conceivably have let four bed-roomed flats to families (which they were planned for)? There wasn't an inch of grass or play-space. Just a lump of concrete the children could play on. And they were badly built in addition to being badly planned. And that was part of St Ann's redevelopment.

Helen Scott. I'm not up-to-date about St Ann's now but I expect some people still feel excluded. When I was involved in some activity and had to book rooms, I often used to think of booking them in St Ann's or Hyson Green [an inner-city low-rise estate built in the 1960s and now pulled down]. These were the two places that people would blink at and not consider going to. I don't remember working with anybody who was ecstatically happy about living in St Ann's. This was 1972-78. A lot of people I knew in St Ann's were moved to Top Valley, and they weren't very happy about that either. Some of their criminal activity increased. For some reason there were new sorts of crime and more opportunities. It was a brand new Council estate, with slightly more open space and air.

Philip Everett. There were more things to do in St Ann's. In the old St Ann's, a lot of people used to say if they were ever bored they would take a walk the length of St Ann's Well Road and there was every type of shop along there. They would just walk along and meet somebody they knew and it was sociable. You couldn't do that in Top Valley, could you?

Helen Scott. I got people that didn't fit in St Ann's. For example, a single woman, ex-Army, living in the middle of Cromer Road. There was a Jamaican family living in two rooms on the second floor of a multi-occupied house on Woodborough Road. I don't recall this community bonhomie.

Joyce Peet. Of course, the people Helen had contact with in St Ann's were all people known to the Probation Service. The people who were probably more community-orientated were not known to the Service. You weren't having contact with old ladies who'd brought up a family and lived there for years and who were very friendly, very supportive with the neighbours. You were dealing with the people who had problems.

Helen Scott. Exactly!

Philip Everett. At the time of the new St Ann's, I was involved in community things. My background was community work. There was the Sycamore Club, and the ARK Youth Club, Adventure Playground and Urban Farm. The ARK burned down unfortunately. A lot of people were involved then. Probation Officers as individuals were involved in things. The Urban Farm in St Ann's is the only one in Nottingham that took off. It's still going strong.

Before we go I'd just like to mention that survey that was done by Coates and Silburn[1]. The people of St Ann's were angry and irritated by it. It painted them in such a bad light. Life for them wasn't about how many bathrooms you had but how good is your next-door neighbour.

My thanks were expressed to John Kay and Barbara Granger and for the appreciated buffet lunch

---

[1] *Poverty, Deprivation and Morale in a Nottingham Community* [Department of Education, Nottingham University 1968].

BRENDA BOGGILD

writes 2000:

I've been a Probation Officer for nearly twenty-eight years. When I first started work as a PO in 1971, I was twenty-three and my first job was in St Ann's. I worked there for six years, the first three during the demolition phase and the next three when many of the larger families were re-housed to larger four-bedroom houses outside the area. Families in St Ann's were learning to adjust to new housing conditions, alongside new material expectations on limited means. Gone was the electricity meter, an emergency fund for a loan, and in was Hire Purchase, the three-piece suite, lots of ornaments and shoplifting. The number of people living in the area went down.

When they learned that I was being interviewed for the Nottingham Probation Service, people said to me: 'Wherever you go, don't go to St Ann's'. It was renowned as being the worst area of the City, the home of appalling living conditions, crime and of 'race riots' in earlier times. As I did not drive and the alternative was Mansfield, I went to St Ann's. I bought a motorbike and used to travel round the patch in a long purple midi-coat, black boots and a white crash helmet on my Honda 90. I later travelled in the comfort of an orange Mini car.

For home visits, walking, my work uniform in the old St Ann's was a mini-skirt and a UPVC Mackintosh, which came in handy when you were not quite sure what you were sitting on! One client said to me: 'Don't sit there, there are mice nesting in it'. Another used to pour bleach down the cracks of skirting boards to kill the mice or rats off. They did not seem to like it! Without the benefit of refrigerators, clients would offer drinks of Camp Coffee with two sugars and sterilised milk. I accepted rather than offend. If it were raining, an umbrella could come in handy too! There would be slates missing from roofs, windows missing, and mould and damp lingered around some of the walls, never mind the electricity!

St Ann's never seemed to me to be 'the worst area of the City' as I got to know the people of the area. Despite the poverty, there were many decent hardworking people who took great pride in their homes. Despite being a Sociology Graduate, I never got round to reading Coates and Silburn's *Poverty: the Forgotten Englishman*. But I remember the days of Ray Gosling and SATRA [St Ann's Tenants and Residents Association]. I was involved particularly with the playgroup committees and Probation 'mothers groups' that involved running a stall during the St Ann's Festival, outings, and part of my role as a PO once included judging a knobbly knees competition.

I feel privileged to have known Nan Bennett MBE, who was the longstanding Headmistress of a local infant school and acted in the capacity of a Probation Volunteer helping with literacy and a crèche after she retired. Rev John Stacy-Marks, Kings Hall Methodist Church, was an impressive pioneer opening his Church to be relevant to the needs of the community. Also I remember Phil Everett, PO, who was into community work before community work was ever invented! He seemed to have worked in St Ann's for eons before I ever got there and everybody knew him.

Margaret Smith was the Senior PO when I arrived and was the proverbial 'mother' of the community and of the office. When I started, she knew of the St Ann's families from when they were children in the Meadows and Broxtowe areas and her patch was half the City. Some POs had children named after them, an indication of how much they were valued by some families. We seem to have gone round in full circle, as Margaret would expect individuals to report as part of a Probation Order, yet she knew the community links to link people into. I used to wonder how she had the uncanny knack of knowing what people's problems were. I now do the same, which comes with experience and expertise, even though we may now see and describe the issues differently.

I guess the fact that landlords knew the area would be demolished meant that previously well-kept properties were lost in the name of change. And cheaper rented properties that had been neglected for many years deteriorated even further. Nowadays, hopefully, such areas would be renovated, and avoid all the disruption of families and discontinuity of the community that occurred in St Ann's. People wanted kitchens, bathrooms and toilets but not necessarily a removal from the extended family and community support that seemed evident in St Ann's.

My caseload was about fifty women with multiple problems involving themselves and their children. As a woman PO, I supervised mainly women offenders. My most useful phone numbers were the health inspector and the rat man and I was frequently writing support letters to assist rehousing.

The wholesale areas of demolition and rubble or the backyards, with properties in various stages of dilapidation, were the play areas for children. Women would bring their children in with them to see me and many interviews were aborted owing to the major distractions of the children. Children were to be seen as a problem if they did not 'sit still', and were described as 'mardy bleeders', and threatened with a belt or indulged in sweets and material things at the expense of time and care from their parents. I soon developed an 'interview kit' of toys, paper and pens etc to keep the children occupied. Issues of inter-generational poverty and breaking the cycle of deprivation seemed very evident amongst such households. Pioneering work done by the NSPCC [National Society for the Prevention of Cruelty to Children] at Kings Hall, working with playgroups for children alongside getting the parents interested in their children's education, seemed to be a way toward change.

Clients then were placed on Probation or imprisoned for prostitution. The most I felt I could do was to help them take less risks to their and other's health and to be someone who listened and cared. Some women saw very little profit from their labours because proceeds went to their pimp. In those days, our role was a befriending one, and many clients were proud to introduce us to their neighbours and we would easily be recognised. Our car numbers were memorised alongside those of the Vice Squad. When I first

St Ann's Nottingham: inner-city voices *by Ruth I Johns* • ISBN 0951696092

started working with prostitutes, I was totally naïve, as I was the product of an all girls' convent education. The reality of these women's lives, often controlled and dominated by men, seemed far removed from mine, as I had always felt I had choices and the benefit of support and a good education, a home and family supports.

I have never forgotten an invitation to a Tupperware party with another PO and that we were the only ones to order anything and pay for them. For the rest, nearly all prostitutes, it seemed a chance to get together. If two girls shared a house, it constituted a brothel, and I even got introduced to their punters as part of their normality.

In the days before Women's Refuges, I helped some women have the courage to leave the violence when it became too much, only to find too often that they would return. In those days, the opportunity to escape when one had dependants was hard and for women, who had such negative images of themselves, alongside feelings of being worthless as a prostitute, I'm not surprised that many would return.

Paying bills on very restricted means has always been a problem in St Ann's amongst our clients. Some had novel ways of saving, such as keeping their money between their cleavage, or making long-term plans, such as breeding Alsation pups that would be due for the next electricity quarter! The dog in question was a most ferocious beast that used to terrorise me as I ventured round the back of the terrace to gain entry. I was allowed in whereas others were not. The visit from the club man or the rent man when there was no money in the pot was a not unfamiliar problem.

Along the bottom of the Promenade, we visited some lively families, one of whom proudly described how she had hit a teacher and it was the best £5 fine she had had! Health and safety of staff, or staff venturing out on home visits, were not considered then. But to prevent a family losing their home for rent arrears, we even went round collecting the rent on occasion. This was dedication in the days before housing benefit and alternative arrangements to avoid family homelessness.

Another shock to me when I started was the number of very large families of fourteen and seventeen children. Having been one of nine children myself, I had never heard of such numbers before. For women still burdened by the risk of pregnancy and the difficulties providing for their children, education and helping them use contraception was a significant part of my work.

Some women offended because they were forced to provide for their children in appalling conditions alongside their partner's alcohol or gambling addiction. You rarely met the partner who was always excused and it was, therefore, difficult to change the overall quality of their lives.

Once the phases of rehousing were done, the new St Ann's brought a new focus. Having got basic housing issues out of the way, it revealed more serious problems within family relationships. In those days we even got involved in matrimonial counselling, family therapy and various forms of group work. We also had a community focus by supporting various community groups.

Issues of race and prejudice were apparent. Unfortunately, the link with prostitution and drugs with a few notorious black families then served to reinforce the prejudice of parents, for example, not wanting their daughters to go out with a black man. Fortunately, attitudes have changed, through education and the experience of a multi-cultural community. Many decent hardworking black families who came to England for work, and sent for their children when they had a stable address, then found problems as their children rejected their values, yet were not best served by the education system. Our work has changed from being able to recognise and understand the different cultures of different ethnic groups to challenging discrimination against black people.

The St Ann's Probation team opened its new purpose-built office in Robin Hood Chase, St Ann's, in the early seventies. Cost and design did not allow a top floor where we hoped to run a group facility. An open-plan entrance and a range of offices around the base is what we got. The focus then was not directly on offending behaviour and risk, as it would be now, but to reach particular group needs. We had a wives' group aimed at support for prisoner's wives or for women on probation. Their children had a crèche. This was a wonderful way for clients to share, support each other and learn. Nowadays, we would not have space for this, and only focus on the offender on their release from prison, and refer families to other community facilities to reduce the stigma.

I ran an adolescent girls' group to give them positive experiences outside the home. The Probation Service has long since lost this group to Social Services and the Youth Court Services. However, I still feel that the time and energy we spent working directly with individuals gave them a sense of community and achievement. I was proud, too, of the Mums' Group when we raised money in a jumble sale and even managed to sell the left-over jumble

St Ann's Probation Office Christmas party c1974. Brenda Boggild is front left and Helen Scott, front right. Photo from Phil Everett

for rags. The proceeds were spent on children's outings to Skegness and Twycross Zoo, where a heavily reclining male primate was likened to one of the women's husbands!

I'm not sure how much has changed in St Ann's today. All the media seems to emphasise is the violence and the use of guns thought to be linked to drug wars between rival gangs in the Meadows and St Ann's. In many ways these undercurrents were always there in the old St Ann's, but in different form. I worked for a further four years making Community Service[1] placements in the community and I was impressed by the resilience of many of my clients who struggled to survive against all odds. I was also impressed by the people in the community who were willing to support and supervise offenders. The community spirit of St Ann's was able to tolerate difference and change and have a common humanity.

ST ANN'S PROBATION OFFICE CLOSES

St Ann's Probation Office on Robin Hood Chase closed in spring 2001. It was put up for sale and was still for sale over a year later. The building stands alone with car park on two sides.

Ellie and I were walking by and met Anthony Williams PO and Beverley Lambert, Senior PO, sorting out and closing the office. Photo: Ellie White 2001

St Ann's Probation Office was purpose-built and opened in 1974. Photo: Ellie White 2001

---

[1] Community Service was introduced in the early 1970s as a possible alternative to a custodial sentence for some offenders, initially via pilot schemes and then more generally.

'RACE RIOTS' 1958

In *Nottinghamshire Constabulary*[1] it states: "There was a more recent example of the City's tendency to rioting in the year 1958 in the slum district of St Ann's, Nottingham, when tensions rose between the black and white population. These were fanned into aggression by the efforts of local hooligans and brought a major policing problem.

"Seen in the light of very serious problems in other parts of the country, perhaps the situation was best summarised in a Press conference comment by the Chief [Captain Athelstan Popkess], who affirmed ***this was not a racial riot:*** *The coloured people behaved in an exemplary way by keeping out of the way. Indeed they were an example to some of the rougher elements.*"

The Rt Hon Norman Manley, Premier of Jamaica, and Dr Carl La Corbeniere, Deputy Prime Minister of the Federation of the West Indies, made a special visit to Nottingham and the St Ann's Well Road area in 1958 after the disturbances with the specific objective of reassuring the West Indian migrants.

Writing of the 'race riots', the *St Ann's Church Centenary Publication 1964* stated there was 'the other side of the picture which does not make headline news'. St Ann's Church had always tried hard to welcome newcomers and the Parochial Church Council's Secretary's Report for 1958 offered a special welcome to West Indian friends. There were a 'fair sprinkling of regulars, from whom have been drawn several sides-men, a member of the PCC and a chorister'.

The disturbances were the first of their kind and the Press throughout the UK and USA reported and commented upon the events in very different ways. In 1958, there were about 2,500 West Indians and 600 Asians in Nottingham.

In a special 20th Century Edition of the ***Birmingham Post*** on June 12th 1999, it reprinted its 1958 report of the St Ann's Race Riots. "It was on a Saturday evening in August that trouble on a larger scale broke out in the St Ann's Well area," recalled Dr Chris Upton.

On the third weekend of the disturbances, the *Birmingham Post* described how Teddy boys gradually 'built up trouble'. As the mood changed: "jocularity gave way to viciousness as the occasional coloured person came along the road. Before long, groups of men were rushing along sidestreets in search of real or imaginary 'niggers'.

"The nastiest incident came in a neighbouring street. Someone (stories varied on who did it) threw a bottle and real anger flared. Windows were smashed, glass littered the street and a van full of extra police moved in to restore order. It was done without a fight but ten minutes passed before the crowd had broken up.

"It was the climax of an hour or more of most unpleasant scenes during which such coloured people as there were had behaved more like English gentlemen than

---

[1] *Nottinghamshire Constabulary* by Bill Withers [Quoin Publishing Ltd. 1989].

the noisy, mocking, swaggering troublemakers who were so proud of their white skins.

"Nevertheless, out of the confusion of insulting yells, barking police dogs and running feet, a definable pattern showed up in relation to the previous Saturday nights.

"On the first Saturday, a public house brawl, spontaneous or organised, developed into a serious fight between white and coloured people and the police called to intervene.

"On the second Saturday, the coloured people wisely stayed out of the way, so that the Teddy boys, having no-one else to fight, fought with police who were already there in large numbers.

"This Saturday, police and troublemakers changed their tactics - the imprisonment and fines imposed last week had made some impression. The police acted with firm caution, refusing to be drawn into a pitched battle. Baulked of easily found victims, the Teddy boys resorted to a noisy demonstration . . .

"The question in Nottingham now is: 'How long will this go on?' There is still much evil in these Teddy boy riots which use racial hate as an excuse."

Time Magazine, September 8th 1958, reported that fist fights "between whites and Negroes have become a common Saturday night feature in Nottingham's slum district around St Ann's Well Road, an area noted for petty crime, poverty and prostitution . . ."

Negative stereotypical terms are still used to define the district. **Time** was decidedly smug about the disturbances being foist on Britain "which clucked over racism in South Africa, gave a friendly welcome to Negro GIs and enjoyed a feeling of moral superiority over Little Rock."

Then as now, in discussing current events, outside agendas dominated. **Time and Tide** [6.9.58], however, took the high ground stating that: "Even among Trade Unionists who previously objected to working with coloured men there is likely to be a sense of shame leading to less colour prejudice . . . In Nottingham and Notting Hill, it was pure hooliganism with the Teddy Boy era arriving at its natural destination. The forces of disorder were seeking victims who could be terrorised and the coloured people were natural targets. If they had not happened to be present some other target would sooner or later have been found."

In his interview, Ralph Needham said he knew a scrap-metal merchant in Newark who helped to set the 'Race Riots' off. Another interviewee was in a vehicle caught up in one of the melees.

Life Stories – Part II

MARGARET

Born 1934

Interviewed in her home 26.1.00

I was born at Woodhouse Street off the Carlton Road, Nottingham, and lived there for the first five years of my life until I was evacuated. My family was mum and dad, two brothers and myself. I was evacuated at the beginning of the War to Costock, nine and a half miles outside Nottingham. I was very young to be away from home and I was a townie. We had running water and electricity at home and at Costock there was nothing. We managed with oil lamps and the lady of the house had to go out to the pump in the garden for water. And every drop of water had to be boiled. I sometimes think her life must have been a nightmare.

I was nine when I came back. I sometimes saw my parents during those years. There would be long waits, waiting for parents to come. We would sit in the cottage at Costock and watch for the bus. You would wait for them to get off the weekly bus, and when nobody came a particular week there was a lot of disappointment. If I hadn't had the chickenpox on the day I arrived home one weekend, I think I would still have been there! But I took ill at home and stayed there.

My first involvement with St Ann's was shortly afterwards because I went to St Matthias Church to a garden party. There was a marching band and a dancing display done by The Query Group Concert Party based at Blue Bell Hill Road and I started going along to that Concert Party. Very soon after, my grandmother died and we moved into her house at 19, Frederick Terrace off Livingstone Street, St Ann's.

There was a good chip shop on Simpkin Street, and a tobacconist newspaper shop on the corner of Simpkin Street at the top. We would come from Gordon Road and go up towards Blue Bell Hill Road and our house was just down that hill a little way. If you went into the City, you caught the No 9 bus back because it stopped on Gordon Road and you only had Simpkin Street to go up. Whereas, if you caught the No 40 or the No 47, you had to walk up that hill. Some hill was Livingstone Street or Southampton Street!

I went to Blue Bell Hill Infant School which, then, was on Blue Bell Hill itself. Later it was moved. It was on the corner of Pym Street and Blue Bell Hill. At school, my life changed. I was very interested in craftwork and there was a teacher who was wonderful, Miss Byers. Nothing was too much trouble for her. She sorted out our projects for us to do, and I took to it like a duck to water. I'm teaching now and I'm still using some of those projects. And I was only at that school for just over a year. Miss Byers woke something up in me.

One of the things we did was felt-work. We made a case in felt to put the Ration Book in. It had the Nottingham Coat of Arms on one side, machine stitched on. My mother kept that for as long as she lived. It was still in her handbag when she died. I remember Miss Byers gave us a piece of felt and she gave us a penny. We drew around the penny and made three balloons in different colours and then embroidered the strings on. I still use that idea to make Pension Book Covers now. We did basket weaving, raffia work, and we worked with wire, very fine wire. We were using the materials that were available then. We used a macramé stitch putting it into bracelets. I think this wire had been something to do with War work.

We made little brooches. Last year we were asking for memories of old crafts and this came back. You wrap wool around and tie it around in certain places to make a little girl and put eyes on.

A disappointment came. Mr Farthing the Headmaster decided I could sit the 11-plus. In those days, pupils were picked out to take it. There was a boy and myself who he felt could pass. By this time, my mother and father had split. My mum said I was the girl and had to work so there was no point in me taking the 11-plus. It was a disappointment and one that I've been able to put right in later life.

I went to the Pierrepont School and didn't like it. I was all right for the first few months and then there was a bad reaction. I'd never gone swimming and the teacher decided that I should be pushed in if I didn't jump. That was in my first term. So I didn't swim. But in the last year at school, another teacher Miss Bickers started to take us for swimming. And in my last month at school I took my Learner's Certificate and my Intermediate. So, again, it's teachers and the way subjects are approached which matters.

But I did well at handicrafts. I did smocking and made blouses. Most people made one. I made three. I made the skirt that we wore. I learned knitting very early in Costock. I can never remember not knitting. With not being so academic, I could really find my feet in the handicrafts. We did a pair of mittens in Fair Isle. I'd finished mine and helped the rest of the class with theirs!

I stayed in the Concert Party from when I joined at nine until I left at eighteen to get married. There was this old lady, she was always old, she lived in a big house called Belle View House on Blue Bell Hill Road and she ran these dancing classes. To start with I was a pupil. Miss Elliott collected people in this house! There was Celia Linton who was a co-teacher with Miss Elliott and who obviously had nowhere else to go. Bill was the lodger, who played piano for us. There was another lady who'd been in Service and had retired to Miss Elliott's house and lived at the top.

After I had problems, I was made a Ward of Court. Mum went into Mapperley [Psychiatric] Hospital and I went to live with Miss Elliott from when I was sixteen to eighteen. We were all a mish-mash, all different backgrounds but it seemed to gel. I remember those years with mixed feelings, but Miss Elliott really was an ogre! I was working and giving her my money. And, of course, the craftwork came into its own. In the attic was a little sewing-machine with a handle, so we made every bit of costume the pupils wore.

Celia was a trained dancing teacher. Miss Elliott got the bookings and saw to the cash side of things. The Concert Party went to all sorts of venues including old people's homes. We thought it was voluntary, I mean the children never got anything for it, but I have a suspicion that Miss Elliott was paid for it. There were about twenty children in the Concert Party, the youngest being around three. They were poor children from the area who just gravitated and came along.

But I enjoyed things. We would go to the pictures when there was a musical on, a Fred Astaire film or anything with dancing in, but we never went on Saturday. Celia and myself used to sit through perhaps four viewings of a particular film. And, by the time we came out, we had got dance steps to teach the children the following week. I hadn't been trained but I was on my toes tap-dancing. Incidentally, I hung up my tap-shoes when I was sixty!

Apart from being evacuated, my first holiday was to Blackpool. Miss Elliott took the children to Blackpool and the Concert Party entertained on the sands. You've heard about the round tent with everybody around and all feet coming into the middle? That's how we were at Blackpool. We entertained around for meals, and different groups fed us.

One thing that struck me in those days. There were a lot of funerals and a lot of cemetery going. People went without food to buy flowers to take to the cemetery and that always struck me as strange. It was a long trek up to Wilford Hill Cemetery at West Bridgford on the bus. My mother, when we went to my grandma's grave, would catch two buses. From the bottom of Livingstone Street, we'd go to the bus station and from there catch a bus to Wilford Hill. That nearly killed my mother: week in and week out she'd do that trek and I'd be with her.

She made me promise that I would never visit her grave. But, she said: 'when I go I'll be at the bottom of the hill'. And she was! When they opened up Wilford Hill Cemetery at the bottom, she was there. But I've never been because of what she said. This was the older generation. If they weren't at the cemetery every week, then it was wrong. And they took flowers every week. When my uncle died, my aunt lived at the cemetery. She lived in Radford and I went to see her and she had no food in. I told her he wasn't at the cemetery. I bought her a little vase and persuaded her to put flowers in the vase at home to remember him.

There was, of course, care in the community between people. Mum didn't go to work but she'd go round seeing people and she helped one old lady in Stanley Street have a bed bath. This is what she was probably doing while we were away in the War years. Everyone came to mum if there was something wrong. For example, a girl down the road got her hands in the mangle, in the cogs on the mangle. Mother just dropped everything and took Rita to the Hospital because her mother couldn't cope with it and my mother spent the rest of the day in the Hospital.

Margaret at the back of Frederick Terrace 1946. She says the blue crepe dress is the only new dress she ever had. The rest were hand-me-downs, like the shoes and the cardigan. It was made for her by Rose at Fisher Gate and worn until it fell apart. Photo: Nottingham Local Studies Library

ST ANN'S NOTTINGHAM: inner-city voices by Ruth I Johns • ISBN 0951696092

Mother never spoke to us about her feelings. I'm finding out more about her since she died. I never had a hug off my mum. There was something that was missing the whole time, and the being let down like when I was waiting for them to come to Costock on my sixth birthday.

There was this boy from schooldays who started taking an interest in me and we walked home from church. And that's when mother went completely berserk hitting me over the head with a copper stick.

Before I was sixteen, I went along to one or two classes which started at St Matthias after the War. I went along with my mum and they were doing crafts. Then we moved from St Matthias to the Congregational Church at the bottom of Alfred Street and I joined the Stanwell Players. It was a drama group and I was in the first play which the Stanwell Players did. I played Sleeping Beauty.

But with all the extra rehearsals we'd had before the day, I fell asleep on the stage and the poor principal boy tried to wake me up! The Stanwell Players are still working today but they are now the Goldsmith Players on Goldsmith Street. A lot of the members I was with all those years ago are still doing drama.

I started working for Boots on my fifteenth birthday. I was so bored. I was just sticking labels all day. When Boots came up and asked if someone could do packing, I did it. That was in the Fancy Department which was at the bottom of Alfred Street near Carlton Road. I was there about six months. I couldn't stick it. But I did learn a lot. I learnt how to pack. Then I went into machining. That was at the bottom of Robin Hood Chase, St Ann's. My Aunt got me a job at Cooper's where she worked as Chief Buttonholer.

They made little children's dresses. They said they would have kept me if they had needed another sample machinist. But they wanted quantity and I wanted quality so we parted company after about a year. This is the time I was having problems and ran away from home. Mother was mentally ill and she finished up in Mapperley and she didn't really come out. She started with Epilepsy and was only fifty-three when she died in 1956, but she looked one-hundred.

Not everyone in St Ann's was poor. When I worked for Myers Tailored Leisure Wear on Alfred Street Central for a while, I used to go home with this particular girl and she'd been on a holiday abroad. I spent a lot of time with her and they were rich.

My younger brother ran away and went into the Army. The elder brother stayed and he married, and lived back home with my mother, and had the house when something happened to my mum. Yes, it was difficult. But if you think that, when I came back from being evacuated, my parents lived in a house that belonged to the Council, a terraced house with only one bedroom that was useable. And there were parents, two boys and a girl. At nine I had to share my parents' bed and they split up very soon after. I wonder why? And then mum never really settled with dad being away. And then people keep talking about the good old days, but were they?

I married for the first time at eighteen and lived with my mother-in-law on Sneinton Road for six months and then we moved to Queen's Drive, the Meadows. I lived in St Ann's for one year later on, in a shared house on the corner of Woodborough Road and Alfred Street opposite what is now the Pakistani Centre. My husband, myself and soon to be born daughter - my first daughter who survived - had a living room, a bedroom and shared a kitchen with two other families.

The landlady, Mrs Bembo, lived on the premises and was very, very friendly. For example, when we arrived there was a fire waiting for us. I got Mrs Bembo's address from the Emergency Accommodation list. I'm still very much in touch with St Ann's. One of my daughters lives on Abbotsford Drive, St Ann's, and one of my brothers lives in St Ann's. I had four children but lost the first and last and have two daughters, aged forty-one and forty-three. And five grandsons and one great-grandson.

My first marriage broke up. He was a man who was dominant who wanted me in the house and he interfered with my daughters. You would think I'd have known. Finally, I left him. I blossomed after my second marriage, went to Clarendon College and got my teaching certificate. I was fifty when I finished. And that was good for me because both my parents thought boys should train and girls shouldn't.

My message for young people in fifty years time, same as now, is that it's never too late. It really isn't. In my first marriage, I wasn't allowed to sing. I was told I would get up on stage and make a fool of myself and I 'took it'. But I know now that it's never too late to start something. Follow your heart. I took singing lessons.

Shortly after my last baby died, I went to work at Sherwood Community Centre as Principal Assistant to Marie Lane, the Warden. That was in 1961. I worked there thirty-eight years and ended up as Acting Manager. When I realised that people were coming out of mental hospitals with nothing much for them on the outside, I fought to get a club going. It was called Chatting and it is still going. There were one or two people in that group who couldn't sit still and so Sherwood Handicrafts was born in 1976, and that's still going. I do a bit of teaching. I've spent quite a lot of my life working with people with special needs. And now I'm spending time looking at the needs of the elderly in isolation. I'm involved in the local United Reform Church and I still go out entertaining.

As kids, we didn't go far. We stayed in one area, the shops on the Street and Sycamore Rec. We didn't have many books in our home. I couldn't believe it when I went to the Library on Dame Agnes Street. You could go in and chose a book and take it home. I joined the Library. We never thought the area was rough. It wasn't a slum to us. I saw that TV programme about St Ann's [at the time of redevelopment]. It wasn't like that. It was a nice place and safe. I've now come back to live in St Ann's. This recollection was given at a late 1990s St Ann's Library Reminiscence Day. Just after this event I happened to meet a young family who have moved into the area as a conscious choice, though they had no previous connections with it.

WORLD WARS

Individual recollections include those of both World Wars. This is a brief summary, which includes some additional material.

A few of the St Annies I've met had brothers in action in both World Wars, and one had brothers who were killed in both. When families were often large, the age differences between siblings could be twenty years or more.

Nottingham was fortunate not to suffer much bombing. In St Ann's, interviewees mention Kings Hall Methodist Mission on St Ann's Well Road being hit and there was a string of bombs up Peas Hill Road. So the direct influence of the Second World War, which a lot of people still remember, was often mainly through its effect on members of the family or of friends in the Armed Services. And of rationing and civil War work.

Some women joined the Armed Services. Many did work of national importance 'on the home front' (for example, Rose Hawley). The Second World War gave many women their first chance to do challenging work and, like Florence Rhodes, they welcomed the opportunity.

At one of the six open workshops I ran at St Ann's Library (1999), I asked about the War. A considerable number of men in the area were in reserved occupations, as miners, engineers, and skilled transport workers. For example, **Cyril Trout** said he was apprenticed as a joiner to the third oldest building firm in Nottingham, Dennett and Ingles (Established 1840). They repaired the roof of the Castle after its historic fire and built the Theatre Royal. He was apprenticed 1925-30. When the War came, a Government Officer said: "You, you and you: report to Lawrence's with your tools".

"We made aircraft wooden petrol tanks. They were dangerous. An airman came and gave us a lecture. Every two weeks during the War I was checked to see if I was doing work for the War [Reserved Occupation]. After the War, I went to the Labour Exchange and to Dennett's with a green card from Lawrence's foreman. I was there until 1974."

He added: "At home, a couple of airmen were billeted on us for about a week. We thought it would be two but they were fetched away and went off to War after one".

But a substantial number of men, and some women, from St Ann's were in the Armed Services. Three of the six women whom Clare Williams, trainee midwife, delivered during her district three months training in St Ann's in 1943 had husbands in the Army or RAF.

The workshop group talked of their knowledge of American soldiers being based at Wollaton Park and Player's Sports Ground, and black American soldiers were based at a factory in Arnold at the corner of St Albans and Mansfield Road. There were also bases at Langar with Canadians and Polish servicemen. Servicemen from all these bases came into St Ann's to the pubs and for entertainment.

Harold Smith said American soldiers drank in the upstairs room of the Napoleon pub in St Ann's. He remembered fights at the Huntingdon Street Bus Depot. The black soldiers were baited by white ones who objected to black soldiers going out with white girls.

Someone recalled having a school teacher who talked of her American boyfriend. She had two children, one with black curly hair and one with straight, something which could cause comment at that time.

Reg Beal said the one minute to midnight train at Victoria Station was packed with American Servicemen.

Children who were evacuated out of St Ann's tended to come back fairly soon. Arthur Beal said when he came back there were four big air-raid shelters in the street. They were made of brick and 6" concrete. They were filled with bunks. "When we had to sleep in air-raid shelters, there was no school next day. We liked that."

Primary age schooling in both World Wars was sometimes reduced to half-day attendance with two schools 'doubling-up' because buildings were needed for other purposes.

There were shelters in many St Ann's streets but nobody has found a photo of one. I'm still hoping! Harold Smith said the shelters stayed up for a long time afterwards: "We did our courting in them!"

He said that people who had cellars in their houses had them strengthened to make air-raid shelters. Arthur Beal added that some houses had joined up cellars so you could move between them. Chickens and rabbits were sometimes kept in individual cellars. Jean Taylor said everyone on Norland Road had cellars except No 24.

Patricia Owen said there was a 'tin hut' on Hungerhill Road and her sister put on a Show for the soldiers.

As part of organised morale boosting in Wartime, Nottingham Corporation Town Clerk's Department issued *Holidays at Home* booklets making known entertainment and sporting events throughout Nottingham, including Victoria Pools, during the summer months. Children's entertainment at Sycamore Rec in St Ann's included Lilliput Follies presented by Leo and Mollie Moore with living marionettes, and Harry Kirk's Punch and Judy Shows. The Victoria Ballroom was open every evening except Sundays.

At the Arboretum, a popular nearby City park with St Annies, there were open-air variety shows, open-air dancing and bands. In 1943, introductory sessions to Square Dancing were started: a development due to American soldiers.

The proximity of the Hungerhill allotments meant that a substantial amount of food was grown nearby and some interviewees record schools using land for growing. The large number of small shops - and the informal trading and exchange arrangements in St Ann's - seemed to render it able to look after itself reasonably well in time of hardship.

The **War Memorial** from St Ann's Church went missing at the time the Church was demolished. The main War Memorial at St Andrew's Church is intact and includes St Ann's names. But, the whereabouts of a bronze War Memorial which was placed in St Andrew's Institute in 1922 is unknown.

There is a Plaque to men killed in the First World War in the now disused Canon Lewis Memorial Hall on Ransom Road. They were members of the St Ann's Church Men's Institute: W Burkitt, C Charlesworth, W Flinders, J Morgan, J Turton, F Thorpe, L Terry, Wilfrid Smith, H Sadler, William Shaw and H Wilson. The building is for sale [2001] and the Plaque has an uncertain future.

KATHLEEN SHAW

Born 1916

From a letter 2000. Kathleen Shaw, who was brought up and who taught in St Ann's, became Deputy Headmistress of Elliott Durham School when it opened in 1966 until she retired in 1976. She contributed to the 1998 book about the school's history, 'Elliott Durham and St Anns'

Nottingham was fortunate in not having the sustained bombing that some other cities had, but we had several quite severe raids and many people lost their lives. In one of them at Sneinton (not quite St Ann's but it affected me), there was an appalling tragedy of a bomb shelter receiving a direct hit and all the people inside were killed, including a large number of children whom I taught.

I was kept busy going out on Air-Raid Patrol [ARP] whenever there was an air-raid warning, which was most nights at one period. I was based at an Air-Raid Warden Centre at the bottom of Robin Hood Chase and frequently we would be walking about under a shower of shrapnel and several times with incendiary bombs falling (including one that hit the roof of our family home at 6, Robin Hood Chase. We moved there from Hungerhill Road just before the Second World War).

People formed firebomb teams and were issued with tin helmets and stirrup-pumps which were a splendid help. One very unpleasant feature of life at that time was the smokescreen. The whole length of Robin Hood Chase was lined with waist-high iron tubs full of filthy oil. When an air-raid was expected, they were lit and sent out dense clouds of black evil smelling smoke which blotted out the landscape. It was impossible to keep windows and curtains clean and we all smelt of horrible oil, but I suppose it hid us from the bombers and perhaps saved us much worse damage, although King's Hall Mission on St Ann's Well Road was hit and the area around the Cavendish Cinema.

The spirit of the old St Ann's remained strong and uncomplaining during rationing and air-raid warnings.

A couple of interviewees mentioned seeing **Zeppelin airships**, but were unable to date these childhood memories. According to Douglas Botting in Dr Eckener's Dream Machine [Harper Collins 2001], at the end of January 1916, nine Zeppelins set off to attack the industrial cities of the Midlands and the North. There were some later, not very successful, flights to try to strike at industrial and commercial targets throughout Britain. In August 1931, The Graf Zeppelin airship made a three-day flight circumnavigating Great Britain after landing at Hanworth Air Park.

JOHN BAILEY

Born 1935

Interviewed at his home 6.12.00. Photos from Christine Davies (nee Bailey)

My earliest recollection of St Ann's was when I was sixteen. I moved up from Lincolnshire with my mother and we lived with her sister, my Aunt Ethel (Et), on 76, Sycamore Road. It was one of those big three storey houses on a hill. You went in the front door straight into the front room and there was one bedroom on that floor. You went downstairs to the kitchen. You'd have your coal cellar and your other cellar where Et used to have a little cooker and then you'd got your little kitchen on the back. It was a kitchen, dining-room cum cellar. On the second floor, you'd got two more bedrooms and an attic right at the top. So it was a very big house. You used to go round to Lavender Street, down some steps and along the passageway to get to the back door. They used to go to Derry's on the corner of Lilac Street for their groceries. Ethel and Philip ran a chip shop during the war.

Auntie Vi came up about 1938. Then there was my uncle, my grandad Palmer and grandma. They came up. Vi had two lads, Donald and Alan and a daughter, Molly. They lived on Dickinson Street, St Ann's. Vi and grandma died and Et moved grandad, Donald and Alan up to Sycamore Road. Molly didn't go. She was old enough to leave home.

Some of the family was still down in Lincolnshire.

There was a little bit of unrest between mum and dad. When mother and I moved up from Lincolnshire, for me it was three in a bed. Donald was two months younger than me and Alan about three years younger. Dad moved up in 1953 after he'd sold everything up down in Lincolnshire.

The family fire-watching team at 6, Robin Hood Chase. Left to right: Kathleen Shaw, her brother Harold home on leave from the RAF, 84-year-old great aunt Nellie Harper, and Kathleen Shaw's parents. The team put out the incendiary bomb that fell on their house. Kathleen was out on ARP duty at the time. Photo from Kathleen Shaw

The top 'Rec' was opposite Et's house. My uncle had an allotment at the bottom and later my dad at the top of Hungerhill Gardens through the 'Rec'.

At first, mother worked nights at the Post Office at Christmas, then Aunt Et got her a job at Player's Number Six factory at Radford. Later she left Player's and went to the Children's Hospital and, after she finished there, she was a Home Help. Then she went to Miss Tibee's on a Saturday and you met her at that time.

Dad had worked on a farm for thirty odd years. He asked if I was going to work on the farm and I said no and he asked why not. I asked what had he ever got out of it, except a double hernia, the cartilage in his knee go and losing a thumb nail? I said I didn't want that. So I started in the Grocery trade at Long Sutton until we moved up to Nottingham.

I got a job at Arthur Barber's at New Basford. It was engineering, bomb lugs and filling plugs for bombs. Swift and Wass were on the other side of the road and they used to poach staff from Barber's and I finished up there until I went in the Forces [National Service]. There were always jobs floating both ways.

Mum moved to 79, Manning Street and she was doing her thing on Tuesday night. Ethel and mother and Phyllis, a cousin, went round different pubs in a darts team. She got a little trophy once.

After we were at Manning Street, I went up to the allotments for some brickettes to make a path at Manning Street. We had a load of brickettes up there and I got one of these haversacks for carrying them. The brickettes were like grey chocolate bars. I used to get a dozen or so in my haversack on my shoulders and take them down the donkey steps to Manning Street, lay them and go back and fetch some more.

Et moved away before St Ann's was demolished, and went to Rosegarth Walk, Old Basford. At the time of demolition, cadgers were all round the area cadging lead off the old buildings. One day my mother said: 'If it wasn't for Mrs Pritchet [a neighbour], my waste pipe would have gone because it's lead'.

I was in the Forces when I first got married and Sheila stayed in Gloucester, then we came up to Nottingham and I went back to St Ann's. That was 1958. Christine was a baby

John Bailey, while in the RAF, with his mother, Lily Bailey

. . . and with grandad Palmer

and we stayed with mother first and then we moved into Chadburn Street near the Dame Agnes pub. Mother came home and she said there was a nice little house for sale up the road. I said I'd have a look at it. It was being sold through Bray on Friar Lane and I had a look at it. It was the middle of three in a terrace. The only thing was all the toilets were in one corner of the yard, so you had the inconvenience of people going across and leaving the gates open.

The house was for sale at £700 and I got it down to about £675 and got a private mortgage. Every three months, I had to pay a bit extra for the interest to go to Mr Lorosky. I got a job in J D Marsden's, on Union Road in St Ann's, smoking bacon and getting bacon orders up ready for the shops.

Then Keith was born. The Health Visitor came and discussed sleeping space. I said I'm not putting any children in the attic. The skylight was right over the stair well. I said if necessary I shall have to go and get another house. So I went down to Bray's again, he was a nice fellow to talk to. He asked me what sort of house I wanted and I said pre-War, about £1,800 in those days back in 1962. The receptionist said why didn't I go and look at a new house in Hucknall. So we got in the Ford Popular and had a look. Going round a corner, Keith fell off the hob in the middle of the back. Next time you'll sit down I said! We saw Sid the Foreman who said everything was in except the fireplace. I said where's my cooker going? There was only a gas socket. I said I had electric so he had to dig a hole in the plaster in the kitchen and put a socket in. We're still here.

I put Chadburn Street on the market. It didn't sell. It wouldn't sell. We had a couple come and look at it. She was a white woman, he was a black fellow. They liked it and then found out it was in the margin for coming down. That was that. Eventually we got an old boy, he lived near Parliament Street bus station and he said he'd had enough of noise from the buses. He bought it at a reduced price, big reduced price, £280 cash. That was 1963. So we lost money on it but, if I'd been renting, it would have cost me that in rent.

When Pauline came along, Christine was at the Elms School on Cranmer Street, St Ann's. Sheila was in hospital after the birth. Keith was three so I'd walk Christine to School and walk Keith home. I'd wash up, get dinner ready, fetch Christine for dinner and take her back and then meet her in the afternoon. Every day they had a pudding. When Sheila came home, the first words Keith said was: 'When are you going back mum. We have pudding every day now dad is looking after us!' I took a week off without pay from the railway. I was working on the railway by then. The social people came down and said: 'why didn't you go on sick for a week'. I said I'd used my savings.

Keith was born at home and so was Pauline. That night I'd just got home because I was push-biking from Victoria Station. Sheila said fetch the midwife. It was raining cats and dogs so I got on my old bike to Cranmer Street, got back and eventually the midwife came. After checking Sheila, she said: 'give us a call if needed'. Twelve o'clock I go and fetch her again, it was still tipping it down and then the following morning we had the doctor come. He came downstairs and said he wanted a hair cut 'before we start'. I said: 'That's all we need'. I did dinner again. With me being a cook in the Forces, it was a big help.

Sheila They gave me something to help make me sleep. By the time Pauline came, I was still half asleep so he [John] had to help deliver her with the midwife.

John Then Sheila went into hospital for a scrape or something and she had to take the baby because of feeding her.

When Sheila was away, my mother was away so I used to go round to Aunt Et and she'd ask how I was coping. I said all right but I'd got some washing and she said: 'Oh, bring it round here'. She had one of those old Rolls washing machines and she'd do it for me.

John Bailey's mother, at the back of 79, Manning Street

The old St Ann's was all right. I'd walk from home to Victoria Station in ten minutes via Brighton Street, Cooper Street, Union Road. But I've not been back there for ages now. When I first came to Nottingham, my cousins said Robin Hood Chase was the select area. There used to be a cobblers at the bottom of the Chase and I went in with a pair of shoes to be repaired. His first words were: 'You're a bloody foreigner!' I said I wasn't. He said: 'Where do you come from?' I said sixty miles up the road, Spalding!

When I first came to Nottingham, they said never buy a house around the Meadows because of floods. Mother was against the move to Hucknall. I think it was dragging me away from her sort of thing. But we still went down to St Ann's on a Saturday to see her. I stood my car up because I was very upset. The Road Tax was £15 and the bloody Labour Party put it to £25 and I said I wasn't paying it. I put the car in the garage and left it there for a year. And we took the bus.

John Bailey's children (left to right) Keith, Christine and Pauline, visiting Grandma and Grandad Bailey in Manning Street not long before it was demolished

John Bailey's eldest daughter, Christine, in the garden of her Grandma Bailey's house, 79, Manning Street, St Ann's

Yes, when I left the Forces, I went to J D Marsden's, like I said smoking bacon, getting bacon orders ready, doing cooked gammons, cooked fore shoulders or fore ends as we called them. In my department, it was boning. I'd got a handful of wart come, because pigs carry wart and I had to go to the skin clinic. They sliced so many off, froze them and sliced them. My hand was very sore.

I went to work for the Railway at Victoria Station as a porter for £7 11s 6d. I was getting £8 10s a week at Marsden's. I got the job through Don Corbet who went to work on the railway after we fell out at Marsden's. There were rumours the store would be taken over. I gave a week's notice. This was about 1960. When I started on the Monday morning, the lads in the Porter Room said: 'What the hell are they setting them on for, they're closing this station down'.

I said to Sheila the other day, I don't know what the old railwaymen would do now because we did everything according to the book. It was done right. I was at the Vic [Victoria Station] about two years and then I went on parcels at the Midland Station. Just before I left Vic, we had a dog on the track. Diesels were coming in and this dog came from Beeston in front of the train. We managed to catch him and get him up on the platform, and I had to take him to the Police Station on Mansfield Road. He behaved himself lovely at the kerb. The police turned round and asked if I'd like to keep him. But living on Chadburn Street he'd be on the road again.

Working on parcels, you used to get a lot of pigeons. The baskets were filthy. But I enjoyed them. My dad used to work on the railway when he came to Nottingham. He started as a porter and then went to left luggage. When they were demolishing Abbotsford Drive, St Ann's, on the way home he got hit and it was his old cheese cutter hat from the railway that saved him. But he was hurt, I think that started his lung cancer.

On the station one day, a big fellow asked me to go over and get this Alsatian dog out of the brake van. It was an Alsatian going to a Melton Mowbray police trainer. The big fellow said he was savage. I got a mailbag off one of the mailmen and pushed it over my arm so if, anything, the dog would get the bag with a biscuit tin in it and not my arm. My method got him out as good as gold. He was hyperactive. We got him to the parcel office. When it came to getting him on the nine-fifteen train at night it was back to number one again because they'd been upsetting him. But we managed to get him on.

If you worked your rest day, your wages were about £14, otherwise it was £11 10s.

I moved to Blanchards, then Frank Bonsor, then Dowty Mining. Then there were the power strikes and we worked a three-night week. You went in eight o'clock at night and came out eight in the morning. The dole made up your money. Freddie Fox was the foreman. I was told I had to have probation. Three months, six months went by and the boss said it's an ordinary storeman's job now. The next week, I found out the previous man had an extra £5.

I found out Boots was advertising and I got a job there in 1973 for £18 plus £3 shift pay. There wasn't much difference between them and the railway. I got into D80 at Beeston. I had one or two skirmishes over the years but you will always get somebody who . . . and you've got friction. But I enjoyed the warehousing itself as I told on my retirement except for the last eighteen months at Ilkeston, which I hated because it was to do with returns.

I was driving forklift trucks for over 30 years at Boots.

I knew John Bailey's mother, Lily Bailey [1909-1993], from the time I started Family First Trust in 1965. She worked part-time as a cleaner for the community and office space at The Croft, Alexandra Park. When I was on holiday, she stayed in my accommodation as the 'responsible' resident person, in a project housing young mums, to deal with out-of-hours queries and emergencies. She sometimes looked after my three children and became a loved granny person who made rice pudding with a crusty top (my daughter's favourite) and apple pie (favourite all round). I stayed closely in touch with her for the rest of her life, after life took me elsewhere and she retired.

Her grand-daughter Christine [who took a History Degree as a mature student] transcribed many of the interview tapes for this book. When she was younger, she and my daughter, Naomi, went on youth activity holidays together. Christine and husband Andy have two daughters, Kathryn and Kirsty.

At the time of St Ann's demolition, I did a 'sit-in' at the Housing Department as a protest at the length of time it took the City Council to offer Lily and Joe Bailey an allocation. They were still in their house in Manning Street long after almost everyone else had left or been moved from the street. Houses were boarded up and vandalised, water was running out of the mains and Joe (as John said above) was injured by a hard object thrown from a disused property. At night it was ghostly. They were given £50 site value for their house, which was beautifully cared for, and allocated a Local Authority maisonette on Highbury Vale. Like other displaced home owners, they became rent payers for the rest of their lives: a poor reward for people who worked very hard for their independence and had completed payments on their own home

---

At a bus stop on Woodborough Road, St Ann's, in June 1992 there was only one other person, an elder Afro-Caribbean man. The bus was a long time coming so we chatted. After the usual pleasantries, he talked about his children and withdrew a large photo from a plastic bag. It was of a daughter, in her twenties, dressed as a barrister. He also showed me four smaller similar photos and said he was going into town to get frames for them. She lived in St Ann's all her life, and had been educated at Catholic State schools until going away to study at Cambridge University. She was currently working in Manchester. He said: 'As a child, she was always working or at church. She sailed through 12 '0' Levels and 6 'A' Levels. She always wanted to be a barrister. She always studied and we worked hard for her. We spent a few days in Cambridge which was great, mixing with everybody.'

St Ann's Nottingham: inner-city voices by Ruth I Johns • ISBN 0951696092

SHEILA MANNERS

(nee Smith)   Born 1936

Written contribution [2000] and letters. All photos from Sheila Manners who was brought up at 31, Festus Street, St Ann's

Unlike the present generation who seem obsessed with spending whether they can afford it or not, I grew up during years of rationing and hardship and so it was only at Christmas, and possibly Easter, that parents made every effort to buy those special treats that bring a smile to children's faces. It didn't take much, believe me!

Mum and dad in the backyard of Festus Street in the early 1950s

This photo was taken with my dad's old second-hand box camera in our Festus Street back yard in the early 1950s. Left to right, Pamela Woodfield, Brenda Miller and my sister Kathleen Weston (nee Smith)

In the those dark days of War and for a long time afterwards, there was also the harshness of outside toilets, bare kitchen floorboards relieved only by hand-pegged rugs, a scullery where mod cons consisted of a sink and a cold water tap, an old gas stove and a built-in copper that you lit a fire underneath on washday. I now realise just how lucky we (supposedly deprived) children were.

There were cobblestone streets on which to play in summer and winter (parked cars were as rare as unpunished misdemeanours). Happiness for me was playing rounders, marbles, pic-cards, hopscotch and best of all whip and top. The latter was invariably bought at Easter or, if preferred, a shuttlecock and battledore. Oh the exhilaration experienced when belting a top up and down the pavement. It was known as the window breaker! We were lucky on Festus Street, St Ann's, because a high brick wall ran up the top of the street from opposite us. So playing whip and top posed no threat to the windows of the houses situated at the top of steep steps placed at intervals on that side of the street.

Again, in sharp contrast to enduring freezing cold bedrooms and early morning treks with my brother Eric (often in snow and ice) pushing a wheelbarrow in order to bring back a supply of coke from the London Road coke yard, there was also the inside of the Cavendish and New Empress cinemas and sometimes the Nottingham Empire. Because treats and goodies were not showered on us, they were all the more enjoyable. My sister Kath was eight years younger than me and too young to go with us. She still lives in St Ann's with her husband and sons.

This is my mum. Doesn't she look lovely? Actually, she's wearing my shoes. I wanted her to look perfect c1953

Most children were required to do some chore or other although, apart from being expected to fetch barrow loads of coke, I don't recall anything set down as a must in our house. The strange thing is, I would often set to and black lead our kitchen fire grate as a surprise for mum when she got back from one of her early morning cleaning jobs. The inner-glow I felt on seeing mum's face was equal to the shine on the fire grate. Both my mum and dad worked hard. My dad was a general labourer working with timber.

Another delight for me was to go with my dad to the second-hand bookshop on Wheelergate in the City Centre.

This was taken outside our home on Festus Street early in 1953. I'm on the left with my best friend, Sheila Parker (nee Merriman), of Twells Street, off St Ann's Well Road

From left to right is our friend George Hallam from Westville Street (top of Festus Street), me and Eric, my brother c1953. Again, the photo was taken with my dad's old box camera

Even today I am in seventh heaven when in the midst of old and dusty second-hand books. Sunday picnics were often taken to the Trent Embankment or Nottingham Castle, also the Arboretum and the Forest [Recreation Ground]. I can still see those soaring kites that dad used to make us. He loved kite-flying and my children have vivid memories of going out with their grandad to fly those much treasured kites of his.

Mod cons are not to be sneered at, nor the availability of an assortment of food and clothes, but I believe we have

This is our backyard in the mid-1960s once the old mangle/wringer had gone. Dad set about making the little garden

lost a lot. In order to feel safe and secure, young and old need rules and boundaries by which to live. Freedom is what young men and women died for in two World Wars. My dad, an orphan at the age of five, would often say to me: 'Give folk an inch and they will take a yard'. Looking around at all our security systems now in place, hidden cameras everywhere, what have we gained? Certainly not freedom.

We didn't have much when we were young but, by and large, we felt safe to walk about. Old folk didn't get beaten up for a few shillings and, as for children wrecking a church or school, they wouldn't dare . . .

My son Glenn Victor at Grandma and Grandad's house, 31, Festus Street. He is in his new school uniform for Grammar School 1968

BROTHER AND SISTER

JAN JARVIS
Born 1939 and

KEN MESSOM
Born 1941

A family gathering at 31, Festus Street in 1969. My daughters, Marie Lynn and Lita Ruth, and my mum who had just come in from the scullery. How did our parents achieve what they did?

My parents, Dora Kathleen Smith (nee Hollinshead) and Albert Ernest Smith at a family gathering in the front room at 31, Festus Street, St Ann's

Festus Street March 1972. It shows the wall Sheila Manners refers to. The arrow points to the only house in the row still lived in. This was an appalling situation which people faced in many streets, sometimes for many weeks, before being rehoused. Photo: Nicholson Photo Archive

Brother and sister interviewed in Jan's home 13.9.00. And conversations. Jan and her husband, John, built two of their homes themselves, the first at Thyra Court in 1969 and in 1973 at Kent Road, Mapperley. Jan and John are moving to Bantry Bay, County Cork, Ireland after retiring [2002] and will be living within fifty miles of where Jan's grandmother's family came from to St Ann's. Ken has moved to Bantry Bay since the date of the interview. Brother and sister will live next door to each other. All photos from Jan Jarvis and Ken Messom

Jan. I was born in the middle of St Ann's on Lotus Terrace but I can't remember anything about it. My first memory of the area was 41, Dame Agnes Street.

Ken. I was born at 41, Dame Agnes Street.

Jan. We didn't know that we lived in St Ann's! We lived near the Woodborough Road. We always caught a 31 bus from what was then called Slab Square [City Centre Market Square]. On the front of the bus it said Mapperley so we thought we lived in Mapperley! We had brothers who are

Jan and John Jarvis, aged sixty-one, taking a short break in Connemara, Ireland, while planning their 'retirement' June 2000

older than us. We lived on the edge of Hungerhill Gardens with wide-open green spaces. Dad had an allotment there. Then there was a top and a bottom 'rec' full of trees and green grass and bushes. Dame Agnes Street ran parallel to the old Sycamore Road which is now called Hungerhill Road.

Ken. The original Dame Agnes pub was just about where we lived on the other side of the road. That's where I met my wife. She was the landlord's daughter. I was nineteen and Vicky (nee Tibbot) was fifteen. I think they came from Liverpool.

Jan. Our mum was married when she was twenty-three to our dad. He had been married before and already had two sons, Billy the firstborn and Herbert. His wife had died. He was in the trenches in the First World War when he was sixteen and said he was seventeen to get in the Army. And there was no pretence he was doing it for King and Country. He said: 'Jan you went in for a warm overcoat, boots on your feet and something in your belly'. He used to say his mum was ignorant, meaning lacking in knowledge, because she had these portraits of King and Country all around the sitting room, and all of her seven sons in the War. Four of them died and she was very proud of these sons.

Ken. Very warm overcoats. I do remember those being on the bed from time to time.

Jan. He used to play with us a lot and he was unusual in his time. He was a man who would be able to sew and cook really well, really look after us materially. He could cobble your shoes. He used to let me sit and comb his hair and we used to do a lot of funning about with my dad.

Mum had five children. Eric [1933-93] was the eldest and he's now died. Then Iris [1935-37] a little girl who died of pneumonia when she was two. Mum always maintained Iris died of a broken heart. In those days children were isolated in hospital behind glass screens and they wouldn't let mum go to her. She was straining to get at mum, crying and straining. Mum didn't see her again. She was dead next time. She said she never came to terms with it. She never had a photo of Iris but she kept a little photo cutting from the newspaper for years because it looked like her.

Jan and Ken's dad working in the 'Gun Factory', Royal Ordnance Factory in The Meadows. He is on the far right c1944

David was born in 1937, the year Iris died. Then me and then Ken.

Ken. Dad was a painter and decorator but he also did building from time to time. It was seasonal work so he would be laid off from time to time and he'd switch to something else. He did seem to us to be streets ahead of most men. He didn't have a very good education and was one of eleven. His name was William Messom. He lived on Meadow Grove, right where the Lady Bay Bridge across the Trent is now. Mum was one of ten.

Jan. He was the best philosopher I've known. He used to say things I thought were outrageous like: 'Parenting is the hardest job in the world and you don't get any training for it. You should have a ragged doll to practice on'. Almost every day through life, there's something that he said. Sound as a drum.

He was the youngest of this load of brothers. And his mum made him this snap sack, or hanging basket thing, which would go round his neck. It was an easy walk to the Cattle Market. He was very little and he used to crawl under the barrows. A couple of onions would drop and he'd put them in his bag. And then a couple of carrots. And he'd get his bag full of vegetables and get them home. His mum would make a soup of them. He was feeding the family.

Mum with us both at the Embankment, Trent Bridge 1946

Ken. He carried on doing that a lot later. He used to take us all fishing in the Trent. Whatever he caught, he'd bring them home. Some were bream and gudgeon which aren't recognised as food. He used to talk about living off the fat of the land. Anything that was going, even potatoes in the fields, he'd dig up. And cabbages and things. He'd gather blackberries.

ST ANN'S NOTTINGHAM: inner city voices *by Ruth I Johns* • ISBN 0951696092

Jan. He was before his time in the way he used to play with us. Sitting down and playing marbles, Beetle Drive and dominoes: all the early number work. And the darts board we had up in the kitchen.

Ken. He'd control us strictly when we were playing darts. You had to add up quickly.

Jan. When he met John [Jan's husband] for the first time, he said: 'By God, I thought I could move fast, but that lad can move faster'.

Ken. Once dad was working in Clumber Street, in the City Centre, when a couple of Shipstone Brewery horses were running without a driver and with a barrel on the cart. He climbed down the ladder and jumped on the cart and stopped the horses. He didn't make a big deal of it. When he was in the Army he was in charge of horses. A few weeks later he got a reward, several guineas, and a letter from Captain Popkess, the Chief Constable. I remember him sitting there saying: 'Well, fancy Popkess writing to me'. Apparently some woman had witnessed the whole thing and wrote about this brave man to the Constabulary.

We had a backyard with a little garden. He was a good gardener. There were Lilies of the Valley and Hollyhocks.

Jan. There was a pond in there with newts and rocks and we had a fish in every corner of the house in Aquariums. Every bit of it was alive and it was such a natural learning environment. We thought everybody lived like that.

We had four bedrooms. It was one of those houses that had a basement kitchen that went off the yard, but the front room was off the street. There were lots of stairs. We also had a cellar that was level with the kitchen but up three steps. When we all moved into this house the cellar steps must have been worn down because dad made a lovely pattern on them after filling them in with concrete or something. I'd go in there and he'd got all these toys laid out, and he had all the tools laid out. I knew all about pliers and the difference between pliers and pincers, all about screws and nails, the big hammer and the little hammer. All the learning work I do with families now was there. Even with the mashing of tea, it was two tea and four sugars!

He had this thing under his bed, an Army chest that he obviously came out of the War with. In it, there would be a 'housewife' with all these little compartments with scissors and cottons. It opened up. And there was this little tin that had chocolate in and it was supposed to give you energy. He'd give us a little bit of this chocolate and we'd jump about pretending we were full of energy. Of course, it was once part of his rations.

He used to tell us stories about the First World War. As you know, our family don't have trouble with talking! Some men could never talk of their experiences. He was in the Battle of the Somme near the front. He got news that the next brother up from him, Sam, was in the next unit just a couple of miles away. He asked permission to go and see him and was refused on grounds of danger. But my dad went anyway! Somebody obviously shopped him. His field punishment was to be tied to the wheel of a gun, crucifix

fashion, and left for twelve hours. But a big battle must have happened and they forgot about him and when they took him down he was stiff. They thought they'd killed him. He could tell you all that. And told us he slept with a nanny goat in a barn in France. He cuddled up for warmth while he was getting over pneumonia.

He said: 'I even shaved in my own water' and I didn't realise this meant his own urine! We were all very politically aware very early on. My oldest brother Bill [born 1924] from my dad's first marriage was a very intelligent man. He went on to be a pacifist and instead of going into the Army, he went down Gedling Pit as a Bevin Boy miner. Then he won a scholarship to Ruskin College, Oxford, and went on to lecture in Maths and Economics at Middlesex Further Education College.

By the time Bill was eighteen he was a communist, when communism was an intellectual big thing. Our house was full of these highly intelligent, very angry young men. John Peck[1] was a regular visitor. Pat Jordan was another. They looked a bit the same with berets on at an angle, looking rakish. And sandals and beards and all of that. We thought that was normal!

Our brother Bill, aged 24, in London 1948

Ken. When we used to go through Market Square, we'd often see Bill on his soapbox. He would always have a large crowd around him. But we weren't proud of him at the time. I remember feeling quite embarrassed. We used to say 'Bill's spouting again!'

Jan. Yes, if anybody from school saw him, I'd 'die'! But dad was there: 'That's my boy'.

Bert, dad's second son [1926] has stayed in St Ann's all his life[2]. He was a builder before he retired. He and Mary, his wife, are well-liked and respected and have five sons.

---

1   John Peck has published his autobiography, *Persistence: the story of a British Communist* [J H Peck, 21, Highbury Vale, Bulwell, Nottingham NG6 9AT. 2001]
2   Sadly he died in 2000. *Jan.*

We don't know very much about dad's dad apart from the fact that he was educated. He was at a little school on Carlton Road called St Luke's. He passed to go to that school. His mum couldn't write her name but he had that chance.

When I was a girl I was going to write a book about my dad, there was so much to talk about. But mum [1910-82] was the strong one. Her name was Blanche Christina (nee Cook). It's hard to remember that we ever thought she wasn't the strong one.

Ken. One thing we haven't mentioned about dad is that he could go to the pub and have a few pints and come back a different man. He wouldn't be happy necessarily, would he? Obviously he was suffering from depression, but he hid it most of the time until he'd had a few drinks.

Jan. I can remember coming home and he was sitting in front of the television. He was quite old. I came in grumbling about some stupid bus conductor who had made a poor man with boots and haversack go upstairs rather than inside. She said: 'In, up there or off'. I was so angry. I came in full of that. And he said: 'I don't want to hear about it, sit down there and you watch this'. It was the Aberfan disaster. He was crying. He'd been on his own all afternoon. There were times when he actually said: 'I wish I was blind, deaf and dumb and then wouldn't suffer as much'. I felt terrible.

Mum was working. My dad was thirteen years older and that makes a big difference as you grow older. He was a charmer when he was young. He met my mum at twenty-three. She lived at that time on St Stephen's Road in Sneinton. She was still a virgin. This man literally walked past her and then decided to come and walk beside her. And that was it. He did all the running as men did in those days. When I was older she told me he was a very exciting man sexually. As she got to know him, he said he would like her to meet his son. He didn't say 'sons'!

Mum and dad were walking along with Billy who turned round and said: 'Aye dad, when's our Herbert coming back?' She said: 'Who's Herbert?' Herbert was three. Mary, their mother, had died.

Eric was born in November and they didn't get married until August.

Ken. I didn't know that Jan!

Jan. Sorry Ken! Eric was born in Castle Donnington. Mum loved that rented cottage in Castle Donnington. I'm not sure why they went from there to Long Eaton. Something happened and they had to do a moonlight flit for some reason. David was born in Long Eaton. If we now think of mum, this is the most staggering story. I'll never get over it. The day of Iris's funeral, this little girl of two, there was a knock on the door and a woman stood there asking for Bill Messom. Mum said they were like two Toby jugs, my mum was a few weeks off having David and there was this younger woman, pregnant.

A separation must have happened at that point because my mum came to her mum in St Ann's after David was born. The break in their marriage must have been at a time when she couldn't cope with any more. But I'm here and Ken's here to prove they got back together!

Dad obviously had to pay maintenance to that woman. We all had jobs to do on Saturday mornings and the jobs depended on how big you were. One of Ken and my jobs was to walk to the Post Office on Woodborough Road, St Ann's, and buy a postal order and registered envelope. I think it was for fifteen shillings and it went to St James Street in Derby, a solicitors. It was mum giving the money out, not dad. He couldn't handle money, he was absolutely hopeless. She was strong, though she was totally un-sensational about everything. After my dad died, she wrote via the solicitor to his 'illegitimate' daughter, Glenys, because she felt his daughter deserved to know about her father. Glenys and my mum became close friends. Glenys was brought up by her mum, who never married, and her mum's sister.

Mum's dad died when she was eighteen from the effects of the First World War. She remembered her mum being interviewed by some official who asked her: 'Can you say your husband's death was wholly due to the War?' And she said 'no'. And my mum at eighteen thought that a disaster because her mum never got any payments. And she had nine children and mum the eldest.

Yes, my grandmother came from County Cork in Ireland, from a genteel background, very Irish. She was called Christine like my mum. Her surname was Manley. She was blind by the time she was fifty, so was her brother. Maybe something in their genes.

Ken. I could never understand what she was saying . . . the accent. I do remember her saying: 'Well, you can't go unless I give you a few coppers'. And she got her purse out.

Jan. Mum said we must never let our grandma know that we knew she was blind. She would touch my head and if I had a little pom-pom hat on or something she'd sit down and wait a little and then say: 'That's a nice hat!' But at one point I must have said she was blind. And she said: 'I can see lovely pictures in my head'. So it was never frightening.

Grandma Christine and her brother Michael Manley married a brother and sister. Christine and Michael's father was one of the survivors of the battle in South Africa, the battle of Rorke's Drift, where 5,000 people met the Zulu warriors and they were saluted by the Zulus eventually for their tenacity.

Mum worked at Bradbury's Paper Bag Factory across the road. She filled those hours in when we were at school. If I came home with homework, she knew the meaning of every word. Where this learning came from we never knew.

Ken. I often think how she could spell. Where did that come from? She could spell words I wouldn't have thought she could have come across.

Jan. She was the one who managed the money. As we said earlier dad could poach and cook, knit, darn socks. Our fire would be right up the chimney so we'd be surrounded by warmth and good food and never feel deprived in any way, shape or form. The country was there at the weekend because we'd go fishing. The 'Rec' was just down the road and we'd have freedom.

Ken. We had one of the first cars in the area. It was a 1937 Hillman.

St Ann's Nottingham: inner-city voices *by Ruth I Johns* • ISBN 0951696092

Kitty and friends who worked with mum at O J Bradbury's Paper Bag Factory which was opposite our house on Dame Agnes Street

Christmas Party at O J Bradbury's Paper Bag Factory c1947. Our mum is fourth in from the left

O J Bradbury's Works Outing c1948. Our mum is fourth from the left, middle row

Jan. We wouldn't have had a car had it been left to dad. Mum didn't earn that much but was incredibly good in managing.

Ken. And we had one of the first televisions because we watched the Coronation and our house was packed with everybody.

Jan. We weren't materialistic, these things sort of happened around us. We were the family in the yard that

Our mum and brother Eric posing in our first family car 1952

everyone came to visit, we were the ones that had this car to go out to Gunthorpe and Sawley, we were the ones that had this garden full of plants, and we were the ones, you and I and Dave, who people would call on to do babysitting, to go and help at the allotments, because we could be relied on. We had a lot of self-esteem. We always felt secure. When we started going to Youth Club, the youth leaders used to come around and talk to dad.

Dave, Ken and I delivered papers for Mrs Bestwick who ran a local newsagents shop on Dame Agnes Street. She always had a dewdrop on the end of her nose and wiped it with her hands which had mittens on! I'd do Alexandra Park and the Mapperley customers quite often. She knew we were reliable.

The boys from the Gordon Boys' Home on Cranmer Street, St Ann's, went to school in their uniform which made them very conspicuous. They had to march everywhere, to meals, to bed and so on. It was run on the Army model. One day, one of the boys came home to tea and clung to our mother's skirt and didn't want to go back. She told him he could come again.

John and I got married from Dame Agnes Street in 1962. The wedding was at John's local church, St John's, Bakersfield.

John Jarvis and Jan on their wedding day June 21st 1962

Ken. And I married Vicky in 1966 at St Peter's Church, Radford, Vicky's local church.

Jan. Dad was quite ill by then. He'd had bronchitis all his life. Ken and Vicky were living in South Africa. It was coming up to the time of St Ann's demolition and dad couldn't have coped with being housed down The Wells Road where the big flats were.

Because dad had this chest and because it was bracing at Skegness we had many family holidays in Anderbury Creek in the sand dunes.

Ken. There was a railway carriage converted into a cottage called the Robin Hood. We didn't always go in the school holidays, because I suppose it was possibly cheaper in term.

Jan. It was wonderful. We'd have three-week holidays and we all had a whistle in case we got in danger.

Ken. My memories are those beautiful white sand dunes and this cottage, even though it was a carriage, nestled in the dunes and marram grass. But in 1953, the floods came and washed it away.

Jan. Then we stayed in this sort of bungalow. Dad thought caravans were crap. But when there was just him and mum, he got a bit drunk one night and was talking to somebody in Chapel St Leonard and together they bought a caravan. By the time they moved from Dame Agnes Street, they had two caravans.

1958 at the Social Club, Chapel St Leonards. We had a couple of caravans there and dad (left) and mum (next to him) used to take Gran and Aunt Amelia (far right) there for long weekends

When it was time for them to move from Dame Agnes Street, John and I went on a search of the area and on Querneby Road we found a terraced house for £650 which had a bigger yard and back garden than they had and a bathroom. Dad died before they'd been there a long time. But he loved it.

Ken. We never felt deprived at Dame Agnes Street. When you consider we were still living there when we were all going to work. There were six of us.

Jan. Mum used to get up and get the sandwiches ready and she'd make parcels of sandwiches for all of us. Where did she dry the washing and all those things?

Ken. Six people getting up and we'd wash in the sink in the scullery. We'd all get washed and dressed and out without any argument.

Jan. And we'd look smart.

Ken. The washing was done in a dolly tub and mangle. I can still hear the sound of the ponch and the ratchet on the mangle.

Jan. We got a washing machine - a Hoovermatic - in 1957. Before that, sheets and towels went to the Bendix place on Beverley Street, bag wash.

Ken. Twenty pounds in weight wasn't it? That would be our job occasionally.

Jan. I used to have my bath on a Thursday night. I'd stay in and wash my hair as well. You'd get the tin bath in and it was no big deal. You'd boil enough water and you'd sit there!

Ken. And there'd be a fire roaring beside the bath.

Jan. Mum's sister Lillian was younger and I was a bridesmaid at their wedding at St Catharine's Church. They lived in a new Council house with a bathroom and they had a pantry and all of these posh things. When I stayed there, there was something about it and I'd want to go home. They didn't have warm beds and their fires were always smoked and no flames, their food felt different. It wasn't really a treat staying there. And yet it was modern and had all these facilities. It wasn't comfortable.

Jan as bridesmaid (aged 6) when Auntie Lillian (her mum's sister) married Uncle Frank in 1945. Left to right: Auntie Alice, Frank's sister; Mrs Ward, Frank's mum; Albert, Frank's brother; Winnie, Auntie Dorothy's friend; ? ; Bridegroom and Bride; Uncle Ted, mum's brother; Auntie Dorothy, mum's sister; my granny (mum's mum); my mum aged 36

Ken. I remember not wanting to be there.

Jan. When we were all working from home, we all went into office work - and in your case apprenticeship - which was unusual in those days because most people went into factories. Ken went to Huntingdon Secondary School. I only went to Sycamore School for a short time before going to the Technical School. I worked at Viyella. David went into office work.

The Technical School was on the back end of Victoria Primary School in Bath Street. It was a pilot scheme. A

Nottingham teacher, Miss Norris had a clear idea that Nottingham City, this textile City, ought to be able to produce people with the practical, technical ability who would go into the textile industry. It was a good principle. We had this badge with latch needles and whatever. We had to give up our art at that point and instead do technical design work.

Ken. And you had a picture in the Royal Academy before I did!

Jan. We learnt to weave on really big looms and learned lace design. We gave up history and geography and did social studies, so it was all like posh different ways, a superb experience. The teacher didn't stand out in front as in secondary schools, and it was not just women teachers. Teachers were Mr Boudler and Patrick Sales. Teachers sat amongst you and invited you to talk and share experiences. In each class there were eight boys and sixteen girls. It was quite expensive I guess, more expensive than your average secondary school. It only lasted eight years but long enough for me to work my way through and come out the other end.

Most of the people in my class, who had great fun at the Technical School, moved into Viyella and we didn't go into design as was intended but into office work. We were still with the lads we were with in school. They'd be in the Mail Room, when we were with Mrs Tanfield and we'd go to the Mail Room in our best frock!

I started there at fifteen and a half. I knew if I went to sixteen at school, I'd got to start doing exams, that's more serious, so a whole bunch of us moved to Viyella. Mrs Tanfield was a wonderful woman and she died of breast cancer when I was twenty. I was heartbroken. She shaped us and we were split up. Two of us were juniors in this office. That's where I met Marge and Theresa and all these lovely friends I still have today.

I left Viyella when she died and Theresa and I went to the Civil Service, at the Depot at Chilwell. At that time all the numbers of every vehicle in the British Army were being put on to computer. We were doing the punch cards, it was very early computer stuff. I couldn't get over how people skived in the Civil Service. There were Unions telling people to go slow and we used to say if we went slower we'd stop altogether! I used to go home and tell dad he'd got it wrong about unions. It wasn't like it was in his day when unions were necessary, and we'd sit and argue.

It was 1961 and I was in the Civil Service and I've never seen waste like it. The boss would say we've got to do this and this, and then there was lots of chatting around machines and falling out and there was wasting of public money to the point I could not believe it. John had been in the Forces [National Service] and we were married in 1962 and I stayed there until 1967. We moved up to Thyra Grove and we were going to adopt a baby and I needed to get used to the idea of being at home before having the baby. John had been working at Hopewell's and by then he was an independent interior decorator.

Ken. David worked at Brown Brothers, Talbot House. I was an apprentice compositor with Wilsons Printers on Mount Street. The plan was that I was going to be a

John and Jan Jarvis with their two children John Paul and Becky c1973

lithographic artist. One of dad's jobs used to be involved in repairing printing machines and he got to know this man who worked at Formans on Hucknall Road. He said he'd organise an interview for me to be an apprentice lithographic artist. I took loads and loads of drawings and mum was all dressed up. The man said the drawings were very, very good and the paintings were very good, but that at the moment it would be difficult for me to be a lithographic artist. But I would be suited to be a compositor. I can remember at the time thinking I don't want to do that.

It was the biggest mistake. I did a seven-year apprenticeship and then worked for a firm called LeButts on Peas Hill Road in St Ann's and then the Ruddington Press which published many magazines. The man who ran it, Guy Waite, lived at Colston Basset Hall, and he said: 'Why is this man a compositor?' And from then I went into the Editorial Art Department, and that was a good start. I was about twenty-three. I had to change Unions from the National Graphical Association to SLADE [Society of Lithographic Artists, Designers and Engravers] and I've been an artist ever since. I'm now working from home, painting, including cards.

Jan. Dad was so proud that his daughter had made it. Mum and dad were living on Querneby Road and John would sometimes employ him when he could. Dad had an allotment on Hungerhill Gardens and say to the other gardeners: 'I'm working for my son-in-law'. He kept the allotment on to the end. He grew flowers - Dahlias, Sweet Peas, Carnations, Chrysanths, Roses. And veg - tomatoes, onions, carrots, lettuce, cucumber. And fruit – apples and pears.

Ken. He'd been to his allotment on the day he died in 1968. He was born in 1898.

Jan. John Paul was six months old. Dad loved him and it was sad. And he would have loved Becky.

Ken. I came home from South Africa for the funeral. I remember this policeman knocking at the door, they wore caps pulled down and sunglasses. He said: 'I've got some bad news from your brother Jan'. And I'd been steeling myself for a big argument over some traffic things when I saw the policeman. This policeman hadn't any skills at all.

I was in South Africa working for four years. At first the political things didn't get to us, but gradually it did and after four years we'd had enough. And Vicky and I wanted a family and thought that was not the place to be.

We had two boys, Christopher and Timothy. As I said earlier, Vicky lived opposite me on Dame Agnes Street when we got to know each other. Then her parents moved to a place in Hyson Green. We were going out together for

Ken and Vicky

Left to right: Vicky and Ken's son Tim with Bess the dog; Vicky and Ken; their elder son Christopher; Dave (with Fred the dog) and Eric, brothers of Jan and Ken

six years. I sometimes worked as a barman there and she was a waitress. Vicky became a social worker. She was incredibly fit and a really lovely person.

She died eighteen months ago of CJD [Creutzfeld-Jacob Disease], not the new variant one but the sporadic type. It was, still is, totally shattering. It's difficult to explain to people how you feel. People try hard to imagine how it must be, but I don't think they ever get it right. Since Vicky died, I don't want to be living in our cottage. I don't want to be seeing the villages where we were looking for a new home. Vicky wanted a big garden.

Friends have been wonderful since Vicky died. I've been on holiday with people and we go out to dinner. Every year I go on a fishing holiday with four male friends. We all fly-fish and usually go to Scotland but this year we went to Ireland. I came back and phoned Jan who said she and John were thinking of a cottage in Ireland.

Jan. We're going to be retiring soon and, you know John, he always wants to be building something. This plan has grown and we're going to get a place in the West of Ireland. We've been surfing the net for details and we've been over several times. We'll miss friends, colleagues and family but they will come out. The place will be big enough. In Ireland, the sort of place we get can't be sold on in order to develop. You can only sell it to family or leave it to family, which is great. Ken will have something near or attached on one end.

Jean Paul is married to Lynne and he works as a web site designer. Becky is a singer and she and her partner Rob[3] have a little girl, Jessica. Ireland is going to be wonderful for all of them.

Ken. What would I pass down for fifty years time? I would find it hard at present to come up with a good answer for that. Vicky and I were so close, and then suddenly total devastation.

Jan. If I focus on St Ann's, I would say we had a very rich life. In our upbringing, we were fortunate in every possible way. I take on board what Ken's saying at this moment. Life takes unusual turns. With hindsight, I realise how special our home was. The layers you get as kids when growing up are what hold you up later.

My professional life has been spent working with special needs kids. I was trained through the nursery nurse route. I remember dad coming down to the 'rec' when I was six. He was calling us in at night. We were always the first to be called in. Ken and Dave and I were playing Dobby. There was a kid who was deaf and dumb and bigger than us and we'd run away from him in a 'different' kind of way and scream at him.

At home, dad gave us a severe dressing down. 'How dare you. Can you imagine how he feels?' I couldn't bear my dad feeling sad over something I'd done. He said: 'Don't you ever let me see you do that again'.

In 1973, I started training as a Nursery Nurse at Waverley Collage, Nursery Nurses Training Centre, on Forest Road, Nottingham. I did my first year's practical

---

3   Becky and Rob married on Valentine's Day 2001 and have two children Jessica and James.

work at the Nursery in Huntingdon Infant and Nursery School, St Ann's, when Mrs Dexter was the Head. Mrs Dexter kept in touch and offered me a post in 1975. From 1979, I worked with autistic children at Sutherland House School for Children with Autism, founded by Dr Elizabeth Newsom. I was a Nursery Nurse with added responsibilities for looking after volunteers and students. In 1987, I became a Portage[4] worker. I love the work as you are only there if parents want you to be. Our team is multi-disciplinary. We need skills more than 'bits of paper'.

Jan is Team Leader of the Portage Early Education Team, Nottingham City Local Education Authority. Jan and John are school governors at St Ann's Infant and Nursery School

---

4   Named after Portage, a town in the USA where a Home Visiting Service started.

Carnival Day at Mablethorpe c1952. Jan and Ken's mum and dad seen standing in front of the crowd nearest the left-hand back of the car

A few more photos from the family photo album

Fishing mates Ted and Bill (Jan and Ken's dad) 1950

At Mablethorpe 1951. Left to right: Cousin Keith, Jan, Auntie Lillian, Cousin Jean and Uncle Frank. Keith and Jean are Lillian and Frank's children

Ken (right) with brother Dave at Hembsy, Norfolk. Ken's photo with 'big fish' behind

VINE HOTEL AND CRAZY GOLF
CHAPEL ST. LEONARDS   117

Jan and Ken's dad sends a message home after his SOS to the family back at Dame Agnes Street to send some money to him when he was on holiday at the Vine Hotel, Chapel St Leonards in 1958

John Jarvis was brought up in Bakersfield but walked to St Ann's from Bakersfield most Sunday mornings to visit his maternal grandparents, Alf and 'Trot' Shepherd, who lived on Moffat Street, off Southampton Street, next door to the Prince Leopold pub. He remembers its mahogany bar with brass fittings and etched glass.

"Grandad was a foundry worker and a major drinker. He used to pass a large white enamel jug through the rear window of the pub every day and it used to get topped up regularly. He was a quiet man always wearing a flat cap and a white scarf.

"I remember the old range in their parlour being black-leaded and drinking tea with condensed milk.

"Grandma used to do lace work from home for my uncle who owned a lace business. She had long hair, which she used to plait and wind around her head into a large bun. She was a real character. After grandad died, she used to take me to Mablethorpe every year."

John Jarvis with his gran from Moffat Street at Mablethorpe

ANON

Interviewed in her home 8.3.95

Before demolition and redevelopment, I lived in Lamartine Street. At the time of the BBC film on St Ann's, people were paid to tear off wallpaper from walls of houses in nearby Plantagenet Street where much of the film was made. The film was a travesty and only showed a tiny fraction of St Ann's life. People in St Ann's brought up their families well. Only one in ten homes caused any trouble.

I had two children. Because of complications with the first birth, I wasn't supposed to have more. When I became pregnant ten years later, my doctor was gruff and I knew how unmarried mothers must feel. But my specialist, Mr Cockayne, was good. He asked if I wanted to go ahead with the pregnancy and I said yes. He helped me. I was in bed for most of the last three months but I'm glad I had my son.

My husband, daughter, son and myself are all interested in CB amateur radio. My husband has worked hard all his life in spite of disability. I am now disabled but get around. Mostly I have worked for people 'without humanity'. But I worked for one boss for ten years who appreciated his workpeople and treated them as human. Most bosses just wanted their 'pound of flesh' and didn't care for people as individuals. But this one was good and let me go early once because of family illness. When his son - who worked in the business - married, his dad gave me his son's car keys, and the staff gave him a right good send off. We filled the car with confetti, tied balloons to it, tied on tins with marbles in so they just touched the road and 'clanked'. And wrote on the windscreen with lipstick underlined with cold cream!

I think social workers have done a lot of harm. On the one hand local people aren't listened to and, on the other, some people are always being 'looked after' by social workers, who don't know what's what.

INNER NOTTINGHAM: inner city voices by Ruth I Johns • ISBN 0951696092

I'm lucky because I have friends my size who are better off than me. They let me pick from their clothes when they are turning out. It's nice stuff. I call myself second-hand Rosie. I help them out with my car when we go swimming.

I've done a lot of youth work in St Ann's. Those in charge of Scouts set out to get more recruits in St Ann's and I told them that sending notes home from school etc wouldn't work. Those methods may work in Wollaton, Mapperley or Sherwood, but in St Ann's you only get anywhere by meeting people face to face.

ANN REDDISH

Born 1939

From correspondence 2000. Photos from Ann Reddish

My father's family, the Hawthorn's were first recorded in St Ann's in the 1891 census. My great grandfather, James, lived at 6, Upper Beacon Street and his brother Lionel at 8, Upper Beacon Street.

We were a lace making family, originally from Sneinton and who moved to France to try to better themselves in 1820. But by 1847, they were back in England where two of the older men ended their days in the workhouse.

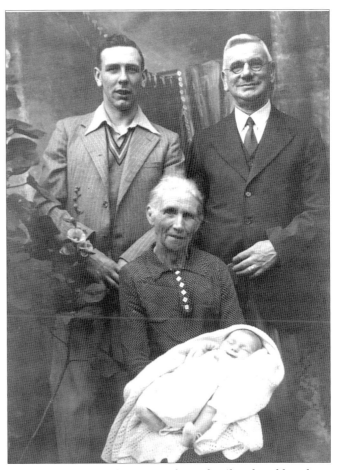

Four generations of the Hawthorn family, the eldest born 1859 and the baby in 1937

James Hawthorn 1858-1925

The brothers Lionel and James who lived on Upper Beacon Street worked for the Nottingham Gas Corporation. I believe they moved to St Ann's to get away from the back-to-back housing in Sneinton where their mother still lived. James's son, also called James (my grandfather), also worked for the Gas Corporation and found a house on Moffat Street, St Ann's, but ended his life at 9, Upper Beacon Street. He retired as Lighting Superintendent. My brother remembers the big clock used by the workers to clock in. The Department was on George Street.

All the houses with the odd numbers on Upper Beacon Street were villa type, with hall, large parlour, living room and scullery, and three bedrooms, one being in the attic. They had no bathroom but a privy at the bottom of the yard. The houses on the other side of the road had no entrance hall, the front door opening straight on the street from the parlour. I believe all had cellars.

The family remained in St Ann's until the area was demolished in 1975. They were Congregationalists, the Rev Ronald K Ross being the Minister for many years.

Ann Reddish sent in a photo of the St Ann's Congregational Church entrance which appears in the Faith section, and a photo of the Fitting Section of Nottingham Corporation Gas Depot, Huntingdon Street. She thought it was taken in the 1930s. No names are identified. An identical photo was given me by Eric and he is identified on it. He says it was taken in 1934

JOHN DUNNE

Born 1943

Interviewed in his home 26.1.00

I was born in Dublin in 1943. My brother was working over here. It's the usual story of Irish immigration. I arrived in Nottingham in 1965 and lived in Stoneleigh Terrace at the top of Canning Circus between Raleigh Street and Portland Road. We were slum clearance there and came to St Ann's in 1972.

We were given a house here by the Council. My two sons and my wife, Anne, and I came down here to have a look. We'd been offered one of the three storey houses with lounge on the first floor. We thought with two young kids, we'd be forever running up and down stairs. So we came by here and the guys were actually painting and I asked one of the painters if we could come in and have a look. We liked the house and we managed to get it within two weeks and we've been happy here ever since. It has three bedrooms.

The house is ideal, we're quite close to town. Once I've finished working, I won't need a car. I've worked at Imperial Tobacco for thirty years. I'm on the security side.

I remember coming down to St Ann's before I lived here canvassing for the Labour Party. This is Harlaxton Walk whereas [before redevelopment] it was Harlaxton Street, Heskey Street and places like that, each with its shop on the corner. There's no shops now. Like all Council estates, there are good sides and bad sides to it. We're quite lucky. Some parts I always think are like a staging post. I mean people come and leave within a year or two. Next door to us we've had about five sets of neighbours in the twenty odd years we've been here. Nobody seems to be putting down roots anymore.

There's twenty-five houses close to here and only three or four of them have people who've been here the same time as us. My children went to St Augustine's, the Catholic School, at the top of the hill. There's a Catholic Church [St Augustine's] at the top of the road. It's a bit of a struggle up the hill when you get older. I go to church on Sunday but I'm more political than religious.

When St Ann's was being demolished, there was the St Ann's Tenants and Residents Association. I started to get involved, putting something back into the community, but then they didn't seem to have any liaison officers with the Council. They got their own club [Pint and Pot] and that wasn't very successful either. It was where the Welcome Inn is now on St Ann's Well Road.

Then we decided that one of the main reasons why not many people turned up to meetings was because they would prefer smaller groups local to them. The Phase 10 Action Group was for the Marple Square area. I used to be involved a lot. We had our ups and downs. Sometimes the only time we saw somebody was when they wanted something. Eventually I got fed up and packed it in. All hours of the day and night, the phone ringing and people complaining that their gate was hanging off sort of thing, when we were looking for bigger things. I used to get frustrated and with working full-time and on shifts . . . Then someone else would come along with a bit more enthusiasm and it revamped itself, and we started again. There's better liaison with the Council now. A few years ago we had some students up from Brookes University, Oxford, and they did a survey for us.

We were assured there was going to be some money to do up this part of the estate, then it fell through, twice. But at the moment it's up and running, so hopefully Phase 10 will be revamped. Alan Hardy is the Chairperson now. Alan's on three or four committees. They've got a good grant coming off. I suppose I should still be there but after being involved for so long, you just tend to give up on it.

I use the pub which used to be called the Mechanics, now it's the Pride of Erin, just up from here. It's run by an Irish family. It used to be one of the few Davenport houses in Nottingham but Davenports the Brewery has gone. I find it relaxing to go up there with people of my own age. It's not one of these plastic imitations where you put a few Irish posters and a couple of Guinness posters on the wall and then call it an Irish pub. The fad is dying out thank God. This is a genuine Irish pub and a lot of Irish people go in there.

I could never understand when I first came to England that you literally hardly knew your neighbours next door. The only people we have any communication with apart from saying good morning or hello is a West Indian lady. We look after one another's house when we're away. The rest you speak to rather than stop to have a chat.

In the 1950s and 1960s there was a lot of unemployment in Ireland. It was the main cause of people coming over. I had a married brother living over here. I went to London, didn't like it, very impersonal and came up where people were very, very friendly. I came from a family of twelve but one of my sisters died, so we were eleven.

I was just watching something on TV before you came and they were on about immigration into Ireland now. It's changed: it's changing. I was over a few times last year. People of my generation used to be friendly. Now with the younger generation, there's an element of greed. And there's racism creeping in. I was crossing the Halfpenny Bridge and there were two guys behind us. They were on about slinging a refugee, Bosnian I think, into the river. That shocked me. I mean you can go into most pubs in Dublin and talk to anybody, you still can. But it's changing, whether it's for the good or not, probably good in the pocket but . . .

I sort of hanker back. But my kids will look back and say: 'Oh! I remember the good old days, the '80s and '90s!' You've probably heard it a hundred and one times, but I think today we lack community. People come in and tend to close the door. I do it myself and keep the world locked out sort of thing. There are people like Alan [Hardy] trying to generate community spirit but I don't think it will ever be the same as when we were kids. We lived just outside Dublin in Dun-Laoghaire, people were

ST ANN'S NOTTINGHAM: Inner-City Voices by Ruth I Johns • ISBN 0951696092

in and out of each other's houses and everybody was in the same boat. It was probably the same over here. Anne's mother lives in Dalkey, about three miles from where I lived. We were going there one day and got absolutely soaked waiting for a taxi. My father says we'll go and ask somebody and he goes and knocks on this stranger's door. The next minute he comes down ready to give us a lift, no problem. That sort of spirit's gone now. We lived in dwellings, two bedrooms. Now they call them cottages, the price is fierce and you couldn't afford to live there.

I think people need tolerance, you've got to be tolerant toward one another, live and let live. All most people want is a job, enough money in their pocket and a bit of security. I think it will be the same in a hundred years time.

I met my wife in 1962 before I came over here. We got married in 1966 back in Dublin. She works for Nottingham City Council in Sherwood. She helps look after elderly or disabled people having respite care.

A Home at the side of where we live here was closed for about three or four years, lying derelict, and we campaigned for that. It has reopened.

In the very near future, the Council is going to start improving the houses round here. What they are going to try to do is to incorporate as much as possible into people's own space. The original plan may have looked terrific on paper, but, for example, this is our front room and it's facing the back! They're going to 'turn' some of the houses so that is reversed and the front room will be in the front. Hopefully it will improve things and people will stay a bit longer and put down roots. Some of the open space and alleyways are invitations to crime, so it should be better when the improvements are done. Using some of the 'open' space to give people carports, brick up a wall here and open up there sort of thing.

You were asking about drugs in St Ann's. I've never seen anyone openly dealing in drugs. It obviously goes on in private estates and it must go on here. It's all about people making money on someone else's misery. What I have seen is two kids standing shivering on the corner and then someone drives up on a motorbike, something is handed over and off they go. And you see the odd syringe now and then.

I've still got one son at home. The other is married and lives at South Normanton. I've got two grandaughters, my pride and joy. You get a second chance I think when they come. Both my sons work for Imperial Tobacco. It's a good company to work for. One is a supervisor and one is a machinist, making cigarettes on the machines. When I first started, Imperial Tobacco [Player's] was based in Radford. They had four factories in Radford and half a dozen outbuildings and employed over eight thousand people. Now they've moved to a single site and it's the only tobacco factory that's left in the whole of England. I don't smoke myself. I do have cigars though.

I was bit apprehensive about this interview but I'm quite happy with the way it's gone.

YVONNE PEACOCK

(nee Bloom)   Born 1944

Interviewed at St Anns Library 11.1.00. Yvonne Peacock and Patricia Owen [also interviewed] met when they lived near each other in St Ann's as young children. They are still close friends. All photos from Yvonne Peacock

I was the eldest of six children and born at 15, National Terrace, Westminster Street, St Ann's. My dad was in the Air Force when I was born. I remember photographs of him but he died when I was only five. He had epileptic fits, but it was an illness when he died. He was only twenty-nine.

My mum (Ivy) managed with great difficulty. In those days you were left to cater for yourself. You got your Widow's Pension and you got Family Allowance and that was about it. Grandma used to live next door and we called her MamMay. Her real name was May Goldby but all the children in the street knew her as MamMay. She was adopted Grandma to a lot of people. She was one of the wise ones. She was my mum's mum and she helped a lot.

Then my mum's sister lived on St Francis Terrace just the other side of Westminster Street. So families were closer together and they did help out in times like that. There were three girls when my dad died. Then, my mum remarried and she had our Robert when I was about nine. I don't think she married straight away which, in those days, was a bit naughty. She had two boys. So we're three sisters (me, Iris and Joan) and two step-brothers (Robert and Raymond) and a step-sister, Beryl. We're still all very close.

As time went on, we used to go potato picking with her. The lorry used to come to the bottom of the street and pick you all up. I asked my mum where they were taking us and it was over Redhill somewhere. And she used to work part-time when it was coming near Christmas at the pickling factory, a little factory at the top of Thorneywood Mount.

I went to the Board School [St Ann's Well Road Infant and Junior School]. Pat [Patricia Owen nee Osborne] lived up our yard at No 9. She was born March 9th 1944 and I

Yvonne Peacock [Bloom]   *Patricia*
From a well-worn photo of the first-year class at the Board School when Yvonne and Patricia were in the same class

---

was born April 3rd 1944. We're still good friends. We're like aunties to our families. We both went to school together. My dad was still alive and he took us both on our first day. My dad died soon after. I remember that day well because it must have been March time to be right for our birthdays. After the first class, we were never in the same class again. I had a nice teacher called Miss Dyer in the Junior School, which was upstairs at the Board School. She taught me to read. I was backward at reading and she was lovely.

When you first went to that school you were in the Infants downstairs. Then upstairs to Juniors in the big hall where the Headmaster, Mr Salt, was. Miss Hayes was Head of the Infants. Miss Dyer taught me as I got on to the second layer. One of my sisters had meningitis and was deaf and dumb afterwards and she went into a Home at Gaulstone, outside Yarmouth. It was arranged through the Air Force to help my mum because she had these little kids. Miss Dyer came from Gaulstone, her mum and dad lived there. She used to go and visit Iris, my sister, for us. Miss Dyer was lovely. We hadn't got the money for visiting days. We used to play all sorts of games on the street, Pat, me and the gang.

Mr Galloway was one of my Form teachers, and when my children went to Seeley Junior School off Perry Road, Mr Galloway was their Headmaster. From the Board Junior School, I went to the Arboretum Open Air School. I was sent there because I was poorly a lot when I was young. I was losing a lot of time from school through sickness and I lost a lot of weight. The Open Air School was a small school at the side of the Girls High School. You went into school from the Arboretum itself.

Yvonne, the middle taller child on the front row, as a bridesmaid at the wedding of Marlene and Ted Felstead (Aunt and Uncle) at St Ann's Church about fifteen years before her own wedding there

I used to travel from Westminster Street across town with school tokens on two buses. There was hot cocoa waiting for you on winter mornings. You were a little bit spoiled. Milk was given to you morning and afternoon. In most schools it was just in the morning.

There were probably about two hundred children, divided into four or five classrooms. I was there until I was fourteen. The doctor used to come and examine me because I had this weight problem with the sickness and stomach problems.

She said: 'We are going to try and get you back into normal school now, because when you leave school you won't get a job if you're still here'. Any child with a handicap went there, so I suppose my handicap was with keep being ill. So I went up to Morley School in St Ann's for the last year.

Television wasn't on the scene for us until we were twelve, thirteen. Pat had gone to Clifton. Vivian Coates we palled about with had gone too. So I started watching television more. As kids we went down to the Pleasure Park by the River Trent. The Hendon Rise Social Club, St Ann's, used to take us on trips there. And we used to go down to Highfields Lido quite a lot.

People found out they could get better homes if they got on a Council overcrowding list and Clifton Estate was being built. There was nowhere to send people before. Some of the homes were overcrowded. Mrs Coates, Vivian's Mum, who lived up the yard at National Terrace had eight kids and two adults in a two up and two down. No bathroom, no running hot water, no real kitchen, it was a sink and a cooker.

My mum is still alive. She stayed in St Ann's until about 1963-64 when they more or less began emptying the houses and she got moved up to Bestwood. I'd left home by then and lived with my Grandma, MamMay, on Hendon Rise, St Ann's. I moved to my Granny's a year after I started work. I didn't get on with my step-dad. The trouble started when I went to work. He was very strict and I wasn't allowed out very much. I used to go to the Pictures on Friday night but I left half an hour before my friends because I used to have to be in so early.

After I left school, I started work with Pat at Gordonia up Stoney Street in the Lace Market. We were twin needling. We were twin needling the binding on pantie girdles and bras. It's still done exactly the same today. We worked lock stitch machines with two needles. You had binding come up from the bottom and the machine with twin needles stitched the binding to the fabric. Next time you look at your bra, you'll see a turning underneath and there's always a binding underneath to stop any frayed edges. It was quite hard work.

I think we started on one pound fifteen shillings a week and they gave us six weeks training at it. After four weeks, if you proved all right, you went up to £2 a week. Then after another two weeks, they expected you to start being able to earn the money piece-rate. They used to pay you by the bundle, so you were working against the clock all the time. You might manage to get up to £3 or even £3.50. That was good money then.

When I started living with my Grandma, I started dancing down at Locarno's. And at the Palais. I liked Jiving, Rock and Roll, Elvis, Dusty Springfield. I was with my Grandma six years before I got married. She was lovely. She was living with Frank, he was all right but I didn't really know him as a person. Her husband, Sam Goldby - my Grandad - was still alive. He couldn't read or write but was quite wealthy. We seemed to know where to find him and he was there if we needed him. When I lived with my Grandma, Grandad Sam used to come regular and she'd

ST ANN'S Nottingham. Inner-city voices by Ruth Johns • ISBN 0951696092

cook him big stew pots and he'd say: 'Florrie can't do stew like you May!' He was living with Florrie.

When MamMay and Sam were together, he used to knock her about. They got on very well apart. He was good to us as kids. At Christmas time, he'd bring all fresh fruit and chicken from the farm. He used to say: 'Go down to Harry Bramley's, there's a couple of nice pieces of pork on Sam'. He had a farm at Epperstone.

During the War, I can remember going up to the farm one day and he'd say: 'Sit and read this paper to me'. He'd pick the paper up and look at it upside down. He's dead now and Grandma's been dead quite a few years.

I was at Gordonia for nine years until I was twenty-four. I'd just got married to Fred when I left. We moved down to Bright Street on Radford Road and I became good friends with Alan Sillitoe's mum. She lived on Salisbury Street. She used to bet on the horses. The reason I knew her was because her grandson was living with her, and he was working with Fred repairing cars down that way. She was a lovely lady. She used to love to dance the Charleston. She said to us one night: 'Come and enjoy yourself'. It was some sort of club and she was dancing the Charleston.

Fred Peacock in his backyard at Stretton Street, Union Road, St Ann's. The toilet is the door on the left

After a while, we bought our own house on Warren Avenue, Haydn Road. It was a big thing to buy a house because we were both brought up to think it was a debt. Later we bought a shop, Fred and Vonny's, on Colwick Road. It was a General Store and off-licence. We did pretty well for about nine years and then the shop next door sold to Kwik Save. So protest as we did, it didn't make any difference and we had to close after a year.

With what money we could salvage from the shop, we could either afford two up and two down inner-city and park your car on the street, or move to Bilsthorpe (where Fred's sister had moved) and get a semi-detached with garage. So that's where we are now. I work part-time back in a general store and off-licence.

We've got two children, Mark who is thirty and Natasha who is twenty-seven this year. They're doing nicely. I think materially, children have it easier today but it's a cruel hard world to grow up in at the moment. They used to say that St Ann's where we lived was a no-go area, but we were always all right and safe. No harm ever came to us. The police used to go in pairs, but I can't remember anything. Whether, when you're children, you don't see these things I don't know. But I wonder where the violence of today is going to end.

I think the old St Ann's had to be cleared away, but it's a shame the way they did it. They would have been better doing it in sections and keeping people together. When they split everything up, and everyone went in different directions, the roots were pulled up. And the values went with them, because we had strong values and great respect for older people.

I don't often come back now. I came to the sessions you ran here at the Library. Fred and I were married at St Ann's Church that was very near where we are talking now. And we had our wedding reception at the old Westminster pub which was knocked down. The first house we lived in on Bright Street, Radford, has gone. So there's only me and our Fred left!

Pat and I are still there for each other. We see each other about once or twice a month, it depends on what's happening with the families.

1967 Wedding at St Ann's Church

Marriage Certificate of Frederick Peacock and Yvonne Jean Bloom April 1st 1967

Yvonne sent photos which also give different aspects of the area around the Church. The first two show the shops on St Ann's Well Road in the background. Yvonne said they could not afford a professional photographer at the time

Yvonne Bloom arriving at Church

Her bridesmaids arriving. From left: Sue (Fred's sister), Beryl and Joan (Yvonne's sisters)

Fred, Yvonne and bridesmaids after the ceremony

Fred's sister, June, and twin brother, John Peacock. Note the bubble car

PATRICIA OWEN

(nee Osborne)   Born 9.3.44

Interviewed in her home 26.5.99

I was born at 3, National Terrace, Westminster Street, St Ann's, the second youngest of five children: three girls and two boys. My eldest sister and brother were born in Gedling: the rest of us in St Ann's. We had quite a happy family life but we were very, very poor.

My father was too old to be in the War and he worked down Clifton Pit, so he would have been exempt anyway. My eldest brother went down the mines, my eldest sister worked at Somnus Bedding just down the road. My mum did not work at that time. My earliest memory is of sitting on my mother's knee when I was three years old. She was teaching me how to tie a bow.

I really did enjoy my childhood on that Street even though we had nothing, absolutely nothing. But every time I think about it, it is all happy memories. I used to play with Yvonne Bloom [now Peacock] at no 15. We played with whipping tops, skipping and we went scrumping a lot on the allotments at the top of the street [Hungerhill Gardens]. We used to do concerts and play tin lurky. We used to tie ropes around the lamposts and swing around them.

Once on the Hungerhills, there was a little shop and outside there was this bike. I watched for ages and ages, and I thought somebody's lost it so I thought I would take it. I took it home and was as happy as Larry with this bike and my mum gave me a good hiding. She said I had found it before it was lost and I had to take it back. We never had anything, never a bike or nothing. I can remember making a doll's pram with a shoebox by tying a piece of string around it and pulling it along with a peg doll. But I did have a doll one Christmas, a pot doll. I just got to the top of the yard and dropped it and it all smashed into pieces on Christmas Day.

ST ANN'S NOTTINGHAM: inner-city voices *by Ruth I Johns* • ISBN 0951696092

I had an Aunt on Cromer Road just round the corner. We used to go around to see her on Christmas morning and take what we had for Christmas. Of course, I had to take my broken doll. All I had left was this wooden thing and you pushed it up and down, a clown.

I must have started school after the Christmas holidays because it was snowing. It was thick with snow. Yvonne's dad took Yvonne and me to the Board School[1]. Mr Salt was the Headmaster. Yvonne and I have been friends to this day. I spoke with her this morning. When I was nine, I went to a new prep department built at Morley School. I was one of those chosen to go up there. And we went into what was called the New Buildings. I was in Prep 2 at nine and I stayed at Morley School until I left at thirteen.

Patricia at Morley School

I went to King's Hall Methodist Mission Brownies. After school, there was a play centre at Board School. That was from half past five to half past six. At Morley too there were after-school events. You could play Badminton. A lot of the boys did boxing and the girls did netball in the summer. In the winter, we could do needlework or whatever. When I hear of schools starting up new ventures after school, I think well that's nothing new, because we used to do it and use all the school facilities.

With my mum having five children at home we had quite a few sweet coupons. I remember having to go to this women who used to buy mum's sweet coupons off her. She hadn't much family at all. When my mum started work as a cleaner at the Eye Infirmary, things started to look up. She used to send us Ice-Skating and swimming. Then we went tap-dancing and ballet-dancing. So obviously some of the money she earned was spent on making up lost time for us. I can remember the neighbours, very friendly, but a lot of fighting as well between themselves. I've no idea over what. When you are young you don't know.

On a Saturday night there was a man with a horse and cart. He used to go round 'call tatting'. When he'd had a few drinks, he'd go around the streets with his horse and cart and you could hear him when you were lying in bed. His name was Alfie Parker and you knew he wasn't very happy with somebody because he'd get his horse and cart and you could

hear them on the cobbled streets. The next thing, there would be a commotion, him fighting. That must have been the anger coming out of him.

Our family was rehoused when I was thirteen and we went to Clifton in 1957 and never liked it. My dad never settled. Right up to his dying day he never liked it. He always said he was going to leave my mum and go back. In fact he had a nervous breakdown. He always hankered to go back to St Ann's. He was born there you see.

Our house in St Ann's was privately rented and I think my mum put our name for rehousing because my brother came out of the Army and we got rehoused because of overcrowding. It was before they started moving people out as part of St Ann's demolition.

My dad had left the pit by then and went to the Ministry of Works, Chalfont Drive, as a stoker. But he was always sick, mentally sick, he was heartbroken. He was born in Sneinton. I remember his mother, my grandma. She lived in Wainwright Street, St Ann's. She wasn't very well off.

We used to go round to Grandma's every Sunday morning. She had plaits around her ears. She used to do lace work. She used to sit there trimming the lace. She was ever so fast. Even on Sunday morning, she would be sitting there, trimming lace.

I remember her fetching the lace work. She used to have these skeins around her arms, probably for underskirts, a few inches wide but in different widths. Then she used to tie it around the middle and then put it into a sort of blanket and then tie it like a knotted handkerchief and put it in the pushchair to take back to wherever she got it from.

I wasn't particularly bright at school, not academically. I found reading and writing difficult. I was good at practical things, PE, art, cookery and needlework.

I've no idea what kept Yvonne and I together. We have always been there for each other. Her family all say I'm the adopted sister! When we were young we played in a gang. There was Vivian Coates, Carol Williams, me and Yvonne. We were in the top of the Terrace. When we had bonfire night, there was top gang and bottom gang. We used to trade each other for bonfire rubbish. We used to take it in turns to keep watch and we would always try and raid the bottom gang and try to climb over the walls and get their things.

Bonfire night was lovely. There was one bonfire at the bottom of the street and one at the top, and two men (one was Mr Varley) poking the bonfires with clothes props. People used to bring all their old rubbish to be burnt. Settees were left to last. Women used to sit round the fire on these settees and chairs and talk and drink. Then when the kids had gone to bed the chairs and things went on. Some of the fires went on until the middle of the night.

Older people used to get more involved then in what children did. They would clear out at that time. I can remember dragging mattresses down The Wells Road. We used to go all around the area asking people if they had any rubbish for bonfire night. We used to go around all the churches at Christmas time. They had parties. And we went to the Salvation Army and the Sunday school at St Ann's Church.

---

[1] People referred to St Ann's Well Road Infant and Junior School as the Board School throughout its history.

There was a beer-off on the corner of our Terrace and I can remember all the people getting their draft ale in jugs. I went with my dad, to the bottom of the street and up some steps and down a dark coal yard, to place a bet at a bookies before betting was legalised. There was a man watching outside, but the police turned a blind eye to it being there.

We had a dog, a terrier of some sort called Spot. We had him from when I was four or five until I was nineteen. I can remember my mum saying that at one time she had a goose when she had a bit of front garden one terrace up from us, Simon's Terrace, where my second brother was born. It used to go to the fence and wait for my dad coming home from work. She said if anyone came near the gate, it got nasty.

My Aunt lived in the first house up from Morley School and then Yvonne went to live yards from my Aunt and she used to pal about with my cousin who was about eight months younger than us. Yvonne and I both starting working the same day at Gordonia up the Lace Market, making bras. She was in the top room and I was in the bottom.

I did a lot of knitting when I was young, and I now knit for my three grandchildren. That cardigan in the photo you've got when I was about twelve, that was the first cardigan I knitted. It was green.

My dad used to go out and play dominos and mum went out Saturday night with him when my older brother looked after us. They either went to the Westminster at the bottom of the street or The Edgar on Peas Hill Road.

Three years ago, Yvonne, my sister and me went on holiday. And when we all meet up we say: 'Let's do this routine'. We can still remember it. When we were young, when we put on concerts one of the songs was Max Bygraves: 'Say what you will, the countryside's still the only place where I could settle down'.

I don't think children have the same opportunities now to create their own fun in their local community. We were quite happy making our own entertainment but I think kids today would be bored with doing that. We were mischievous but we didn't vandalise anything. I remember standing outside this hedge, and Yvonne was inside getting the apples and, if I whistled, it meant there was somebody coming. But we wouldn't break the branches of the trees to get the apples. It was done nicely, by one person sitting on another person's shoulders and things like that to shake the branches, but not to break them.

My Uncle was a policeman in the area. We called him Uncle Walter but he was my sister's brother-in-law. My sister was a lot older than me. I remember him going round the streets with a cape on.

Yvonne was ill when she was young and she was once in hospital in Leicester. I remember going outside this telephone box with four pennies which we had collected to buy her some sweets when she came back. We spent two pennies on sweets and two to phone her up. We didn't know which hospital and we got this hospital through the operator. In the end we got to speak to somebody who knew Yvonne there. But she never got her sweets. We ate them!

GILL WEST

Born 1944

The following contribution was sent in, plus additional material from letters, 2000 and 2001

My maiden name was Pettitt and our address was 94, Beverley Street, St Ann's. My dad was born in that house and, like his allotment, he took tenancy of it when his parents died. My mother came to Nottingham from Wales in 1926 and she met and married my father in 1929 when she had finished her nursing training at the Coppice Hospital. They had six children, Philip (1930), Eirwen (1932), David (1935), Margaret (1940) and twins John and me, Gillian (1944).

We twins were born premature, John weighing three and a half pounds and myself weighing two and a half pounds at birth. I think my mother was a remarkable lady as she reared us at home with no incubators or special baby unit but using her nursing skills. We were kept in a clothes-basket wrapped in cotton wool and muslin soaked in olive oil for the first three months of our lives. Not bad for 1944! Because my mother was a nurse, people were always knocking on our door for her to help to deliver a baby or lay someone out.

John and Gill Pettitt at about eight months old

I always went to the Boys' Brigade because my mam ran the canteen for the lads and my three brothers were members. No Big Macs or pizzas in those days. Jacket potatoes, cheese on toast or morning coffee biscuits served with tea or coffee.

Our holidays were always spent on the allotment on Hungerhill Gardens. This is what we did on a summer Bank Holiday. We would start by having a ride in dad's wheelbarrow. The first stop was the Valley Dairy where we would buy Colwick Cheese, a tub of cream and a bottle of orange. When we arrived at the garden, mam would make a fire in the small fireplace in the tin hut and then the kettle would be put on. It was on all of the day. We all had our jobs to do, weeding, watering but, best of all, was picking the soft fruits, raspberries, blackberries, gooseberries. When my brother had that job, my mam

St Ann's Nottingham: inner-city voices *by Ruth I Johns* • ISBN 0951696092

made him whistle while picking so we all got a full dish of fruit each!

The salad was picked and washed at the communal tap in the garden avenue. Time for our picnic: Colwick Cheese and cucumber sandwiches, fresh salad and, for afters, the soft fruits with one spoon each of the cream. I don't know whether it was because I was young that things seemed larger than life but dad's raspberries were bigger than strawberries and so sweet. There was lots of time to play. We had a swing and a rope tied to the apple trees at the bottom of the garden and, if you went high enough, you could see the Coppice Rec.

By mid afternoon you were ready for more food and that would be rhubarb and sugar. It's now time to put the garden produce into dad's barrow to take home. There was no room for a ride, but dad would tell us a story of fairies that lived in the gardens and, if you worked hard, they would leave a shilling on the tree stumps on the main avenue. Unbeknown to us, he had put it there on the way to the garden that morning. So my brother and I would feel on all the tree stumps until we found the shilling and it was always spent on a block of ice cream from Staple's and taken home for tea.

My mam was a wonderful cook and made full use of the produce by making jams and pickles and the lovely Russet apples were put in a chest-of-drawers for Christmas. As an adult I now realise, although we were poor, we lived like royalty on the produce from dad's garden.

Nights at the Northampton Street Boys' Brigade Youth Club were wonderful. The week was taken up getting ready for Friday night. Our skirts were three yards of gingham from Harry on the Market and two yards of net from the net stall, then black patent shoes from Quality Street, a white shirt and a black wide belt. We looked a million dollars.

The late John Jacques and Len Adey were at the Club to make sure it was run in an orderly way. We were encouraged to run it ourselves. We had dancing-the-night-away, snooker, table tennis and chess for those who wanted it. My husband and I remember fourteen couples who met and married from that Club. That speaks for itself! To end the night, we all had fish and chips from the Chase chip shop. It had to be there because Angie was in love with Jack, the owner's son. He looked just like Tommy Steele.

I started my working days as an apprentice hairdresser with Lilla Wakelin, a well-known shop in St Ann's. I worked there for nine years until I left to have my first baby.

I married Peter West who also came from St Ann's. It wasn't until I was married and moved away that I realised St Ann's was 'slums'. We never locked the door and everybody was friends, even Bobby Briggs the local policeman.

John and Gill Pettitt and brother David c1950

Gill West's dad with his grand-daughter up on the allotment c1958

My father died in 1970. My mother, who is ninety-six years old, is now in a nursing home and I go most days to see her.

RALPH NEEDHAM

Born 1946

Telephone interview 1999 after meeting in St Ann's

My grandfather George James Needham played for Nottingham Forest 1906-15. The professional footballer's wage was £2 a game. I've talked to people who saw him play.

My father worked with my grandfather running a pub, the Old Volunteer, Burton Road, Carlton. When grandfather retired, my father didn't wish to continue and he tried various things before deciding in 1953 to run his own business, which is why he got a newspaper shop at 35/37 Corporation Road, St Ann's. I was seven at the time and moving there, from a quiet part of Netherfield, was a total culture shock!

I changed from the Sacred Heart School, Carlton Road, to Sycamore Infant School on Sycamore Road [now Hungerhill Road] for about a year and I remember 'little' Miss Berber, a Jewish teacher. Then I went to the Elms School, which was the rebuilt Alfred St School and I was in Miss Burney's class. Other teachers included Mrs Smith and Mr Christine who looked like a Scottie terrier in a dark three-piece suit.

Class photo while Ralph Needham was in Mrs Smith's Class at Elms Junior School, July 1976. Mrs Smith on the left of the photo. Ralph Needham is next to her on the back row. Names he remembers include: back row (left to right) after him: ? , Tony Dawson, David Savage, Brian Ready, ? , Malcolm Gill, ? , ? , Colin Gilbert. He remembers a few of the others, including June Russell, third girl from left sitting down: and Sandra Bacon fifth from left, same row

Teachers were characters you held in great awe. Mr Bore was disliked. He was tall and always wore a tweed jacket, light coloured trousers, round metal framed glasses and hair slicked right back. Miss Holt was very short, very fat with a voice that could break glass. Miss Hilda Singleton, Head Teacher, was killed in a car crash whilst I was at school. She and her sister were motoring together and were both killed. She was a really nice person. You could always talk to her. It was difficult to accept that she wouldn't be there any more.

My family left St Ann's in 1957. My parents got a newsagent's shop next to the Duke of Cambridge pub on the Woodborough Road in nearby Mapperley, but I continued at school in St Ann's. It was decided when you were at Junior School who was or who wasn't likely to pass the 11-plus exam. We were segregated into three sections. The top were given all the attention because they were singled out for passing the 11-plus and getting to Grammar School. The middle section was considered as including a couple who might pass the 11-plus. And in the bottom section were the rejects. I was there! I was not surprised when I failed my 11-plus.

I should have gone to Huntingdon Street Secondary School. But it was a very tough school and I wouldn't have survived. I wasn't tough. So my parents fell back on our religion and I went to St Augustine's R C School on Northville Street (where you could start as an infant and leave as a senior). Part of the school consisted of one long room divided into three classrooms by removable partitions, which were sometimes opened up to make a hall.

The school was run by nuns [Sisters of St Joseph of Peace] from the Sacred Heart Convent on Mapperley Road. I started with Mr Bowne. Sister Francis was Head of the whole school. Sister Cyprian was Head of the infants. I also remember a nun called Sister Patricia. The nuns kept us very much in line. If you upset them they could be vicious. Mr W A 'Bill' Clark was Senior Teacher. Bill Clark came to school on his motor bike, an Excelsior, powered by a 125cc Villiers engine, and put it in the bike shed and nobody dared touch it. One brave soul, Patrick Costello, kicked the starter, the engine roared into life, the throttle stuck open and the noise was deafening. Patrick didn't know how to stop it. Mr Clark came running out of the classroom and all hell let loose. You didn't touch Sir's bike. I'd still call him Sir if he appeared today! Later, he got a grey Austin 'rounded' car. Tony Clark, Bill Clark's nephew was in our class. It was a real disadvantage being related to a teacher.

Children were expected to be at church in front pews on the left hand side on Sunday. One of our teaching nuns used to be there to keep us under control. If you were not at church, you were 'hiked out' on Monday and asked why. I was at that school for one year when Corpus Christi School opened in Ruddington and my parents had me transferred there. We were bussed out there by a bus which left from the side of the Council House in the City Centre. I hated it. The School's catchment area was the whole of Nottingham and children from different areas didn't get on. They tried to establish a pecking order. I stayed for about eighteen months and then just stopped going and truanted. So I went back to St Augustine's and left in 1961. During my absence Mr Bowne had left and been replaced by Mr Byrne.

In 1960, my family moved to Plains Road, Mapperley, but I've always regarded St Ann's as my home area. After the initial culture shock when I went there at seven, I always fitted in rather well. The community had been established a long time. There was a lot of poverty, but they were a happy crowd and nice people. There was a sense of morality. Nobody died alone, thumping women was not approved of though you might get your meter robbed. There was tut-tutting if an unmarried couple lived together.

On New Year's Eve I would hang out of my bedroom window as the steward of the Robin Hood Social Club, Freddie McCummings, ex-RAF, would come out of the Club with everybody behind him in crocodile. He'd be banging the lid of a crisp tin. He'd march down Corporation Road into the General Cathcart Pub at one door and out of the other with everybody following. Then go to the Broad Oak pub and pick up their customers and back to the Club.

We children used to build trolleys with pram wheels at the back and push chair wheels at the front, a broad piece of wood to sit on and a narrower piece of wood up the front. There would be string from the front axles to our hands for steering, or we did it with our feet. We used to have races from the Broad Oak pub round the streets and back to the pub.

Entries were a favourite place for playing in. Each group of kids had 'their' gas lamp to meet under, to chat and plan. 'Our' gas lamp was outside the Broad Oak Pool pub. I remember it was a great place for playing marbles. Sometimes we would have gang fights against a rival street. Each side would consist of about 10-17 seven to eleven year olds. We would invade the enemy's territory. This was called a raid and we armed with dustbin lids and pieces of wood. Most of it was staring and shouting abuse. I never remember anything serious, maybe a scratch or two. Then a little old lady would come out and shout for you to go away and it was all over.

My best friend was Philip Scullion who lived at 21, Corporation Road. I still see him from time to time. Another friend, Vincent Mullins, lived further up Corporation Road. I remember the Holland family of 29, Corporation Road. They were poor but very cheerful. Harry Holland was a lorry driver for British Road Services. Sometimes he'd bring a lorry home overnight and we'd climb all over but never did any harm.

I remember a family called Carter who lived at 26, Corporation Road. They had a son, Lawrence, and several daughters. They sometimes used candles long after electricity was normal. But they were a happy crowd. Where I'm living now they are a miserable lot! My mum came from London and she wasn't quite so fond of St Ann's.

We played football on the Ransom Road 'Rec'. If you got to the bank at the Caunton Avenue end, you could dig up lead bullets. The Robin Hood Rifles, Nottingham's Volunteer Regiment, used to practise there in the 19th Century.

I pestered my parents for a real sledge I had seen. It was seven shillings and six pence in a second-hand shop at the top end of Abbotsford Street. It was all wood with steel runners and I had it for years. When you went sledging down Robin Hood Chase, you could get up quite a lick. The gratings ran across and you had to be careful

to 'hit' them at an angle or the runners of the sledge would get caught.

Favourite children's pastimes included tying doorknobs together, then knocking on doors to see what happened! Also, spirit-tapping. Put a button on a thread and hang it from a downstairs window. With a thread from an entry opposite, pull the thread so the button taps the window. Or tie a milk bottle (empty) to a doorknob and place it on a windowsill so it crashed over when the door was opened.

At the side of our shop was an entry with a gate, which was unusual. The other side of the entry was a grocer's shop. It was run by Mrs Holmes who had a daughter, Susan. Mrs Holmes claimed she was the mother of the actress Joan Rice. I think it was true. The story was she had been put in a Children's Home. She was a J Arthur Rank starlet and played Maid Marion in the post-War Robin Hood film starring Richard Todd.

Around the corner from the Broad Oak Pool pub on Dame Agnes Street was a butcher's shop owned by Freddie Abel. He was an officer in the RAF during the Second World War and had been on the famous Dambuster raids. He was awarded the Distinguished Flying Cross medal. A few doors further up Dame Agnes Street lived an old gentleman on his own. When a soldier during the First World War, he had been blinded by a German hand-grenade.

I remember the Pownall family. John Pownall had a scrap-yard at the end of Alfred Street South, St Ann's. He was very tall and well-spoken and looked more like a teacher. It was a very long narrow yard where you could find all sorts of things including bits of aeroplanes. His brother Ken had a rag and bone shop on St Ann's Well Road with a scrap-yard at the back. He was a soldier in World War Two. Everybody knew where interesting things could be found. Philip Scullion said he knew of a yard with German helmets in. I gave him nine pence and he got me one.

In the 1950s when Germany was beginning to be allowed weapons, halfway up Dame Agnes Street on a wall I remember graffiti saying: 'Merry Christmas, no arms for Nazis'. Anti-German feeling was still high.

I knew a chap from Newark, a scrap-metal merchant, who helped to set the St Ann's race 'riots' off [1958]. He said: 'immigrants carried knives. It wasn't a British thing to do. The Brits would hit you with a house brick. Teddy Boys carried razors'.

I did a lot of different jobs. It was easy to get work: mine included the lace trade and the mines. For two years I worked for a St Ann's lad made good, John Carter. He used to buy all the ex-Granada rental TV sets. We started at 9.0 in the morning. He said nobody should be required to start earlier. I was a lorry driver then. I married for the first time at St Augustine's in St Ann's.

At the time of redeveloping the area, one of the most stupid things was to move people to Clifton, Broxtowe, Aspley . . . A lot of the old people died. The area became soulless.

For a living, I do historical presentations in period costume. I play fourteen different characters in history, often for English Heritage. For example, I play a Victorian Recruitment Sergeant, a Nottingham Policeman 1897, one of Robin Hood's outlaws. My house is full of costumes and items to do with the period of a character.

I remember my time in the old St Ann's with great fondness. It is part of my life I would not have missed.

A photo Ralph Needham found from his St Ann's time. Children's Fancy Dress event, Emmanuel Church Parish Hall, Woodborough Road c1955

CHRISTINE ALTON

Born 1947

Written contribution [1999] and conversations about a 1960s wedding in St Ann's. Christine Alton lived at 34, Caroline Street. All photo are hers

Charles and I met in April 1964 when I was sixteen and he was twenty. Our first meeting was at a twenty-first birthday party in the old Emmanuel Church Hall on Woodborough Road. He thought I went out with someone else!

Charles was in the Boys' Brigade and I was in the Girls' Life Brigade 1st Nottingham Chase Mission Baptist Church. Charles used to go to the lads night at the Mission so we both knew the boy whose party it was. A few weeks later Charles and I met on the street where I lived, Caroline Street, St Ann's. He was working for the Gas Board and lived on Westdale Lane, Mapperley.

We dated and after eleven months we became engaged. We got rings from Poysers on March 20th 1965. His was £7.10s and mine £23.00.

We met his family in the Gardeners pub at the bottom of The Wells Road to celebrate. In December we bought a house in Querneby Road just outside St Ann's in Mapperley, for £1,900. On April 2nd 1966 we married at St Ann's Church. Everyone was wanting to get married before the end of the tax year to get the rebate (so romantic!), so there were weddings every hour from ten in the morning until four in the afternoon. Ours was 3.00pm. The Vicar was the Rev Rawlinson.

The arrangements were quite simple as I did them all myself (my mother had died in 1964). The reception was

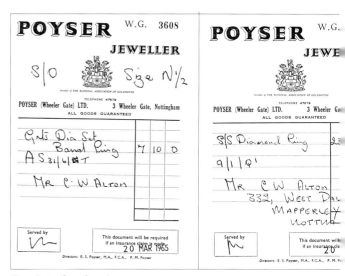

Receipts for the rings

Family group outside St Ann's Church after our wedding. Left to right, Charles' parents, Ruth and Joseph Alton; best man John Shipman; chief bridesmaid Sharon Cooper; us; sister Joan; my dad, George Bramley. In front (left) is niece Ann Duriez and second cousin Elaine Webb

held at the St Ann's Well Inn, on the corner of Peas Hill Road and St Ann's Well Road. It was the nearest pub to the Church. Nobody had cars then. We only just got this, because the couple who married an hour before us wanted it too! The girl lived on the next street to me, Brighton Street.

The wedding cars were black and white taxis from the local owner-driver on Cooper Street. The photographs were taken by a policeman from Sneinton, Bob Rosamund.

Flowers came from the Fruit & Flower Basket, Trent Boulevard, for a total of £8 12s 6d.

My dress was bought for £5.00. It was third-hand and my sister altered it for me. A lady I worked with, at Aldred's on Union Road, St Ann's, made a veil for me. My shoes were bought in the January Sales. My sister made dresses for the two small bridesmaids and the Chief Bridesmaid wore the one she had worn a few weeks earlier.

The cake was a present from one of my aunts. We didn't see it until the day and it was beautiful. The Catering was by M Lacey of Whitemoor Estate. Fifty-one adults at 8s 0d and seven children at 5s 6d. Total of £22 6s 6d.

ST ANN'S NOTTINGHAM: Inner city voices by Ruth I Johns • ISBN 0951696092

Charles and Christine Alton outside St Ann's Church with St Ann's Well Road in the background

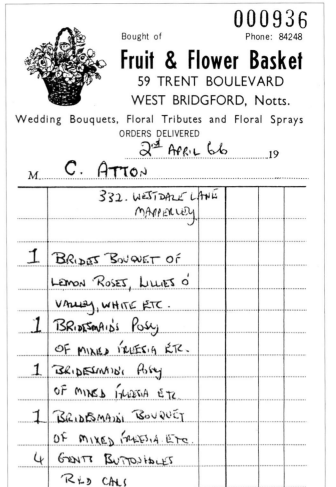

Receipt for the flowers

A friend of my mother-in-law played the piano at the reception. Two barrels of beer were provided by the two dads plus sherry for the toast. I had Friday afternoon off work to prepare for the big day, cleaning the house and shopping for my dad. Saturday morning to the Public Baths on St Ann's Well Road, take the bridesmaids and myself to the hairdresser. While we were there it started snowing! Back home to make dinner, then get ready with my sister crying all over the place.

We went to the reception room the night before to put daffodils on the table. Everyone wore spring suits so they froze! When we arrived at the reception, there were two huge coal fires. Most of the people we used, like the caterers, were used by other couples we knew.

My husband's elder brother took us to Matlock for our honeymoon, two nights. We couldn't move into our house for about four weeks so we stayed at my dad's. I've still got the newspaper with the wedding picture in.

Earlier, I had been to Shelton Street Infants School, Huntingdon Junior School and Sycamore Girls Senior School. I worked at A C Gill in the Lace Market for sixteen years. I now work at a travel agent. I'm now Chair of the Harlequins which meets at Nottingham Mechanics and is the former Women's Gas Federation. I did a lot of voluntary work for Family First when my children were young, and am very interested in family and local history.

2002. Christine Alton now works at a Solicitor's office. She adds: "I was recently asked by my sister-in-law if I would talk to the children in her class at Sycamore Infant School on Abbotsford Drive, St Ann's, about what it was like living in St Ann's in 'the olden days'.

"The school virtually stands on the site of Caroline Street where I used to live.

"I took along lots of artefacts, including toys and games, but the thing that amused them most was the fact that the toilet was 'across the yard' and, when it rained, we had to put an umbrella up because the roof leaked! And, at night, we had a chamber pot (poe) under the bed. This caused great shrieks of laughter. I never dreamt that I would be giving a talk to children in the 21st Century about my childhood, and that they would find it so interesting. I thoroughly enjoyed the whole experience of bridging the generation gap."

Some photos from Christine Alton's album

My maternal grandparents, also of St Ann's. Henry Webb and Harriet (nee Yeomans)

Alice, my mum, in the middle with her sisters Mary (left) and Ada. Alice's family lived on Providence Street, St Ann's. She was the youngest of sisters Amelia, Hannah, Harriet, Ada and Mary. There were two brothers Harry and Harold and possibly a third. Mary lived on Providence Street until it was demolished. Harold and his wife Lily and three sons Harold, Arthur and David lived at 2, Providence Street

Photo of my dad and Uncle Harold in the Mansfield Road Wesleyan Cricket Club. Dad is on the middle row third from right and Uncle Harold front row third from left

This is my mum, Alice (nee Webb) and dad George on their wedding day. They were married at St Ann's Church

My mum cleaned for Dr Adams on St Ann's Well Road, and then he and his wife, Ann, moved to Fairlawns, Lucknow Drive, Mapperley. Ann was my godmother and I did a lot of growing up in their house while mum was working and as god-daughter. This photo of me on the potty on wheels is at their Lucknow Drive home!

ST ANN's NOTTINGHAM: Inner-city voices by Ruth I Johns • ISBN 0951696092

Me and my big sister Joan on holiday. She was eleven years older and brother George sixteen years older

I was bridesmaid on five occasions, three of them in St Ann's. This picture is at a cousin's wedding at St Ann's Church. I remember the dress. It was blue satin with hand-made blue roses. I was about four

This is at a Coronation celebration at Emmanuel Church Hall 1953. I've no recollection of what happened!

Caroline Street backyard. I was about two. The remains of the air-raid shelter is in the background. I played in it. Dad built rabbit hutches

21st Celebration of the Cavendish Cinema Saturday morning club. There's me with the key. I won the fancy dress competition so received free entrance for a year. Members from Notts County Football Club and Nottingham Panthers Ice Hockey players were present. Back left is Ann Swinscoe and bottom left Ann Gibson

This is at Shelton Street Infant School. I'm in the middle with the bow. Miss Wallis was Head Teacher and Miss Reynolds my first teacher

Charles and me on holiday in Skegness: 'Nottingham by the sea.' 1964

THREE GENERATIONS ON PEAS HILL RISE

by **Dave Bowring**

Born 1947

Dave Bowring heard about this book from the Nottinghamshire Family History Society Journal. He wrote this in 2000

My grandparents, Ernest and Annie Bowring, moved to the St Ann's area in 1937 with my father, Leonard (13), Phyllis (9), Eileen (5) and his brother Sidney (3). They moved from Corby Glen in Lincolnshire, a mainly rural area, to seek better employment opportunities. Ernest originally lived in the Radford area of Nottingham, and moved to Corby Glen when he married and took up work as a builder. When they moved to St Ann's, Ernest returned to the textile industry as a twist hand but later became a builder again.

In St Ann's, they lived at 11, Peas Hill Rise which ran between Peas Hill Road and Robin Hood Chase. The Rise was a continuous row of terraced houses on both sides of the street. Number 11 had two main rooms downstairs and three rooms upstairs. The front door was down an enclosed 'entry' and led into a small hallway. The front room was on the right as you went in and was only used on high days and holidays. It contained the best furniture and family treasures, including the inevitable upright piano. The stairs to the first floor were directly opposite the front door.

To the left of the hall was the living room where the family spent most of their time. It was furnished with dining table and chairs, an easy chair, a settee and a sideboard. The focus of this room was the range. Originally this would have been the only means of cooking and heating water. The fire grate was in the centre of the range with a boiler on one side and an oven on the other. My grandmother meticulously cleaned and blacked the range every week. My grandfather stood by the range every morning with his shaving mug, brush and cut-throat razor, trouser braces draped by his side, scraping away at his stubble in the warmest spot of the house.

The coal for the fire was stored in a cellar reached by brick steps down from a door off the living room. The cellar was under the front room and the coal was delivered through a grating at the front of the house. The coal delivery was always a cause for excitement. The coal wagon was pulled by a horse, which was given a nosebag to feed from, while the black-faced coalman dragged coal in strong canvas bags onto his back and dumped the contents through the grating hole into the cellar.

We children were fascinated by the horse, daring each other to stroke its neck or pat its side. Others were watching for anything that might be ejected from its rear end! Anything which did appear was immediately scooped up on a dustpan and deposited on the diminutive strips of earth that constituted the gardens, one running across the front of the house and the other down the side of the backyard.

The same happened when the rag and bone man appeared with his horse drawn cart. He would sit on the front of the cart filled with all manner of junk calling: 'Ragbone, ragbone' until people appeared carrying their bits of scrap and old rags. Money rarely changed hands. The scrap dealer handed out cheap plaster of Paris ornaments or pots and pans instead!

Horses played a large part in those times. We used to watch in awe as the pairs of massive shire horses from Shipstone's Brewery clattered along Peas Hill Road hauling their load of wooden barrels on the brightly painted and polished wagon to deliver beer to the area's pubs. What a sight! All brass and leather, clinking away as the driver, dressed in apron and Bowler hat, whip in hand and foot resting on the huge brake lever, steered these magnificent animals through the streets. But back to Peas Hill Rise . . .

My grandparents' house had undergone some modernisation, the addition of a scullery extension to the living room. This provided sufficient space for a gas cooker, a sink, a wall-mounted heater ('geyser') and a larder cupboard. A door from the scullery opened into the yard, which was enclosed by a six-foot high wall. At the bottom of the yard were the toilet and the washhouse complete with coal-fired boiler and dolly tub. A gate from the yard led on to the cobbled alleyway between the backs of these houses and those of Edgar Rise.

Upstairs the house had three bedrooms. As you went up the stairs the main bedroom was on the right. To the left was a small bedroom and if you doubled back on yourself there was an even smaller bedroom.

My father was still of school age when the family returned to Nottingham. He went to Huntingdon School, St Ann's, for his final year, leaving at the age of fifteen. He went to work in the warehouse of lace makers (Birkin's I think) for ten shillings a week. The work didn't suit him and he left to become a builder. He remained a builder until he retired.

England had been at War for three years when my father was eighteen and was conscripted into the Army in 1942. He was sent to Scotland for his basic training and he met my mother, Margaret Peters. Romance blossomed and they married in my mother's home town of Farnworth in Lancashire on June 9th, 1945. They decided that Nottingham was the place where they wanted to set up home so, while my father returned to the Middle East, Margaret moved into two rented rooms at 19, Peas Hill Rise, a few houses away from my grandparents.

After my father's demob, they both lived in these rooms until their landlady died and they were offered the rental of the whole house. It was very similar to my grandparents' house except for the scullery extension. Instead, there was a tiny area off the living room with just enough space for an oven and kitchen sink. I think this house had been built later than my grandparents' one because it didn't have a range in the living room. There was a tiled fireplace and hearth.

Dad returned to his old trade as a builder and mum went to work for Boots before training to become a nurse and gaining her State Enrolled Nurse qualification.

One of my earliest memories was about 1951. I had been sent upstairs for my afternoon sleep (quite common for infants in those days). I was woken by the sound of commotion and dad's voice: unusual, because he wouldn't usually be home at that time of day. I came downstairs to find dad with his arm strapped up and looking in much pain. He had been working on the building of Staythorpe Power Station near Newark. While carrying out some final bricklaying work on one of the tall chimneys, a piece of scaffolding had become loose and he fell from it. Fortunately, other scaffolding broke his fall and he came away with nothing more than a painful dislocated shoulder, an amazingly lucky escape which nevertheless kept him off work for some weeks.

I went to Shelton Street Primary School, a relatively short walk away from Peas Hill Rise. The things that seemed to occupy most of our time outside school were marbles, played in the cracks of the cobbled alley, and cricket with stumps chalked on the wall of the yard. The dairy on the corner of Peas Hill Road and Edgar Rise was a favourite haunt. Here, we could buy cream ice-lollies straight from the mould and orange drinks that had been frozen in their packets. Butter was bought loose, the required amount being cut from a yellow mound, weighed and deftly patted into shape with wooden paddles. The dairy had its own characteristic and peculiar smell: a mixture of vanilla and cream and an ever-so-slightly-rancid undertone.

Across the road from the dairy, on the other side of Peas Hill Road, was a road (the name of which escapes me). But down this road was the Corona Depot. Every week the Corona man would deliver Orangeade, Cherryade and Dandelion and Burdock in their distinctive bottles with porcelain stoppers held on with an ingenious system of wire levers and red rubber seals.

Bonfire night was a time of great excitement. Bonfires would be built in the alleyway every ten houses or so. It was a matter of stiff competition to see which bonfire would have the best-looking Guy. I have no idea where the wood and fuel for these bonfires came from but it appeared from somewhere. Our bonfires were relatively small affairs compared with the huge beacon that was built in the neighbouring Edgar Rise.

Robin Hood Chase was at the outer reaches of our play area. Here there were trees and grass and tarmac walkways that provided a wonderful surface on which to race Matchbox Ferrari and Maserati model cars. The houses here seemed much posher than ours and we didn't really mix with the children who lived in this rarefied atmosphere.

Every Saturday, we would go to the Cavendish Cinema for the morning matinee. Sixpence bought the opportunity to lose ourselves in a world of adventure, laughter and cliff-hanging suspense. There would be a comedy, either Laurel and Hardy or Old Mother Riley, a cartoon and the Serial. This was guaranteed to leave the hero in an impossible situation from which there could be no possible means of escape, and ensured that you would be first in the queue for the next week's episode which, strangely, would have a much more mundane beginning than the previous week's ending. So the hero escaped after all! At Christmas there would be a special matinee that included a real clown or comedian and possibly even a competition to see who could do the best yo-yo tricks! We were given an orange and some sweets and a good time was had by all.

We were one of the first families in the street to own a television, a brown walnut cased instrument with a tiny screen. On the day of the Coronation in 1953, I think virtually the whole street crammed into our living room to watch black and white, slightly fuzzy, pictures of the young Queen waving from her carriage, walking regally down the aisle at Westminster Abbey and eventually receiving the crown from the Archbishop of Canterbury. Everyone was straining for a view. Being a child had its advantages. We were able to sit crossed-legged at the front and had an unobstructed view.

After the ceremony, we all went out into the front road for a street party. This in itself was unusual because nearly all the socialising, and certainly our playing, used to take place in the alleyway at the back of the houses. I suppose it was the equivalent of only using the front room on special occasions, and this was a very special occasion. Trestle tables, decorated with red, white and blue crepe paper, had been set in a row down the whole length of the road. There were hats and streamers, *meat* sandwiches, jelly and pop, and jugs of beer for the grown-ups. Someone brought out a wind-up gramophone and people just danced and sang.

I don't know how long this went on for. This was June and the days were long but the gas street lamps, with their glass panelled tops and ornate criss-cross pieces, came on and cast a greenish glow over the continuing celebrations. I can't remember how it ended but I think we were carried sleeping to our beds.

Another incident, vividly remembered for very different reasons, were the race riots in the late 1950s. By this time our family had moved away from St Ann's. My father was now a self-employed builder and had, over a couple of years, built us a new house in Carlton. We moved there in 1955 when I was eight. We still regularly visited my grandparents in Peas Hill Rise, travelling in dad's recently acquired van, a green Commer Cob.

One evening, after one of these visits, we all got in the van to go home: mum and dad, my younger sister Heather and myself. As we pulled out of Peas Hill Rise on to Peas Hill Road we were confronted by a huge mass of people. It was dark and very noisy. We drove slowly towards St Ann's Well Road but eventually the crush of people became too great and we were unable to move any further. People were fighting and shouting and banging against the van. I had never seen so many people in one place and we were stuck right in the middle of them.

I don't remember being particularly afraid. I suppose I was too young and too interested in what was going on to realise that we might be in some danger. Suddenly several large black police vans pushed their way through the crowd of people on St Ann's Well Road. The back doors opened and what appeared to be dozens of burly, uniformed policemen leapt out, truncheons drawn, and threw themselves into the crowd. I recall one particular policeman well. He was very tall with a great bushy moustache and was wearing black leather gloves. He wasn't holding a truncheon. I remember dad saying: 'Here come the police boxers, we'll be OK now'.

Eventually, the police cleared a path for the van and we were able to turn and make our way up St Ann's Well Road. I don't know how long we had been stuck in the crowd. To me it seemed ages. Amazingly, the van was completely untouched and we were able to make our way home without any further hindrance. I believe from conversations I recall that there had been several people injured, some with knife wounds, and many arrests were made. It was a sad episode in the history of St Ann's [1958 'Race' Riots].

Our family never really left St Ann's. Dad's eldest sister, Phyllis, married Sydney Taylor at King's Hall Methodist Church on St Ann's Well Road, where my grandparents were enthusiastic members of the congregation. Phyllis and Sydney moved into a house at the bottom of St Ann's Well Road, where they brought up five children between 1953-1962. Dad's younger sister Eileen married Keith White, again at King's Hall Methodist Church, in 1954. They moved into our old house at 19, Peas Hill Rise bringing up three boys there between 1956-1962, thus continuing the Bowrings' three-generation occupation of Peas Hill Rise!

The wedding of Phyllis Bowring and Sydney Taylor at King's Hall Methodist Church. Dave Bowring is the page boy in the front. Everyone in the photo are close relatives. Photo from Dave Bowring

My grandmother died there in 1969, in the house she had lived in for thirty-two years. Grandad stayed on in the house until it was due to be demolished. He was moved into one of the new maisonettes built to replace the terraced housing. He died there in 1975.

Eileen and Keith stayed at 19, Peas Hill Rise until they too were rehoused. They still live in St Ann's today.

I have read reports about the redevelopment of St Ann's, describing it as a 'slum clearance scheme'. These were never slums in the accepted meaning of the word. The houses may have been cramped and lacking in what we now call 'facilities' but they were home to a close-knit warm community, where everyone knew their neighbour and they all looked out for each other, something very rare in today's modern housing developments.

JEAN TAYLOR

(nee Morley)   Born 1951

Interviewed in her home 22.6.99 and conversations at other times. Jean has written prose and poetry about her life in St Ann's. All photos from Jean Taylor unless otherwise stated

I was born on Clarence Street, St Ann's. My mum, dad and sister were lodging with Lily Wood (nee Goddard) who died this year. She was an old school friend of my mum. From there we moved to 4, Norland Road, off St Ann's Well Road. We stayed there until our street was cleared and later pulled down. When I was fifteen we went to Sherwood. But I've gone back to St Ann's many, many times to the Library, to see friends, to local pubs. There were another two sisters younger than me so we were four sisters: Sue, me, Elaine and Vicki.

My mum 1952 on the back step at Norland Street

My mum and dad were really lovely, lovely people. Any child on our street could come to our house for tea or could come and play or go on holiday with us. We always had a week in a caravan in Skegness. We once went to Yarmouth when my sister was working there. I still go to Chapel St Leonard's every year. I like it.

Generally, we had a really nice time as children. We were bad off like most families. My mum, Mavis (nee Maltby) was a very hard worker. She did a little job, lace

Me on holiday at a caravan site in Skegness 1959

work, cleaning, anything that made us look special and nice. Also I was privileged because my mum and dad won on the Football Pools, £110. In those days that was a lot of money. Me and my sisters happened to be the best dressed kids out, but the money went into other families to help them get along in life as well. So I think we missed out! We would have been quite rich.

My mum came from off the Carlton Road and my dad came from Sneinton. They married in 1948. My dad was a bus driver and my mum was a conductress. That's how they met.

Later, when she did lace work at home, we used to fetch it from Mrs Simmonds on Crown Street, off Blue Bell Hill and bring it back to our house. Different friends would come and we'd draw the threads together. My mum wasn't very good at it and sometimes we'd go to Auntie Pems at Bestwood and she was extra good and we'd work together pulling threads.

It wasn't well paid at all and you were sort of scared in the house because you dare not put your feet on it or you'd be in trouble. Any marks on it and you wouldn't get the money for it. I remember sitting with a little block shining the lace so my mum could pull the threads easier. The lace work was all in one big piece and there were certain threads that separated it into small strips, which you would then roll up. The strips were the lace that afterwards went around tablecloths, pillowcases and petticoats. Mum said lace work wasn't a good name for it. It should have been called hard work!

I went to St Ann's Well Road Board School until I was eleven, then on to Sycamore Secondary School. For my last year I went to Elliott Durham School[1]. I really enjoyed that and hoped to stay on but once we moved to Sherwood it was a bit of a long way to go and I decided to leave and go to work.

---

[1]   Jean Taylor writes about her experiences at Elliott Durham in *Elliott Durham and St Anns: the comprehensive school on the hill in inner-city Nottingham* [Plowright Press 1998].

At Board School, I mostly remember Mrs Hayes and Mr Salt. They were very kind. Sadly I remember a Miss Smith who made me drink sour milk and slapped me for no reason.

Board School 1960. I'm absent. Left to right back row after Mr Salt: ? , Ida Hurst, John Craven, Susan Gillett, ? , Michael Gough, Margaret Farmer, Arthur Pearson, Valerie Dobney, John Lancaster. Middle Row: Dennis Fisher, Alan - , Susan Buckley, ? , Linda Bamford, Jean Gulvier, Susan Peck, Steven Bird, ? . Front row: ? , ? , ? , Susan Lawson, Jessie Thomson, ? , Linda - , ? , Steven Cranfield, Steven Brown, John –

An earlier photo. Board School Infants' Class with me fourth girl from the right, middle row

Miss Smith was a Scottish dance teacher and really she was very nice. I don't know why, but teachers have pets. My friend Susan Peck was her pet. But no matter what I did or showed her, it was rubbish and I had to go away.

The caretakers were kind Mr and Mrs Carnelly. 'Go up and eat your nice dinner up', they would say with a smile. Treacle cornflake cake and caramel puddings were my favourites. There was a lad called Malcolm Bingham, who came in handy because he was a good eater and liked most foods the other kids didn't. 'Pass it up here', he would say.

My mum went up to school to tell off Mr Hamlin. It was always a funny thing for my friends, because he was just reading about Robin Hood and his Merry Men coming when in walked my mum and my Aunty to tell the teacher off! After that, my mum had a bit of a nickname as one of

Robin Hood's Merry Men. My big memory of Mr Hamlin is him asking me if I'd like to join his class to see *Busy Doing Nothing* at the Co-op Arts Theatre in George Street. He was always kind to me, but I think my mum had something to do with it.

I never did very well at school. I always liked to do a bit of everything but weaving was the only subject I loved. I didn't have help with things like spelling at the time. I'm self-taught as the years have gone on. At school I was sent away to try again and I didn't go back. It was terrible really. I should have had help. If that had happened, I might have been writing little verses for cards because I used to do it as a child for family cards but nobody ever thought to tell me I might have a little talent. Everybody's got a small piece haven't they? But finally I have the pleasure of what I write today.

When I wasn't in school, I used to go to the play centres, youth clubs, cafes, pictures. I would go anywhere where there was an outing! We used to take bottles off window-sills to get the pennies to go to the Baths. Both the Board School and the Sycamore School opened up two evenings a week so you could play cards, dominos, paint, draw, do what you liked, it was very nice. There would be two teachers and two helpers who would give time to come in so you could do these things. It was all free. Yes, everything was free. That was why it was so nice. If you wanted to, say, paint a picture of a tree or something, a teacher would show you how to do it. Nowadays you would have to pay for that knowledge, wouldn't you? I enjoyed it more than school.

We'd play around our area. One of my memories, which I think is terrible looking back, is about us 'helping' the dustbin men. They used to come around the house backs to collect the dustbins. The dustbin lorry wasn't like it is now when everything is tipped in and not seen. There was like a big tray that pulled forward and the rubbish would go behind it. They kept pulling it forward and the rubbish kept falling behind. Me and my cousin Susan used to stand clinging for life on the back of the lorry up and down the streets. It was good fun and we were never told off. We'd help the men if they had a box of glass or something they couldn't bring at the moment, we'd go and fetch it. Just think of that! Nobody ever said: 'get away'. Oh dear!

I was a Brownie for two years, then a Girl Guide, at St Ann's Church. I became a Brownie Leader myself in Arnold for a few years when I was about thirty. I stayed there until my daughter went to Guides. I didn't go away to camp when I was a child. We didn't have money to do things like that. We had days out. From Elliott Durham School I was going to go to Devon but I never got there because I wasn't well.

My elder sister Sue went for a week or so with her class to Rosebury House on Lumley Avenue, Skegness. It was 1958. A lot of poor children also went. All the girls wore brown gabardine macs and berets and hated them. They had to copy a letter to send home: 'Dear Mum and Dad, having a lovely time' while a lot of tears were being shed as they wrote. It really was awful. The teachers were mean. She said a large Easter Egg was donated and they had their photo taken with it. The place is still open and, nowadays, the children have a great time.

My dad, Ernest Morley, left the buses and became a lorry driver all his life. He enjoyed that. Children in those days were allowed in the lorry so we had days going all over with him. Sometimes, he'd also take a couple of my friends off the street and we'd all sit in the lorry. No seat belts then! I was about eight when he used to take us to Skegness if he was that way and we'd have to duck down when he was delivering the coal or something. Or he'd drop us at Butlins or somewhere, let us have the day while he did his work and we'd have a time to meet him on the way back: there was me, aged nine, my sister would be twelve, my cousin fourteen and my friend nine. He would just leave us and it was the done thing then.

He drove for Smith's on Canal Street. I would go down to Smith's and the wages lady, Dora, would pin dad's wage packet into the pocket of my navy blue school knickers. Some nights he would bring the lorry home and park up on a wide piece of the road at the top of our street, facing the Sir Rowland Hill pub. When coal fell off, neighbours came to collect it in buckets. He worked until he was sixty-six and died at sixty-seven.

We had some lovely neighbours. One was George Cranfield and they had had an apple tree in their garden, which was very unusual, but it didn't bear any fruit. Apples at that time had very hard stalks and he would tie them on to his tree with cotton and then say: 'Come and scrump my tree!' I'll never forget him for that. The street I lived on, I can still go in and out of each house and tell you who lived there and what children they had.

Most of the street had relatives living in several of the houses. We lived at No 4. A Mrs Roberts lived at No 12 and mum always did extra food and she would ask me to: 'take this basin of stew to Mrs Roberts'. Josephine Smith lived at the top of the yard, No 20. I still see her, she lives in St Ann's. I always thought she was posh, because they had an Ascot for hot water. She had relatives at No 10, Mr and Mrs Shepherd.

Eileen and Jack Ashton lived at No 16 with their children John, David and Sandra. Sandra always came on holidays with us. Grandad and grandma Ashton lived at No 22. At No 2 were the Cranfields: Pauline, George, Steven, Tony and David were the family still at home when I lived there. At No 19 there was Sue and Les Davey. Les writes poetry and I often see his work. Four Davey brothers married four sisters: all smashing people.

Harold and Kathleen Newman with children Doreen, Marjorie, Kath, and twins Frances and Billy lived at No 36. Mr Newman had an allotment and would spend hours growing fruit and vegetables. He made his own square barrow and was often seen pushing it from the Hungerhill Gardens. He also had a beautiful aviary there where he would breed birds. He sometimes let us use his barrow for fun. The Sunday after Goose Fair, a crowd would take the barrow there to see what could be found.

Our next-door neighbour was a girl called Irene Raynor and she had a daughter, Susan. Now, in the house facing Irene was her mother Annie and brother John and next to

At the Garden Gate pub after an outing 1966. My mum and dad are fourth and fifth in from the right. Little Mickey Monkey, on the laps on the left, is still in my loft!

And a ladies night out. It's easy to see my mum

Annie was Mrs Bignall, Annie's mother. And that's how it went on in the street. My Aunt Eliza Richardson lived at No 14 and when she moved out my cousin Audrey moved in. Across the road from No 14, there was a young girl, Jean Frost, who married a cousin of mine, Ernie Richardson. So the street all seemed to be mixed up with each other. There were about four Bestwick families all facing each other. I think Nos 1-30 were rented from Hawksley and Haslin, which were in town near Clumber Street. That was where I used to go to pay the rent. I still have the rent book. When we left in 1967, the rent was nine shillings and eleven pence. The rent place was spooky – all brown wood.

That was the time of the clearance. A couple of friends owned their houses and they only got £50 for them. We had to move because of the clearance, to a council house in Sherwood. It had a big garden back and front and I remember thinking we were in the country. I know it sounds silly, but I didn't like the change. I liked taking my jug and bowl upstairs for a wash. And I liked going across to the toilet. My mum was very clean so the house was a lovely spotless little place. People didn't bother in those days to match things up, but my mum did, and I can go right through the house and the memories are wonderful.

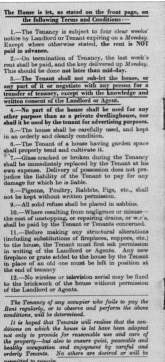

Cover and inside of our Rent Book up to the time we had to move from St Ann's

It was a three-storey house. There was a front room and a kitchen: a bedroom and landing on the first floor and spiral stairs to another bedroom and landing. And when you talk about landings, they were the size of bedrooms, as big as this room we're sitting in. The backyard was fairly small. Different neighbours would swill the yard down and scrub down. It was a shared yard for twelve houses and it went in sections of three or two. We had our own toilet. There was an outhouse and toilet, then our toilet and outhouse and that's how it went up the yard. Dad used to whitewash the toilet and we did have newspaper on a string and the bath hung in the yard. If you went to Quality House for a new pair of shoes, mum would ask for an extra bit of tissue paper because, if you were having visitors, you could have a bit in the toilet for them. I think about that now, so simple, so nice.

We had a dog that ran on to the road and died. After that mum and dad said we'd have to wait until we had places of our own. We had a small garden, which a lot of houses didn't, but the dog wouldn't stay in the garden. On the front garden, we had two marble wash tops. They made our little boundary line with the soil behind it with Michaelmas Daisies, and the rest was just hard soil that had crusted over the years. When it rained heavily, because we went down a step to our front door, the water would come in the door. We had to have piles of newspapers and towels to stop sludge and stuff pouring through the door. But dad did make a little fence and one lady used to steal the fencing for making fires. It was a known thing that people used to break a little bit of fence. She earned herself a nickname Mrs Take a Fence! At the top of the road, there was a lady called Mavis. She had lots of cats and was called 'Cat Woman'.

There were at least two bonfires each year on the street, one in the middle and one at the bottom of the street. We'd go to both. There were lots and lots of fireworks. One boy on the road, Petro Mantarno had fireworks in his pocket and as he went to throw one, a spark caught those in his pocket and blew a hole in his leg and it was the following summer before he came out of hospital. But he was fine. Even then, the medical profession managed to save his leg.

I'm in the front with my mum's hand on my shoulder. Left is cousin Beryl holding her niece Kim. On the right are my cousins Pat and Raymond. Taken on the steps of my aunt's house in Talbot Street [not St Ann's] 1960

But there was one girl on the street and a firework went down the top of her dress and caused a nasty scar. I think each household could tell a different story about their families and what they did. One family that left our road, the lady was murdered and that was sad.

My dad's sister Eliza had eleven children in a house on Norland Road and she left there to live in a rather bigger house on Talbot Street but she brought up the family in Norland Road in a house no bigger than ours. I think a lot of those children went top to toe.

As children, we'd go out in a gang. And if anybody spoke to you who shouldn't, you'd all hurry along together. Nobody would leave each other. It was a gang out for fun. I don't remember anybody doing any vandalism, they were cheeky, yes, or might shout after someone but I don't remember anybody, say, wrecking a bus shelter or anything like that. Anything that got damaged was just wear and tear.

I was always one of those children that wanted to help. I was happy washing pots and cleaning down as any of my cousins will tell you. They used to nickname me, and I don't know why, 'sludge bump'. Now I never had to do anything. But if my mum said she was going to get the washing ready for the laundry, I'd want to do it. If she was going to wash pots, I'd say the same. I just seemed to have this protective thing over my mum and dad and it's something that stayed all my life.

We did have little chores like cleaning our bedroom and: 'No she can't come out until she's done her room' and: 'Don't think you can do it quickly, because you know it's got corners'. I loved nothing more than scrubbing the window sill and step. I do remember getting into trouble when my mum had left everything in her dolly tub. She and my dad were going out. I was there with my sister and friends having a little concert and then I said I was going to do mum's washing. I put it all through the mangle and pegged it all out. Next morning I got into trouble because all I'd done was mangle it and peg it out, it had never been washed! I just assumed that because it was in water that it had been done.

Higher up the road were a very old couple and when I was nine I had Saturday morning work there for six months for one shilling. I used to wash their step and windowsills, clean the front room floor and go to Penrose's Beer-off for two jugs of Ale, and some extra jobs were added. A lot of shops put things 'on the slate': Cook's Beer-off, Ayre's Newsagents, Bombay Groceries, Trott's Hardware, Mason's Butcher, Finise's Greengrocer.

We had regular concerts on the backyard steps. Sheets pegged on the line were stage curtains.

We had a piano, which was very unusual. My dad could play by ear and he was a lovely singer. This is a true story. My Auntie Connie and Uncle Alf came to see us with their three children for Christmas and they had such a good time they didn't go home until Easter! And they only lived in Sneinton. They used to walk over Donkey Hill and go back to Sneinton and get changes of clothes and things and come back and continue to stay with us. But my mum and dad did have this special thing where our house was open

St ANN'S NOTTINGHAM: Inner-city voices *by Ruth I Johns* • ISBN 0951696092

house. Any friends are welcome, they don't come to see what you've got, they come to see you. And what we've got anybody can have if we can afford it. I think in some ways mum and dad were unique.

I must tell you about my mum. With me and my sisters, she would stroke you on the arm and you might say: 'Oh, is there something there?' And she'd say I'm touching you because I love you and don't ever forget it. I didn't think anything about that then, but now I think all those lovely things stemmed from her not having a very great life growing up herself. She had this thing that when she grew up and had children, they were going to be very, very happy and she did a good job.

And I remember my dad worn out from working and his hands all cut and I'd say: 'Why are your hands all dirty?' And he said: 'Always remember Jean I go to work to get these hands dirty to keep your hands clean and if you just do good by that you won't go very far wrong'. I've got lots of these things I keep in my mind.

As a child, for a few years I went to a church, which was a tin hut at the top of Norland Road. The congregation were mainly Jamaicans with tambourines and all their chants of hallelujah. They sang songs very different to our ordinary Church of England church and it was jolly and dancing and colourful. I won a Bible for remembering the books of the Bible and singing on stage. I've still got the Bible and am very proud of it. I had a month to learn the books of the Bible and recite them in correct order. I managed to do it until about four from the end, which I couldn't remember but I was still given the Bible. I've still got the little card for attendance that they gave me every week.

The tin Church at the top of Norland Road [1969]. Photo: Nottingham Local Studies Library [the same tin Church is shown in the Faith section. This photo was taken after Jean's family - and some others - had moved out]

I remember, one of the Jamaican ladies shouted Hallelujah, praise the Lord, and fell to the floor and I jumped up and ran to her and said: 'Quick get help'. The man in charge, Mr Allsop, said just leave her, she's very, very happy. She's just chanting to the Lord. I was quite amazed by that. Anyone could get up and preach.

At Sycamore School, it was Mr Darrington and Miss Shaw was the Deputy Head and then she became the Head. When the secondary school parts of Sycamore, Morley and Huntingdon Schools went to the new Elliott Durham School, Miss Shaw became Deputy Head there. I always found her very, very fair. I don't think she had any favourites. The same really with Nellie Hayes, Head of the Board School. Some people say Mrs Hayes whacked their legs or arms, but she never hit me.

While I was at Sycamore, I remember being shown round where there had been a swimming pool in the basement. I heard a rumour that there had been an accident there and that is why it closed. The Caretaker showed a group of us children around the rooms down there with baths in, with old-fashioned legs. The School was a good one. Some huts came for extra classrooms because there were quite a lot of Jamaicans and Asians in that area then.

I had quite a few friends among them, including a Jamaican girl called Elaine Deer and Barpinda Kaur. They told you about their own town and how they lived and it gave you an insight and I think that was good for us. At that time, I don't think there were many of my age group who were prejudiced. I think we just accepted things and we were all friends together. My other friends included Pauline Fedoriwskyi, Linda Bamford, Kathleen Dunmore and Janet Watson.

I used to chat to a Pakistani man who lived on the road. Quite a lot of people lived in that house. Sufi used to sit on the step. One day his beard was ginger. I said: 'Sufi you've dyed your beard'. He said, in broken English: 'Me dye my beard, you dye next week!' I thought he meant 'die' and ran home. He was a lovely friendly man.

This is a page of the attendance card and you'd stick in an attendance stamp each week

One neighbour delighted in getting children into trouble. She told my mum the children were causing nuisance and needed a good hiding. Mum made us come in. Once we were behind closed doors, mum said the lady didn't like children. Then mum told us to wet our eyes and give them a rub and look sad and then told us to go out to play and don't let her down. She said: 'I'm not hitting you for nobody'.

We always put old bread on the windowsill for the pig man who lived half way up the street and kept pigs on the Thorneywood allotments.

When I was about eleven, I suddenly had a bad cough and then I found this blood in my mouth and mum took me to the doctor to have it checked. And because my grandmother, Edna Maltby, had died at thirty-seven with Tuberculosis, it was a *must* that I was checked. So I was sent to the City Hospital and I was under Dr Linton and some other doctors from then until I was fifteen or sixteen. I was in and out of hospital having operations, bronchograms, bronchoscophies . . . the last operation I had was a heart-o-graph where they did six stitches in my arm and threaded a tube through. We had to sign that I was a guinea-pig for it and it was all very serious and they didn't know what was going to happen to me. They thought I'd got clots on the lungs and one thing and another.

Then one day, I was seriously ill and mum, dad and a Vicar were called in, and they then found they'd given me some drugs and I was allergic to Penicillin. After this, another doctor came and checked me over and he looked at my nose and throat and said he thought he knew what was happening. They would monitor me all night with the bed tilted. What happened was that when I sniffed, a little blood vessel burst and in the morning the blood would come into my throat. So I had five years in and out of hospital, operations and missing a school trip, and there was nothing wrong with me. And then they told me, with being a guinea-pig, I could end up with severe Asthma but that never happened, thank God. So, I was never at school but I've never been off work!

When we had to leave St Ann's and I started work, in those days you could walk round town and choose where you were going to work. I decided to go to Farmers at the top of Exchange Walk. Mr Dean, the boss, interviewed me and asked me to call back next day. Next day he said: 'I'd like you to start on Monday'. It was a forty-hour week for four pounds, four shillings. I was lucky because I worked at every department in the shop to fill in, so I was on Soft Furnishings and then someone was taken ill and I was on Haberdashery, then Wedding Materials, Patterns and Coats . . .

That building was very big and had lots of rooms that people didn't know about, where staff lived years before. Behind the shop's departments, we used to have Emily in the sewing room, there was a corset room . . . but our stockroom was in the old Eight Bells pub at the bottom of Exchange Walk. It is no longer there of course. I once went to get some cushions out of a box there and all these rats jumped out. I was so scared and in shock, they had to send me home. In all the time in St Ann's when people had spoken about rats and mice, I'd never seen one. I never visited the stockroom again! I stayed at Farmers three years.

I left to go to Minsons on Stoney Street where I became a folder, folding net curtains and I loved that. The reason I was there was because my sister was there and friends. From that point of view I loved factory life. I appreciate all people's jobs really. I know what shop assistants go through and what factory people go through.

I got married in 1971 and worked part-time in the Co-op in Arnold and my daughter was born in 1973. I didn't work then until 1978 when I became a Care Assistant, which I was for twelve years and then I was a Warden in a retirement complex for ten years and now I've been nursing for a year at the City Hospital, Jenner Ward. I love it. I seem to be doing all the things I always hoped I could do. I can't do drugs and injections because I don't have the training. I'm the proud mother of a Staff Nurse.

1999 and I'm an Auxilliary Nurse and my daughter, Clare, a Staff Nurse at the City Hospital

I go back to St Ann's because I stayed with the Library and I change my books there. And me and my sisters, we like to go round and reminisce. I don't like the new St Ann's as much as I did the old. But at the end of the day I can't dislike it because people live there now and it is lovely to them. When I was there, what was called a slum was lovely to me.

"Who being loved, is poor?" Oscar Wilde

MEMORIES OF ST ANN'S
by Jean Taylor

I'm outside the Palais with time on my hands:
I'd stroll with my friends where I lived in St Ann's.
From the top end of town we decided to go
To Central Market with stalls row by row.
We'd walk through just browsing, so much to see:
Materials, pots and confectionery.
There were lots of stalls selling clothes,
In the fish market, I'd hold my nose.

St Ann's Nottingham Inner City Voices by Hugh I Johns • ISBN 0951696092

Out of the doors on to Huntingdon Street,
Visit Bath Street park, an extra treat.
We'd sit near the lion on Bendigo's[2] grave.
Read all about him, wasn't he brave!
Back at the Empress Cinema, too late to go in:
Ah! Missed the latest: it was Tales of TinTin.
Up St Ann's Well Road, it was bustling with folks,
The barbers were busy cutting hair for the blokes.
Saturday, everyone seemed to be out – or just doing
     weekend chores.
Opticians for glasses, jewellers for rings, even
     perambulator stores.
Snack bars, shoes shops, dry cleaners (about four)
Back in two minutes was a sign on the door.
Bamfords large windows, don't look inside
In those days it was hushed if someone had died.
Gents and Ladies Outfitters at Plunketts or Deans
Then Cavendish Picture films on the big screen.
Olive's sweet shop where all the kids queued
Getting toffees before the film they viewed.
There was fancy goods, grocers, fishmongers and more
Drapers and fruiterers and Boots Chemist Store.
Eric Bishop your boots he'd repair
Scrimshaw pork butcher, get your meat there.
Bendix launderette gets the weekly wash done
Or do things by hand and get them spun.
Pownall's waste merchants, we took our rags,
Extra coppers for wool in bags.
Then McCarthy[3] the decorator, he does a great job,
Make your room nice, spend a few bob.
School Headmaster Mr Salt: lovely man who didn't pick
     fault.
Headmistress Mrs Hayes always kind, giving praise.
The school was Juniors and Infants, we studied the
     three 'R's.
Playtime was exciting although we had only two bars.
Oh! Albert Lover sold sugar in little blue bags
Butter out of the barrel and packets of fags.
Mr Peace, Waydecor, Norland Road, my abode
Mr Cook, our beer-off, where Shipstone's horses
     unload.
Rawson's, local chippy, Saturday nights were a treat.
Fish, chips, pies, roe, they'd queue out in the street.
Mr Ayres newsagent sold papers, comics and books
While Mrs Trott next door sold ornaments and cups.
Lotus Street, Queen's Arms pub plus another drapery
     store.
Holmes was the tobacconist, Bonfire Night we saved
     with him for.
Sanderson's, Beighton's, Bramley's, Tracey's chips
     you'd adore,

Co-op, George Smith, Reg Jones, Henson's, the bus
     terminus near their door.
Having reached Westminster Street, I'll have to rest my
     aching feet,
Across Coppice Road to Elsie's café, Tizer or Vimto and
     have a laugh.
I cross over to the other side, oh how I love this road!
Barber Bullocks, Lees machine shop, Miss Exton's shop
     was old
Bombay, Ronald Martin, Speed Electrics, Cox's to name
     a few.
Strecker's pork butcher, who everyone knew.
Meadow Dairy, Public Baths, Douglas White hardware,
The Post Office, Marsden's, Frank Tetley were all there.
The King's Hall Church, local police and pubs,
We did have parks and fun at youth clubs.
My memory's been back to when I was young,
St Ann's Well Road, oh wasn't it fun!
At Quality House I got my shoes,
The Havelock, the nearest booze.
Lily Wakelin for your hair. Northampton Street: get
     your bath there.
Mr Chettle, the dentist, took out my dad's teeth.
Next door was Dewhurst's, get the braised beef.
Taylor's opticians it is the last one
But you know there's more, let your memory live on.

STEVE HARRISON

Born 1951

Interviewed in St Ann's Library 14.9.99

I used to live at 100, Robin Hood Chase, St Ann's. My
family moved in there in 1961. I was the fourth out of five
lads and three girls. We moved from Radford because we
were being demolished there.

And then Mrs Eyers next door at No 98 said Robin
Hood Chase was going to be demolished within about nine
years. My parents were renting the house from the Council.

But all the houses in Robin Hood Chase at that time
were being renovated, having bathrooms put in and the
outside toilet demolished.

I've quite a lot of good memories of that time. Mrs
Eyers' house was a guest house and she would give us
things like left-over soup. She used to have gentlemen stay
over for Bed and Breakfast.

In the early 1960s things were quite bad. My parents
were hard up. My dad was a lorry driver with Walter Danks
on London Road.

I went to the Elms School and then to Morley School. I
had to give evidence to the police while I was at the Elms
about a teacher's sexual molestation of some of the
children. He would have a child behind his high desk
whilst continuing to teach, but the class couldn't see what
was happening.

I was bullied at Morley School and left unable to read or
write. My dad went up to school in his lorry to tell the Head
to stop me being picked on, but my dad was rough with us

---

2   On Sunday mornings we'd get up and always go to visit Grandma and Grandad's
    in Sneinton. If the church band was on parade, we'd march with them down St
    Ann's Well Road (before I joined the Brownies and Guides). When we got to Bath
    Street, we'd go into the Rest Garden park and visit Bendigo's grave. 'He lived like
    a lion and died like a lamb.' He died in 1880, aged sixty-nine. He was one of a
    large family and lived on Trinity Walk off Parliament Street. He was a champion
    bare-knuckle prize fighter. Dad used to say he was some way-back relation. Dad's
    brother Alf was a boxer at one time. Bendigo was a well-known local preacher.
    JT.
3   Dennis McCarthy's dad.

Elms School April 1959. The teacher is Mrs Byers. Photo from Steve Harrison

at home as well and used to shut me in the cellar. I learnt to read and write through my own efforts around 1980 and later got an old typewriter and taught myself to type.

I was in the last class to leave Morley School in July 1966. Some of the kids smashed up the school and about six to eight youths were reported to the police. The Head, Mr Pearce left around 1965 and the Deputy Head, Mr Martin, took over until the school was closed.

I used to go scrumping up Hungerhill Gardens and sledging down Robin Hood Chase. I remember all the shops and names of the people, like Frank Vincent who owned the hardware stall as you came down Abbotsford Street facing the pub, the Adelphi pub. He used to sell a few bits of second-hand things as well and then go into the pub for a few drinks. That was his life. He lived to a very old age. Mary Lamb's shop was on the corner of Abbotsford Street where it joined up with Rosslyn Street. In the early 1960s, her mother was still serving at the age of ninety. She always used to get the change mixed up.

I remember Brighton Street as being a very clean street, much better than some of the neighbouring streets. I've never seen photos of some of the old shops including Mary Lamb's grocery shop, Severn's Newsagents on Dame Agnes Street, the Co-op Grocery on Dame Agnes Street and Dowties Beer-Off, or of the Adelphi pub. My film collection includes 'All around Nottingham' and 'Goodbye to old St Ann's'.

I was always late for school because I used to watch the BRS lorries leaving the BRS [British Road Services] depot on The Wells Road, because my dad was a lorry driver. I used to go out with him to deliver baths to customers.

When I left school, I went to work for the PDSA [People's Dispensary for Sick Animals] jumble which was in Broad Marsh. That was in 1966. My wages were £3 11s. I used to have to go knocking on people's doors asking for jumble to sell to help animals. PDSA was a charity.

I can remember the time before we moved to Bilborough. My dad chopped up all the old furniture we wouldn't be taking with us to make firewood for the winter. It was very strange because we all slept downstairs then. I think Robin Hood Chase was nearly last coming down because I visited it 1971/72 and Mrs Eyers was still living there. I noticed that our house had all its windows

smashed in. I didn't see any of the area where I used to live as a ten year old child. I didn't actually see it being pulled down. I'm really glad I remember it before that time. I was growing from a child into a man.

When we moved to Bilborough, the housing was better but the neighbours weren't very good. It wasn't so close as St Ann's where people helped each other. We used to clear snow for people, run errands for people. There was an old chap lived three doors from us and I used to go and fetch his medication. They'd pay us pennies and if you refused they were insistent that you took it.

After the PDSA, I worked for Marathon Knitwear. I left the PDSA because I got beat up by one of the lads. My neck was all bruises. At Marathon Knitwear my job was in the stores unloading lorries and putting away, that sort of thing. I was there five and a half years, then went to Blanchards Bakery, on Watnall Road.

I've been unemployed now for fifteen years. I'd rather work but I'm told that the longer you're out of work, it becomes difficult to set you on. I spend my time looking at archives, old photographs, films. I collect old films and show them to friends. I'm in Sneinton now. With the houses being close together, you get to know your neighbours, whereas at Bilborough the houses were more spaced out.

I think St Ann's was ruined. I've had these dreams over the years, more like nightmares. I go to bed at the right time and I'll have a dream and the old St Ann's crops up, whereas they haven't knocked it down at all, all they've done is put new lamposts up, new walls, new window frames. And then there may be another dream where we've left our house and then gone back to it and moved in. Or after a number of years the houses have broken windows and I've actually moved in and done it up, you know that sort of thing. You know we never had any damp in our house in Robin Hood Chase.

If you go up Robin Hood Chase there is a flyover. Well that was out of Caroline Street. I've got maps of the whole area. Our house, No 100, was by the second or third tree on the right facing the Baptist Mission. I was in the Boys' Brigade at the Baptist Mission, the 41st in Nottingham. I used to enjoy marching up the road and everyone looking at you. Every Friday, we had a club night and play darts, dominos and things like that. I was the only one of the family that went. I did boxing but it didn't last long because I got boxed in the ears.

My brothers and sisters? We were always fighting. Still fighting and arguing even today!

I don't think big families stick together in old age, they spread out, so the only contact you have with your brothers and sisters is through your parents. As I say to my mum and dad, it's not nice but, when you two have gone, I won't see my brothers and sisters. My mum and dad are in their 70s.

I live on my own. All I've got is next door's cat moved in with me and the family don't come. It's always excuses. They say if anything happens to me they will just come and dump my archives in a skip. I know they won't. If there are any films going cheap in Nottingham, I buy them from Film Fairs. I filmed Boots Island Street before it was demolished.

St Ann's Nottingham. Inner-city voices by Ruth Johns • ISBN 0951696092

After completing National Service in the Armed Forces in the late 1940s and early 1950s, a group of five young men set up a **Judo Club** in St Ann's. A Sheldon, who writes elsewhere in this book about Les Townsend, Manager of Butler Morris Ltd, St Ann's Well Road, told me that the Club was to be found across a small courtyard in Blue Bell Hill Road on the upper floor of a small factory. He was one of the founder members and is seen standing in this photo. At one time, the Club had sixty members of both sexes and had to restrict the number of enthusiastic recruits until more members reached certain standards of skill. Photo from A Sheldon.

A young woman resident [1999]: "I've never had a problem with St Ann's. When I was still at Primary School, I used to take my younger brother to school [mid-1980s]. As kids we used to go all over, we weren't kept in the garden or anything. That was before St Ann's was 'done up'. There was just the park and stuff. We used to build tree houses. We did use the Adventure Playground but didn't like it because it was so ordered. I suppose it was because we were kept in there once we went up there, and we were used to being free. But it's great for kids. There wasn't as much stuff as there is now. We just had the inflatable and a little table football game."

STEPHANIE WILLIAMS

Born 1953

Interviewed in her home 6.10.99

I was born at Robin Hood Chase, St Ann's. I was there until I got married at seventeen. I moved before the area was demolished, but my mum had to move and they moved her to Sherwood. My mum and dad were Roy and Dorothy Nicholls.

There were two doctors on Woodborough Road, Dr Everton and Dr Want. Dr Everton brought me into the world at home. I was very small, not more than three pounds and placed into a chest of drawers because there was no cot. We were all under three pounds, one sister was two pounds. We were just wrapped up and put in a drawer. I was the youngest of five. I've got two brothers and two sisters.

I started at the Sycamore Nursery at the bottom of Sycamore Road, then I went to Sycamore Infants, then I went to the Elms Junior School and then the Sycamore Secondary School.

I went to the Nursery because mum and dad were working full-time. I remember being in my pram with big wheels and I remember breaking my wrist walking up the little concrete steps on to the garden where we used to have a nap in the afternoon. My dad was a Trent bus driver in the old Huntingdon Street Bus Station and mum worked at William Bancroft's which are still there today [Robin Hood Street]. She was a machinist.

My dad's mum and dad lived on Eton Street, which isn't there any more, at Mapperley. And my mum's mum and dad lived on one of the streets off Peas Hill Road, St Ann's. I didn't know my grandparents on my mum's side. When we were kids we went scrumping on the Hungerhill Gardens off Sycamore Rec. Once we were caught and all my friends fled and I was caught up this tree and tore my dress. I implored the man not to hurt me. We got up to a lot of mischief but were respectful of what adults said.

We used to go to Len's chippy on a corner in Westville Street because we always used to have sixpence every night on the mantelpiece, and that was called 'your supper money'. We couldn't touch it until I'd set up tea for all the family when I came home from school. We got into the routine of getting some bread and butter and then sitting in Len's chip shop and they used to pour batter bits over the top with salt. With sixpence, we used to have a bag of chips and batter bits and as much salt and vinegar as we liked. We probably had a penny left to get four chews. That was our treat. Then we'd go home and have a whale of a time.

I used to have a key on a ribbon round my neck. Many a time I would lose it, so I had to give it to my teacher. This was at Junior School. If I lost the key I used to shimmy up the drainpipe on to the bay window, go through into my mum's room and come down and unlock the door. The rest of the family gradually used to come home from school and work. I would set the table with cups, saucers, side plates, knives, forks, place mats, teapot on the chrome stand with the little white plastic knobs on the legs, milk jug, sugar bowl. My mum prepared the dinner on the stove and I used to light it as I came in so it would still be cooking for when my mum came home ready to serve up.

We left school at ten past four from the Elms Junior School and I got home at quarter past because it was straight down Corporation Oaks across Woodborough Road into Robin Hood Chase. I could never remember the number of the house. I know it sounds strange but I used to have to count the trees down to my house. I was always the first one home. My brother was at the same school but he used to run off and play, football and things, so he wouldn't have the key. It was left to me to open the house. Tea for the younger ones - my brother and me - was generally bread and jam, but we knew the sixpence was there.

The tea was mainly for the older ones that came in from work, Kathleen, Susan and John. Dad would come if he was on the right shift, otherwise his dinner would be well cremated in the oven or on a pan of hot water to keep it warm. The sixpence was for the kids left at school. In the end, that was me and my brother. When we were home from school, my brother and I used to fight. We used to have shillings to put in the gas meter in the cellar. If I went down to put one in, he used to lock the door and turn the light off. I'm petrified now of closed spaces. I suppose that comes from that time!

When the older ones left school, they earned their own money and tipped all their wages to mum. I did when I started work. You just gave your mum all the money and then they made sure you got your snap or your dinner money for work and your clothes were bought out of what there was. But all the money went in together.

We used to play hundreds of games as kids. Mum's washing-line was a skipping rope, mum's pegs were aeroplanes, take my mum's stockings or tights and put a tennis ball in . . . There was two-ball, marbles, general skipping, conkers, knocking on doors and tying door knobs. We used to tie all the doorknobs together criss-cross all over the terrace at the back and we would hide underneath the knobs and all at once knock on the doors. Then we'd run as everybody would try to open their doors! We used to go out the back, out of our yard, which was sectioned with a gate into Northville Terrace. We'd play tennis and we always broke a window and it was always Mrs Laycock's window. You used to run then.

There was a grocer's shop on the corner of Northville Terrace and I played with the daughter of the people who owned it. I suppose we were little rogues really, tying string round milk bottles on Mr Raynor's shop window so when they opened the door the bottle would fall off and smash. It would be empty. And there was hide and seek, tagging and climbing walls and jumping over walls and through entries. We used to have a section between Woodborough Road, Raglan Street and Peas Hill Road and Robin Hood Chase. In that block you did all your running, hiding . . . If you got caught you came all the way back to Northville Street and stand at the lampost waiting for someone to come and tag you so you could be free again. We covered miles.

For bonfire night, someone would cut a tree up and put it outside Len's chippy and the beer-off on Westville Street. I can remember an old piano we had used, and we were taking it to the bonfire. We sat on top and someone pushed it so it would crash into the bonfire. We used to think it was wonderful but you didn't realise the dangers. It was just having fun.

Our house was rented. We had the whole house. It was three storeys, bay windows. We had a bathroom upstairs with a toilet and an outside toilet. We were called posh. We were allowed to use only the outside toilet in the day. We used the upstairs one once we went to bed. Half past seven you were in bed, you just didn't argue, you went to bed. It was a really big bath but it was cold there, because there was no heating. All you had was the coal fire downstairs. The bigger ones had that bath, the little ones we had the tin bath and then earlier it was in the sink. We had a fairly big front garden on to the Chase, with blackberry bushes in.

I still remember friends from those days: Gillian, Pauline, the Thompsons, Audrey, Sylvia Laycock who was my sister's friend, and Janet Baker who I haven't tracked down. We were always together. We used to toddle off through the alleyway on the Chase that came on to Dame Agnes Street, then we used to cut through the back of the terrace where there was a newsagents shop. Everybody knew everybody. If mum and dad weren't in, there was always somebody there for you. That's how I was brought up and, in my life, I've always helped everyone and looked after each other's children.

And everybody was more or less the same. I suppose we were one of the first to have a television but you weren't allowed to watch it unless your parents said you could, like the Wooden Tops and things like that. We had budgies, hamsters, mice and we found a stray dog and we used to go to the vets[1] which are still there on Woodborough Road. All my pets have gone there. I've got a Pekinese now.

We had new outfits at Easter. With mum being a machinist, we girls would all have dresses the same, and new shoes. On a Saturday, we used to go down the old Central Market on Huntingdon Street and get fabric. She had a treadle Singer machine at home. She baked everything by hand, it was all fresh done from scratch.

I did enjoy school. I was top of RE [Religious Education]. At Sycamore Secondary, I was in the top five for Maths. Most of all, I enjoyed writing my own stories, because my imagination was out of this world. I remember the teacher who used to live on one of the streets off Cranmer Street. We used to carry books and things home for her. She was a young teacher and we got on really well with her. The first words Miss Shaw, the Deputy Headmistress, said to me were: 'I hope you're going to be more like Susan than Kathleen, but we'll just wait and see'.

It made me feel I was singled out straight away. But, I suppose they did have an eye for it, because generally I do tend to be more like Kathleen than Susan. But I wasn't a

---

[1] See Alan Swift's interview re this Veterinary Practice.

naughty child, I got on with my work, I used to sing in the School Choir and got awards all over the place from Sycamore School.

My Auntie Hilda lived at the Vicarage, as they called it, at the top of the Chase. That's not there now. Where she lived was like a wall with little windows in and a door and it was something to do with the Vicarage. Two cousins lived there as well and they were in the Church Choir like me.

After I left school, I went to work at Ericson's in Beeston and went to College for night-school in shorthand and typing once a week. Then I caught for my son, and I got married and that was that. You had to marry, there was no question. I was seventeen and had no choice. I think it was something to do with the neighbours at that time and shame on the family, plus he was Italian and it was the same for him. We lived in his father's house in Arnold, he had an Ice Cream Factory there.

My dad took me aside and said I didn't have to marry him if I didn't want to, and then I looked at mum's face and thought, yes I do. There was a bad time when my sister got pregnant and she got the brunt of it. She ran away and lived with him. When I got pregnant it wasn't quite the same. How can I put it, the sting went out of it. I wasn't chastised. It was: 'You've made your bed my girl, now lie on it'. My father never took a hand to us except when my sister was pregnant. Looking back, it was amazing that, in those days, we simply didn't know about sex and babies. Mum never told me anything and referred me to my sister.

My marriage only lasted about two years. I went back home to my mum and dad who had a house in Sherwood then and you just did what your parents said even though you had been married and had a son. I was still the baby of the family. It was a case of, come home, yes, but you go to work and provide for your son, we don't provide it for you. And you just got on with it. I worked twelve hours in a flower-packing factory, six hours in the morning and six at night.

And then I worked behind a bar on and off for years. Because my mum was a barmaid after she retired from Bancroft's because of her eyesight. She'd been machining all her life working close and it affected her eyes. So I followed mum's footsteps and became a barmaid, which I thoroughly enjoyed. After the birth of my son, I was told I couldn't have any more children because I was ill with cancer, but fourteen years ago I had another son against all the odds.

My mum died just after he was born and my dad a few years before. I had a tiring time looking after them. It was always left to me to look after them. I remarried about three years ago and came back to live in St Ann's about a year ago, but we are hoping to sell and move out to Lincolnshire. My husband's family originally came from out there and his parents moved over to Nottingham to give his brother, sister and him a better life. My elder son is now a Chartered Management Accountant and my younger son is still at school.

I still remember the old St Ann's, cobbled streets, Shipstone's horses coming up and down, the coal man arriving, then the little man on his bike who came to sharpen your knives. We used to run out and get a balloon off him. I wasn't there at the time of demolition. I used to go to Sunday school at Emmanuel Church and I was quite upset that it had been pulled down. We had Sunday school, Choir practice Fridays and weddings on Saturdays and at church all day Sundays. It was the main thing in your life. The Church had a Girls' Friendly Society in a hall that ran across the bottom of the Church down Woodborough Road. And they used to have jumble sales there. But that's not there anymore either.

My mum was quite religious. My dad was an atheist. Mum had the family Bible. She didn't go to church. I think in those days it was a matter of getting the kids off to church, out of sight, out of mind sort of thing. When I got confirmed she came and now and again she would pop to church. But she was that busy with five children, my dad, getting Sunday dinner prepared, getting the washing and ironing done. I mean it was the old dolly tub and ponch, no washing machine.

If they [architects and planners] had the knowledge they have today they would have made grand houses out of some of those houses in St Ann's that were pulled down. They would have revamped them, put central heating in . . .

Some people who live in St Ann's feel trapped by its bad reputation. The following are comments from four St Ann's people [1990s].

- "My family don't like visiting me here though I've never experienced any kind of trouble." [sixty-six year old woman in sheltered accommodation]
- "My son tried to get a job but when they saw St Ann's on the address, that's it, no interview. So he's started putting Mapperley"
- "People think we live like animals in a slum but they've never been here". [woman in her fifties]
- "I'm *still* angry at the way that report was turned into a film [referring to the BBC film made following the Coates and Silburn survey on St Ann's when the area was suffering planning blight]. There was poverty, yes, but people were clean even though it was a lot of hard work. St Ann's got a terrible reputation it didn't deserve. It stuck." [woman in her seventies]

On the No 50 bus route [mid-1990s], a mother with two young children on the bus on her return to women's refuge accommodation in St Ann's said she was there because a neighbour, from her 'home' area raped and attacked her and she fled. The police wanted her to press charges but she feared reprisals if she did. She just wanted to keep her children safe and was to be settled in a new area outside Nottingham. Her partner had left them the previous year.

She said she'd always remember her weeks in the Hostel in this "all right area" St Ann's.

JOHN B HIBBITT took these photos when he lived in St Ann's

Triumphal procession in Alfred Street South on Saturday, May 2nd 1959 after Nottingham Forest won the F A Cup

The Greyfriars [Hunt Street/Flewitt Street] Pipe Band 1959 on Blue Bell Hill, St Ann's. The Greyfriars Pipe Band has recently started again. See Index

1960. Back of 66, Flewitt Street with Lytton Street in the background. Kevin White, aged two, in the garden of his grandfather, Jack Brown. Sunlight shines on the toilet block. "From their bedroom windows in good weather, neighbours would chat whenever one went to the toilet. You really did know everybody's business! "

Gordon Road, St Ann's, 1972, looking toward the City and Victoria Centre flats with Sketchley Street on the right

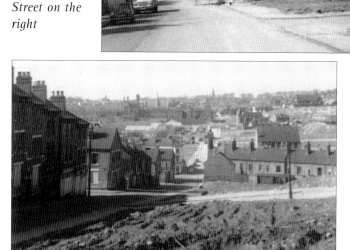

The new block of flats, Kendale Court, at the bottom of The Wells Road 1968. This photo was taken from Porchester Road

The remains of Alfred Street Central 1971 looking toward the new Victoria Centre flats

Pym Street, St Ann's, 1972. St Ann's Well Road runs across at the bottom of the hill and Peas Hill Road is opposite Pym Street. In the near distance Turner Street is on the left and Moffat Street on the right. St Andrew's Church spire is ahead in the distance

St Ann's Nottingham Inner City Voices by Ruth Johns • ISBN 0951696092

MARIO McKAY

in search of friends from his childhood

One fine summer afternoon in 1999, Mario McKay, in an open top sports car, was in Manning Street, St Ann's. He had come over from Peterborough. He was bewildered at the change in the layout of the streets. He was last in St Ann's before the time of demolition and rebuilding. He was looking for a family called Langham, who had lived on the corner on Lilac Street when he was a boy. We chatted about his interesting reasons for wishing to trace the family. I explained about the changes to the street layout. I suggested he went to Nottingham Local Studies Library.

Later that day, he did some research in the Library. Through the Electoral Register he found the name of Langham at 12, Lilac Street and at 17, Lilac Street and discovered, later, that the two didn't know each other. But by 1970, No 17's Langham wasn't listed and in 1971, No 12's Langham wasn't listed so he assumed the family had moved out due to redevelopment. As a last resort, the Library staff suggested he look up the 1970 Telephone Directory, but no Langham with the correct initial there. But a look at the current Directory and one phone call, and he found who he was looking for!

Mario McKay wrote and told me of his successful search. He added:

"You may remember I told you that I was taken into the National Children's Home at Springfield, the Crescent, Alexandra Park in 1959 when I was five years old. I attended the Elms Infant and Junior Schools in St Ann's before going to Claremont Secondary School. My connection with St Ann's was also going to Cubs and Scouts at Sycamore School, and the minor skirmishes with children from the Rec at the bottom of Sycamore Road [now Hungerhill Road].

"At the time, we in the Children's Home were considered 'different' by these kids and they would occasionally come into the field below the Home to taunt us. I can now understand why they thought us strange. We had a mixture of accents, my own then was broad Cockney and, before 1967, it was all boys. We all went to a little barber's shop on Dame Agnes Street opposite Lilac Street for our regulation short back and sides, which I absolutely hated.

"On reflection we were dressed a little smarter than they were and we were somewhat isolated. I am pleased to say these skirmishes never amounted to much."

[1999] Sitting next to me on a bus from the City Centre, a man of seventy-three said: "Life is all memories, isn't it duck? I used to call out for my mam when she was dead. Now I cry out for my wife who died of breast cancer at forty-five." As we passed Shelton Street, St Ann's, he said: "We used to have a house down there [long before demolition time]. It cost £359 and people wanted to know how a working man could afford it."

BROTHERS: BORN IN JAMAICA AND BRITAIN

LINBIRD N GREEN

Born 1955

Interviewed in his home 23.11.99

I was born in Jamaica and I came to this country in 1967 when I was thirteen. My parents were already here and I came over with three of my sisters. One was older and two younger than myself. My eldest brother was already here. My younger brother, Glenford, was born in this country.

In Jamaica, we were living with our grandmother. She was taking care of us. But she was getting old and it was difficult for her. So my mother, Pearly Green, decided to send for us. And if she didn't send for us at that time, it would have been more difficult for us to come over because immigration policy was changing.

I hate to see people suffer. It goes back to the way I was brought up in the Caribbean to care about people. In some ways it was a tough childhood. We had a struggle to make ends meet. We were living in the countryside and had people all around us showing off because they had all these things and we didn't have much. I was a sick child and my grandmother used to do everything she could to cure me and I miss her very much. I still see her as though she is living.

The rough time I had there gives me a sense of responsibility to know what people have to go through and I'm sensitive to people's feelings and their social environment. I was brought up in the Church in the Caribbean, the Pentecostal Church. When I came over here, I used to attend church but I don't now. But I still believe in God. I'm not bitter about any problems I've had. I think they make me stronger.

When we came to Nottingham, we were living at 275, Woodborough Road, St Ann's. Then we moved to 89, Woodborough Road. So I have been living in St Ann's all along. I went to Elliott Durham School before it became a Comprehensive School. People were very friendly then, we had a very close community and people supported each other. Since demolition, people you knew disappeared because the Council had to find places to house them elsewhere.

At the time of demolition, I was too young to know whether demolition was a good idea. But it has altered everything in terms of solidarity, in terms of living as good neighbours. That spirit has rather gone. While we were living at 89, Woodborough Road, they were starting to demolish the area nearby and then they wanted to demolish our house and they decided to move us to this house. And we've been here since 1973. Some of our neighbours were European and some African Caribbean. We all got on extremely well.

Since then, some of our neighbours have died because of illness or old age, and some have moved out of the area. Then new neighbours moved in and they are not as friendly. I don't know why except since Mrs Thatcher came

Linbird Green 1969 while at Elliott Durham School

Linbird Green 1992

to power and people changed to think of themselves and not really think about community and others living around them. People have become selfish and isolated.

I left Elliott Durham in 1970 and went to Basford Hall College for a year to help me develop my education. When I came from Jamaica I was a bit rusty with my reading and writing. After that I was unemployed for some time.

I've done various jobs, working in a toy shop, for the Family Practioner Committee, as a warehouse assistant, as a messenger at the Department of Trade and Industry on Cranbrook Street, as a dispatcher, as a cutter at a firm in the Lace Market, then as a cutter for a firm on Vernon Road, and then I was unemployed again.

Then I went to work at Sycamore Youth and Community Centre in St Ann's. For five years I was a youth worker and I found that really interesting. While I was there, I decided to do a part-time Certificate in Youth Work. I thought I would go on to study for social work and went to Birmingham Polytechnic [now University] to study for CQSW, but I left after about twelve weeks because I found it very stressful having to leave Nottingham and live in Birmingham. I got homesick.

For a while I had a temporary training place with JIPAC [a project in St Ann's] as an education worker and then they moved me to a position of supervisor. After that I did a spell of training in a residence for young people with severe emotional problems. The officer in charge thought I was standing up for the children too much instead of supporting the staff. I think I was more on the children's side.

I was in and out of jobs and unemployment, but I always did a lot of voluntary work. In the early 1990s, I started a local Tenants and Resident's Association. It was called St Augustine's TRA because the St Augustine's Church was the only long-serving building in the area. I used to edit newsletters, meet all the residents, elderly and young, and tried to help them. The group ran for about four years and then, as I said earlier, people moved out of the area and there were not enough people to share the workload. I'm hoping to help start this up again, and to try and involve the newer people.

I attended an Access Course at People's College when I was about thirty-seven and got O Levels and A Levels then I went for teacher training in Derby and I passed the course academically, but was not successful with my teacher placement report. There are reasons why I contested that. Now it's at the European Court of Human Rights and I am waiting to hear. While I was studying at Derby, my youngest sister died and that did affect me. I came over from Jamaica with her.

At present I am having a wonderful time on a Counselling Course at the University of Nottingham. The teachers and students are great. At the moment I am doing voluntary work. I'm Chairperson of this group called Concerned Citizen Group. It is a group interested in African Caribbean young people's development in education and social skills.

And I'm setting up an Association for supplementary schools. I used to work for five years as a supplementary [Saturday] school co-ordinator and teacher in St Ann's. It was held on Cranmer Street.

St Ann's Nottingham: Inner-city Voices by Ruth I Johns • ISBN 0951696092

There were about fifty children attending, mostly African Caribbean and some white. That supplementary school has closed down now. I thought there should be an Association to safeguard the interests of supplementary schools. There are thirty-six supplementary schools in Nottingham. Most are for African Caribbean and Asian children, also Polish, Ukrainian, Greek, Italian and Vietnamese. My interest in supplementary schools started when I was working with JIPAC.

There are politics involved with supplementary schools. I wrote to David Blunkett [then Secretary of State for Education] and one of his educational advisers got in touch with me. He sent me this booklet explaining they are trying to pump more money into supplementary school education and I think they want to take them over and run them the way they would like to see them operate. But I see a danger in this. If the Government then decided to withdraw the money, then supplementary schools would suffer. Do you see why I think an Association would be a good idea? It would safeguard supplementary schools. I think one reason why the Education Department do not want an Association is because they want everything under their control. At present the Government is helping just with funding.

To young people in fifty years time, I would say I was brought up in St Ann's and see it as a beautiful place to live because you meet so many different people. The area is developing, it's improving. City Challenge [from 1992] helped. Thousands of pounds were put in to improve the houses and they are nice houses now. I love the area and even when I reach the age of sixty to seventy-five, I shall still be in St Ann's. I live here with my mother and younger brother, Glenford.

2002. Linbird Green writes: "I have now received my Advanced Certificate in Counselling from Nottingham University. I am doing my Diploma in Professional Counselling at Nottingham Trent University, a two-year course. In October 2001, I started working for the National Institute for the Blind as a part-time telephone fund-raiser"

PEARLY LOUISA GREEN

I came over from Jamaica in 1963. We lived in Birmingham and my husband was working nights, piecework, making cars. I had a sister in Nottingham so I left him in Birmingham and came to Nottingham later in 1963. I worked at a factory on Queen's Drive. They made fabric. I was there for about five years. Then I worked in a factory at Netherfield doing the same. That factory closed down.

My six children are Evan, my first son, then Alva May, then Joylee and Linbird. Then Mable who died and the last one Glenford, he's born here. He's thirty-two, studying law. He's studying to go further up to be a lawyer.

St Ann's here was nicer at first, friends around. A lot of them have passed away and some strange people have come. But anyway, it's peaceful, it's all right, sometimes lonely. I go to the New Testament Church on Ilkeston Road.

GLENFORD GREEN

Born 1966

Contribution sent 1999

I was born at 275, Woodborough Road, St Ann's, and I still live in St Ann's across the road from where I was born.

My father was Cleveland George Meilkle, known as Mr Meilkle. He was born in Johns Hall in Jamaica. He died in 1984 in Jamaica. He was an employee of Brush Electrical Engineering, Loughborough, for over twenty years.

My mother is Pearly Louisa Green. She came to England. My mother was trained in tailoring and machining in Jamaica and was involved in the Church in Jamaica. She worked as a care assistant at an old people's home on Sneinton Dale, Nottingham.

I have two older brothers in England, Linbird Green and Evan 'Winston' Green, and two older sisters Alva and Joylee. I also have another older brother from my father's side, Mac, who lives in America, and two older sisters who live in Jamaica. My younger sister, Mable Johnson, sadly died in 1993 in Nottingham.

I went to Huntingdon Infant and Nursery School in St Ann's. Huntingdon Junior School is famous for being the first school in Nottingham to introduce a steel band. Mr Vaughan was one of the first black teachers I ever saw. He gave steel band lessons in the evening after school.

My best memory of going to Huntingdon was when I played the part of Mr Bumble in the school play Oliver Twist. The thing that was different about me playing that part was that I used a Jamaican patois dialect. Old school friends remember this.

I enjoyed art, playing football and music at Huntingdon. Mr Groves and Mr Tiplady would take us for football practice. Although I was good at football, my mum did not like the idea of me playing and getting hurt. Although I enjoyed playing football, I did not enjoy being

Glenford Green

put under pressure by the teachers to play for the school team. There was an incident when the school had an important football match on Saturday morning and I did not turn up. On Monday morning, I was in trouble and had to stay behind after school to see my Sports teachers.

They shouted and accused me of letting the school down. I was frightened and began to cry. It was beginning to get late and I heard someone walking quickly toward the classroom. It was my mum. At that moment, I was allowed to go home. My mother gave both teachers a good telling off. I was never asked to play for the school football team again.

At eleven, I went to a Catholic School, St Bernadette's on Sneinton Dale. A lot of kids from St Ann's went there. My best subject was art with Mr Ash my Art Teacher. He said I was gifted in art in my school report. I enjoyed most sports especially football and basketball. Mr Burgess, my Sports Teacher would try to get me to play for the football and basketball teams. If you did not play for one of his teams, he would make school life difficult for you.

One thing that concerned my parents and me was that I was encouraged in sporting activities but not with my education.

As a young teenager, I was involved in the church. I used to attend a church on Heathcoat Street in the City. I would bring my electric guitar to church to play. I was taught by Mr Bennett, also known as 'Money Man' who died a few years ago. He lived in St Ann's. I used to go to his house every Saturday evening for guitar lessons. I became the church musician and played my electric guitar on a regular basis at church conventions and services. But after a couple of years my Pastor, Pastor Peddy, emigrated to America. The church closed and I stopped going to church.

As a child I watched brother Johnson, the church guitarist, and that's the reason I started to play. Later, he married my sister Mable. At that time I was attending the United Holy Church of God, Ilkeston Road.

I left school in 1982 aged sixteen. I passed a few CSE exams obtaining my best grade in Art. I was sad at leaving school and decided to apply to College.

At that time, a new dance craze was just reaching England: body popping. I saw Jeffery Daniels body popping on Top of the Pops and I was very impressed. He was one of the singers from the American Soul Group Shalamar. I started to get into this dance craze and would practise almost every day. Break dancing was also just starting to appear. The record Buffalo Girls was in the charts and the video featured an American break dance crew called Rock Steady Crew. After a couple of months I actually began to get good at body popping.

I used to attend the Sycamore Youth Club in St Ann's. My brother Linbird was the youth worker there. Most of the kids who came were into the reggae scene. I attended the Rock and Reggae Festival on the Forest Recreation Ground in 1983. The DJ was playing Rocket by Herbie Hancock. There was a man doing some body popping in a crowded circle. I asked him what his name was and he said: 'Leyton'. I invited him to the Youth Club and, after that, he would regularly DJ at the Youth Club.

Each Thursday, break dance crews from all over Nottingham would come to Sycamore Youth Club in St Ann's to practise. The Club became very popular as a place to practise break dancing. But around 1987, the break dancing craze began to slow down. I decided to go back into education. I attended night-school and studied A Level Art.

In 1988, I went to Buffalo, New York, to visit Uncle Zedie. Before going, I took a temporary job at Raleigh in the wheel shop. After I was laid off, I started employment training with JIPAC [Joint Indian, Pakistani and Afro-Caribbean Project] Print on Hungerhill Road, St Ann's. I was there a year. At the same time I studied O Level English at People's College. I gained a Grade C. I completed my employment training with an NVQ in Offset Printing.

I applied for a warehouse job at John Menzies Library Services and worked there until 1991 when I was unexpectedly made redundant.

My brother Linbird suggested I should go on an access course to Clarendon College. I started in September 1991. My favourite subject was African history. I completed a full year at College. When I received my exam marks, I was quite surprised to find that I had failed all my exams and course work. I decided to put what happened at College behind me and decided to go on the Gateway to Teaching course at People's College.

Whilst studying at People's College, my brother-in-law died suddenly from a heart attack at Christmas 1992. In the summer of 1993, our younger sister Mable died suddenly. We are a close-knit family and could not believe what was happening. My brother Linbird and I care for our elderly mother.

I was told I failed my course by two marks. I gained a place at Nottingham University but lost it because of this. I was the only student out of thirty-two not to pass. I made complaints about my experiences at both Colleges but both cases were struck out. Eventually, Linbird encouraged me to go and study law. I enrolled at Arnold and Carlton College in 1995 to study A Level Law. I was nervous at attending College again but was determined to succeed. I passed.

I was offered a place at the University of Derby to study Law (LLB Law part-time for four years). In June this year I passed my Law degree after four years of study. I was very pleased but, at the same time, I was shocked. The course was part-time and I had to pay for the course fees. Most of the time I had to borrow from my mum.

From my own experience and studies, I decided I would become a lawyer. I applied for a place on a Legal Practice Course and was offered a place for September 1999. The only problem was you would have to pay your own fees, which was £6,000 for two years. I applied to the Law Society in London for financial assistance and was one of twenty selected from the UK for interview. At the interview I was asked why did I want to be a lawyer. I stated that I liked to help people. I also mentioned that I came from St Ann's in Nottingham and was proud that I came from that area. A few weeks later I received a letter stating that I would not receive any financial help. At present I am

ST ANN'S NOTTINGHAM. inner-city voices by Ruth I Johns • ISBN 0951696092

looking for a training contract and help to pay for the Legal Practice Course.

My brother Linbird, my mum and me were involved in a campaign to save Nottingham's first Afro-Caribbean Church, the United Holy Church of God on Ilkeston Road. My mum came home from Church one day crying that the Church was going to be sold. Linbird and I decided to take action. The Church elders seemed determined to sell. I decided to get the media involved and contacted the *Nottingham Evening Post* and the BBC. I was often stopped in the street and asked if I had saved the Church.

On the Monday after my mother and I appeared on the News, my mum got the message that a sale sign had been put up on the Church. We caught the bus and went to see if this was true. It was. The next day, I went back to Radford looking for my brother-in-law, brother Johnson who was one of the original members of the Church back in the early 1960s. He was Caretaker working at All Souls Church and Community Centre. He was not very pleased a For Sale sign had gone up. The next day, the sign had mysteriously been taken down. The Church elders decided not to sell the Church. Brother Johnson died in December 1998.

In 1997, I decided to enter Politics and joined the Liberal Democrats. I stood as a candidate for St Ann's in the local elections, the first England born Afro-Caribbean to represent the Liberal Democrats in local Politics. I believed I had something to offer the St Ann's community.

Another reason for entering Politics was that I and my family had been experiencing some antisocial behaviour in our neighbourhood. Each time we complained to the Council, they did not seem to take our complaint seriously.

The Liberal Democrats came second to Labour and beat the Conservatives. I gained over 700 votes at my first attempt in local Politics.

Glenford Green

In 2001, Linbird and Glenford Green were banned in the High Court from taking any further legal actions after thirteen unsuccessful law suits over four years. A spokesman for the Lord Chancellor's Department said: "There's no real benchmark for when someone has taken enough actions to be considered vexatious, but if you have upward of six cases which are struck out then you are looking at it becoming a possibility." Nottingham Evening Post 21.7.01. Glenford Green [2002] is still planning to become a solicitor providing the Law Society allows his legal training to progress

A life story on part of its journey! St Ann's Well Road on St Valentine's Day 2001.
Photo: Ruth I Johns

I came from Jamaica in the mid-1950s a few years after my husband. I was twenty-three. Originally we wanted to go to America but that meant having £2,000 in the bank. We just couldn't manage that, so it was Britain instead. When I arrived I lived in an Indian house. It was very cramped at first. I came back to St Ann's when it was rebuilt. In Jamaica I ran a shop but it didn't sell for more than £700. I worked hard here and brought my family up.

Things were bad when we first came over but once the white people in St Ann's knew you, they were your friends. I always got on well with Irish people. They were disliked by some people.

I visit Jamaica and have land there but here is home. I want to die and be buried here [Member of Chasewood Baptist Church 1999].

Local Councillors

St Ann's district is a substantial part of St Ann's Ward and of Manvers Ward. There are interviews with both councillors from St Ann's Ward, Councillors Jon Collins and Des Wilson. There is also an interview with one of the councillors from Manvers Ward, Councillor Betty Higgins. Councillor David Liversidge is the second councillor for Manvers Ward and quoted elsewhere in this book.

A small part of the district is in Greenwood Ward. Greenwood Ward's proximity to St Ann's Ward and Manvers Ward is shown in the 1995 City unemployment map in the 'Things we did then: many we still do' section. Councillor Jon Collins, in his interview below, indicates how ward boundaries are soon to change.

Past local councillors are referred to in individual recollections in this book. In this section, there is an interview with one former local councillor, Peter Burgess, who became Lord Mayor of Nottingham and also Chairman of Nottinghamshire County Council. He lives in St Ann's.

PETER BURGESS

Born 1921

Interviewed in his home 10.5.00. Peter Burgess has been **Lord Mayor of Nottingham** *and also* **Chairman of Nottinghamshire County Council**. *Nottingham City lost its unitary status in 1974 and regained it April 1st 1998*

I was born in a place called Hellingly near Hailsham in Sussex. It was a railway town. I was born as a child of a one-parent family. My mother was sixteen and I was born in Miss Bucks stall on the railway station. There was no such thing as legal adoption in those days, but in less than a year a Mr and Mrs Burgess took me over and brought me up as their child. They were mum and dad, although I did know my real mother because I went to school with her other sons.

I was brought up on Romney Marsh at Brenzett. It was a harsh life for the family there. Dad was a farm worker, a sort of labourer cum foreman on a massive farm with mainly sheep. We had a few cattle. I spent my early days on the farm sitting on horseback to feed the cattle. I could shear a sheep by the time I was twelve and look after cattle.

I went to Brenzett School, a small village school which is still standing. I passed for the Grammar School at New Romney but I wouldn't go because they wore tassels on their hat. So mum sent me to a private school where I used to get in trouble. We moved to Bilsington, which is off the Marsh on the hills. And then I went to Ashford South Central School.

My wife, Dolly, went to North Central School. Dad had a smallholding and wanted me to work on it when I left school. I didn't like farming. At fifteen my mother apprenticed me to the Merchant Navy. I went to Gravesend Sea School, which I visited in 1994 when I was Chairman of Nottinghamshire County Council.

My first trip was to Australia as a laundry boy in 1936 on a 20,000 tonne liner. It was a hard life. I was seasick. I got back for my sixteenth birthday and my mother got me a bike and I was out on my bike with my friends in the village of Bethersden where they'd moved. That evening there was a message on the wireless (as we used to call radio then) saying: 'Any passenger or ship's company of SS Orama please report to your nearest medical health officer'. I did that next morning and was rushed to hospital with typhoid fever, caught from the water in Bombay. I spent six months in hospital paralysed down one side, but I'm all right now.

I did all sorts of jobs. I started in a garage and broke a window of a Rolls-Royce and got the sack. I went round the corner and got a job as a cinema boy and got in trouble because I was fighting. I worked for a greengrocery shop, and got into trouble because he was always picking on me, so I locked him downstairs in the cellar and left the shop and went home.

Early 1937, I went off to Chatham and went into the Army recruiting office. I was just seventeen and they asked if I had my dad's permission. I went to the RAF place and they wouldn't have me. I went to the Royal Navy place and they said I was the sort they needed. I did an examination: oral, mental, physical, the lot. A fortnight later a buff envelope arrived which said Mr W G Burgess with OHMS [On His Majesty's Service] on it. Dad slit it open, looked at it, read it, signed it and then said: 'You're in the bloody Navy, now perhaps you'll do as you're told.' They were a wonderful mum and dad.

The Navy sent me to Devonport. I did my training and the War broke out and I went on my first ship HMS Carlisle out to the Mediterranean. I went to Norway and helped to evacuate the British troops when the Germans came through Norway, back to Scapa Flow, and back to Devonport. Then I found myself down in Aden, then Italy came into the War and we went down to Colombo where I was put off the ship as I was a troublemaker again. I argued with an officer, nothing serious, and I went to a wireless station in the jungle for nearly four years outside Colombo.

It was a big wireless station covered with trees all around for miles. I learnt to play hockey and represented the Navy. Dolly used to write to me. When I got back to England I had fifty-six days leave so I thought I better look Dolly up. She lived at Westwell near Ashford. She came to the door with a baby in her arms and quickly said: 'It's not mine. It's my sister's.'

My dad then kept a pub at Lympne called the Welcome Stranger. It was 1944 and I'd been away since 1938. I went in, nobody in the bar, then a little old man came to the counter and asked what I wanted, looked again and then shouted: 'Mother he's home!'

Dolly and I were married by special licence in February 1944 and we had a fortnight's holiday in Kent. You couldn't go anywhere in those days. I went back to Devonport, then to Milford Haven up to D-Day, then to Australia via the Panama Canal. I picked a ship up in Sydney, HMS Wrangler, a destroyer, and finished the War in the Pacific, in Tokyo Harbour on VJ Day. Then I worked my way home.

I did all sorts of jobs. For ten years I was in the Kent Fire Brigade. I was never a full-time fireman but retained. The one job I enjoyed was the Fire Brigade. We lived at a place called Charing outside Ashford. Eventually a friend of mine who'd moved to Nottingham said he'd got a job for me there. So Dolly and I came here April 9th 1959, the year Forest won the Cup, 1959.

We stayed at first in North Sherwood Street and I was working for a construction company. My furniture was in store on Huntingdon Street. I'd only been there three or four weeks and they said they'd like me to go to Scotland. I didn't want that. So I got my cards. Next day a chap said there's a dying job available, Lambert's on Talbot Street.

I thought it was a big place for a mortuary! I didn't realise it was textile dyeing and finishing. It was the worst place there was, long hours, low wages, deplorable conditions. I worked there three years and Dolly got a job at Sketchley's. I left and went to Henry Ashwell on Radford Road, and moved up a peg into real technical dyeing, women's garments and hose and men's shirt material. The real professional side. I was made redundant in the 1970s.

After North Sherwood Street, our daughter and Dolly moved up to Pleasley, and I found lodgings on Goldswong Terrace, St Ann's. We had a terrible landlord and the other tenants . . . it was murder. We phoned the man who stored my furniture and he said he had a place on Egerton Street, St Ann's, on Alfred Street North. We did a moonlighter from Goldswong Terrace one night owing a month's rent, I wouldn't pay. He was a bus conductor and we had words once or twice. I threatened him with a good hiding if he kept pestering me.

We lived on Egerton Street until the slum clearance. By 1971, I was a councillor for Manvers Ward so I was into politics, Labour Party. I'd been a Trade Union Official for years including Secretary of the Dyers and Bleachers Union

PETER
BURGESS

BETTY
HIGGINS

PETER BURGESS

BETTY HIGGINS

2 LABOUR CANDIDATES

THURSDAY, 13th MAY 1971

PLEASE DISPLAY IN YOUR WINDOW

Published by G. Edwards, 153 Pym St. Nottm.
Printed by W. J. Butler & Co. Bulwell Nott.m

Peter Burgess and Betty Higgins poster for Manvers Ward 1971

St ANN'S NOTTINGHAM: inner-city voices *by Ruth I Johns* • ISBN 0951696092

of Nottingham with some 8,000 members. That dwindled as the textile trade slowly dwindled away. I was there until I became redundant and then I got talked into joining the Labour Party and becoming a councillor. I had no idea what a councillor's job was. It wasn't as harsh as it is today. I won the election at the first attempt with Betty Higgins who is still a Councillor.

Peter Burgess, Lord Mayor of Nottingham 1982-83

Peter Burgess, Lord Mayor of Nottingham, with his wife Dolly Burgess, the Lady Mayoress 1982-83. Photo: source Peter Burgess

After a short session at Manvers Ward [which includes part of St Ann's], when the first part of the slum clearance was going into full sweep, I moved over to St Ann's Ward with a majority of one. I had sixteen years as a councillor here until 1984 when I wasn't selected as they wanted a black candidate. I was Lord Mayor 1982-83 including giving Torvill and Dean the Freedom of Nottingham.

After leaving the textile trade, I took a year out and then took a job as a cleaner at Nottingham Co-op and had ten years there. And then I thought I would retire through the [Government's] Job Release Scheme. Then I changed my mind and the Chief Executive said I could continue in my job providing I spent eight hours a day doing it instead of being stuck down at the Council House. So I retired and have been my own master ever since.

Later, I was asked to stand for Strelley, in Broxtowe, and won at the first attempt so became a Nottinghamshire County Councillor for nine years and took retirement because of the change to Unitary Status of Nottingham City. In 1994, I became Chairman of Notts County Council. The other thing I was very involved in was East Midlands Airport.

When I became councillor for St Ann's, one of the most pressing issues was the District Heating Scheme [which services the properties built in St Ann's after demolition]. I was very involved. The Eastcroft District Heating was the cheapest sort of heating then, and it is now. I was a champion of the heating scheme ever since I've lived here when we moved from Egerton Street in 1972. There are a lot of news cuttings there [in a scrapbook] about the battles to sort out the heating. It started as a blow air system and is now a warm radiator system. I sat on the Heating Committee for many years.

We're now living in an environment worth living in, a smokeless zone, no more smogs and fogs. When Dolly worked at Sketchley at Basford, she used to have to walk home in the fogs to Egerton Street.

Dolly Burgess   I couldn't find my house one night, I kept walking by it.

Peter Burgess   The trouble with the slum clearance was that it was going very, very fast. Once you start a rolling programme, there were going to be people who were disenchanted with the fact that they had to be moved somewhere else like Strelley and Broxtowe. Many have come back. I met an old lady last week, in her eighties, she's come back. When I was a councillor over there, many remembered me from St Ann's and they said they wouldn't want to come back into the system built houses of these [small] sizes.

Home owners probably got £50 site value compensation under the compulsory purchase scheme. Tenants got a disturbance allowance. About £400. Tenants who were put into the area as a temporary measure didn't get an allowance. The disturbance allowance was for long-standing tenants, and it was worked out by officers in the Treasurer's Department. Some got more than others.

We have a grandson living nearby on the Metropolitan Housing Estate. He's twenty-six. He comes down regularly. Our daughter lives on Carlton Road.

I'm still very active including being put back on the Race Equality Commission as a Co-op representative. I represent the City Council on the Community Health Council. It's very interesting. It's being involved with people. I couldn't just live here and do nothing. I'd go mad.

My thoughts on how St Ann's is now to what it used to be? In the new St Ann's, if you're not a friendly character you are isolated in a way you wouldn't have been in the days of going out and scrubbing the front doorstep, meeting your neighbour, leaving your door open and chatting to people. Those days are gone. To a certain extent it's now everyone for themselves, but I think St Ann's is a good estate. I disagree with people who say it's not safe to walk about the streets, you can. By and large the people are friendly. I don't use the pub like I used to. I go once a week. But I can go down to the Precinct [on Robin Hood Chase] and chat to people, I know people down there. It's still very much a family estate with mother, sons and daughters, and grandchildren all living around the estate. I think it's getting back like that. I wouldn't move. I'm quite happy.

There are a few problems. For example, we've seen three generations of kids around here. There's always kids about. When St Ann's was planned, they had a wrong conception. They said old people liked to see children around them and I went along with that. So, where we are, they built flats in the middle of houses. The flats should have been one side with the two rows of houses in front, so children's noise wasn't all around the flats.

Yes, the allotments are longstanding. There were a number of allotment sites. There's the big one still here, the Hungerhills. There was one where the Metropolitan Housing Estate is, that was originally all allotments. There were allotments over the other side of St Ann's Well Road, the estate at the back of Gordon Road was allotments. Around here was one of the biggest allotment sites in the country. I'll get you a list of allotment sites now.

I'm President of the Hungerhills Allotments site, I took it on years ago. The Bridge Trust own them and there's a clause to say they are for perpetuity and cannot be sold off. We have to be very wary of that. Terry Brady is Secretary of the Hungershills Allotment Holders. I have an allotment. I grow basic vegetables for cooking, runner beans, peas, I've just planted 500 sets of shallots, I've got beetroot, parsnips, basic stuff. I grow one row of early potatoes. I don't grow a main crop: you can buy them cheaper. I'll plant leeks. I haven't got a massive allotment. I took it on when I was about sixty.

I've got an old asbestos hut which has been broken into three times. After the last time, I left a note on the door saying: 'Please close the door when you leave', and they've not been back since. My garden isn't posh, I've got dandelions, and stinging nettles round the outside. And I've got one side where I've got four rose bushes and some self-grown raspberry bushes. And on the hedge, I've got a blackberry bush that has lovely blackberries.

Last week, a widow neighbour downstairs, Dolly and I took a stroll up the garden on Sunday. I've got three deckchairs up there and we sit in the summer for two or three hours, listen to the birds, hear the kids screaming down here while we're up there. It's a nice afternoon out. I go up when I can but I've not been up this week. I've got to go and do some watering.

I've been a Governor of Elliott Durham School since the 1970s and I've seen five Head Teachers, the bad days and the good days. I'm also a Governor of the Elms School in St Ann's. I like to see kids improve themselves. I don't live up at the schools but today we've got a child round here who's on exclusion and I'm involved in that. I'm on the Exclusion Panel.

In fifty years time? There will be a more technological life in St Ann's and they will look back and say: 'Good Lord, is that how they lived fifty years ago? It must have been a hard life!' Schools will have gone and there will be technical colleges because everything will be computerised. Every child will sit at a computer as they do at the City Technology College now. I think the heating system will have gone. And there'll be another form of heating. I don't think it will be the same form of policing. We might be going along the style of the American State Troopers, I don't know.

I hope the Hungerhill Gardens will still be there. It does amaze me today to think there are so many gardens which are vacant. You have young men today who don't have a job and they could get a garden up there at an unemployed rate, grow their own stuff, save the wife going to town shopping, and getting green stuff. They don't want to know because it's work. It's hard work to dig a garden. Most schools don't teach gardening any more. Elliott Durham School has the land with fields right the way to the bottom. Why don't they have a School Garden and teach boys and girls about garden produce, how stuff is grown? Unless you do the manual side of it you'll never learn. Then probably they would take it up when they leave school. There is still work to be done manually. They have no concept of manual work.

If some of the allotments were taken by young families with people out of work, we would get less vandalism up there. We still suffer with vandalism. Last year, one bloke's shed was stripped of all his onions, all his carrots, all his stuff, the whole lot. Now you can't blame kids for that. Somebody with a vehicle took that at night. Some of the vandalism is by kids of twelve, thirteen and fourteen when they get hold of their parents' special key.

Dolly Burgess I was manager of a shirt unit at Sketchley's. People used to send their shirts in. I packed it in when they got rid of the unit. During the War, I worked in the Ashford Railway Works in Kent, hotting the rivets. I used to enjoy it. After the War before coming up here I used to work in the fields.

Peter Burgess In the fruit season, we used to do it with the family, didn't we? Cherry picking, blackcurrant picking. Her brother had a van. Her mother, me and all the rest used to do the fruit picking.

Dolly Burgess When I was a kid, we went hop picking and I didn't like it. When it was wet, they'd pull the hops down and you'd get drowned in water.

COUNCILLOR BETTY HIGGINS

Born 1926

*Interviewed at the Council House, Nottingham 31.1.01. Councillor Betty Higgins has represented **Manvers Ward** and **St Ann's Ward** for many years and was formerly Leader of Nottingham City Council*

I was first elected to Nottingham City Council in 1971 and, apart from three years, I have been a councillor ever since. In 1971, I represented Manvers Ward which postal-wise and community-wise includes part of St Ann's. Around 1974, I moved across into St Ann's Ward. At that time we had annual elections. I lost the 1976 election when there were two Labour candidates, one was Peter Burgess and one was me. Peter ran a campaign against the Coal Board and the District Heating costs. I couldn't legally do that because I didn't live in the area served by the District Heating. He just slid through. I spent the next three years helping to print and deliver *Chase Chat*, the community magazine.

October 1974   3p

HASE CHATTING

n's ...... Politicians ....Heating....... Chase Chat

YOUR VIEWS

A clip from one 'Chase Chat'. See the others at St Ann's Library or Nottingham Local Studies Library

Later, I came back representing Manvers Ward. I like to think I've always been interested in St Ann's. I was very involved with the SATRA [St Ann's Tenants and Residents Association] Club which later became the Pint and Pot [now the Welcome Inn]. They were heady days. There were various live wires like Ray Gosling, and Sid Lighton who decided they wanted more than just a SATRA Association, they wanted premises. He and his wife Audrey lived on Warton Avenue, St Ann's. Audrey was very lively helping tenants in the area at the top end of The Wells Road, and Sid became active in the Club. They helped run the SATRA Tote for many years. They left Nottingham about ten years ago.

Everybody was enthusiastic about the Club but over the years, of course, they had to pay the Brewery back, and they had to make a go of it and it just never 'washed its

face'. The City Council were involved to an extent and both Peter Burgess and I sat on the Committee to try to get them out of trouble. Eventually it was privatised. During that time there were street warden schemes, where volunteer wardens and police met about helping the community in various ways.

I remember quite a lot about the time of St Ann's demolition and rebuilding. It was my grounding into politics. I'd been a member of the Labour Party since around 1948 and I'd never thought about becoming a councillor. Someone at a branch meeting I wasn't at moved me for the panel for Council. My husband came home and told me and I said: 'Don't be stupid!' Anyway, eventually I decided to have a go. Demolition and rehousing was a difficult stage for people to go through which meant tough political arguments. I fought different wards from 1965 until I was elected for Manvers in 1971 with Peter Burgess as my co-councillor and John Carroll and my husband in St Ann's Ward.

At the start of my time, the St Ann's area around Storer Street, Clarence Street and Lowdham Street were being pulled down. After the demolition started, it was a fashionable thing for people to say it shouldn't have happened and that we should have demolished bits, improved bits and left bits. And, to some extent, I can see the logic of that. But having said that, the bits that SATRA fought for, the Ransom Road area and the top of Blue Bell Hill, are now pretty well ready to come down. I suppose a lot of it lasted a long time. It gave a choice to people who didn't want to live in marvellously well-heated and well-built flats and houses. But now those areas are a bit of a headache because landlords who weren't living in the property neglected them quite badly.

Yes, Cromer Road is one of those roads. Quite a lot of the houses have been sold back to the Council so there's very mixed ownership. And the Council isn't geared up to

Councillor Betty Higgins (right) in the early days of her representing St Ann's people. Seen here talking to Jean Sparkes and a group outside the former Blue Bell Hill Junior School building, some of which came down in the redevelopment. The part which was spared became part of the Blue Bell Hill Community Centre. Photo: source Betty Higgins, Charles A Noble

look after that sort of property really. It's best to do a complete improvement. Otherwise it leads to 'pepper potting', some good and then a patch of bad. I was at a meeting last night about some houses along Blue Bell Hill Road. Part of the reason they were left originally was because they were owned by St Mary's Church. But now some of them are a real nuisance because they are now owned by absentee landlords whom we cannot contact. It was a teacher from St Edward's School saying these houses lead to a lot of neighbourhood trouble because of vandalism when they are empty. We [the City Council] are working on it, to find a way to wrest the houses off those who've got them and get them back on the market.

It's a long struggle. Housing Officers are too busy looking after the general melee of properties, and everything else that goes on, to fight a long battle with somebody who might be living in Zanzibar or wherever. Absentee landlords don't care. They're just getting money for their houses and they do that through an agent who couldn't care less very often.

There's another thing that has crept in. The Council managed to buy properties and sold them on to a Housing Association because the Council didn't have the money to do the full refurbishment and Housing Associations got bigger Government grants and loans. But, unfortunately, in order to pay those back, their rents are higher. Sometimes this means additional pressures which prevents people being good neighbours.

I really don't know what the solutions are. Local Authorities have been starved of money for some years in favour of Housing Associations. That was a political move by the Opposition Party but it hasn't been reversed by this Government, which is sad. I do believe in Local Authorities owning houses. Originally, some Housing Associations, notably Nottingham Community Housing Association, were founded to meet specific housing needs, to house the refugees of that time.

At one time, when I was Chair of Housing, the Council had fifty thousand housing units, now it is just over thirty thousand. Which is still more than similar size authorities, which sold more properties on to associations, because we've been very stubborn. We've consulted tenants carefully and they've said they prefer us to be their landlord.

There's a great deal of tenant participation now. There's a lot of pressure from Central Government to consult. Before the Council had tenant liaison support, there were about a dozen tenants groups, now there are about sixty. That paid support helps a lot.

Government support is changing. There are more tenant liaison workers. But community development work, which is part of the Leisure and Community Services Department, is not getting a lot of Government support. Yes, several Community Development Workers have lost their jobs, including two in St Ann's. There has been a change of thinking about the nature of community development work and whether workers actually 'nurse' groups and work in their premises or not. I'm not sure that I go along with some of the new thinking but that's what's

Councillor Betty Higgins when Leader of the City Council. Photo: Nottingham City Council Annual Report 1991/92

happening. I know of at least one neighbourhood community association that has lost their warden. Lots of people were working really, really well but they just needed that bit of support.

In my years as Leader of Nottingham City Council[1] and leader of the Labour Group, I worked hard with local authorities in similar situations to make sure we became a city with its own Social Services, Education and Planning functions which we lost with reorganisation in 1974. Our relations with the County Council were a bit 'fraught' during that time but my aim was achieved in 1998. It's much too remote to have these things dealt with by the County Council. In 1993, John Taylor became leader of the City Council for two years and then Graham Chapman.

I've been a Governor of the Elliott Durham School, which serves St Ann's, for a very long time, since Wyn Davies was its first Head Teacher. When the County Council was responsible for education, they didn't mind if children went out to suburb schools because it was all in

---

[1] In Nottingham City Council's Annual Report 1991/92, Betty Higgins, Leader of the Council said that winning City Challenge was a positive achievement at a time of 'prolonged recession'. City Challenge started in 1992. It resulted in £37.5m worth of Government funding, which aimed to attract a total of £150m worth of investment through private sector and other grant sources. The aims were to promote self-sustaining economic and social regeneration in Sneinton and St Ann's.

the county. Now, the City schools are still losing some of their brightest pupils and we have to change it. People like Jane Todd, Director for Development and Environmental Services for Nottingham City Council, and Alan Simpson MP, educated their children at Elliott Durham and speak highly of it. The Education Department is now giving a lot of support to Elliott Durham. Councillor Mike Edwards is a good ambassador for the school.

Talking about how myths are created, I remember talking to associates of Ken Coates and Bill Silburn who used to say the heart's gone out of St Ann's because you've broken up the community, there's none of the community feeling left. Yet, as I was going round canvassing, talking to people, that feeling was there but they wouldn't recognise it because they'd got this theory that it wasn't there any more. I really feel quite bitter the way people were 'put down'.

In some ways the drug culture thing has been a real setback. It's what people talk about, for example saying: 'That's the phone box where they exchange drugs you know.' It's across all areas of the City, including even West Bridgford.

I would like to think that in fifty years time people are free to go about their everyday business feeling no undue pressure from crime. I am worried about the number of bars in Nottingham and the Saturday night situation.

I feel people need to have a community there that will support them. In order to do that I think extreme poverty has to be tackled. People have got to be prepared to accept that some people at some time in their lives do need support. Schools and other institutions, including Local Government, can help attitudes to encourage people to become more neighbourly.

I was born in Southwell and moved to Nottingham in 1949. My husband was also a City Councillor. We split up some years ago. I have two children and two grandchildren. For twenty-two years I was a teacher. I will always remember my first day as a supply teacher at a junior school and being asked to referee a football match. It rained and I was so grateful!

St Ann's is a rewarding place to work. If you are a politician you do get branded as the 'lowest of the low', but pull back the skin and people do appreciate what you try and do for them. I've always thought people in St Ann's and Manvers Ward have responded very well. I'm also a Governor for Sycamore Junior School, St Ann's.

I've got a public meeting tonight about the closure of Long Hedge, an elderly persons' home near St Matthias Road, St Ann's. It's the way things are going. We tend to get pushed down this path. There's very little money coming in to support old people's homes. But equally there is a good case for saying people prefer to live in their own homes and I feel like that. But some people no longer have homes and are living in residential homes and their relatives feel very strongly that we are wrong in closing Long Hedge.

It's a commonly held misconception that the Council put 'rubbish people' (their phrase, not mine) in certain areas. For example, a long time ago before Caunton Avenue flats off Ransom Road were pulled down, a lot of people said we put 'rubbish people' into Caunton Avenue. I think this attitude starts because people who can afford to wait will wait for the property they want. Those who are desperate will go to what is available and that is where that mythology starts. We obviously don't deliberately put unsociable people together. And, of course, now we have a firm policy of evicting antisocial tenants.

But, though the Council does not have to rehouse them, they will find accommodation, probably with a private landlord.

With this Government we did feel we would be getting the support we needed as a Local Authority. They are now saying: 'We know better than you and you'll do it this way. And then we will give you the money.' Or: 'We don't really trust you anyway and we'll make the money available through, for instance, Sure Start.' I've deliberately involved myself with Sure Start locally, because they will offer a service to local people, but at the same time we (the Council) are closing Family Centres. I sometimes wonder!

We've actually received a very bad settlement this year (2001-2002). We would otherwise have spent more time reviewing the Family Centre Service. But, with the shortage of money, we're likely to rush that ahead and it will be seen as a lack of forethought and consultation.

Discontinuity is not what is needed.

COUNCILLOR JON COLLINS

Born 1960

Councillor for **St Ann's Ward** *interviewed at the Council House, Nottingham 22.3.01. Jon Collins is Chair of Nottingham City Council's Education and Employment Board and Chair of the Renewal Trust*

I was born in Croydon and spent most of my young life in Watford. I studied Biology at Southampton University, worked for a short while for the Greater London Council and then applied for a job working as a full-time officer for Nottingham Area Student Council. I got the job and have been in Nottingham ever since.

Later I worked for Nottingham Community Transport for two years, was a Public Relations Officer with Derbyshire County Council for a number of years, then worked for Nottinghamshire County Council as a Homelessness and Housing Development Officer. About four years ago I did a part-time MBA degree in Birmingham and worked part-time. Then I worked full-time for the consulting firm Enterprise plc and now, under the new political arrangements in Nottingham City Council, I work four days a week as Chair of the Education and Employment Board and try - with mixed success - to do a day a week freelance consulting. My partner and I have two daughters.

I first got interested in St Ann's because when I moved to Nottingham, after living on Bentinck Road, I moved to the Woodborough Road, St Ann's, for a number of years:

on the part between Cranmer Street and St Ann's Hill. I was elected to Nottingham City Council in 1987 when it was a District Council, and the year I got elected Labour lost control so I was in the opposition. The Conservatives had a tiny majority and they lost a couple of by-elections and Labour took control with the help of John Peck, the Green Councillor.

I had been active in the Labour Party for a long time, back to University days. I got involved locally and, looking back, perhaps rather arrogantly thought I could do the job as well if not better than the two sitting Councillors. That was true of one of them, Frank Higgins, but was pretty unfair on the other, Peter Burgess, who lived in the area and did a lot of good work particularly for people on the estate. I've represented St Ann's all the time since being elected. Before I'd been Secretary and Campaign Manager for the Ward.

One side of a leaflet about St Ann's Councillors' Advice Surgery 1994

St Ann's Ward is quite diverse. It includes the Aboretum, a bit of Mapperley and about half of St Ann's, the half on the Robin Hood Chase side of the St Ann's Well Road. But the boundaries are about to change again. After the last Boundary Review, the City Council is basically forced to having three-member wards, so there will be twenty wards in the City with three members. So St Ann's Ward will become the whole of St Ann's as people know it and lose the Mapperley bit and the Aboretum bit and it will gain a bit of Windmill Lane in Sneinton.

The selections will be next year some time and I will try for selection to the St Ann's Ward. When I first came into local politics, for me it was about making a decent job of representing local people, doing the casework properly. There were campaigns around the District Heating Scheme which I supported, and there was work being done at the Chase Advice Centre. In the Phase 10 area, people were trying to get improvements secured for the Marple Square area, which includes Cheverton Court which is sometimes called the ski-run because of its roof design.

Cheverton Court never recovered from the decision to open the Housing Allocations policy there. Previously,

allocations were on the basis of references and for people who were working. When it became general accommodation, it wasn't suitable. Turnover grew and the attractiveness of the accommodation fell through the floor. I think the next stage will be to demolish it. There are some structural problems as well.

Yes, it's a design that got into the architectural journals, but, it's funny isn't it how architects never ever seem to want to live in the places they design?

It was a coincidence that there was £18m available for St Ann's through the Estates Action Programme at about the time that City Challenge, a Government programme, came to the City. So people tended to equate the two projects. The Estates Action money covered improvements for about a third of St Ann's, focusing on the worst first. The programme came to an end in 1999 and, since then, we're keeping progress going with improvements. At the moment it's Rushworth Close.

The Phase 10 Marple Square area was a bit of a saga. City Challenge didn't have enough money for that, but it did cover all the consultations and came up with a blueprint. After the Government ended Estates Action, a submission was made for SRB [Single Regeneration Budget] funding. We didn't get SRB 1 for the City. It was devastating. There were promises for SRB 2 but then Government officers, because the amount of money was relatively small, told the Council to drop it. Des [Wilson] and I made a lot of fuss about the fact that it had been dropped, and Phase 10 was built into various Council priority lists for the next large amount of capital resources. The next time was New Deal for Communities so we argued strongly that the area should be included, but St Ann's Phase 10 wasn't. Partly as a result of lobbying, it was agreed that the City Council's Capital Programme meet the £12m scheme to improve the area.

It will probably take another three to four years. One of the difficulties of the area is that although the houses are actually quite good, the area design is lacking. We don't want a tarting up job. We want to find a way that will actually make a difference so there is a long-term future for the area. Which is why I think Cheverton Court needs demolishing and a good chunk, at least two sides of Marple Square needs to go as well. The side that would be retained would be the one over by Balisier Court and the old Ukaidi building. The other two sides would give opportunity to create a new road with bungalows and houses and we would be able to do extra bungalows and houses if we then demolished Cheverton Court.

There needs to be a general shop with frontage to the Woodborough Road because otherwise it won't be viable. And the Housing Office and the Resource Centre need to be included in the design.

You are asking me about allocations policy because people believe St Ann's can be used as a 'dumping ground'? You could go to any housing estate in the City and that's exactly the same point that is made. It's made in Broxtowe, Bestwood, Bilborough, Edwards Lane, everywhere says they are a dumping ground. It's not true. But what I would say is that we have an allocations policy that is being reviewed. I have concerns about the existing policy because it is a laissez-faire policy. Now, availability determines where people go. If you have a priority system where people in the greatest need get the highest priority, and you know their preferences will presumably be areas where there is housing opportunity (where there is the highest turnover), then these areas will get concentrations of people with greatest need. It's like market forces.

I think the allocations policy should be based more on building communities, and actually having a view about what creates a stable community. I know it sounds like social engineering, trying to get a balance between old and young and between families and single people and couples. So rather than being in a situation where people with high priority get the first property which comes up, they should be given added priority for accommodation within an area, say, if they have other family living there, so we can keep the community together and build on it. At present a son or daughter, with family now of their own and who want to stay in St Ann's near their parents, stand no better or worse chance of being housed in St Ann's than anywhere else. I would argue they should have a much better chance of being housed in St Ann's than anywhere else.

If the community is right, if you get those links, it makes an area more cohesive, reduces turnover, increases commitment, increases community activity. That's the only way forward. What isn't good for an area is high turnover, lots of transient people without commitment or a stake in the area. That's not to say that incomers won't develop that stake because I think they can. It's a matter of balance. The Estates Action improvements have helped to make properties more secure and turnover has reduced, but more needs doing.

I'm not minimising the crime worries in the area but it's not as bad as the myth about it. Issues like car crime and burglary are being effectively focused on. Some of the improvement works and CCTV have helped. The biggest concern is drugs. I'd be a fool to say there isn't a drug issue in the area. But the drug culture doesn't necessarily impinge directly on the lives of the majority of people in the area. It does impinge on some, and some are affected indirectly because they are worried.

There is a gap in provision for teenagers in St Ann's. I think we're trying to respond to it in several ways. The schools are important. Elliott Durham Comprehensive School is reasonably well placed to go forward now. They've got a good Head Teacher [Rob Boothroyd] and we are proposing to work as an Education Authority with them to develop a sports and leisure facility at the school, which I think youngsters in the area will find attractive. It will offer an extended day so, after the end of the formal school day, there are a range of activities. There's a lot of equipment there like computer suites. There can be opportunities to do things which may not be available at home.

After City Challenge ended, the City set up the Renewal Trust. It is an entirely separate Trust but it has the continuing income from the assets of City Challenge. I'm Chairman of the Renewal Trust. One of the biggest projects that the Trust has been involved in is the Sycamore Centre, on Hungerhill Road, St Ann's. The building complex was taken back from the County Council. The sports block was refurbished with money from the Millennium Trust and there's a café there. Then the front block has an office and workshops to generate income to support the sports programme. It is beginning to take off. It will take time before we get the youngsters involved in the managing and activities of the Sycamore Centre. It's got to be done in a controlled, managed way so that we have the appropriate levels of staff there.

The Chase Neighbourhood Centre too has done good work with youngsters. Part of the difficulty has been the City Council's apparent withdrawal of Youth Services from key areas and Community Services and it is a problem. People make the difference and having people on the ground is particularly important.

Councillor Jon Collins (right) at a Chase Neighbourhood Centre event. Photo: Chase Action Group Ltd

The recent reorganisation of Community Services was done partly to identify resources to put into the Youth Offending teams. The whole thing was done badly without proper consultation. It was also about trying to provide an additional member of staff for each of the area committees. Areas like Sneinton and St Ann's which were well-provided with community development workers ended up with the same number of staff as less well provided areas. [Two staff who lost their jobs in St Ann's were Community Development Workers Phil Jackson and Steve Lack.]

One of the reasons I am committed to the Renewal Trust is that when it comes to active support for the community and encouraging community activity, my view is that the area shouldn't be beholden to the Council because you can't rely on Council provision continuing to be there. It's far better that people do it for themselves.

The Renewal Trust is nothing to do with the Government, it is a Community Development Trust, a charity. It has guaranteed income from the Council but this guaranteed income simply reflects the income from certain assets, Sneinton Market and one of the buildings on the

Island site, which I negotiated as Chair of City Challenge. This income is bequeathed to the Renewal Trust for ninety-nine years after the end of City Challenge. The Renewal Trust has an independent board made up of one-third from the community, one-third City Council and one-third local business.

It uses the resources it gets to match against external funding programmes whether from Charitable Trusts, the Lottery, or European Funding for example. It employs outreach workers who work in Sneinton and St Ann's including one for the Afro-Caribbean community and one for the Asian community. It has set up secure funding for the running of the Sycamore Centre. It is the accountable body for Sure Start II which covers the St Ann's area. We employ the managerial staff for that. And hopefully managerial staff for Sure Start VI, which will be in Sneinton.

The Renewal Trust has a Community Chest of about £15,000 a year and it allocates small grants fairly flexibly to organisations. We jointly fund TANC [Technical Aid to Nottinghamshire Communities] to work in the area, the St Ann's allotment campaign [STAA] and so on. We've put support into the Chase Action Group. We're in the process of leading a bid for a Healthy Living Centre for the area. We have secured some IT funds through the Capital Modernisation Fund for an IT network in the area. I think we sometimes underestimate the amount of IT awareness in the area. The idea is to have a network of links, web pages for voluntary groups in the area. So people can find out what is going on, what the facilities are, what the background is and address some issues.

The Council, through its area committee [Area Five] and the Renewal Trust, tried to sponsor a magazine *East Side West Side* but it only did two editions when, due to reorganisation of Community Services, the person concerned was moved from the area. We hope to get that going again. But people don't necessarily read Newsletters. But we do need to communicate better.

That goes back to one of the points you made earlier. In the Renewal Trust, I didn't want it to start in a blaze of glory, we're going to do this, that and the other and change the world, which is what all initiatives have said. I wanted it to build up a track record of actually doing things, and then trying to communicate to people that it is actually their organisation. We have an annual general meeting that any resident can come to. It's open and accountable.

One of the things we should be really pleased about in St Ann's is that we have some absolutely fantastic primary schools. St Ann's Well Infant and Nursery School is a beacon without any doubt, it's probably one of the best primary schools in the country. Both the Sycamore Infant and Junior Schools are good. Huntingdon School, having been at the point where it was almost closed, is improved out of all recognition and is first rate. Elms School has always been a reasonable school and is now one of the most improved schools. St Augustine's has always been a first rate primary school, and continues to be. Morley School has just come out of Special Measures. And there are other schools on the other side of St Ann's outside my

ward [for example, Blue Bell Hill Infant and Nursery, and Junior Schools and St Edwards RC Primary and Nursery School].

The quality of that provision is first rate, and it underlines our belief that all youngsters can learn and all can achieve. Nottingham has been an Education Authority for four years [after the City Council became a Unitary Authority again. It lost that status in 1974]. The improvements at primary level have been dramatic, the secondary level City-wide has seen some improvement but the scale of improvement needed is very significant. The Elliott Durham School, after going through a rocky patch, is showing strong signs of improvement and I think the school is much better than its reputation. There is a problem that parents are not even opting to go and have a look at the school and they should. I won't name names, but I would argue that the quality and breadth of its provision and the support the youngsters get makes it a better school than some 'preferred' ones.

As I mentioned earlier, there will be opportunities for after-school provision so the youngsters can stay on site until five-thirty or six o'clock. It would help parents and improve the educational experience for the kids. They can use the facilities, we can develop the sports side with the school fields and the swimming pool.

No, St Ann's Ward doesn't cover the Metrazone [community building of the Metropolitan Residents and Tenants Association] but it will when the new ward boundaries come in. Metrazone was funded by City Challenge.

Councillor Betty Higgins chaired City Challenge for the first years and I did for five years. It was 1992-97. It had an impact. It made mistakes and I could point to them as well! The budget was £37m over the five years for St Ann's and Sneinton. That money enabled more to be levered in and the total was £120m spent.

In St Ann's, it funded the Chase Neighbourhood Centre and the revamp of Robin Hood Chase which was good, and the car park at the back of the shops. It funded new secured door and window locks for every property on the estate. It paid for improvement works on Broad Oak Close and Norland Close, which were of benefit. It supported projects like Brake Away which is going strong. And the Adventure Base (at the back of the Sycamore Centre) which was good for a while but which was let go by the County Council and now needs a total revamp. City Challenge funded it and the County Council gave a commitment to staff and to resource it. In the run up to local Government re-organisation the County Council disinvested in the City, and any savings were made in the City. City Challenge improved bus stops, lighting, CCTV . . .

City Challenge was direct Government money and some money was spent on things that should have been funded from elsewhere. We did manage to divert quite a lot of money away from those types of scheme, like more money to Housing Associations to build houses which they could get funded by the Housing Corporation. Some of the District Heating Improvements were funded by City Challenge. There was a bit of quid pro quo on that. That

St Ann's Nottingham: Inner City Voices by Ruth Johns • ISBN 0951696092 was funded for the Council and then the Council funded £1.5m worth of improvements on St Ann's Phase 10 after the end of City Challenge. At the end of City Challenge, the Government evaluated its success according to three categories and Nottingham was in the top one. On the Sneinton side, funded projects included moving the wholesale fruit and vegetable market to Meadow Lane and thus ensured keeping jobs in the area. The alternative was Long Eaton.

I would want people in fifty years time to know that there were a lot of good things going on in St Ann's now. It is an active, vibrant community. There are some bad things going on too, but it's a living community and a lot of good people live in it. It doesn't deserve its reputation and things are improving. It has the reputation because a small number of people are involved in newsworthy activities like drug dealing and violent crime. But it is only a small number of people and it happens almost parallel to everyday life for the majority of people. If I had a choice of which estate to live on, it would be St Ann's. There is also easy access to the City Centre and all that has to offer as well.

COUNCILLOR DES WILSON

Born 1939

Interviewed at the Council House, Nottingham 16.1.01. Des Wilson was Sheriff of Nottingham 2001/2002. He is a councillor for **St Ann's Ward**

I settled in Nottingham in 1957 and have been a councillor for St Ann's Ward for about ten years. I used to live in St Ann's in the 1950s and 60s but I moved because of demolition and rehousing. I was in St Ann's at the time it was pulled down.

To me in those days it seemed a more closely-knit community. When a stranger passed through the area, people would observe that the person didn't live or associate with anybody in the area. It made criminals less privileged then. The demolition didn't affect me much as a youth. I didn't take much notice. I lived on Cranmer Street for a time then on Little John Street off Peas Hill Road, and then moved out to live in Lenton. I have two children.

I became a councillor because, through my community activities and looking at service delivery amongst people from the ethnic minorities, I felt there weren't enough voices in the right places to champion the causes of these people. That gave me an urge to play a part in active politics.

Over the years, I've been involved in a lot of organisations that take on board the cultural and social needs of people from the Afro-Caribbean community and, on occasions, with Asian communities. I was involved in the early stages of the Afro-Caribbean National Artistic Centre [ACNA].

I was elected to the Council in 1991. I think there were thirty-seven Labour councillors, seventeen Conservatives and John Peck as a Green Party member. In St Ann's, one of the things people have always been concerned about is crime. Crime in St Ann's escalated because of the way the new St Ann's was redeveloped. There were too many thoroughfares. Mostly elderly people got mugged and nobody knew where the perpetrators disappeared to because there were so many routes in and out of St Ann's.

The Phase 10 area was one of the worst because of the number of thoroughfares through it and a mugger could be at Victoria Centre in the City almost within seconds. In the old St Ann's, houses used to have alleyways at the back of them but there was no exit. So if someone went down an alleyway, they had to come back out. We've now had City Challenge, which has done a lot of environmental improvements. People feel more secure because of the environmental and security improvements. But at the same time, within the City Council, we are not complacent and are still trying to improve conditions within St Ann's.

I think one of the things which caused a lot of deterioration in St Ann's is the introduction of Care in the Community. St Ann's is an area which seems to get a lot of people with mental problems rehoused in the community. From my personal observations I think it was because Mapperley Hospital[1] was more or less on top of St Ann's and maybe people based at the hospital had links with St Ann's and tried to get housed within St Ann's when they went into the community. It has been one of the biggest problems in the area. Where a lot of people with mental problems have been rehoused within the community, it makes things difficult for residents in St Ann's. They don't know what the conditions of those individuals are, if they do not take their medication they might go off the edge and this creates problems.

One of my concerns is the rising mental health problems within the City, especially among Afro-Caribbean people. And health problems in St Ann's will remain at the top of the agenda. It is essential to pool resources to get the best possible service in an area. The City Council ought to be working hand in hand with the Health Authority and we're moving in that direction as we have a more inter-agency approach to service delivery.

There are people in St Ann's who are committed to the area and who have lived there for years. It is because of them that the area maintains its credibility. But there is also a high turnover of people. When research was done on the area by Trent University around 1993, it revealed most of the things I had concerns about.

We have councillors' surgeries in St Ann's every Wednesday at St Ann's Library on the Chase between six and seven o'clock, and at the Phase 10 Community Centre, Marple Square, on the first and third Saturdays in the month between ten and eleven o'clock. The ones at the Chase are well attended, but not so much at Marple Square but occasionally you pick up some important cases, which need dealing with.

Jon [Collins] and myself are putting a lot of pressure on the authorities to generate resources in this area. The Architect's Assistant is working with residents to come up

---

[1] Former psychiatric hospital on Porchester Road.

with the design for the shop frontage on Marple Square when it is redesigned. There is a four-year programme in Phase 10. Already some of the houses have been 'turned round' in conjunction with residents wishes.

I think one of the major improvements appertaining to service delivery, within not only St Ann's but within the City generally, is residents' participation. I've always been an advocate for consultation. Jon and I have always encouraged Council officers to consult with residents. I think that is a culture evolving across the City now. Residents' participation pertaining to service delivery makes a hell of a lot of difference to individuals who have got to live with whatever the end product is.

A lot of money has gone into St Ann's. There was City Challenge from 1992-97. As I said, a lot of money went into environmental and security improvement and into training. A lot went into supporting projects and to improve activities. One of the big problems about pots of money like that when they are brought into areas is that, when the finance period ends, the City Council is left trying to decide which of those projects it can take on to its mainstream programme. Projects that do not get continued funding have to look elsewhere because there are different pots of money available, European Social Fund, the Lottery . . . The Renewal Trust picks up some of these activities and also drip-feeds some of the organisations that are doing good work within the area.

This Government has made dramatic changes because you find that money going into an area has an effect on the infrastructure of the area. Before that, there was a situation that a pocket of money going into an area like St Ann's was being used just to stabilise the unemployment. Most people, as soon as they got jobs or were trained, moved out of the area. And people moving into the vacant properties were unemployed, so unemployment doesn't come down, it stabilises.

I look at St Ann's as part of Nottingham and Nottingham has a great history over the years. I don't think most people who were born and grew up here realise and appreciate some of the history of this City. St Ann's is part of it. I feel proud to be part of what's happening in Nottingham over the years I've been here, and even

prouder over what has transpired in St Ann's over the last ten years. I hope young people several generations on will realise that St Ann's is an influential part of the City.

I've lived and worked in Nottingham for forty-three years. I'm General Manager for Positive Action Training Agency [PATRA] within the East Midlands region. The main objective is to get people from ethnic minority communities into employment where there is under representation within the workforce. I've been involved with the organisation since 1993. We've had more enquiries from organisations recently wanting us to work with them to meet the targets set by the Government and through the McPherson Report.

I arrange most of my Council activities and community activities around the evenings and weekends unless I'm away on a conference or something. Then we have structured days for what are now called Strategic Board Meetings in the City Council. They are no longer called Committee meetings. And maybe half a day a week when lead members and senior officers get together to look at policy issues.

*In May 2002, Councillor Des Wilson became **Lord Mayor of Nottingham** for a year. He is the first Afro-Caribbean Lord Mayor of the City. He is seen here in front of Nottingham's Council House with the Lady Mayoress, his niece Lisa Henry. Photo: Nottingham Evening Post*

Endpiece

St Ann's is one of many areas in Britain with communities whose rich and evolving history, roots, cultures and built environment were wrenched from them with permission neither negotiated nor granted. The 'new' St Ann's, like many other redeveloped districts, has become stereotyped as an area of 'multi-deprivation'. This stereotype echoes the description of 'slum' placed on the 'old' St Ann's with its vibrant, diverse and resourceful community.

Gathering a history of St Ann's in living memory has been an absorbing, enjoyable and long task. I am angry that St Ann's people, of all ages, are not afforded more respect for what they have achieved, and because St Ann's is too often defined only in terms of the bad things which happen in it.

As shown in these pages, there are people who, from choice, live and/or work in the inner-city. I rewrote this endpiece after having another encounter with someone influential who believes that brutal market forces should be allowed to overrun districts like St Ann's so they become part of the so-called 'mainstream'.

Many St Annies do not move out of the district, although their circumstances would allow them to do so. They like the way of life in St Ann's. It is their home, their place. There are also people in St Ann's on too low an income, whose lifestyle would further suffer if the district were gentrified.

I hope that voices in this book may do something to convince the 'mainstream' that there are values and aspirations within St Ann's that are worth understanding. I believe there is ample evidence to suggest that - at some future time - 'mainstream' society will have cause to look at areas like St Ann's to re-learn some basic way of life values which are not determined by the ideology of maximising profit.

It is extremely important that the small minority of people who do bad things in St Ann's are not allowed to define it.

At the beginning of this book, I mentioned working with St Ann's young people who knew little of the district's history. When given opportunity to find out, they were very interested. I hope the voices in this book will assist young people to feel a sense of belonging to a place with a history and a positive future.

I have not edited people's voices into a framework that fits into any particular current agenda. To do so might have banished the content most likely to be of future interest and value. Perceptions change over time, sometimes very quickly.

Appendix I

SAINT ANN'S WELL

by **Patrick Fleckney**

Patrick Fleckney lives in St Ann's. He started researching written material about the history of St Ann's after archive and photographic material about the heritage of St Ann's was lost in a fire at a district library. Whilst the Local Studies Library, Angel Row, held newspaper clippings, maps and some photographs, much work needed to be redone. Among other things, Helen Blackmore, then community librarian, and staff at St Ann's Library decided to hold a 'Day of Memories' where former residents of St Ann's could meet up and re-live their memories. Patrick Fleckney set about gathering a concise history of St Ann's from the Local Studies Library and Nottingham Archives. Patrick Fleckney's booklet on the history of St Ann's was available at the first Reminiscence Day at St Ann's Library in 1993

King Henry IV visited Nottingham and on a number of occasions visited the area of Saint Ann's we know today. He was born at Bolingbroke in 1366. He was King of England 1399 -1413. In his later years, he had much ill health through leprosy. After his visits to Oswell, the original name for the St Ann's Well, and finding that it was a religious site, in 1409 he gave money to the monks for a chapel dedicated to Saint Anne, the patron saint of pregnancy, to be built on the site of their hermitage. Searching the Nottingham archives we find the historical works of the Reverend John Orange. He wrote about Saint Ann's Chapel and Hermitage for the period 1500 - 1618 and he takes our story further:

" . . . our Nottingham historians have strangely failed to grasp the significance of the ancient foundations at Saint Ann's Well. The historian Deering [Deering's work *Nottingamia vetus et nova,* 1751] merely says: 'Near this Well there stood anciently a chapel dedicated to Saint Anne, whence the Well obtained the name it bears'. All subsequent writers follow suit. As a matter of fact there can be no doubt whatever that the institution was really a hermitage, where the chapel was the most prominent feature. We have an instructive parallel in the case of the much more important establishment in Nottingham Park, which was always known as the Chapel of St Mary In the Rock.

"The Spring called Saint Ann's, evidently under the earlier name of 'Oswell' meaning 'the source of the Nottingham Beck[1]', must have been a holy well from an early period. Even if it were not previously so, the foundation of the hermitage would certainly sanctify it. Unfortunately there is no record as to when the latter event took place.

"What we claim to be the earliest known allusion is represented by Dr Charles Deering's note that William Chaundeler of Nottingham, keeper of St Leonard's 1357 - 1358, made an encroachment of half an acre of ground 'in the King's domain, within the court of the town of Nottingham, in the ermitage that is called Oswell'.

"Whether there was any sort of connection between the Leper Hospital and the hermitage, it is now impossible to say.

"Again, in a forest record of the same date, we read that 'William of Capole, clerk, that now is dead, held as assert of old time, that is called Hermitage Wong, within the covert of the King's wood [The Coppice] of Nottingham, of 20 acres of ground'. Of course, the hermitage itself, thus incidentally mentioned, may have existed prior to 1357.

"The above 'Hermitage Wong' was probably with the later close called 'Le Hermitage' mentioned in 1513 and subsequently in our Borough records.

"In 1552 the wood and trees in the 'Harmytage Closse' were sold by the Corporation for over £50. It must be confessed that nothing of the medieval history of Saint Anne's Well and its hermitage has really survived to our day. We know the latter was founded and that the old hermits, living their quaint secluded lives, succeeded each other for centuries, but not even their names remain to us.

"Though not actually recorded, we may be quite sure such a romantically situated spot was a favourite little pilgrimage for the people of Nottingham, and that the healing properties of the water obtained early renown. And no doubt people of position, as well as ordinary towns folk occasionally resorted there if only in connection with the sports of the chase.

"In direct evidence here of seems to be afforded by the discovery at St Anne's Well about 1850 of a gold ring of the time of Henry IV, bearing devices and a motto. It would

---

[1] The 1881 Ordnance Survey map shows the source of the Beck actually lies in the nearby grounds of the Coppice Lunatic Asylum, which meanders down, over and underground to Oswell, where it rises to the surface far more prominently.

seem probable that the original chapel of this hermitage was a humble wooden erection, and judging from the reference of 1357-8, possibly there was no formal dedication to Saint Anne until the permanent chapel of stone was reared.

"With regard to the date of this event, the only evidence that we possess is represented by Deering's record of a date stone inscribed with the year 1409, but this testimony will not be regarded as reliable in the present day. Nevertheless, in default of better information we are unable to supersede it.

"The earliest contemporary allusion we possess to the dedication of Saint Anne at this spot goes back no further than 1503 - 1504, and then it only relates to an adjacent field called 'Seynt Anne Close'. However, it is clear that the name was derived from the previous existing name of the chapel or Well.

"Unfortunately, we find no actual allusion to the chapel until after it had probably ceased to serve its proper purpose, and when it was being adapted by the Corporation for secular uses. In the municipal accounts for 1543 - 1544 it is recorded that the sum of 3s 6d was 'paid to William Rose and his fellow for workmanship at Saynte An' Chapelle'. And a further sum of 2s to 'Deonyse Cowper for workmanship at Saynte An' Chapelle'. The proceedings, added to the following extract from the *Mickleton Jury* of 1577, are the only contemporary notices we have:

" 'Master Mayor, we desire you and your brethren that there may be a cover made at Sent Anne Well, as you and your brethren may desire as concerning, either at the Chapel end or at some place convenient where you shall think good.' The old chapel probably remained standing down to 1617 -1618, when a house of entertainment on a lavish scale was built at the Well, laying the foundation of its popularity as a great pleasure resort.

"Deering's evidence tends to show that the chapel was most likely pulled down to make way for the new house, except that a piece of old wall was grafted into the latter . . ."

The history of Saint Anne's now sees another royal visitor, Anne Queen of England, Ireland and Scotland. Anne was born in 1665, the daughter of James, Duke of York (James II) and his first wife Anne Hyde. She received a Protestant education and in 1683 she married Prince George of Denmark. Sadly all of their children died young. When William of Orange (the future William III) invaded England on November 5th 1688, Princess Anne fled to Nottingham and remained until 1702. She stayed at Thurland Hall in the City Centre, and later Columber Park. The original Thurland Hall was demolished in1831 when the modern Thurland Street came into being.

She may also have stayed for a while in Nottingham Castle as this short passage from Celia Fiennes *Through England on a side saddle in the time of William and Mary* [1888] states:

"In Nottingham Castle . . . the Chamber of State is hung with a very rich tapestry so much silver and gold in it that the 3 pieces that hung in the roome cost £1500. The bed was railed in as the present chamber used to be, the bed was damaske; the floor of the room was inlayed with Cyphers and the Coronet, and here the Princess Ann lay when she fled in King James's time. . ."

The Princess also visited Saint Ann's Well, so here we have a real Princess, later Queen of England, with the name of Anne who we can associate with this place in Nottingham. Also the unfortunate fact that many of her children died young links in with the Well being named after the patron Saint of pregnancy.

In the reign of Queen Anne 1702 - 1714, Roburt Purcell, a native from Ireland, came to Nottingham to cultivate waste lands and to grow the field potato. Before that time, this root had only been grown in the garden. He took up abode at the house of Saint Anne, then a public house, and kept by Mrs Blee. The Irishman had permission to clear away the underwood of a piece of land in the Coppice. His crop was abundant and he realised great profits.

It was in the ground of this house that a murder took place which shook the people of Nottingham. On the morning of September 22nd 1741 just after Midnight, John Clarke, a young servant with widow Blee, heard a noise among his Mistress's poultry in the farmyard. He got up and went down into the little yard. A gun was fired at him killing him instantly, but the murderers escaped detection. Twenty-six years later, in 1767 a framework knitter of the town, John Shore, gave information to the magistrate, that to his knowledge the murder was committed by John Wilkins, James Cuff and two brothers, all soldiers on General Churchill's regiment of Dragoons then, in 1741, quartered in the town. They had been out deer-stealing but, having been unsuccessful, were determined to have some of Mrs Blee's geese on their return. In this they were disappointed by the appearance of the unfortunate servant, John Clarke.

Wilkins and Cuff were arrested in the neighbourhood of London, then being outpatients of Chelsea Hospital. As other parties were dead who might have been witnesses, there was not sufficient evidence to convict. Soon after, on his deathbed, one of them confessed his own guilt and that of three of his companions.

In time, the public house at Saint Ann's Well saw frequent brawls and the old tavern eventually lost its licence in 1824 for unruly conduct.

The river Beck originated from its source at the nearby Coppice Lunatic Asylum and percolated up out of the ground at Saint Ann's Well, formerly known as Oswell, and then flowed down hill following the curvature of the Beck Valley which today is St Ann's Well Road. It was a stream of natural spring water from which many a horse would stop for refreshment after pulling his heavy cart and master along the valley.

The Beck then followed a winding path along Beck Street and through the outskirts of Nottingham borough, before flowing into the Nottingham Canal at the former Boots Island on London Road, since demolished.

As St Ann's expanded, the River Beck was made to flow through a sewer culvert under St Ann's Well Road, a painstaking and muddy task which many people disliked.

Many people believe that the site of St Ann's Well lies below the foundations of the north abutment of a double-arched rail bridge which crossed St Ann's Well Road, under the shadow of the Gardeners Public House. It has emerged that the architect, Mr Tarbottom, built a monumental structure on this location, which he designed himself, to commemorate St Ann's Well so it would not be forgotten. In doing so the structure was constructed seven metres forward of the actual well site. Therefore, St Ann's Well lies on the left side of the garden at the rear of the public house.

With the commencement of the Great Northern Railway in 1886, the Tarbottom structure was demolished and the site was excavated to a depth of 30 feet for the foundations of the north abutment of the rail bridge. As a consequence, Oswell was no more. During these excavations, a half-crown dated 1685 and some old bones were found. Today

the fifteen foot embankment which lies over the site of Saint Ann's Well lies under the shadow of The Gardeners public house.

The shape of the monumental structure destroyed for the needs of the railway has come to signify St Ann's Well, and has sometimes been used as a logo for St Ann's events

Appendix II

THE MAZE NEAR ST ANN'S WELL

from *Tales of Old Nottinghamshire by* **Polly Howat** [Countryside Books, Newbury 1991]

The maze known as the Shepherd's Race, or Robin Hood's Race, was cut on top of a hill close to St Ann's Well . . . These winding labyrinths were once a common feature throughout Britain. Many of the ecclesiastical ones were cut in the Middle Ages. For some curious reason mazes are enjoying a remarkable resurgence. There are now more than 100 in this country, compared with about 40 a few years ago.

The Shepherd's Race is estimated to have had a diameter of some 21 yards and the extreme distance between each projection was some 34 yards. Its winding path was about 536 yards long. Nobody can say for sure when it was built or by whom, but it was an unusual shape, being circular and with four horseshoe shapes forming a 'square' maze.

Sadly it was ploughed up on 27th February 1797. Later [c1838] a facsimile was cut in the grounds of Poynters Tea Garden which stood on Blue Bell Hill, overlooking the valley of St Ann's Well and not far removed from the original 'Race'.

This authentic miniature was shaped by box hedging, and the paths were narrow and covered by Beeston gravel, which made running impossible. The Poynters had a half-clipped standard poodle which had been trained to run the maze for a penny. Being an untrustworthy dog he often took short cuts, yet always demanded payment from his onlookers. He would rush off to his mistress with his coin in his mouth, which he exchanged for a titbit. The Poynter's smart poodle was an added attraction to the tea garden.

However, the model could never have offered the same fun as the real thing, as described by the local historian Blackner, in the 19th century, who lamented its destruction.

Further information and sketch of the maze near St Anne's Well in *Old Nottinghamshire*, Edited by John Potter Briscoe 1881. Available in Nottingham Local Studies Library, Angel Row

Appendix III

WHAT HAS ST ANN'S TO DO WITH THE UPKEEP OF TRENT BRIDGE?

Allotment land in St Ann's is owned substantially by the Bridge Trust and Chambers Estate. It is rented and managed by the City Council (see the Allotments section). This was not generally known until recent years. When he discovered this, Vernon Hawley researched the Bridge Trust

by **Vernon Hawley**

The Bridge Estate was set up centuries ago to acquire and manage resources - mainly land - to provide income for the maintenance of Trent Bridge. The role of the Local Authority as Trustees of the Bridge Estate, a Charity, was separate from the role of the Local Authority.

In 1973 it was discovered that there had been unlawful appropriations of Bridge Estate land, including valuable sites in St Ann's, for Local Authority purposes in recent times. Therefore, this matter had to be rectified by substantial payments by the Local Authority to the Bridge Estate.

According to Nottingham City Archives (4176) in Letters Patent of Edward V1 February 21st 1551, there was the granting of possessions of Chantry of St Mary in St Mary's Church and of the Hospital of St John, Nottingham, to Nottingham Corporation toward the sustention of Trent Bridge. Unfortunately this grant does not detail the lands involved. So it is not possible to distinguish the new royal gift from the previous private gifts. However it is possible to guess. This is because the biggest acquisitions of 1551 appear to be the Hungerhills, Gorsey Close and the New or Far Coppice.

None of these are mentioned in the Corporation records prior to 1551 as belonging to the Corporation. But all are being administered by the Corporation shortly after 1551. They were all 'entire' (i.e. non-commonable lands) and did not form part of the open fields.

Instances of the Bridge Estate land in St Ann's being used by the Local Authority's Housing Committee without proper payment at the appropriate time included 490 sq yards of land at Corporation Road [Council Minute 3.2.1969], 0.348 acres at Kildare Road [7.11.1966], 1.320 sq yards at Westminster Street [2.3.1970], 1.515 acres at Westminster Street/Hungerhill Road [2.3.1970], 1.189 acres at The Wells Road [6.4.1970], and 0.910 acres at Shelton Street [6.12.73]. And the Education Committee used 10.279 acres of land at Coppice Vale [6.2.1961].

For more on the history of Trent Bridge, a good start is in *History of Nottingham* by W Howie Wylie and J Potter Briscoe [Frank Murray, Nottingham. 1893].

Index

ST ANN'S Nottingham: inner-city voices by Ruth I Johns • ISBN 0951696092

ST ANN'S NOTTINGHAM: inner-city voices, by Ruth I Johns • ISBN 0951696092

ST ANN'S NOTTINGHAM: inner-city voices *by Ruth I Johns* • ISBN 0951696092

St Ann's Nottingham: Inner-city voices *by Ruth I Johns* • ISBN 0951696092

ST ANN'S, NOTTINGHAM: inner city voices by Ruth I Johns • ISBN 0951696092

St Ann's Nottingham: inner-city voices by Ruth I Johns • ISBN 0951696092

ST ANN'S, NOTTINGHAM: inner city voices *by Ruth I Johns* • ISBN 0951696092

St Ann's Nottingham. Inner city voices, by Ruth I Johns • ISBN 0951696092

ST ANN'S NOTTINGHAM: inner-city voices by Ruth I Johns ● ISBN 0951696092

St Ann's Nottingham: Inner City Voices *by Ruth I Johns* • ISBN 0951696092

St Ann's Nottingham: Inner city voices, by Ruth I Johns • ISBN 0951696092

Titles from Plowright Press

PO Box 66   Warwick CV34 4XE

'ORDINARY' LIVES SERIES

(Laminated PB. Stitch bound)

- **Bill of Bulwell** by Bill Cross. ISBN 0951696017. £9.95. Autobiography of a Nottingham miner born in 1918. Already a must for social history students. 2nd Edition [1998]. 208 pp including photos.

- **Alice from Tooting** [1997] by Alice Mullen (1879-1977). ISBN 0951696041. £8.95. Few working-class women of Alice's generation wrote their life story. Hers was found in a hard-backed notebook after her death. The book is 'biography, local history, social history and a lot more' *Journal of Kent History*. 208 pp including photos. Edited by Anne Bott.

- **Flo: Child Migrant from Liverpool** [1998] by Flo Hickson. ISBN 0951696033. £9.95 (Aust $32.00 post free). First published autobiography of a woman 'child migrant'. Flo, aged 7 in 1928, was sent involuntarily - like thousands of children from Britain to Australia - to add to 'good white stock', even though she had relatives willing to care for her in Liverpool. Good reviews in major Australian Press, including the *Canberra Times*: 'We all know about the Dunera boys but we need to learn more about the Flo Hicksons'. 224 pp including photos. Edited by Anne Bott.

- **Geoff: 44 years a railwayman** [2000] by L Geoffrey Raynor. ISBN 0951696068. £9.95. Starting as a Messenger Boy at Nottingham Victoria Station in 1939, Geoff rose to be Signalman, Controller and Senior Accident Clerk. His railway life is told in the context of the rest of his life, including his wife's thirty-three year struggle with cancer. 208 pp including photos, maps and details from BR Rule Books. Edited by Anne Bott.

- **Vic: from Lambeth to Lambourn** [2001] by Victor Cox. ISBN 0951696084. £11.95. Vic's pre-1920 childhood in Lambeth, London, gives a rich insight into the time. Vic started work at 14 and worked as a waiter at the famous Waldorf Hotel, in London's Aldwych, haunt of the rich and famous. 304 pp including photos. Edited by Anne Bott.

This Series has four broad, but overlapping, readership groups:

- elders who like life stories about 'ordinary' people with whom they can identify directly or vicariously

- students and social historians looking for first-hand accounts and reliable detail

- those interested in place-specific events and people

- a growing readership who love this Series simply 'because they do'! They sometimes write and say why they like the books' content, their friendly feel and clear print. They welcome the 'Ordinary' Lives Series as an antidote to the commercial world's obsession with celebrity

'Just a note to let you know how much my husband and I have enjoyed the books in your 'Ordinary' Lives Series. We have found them interesting, educational and, at times, sad. We look forward to your next publication.'

J M, Streatham

ALSO ABOUT NOTTINGHAM

Elliott Durham and St Anns: the Comprehensive School on the hill in inner-city St Anns [1998]. This School opened in 1966 with pupils from three schools which were closing in the area. Like many comprehensive schools, it had no recorded history of the school before work on this book started. 76 pp with many photos. Laminated cover. PB. Edited by Ruth I Johns. ISBN 0951696025. £6.50

Radford Care Group, the story of over thirty years of an independent day care centre for elders in inner-city Radford: told by elders, staff and volunteers [2000]. Photos and background information about Radford, where Player's and Raleigh once dominated. The Radford Care Group was initiated to meet the needs of elders in Radford after much of the area was redeveloped and many young families left. Foreword by Alan Simpson MP, who says the book is a celebration of what can be done when people stand up and work for a society in which people matter because their humanity has no 'sell-by date'. 112 pp. Laminated cover. PB. Edited by Anne Bott. ISBN 0951696076. £6.50

Plowright Press [1995] is a member of the Publishers Association. It is one of a growing number of professional, small independent and specialist publishers. It is a not-for-profit company. Reader feedback is very positive

Plowright Press books are available through libraries, bookshops, Amazon.co.uk or direct from the publisher at PO Box 66, Warwick CV34 4XE

BOOKS IN PRINT BY THE SAME AUTHOR

Ruth I. Johns' book **Life Goes On** *was published under the Unknown Publisher imprint after two major publishers wanted to amend her text to a high-selling 'guru' blueprint for running a self-help organisation. Believing that such blueprints are damaging to community self-sustainability, she refused. In defiance, in 1982 she published under the imprint of the Unknown Publisher! Her book received twenty-five excellent reviews*

Life Goes On [1982] outlines the philosophy and practice of the first ten years of Family First Trust, a pioneer Nottingham housing association and community organisation which the author started in 1965. Family First provided independent housing for disadvantaged groups. For example, it housed lone unsupported parents for whom adoption or placing children in care were then often the only 'solution'. Family First worked in appropriate local ways, including the provision of a day nursery, furniture service and day workshop 'in the community' for patients of Mapperley Hospital. 192 pp. Laminated cover. PB. ISBN 090789500X. £10.00

The Job Makers [1984] is a case study of a Nottingham working community of small firms. Twenty-six of the thirty-seven firms studied, during a period of four and a half years, were new ones. The study records what can be done through private small-scale investment, but seldom is. In his foreword, Professor Jack Willock says: "This book offers a wealth of case information to lead into debate about the relationship between wealth creation - in terms of people being able to provide not only their own employment but to give or create work for others - and short term maximisation of direct profits." 146 pp. Laminated cover. PB. ISBN 0907895026. £8.00

Company Community Involvement in the UK [1991]. *Employment Gazette*: "A thought provoking and distinctly different look at the role of business in the wider community." *Accountancy Age*: "This study shows there can be no 'quick fix' and argues that too much UK company 'socially responsible' activity is taken up with imposing central government ideas". Still very topical! 87 pp. Ring-binding. ISBN 0951696009. £15 companies and statutory bodies. £5 community organisations and individuals

A PROJECT OPEN TO ANY ELDER LIVING IN THE UK

RUTH'S ARCHIVE gathers first-hand accounts of individuals' community involvement. One method used is through a special fill-in book. This fill-in book offers some structure to help people to write their experiences. The returned, completed books describe individuals' participation in extended family, neighbourhood and community life. This is a way of placing 'on the record' the things that YOU feel have been and are important in your life. Completing the fill-in book can be done in any way to suit yourself. There is no 'correct' way! The ARCHIVE will become publicly accessible at no charge in 2009. The fill-in books on archive quality paper are £6.00 post free from PO Box 66, Warwick CV34 4XE. Further details on request

Ruth I Johns started work at sixteen as a cub reporter on a Newton Abbot weekly, before joining the staff of the *Western Morning News* at Exeter. She was a founder member of the National Pre-School Playgroups Association [PPA] when her three children were pre-schoolers. As PPA area organiser in Lichfield, she campaigned for play space on a Birmingham overspill high-rise estate, and ran a playgroup herself. When she moved to Nottingham, she became the first PPA representative in the city.

In 1965, she founded Family First Trust, a pioneer housing and community self-help organisation in Nottingham and worked with it until moving to London for family reasons in 1976. Ruth became National Director of Action Resource Centre, which mainly supported local community initiatives to provide appropriate permanent employment. It worked through local staff in thirteen UK cities, including Nottingham. This job brought her closely in touch with Government, major institutions and companies as well as local communities. The experience fuelled her determination to make the voice of local communities better heard.

Over some difficult years following medical injury and paralysis in 1984, Ruth slowly regained mobility; went to Bradford University and gained an MA in Peace Studies: then became a community historian. Her role of community historian is from the perspective of belonging, and helping to gather the history of a local community through the voices of its own people. Ruth lives in the West Midlands and St Ann's, Nottingham.

An author, Ruth also writes for newspapers and journals. She was Midlands Regional Whitbread Volunteer of the Year in 2000 in recognition of many years voluntary work in the West Midlands and Nottingham, including work on this book.

Further history/photos of St Ann's, Nottingham, may be sent to Ruth at Plowright Press, PO Box 66, Warwick CV34 6XE. She would also be interested to hear of people's experiences of redevelopment in other places.